TERRORISM IN INDIA'S NORTH-EAST A GATHERING STORM

TERRORISM IN INDIA'S NORTH-EAST
A Gathering Storm
(In 3 Volumes)
(Volume-1)

Col. Ved Prakash

PUBLICATIONS

KALPAZ PUBLICATIONS

DELHI-110052

Terrorism in India's North-East
A Gathering Storm

Rs. 2500 (Set)

ISBN: 81-7835-660-0 (Set)
ISBN: 81-7835-662-7 (Vol. 2)

Published in 2008 in India by
Kalpaz Publications
C-30, Satyawati Nagar,
Delhi-110052
E-mail: kalpaz@hotmail.com
Phone : 9212729499

Laser Type Setting by: Quick Media, Delhi
Printed at : Singhal Print Media, Delhi

DEDICATED TO

My grandson, Aryan Sharma,
with
a fervent plea to the present generation to
render his generation the world over
safe from the scourge of terrorism

Contents

Preface

The humanity today is in the virulent grip of a pandemic—the scourge of terrorism. Several groups and outfits are engaged in this 'War through terror', a low-cost option for the inhuman desperados; but the most potent and wide-spread threat to the very existence of this world as we know it comes from this insiduous war being unleashed by the Islamist groups perpetrating this heinous crime against the mankind in the countries spread from the Philippines to the United States.

It is only apt that the then senior most servant of the world community, Mr. Kofi Annan, who served the UN as its Secretary General for eight long years (1998-2006), is quoted on the issue. He said on 4 Oct. 2002 :

> "Terrorism is a global threat with global effect; .... its consequences affect every aspect of the United Nations agenda from development to peace to human rights and the rule of law. By its very nature, terrorism is an assault on the fundamental principles of law, order, human rights and the peaceful settlement of disputes on which the United Nations is established. The United Nations has an indispensable role to play in providing the legal and organisational framework within which the international compaign against terrorism can unfold."
>
> [Terrorism Prevention Branch
>
> United Nationals Office on Drugs and Crimes
>
> Vienna International Centre, PO Box 500
>
> A – 1400 Vienna
>
> Austria]

We have just been though the human history's most violent century. Curious, if interesting, trends have marked the era. If in the early years of nuclear age, which commenced with the Hiroshima blast, the world lived under the shadow of a nuclear holocaust, by the end of the Cold War the probability of a nuclear war and exchange was lower than ever before. Likewise, after the Second World War the likelihood of the clash of arms between any two major powers divindled progressively. In a manner of speaking, the 1991 Gulf War may well be the last classical war for a long time to come. The 2003 US invasion of Iraq was hardly a conventional war. It was a case of technology defeating the 'mighty' Army of President Saddam Hussain. But what is more significant is that when the Iraq war is entering the fifth year on 23 March 2007, the US military machine and coalition forces are losing it—almost—to the practitioners of an unconventional warfare : War through terror.

So in the recent years, the nuclear and classical inter-state wars seem to be becoming less likely, and the phenomenon of sub-conventional war and transnational militancy and terrorism have been on the rise. The latter belongs to the genre of "Low Intensity Conflicts" (LIC). The term LIC has emerged only in recent decades, with the US Pentagon's description of the spectrum of conflict consisting of 'high', 'medium' and 'low' intensity levels, in Klare and Kornbluh (ed), *Low Intensity Warfare*, 1988.

Contemporary warfare has begun to lean extensively towards the 'low intensity' variety. Since 1945, the world has seen some 160 or so conflicts. Of these, three-fourths have been low intensity. 'Terrorism' is the most dominant and most widely practised form of the LIC today. It is perpetrated by the non-state actors and its targets mostly are innocent civilians, including women and children. The real tragedy lies in the fact that the victims even do not know why they are killed so mercilessly. Some other compelling facts and data are recorded here :

- Only four of the 82 conflicts recorded between 1989 and 1992 were of the classic inter-state character, and every year since 1991, there have been at least ten internal conflicts around the world that caused the deaths of more than 10,000 where the primary weapons of war mere light weapons—mostly used by the terrorists.
- Non-state actors appeared to have little difficulty in accessing either the weapons or the ammunition, as prices dropped to as little as $ 8 for an AK-47 assault rifle—a prized possession of a terrorist.
- In all of the intra-state conflicts being waged today, light weapons are the primary weapons of war of both the combatants—the State and the non-state actor.
- The rise in sophistication was accompanied by a corresponding increase in the casualty rate in most conflict areas. The path from the .303 to the assault rifles and rocket propelled grenades (RPGs) has been a bloody one.
- All wars in Asia and in some other parts of the world are funded wholly or in part by narcotics movements—popularly known as nacro-terrorism.
- Besides an inordinate number of casualties suffered by the civil society, the terrorism also causes huge refugee movement. By the end of the 20th century, the various conflict zones the world over had over 120 million chronically malnourished people, while there were

over 28 million refugees and displaced persons, an eleven-fold increase since 1970 (Human Development Report, 1999).

- In more specific terms, in Sudan's Darfur region alone, an estimated 200,000 people have been killed and over 2 million rendered homeless in the terrorism-related upheavels during the past half-a-decade period.

What should be a matter of serious concern to the international community is its inability to craft a joint, concerted and effective policy frame-work to confront and defeat terrorism. A western scholar has asserted that what the world is witnessing and experiencing today is a "clash of civilizations". Radical Islam is not only pushing hard to dominate the ummah, but also bent upon destabilising the countries it deems as its 'enemies'.

Presently, terrorism is perpetrating mindless violence—horrendous killings and wanton destruction of property. A Pakistani Army Officer Brig S.K. Malik, *Quranic Concept of Work* (Wajid Alis, Lahore), 1979, P. 59, has put it like it is :

"Terror struck into the hearts of the enemies is not only a means, it is the end in itself."

Besides the Islamic outfits, some other terrorist outfits are active in Sri Lanka, North Ireland, Europe, Japan and South America. Not to speak of a joint fight against the terrorists, the UN has not succeeded till date to resolve the definitional hurdle in the counter-terrorism stakes.

The Author has the hands on experience of fighting the insurgency and terrorism during his two stints of service in India's North-East. When he joined as a newly-commissioned officer his unit, an Infantry Battalion (3 Sikh), in 1957, he was blooded into the active battle, so to say, as the Phizo-led Naga insurgency was at its virulent worst. During this tenure (1957-61), as young officer he led his platoon in attacks on the rebel camps in the jungles and cavernous hills of Nagaland, then merely Naga Hills district of Assam. Once tragedy struck his patrol and he saw one of his men fall to a bullet fired by a Naga rebel. The patrol fought its way out of the ambush sprung by the ultras. It has been aptly said that no one understands the pains and pangs of the battle/war better than the soldiers. In counter-insurgency operations, the action is generally at the level of platoon and company. The operations, thus, are led by the junior leaders.

His next tenure was the Mizo Hills, 1984-87, when he was commanding officer of an Infantry Battalion (18 Assam Rifles), deployed in the area along the Mizo Hills/Burma (now Myanmar) border. It was during the active-phase of Laldenga-led Mizo rebellion. It was again a rewarding experience, involving as it did, planning counter-insurgency operations in various areas under his command and liaison with senior civil and police officers.

A word of praise is due to the Naga and Mizo militants. Not only were they brave and doughtly fighters, they observed a certain code of honour. They usually targeted uniformed men, soldiers and policemen, and seldom the civilians. Of course, the perceived 'informers' were indeed targeted. They indeed were worthy 'enemies'—far removed from today's mindless murderers.

It may not be out of place here to mention some 'trivia' which will be of great interest to any Indian interested in the subject. It, of course, relates to the Author's two tenures in the North-East. During his first (1957-61) tenure, his unit was headquartered at Khonoma, the village of the legendary Phizo, who was then leading the insurgency against the Indian state. Some details deserve a mention. The Officer's Mess of his unit, 3 Sikh, was occupying the Dak Bungalow once home to a Japanese unit commander. The Bungalow, 13 km south-west of Kohima Garrison, which stubbornly thwarted the advance of Japanese forces to Dimapur and Gawahati, marked the limit of their penetration into Indian territory during World War II. More interestingly, this Bungalow was skirting the base line of a 650-meter long ridge on the top of which stood Phizo's house, occupied by his wife and children. Ironically, the Assam police was guarding and protecting the family of the rebel leader, Phizo, while the soldiers of 3 Sikh were hunting his Naga rebel warriors in jungles. Phizo by then, of course, was comfortably ensconced in a safe house somewhere in Pakistan, arranged by its intelligence agencies.

During his second tenure (1984-87), the Author's unit, 18 Assam Rifles, was located at Lungleh (now spelt, Lunglei), the village of equally legendary Mizo leader, Laldenga. His house was located near the Headquarters of the Infantry Brigade. Needless to say, his family too was given security by the Indian State of Assam. Another 'trivial' detail may be of interest to the lay reader. One late might, when the Author was returning to his unit after attending some function at the Brigade Headquarters, his vehicle was 'nearly' ambushed by the insurgents near Laldenga's house. This he learnt next morning from an officer who was travelling in his own jeep some distance from Author's : "Well, last night it was a close call for you. There were a couple of Mizo ultras well-concealed and all set to spring an ambush. After all, a Commanding Officer is an attractive prize for them. As soon as they saw the lights of my vehicle, they melted into the jungle."

That the Indian State was guarding the families of the top Naga and Mizo leaders in the 1950s and 1980s is a tribute to Indian democracy and reflective of its innate strength! And the tradition continues till date. All the Kashmiri secessionist leaders are being provided security today while they are carrying out vicious campaigns to violate India's sovereignty and integrity. The latest episode in this saga of generosity displayed by India came yesterday (20 March 2007) when the most passionate, some would say, 'vicious' among the hard liners, was granted visa to proceed to the US for treatment of a serious medical condition. This is not all. An opponent of this secessionist leader, Prof. Bhim Singh, Chief of the Panthers Party, offered to bear all the expenses for this treatment! Three cheers for the Indian culture, civilisation and tradition!

We must remember that never before in the history of civilization were human beings so much exposed to terrorism as they have been during the last couple of decades. Extremist, fundamentalist, and disruptive forces the world over are focussed single-mindedly to destroy its peace and harmony through wanton violence unleashed by their foot soldiers, blinded and indoctrinated by religious and ideological passion. The mindless death dance is not only targeting mostly the innocent people including women and children but is also transforming the tender youth into hardcore terrorists—the unthinking killing machines. The suicide bomber is the latest and the most lethal addition to the armoury of the planners and perpetrators of the terrorism. It is beyond comprehension how the fanatic, fundamentalist clerics and the narrow nationalist ideologues can easily convert simple youngman into human bombs alluring them with an after-world of living with given number of virgin nymphs and other luxuries they could have only dreamt of during their sojourn on the earth. The counter-terrorism policies and strategies of the West (the USA, the UK etc.) and East (India and Isreal etc.) do not seem to have an answer to this unthinking robot-like machine—also known as the human-bomber.

Incidents like the attack on the Indian Parliament, the largest democratic institution of the world; repeated attacks on transport systems and commercial hubs of Mumbai, the economic capital and nerve centre of the largest democracy in the world; the destruction of World Trade Centre of the US, popularly known as the Nine-Eleven; blowing up of a hotel on a Bali beach in Indonesia; ruthless killings of passengers on Metro trains and stations in London; similar attack on Madrid (Spain) trains; and the tragedy in a Moscow theatre are only some examples to prove that we all are vulnerable targets of terrorist depredations at any time, no matter which part of the world we live in. The elder statesman of India, AB Vajpayee, put it succinctly this way when he addressed the US Congres as India's Prime Minister in September 2002 :

> "No country in the world could enjoy immunity against terrorism on account of distance or geograpphy."

Majority of the material in this book is from open sources : the print and visual media, the internet, and personal discussions with the reputed experts and journalists involved with the subject. I owe a deep debt of gratitude to the Institute for Conflict Management, headed by a great Indian who retrieved the Punjab for India when it had 'nearly' gone under. At a more personal level, I am grateful to a senior Research Scholar at this Institute who not only sent me a particular monograph, but also offered to download for me any data/material I needed for my book. I thanked him profurely and told him that I would not like him to give him so much bother and would ask my son/daughter to download all I needed from the South Asia Terrorism Portal (SATP).

This book, a multi-volume, comprehensive study, aims at spreading the awareness among the civil society about the dangers posed to the international community by the ever-spreading phenomenon of the deadly pandemic of terrorism. It covers all aspects of terrorism in various corners of the world including India, West Asia, Asian countries to the east, Europe and America. It explains the ground realities in a lucid style sans any academic and professional jargons.

Encyclopaedic in scope, the book will have served its purpose if it enables the reader to see the issues relating to terrorism in perspective and appreciate the implications of the threat it poses in clearer terms.

With this, I rest my case, hoping that the reader would find the book worth a read.

Ved Prakash

Abbreviations and Acronyms

AA	Asian Age
AAC	Awami Action Committee (J & K)
AAJM	Anjaman-e-Auqafi Jama Masjid
AASU	All Assam Students Union
ABDR	Al Badr (J & K)
ABQ	Al Barq (J & K)
ABSU	All Bodo Students Union
ADC	Autonomous District Council
AEH	Ahal-e-Hadis
AESS	Anjuman-e-Sipah-e-Sahila (J & K)
AFF	Al Fatah Force (J & K)
AFIS	Automatic Fingerprint Identification System (USA)
AFSPA	Armed Forces (Special Powers) Act
AHAB	Ahl-e-Hadith Andolan (Bangladesh)
AIPRF	All India People's Resistance Forum
AJF	Al Jihad Force (J & K)
AJKEC	All Jammu and Kashmir Employees Confederation
ALI	Assam Light Infantry
AMF	Al Mujahideen Force (J & K)
AMFI	Al Mujahid Fil Islam (J & K)
AMLT	Assam Muslim Liberation Tigers
AMU	Aligarh Muslim University
AMULFA	All Muslim United Liberation Front (Assam)
AMUS	Al Mustafa
AMYA	Al Madad Yalgar-e-Ali
ANLA	Adivasi Nationalist Liberation Army
ANVC	A'chik National Volunteer Council (Megh)
APHC	All Party Hurryat Conference (also, KJHC)
AR.	Assam Rifles
AS	Adam Sena (Islamic, Asm)
ASI	Archaeological Survey of India
ASR	Assam Secretariat Records

ATGR	Allah Tigers
ATI	Anjaman-e-Tablig-ul-Islam
ATTF	All Tripura (Tribal) Tiger Force
AUC	Al Umar Commandos
AUI	Ansar-ul-Islam
AUM	Al Umar Mujahideen
Baharistan	Baharistani-i-Ghaibi, a contemporary account of events in the reign of Jahangir (1605-27). It has information on certain Muslim invasions of Assam (Jadunath Sarkar's trans, 1905)
BDR	Bangladesh Rifles
BdSF	Bodo Security Force
BIMSTEC	Bangladesh, India, Myanmar, Sri Lanka, Thailand Economic Cooperation
BJP	Bengal Judicial Proceedings (also, Bharatiya Janata Party)
BKI	Babbar Khalsa International
BLT	Bodoland Liberation Tigers (Asm)
BLTF	Bodoland Liberation Tiger Force (Asm)
BNLF	Bru National Liberation Front (MR)
Brig	Brigadier
BSF	Border Security Force (India)
Capt	Captain
CBS	Central Broadcasting Service
CEM	Chief Executive Member (of the ADC)
CFR	Council of Foreign Relations
CHT	Chittagong Hills Tract
CI	Center-Insurgency
CIA	Central Intelligence Agency
CKRF	Chin-Kuki Revolutionary Front (MPR)
CNLA	Chin National Liberation Army (Myanmar)
CO	Commanding Officer (of an Army Unit) also, OC)
Col	Colonel
COMOA	Coordination Committee for Minorities of Assam
CPI	Communist Party of India
CPI (M)	Communist Party of India (Maoist)
CPI (ML)	Communist Party of India (Marxist-Leninist)
CPM	Communist Party (Marxist)
CRPF	Central Reserve Police Force

CRS	Congressional Research Service (USA)
d	Inactive, and perhaps, defunct
DEA	Drug Enforcement Administration (USA)
DEM	Dukhtran-e-Millat (J & K)
DGFI	Director General Field Intelligence (Bangladesh)
DHD	Dima Halam Daogah (Asm)
DoD	Department of Defence (USA)
DoS	Department of State (USA)
EAM	External Affairs Minister
EC	Election Commission
Ed/ed	Edited, Edition
EM	Executive Member (of the ADC)
Encyclopaedia	All references in this book are to the *Encyclopaedia Britannica,* 15th Edition, 1984
Epigraphia	*Epigraphia Indica*
Exp	Indian Express
FALN	Fuerzas Armadas de Liberacion National (Venezuela)
FAR	Fuerzas Armadas Rebeldes (Guatemala)
FATA	Federally Administered Tribal Areas (In popular imagination, these areas in Pakistan's NWFP are self-governing)
FLN	National Liberation Front (of Algeria)
FPC	Foreign Political Consultations (British Indian Records/ correspondence with foreign countries)
Gen	General
GOC	General Officer Commanding (of an Army 'division' or a 'corps')
GOC-in-C	General Officer Commanding-in-chief (of an Army 'Command')
GoI	Government of India
GR	Gurkha Rifles
GWOT	Global War on Terrorism
HAJC	Hamin Al Jihad Commandos
HALC	Hynniewtrip A'chik Liberation Council (Megh)
HEI	Hizb-e-Islami (Gulbuddin Hekmat Yar's outfit in Afghanistan)
Hizb	Hizbullah
HKEI	Harkat-e-Islami

HKMN	Harkat-ul-Musalmeen
HM	Hizb-ul-Mujahideen
HMM	Hizb-ul-Momineen
HNLC	Hinniewtrip National Liberation Council (Megh)
HPC	Hmar People's Convention (MPR, MR)
HT	Hindustan Times
HUA	Harkat-ul-Ansar
HUJ	Harkat-ul-Jehad
HUJI (B)	Harkat-ul-Jihad-al-Islami (Bangladesh)
HUM	Harkat-ul-Mujahideen
HUT	Hizb-ul-Tehrir
HVC	Hmar Volunteer Council (MR)
IAEA	International Atomic Energy Agency
IAS	Indian Administrative Service (successor service to ICS)
ICG	International Crisis Group (Belgium-based)
ICI TAP	International Criminal Investigation Training Assistance Programme (USA)
ICS	Indian Civil Service (predecessor service of the IAS)
IDP	Internally Displaced People
IDSA	Institute for Defence Studies and Analysis
IED	Improvised Explosive Device
IIC	India International Centre (New Delhi)
IISS	International Institute of Strategic Studies
IJ	Islami Jung; also Islamic Jehad
IJET	Islami Jamaat-e-Tulba
IKL[d]	Ireiba Kanba Lup
Ikhwan	A counter-insurgency outfit in J & K, mostly of former militants and supported by the State Government. Its best known face and chief was Kuka Parrey
ILAA	Islamic Liberation Army of Assam
IMU	Islamic Movement of Uzbekistan
IOJ	Islamic Oikya Jote
IPC	Indian Penal Code
IRB	India Reserve Battalion
IRF	Islamic Resistance Force
IRP	Islamic Resistance Party
ISAF	International Security Assistance Force (Afghanistan)

ISFI	Islamic Security Force of India
ISI	Inter-Service Intelligence
ISL	(International) Islamic Students League
ISS	Islamic Sevak Sangh
ISYF	International Sikh Youth Federation
IUM	Ikhwan-ul-Musalmeen
JAH/JAEH	Jamaat-e-Ahl-e-Hadis (J & K)
JAKLI	Jammu and Kashmir Light Infantry
JEH	Jamaat-e-Hamdania
JEI	Jamaat-e-Islami
JEI (A)	Jamaat-e-Islami, Assam
JEM	Jaish-e-Mohammad
JHU	Jathika Hela Urumaya (Sri Lanka)
JKIF	Jammu and Kashmir Islamic Front
JKJEI	Jammu and Kashmir Jmmat-e-Islami
JKLF	Jammu and Kashmir Liberation Front
JKLT	Jammu and Kashmir Liberation Tigers
JKML	Jammu and Kashmir Muslim League
JKMLA	Jammu and Kashmir Muslim Liberation Army
JKPL	Jammu and Kashmir People's League
JKPL (R)	JKPL (Rehmani)
JKPL (S)	JKPL (Shabir) or (S. Hamid)
JKPPF	Jammu and Kashmir People's Political Forum
JKSF	Jammu and Kashmir Students Federation
JKSLF	Jammu and Kashmir Students Liberation Front
JKUPL	Jammu and Kashmir United People's League
JMB	Jamaat-ul-Mujahideen (Bangladesh)
JMJB	Jagruti Muslim Janata (Bangladesh)
JS	Joint Secretary
JUD	Jamaat-ul-Dawa
JUI/JUUI	Jamaat-ul-Ulemah-e-Islami
JUIH	Jamaat-ul-Islam-e-Hind
JUM	Jamaat-ul-Mujahideen
JUMA	Jamaat-ul-Mujahideen Almi
JUUI	Jamaat-ul-Ulamah-e-Islami (Pakistan)
KAB	Kashmir Awareness Bureau
KAC	Kashmir Action Committee

KAF	Kashmir Army Force
KBA	Kashmir Bar Association
KCF	Khalistan Commando Force
KCP	Kangleipak Communist Party
KDF	Kuki Defence Force
KDM	Kuki Democratic Movement
KFS	Kital Fi Sabilillah (= armed movement for Islam = Establishment of Islamic Rule)
KJC	Kashmir Jihad Committee (Pakistan)
KJF	Kashmir Jihad Force
KJHC	Kul Jamaat Hyrryat Conference (also, APHC)
KLC	Kashmir Liberation Cell
KLF	Kashmir Liberation Force
KLO[d]	Kangleipak Liberation Organisation
KLT	Kashmir Liberation Tigers
KNA	Kuki National Army
KNF	Kuki National Front
KNO	Kuki National Organisation
KNU	Karen National Union (Myanmar)
KNV	Karbi National Volunteers (Assam)
KRPC	Kom Rem People's Convention (MPR)
KSF	Kuki Security Force (MPR)
KYKL	Kanglei Yawol Kann Lup (MPR)
KZF	Khalistan Zindabad Force
LEJ	Lashkar-e-Jabbar
LET	Lashkar-e-Tayyaba
LITF	Liberation Islamic Tiger Force
LMG	Light Machine Gun
LOC	Line of Control
LSI	Linguistic Survey of India
Lt	Lieutenant
Lt Col	Lieutenant Colonel
Lt Gen	Lieutenant General
LTTE	Liberation Tigers of Tamil Elam
Maj	Major
Maj Gen	Major General
MBT	Main Battle Tank

MC	Muslim Conference
MDI	Markaz Dawa-ul-Irshad
MEA	Ministry of External Affairs
MeA	Mahaz-e-Azadi
MEI	Mujahideen-e-Islam
MG	Machine Gun
MHA	Ministry of Home Affairs
MIM	Majlis-e-Ittehad-ul-Musilmeen
MJAH	Markazi Jamaat-e-Ahal-e-Hadith
MJC	Muttehida Jihad Council (also UJC)
MJF	Muslim Janbaaz Force
MKM	Muslim Khwateen Markaz
MLA	Muslim Liberation Army
MLFA	Manipur Liberation Front Army
MLFA	Muslim Liberation Front of Assam
MLTA	Muslim Liberation Tiger of Assam
MM	Muslim Momineen
MM	Muslim Mujahideen
MMA	Muttehida Majlis-e-Amal
MMG	Medium Machine Gun
MNA/F[d]	Mizo National Army/Front
MOD	Ministry of Defence
Mohd	Mohammad/Mohammed
MoS	Memorandum of Settlement
MoU	Memorandum of Understanding
MR	Maritime Reconnaissance
MSA[d]	Meitei State Army (MPR)
MULFA	Muslim United Liberation Front of Assam
MULA	Meghalaya United Liberation Army
MULTA	Muslim United Liberation Tigers of Assam
MVF	Muslim Volunteer Force
n	Note/Notes

Muslim Terrorist Outfits in Assam

AS	COMOA		MULTA
HUJ	JEI (A)	MULFA	
ILAA			
HUM			
ISFI	LITF	MVF	
ISS	MLTA	SIMI	
	MLA	URPA	

NAM	Non-Aligned Movement
NC	National Conference
NDFB	National Democratic Front of Bodoland (ASM)
NECA[d]	North-Eastern Council Army (MPR)
NEHU	North-Eastern Hill University
NFG	(Also FNG) Naga Federal Government
NLFT	National Liberation Front of Tripura
NLG	Nagalim Guard (MPR)
NNC (A)	Naga National Council (Adino)
NNC (K)	NNC (Khodao)
NPC	Naga People's Council
NSA	National Security Adviser
NSC	National Security Council
NSCN (I-M)	National Socialist Council of Nagaland (Isaac-Muivah)
NSCN (K)	NSCN (Khaplang)
NWFP	North-West Frontier Province (Pakistan)
OC	Officer Commanding (also, CO)
NIC	Organisation of Islamic Conference
Op	Bluestar Operation Bluestar
PC	People's Conference
PCC(I)	Pradesh Congress Committee (Indira)
PEI	Pasban-e-Islam
PFLP	Popular Front for Liberation of Palestine
PISCES	Personal Identification Security, Comparison and Evaluation System (US)
PLA	People's Liberation Army (MPR)
PLO	Palestinian Liberation Organisation
POK	Pakistan-Occupied Kashmir (To Pakistanis, it is Azad Kashmir)
PPT	Pir Panjal Tigers
PRA[d]	People's Republican Army
PRE PAK	People's Revolutionary Party of Kangeipak (MPR)
PS	Police Station
PULF	People's United Liberation Front
QMC	Quranic Muttehida Council
R	Reprint (of a book, with the year)
RBA	Royal Bhutanese Army

RDX	Research Department Explosives. RDX, in fact, is the popular name for cyclotrimethyle netri nitromine compound.
RGM	Revolutionary Government of Manipur
RJC	Revolutionary Joint Committee
RL	Rocket Launcher
RPF	Revolutionary People's Front
RPFK[d]	Revolutionary People's Front Kangleipak (MPR)
RPG	Rocket-propelled Grenade
RSF	Rabha Security Force
SAARC	South Asian Association for Regional Cooperation
SAIR	South Asia Intelligence Review
SC	Scheduled Castes
SEJ	Shora-e-Jihad
SF	Security Forces
SICC	Somalia Islamic Courts Council
SIG	Special Investigation Group
3 Sikh	3rd Battalion of the Sikh Regiment
SIMI	Students Islamic Movement of India
SLFP	Sri Lanka Freedom Party
SLI	Sikh Light Infantry
SOG	Special Operations Group (of J & K Police)
SP	Superintendent of Police
SSF[d]	Special Sacrifice Force (Kuki) (MPR)
S/S capt	Self-styled Captain
ST	Scheduled Tribes
TADA	Terrorist and Disruptive Activities Act
TEHK	Tehrik-e-Hurryat Kashmir
TEJ	Tehrik-e-Jihad
TEJI	Tehrik-e-Jihad Islami

Terrorist Outfits: Arunachal Pradesh

ULAA	ULVA
ULMA	UPVA

Terrorist Outfits: Assam

BdSF	NDFB
BLT/F	ULFA
DHD	
KNV	UPDS

Terrorist Outfits: Manipur

CKRF	KYKL	RJC
HPC	MLFA	RPF
IKC[d]	MSA[d]	RPFK[d]
KCP	NECA[d]	SSF[d]
KDF	NLG	SSF[d]
KDM	NSCN (I-M)	THADC[d]
KDM	NSCN (K)	UILA[d]
KLO[d]	PLA	UNLF
KNA	PRA[d]	VNO[d]
KNF	PRE PAK	ZRA
KNO	PULF	ZRO
KRPC	RGM	ZRV
KSF		

Terrorist Outfits: Meghalaya

ANVC
HALC
HNLC
MULA

Terrorist Outfits: Mizoram

BNLF	HVC
HPC	MNA/MNF[d]

Terrorist Outfits: Nagaland

NSCN (I-M)	NNC (A)
NSCN (K)	NNC (K)
NFG	
(Also, FNG)	

Terrorist Outfits: Tripura

ATTF
NLFT
TNV
TUJS

THADC[d]	Thangjing Hill Area Defence Council
TMK	Tchrik-e-Mazahmat Kashmir
TNFJ	Tehrik Nifwa Fiqa Jaffaria
TNRF	Tiwa National Revolutionary Front
TNV	Tripura National Volunteers

TOI	Times of India
Trans	Translated, Translation
TUJS	Tripura Upjati Juba Samiti
TUM	Tehrik-ul-Mijahideen
UBGL	Under Barrel Grenade Launcher
UILA[d]	United Islamic Liberation Army (Asm)
UILAA	United Islamic Liberation Army of Assam
UJC	United Jihad Council (also, MJC)
ULAA	United Liberation Army of Arunachal
ULFA	United Liberation Front of Assam
ULFSS	United Liberation Front of Seven Sisters
ULMA	United Liberation Movement of Arunachal
ULVA	United Liberation Volunteers of Arunachal
UMFA	United Minorities Front of Assam (Islamic)
UNHCR	United Nations High Commissioner for Refugees
UNIMOG	United Nations International Military Observers Group (in J. and K.)
UNLF	United National Liberation Front (MPR)
UNO	United Nations Organisation
UNP	United National Party (Sri Lanka)
UPDS	United People's Democractic Solidarity (ASM) (The DHD, KNV and UPDS are mainly active in the two Hill districts of Assam)
UPI	United Press International
URPA	United Refermation Protest of Assam
UPVA	United People's Volunteers of Arunachal
USI	United Service Institution (of India)
VDC	Village Defence Committee (J & K)
VNO[d]	Vaiphei National Organisation
WKFM	World Kashmir Freedom Movement
WMD	Weapons of Mass Destruction
ZRA	Zomi Revolutionary Army (MPR)
ZRO	Zomi Re-unification Organisation (MPR)
ZRV	Zomi Revolutionary Volunteers

ABBREVIATIONS SPECIFIC TO THIS BOOK ONLY

Newspapers

AA	Asian Age
HT	Hindustan Times

Ind Exp	Indian Express	
TOI	Times of India	

North-Eastern States

	ArP	Arunachal Pradesh
	Asm	Assam
	Megh	Meghalaya
	MPR	Manipur
	MR	Mizoram
	NL	Nagaland
	TPR	Tripura
PS	Police Station	
SF	Security Forces	

1

Insurgency/Terrorism in India's North-East: A Quagmire or an Opportunity

The insurgency in Kashmir (more correctly, in Jammu and Kashmir) occupies centre-stage in most of the security related studies concerning India, amongst strategic community both at home and abroad. This could be due to a variety of reasons: strategic importance of the region, involvement of Islamist terrorists from several countries; its impinging on India-Pakistan relations; and its concurrent spill-over into India's other regions, posing a serious threat to its stability. All these factors notwithstanding, what is generally not realised by most countries is that India also continues to face major security challenges in its North-East Region.

Some of the seven states in the region have faced a series of insurgencies since India's Independence. In fact, all the seven states presently are facing one or more insurgent movements within their borders. In some ways, these insurgent movements and homeland demands may prove even more intractable problem (compared to Kashmir's). Given the extremely complex political and social environment, river by sharp ethnic rivalries and aspirations, the competing political demands with the ostensible aims of preserving their individual identities, the sheer number of insurgent groups (over a hundred, according to the South Asia Terrorism portal), each with different agendas and inter-linkages of these groups, is proving to be a challenging task for the security establishment of India. Even more curiously, the counter-insurgency operations in the North-Eastern region have always suffered due to happenings in other parts of the country : be it the 1971 Indo-Pak War, 1989 Punjab insurgency; or the subsequent worsening insurgency situation in Jammu and Kashmir, and 1999 Kargil operations. Much needed troops engaged in counter-insurgency tasks in the North-East are shifted/removed to deal with security threats in other regions.

Observers have noted that there does not seem to have been any consistent application and continuation of counter-terrorism measures in the

North-East, with a result that the insurgent outfits in the region have expectedly taken the maximum advantage of this situation and have succeeded to spread their tentacles in all the seven states, as stated above through an effective network/linkages.

India's North-East, located in the extreme north-eastern corner of the Sub-continent, shares international frontiers on its North, East and South with four nations—Bhutan, China (Tibet), Myanmar and Bangladesh and is connected to the rest of the country on its west through the 28 km Siliguri panhandle. It lies, geographically, between 22° and 29° North Latitudes and between 89° 46′, and 97° 5′ East Longitudes. In political terms, the region comprises of 7 States of the Indian Union, popularly and affectionately called "Seven Sisters".

Essential statistical information about these seven states is contained in the table below :

North-East's Seven Sisters : Comparative Figures

		Population			*Area*		
S. No.	*Name of State /Entity*	*2001*	*Rank in*		*Sq km*	*Rank in*	
			North-East	*India*		*North-East*	*India*
1.	Arunachal Pradesh	1,097,968	6	24	83,743	1	13
2.	Assam	26,655,528	1	13	78,438	2	14
3.	Meghalaya	2,318,822	3	20	22,429	3	19
4.	Manipur	2,166,788	4	21	22,327	4	20
5.	Mizoram	888,573	7	26	21,081	5	21
6.	Nagaland	1,990,036	5	22	16,539	6	22
7.	Tripura	3,199,203	2	19	10,486	7	23
8.	North-East	38,495,089	2.69 per cent of India's	—	255,088	7.75 per cent of India's	—
9.	India	1,027,015,247	—	—	3,287,263	—	—

The region has external borders with Bangladesh (4096 km, including 2216 km between West Bengal and Bangladesh), Myanmar (1643 km), Tibet (1035 km), and Bhutan (515 km).

The North-East was always remote and distant. It forced its way into national consciousness when some of its more vigorous and restless ethnic groups refused to be part of the celebrations when India gained her Independence in 1947. The first daunting task the hastily-divided fledgling armies of two nascent nations handled was the supervision of 7-8 million people who crossed the newly-created borders in either directions. Perhaps 200,000 of these did not complete the journey, slain on the way by the frenzied partisans. The Indian Army was still strong on the borders as also stretched in internal security duties when it was called upon to fight the Pak invasion in Kashmir under the facade of tribal incursion. With cease-fire signed on 1 January 1949, it looked forward to a well-deserved interregnum for rest, refit and reorganisation. It was not willed that way, because not long after that, the tribal upsurge in the North-East demanded Army's deployment there early 1950s. If the external aggression fomented the troubles in Kashmir, the internal dissonance was behind the eruption in the North-East. Thus it was that men in uniform came into close contact with the region. "But to a common Indian, the North-East had a romantic ring about it; it was a rainbow country, extraordinarily diverse, colourful and mysterious"; and to the well-read and the cloistered academia, it was a troublesome frontier for all too many and a strange land where the 'wild tribes' still ruled the roost. But this was the picture soon after Independence. Thus it was not a happy augury to begin with. The nation had to send troops to cool some hot heads in the region. But that was unavoidable for the process of nation-building. But today, the picture is vastly changed, compared to those turbulent days. The region is on the march; even if the insurgency continues, it is much reduced in extent and virulence, barring perhaps in the case of Bodo insurgents. The change is discernible.

From this general, broad brush picture of India around the time of 1947 Independence, we move to the specifics of the region, known as India's North-East, starting with the number of terrorist organisations in the region.

Terrorist/Insurgent Outfits in North-East : Nov. 2006

The table below has the detailed information :

Terrorist Groups in North-Eastern States : Nov. 2006

States	*Number of terrorist, insurgent and extremist groups*
Assam	36
Manipur	39
Meghalaya	4
Nagaland	3
Tripura	30
Mizoram	2
Arunachal Pradesh	1

Source : *Frontline*, 15 Dec. 2006.

General

Few countries can claim to have faced problems of secessionism and insurgency as serious as those of India. She faced such problems right at its birth in 1947 in Hyderabad and in Naga Hills. Soon after that, the state faced the problem in the then Madras Province and Telengana. In the succeeding decades surfaced insurgency, terrorism, and militancy problems in the Mizo hills, Kashmir, Assam and Punjab. Before launching into specific details of the issue under discussion, it will be useful to view it in contemporaneous perspective. The immediate instrument available to the state at that point in time to combat those disruptive forces was the Indian Army. But the nation and Army then had no model to look up to, no precedent to follow, and no locus classicus to study and learn from. The most recent example was that of the British Army fighting Malayan insurgency. But that was a case of a colonial army dealing with a subject people and its harsh paradigm could not have been an apt model to be followed by a democratic disposition dealing with its own citizens. The goal was clear, but to reach it, the army had to work its own devices and determine its own parameters of operations against the insurgents. So was the National Government required to undertake on-the-job-training exercise. But first a focus on the area we are concerned with and its situation.

The North-Eastern region of India is strategically located. It has immense regional geopolitical significance. This importance stems from the fact that it is the eastern part of a region that is dominated by the head-waters of some major rivers like the Hwang Ho, Yangzekiang, Sinkiang, Irrawaddy and the Brahmaputra. A rough and fractured topography dominated by dense forests, its accessibility conditions are very limited. It is inhabited by large number of tribes, some well-known, others not so. Most of the tribes are known to history for their antagonism towards the established central authority and on several occasions have asserted their autonomy and independence. The 19th century political circumstances brought them under administrative control of major powers, consequently dividing them politically.

Post-1947, in keeping with their traditions, some tribes took recourse to violent means to express dissent. Thus in the first three decades or so of India's independence, the North-East was characterised by socio-political instability and economic backwardness. But New Delhi's policy of winning them over through politico-military means has been seen to be succeeding. Liberal economic packages also are helping the region to come out of its isolationist attitudes.

It is to be noted that the extension of administration and its systemization in the region was a post-Independence phenomenon. Even this spread was viewed suspiciously by certain extremist elements, and condemned as an interference in the social, political and economic mores of their tribes.

In spite of the sustained and sincere endeavour, India has not solved the problem of violence fully. Though some tribes have come round and settled to democratic ways within India, some others are still carrying out their movements. The Chapter examines the course of insurgency in the Region and its present status.

The Genesis and Causes of Insurgency

The roots of emergency in the Region goes back to pre-independence days. The British deemed it prudent not to bring the tribes under a strict regime of political control and rigid regulations. Their tribal policy and Christian education and influence were also believed to have queered the pitch for Independent India. But cutting back to Simon Commission days, the clamour for autonomy that greeted it during its visit to the Region in January 1929 should not have been a surprise to the cognoscente. 27 memoranda were presented to it at Shillong by various groups, including the (1) Bodos and other Plains tribals, (2) Goalpara groups, (3) Kacharis, (4) Naga Club of Kohima, (5) Nagas of Mokokchung, (6) Khasi National Durbar, (7) Representatives of Khasi and Jaintia Hills. Dr J.H. Hutton, long-serving Deputy Commissioner of Naga Hills District and author of several authoritative books on the tribes, submitted a memorandum on behalf of the Assam Government, which pithily demanded: "The Hills should not be tied politically to the advanced plains." The Naga Club went a step further, telling the Commission: "Just leave us alone!" Indians blame the Hutton ancestors and their ilk for sowing seeds of separation among the tribes. Expectedly, the Nagas refused to be a part of India on 15 August 1947, declaring their own independence on the preceding day; refused to accept an ADC under Schedule Six; and were the first to raise the flag of insurrection early 1950s. Government of India acted wisely by granting autonomy to many ethnic communities who perceived their ethnic and cultural identities threatened by a mega-identity called India, and thus doused some potential conflagrations. But Assamese political class displayed certain insensitivity towards the ethnic insecurities and sensibilities of the tribal minorities. Some inconsiderate measures—the Official Language Bill of 1960 foremost among them—aggravated those fears. The Mizos went the Naga way a decade later, the two posing the most serious challenge to India's integrity till date. The others were to follow in due course.

At another level, rising aspirations of the people did not match up with the pace of economic development, and the consequent frustrations fuelled the discontent. Administrative apathy and economic dominance of up-country businessmen (particularly in Assam) was the right breeding ground for the growth of militancy.

Justice for the Tribes Still Awaited

Ideologically inclined scholars assert that the rights of the tribals have been curtailed, even taken away in some cases, by the demands of progress of the modern society.

1993 was observed as the "International Year of the Indigenous People". Their plight was highlighted in 1992 during the 500th Anniversary of Columbus' voyage of discovery and colonisation. As an angry activist put it: "....Apart from a couple of national tribal conventions, the 70-million tribal community in India, the largest indigenous population in the world, has little to look back on."

"The tribals are yet to secure their full rights", feel the sympathetic activists. The origin of the conflict between the tribals and the State can be traced to the colonial times. "The advent of the British brought about major changes in the pattern of resource use as the natural wealth of India became cheap raw material for British industry." The setting up of "Reserved Forests" led to the loss of tribals' control over natural resources. The "Rights and Privileges" of the tribals under the Forest Act of 1927 were further reduced to "Rights and Concessions" by the Forest Policy of 1952. So the Governments, whether of British India or of Independent India, have always encroached on the rights, lands, and forests of the tribals, nay, on their very lives. The National Commission on Agriculture suggested in 1976 that these rights should be abolished. The latest Forest Policy promulgated in December 1988 retained the concept of exclusive state ownership of forests. While industrial requirements were termed "national needs" in the new policy, the rights of the tribals and other forest dwellers were reduced to "people's needs", rendering the tribals encroachers in their own habitat. The crisis has been acknowledged by the 29th Report of the Commission for Scheduled Castes and Scheduled Tribes.

The resolution[1] adopted by the Indian Confederation of Indigenous and Tribal Peoples during the International Year celebrations in New Delhi admirably sums up the Tribal psyche:

> "We do not want to be museum pieces for the enjoyment of the tourists. Efforts are made to integrate us, who have lived in an egalitarian and classless society, into the mainstream as a low caste. Our culture is looked down upon and the dominant culture with its caste-based inequalities is imposed upon us."

The above is a good picture of unjust treatment meted out to the tribals by their "civilised" brethren. Now a word on "civilised" and "uncivilised" people. It was natural for European officers and scholars to describe these "unkempt and unwashed" tribals living in the remote and isolated hills as "uncivilised" or "less civilised". The use of such terms must have pained Dr Elwin in his lifetime for he considered the tribals as much, if not more, civilised as the so-called "civilised". It is therefore no surprise that Guha's recent book on his life[2] has been aptly titled "Savaging the Civilised", which accurately sums up Elwin's ideas and philosophy on the tribal people. But Elwin's understanding and empathy for the tribals had distinguished ancestry. Jean Jacques Rousseau (1712-78) was the first to apply the much-celebrated and much-used phrase, "noble savage" to the tribal.

It is Universal Truth that in the newly-emerging nations, the tribal populations are adversely affected by Government-initiated internal migration, presence of bureaucracy and SF. The reasons for insurgency were a combination of ethno-cultural factors, faulty nation-building strategies, and an inappropriate development approach/path. All these factors generally reduce the tribals to "a hopeless minority not only in religio-cultural terms but also in the power structures at the Centre and States".

In India's North-East, insurgency is an ethno-cultural phenomenon, in the sense that perceiving their ethnic identity threatened, they seek political power to preserve it and then develop their lands by their own genius. So, the insurgency is a political war, and it is amenable to political solutions only. Initially, State power is essential to convince the insurgents that their unlawful violence would not pay. It is only then that they come to the conference table for a political dialogue.

Ethnicity and Tribal Revolts/Movements

There was an unprecedented world-wide upsurge of ethnicity in the 1970s and 1980s. Ethnicity and autonomy movements are closely inter-connected. Political anthropology was born as a branch of social and cultural anthropology only when Fortes and Evens-Pritchard published their classic paper on the African political system as a part of synchronic studies in 1940. Social and political movements can be described as collective action by people either to promote or resist a change. Many Indians look askance at the spate of tribal revolts and movements in the North-East, particularly the one with secessionist overtone, taking them to be unique phenomena. This obviously is a misperception, flowing from ignorance. V. Raghavaiah chronologically listed as many as 70 tribal insurgencies during 1878-1971 period in his "Tribal Revolts" (Nellore, 1971). Again, "Man in India", 125(4) of December 1945, had four papers on various tribal movements. But what is noteworthy is that both these references dealt with the tribal revolts in Central and East India, and not in the North-East; essentially because there was no information available on the latter. It is a fact thus, that very few studies were conducted on the subject in the North-East during the pre-Independence period. Perhaps earliest such studies were by Stephen Fuch whose "Kabui", 1965 is a rather sketchy study and by Gautam Bhadra in 1975, who contributed a valuable paper *"The Kuki Uprising (1917-19): Its Causes and Nature"* in "Man in India", 55(1), January-March, 1975. Before giving details of various other post-1947 studies on the Tribal Revolts in the North-East, a brief look at the tribal situation there and the attendant causes that gave rise to these movements should be of interest.

Many tribes living on the international boundaries acted as bridge or buffer communities and shared cultural and ethnic affinities with tribesmen across the frontier until the advent of colonialism. The situation underwent a sea change with the British take over of Assam in 1820s. Not only was the cross-border intercourse discouraged as a result of the Yandabo Treaty, even the Hills-Plains contacts got regulated through policy measures like the Inner Line Regulation II of 1880. What was even worse was the designation of most of the hill areas as "Backward" under the 1919 Act and then as "Excluded Areas" under the 1935 Act. Intended or otherwise, these measures broadened the gap between the Hill and the plains people. The spread of education and activities of Christian missionaries were largely held responsible for awakening of the people regarding their individual and ethnic identities, or "nationality consciousness". The growth of nationality consciousness among different communities inspired several movements. Even the introduction of money economy to replace traditionally self-sufficient economy of the tribes "proved disastrous as it shattered the very basis of the tribal society in the long run, since it was not at the same time accommodated in the modern economic system".

The pre-Independence revolts, in the main, revolved round the land: land alienation, usury, forced labour, minimum wages, land grabbing, etc. The tribal resentment forced them into violence and protest movements. The influx of non-tribals and advancing tea plantations made the situation intolerable. It needs to be understood in these circumstances that the occasional tribal raids on the plains men were not always actuated by rapine and blood thirst. So it was not surprising that during the British rule, several tribes launched movements demanding autonomy to manage their own affairs, since they were convinced that the alien administration and the outsiders were ruining their culture and economy.

Because there are meagre studies on the subject of Tribal Movements in the North-East, it would be misleading to conclude that there were none before 1947. If that was the case, why did they invite repeated punitive expeditions? The movements might not have been well-led and well-organised, but they were very much there, resisting every British advance into their lands in any form. Besides ethnicity, language became an important divisive issue to start and sustain a movement in the post-1947 India. The demands for secession and autonomy in India's North-East gained geopolitical dimensions because of creation of (East) Pakistan in its neighbourhood. Some of the studies carried out on the post-Independence Tribal Movements are detailed in the table below for the interested readers to make his pick and for a concerned scholar to launch on a comprehensive study on the subject.

Tribal Movements in the North-East

	Author	*Year*	*Title*
1.	Anand, V.K.	1980	"Conflict in Nagaland." Analyses reasons for the conflict, and found psychological factors in geo-political context to be mainly responsible for it. The insurgency acted as an effective instrument to fulfil their demand.
2.	Bhattacharjee, S.R.	1989	"Tribal Insurgency in Tripura." Various aspects of the subject discussed in the book are listed below: 1. Inequality of economic opportunities and matters economic. 2. Sharing of political rights. 3. Changing demographic profile, with the percentage of tribal population falling in each successive count. 4. Urbanization. 5. Immigration. 6. Land alienation. 7. Cultural and political domination by non-tribals.
3.	Bhattacharjee, Suchintya, R.	1990	"Genesis of Tribal Extremism in Tripura."
4.	Bhuyan, P.C. (ed)	1989	"Political Development of the North-East." It has 17 papers of which 5 deal with tribal movements for autonomy in Assam.
5.	Bhuyan, S.K. (ed)	1951	"Kachari Buranji" (in Assamese), Second Edition. Deals with Kacharis, a branch of Bodo race, under the following heads:

Author	Year	Title
		1. Legend on origin of Kacharis. 2. Their Kings and Kingdoms. 3. Comprehensive history of Ahom-Kachari relations from end of the 14th century upto the beginning of the 18th. The work is an important reference on the Kacharis.
6. Chaube, S.K.	1973	"Hill Politics in North-East India." It points out major factors and root causes behind the political turmoil in the North-East, as listed below: 1. Concept of nationalism that partially ignored the smaller identities. 2. Territorial boundaries that criss-crossed the ethnic consolidations. 3. Process of industrialization, unconcerned with or unmindful of the traditional tribal economy. Though the subject was essentially political, yet, the historical, geographical, and sociological aspects were given due importance.
7. Chatterjee, Suniti Kumar	1974	"Kirata Jina-Krti" (Second Edition). It is a profound work in the Indo-Mongoloid tribe, the Kiratas. It focuses on Kiratas in general and particularly on their presence in the North-East.
8. Daimary, V.K.	1986	"Boro Movement since Independence." (M. Phil Dissertation, North-East Hill University, History Department, 1986. Unpublished.)

	Author	*Year*	*Title*
			A useful study on Bodo demand for a separate state, though limited in its approach and contents.
9.	Datta, P.S. (ed)	1990	"Ethnic Movements in Poly-cultural Assam." It has four papers, three of which deal with the people of Mongoloid origin and question of identity crisis. Its strength lies in its emphasis on ethnic connotation inherent in their movements which has not as yet been analysed adequately.
10.	Datta-Ray, B.	1989	"Tribal Identity and Tension in North-East India."
11.	Endle, S.	1975	"The Kacharis". A monograph that comprehensively details the social and domestic life of the Bodos.
12.	Goswami, B.B.	1979	"Encyclopaedia of Social Sciences (Vols. 11 and 12) The Mizo Unrest."
13.	Guha, U.C.	1971	"Kacharer Itihritta" (in Bengali). It is an indispensable source book for Cachar and Kacharis.
14.	Misra, Udayan	1988	"North-East India: Quest for Identity." It deals with contemporary development in North-East in two parts. Part 1: Nagaland question and typology of Naga nationalism. Part 2: Assamese national question.
15.	Nag, A.K.	1984	"Mizo Dilemma." It draws attention to certain issues raised by the growing ethnic aspirations and how they pose a threat to national integration. It also focused on the role of the Church in the imbroglio.

	Author	Year	Title
16.	Narzi, Bhaben	1985	"Bodo-Kachari Samaj Aru Sanskriti" (in Assamese). An admirable work on social life and culture of Bodos. The demand for a separate state to secure an independent entity for Bodos has received little attention from professional researchers.
17.	Nibedan, Nirmal	1981	"North-East India: The Ethnic Explosion." It dilates on the ethnic and nativistic aspects and factors behind the explosive situation.
18.	Paul, M.C.	1989	"Dimensions of Tribal Movements in India: A Study of Udayachal in Assam Valley." It attempted to interpret the theoretical framework of the demand for a small state.
19.	Sanyal, C.C.	1973	"The Meches and Totos of North Bengal." Monographs on two sub-Himalayan tribes, believed to belong originally to great Tibeto-Burman Bodo race. The two are much influenced by the Assamese and Bengali cultures and are now making desperate effort to preserve their linguistic and cultural identity.
20.	Sarin, H.K.	1980	"Insurgency in North-East India: A Study of Sino-American Role." It studies the role played by these two foreign countries. The North-East will continue to remain vulnerable to foreign pulls and pressures because of its geography. The fire of insurgency first lit in Nagaland spread to other states in the area and the consequent unrest provides excellent opportunities to other nations to strike fires of

	Author	*Year*	*Title*
			conspiracies against India on its own soil. The author seems to have overlooked facts and feelings that led the people into revolt in the first place. The outsiders can at the best only stroke the fire, not create it. A similar study was carried out by V.I.K. Sarin also.
21.	Sarin, V.I.K.	1980	"India's North-East in Flame." The book stresses the geo-political importance of the region and clearly states that transition from traditional barter economy to modern economy created an upheaval in the tribal societies. The issue of immigration was examined with its consequent ill effects on the tribals, including their alienation from land. "Some groups chose path of insurgency with help from foreign powers." The author gives an outline of counter-productive efforts made by the Government of India to resolve the ethnic problems that further whipped up the parochial sentiments.
22.	Singh, G.P.	1990	"The Kiratas in Ancient India." It is an admirable attempt to study this ancient tribe, widely spread in North and North-East India. They reputedly lived in the Mahabharata period. The author relies on the historical, anthropological and archaeological data to exhaustively deal with the origin, antiquity, identification, and expansion of the Kiratas in ancient India.
23.	Singh, K.S. (ed)	1983	"Tribal Movements in India." Volume I covered all tribal movements in the North-East region, except the Kuki uprising, concentrating on the movements in post-Independence period.

	Author	Year	Title
24.	Singh, N.J.	1992	"Social Movement in Manipur, 1917-51." The author draws a conceptual framework of social movements and avers that the Kuki Rebellion (1917-19) and Zeliangrong movements (1930-32) were two of the foremost and well-organised anti-imperialist and anti-feudal tribal Movements.

These studies on different tribal movements in North-East India reveal broadly similar causes/factors responsible for these Movements, even if they seem to differ by nature and in matter of details.

In view of what has been described above, the causes of tribal unrest and consequent militancy/insurgency are easily understandable. The insurgency thrives when ethnic minorities see a threat to their identity from a "brute" majority. This threat could be perceived in cultural, economic, or political spheres. The perception is compounded if it is combined with a feeling of being neglected or discriminated against. Even imaginary discrimination can be exploited in the cause of insurgency through skilful propaganda. Lack of good governance, economic deprivation and large scale unemployment can be cited to support the neglect, and discrimination theory. If a hostile neighbour extends moral and material support to an insurgency, it can greatly strengthen it and prolong its life, if not ensure its success which would largely depend upon the quality of its leadership—steadfast and dedicated—and popular support.

A charismatic leader, of course, is a *sine qua non* for the success of an insurgent movement. Che Guvera's is one of the finest examples of such leadership in 20th century. In their own way, Phizo and Laldenga could be said to belong to this category.

The causes of the unrest may differ, but the process is similar. Some analysts feel that in one form or other, it is a reaction to the homogenizing state and control over livelihood. When the external control results in less land and fewer jobs, they are then reduced to fight among themselves, e.g., the NSCN factions, Nagas and Kukis, Bodos and Adivasis, *et al.*

Two Experts Speak Out

Two Indians' testimonials, who have dealt with the insurgency situations in their times, should be of interest. First, Lt. Gen. VK Nayyar, who while in service commanded Army formations engaged in active counter-insurgency operations in the North-East and after retirement was Governor of Manipur in the 1990s and resigned, nearly accusing his Chief Minister of collusion with the insurgents, says rather bluntly: "The problem here is about social, economic, ethnic and political deprivation. These people are not anti-India, only anti-establishment. They have been exploited by wily politicians in league with the rebels, and sense of alienation has deepened.... The money for development never reached the target villages. The corrupt politicians divert the public money to insurgents to buy security...." Now Ved Marwah, a distinguished policeman who served as IGP Mizoram during its worst phase of insurgency, speaking in 1999: "Things are worse than ever before as recent killings and blasts show. The NSCN and ULFA are never short of the recruits as educated youth is swelling their ranks.... All this coupled with infiltration from Bangladesh, drugs, role of the ISI, has complicated the problems." Then he gives some instances of display of insensitivity and ignorance about the Region: "Prime Minister Desai reprimanded the Mizo officials and lectured them about the naturopathy when they asked for more hospitals. It all ended in bruised egos. Expectedly, he was given a cool send-off. His Home Minister, Charan Singh, once asked a Chief Minister from the Region the name of the capital of his State...." Even Nehru seems to have gone amiss in the sensitivity stakes. To wit, here is what the former Nagaland Chief Minister Vamuzo says: "In 1953, Nagas turned their backs on Nehru after he refused to meet them.... This alienated common Nagas."

Role of Middle Class

Main feature of style of middle class politics is characterised by certain universalist ethos. The fact of being middle class becomes far more important in shaping the style of its politics than anything else (like its being affiliated to a particular ethnic group). Viewed in this light, the middle class politics the world over is seen to cut across the particularistic ethnic affiliations and loyalties.

But that does not seem to be the case in India, and more so in its North-East. Here, the middle class politics does not seem to be infused with such a universalist ethos, not in the long run in any case. Here the emergence of classes does not result in the obsolescence of ethnic communities. Thus in Assam, when we refer to a middle class, we invariably refer to an ethnically afflicted-middle class: an Assamese middle class, a Bodo middle class, and even a Bengali one at that. That ethnic difference there are so pronounced that they seem to be "at the root of separatism". So, it is not surprising that the middle class is not an homogenous entity here; it seems to be ethnically fragmented in character. The other striking feature of the middle class politics is its "movemental nature". The Assamese middle class is commonly designated as "agitationist" and sometimes, less charitably, as "xenophobic" (Das, A., 1991).[3] As per "recent studies, there are as many as 19 ethnic (10 in Assam itself) movements demanding further reorganisation (of Assam)" (Chattopadhyay, 1990). Obviously, the middle class ethos did not subsume various ethnic identities within its fold.

Rats are the Culprits

It is popularly believed that rats were responsible for the birth of the Mizo National Front (MNF), the progenitor of the Mizo insurgency. Mizoram experiences flowering of the bamboos (*Mautam*) once about every 40-50 years. The rats are known to multiply fast after feeding on these flowers. Subsequently, the armies of these rodents destroy the standing crops in the fields and then attack the granaries. This causes acute food shortage and famine. Mizoram experienced *Mautam* and consequent famine in 1957. It was Laldenga's Mizo Famine National Front (MFNF) that helped the suffering Mizos during those dark days. Subsequently, MFNF was converted into MFN by dropping one 'F' from it. The rest, as they say, is history. It took three decades of death and destruction before peace returned with the June 1986 Accord.

Scared of the *Mautam* and its consequences, Mizoram and Manipur had declared a war on the rats in March and April 1999. Mizoram Government had offered Re. 1 for each rodent tail. "Till 25 April 1999, 90,000 tails had been collected" (*Times of India,* 27-4-1999).

Insurgent Outfits in the North-East and their Aims

Every State in the Region has a number of insurgent groups, though not uniformly active. Some of them have been around for decades, others of more recent origins. Some may have been floated, as some hard-nosed journalists like to suggest, by Indian Intelligence, to encourage splits and create confusion. The table below is merely illustrative, based essentially on published sources.[4]

A new element in the murky politics of insurgency in Manipur is Kuki insurgency under an outfit called Kuki National Council (KNC) and its armed wing, the Kuki National Army (KNA) (both raised early 1990s), not to be confused with another KNA, acronym of a recognised regional party called the Kuki National Assembly. The KNC, which is engaged in bloody clashes with NSCN(I-M) is believed to be an ally of NSCN(K), a natural alliance, given the enmity between the two factions of the NSCN. Another Kuki-Chin outfit, called the Chin Liberation Front (CLF), which like the KNC is based both in Burma and Manipur, is believed to have links with the NSCN(I-M). The UNLF, the oldest insurgent groups in the valley, is formally a part of the IBRF[5] but supports closer coordination with all the insurgent groups. Other Valley-based insurgent groups like the RPF, the KCP, and PREPAK have close relations with the NSCN(I-M) but these must be viewed in the context of the complex relations between the Meiteis and the Nagas and the fact that the fulfilment of Naga Nationalist aspirations for Greater Nagaland, under any appellation, are predicated on the disintegration of the present geographical entity of Manipur—something no insurgent group in the valley can support.

Assam

Sl.No.	*Name*	*Abbreviation (Acronym)*	*Cadre Strength (2005-06)*
1	*2*	*3*	*4*
1.	**United Liberation Front of Assam** banned since 27 November 1990. Both ULFA and BdSF, which are closely linked to each other, also seek close links with all other insurgent groups. Indeed, ULFA is formally committed to the "Liberation" of the whole Region, not of merely Assam. But given the contradictions between and within the groups, the goal is highly unrealisable. The most lethal of the North-Eastern militant groups, and wild child of the Assam movement, ULFA is now linked to Islamist groups in Bangladesh. Over 5,000 have surrendered since 1992. Responsible for 15-8-2004 blast that killed 13 children. (Details in Chapter 19)	ULFA	1,600
2.	**National Democratic Front of Bodoland.** Some Intelligence report held it was formerly BdSF. Banned since 1992. Founded in October 1986 as Bodo Security Force (BdSF). It was renamed as NDFB in 1994. Responsible for the 2 and 5 October 2004 blasts that killed 60 people. Over 1,000 have surrendered since 1992. Demand: Sovereign state for Assam's Bodo people. (Details in Chapter 5)	NDFB	500

1	*2*	*3*	*4*
3.	**Bodo Security Force** Armed Wing of the NDFB (see Chapter 5).	BdSF	600
4.	**People's Democratic Front**	PDF	NA
5.	**Bodoland Liberation Tiger Force** (see Chapter 5) banned since 1997, but has declared ceasefire with the Government since early 2000.	BLTF/BLT	NA
6.	**Assam Tiger Force** Police claims it is ULFA's red herring.	ATF	?
7.	**Islamic Militant Outfits.** Police has dossiers on 25 such outfits, formed mostly by criminals and ISI-backed fanatics. Mainly based in Assam; some of them have tentacles reaching out to Nagaland, Mizoram, Manipur etc. 14 of them are named here:		
	1. Muslim United Liberation Tigers of Assam	MULTA	
	Believed to be backed by Pak ISI. It sends batches of young boys to Bangladesh for arms training. Circulates fake currency. **Strength:** Not known. **Demand:** Greater Islamic nation comprising the North-East and Bangladesh.		
	2. Muslim Volunteer Force	MVF	

1	2	3	4
	3. Islamic Revolutionary Force	IRF	
	4. Students Islamic Movement of India	SIMI	
	5. Indian United Liberation Army	IULA	
	6. Assam Minority Liberation Army	AMLA	
	7. Muslim United Liberation Front of Assam	MULFA	
	8. Muslim Liberation Front of Assam	MLFA	
	9. United Special Return Army of Assam	USRAA	
	10. Minority Liberation Tigers of Assam	MLTA	
	11. Tiger Liberation Front of Assam	TLFA	
	12. Islamic Revolutionary Army	IRA	
	13. Saddam Bahini	SB	
	14. Islamic Sevak Sangh	ISS	
8.	**Bengal Tiger Force.** It was floated to protect the Bengali Hindus who were targeted by ULFA and Bodo militants.	BTF	
9.	**Dima Halam Daogah.** Founded in December 1995, it has its origins in the now-defunct Dimasa National Security Force (DNSF). Espouses the national aspirations of Dimasa people. One of the two Hill Tribes of Assam (other being the Karbi, mainly in Karbi-Anglong District), Dimasas	DHD	

1	2	3	4
	are mainly concentrated in North Cachar. Its demand is Dimaland based on Dimapur and comprising of North Cachar Hills and other Dimasa areas of Assam and neighbouring States. It has links with NSCN(I-M) and is currently honouring cease-fire with the Government.		
10.	**United People's Democratic Solidarity,** a corresponding outfit based in Karbi-Anglong District, is presently observing a cease-fire and engaged in negotiations *(Frontline,* 27-11-2002). Founded in 1997, it also has links with NSCN(I-M). **Demand:** UT status for their district, where they form majority.	UPDS	
11.	**Karbi National Volunteers** (Karbi Volunteer Corps) Perhaps armed wing of the UPDS, or allied to it.	KNV/KVC	

1	2	3	4
	Nagaland		
Sl.No.	*Name*	*Abbreviation*	*Cadre Strength (2005-06)*
1.	**National Socialist Council of Nagaland (Isaac Chisi Swu - Thuingaleng Muivah Faction).** Banned, but it has declared truce with the Government since August 1997. The cease-fire does not extend to Manipur, Assam and Arunachal Pradesh. Founded by the duo (Swu and Muivah) in 1989 in the wake of the Shillong Accord between New Delhi and Phizo's NNC. It split into two factions of (I-M) and (K). Presently talking to the Government. **Demand:** Nagalim comprising of Nagaland and other Naga-inhabited areas in the contiguous States of Manipur, Assam and Arunachal and in border areas of Burma.	NSCN(I-M)	2,000
2.	**NSCN (S.S. Khaplang faction)** Banned; Sibling arch rival of NSCN(I-M). It is based in Burma. Its demands area same as that of the senior and more powerful (I-M) faction. It is in ceasefire with New Delhi since 1999.	NSCN(K)	1,000
3.	**Naga Federal Government**	NFG (also FNG)	
4.	**Naga National Council (Adino)** Military wing of the NFG	NNC(A)	
5.	**NNC (Khodao)**	NNC(K)	
	NSCN(I-M) and NSCN(K) are presently active in the field, the former being more powerful of the two. The rest are irrelevant.		

1	*2*	*3*	*4*
	Manipur		
Sl.No.	*Name*	*Abbreviation*	*Cadre Strength (2005-06)*
1.	**People's Liberation Army** Founded in September 1978 by N. Bisheswar Singh. Its political arm, Revolutionary People's Front (RPF) was born in 1989. It has bases in Bangladesh. **Strength:** 1,500 (2004). **Demand:** Wants a Revolutionary Front covering entire North-East, uniting all ethnic groups like Meiteis, Nagas, Kukis, to liberate Manipur.	PLA	1,000
2.	**Revolutionary People's Front.** Political Wing of the PLA.	RPF	
3.	**United National Liberation Front** The oldest (Meitei) insurgent group founded in November 1964. Initially took East Pakistani help. Supported Pakistan during 1971 war. Sent cadres for training in China. Floated Indo-Burma Revolutionary Front (IBRF) with ULFA, NSCN (K), and Kuki National Army (KNA) in 1990. **Strength:** 1,000 activists (2004). **Demand:** Independent Socialist Manipur	UNLF	1,500
4.	**UNLF (M Oken Faction).**	UNLF(MO)	600
5.	**Peoples Revolutionary Party of Kangleipak** was founded in October 1977 by R.K. Tulachandra who was killed by SF in 1986. Part of Manipur People's Liberation Front (MPLF) with PLA and UNLF. Got initial training from NSCM (I-M). Also has links with Kachin Independent Army of Myanmar. **Strength:** 1,000 (2004)	PREPAK	1,000

1	*2*	*3*	*4*
	Demand: Ouster of all "outsiders" from Manipur. (There are ten other groups, with an uneven spread of sophisticated weaponry and cadre strength from 200 to 500. These are listed below serials 6 to 15.)		
6.	**NSCN (I-M)**	NSCN(I-M)	
7.	**Hmar People's Convention**	HPC	NA
8.	**Kuki National Front**	KNF	100
9.	**Kuki National Council**	KNC	—
10.	**Kuki National Army.** Armed wing of the KNC	KNA	—
11.	**Kuki National Organisation**	KNO	500
12.	**Kangleipak Communist Party**	KCP	
13.	**Kanglei Yawol Kanna Lup**	KWKL or KYKL	250
	The name means "Organisation to Save the Revolutionary Movement in Manipur." Formed in 1994 by merger of three groups: Oken faction of UNLF, Mciraba faction of PREPAK, and Ibo Pishak faction of KCP. Has links with both factions of NSCN.		
	Strength: 1,000 (2004).		
	Demand: Cleansing Manipur of corruption, drugs and immoral activities.		
14.	**United Kuki Liberation Front**	UKLF	
	It is the latest name to join the Manipur fraternity of militant outfits. May be a front of already existing groups, or could be a new outfit (*The Hindu*, 11-10-2002).		
15.	**Manipur People's Liberation Front**		
	It is an alliance in action of three of the oldest valley-based insurgencies of Manipur: UNLF, PLA and PREPAK (*Frontline*, 27-11-2002).		

There are about 14 other groups in Manipur, with an uneven spread of sophisticated weaponry and cadre strength between 200-500.

Tripura

1. Tripura National Volunteers (Extinct) TNV
2. National Liberation Front of Tripura NLFT 150

   Founded in 1989 by Dhananjay Reang, former Vice-President of TNV, has camps in Bangladesh. Currently (2004?) in talks with the Government. This averment is of doubtful value. In 2005, the outfit is continuing with its violence, killings and extortions. Only a faction (Nayanbashi) came overground.

   Demand: Independent Tripura, free of Bengali migrants.

3. All Tripura (Tribal) Tiger Force ATTF 300

   Founded in 1990 by the renegade TNV after its main group signed an accord with the Government in 1988. In 1997, about 1,600 surrendered, but the core group continues with its violent ways. Has 16 camps and HQ in Bangladesh. Has links with ULFA.

   Strength: 600 (2004)

   Demand: Expulsion of all Bengali-speaking migrants of East Bengal/ East Pakistan/Bangladesh origin who entered after 1949.

4. Tripura People's Democratic Front—TPDF

   After signing of an accord in August 1988, TNV ceased to exist. Some remnant of the TNV had organised themselves as NLFT under Dhananjay Reang. However Reang and some others surrendered in 1993. The remainder NLFT, renamed TPDF, is still a force to count within Tripura and has continued its links with NSCN (I-M).

Mizoram

1. Hmar People's Convention	HPC	Hmar issue
2. Hmar Volunteers Council	HVC	settled
(Armed wing of the preceding)		
3. Mizo National Front	MNF	(Defunct)

HPC was active in Mizoram, Manipur's Churachandpur district, and North Cachar Hills District of Assam. Militants of the HVC and the NSCN(I-M) were known to have engaged in joint operations in Assam's NC District. The demand of HPC for creation of a "Hmar Autonomous District Council' in North-East Mizoram was conceded by the State Government, and peace has prevailed in the area ever since. A rather peaceful environ prevails in Mizoram. The Mizo Accord of June 1986 remains the only accord till date that succeeded in bringing peace to the state and harmony between the high parties.

Having said this, it must be remembered that the Chakma issue keeps popping up off and on.

4. Bru National Liberation Front BNLF

Brus are a small group, which occasionally suffers ethnic violence at the hands of the majority Mizos. BNLF has potential to foment trouble as consequence. It has some ethnic links in Tripura. They are presently agitating for creation of an ADC.

Demand: An ADC for the Brus in Mizoram. They are akin to original tribes of Tripura.

Meghalaya

1. A'Chik National Volunteer Council ANVC

   Banned November 2000
2. Hynniewtrep A'Chik Liberation Council HALC

   Banned November 2000
3. Hynniewtrep Volunteer Force HVF
4. Hynniewtrep National Liberation Council HNLC

   Founded in 1992 after the split of the HALC, the first militant group of the Meghalaya, Hynniewtrep, draws its members from the Khasi and Jaintia tribes. Has bases in Bangladesh. Known to circulate fake currency at the behest of the ISI.
5. A'Chik Liberation Matgrik Army ALMA
6. People's Liberation Front of Meghalaya PLFM
7. Bru National Liberation Front BNLF
8. Meghalaya United Liberation Army MULA
9. A'Chik National Volunteer Council ANVC

   Formed in 1995, the outfit has links with NSCN(I-M), ULFA, NDFB. Signed a cease-fire agreement with the Government but armed acts are still reported. (2004)

   Strength: 500

   Demand: A separate state for the Garos in Meghalaya's Garo areas and adjoining area in western Assam.

The situation in Meghalaya can be described 'iffy' as the insurgencies go, but less so than in Arunachal Pradesh. Most of the above outfits, the Police see, as ganging up of the criminal elements; but the first two occasionally grab the headlines, with some violence against the foreigners. Understandably, given their location and geography, they have tried to link with the NSCN(I-M), earlier known as NSCN (South), or NSCN(S). But given its distant location and salubrious climate, Shillong have often played host to insurgent groups from Assam, Nagaland, Manipur etc., whose members occasionally come here, as per the Intelligence agencies, to rest, refit, and re-think their strategies and coordination. It is overall a peaceful State but for an occasionally anti-outsiders riots, an affliction not restricted to this State of the Union only. Larger States like Maharashtra and Karnataka and smaller ones like Assam and Arunachal have also suffered and are still suffering from it. The outfits at Serials 1 and 4 above are demanding a separate Khasiland. Little is known about the outfit's at Serials 6 and 7.

12 major militant/insurgent outfits in the North-East are ULFA, NDFB, UNLF, NSCN(I-M), NSCN(K), PLA, PREPAK, ATTF, NLFT, KCP, KYKL and BLT.

Arunachal Pradesh

1. United Liberation Army ot Arunachal ULAA
2. United People's Volunteers of Arunachal UPVA
3. United Liberation Volunteers of Arunachal ULVA
4. United Liberation Movement of Arunachal ULMA

Its long-serving Chief Minister (Apang) had justly claimed his state to be an "island of peace" in the region. But during the recent years in the late nineties the presence of the long-settled Chakma refugees did create some dissonance, even mild violence occasionally. The first two groups have some militants in their fold, but the latter two have remained on paper. Some members claiming to belong to both ULAA and UPVA had surrendered in early 1990s, but some still occasionally surface making claims on the parochial lines. ULAA did try to link with the NSCN(I-M) and UPVA with NSCN(K), but there has been no Intelligence confirmation. It certainly is peaceful State till the anti-Chakma riots spoiled the idyll. For the last couple of years, say since the 1999 or so, the State has become a safe haven for Assam and Naga militants.

It may be noted that the States have been placed in the descending order of the intensity and virulence of the insurgency movements, and the last three are once again largely free from the virus, particularly so, Mizoram.

North Bengal

1. Kamatapur People's Party KPP

Active since the last 10 years, is demanding a separate state of Kamatapur, comprising of five districts of North Bengal and adjoining areas of Assam.

2. Kamatapur Liberation Organisation KLO

Armed wing of KPP, has become almost sole representative of the Rajbongshis whose party KPP is, and more worryingly, the KLO has developed secessionist orientation.

3. Some Muslim outfits are also operating here, but these has been discussed elsewhere.

KPP

It was set up in January 1996 by Atul Roy who ironically heads a break away (minority) faction presently (2005). Nikhil Roy is the President of the

KPP. Both the factions share with the more militant outfit, KLO, the demand for a separate State of Kamtapur (also spelt Kamatapur) in the region, to be carved out of North Bengal, comprising essentially its five districts, and some areas of the contiguous Assam. This demand of late (since 2001 or so) has taken the shape of Greater Cooch Behar (GCB) spearheaded by the Greater Cooch Behar Peoples' Association (GCBPA).

They Want Greater Cooch Behar Now

Though in a different guise, separatist forces are "making re-appearance in the political foreground in North Bengal, stoking ethnic sentiments and threatening peace in the nation" (Marcus Dam, *Hindu,* 22-9-05). The emergence of a new political entity the GCBPA, was announced loudly, rather too loudly and even violently by the mindless violence perpetrated by the demonstrators ('mobs'?) at Cooch Behar on 20-9-05, in which three policemen were killed, including one whose eyes were gouged by the "irate"(?) crowd, as one daily put it as if to provide some justification. The agitation is obviously carried out by the Rajbongshis, a majority in the North Bengal area, and particularly in Cooch Behar, an erstwhile princely State which became a part of West Bengal in January 1950. For West Bengal State Secretary of CPI(M) Anil Biswas, the demand for a GCB is both "meaningless and unacceptable". As is typical of the Indian political class, for this very reason, the demand is "a debatable issue" for the TNC leader Pankaj Banerjee, who blamed the "trigger-happy" administration for the 22-9-05 violence. How one wishes the political class could rise above the party interests, even if to ask them to soar into idealistic orientation while dealing with such issues will be asking for too much!

Chief Minister Buddhadeb Bhattacharjee, "due to address a public rally at Cooch Behar on 24 September 2004, in the post-20 September violence context, will have to address the separatist forces of his State in the backdrop of the changing political scenario". On the 19th, he warned that the KLO was engaged in a fresh attempt at reorganising itself in the North Bengal. Having been driven out of its camps in southern Bhutan by the 2003-04 Royal Bhutanese Army, most of what remains of the KLO leadership is sheltered in camps in Bangladesh, evidence of which was supplied by the BSF to the BDR early in September 2005. But one Intelligence report should worry Bhattacharjee: Separatist forces in North Bengal enjoy the support of the Maoist rebels in Nepal.

Violence Unlimited: 20 September 2005

On 20 September 2005, thousands of agitators took to the streets at Khagrabari and Chakchaka, outside Cooch Behar town on the call of GCBPA, spearheading a Movement for a separate State. The situation went out of hand when the agitators tried to break through the police barriers to enter the town to begin a fast-unto-death outside the District Magistrate's office to press for their demand. Lathi-charged and tear-gassed, the enraged mob which outnumbered the SF, isolated "two constables (Jogesh Sarkar and Gour Chandra Dhar) and mercilessly tortured them to death. Two women Sub-Inspectors (Tanushree Biswas and Mumtaz Begum) were mercilessly assaulted by the mob and both of them are in critical condition" (Parwez Hafeez, AA, 22-9-05). Kalimpong ASP Mushtaque Ahmed too was lynched to death. He was buried at Bagmari in Kolkata on the 23rd with full state honours (The violence was alluded to in the preceding two paragraphs).

The killing of Ahmed reminded a newsman of killing of Kolkata (Ports) Deputy Commissioner of Police Vinod Mehta by a mob in Garden Reach area in 1994. Two agitators were killed in the police firing.

Profile of Leadership and Weaponry

The information on the five worse-affected States is given below:

Assam		
ULFA	1. Arbinda Rajkhowa, Chairman	AK Rifles - 200
	2. Paresh Barua C-in-C	RPGs - 20 (Rocket propelled grenades) Rifles Sundry - 400
	3. Pradip Gogoi, Vice President (In Guwahati jail since 1998)	
	4. Anup Chetia, Secretary	(was awarded a jail term in December 1997 in Dhaka, on completion of which, he was released in 2004. Dhaka has refused to hand him over to India, citing another court case pending against him.)
Bd SF	Ranjan Daimary (1999)	AK Rifles - 50 Rifles Sundry - 100
NDFB	Ranjan Daimary, Chairman (2003)	
Nagaland		
NSCN(I-M)	Isaac Swu, Chairman Muivah, General Secretary	AK Rifles - 400 RPGs- 50 Rifles Sundry - 900
NSCN(K)	Khaplang, Chairman	AK Rifles - 200 Rifles (Sundry) – 350

Meghalaya		
HNLC	Julius K. Dorphang, Chairman	AK Rifles - 200
ANVC	Dilash R. Marak, Chairman	
Manipur		
UNLF	Chairman - Rajkumar Meghen General Secretary - T. Sanachou	AK Rifles - 200
PLA		A K Rifles-150
PREPAK	Chairman - Achamba	
KYKL	Chairman - Achou Toijamba	
Tripura		
TPDF	Tripura People's Democratic Front, (Political face of ATTF) Ranjit Debbarma, (President)	AK Rifles - 50
NLFT	Nayanbasi Jamatia	AK Rifles - 50

Coordinating Their Activities: Insurgent Outfits

For better results, various groups have joined hands against the State. The linkages, not made public, are prised open generally by the Intelligence.

Being oldest in the business, and mother of all insurgencies in the area NSCN, presently split into two factions, is central to such coordination, and over the recent years, has been aided and abetted by the Pak ISI. For this reason, most of the insurgent groups have gravitated towards one or the other of the two factions.

Beyond this, there have been attempts to float broader structures to coordinate the insurgent activities. Early 1990s, S.S. Khaplang of NSCN and John Khaw Kim Thang, President of Chin National Front reached an agreement to bolster the insurgency astride the Indo-Burma border with the active support of KIA. On the same lines was born the Indo-Burma Revolutionary Front (IBRF) on 22 May 1990—its founder members being Khaplang of NSCN(K), Paresh Barua, C-in-C of ULFA, and Sama Yaima of UNLF. The IBRF forbade any individual constituents from holding parleys with the Centre or States. Several factors have conjoined to bestow a position of hegemonic dominance on these outfits on the Indo-Burma border in the Region: these are the strategic importance of this border area, favourable topography for guerrilla warfare, existence of ethnic affinities across the border, and long experience of running underground movements by so many insurgent outfits on either side. These Fronts offer best chance to fight their secessionist battles against New Delhi (and Yangon). Though NSCN(K) was the first off the mark, NSGN(I-M) was to follow soon and formed more than one front. Its first attempt, soon after the May 1990 formation of the IBRF, was to form

Indo-Burma Liberation Front (IBLF). Its members, besides the prime mover NSCN(I-M), were the Revolutionary Joint Committee (itself an apex body comprising of RPF, KCP and PREPAK, all of Manipur), HPC of Manipur and Mizoram, BdSF of Assam and surprisingly ULFA, with a foot already in IBRF. If the IBRF aimed at creating an independent nation comprising of territories astride the Indo-Burma Border, and the Brahmaputra Valley under the Bra-Chin (Brahmaputra-Chindwin) Plan, the IBLF merely planned a coordinated effort. But if the former died a premature death, the latter proved a case of still-birth.

In 1993, NSCN(I-M) formed the United Liberation Front of Seven Sisters (ULF-SS). Some assign 1992 as its date of birth in Bangladesh, under the guidance of the ISS. It too was a failure. Not giving up, the NSCN(I-M) then formed a Front, with the jaw-breaking acronym SDUFSEAHR (Self-Defence United Front of South-East Asian Himalayan Region), on 30 November 1994. Its 23 members include the new insurgent groups of the 1990s like HALG; KNV and NDFB; HPC of Mizoram; and some groups from Manipur like the KYKL, UNLF (Okan faction), KCP (Isopishak faction), and PREPAK (Khamba faction) leaving out other factions. Even the ULF-SS, though virtually split, is not with the Front, the excuse that its leaders could not attend due to logistics problems notwithstanding. With so many factions within and more outside of it, the Front fared no better than the earlier ones considering that the KNV and NDFB were reportedly 'anti-social' elements and that the HPC had already signed a memorandum of understanding with the Government of Mizoram (B. Pakam, at the North-East India Political Science Association, Fourth Session, 1995 and *The Shillong Times,* 3-2-1995).

Much earlier, there were reports of joint meetings for strategic cooperation, in Dhaka during the 1970s, of outfits like the MULA, PLA, ATTF, NSCN(I-M) and MNF. All of them had their training camps in Bangladesh.

Shillong: A good host and safe shelter. Perhaps largest cosmopolitan town of the Region, with large number of settlers from all its states and beyond and very little Army presence, Shillong proves a safe haven for the insurgents of all hues. "It is well-known that the ultras of various groups from major affected states, including ULFA, NSCN, UNLF and PLA meet here regularly" to plan their joint operations.[6] In addition, these groups also send their members for medical treatment to Shillong, and hospitals, mostly private and at times even Government, are forced to treat them free of cost.

The latest to join forces seem to be the ULFA and the much older UNLF of Manipur. The alliance, latest of several such constantly shifting and cross-cutting linkages, is indicated by the fact that the bandh and boycott call against the Independence Day 2002, which had been announced from Guwahati since the Republic Day 1968, emanated from Imphal.

Earlier in the year, about 12 banned armed groups of the Region, including ULFA and NSCN(K) had called for a general strike and boycott of the Republic Day celebrations on 26 January (2002), according to a statement published by them in *Freedom,* ULFA's mouthpiece *(Indian Express,* 18-1-2002).

Nexus: A Summary

Insurgency and militancy have ushered in greater co-operation, co-ordination and nexus between various insurgence groups both within and without the region. At times, the pact could be symbolic or ideological. The nexus often involves arms supply, financial support and logistical assistance. Prominent secessionist groups such as NSCN, ULFA, PLA , UNLF, BdSF and KIA have at one time or other have/had reached close understanding among themselves [See Table below]. Some even established links with outfits such as the Liberation Tigers of Tamil Eelam (LTTE). Capitalising on the geographic proximity, a number of extremist established base and support facilities in the neighbouring states of Bangladesh, Myanmar, Nepal and Bhutan.

Nexus Amongst the Rebel Outfits : Around 2004

State	*Militant group*	*Partners*
Assam	ULFA	ATTF, NSCN(K), KIA, LTTE
Assam	NESO	AASU, APSU, AMSU, NSF (Nagaland), KSU (Khasi Students Union), MSU (Mizoram)
Assam	Dima Halao Daagah (Cachar region)	NSCN(I-M)
Assam	Bodo	NSCN(K & I-M), KNA, PLA
Nagaland	NSCN(K)	ULFA, UNLF, IBRF (Indo-Burma Revolutionary Force), Indigenous People's Pact (ORG, Bangkok)
Nagaland	NSCN(I-M)	BdSF Camp in Bhutan and Manas Tiger Sanctuary, Asian Indegenous People's Pact (ORG, Bangkok), Hmar People's Convention (demanding autonomy in Mirozam); NLFT (North Tripura close to NSCN route)
Tripura	TNV	NSCN, MNF

Networking and Linkages of Insurgencies in North-East: Current Status

In this age of internet and advances in technological field, the simple nexus of yesteryears have graduated to sophisticated networking and linkages of/among insurgents operating not only in a particular country but also beyond its borders.

So the insurgents in India's North-East could be networking not only with their counterparts in the contiguous countries like Bangladesh, Myanmar etc. but also with Al Qaeda operating far away. Consequently, the insurgent groups in this region have taken the maximum advantage of this and have managed to spread their tentacles in all the seven states of the region.

Of late, analysts have been arguing that the linkages of North-Eastern insurgent groups are heading towards a dangerous direction. With the supportive and active role being played by the Director General Field Intelligence (DGFI) of Bangladesh and Inter Service Intelligence of Pakistan in North-East India, successful attempts have been made to link these groups with Al Qaeda network. This is something the Indian Intelligence must concern itself diligently and uncover the sinister conspiracy for the world at large. "Then, there is also an attempt being made inside Assam by external forces to create a situation similar to Jammu and Kashmir."

In a wider context, one can see a broken pattern of emerging insurgencies, violence and poor governance. Ultimately, the consequent uncertainty along with human destabilisers who exploit the situation for their objectives create a vicious circle of hate. The armed non-state actors/groups are undermining the nation-states' physical capability to govern, and ultimately question and challenge even their moral right to govern. Generally speaking, "the near chronic political chaos can be seen propagating its respective form of instability and violence in large parts of North-East presently. The two current instances of political instability, generated by personal ambitions of the rival state leaders and consequent stage-managed rebellions by their minions in the legislatures forcing the current Chief Ministers to resign, have just been seen in Meghalaya (March 2007) and in Arunachal Pradesh (April 2007). Both these States are facing ethnic terrorism and the politicians involved in these shenanigans are possibly not even aware that by their actions they are helping the terrorist outfits in their states to exploit the political theatre of the absured played out as consequence of their skullduggery.

The rise of new war-making entities, helped by a variety of narco-traders, economic offenders and trans-national non-state actors, should be a matter of serious concern to the nation-states. It must be clearly understood that as a result of this phenomenon, various insurgent groups in the North-East are much more than mere stateless gangs. These new network insurgents possess "standing armed groups, treasury, revenue resources, their own intelligence services and ability to make alliances with other non-state entities and intelligence agencies of other countries." They also promote a common vision by promulgating the policy, laws and most importantly, war against the state. Brain M. Genkins, in an insightful essay, "Re-Defining the Enemy : The world has Changed But Our mindset has not" (RAND Review, Spring 2004) describes the distinction between war and crime, which continues to result in a policy quandary where we underestimate the power of militarily inferior foes (insurgent), difficult terrain, unceasing hostilities, and other unconventional measures of power.

Indian security planners must factor in such advanced technological innovations available to the simple terrorist of the yesterdays, which multiply his already formidable capabilities, to work out more effective counter-strategies to defeat the combine of transnational terror, crime and drug merchants. It is not a call for pessimism and despondency. India has been fighting the terrorism/insurgency for the past half a century by employing its military in a responsible manner, seldom taking resort to gunships, bombing the insurgent strongholds, or endangering civilian lives. It is also reasonably certain to aver that insurgent, terrorist, or militant outfits are aware that they cannot defeat India by mindless murder and mayhem.

What is called for is India finding ways to counter the sophisticated networking and linkages created by several insurgent groups in the North-East as a whole. These related issues have been discussed above in their theoretical and conceptual aspects as far as they concern the North-East. The details of linkages and network in respect of individual states of the region will be discussed in the respective chapters dealing with the terrorism in those states.

It bears repetition that tribal communities in the region are all zealously guarding their ethnic identity. India's Northeast is one of South Asia's hottest trouble spots, not simply because the region has more than 50 active armed insurgent organizations operating and fighting the Indian state, but because trans-border linkages that these groups have, and strategic alliances among them, have acted as force multipliers and have made the conflict dynamics all the more intricate. These linkages could be tactical, operational linkages or for financial benefits, as will be seen with the linkages in different states.

The inter-group linkages and networking in this region are heading towards a dangerous trend. This will be obvious if one studies the pattern of networks of terrorist outfits in individual states constituting the North-East. Most of these groups have linkages with other insurgents groups in some way or the other. The smaller insurgent groups have joined hands with bigger groups for support in case of need. The smaller groups provide safe sanctuary and passage to the bigger groups whenever required. In case of operations by the security forces against bigger insurgent groups; these groups fall back on the support cover and safe havens provided to them via small groups and vice versa. These linkages prove hazardous to the security forces in their operations. Gaining information about the insurgents would not only become difficult but also confusing.

The *interest groups,* as brought out earlier have already entered Assam. Their attempt to pierce into other states should be prevented by immediately taking the appropriate counter measures. There is also an attempt being made inside Northeastern Region by external forces to create a situation similar to Jammu and Kashmir. Unless innovative steps are undertaken to address the issue, the process could prove irreversible. It is expected that the Government of India would address the question more forcefully. The imperative of development buttressed by a security angle for the North-East Region should be uppermost in the Government's mind. Unless a pro-active role is taken by the government, this region could be infested by networked insurgent groups, shaking the edifice of Indian democracy.

The construction work of the border fence along the Indo-Bangladesh border has to be completed on priority so that a check is imposed on the inflow of Bangladesh nationals inside India. Constant pressure has to be mounted on Bangladesh government to take appropriate action against the India's North-East insurgent camps inside that country. Nepal may also be informed to keep a look out for any new linkages being established by the North-East insurgent groups.

Demonstrative Show of Force: July-August 1999

Over the years, the insurgents in the North-East plan special death dance around the Independence Day for its demonstrative effect. The Intelligence reported a meeting of several outfits—ULFA, NDFB, NSCN (both factions), PLA, PREPAK, UNLF, KCP, NLFT, TPDF and ATTF—in July 1999 at a place in Burma close to Manipur border to plan attack on the SF and communication arteries and also on production units, around 15 August. The meet was also meant to revive the fortunes of the IBRF not so active over the years. The ULFA Chairman on 6 August called upon all rebel groups to boycott the Independence Day. The other groups likewise issued warnings to citizens not to fly National Flag on the day. Major incidents, including acts of sabotage are summarized here:

1. *14 July.* A JCO killed and 7 soldiers injured when PLA ultras ambushed an Assam Rifles convoy at Pundongbam in Imphal East District, Manipur.
2. *3 August.* 5 policemen killed in a NSCN(K) ambush in Karbi Anglong district, Assam.
3. *4 August.* Bodo militants blow up a portion of rail track between Barpeta Road and Sarupeta Stations.

4. *5 August.* An attempt by ULFA to blow up oil facilities foiled with the killing of Bablu Ingti, ULFA Action Group Commander for Gauhati and Kamrup districts, at Gauhati. Quantities of RDX seized.
5. *7 August.* Two Power Grid Corporation pylons collapsed in a blast in Barpeta district.
6. *8 August.* The Arunachal Express also targeted but had a narrow escape when the explosives planted in one of its coaches were detected and defused minutes before its arrival at Bongaigaon.
7. *8 August.* A bomb was detonated under Sapkata bridge on NH No. 37, but security men foiled an attempt to blow up a rail bridge at Salakati Station.
8. *8 August.* The passengers on Gauhati-bound North-East Express had a narrow escape when a bomb blast derailed a pilot engine between Bijni and Patildaha Stations, near Bongaigaon.
9. *8 August.* A possible case of mistaken identity saves the Gauhati-bound Rajdhani Express. A goods train, 15 km ahead of the Express, absorbed the impact of the IED explosion by Bodo ultras under a bridge between Kokrajhar and Salakati Stations; 5 persons including 3 RPF men, injured when the explosion derailed it.
10. *8 August.* Most prominent incident. The Assam Police arrested two officers of the ISI—Mohammed Fasihullah Hussaini and Mohammed Javed Wakhar—and two operatives of 1 Harkat-ul-Mujahideen (HUM)—Maulana Hafiz Mohammid Akram Mallick and the totally blind Qari Salim. Qari, hailing from Muzaffarabad, was one of the four founders of the Lashkar-e-Babri, UP wing of HUM, and "one of the most dangerous operatives of the LSI in India". The arrest of these four ISI men had its fallout in other spheres, with police nabbing 27 other members of various Pro-Pak outfits, subsequently. The following two recoveries were the result of these four arrest:
    (*a*) 16 *August.* The State Police recovered 14.65 kg of explosive AMFO (ammonium nitrate mixed with fuel oil), from Platform No. 8 of Calcutta's Sealdah Railway Station. The Police believed this explosive was part of the main consignment from Bangladesh which was delayed/diverted after the 8 August arrest of the ISI officers.

    (*b*) *16 August.* 6 kg of RDX seized in Phulbari in Jalpaiguri district of North Bengal. It also possibly was part of the main consignment mentioned above.

The arrests and subsequent seizures should show continuous nefarious designs of Pakistan and its agencies to destabilise India.

11. *11 August.* NLFT ultras kill a police officer.
12. *12 August.* NLFT rebels, coming from Long Larai hill ranges gunned down 6 non-tribals in Shib-bari village of Dhalai district, Tripura, with their AK-47s.
13. *12 August.* The NDFB blew up with IED, an Army vehicle at Rajgarh (Sonitpur district) on Assam-Arunachal border, killing 3 soldiers.
14. *12 August.* A CRPF convoy had a narrow (miraculous!) escape when the IED planted at Bilpara in Nalbari district of Assam by ULFA, went off seconds after the convoy crossed the spot.
15. *15 August.* 3 CRPF men killed when armed militants ambushed two vehicles of 82 CRPF Battalion at Khabirakpam in Bishnupur district of Manipur. 31 others, including 17 CRPF, were seriously injured.
16. The following two events may be part of the 15 August-related death dance:
    (a) A series of blasts in the first 10 days of August 1999 prompted the Railways to suspend train services after sunset in Assam from 11 to 15 August.
    (b) In August, NLFT ultras kidnapped M. Debnath, father of Ranjit Debnath, Senior CPI(M) leader and former Transport Minister, from his Bangalipara residence in South Tripura.
17. *15 August.* The Bodo-dominated Lower Assam remained strike-bound.
18. *15 August.* A happenstance or a design? Over 200 ULFA and Bodo ultra surrendered to the Army in different parts of Assam; and handed in their arms, including AK-47s, grenades and revolvers. Among the welter of explosions that disturbed the peace around 15 August, did these surrenders make a statement?[7]

Unique Bomb

A blast at New Jalpaiguri Station killed ten people. It was unique in the sense that a new kind of bomb, nitro-based, was used for the first time in India. This explosion, unlike the one caused by the RDX, "cause more deaths in covered and semi-covered areas".

Aims and Methods of the Insurgents

The insurgency movement generally aims at challenging a nation-state and undermining its sovereignty. The political propaganda barrage is mounted to subvert the loyalty of the citizenry and cause disaffection among the masses. Besides the political mobilisation, instrument of mindless violence is employed to target the ruling classes, SF, and elitist sections to create all-round panic and fear psychosis. Finally, the innocent civilians are targeted to cause social disharmony; and selective killings are resorted to for causing religious, communal, or sectarian tensions and conflict. But an equally effective mean to subvert the will of a nation-state is to hurt it economically by attacking its economic sinews and communication networks. That will not only cripple the economic growth of the country, but also cause security problems for it by hindering the movement of its SF from one part to another when required for strategic and operational reasons; and this indeed was done in the Kargil conflict in 1999 (for some reasons, the Government did not want to call it the Kargil War).

To cripple the economic development of the Region, the militants have been targeting the railways and roads, oil installations and refineries, and hydro-electric plants. Here is just one example of sabotaging hydro-power development. The North-East is estimated to have a hydel potential of 40,000 MW of which only 1 per cent has been harnessed so far. "The Union Government has already cleared development of 20,000 MW hydel capacity for the Dihang and the Subansiri Projects in Arunachal, by the NHPC" (Vinay Pandey in *Times of India,* 25-1-2000). This is billed as the largest hydel project in the world. But the killing of S.C. Sher, CE, NHPC Loktak (Manipur) Project by militants cast a long shadow on the successful completion of the hydel plans in the North-East.

The Loktak project has 1200 workers, of whom over 50 per cent are non-Manipuris. They were panic-stricken. Railway Board Chairman told the press on 6-2-2000 that rise in terrorist violence has resulted in low morale of the employees of the NF Railway. Some instances of blasts on the rail track and coaches have been given in the preceding pages.

Fighting the Insurgency and Hurdles in the Way

Fighting insurgency is a complex, time-consuming, and strenuous exercise, which needs patience, understanding, and political skill of the highest order. Economic measures and anti-insurgency operations must go hand-in-hand. Once considerable progress have been made in the twin tasks, and particularly when the militant leadership is convinced that the violence would not pay, it is the time to repair to the High Table.

Economic Development

Economic development is the answer to the sense of deprivation and neglect of the Region by the powers-that-be. Consequent employment opportunities should draw the educated youth away from the enticements and blandishments offered by the insurgent groups. Prime Minister's economic package and the Shukla Commission's Report are meant to put the North-East on way to economic recovery. The Government have already accommodated the micro-identities and sub-nationalities with finesse and dexterity, essentially through the instrumentality of Sixth Schedule and subsequent elevation of certain ethnic minorities' territories into statehood.

The States in the Region have too been taking certain policy decisions to ameliorate the lot of common man. They are discouraging jhum cultivation and offering incentives to develop alternate methods to minimize the degradation of the land and environment caused by the former. Horti-flori- and herbi-culture and plantation have potential with every type of agro-climatic zones available here. But some problems of land, labour, capital and marketing intrude, which are being addressed.

Counter Insurgent (CI) Operations

It is an over-wrought cliche by now to say that force alone cannot root out insurgency. Perhaps it would be truer to say that no political solution is possible till the insurgents are made to realize that they cannot have their way with the gun. And force is the only language they understand. Stage for political negotiations would follow. Some of the musts for a successful CI operations are:

1. The operations of various SF involved must be well coordinated to avoid duplication and wastage of resources.
2. A unified command set-up has proved a success in the recent years. It must be headed by an appropriate political leader.
3. An effective intelligence network.
4. The State Police and Para-Military forces must play their role in these operations, and not be reduced to secondary positions.
5. Politics and political interests of parties and individuals must not intrude into the scene.
6. The police must get improved weaponry and better radio sets.
7. No undue harassment/excesses against the locals.

Banning the Underground Outfits

Banning the secessionist groups is deemed helpful in fighting them. Some of the outfits so banned are NSCN (both factions), ULFA, PLA, UNLF, etc. They are declared "unlawful associations" under the Unlawful Activities (Prevention) Act, 1967. To facilitate the operations of the CI forces, the Government in a related move, has declared the whole of Manipur, Nagaland, Tripura and Assam as well as Tirap and Changlang districts of Arunachal as "disturbed areas" under the authority of the Disturbed Areas Act, 1950.

The last groups to be banned were ANVC and HALC of Meghalaya in November 2000.[8] Some feel it will only help to glorify these two ragtag outfits, which police think are nothing more than criminals posing as gun-toting patriots even if the ANVC is fighting for creation of a separate Garoland out of Meghalaya. The policy of outlawing a militant outfit in order to discredit it or smash it cuts both ways, argues the analysts. If on the one hand, it enables the State to take effective and prompt action against it, the banning bestows an aura of martyrdom on the outfit, elevating the 'extortionists' to 'freedom fighters', on the other. It seems the politicians are still able to maintain contacts with the banned outfits to safeguard their turfs. If a Nagaland Chief Minister (S.C. Jamir) had allegedly close relations with NSCN(K), his counterpart in the neighbouring Manipur (Rishang Keishing) had similar links with such groups in his State (*Times of India,* 26-1-1997), which prompted its Governor, a retired Lt General, to send his resignation to the President in disgust. Again in Assam, the AGP and the Congress have accused each other of nursing ULFA.

Need to Staunch the Flow of Funds to Insurgents

Insurgents are known to be flush with funds, with some of their leaders ensconced in luxury hotels abroad. When the State gets weak, the insurgent outfits collect large amounts through taxes, "Voluntary" contributions (read extortions), coercion and intimidation, and plain robbery. In the recent decades, the narco trade is filling their coffers. Worse still, the politicians, bureaucrats, and contractors/the wealthy are known to pay the security money to the terrorists. In some areas, the insurgents are reportedly running a parallel Government. To staunch this flow, the Government must ensure safety of its citizens and employees through effective governance. Then comes the time to win the battle of minds, first of its own people and then of those gone astray.

Political Parties and Insurgency

The process of integration and development has generated the subjective sentiment of relative deprivation among some ethnic groups in the region, and that in turn has created an objective material condition for ethnic unrest and militancy in those groups. Simultaneously, it is necessary to evaluate the contribution of different political parties for the growth and perpetuation of violent ethnic movements to further their own electoral prospects.

A close observation of political developments in Tripura during the eighties and nineties should reveal the unholy nexus between the insurgency and electoral politics. The comparative backwardness of the tribals and the consequent tribal militancy have skilfully been exploited by the parliamentary forces for their electoral benefits. It is widely believed that the genocide perpetrated by the TNV before the 1988 Assembly elections at the behest of the Congress (I)-Tripura Upajati Juba Samiti (TUJS) combine brought the latter into power (*The Statesman,* 27-10-1994). The signing of the Peace Accord between the Congress (I) Government at the centre and the TNV after the elections to create some political space for the latter is proof enough of a clandestine understanding between the two. Similarly, the massacre committed by the ATTF on the eve of the 1993 elections is believed to have helped the

CPI(M)-led Left Front to regain power (*The Shillong Times,* 9-9-1993). It was reported that while the ATTF and the Tribal Youth Force (TYF) were floated by the Gana Mukti Parishad, a CPI(M) tribal wing, the Tripura Tribal Volunteer Force (TTVF), the Tripura Tribal Development Force (TTDF), and the Sangrak enjoy the tacit support of the TUJS—an ally of the Congress (I) (*Statesman,* 9-9-1994).

Thus it appears that the opposition parties, in order to capture power, not only patronise the militant outfits, they, at times, even float such outfits to destabilize the ruling dispensation through disruptive incidents by the latter. Another ploy of the opposition parties, as soon as they come into power, is to stage a surrender drama with much fanfare which gives the surrenderees double benefits; general amnesty and economic rehabilitation. The Left Front assumed power in Tripura in April 1993, and over 2,000 ATTF cadres surrendered on 9 September 1993 (*Anand Bazar Patrika,* 21-9-1994). A similar incident took place during the earlier stint of the Left Front when the activists of the All Tripura People Liberation Organisation (ATPLO) led by Binanda Jamatia came overground. The play-acting enables the political party to claim credit for bringing normalcy and peace to strife-ridden socio-political environment, and for the cadres, it ensures the Government jobs, licences, permits and respectability.

In certain cases, political parties ensure the longevity and perpetuation of the insurgent movements for their own political security and survival. It is well-known that the possibility of a negotiated settlement was bright in early 1990s as a result of several round of talks between the Central Government and the ULFA. But the move was allegedly sabotaged by the ruling party under Hiteswar Saikia, since they feared the settlement might oust them from power as indeed had happened earlier consequent to the Assam Accord (1985) and Mizoram Accord (1986).

The analysts assert that had an accord been signed with the undivided ULFA, the insurgency problem in Assam would have been solved once for all, as it happened in Mizoram. Any agreement signed with a section of a movement has never been successful, as was seen in case of Shillong Accord with Nagas and Rajiv-Longowal Agreement. The ruling elite at Gauhati engineered a vertical split in the ULFA through large-scale surrenders, and followed the policy of divide and rule to secure their own political fortunes. They brought the movement down to such a level that it could remain under control but did not put an end to it. It was obviously aimed at perpetuating its presence to ensure their indispensability in state politics.

These may be partisan rhetoric, but it is widely believed.

Divided Communities

Colonial encroachments created artificial boundaries. The Singphos in India have their kin in Jinphos in Myanmar, South China, Thailand and Laos.

The Mizo-Kuki-Chin group of tribes, some of the Naga tribes and the Meghalaya tribes, several tribes in Arunachal Pradesh, and even the plains people, Meiteis have their counterparts across the borders. All of them had dual—sometimes, multiple—cultural orientations, social and economic linkages and shared political beliefs in customs, traditions and mores. The divided communities syndrome continued even in the post-colonial era in the sphere of domestic reorganisations of the political boundaries as a result of agitations actuated and fuelled by the ethnic aspirations and identity crisis, actual or perceived, and consequently, the tribes, like the Nagas, find themselves in more than one state.

Insurgency as an Industry[9]

Were Phizo and Laldenga, the archetypal rebels, men informed by ideology and fired by apocalyptic vision? After all, they too spent long years abroad. But it is perceived by some that militants in the North-East "were not strong on ideology". The insurgents there are ethnic-separatist by inspiration. If they have more staying power, it is because they can draw on a large reservoir of public support, as also on a 'benign' foreign hand. In course of time, it becomes an industry which thrives on regionalism, rather ethno-separatism.

The pattern is similar by now. Having attained power through 'deals'—a cynical expression for 'accords'—with the Union or State Governments, the leaders who once fumed about independence, sovereignty, self-determination, ethnic identity and colonial syndrome, are now content to live on the Central doles, called grants. Again, a cynical view is that not only do they get coopted into the system, but also get used by the Centre as regional satraps to control the region for the central leaders. But somewhat surprisingly, even when some such leaders get sucked into the system, whether through persuasion, cajolery, inveighment, or cooption, the insurgency has endured. It seems clear that the ideology, if at all, of ethnic identity, or the colonial mind-set of the ruling classes, are not the sole—or even the main—motives that sustain the appeal of the insurgency. There are perhaps more pragmatic and mundane causes for this phenomenon; namely, personal ambitions, personal gains not only of monetary kind or even ego-mania. But for these not-so-idealistic causes, the plethora of Accords[10] signed by the Centre and State Governments with various militant outfits should have rooted out the insurgency situation from the North-East. All these accords failed to bring accord between the parties at the high table, at least not as yet; the Mizo Accord being the sole exception which only proves the rule.

So, it may be a truism to say that after a certain stage, the insurgency continues, rather, is sustained, not for the idealism and original causes, but for other reasons. At this stage, it is insurgency for the sake of insurgency. Not only it has to be sustained for the benefit of the rebels, but also for the gain of those ranged on the other side—politicians, SF, bureaucrats and the police. So goes the cynical wisdom, or is it? The Press and the public write and read widely about the "games politicians play". But are they the only ones playing games in this theatre of the absurd? No, there are so many other players, as named above. It may be surrealistic, it may even be macabre setting, but it is true! If there is "leakage"—an innocent euphemism for crass corruption and crafty manipulation of Government money—in the development funds, it is not because it cannot be staunched, but because so many are interested to see that it is not plugged. It is here that they play games with the public money—so adroitly and so deftly. Is it any surprise that the insurgency at certain stage becomes an industry, benefiting multiplicity of "industrialists" on both side of the divide? It is no surprise that a resident watcher told a journalist in January 2000: "The goal here is not identity any more, it is money.... If a gun is pointed, it is for the good time, not for the separatism" (Verghese, 1996). The politicos too may have a case. The Chief Ministers of Nagaland (S.C. Jamir) and Arunachal (Mukut Mithi) claim they are under the threat from the NSCN(I-M). It has been pressing Jamir's ministers and MLAs to withdraw support from the former in the Assembly elections due next year and targeting ministers from Tirap and Changlang districts because its members are insecure with the new Arunachal Pradesh Control of Organised Crime Bill, 2002 (*The Week*, 22-9-2002).

A word on the splitting games. Splitting is a legitimate weapon in the political field. But when the politicians extended the tactic to the insurgent outfits, it resulted in disastrous consequences. If the aim of splitting was to weaken or decimate a movement, it does not seem to have happened in most cases. In fact, the end result has been quite the opposite: the faction that stays the course emerges even stronger and more virulent. Whether it is Saikia splitting the Bodos or Rajiv Gandhi playing footsie with a faction (Longowal's) of the Akalis, results were opposite of the desideratum. On the other hand, the militant outfits are frequently splintered by internal dynamics fuelled by some leader's self-serving ambitions. Often, the factions try to outdo each other through incremental and competitive violence. Somewhere along the way, today's moderates become tomorrow's extremists. So some critics dub this splitting game as sharp practice. They ascribe mushrooming of militant groups in the Region as an "inevitable result of Government's efforts to solve the North-East's problem on the cheap". Whether caused by the shrewd politicians or by internal skullduggery, perhaps more by the latter, there are too many splinters for comfort; *viz,* NSCN(I-M) and NSCN(K); NNC(A)[11] and NNC(K)[12], latter closer to NSCN (I-M); the Meiteis have half a dozen valley-based militant groups including UNLF, PLA and PREPAK; and the Kukis have KNF, and KNA and the latest UKLF.

Now to the leakage of funds. It is axiomatic that most insurgency movements in course of time come to thrive on political patronage. Perhaps rightly, analysts have seen a symbiotic relationship between the politicians and militants—each drawing sustenance from other. Some linkages have been mentioned above. One time Nagaland Chief Minister Vamuzo had accused S.C. Jamir of supporting one group and trying to eliminate the other. In Tripura, if the ruling Left Front is alleged to have propped up the ATTF, the Congress is said to be sustaining the NLFT. In Assam if P.K. Mahanta is accused of being soft on ULFA, the Congress is blamed for creating BdSF to counter the AGP (*Times of India,* 26-1-1997).

Over the years, insurgency movements in the North-East seem to be characterised by killings, extortions, rapine, money-laundering *et al.* It is mindless violence all the way, perhaps actuated by the lust for power, pelf and naked ambition. It is no surprise that presently in large measure the militancy came to be sustained by money power alone. They have found ingenious ways to ensure that cash keep flowing, filling their coffers: narco-trade, cuts and commissions from the contracts, selective taxes levied in their areas and extortions. "The ruling politician, Government officials and businessmen divert Government funds as their contributions into the kitty of the militant outfits. Insurgents never seem to be short of money. How often does one see advertisements in Nagaland dailies, wooing the youth to join militants on a monthly salary of Rs. 15,000?

What kind of money is involved here? One computation has it that in a period of 25 years (1970-95), the Centre has spent over Rs. 30,000 crore in Nagaland alone. That works out to Rs. 25 lakh per person for a population of 12 lakh. This comment by a local academic sums up the scandalous situation: "If in the rest of the country only 15 paise from each rupee reach the target people, in the North-East it is 2 paise!" Some leakages, this! This illustrates effectively how the politicians, rebels, officials, contractors, *et al.* sponge on the Central grants and development funds, leaving the common man high and dry. All this must change drastically if we are to win the war.

In June 2003, Arunachal also came under the scanner for the politician-insurgent nexus; when the Deputy PM Advani ordered an Intelligence inquiry into the allegations of nexus between 6 ministers and 5 ruling Congress MLAs and the two factions of the NSCN (*Express,* 30-6-03).

A Different Game

The then Assam Chief Minister P.K. Mahanta's ambivalent attitude on setting up of the Unified Command to ensure better coordination between the Central forces and civil authorities was publicly commented upon. This is what a reputed national daily wrote, editorially castigating him for his dubious ways to sideline the real issues: "Centre's decision to launch joint operations was long overdue. It would have done good for Mahanta and his party if he had taken charge of the Unified Command instead of leading an All Party delegation for talks with the Central leaders on 'law and order' situation in Assam—essentially a state subject. His equivocal attitude in dealing with the insurgency in the State is an embarrassment for Mahanta as he is also a member of ruling coalition at Centre". (*The Hindu,* 18-1-1997).

Making Surrender Worthwhile

The Union Home Ministry offered a worthwhile surrender-cum-rehabilitation package in April 1998 to persuade the militants in the North-East to give up the path of violence. The scheme offered a number of monetary incentives and benefits to the militants to ensure that they don't return to the jungle again, including the vocational training to equip them to start life afresh. Each weapon handed in will be paid for at a fixed scale, but not in cash but in the form of a fixed deposit in the joint name of the surrenderee and a nominee of a NGO/State Government. The surrendered militants would be paid a monthly stipend for a year at a graded scale, the minimum being Rs. 2,000 a month. The surrenderees will be lodged in a Rehabilitation Camp for a year, with free boarding and lodging, and provided training in a trade or vocation of their liking. Subsequently, effort will be made to settle them in civil society.

Till 10 November 1999, 714 militants from Nagaland, Assam and Tripura had surrendered.[13]

The table below indicates the payment for each weapon/equipment handed in by the surrenderee, under "give up-and-gain" criterion.

Cash for Surrendered Arms (1998)

Weapon/Equipment	*Payment Per Piece Rs.*
Rocket launchers	25,000
Sniper Rifles	25,000
Assault Rifles of AK 47, 56 and 74 Series	15,000
Pistols/Revolvers	3,000
Rockets	1,000
Hand/Rifle Grenades	500
Remote Control devices	3,000
I ED	3,000
RDX etc.	1,000 per kg

Response by the Government

An important aspect that government might consider is about incentive that should be provided to a group that seeks to cease the hostilities. Whereas the latest rehabilitation package which came into force from April 1, 2005, provides for monthly stipends and a one time grant in the end of a monitored three year period for surrendered, nothing is being provided to an insurgent group that comes over ground after instituting a ceasefire. The government has to put in dedicated efforts at all fronts to counter the dangerous networks and linkages operating in the northeast region.

Costs and Means of Fighting Insurgency

The nation has paid a heavy price in human terms, leave aside the material and financial costs for fighting the scourge of insurgency in the North-East. Some relevant information on the North-East as a whole and state-wise break-up/tally for worst-affected States for 10-year[14] (1989-98) period are adduced on the following pages. The toll had crossed 8000 (lives) by 1998 and has been rising ever since.

Some Select Facts for the Entire North-East

1. In 10 years (1989-98), over 15,000 insurgents have been arrested and more than 6,700 weapons recovered.
2. In 1996 alone, 2617 people were killed, including 374 Army men. Of these, 734 were killed in extremist violence in Assam alone, of which 210 were the victims of the Bodo-Santhal ethnic violence in May 1996. The BLTF topped the list in Assam, killing 129 in 104 violent incidents.
3. The Centre gave a grant of Rs. 260 crore to Tripura to defray its insurgency-related expenses for 3 years (1994-96). The amount was meant to rehabilitate 5000 rebels who had surrendered and to provide them employment.

Assam

1. Over 2700 killed.
2. 385 killed in Bodo-Santhal clashes alone.
3. If the Bodos want a separate state, so do Santhals.
4. Bodo Accord of 1993 is stalled over the issue of villages/ area to be included in Bodo Autonomous Council Jurisdiction.
5. The abductions and extortions have never ceased.
6. Army has lodged FIRs against senior ministers for their nexus with the insurgents, for often giving them shelter.

   The officials and contactors are known to be passing money to the insurgent outfits.

7. Cases have been filed against some tea companies for funding some outfits.
8. ULFA will have nothing short of independence.
9. Both its hill districts, Karbi Anglong and North Cachar, are agitating for Union Territory status.

Nagaland

1. Over 1500 killed.
2. It is the longest-running violent but fractious movement. Ironically, the Naga Agreement of November 1975 itself caused a split among the insurgents.
3. A cease-fire agreed with NSCN(I-M) is in place since 1 September 1997 and periodic talks have been held with their leadership by the Government of India representative in some foreign capitals, and of late in New Delhi.
4. NSCN(K) too is observing *de facto* truce.
5. Both factions desire independence.
6. All factions also want the Naga-inhabited areas of Manipur, Arunachal Pradesh and Assam (essentially in North Cachar Hills) to be merged into a Greater Nagaland.

Manipur

1. Over 3000 killed.
2. In the Naga-Kuki clashes alone since 1992, over 750 people have been killed and 4100 houses burnt.
3. Since June 1997, 270 have been killed and 3550 houses burnt in the Kuki-Zomi clashes.
4. The Meiteis fear balkanization if their state in the face of the Nagas demanding merger of Naga areas of the state into the Greater Nagaland.

Tripura

1. Over 1600 killed.
2. NLFT and ATTF are still maintaining bases in Bangladesh.
3. NLFT depredations are on the increase, and 27 Police Station areas have been declared as "disturbed".
4. Abductions by NLFT are up by over 30 per cent during the last two years of the decade in question.
5. There is increased tension between the tribals and non-tribals.
6. The tribal militancy is gaining more virulent edge.
7. In August 1988, an Accord was signed with the TNV. Consequently, the TNV ceased to exist, but its die-hard core gave birth to NLFT.

8. The one-time majority tribal population is an aggrieved party after it was reduced to a minority consequent to a post-1947 influx of immigrants from East Pakistan/Bangladesh.

Forces Deployed in CI Role

1. The Army deployment is seldom made known to the public. The following seems plausible information from the published sources:
   (*a*) Tezpur (-based) corps is responsible for counter-insurgency operations in Assam. It has one to two Army Divisions at its disposal for the task; approximately 20,000 troops.
   (*b*) Dimapur (-based) corps has more onerous charge of controlling insurgency in Tripura, Manipur, Mizoram and Nagalard. Its main job lies in the last two states. Besides the two to three Army Divisions, the BSF and Assam Rifles contribute considerable strength for the task.
2. Unlike the Army, the Para Military Forces (PMF) generally keep announcing the quantum of their forces deployed in different states. Some illustrative figures of PMF deployed in Assam in December 1996 are given below:
   (a) CRPF - 138 companies
   (b) BSF - 20 companies.
3. A little earlier (July 1996) Chief Minister Mahanta had announced (*The Hindustan Times* of 29 July 1996) that there were 57 companies of PMF, 37 of Assam Police, 5 from Karnataka and 15 from Bihar. He also disclosed that during the elections (early 1996), there were in all 157 companies.
4. CRPF told the press (June 1997) that it had a total of 350 companies in the North-East, of which 156 were in Assam to operate against the ULFA and Bodo militants. Its force was divided into three sectors (their term was *clusters*): Gauhati, Agartala and Imphal
5. Reality and Fantasy. On the poll eve in February 1998, there were 69 companies of PMF against the projected demand of over 600 companies! An angry Mahanta told the press on 12 February, four days before the poll: "No additional forces promised to us have come.... If the forces come 36 hours before the polls, they will be of no use."[15]
6. Additional Units Raised. Home Minister Inderjit Gupta informs the Lok Sabha in January 1998 of the Government decision to raise 12 India Reserve Battalions for anti-insurgency duties in the North-East. The figure was raised to 13, Home Minister L.K. Advani informed the

meeting of the Consultative Committee of his Ministry, in December 1998. The State-wise allotment indicated was:

Assam	– 4	Manipur	– 2
Tripura	– 2	Arunachal	– 2

Meghalaya, Mizoram, and Nagaland – 1 each

North-East : Post 2001 Scenario

New Delhi's attitude towards Engaging the Militants : A critique.

Two entities signing a ceasefire should usually amount to a commitment to talk. But New Delhi seems to be dithering in its resolve on this score. One instance that comes to mind in this connection is the Centre's invitation for talks to the National Liberation Front of Tripura (NLFT) in 2004 by the then NDA regime. In response to the call to eschew violence, two splinter groups of the NLFT surrendered, led by Nayanbashi Jamatia and Mantu Koloi respectively. But the dominant group led by Biswamohan Debbarman refused to fall into line and continues, alongwith the All Tripura Tiger Force (ATTF), its defiant posture. The common objective of these two outfits is to cleanse the hills of the non-tribals who settled in the region after 1949 when Tripura state was merged with the Indian Union.

So far the Centre has made no move to contact the leaders of two factions of the NLFT who surrendered and to talk to them. Is it any surprise that within weeks of surrendering, when he was simply ignored by the authorities, Jamatia reportedly went underground in Bangladesh.

The Garo Hills-based Achik National Volunteer Council (ANVC) is a major security risk because of its nexus with ULFA and Bodo militants and its objective of securing a Greater Garoland obviously after achiving the disintegration of the present State of Maghalaya. It had got its image tarnished because of abductions, extortion and murders. So it surrendered in 2003, coming clean in the bargain. After surrender, its cadres killed boredom by playing cricket and football with locals until the Meghalaya Government perceived it as a violation of ceasefire codes and isolated them. It obviously miffed them. And to know that they were said to have gifted an ambulance van to a charitable organisation and also contributed towards the tsunami fund. Why do the authorities have to be so supercilious in such minor matters?[16]

It is not suprising, therefore, that the Khasi-dominated Hinnietrep National Liberation Council (HNLC), formed in the early 1990s with the blessings of the NSCN (I-M) and responsible for killing a number of non-tribal traders in Shillong, has refused to sue for peace. Its leaders, too, are in Bangladesh. Surprisingly, when the smaller ANVC has been proscribed, the HNLC bears no such stigma.

Both the United People's Democratic Solidarity (UPDS) in Karbi Anglong district of Assam and Dima Halam Daogah (DHD) in North Cacher Hills are at peace with the Centre, consequent to a ceasefire agreement, since 2003, even if not between themselves. In 2005, as a result of clashes between the two, as many as 90 people mere killed. The figure for 2006 was not very different either.

It is not that New Delhi has easy options. Still it must have clear cut and transparent policy on the issues involved on such subject, NSCN(K) faction has truce with the Government for years but has not as yet been invited for negotiations. It is known that the NSCN(I-M) comes in the way of such talks. The latter has been talking to New Delhi for years all over the world but the two are nowhere near an agreement. How long will the NSCN(K) hold patience? To express its uneasy feelings it occasionally engages in bloody street fights with the NSCN(I-M).

Similar logjam exists in New Delhi's relations with the Bodo outfits. Consequent to an accord with the Bodo Liberation Tigers (BLT) leaders, they are presently controlling the leavers of power in the Bodo Territorial Council (BTC) set up under the 6th Schedule. But the National Democratic Front of Bodoland (NDFB), rival of the BLT, is still waiting in the wings after signing the truce in 2005.

As for the Centre concluding peace accords with the militants in the North-East, the 1986 one with the MNF in Mizoram was the only success story so far. As a result, Mizoram remained peaceful for years. But alas even that no longer holds true. That distinction stands shattered as the state Government did not display due sensitivity towards the aspirations and ethnic identity of the Reangs. The Mizos obviously have forgotten their oven struggle of the yore. But the smaller tribes have learnt their lessons from that very struggle. The Bru National Liberation Front (BNLF), spearheading the agitation of the Reangs for a separate state since 1996, also adopted terrorism to achieve its aims. Conceding its demand, Aizawl signed a truce with the BNLF in Oct. 2005. But unfortunately, a splinter group, Bru National Front of Mizoram, emerged to challenge the truce. The worse is that even after truce with the NBLF, thousands of Reang refugees are still living in the camps in Tripura.

It is necessary, even urgent, that the Government crafts a coherent policy to conclude agreements with the militant outfits in the North-East and have required machinery in place to ensure its implementation. New Delhi must find time for this implementation. Otherwise, the youngmen languishing in the camps will be facing frustration again and consequently may get sucked into the vortex of terrorism and violence.

North Bengal Situation : Still Violent and Worrisome

Peace seems to be nowhere in sight in this region. Only on 5 Feb. 2007, the Howrah-Dibrugarh Kamrup Express had a narrow escape when an explosion took place at Kamakshyaguri railway station neighbouring Aliduar in Jalpaiguri district within moments of the train leaving the platform. Seven people were hurt when a bomb kept in a stray bag on platform no. 2 exploded in the afternoon.

A similar blast suspected to have been triggerd by an ULFA/KLO chique late last year inside a passenger train at Belakoba station, also in Jalpaiguri district, snuffed out seven lives.

It is indeed a matter of deep concern that in a span of five months, Oct. 2006 to Feb. 2007, North Bengal has witnessed three bomb blasts. Of these two went off at two railway stations and one explosion occurred in a market place along the Assam-West Bengal border. The toll : Eight dead and many more injured.

All that indicates that a tumultuous time is set to disturb peace in the region, lying at the junction of Assam, fighting insurgency for the past 25 years, and North Bengal, centre of Kamtapur agitation. The vulnerability is only increased by the fact that the region shares international boundaries with three countries : Nepal (just coming out of the throes of the Maoist insurgency and the anti-king political agitation), Bhutan (ULFA and Bodo militants are again attempting to establish a foothold there) and Bangladesh (breeding ground for the ultras operating in the North-East).

The KLO is the main source of the violence in the area. A local outfit, it is spearheading a movement for establishment of a separate homeland for the Rajbanshis of North Bengal and four districts of adjoining Lower Assam. It had unleashed a massive spate of violence till 2003 when Bhutan carried out operation Flush Out against Indian terrorists camping on its soil. Since that year, the North Bengal police has taken its gaze off the KLO, as majority of its cadres had surrendered.

It was obviously a miscalculation on the part of the State police. Even if its backbone had been smashed, the KLO could hardly die this way. Besides the ideological motivation behind this outfit, the outlawed ULFA would never allow the KLO to die, after all, it is its strategic partner and it would sustain it for its own cause. Simply put, ULFA needs an ally in this part of West Bengal to provide its cadres all the logistic support they need. It also helps it to access the camps in the neighbouring countries using the North Bengal corridor. In the bargain, the KLO also gets reciprocal help to wage its own war for Kamtapur. KLO cadres are trained, equipped and lodged in the ULFA camps in Bangladesh. Intelligence reported that a new armed group of the KLO cadres trained in the Chittagong Camps sneaked into North Bengal in mid-2006.[17]

Intelligence inputs suggest that the renewed violence, mentioned above, indicates the strategy of "minimal risk, maximum gains". They avoid direct confrontation with the security forces, and instead target the public zones. Attacks on the two railway stations (Belakoba and Kamakshyaguri) and at Barovisha market stand testimony to the new strategy. Is the State, and particularly its police, aware of this changed policy adopted by the outfit? Their inaction so far shows it is not.

For effectively countering the KLO violence West Bengal must share intelligence with Assam as this outfit has partners-in-crime operating in the latter's territory, like the ULFA.

It is essential to convince such outfits that they cannot bend the state to their will and only offensive operations launched by its security forces can do this job. Only then will the KLO feel compelled to come to the negotiations table.

Besides looking at this region in the context of insurgency-related violence, there is also a foreign policy angle to it. The recent (around the close of 2006) spurt in the incident of firing from across the Bangladesh border aimed at aiding the intrusion of militants into North Bengal and Assam has made the security experts to sit up and take a serious look at country's threat perception vis-a-vis our existing foreign policy stance of reconciliation in regard to India's immediate neighbours. Unprovoked firing by the BDR in Assam's Cachar sector and along the North Bengal frontier encompassing the sensitive districts of Jalpaiguri, Cooch Behar and North and South Dinajpur will give sleepless nights to North Block officials dealing with the internal security.

The use of RDX in the 20 Nov. 2006 explosion in the Haldibari-New Jalpaiguri passenger train at Belokoba in North Bengal (already mentioned earlier) should persuade the MHA to reorganise the operational blueprint designed for the Eastern/North-Eastern region. It is worth remembering that the Chicken's neck located in this region is strategically significant for India's security as this 29 km panhandle joins the entire North-East to the mainland. A few dozens of determined terrorists, stiffened by some suicide bombers of whom there seem to be no shortage of late, could effectively disrupt this connectivity.

Even more worrisome is the fact of India having a long and porous international border with Nepal, Bhutan, Myanmar and Bangladesh, which only encourages our adversaries to try and dominate the region by sponsoring or helping the insurgent movements in the area. It has already been stated that situation in Nepal and Bangladesh can cause concern to India's security minders (The caretaker government in Bangladesh has taken some tough anti-terrorism measures in Feb.-April 2007 period, but they could turn out to be short-term palliatives). Even if the intelligence has held the KLO (in association with the ULFA) responsible for the Belakoba blast, there are other sources of worry as well. The leaders of groups like the ULFA, KLO, ATTF, NDFB and others are in touch with HUJI-B and Jamaat-ul-Mujahideen (Bangladesh) and are supported by Pakistani ISI. ULFA leader Paresh Baruah's recent (late 2006) visit to Pakistan only fortifies such claims. Yet again, it is believed that KLO Chief Jeevan Singh had taken refuge in ULFA training camps in Chittagong in order to arrange more recruits for his own outfit to spread terror in his "area of operations."

With terror groups like the LET and Al Oaeda having set up links with the insurgent groups, West Bengal has turned out to be a safe haven for jihadi outfits. The State has not taken seriously the advisory from the MHA to strengthen security apparatus at the railway stations and other vulnerable areas.

To prevent any further flare up particularly in West Bengal, counter-intelligence agents must be deployed in sensitive border districts, with back-up from the special forces. Observers feel "the ruling party in West Bengal must realise the harsh fact that a police force deployed in self-esteem and politically browbeaten can never be an effective tool against insurgency."[18]

MHA Worried over Violence in North-East : 2006 Report

The MHA report reviewing the internal security situation in 2006 says :

> "In Assam and Nagaland, the violence has gone up due to increased activities of the ULFA and factional clashes between the NSCN(IM) and NSCN(K). But the overall situation in the North-Eastern states has shown signs of improvement. There has been a decline in violence in Tripura, Manipur and Arunachal Pradesh. In Meghalaya, violence has been contained. Mizoram and Sikkim continue to be peaceful."

The report says after a temporary/unilateral suspension of operations against the ULFA, the counter-insurgency operations have been resumed because there was no direct response from it.

In Nagaland, fratricidal clashes between the rival NSCN factions have claimed at least 200 lives during the past five years.

Current Situation in North-East : A Review : March 2007

About 30 organisations described variously as terrorist, militant or insurgent, are active in Assam (presently 'Asom') and other states in North-Eastern India. The South Asia Terrorism Portal (SATP)[19] actually identifies over a hundred 'terrorist/insurgent groups' in the region. Most of them are admittedly little more than names and sign boards with poorly written constitutions, manifestos and charters of demands, engaged essentially in extortion and racketeering. Many of these are nearly moribund/defunct. Others, with a little more substance to them and boasting of 'greater autonomy' agenda are engaged sporadically in violent activities alternating with some kind of negotations with the State/Central governments.

About a dozen of the 30-odd active outfits are engaged in 'armed struggle' against the Union of India. The most prominent of these outfits are the ULFA and the NSCN. While the ULFA seeks to restore the sovereignty of Assam lost as a result of the 24 Feb. 1826 Yandabo Treaty, the NSCN (IM) demands an independent Nagaland, as "the Nagas were never part of India—British or Independent". In fact, the Nagas under ZA Phizo 'declared their independence on 14 August 1947, a day before India's'.

The oldest organisation engaged in 'armed struggle' in Manipur is the UNLF, even if 3-4 other outfits are engaged in similar struggles for restoration of Manipur's lost sovereignty as a result of 'the undemocratic and inequitable' Merger Agreement of 15 Oct. 1949.

But these sovereignty claims by various insurgent outfits on the territories they aspire for themselves are complicated by the district and state boundaries drawn and redrawn by the British India as dictated or demanded by the administrative convenience or constriants. As a result, the history and geography of the territories concerned being what they are, there are inescapably conflicting territorial issues involved in, and indeed integral to, the sovereignty aspirations. "Ironically this interface between sovereignty and territoriality impinges on all the states where these organisations are active, highlighting the fundamental contradictions of these sovereignty struggles.

The ready and an apt instance that comes to mind is the NSCN(IM) demand for Nagalim (= Greater Nagaland), which is the most intractable difficulty blocking the resolution of the long-outstanding Naga problem, as also any further progress in the sustained 7-year long negotiations between the NSCN (IM) and New Delhi. The conceding of this contentious demand will simply mean disintegration of the three Indian states—Manipur, Arunachal Pradesh and Assam—and the latter will just not hear of it. Nor is the Centre in a position to force it on them. The constituent states of India guard their constitutional and jurisdictional rights rather jealously. A remote and an indirect hint of New Delhi giving in on Nagalim demand some years back created a conflagration all over Manipur.

Can the leaders demanding sovereignty ever hope to succeed, considering their adversary is the Indian state? Sophisticated and well informed as these leaders are about history, the answer must be clear to them. India is too big and too powerful to be defeated in war, or allow foreign occupation. Their aim in continuing with these meandering negotiations is rather simple: To get maximum out of India for their 'dream lands'. They know India would not bend beyond a point. Negotiations in any case is their best bit—for the age-ing leadership in some cases. Even then, they want to continue nurturing the hope however slender the thread.

All human beings have a right to dream. The modest and continuing gains made by the Catalonian autonomy movement and rather more dramatic success by Montenegro, which in the May 2006 national referuendum voted narrowly for secession hold promises for separatist movements in the region. Neither the example of Kosovo is lost on them. But it is equally clear to them that India is neither the (now defunct) Soviet Union nor Yogoslavia. You cannot fault them for unrealisable dreams!

A mention must be made here of a new demand in Manipur : the current campaign for a plebiscite on the issue of Manipur's independence, proposed initially by the UNLF and since then taken by several 'civil society' groups. Some analysts have noted that it "followed closely, indeed almost coterminously, in the wake of referendum in Montenegro." Interestingly but surprisingly, if not omenously, it drew an assortment of eminent speakers for its 6 June 2006 meeting in Imphal. Some of them should have displayed more discretion than attending this meeting on plebiscite, opined a scholar. Some of those who addressed this meeting were the titular king of Manipur, a former Lok Sabha member, a former Human Rights Commissioner, the President of the Manipur Working Journalists' Union, leaders of political parties and several women leaders—always a potent force in Manipur.

Coming to the latter half of the year 2006, a ceasefire arranged through the exertions of a civil society group led by eminent author Indira Goswami collapsed as the ULFA refused to come to the negotiations table for the direct talks with the Centre. Subsequently, it resorted to doing what it is justly infamous for : killing innocent civilians, mainly non-Assamese Hindi-speaking Biharis. By way of reaction, the Government mouthed the usual, inane shiboleths—"culprits will be brought to book", "it shows the frustration of ULFA", all necessary measures will be adopted to prevent the recurrence of such ghastly act", *et. al.,* which are best forgotten till the next outrage.

So after that brief lull of cease-fire period, Assam was in turmoil once again by Jan. 2007. An analyst put it rather bluntly on 19 Jan. 2007: "The killing of innocent civilians by rampaging insurgents, as a malleable' Centre desperately calls for a truce to rescue the forthcoming National Games (in Guwahati) from the scourge of terror, and reluctant to act tough on the illegal migrants, goes on to prove that the North-Eastern theatre is on the verge of ignition."[20]

The NSCN(I-M) held its latest round of talks with the Government of India at New Delhi in March 2007, which "made some progress", as Muivah put it.

Notes

1. *Times of India,* 26-1-1994.
2. Ramchandra Guha is the author of the book *Savaging the Civilised; Verrier Elwin—His Tribals and India,* OUP, March 1999.
3. These observations seems to be particularly applicable to the AASU agitation (1979-1985) in Assam.
4. Collated from the *Frontline* of 11-2-1994; *Times of India,* 1-1-1997; *Sunday Observer,* 19-1-1997; *Outlook,* 1-2-1999; and *Hindu* of 23-8-1999 and 25-11-2000.
5. Indo-Burma Revolutionary Front (IBRF) is a conglomerate of multiplicity of insurgent outfits in India's North-East and Burma's Eastern regions.
6. *The Indian Express,* 26-9-1999.
7. The details in 1-18 serials are from the *Hindustan Times,* 10 and 21 August 1999, and *Frontline* of 10-9-1999.
8. *The Hindu,* 25-11-2000.
9. This heading is inspired by a story penned by that indefatigable journalist (now a Minister at the Centre), Arun Shourie in the early 1980s on the politicians and their corrupt ways, on the front page of the *Indian Express,* under the heading "Politics as Commerce".
10. Here is the list of major accords signed in the Region: (1) 16-Point Agreement with the Naga People's Convention in 1960, (2) Naga Accord, Shillong, 1975, (3) Assam Accord, 1985, (4) Mizo Accord, 1986, (5) TNV Accord, Tripura, 1988, (6) Bodo Accord, 1993. Half a dozen minor accords signed within the Regional States are not enumerated here. Also not included is the first written understanding Sir Akbar Hydari had with the Nagas in 1948.
11. After Phizo's daughter, Adino, who leads this faction.
12. It is led by Khodao (K) Yanthan.
13. From the *Outlook Weekly,* 1-2-1999 and some dailies.
14. *The Hindu,* 23-11-1999.
15. *The Outlook,* 23-2-1998.
16. JB Lama, *The Statesman*, 26 March 2007.
17. Bappaditya Paul, *The Stateman*, 20 Feb. 2007.
18. Seema Sengupta, *The Pioneer*, 5 Dec. 2006.
19. MS Prabhakar, *The Frontline*, 22 September 2006.
20. Seema Sengupta, *The Pioneer*, 19 January 2007.

2

Foreign Nations are Muddying the Waters

If Russia and the now defunct Soviet Union were playing the great game with the British India before and till 1947 on the latter's North-Western frontiers, China quietly 'devoured' Tibet soon after that year. Post-Indian Independence period saw her neighbours—Pakistan, Burma (part of the erstwhile India), and later Bangladesh—nibbling at India's sovereignty and integrity by training, equipping and offering safe heavens to its insurgent outfits in the North-East.

Foreign Hand in Indian Insurgency

An insurgency movement challenges a nation-state and aims at undermining its sovereignty. When it finds an external (a neighbouring country usually) sponsor or supporter, it tends to become at one level a part of inter-state conflict. It is a form of an indirect aggression against the nation-state by that neighbour, made attractive for it by the inability of the former to use its conventional military power. For the neighbour, this war—popularly called 'low-intensity conflict' (LIC) is a low cost, cheaper option to destabilize, bleed and even defeat the nation-state. This in brief is the theory and reality of a foreign hand aiding and abetting insurgency in another country.

The extent of material and moral support by an external power is one of the important factors for the success of an insurgency. The geography of the North-East consequent to 1947-Partition of India, renders it eminently well-placed for the insurgent groups operating in the area to receive such help and support, sharing as it does its borders with four external powers—Bhutan, China (Tibet), Myanmar and Bangladesh (earlier East Pakistan).

Foreign Hand was always there Ubiquitous

So it should be no surprise that a foreign hand of one shape or the other has always aided and abetted the insurgent movements in the Region (and the country beyond) almost since 1947. If it was China in the North-East during the 1950s through 1970s, it was Pakistan to start with in Kashmir, later in Punjab, and finally (perhaps, post-1971 tragedy) in the North-East through its 'famous' ISI. Bangladesh and Myanmar too had added fuel to the insurgency fires at one time or the other.

It is no consolation to India if analysts ascribe racial and ethnic reasons for the external involvement. The North-East is inhabited by the Mongoloid tribes who have close ethnic and cultural ties with the tribes in China, Tibet, Burma (and even Bangladesh). Barring Khasis and Jaintias of Meghalaya, almost all hill tribes belong to the Tibeto-Chinese fold and to the Tibeto-Burmese family of languages. It was this affinity, they argue, which led some of the tribal groups to turn towards their own stock, across the border than towards the country they resided in. The strategic location of the North-East and the access of the disaffected groups to China, Burma, Bangladesh and Bhutan together with material and moral support of foreign Intelligence agencies have facilitated insurgency in the Region.

They also cite the historical reasons for the foreign interest in the Region. "Like India, its neighbours like East Pakistan (Bangladesh) and Burma, are bound to have 'permanent interests' in the Region with which all of them have had closer historical links." Assam, once invaded and occupied by Burma before British annexation, was an administrative part of Bengal Province (1826-74), and again of East Bengal and Assam province (1905-12). They might as well add that it was repeatedly attacked by the Muslim rulers of Bengal and Delhi. Again it was under a Muslim League Ministry during April 1937-September 1938 and November 1939-December 1941. The counter view is that these historical reasons for permanent interests are a mere sophistry for their nefarious designs on Assam by the Muslim fundamentalists. It needs to be remembered that Assam figured as an integral constituent of the yet-to-be-born Pakistan in the scheme of things vigorously espoused by the ideologues of the Muslim League. As if by way of wish-fulfilment, the Cabinet Mission Plan placed Assam and Bengal in Group C in 1946. Muslim League was not to be blamed if it had visions of Assam as part of future Pakistan "to act as a Lebensraum for its East Pakistan compatriots" (Assam was saved for India by fierce, stout and unceasing endeavour by her great son and a great Indian, Gopinath Bordoloi with unstinted support and blessings of Mahatma while the rest of the leadership of the great INC—including Nehru and Patel—had acquiesced). Another factor that placed Assam in an inextricable association with East Pakistan/Bangladesh was a continual influx of Bengali immigrants, legal and illegal, that started from Day one of its take-over by the British in 1826 and "continues till date in spite of the bitterness and political storms it has created over the years". Subsequent emergence of Bangladesh and consolidation in that country of a unilingual and virtually unireligious nationality which had historically been in an adversarial relations with the Assamese-speaking people, have only sharpened the anxieties and expectations arising out of these facts, on the respective side of the border.

That the Intelligence agencies of the countries of the Sub-continent, given the background mentioned above, would be active in the Region in a manner and with an intent going far beyond the legitimate intelligence gathering, was hardly unexpected. Specifically in the North-East, where several insurgencies have been active for over half a century, Pakistan has always been fanatically active, keeping track of them and extending full help. On the eve of emergence of Bangladesh, East Pakistan figured prominently as a sanctuary for both Naga and Mizo insurgent; their leaders were sheltered in East Pakistan and travelled to third countries on Pak Passports. The insurgents' camps located there came to light after creation of Bangladesh.

India Better Watch Out: Conspiracies Galore

Certain interests were already at work even before 1947. Some British officers, including the then Governor of Assam, were planning creation of a 'Crown Colony', comprising hills areas of both India's North-East and Burma's West and North-West which in due course would be an independence state—popularly called Coupland Plan.[1] Macdonald, Political Officer, Lushai Hills, mooted another scheme for carving out an autonomous state comprising of Lushai Hills and parts of Chin Hills of Burma, as a British protectorate, since "the tribes were not Indian—neither in origin, nor in language, nor in habits, nor in looks...and it would be unfair to allow this great body of non-Indian Animists and Christians to be drawn into the struggle between the Hindus and Muslims". The conspiracies have not ceased since!

India be better beware of the games the West want to play with and in its North-East. As early as 1966, the Agenda International de Prensa (International Press Service—IPS) circulated reports datelined Dhaka that there were efforts to create a united and independent Bengal, comprising East Pakistan, West Bengal, Assam, Nagaland, Manipur, Tripura, *Sikkim* and Bhutan.[2] An excerpt from the IPS Report: "The separatists are counting on USA and other western powers to give them necessary assistance. They are confident that these powers would be interested...in such an independent state in South-East Asia...which could provide shield against the Chinese aggression."[3] And there is more of the same designs!

The US International Communications Agency's June 1979 circular, entitled "Project Brahmaputra" is equally significant, perhaps sinister in its intent. Sent to all its branches in Delhi and Calcutta, it disclosed that the Special Research Cell of George Washington University, with the approval of the State Department, had detailed several teams of investigators to conduct research in the North-Eastern States, Sikkim and Bhutan. And pray, what was the purpose of research? "To throw light on the public opinion in the region to establish in what measure the present status of these states remain acceptable or whether there are indications that the formation of a 'New State' is a current problem."[4]

The above is somewhat elaborate picture of India's North-East and her neighbours' envy! It shows up the permanent interests of these neighbours! What follows is brief, very brief description of individual neighbour's perfidy to muddy India's North-Eastern waters. Briefly because it is recent, even current, history and facts are too well-known for detailing.

PAKISTANI SHENANIGANS

Pak abetment of the insurgency in the North-East has been blatantly direct. When Army was called out in 1956 to fight the Naga insurgency, Phizo crossed over to East Pakistan and was welcomed with open arms. After a 3-year stay in Dhaka, he was flown to Britain under a Peruvian passport (and he died there in exile on 30 April 1990). While in Dhaka and London, he was given all help to procure arms and raise the Naga issue at various international fora.

Between 1962-68, at least 10 underground Naga gangs, totalling over 2500[5], crossed over to East Pakistan and were trained in camps located at Rangamati, Ruma, Bandarban, Rangkhiang Ali Kadam[6], all close to Indian border in Chittagong Hill Tract. They returned with arms (including LMGs, RL, Carbines, and 2" mortars) and ammunition. The attempt to send any more batches for similar training did not seem to have succeeded. Mowu Angami-led band to East Pakistan was intercepted by Burmese Army.[7]

To show their solidarity with Pakistan, during the 1965 Indo-Pak war, the Naga leadership issued a statement calling upon Government of India "to take immediate steps to disengage the services of any Naga...".

The Pakistani help to Mizo rebels was even more crucial. Apart from the advantage of having a long, nearly unguarded border with East Pakistan/ Bangladesh that offered a choice of several infiltration routes, the Mizo rebels had an ideally-located sanctuary, just across the border, in the Chittagong Hill Tract (CHT). Laldenga, the Mizo leader, seemed to have done his homework rather well. He crossed the border in first week of December 1963 and was eagerly received by the Pak agencies. Quantities of Pak arms and ammunition were dispatched from Chittagong via the Dohazari Railhead to the CHT, whence the rebels moved them to safe places within Mizoram by January 1965. The Mizo uprising started on the night 28 February/1 March 1966 and the rebels made effective use of the Pak 'gifts'. Assam and India were taken by surprise and the Indian Army took more than a month to retrieve the situation.

After the Army crackdown, Mizo underground shifted their operational base to the safety of jungles in Burma and CHT. Interestingly, Laldenga's liaison officer on behalf of Pak Army in the late 1950s was a certain Capt Ershad, later General and Bangladesh President. At its peak, the MNA had over 7000 men and women under arms, majority ensconced in East Pakistan. Well supplied with weapons and victuals, they virtually had a free run of the land.

China and Indian Insurgents

Chinese entered the field late, but ever the pragmatic, their help to the rebels was comprehensive and they did not help the Nagas only; they took the Mizo and Meitei rebels also under their wings. For Nagas, the support from China, the inspiration for the revolutionary groups in many parts of the world in 1960s, would bring international spotlight on the Naga 'freedom fight' and consequently boost the morale of both the leaders and the led. The Chinese help was also a necessity "because, of late, Indo-Pak border had come under an increased surveillance". But China had its own calculations: A level of support to the Naga and other rebel outfits would keep some Indian Army formations engaged in CI operations which would cause some attrition in the process—greater, the better for the Chinese Army.

The Nagas started getting the active Chinese support from 1966 only. The guerrilla and subversive warfare training for their cadres was arranged in the Yunnan Province of mainland China, and later in Lhasa in Tibet.[8] Muivah, who had led the first batch in November 1966, had stayed back and was taken to Beijing and later to Hanoi to take some lessons on ideology as also in the art of guerrilla tactics against the modern weapons[9] (His batch had taken 3 months' arduous journey through jungles of Arunachal and Burma to reach Yunnan).

The Mizos and Meiteis also received some help and training from the Chinese. Three Mizo groups were sent to China during the May 1975-early 1976 period. Laldenga also visited Beijing and met Chou Enlai. The Meitei insurgents under Bisheswar took an unconventional route via Nepal to make it to Lhasa. The Meiteis were ideologically Left-oriented and were the first to bring with them the techniques of Urban Guerrilla warfare, aimed at engaging Indian troops in built-up areas in Imphal.[10]

In mid-1969, China and Pakistan evolved a joint strategy to train various rebel groups operating in India's North-East and to coordinate their activities to improve their functional and operational efficiency. A Guerrilla Training School was set up in East Pakistan with the Chinese instructors to train the Naga, Mizo, Meitei and Kuki cadres. A small air strip was also built at a place 15 Km off Rangamati.[11]

From the late 1970s, the Chinese support to the North-East Insurgents declined mainly because the cadres could be adequately indoctrinated within their respected areas by their own instructors and the realisation and emphasis on desirability and principle of sustaining a revolutionary movement with internal resources and mobilization at local level. A contributory factor for this decline in external support could be the Chinese concern at the large scale surrenders by the Nagas in the 1970s. Consequent to the Governor's call during his address to the Budget session of the Nagaland Assembly, 1049 Naga cadres surrendered in 1969 alone.

Bangladesh and North-Eastern Insurgents

When Bangladesh emerged from its travails of West Pakistani oppression and became a free nation in December 1971, with some help from India, it was expected all help extended to the North-East insurgents by the erstwhile East Pakistan would dry up and it indeed did for a time. The things started returning to the old ways after the assassination of Sheikh Mujib-ur-Rahman on 15 August 1975. The Mizo rebels regained some of the lost ground in CHT, not as an associate of Chakma militants but as collaborators of the local authorities, helping them in settling Bengali Muslims in CHT (at the cost of the interests of the indigenous Chakmas who had fled to India) and ensuring their own (Mizo rebel's) safe refuge in return[12] (The Mizos helping the enemies of the Chakmas is quite natural and logical, after all the latter were an unwelcome presence in Mizoram, and thorn in the flesh of excessively chauvinistic Mizo sections in Mizoram).

Besides the Nagas and Mizos, the cadre of Tripura Volunteer Force (TVF) also found patronage in Bangladesh. But the Bangladeshi help to Tripura insurgents was partially a *quid pro quo* to the support India was extending to the Shanti Bahini, a Chakma rebel outfit fighting the Bangladesh Government in CHT. Ashok Tandon, DG, BSF, in his annual press conference on 21 November 1997 asserted that both the ATTF and NLFT continued to get support from Bangladesh. Indian protests failed to persuade Bangladesh to close down rebel camps in its territory.[13] A 10-page Press Note released on the Raising Day of the BSF in November 1995 had details on the involvement of Bangladesh Government with the North-East rebel groups and help extended by it to them. It disclosed that most insurgent groups were obtaining sophisticated weapons from Thailand with the active connivance of Bangladesh Intelligence. It also talked of the nexus between Pakistan's ISI and Bangladesh Intelligence agencies. India's Home Minister at the time, Indrajit Gupta, disclosed as much in his reply to a starred question in Lok Sabha on 3 December 1996[14] (By this time, Sheikh Hasina had become the Prime Minister of Bangladesh).

The links of Manipur rebels with East Pakistan/Bangladesh go back to decades. The training camps of Manipuri insurgents were reportedly located in the Srimangal, Bhanugach and Dhamai areas in Bangladesh close to the border.[15]

Can Fencing be the Answer?

Foreign Secretary (FS) level talks held in June 2005 at New Delhi failed to bridge the gap between India and Bangladesh on the fencing issue. Bangla FS Mohammad Hemayetuddin reiterated his country's opposition to the border fencing that India is erecting as an anti-infiltration measure. India holds the fencing does not violate the 1975 border guidelines, with which Bangladesh disagrees. The two sides agreed to simultaneous patrolling of the border including the riverine stretches by the BDR and BSF. The Bangla delegation provided details of recent operations against the Indian insurgents and criminal groups but the Indian FS Shyam Saran urged them to share the details of those killed and apprehended.

Bangladesh proposed three new bus routes: Dhaka-Siliguri, Dhaka-Guwahati, and Dhaka-Shillong *(AA, Hindu, Tribune,* all of 23-6-05).

Bangla FS said ULFA leader Anup Chetia, though he had served his term in jail, could not be sent to India as he had one more court case against him. The Bangla FS denied the existence of the Indian insurgents' camps in his country and assured the Indians that they would not allow any anti-Indian activities on their soil.

The work on fencing, and the road along it, has not been as per schedule, mainly because of poor funds situation. The target for completing the fencing along the Assam-Bangla border was fixed for 2003 but has been extended to 2006. Again, only 578 Km of fencing along the Tripura border was completed by 1996 against the target of 896 Km (*TOI*, 19-12-96).

Assam-Bangladesh Border Fensing : Status Dec. 2006

It is indeed a story of "another year, another target", as the Indian Express of 1 Jan. 2007 put it. Nothing illustrates this truism better than the mid-Dec. 2006 statement by Minister for Assam Accord Implementation Bhumidhar Barman in Assam Assembly : "on 31 March, 2007 a barbed wire fence will finally mark the Assam stretch of the Indo-Bangladesh border. It is the last and final target date for completion of this long-pending project." It is for record that at one stage, the fencing (and the accompanying road) was targeted to be completed by 2003, which, subsequently, through several changed target dates, was shifted to 2006. Now, as per the Minister, 31 March, 2007 is the "last and final target date."

But as of now, as Barman himself said, 17.80 per cent of the border length under the Assam Public Works Department remains to be fenced. In real terms; it works out to 43 km of the 263-km border in the state. The Centre however has sanctioned fencing of only 223 km, as the remaining part is across rivers including Brahmaputra. The total length of the Indo-Bangla border is 3,286 km.

It may be mentioned in passing here that on 29 July, 2006 the Union Government had told a tripartite meeting (attended by representatives of the AASU, Assam Government and Central Government) that "the gaps (in the border fence) will be filled up by Dec., 2006."

As is well-known, it was AASU which made New Delhi agree to fence the Indo-Bangladesh border and had it included in the 1985 Assam Accord it signed with the latter in that year. The AASU has been sore with New Delhi for the tardy implementation of this urgently-needed project. On the Minister's setting a "last and final target date" of 31 March, 2007, Samujjal Bhattacharyya, Adviser to AASU, said: "We are happy that at least it is nearing completion... It will prevent further influx from Bangladesh, and put an end to the cross-border activities of the ISI and various fundamental Islamic militant groups which have their bases in Bangladesh."

Here is the Adviser's lament on the delay and changing target dates :

> "The saddest part is that the Government never had a time schedule for completion of the fence. Even when the Assam Accord was signed and the Government agreed to fence the border, there was no mention of any target. It was only in the first tripartite talks on the Assam Accord on 5 May, 2005 that the Government fixed a time frame, the target being Jan. 2006. But that was missed. The next tripartite meeting, attended by Home Minister Shivraj Patil, extended the deadline to Dec. 2006, which was reiterated in the next meeting on 29 July, 2006. We do not understand how the Government has now extended this to March (2007)."

One reason for the delay deserves a mention. Initially, the Assam PWD was assigned the task of constructing the border road and border fence. By the time it completed first stretch of 41-km of the job, its pace was found unsatisfactory, and the project was transferred to the NBCC.

The AASU, and for that matter, the AGP, BJP and all those who have been passionately vocal against the influx from Bangladesh, all are unanimous on the "irreparable" damage done by the delay in completion of the border fence. To wit, the state BJP President Ramen Dika: "The demography of Assam has already been changed, and no power on earth can revert it to the pre-Bangladesh times."

Now for the two statistical pieces of information :

- Rs. 198 crore have been spent on constructing the 179.91 km fence and the 263-km border road.
- Rs. 99 crore will be required to complete the remaining work according to government estimates.

Now this leaves only one question on the fencing : How effective will it be when completed to stop the influx of the Bangladeshis into India, especially Assam and West Bengal? To assert that it will make no difference and the infiltration would continue as hithertofore, as some analysts indeed do, would be height of pessimism, or conceding too much to human ingenuity. The more accurate answer will be : The fencing will definitely thwart, if not eliminate, the influx. It may be apt to mention here that the US is fencing its Mexican border as is Pakistan doing its Afghan border.

The Denials Notwithstanding

When the Indian Home Secretary Dhirendra Singh visited Dhaka in September 2004, he gave a fresh list of training camps being operated in Bangladesh by various Indian insurgent outfits: ULFA, NDFB, NLFT, etc. During his meeting with his BDR counterpart in August 2004, the DG BSF had given a list of 195 camps run on the Bangla soil. The September 2004 letter was an essentially updated version of the August list. India also demanded that Dhaka hand over fugitive insurgent leaders like Arbinda Rajkhowa, Paresh Barua, Anup Chetia (all of ULFA), Dev Burman (NLFT). Like the DG, BDR, Bangla Home Secretary also denied the existence of any such camps in his country.

In mid-2004, a 5-part article in a prominent Bangla daily *Prothom Alo* disclosed that the banned Bangladeshi Islamic extremist outfit, Harkat-ul-Jehad-al Islami (HUJI)—declared a terrorist outfit by the US State Department for its links with the Al Qaeda and Taliban—has established an active network through madrasas and local NGOs. The HUJI was also suspected to be "behind the recent attack on Sheikh Hasina at a rally in Dhaka". The article also said it "is imparting training to the insurgents from Myanmar and India" *(Hindu,* 9-3-04).

As an analyst put it (Exp, 3-2-05), "for several years now, India has been conducting a dialogue of the deaf with Dhaka, with bilateral relations deteriorating...". New Delhi has been consistently telling Dhaka to crack down on as many as 1174 terrorist camps housing cadres of not only of Indian insurgent outfits (Like ULFA, NDFB, NLFT, KLO) but also of Al Qaeda, Lashkar-e-Tayyeba (LeT), HUJI, Islamic Oikya Jote (headed by Mufti Fazlul Haq Amini), Jagrata Muslim Janata (JMJ) of Bangla Bhai.

By way of a smart riposte, Dhaka not only sought specific-addresses and telephone numbers of these so-called camps but also offered to ferry senior Indian officials by helicopter to the "alleged" sites to "prove" no camps exist. Unlike the more fixed structures in PoK, these camps are said to comprise hastily constructed bamboo structures that can be removed in minutes. In a constant denial mode, Dhaka has stubbornly refused to accept Indian Intelligence reports on the camps, countering them with the lists of criminals who, fleeing from the local criminal justice system, have sought refuge in West Bengal and Tripura.

After the 1992 Bombay blasts, operations by the extremist Islamic terrorists/jehadists have shifted from the western coast to the eastern regions—with the gun-running, camps, and clandestine anti-India activities concentrated along the CHT, the Siliguri Corridor and Myanmar.

There is enough evidence, if the evidence was required at all about the "cyclical rise of Islamic fundamentalism" since the return of the Khalida Zia's BNP to power in October 2001, followed by the familiar incidents like the mass exodus of Hindus from the villages and countryside; violence against the opposition leaders and minorities; and spate of explosions. All this should not come as a surprise as an extremist Muslim outfit is a partner in the Coalition Ministry as also Khalida's repeated anointment of India's North-Eastern insurgent groups as freedom fighters!

As for targeting the opposition, "there were over 100 blasts at political rallies with more than 200 casualties, the most recent being the killing of SAMS Kibria, a former diplomat and finance minister.... Blast within high security zone in Dhaka days before the (aborted) SAARC Summit further raised New Delhi's concerns" *(Exp/Hindu,* 3-2-05). 'Casual' violence aimed at political workers "has claimed over 1100 lives in the past three years (2002-04)." An analyst says "the present dispensation in Bangladesh is using Islamic militants to target their political opposition. On balance, it is absolutely clear the Government is involved." For the Indian Officials the 'Commando-style attack' on Hasina in August 2004 and the 'murder' of Kibria showed how "systematically the democratic, secular fabric of the country" is being eroded.

Inter alia the above para, the Intelligence reported July 2005 that "the ruling coalition in Dhaka has outsourced" the job of tackling its political rivals to the Indian insurgents it continues to shelter, all the loud disclaimers notwithstanding" (*TOI*, 5-7-05). Investigations into the recent attacks on Awami League (AL) leaders as also the 'huge arms haul' in April 2004 confirmed the suspicions of an unholy nexus between the ULFA and ATTF insurgents and the ruling coalition in Dhaka which includes the fundamentalist Jamat-i-Islami and has often been accused of intolerance of political rivals. This collusion got confirmed when the investigations disclosed that some of the grenades used in attacks on the AL leaders were supplied by the Indian rebels (Bangladesh's *Daily Star,* 29-5-05). Concerned about the fall-out of the disclosure on its ties with India and on its global image, in view of the post-9/11 heightened international anti-terrorism sensibilities, Dhaka ordered immediate suspension of the investigations. To deflect attention from its discomfiture and the real issue, the Zia Government resorted to the familiar ploy the governments the world over placed in such embarrassing, compromising situations often do: Launched propaganda blitz accusing the Awami League and the ubiquitous 'foreign agents' (read Indians) of engineering these attacks!

As for the denial of the Indian rebels' camps on Bangla soil, here is what ABM Mohiuddin Chowdhury, a senior AL leader and Mayor of the port city of Chittagong said at a press conference (10-4-04) at his office: "The Indian secessionists are running 50 to 60 training camps in the CHT and the huge cache of weapons seized on the night 1/2 April were meant to arm these rebels under a sinister conspiracy to create unrest in India and to destabilise the sub-Continent.

How come the Huge Arms Haul?

"The fire power involved may be enough to keep an army brigade in fighting fettle for a year." Another analyst thought "the largest ever illegal arms shipment in South Asia was enough to equip a division". They both were talking about the massive arms haul made in Chittagong on 2 April 2004. Its sheer size was mind-boggling.

AK-47s	1290	Rocket launchers	150
Rounds	1.1 m	Grenade launchers	2,000
Grenades (T-82/2)	25,020	Night vision devices (goggle sets)	3,550
Rockets	840		

The fact of Bangladesh coast emerging as a major avenue for arms smuggling is known, but the nature and size of this arms seizure has sent the *Intelligence* officials reeling: "We have never seen any thing remotely like this big before!" No one single insurgent group in the Region—not ULFA, not Nepal Maoists—could afford to pay for this shipment by themselves. The cache was obviously planned to be parceled out to different groups. The fact that this kind and level of coordination is being planned is itself worrisome. A radio intercept suggests a part of the consignment was for the ATTF, but then, who were the other recipients? The trucks hired to carry the cargo were due to go to Sylhet and Maulvi Bazar, bordering Meghalaya.

Even more worrying is the fact that the discovery was serendipitous. A policeman spots two trawlers pulling in at a jetty. Large crates are unloaded on to 10 trucks. Most superiors ignore his urgent calls but one inspector arrives with a large force at 4 AM (2-4-04). The consignment is seized but no arrests are made. Months after the seizure, no one knows who sent the arms, or for whom. Indian officials were rightly indignant: "These weapons were meant to be used in our country and we have a right to know who were involved. Until that happens, there will be little contact between us." In specific terms, the Prime Minister's (whosoever he or she may be post-April 2004 poll) visit for SARC Summit and others by the officials/ministers were no-no. But in the following months, Manmohan Singh did not go as the SAARC Meet was cancelled, but the rest did make the trips, viz the Home

Secretary in September 2004 and Union Ministers Kamal Nath (August 2005) and P.R. Dasmunshi (September 2005), even when the Indians are in the dark as to what all information Dhaka has provided to New Delhi. Going by the past record, the picture could not be too rosy. After all, India still docs not know what happened after the Bogra arms seizure in June 2003 when the Bangla police arrested Jogesh Dev Burman of the Tripura Cooperative Association, a front for the ATTF, along with 200 Kg of explosives and 1,00,000 bullets.

It is necessary to record that the Indian officials had been concerned at the possible involvement of leaders of the ruling BNP in the arms haul case. The Intelligence was then speculating about the involvement of some ships owned by BNP leader Salahuddin Qader Chowdhury's QC Shipping Lines which were in Chittagong port at the time. "We know the two trawlers received the weapons from a ship in anchorage." As the long arm of the ISI stood proven, knowing the past cases, the sleuths were worried that a part of the haul could be for the distant Kashmir-based terrorists (Siddharth Varadarajan, *TOI*, 10 and 12 April 2004). Here is what Chittagong Mayor Chowdhury says on the arms haul: "These arms were shipped from USA and Pakistan in sinister conspiracy to destabilise India by arming her rebels." A letter written in Urdu from Batsebawui in Pakistan was seized from near the weapons consignment, raising speculations about Pak connection with the incident.

New Islamic Outfit

India expressed concern over the emergence of an Islamic outfit, Jagrata Muslim Janata (JMG), led by one 'Bangla Bhai' in the country's northern region adjoining West Bengal. While secular politicians are blaming Khalida Government for its links with what they dub as "Bangladeshi Taliban", the press carries reports on the "unlawful activities" of Bangla Bhai, a trained middle-aged fanatic whose private army, JBJ, described as the "vigilante force to annihilate left extremists", has established its own administration in the Rajshahi region. Christina Rocca, US Assistant Secretary of State for South Asia, had expressed her concern at Bangla Bhai's activities "during her recent visit" *(Hindu,* 31-5-04).

Bangla Bhai, selfstyled 'commander' of the JBJ having thousands of volunteers, many of whom are the activists of the ruling alliance is operating with the alleged blessing of a powerful lobby in the Government. Despite an 'order of arrest' from the Prime Minister, Bangla Bhai "is still at large" and non-challantly commanding his 'army'.

Dhaka Acts, Finally

The BDR detained 18 suspected Indian militants near Habibganj town of Bangladesh on 4 October 2004, all newly recruited cadres of ATTF from

Tripura. The Bangla officials arranged wide circulation of the news, to extract political mileage from the first crackdown on the Indian insurgents, so long demanded by New Delhi. Some analysts see it as a cosmetic exercise to win Brownie points with India, and the world beyond *(Hindu,* 13-10-04).

"Tiny Packs Sniff of Big Terror Plan"

The *Indian Express,* (Sakkyasen Mittra), 22-6-03, carries a sensational news story under this headline. The Bangla Security forces seized 225 gm of "semi-processed explosive grade" Russian made Uranium. As this is not the first time that such a seizure has been made, and the seized material is Uranium, has put the West Bengal *Intelligence* agencies on alert. The explosive is packed in 225 gm protective packets complete with a user's manual, and has so far been seized from a particular zone along the Indo-Bangla border. If the recent catch was made in Puia in Bangladesh's Nowgaon district on 30 May 2003, it was identical to the one seized earlier in Balurghat in West Bengal's North Dinajpur district in August 2002. And Puia is 35 Km from Balurghat.

That the Uranium could be misused is clear from the 23 page manual accompanying each packet that provides details of how to extract its reactive quality to make explosives and charge them with nuclear tips. The officials are baffled as to how the Russian-made uranium made its way into India. But they are certain that the mineral is not from mines in Jaduguda in Jharkhand. The packets are marked from Kazakhstan and dated 1988. Earlier the agencies thought the uranium was being sent to Kashmir through Bangladesh. Now the Officials feel it is going to the rebel groups having bases in Bangladesh.

Bangladesh arrested two couriers of terror outfit Shahadad-ul-Hikma who allegedly confessed that the packets were coming out of India. Security Officials aver that the repeated arrest of ultras and hauls of incendiaries and arms have established that West Bengal is being used as a conduit by the subversives backed by the hostile operatives. They even claim to have discovered Pak plans to shift their focus from heavily guarded western frontier to the near-porous eastern and north-eastern borders.

ULFA's Foreign Hands Extend into Bangladesh

The ULFA first made contacts with the KIA and Naga rebels in 1986. By end-1988, it had established contact with Pakistan ISI operatives in Bangladesh. Going beyond, it established liaison with the Afghan Mujahideen in Pakistan. In March 1994, Assam Assembly was informed that ULFA cadres had been trained by the ISI of Pakistan, many of them in Afghanistan. ULFA had also established contact with Bangladesh FIU (Field Intelligence Unit) in Dhaka, and was allowed to establish bases in Bangladesh.

Top ULFA leadership was located in Bangladesh till the mid-1990s. They had training camps in Mymensingh district at Bhemugach, Nilfarmani and Dhamai, all located in Maulvi Bazar area.[16] The Sheikh Hasina Government came to power in 1996 and decided to freeze all help to the outfit. Subsequent to the crackdown, ULFA shifted its operational headquarter and bases to the jungles of South Bhutan, close to India's borders, and some camps in Assam's Manas Reserve Forest.[17] The situation could change adversely for India if an unfriendly and fundamentalist regime comes to power in Bangladesh, as many of opposition leaders including Begum Zia, have called the North-East insurgents as "freedom fighters".[18]

Situation did improve when Hasina took over in 1996. But in spite of her assurances, the Intelligence confirmed that there were 35 camps in 1998 of different outfits, operating in the North-East Bangladesh close to Meghalaya border. Later, she did initiate action against them.

Hopefully, there seemed some change in the hardline stance of Khalida Zia Government. At the February 2002 conference of their Foreign Secretaries, Bangladesh assured India of its commitment not to allow its territory to be used for any activity detrimental to India's interest *(Times of India,* 20-2-2002). "Whether the undertaking would be honoured is yet to be seen, as Indo-Bangladesh relations are subject to extreme fluctuations caused by the domestic situation, with the Islamic extremists often queering the pitch."

The porous nature of 4096 Km Indo-Bangladesh border makes things difficult for India, as the ultras can move across it without any serious difficulty. The situation gets aggravated along the riverine stretches of the border. Unless Bangladesh cooperates by stopping this cross-border traffic and closing the camps inside its territory, India's task of fighting insurgency in the neighbouring areas would become even more difficult.

The Narco-Arms Cartel

It is axiomatic that the most virulent form of insurgency is sustained with the weapons obtained from individual foreign countries. Over the years, the international cartels took over the role of major suppliers of the contraband; they perfected the art of gun-running and the lucrative narco-arms trade.

The LTTE over the years has come to occupy a leading position in the field because of its expertise in high-seas operations. Expectedly, the ISI joined hands with it to ferry arms into the North-East. The LTTE helps in transporting them upto the Cox Bazar and CHT ports from the sources in Golden Triangle. From there the ISI and Bangladesh agencies take over for their overland journey to the North-East. Interestingly, the arms-running through the sea off the Andamans, which had been reduced to a trickle by 1995-96, increased manifold since the late 1997. The US Intelligence Reports on the LTTE say that sea route from the Golden Triangle to Burma is a key conduit for arms and narcotics. "Almost 80 per cent of heroin in the world is channelised through this route", which is corroborated by the widespread drug addiction in large parts of North-East, especially in Mizoram. Most of the sophisticated weapons with the insurgent groups in the Region can be traced to the Far East market. The narco-arms dealers obviously have a free run of and an easy access to this arms bazar. That most of the arms consignments take this route and can be intercepted in the high seas off the Andamans was shown by the successful Tri-Service "Operation Leech"[19] in February 1998. The SF killed 6 gun runners, arrested 73, and seized a huge consignment of arms including 140 AK series rifles. The end-users of this particular consignment were NSCN(I-M) and ATTF in India's North-East and Chin National Army in Burma.

The Government of India were reticent for whatever reasons about the ISI activities in the North-East. But Dimapur-based Corps Commander had reportedly written to Army Headquarter in 1996 about the militants getting arms from the groups like Khmer Rouge.[20] His counterpart at Tezpur, heading the Unified Command in Assam, confirmed the elementary truth about the ISI, to the Press in October[21] 1997. By early 1990s, the LTTE had established links with the NSCN and ULFA, and in the recent years, perhaps by mid-1990s, the ISI had spread its tentacles in some North-Eastern outfits which came to light in case of BdSF during the Indo-Pak conflict in Kargil sector and of ULFA with the arrest of four ISI operatives on 8 August 1999.

The ISI, assert Indian Intelligence, is targeting the entire border belt from Kashmir through Nepal to Tripura. Having played havoc with India's national fibre in Kashmir, it is now hyper-active in the North-East. Besides arming the ultras for acts of sabotage and violence, the ISI is playing deep game of ensuring large scale bloodshed in the name of "ethnic cleansing", with the ISI pumping in arms and explosives for the insurgents on the one hand and the targeted non-tribals arming themselves for retaliation, on the other. Their prognosis came true in November-December 1999 when the ULFA ultras targeted the Bihari people in Assam.[22] "This should worry the nation" because the Intelligence circles foresaw "a hundred Nellie-type massacres". What should cause greater concern "is that even diplomatic bags are being used to ferry India bound RDX via Kathmandu while consignment of illicit arms have reached North-East through Bangladesh and Burma", as per the 1997-98 press reports.[23]

The Bodos and ULFA of Assam art not alone in letting the ISI in. The ultras in Nagaland, Manipur and Tripura too have discarded the abhorrence for the outsiders. The help from China and Burma till 1970s was welcome on the grounds of ideology and of ethnic affinity across the borders. Today, idealism is out as the golden triangle of cash-crime-corruption is in "in tune with the macho image of an insurgent". If foreign travels and luxurious, extravagant lifestyles are hall-mark of the leadership, the gypsies, girls, drugs, and a non-challantly strung AK-47 add upto a glamorous insurgent.

That ISI is planning subversion and mayhem is obvious from the interrogation of their four operatives arrested on 8 August 1999: Cause dismemberment of India's North-East through bloodshed incited by incendiary riots, communal and ethnic. Part of explosives, subsequently, were meant for blasting crucial Leh-Manali Highway, only alternative to the much-threatened Leh-Srinagar Highway, life line of troops fighting Pak aggression in Kargil. Imagine the explosives being shipped from Assam across the vast sub-continent for use in Leh.[24] Some confidence, this! The reach of the ISI is truly amazing. If Oari Salim is from Muzaffarnagar, UP, Mallick is from Kupwara, Kashmir. These operatives had flown from Islamabad to Dhaka and thence crossed into Assam through the porous border. Consequent to their interrogation, 31 Harkat activists were arrested from Assam. Though these are first arrests of actual ISI operatives in the North-East, the Agency has been involved in the area for at least a decade, when it established contact with ULFA and helped it to secure bases in Bangladesh.

It was long suspected that besides the ISI, Bangladesh Intelligence was also active in the North-East. On 31 December 1996, Home Minister Inderjit Gupta named the Directorate General of Field Intelligence of Bangladesh in this connection. On 16 December 1996,[25] Foreign Minister Gujral announced: "Bangladesh Prime Minister Sheikh Hasina has acknowledged the existence of the insurgent camps on her soil...and promised to throw them out."[26] It is obvious the Indian insurgents had the run of the country during her predecessor Khalida Zia's regime. In her second coming, things have only worsened, with the Time of USA reporting (October 2002) that Dhaka is den of anti-India extremists. The involvement of Bangladesh with the insurgents in the Region was detailed in a 10-page Press Note issued by the BSF on its raising day in November 1995:

> "Most insurgent outfits in the North-East (ULFA, NSCN, PLA, etc.) were getting weapons from Thailand with active connivance of its Intelligence agencies.... They were coordinating with ISI to ferry arms from Bangladeshi soil into North-East, bringing Kashmiri youth into the country to motivate its citizens to join Jihad in the Valley. Bangladesh is not doing enough to stop the exodus of its national into Assam. Are they trying to solve their population explosion on the cheap?... There are already 8-10 million Bangladeshis living illegally in India."[27]

Having studied the problem and alarmed by its dimensions—an annual influx of 300,000 as per Intelligence—"Gen Sinha, Governor of Assam submitted a report on the "Illegal migration into Assam" to the President in November 1998, suggesting among other measures, annulment of the IMDT Act.

One of the operatives arrested on 8 August 1999, Hussain, disclosed "that over 300 ULFA ultras had received training in Pakistan over the past few years. In addition, the ISI also trained over 100 youth recruited from Assam by the Harkat-ul-Mujahideen, Lashkar-e-Toiba, and Harkat-ul-Jehad".[28]

It is widely believed that a lot of the ISI subversive activities are funded by drug money. It is also given that the "Pakistani Drug Syndicate runs a parallel economy in Cahoots with political and military establishment to destabilize India. The Pak heroin industry, says a UN Report, in terms of turnover is estimated at Rs. 74 billion, i.e., 5 per cent of its GDP of 1992-93, which is 20-25 per cent of the total estimated shadow economy. Pakistan reportedly earned $ 1.5 billion from the heroin export in 1992 (For detailed account of drug economy, *See* Inam-ul-Haq's *From Hash to Heroin,* Lahore, 1991).

BHUTAN : A HELPLESS NEIGHBOUR?

The Hindu of 23-12-2000 published an evocative photo illustrative of changed times. It showed the Army men on bicycles patrolling the fields along the Indo-Bhutan borders in the Nalabari district of Assam, "where vigil has been stepped up and night curfew imposed". It is a sea change for an international, so-far-off border.

Whenever under pressure, the militants in India, Myanmar and Bangladesh simply crossed over to the jungle sanctuaries of South Bhutan. The first influx came when the Indian Army launched Operation Rhino early 1990 against Assam ultras. By early 1992, there were as many as 21 camps between Kalikhola and Daifam. There was spurt again when ULFA terrorists in Bangladesh came under pressure in 1996-97 following Sheikh Hasina's ascension to power. In spite of repeated requests Bhutan seemed reluctant to proceed against ULFA and Bodo terrorist, then numbering around 2000. Bhutanese Home Minister Lympo Thinley Gyamtsho held two rounds of talks with ULFA, on 20 November 1998 and 7 May 1999. In second round, Paresh Barua, ULFA's Army Chief, offered to reduce the camps but expressed his inability to leave Bhutan before another year and half (say, before end 2000). Barua and his Chairman, Arbinda Rajkhowa, invited for third round, simply failed to show up. Similar talks were held by the Minister with Ranjan Daimary of NDFB bur the latter turned down the request to leave, *citing security reason.*

The Bhutanese National Assembly (BNA) did not sanction the Indo-Bhutan joint operations against the rebels at its 78th session in July 2000, and wanted Royal Bhutanese Army (RBA) to do the job itself. The stance hardened when senior rebel leaders Rajkhowa and Daimary ignored invitation for talks in Thimpu. Consequent to July 2000 decision of BNA, RBA raised two additional battalions, and 8,000 troops were deployed by December 2000 in Kalikhola-Daifam area "on the east of which are located the rebel camps. 2,500 ULFA and Bodo rebels were reported to be in Bhutan, with a large arsenal. G.K. Pillai, JS, North-East, revealed that "2,000 soldiers of RBA have already been trained by Indian Army in CI operations. The Campus of the Royal Technical Institute at Demathang was got vacated, and taken over by the RBA. Security posts were located at Bhurkhola and Dholkhola to guard two vital bridges on Sarphang-Gelegphu highway. All supply routes to the rebel camps were blocked. Meanwhile, exerting pressure on the rebels in the manner of Burmese Army, RBA forced ULFA in February 2000 to shift a key camp near Phukapthong towards Tshelingkhar in North-East of Bhutan, near Arunachal border.

The Intelligence reported that ULFA leaders converged at their Central Headquarters in Bhutan on 15-18 February 2000 to plan series of attacks in Assam, to take advantages of "lack of coordination and cooperation" among the constituents of India's Unified Command structure there. But for the killing of Assam's PWD and Forest Minister Nagen Sarma, ULFA failed, it failed to notch any spectacular successes, mainly because of its troubles in Burma and Bhutan. If RBA forced ULFA to close/shift a major camp in Bhutan, joint operations by Dimapur-based 3 Corps and Burmese Army forced the militants to move towards south-west Burma, bordering CHT of Bangladesh.

During the April 2000 visit of Bhutan's Foreign Minister Lympo Jigme Y. Thinley, some Assam officials raised a controversy, saying "the Indian rebels have Bhutan Government's patronage". One source claimed the "king had breakfast with rebel leaders on at least three occasions". A Bhutanese official said at New Delhi on 27 April 2000 that if 700-2000 ultras do not leave the country peacefully as a result of talks underway, RBA will use force to evict them. On his return from New Delhi on 22 April 2000, Chief Minister Mahanta was not diplomatic: "...Government was helping the rebels.... Militants are being imparted training by the ISI in camps located in Burma, Bangladesh and Bhutan".

As a part of mindless violence unleashed by ultras of all hues, the outlawed NDFB killed ten Bhutanese nationals at Laki Bazar area in Barpeta district, close to the Bhutan border, on 21 December 2000.[29] The victims had come down from Namlang, 7 km inside Bhutan, to sell their merchandise in a weekly market. This attack came on the heels of similar attacks on Bhutan national at Kokrajhar, Barpeta and Bongaigaon on 19 and 20 December, in which two people were killed and two Bhutanese vehicles set ablaze.

Realising that militants had no intention of quitting its soil and singed by the heat of these attacks Bhutan signaled its readiness to India not only to act more vigorously against the militants on its soil but also for joint operations to flush them out. There was no immediate formal agreement with Bhutan for joint operations, but India "has formed at an informal level a 'Regional Initiative' with Bangladesh, Burma and Bhutan to check the influx of arms and narcotics and to destroy the insurgent havens in these countries.[30]

Long last, losing all patience with the Indian rebels, who had enjoyed, and even exploited its hospitality on her soil for the long 12 years, the RBA launched its operations on 15-12-03 against the Indian insurgent camps in its territory. Bhutan explained it had held final talks with the ULFA in October and NDFB in November, while the KLO had failed to turn up for the talks. The Bhutanese move was widely hailed. Indicative of its pride and self-confidence, the RBA did not seek any help, logistic or operational, from the Indian Army which as a matter of abundant caution, sealed the border on the Indian side.

The "RBA had gone to war after 138 years, for us", gushed the *Indian Express,* 21-12-03. Bhutan announced 20-12-03: "All militant camps dismantled. The number dead was between 120 and 150." Apparently, the ultras were on the run, helter-skelter. The RBA, personally led by king Jigme Singye Wargchuk and his son, went into action professionally. It handed over to India the first batch of seven captured insurgents. ULFA openly declared of its being surprised. Dealing a serious blow to ULFA, its adviser and think-tank, 70-year old Buragohain injured in the first day of the offensive, died on 18-12-03. Besides the ideologue, other senior leaders killed included Apurba Deka, Satish Hazarika and Ranjit Hazarika. Among those arrested was Bening Rabha, a top leader of the ULFA's military wing and in-charge of the ULFA camps in Bhutan. A Bhutan official said 20-12-03 that "19 of the 30 rebel camps have so for been destroyed". He disclosed that the King was in constant touch with Prime Minister Vajpayee and senior Indian Army officers.

Reeling under the offensive, and Thimpu rejecting their ceasefire appeal, the rebel groups (ULFA, NDFB and KLO) called for a 48-hour strike in Assam and North Bengal, which got little response from the public.

The operation had been launched after much planning and preparations for which it elicited ungrudging admiration of the Indian Government and its military. India viewed it as an example for other neighbours, particularly Bangladesh, where, too 110 camps of insurgents from India's North-East have been operating. Apprehending negative security and diplomatic implications, the Bangla media even blacked out the developments taking place in Bhutan.

It was all over within three weeks.

Three weeks after Bhutan had cadres of the outlawed ULFA, NDFB and KLO on the run from the kingdom, "Myanmar troops have begun targeting North-East insurgent camps in north-west Myanmar, responding to the pressure from New Delhi", said the *Indian Express* of 6-1-04.

There was domestic fall-out also following the RBA action in 2003-04. As ULFA ultras joined Bodo outlaws and carried out a wave of attacks for the second successive day on 3-10-04, killing another 13 in as many attacks, Assam sent an SOS to the Centre: "Get Bangla and Myanmar to do a Bhutan soon." They wanted India to lean on its two neighbours to act against Indian rebels, as Bhutan did.

Bhutan again Assures Assam : Dec. 2006

"It goes without saying that we will not allow any insurgent groups to set up camps inside Bhutan". This is Mr. Dago Trering Wangda, Joint Secretary (Home), Royal Bhutanese Government speaking to the media after leading a delegation of Bhutanese officials to talks with the Assam Government. After assuring Guwahati that Bhutan will not allow the ULFA insurgents to smuggle themselves into its territory, it made it clear that there should be effective patrolling on the Indian side by the security forces in Assam and Arunachal Pradesh.

He said the presence of ULFA and other groups in eastern Bhutan between the 1991-2003 period had devastated the Region's economy because during the Dec. 2003 anti-terrorism operations by the Royal Bhutanese Army, the Bhutan-Assam border was closed due to security concerns. That led to a sharp escalation in the cost of goods since they had to be transported long distance to the main entry point in West Bengal.

But he said the captured ULFA leaders had been handed over to the Indian security forces. ULFA insists a number of their leaders disappeared after being held and has been demanding that New Delhi and Thimpu clarify their status. Wangda's statement puts the onus on India.

MYANMAR (BURMA)

India shares 1670 km land and 200 km maritime borders with Burma. People on either side share ethnic affiliations, and some are fighting their respective Governments. Going back in history, insurgent groups like the Naga, Mizo and Meitei, had bases in Burma at some point in time. Mid-1996, the NNC established contact with the KIA (Kachin Independence Army) in Kachin Hills, and Indian groups found sanctuary in the lightly administered border areas of Burma.[31]

Some Burmese tribals of Kuki Chin group have been fighting for the merger of their land with India.[32] Some other Burmese insurgents outfits are Arakan Liberation Party (ALP), Burmese Communist Party (BCP), etc. The underground Zoomi Liberation Front (ZLF) in Burma used to recruit its cadres for guerrilla war there. When the Military Junta cracked down on the Project-democracy supporters, many of these rebels took shelter in Manipur and Mizoram. To show its unhappiness, they started giving support to India's PLA. Moreover, it is easy for the outfits (like ULFA, NSCN, KIA, BCP and ALP) of either side to move across the Indo-Burma border as there is free passage between Moreh and Tamu. Expectedly, all these groups are involved in drug trafficking, using the money for purchase of weapons.

India's cool attitude to the Junta in 1988 put Indo-Burma relation on a downswing. This unhappy phase was reversed when the two nations launched "Operation Golden Bird"—a joint military action against the ultras on both sides. Things changed qualitatively when the two joined BIMSTEC, around the time Burma was admitted into ASEAN in 1997. The periodic interaction between the two sides was institutionalized in the annual national level meets between their civilian border authorities; 6th and 7th rounds were held in July (28-31) 1999 and August (28-31) 2000. An important subject in these meets has been insurgencies in the two nations, particularly the nexus among some of the outfits operating from the either side of the common border between two nations, particularly in Manipur and Nagaland. The mutual relations further improved when Gen VP Malik visited Burma in mid-1999 and July 2000 and Gen Maung Aye, No. 2 in State Peace and Development Council, received a red carpet welcome during his November 2000 Shillong visit. Gen Maung disclosed that 5 NSCN(K) camps had been eliminated during 1999. The inauguration by Indian Foreign Minister Jaswant Singh of the 160 km Tamu-Kalewa-Kalemyo Road marked an important milestone in Indo-Burmese relations. To be extended soon to Mandalay, second largest city of the nation, this road would link Moreh in Manipur to Central Burma.

It is well to record that large quantities of contraband (arms and drugs) reached India's North-East by the overland route through Burma, especially till the mid-1995 when the supplies shrunk because of Burma's crackdown on the illegal trade and her agreement with the 17 rebel groups barring the Kachins.

1643 km Indo-Burma border is sensitive area, as the ethnic groups on either side have been waging war against their respective Governments. Yangon's situation is not easy as it is fighting several insurgent groups like Chin National Front, KIO, Karen National Front, New Mon State Party, Wa National Organisation, BCP, NSCN(K), NSCN(I-M), etc. Two nations are tackling the insurgents by politico-military measures. India is already negotiating with the NSCN(I-M) since 1997, and trying to bring NSCN(K), ULFA, PLA and Bodo groups into the mainstream. The ruling SPDC of Burma has reached peace agreements with 15 armed groups including KIA (*Hindustan Times,* 13-2-2002). While this has brought peace to northern and eastern parts of Burma, it still has not been able to control Karen, Arakenese and Chin insurgents active on its border with India. It is these groups who provide shelter and arms to Indian insurgents. It is this North-West hilly frontier of Burma which is used to channel narcotics and arms to India via Cox Bazar.

Both sides are coordinating their CI operations. It is known that NSCN(K), whose cadres are Burma-based Hemei Nagas, have camps in Hongyat, Chamyu, Longko, Bonyo and Wayok areas across Nagaland. The NSCN(I-M), UNLF and PLA have camps around Tamu, Mintha, Somra, Namphalong and Chikka-Phaisat stretch across Manipur. The two Nations must coopt Thailand Government in their battles as that country "is centre of activity for the Indian and Burmese insurgent groups". Secondly, majority of arms purchases by these groups are made in Bangkok, Ranong and Chiang Mai in Thailand, and reach India via Bangladesh route. The two nations are sharing Intelligence to thwart the insurgents. In the past two years (2000, 2001) particularly, there have been efforts by Yangon to ensure that its territory is not used by the Indian insurgents. In fact, February 2002, Burmese Army conducted CI operations in Onamyu area, killing 6 NSCN(K) and 10 ULFA cadres. The things should improve in this field with the increased politico-economic interaction between New Delhi and Yangon.

Myanmar's Top Leader Visits India: October 2004

It was as a result of greater understanding shown by India towards the military leadership of Myanmar that the latter's top man, Senior General Than Shwe, Head of the Military Leadership and the State Democratic Peace Committee of Myanmar paid a 6-day (historic) Official visit to India in October 2004, the first by the Head of State/Government during the last 17 years.

The MoU signed between the two nations on the non-traditional security issues on the 25th October would tighten the noose around the North-Eastern insurgent outfits operating from outside the country. During their talks, Manmohan Singh expressed serious concerns about these groups, and Gen Shwe assured him that he would not allow Myanmar to be used for anti-India operations. He also said Myanmar was willing to mount offensive against these insurgent groups in concert with India, and beef up the vigil along the border with India. The two countries decided to exchange operational intelligence and personnel too.

Barely three months after the visit of Senior General Shwe, a high level delegation arrived in India in February 2005. The two sides agreed on measures to strengthen co-operation in combating terrorism, narcotic trade and arms smuggling under the broad rubric of non-traditional security issues.

The first action under this understanding was taken by India when it proceeded militarily against the Myanmarese militant outfit, Chin National Army, in the Jungles of the southern district of Mizoram, Saiha, on 5-7-05, under Phase II of "Operation Hailstorm". Subsequently, acting on the instructions from the MHA, Mizoram Government closed the Indo-Myanmarese border at Champhai in eastern part.

Myanmar Fights Indian Rebels : Dec. 2006

Myanmar launched a military crackdown against an Indian tribal separatist outfit, SS Khaplang faction of NSCN, camped in that country, with heavy fighting reported between its troops and militants, said NSCN(K) spokesman Kughato Mulatonu on 29 Dec., 2006.

"A brigade of the Burmese Army with heavy weapons launched the assault in Burma's Hkamti district of Northern Sagaing Division, targeting our cadres for the past three days (26-28 Dec.)". (This was conveyed by Mulatonu to the AFP by telephone from an undisclosed location).

There was no immediate confirmation of this offensive from Myanmar with which India shares a 1640-km unfenced border. The last crackdown on Indian rebel camps was in Feb. 2006. The NSCN(K) has at least 50 camps with a total of around 5,000 militant fighters in Sagaing, according to Indian estimates.

Incidentally, SS Kahplang, leading his faction of NSCN for creation of an independent Naga homeland in India's North-East, stradling the Myanmarese border, is a Myanmarese by birth!

Myanmarese Shadow over India's Domestic Scene : March 2007

Myanmarese refugees in India held a silent rally at Jantar Mantar—India's Hyde Park—near Delhi's famous Connaught Place on 26 March, 2007.

The rally was held as "Global Day of Action Against the Shive Gas Project in Burma", informed a banner slung high on a pole. Its sponsors called themselves : 'Shive Gas Movement—India'.

It was obviously a multi-purpose rally which brought together various groups among the Burmese refugees in India. The Kuki students in the rally were holding a silent protest—the demonstrators had a black band sealing their lips—against "atrocities being committed on Kuki villagers on the Indo-Myanmar border by the Myanmarese Junta" A banner held aloft was reflective of their 'cry of anguish' : "Lathis, Tear Gas, Jail Hospitals—what more?"

It is rather curious that some Myanmarese refugee groups in India still want to call their nation as 'Burma'.

NEPAL

The 1800 Km Indo-Nepal border is an open one and hence poses no problem to insurgents or their friends like the ISI. In the recent years, there is an increasing evidence of the Agency expanding its anti-India operations in Nepal. Several subversives arrested in the recent years disclosed their flying into Nepal and then entering India over the land-borders. "The reverse route is also being used by the ISI to smuggle its agents to safe havens in Nepal after committing crimes in India." The most well-known case of this kind was of Yaqoob Memon, one of the 1992-93 Bombay blasts accused being tracked down in Kathmandu.

Reports of numerous new madrassas and mosques springing up in the recent years—mid 1990s onwards—in the Muslim-inhabited areas of Terai, near the Indo-Nepal borders, should be a cause of concern to the Indian agencies. Some extremist elements are suspected to make use of this situation to foment anti-India sentiment. The ISI agents operating from the Nepalese soil have been worrying New Delhi. The hijacking of an IA plane from Kathmandu on 30 December 1999 was an unpleasant reminder of that Agency's operational success in Nepal

THAILAND

Thailand seems to be the latest country to have provided succour and shelter to North-Eastern rebels, as also operational bases. The MHA Report on the insurgency in the Region speaks of Thailand's flourishing, clandestine arms bazars located in the 3-Pagoda Pass area opposite Burma's Karen State, and another along the Ranong Goast adjoining the Tennaserim Division of Burma. Both the areas on Burma's borders are controlled by ethnic rebel groups. In both the markets, arms and communication equipments of wide variety are available for the asking. The real worry for India starts when these arms are transhipped from the southern coastal strips of Thailand and Burma to the coastal areas of Bangladesh in fishing vessels operated by Burmese rebels. India's "Operation Leech" was launched to thwart this type of the deadly cargo. From the Bangladeshi coastal rendezvous, the gun-runners ensure it reach the end-users in the North-East through west and north Mizoram. At times, arms for ULFA are stored in Meghalaya. It is ironic but true that courtesy such markets, the insurgents have better arms and equipment than the SF fighting them.[33]

History of interaction between the insurgents of the Region and Thai arms dealers tells us that the NSCN was the first group to register its presence in Thailand in 1987; followed subsequently by the Bodo ultra to negotiate arms purchase.

The NSCN leaders seem to favour Thai 5-star and luxury resorts for rest and refit—spending considerable time there for business and pleasure. In a queer twist of fate, NSCN(I-M) leader Muivah was arrested by Thai police for travelling on false documents; and later it produced him before a court in handcuffs.[34]

The above explains why Thailand has to have a place in India's plans to fight insurgency and other anti-national forces at home. To re-emphasis, Thailand—and Bangkok in particular—has long been the staging ground for all kinds of operations impacting India. After all, almost all insurgent outfits have a presence here. The Nagas have an office in Bangkok. ULFA leaders lived here in exile and the Bodos made frequent trips to it and the ISI distribute fake Indian currency there. On the crime side, India's dons like Chhota Rajan (involved in a shoot out early 2000), Chhota Shakeel, Dawood Ibrahim *et al.* are involved in their gang wars there. Even more significantly, Chiang Mai has maintained its leading position in the international drug trade, and the Intelligence confirms that very large percentage of drugs smuggled into India through its North-East emanates from there. These facts were pressing enough by themselves for interaction between the two nations. With Thailand emerging as an important economy in the ASEAN region, the Indian Prime Minister making an early visit was on the cards. Manmohan Singh was in Thailand in July 2004, for BIMST-EC Summit, soon after taking over the reigns.

But the situation has changed after the 9/11 and the Bali bombings. Early 2004, Thai forces killed over 100 Muslim extremists in the country's south, near the resort town of Phuket, "and the Thais are intensely worried that Islamic Militancy could wreck the country's image as a tourist paradise" (Vir Sanghvi, *HT,* 31-7-04), and may even thwart its rising economy. So while the Prime Minister discussed high policy with his counterpart Thaksin Shinawatra, K. Padmanabhaiah engaged the Swu-Muivah duo in peace talks at the Thai hill resort of Chiang Mai, 500 Km from Bangkok, and consequently, the cease-fire due to expire on 31-7-04, was extended for another year on the 30th.

In spite of the 9/11 and the understanding shown by the Thai Prime Minister, owner of one of Thailand's largest industrial conglomerates, some worries remain. The drug-mafia in the Chiang Mai region still flourishes. "And there is evidence that the officers in Thailand's notoriously corrupt Army are still willing to sell arms to the separatist groups." It was issues like these that were addressed by India's NSA, J.N. Dixit, accompanying the Prime Minister, in his talks with his Thai counterpart.

Needless to say, India looks more optimistically at its future relations with Bangkok.

Some Latest Developments

Pakistan does not Relent

With the emergence of Bangladesh in 1971, the Mizo and Naga rebels lost the use of their bases there at least for the initial years. The Mizos travelled West via Rangoon to reach the rump Pakistan and developed future ties with it. The MNF also strengthened its ties with the BCP, and managed to reach Yunnan through the Kachin Corridor. Bhaumik (1996) opines that it is only after China's overt support of Naga rebels and concurrently of Mizo outlaws that the Pakistanis devised a strategy of linking up the rebel tribal outfits under one 'joint command'.

From 1980s, there has been a quantum jump in covert operations by the ISI. It has not only fostered the destructive power of ULFA and Bodo groups by giving them arms and guidance, but also spread its deadly tentacles in Bangladesh and Nepal with the sole, singular aim of weakening India's internal security system and to sap the nation's will to defeat Pakistan-launched terrorism-driven low-intensity war in Kashmir. For this purpose, Pakistan has effectively exploited the prevailing communal divide in the Region. At least 18 separatist Islamist groups[35] have so far been identified by the Intelligence. Islamic fundamentalists have targeted India in the recent years, and have managed to find willing accomplices/sympathizers from these outfits. It is time, warn Indian strategic analysts, to take Osama's threat seriously as published in *Jang* (of Pakistan) of 16 September 1999, calling for the first time, an all out Jehad against India: "India and America are now our biggest enemy...."[36] Recent interrogation of Harkat-ul-Mujahideed (HUM) activists revealed that the "ISI plans to train 10,000 people in Assam for jehad to liberate Assam and establish an Islamic country comprising Assam and certain other parts of North-East".[37] The HUM, based in Yatrabari, near Dhaka, is operating in Eastern parts of India. Their operational nerve centre is Noorani Madrassa where they 'train' acolytes from Assam and Bengal.[38]

The role of ISI in the arms-drug trafficking into India is well-known and documented, but its blatant extent can be judged from Nawaz Sharif's interview to the *Jang,* a reputed Pak daily, in its 13-9-1994 issue: "...3 months after my election as Prime Minister in November 1990, Gen Aslam Beg, then Army Chief and Gen Durrani, ISI Chief, told me that military needed more money for covert foreign operations and wanted to raise it through mega drug deals. Durrani said the blueprint was ready for my approval. I was flabbergasted...." A few days later he told the Army not to launch the drug trafficking plan. Incidentally, by 1999 "the so-called Golden Crescent which lies along Afghanistan, Pakistan, Iran, almost replaced the Golden Triangle as the world's biggest drug producing region." The 1994 Report of the US State Department says: "About 70 tonnes of heroin is produced in Pakistan annually, a third of it smuggled abroad, mostly to the West." The UN says 80 per cent of heroin in Europe comes from the region. It has been rumoured for years that the Pak military, especially ISI, is involved in the drug trade.[39]

Some reports suggested that the ISI base camp in Dhubri area was being used as a centre for smuggling of *ganja* and brown sugar *(The Sentinel,* Guwahati, Assam, 10-3-2000).

With a major blast at New Jalpaiguri Railway Station on 22-6-1999 (details discussed above), killing 9, including 5 soldiers, Pakistan signaled its success in penetrating West Bengal as well.

It seems Gen Parvez Musharraf does not play host to Kashmiri ultras and Afghan mercenaries only; he has extended his hospitality to the militants in the North-East also. The Indian Intelligence says he has hosted several batches of ULFA and NDFB taking them round the country and training them in terrorist camps in POK and Afghanistan run by the ISI. These terrorists have been flown out of Dhaka to Islamabad via Karachi, and thence to their allotted camps. Besides, activists of some Islamic outfits in the Region have also been to Pakistan, including 30 Muslim youths from Western Assam *(Hindustan Times,* 29-6-2002).

Can China be Friendly with India?

In the 17 April 2000 Note, Arunachal Government informed New Delhi and the Army about 2000 Chinese laying the road track opposite Asaphila area in Tawang district. If this was cause of concern, more ominous disclosures were made during their interrogation by Lohit Dewri, a senior ULFA commander and ULFA rebels who had surrendered on 14 August 2000, including the hitherto unknown ULFA connection. The Intelligence reports that the Chinese resumed/stepped up their anti-India activities after the May 1998 Pokhran Tests, including supply of arms to the North-Eastern rebels but carefully avoiding direct hand. "They operate through a mysterious entity, called 'Black House', which delivers the arms after erasing the Chinese markings."[40] But the trail goes to the earlier past. The ULFA leaders, who had gone to China in 1993 for arms and indoctrination, had met Chinese Army officers. The contacts were renewed in 1997 This in spite of the two so-called landmark agreements of 1993 and 1995.

Pakistan ISI : A State within a State

Perhaps no Intelligence agency in the world can match the freedom of action enjoyed by the ISI. It is not only autonomous but nearly sovereign. It is no secret that it formulated Pakistan's Afghan policy and drives all its moves in Kashmir. It was Pak IB's poor performance in the 1947-48 war over Kashmir that resulted in the decision to create the ISI with an Indo-centric focus in 1948. Its pivotal role in the internal politics of Pakistan can be judged from the fact that the ISI under Lt Gen Hamid Gul was the prime mover in the formation of Islamic Jamhourie Ittehad (IJI) or United Democratic Front (UDF), to counter Benazir Bhutto's PPP in September 1988. For first three decades, it concentrated more on the internal intelligence; with limited external agenda, largely Indo-Centric, essentially because Pak fought three wars with India. Consequent to the Soviet advent in Afghanistan, the ISI evolved a greater external orientation from the late 1970s. It was closely involved with the guerrilla warfare against Soviet troops. Even then, it retained its internal orientation due to compulsions of military rulers who wanted it to keep a tab on the civilian politicians for their "subversive activities"!

The proxy war launched by it in 1989 continues to take its toll in J and K. The haul of 30 kg of RDX from the Indo-Bangladesh border and seizure of 63 kg RDX in Delhi during the three weeks (14 August-2 September) in 1999 is indicative of the penetration made by the ISI-backed militant outfits in the post-Kargil situation. The MHA assessment says the ISI has established its network in Western UP, North Kerala, Tamil Nadu, some pockets in Andhra and Karnataka, Indo-Bangladesh border, especially the Siliguri Corridor, and North-East, besides Jammu and Kashmir. It trained and funded mercenaries from 14 countries and pushed them into Jammu and Kashmir. Authoritative figures show that of the 1037 foreign mercenaries killed in Jammu and Kashmir during 1990-98, over 400 hailed from Pakistan.

"Besides the sabotage and usual killings, the ISI is now planning to foment communal riots in the country, especially in the so-far-quiet South." A little known Muslim sect, Siddique Deendar Anjuman, ostensibly a religious organisation "committed to promoting peace and harmony", was found to be involved in subversion+causing series of explosions—12 in all—that "had rocked churches, temples and a mosque across the peninsula from Andhra through Karnataka to Goa since 21 May 2000". Its aim was to trigger communal violence and tarnish India's image. A serious act of sabotage was aborted by an accident on 9 July 2000, when a blue Maruti Omni exploded off the JC Road in Bangalore, killing two of its occupants."[41] The MHA gave the following information/statistics to its Consultative Committee of MPs, on the magnitude of the ISI sponsored terrorism for the 1989-1998 decade:

1. 29,151 civilians and 5,101 SF men killed.
2. Public/private property worth Rs. 2000 crore destroyed/ damaged.
3. Nation incurred an expenditure of Rs. 46,000 crore on Army and PMF employed on IS (internal security) duties.
4. Rs. 18,500 crore spent on awarding compensation to the victims, erecting border fencing, and raising counter-terrorist forces.
5. High grade explosives, mostly RDX, quantity 51,900 kg smuggled into the country, of which 43,750 kg was recovered (what this quantity means can be realized by the fact that in a chain of 21 blasts that wrought havoc in Mumbai in 1992-93, only 3.5 kg RDX was used).
6. During this decade, 7,125 Paki and foreign saboteurs infiltrated into India, and 19,800 Indians were trained by the ISI in Pakistan, POK and Afghanistan Camps.[42]

The White Paper on the ISI activities in India, promised by Home Minister L.K. Advani in 1998, was never published, due to a variety of reasons. But what worries experts is the level of success achieved by the ISI in networking the militant groups in different parts of India, exploiting their ethnic, communal and anti-establishment sentiments. The threat from such a wide network of recalcitrant groups can be assessed from the massive haul of 4000 kg of RDX from the suspected agents during 1999 alone. The extent of spread and reach of the ISI should be judged from the fact that India busted 161 modules, Home Minister Advani told the Press on 17-10-2002, during the last three years (2000, 2001 and 2002).

Siliguri Corridor and Demand for Kamatapur State

The 28 Km wide Siliguri Corridor, also called the Eastern Chicken's Neck, is a sensitive area which has drawn attention of the ISI in recent years. A serious internal disruption, fomented externally, can cut off the North-East from the mainland. The situation has taken a serious turn with the violent activities of the Kamatapur Liberation Organisation (KLO) for a separate Kamatapur State, over the last few years. KLO is the armed wing of the Kamatapuri People's Party (KPP), essentially of the Rajbongshis who constitute 31 per cent of 12 million population of 5 districts of North Bengal.

The Rajbongshis also comprise a substantial section of the non-Bodo population in the proposed Bodoland. So the KLO also wants parts of Assam contiguous to North Bengal to be part of their Kamatapur. The KPP has been demanding a separate state for over 30 years, but has not made much progress as they do not have an outstanding leader to guide them. For the last few years, the KLO has taken over the movement, and it seems to have developed secessionist orientation, after coming closer to the ULFA. They too have started extortions and looting. On 22 November 1999, the two jointly looted cash from the Railways, near Siliguri. The worst outrage was their killing of five CPI(M) activists at their Dhupguri office in a dusk operation on 17 August 2002. In July 2000, they had killed two supporters of CPI(M) in same area. Their first strike was in May 2000 when they killed CPI(M) leader Pranesh Pal at Barobisha in Jalpaiguri.

Since 1996, KLP ultras have been visiting ULFA camps in Bhutan. They themselves are reported to have set up camps in Bhutan, just 3 miles from the border. Of late, KLO has an alliance with ULFA, in turn allied with NDFB.

Christian Terrorism in India's North-East?

This is not something that is widely talked about, nor is the Christian terrorism known to have been discussed in the rarefied policy circles of India. But there is indeed on entry on the subject on the internet, which is reproduced at the appendix below without any comment, and for whatever worth it is.

Appendix

Christian Terrorism in Northeast India

In our attempt to help promote peace in the world for mutual and social spiritual development, there are nonetheless areas and organizations that are devotedly working against that goal. Because of their own allegiance to a particular ideology, usually based on a religion, they threaten the freedom and challenge the well-being of those of other religions. And one area where this is taking place is in India's northeastern states, such as Assam, Arunachal Pradesh, Nagaland, Manipur, Tripura, etc. Because of wicked terrorist tactics and even "gun point conversions", some people are being forced to give up their traditions. This is something that much of the world, and even many Indians, are not aware of. And since I have personally traveled in this area to give lectures to promote the preservation of the culture there and met many wonderful people, it is region in which I have a special interest.

Here on this page you will find several reports and news items on the shocking amount of terrorism caused by the Christian militant groups in Northeast India, how they operate, where they get their funds, and the thousands of people who have already died because of it. It is primarily due to those who want to make the whole region into a separate Christian state at the expense of those who would prefer to follow their own indigenous and Hindu cultures.

Christian Terrorists Massacre Eight Hindu Civilians in India

Christian Terrorists Kill 44, Wound 118 in Attacks in Northeast India

Baptist Church Backs Terrorism in North-East India

Terrorists in North-East India get American Support

Christ and North-East India

Mahatma Gandhi on Conversion

Thirteen Years of Killings in Tripura

My Northeast India Mission

Preaching in India's Northeast for Cultural Preservation

Save Your Culture

[Home] [The Books by Stephen Knapp] [Book Reviews]
[CD Slide Shows] [Order Form]
[The World Relief Network] [Articles to Read] [Seeing Spiritual India]
[A Little Book of Prayers Mantras & Gayatris] [Krishna
Darshan Art Gallery]
[Vegetarian Recipes and Resources] [Stay in Touch with Us]
[Links to Other Websites]
[Jokes and Anecdotes]

(Source: http://www.stephen-knapp.com/christian terrorism_in_northeast_india.htm)

The Naga Talks : Hopeful Signs

After decades of dark clouds, there is some hope on the horizon. The Centre has been holding talks periodically with the NSCN(I-M) and the cease-fire has been holding since 1 September 1997. The talks so far held in the foreign capitals like Bangkok, might be shifted to a venue within India. Mizoram Chief Minister said on 21 October 2002 that NSCN leaders "are ready to visit India if the ban is lifted on the outfit. The MHA sources indicated the ban, due to lapse on 26 November 2002, "might not be extended", to enable Muivah and Isaac to visit India *(The Hindu,* 22-10-2002). Their first visit to Delhi indeed came in January 2004.

In March 2001, Home Minister Advani visited the Region and met Government representatives and leaders of outfits other than NSCN(I-M). The operations against these outfits were suspended. Advani informed the Rajya Sabha that "militant outfits in the North-East have responded positively to the suspension of operations and the call for dialogue" *(The Frontline,* 13-4-2001).

September 2005. The press reported that NSCN(I-M) wanted a firm assurance from the Centre on the integration of the Naga-inhabited areas before the next round of talks, likely to be held in October 2005. They also expressed their willingness to hold talks with the Governments of Manipur and Assam to find a way out of their opposition to part with any of their areas for Nagalim *(Exp* 21-9-05). More details on the subject will be found in Chapter 16 and 17.

Five Militants are Lynched

Five militants of NDFB were lynched to death on 8-11-03 after they threw grenades at the villagers following a scuffle with them. The villagers were from Aikata, on the border of Goalpara and Dhubri districts and Sialkunda in the same area. The ultras possibly entered the district from Meghalaya. 3 villagers also lost their lives.

Abductions Halt Trade

A spate of abductions—one customs inspector and six coal exporters were abducted in Meghalaya by the armed militants in March 2003 belonging to various militant outfits in the State-brought trans-border trade between India and Bangladesh in the north-eastern sector to grinding halt by the end of the month. As many as 10 customs stations (two in Meghalaya, four in Tripura, one in Mizoram, and three in Assam) will be closed until these States devise adequate security measures *(Exp.,* 6-4-03).

Gandhi Jayanti 2004—Terror Strike : 7 Blasts, 48 killed

A series of explosions and militant attacks in the North-East— 5 in Assam and 2 in Nagaland—killed 48 people on 2-10-04. Details follow:

> **Assam:** NDFB behind all five (1) At 5 PM armed ultras opened fire at the weekly market at Makrijhar, 25 Km from Dhubri, close to the Bangladesh border, killing 11 persons on the spot. (2) Two persons were killed in grenade attack at Abhaypuri in Bangaigaon district close

to Dhubri. (3) 5-30 PM, grenades lobbed by the ultras at Baihata Chariali Police Station (PS) in Kamrup district left three people dead and at Jagi Road PS in Morigaon district injured two policemen. (4) Mid-day, IED explosion at Shantipur village market under the newly-created Chirang district left two dead and six injured.

"Tomorrow (3 October) is the raising day of the banned Bodo outfit (NDFB)," which has demanded a sovereign Bodo tribal state *(Exp.,* 3-10-04). It was only on 30 September that Assam Chief Minister Tarun Gogoi had offered to declare a cease-fire against the NDFB and ULFA from 15 October if they came to the negotiations table abjuring violence.

Nagaland: Two simultaneous explosions rocked Dimapur, the commercial hub of the hill State at 9.35 AM: (1) at the Platform No. 1 of the railway station when hundreds of passengers were waiting for the delayed Lumding-Tinsukia Passenger train.[43] It created a huge crater on the platform and left its roof collapsed; (2) at Hong Kong Market on Marwari-patty Road, just 200 mtrs away. The blasts left 32 dead.

It was the first major blast in any public place in strife-torn Nagaland in the last ten years. No wonder Nagaland Chief Minister Neiphiu Rio rushed to Dimapur.

Manipur: Far from Peace: 11 Jawans of 5/8 GR were killed and 6 others injured when they were ambushed by the KYKL on 19-9-05 at Upper Ngarian in Bishenpur district, 45 Km from Imphal. The next day, one havildar of the 26 Assam Rifles was killed and four others injured in an IED explosion set off by the PLA, near Jiribam/Jirighat tea estate along the Manipur-Assam border. Defence Minister Pranab Mukherjee arrived next day on his first 2-day visit to the North-East since he took over (on 20-9-05).

NOTES

1. It has been discussed in some detail in this book. Also *See* Urmila Phadnis, *Ethnicity and Nation Building in South Asia,* 1989.
2. The Cabinet Mission Plan had placed Bengal and Assam together in Group C. This here is the enlarged Version, with the addition of Bhutan and Sikkim.
3. Cited by Brig SP Sinha, "Insurgency in North-East India: The External Dimension", the *USI journal,* July-September 1998.
4. Urmila Phadnis, 1989, Note 1, and V.K. Sareen, "India's North-East in Flames", 1980. Sareen gives a lucid account of CIA activities in the North-East in the early 1970s.
5. The first batch of 200 ultras led by Kaito Sema, C-in-C, Naga Home Guards (the then name of the underground Naga Army) went for training to East Pakistan early 1962 through North Cachar Hills, and returned in March 1963. Another group of *500* under Dusoi Chakhesang trekked to Pakistan through Chin Hills of Burma in October 1963 and returned in May 1964. The largest

group of 1000 insurgents was led by Zuheto Sema in October 1964, after suspension of hostilities negotiated by JP-led Naga Peace Mission. The group reinfiltrated into Nagaland during August-September 1965 through Burmese Somra Tract.

6. The MEA Press Note dated 3-10-1968, cited by Parkash Singh, "Nagaland", 1972.
7. Hazarika, Sanjoy, 1995.
8. The first batch of 300 Nagas under Muivah and Thinsuelie crossed the border into Burma in November 1966 and trekking 1000 Km, reached Yunnan in January 1967. The second batch of nearly 500 strong was led by Mowu Angami and Isaac Swu in December 1967. Throughout 1968, small groups were trekking back into India.
9. Parkash Singh, *op. cit.*
10. For Naga, Mizo, and Meitei insurgents' links with China. *See* Nibedon, 1981.
11. Parkash Singh, *op. cit.*
12. *Times of India,* 1-10-1984.
13. *Hindustan Times,* 29-11-1997.
14. *Times of India,* "Will Bangladesh now cut off support to North-East Insurgent", 19-12-1996.
15. *Frontline,* M.S. Prabhakar, 11-2-1984.
16. Hazarika, *op. cit.*
17. Verghese, 1996.
18. For a detailed analysis of external factors in the spread of insurgency. *See* Urmila Phadnis, n. 11.
19. That some such operation did hand down polemical missiles to the doughty warriors—Defence Minister Fernandes and Admiral Bhagawat—to engage in a no-holds-barred duel, is a matter of recent history.
20. Nitin Gokhale in *Outlook,* 1-2-1999.
21. *Ibid.*
22. It provoked a sharp reaction from the Assam Governor, himself a Bihari, and a retired Lt General. He had asked the victims of the senseless attacks to defend themselves, using all means at their disposal. That the Governor's strong comment came under sharp attack from a spectrum of political parties—the usual Left-Centre Combine—is indicative of a fractured Indian polity.
23. This was happening in spite of our improved relations with Burma since 1995 and Bangladesh since "the Vajpayee Regime took over (February 1998)". India did get cooperation from these countries depending upon the hue of their Governments. In April 1995, Indian and Burmese armies jointly launched "Operation Golden Bird" on Manipur-Burma border when over 40 ultras of two countries' insurgent groups were killed and huge cache of arms recovered. Later years, India got necessary help from Bhutan and Bangladesh. Earlier years also had seen such collaborative operations—published or unpublished. Col PV, a contemporary of this Author during his 1975-78 stint in Mizoram, informed him of a joint operation carried out by the troops of the three nations in 1977 in the area around the Indo-Burma-Bangladesh injunction.
24. *The Outlook,* 23-8-1999.

25. It is important to note that on this date (16-12-96) the two nations signed the Indo-Bangladesh Treaty on sharing of the Ganga waters.
26. *Times of India,* 19-12-1996.
27. Cited by Dincsh Kumar in *Times of India,* 19-12-1996.
28. *The Frontline* 10-9-99 and *The Hindu,* 28-8-1999.
29. Assam and Bhutan got involved in a public spat over killing of these ten 'Bhutanese'. Mahanta claimed the culprits were NDFB ultras, ensconced on Bhutanese' soil, who killed the victims across the border and then dumped their bodies on the Assamese side. Bhutan claimed it was the handwork of the ultras of BLT (who were then negotiating peace with the Assam Government) who killed Bhutanese nationals on the Assamese soil, and "we want Government of India to pay compensation for these deaths".
30. For further details, *see Hindustan Times* of 24-7-1999, 12-3-2000 and 26-4-2000; *Hindu* of 28-4-2000 and 23-12-2000; *Indian Express* of 24-12-2000; and *Frontline* of 19-1-2001.
31. *Deccan Herald* of 25-10-1998.
32. Phanjoubam Tarapot, *Insurgency Movements in North-East India*, 1993.
33. *Assam Tribune,* 4-7-1999.
34. An over-sympathetic 'North-East expert' was moved to an angry outburst over a press photo of a hand-cuffed Muivah: "It is a matter of shame that a leader of a movement, of Muivah's stature, was shown in such pathetic condition, hand-cuffed like a common criminal...." It seems to be a case of misplaced, even wasted sympathy! One can't understand this expert's anger and piety on seeming such a photo, until he belongs to ultra-liberal and bleeding hearts brigade who just cannot countenance even mildest of the inconvenience suffered by the most hard-boiled of the anti-national insurgents, who have blood of countless innocent civilians, including women and children on their hands. I have seldom seen them angry on the death of the soldiers fighting these ultras.
35. Some of the names are MULFA (Muslim United Liberation Front of Assam), MULTA (Muslim United Liberation Tigers of Assam), PULF (People's United Liberation Front), SIMI (Students Islamic Movement of India), Adam Sena, Jehad Council, etc.
36. Cited in *India Today,* 4-10-1999, by Jason Burke and Harinder Baveja.
37. *Deccan Herald,* 16-8-1999.
38. The recruits from Assam, for training at their seminary in Bangladesh, cross the border at Karimganj, and reach Sylhet through Zakiganj; those from Bengal cross the border at Dinhat in Cooch Behar *(Asian Age,* 23-5-1999).
39. *The News of Pakistan,* 13-9-1994.
40. *The Hindu,* 19-8-2000.
41. For detail, *see India Today* of 31-7-2000.
42. Vinod Kumar in *The Hindu* of 5-9-1999.
43. Army men, more than any other professionals, love to live by fond memories. I vividly remember the contours and outline of this Platform No. 1 where I landed on my first commissioning on 12 January 1958, like the back of my hand.

3

Turbulence in Assam

Assam is the most populous state among the seven sisters, but has been pushed down to No. 2 position in area.

Key Statistics : Assam State

Date of formation	26 January 1950
Area	78,438 sq. km
Population	26,655,528
Capital	Dispur
Principal Languages	Assamese
	Bengali
	Bodo/Boro
Major Religions	Hinduism
	Islam
	Buddhism

Before going into other details, an overview of Assam's terrorism situation (Assam Backgrounder) and a brief look at the year gone by (Assam Assessment 2006) are considered useful for the lay reader.

Assam Backgrounder

The problem of militancy in Assam has its origin in the large-scale migration of refugees from East Pakistan—what is now Bangladesh— since India's Partition in 1947. A continuous flow of illegal migrants across the borders has disturbed the local demography and brought much of India's Northeast to the knife-edge of violence. In July 1979, the All Assam Students Union (AASU) and the All Assam *Gana Sangram Parishad* (AAGSP) launched a mass movement for the detection of illegal immigrants, their deletion from the voters' list and their deportation to Bangladesh. The agitators demanded that the process of detection should cover all migrants who had entered India since 1951. The Central government agreed to the policy of deportation, but insisted on a 'cut-off' date of 1971 for the identification of illegal aliens. Irrespective of the cut-off date, it is a fact that a minute fraction of the illegal migrants has actually faced deportation and the processes of identification have, even now, barely begun. However, talks between the Central government and the AASU-AAGSP agitators broke down on this point, and the agitation gathered momentum towards the end of November 1979, when the entire State administration was brought to a halt as government employees joined the movement. In December 1979, Assam was brought under President's rule.

The anti-foreigners agitation soon took a violent turn and began to display secessionist tendencies. A militant organisation, the **United Liberation Front of Asom (ULFA),** was established on April 7, 1979, under the leadership of Paresh Barua. While secession from India was the declared goal, the organisation adopted an anti-foreigner plank since this was the popular issue gripping the masses in Assam. Pushing its objective of secession to the background, the ULFA operated within the AASU-AAGSP's agitation.

On March 28, 1980, the army was deployed in the State to restore law and order. The entire State, with the exception of Cachar and the North Cachar Hills districts, was declared a disturbed area and was brought under the Assam Disturbed Areas Act, 1955, and the **Armed Forces (Special Powers) Act, 1958,** on April 6, 1980.

Several rounds of talks were held between the Central government and the leaders of the Assam agitation over the period 1980-83, but they failed to make any headway. Despite a call for a boycott by the agitators, the Central government decided to hold elections to the State Legislature in February 1983. On February 18, over 600 Bangladeshi settlers, including women and children, were massacred in Nellie, Nagaon district. Nevertheless, elections were held. The Congress (I) under Hiteshwar Saikia, came to power, and, while the agitation continued, a measure of order was restored in the State.

Talks between the Centre and the leaders of the agitation were resumed when the Rajiv Gandhi government came to power in Delhi, and on August 15, 1985, the **Assam Accord** was signed. According to the terms of the Accord, all foreigners who entered Assam on or after March 25, 1971, were to be detected and deported.

After the Accord, a new regional party, the Asom Gana Parishad (AGP) was created, bringing together many of the prominent leaders of the agitation. Elections to the State Legislature were held in December 1985, and the AGP was swept to power, with Prafulla Kumar Mahanta as the Chief Minister.

At this stage, the ULFA, emphasised its basic objective i.e., to 'liberate Assam from Indian colonial rule' and to form a 'sovereign, socialist Assam' through an armed struggle. As the Assam Accord and the subsequent political settlement were inimical to this objective, the ULFA continued with its violent activities even after the AGP assumed power in the State. By 1986, the ULFA had established contacts with agents of Pakistan's Inter Services Intelligence (ISI), as well as with militants from the National Socialist Council of Nagaland (NSCN) and the Kachin Independence Army (KIA). Its strength then was estimated at 3,000 militants with access to some 2,000 weapons of various makes. The ULFA created terror in the State, disrupting communications and hitting various economic targets, kidnapping prominent businessmen for ransom and killing government officials. Its activities escalated, reaching unprecedented heights in 1990. As the AGP government lost control of the situation, the State was, once again, brought under President's rule on November 28, 1990 and the ULFA was banned under the **Unlawful Activities (Prevention) Act, 1967.** The army had been re-inducted in the State and *Operation Bajrang* was conducted between September 1990 and April 1991. 209 hardcore militants were arrested during this operation and a large quantities of arms, along with Rs. 48 million in cash—the proceeds of extortion—were also recovered.

Operation Bajrang succeeded in restoring a measure of normalcy in Assam, and elections were held in June 1991 to the State Legislature. The Congress (I) defeated the AGP and Hiteshwar Saikia was, once again, sworn in as Chief Minister on July 1. ULFA resumed its violent campaign almost at once, and the army launched *Operation Rhino* in September 1991. Over the succeeding four months, 2,578 hardcore militants were nabbed, along with large quantities of arms and Rs. 780,000 in cash. The army also destroyed 15 ULFA camps. However, in January 1992, the Saikia government suspended army operations and announced an amnesty for all militants who were willing to surrender. By March 1992, some 4,000 ULFA militants had surrendered to the authorities.

The ULFA, however, proved extremely resilient and restored its strength and activities, acquiring new military hardware and establishing a chain of training camps across the border in Myanmar, and later in Bhutan. In April-May 1995, the Indian and Myanmarese armed forces jointly launched *Operation Golden Bird* along their border. 50 militants were killed during this operation and huge quantities of arms and ammunition were recovered.

The AGP returned to power in the State Legislature elections of May 1996. Counter-insurgency operations continued, and on January 20, 1997, a Unified Command structure was set up to co-ordinate the functioning of the various forces carrying out operations against the terrorists. Since then, continuous military and para-military operations have considerably weakened the ULFA, driving its senior leadership into exile. A disturbing trend, however, is the widening network of extortion, criminal and quasi-legal operations that this leadership-in-exile now commands in Assam, which not only fuels and finances militancy, but, more significantly, has had an extremely corrosive impact on democratic institutions and structures in the State and a deeply corrupting influence on increasingly collusive government officials and political leaders. With this, there has also been a continuous process of 'lumpenisation' among the rank and file of the ULFA cadres, as increasing numbers of criminals join in the extortionary and other illegal activities of the organisation.

The emergence of a Bodo insurgency in the State has become another major problem. The Bodos, a major tribe of plainsmen, are one of the earliest settlers in Assam. They have been demanding better social, political and economic conditions since independence. There has been a long history of tensions between the Bodos and the Assamese. The former feel that they have been neglected and exploited by the latter. The All Bodo Students Union (ABSU) was formed in 1967 to represent the Bodo cause. In the early 1980s, the ABSU emerged as a potent force under the leadership of Upendranath Brahma.

A militant organisation, the Bodo Security Force (BSF) came into being in 1989 under the leadership of Ranjan Daimari. The BSF, later renamed the **National Democratic Front of Bodoland (NDFB),** resorted to terrorism in order to secure an 'independent Bodo nation' north of the river Brahmaputra. A very large proportion of violent activities in the State, including killings, explosions, arson, and attacks on police stations, have been carried out by the NDFB. This is an organised and well-trained militant group with a strength of about 900. It has established a 'working arrangement' with the **NSCN - isak-Muivah (NSCN-IM)**.

Another terrorist group, the **Bodo Liberation Tiger Force (BLTF),** headed by Prem Singh Brahma, has been fighting for a separate State of Bodoland within the Indian Union.

An accord was signed on February 20, 1993, between the Government of India, the Government of Assam and Bodo leaders, creating the Bodoland Autonomous Council (BAC) within Assam. However, since Bodo villages are not contiguous, the demarcation of the jurisdiction of the BAC has remained a problem. Both the NDFB and the BLTF have condemned the Bodo Accord, and have, since the mid-1990s, been engaged in a campaign of violence directed against other ethnic groups within 'Bodo areas'. Large scale attacks were carried out against Santhal tribals in May 1996, displacing tens of thousands of people. A second wave of attacks in May 1998 displaced another couple of thousand Santhals. The Santhals and other non-Bodo communities have also begun to arm themselves and fight back. This has resulted in significant displacement of the Bodo population from areas where they are a minority.

These trends in retaliatory violence are not restricted to the Bodos. Muslim migrants in Assam have also shown signs of incipient militancy. The

Muslim United Liberation Front of Assam has been constituted. A demand for a separate State bringing together the five border districts in Assam, which now have a Muslim majority, has been already voiced.

The recent history of the fissionary trend in which every tribal, linguistic, religious or cultural sub-group demands separation from the others, compounded by the rhetoric of ethnic sub-nationalism, radical demographic shifts and a long history of poor governance, make this State, perhaps more than any other region in the country, a potential source of increasing mass strife over the coming decades.

(Source: South Asia Terrorism Portal, SATP, of Institute of Conflict Management, New Delhi.)

Assam Assessment 2006

In the year 2006, a total of 86 people have been killed in militancy-related incidents in Assam, which includes 48 (55.82 per cent) civilians, 16 (18.60 per cent) security force (SF) personnel and at least 22 (25.58 per cent) militants.

Fatalities in Terrorist Violence - 2006

	Civilians	*Security Force Personnel*	*Terrorist*	*Total*
January	5	1	2	8
February	10	1	1	12
March	3	0	0	3
April	4	0	3	7
May	1	1	0	2
June	13	6	5	24
July	7	0	3	10
August	5	7	8	20
Total	48	16	22	86

Source: Institute for Conflict Management database.

Among the major incidents of terrorist violence in 2006 are:

January 20: Ten persons, including eight CISF personnel, are injured in a grenade attack by United Liberation Front of Asom (ULFA) at the entrance of Guwahati Refinery at Noonmati in Guwahati city.

May 9: Two SF personnel are killed in an ambush by the ULFA near the Borahibari railway station in Sibsagar district. Five persons, including the former State Transport Minister and senior Asom Gana Parishad leader Pradip Hazarika, are wounded in the attack.

June 8: ULFA triggers a series of grenade explosions, while targeting SF personnel, at various parts of the State leaving at least 25 persons wounded.

July 11: Two ULFA cadres, Pradip Rajbangshi and Mrinal Rajbangshi, are killed in an encounter with the SFs at Baglamari village in the Nalbari district.

On August 13, 2006, the Union Government suspended Army operations against the ULFA at a time when the militant group was engaged in a routine stepping up of violence ahead of Independence Day (August 15). Specifically, the announcement came hours after ULFA cadres shot dead a petty trader in the Joypur town of Dibrugarh district, hurled a grenade at the private residence of a senior Assam minister at Digboi in the Tinsukia district (the minister was present but there was no casualties), and made an abortive grenade attack on the Police in the western district town of Nalbari. In ten days, beginning August 4, 2006, the ULFA had launched several grenade or bomb attacks, killing a dozen people, including six SF personnel, five of them of the Assam Police, and injured up to 40 others.

The Union Government, subsequently, decided to extend the suspension of counter-insurgency operations against the ULFA by 15 days. A decision to this effect was taken at the meeting on August 23, 2006, between the Government and the ULFA-backed People's Consultative Group (PCG) to decide modalities for direct negotiations with the outfit.

There have, however, been several roadblocks thus far, obstructing a possible face-to-face meeting between the ULFA and the Government of India:

- New Delhi has asked ULFA to name its negotiating team. ULFA says the team cannot be named unless five of its top detained leaders are freed.
- New Delhi has asked ULFA to give its consent for the talks in writing. ULFA responded by saying the Government must also state in writing that it would discuss the group's key demand of 'sovereignty'.
- ULFA has demanded information on the whereabouts of 14 of its cadres 'missing' after the Bhutanese military assault in December 2003.

In 2006, the ULFA continued with its depredations, bombing markets, oil and gas pipelines and other installations. And it sent alarm bells ringing in the State's industry and security establishment by slapping an INR 5 billion (USD 112 million) extortion demand on the state-owned Indian oil major, Oil and Natural Gas Corporation (ONGC) in January 2006, forcing the authorities to intensify vigil on oil and gas installations. Also on July 3, 2006, the Reserve Bank of India, the country's central bank, was served an extortion demand for INR 1.5 million by the ULFA.

On the other hand, the first round of talks between the Union Government and National Democratic Front of Bodoland (NDFB) was held in New Delhi on May 27, 2006. Both sides agreed to extend their cease-fire agreement for another one year with effect from June 1. However, the group reportedly continues to carry on its extortion and violent activities in its areas of operations even as it indicates its willingness to resolve its problem through negotiations. The Centre and NDFB had entered into a one-year ceasefire agreement in May 2005.

On the political front, the election results of May 11, 2006, brought in new, though not unanticipated, power players into Assam's Legislative Assembly and into the State's Government; players, who were, not long ago, designated as terrorists, and had relentlessly waged war against the state and the democracy that has now catapulted them into the arguable position of 'kingmakers'. The Hagrama Mohilary faction of the Bodo People's Progressive Front (BBPF-H), with its leadership comprising principally of surrendered militants of the Bodo Liberation Tigers (BLT), secured an overwhelming victory in the Bodo Territorial Council (BTC) areas, capturing 12 out of the 18 seats it contested in the 126-member Assam Assembly. The centrality of this victory is underlined by the fact that Chief Minister Tarun Gogoi's Congress Party has returned to power with drastically reduced margins, and just 53 seats in the Assembly, well below the halfway mark, making it dependent on BBPF-H's support to form the Government.

Casualties of Terrorist Violence in Assam - 2006

	Civilians	*Security Force Personnel*	*Terrorist*	*Total*
January	6	0	3	9
February	1	0	7	8
March	3	1	7	11
April	3	0	9	12
May	5	2	10	17
June	3	2	15	20
July	1	1	5	7
August	12	1	2	15
September	10	1	5	16
October	81	0	12	93
November	10	1	4	15
December	14	1	4	19
Total	149	10	83	242

Source: Institute for Conflict Management database.

Comparative Levels of Violence, 2001-2005

Year	*Civilians*	*Security Force*	*Militants*	*Total*
2001	264	59	283	606
2002	138	32	275	445
2003	212	12	281	505
2004	194	24	136	354
2005	149	10	83	242

Source: Institute for Conflict Management database.

Following is the sampling of the major incidents of violence in Assam during 2005.

January 11: Fourteen civilians, induding a nine-year-old girl and four women, are injured when suspected ULFA terrorists trigger an explosion at the Marwaripatty area of Jorhat town.

February 23: Willingson Timung, the KLNLF 'commander-in-chief, is killed along with two other cadres by cadres of his own outfit inside the Langlakso forest area in Karbi Anglong district.

June 16: Four ULFA cadres, including three women, are killed in an encounter with the police at Doloni village in Dibrugarh district.

June 19: Four ULFA terrorists and one SF personnel are killed during two encounters in Nalbari district.

August 7: Four persons are killed and 12 others sustain injuries in an explosion detonated by the ULFA at a bus stand at Boko in Kamrup district.

September 14: Eight persons are killed and several others sustain injuries as suspected Kuki Revolutionary Army (KRA) militants open indiscriminate fire at Thekerajan village in Karbi Anglong district.

October 2: Five members of a family are killed by unidentified militants at Hemari Terang village in Karbi Anglong district.

October 8: Suspected militants kill five Karbi villagers at Borsing Bey village near Diphu town in Karbi Anglong district.

October 9: Unidentified gunmen kill at least six persons at Bura Fanchu and Longsing Engti villages in Karbi Anglong district.

October 21 : Suspected DHD militants kill nine UPDS cadres at Tamulbari under Diphu police station in Karbi Anglong district.

December 2: Four civilians, including a two-month-old infant, are killed by DHD militants at Sirkangnep village in Karbi Anglong district.

It was on September 7, 2005, that the ULFA announced the setting of the People's Consultative Group (PCG), a hand-picked 11-member team comprising journalists, rights activists, lawyers and academics. The group is led by writer Indira Goswami, who has been acting as the mediator between the outfit and the Government in New Delhi for some time now. Rebati Phukan, a former football player from the State, supplements Goswami's efforts. The PCG's mandate was to clear the roadblocks and prepare the grounds for direct talks between the ULFA and the GoI. The PCG has held three rounds of talks with the federal authorities in New Delhi so far, the first meeting on October 26, 2005, chaired by Prime Minister Manmohan Singh. The second PCG-Government meeting was held on February 7, 2006, and the last on June 22, 2006. However, the constitution of the PCG has had little impact on the continuing violence in the State.

During 2005, the ULFA reportedly reorganised its units in its traditional strongholds, forming new 'battalions', and moving into hitherto unexplored territories, both within Assam and in adjoining States. On April 20, 2005, the Police demolished a well-equipped camp of ULFA's newly-formed '27th battalion' in Karbi Anglong district, an area where the organisation's traditional influence has been low. The camp was established in the first week of April 2005 and was led by a middle level cadre, Dandi Bora. On April 21, 2005, six ULFA leaders, including a woman 'sergeant major', were arrested by the Army at Sesupani in Tinsukia District as they descended into Assam from their Changlang camp in neighbouring Arunachal Pradesh. Movements of ULFA cadres drawn from its '28th battalion' have been noticed in the Jonai area of upper Assam's Dhemaji District and also in the Poba reserve forest area spread over a 100 square kilometers along the borders with Arunachal Pradesh. Each of these is a territory that has remained untouched by the group's terror and extortion in the past. Meanwhile, ULFA cadres continue to use the neighbouring State of Meghalaya's Garo Hills area for transit and as an arms dump. On May 14, Police recovered two universal machine guns, three magazines and 60 rounds from an ULFA hideout at Masuk in the West Garo Hills district.

There was a series of macabre killings spanning almost a month (October 2005) in southern Assam's Karbi Anglong District. An analysis of official statistics relating to the violence revealed unexpected dimensions of the violence, suggesting that a particular community - surprisingly the majority in the District - bore the brunt of the merciless raids, suggesting that this was not, as has been widely projected, an 'ethnic war' that has been witnessed. Rather, the attacks had the character of an organized expansionist campaign by a particular ethnic militia, capitalising on absence of pressure from counter-insurgency forces as a result of the prevailing ceasefire with the authorities. As on October 29, 2005, a total of 88 people were officially reported killed, of whom 76 belonged to the majority Karbi ethnic group. The others killed include nine Dimasas, one Bodo, one Nepali and one Assamese.

On its part, the Government has admitted the role of local insurgent groups in the violence. Two rebel groups operate in the District: the United People's Democratic Solidarity (UPDS), pushing for 'self-rule' for the Karbis; and the Dima Halim Daogah (DHD), primarily based in the neighbouring North Cachar Hills District, fighting for a separate Dimaraji State for the Dimasas. Incidentally, both UPDS and DHD had entered into a cease-fire with the Government - the DHD truce came about on January 1 , 2003, and the UPDS cease-fire on May 23, 2002. Obviously, the UPDS cannot be behind the slaughter of the Karbis. The slaughter of the Karbis is believed to be the work of the DHD and its supporters or some other shadowy Dimasa forces. Some of the major incidents of violence that broke out in the Karbi Anglong district in October 2005 are:

October 2: Five members of a family are killed by unidentified militants at Hemari Terang village under Diphu police station.

October 9: Six persons from the Bura Fanchu and Longsing Engti villages are killed and hundreds of houses are set ablaze by unidentified terrorists in separate incidents under Diphu and Bokajan police stations.

October 10: Six Dimasa civilians are killed at Kheroni village. Nearly 60 houses also set ablaze by the miscreants.

October 17: Suspected Dimasa militants waylay two passenger buses traveling from Zirikinding at Charchim under Kheroni police station and kill 23 persons, including nine women, belonging to the Karbi tribe.

October 18: Six persons are killed at Doyangmukh area under Diphu police station.

October 21: Suspected DHD militants kill nine UPDS cadres at Tamulbari under Diphu police station.

The high hopes of the Bodos following the formation of the BTC were quickly shattered when former BLT leaders fell out with the former leaders of the All Bodo Students' Union (ABSU) in their bid to control Bodo politics. The nascent BBPF, formed at Kokrajhar on April 12, 2005, at the behest of the ABSU and former BLT militants, underwent a sudden split on the eve of the Council elections held in May 2005. The divide in the BPPF came mainly as a result of Hagrama Mohilary's support to some former militant comrades who had contested the Council elections as independent candidates against official candidates of the BBPF. Manoj Kumar Brahma, one of Hagrama Mahilary's close associates, for instance, was pitted against Rabiram Narzary, the founding president of the BPPF, at Banargaon. Nevertheless, on June 2, 2005, an 11-member Executive Council headed by Hagrama Mahilary was sworn in at Kokrajhar, to run the 46-member BTC. Post-poll violence continued to rock the Bodo heartland of Assam with two rival BPPF factions engaged in violent clashes - attacking villages, torching houses and indulging in vandalism.

The split in the BPPF and subsequent clashes between the supporters of the two factions have been a boon for the NDFB, which has consolidated its lost position among the Bodos. Its cease-fire with the Government has also raised hopes that the outfit might be able to secure a better deal than the present BTC - though it is difficult to see what more the Government could offer. When the NDFB signed the cease-fire agreement with the Union and State Governments on May 25, 2005, there was jubilation within a large section of the Bodo community. However, the proposed negotiations are expected to be difficult, since the outfit is yet to give up its original demand for a sovereign state of Bodoland.

With the BPPF having secured dominance in the BTC and now gaining a stranglehold in the Governing coalition at Guwahati, its power in Bodo politics will be difficult to challenge for the next five years. Other political formations will, consequently, be increasingly tempted to violence to undermine this influence, even as the Government will have little to offer the surviving Bodo militant group, the NDFB, to secure its return to democratic politics.

Assam was gripped by both euphoria and fear after the country's Supreme Court, on July 12, 2005, struck down as unconstitutional an immigration law that was in force only in the State. While certain groups welcomed the apex court's verdict thinking it would now be easy to detect and throw out the 'hordes' of illegal Bangladeshi migrants, others fear the exit of the special piece of legislation could lead to genuine citizens belonging to the minority communities being victimized or harassed in the name of detecting Bangladeshi aliens.

The Illegal Migrants (Determination by Tribunals) (IMDT) Act, a federal legislation, was introduced in Assam on October 15, 1983, at the height of the 'anti-foreigner' (anti-Bangladeshi migrants) uprising spearheaded by the All Assam Students' Union (AASU). With the introduction of the IMDT Act, Assam became the only State in India where the Foreigners Act was not applicable.

Over the past two decades, just about 1,500 'illegal Bangladeshis' have been expelled, according to official records. Even for this number, however, there is no evidence that Bangladesh has officially accepted their return.

It was in 1998 that the All India Lawyers' Forum for Civil Liberties filed a public interest litigation (PIL) in the Supreme Court seeking a direction to the Centre and the State Governments in Assam, Meghalaya, West Bengal, Mizoram, Tripura and Delhi to deport all Bangladeshis living illegally in India.

Then, in 2000, former All Assam Students Union (AASU) president, and currently member of the Lok Sabha (Lower House of Parliament) from the AGP, Sarbananda Sonowal, moved a PIL seeking the quashing of the Act itself. After a five-year legal battle, the Supreme Court's verdict came on July 12, 2005. The Court's observations were interpreted by the AASU, AGP and the BJP as a vindication of their stand.

Significantly, however, the Supreme Court's order said: "All the tribunals and appellate tribunals under IMDT Act shall cease to function. All cases pending before (these) tribunals shall stand transferred to Foreigners (Tribunal) Order and be decided under Foreigners Act." The ruling Congress in Assam found this a great relief. "The positive aspect of the Supreme Court verdict is that it did not leave detection of foreigners to police and directed constitution of tribunals under the Foreigners Act," Assam Chief Minister Tarun Gogoi was quoted as saying. He said the Congress party was all along demanding that the foreigners should be detected through a judicial process and that the matter should not just be left to the police machinery. So, it seems clear that the exercise of detecting and throwing out illegal migrants is not going to see results overnight even under the new arrangement

Assam : Too many Autonomy Movements

In its diversity, Assam epitomises India. It is not without reason that it has been called an ethnic and cultural mosaic, embracing in its fold the *Ahoms, Bodos/Boros, Rajbongshis, Mishings, Miris, Deuris, Hojais, Meches, Lalungs (Tiwas), Kacharis, Rabhas* and several other smaller groups in its plains, with a significant presence of the *Bengalis, Biharis, Oriyas, Santhals, Punjabis, Sikhs, Nepalese, Bhutanese, Sikkimese;* and of late, a smattering of the people south of the Vindhyas. To complete the picture of this bewildering diversity, the two autonomous hill districts alone are inhabited by the tribes like *Chakma, Dimasa, Garo, Hajong, Hmar, Khasi, Jaintia, Synteng, Pnar, war, Bhoi, Lyngngam, Kuki* (tribes), *Lakher, Man* (Tai speaking), *Mizo* (tribes), *Mikir* (now, Karbi), *Naga* (tribes), *Powi*, etc. Physiographically, Assam is land of great plains, great hills, and verdant valleys. But unfortunately, this land of bounty and beauty has been wrecked by inhuman levels of continual violence unleashed by various militant and insurgent outfits since the dawn of India's Independence.

Differences: Natural and Man-made

The militancy in Assam did not develop suddenly, nor did it spread to all parts of the North-East simultaneously. But it certainly had its origins in Assam for a variety of reasons. The initial impetus came from the ethnic resurgence and identity assertion in the wake of our Independence, which ultimately led to the vivisection of the Region. Some analysts aver the downslide could have been addressed promptly and effectively when they initially raised their head in the *Naga* and *Mizo Hills.* Others feel that disintegrative forces and separatist proclivities were in-built in the history of the Region, and unraveling of the pieces was almost inevitable. Still others hold the huge influx of human beings into the State from East Bengal/Pakistan, later Bangladesh (foreigners) and other parts of the nation (outsiders) as a major cause of troubles in Assam today, and more potentially dangerous, tomorrow!

Then there was certain hiatus between the inhabitants of the *Hills* and the *Plains*. Some scholars blame the British for keeping the *Hill* people away from the plains people through the instrumentality of certain deliberate policy and administrative measures, already discussed. That restricted the social and political interaction between the two peoples (Singh, S.N , *Mizoram, Historical and Geographical,* 1994). This created and then widened not only the physical but also the mental hiatus between the two communities. The natural process of social and cultural assimilation at various levels came to be thwarted. The march of time and exposure to modernity, changing lifestyles, social ethos and political perceptions, all added to the chasm. *Mutual distrust* was the natural outcome. If the hill tribals were nomadic, uncivilised, and even barbarians to the plains people, the latter were dubbed as 'grasping' and 'rapacious' outsiders; and interestingly, most, if not all, tribes had their own nomenclatures for the outsiders, like the *Dokhar (Khasi), Vai (Mizo), Mayang (Manipur),* etc.; and all these terms were disparagingly dismissive pejoratives for these not-so-loved outsiders.

Man and nature, it seems, complimented each other in creating and nurturing an unhappy picture. Physiographic constraints, geographical distance and isolation, and inter- and intra-tribal hostilities of the early times were the realities of situation before the Ahoms and the British tried to extend regular administration to the hill areas. Subsequently, peripheralisation of the Region, yawning communication gaps, long years of neglect, indifference of the nation to the hardship and concerns of their compatriots in the strategic Region, "unimaginative" Government policies, and gross ignorance of the tribal ethos and susceptibilities, created among the Tibeto-Burman people a sharp awareness of their ethnic and cultural differentiation between the "so-called" mainstream and themselves—or so have written some analysts. It is only the natural next step if "they tilt towards making closer affinities in the Shan and Kachin States of Burma and in the Chittagong Hill Tracts of Bangladesh".

The *Assamese* middle class has been described earlier as fractious, and divided along the ethnic, communal, regional and linguistic lines. It was, perhaps justifiably, dubbed as 'movemental' and 'agitationist' and at times, less charitably, as 'xenophobist' (Das, A., 1991; cited in *Reorganisation of*

North-East India, 1996). A 'Study' (Chattopadhyay, 1990) established that there were as many as 19 (10 in Assam alone) ethnic movements in .North-East, all demanding further reorganisation and division of the Region.

Revivalist Organisations and their Variants

Assam has faced a number of revivalist organisations, including some revanchist ones, from fairly early times. Elites of ethnic groups, which lamented their sinking to insignificant positions from their erstwhile dominance, thought of reviving their old glories to reclaim their due share in the power structure, through organisations like:

1. Ahom Association 1893
2. Koch Rajbhongshi Sanmilan 1912
3. All Bora Chhatra Sanmilan 1918
4. Kachari Sanmilan 1921
5. Kachari Students Association 1922
6. Boro Maha Sanmilan 1924
7. Mattak-Moran Sanmilan 1937

What follows are a variety of literary, socio-cultural and students organisations.

Literary Organisations

1. Assam Sahitya Sabha
2. Bodo Sahitya Sabha
3. Rabha Sahitya Sabha
4. Deuri Sahitya Sabha
5. Mishing Sahitya Sabha
6. Tiwa Sahitya Sabha

Socio-Cultural Organisations

1. Tai Historical and Cultural Society
2. Mising Bane Keband
3. Banak Puplik Maung Tai
4. Chutia jati Sanmilan

Students Wings of most Ethnic Groups

1. All Assam Students Union—AASU
2. All Bodo Students Union—ABSU
3. Kachari Students Union
4. All Rabha Students Union

5. Moran Students Union
6. All Tai Ahom Students Union
7. Karbi Students Union
8. Tea Tribes Students Union
9. Mishing Students Union
10. Tiwa Students Union
11. All Tribal Students Union

Several Students Unions have played a leading part in various movements in Assam, e.g., AASU Movement against foreigners in Assam and ABSU's for establishment of Bodoland.

Another point of note is that till the late 1960s, there was no Minister of Cabinet rank in the State Ministries from members of *Ahom-Tai Mongoloid group*. This and other such 'neglects' are cited as evidence of discrimination against the concerned group or community and come handy as justification for starting an agitation or launching a revivalist or identity-related organisation or movement.

Political Platforms

The nature of middle classes and differences, natural and man-made, among the communities have given birth to a variety of dissonances, first in the entire Region and later (presently) in Assam as it exists today, giving rise to issue-based or demand specific movements and platforms, at one time or other. Some of these are listed here:

1. Ahom-Tai Mongoloid Rajya Parishad (Later, to be renamed Ujani Asom Rajiya Parishad); Ahom Movement
2. Plains Tribal Council of Assam (PTCA)
3. Bodo People's Action Committee (BPAC)
4. Assam Movement (against foreigners) led by AASU and (1979-85).
5. United Tribal Nationalist Liberation Front
6. ULFA
7. Assamese agitation leading to the Official Language Bill of 1960
8. The above Bill, declaring Assames as official language of Assam gave birth to two organisations in Bengali-speaking Cachar (Barak Valley) to safeguard its linguistic interests and to espouse the cause of its Bengali population:

   (a) Nikhil Asom Banga Samiti

   (b) Cachar Zila Gana Sangram Parishad

9. Medium of instruction movement launched by other linguistic minorities in 1972
10. Autonomous State Demand Committee (ASDC) for UT status for two Hill Districts of Assam
11. Tiwa agitation for an ADC for their tribe
12. Rabha agitation for an ADC for their tribe
13. Mishing agitation for an ADC for their tribe (The above three are respective Movements by Rabhas, Tiwas and Mishings)
14. Bodo Movements for autonomy and secessionism.
15. The agitations mentioned at Ser 8 above led to the Cachar Movement.
16. Bishnupriya Conundrum
17. Islamic Militancy

We have seen "larger Assam" being divided into Seven States, the "present Assam" being just one of them. If some have chosen to call this unhappy denouement as the end result of "the ethnicity run amok", others justified it as the logical culmination of a process set in motion by ethnic assertions and people's urge for self-identity. But this does not seem to be the end of troubles for the rump Assam. Its troubled history seems to be intent upon continuing on its perilous path, "bent upon causing further self-inflicted injuries to its soul. Its integrity is still under various kinds of threats: Some immediate ones of the ethnic variety; others medium-term, of racial variety; and third, long-term, of religious variety. If the demand for Bodo Land and UT status for two *Hill* districts belong to the first category, the demand for separation of Barak *Valley* from Assam, presently waiting in the wings, answers the second category.To the third category belong the two threats, which will cause grievous hurt to Assam with sinister implications for the Indian *Nation* as a whole: ULFA's desperate struggle for secessionism which in turn, will inevitably give a fillip, at a certain future stage, to the secessionist yearnings of sections of large Muslim population in the Region, which is increasing disproportionately due to natural increase and more dangerously, because of continuing immigration (some Assamese and Indian academics call it infiltration). The latter will no doubt be helped by Pakistan and other members of the "Ummah", as has been seen in the recent years in case of Chechen and Kashmir imbroglios. Some of these movements are discussed hereafter, bar the ones at Sers 6 (ULFA) and 14 *(Bodos),* discussed in Chapters 4 and 5 respectively.

Militant and Insurgent Outfits Operating in Assam

What follows is the list (for record) of terrorist/militant/ insurgent outfits operating in Assam alone as downloaded from www.satp.org on 30 September 2005.

Groups Proscribed under POTA

1. National Democratic Front of Bodoland—NDFB
2. United Liberation Front of Assam—ULFA

Active Terrorist/Insurgent Groups

1. Adivasi Cobra Force—ACF
2. Dima Halam Daogah—DHD
3. Hmar People's Convention-Democracy—HPC(D)
4. Kamatapur Liberation Organisation—KLO
5. Muslim United Liberation Front of Assam—MULTA
6. United People's Democratic Solidarity—UPDS
7. Harkat-ul-Jehad—HUJ
8. Harkat-ul-Mujahiddin—HUM
9. Karbi National Volunteers—KNV
10. Karbi People's Front—KPF
11. Islamic Liberation Army of Assam—ILAA
12. Koch Rajvanshi Liberation Organisation—KRLO
13. Muslim Tiger Force—MTF
14. Muslim Volunteer Force
15. People's United Liberation Front—PULF
16. Rabha National Security Force—RNSF
17. Tiwa National Revolutionary Force—TNRF
18. United Liberation Front of Barak Valley—ULFBV
19. Dimasa National Security Force—DNSF
20. Bodo Security Force—BdSF
21. Kuki Revolutionary Army—KRA

Inactive/Dormant Outfits

1. Adam Sena—AS
2. Adivasi Security Force—ASF
3. All Assam Adivasi Suraksha Samiti—AAASS
4. Barak Valley Youth Liberation Front—BVYLF
5. Bodo Liberation Tigers—BLT
6. Gurkha Tiger Front—GTF
7. Islamic Seva Sangh—ISS
8. Islamic United Reformation Protest of Assam—IURPA
9. Muslim Liberation Army—MLA
10. Muslim Security Council of Assam—MSCA

11. Muslim Security Force—MSF
12. Revolutionary Muslim Commandos—RMC
13. United Liberation Militia of Assam—ULMA
14. United Muslim Liberation Front of Assam—UMLFA

Aasu's Anti-foreigners Movement (1979-85)

The Anti-Foreigners Movement had spawned a considerable amount of literature books, magazine features and newspaper articles, scholarly theses, *et al.,* which attempted to analyse its course, context and character as also the causes that led to it.[1] The agitation, launched and run by the AASU, with AAGSP as junior partner, can easily be termed as one of the greatest mass upheavals in the history of post-1947 India. It should be useful to mention briefly the causes that led to it.

The long-festering problem of continued influx of the immigrants and infiltrators from across the border, and consequently, the ever-increasing pressure on land, coupled with the fear of the Assamese losing their socio-political identity, seemed to be the immediate, motivating factors, or provocations for the Movement. But some analysts would like to think that the real reason lay deeper in the history of Assam going back even to the British days. In fact, the real cause of this popular outburst was the decades of economic neglect of the State by the Independent India, and even worse, its continuation of policy of imperial exploitation of Assam's resources followed by the British (1826-1947) period. It is significant that the most-recent popular movement that preceded the Assam movement was the one of the 1974 led by the AASU protesting the economic backwardness of the State. There was great paucity of productive capital in the State and its annual growth rate during 1970-1980 decade was a mere 0.4 per cent against All-India average of 1.43 per cent. The number of the unemployed rose at an alarming rate during the 1971-1981 period, with the applicants on the live register of the Employment Exchange increasing as much as 270 per cent. More significantly, during the same period the educated unemployed increased by 343 per cent. Of the total number of job-seekers in December 1980 (3,50,000), as many as 1,50,000 were post-matriculates and the ITI and Engineering Diploma holders. Against this rising demand, unfortunately, the job sector in the State Government was virtually stagnant, "while the PSUs under the Central Government were known for their discriminatory attitude in the matter of appointment of the local candidates, particularly, the Assamese and tribals".[2] This discrimination was certainly rankling the mind of the Assamese educated middle class, a class that really mattered. "Such feelings spread poisonous seeds, creating further socio-economic tensions." Some analysts wrote that those in authority were taken in by the stillness that preceded the storm and earthquake.

The theorists of discrimination cited the patterns of employment, as on 21 February 1976, at the NF Railway Headquarters at Maligaon, Guwahati. Of the total of 4,474 employees, 59 per cent had their birth-places outside Assam; and of these, 57 per cent came from former East Bengal (now Bangladesh) and 22 per cent from West Bengal. Only 41 per cent (numbering only 1830) came from within Assam. The Bengali factor always weighed heavily on the Assamese mind, and in this case, 79 per cent of the outsiders were Bengalis, and this does not include the Bengalis, within Assam. This was only the proverbial tip of the iceburg, they asserted, for the situation in the State's coal, tea, oil and plywood industries was even worse. In the 1970s, the realisation was dawning that barring the coal, the latter three industries seemed to be having little impact on the economy of the State, and consequently, on the economic prosperity of the common man.

One scholar[3] thought that the tea industry which had grown up with unduly large concessions from the British rulers had done almost nothing for the welfare of the people of Assam.[4] Enormous profits made by the British and Indian companies were invariably channelised outside the State. Even in the matter of sales tax, Assam got only about half the amount secured by West Bengal by virtue of the fact that head offices of most of the tea companies were located in Calcutta. The *Assam Tribune* (15 June 1980) reported that for the year 1979-1980, *Assam* got only Rs. 22 crore as sales tax on the tea produced in the State, against Rs. 42 crore that went to *West Bengal*. A quick survey of profits made by the tea gardens in Assam in the years preceding the AASU Movement showed that the 175 Agency House gardens which had foreign capital involved, posted gross profits ranging between 1 and 12 crore. Transfer of ownership of tea gardens from British to the Indian hands made no difference to Assam's economy as not only the profits kept flying outside the State but the new Indian owners also brought the outsiders to man the managerial positions. 82 per cent of the managerial posts in Assam tea gardens were held by persons from outside the State.[5] A recurring heartburn for the *Assamese* is that despite the fact that 756 tea gardens of Assam produces 55 per cent of the country's tea and earned an annual foreign exchange of over Rs. 500 crore for the nation, not only most of the head offices of the tea companies continues to be located in Calcutta but even the main office of the *Tea Board*, the highest authority of the tea industry, continued in that city. One estimate placed Assam's annual earnings during 1962-1976 at $ 5,250 million, with an average annual production of 250 million Kgs, at tea price of $ 2.50 per Kg. But the industry's "role in the State still remains predominantly colonial, with not even marginal investment being made to develop the economic infrastructure of the region".[6]

The situation was no different for the plywood extracted from the State. Assam's share of the proceeds was a mere Rs. 35 lakh against the Centre's Rs. 80 crore.

A look at the oil industry also presents a dismal picture as far as Assam's economy is concerned. *Assam's* only private sector oil wells at *Digboi*, operating since 1890, produced some 0.1 million tonnes of crude annually, till 1962. The production expanded sharply from the late 1960s, with discovery of oil in several areas of *Upper Assam,* when it touched an annual figure of 3.5 million tonnes. 1970s onwards, it was 5 million tonnes a year. But the royalty paid by the *Centre* for the *Assam Crude* on the eve of the popular upsurge of 1979 was a mere Rs. 42 per tonne. It was only in the mid-1980s that the rate was raised to Rs. 325, and subsequently to Rs. 578 per tonne. The *Assam Government* demanded much higher rates, 20 per cent of the posted price of equivalent *Middle East Crude* in India, but *Centre* did not accede. Even in the matter of sales tax on the Assam crude, the *State* got only Rs. 574 per tonne, whereas the Centre got Rs. 991 per tonne.[7]

It was an unhappy scene on the kerosene front as well. The sales tax on it amounting to several crores went to *West Bengal* till 1979 since the marketing division of the product was located at *Siliguri*, the kerosene from the *Assam* refineries was carried there by one of the world's longest pipelines. In the matter of natural gas, of which Assam has an estimated reserve of over 60 billion cubic metres, the *Centre* displayed an even worse sort of indifference. "Over 50 million cubic feet of natural gas are flared up daily in Assam's oil fields[8], whereas its proper utilization would have turned the *State* into one of the richest in India in the matter of power generation, and production of various industrial goods like a variety of rubbers, nylons plastics, polyester fibres, paints and dyes, lacquers, pesticides, and other sundry *Chemicals.*[9]

Considering the facts about tea industry the regional scholars aver that "there is much gist in the allegation that this industry in *Assam* is part of the overall colonial exploitation of the State by big industry and the Centre". They believe that with a little bit of sympathy and positive attitude towards the *State* and its economy, both the tea and oil sectors could have contributed substantially in achieving the desideratum of improving the overall condition of the people of the region, "thereby keeping both the growth of secessionist ideas and forces espousing them, in check".

Adding to the growing feeling of colonial exploitation was the problem of ever-increasing influx and consequent pressure on land. Not only was there some jugglery over the influx figures in the state, with scholars either exaggerating or underplaying the crisis caused by such influx, depending upon which side of the fence they stood, there was also an effort to over-paint the benefits accruing to the State from the labours of the immigrants. The influx from East Bengal had been a common phenomenon in the early decades of the 20th century; and undoubtedly, the migrants had added to the State's economy by opening up difficult waste tracts and riverine belts for cultivation, which the local Assamese had been unable or unwilling to do. The immigrants, land-hungry, hard-working, and hardy lot, did prove their usefulness in the initial stages. But beyond a point, their presence was bound to be resented, making them unwelcome guests. This is what exactly happened as the immigrant pressure on the reserved tribal belts and blocks and the grazing areas increased; and the Assamese public opinion swiftly veered against immigration. The immigrants were seen as encroachers on the lands of the Assamese cultivators and the Government lands, and the reserved forests. To stem any further tensions between the sides, the British Government introduced the line system in 1920 to restrict the immigrants, mostly Bengali Muslims, to certain areas. But the measure does not seem to have produced the desired results. The 1951 Census revealed that the number of settlers had risen from 3 lakhs in 1921 to 5 lakhs in 1931. Attempts by Assamese members to legislate laws to prevent any further settlement of immigrants met with little success during the 1920s. Consequently, during the 1930-1936 period, as many as 59 grazing, forest, and village reserves were thrown open, de-reserved, so to say, in Nowgong district alone to the immigrants under the Colonisation Scheme.[10] Citing data from Nowgong district, a researcher[11]! points' a grim picture of threat posed by the immigrants to the Assamese people:

> "Out of the District's total occupied area of 5,41.160 acres (sown and fallow) in 1936, 2,04,078 acres, or 37.7 per cent, were under the immigrants' occupation, as against 62.3 per cent still in the hands of the indigenous people. The cultivable waste lands other than fallow in the district amounted to more than 1.4 million acres. The land-hungry Muslim immigrants, segregated and pitted against all odds never appreciated the Assamese point of view. If all men were equal in the eyes of Allah, why should thousands of acres of land remain waste, particularly when men in search of livelihood and lebensraum were available to turn them into smiling fields.... They wanted the Line System to go."

This was the threat the Assam movement was to highlight during its agitation against the foreigners, for the simple reason that immigration from across the border had continued even in the post-1947 period. The land alienation was adding to anti-immigrants sentiment among the Assamese people. All immigrants were coming to be perceived as hostile presence.

Land is another emotive issue that impinges upon the common Assamese. Decrease in the average size of ownership holdings, very high percentage of households owning no land (and to know that there was practically no problem of landlessness in pre-1947 Assam), reduced forest cover, etc. and resulted in pressure on the land. It needs emphasis that the land question in Assam is an extremely complicated problem, and it is this question, which more than the "ethnic" dimensions and "threat to identity" invested the Assam Agitation with a measure of legitimacy.

It was only natural that in course of time the students' demand for economic development of the State would be shifted to the unwelcome presence of the foreign migrants who were seen as the ones mainly responsible for the present unhappy state of affairs. The Assamese people became even more apprehensive when it dawned upon their mind that the migrants, particularly the immigrant Muslims, constituting easily the largest single vote-bank of the State, were about to emerge as a viable political entity. The long-built Assamese fear of being outnumbered and out-voted in their homeland found official confirmation in the statements of the Chief Election Commissioner (CEC) Shakdher, who expressed serious concern over the fact that the foreign nationals, constituting a sizeable proportion of the voters, would be affecting the outcome of the poll verdict. It was an obvious and unacceptable infringement of India's sovereignty. To ensure that the foreigners do not participate in the polls, the CEC urged upon the Union Ministry of Home Affairs to issue Identity Cards to the genuine voters of the State. For reasons administrative, political, or whatever, the CEC's warnings fell on the deaf ears in New Delhi. The advocates of autonomy/Swadhin Asom saw the Centre's response as arrogant indifference towards Assam's interests and sensitivities. The Assamese intellectuals of the Independence period had come to associate such arrogance and insensitivity with leaders like Nehru, and they perceived the current crop as no different.

The final shove of the Assam movement on the foreigners' issue came from the event of updating the rolls for the Parliamentary bye-election to the Mangaldoi constituency caused by the death of a sitting member. The tribunal set up by the State Government for the purpose declared as many as 45,000 voters in an electorate of 6 lakhs as foreigners. The foreign infiltrators had thus finally emerged as a major electoral factor in Assam's polity. Something had to be done to stem the tide. It was this aim and under these circumstances that a plan for united action among the All Assam Gana Sangram Parishad (AAGSP) composed of some regional parties, the Asom Sahitya Sabha, and the AASU, was born at Dibrugarh on the initiative of the AASU in August 1979. Within three mnths, Assam Movement had begun.

It should be relevant to mention some of the salient features of Assam Movement, whose very success seemed to have helped the demand for Swadhin Asom, subsequently spearheaded by ULFA. The Movement was, by and large, a democratic[12] agitation. But for its wide popular base, the Movement could not have sustained itself for five long years, in the face of vigorous (repressive) measures adopted by the Government to suppress it, claim its supporters. They also postulate that given the scale of people's participation, it must be conceded that there was a great degree of "national" content in it. The Assamese middle class, no doubt, played a leading role in the agitation, but its success must be ascribed to "the strong degree of support it received from the rural masses, both Assamese and tribal". The "civil disobedience programmes", "Janata Curfews", oil blockade, and finally, the boycott of the 1983 polls would not have been possible if the rural population of Assam had not overwhelmingly responded to the call of the AAGSP (The counterview that the coercive measures and violence threatened by its leaders could have silenced the opposition, or even forced the reluctant to join in, need not necessarily be dismissed as untrue. The "Swadhin Asom" (=Independent Assam) exponents aver that certain organisations supporting secessionism were also active partners in the movement.

It is also averred that by the time the Assam Accord was signed in August 1985, people's confidence in the Centre had been shaken, "because of the excessive force used by the Government during the agitation to suppress it, creating a vacuum in the political space with the virtual nullifying of the Congress which had ruled the State almost uninterruptedly since 1947. The "Independent ..Assam" theorist posits that this vacuum was sought to be filled in by forces which propagated separation from India through an armed struggle. And this space and opportunity, ironically offered by the success of AASU, was exploited by the ULFA to strengthen itself and its secessionist platform.

Subsequent to the success of the Movement, certain yearnings for Swadhin Asom resurfaced when the realisation dawned on the section of the youth that despite the massive involvement of the people, nothing very tangible had been gained by them. The disillusionment was further strengthened when the AASU-spawned AGP Government failed to achieve any success on the issue it had waged the long, acrimonious war for. The number of illegal foreigners the Students Ministry expelled from Assam was negligible. It was not surprising then that the ULFA increased its influence among the people during the Mahanta (1985-1990) Ministry. Some analysts claim that the extremist and irreconciled elements of AASU were the ones who provided leadership to the ULFA!

The above is an account of the causes that led to the Agitation, in broad terms, and some views about it being democratic or otherwise. What follows are some additional information on the Agitation, fleshing out some details on the aspects already mentioned above.

Assam Accord: Some Prominent Features

Some prominent provisions of the *Accord* signed on 15 August 1985 are mentioned here:

1. For purpose of detection and eviction of foreigners, 1-1-1966 shall be base date and year.

2. Foreigners who came to Assam after 1-1-1966 and up to 24-3-1971 shall be detected as per provisions of the Foreigners Act, 1946 and their names deleted from the Electoral Rolls. After expiry of 10 years, their names shall be restored to the Rolls.
3. Foreigners who came to Assam after 25-3-1971 shall be expelled as per the law.
4. The Government will give due consideration to certain difficulties expressed by the AASU/AAGSP about the implementation of the IMDT Act, 1983.
5. International border shall be made secure against future infiltration by erection of barbed wire fencing and... construction of a road...along it.

Violence Indeed was Part of the Movement

The impact of demographic changes as an important conflict-generating cause had come to the limelight in the two decades of 1970s and 1980s. However, the resentment over the large scale unchecked migration into the region from foreign countries East Pakistan/Bangladesh in the main, and Nepal and Bhutan on smaller scale had been brewing much before the anti-foreigners' agitation burst out in the late 1970s, subsequently engulfing various parts of the State. But when the immigrant population impacted upon the electoral processes of Assam, it became an explosive mixture. When many non-Assamese were elected to the State Assembly in 1977, the indigenous Assamese got apprehensive about their position in their own home. It was this spark, say some analysts, that started the movement in July 1979 for the eviction of these foreigners from Assam. The joint AASU-AGSP agitation was indeed peaceful in the initial stages, "and they even appealed to the Army not to use its guns against the volunteers of the Movement, whose sole objective was to protect Assam, and hence, protect India's sovereignty and independence. The agitation gained momentum fast and by the end of November 1979, all organs of the Government were infiltrated into". The oil production and distribution had been taken over by them; NF Railway took order from them, transport was controlled by them; the AIR Gauhati was broadcasting their programme; and the local media was fully supporting their cause. "All being terror-stricken, nobody dared to challenge them in the State", said a contemporaneous report. "It was the stage when they ran a parallel Government, a la Sheikh Mujib in East Pakistan before its formal demise on 17 December 1971." The State Government being near defunct, President's rule was imposed in December 1979.

In January 1980, the agitationists resorted to mass violence and terrorism, in which many people were killed and about 15,000 rendered homeless due to fear and arson, who were moved into relief camps. It was about this time that the minorities started losing confidence and began to separate themselves from the students' agitation. The Army was called in and given responsibility for internal security from 28 March 1980. The entire State, excluding the North Cachar Hills District, was declared a disturbed area under the provisions of the Assam Disturbed Areas Act, 1955 and the Armed Forces (Special Powers) Act, 1958, which were promulgated on 6 April 1980. The Gauhati High Court stayed the implementation of this notification on 8 April. Later, the Court modified the stay order partially and enjoined that the stay order would remain in respect of Section 4 of the Assam Disturbed Areas Act, 1955 and Section 4A of the Armed Forces (Special Powers) Act, 1958. "This partial stay constrained the powers of the forces to a considerable extent and put them at a serious disadvantage."[13] Subsequently, the Government had to approach the Supreme Court for necessary relief. During this period, the Army was also charged with the responsibility of flushing and production of oil that they did successfully, which in turn affected the image of the agitators. Consequently, a popular Government was formed on 6 December 1981. Due to the loss of support in the Assembly, the Government resigned and President's Rule had to be once again imposed on 30 January 1982.

During the period 1980-1983, a number of rounds of talks were held between the Centre and the agitation leaders, but without any positive outcome. Election had to be held before March 1983 to fulfil a constitutional requirement. The Student leaders demanded complete revision of electoral rolls before holding of the elections in order to delete the names of the foreigner; from these rolls. That being not possible due to immensity of the task, the Government scheduled the elections for February 1983. The agitationists made every effort to thwart these polls, resorting to intimidation and assassination of the candidates, threats to the Government employees engaged in the poll process and the voters, kidnapping, rapine, *et al.* There was widespread violence, causing death and destruction. The worst was on 18 February 1983 when over 1700 lives were lost in the worst-ever acts of mindless violence in Nellie and some other places. The February 1983 Poll was most violent ever. Consequently a popular Government under Hiteswar Saikia came to power. The SFs were able to restore order, and Government initiated steps of prevent further infiltration.

The Rajiv Gandhi Government signed an Accord with the AASU-AGSP Leaders on 15 August 1985 (discussed elsewhere). An organisation, known as ULFA, had been formed in April 1979, which constituted the armed wing of the AASU-AGSP combine, and was raised to support their struggle, some analysts had suggested. Their activities assumed menacing proportions when the AGP Government came into power in December 1985, with Mahanta as Chief Minister, as a result of the said Accord in August that year. During the

AGP Rule, the minorities felt insecure and demanded greater protection. On the other hand, the tribal communities, viz, the Bodos, Karbis and Cacharis, started demanding autonomy and separation from Assam. A reign of terror and violence was let loose by the ULFA and Bodo militants in the latter half of the Mahanta Rule, and the worst hit were the tea plantations. Due to its utter failure to maintain law and order in the State, the Mahanta Government was dismissed on 28 November 1990, ULFA banned and President's Rule was imposed once again. The Army had launched operation Bajrang in September 1990 to clean up the mess. Consequent to the June 1991 Election, Hiteswar Saika's Congress came to power, and the Ministry was sworn-in on 1 July 1991. ULFA again resorted to its violent activities. The Army launched Operation Rhino on 15 September 1991 against the militants, this time achieving better results compared to operation Bajrang. Chief Minister Saikia was able to lure large number of ULFA cadres into surrender but Paresh Baruah succeeded in fleeing to Bangladesh with his considerable strength intact. In 1996 elections, Mahanta's AGP again came to power, for a second stint.

Students in Power and Foreigners Issue

Having won the victory, the AGP-AAGSP combine during their first stint in power (1985-1990) faced problems from the Bodos, their one-time acolytes. If the Bodos were proving most recalcitrant, other tribes too were picking up the ropes fast. Plains tribes by then were clamouring for autonomy. In the 1989 Karbi Anglong District Council Elections, Marxist-led ASDC eclipsed the AGP, the ruling party, spawned by the powerful AASU in 1985, after the conclusion of the 15 August 1985 Accord and on the eve of taking over power. AGP thus was the political wing of the AASU. But they were finding it difficult to find their feet in political management of the State they had taken over. For the "experienced agitators" but the "inexperienced administrators", it was even more worrisome that some of their erstwhile colleagues and the AASU hardliners were veering towards the ULFA, an outfit which later grew to menacing proportion and unleashed unprecedented violence on Assam; and it had to be finally banned for espousing secessionism.

The Students' Movement and its Government suffered crisis of confidence when they failed to come up to the high expectations raised by their victory, as also their failure to deliver on the provisions of the Accord. They also could not provide an honest and efficient governance to Assam. On the other end, Rajiv Gandhi himself was on the defensive beset by his own domestic problems: Punjab terrorism, Shah Bano case and Muslim Women's maintenance case, reservation issue in Gujarat, Bofors Gun scandal, etc. Mahanta Ministry's worst failure was its inability to achieve any success on the hot issue of illegal influx—the very subject on which the whole edifice of

Students' Movement had been built. The allegations of unabated influx continued to be made, despite the construction of border roads and fencing. Even the AASU was unwilling to buy the AGP Government argument that "it was not possible to man every inch of the border and seal it against the determined infiltrators", particularly the 180 km riverine sector. In face of the strident criticism, the AGP Government shifted the blame for their own failure to the existing laws and the regulatory procedures, particularly the Illegal Migrants (Determination by Tribunal) Act, IMDT Act for short.

The crunch came because of its failure to control ULFA and Bodo militancy, and its running amok among the tea gardens. Consequently, the first Mahanta Ministry was dismissed by the President in November 1990, and ULFA banned as an illegal organisation.

The power had corroding effect on the AGP leadership even before they completed their five years in office; it was an open secret that Mahanta and his No. 2, Bhrigu Phukan were pulling in different directions. It was no surprise when the AGP was handed down a humiliating defeat in the 1991 Assembly Elections, and Saikia-led Congress came into power (1991-1996).

During the 1985-1990 period, Mahanta Government "could not detect more than 347 foreigners, and what was even worse, could not deport even one of them". Chief Minister Saikia created a huge controversy early in his tenure (1991-1996) by declaring that there "are no (later amended to 'no new') foreigners in Assam". Possibly to spite the AGP for its loud and noisy agitation against the foreigners, he cited the 1991 Census figures to make a point: Assam's population grew by only 53 per cent during the 1971-1991 period, one per cent fewer than the national average. He even claimed to have pushed back 48,000 foreigners—"a figure too neat and trim for belief".

Another issue that invited notice (in 1994) during the Saikia term (1991-1996) was the revision of electoral rolls, again an offshoot of the contentious foreigners issue. The revision was to be carried out in 1994-95 with 1 January 1994 as the qualifying date for the next Assembly election, "then due in mid-1996." The Election Commission (EC) wanted extensive revision under its special Revised Instructions which classified the voters into List I (valid voters) and List II (suspect or doubtful voters whose names were to be marked as such on the Rolls). All Assam Muslim Students Union (AAMSU) and United Minorities Front (UMF) were stoutly opposed to these special guidelines. The revision was carried as per the EC guidelines and AAMSU and UMF have ever since been agitating to upgrade the names in List II to the status of valid voters.

Another issue belonging to this genre also cropped up in 1994-95. As per the 1985 Assam Accord, some 18,294 foreigners of 1966-71 category whose "names had been deleted from the electoral rolls for 10 years, would be re-eligible in 1995, rendering them qualified to vote in the 1996 polls. Both issues had to be put on the hold during those polls.

Mahanta with his AGP was back in power for a second stint (May 1996-May 2001). His second innings was not any the more happier experience. He was accused of having forgotten the foreigners' issue. "He is only interested in saving his chair", was another uncharitable jibe hurled at him, clinching the issue with the question: "Is not he holding on to power with the support of the very people who are even denying the presence of any foreigners in Assam"? The issue indeed seemed to have been put on a back-burner, if not forgotten, when Assam's energies were spent on combating the lawless violence unleashed by the ULFA and Bodo ultras. To cite statistics, the extremist violence had cost 1370 civilian and 2201 police lives in Assam in the 10 years (1986-96) following the 1985 Accord. Moreover, things have only worsened after 1996, as shown by the statistics cited elsewhere. Even at the end of their second stint in power in 2001, the main issue that spawned a fairly violent movement (1979-81) and put its protagonist in power, is no nearer the solution than it was at the start of it. It is an accurate indictment of and a sad reflection on the performance of the Students in power. In fact, it is worth examining if they were any different from other politicians in exercise of power. Did the one-time starry-eyed, idealistic Students use power to ameliorate the lot of the common man?

Students in Power: Were they any different?

Two student leaders, P.K. Mahanta and Bhrigu Phukan, who successfully led the movement, were the leading lights of the Government that came to power consequent to the December 1985 elections, being its Chief Minister and Home Minister respectively. The nation, celebrating the victory of the idealistic young people, had high hopes from them. They had shown their organisational and mobilisational skills during the long, bitter, and often violent movement, and captured political power in the geo-strategically important State in India.

Here are some heart-warming and interesting statistics on the leaders elected in the 1985 polls:

1. Mahanta at 32 became the youngest ever Chief Minister in India.
2. With an average age of a little over 30 years, the AGP was India's youngest ever legislature party to occupy the treasury benches in a State Assembly.
3. Only 4 of the 109 AGP MLAs had ever contested an election earlier. Only one, Atul Bora, whose father was once a Minister, lost narrowly from Marigaon.
4. There were 50 MLAs with Bachelor's degree or more; just two without any formal education.

5. By contrast, AGP members in Lok Sabha were a senior lot, headed by Dinesh Goswami. The youngest MP among them, Gokul Saikia, at 34 just fell short of becoming the youngest ever MP from Assam, yielding the honour to another Assamese, the "Venerable" D.K. Barooah who, had first entered the Lok Sabha at 33.

As is its wont, the Press went overboard; Mahanta was the idealist; Phukan, strong and silent, Sardar Patel II. But even before the mid-way mark, things soured, rivalry between the two coming out in the open. Then there were hints of corruption and nepotism taking over the idealism of the youth. Phukan accused Mahanta of not being serious on implementing the 1985 Accord, the very basis of AGP' ascent to power. Mahanta returned the honours, accusing his own Home Minister of failure to contain ULFA's demand for a Sovereign Assam. But somehow, they continued in an uneasy relationship. Two years in power, internal dissidence had become serious, compelling Mahanta to drop 12 ministers (1987). Then on, the Government was always teetering on the brink. It had failed to confront the ULFA head on; some even accused it of pro-ULFA leanings.

The crunch came on 29 July 1990 when Phukan resigned, owning moral responsibility for the killing of the Dibrugarh SP in an ambush. The real reason lay elsewhere, he believed Mahanta was spreading rumours about his links with ULFA. General Manager of the Gauhati Refinery had been abducted, along with his son and driver, and the word was going round that the Home Minister was negotiating with the militants secretly and in his personal capacity. "On a certain clarification, he decided not to press his resignation."

By design or otherwise, the Mahanta Government had failed to control and crush the militancy, and it was already in the last year (1990) of its first term. It had failed in the primary responsibility of ensuring safety and security of its citizens. It was disgrace abounding when unable to meet the rising demands of ULFA and Bodo militants, the Doom Dooma India, a subsidy of Unilever Group, airlifted its executives and their families out of Assam. It was this 'infamous' evacuation by air that highlighted the utter failure of the Government in fighting the insurgency which brought the Chandrashekhar Government to the end of its tether—and patience. In November 1990, the Mahanta Ministry stood dismissed.

Even the dismissal was not chastisement enough for the factious leaders. In 1991, Phukan revolted against Mahanta, and in an attempt to dislodge him from the Party Presidentship, charged him with corruption, nepotism, treachery and hunger for power—some charges, these! Mahanta hit back, by expelling Phukan and six other senior dissidents. The latter formed the Nutan (new) AGP (NAGP), and Party stood formally split. It helped Saikia-led Congress returning to power in June 1991 Poll, winning 66 of the 126 Assembly seats, with the AGP getting only 19 and NAGP just 5. The wilderness taught them a lesson, as the two factions united to win the May 1996 Assembly polls (some comments were unambiguous that the AGP captured power with the active support of ULFA, but more on it later). A 5-Party Coalition under Mahanta came into power. Phukan and his supporters did not find a place in the Ministry. At the Third General Convention of the AGP held at North Lakhimpur in October 1996, Phukan's marginalisation was complete when he was even dropped from the AGP Executive. Later in a clever move, he was suspended from the Party, rendering him unable to float a new party, because if he did, he would have lost his Assembly seat under Anti-Defection Act. If expelled, he faced no such handicap. So the students were no less adept in the art when it came to playing games. To embarrass Chief Minister Mahanta, Phukan had been stridently demanding scrapping of the IMDT Act which, it was generally believed came in the way of expelling the illegal immigrants; and also wanted opening of talks with ULFA, even if the latter was disinclined to do so till that time.

So this is the tale of two young student leaders who, having worked successfully together to lead a long movement, could not put their heads together even for five years for the common good of their cause and State, unable or unwilling to rise above their personal egos and petty quarrels. So, they too proved, that in politics there is place only for one on the top. With what high hopes their people had put them in power in December 1985! Having seen these students, should the public and press still be too harshly condemnatory of the professional politicians for their "hunger and lust for power"? But having finished his rival and challenger, did Mahanta give a clean, efficient governance to Assam?

AGP's Second Stint in Power: 1996-2001

The question of AGP's links with and soft corner for ULFA had always been a matter of serious speculation and comment. On 7 June 1997, Mahanta had a narrow escape when an IED exploded just as the Chief Minister's cavalcade passed by the much-revered Kamakhya Temple in Gauhati. He ordered a crack-down on ULFA. Within ten days, it was realised how tough and even embarrassing decision it had been. Surely, realised Mahanta could not have been unaware of ground realities in his own capital, where the ULFA had not only penetrated the administrative apparatus but also established a strong grip on the people by persuasion or coercion. Mahanta was scheduled to address a public meeting in his home constituency of Barhampur in Nagaon district within a fortnight. Then happened something providing a stunning proof of ULFA's influence in the State! On 17 June, the Nagaon Unit of the Ruling AGP had to sign an agreement with the Convener of ULFA's Kalangiri Council to ensure a violence-free meeting of the State Chief Minister!

Here are some interesting clauses from the Agreement:

1. ULFA, AGP, and AASU—obviously in the same order—will fight jointly against the Unified Command structure in the State and for the withdrawal of the black (read, anti-terrorism) laws.
2. The promise to struggle for the self-determination of Assam will be delivered. And this will also have to be done jointly.

Mahanta finally addressed his meeting on 20 June but not before the militants had rubbed his nose in the dust, and reduced his Party to the situation faced by the numerous tea gardens in the State—helplessly obeying the diktats of ULFA. The AGP's reaction? Same as non-combatant civilians: It acquiesced. The Press was very critical of the 'Agreement'. It was published in detail. It was widely commented that Mahanta was using the Tata Tea imbroglio (they were being blamed for helping the rebels) to obscure his own Party's links with ULFA, and his own Government's failure to fight the insurgency. It was an ultimate ignominy for the political class in general and AGP in particular that a Chief Minister had to seek permission from an avowedly secessionist outfit to hold his public meeting. But Mahanta told a Weekly that "such things (documents on Agreement) can be easily fabricated".[14] But he failed to explain why his Government flinched from taking legal action against these fabricators.

Nor was the Students' Ministry above the charges of graft and corruption. The 400-crore LOC (Letter of Credit) scam, regarding 12 cases of fraudulent withdrawals from the State treasury and subsequent disbursement of the money through the Veterinary Department without proper bank guarantees, hit the headlines in 1993, and case handed over to the CBI next year. 11 charge sheets had been filed by the end of 1997, and Mahanta was suspected to be involved in the 12th case. In 1998, the CBI approached the Governor, Lt Gen Sinha, for permission to prosecute Mahanta but Sinha rejected the request on 5 February 1999. But Mahanta's troubles were not yet over. Nabin Chandra Kalita, a poor cultivator from Hajo,[15] filed a public interest petition on 19-9-1999 in Gauhati High Court to reopen the case. The case had gone nowhere till date (November 2002).

There was a spurt of nepotism-induced dissidence in 1998 when Mahanta gave Lok Sabha ticket to his wife, Jayshree, for the General Elections that year. Mahanta somehow weathered the storm by parading a majority of MLAs at his press conference on 28 May.[16] Ironically, at the end of it all, Jayshree lost the election. But refusing to let up, Mahanta nominated Jayshree for a Rajya Sabha seat. Winning the seat, she was sworn-in in October 1999 as a member in the 197th session of that august body.[17] The following press comment should be an apt summing up of Mahanta's progress from a student leader to a politician:

"...what ULFA and Mahanta's closest colleagues now realise is that he has changed.... He is intent on keeping his chair. But like ULFA and Tata Tea, the Ministers now realise they are not dealing with a starry-eyed Mahanta. He is now Party's sole power centre, and Party's culture, once touted as revolutionary, has changed.... Staying in power takes a top priority now. Sycophancy and patronage have been imported from the Congress, Mahanta has kept all of 24 departments with himself, and with reason. 'When you have so many portfolios, it is that much easier to dole them out when people have to be won over', says a senior Minister.... As for implementing the main provisions of 1985 Accord on expelling the illegal immigrants from Assam, we can forget about it.... He is ruling Assam presently with the support of a party[18] which is fiercely pro-immigrants, legal or illegal."[19]

What was Mahanta's record in other fields? As for its financial health, Assam was virtually bankrupt. It owed over Rs. 7000 crore (till end 1997) to the Centre and PSUs. He pleaded with New Delhi for waving Assam's over Rs. 4000 crore debt and sought reimbursement of insurgency-related expenditure of Rs. 400 crore.

On the militancy front, ULFA was unrelenting in its depredations, even though the AGP had signed a virtual pact with ULFA in June 1997. Militants had killed till June 1997 over 1100 people since Mahanta took over in May 1996; the figure had climbed to 1490 till September 1997.

In view of the so-called 'Pact' AGP had with ULFA, Mahanta's attitude towards the Unified Command (UC) came as no surprise to the people. The UC was set up on 4 January 1997 under the Tezpur Corps Commander. Although Mahanta denied reports on the 8th that he was opposed to setting up of the UC but refused to acknowledge that such a Command has already been set up (four days earlier); he merely, blandly announced "that some proposals have been received". The Press reported his refusal to head the UC. In fact, he led an All-Party delegation to Delhi, met Prime Minister Deve Gowda and Home Minister Inderjit Gupta, discussed law and order situation of Assam (patently, the State subject) with them, and urged them to take necessary measures to control insurgency and find a political solution to ULFA's demand for independence. He was obviously politicking, and his Delhi visit was impelled by demands of the internal politics of the AGP—to impress the dissidents within his party. As a daily advised him editorially, "he should have followed Farooq Abdullah's example by taking over the UC", instead of an escapist visit to New Delhi.[20]

It all added up to a hopeless situation for Mahanta and his AGP. Out of 14 Lok Sabha seats for Assam, AGP did not win a single in the two general elections of 1998 and 1999. Then, the all-important question of illegal immigrants and their deportation seemed to have been forgotten. A 'cynical' question is: "Is any one interested?" The AGP was spending all its energies in retaining power. They could not get the IMDT Act amended/repealed. In two terms, the critics say, whatever number they claimed to have deported, which in any case, did not cross the three figures, "have already returned to Assam". This, in brief, is what the AASU Movement was all about, and what the AGP Government, spawned by it, had achieved in 10 years, split over its two terms of 5 years each, separated by the Saikia interregnum of 5 years (1991-96).

Finally, the inevitable question: How different were the 'Student' politician from the 'professional' politician? Does one need to give an answer!

Last Word on the Unhappy Situation

The last word on the AASU, AGP, and the present situation should belong to the two most eminent sons of Assam; one a poet and other, a historian.

In a 1998 Song, Assam's Poet Laureate, Bhupen Hazarika, asked in anguish and despair: "If we seek the sunrise, then why do we rush to embrace the sun-set?"

Assam's Historian Laureate, H.K. Barpujari,[21] is more direct if less poetical than the Bard quoted above. Says the Historian in an interview: "This phase since the Assamese movement began in 1978-79 is the worst I have seen.... The ruling AGP is its errant child, and ULFA the illegitimate grandchild ."

Mahanta's Fortunes: Ebbing

It seemed Mahanta had survived all the dissidence in his party when he was elected President of the AGP for the second time in a row since 1995 at the end of the Party's four-day fourth convention at Nagaon on 1 February 2001. When he was re-elected the AGP Chief for the second consecutive term, his wife too had been elected as one of the eleven Vice-Presidents of the Party.

The AGP came to power in Assam after signing the historic Assam Accord (1985) following a six-year agitation to flush out illegal Bangladeshi immigrants from the State. "It has been 15 years since. The AGP has ruled the State for two terms but seems to have forgotten about the Accord" *(Hindustan Times,* 29-4-2001). The Party's manifesto for May 2001 Assembly Poll released on 27 April made no mention of the unfulfilled clauses of the Accord! AGP lost the polls to the Congress.

Within three months of its rout in the Assembly Polls, the AGP, "which is the strongest regional party in Assam and has ruled the State for 10 years, suffered successive blows, with three of its former Ministers, including former

Chief Minister Mahanta, figuring in scandals involving women". In her interview published in an Assamese Weekly on 15-8-2001, Sanghamitra Bharali, a language officer in the Assam Assembly, claimed that she and Mahanta were married on 11 March at the Bigneshwar Ganesh Temple in Mumbai. Stung by the bigamy charge, Mahanta handed over charge of the party presidentship to Biraj Sharma, until October. The other former ministers involved in the sexual escapades were Rajendra Mushahary and Jatin Mali (For details, *see* the *Frontline* of 14-9-2001 and *India Today* dated 3-9-2001).

As if the bigamous scandal was not enough to make a dent in his personal graces, some months later, his wife lodged a FIR with Delhi Police that Mahanta had physically beaten her. Then came the unkindest cut of the political kind. The AASU accused Mahanta of "being the greatest traitor the State has ever seen" for betraying their agitation against the Bangladeshi migrant. AASU advisor, Samujjal Bhattacharya says "Mahanta has 'done nothing' to get the IMDT Act revoked when he was in power for two terms." Mahanta hits back saying his Government had filed petition in the SC in 1999 praying for revoking of the Act. Incidentally, the new Congress Government of Assam under Gogoi, after coming to power in May 2001, changed its stand and submitted a revised petition before the Apex Court, saying the State Government was against scrapping the Act (*Indian Express,* 22-8-2002). Incidentally, the betrayal charge came soon after the return (July 2002) of Mahanta from his 11-month self-exile consequent to the bigamy charge on 15 August 2001.

Once a darling of the Assamese people who led a sustained 6-year Anti-Foreigners Agitation of the AASU and twice was the Chief Minister of Assam Mahanta had—or, so it seems as of now—a sad end of his political career. After years of intra-party blood-letting, he was publicly called a 'betrayer' by his party, first suspended and then expelled from it in July 2005. Presently he heads his own party, a faction of the mother organisation.

ASSAM'S HILL DISTRICTS: THEY WANT AUTONOMY

(Karbi and Dimasa Movements)

Presently, Assam is left with only two Hill districts in its fold: Karbi Anglong (KA) (earlier, Mikir Hills district) and North Cachar Hills (NC, for short) district; the former has some distinction, located as it is at the junction of the two geographically undemarcated segments of Assam, popularly known as the Upper Assam (UA) and Lower Assam (LA). Further, this district, the largest in Assam, is formed of two discontinuous parts: the large one to the east (Diphu Sub-division) where the district capital, Diphu, is located, is separated from the smaller one to the west (Hamren sub-division), by a strip of NC Hills and a pan-handle of Nagaon district.

Mikir (Karbi) Hills were taken over by the British in 1838 and NC Hills in 1854. The Mikirs were the more active of the two, even as they are today. The Mikir-Dimasa (NC) Tract was designated as 'backward" under the provisions of the Scheduled District Act, 1874. Again the two tracts, Mikir Hills and NC (Dimasa) Hills, were designated "backward tracts" under the Government of India Act, 1919. As recommended by the Simon Commission (1928-29), the two areas were given a slightly different status under Section 92 of the Government of India Act, 1935: NC Hills were placed in the category of "Excluded Areas" (EA) and Mikir Hills under the "Partially Excluded Areas" (PEA) category. Thus these two areas were treated as special categories, which was not the case, say, with the Bodo-Kachari areas. This special treatment in the historical context is cited as justification for autonomy by these two areas. As the two had shared a common history, hence the joint struggle for a place in the sun. But it needs to be noted as well that the Mikir (Karbi)-Dimasa demand for a separate entity came much later than the Ahom and Bodo aspirations raised in their representations to the Simon Commission in 1929.

Political aspirations grew as the Mikirs got the PEA status. They were allowed limited political activities, from which emerged some prominent leaders in the mid-1930s: Samson Singh Ingti, Seng Bey, Khor Sing, Terang, etc. In 1937, these leaders, in a memorandum to Assam Governor, Sir Robert Neil Reid, at Mohungodijua, demanded a separate hill district for Mikirs. To mobilize public support for their cause, they held two conventions, at Kathalguri in 1945 and at Hawaipur in 1947. At the latter convention, a regional political forum, called Karbi-A-Durbar, was formed to intensify the movement. These stirrings and consequent demand for a separate district with functional autonomy, can be deemed to be the genesis of the latter-day agitation for the UT status for the two hill districts of Assam. But the Mikirs failed to get their district under the Raj. The two, Mikirs and Dimasas, got their wishes fulfilled with the creation of a composite, United Mikir and NC (UMNC) Hills district on 17 November 1951. The new district covered the areas of Mikir Hills Tract and its contiguous Mikir-inhabited areas of the then districts of Nagaon, Sibsagar and United Khasi and Jaintia (KJ) Hills; and the NC Hills. Its total area of 15,237 km^2 was divided into two sub-divisions of Mikir Hills and NC Hills. The UMNC District got its ADC on 23 June 1952 under the Sixth Schedule. The Mikir and Dimasa Chiefs who had ruled till then in Mikir and NC Hills respectively, yielded place to the people's elected representatives.

The search for autonomy continued even after they got the ADC for themselves. The Official Language Bill of 1960 also caused some fears among the Mikirs about their own ethnic identity, and consequently the Bill gave a fillip to the autonomy demand in the two hill districts. The Karbi-A-Durbar, the ruling political party in ADC which had accommodated dissent in its fold till then, faced some turbulence in 1964. A section of the Durbaris began to speak the language of the opposition, which stood for: (1) Naga Hills and NC Hills merger movement and (2) Mikir and K-J (Khasi-Jaintia) Hills merger movement. This meant the Mikirs (Karbis now onwards) and Dimasas going their own ways—the Karbi-Dimasa unity was under serious threat from these dissenters. To counter this threat, a new body, Riso-A-Durbar was formed; it was a youth body raised by those opposed to the dissenters.

The hill leaders felt the ADC did not have adequate powers to develop the hills. On 1 June 1970, 30 development departments/subjects were transferred to the ADC of UM-NC District, in addition to the 29 handled by it under the Sixth Schedule.[22] The addition, meant to keep these hills away from the separatist movements in other hill districts, failed o satisfy the Karbi and Dimasa leaders, only whetting their urge for more. In a 1973 Memorandum to Prime Minister, they complained of continued Assamisation in the wake of "Medium of Instruction" order. The leaders demanded an autonomous state under Article 244-A of constitution which had been expressly added to it to create an autonomous/associate (Meghalaya) within Assam in April 1970. They also demanded "500 M^2 of contiguous areas from Assam plains".

2 February 1976, the UMNC district was split into two districts. It simply meant upgradation of the two sub-divisions, Mikir Hills and NC Hills, two separate geographical entities in any case, to the district status. Some relevant details on the newly-created districts are given in the table below:

Mikir Hills and NC Hills Districts Compared

Name of the District	*Area (Sq km)*	*Population (1971 Census)*	*Main Tribes*
Mikir Hills	10,332	6,55,415	Mikir (Karbi) in clear majority, Dimsa.
NC Hills	4,890	1,49,346	Dimasa in clear majority; Zemi and other Naga groups, Hmar and Kuki.

Both districts have mixed populations, dominated by a single, specific tribe; and both have substantial non-tribal populations. Needless to say, the two districts got their own ADCs after the split.

In October 1976, Mikir Hills district was redesignated as Karbi-Anglong (KA, for short in this part of the book) district.

It needs to be mentioned that these two hill areas did not join Meghalaya when it was created as an Associate State in April 1970. They were apprehensive of being swamped in a more advanced and Christianised

Meghalaya, inhabited as these two areas were by the more Hinduised and backward tribes. Or, may be, they were persuaded to stay with Assam, with promises of greater autonomy by the Assamese leaders. The fear of subsumption war fostered for ulterior motives, perhaps! After all, it does not need deep prescience to realise that their going out of Assamese would have physically severed the Barak Valley from the Assam Valley. In any case no one—a state or an individual—acts altruistically in political field. Both sides must have seen their own interest in the *status quo.* But this limited option available to the Karbi and Dimasa leaders—of either joining Meghalaya or remaining within Assam—rankled them. After all, all the hill districts of Assam had gained either statehood or UT status. Then why this discrimination against them. Their logic was simple and straight: Both Congress and non-Congress parties had supported their movement for autonomy. That is how they gained strength. No one can charge that their demand for a separate state was handiwork of some disgruntled elements since their leadership was essentially comprised till 1982, or loosely till 1985, of Congress or Congress-related political parties.

After the 1973 Memorandum, the next one came in 1980, in which the leaders complained to the Prime Minister that their identity was under threat from the AASU-AAGSP Agitation which was out to destroy the language, culture and traditions of the tribals and minorities. The protagonists of a separate State made a powerful statement when they scored a massive victory in the Hills in the December 1980 polls. Now follows the further progress of the movement:

1. *1981.* Separate State Demand Committee (SSDC) formed under Presidentship of Dhani Ram Rongpi; a memorandum submitted to the Prime Minister for a separate state comprising, the two districts.
2. Their 1982 Memorandum accused the Assam Agitation of preventing the conduct of 1981 Census in order to thwart the planned development of their area; and that the election to the two reserved Parliamentary seats too was not allowed for the same reasons. They went further: "Assamese Language Policy came in the way of the tribal students learning English and Hindi, so essential to forge links with India and the world beyond.... The tribals were also being prevented from joining the NEHU at Shillong."
3. By 1985, academics were praising the maturity of the SSDC Movement leaders for asserting their self-identity rather than railing against the Assamese hegemonism, as the ABSU and BPAC leaders were doing. But still, there was opposition to the demand within the hills, as will be seen shortly.
4. When the Autonomous State Demand Committee (ASDC) came into being in 1986 under the CPI(ML) leadership, the movement became mass-based. Expectedly, its 1987 Memorandum to the Prime Minister

was much more outspoken and jargon-ridden.[23] They demanded statehood for the two districts, together with the Inner Line restrictions.[24]

5. Karbi Students Association (KSA) joined hands with the ASDC, and the Movement became more strident in the post-reorganisation Assam (In February 1987, the Region stood divided into 7 States).
6. The joint ASDC-KSA Memorandum of January 1990 reasserted demand for a State; at the very minimum, a UT.
7. *March 1990.* Ultimatum to Assam Chief Minister: Concede demand or face agitation.
8. *1991.* United Peoples Conference emphasised a full-fledged State.
9. KA District ADC members' 1991 memorandum to the Bhupinder Singh Committee narrated its own litany of woes: (1) The ADC was dissolved four times in the past decade, and consequently development suffered. (2) Lack of police powers came in the way of maintaining peace. (3) Processing of all projects through the Deputy Commissioner gave him discretion to delay the decisions.[25]
10. NC District ADC memorandum to this Committee had a similar ring. It too had been superseded five times between 1978 and 1990. It accused the State Government of disbursing the Positive Hill Area Financial Assistance among all districts of Assam whereas it was meant for just two Hill districts.[26]

In 1992, State Government transferred some additional subjects to the two ADCs. The ASDC-KSA combine appreciated the gesture but refused to withdraw the State plank. Meanwhile the KA District ADC where the ASDC had huge majority, was dissolved by the Saikia Government in November 1992, provoking all-round resentment. But what was the level of support for the demand in each of the two districts?

KA District

Though the movement is on in both the districts, the ASDC is more active and influential in KA District. Of course, there is opposition to the demand within the district. But more importantly, the demand, though similar, has different ramifications for the two districts. The non-Karbi groups in this district formed a Citizen Rights Protection Committee (CRPC) and accused the ASDC of practising discrimination against non-Karbis and non-tribals who, they claimed, constituted a majority in the district. They also accused the ADC of collaring lands, appointments and funds, which led to the corruption and deforestation. The ASDC promptly dubbed the CRPC as Government agents and front for the Congress Party.

The religion also came in handy in this welter of accusations and counter-accusations. 40 per cent of the Karbis are Christians, the Church having played a major role in education and politicization of the community. The CPI(ML)-led ASDC, founded in 1986 as an offshoot of the KSA, has been accused of being anti-religious, despite having been sponsored by the missionaries. The ASDC dismisses the charges out of hand.

Violence was born about mid-1990s. Subsequently, the Karbi National Volunteers (KNV) and Karbi People's Force (KPF) have been active in the district since 1996-97. It is reportedly in cahoots with the NSCN. On the other hand, the Kukis and Bodos in the district are believed to have links with KNA and BdSF respectively.

NC Hills District

The situation here is more complicated because the district is home to large number of ethnic groups, and also because of its geography. The two factors render it prone to much ethnic activity and political turbulence. This district has come to occupy particularly the Jatinga[27] Valley (famed the world over for its mass suicide by the winged species) and Barail Hills, a geo-political significant place of its own in the current insurgency scenario in the Region. This is because the territory provides a corridor for the ultras from Nagaland, Meghalaya, Manipur and the Barak Valley districts of Assam to reach Bangladesh (Sylhet) areas. Even more importantly, the area constitutes a hiatus in the continuum of insurgency network spreading from Upper Myanmar to the CHT (of Bangladesh), covering most of the tribal pockets in Myanmar, (North-East) India, and Bangladesh. The NSCN is making clever, effective moves to fill this gap.

The ethno-religious political contradictions in the area offers a convenient, and ideologically suitable opportunity for the NSCN to make a success of its ethnic aspirations. It needs to be understood that the NSCN inroads in the North Cachar Hills are of different hue and intent from its exertions in Assam, Meghalaya, or Arunachal. In the latter areas, it is carrying out its operations to stretch the SFs and/or to secure a safe passage to Bangladesh; but in the former case, it has territorial ambitions. It is for this reason that the area North of the Railway Line in North Cachar figures significantly in the NSCN maps of Greater (Sovereign) Nagaland, or Nagalim. This move is a direct threat to the Dimasas, the dominant majority in the district. But it is well-known that the NSCN has been able to coopt certain Dimasa extremist elements to further its aims. So, the NSCN is able to rope in various ethnic groups of North Cachar Hills and Karbi Anglong districts under the promise that in the event of the creation of the Nagalim, their aspirations will be legitimately accommodated. The NSCN has been particularly solicitous towards Zeliangrong *(Zemi+Liangmai+Rongmai)* group of Nagas and others around Haflong, Mahur and Maibong—assuring them of a "Homeland of the dreams of their legendary Rani Gaidinliu."

The Nagalim ideologues are casting their gaze far beyond the immediate. Once the North Cachar Hills are incorporated into the rebel-controlled Nagaland-Manipur block, they will start exploring the possibility of a corridor connecting it to the sea via the Arakans. They do not see much difficulty in making Meghalaya, particularly its uranium rich areas, part of this dreamland; and they feel the incipient insurgency, that occasionally raises its head there, can always be reinforced for achieving their desideratum.

A word on the District. The dominant Dimasas are Kacharis, who speak Dimasa written in Bangla script, not a recognized language as yet. The medium of instruction here is Bengali, Assamese, or English, though the lingua franca is a pidgin, called Haflong Hindi, used by the local station of the AIR. The district has 500 km^2 under Reserved Forest and the remaining 4500 km^2 is unclassified State Forest which can be used or misused by various militant outfits operating in/throuph it. In the recent years, the district has become a transit for NSCN(I-M) and Meitei outfits movements to Bangladesh which has replaced Burma as a sanctuary, staging area/post, and conduit for arms and training.

Its contiguity with Nagaland poses threat to the integrity of the district, particularly because it has a considerable population of Zemi Nagas. The Zemis, also found in Nagaland, are ethnically allied to Liangmeis and Rongmeis, found both in Manipur and Cachar district. The three closed ranks to create a larger grouping, impressively designated Zeliangrong, the term coined by joining the first syllables from the names of these three tribes (ze+liang+rong). Thence, the three tribes demanded creation of a separate district by merging contiguous (Naga) areas from NC (Assam), Manipur and Nagaland, as these are inhabited by their kin. For form, the three states have rejected the demand as it would mean dismemberment of their territories; but those in the know believe the move is a clever plant by the NSCN(I-M) and even Nagaland Government to further the cause of Nagalim!

The district is presently in the grip of tribal extremism. The NSCN (I-M), historically powerful in Nagaland and Manipur, spread its wings here during the 1993-95 period. Surprisingly, the outfit found allies among the sections of the youth of the Dimasa tribe, largest in the district, "numbering 1,60,000, divided into a dozen communities".

It was not that the Dimasas needed any instigation from the Nagas to engage in violence. They were no novices at the game. In 1990, they had raised a militant outfit, called Dimasa National Security Force (DNSF), then the latest entrant at the revivalist stakes. It wanted restoration of the lost glory of Dimasa Kingdom, which once had its capital at Dimapur. It was reportedly demanding ransom from the rich. Not to lag behind, the students set up All Dimasa Students Organisation (ADSO), early 1991. It wanted

Dimaland and was "reportedly set up by Assam Congress to counter the ASDC". Wheels, within wheels, perhaps!

By mid-1990s, it had not gone beyond the wall-writing; and even subsequently, it was unknown beyond the confines of the district.

The NSCN(I-M)-Dimasa alliance suffered a set-back in November 1994 when most members of the erstwhile DNSF, led by Bharat Langthasa, surrendered. But subsequently, the NSCN(I-M) managed to bring together all those who did not surrender into a new outfit called the Dima Halam Daogah (DHD). Numerically a small force, its importance lied in the fact of it being a local agent of NSCN(I-M). The two joined hands to extort large sums as house-tax in their area and as security-money from the businessmen. It was reported that Assam's Minister, Gobinda Langthasa paid Rs. 7 lakh to buy the security of his family in late 1994. If some officers were known for not paying, a large number paid out willingly or otherwise.

There are easily discernible reasons for NSCN(I-M) focusing on this district: (1) Its border with "Nagaland and Manipur is porous, guarded now by only 4 check points against twenty in the 1970s and 1980s during the anti-Phizo drive" (A February 1996 Report in a weekly). When under pressure in Nagaland and Manipur, they crossed into North Cachar Hills: when things eased off they returned. (2) It is shortest and safest transit route between Upper Burma;and Bangladesh. It is also shorter route for weapons they received at Cox Bazar by sea or in Burma by land route from markets in some South-East Asian nations. (3) The Nagas, insurgents and moderates alike, have not stopped thinking of some areas of North Cachar Hills and Bhuban Pahar area of Cachar district, both of which have some Naga population, as parts of their dreamland, Nagalim (=Greater Nagaland).

But the North Cachar Hills are not an easy world for the NSCN (I-M). Several non-tribal groups, like Bengalis, Assamese, Nepalis, Hindi-speaking people, are not its friends. The Dimasas, its largest tribe, are Hindus and culturally close to Bengalis, who make up a vast majority in Cachar area. The NSCN's pronounced Christian identity cannot endear it to the Dimasas. The Kukis are Naga group's enemy, locked in lethal combat with them in Manipur. The Baites having a small number in the district, belong to the Kuki group, as do the Halams, Vaipheis and Khelams.

Who are the potential allies of the NSCN in NC Hills? Hmars, who struggled for a separate state in North Mizoram and later settled with the State Government with an accord in 1994, could join hands. Zeliangrgng Nagas, numbering 9-15,000 in the district, could be of help. But the Zemis, vast majority in the combine, are very different from the Tangkhul and Sema Nagas, the backbone of the NSCN. Being backward in comparison, they may not feel comfortable with the NSCN. Religion is another factor setting the Zemis apart from the NSCN, because only 40 per cent of the former are

Christian. Others suggest they are one with the NSCN, flaunting of differences is a put-on!

Besides the NSCN and Dimasa militants, the KNA and HPC ultras were/are also active in certain areas, often taking shelter in the respective village of their kinsmen.

The insurgent activity was on the rise from the end of 1980s, continuing through the 1990s. Insurgency-related crimes grabbed the headlines off and on, with reports of loyalty-tax payments, kidnappings, ransom killings, extortions, etc. The period 1992-95 saw, increased attacks on the SF. In a daring ambush, 13 BSF men were killed in Mahur area, near Nagaland border, in late 1992.

Chess Board Moves and Counter Moves

The Political Report of the CPI(ML) for 1993 had promised a broader front called North-Eastern Tribal Peoples Front as an ideological counter to the Indian ruling class's perception and solution of the problem of integration of the North-East with the mainstream of the Indian polity. The wider political alignment promised and envisioned by the ASDC in the KA District ADC in the shape of this "Broader Forum" proved a case of early death with the signing of Memorandum of Understanding (MoU) between Chief Minister Saikia and the leaders of ASDC (from both districts), KSA, Dimasa Students Union and NC Hills Students Federation, at New Delhi, on 1 April 1995. Under this MoU, the ASDC agreed to accept enhanced powers much beyond those available under Sixth Schedule and gave up its insistence on Sub-State, Associate State, or Autonomous State under Article 244-A of the Constitution, a la Meghalaya of April 1970. Not only were the two ADCs to be granted vast powers, they were also to be upgraded to the status of "Autonomous Councils". The MoU had generated high hopes: "New Councils would enjoy substantial devolution under the Sixth Schedule through a unique combination of powers vested in a Sub-State, UT, ADC and Deputy Commissioners: a degree of autonomy unknown so far.... The new experiment, granting the structure vast powers...including access to Governor and Planning Commission, will be watched with interest by many organisations and groups waiting in the wings, harbouring hopes of a State or UT status for their areas." The new AGP Government, that had replaced Saikia's in May 1996, handed over 30 additional subjects to the two ADCs on 31 December 1996. But as the respected daily *Hindu* was to) editorialise (31-5-1997): "This failed to satisfy the ADCs." But it all was to prove a false dawn. Move for Autonomous State was revived.

Events of May 1997

25 May. ASDC revived the demand for an Autonomous State within Assam under Article 244-A of the Constitution, at its General Body Meeting at Haflong.

28 May. Holiram Terang, Leader of 5-member ASDC group in Assembly announced withdrawal of his party from the 5-Party Ruling Alliance of Assam,[28] led by AGP (other three being CPI, CPM, UPFA). He accused the Chief Minister of not implementing the MoU. He grandly announced the formation of an alternative political front, Assam People's Front.

29 May. Dr Jayanta Rongpi,[29] MP and Chairman, ASDC, publicly announced revival of the old demand for a Sub-State, thus completing a full circle.

These are the games they play on the political chessboard.

They Want Two States Now—Not One!

The game goes on. The ASDC ascribes absence of the job opportunities and lack of economic development to the inadequacies of the ADCs and the Assamese machinations and manipulations! So it wants sub-State despite the opposition by the smaller tribes and minorities. And now comes the ultimate truth: Being conscious of their own deficiencies *vis-a-vis* the Karbis, the Dimasas have demanded two States, one for each district, and nor one which would surely be dominated by the more advanced Karbis.

ASDC Splits

The ASDC, ruling party in the two ADCs and having one MP, split on 25 July 2000. The followers of Dr. Jayanta Rongpi, MP and Chairman ASDC, adopted a no-confidence motion in the KA.

Council, against Jetson Bey, Chief Executive Member. Babu Rongpi, Council Chairman, was prevented from presiding over the session, which was conducted by Daniel Terang, a Dr Rongpi loyalist.

The crisis had been brewing for sometime. Most ASDC leaders are members of the CPI-ML (Vinod Mishra Group). Sometime before the October 1999 General Elections, ASDC decided to contest these elections in the name of CPI(ML) and that the ASDC would contest the District Council poll. It must be noted that "the CPI(ML) Karbi Anglong Party Committee is not affiliated to the Assam State Committee, but to the Central Committee" (*The Hindu,* 27-7-2000). The decision was not liked by the rank and file of the Party. In June 2000, Holiram Terang, Leader of the 5-member ASDC Group in Assam Legislative Assembly, raised the banner of revolt, accusing Dr Rongpi of corruption. On 21 July 2000, Terang and his supporters requested for postponement of the Standing Committee meeting that day at Diphu. When the proposal was rejected by Dr Rongpi group, they walked out of the meeting. The split on the 25th was the next logical outcome.

The events only show that the politics at the district level apes the politics at the State and national levels.

Mindless Violence Enters the Scene

We have read the comment about "maturity" of the Karbi and Dimasa leaders of ASDC in conducting their movement. Again a respected scholar/

political scientist praised the leadership for their sobriety. But alas, of late the idyll stands shattered in the late 1990s.

The United People's Democratic Solidarity, UPDS (a rather unlikely name for a militant outfit) and Dima Halam Dauga (DHD) are two outfits behind the depredations, murders, and mayhem, indicative of the latest recrudescence of violence in the two Hill districts, helped no doubt by the NSCN and ULFA, both long-reputed merchants of death and destruction in the name of their wars for the rights of their respected people—the Nagas and the Assamese. The UPDS was formed in 1999 when, two smaller outfits—Karbi National Volunteers (KNV) and Karbi People's Force (KPF)—merged to strengthen the Karbi Statehood Movement being conducted by the ADC for the last decade or so. The DHD, a militant outfit of *Dimasa* is in a manner of speaking, the counterpart of UPDS in NC District. Of late, as the Dimasas veered to have a state of their own, the DHD too stepped up their depredations during 2000 in demand of a separate Dimasa State.

Initially, these two outfits were aided and trained by the NSCN(I-M) as it was keen to make inroads into the area for its own strategic considerations. Since it signed peace with the Centre in 1997, UPDS turned to ULFA for help and guidance. Indicative of ULFA's desire to help the militants in this area were two Intelligence reports of its supplying arms to UPDS: 16 advanced model AK-56s in April 2000 and some small arms and ammunitions a little later. There had been periodical militant-perpetrated crimes in the two districts earlier also, particularly in KA District, but these killings assumed sinister colours in 2000. On 9 April, UPDS cadres shot dead timber workers at Langatso in KA District. All the victims were Biharis, that is, Hindi-speaking people. It did ring up alarm bells. On the 19th, UPDS, helped by DHD, struck again, mowing down 11 Nepalis—again non-Assamese people—in a remote village of the same district, under Baithalangso police station. So, the sinister ethnic cleansing was under way. Emboldened by its success, the UPDS forced the Government of KA-NC Hills Self-Rule Territory (GKN-SRT) to get rid of all outsiders. This violence brought the focus on UPDS which, it needs notice, started the ethnic cleansing in two Hill districts 6 months before the ULFA and NDFB started similar operations in other parts of Assam. After these two killings, the Hindi-speakers continued to be targetted by UPDS and DHD in the two districts till September when some unidentified gun-men killed relatives of two senior UPDS ultras. "The killings stopped immediately" (*Hindustan Times,* 30-12-2000). After a deceptive lull of two months, the troubled KA District reverberated with gun shots again when UPDS killed 8 Biharis again at Rangnagar village. It was obvious that NSCN-trained UPDS had joined hands with ULFA which "planned to target non-Assamese Hindi-speakers in some 2000 sensitive pockets of Assam". This dispersed area is unofficially referred to as "Hindi belts". The UPDS had reportedly divided the non-Karbis into two categories of affluence: rich and very rich, charging from them

Rs. 5,000 and Rs. 10,000 as taxes respectively. Clearly, there were no poor among the non-Karbis.

The non-Assamese selected by the militants for ethnic cleansing are attractive targets; Nepalis inhabiting the hills in Hamren Subdivision and the Hindi-speakers farming in Kheroni, Howraghat, and Baithalangso areas. So are the outsiders living in the foothills of the two districts. Besides being fertile, these areas have prospered because of their proximity to the markets in the plains. Unfortunately, the people in these Hindi belts had earlier been at the receiving end of the Naxalites who held sway in the KA and NC Hills, for refusing to toe their line, the officials told the media.

In December 2001, suspected DPDS ultras killed 8 persons of a polling party in an ambush near village Langlokso under Howraghat PS. The polls for the ADCs of the two Hill Districts "are due on 5 December 2001" (*Times of India,* 4-12-2001). 5 persons belonging to an ONGC drilling party, including a Senior Scientist and an Assistant Engineer were killed in an ambush by suspected DHD militants on 24 June 2002.

Ethnic Violence in North Cachar

Hmar-Dimacha clashes in April 2003 were worst in the recent memory. Eight persons were killed during sporadic clashes at several places on the 9th. Panic-stricken 3,100 families belonging to both tribes were either rendered homeless or fled their homes. Curfew was clamped in the entire district after hundreds of Dimachas, dominating tribe of the district, allegedly armed with 'lethal weapons attacked two Hmar settlement and set over a 100 houses afire. "The Dimachas and Hmars have been at war for more than a month now", *Express* 11-4-03. On the 10th, the leaders of the DHD and the Hmar Inpui and Hmar Church met for peace talks at Haflong. The officials accommodated about 1500 Dimacha and 1600 Hmar families in five relief camps. Besides, while 200 Hmar tribals took shelter in Lumding in the adjoining Nagaon district, another 200 had fled to Meghalaya who got shelter at the Evangelical Free Church of India campus in Shillong. It was only on the 7th that Chief Minister Gogoi had visited strife-torn tribal villages in the district following the massacre of 28 Dimachas and had announced a relief of Rs. 1 lakh to the next of kin of each of those killed. The 28 victims were abducted and gunned down by the HPC ultras in the neighbouring Cachar district on 3-4-03.

In the renewed ethnic violence in the disturbed NC Hills district on 12-5-03, Narmendu Langthasa, 35, son of senior minister and veteran Congress leader Gobinda Chandra Langthasa, was shot dead by suspected HPC ultras in the heart of Haflong when he had gone to pick up his son from his school. Narmendu's elder brother Purnendu, is the CEM of the NC Hills Autonomous Council. At 10.30 AM, a little before the murder of Narmendu, Phani Lal Liengjao, an accountant in the Haflong DFO's office, was gunned by the DHD ultras.

Violence in Karbi Anglong (KA) District

29 November 2003. Six Karbis, including a 5-year girl, were gunned down in villages Piti Atong and Jilangso under Bokajan PS by Kuki Revolutionary Army (KRA) militants. 116 Karbi houses were burnt.

There was violence as the anti-talks faction of the UPDS (re-named itself as Karbi Longri [NC Hills] Liberation Front, KLNLF, in 2004, and its armed wing as Karbi Long NC Hills Peoples' Resistance, KNPR; *see Sentinel,* Guwahati 16-5-04) gave a call for 120-hour bandh on 25-12-03 in the two Hill districts, in protest against clause 8 of the Bodo Territorial Council Accord which promises to "consider sympathetically" the grant of tribal status to the Bodos settled in the two Hill districts. Karbis are dead set against it. The UPDS, created in March 1999 with the merger of Karbi National Volunteers (KNV) and Karbi Peoples' Front (KPF) with proclaimed objective of purging KA of the Non-Karbi population (including Marwaris Biharis, Nepalis, Kukis and Bengalis), got split when a faction came out for talks with the Government in 2001.

3-12-03. The KRA was formed in December 1999, with the help of NSCN (I-M), with declared objective of creation of an Autonomous Kuki National Council for the Kukis in the KA district. Its three leaders are: (1) Thangkeng Hangshing, Chairman, (2) Zet Kuki, Publicity Secretary, (3) D.T. Haokip, Information Secretary. Its 50 cadres killed three people and burnt 30 huts when they attacked a remote Karbi village, Menterang.

5-12-03. The UPDS militants made an abortive bid on the lives of the DC (Anurag Goel) and the SP (Abdul Kuddush) at the village of Hidim Terang, KA district.

24-3-04. 31 Karbi villagers were killed by KRA militants in attacks on four villages during 36 hours: (1) Udematisso under Dilai police out-post, (2) Two adjacent villages Sarpoteron and Sarkhe-Engleng, 20 km from the first, (3) Jariteron, close to Diphu. Surprisingly, not a single woman or child was killed in any of these attacks. The men were called out, lined up, and gunned down or hacked to death. These killings "were in retaliation to the 19-3-04 incident when the UPDS gunned down six Kukis at the remote village of Thangbong, 45 km from Diphu".

This was the second major insurgent killing in the Hill District since it was rocked by a fierce gun battle between the KRA and UPDS which left nearly 50 people dead from both the communities (Kukis and Karbis) in October and November 2003. Several hundred people were injured, with over 1000 villagers from two sides rendered homeless.

The two hill districts "have been witnessing sporadic internecine clashes for the past one year, with the Kuki group that had entered the State from Manipur regularly targetting the original tribes of the two districts, the Karbis and the Dimasas (of late spelt as Dimachas)"— *Express*, 25-3-04 and *Hindu*, 25-3-04.

21-7-05. The police arrested 15 adivasis in connection with a clash on the 18th which left 5 Biharis dead and over 40 houses torched in the KA district.

The Cold Statistics: Karbi Anglong District

A study disclosed that the clashes between the KRA and the anti-talks faction of the UPDS(K) during Oct 2003-Mar 2004 killed 85 persons mostly men, which included at least 23 Kukis and 54 Karbis. Again, Guwahati's *Assam Tribune* said on 28 Dec 2003 that the UPDS(K) and KRA had killed 35 persons, including 17 Kukis and 15 Karbis since Nov 2003 in KA district.

The 24-3-04 incident (mentioned above) is an instance of the highest civilian casualty (the later toll stands at 34 killed) in Assam in a terrorist incident in a single day (Praveen Kumar, Strategic Analysis, Apr-Jun 04, an IDSA publication. Again it is the largest civilian casualty in the district since the Pro-Talks UPDS faction under Horen Singhey Bey signed the cease-fire agreement with New Delhi on 23-5-2002. H.E. Kathar, the UPDS General Secretary, opposed to the talks, leads the anti-talks fraction: UPDS(K).

A word on the KRA- The outfit claims a cadre strength of 540 (2004), 180 of these being in KA district. Based in the Saikul area of Manipur's Senapati district, the KRA claims to have linkages with UKLF and (KNF-MC); NSCN, both factions of (I-M) and (K); and NDFB and DHD. It is the sole militant Kuki outfit claiming to safeguard the Kuki interests in the KA district.

Ethno-political dynamics and desperate endeavour to control the underground economy of the KA district have pitted the KRA and UPDS against each other. The Karbis are the largest tribe in the district and the Kukis claim to be in majority in its Singhason hill area. The Kukis roam in pursuit of Jhum cultivation in the district, but their main (largest) concentration is in Manipur (15 per cent), says the *Shillong Times* (Internet Edition) of 3-12-03 (Its "Demand for Regional Council could aggravate Kuki-Karbi Clashes"). Karbi groups, including the UPDS, dispute KRA's projection of the 'indigenous' population at more than 35,000 in the Singhason hills [*See* "UPDS says No to KRA's Peace Proposal", *North-East Enquirer* 2(18), 22 Dec 03-6 Jan 04, at http://www.nenanews.com/ NEE/20/Dec 22-Jan 6/2004/ oh11.htm]. They say the Kukis are no more than 2,000 in that area, and the hugely exaggerated figure of 35,000 is KRA's 'tactic'—just a clever ploy—in justification of their demand for a Kuki Autonomous Council in the district. In a manner of speaking, both are vying for a place in the sun: if the Karbis demand a 'State' to be carved out of Assam, specifically from its two hill districts, the Kukis want an Autonomous Council for themselves to be carved out of this 'State'. Then intervenes the 'foreigners question' in this imbroglio.

Citing the examples of foreigners displacing the indigenous tribals in Tripura and threatening to do the same in Assam, the UPDS ideologues express fears that the Karbis would be outnumbered in the district by the Kuki influx that started following the Naga-Kuki clashes in Nagaland and Manipur in 1992 (For details *see* M.S. Prabhakara, "Outrage in Assam", *Frontline* at http:// www flonnet.com/fl2025/stories/ 2003 121 9006800800.htm and "Karbi-Kuki Imbroglio: Ultras Blamed for Clashes", *Assam Tribune* 30-12-03).

There are differences between the Kuki National Assembly (KNA), the apex political organisation of Kukis in the KA district and the ASDC which is fighting for a Karbi state. The KNA had first demanded an Autonomous Regional Council for the Kukis in 1992 through a memorandum to the State Government. Two rounds of talks were also subsequently held in 1997 and 1998. The ASDC split in July 2000 due to differences within the local leadership that allowed the Congress to control the Karbi Anglong Autonomous District Council. Later a faction called ASDC-United (ASDC-U) endorsed KNA's demand for a Kuki Council, obviously to widen its support base against the rival faction of ASDC-Progressive (ASDC-P), an ally of CPI(ML) that represented the area in the 13th Lok Sabha. But interestingly the ASDC(U) is now against the KNA's demand.

Besides the ethnic factors, another reason for both the outfits—KRA and UPDS—fighting for supremacy over the Singhason hill area is 2000 MT of high quality ginger it produces annually. While both the outfits lean on the local tribal populace to extort their share from this lucrative trade, the UPDS considers the area as its exclusive turf. Hence the bloody rivalry.

Stirrings Among the Rabhas, Tiwas and Mishings

It was but a matter of time before other major plains tribes like Rabha, Mishing and Tiwa would follow the path traced by the Bodos. All these three tribes are predominantly Hindu, and speak Assamese, though Mishings and Tiwas have their own Tibeto-Burman languages, the former being of the Bodo group. Here are some other relevant information:

1. *Rabhas.* Mostly found in Goalpara and Kamrup districts on the south bank and in the Darrang district on the north, they constitute a minority in Bodoland. There were 1,38,630 Rabhas in 1971, including those in Meghalaya (No census was carried out in 1981).
2. *Mishings* (Miris). One of the larger tribes on north bank, it is concentrated in Dhemaji, Lakhimpur, Sonitpur districts and Majuli Island. They enumerated 2,59,551 in 1971.
3. *Tiwas (Lalungs).* Mainly inhabiting Nagaon and Marigaon districts, they counted 95,609 in 1971.

There are some other smaller tribes also in Assam:

1. *Deuris.* Mostly inhabiting Dibrugarh district, they enumerated 23,000 in 1971.
2. *Sonwal Kacharis.* They are a larger group, but scattered over the Eastern parts of the north bank.
3. *Meches.* They belong to the large Bodo-Kachari group and are found in certain areas of Assam and North Bengal. In Assam, they are a miniscule community, generally inhabiting Goalpara district and Hojai area. They number a mere 12,919 (1971).

The Assam Government feels local autonomy to the Rabhas, Mishings and Tiwas should go a long way to assure their cultural identity. Each of the three tribes has its Student Union and Sahitya Sabha. These tribes presently feel discriminated against and suffer from a sense of deprivation and exploitation. Formation of District Councils would allay discontent through a variant of Panchayat Raj introduced under the 11th and 12th Schedules (Amendments No. 72 and 74) of the Constitution. This measure, introduction of local self-rule, will ensure socio-economic development, and more importantly, direct popular energies from agitation to constructive pursuits, with insecurity yielding place to self-assurance. Conceded in time, and that is important, such politico-administrative measures should stem any fears of fragmentation, revivalism and balkanization. The Government is not willing to grant them certain concessions earlier bestowed on the Bodos. For example, in Bodoland, minority villages with as low as 10 per cent population were included in the jurisdiction of the Bodo Autonomous Council (BAC) to provide contiguity to the adjacent Bodo majority pockets. Government's unwillingness to extend the same understanding attitude to these smaller and more scattered tribes is resented by them. The powers prescribed by the Bhupinder Singh committee, however, have been adapted within 2-tier structure.

The Government constituted a ministerial committee to process formation of the three District Councils. The Rabhas, Mishings and Tiwas, meanwhile, have pressed their claims to 862, 1600 and 371 villages respectively. All three are demanding some intervening villages to establish contiguity, especially because these areas were initially tribal belts and blocks, surreptitiously usurped by others (read "outsiders" or "foreigners") or diverted for other purposes. One cannot put the issue more succinctly than Verghese (B.G.), 1996: "There is a weight in these arguments, in spite of some exaggeration and inflation of figures of tribal population. Whatever be the truth, unscrambling of the omelette can be debated, but not undone."

The Rabhas

Rabhas have been politically more conscious and active among these three tribes. Their movement demanded Rabha Hasong (Rabhaland)

Autonomous State within Assam on south bank, extending from Joyrasmukh in Goalpara to Rani in Kamrup. Their other demands include:

1. An autonomous district in Darrang on the north bank,
2. District councils in yet four other districts with Rabha pockets,
3. Rabha village councils in several districts, and
4. Five reserved seats in BAC.

They seem to have flirted with violence and nurtured ambitions of organising some terrorist outfit. The press had reported the existence of Rabha Security Force (RSF), which reminded the observers of the depredations of the BdSF. The former seems to have made to the pages of the newspapers, with an occasional act of terrorism. To wit, the RSF kidnapped a Construction Engineer (Naresh Lalwani) on 24 December 1998 while working on a site on the 142 km second broadgauge line from Bongaigaon to Gauhati along the south bank of the Brahmaputra. Panic-stricken labour fled, rejoining only when RPF was deployed in the affected area between Goalpara) and Mirza for its protection. Because of such attacks, the project could not be completed as scheduled by 31 March 1999. This is just one instance of militancy adversely affecting the economic development.

The 7th Annual conference of All Rabha Students Union (ARSU) in 1994 demanded more Rabha Primary Schools and concerted measures to promote Rabha language and culture.

10 March 1995. A Memorandum of Understanding was signed, constituting Rabha Hasong Autonomous Council, an apex body, with "discontinuous satellite areas" and Rabha Hasong village councils in rural areas with not more than 50 per cent tribal population. The villages in the reserved forests were to be included after clearance from Ministry of Environment and Forests. Interestingly, Meghalaya issued a cautious warning against inclusion of disputed villages on the boundary. An interim Rabha Hasong Council was set up pending elections. The village councils were to have executive powers over 29 subjects (Shades of District Councils under 6th Schedule), and the Apex Council, over 39 subjects.

Understandably, similar Accords were signed with the Tiwas on 13 April 1995 and with the Mishings on 14 June 1995.

The Tiwas

The Tiwas were fast learners. When the Assam Students were running their anti-foreigners campaign in early 1980s, "a tribal community in the Centre of Assam was airing its own grievances from their house-tops literally", wrote a journalist in a Gauhati Daily. Travelling through Nagaon district, a visitor could see some posters on any likely place available (tree trunks, walls of the houses, telephone poles, way-side shacks and shanties), loudly protesting the neglect of the Tribe by the Central and State Governments and consequent lack of economic and social development, "more than three decades after the Independence". They seem to have been the first to learn from the AASU Movement the practical ways of registering their protests and grievances. It was an effective PR Job! Though they seemed to have started their protest about the same time as the Bodos, happily, they did not go the Bodo way! Even more happily, they seem to have shunned the example of the Rabhas too, who did register their presence in the field of violence through desultory acts of terrorism, like kidnappings and killings.

In 1967, the Tiwas first demanded autonomy around the same time as Bodos. They were generally peaceful apart from that frenzied outburst at Nellie in 1983 against the immigrant settlers. They demanded 3264 km^2 area for their "homeland". Their complaint: "The Assamiya chauvinists had under-enumerated us." Here is the famous outburst by Tulsi Bordoloi, convener of All Tiwa Students Federation (ATSF): "Bordoloi is not my real name. In our schools, Assamiya teachers changed our names without discussing anything with us" (Biswas, Ashish K., 1995).

Two-tier Tiwa District Council comprises of 144 villages, with the Autonomous Tiwa District Demand Committee claiming additional 175. The Tiwas Sahitya Sabha (TSS) wants acceptance of the Roman script only for Tiwa language, presently written in both Assamese and Roman scripts. This is perhaps to ensure that their language is not at some distant future subsumed by the Sanskritised Assamese language. This is the best way, feels the TSS, to ensure the continued existence and autonomy of their language.

The Mishings

Mishings felt aggrieved at non-inclusion of certain forests and other villages in the Mishing District Council. They rejected the majority-village principle insisting on inclusion of all villages with more than 33 per cent Mishing population. The proposition is unlikely to be accepted, going by the reaction in BAC areas, where non-Bodos resented being sacrificed in the interest of greater Bodoland.

AHOMS: YEARNING FOR PAST GLORY

The Ahoms, having been the rulers for 600 years, had always nursed a grievance during the British Rule that they had been marginalized in favour of the Assamese and Bengali Caste-Hindus. A section of the Ahom elite had been insisting that the Ahom identity had been under threat from Hindu Aryan culture. But unfortunately, their representative body, the Ahom Association, formed as early as 1893, was unable to make much headway among the Ahom masses, since they had largely integrated with the broader Assamese Community and accepted Sankardev's Mahapurusia Vaishnavism.

The Ahom Association, which till 1910 was known as Ahom Sabha, continued its efforts to claim a separate identity for the community. When the national movement spread in Assam, gaining greater momentum and larger adherents the Ahoms felt further marginalized and jittery, since the Congress leadership was largely drawn from the caste-Hindu sections of the Assamese Society. Dubbing the Congress as a caste-Hindu organisation, a section of the Ahom elite started demanding a separate, sovereign status for Assam, where the Ahom would once again be the major cohesive force in the Assamese society. They firmly believed that only through an independent Assam could the identity of the Ahoms be safeguarded and strengthened. In its meeting in September 1944, the All Assam Ahom Association (AAAA), Sibsagar declared: "In view of the peculiar position of Assam, both geographically and otherwise, and the great preponderance of the Mongolian races with their distinctive languages, cultures and religions in the population of the Province, Assam without Sylhet, has a legitimate claim for free and independent existence in the event of India being divided territorially into Pakistan and Hindustan Zones.[30] The demand for a sovereign Assam was also raised in several other Ahom-dominated areas of Province. It is obvious that the Ahom demand for a sovereign Assam and the Swadhin Asom demand by other segments of Assamese population had a lot in common. In either case, the protagonists harked back to a glorious, independent past: the former to their recent 600-year rule and the latter to the legendary Kamarupa days. It was also consistently maintained that Assam belonged ethnically to the Mongoloid race and that its culture and civilisation were a part of the glorious heritage of South-East Asian region, the Province sharing little with the rest of India. (But the matter did not end there. Today also, this argument forms a major plank of the thesis offered by the ULFA's ideologues who assert vehemently that Assam should look East, and not towards India, for inspiration and sustenance, as it historically forms a part of the great Mongoloid fraternity.)

But there is an inherent contradiction in the stance of organisations like the Ahom Association demanding an independent Assam, fearing the Hinduisation of their culture and polity. It is that Hinduisation in the first place was brought and promoted in Assam by the Ahom rulers themselves. Like the Ahoms, the protagonists of Swadhin Asom too could not wish away the Hindu connections of their "glorious" past, so fondly referred to, and repeatedly. The Kamarupa empire was well-known for its cultural and civilisational links with the rest of the Indian Sub-continent with its predominant Hindu ethos. If the Ahom separatists tend to completely sweep part of their own past under the carpet while pleading their case for independence, the proponents of *Swadhin* Asom do the same, intentionally failing to see that Pragjyotisha and Kamarupa were not only part of wider India civilisationally, but also politically, it would seem. After all, Bhagadatta had participated in the Epic war, and Bhaskar-Varman was an ally of the Great Harsha, the powerful King of Kannauj. These strong cultural and historical links, which both pre-Ahom and Ahom Assam had maintained with the rest of the country, goes a long way to explain the quick acceptance of Gandhi and the Congress in the Province. Ahom's stress on Assam's Far- and South-eastern connections, especially with Burma, was bound to evoke the frightful memories of the Burmese occupation of the land. The pro-British and occasionally, even pro-Muslim League posturings of bodies like the Ahom Association,[31] alienated them from the broad mass of the Ahom people, who, in any case, having joined and become indistinguishable from the Indigenous Assamese, went along with the Congress in the fight for freedom from the British Raj.

Failing to see any possibility of success, Ahom Association climbed down from its high horse of "Independent Assam", and started demanding creation of a separate Ahom State comprising the Upper Assam districts. They were also exploring the possibilities of establishing contacts with the Shan States beyond the Patkais.[32]

Having never been a powerful body, and failing to battle the Congress on the election front, the Ahom Association lost much of its relevance in the recent years.

Now, to flesh out some details about marginalisation of the Ahoms.

Degradation/Fall of Ahoms

It is a fact of history that the Ahoms had been enervated due to a long stay in the fertile, humid and luxury-inducing Brahmaputra Valley. Additionally, the self-destructive, internecine civil war among the Princes during the last 50 years of their rule nearly emaciated the ruling class and middle classes. The Burmese occupation subsequently completed the ruin of the masses. The abolition of the *paik* system by the British ruined the land-owning classes as they were unable to cultivate their lands. All this spelled their economic ruin. The aristocrats became destitutes overnight, so to say. The British policies reduced the Ahoms to penury, kept them away from power and position, and simultaneously ensured the emergence of a new middle class. It is recorded that most of the noble families were compelled to sell or mortgage their properties to meet their revenue arrears. Part of the property of Kandarpeswar Singh, the Ahom King was auctioned at Jorhat.[33] The British recruitment policy also contributed to the economic backwardness of the Ahoms. The Ahoms, erstwhile ruling class, unable to reconcile to the loss of power, tried to regain it through local rebellions and conspiracies. Consequently, the British distrust barred their entry to any important position—bureaucratic and political. They mostly imported clerks and officials from Bengal.

Their situation became even bleaker when the British made the formal western education a pre-condition for entry into jobs because during their rule, education was never considered important or even necessary as their livelihood depended upon their status.

Thus, the Ahoms deemed it derogatory, or at the very least, unnecessary to educate their children unless their forefathers were the class of Kakotis.[34] For these reasons, the Ahom society was conspicuous by absence of any formal education till 1826. Even after the British take-over, they did not take corrective steps almost till the end of the 19th century. It is on record that in 1851-52, there were only 39 Ahom students in a population of over 150,000. The picture was hardly encouraging in the last two decades of the 19th century as can be seen from the comparative positions of various communities in the two tables (on the following page) based on the Census Reports of 1891 and 1901.

The inadequacies and disadvantageous position of the Ahoms *vis-a-vis* some other communities, illustrated by the two tables, goaded their elite into organising themselves to articulate their grievances and demands for a better future. That is how the All Assam Ahom Association was born in 1893.

Ahoms Organise Themselves

AAAA was the first endeavour by the down and out Ahoms to ameliorate their socio-economic status. It was also indicative of the first revivalist stirring of an agitated community. It is also tempting to see it as something of a movement for an identity assertion. It may be a far-fetched proposition (or, may not be so), these end-19th century stirrings showed that the community realised the value of formal education for their socio-economic-political advancement. The 1921 Census figures in the table below prove the point.

The 1921 Census did show that the Ahoms registered some advance, but they were far outdistanced by other sections of the upper caste Assamese, as admitted by Gurdon: "In educational matters, Ahoms are more backward than even the ordinary Assamese Hindus, which is saying a great deal." The fact was further confirmed by the British Census Commissioner, C.S. Mullan, in his Report on the 1931 Census: "Looking at the 1931 figures, we see at once that the Baidyas and Brahmins show a long lead over all other Hindu castes in the matter of literacy, as they did in 1921. Among the Ahoms, 24.6 per cent of their males are literate but only 1.4 per cent of their females can read or write." This was possibly because of their 'royal vanity' and indifferent attitude towards education.

Literacy Ratings: Ahoms and others: 1891

Caste	*Male*			*Female*		
	Total	*Students*	*Literate*	*Total*	*Students*	*Literate*
Ahom	78840	990	4559	74673	17	57
Baidya	2600	545	1279	2066	39	249
Brahmin	52934	6157	23498	44042	224	506
Kalita	115978	2284	7498	106621	93	327
Kayasth	48731	5832	16346	43619	398	1226
Dom (Patni)	101139	1264	3155	100914	6	4

Source: Report on 1891 Census.

Literacy Ratings: Ahoms and others: 1901

Caste	*Literate in Non-English Languages*				*Literate in English*		
	Population	*Total*	*Male*	*Female*	*Total*	*Male*	*Female*
Ahom	178049	4588	4461	127	893	882	11
Baidya	5154	1401	934	467	757	740	17
Brahmin	109446	28941	27652	1289	3616	3577	39
Kalita	203108	9227	9062	165	865	858	7
Kayasth	86918	19967	17740	2227	4287	4250	37
Dom (Patni)	194852	3752	3587	165	97	97	–

Source: Report on 1891 Census.

Literacy Ratings: Ahoms and others: 1921

Caste	*Population*		*No. per 1000 aged 5 and above who are literate*					
	1911	*1921*	*1911*			*1921*		
			Persons	*Male*	*Female*	*Persons*	*Male*	*Female*
Ahom	197000	216000	73	136	4	109	197	11
Baidya	5609	7210	654	833	437	704	817	570
Brahmin	137000	160000	375	623	64	438	721	111
Kalita	222000	235000	95	174	6	145	255	20
Kayasth	82000	12000	413	644	138	429	629	187
Dom (Patni)	63281	18000	45	85	4	41	78	4

Source: Report on 1921 Census.

It is to be noted that even a section of Ahom elite believed that apart from the British policies, the Ahoms themselves were to an extent responsible for their degradation, attributing three factors for the same: distorted

Hinduism, false pride, and excessive use of opium. One opinion is that the 55 years, from the disappearance of Purendar Singh's Kingship (1838) to the first stirrings of awakening among the Ahom elite symbolised by setting up of the revivalist AAAA (1893) was the most despondent period for the community. It was not only poverty in abstract economic terms, but also a drain of their moral, physical and intellectual resources as a whole that relegated a race with six centuries of dynastic rule to utter insignificance—socially, economically, educationally and politically. This collapse awakened them to the realisation that the development and prosperity of their own community must rest in their own hands, and for that they must establish and maintain a distinct identity within the larger Assamese society. Hence the birth of AAAA, with the aims explained above. This was the beginning under the leadership of a great Assamese litterateur, Padmanath Gohain Baruah. Subsequently came some other organisations into being to fight for their rights.

The Ahoms had been presenting their case before the concerned authorities. Some of their demands were conceded, and included in the 1909 and 1919 Reforms. It is for note that the British considered them a backward community within the Hindu fold. The Ahoms had asked for recognition as a separate, distinct entity and pleaded for a separate geographical area and autonomy for themselves before the Simon Commission (1929), like so many others in the North-East. The Commission did not accept their case, though it included them in the list of high caste Hindus. It is indeed ironic that because of being exalted to higher classification the Community did not find a place in the list of Excluded Areas of either of the two categories, as did the backward communities of the Lushai, NC, Mikir Hills, etc. Consequently, the 1935 Act excluded them from the list of minority communities (and consequently they did not receive any privileges under the Communal Award). So, it was during the 1930s that the need for political activism dawned on them. That is how the AAAA aligned with the Indian National Congress (INC) to fight for nation's independence; and after it was achieved, it merged with it, almost in the manner of the Tribal League (TL) of Assam. Both had unhappy experience of joining hands with nation's premier political formation. So, when the Government announced its decision to set up the SRC in mid-1950s, so the two, AAAA and TL, revived themselves under new names, All Assam Tai Sabha (AATS) and Plains Tribal Council of Assam (PTCA), respectively, to fight for the socio-cultural development of their communities, though deep down, the aims were political. If the PTCA pleaded for a separate state for the Plains Tribals, AATS wanted a separate state for Ahoms in Upper Assam comprising the districts of Dibrugarh, Lakhimpur and Sibsagar. The Commission even-handedly, rejected both!

From the late 1960s, several Ahom organisations are in the field, striving to achieve what they call their "legitimate share" in the administration of the State; an aim considerably watered down from the one they originally set for themselves, viz, "identity assertion"—a phrase that has unfortunately come to gather sinister connotations in the North-East. Some of the organisations—important, not so important, and even defunct presently—that worked at different times with the express aim of safeguarding and promoting the ethnic, cultural, social, and so far undeclared, political interests of the Ahom are mentioned below:

1. Ahom Tai Mongoliya Rajya Parishad
2. Ban Puplik Mioung Tai
3. All Tai Ahom Students Union
4. Tai Ahom Council
5. In 1960s, an attempt was made to revive AAAA, but it never could be revived to be a force to be reckoned with.
6. In 1970, the nearly defunct AATS was revived and re-christened as Ujani Asom Rajya Parishad (UARP), again aspiring for a state of its own within the Indian Union. It did engage in some political activity in the early 1970s, but without any singular achievement.
7. Another organisation formed by a section of the Ahoms is Phuralung Buddhist Council of North-East India. It obviously seems to be a religious platform.

The North-East has remained a battlefield, to put it tersely, ever since our Independence. Nagas even declared their independence 24 hours before India's. Luckily for the nation, the others did not follow their lead as violently and as single-mindedly as the Nagas, even if they concealed and carried a hurt. The Ahoms kept along the path of peaceful agitation. But their attempts to regain their ethnic identity through several organisations formed for the purpose did not succeed.

But unfortunately for them, their identification with the larger Assamese identity is nearly so complete that none of their several movements aimed at identity assertion really took off.

Their last attempt at tribal revivalism was in the 1970s when they rechristened A ATS as UARP to espouse their cause for a separate state within India. It also turned out to be a tame affair, like the earlier ones. It was also in character that when in the wake of violent Bodo agitation, Chief Minister Saikia (1991-96) was bestowing (some cynics thought "forcing" was the right term) autonomy on other ethnic groups like the Rabhas, Tiwas and Lalungs, and also the Karbis, perhaps as a pre-emptive move to dissuade them from adopting the violent ways of the Bodos, the Ahoms were kept out of his bounties. It should cause no surprise if a casual observer to the area finds that the Ahoms are reconciled to their present situation—almost.

BISHNUPRIYA CONUNDRUM

The Vaishnavite influence which spread from Bengal to the North-East centuries ago—it possibly started spreading even before the putative date of the 15th century—has left scattered Bishnupriya communities in Tripura, Manipur and Assam (mainly in Cachar valley). This community has become a cause of tension in Assam in the recent years, with implications far beyond its borders since it is also found in certain neighbouring States as mentioned above. For the present, the Assamese-Manipur row over the subject is very prominent, threatening to vitiate the relation between the two neighbours.

The "Bishnupriya Manipuris" in Cachar have been seeking official recognition for their language, which they have started teaching in Silchar along with some other minority languages like Dimasa and Karbi. They have been carrying on this campaign for years. Interestingly, but not surprisingly, the Manipur Government has been objecting to the Bishnupriyas of Assam using the suffix 'Manipuri' with their community's name, harbouring some apprehensions and even forebodings flowing from this association. The issue has been causing some uneasiness in relations between Assam and Manipur.

"Assam Chief Minister P.K. Mahanta has invited more trouble by recognizing the Bishnupriya language as 'Bishnupriya Manipuri'. This has led to strong resentment being expressed by Manipuris in the State and in Manipur" (Kashyap, Samudragupta in the *Indian Express* of 2-6-1999).

It all started with the Assam Government announcing its decision in May 1999 to recognise Bishnupriya Manipuri as a language of instruction at the primary level acceding the longstanding demand of the Bishnupriya community of the State. The Manipur Chief Minister, W. Nipamacha Singh, reacting strongly, criticised Assam's decision, asserting that the Bishnupriya community was not part of Manipuri community. He emphasised that Manipuri and Bishnupriya were two distinct and separate linguistic groups, as the former belonged to the Tibeto-Burman family of the languages while the latter language was part of the Indo-Aryan linguistic group.

The scholars did not lag behind the politicians to safeguard the interests of their language and the State. Manipuri Sahitya Parishad of Assam threatened to launch an agitation against the decision. The Manipur Government has lodged a protest with the Centre and urged it to press Mahanta to drop the suffix Manipuri from the term.

Sounding reasonable, Nipamacha Singh said that while his Government and community had no objection to the Assam Government recognizing

Bishnupriya as a language of instruction, the suffix Manipuri should be immediately dropped. Sensing strong sentiments, Mahanta was compelled to hold discussions with leaders of both communities and assured the Manipuris of an amicable solution, which is still to see the light of the day.

But why this strong position on the issue by Manipur? Is it only born out of unwillingness to confer the privilege of Manipuri identity on the false claimants? Or, is it something deeper and more sinister that troubles the Manipur State and its people? Is it the fear of disintegration of their State that is looming large in the Manipuri psyche? Already facing claims to the northern parts of their State from the Naga insurgents and Nagaland Government to fulfil their dream of Greater Nagaland, do the Manipuris perceive the Bishnupriya's insistence on the suffix (Manipuri) as a ploy for use at some future date? The unstated fear is that the Bishnupriya Manipuris could be thinking of laying claims on western part of Manipur, on the plea of it being inhabited by their compatriots. A worse scenario is also imagined. If the Barak Valley succeeds in achieving the UT status/statehood somewhere in the future (say, Purbanchal of their dreams), thence they might start clamouring for a Greater Purbanchal a la Nagaland — greedily eyeing areas in western Manipur. The fears might be far-fetched, but the scenario envisaged here is within the realm of possibility. Manipuri fears are not unfounded; and in any case, the fore-warned is fore-armed!

Islamic Militancy and its Implications for Assam

Of recent years, a new kind of religious threat has raised its head in the North-East, report certain concerned Intelligence agencies. While the official agencies and the Government have been busy fighting and controlling politically and ethnically-impelled insurgency/militancy in the North-East, Islamic militancy has been unobtrusively consolidating itself there. In Assam, the Muslim community and Bangladesh infiltration/immigrants are sensitive subjects, more so than the rest of India. Again, as in the rest of the country in Assam too, according to the analysts who study the subject, the Militancy and Islam have been used, misused, or exploited for political purposes by most political parties, if not all, but ironically each party blames the rest of them for the sin. The issue is especially contentious during the election time. And the question of presence of "illegal immigrants" on the electoral rolls makes the situations explosive at the elections, sometimes even "unmentionable". The related issue have been discussed elsewhere in this book, here only the limited question of newly emerging threats to India's sovereignty and integrity from the Islamic militancy will be looked into briefly.

SFs for some years have been reporting the existence of Islamic militants in Assam, as discovered by the Intelligence agencies, but the analysts aver the Governments and political parties have been smug about the subject for reasons of their own. The "blatantly blunt" Hindutva formations are blaming all "secularist" parties for playing politics of appeasement. A large number of Muslim fundamentalist organisations are now active in the region and the SF and Police have been arresting some of their members for anti-national activities. But more importantly, "what has been an open secret for a decade or so," received official confirmation when Chief Minister Mahanta admitted during the Budget session of Assam Assembly, 2000, that "the Islamic militancy has been menacingly active in Assam". For years the SF have been pursuing these extremists to control the situation in Assam, "it is now that the Chief Minister admits the growth of Islamic militant organisations in the inaccessible Char (riverine) areas of Muslim-dominated districts of Central and Lower Assam". "They grow away from the civilisation and scrutiny of the SFs." What is of greater concern to the State and its security agencies is that aided, abetted, guided, rather manipulated, by the ISI, this religion-driven militancy is on rise, and has become a potent force for spread of extremism and fundamentalism of obscurantist variety. Large number of youth belonging to these outfits have visited Pakistan for armed training under Harkat-ul-Mujahideen and Lashkar-e-Taiba, the two most rabidly fanatical, anti-India formations.[35]

The gravity of the Islamic fundamentalism and the existence of the ISI controlled and operated network in the North-East hit the media headlines and Indian public alike when Chief Minister Mahanta announced the arrest of four militants including two Pakistani militants in Gauhati in July 1999, viz, Mohammad Fasih Ullah Hussain from Hyderabad Sind and Mohammad Javed Wakhar from Karachi. Arrest of the ISI argent, Qari Salim Ahmad alias Abdul Hamid with three others, revealed that their mission was to hand over a large quantity of RDX to the Assamese insurgents to carry out subversive activities on the eve of Independence Day, 1999 (*India Today,* 23 May 1999). Further investigations disclosed even more sinister aims of the Pak Intelligence. Part of the deadly cargo was to be taken to North-West India to blow up bridges on the Kulu-Manali-Leh Road to disrupt the only alternative artery to the much-threatened Srinagar-Kargil-Leh Road. If successful, the plan would have completely cut off and isolated the Indian SF in Ladakh, "to be starved into submission", the expression used by the Pak think tanks. Need more be said about the long arm of ISI and Pakistan's morbid anti-India intent, obsession and hatred.

Some 17 of the Muslim fundamentalist organisations working in region are listed here:[36]

1. Muslim United Liberation Tigers of Assam (MULTA).
2. Muslim Liberation Tigers of Assam (MLTA)
3. Islamic Liberation Army of Assam (ILAA)

4. Muslim Liberation Army (MLA)
5. Students' Islamic Movement of India (SIMI)
6. United Reformation Protest of Assam (URPA)
7. Jamaat-e-Islami, Assam (JEI, A)
8. People's United Liberation Front (PULF)
9. Muslim Volunteer Force (MVF)
10. Muslim United Liberation Front of Assam (MULFA)
11. Adam Sena (AS)
12. Islamic Sevak Sangh (ISS)
13. Harkat-ul-Mujahideen (HUM)
14. Islamic Security Force of India (ISFI)
15. Harkat-ul-Jehad (HUJ)
16. COMOA[37] (Coordination Committee for Minorities of Assam)
17. Liberation Islamic Tiger Force (LITF)

The objectives of these organisations, as analysed by the Intelligence, are two-pronged (1) To spread the fundamentalism in the entire North-East and thus prepare and use the immigrant Muslim community for Pan-Islamisation of the region. (2) To foment serious political and religious riots in the area, compelling the Government to rush the SF, especially Indian Army, to control the situation. It will not only create anti-Army and anti-India sentiment when Army was forced to suppress the riots, thus giving further scope for creating disquiet and disafetion in Assam, but also weaken India's anti-terrorism capability in Jammu and Kashmir, giving greater opportunity to Pak-trained foreign immigrants to convert the situation in their favour, to sever the valley from India. This in simple terms, is the dimension of the threat to India's sovereignty and integrity, both in North-East and North-West. Reports with the Intelligence agencies indicate that almost all these organisations operating in Assam are working for a common cause, spelled out here, and have approached several Muslim countries and organisations like the OIC, with the active connivance/even help of the ISI, and they are getting material help of all kinds to achieve their aims. Of the fundamentalist organisations listed above, HUM and HUJ are most fanatical in their ideology and functioning, hence most diabolical and dangerous, having been directly raised as they have been, by the ISI. The members of these organisations are reportedly trained by the ISI personnel at their Bangladesh Camps, located in Cox Bazar and in Rangpur district. Though the activities of some of these camps are reported to had been scaled down under pressure from the Hasina Government, but the stranglehold of the fundamentalist elements in Bangladesh's political, economic and social fields, is so strong that it will need much bigger reserves of endurance, determination and patience than employed so far to break it. The Government's job is extremely difficult if not impossible in view of the opposition's known soft-corner for these anti-India forces; in fact, while in power, Begum Zia had not only spectrally supported these powers in their anti-India work and plans but had indulged in anti-India tirade herself.

It seems more than likely that there will be a spectrally shift in militancy profile in Assam, when the neighbouring countries like Bhutan, Myanmar and Bangladesh throw out Indian insurgent outfits from their soil as a result of India's diplomatic initiatives and they in turn are controlled, reduced and finally eliminated by the Indian SF. But meanwhile, the Islamic fundamentalism and militancy would have considerably added to its strength. Afghanistan supported world-wide Islamic extremism in the past, in concert with various similar organisations in several Muslim nations. But for the cliched nine-eleven, the macabre game would have continued. The recent recrudescence and mobilisation of Islamic Jehadis the world over to support the ongoing Palestinian resistance will provide a fillip to the fundamentalist mobilisation in Pakistan, Bangladesh and Bangladeshi migrants in Assam (And let woolly-headed Indians be warned that a similar mobilisation of Islamic Jehadis could take place on the issue of Kashmir in not too distant a future, if Indians do not wake up to the dangers). All these developments will have anti-India ramifications, positively inimical to its integrity and sovereignty. It will be an ideal situation for the ISI to fish in the troubled waters of North-East by fomenting subversion and terrorism in the Region. Given the population mix of Assam, it will be a sure-fire formula to generate communal conflagrations in India that could lead to its destabilization and ultimately, to its disintegration, a desideratum the ISI is working for. This might appear to be an over-drawn picture of dangers posed to the Indian State, "impelled by fervid imagination of some Intelligence hands", as some scholars, particularly of Left variety, are sure to assert, but Islamic fundamentalism in Assam is something the Indian security apparatus must devote sometime to. The DG, BSF was not exaggerating when he said on 7 April 2000 that "5 to 10 km belt (in depth) in West Bengal along its border with Bangladesh has already become a Bangladeshi and Muslim-dominated territory. This area is being exploited by the ISI for infiltration of subversive elements into India". A surer foothold could not have been asked for by a foreign Intelligence agency.

It bears re-emphasis, in the context of the foregoing, that some years back, the far-seeing Henry Kissinger spoke of one or more Muslim nations emerging from the North-Eastern region of the Indian Sub-Continent.[38] Within the country, tremours have been felt far-away from the North-East.

DGP of UP told a daily in October 2000, disclosing the role of SIMI in anti-national activities, that time bombs had exploded in the State for the first time on the eve of Independence Day 1999, and "the plan was hatched in Aligarh in which SIMI's role has been established[39].

Some of the Movements/insurgencies in the North-East are externally helped and New Delhi is close to bringing them around. The Islamic militancy is the only one externally-generated and guided, essentially, by the ISI, and hence should be a cause of serious concern to India.

Current Scenario : 2005-2007 Situation

The presence of Islamic militancy in the North-East and dangers inherent in its further spread has been discussed in the preceding pages. It also shows that certain extremist outfits are already active in the region and are spreading their wings under active guidance from the ISI. The Islamist threat to the North-East is assuming more serious proportions as there are elements among the Bangladeshi migrants who are bent upon spreading disaffection among the Assamese Muslims. The growth of multiple Islamist organisations in the North-East and their metastatis are a cause for serious concern. The Government does not seem to be paying adequate attention to the security threat to India's North-East due to continuing ingress of foreigners, even when some of the Islamist outfits have, of late, started demanding creation of a Muslim nation in the region. Sounds of the Kissinger warning, mentioned earlier here.

Meanwhile, Islamist organisations like the MULTA, HUM, MULFA, MLA, MV, ILAA, LITF, MLTA, USRA (United Social Reform Army), ISS, URPA, SIMI, PULF, SIO (Students' Islamic Organisation) and ILA (Islamic Liberation Army) have spread their tentacles across the North-East. These groups are known to have been entrusted with the job of creating instability in the region.

Four of these outfits are seen in a little more detail in the pages that follow :

- MULTA

It was raised in 1993 with the objective of protecting the interests of Muslims in Assam, especially the illegal migrants from Bangladesh who continue to be its main support base. "It must endeavour towards carving out a 'rightful place' for Muslims in Assam. The outfit is attempting to have a separate Islamic homeland in Assam comprising the districts of Nagaon, Dhubri, Kamrup, Karimganj and Hailakandi. There are reports of MULTA cadres getting training for its assigned tasks.

A group of 13 MULTA cadres were trained by the ISI in Bangalmara, North Lakhimpur district. A joint group of 160 MULTA and MULFA cadres underwent three months training at Chetak and Jayantipur in Bangladesh under the supervision of two ISI officers (Maj Nizamuddin Shah and Capt Iqbal Ali) during the period 1999-early 2000.[40]

Besides training the MULTA cadres, Al Qaeda and Bangladesh are also channelling arms and ammunition to Islamist outfits from the temporary headquarters set up by the ISI in a mosque at Hathijan in Cox Bazar.

In early May 2002, nine Islamist groups assembled at a camp near the Bangladesh town of Ukhia and created the conglomerate Bengladesh Islamic Manch (BIM). The new umbrella organisation, in a bid to expand/ strengthen Islamic solidarity in the North-East, has also admitted non-Bangladeshi fundamentalist groups like the Rohingya Solidarity Organisation (RSO) and Arakan Rohingya Islamic Front of Myanmar (ARIFM).

Incidentally, MULTA is also a member of the BIM whose declared aim is to create a Brihat Bangladesh (= Greater Bangladesh) by merging areas of Assam and Myanmar's Arakan province. BIM has been formed at the initiative of HUJI-B and is reportedly being chaperoned by the usual suspects ISI and Al Qaeda.

Here are interesting nuances to MULTA's duplicious intentions. It does not qualify its stand on the issue of "separate homeland", refusing to clearly state whether it is to be a sovereign state or the one within the Indian Constitution. But because the Constitution does not cater for/ allow an Islamic state within its ambit, it is, therefore, reasonable to assume that MULTA indeed desires to carve out a sovereign state in India's North-East! Shades of Kissinger's prophecy, once again.

- HUM

It was formed in 1998-99 with the objective of fighting anti-Muslim forces for the creation of an Islamic state and safeguarding the interests of Muslims in Assam.

- MULFA

Formed in 1994, it demands the creation of a separate Muslim state, protection and preservation of Muslim Personal Law and 30 per cent reservation for Muslims in government services and educational institutions. The outfits has a well-accentuated link with the ISI.

- MVF

It was formed with the objective of safeguarding the interest of Muslims in Assam and fighting anti-Muslim forces.

Now to the looming dangers for India's security and sovereignty in the not-too-distant a horizon. After its ouster from the Bhutan soil, it is not too happy a situation for ULFA which by force of circumstances was compelled to break bread with anti-Indian Islamic outfits. After its request to China for sanctuary in its territory met with a curt rejection, ULFA shifted its base and camps to the jungles of Bangladesh. Presently, it is not only a welcome guest there, it is running an affluent empire of commercial and industrial enterprises.

Hence its compulsions of supporting anti-India Islamic outfits, whose support base is essentially among the Bangladeshi (illegal) immigrants (After all, it is well-known fact that the Assamese Muslim, long-settled there, have lived peacefully with their non-Muslim compatriots). As a consequence to its changed circumstances, it should come as no surprise to the cognescenti that ULFA's (new) definition of real 'illegal migrants' does not include the Bangladeshis! Some late wisdom, this!

It is time that Indians realise that it is already too late to stem the tide of Islamist foot soldiers belonging to various militant/terrorist outfits coordinating with each other and facilitating the spread of anti-India sentiment in North-East unless the Government at New Delhi and in the North-Eastern States show some stead fastness and take counter-measures to stem this tide. One is not optimist of such a thing happening in a hurry, as Indian polity's record of acting fast on countering terrorism in the country has been rather dismal. We are still to see our Government crafting an effective, no-nonesense anti-terrorism policy, especially the current dispensation, dominated by the left and weighed down by 'political' considerations on the issue.

An analyst says : "The entire North-East has become a seething-cauldron on account of persistent insurgency and the menance of illegal migrants has further compounded matters.[41]

If security fraternity and academics are worried on this score, they have a reason to nurture a degree of pessimism : "unfortunately, the Indian State has a habit of letting a problem fester to such an extent that it becomes intraceable in course of time."

If the security scenario remains unaddressed indefinitely, political, social and economic instability will follow in its wake. This is the law of the nature. By then, national security would have been damaged irreparably.

CACHAR MOVEMENT FOR A STATE

Cachar[42] is predominantly Bengali-speaking area, essentially because of its cultural affinity and physical contiguity with the Sylhet region of East Bengal. The two valleys, viz Cachar/Barak and Brahmaputra, have been in proverbial rivalry from day one when Cachar was merged, along with Sylhet, with the newly-separated and created Chief Commissioner's Province of Assam in 1874. Till then, Assam had been a part of Bengal as a Commissionership. For these 50 years (1824-74) since the advent of the British, Assam had been dominated by the Bengalis because of their ruling the roost in its administration and professions. To make matters worse for the Assamese pride, Bengali was made, on the advice and insistence of the well-placed Bengali-elite, the language of the courts and administration in mid-1830s. By the time the British undid the injustice in 1874, the anti-Bengali sentiment was already well-entrenched in Assam. The hurt and rancour was to continue for long, long-time—perhaps never to be forgotten or forgiven.

Because of its majority, the Bengalis dominated the administration in Cachar, even when merged with Assam in 1874. That was enough to cause a sense of an unease and jealousy among the Assamese, and an open display of arrogance and racial superiority by the Bengalis only made the matters worse. And some thought the Bengalis of Cachar and Sylhet, post-1874, were even more supercilious in their attitude. So the two valleys not only remained antagonistic throughout the British rule, the rivalries continued even after Independence. Occasional anti-Bengali riots continued after 1947, in spite of the fervent appeal by the much respect Governor Sir Akbar Hydari (1947-49) during his address to the State Assembly in November 1947:[43] "Please give the strangers in our midst (Bengalis) a fair deal." The anti-Bengali sentiment continued just beneath the surface to erupt in worst riots in 1960 which left many innocent dead and houses and property burnt/destroyed.

It is not only geography that separates the two valleys, the two hill districts separating the two. The physical separation is further accentuated by cultural and linguistic differentiation between the two entities. The Cacharis simply could not see them as part of the larger Assamese family. Not welcome in Assam, the Bengalis of Cachar pleaded before the SRC for creation of the Purbanchal State, that was rejected by the latter. But they did not give up. In 1967, their then representative body, the Jan Mangal Parishad demanded that Cachar be made a federating unit in Assam, echoing the one-time sentiment of hill districts of Assam under the leadership of the APHLC. Six years later, the Cachar Gana Parishad in their memorandum (1973) to the Prime Minister sought UT status for their area. Strangely enough, it made use of the Governor's words—"strangers in our midst"—cited above, to justify separation. The 1980 and 1986 memoranda cited the reasons proffered by the less developed hill tribes around the Assam Valley to demand separation, viz, discrimination in language, employment and development. Further, they asserted that all the promises and concessions made in the Assam Accord were in favour of the Assam Valley, constituting a positive discrimination against the Barak Valley. But the Centre rejected the proposition, asserting that (1) Bengali was an associate language in Cachar; (2) there were regional Medical and Engineering Colleges; and (3) "recently, a Central University has been sanctioned for them".

It is no surprise that they have been harbouring separatism for long. Months after Independence, they drew up a scheme for separate administrative unit, nomenclated Purbanchal to include the two districts of the valley (Cachar and Karimganj), NC District, and sub-divisions of Hojai and Hamren. The 1948 Memorandum on the subject adduced the following reasons for separation:

1. Cachar did not form part of the mainland of Assam. British took it over in 1832, eight years after their occupation of Assam. It remained a part of Bengal till 1824.[44]
2. After its merger with Assam in 1874, it was administered by a separate Divisional Commissioner, with his headquarters at Silchar.
3. The 100-mile long Barail Range severs it from the mainland of Assam.
4. Number of Assamese in the Cachar region of Assam was rather small.

The protagonists of separation have not succeeded as yet. But they are still optimistic, watching with keen interest the Movement for UT status being carried out by the Karbis and Dimasas of the two Hill districts of Assam. If they succeed, Assam will find it very difficult to keep the Barak Valley within its fold, disconnected as its would then be from the Brahmaputra Valley.

NOTES

1. Among the prodigious writings in the contemporary press, regional and national, the most interesting, well-informed, and deeply-reasoned, debate was the one that figured on the pages of *The Economic and Political Weekly (EPW),* Bombay.
2. Barua, Srinath, *Employment Problem in Assam,* 1983.
3. Borgohain, Homen, *Aupanibeshak Soshamar Biruddhe Asomar Sesh Sangram* (Assamese), 1980; cited, Misra, Udayon, 2000.
4. The Assamese authors assert that till the ULFA came on the scene, extorting money from the tea industry or forcing them into launching some measures to improve the lot of common Assamese, this industry had done almost zilch by way of social responsibility towards the Assamese citizens. If at all anything was attempted in this direction, it was more of cosmetic in nature than substantive.
5. 5th Report of the 'Employment Review Committee' of the Assam Assembly, 1976.
6. Misra, Tilottoma, "Assam: A Colonial Hinterland", *EPW,* 9 August, 1980.
7. *Ibid.*
8. A part of such arguments and assertions must be ascribed to an overheated partisan rhetoric. If gas for years was flared or head offices of tea companies were not shifted to Guwahati, it was not just because the Centre was being cussed, or imperialist in its approach to Assam, as many of them like to believe. The inability or delay flowed from reasons of economics, non-availability of requisite technologies in some fields, or even political. The Centre itself was hamstrung due to the resources crunch. Even then, it must be conceded that a more sympathetic-approach could have moved the things a little faster.
9. Misra, Tilottoma, *op. cit.*
10. Under the Colonisation Scheme, 20 bighas of land were given to each immigrant family against the payment of a nominal sum.
11. Guha, Amalendu, *Planter Raj to Swaraj: Electoral Politics in Assam,* 1826-1947, 1977.

12. Certain reservations have been expressed by social analysts and scholars about the democratic content of this Movement. Midway through the Movement, the non-Assamese constituents of the AAGSP, namely the Plains Tribals, the Hillmen, the minorities, ethnic and religious, were disenchanted by the way the Assamese majority was conducting the movement. Much before its end, the former had practically dissociated themselves from the Movement. Then, despite its Gandhian claims, anti-foreigners Movement was not without its communal outbursts of violence. Even if the killings at Nellie might have been immediately provoked by the kidnapping and rape of tribal Lalung girls by the immigrant Muslims, yet the large-scale nature of killings where women and children "were mercilessly butchered, should clearly reveal strong communal overtones." Communal violence on large scale also took place in several areas of Kamrup and Darrang districts. In these outrages, not only the immigrant Muslims were attacked Bengali Hindus also became the target of mindless violence.

13. Gen (Retd) KV Krishana Rao, PVSM, former COAS, in his National Security Lecture, 1997, delivered at the USI, New Delhi, on 12 December 1997; excerpts from it were published in the *USI Journal,* April-June 1998.

14. In the interview Mahanta gave to *India Today* (20-10-1997) staffer Avirook Sen.

15. But Kalita, who engaged a Supreme Court lawyer, is an unlikely politician, and "appears to be a mere pawn in an elaborate game of chess being played between Mahanta and senior AGP dissident leaders Phukan and Atul Bora. "How does one otherwise account for the lawyers' frequent trips by air to Gauhati to pursue the case?," asks a Fortightly dated 30-9-1999. The Petitioner would have to field some uncomfortable questions, such as where did he get the funds from to engage an expensive lawyer and pay for those frequent trips. "The distraction, Mahanta's friends hoped, will lead the case where they want it to go: Nowhere!" And, they were right (For details, *see The Frontline,* 30-9-1999).

16. Taking advantage of Atul Bora's opposition to Jayshree's nomination, Mahanta stripped him of his PWD 'fiefdom', and Bora quit in a huff. Thence, Mahanta sacked another Minister for supporting Bora. It was a dangerous mix when Thaneswar Boro, Party's venerated stalwart and Education Minister, resigned and the Phukan-led dissidents proposed him as Chief Minister. But Mahanta won the day with his press conference.

17. She will be member till 2005, as the member of Rajya Sabha has 6-year term compared to Lok Sabha's 5 years. So she got an extra year as a MP, without going through the hurly burly involved in fighting the Lok Sabha election.

18. The hint is for the United Minorities Front.

19. *India Today,* 20-10-1997.

20. *Times of India,* 9-1-1997.

21. At 86 (in 1999), he is the oldest historian of the North-East with 50 books and over 50 years of research to his credit. He has the distinction and honour of having learnt his craft at the feet of that famed teacher of Indian history, R.C. Majumdar. In an article in a periodical, the Historian has lamented the fact that no library in India has the oeuvre of his works for study or reference but the Library of Congress (in USA) has deemed it necessary and worthwhile to have all his books on its shelves! He clearly implies through this statement a certain neglect and unconcern for the North-East and Assam in particular in the rest of India. My own personal experience confirmed this unconcern. I had read a review of *Comprehensive History of Assam* by H.K. Barpujari (ed) in some daily. All my persistent, even frantic efforts to obtain in a copy of this book (Vol. 1) from several Delhi colleges and universities, including Delhi and JNU, through some students and professors bore no results. The frustrating counter query was: "A book on Assam's history? Is there one? Never heard of it!" I had given up all hope when finally and luckily I secured a copy from an important functionary in the Lok Sabha Secretariat through a well-placed Army officer, and "strictly for one week, that is 7 days!"
22. The subjects that still remained outside the jurisdiction of the ADC were law and order, supplies, excise, elections, census and District Rural Development Agency.
23. The ASDC "castigated the arrogance of the plainsmen, their condescension towards the Indo-Mongoloid tribes of the North-East. The Hill areas have been turned into the sanctuaries for overflow of job-seekers, contractor and businessmen.... The locals were discriminated against" (Datta, P.S., 1993).
24. Datta, P.S., 1993.
25. Bhupinder Singh, *et al.,* 1992.
26. *Ibid.*
27. Jatinga is 8 km from Haflong, the District capital.
28. Chief Minister Mahanta was unfazed. After all, his coalition had 77 MLAs in the 126-member Assembly, excluding the five of the ASDC.
29. Dr Jayanta Rongpi belongs to the Vinod Mishra group of the CPI(ML).
30. In a resolution passed by the AAAA at Sibsagar in September 1944. *See* Proceedings of the Executive Committee, Sibsagar, 1944.
31. Bhuyan, A.C., ed, *Political History of Assam,* Vol. I, II, III, 1977-78; and Phukan Girin, *Assam's Attitude to Federalism,* 1984.
32. Barpujari, H.K., ed, *Political History of Assam,* Vol. I, 1977.
33. Fort William Archives; Judicial Proceedings, 24 July 1859.
34. During the *Ahom Rule,* class of people who were entrusted with the responsibility of keeping written records of land and of revenue administration, was called Kakoti.

35. *North-East Sun,* "Threat Perceptions: Assam's Concern" 15-31 August 2000.
36. *Hindustan Times,* "Pakistan's Dhaka Mission has links with ULFA: Mahanta", 8 April 2000; cited by Dinesh Kotwal, in his "The Contours of Assam Insurgency", in the IDSA monthly, 'Strategic Analysis'.
37. Coordination Committee for Minorities of Assam (COMOA) is a political organisation. It has several affiliated bodies, some of the prominent ones being UPPA, UMF, Linguistic Minorities Forum (LMF), and All Assam Nepali Students Union (AANSU).
38. Henry Kissinger in his "White House Years".
39. *Hindustan Times,* "The UP DGP Hits out at SIMI", 15 October, 2000.
40. Seema Sangupta, *The Pioneer*, 19 Jan. 2007.
41. *Ibid.*
42. Presently, the Cachar Valley stands divided into three districts of Cachar, Hailakandi and Karimganj.
43. Datt, P.S., 1993.
44. In fact, the Cachar district was transferred to the Dacca Division of Bengal in 1836, and stayed as such till restored to Assam in 1874.

4

ULFA : A VIRULENT OUTFIT (But a Financially Rich 'Corporation')

ULFA presently is the most virulent terrorist organisation, espousing secessionism. With the NSCN(I-M) honouring cease-fire since 1997, this outfit remains most potent threat to India's integrity, with the NDFB being a distant second.

Origin, Growth and Objectives

ULFA was formed on 7 April 1979 at a meeting of its initial think-tank at the Rang Ghor; the 17th century amphitheatre of the Ahom Royalty, near Sibsagar. The group that morning included Arbindo Raj Khowa, Golap Barua alias Anup Chetia, Pradip (Samiram) Gogoi, and Paresh Barua. Their professed aim was liberation of Assam from the "Indian Colonial rule" and setting up of an independent State, through armed struggle if necessary. The slogan of "sovereign, socialist Assam" lent certain intellectual underpinnings to their ideological dreamland which did bestir the rural masses and a section of the intelligentsia. Most leading lights of the leadership at that time were of Muttock origin, belonging to Upper Assam. Could anyone have imagined at that point in 1979 that the event staged by these starry-eyed, young idealists would give birth to a major, secessionist force in Assam? By November 2002, after three spells of President's Rule and ten Chief Ministers, Assam and the country were still groping in the dark for reigning in the monster it has become for the last two decades and more. At its birth, Assam was passing through a spell of instability. The post-Emergency Janata Party Government of Golap Barbora had fallen, whence followed three Governments within a short span of 28 months.

The founders blamed exploitative policies of New Delhi for Assam's troubles. Like any ideologically-driven movement, they stood for a revolutionary purge of society. They had convinced themselves that Assam was never a part of India. It had forcibly been made a part of Indian polity by some Hindu and Muslim rulers at various periods of history. Till then the Assamese nationality grew in isolation and the people of Assam are proud possessors of a heritage—historical, racial, ethnic, and cultural—totally distinct from that of Metropolitan India. Assam was annexed by the British under the 24 February 1826 Yandabo Treaty, and it came under the unified Indian administration. But the Treaty itself was bad in law hence, the annexation under it itself became null and void as it did not have concurrence of the people of Assam, nor was it ratified by the Ahom rulers. So ran the ULFA argument. So on 15 August 1947, Assam reverted to its status of an independent country; the Indian Independence Act of 1947 only joined it artificially with India through a narrow strip of land (Siliguri Corridor). Moreover it contends that various laws and constitutional prohibitions and bindings about the migration of foreigners have by default been rendered inoperative, resulting in illegal in-migration of millions from the neighbouring Bangladesh, which has destroyed the distinct ethnic character of Assam. Therefore, as an ULFA publication explains, "to create an exploitation-free society, our next step (must) be a national war of liberation.... We have no alternative to armed revolution".[1]

ULFA objective, therefore, was and still remains the creation of an Independent Assam, intended to resuscitate the glory of the ancient Assam and Ahom civilisation.

It should be of interest to trace the lineage of sovereignty from earlier times, even if nurtured by a section of intelligentsia. In that sense, ULFA is not the progenitor of the *Svadhin Asom* (=Sovereign Assam) as it had already been dreamt of by earlier generations. The peasant struggles in Assam in the latter half of the 19th century were unique in the sense that, unlike the similar struggles in the rest of India, a common front was put up against the British Rule by both the land-owning class and the middle and poor peasantry. This was possible due to various factors: (1) nature of land settlement under the long Ahom Rule; (2) strong tribal content in the Assamese society; (3) predominance of the small land-holding farmers; and (4) absence of the zamindari system.

Different struggles during the period of British Rule by themselves were not a fight for "Assamese identity" or "Assamese nationality"; they were simply stages in the mobilisation of a people, who would in years to follow be involved in a larger national struggle where the peasantry would play the pivotal role. The different ethnic groups, which constituted the social fabric of Assamese society on the eve of British advent, were yet to be brought together on the common platform of the Assamese linguistic nationalism. The struggle against the British Rule led by the Assamese middle class, which had got a head-start over the other smaller nationalities of the Region, gave it a position of hegemony that was to continue till 1960s, and 1970s when the emerging middle classes of these nationalities started asserting their rights, and a schism began to appear in the facade of a monolithic Assamese nationalism. It was during the initial years of consolidation of Assamese nationalism in the 1920s and 1930s that the idea of *Svadhin Asom* began to fire the imagination of a section of the middle class. Incidentally, that ULFA ideologues claim to take the inspiration for their movement from this period.

Modern political consciousness in Assam may be deemed to have commenced from around 1853 when Maniram Dewan and Anandaram Dhekiyal[2] Phukan submitted their memorials to Moffat-Mills. It would take another 70 years or so for this consciousness to develop and give shape to the Assamese nationalism, with the INC establishing its unit in Assam in 1921. "By 1870s, non-indigenous element constituted at least a quarter of the population of Assam proper."[3] Added to this was the serious imbalance between the fast-growing modern sector of tea and extractive industry (oil and coal) and traditional agricultural sector. Almost the entire surplus from the former was being remitted to Britain. The colonial exploitation was on the rise. It was against this background that the Assamese students in Calcutta formed the Assamese Library Society (ALS) in 1872, supplanted by the Asomiya Bhasa Unnati Sadhani Sabha (ABUS) in August 1888. It published the catalogue of Assamese manuscripts in 1897 and the journal, *Jonaki* which ushered in a hew era of Assamese literature. The articles in Jonaki harked back to the glories of the past when Kamarupa held sway up to the borders of Bihar and bemoaned the loss of economic autonomy. Kanak Lal Barua[4] blamed the British for the decay in Assam's handloom industry. An argument for economic independence is but one step away from advocacy for political independence, given the socio-political scenario at the beginning of the 20th century. Kamala Kanta Bhattacharya[5] insisted that Assam should constitute an independent self-reliant nation and warned that with the development of transport and communication means, foreigners would pour into fertile soil of Assam and jeopardise our "distinct identity". Lakshminath Bezbarua[6] did not plead for political emancipation but worked for cultural resurgence of the Assamese. Noting the non-mention of Sankaradeva in the histories of Indian/ Bengali saints, Bezbarua says: "It only proves that Assam was till the other day an independent country." Although Bezbarua's Assamese nationalism (Asamiya Jatiyatabad) was part of broader Indian nationalism, still in his writings *Assam Desh* is an autonomous socio-cultural and political entity. His poem, *Mor Desh* (= my country) written in 1910, today is Assam's Jatiya Sangeet (national anthem), and sung on all public occasions along with India's National Anthem. The writings in *Jonaki* and other journals of the period show the existence of two types of nationalism, regional and national, side by side, in Assam. Scholars posit "it was a common phenomenon throughout India".[7] But in the case of provinces like Assam, not to speak of its hill regions which came under the British Rule much later than most of other parts of India, the Regional brand of nationalism got the better of pan-Indian nationalism whenever the Region and the Community faced a crisis—cultural, economic, or political. Geographical and historical factors often counted for pan-Indian nationalism to be overshadowed by regional nationalistic emotions in Assam and other regions in the North-East. Thus, for the understandable reasons, the struggle between the two strands of nationalism have formed an important part of Assam's history right from the days of the advent (1921) and consolidation of the Congress politics in Assam to the post-independence period when cries of "Colonial exploitation" of Assam rich natural resources by the Centre started becoming increasingly strident.[8]

As the Assamese joined the 1920-21 Non-cooperation Movement in large numbers, it resulted in swift politicisation of the masses. Consequently, a variety of socio-political organisations sprung up in Assam, ranging from the Assam Sangrakshini Sabha (ASS) founded by Ambikagiri Roy-Choudhury[9] (later, Asom Jatiya Mahasabha, AJM) to dozens of Krishak and Ryot Sabhas, dedicated to voicing the peasants' demands. In May 1920, Chandranath Sharma, virtual founder of Assam Congress, voiced his concern on the threat to Assam's identity from the unchecked infiltration, particularly from (West), from Bengal. It was in these circumstances that the Assamese middle class intellectuals like Roy-Choudhury and Jnananath Bora wrote on the need to defend Assamese homeland against "foreign" incursions. As mentioned above, Chandranath Sharma also harboured similar apprehensions about the fate of the Assamese nationality. Roy-Choudhury, who was no Assamese chauvinist (as he is often made out to be) and in fact was a senior Assam Congress leader (1926), initially advocated the concept of an Indian Federation of (equal) linguistic nationalities. But in the later years, it was the failure of the Indian National Congress (INC) to take an unequivocal stand on the issue of continued influx of foreigners threatening the very identity of Assam and its attempt to force Assam to accept the Cabinet Mission Plan[10], that would have resulted Assam going to Pakistan, were the reasons that pushed Roy-Choudhury and his AJM to express sentiments bordering on a demand for an independent Assam. As early as November 1937, he had submitted a memorandum on behalf of the ASS to Nehru, emphasizing the following:

1. If the line system segregating the autochthons and immigrants was withdrawn, it would lead to fresh tensions emanating from further occupation of Assamese-held lands by the immigrants.
2. A considerable section of Assamese intelligentsia feels that if the full leadership of the Congress did not view their fears regarding Muslim influx seriously, then Assam should secede from India.
3. The support for the Congress in Assam would depend upon the two issues that deeply trouble the Assamese: one, Sylhet and Cachar be separated from Assam; two, mass immigration into the Brahmaputra Valley be stopped.

In the June 1946 Memorandum to the All India Congress Committee, Roy-Choudhury's AJM accused it of not seeing the threat caused by the Grouping Plan[11] to Assam's identity and "the Assamese were prepared for a desperate struggle for national existence and emancipation. He even built up Asom Atmarakashi Bahini to save Assam from the designs of Muslim League, which had caused the widespread riots in the East Bengal districts, and "the victims of the Noakhali disturbances are entering Assam".

When after Independence, Assam's Congress Government failed to provide adequate checks against the infiltration from the newly-created East Pakistan, the AJM in a meeting on 1 January 1948 declared that "Assam should come out of Indian Union and become independent like Burma". It must be noted that the AJM's (Asom Jatiya Mahasabha) consistent demand that Sylhet be separated from Assam and opposition to the CHT being incorporated into it (Assam) were motivated by an urge to have a homogenous Assamese territory "distinct from the Indian mainland" But luckily for the nation, Roy-Choudhury, and others of his ilk, remained a lonely voice in the first two decades or so of the post-Independence Assam which, dominated by the Congress ideology and politics, veered sharply towards the pan-Indian nationalism. The success of Bordoloi in thwarting the Grouping Plan and separation of Sylhet (bar its Karimganj sub-division) had largely eased the Assamese fears of losing their identity. Thus, from 1947 till the 1960s, regional nationalist forces had to take the back seat. "It was from the early 1970s, that Roy-Choudhury's ideas started finding favour with sections of the post-1960 generation of Assamese who had become increasingly aware of the colonial pattern of exploitation of Assam by the Centre as well as the growing threat posed by the influx of foreigners into the State." Jnananath Bora was another intellectual who advocated for a sovereign Assam during the 1930s. He asserts the British forcibly incorporated Assam into British India and on that basis, "the educated amongst us have been trying to prove that Assam is a province of India."[12] This argument is very similar to the ULFA's present stance regarding the role of the intellectuals in Assam, who are dubbed by it as the 'Indian agents'. Bora's writings, forgotten for decades, have now been resurrected by the proponents of the *Svadhin Asom* who have been trying to use them to garner people's support for the ULFA's cause.

In spite of their large scale participation in the 1942 Quit India Movement, the Assamese felt let down when the Congress Working Committee accepted the Grouping Plan on 10 August 1946. Assam's fears were not unfounded as Bengal with its huge majority could/would impose its will on it.[13] In view of this betrayal by the Congress, some scholars ask as why the *Svadhin Asom* proponents did not push their case more aggressively. One of the main reasons for their low profile during this period could be the fear of Muslim domination resulting from the inundation of the indigenous Assamese in the flood of in-migrants from across the border and hence the need to stay with India. It was easy to see, given the demographic realities and the experience of the recent past with the Saadullah Ministries,[14] that a *Svadhin Asom* would be even more vulnerable to and fall an easy prey to the machinations of the Muslirn East Pakistan. The Hill leaders too were well aware of the need to stay with India to avert a Muslim take-over. Nichols-Roy,[15] the eminent Khasi leader declared: "We know what the policy of Muslim League is in Assam. Even now, the Muslim League in Bengal wants to send thousands upon thousands of immigrants into Assam."

It may be fair to say that the fear of Muslim Pakistan and the demographic challenge posed by it through an aggressive migration policy pursued by the Muslim League and supported by it, attenuated the fervour of the *Svadhin Asom* proponents. Moreover, once the Muslim majority district of Sylhet voted itself out of Assam, the CHT did not get tagged to Assam, as some had reared, and Assam joined India on 15 August 1947; all existential fears of the Assamese seemingly evaporated and the concept of Svadhin Asom also petered out.

This is a brief, broad brush survey of *Assamese* 'nationalism', and urge for 'sovereignty', during the British days. The ideas on sovereign *Assam* may not have been widespread, but the germs were always there all be it just below the surface. Happily for us all, its espousal was restricted to a few eminent individuals, academics, intellectuals and leftists. The feelings of separateness persisted till the 1930s and even 1940s. To cite just one instance, a mere one month prior to the Independence, one of the leading intellectuals of *Assam*, Birinchi Kumar Baruah, a known authority on Assamese literature and culture, who subsequently became the Dean of Faculty of Arts, Guwahati University, said in a public lecture: "culturally, socially and linguistically, every non-Assamese is a foreigner, in Assam"...It speaks of India's strengths that all such individuals are happily doing their duty by India's cause. It is a tribute to *Indian* civilisation's all-encompassing nature that India exists as a multi-cultural, -linguistic, -religious and -ethnic nation, a pulsating democracy amidst a sea of autocratic and fundamentalist regimes.

The demand for autonomy—nay, sovereignty—was to resurface some forty years after it had subsided (if not died) at Independence. But this time around, it was to be backed by an adequate infrastructural support in the form of an armed outfit (ULFA) to wage the battle violently and on an en otive, sensitive issue of "colonial exploitation" of Assam (and the North-East) by the "Imperial India"; it was a war in the field of ideas and ideology.

The above should sum up the ideological and motivational basis in history that the ULFA leadership has intelligently, if cleverly, used to build and sustain their case for secessionism.

Graduating into a Virulent Movement

The ULFA remained rather dormant for some years after its formation in 1979. During the AASU Agitation (1979-85), some militant groups like the Assam Fighters Union (AFU) and Assam People's Liberation Army (APLA) came into being which lent some belligerent touch to it, from the sidelines. Subsequently sprang up some parochial organisations like Assam Jatiyabadi Dal (AJD) and Purbanchaliya Lok Parishad (PLP) which also occasionally shouted some belligerent slogans for effect. ULFA was, besides these four groups, another outfit that played on the sidelines of the Assam Agitation, but with a difference. Some saw it as B team of the AASU during the Agitation. With its brazen advocacy of Assamese Chauvinism, ULFA represented the extremity of xenophobic ideology, the bedrock of this Agitation. The AFU, APLA, AJD and PLP declined and fizzled out after the Assam Accord was signed in 1985. But the idea of forming a violent underground with the sole objective of liberating Assam did not die down. It stayed alive and was nurtured by ULFA.

There are interesting speculations on the AASU-ULFA relationship. Some feel the ULFA had watched the AASU Movement from close angles and learnt some lessons in organising and conducting such movements. In fact, the ULFA had ingratiated itself with the AASU hierarchy. It was not an unexpected development or difficult task, as the leadership of the two organisations was comprised of the idealistic, educated youth, having similar social and economic background. This was but a simple fact of life, even if the analysts have engaged in semantics on the issue. If some posited that ULFA was an offshoot of the extremist fringe of AASU, others counter it by saying that it was born at least 6 months before the AASU Agitation took off. A certain symbiosis between the two during the agitation is widely acknowledged. But once the AASU ascended to power as AGP, the chasm between the two was inevitable. Hence the postulation that the AGP lost the 1991 Assembly poll due to ULFA's antagonism, and returned to power in 1996 with its support. Some analysts assert that even when the two organisations are firmly pitched on the opposite sides of the fence, there is a degree of mutual admiration and kinship of ideas and interests between certain identifiable sections of the two camps.

The 1983 Assembly polls were excessively violent because they were held in the wake of the boycott call by AASU, since it alleged that the electoral rolls prepared in 1979 contained the names of over 4 million aliens who, if allowed to participate in the polls, would vitiate their sanctity. AASU deemed the Saikia Government that came into power as a result of these polls as illegitimate. It was during these un-popular elections and the tenure of the Saikia Government (1983-85) that rose to power in consequence that ULFA cut its teeth in agitational politics and made significant inroads into the body politic of Assam. It assiduously built its case of exploitation theory: India was not concerned with Assam's interests, but only in its resources. Hence its stubbornness in holding polls against fierce opposition of the Assamese. Spreading this sentiment adroitly, it built and expanded its support base among the educated, unemployed youth.

ULFA had infiltrated some departments of the Mahanta Government. Mahanta did not act even when he knew that the ULFA activities were harming his Government. By 1987-88, their depredations had reached menacing proportions. Towards the end of 1980s, situation reached a point of no return. AGP Government not proceeding against the ULFA cadres was understandable, "after all, they were our boys", but even the V.P. Singh Coalition at the Centre failed to act, hobbled as it was by its internal troubles; and in addition, AGP was part of the Coalition. Then came the infamous airlift of the Doom Dooma Tea Executives and meanwhile Chandrashekhar had taken over who dismissed the Mahanta Ministry on 27 November 1990. The Union Minister of State, Subodh Kant Sahay put it tersely: "The whole State machinery is with the ULFA".[16] ULFA was banned the same day. The next day (28-11-1990), Army launched operation Bajrang. The ULFA leadership escaped the dragnet as the word had leaked about the impending operation. The first camp to be struck was at Lakhipata, a short distance from both Digboi and Dibrugarh. It was the case of Army reaching and searching the just-abandoned camp. The same story was repeated elsewhere. The mass graves in some of the camps told their own story of gory torture and death. ULFA was in disarray, but far from being broken, as the educated youth was available and willing to join it.

"The elections of 1991 were completed despite ditching by those charged with responsibility to conduct them." These elections were completed courtesy ULFA, as some critics asserted. Though ULFA was seen as a half-brother of AASU, but it reportedly helped the Congress, covertly. The Saikia Ministry was sworn-in on 1 July 1991 and perhaps to remind him of the promises, it struck the same day. 14 officials and some others were taken hostages. In the ensuing negotiations, the Assam Government agreed to the following: (1) Amnesty for ULFA leaders and cadres. (2) Over 400 cadres released. (3) Operation Bajrang was called off much against the Army's advice. With a single stroke of pen, Saikia undid what the SF had achieved at some cost to them. All his was done against a mere promise of release of hostages. Paresh Barua went to Bangladesh to persuade Arbindo Rajkhowa, Anup Chetia and Pradeep Gogoi and their cadres to join the peace process. Not only they did not return, they issued a call from Dhaka for renewing the armed struggle. In a perfidious move, they killed some hostages and went on a rampage. Utilising the peaceful interregnum, they regrouped and rejuvenated their outfit and unleashed an orgy of violence. Within a period of 11 weeks, 166 innocents were killed and another 252 kidnapped. Singed by their perridy, the Government called out the Army again. Operation Rhino was launched on 14-15 August 1991. This is the story of ULFA during the first decade of its existence.

It needs re-emphasis that its initial success in building up and sustaining its mass base was because of its ideology-driven motivation. In its letter to the UN Secretary General dated 20 October 1990, it shunned all forms of disruptive violence. When the ISI wanted ULFA to "disrupt communications and economic targets like oil refineries and gas fields, and create chaos to pave the way for a general uprising against the Government", both Paresh Barua and Sunil Nath, two of ULFA's top leaders, expressed strong opposition to any major attacks on Government property, "as that would alienate us from the people...." This was early stage. The streak of idealism was still intact and they were keen to retain the sympathy of masses. The success in the initial stages could be seen in the way it was able to infiltrate the police, AGP, and other branches of the State administration. That should explain the fiasco in which Op Bajrang had to end, as ULFA had been tipped about it a week in advance. But this should not have been a surprise for the people in the know. After all, ULFA was the brain child of the extremist section of AASU and a certain symbiotic relationship must have continued to exist between the two. An analyst was not far off the mark to say: "AGP had become a cloak for ULFA's activities." Even more significantly, ULFA was able to create a space for itself in the public life viz, civil society, independently of the overwhelming State apparatus. That should explain the birth of organisations like Manav Adhikar Sangram Samiti (MASS) and hydra beaded growth of newspapers like Budhbar and Sadin, generally acquiescing in ULFA's violence but loudly protesting the State's so-called excesses.

So, initially at least, ULFA had ideological moorings, even if mixed with nationalistic cliches. At that stage, it indeed was ideologically-driven movement. But all that was given a go-by when, mid-1990s onwards, its leadership under pressure from Army, resorted to mindless violence. Its mass support really suffered with its pro-Pak stance during the 1999 Kargil war and communal killings in end-2000 period. It was simply violence for violence, sans any ideology.

Political Games

It is an accepted fact that ULFA came into its own only after its cadres were put through their paces in the NSCN training camps. It opened its account in the violence trade with a bank robbery at Namrup in Upper Assam in 1985. Saikia was in power then (1983-85). Some observers feel the wily Chief Minister built up ULFA to even out with AASU, which was then in the mid-course of its own agitation. In such situations, it is always difficult to know the "facts". But it does seem true that they gained strength during the first Mahanta Ministry.

Several batches of ULFA recruits got trained in Nagaland and Manipur in the NSCN camps. Subsequently, senior leaders began establishing camps within Assam as Mahanta, a youthful tyro, was struggling to pick up ropes as Chief Minister. As already discussed, he was unwilling or unable to confront ULFA in this term. ULFA Chairman Arbindo Rajkhowa (real name, Rajiv Rajkonwar; a school teacher and son of a freedom fighter from a place near Nazira) appointed Paresh Barua (a football player and a railway employee) the chief of ULFA's Military wing. It was around this time that the killings began, slowly but steadily. The Chairman of the United Minorities Front, a pro-migrant Muslim outfit in 1986, was among the first targets.

The initial training in Burma was arranged by ULFA for its cadres from the KIA in 1986. This needed hard cash which set in motion a train of extortions, kidnappings, and demands for ransom. The message was soon to reach a wide circle of traders, businessmen, tea garden executives, and Government employees/officers with a mixture of hype, effrontery, and selective strikes. Thus, it was that ULFA became a dreaded name by the closing years of the 1980s. "During 1989-90, they managed to extort Rs. 20 crore from traders in Jorhat alone." They had arrived on the scene with a big bang. But far more impressive were their pickings from the tea industry (details later):

> By 1989 the ULFA was a grown-up! It had started taking journalists to its hide-outs to draw some publicity mileage. Meanwhile the killings increased as did the extortions. They established links with the ISI, enabling them to obtain the Pakistan and Bangladeshi passports for travels abroad. It was only when their depredations reached tea gardens that the Centre sat up. In the latter half of 1990, Surendra Paul, Director, Assam Frontier Tea, was killed and many others were abducted. When the Doom Dooma executives were airlifted to safety outside Assam, the Chandrashekhar Ministry dismissed Mahanta (November 1990) only weeks before completion of his term. The press reports said he was compelled to take this step by the Congress which, angling in the troubled waters, had espied a political opportunity.

If Mahanta during his first term (1985-90) in office failed to see the threat posed by the militants to the nation's integrity, the Saikia Government (1991-96) proved even worse. The split engineered by him in 1993 proved counter-productive. The residual faction turned stronger and even more ruthless and SULFA proved an obstreperous child even to its own parents, indulging in its own little games of revenge and extortions. While Saikia spent more and more time guarding his political flanks, thousands of SULFA cadres turned out to be a new pack of anti-socials. The fiasco was mainly because not only Saikia failed to make them surrender their weapons but his Government was lacklustre in providing them any worthwhile alternative employment as promised and planned. The slip-shod policy resulted in huge amount of money given as loans for rehabilitation, remaining unrecovered. And to imagine that 50 per cent of ULFA's cadre strength—amounting to about 3500—had surrendered by 31 March 1993 and Saikia had publicly said that "ULFA stood neutralised and as a result it would now call for peaceful negotiations". The subsequent events showed that Saikia's remained a vain hope, and there never was greater hiatus between hope and reality! In the end, ULFA emerged stronger, since it became more selective and stricter in recruiting the youth; and going by reports, over 600 joined its ranks and received arms training in Bangladesh, Myanmar and even Bhutan during *Saikia's* term. More unfortunate was the anti-SF sentiment resulting from the vociferous human rights activists. Large-scale corruption helped ULFA to fill its coffers with large amount of money resulting from the leakage of development funds.

The anti-Army sentiments was so strong during the 1996 electoral rhetoric that Mahanta had promised to send the Army back to barracks and withdraw the black laws.[17] There are two views about reasons for this unwise promise. One, his pro-ULFA leanings led him to this statement. Two, quite to the contrary, others felt he did so under direct pressure from ULFA. It is an irony that Mahanta had to eat crow, and call out the Army urgently to bail him out as the ULFA unleashed a vicious violence on the very day he was sworn-in (15 May 1996) for his second term. Midway through this term, he felt threatened enough with ULFA's depredations and fearing the fall of his Government, that he even wanted to requisition the services of K.P.S. Gill to help him weather his battle against ULFA.[18]

What are the political leanings of the ULFA? It is a difficult issue to tackle. Its support to the AGP resulted in Mahanta winning 1985 and 1996 Assembly polls; or so says the grapevine. The party lost to the Congress in 1991 elections due to its opposition. On similar grounds, it lost the 1998 and 1999 Parliamentary polls. But all this may be too simplistic, as if the AGP's own performance in power had no role to play. But there is another view to the scenario. Public pressure was seen to be building up against ULFA by 1997-98. Particularly after the cold-blooded murder by ULFA of Sanjay Ghose, a dedicated social worker who had brought hope and light in the lives of the Mujuli Islanders, there was a groundswell of anger against the outfit. If the political class had acted in national interest, the Mahanta Government showing the will to act and the Congress Party resisting the temptation to pull it down by fostering dissensions in the *AGP* ranks, ULFA might have openly come forward for talks.

All said and done, the AGP suffered due to its proximity to ULFA, perceived or otherwise. It was perceived to be pro-ULFA. After all, Mahanta had accused his own Home Minister (Bhrigu Phukan) of pro-ULFA stance during his first Ministry. Mahanta's own flip-flops could hardly assure the people of his hands-on determination to confront the secessionist outfit squarely. His anti-Army rhetoric in the run-up to the 1996 poll and subsequently eating his words, belong to the pages of history. It is also widely believed that he held a public rally in Guwahati in the 1998 elections after an agreement with the ULFA. Again, it is well-known that he dragged his feet for months after taking over as Chief Minister in May 1996 on setting up a Unified Command structure for efficient and coordinated conduct of CI operations in his State. "Even when forced down his throat early 1997, he refused to take command",[19] as some news reports claimed, and only agreed to a convoluted structure for Unified Command: a Strategic Group under his Chief Secretary and an Operational Group under the local (Tezpur) Corps Commander. But his distaste for the Unified Command did not end with the creation of a frayed and truncated structure. Late 1997, capital of Dispur (along with Jorhat) was taken out of the purview of the Unified Command. Was it any surprise that Guwahati witnessed a series of violent incidents in the months following this decision, asked a concerned citizen? It is also held that Saikia was no different from Mahanta for playing political games of his own. He had reportedly reached a tacit understanding with ULFA on the eve of 1991 Assembly poll (Did this ensure his victory?). It was his failure to deliver on some unwritten promises that forced the outfit to resort to large-scale kidnappings on the very day he was sworn-in on 1 July 1991. His soft-corner for ULFA was obvious from the so-called conciliatory offerings he made to it during the ensuing negotiations for release of hostages. The perfidy of ULFA, in killing some hostages, including the Russian Engineer, did not seem to have overly dismayed Saikia as he continued dealing with it "to persuade it to come to table for peace talks". As for the post-Saikia Congress' relations with ULFA, Chief Minister Mahanta (1996-2001) persistently accused it of a clear nexus with the outfit. After the October-December 2000 minority massacres unleashed by ULFA, Mahanta claimed in the Assembly that he had documentary evidence on this nexus, and claimed it was aimed to destabilise his Government.

Having said it all, how is the following news item as dessert?

> "The ULFA has decided to help the Congress (I) in the (September 1999) Lok Sabha elections, like in 1998. It has already issued instructions to this effect to its units, reliable sources said here today." (*The Hindu*, 10 September 1999, Guwahati). The sources hinted that some Congress (I) leaders, mainly in Upper Assam, were in touch with the ULFA. An affluent

former MP was likely to provide the necessary "inducement" to the ULFA to help the Congress (I).

It is an issue where no analyst can talk in terms of certainty. There are shades and shades between black and white. May be, it is fair to say that in this game, no political party can be pure evil or milky white. It is good enough to mention the possibilities and potentialities, and let the matters rest there. It is Herculean task to draw conclusions from the unedifying mud-slinging indulged in by different political parties.

VIOLENCE BY MILITANTS

1991

1 July	The Saikia Ministry was sworn-in this day and it was the day when ULFA kidnapped 14 people from different places in Assam. Most of them were officials from the oil industry, including a Russian Engineer. They were kept in captivity for long period. They killed three of them in cold blood, including the luckless Russian. How Chief Minister Saikia walked into the trap of negotiations with ULFA has already been recounted.

1993

5 Oct.	Rs. 2.34 lakh looted from the employees of Agricultural Training Centre at Amoni Tenali, near Tezpur.
17-18 Nov.	ULFA took away Rs. 50 lakh in cash from the ONGC central workshop, near Sibsagar.

1994

28 May	Kokopathar Tea Estate (TE) under Dibrugarh Police Station receives an extortion notice for Rs. 20 lakh.

1995

30 Dec.	15 militants sprayed a volley of bullets on the convoy of Assam Health Minister Bhumidhar Burman, killing 10 and injuring 3 policemen.

1996

7 Jan.	SP Nagaon's caravan fired at indiscriminately.
20 Jan.	Lachit Kalita, President of Assam Youth Congress shot dead in Guwahati.
12 Feb.	Two passengers on a Guwahati-bound bus shot dead near Golaghat.
21 Feb.	Mohd Haque son of Assam Minister R. Haque, kidnapped along with his three friends and his driver.

	All set free, except the Minister's son, who was released much later, at 10 PM on 5 April, probably after taking ransom.
29 Mar.	A.K. Brahma, a SULFA cadre, gunned down near village Balabari.
25 April	Binu Chetia, Congress candidate in Assembly Election (due in May) along with his 3 PSOs (Personal Security Officers) shot dead, 3 km from Margharetta.
28 April	Lt Col Devan Tyagi shot dead and Lt Col AD Ghosh injured at the Kamakhya Temple.
6 May	Assam Minister Nagon Neog shot dead along with 9 of his security men while returning from Golaghat.
15 May	Bodo and ULFA ultras unleashed an orgy of violence on this day. Mahanta is sworn-in second time as Chief Minister.
16 May	SP, Tinsukia and 4 others shot dead.
31 May	Rs. 5 lakh snatched from the Union Bank of India Manager (The loot from different incidents during the month totalled Rs. 12,65,780).
9 Sept.	IGP, S.K. Deb, shot dead in the heart of Guwahati city from a point-blank range.
28 Nov.	Oil pipeline to Baraumi blown up by ULFA, near Bijulighat in Nalbari district. The blast completely damaged the pipeline over river Pagladiya. The impact was heard as far as Nalbari town, 10 km away.
30 Dec.	The Brahmaputra train blast.
	Parag Kumar Das, General Secretary, Manav Adhikar (Human Rights) Sangram Samiti (MASS), was murdered brutally. He was the Editor of a Guwahati Daily and a ULFA ideologue. "Army had no hand in his murder, nor did the Police for that matter, particularly so after an ignominious departure of senior Police and Civil officials like DGP Ranjan Das, IGP Ashim Roy, and Chief Secretary Arunoday Bhattacharya, by the first available flight."

1997

16 March	Lt Col KS Kalra shot dead at Tezpur where he had gone with his family for worship at the Ganesh Temple.
8 June	ULFA tried to eliminate Chief Minister Mahanta by exploding an IED while he was on his way to the city from Guwahati airport.

23 June	A CRPF vehicle going to town from Guwahati airport ambushed; 4 men were killed and 5 injured.
3 July	Rs. 1.26 lakh snatched from the accountant of the Purabi Dairy in Kamrup district.
August	The re-charged ULFA and Bodo militants staged a death dance on the eve of Independence Day, 1997.
6 August	ULFA confirms the death of Sanjoy Ghose, claiming he slipped from a cliff top in Arunachal Pradesh.
8 August	Brig TDS Vishakhan and his staff officer are gunned down in Guwahati, with his daughter witnessing the killing.
8 August	The Bodo rebels blow up two bridges. 7 BdSF rebels killed. Army recovers 8 Kg of RDX.
11 August	A powerful blast 10 metres ahead of the Rajdhani Express near Sarupeta in Lower Assam, over 300 lives lost.
12 August	Bengalis lined up and shot dead by BdSF at Rangiya.
14 August	A bomb blast derails a passenger train near Siloni in North Lakhimpur district, killing 7 and injuring many more.
	Violence in Tea Gardens. The acts of ULFA violence during the period 1988-90 and 1992-96 are covered separately, on the next page.

1998

11 February	ULFA targeted many AGP candidates during the 1998 Parliamentary Election. Its Vice-President Biraj Sharma is attacked, but escapes with serious injuries.

1999

August	ULFA and Bodo militants launched a number of subversive attacks on the trains, bridges, and SF personnel (discussed in detail separately).

2000

Oct.-Dec.	A reoriented ULFA, moving away from its ideological moorings, launched vicious violence against the non-Assamese Hindi-speaking minorities (also discussed separately).
27 February	The Assam PWD and Forest Minister Nagen Sharma and 4 others were killed around 1.45 PM when the ULFA militants blew their vehicle by a remote-controlled IED at Nij Bahjani village in Nalbari district. The village is considered one of the strongest bastions of ULFA, though the district itself is dominated by this outfit. Sharma, a senior AGP leader, was its seniormost General Secretary

Summarised Information on Violence. ULFA violence claimed the lives of 1370 civilians and 20 SF men during the 1986-95 period. Details of killings and kidnappings for three years follow:[20]

Year	*Killed*	*Kidnapped*
1995	30	29
1996	107	36
1997	118	40

Here are the official figures[21] of human cost of violence perpetrated by ULFA.

Persons Killed by ULFA

Period	*Incident*	*Total*	*Persons Killed*	
			Civilians	*SF*
1996	141	107	59	48
1997*	79	60	41	19

*(1 January to 7 May 1997)

Poor Show by MHA

Fuller accounts of incidents of killing, kidnapping, and extortion are available in the 36-page pamphlet distributed by the MHA officials during the 16-17 October 1998 meeting of the NEC at Shillong. Coming from an exalted Ministry, it is a shoddily document; with poor grammar, poorer syntax, and careless editing. More surprisingly, it singularly lacks felicity of expression, generally a strong point with the IAS/IFS community, which must have drafted the document.

Assam Tea Tastes Bitter

If Assam tea has made a name for itself for its quality and flavour the world over during the last 150 years, it also made news in the recent years but for different reason. By the end of 1980s, it had become a milch cow for terrorist outfits like ULFA and BdSF. Crores of rupees had been extorted from the executives of various Tea Houses on the pain of death threats. Anyone daring to be defiant was dispatched without remorse. When extortions crossed the limits of forbearance, one company (Doom Dooma) decided enough was enough and flew its executives out of Assam. How this resulted in the dismissal of the first Mahanta Government in November 1990 has already been discussed. Subsequently, for some years, the tea did not boil over, even if it was simmering below the surface. But when a tea major (the Tata Tea Limited-TTL) got enmeshed in a major controversy in 1997, Mahanta again was in office and this time around he was determined to make political capital out of that company's discomfiture. Being recent events, they will be discussed in outline only.

The TTL vs Assam Government controversy grabbed the headlines following the arrest of ULFA's Culture Secretary Pranati Deka at Bombay on 22 August 1997. Her interrogation revealed TTL had defrayed her medical expenses after she had given birth to a baby boy a fortnight ago at Bombay's upmarket Jaslok Hospital. DGP, Assam told the *Frontline:* "Deka was living with her husband, C. Hazarika, Finance Secretary of ULFA, in a safe house in Bhutan. She boarded the flight for Bombay from Bagdogra in Siliguri district on 22 May, accompanied by Dr Brojen Gogoi, a manager with TTL." TTL had paid for her air tickets. The Assam Government adopted a tough stance against the Tea Companies, particularly the biggest of them all, TTL (with interest spread over 21 estates, employing 170 managers and 20,000 workers), following the allegations that they aided and funded militant outfits in the State. It was revealed that the tea companies were making regular payments to ULFA, NDFB, etc. How did it all start? The State CID disclosed that the whole thing resulted from the recovery by the Army of copies of the audited balance sheets of the NDFB for 1994-95 and 1995-96 in course of a CI operation in Darrang district in December 1996. The Army had lodged an FIR on 2 January 1997. The Mahanta Government never explained as to why it waited for full 9 months (till 2 October 1997) to hand over the case to CID. But critics argue it is easy to blame the tea companies but did they have a choice? ULFA had gained strength 1987-88 onwards, as did the violence unleashed by it. Killings in tea estates had started early 1989 for extortions and taxes. The brutal murder of Surendra Paul in June 1990 had completely unnerved the industry. The, Mahanta Government was unable or disinclined to protect its employees. ULFA and to an extent, BdSF were running parallel Governments in their respective areas of influence. So when ULFA summoned in June 1990 representatives of tea companies to a meeting at a garden outside Dibrugarh, leading lights of the industry responded. Under a compromise, they agreed to 'contribute' to ULFA's war chest. It should be no surprise that Assam's tea industry, with an annual turn-over of over Rs. 2,200 crore, had been prime target of militant groups like ULFA and NDFB. Some reports said the NDFB levied 'tax' at Rs. 2,500 per hectare. With 2,30,000 hectares under tea cultivation, their rakings-in must be staggering. And competing demands by different outfits must have squeezed these companies to unbearable limits. The faithfully-maintained balance sheets revealed that the fear of insurgents had penetrated deep in the official hierarchies. Various department officials manning the Srirampur check-post at Assam-West Bengal border were making regular monthly payments to the banned outfits since 1994, ranging from 3 to 5 lakhs. A list of 100 such officials was prepared who were thus funding the militants. The CID had arrested 6 such officials who had subsequently got bail from the High Court (1995-96). The payments made by various entities are given below:[22]

		In Lakhs
1. Bhergaon Tea Estate (TE)	—	25
2. Willamson Magor TE[23]	—	24
3. Nandan Nayar TE	—	10
4. Badlapur TE	—	9
5. Chandana TE	—	5
6. Ambika TE	—	3
7. Motor Vehicles Department	—	4.5
8. Forest Department	—	4
9. Sales Tax Department	—	3
10. Heavy Industries	—	3

Now follow two tables listing the persons from the tea companies abducted and killed since 1992 and 1989 respectively. Reading the lists, can one fault the Tatas for adopting a certain course in dealing with the insurgents to safeguard their interests and save the lives of their employees in tea estates? Some comments commended the Tatas, India's largest industrial group with a combined net turn-over of Rs. 31,000 crore, for adhering to a principle (of not paying cash) in dealing with the insurgents. Two Tata executives,[24] who had attended the Dibrugarh meeting, and as they disclosed later, had guns pressed against their heads as they were served a notice to pay a tax of Rs. 95 lakh. Tatas refused to yield (as did the Doom Dooma). Three years later, Bolin Bordoloi, TTL's Deputy GM, was kidnapped by the BdSF, who slapped a ransom demand for $ 15 million (Rs. 54 crore). The Company chose to stick to its policy of not paying up. This angered the then Chief Minister, Saikia, who was under pressure from Bordoloi's mother, widow of Assam's first Chief Minister, G.N. Bordoloi, to secure his son's release. It was during the Bordoloi incident that B. Gogoi, a doctor serving the Tatas since 1975, gained prominence as a negotiator. Known to ULFA C-in-C, Paresh Barua, who always referred to him as an elder brother, he established contacts with BdSF through ULFA channel. BdSF finally lowered the demand to Rs. 5 lakh, passed off as "the expenses incurred in maintaining Bordoloi in captivity". Even that demand was refused. But significantly, the TTL decided to set up a Rs. 7 crore, 65 + bed hospital at Chabua Tea Estate for the good of the common Bodos. This crisis helped creating a working relationship between the TTL and IB. The former are believed to have kept the IB informed on their contacts with the insurgents. The Tatas troubles were not over yet.

Tea Estate Persons Abducted Since 1992

Sl. No.	Name/Particulars	Date of Abduction	Date of Release
1.	Subir Ray, Manager Dimakshi TE (Williamson Magor)	18-3-92	7-4-92
2.	K.K. Mital, MD, Manabari TE	Dec. 92	No trace
3.	S.K. Barooah, MD, Bhergaon TE	23-3-94	30-3-94
4.	Bolin Bordoloi, Deputy GM, Tata Tea (He is younger son of Assam 1st Chief Minister, Gopinath Bordoloi)	8-4-93	11-3-94
5.	J. Choudhuri, MD, Fatemabad TE	12-6-93	13-7-93
6.	R.K. Gohain, Asst Manager		
7.	D.V. Singh Manager and A. Datta, Asst Manager, Nonoi TE (TTL)	17-10-95	Rescued Next day
8.	O.P. Siwal, Asst Manager, Tyroon TE	19-10-95	26-10-95
9.	N.N. Kilpadi, Manager, Saola TE	26-1-96	30-1-96
10.	D.K. Baruah, Bhergaon TE	17-9-96	3-4-97
11.	Arup Bhaduri, Owner, Sonapur TE	29-1-97	26-9-97
12.	P.K. Chowdhary, Menoka TE	29-7-97	8 Aug. 97

Tea Estate Persons Killed Since 1989

Sl.No.	Name/Particulars	Date
1.	D. Chowdhary, Asst Manager, Ledo TE	15-2-89
2.	Amal Baruah, Field Clerk, Corramore TE	5-8-89
3.	P.C. Scaria, TTL	13-3-90
4.	Surendra Paul, Director, Assam Frontier Tea	7-6-90
5.	Jawahar Lal Jain, Manager Dheria TE	19-10-90
6.	D.K. Choudhury, Manager, Romai TE	12-2-91
7.	C. Chakrabortty, Manager, Panbari TE	4-4-92
8.	Rameshwar Singh, GM, Assam Frontier Tea	15-2-94
9.	Koilee Baisnav, Worker, Attrekhat (case of Mistaken identity)	15-10-95
10.	Tejinder Kaur, wife of S. Singh, Manager, Nagrijuli TE	3-3-97

On 15 December 1995, an ULFA letter demanded a supply of 100 Walkie-talkies. The Tatas refused and informed the Home Secretary of Assam of the

ULFA demand in their letter dated 1 January 1996. Meanwhile, they continued talking to ULFA through B. Gogoi and B. Bordoloi. After repeated warnings, the last one on 17 June 1996, the Tatas evolved a Medical Aid Scheme under which the Company would pick up the tab for hospital costs of people recommended by ULFA. Gogoi was selected to sell the package to ULFA chief in Dhaka at a July 1997 meeting. Again, Gogoi it was who had accompanied Deka. Hence the ire of Assam officials against him. IGP of Assam (Int) was convinced: "Gogoi is an active member of ULFA." He was arrested on 24 September 1997. Another damning charge was that TTL had made payment in foreign currency to the banned outfit in London in 1997. Mahanta was firm on crackdown on tea companies. Had he found a whipping boy for his party's and his own soft corner for the ULFA? But when Assam Government was riding a high horse against the anti-national activities of tea companies, the Army engaged in CI operations in the State lodged an FIR at the Mangoldoi PS on 23 October 1997, suggesting links between a senior (Revenue) Minister/colleague of Mahanta and ULFA. "Law will take its own course" was all that Mahanta said by way of response and refused the Minister's offer to resign.

To cut it short, the story took a murky twist when the *Indian Express* 5 October 1997 published transcripts of "illegal tapes" of telephone conversations among Ratan Tata and some of his corporate friends. It had some indiscreet remarks. Some wrote the Tata's troubles with Assam Government were the result of intercorporate rivalries. Others thought Mahanta had some interest in intra-Bombay House battles? Some asked who was behind the tappings, and why did the Express indulged in 'despicable' act of publishing the tapes? In an open letter, Ram Jethmalani asserted that successive Governments had failed to rid Assam of curse of terrorism. Some even doubted his sincerity of purpose. Lt Gen KS Brar, Eastern Army Commander early 1990s, handed down a stinging criticism of political class, Mahanta and his successor and predecessor Saikia included: "...By early 1992, we had captured top ULFA leaders and literally broken the back of the movement.... The Government got the leaders released as the IB and RAW had contacted them for talks.... It was a trap and Saikia Government walked into it.... Against our advice, operation Rhino was called off.... They regrouped and resumed fighting. As for the AGP, while in opposition, it used ULFA against the Government, like the Akalis (in Punjab).... AGP was born of AASU agitation, as was ULFA. Problem arises when those who hobnob with terrorists come to power" (*Sunday Observer*, 21-9-1997).

Finally an ominous truth and potential reality which cannot be ignored by those, including the businessmen, who are confronting the insurgents. Today's terrorist could well be tomorrow's Chief Minister, a la Laldenga. Can

TIL be hanged even if they had given cash to the ULFA, which in any case they deny? At the end of it all, it is fair to say that in such complex situations, the truth cannot be monopoly of any particular player. Either or both sides could be acting too pious![25]

After the 1997-98 events, things remained comparatively quiet on the tea front. The ULFA seemed to have gone into lower gear. In fact by 2000, SF had started talking rather loudly about their success in having controlled, if not defanged, the monster. It all proved premature when ULFA struck with a vengeance at the non-Assamese Hindi-speaking people in the last quarter of that year. But the militants had opened a new front in Cachar area in 1999. From the speeches made at the 99th AGM of the Surma Valley Branch of the Indian Tea Association on 4 February 2000, it seemed the tea gardens in the south were facing the troubles its counterparts in Upper Assam had gone through in the earlier years of the 1990s. Several terrorist outfits had been active since 1999 or so killing, abducting, and extorting. The abduction and killing of Rajat Banerjee, a manager with Pathemara TE sent shock wave in the Barak Valley tea gardens. There were 9 cases of abduction of managerial staff in 1999 alone, including that of Banerjee. The depredations continued throughout 2000. The outfits involved are DHD, KNV and NSCN(I-M); in that order. Most of the affected TEs are near the Manipur-Cachar border, totally isolated; giving the desperados a free run over them. Early 2000, a new militant outfit of Manipuri and Bengali Muslims, calling itself 'People's United Liberation Front' (PULF), appeared on the scene.

Important CI Operations

To ensure cooperation between the SFs fighting the ultras as also between them and the Intelligencies agencies, a United Command was set up in 1997. Three operations are discussed here:

1. *Op Bajrang.* Launched on 28 November 1990, it yielded less than satisfactory results as the timing had been leaked to the militants. The troops mostly found just-abandoned ULFA camps.
2. *Op Rhino.* Launched on the night 14-15 September 1991, the Army was able to achieve a surprise this time, leading to a great success. In the bag: 431 hard-core cadres, including 46 top and middle rung leaders, besides the 299 supporters and trainees. Army destroyed 16 ULFA camps, recovering quantities of arms and ammunition and some important documents. The latter established ULFA's links with KIA, NSCN and even LTTE; and its sanctuaries in Bangladesh. The Army landed Rs. 5 crore in cash and 32 gold bars some of it certainly from the narco-trade, fruits of illegal transactions. The records showed purchase of weapons and equipment: automatics at Rs. 50,000 a piece, pistol at Rs. 40,000, and VHP radio set at Rs. 45,000.

- During Op Rhino, Army launched a civic action drive, to win back the hearts and mind of the people.
- An Inf Bde organised an Army Samaj Seva Mela at Naharkatiya, 80 km from Dibrugarh, in August 1994, providing medical facilities in various disciplines to the people at their doorsteps.

3. Joint operations, code named 'On Golden Bird', launched by the Indian and Burmese Armies (April-May 1995). As a result of major engagements in the Chimtuipui and Champhai sectors of Mizoram borders, 52 ULFA and PLA cadres were arrested and 45 killed.

Surrenders, ULFA vs SULFA and Peace Talks

The surrender by one-time ruthless and lawless insurgents makes for an interesting subject. And there are surrenders and surrenders. Reasons? Any of the following:

1. They are induced into it (surrender) for political or economic gains.
2. They find themselves unequal to facing continued hardships and privations of an uncertain life.
3. They have realised the futility of their battle against the State apparatus, and hopelessness of it all.
4. Some might have seen the wrongness of their cause at some stage. Horrendous blood-letting caused/witnessed by them could hasten the day.
5. Dissensions within leadership and consequent in-fighting within the ranks.

The phenomenon of surrender by ULFA ultras really started during the Saikia tenure (1991-96). ULFA had gained strength during Mahanta's first stint (1985-90); and became notorious for killings, abductions and extortions by the end of 1980s. Moreover, they had no reasons to surrender in this period; after all, they were half-brothers to AASU/AGP. Their excesses in the tea gardens had led to Mahanta's dismissal in November 1990 and Saikia knew it. On taking over in July 1991, he started working on it and shrewd as he was, he achieved early success, creating factions within ULFA. With Saikia announcing amnesty in March 1992, Sunil Nath, ULFA's Publicity Chief, led over 3,500 youth overground. Later, outfit's Dy C-in-C and Foreign Secretary also surfaced to swell the ranks of the surrendered, popularly, SULFA. It was a singular success, and there is no reason to deny credit for it to Saikia, even if the success turned sour subsequently. His critics castigated Saikia for splitting the ranks of ultras, as if it were a cardinal sin. It was a success story gone awry. The Army had broken its back (during Op Rhino) and ULFA was pushed to the wall. It was at this precise moment that Saikia got the ULFA cadres released from the Army custody and the latter rightly accused him of playing into ULFA's hands, acting credulously on its promises. How the perfidious ULFA was subsequently dealt with has been discussed above. Returning to surrenders, it must be acknowledged that at the time, ULFA had as yet not lost its sheen accruing from an ideologically-driven movement and made up its losses quickly through a vigorous recruiting drive and returned to its violent activities with a renewed vigour. But in spite of the setback, Saikia did not give up, garnering even larger successes in the following years, through liberal terms offered to the surrenderers: a cash incentive of Rs. 50,000 and a loan of Rs. 200,000 per head. By end-1995, 4,860 ultras[26] had surrendered, of which 4,015 had chosen to avail of the incentive scheme.

Following the loss of its cadres, ULFA rewrote its constitution to re-energise itself, laying greater stress on the civic aspects of its policies and operations to win over the common Assamese to its side. Its leadership reiterated in October 1993 its demand for an independent Assam outside the Union of India. After re-working its philosophy and rejuvenating its cadres, it started working from its sanctuaries in Bangladesh and understandably became even bolder in its depredations. It was in this period that ULFA created and reveled in its image of Robin Hood, robbing the rich to help the poor. The image, actions and ideology gained it popularity and a constituency for sometime. But it started losing people's respect and sympathy when its cadres launched on a course of mindless violence May 1996 onwards. It suffered further decline when a popular social activist like Sanjoy Ghosh was killed next year. Towards the end of 1990s, its image stood tattered for several reasons: (1) the Robin Hood was dead; (2) Youth's enthusiasm to join ULFA flagged; (3) lack of funds; (4) Lavish style of living enjoyed by its leaders, ensconced in 5-star hotels abroad, their children studying in expensive colleges in these countries, and people seeing the pictures of these leaders wallowing in luxury and affluence splashed on the pages of the dailies; and (5) the success of the CI operations by the SF. To repair the dented self-image and to restore the sagging morale of their cadres, the leadership decided on an expedient short-cut. Discarding their ideology and ideals, they launched vicious attacks on minorities to divide the Assamese (last quarter of 2000).

As for the SULFA (surrendered ULFA) cadres, they were an Intelligence asset in the initial stages, say during 1993-95 periods. Then came the time when they were a cause of serious concern to civil and military authorities, becoming a law unto themselves. They indulged in looting, extortion and even killing to settle personal scores, all made possible since they had been allowed to retain their arms for reasons of personal security. But the things became really dangerous with the ULFA-SULFA clashes, which were not unexpected, as SULFA were the main source of Intelligence on their former colleagues. The fratricidal clashes assumed horrendous dimensions in the late 1998, with 25 ultras from two sides fell to one another's bullets during the two months' period of the year, mid October-mid December. Some analysts thought the

Government/SF were encouraging these clashes, which had started when ULFA felled Tapan Datta in the heart of Guwahati on 10 August 1998. He was a prominent Dibrugarh businessman and a SULFA activist who had surrendered in 1998 and had been accused by ULFA of misappropriating huge amount of outfit's funds. The SULFA retaliated by killing relatives of top ULFA leaders. In August itself, Arbindo Rajkhowa's brother and five relatives[27] of ULFA's Publicity Chief were done in. Some of the prominent killings on either side during November-December 1998 are listed here:

- *13 November.* Prominent SULFA and ex-Assistant General Secretary of ULFA at Guwahati. Not only had he criticised ULFA leadership for betraying the original ideology, he had also led 195 cadres into surrender in early 1998.
- *21 November.* Key ULFA hitman, Alok Goswami, in Silchar.
- *3 December.* Prominent SULFA, Diganta Barua and his two bodyguards in Guwahati in a well-planned operation.
- *8 December.* An ULFA unit commander, in an encounter, near Guwahati.

Reworked Surrender Package

The extravagant surrender package did not prove a success; and moreover it was "misused and exploited by certain non-genuine persons, in connivance with some smart operators, including politicians and officials". In particular, bank loans advanced to the SULFA were hardly paid till 1998. The Tezpur Corps Commander suggested in August 1998 that "the first two batches, totaling 210 militants, who recently came over ground, must be given jobs in the Central Security Forces as promised".[28] On 2 April 1999, Union Home Secretary B.P. Singh announced the new rehabilitation package, that included cash incentives[29] for militants surrendering with weapons. It was to start with the two batches of 400 and 150 militants "who had surrendered recently".

Cash Incentives for Different Weapons

1.	Rocket Launcher	Rs. 25,000
2.	Rifle AK-47	Rs. 15,000
3.	Pistol/Revolver/Remote control device	Rs. 3,000
4.	Wireless sets (short to medium range)	Rs. 1,000 to Rs. 5,000
5.	Explosive (Each Kg)	Rs. 1,000
6.	Rocket	Rs. 1,000
7.	Grenade	Rs. 500

Cease-fire and Hopes

SULFA did create problems at times, but "it seemed to be the only hope for the nation to do business with the still powerful ULFA", went one line of thinking. The cease-fire observed by ULFA during the festive season of Bihu in April 1999 was in response to an appeal made by the SULFA leaders led by Sunil Nath, ex-Director Publicity, who had surrendered in March 1992. It turned out to be the first positive sign of peace in the bloodstained saga of a long-running militancy in Assam. More heartening was the news that ULFA was in touch with the Centre. GOC4 Corps at Tezpur, Lt Gen DB Shaketkar, told the press at Guwahati that "a top ULFA functionary had contacted him on 14 April,.... And if they take one step for peace, Army would take four."[30] Besides suspending its operations, Army also sent gifts to the kin of some top ULFA leaders.[31] Army also announced on 16 April that as a goodwill gesture, the troops had been ordered to allow safe passage to the ULFA militants who came unarmed to meet their kin during the Rangoli Bihu. Gen Sinha, Assam Governor also promised a safe passage during the Bihu and Diwali (7 November 1999). Mahanta did one better announcing a "millennium offer to the ULFA cadres", allowing them to meet their families between 21-31 December 1999.[32] Certain optimism was in the air.

ULFA leaders were not keen to sit with Mahanta, who asked for tripartite talks; they wanted to talk to the Centre only. "They opened a line of communication with New Delhi in June 1999." It was a significant first! Later, the Government officials reportedly met ULFA leaders outside India for informal talks; "Arbindo Rajkhowa in London, and Paresh Barua in Karachi were in direct contact with Home Ministry officials." Having earlier spurned all such offers of talks, why did ULFA had a change of mind in mid-1999? Likely reasons: (1) People were losing respect for it. ULFA cadre Amit Bhuyan was lynched by villagers of Kukrachara in Sibsagar district when he came to extort money on 7 July 1999 and threatened to blow up the locality if his demand was not met. They were really sick of "our boys"; (2) A spate of armed surrenders in the recent months, particularly since mid-1998 possibly unnerved the leadership, compelling it to clutch at the BJP's offer; (3) "ULFA's close liaison with the ISI and its support for Pakistan during the Kargil War made it extremely unpopular."[33] (4) It was under tremendous pressure from public, Army and Government; and (5) Bangladesh and Bhutan had possibly taken action against ULFA cadres who were in camps and hide-outs on their soil.

Spate of Surrenders

There was certain disillusionment discernible among the lower ranks, as indicated by certain events. The surrender by 22 activists, some with AK-47s, and led by Sgt Maj Khirod Gogoi in August 1999 at Joysagar in Sibsagar district was significant. Gogoi said they returned to the mainstream, realizing that the "attainment of sovereign Assam was impossible.[34] ULFA leader Akash Bora, in his letter of 28-7-1999, told the SP Sibsagar: "Leaders are only interested in mortgaging the state to the ISI and Pakistan.... They lived luxurious lives while the cadres were forced to lead a life of hardship."[35] But it is obvious that no forward movement was discernible till the end of 1999, even though some initial contacts were made during the year and some informal talks about the talks were held. Two relevant stories from a respected daily are excerpted below to indicate the realities of life at that stage.

The Hindu, 11 September 1999

> "Pressure is mounting on ULFA leaders from their armed ranks to start a dialogue. In Nalbari, many ULFA extremists are planning to surrender. Apparently to prevent this, some middle-rung activists were summarily executed by the outfit a few days ago. Gunning down of a prominent AGP leader yesterday at Barama in Nalbari district is believed to be a warning to the Party not to encourage surrenders."

The Hindu, 25 March 2000

> "18 ULFA cadres have deserted the outfit, come over ground, and are seeking 'to live freely'. The process of disillusionment with the ULFA started long ago, but the killing of the PWD Minister, Nagen Sharma, at Nalbari on 27 February, was the breaking point."

Before examining the talks front during 2000, a look at the surrenders front (1998-2000) should be useful.

1998

1. *24 July.* 51 at Thakurbari
2. *14 August.* 133 at Mariani.
3. *31 December.* 36 at Dispur.

1999

1. *21 January.* 159 at Tamulpur in Nalbari district.
2. *25 May.* 102 at Nagaon.
3. *16 August.* 178 in total, at nine different locations.

2000

1. March. "A spate of surrenders in the recent weeks has hit the outlawed ULFA", reported *Indian Express* of 28-3-2000. The General Council was alarmed enough to convene its meeting after a gap of 3 years to discuss the issue at its Bhutan hide-out on 4-5 April. These leaders had converged on the hide-out to take part in the Foundation Day Celebrations on 7 April. On 27 March, a group of 13 senior functionaries of ULFA, belonging to Nalbari district announced their decision to shun violence. They included Mintu Dutta alias Nagon

Haloi, Chief Political Advisor (Commissar) of ULFA's units in Lower Assam Zone, and Bikash Dutta, Organising Secretary in the same zone. The former, with ULFA for over 14 years, accused the leadership of straying from its ideology.

14 senior cadres at the zonal and Anchalik levels had surrendered during first two weeks of March. The total figure for the month rose to about 52, including Abinash Bordoloi, Chief of the Armed Wing for the three Lower Assam districts of Nalbari, Dhubri and Kamarupa.

2. 532 surrenders on 4 April. They laid down their arms before Gen Sinha at Rang Ghar, the very venue where ULFA was born 21 years ago, on 7 April 1979.

It was the largest surrender on any one day. The Governor assured them that the inadequacies in the Rehabilitation Package would be removed. Chief Minister Mahanta asked the ULFA and NDFB to come forward for talks, as the NSCN(I-M) was already talking to the Government. The leader, Lt Phukan charged that Paresh Barua was dictatorial, and using ULFA to serve his own interest. The breakdown of 532 ultras who surrendered on 4 April: ULFA-436, KNV-77 and NDFB-19.

3. 288 surrendered before Chief Minister Mahanta at Guwahati on 14 August. It was the 15th such ceremony in the State since the Unified Command came into being mid-1997. Their leader was ULFA Capt Lohit Deuri, who had served as General Staff Officer at ULFA's GHQ in Bhutan. He had been with the police for a while, helping them to track down ULFA activists. Joining ULFA in 1985, he had set up the first ULFA camp in Bhutan in 1992. The 288 had been under police protection for a long time, were getting monthly stipends, and had undergone training in different crafts under the Centre's Rehabilitation Scheme. This figure of 288 surrenders on 14 August brought the total number of surrenders since April 1998 to 1994.[36] Mahanta told the surrenderees that State Government had earmarked 300,000 bighas of land for distribution among them.[37] The break-down of the 288 surrenderees: ULFA-242, UPDS-25, RNSF-12, NDFB-5, DHD-2, and MULTA-2.

4. How vastly different was the Independence Day eve of the year 2000, compared to the one of the year before! In 1999, ULFA had unleashed an orgy of violence, killing many innocents, blowing up several rail and road bridges, dynamiting sections of railway tracks, bombing industrial plants and oil refineries, etc.

ULFA Surrenders: Official Figures

Yearly Surrender of ULFA Cadres

Sl.No.	Year	Number
1.	1998	227
2.	1999	970[38]
3.	2,000 (Till October)	1186[39]

1998-2000: ULFA at the Cross-roads

Beginning 1979, by end-2000, ULFA seemed to have reached at a certain cross-roads in its quest. It must have had its highs, troughs and lows during this journey. Its first test came in November 1990 during Op Bajrang but it escaped with minor losses since it was able to get advanced information of it. But was not so lucky during Op Rhino, launched in September 1991, suffering grievous losses consequently. But the crafty leadership earned a reprieve when Saikia Government, in power since mid-1991, 'forced' or 'persuaded' Army to suspend operations against it on a mere "assurance that it would abide by the Indian Constitution and abjure violence". But it then took advantage of the situation, regrouped and rethought its strategy, and then cocked a snook at Government of India. In May 1992, Chairman Rajkhowa announced that "ULFA never committed itself to talks on India's terms". By end of the year, it was ready for the fight. But then it was defeated not by the might of Army, but by "the guile and shrewdness of Assam's Chanakya (Saikia)"'. In 1993, he had lured close to 5000 ULFA cadres, perhaps majority of its strength at that point in time, into surrendering to join the mainstream. The main reason for that singular success might have been the fact that large part of the cadre then was of fresh recruits enlisted during the suspension of Op Rhino in 1992. This time again, ULFA was able to make up its losses quickly; and relaunched on its violence trajectory. Subsequently, it grew in size and strength, with the hardline leadership expanding its base of operations from Upper Burma to Bangladesh, and still later to Bhutan.

This accretion to ULFA's strength made it most feared outfit in the Region. Through skilful negotiations, it strengthened its ties with other such outfits in the North-East. Expectedly, at a certain stage, it struck an equation with the ISI, becoming a bigger headache for India. Some analysts assert it is totally under the thumb of the ISI and somewhere along the way, it has lost its moorings in the ideology of ultra nationalism. Once the ISI started training its cadres on the Bangladesh soil, peace eluded the Region. With its violent movement, ULFA cannot continue to remain popular and retain people's sympathy for ever. From mid-1990s, it seemed to be indulging in mindless violence. Of late, Bhutan and Bangladesh have taken initiatives to flush out its cadres from their soil and Unified Command has been closing in on ULFA; and consequently, it has been on the downslide. In the 1997-98 period, it had been fast losing people's support as the sole aim of its mindless violence seemed to be killing of people. If the killing of Sanjoy Ghose cost it the sympathy of socially-conscious common man, the killing of Assam's PWD Minister Nagen lost it the support and understanding of the intelligentsia and politically conscious class. In this situation something had to give in. It came in the shape of spate of surrenders, particularly April 1998 onwards. Consequently, by August 2000, with large scale surrenders and desertions, ULFA was certainly standing at the cross-roads. In the past two years or so, a number of senior posts at zonal and Anchalik levels had fallen vacant. The Army's CI Operations too had taken their toll. It was a frustrating period for the leadership. It was a discomfiting situation to be in. It must stem the rot or go under. The latter option does not come easy to the coarsened outfits like the ULFA. Having lain low for about two years, or so the SF thought, barring some attention-grabbing, high-profile killings, it decided to resort to something drastic to boost the sagging morale of its cadres, as also to announce the arrival of a reoriented ULFA. Forsaking the moral high ground claimed on the strength of its ideology, the desperate leadership unleashed the vicious killings of the non-Assamese Hindi-speaking people, to divide the society on communal lines and then to regain the support of the ethnic Assamese. This was the re-oriented ULFA, sans ideology, sans nationalistic philosophy! The October-December 2000 orgy of violence was meant to convey a message to the Government: ULFA was well and alive, and back in business. This was the route chosen for immediate gains and immediate attention for itself. The other way led to the peace talks. Having taken some halting steps in this direction in 1999, and registered its presence by end-2000, will it now seriously smoke the peace-pipe?

So, the question really is: will they come to sup? Gen Sinha and Mahanta, and now Gogoi (2001-) have been trying to create situation conducive for talks. The Government had offered safe passage to the ULFA cadres wanting to meet their kin, particularly during the Bihu festivities in 1999 and 2000. Their cold response notwithstanding, Mahanta repeated the good gesture during the period 21 December 2000-17 January 2001, as a millennium offer. Mahanta told Prime Minister Vajpayee during his 23 January Shillong visit that "the offer was availed by many militants". Similar offers were made by the two during 1999.

A back grounder to the 1999 offer is of interest. Gen Sinha flew into Lakuma, a small village in oil-rich eastern District of Sibsagar in October 1999 to call on the ailing Umakanta Rajkhowa, a veteran freedom fighter, recipient of the Tamrapatra and father of ULFA Chairman Arbindo Rajkhowa. It was after this visit that he announced the safe passage offer, and Mahanta followed suit. ULFA had rejected both. In spite of the October-December 2000 communally divisive carnage, Gen Sinha repeated the offer of a free passage on 9 December 2000 at Guwahati. "Gen Sinha feels it-is right moment for talks". He said on 23 January 2000 at Shillong that the middle and lower level cadres were in favour of talks but "the top levels are yet to respond. On 16 July, reverting to the theme, he said: "There was attitudinal change among the people, as they are now opposing the militancy." He claimed that "there has been marked improvement in security scenario; people are taking part in large numbers in the peace rallies and processions". On the economic front, Assam achieved foodgrains sufficiency for the first time in 2000. The Army, through the Unified Command experiment, has done its bit to chastise ULFA. In the three years (mid-1997-2000) 700 ultras were killed, over one crore rupees seized, and 2,000 weapons recovered. Now what was ULFA's response to this peace overtures? ULFA's three pre-conditions for the talks are well-known and oft-repeated:

1. Talks should be held in a foreign country.
2. They should be held under the UN supervision.
3. They should focus on sovereignty only.

In November 1999, Paresh Barua called up newspaper offices in Guwahati, and voiced his demand for a UN-supervised plebiscite in Assam on the question of sovereignty, outrightly dismissed by the Government as preposterous. The timing of demand was ill-considered, coming as it did within a month of the Lok Sabha poll (September-October 1999) in which 70 per cent of Assam's 1.4 crore voters had exercised their franchise in defiance of ULFA's call for its boycott. This was Assamese way of expressing distaste and disapproval of ULFA's support for Pakistan during the Kargil War earlier in the year. Thus ended 1999 and the year 2000 hardly saw any movement on the talks front. The next year began with some interesting stories. In his interview to a local daily in January 2001, ULFA C-in-C said if New Delhi's talks with NSCN(I-M) succeeded, he too would fall in line. He further mouthed standard vocabulary: "Government of India is only interested in bringing peace to Assam and not in solving real problems of its people.... We too want solution but not the one dictated by the Government.... The discussions must have some 'scientific basis', whenever they are held."[40] In the second interview to another local daily (cited by *Indian Express,* 15-1-2001), ULFA dropped first two of the three demands listed above and it was ready to discuss the issue of sovereignty alone. Barua disclosed "this stand has been conveyed directly to the PMO in December 2000". The Centre's pre-condition that ULFA must give up violence before the talks start was not acceptable to Barua. On 16 January 2001, at Guwahati, G.K. Pillai, JS, NE, in MHA, offered unconditional talks to ULFA.[41] So did Home Minister Advani at a public meeting at Nagaon on 5 February 2001, but asked the "banned outfit to lay down arms".

ULFA Leadership

The contrast between the living standards of the leaders and the led, even in Bhutan has been commented upon. The cadres in jungle camps of Samdrup Jongkhar, Deothang, etc. and hide-outs along the Manas Forest Reserve "are facing acute shortage of food and medicine, often leading to low morale. But their leaders are staying in classy hotels and well-appointed guest house in Thimpu and Phuntshoeling, with foreign cars and mobile telephones.

Recent mindless violence (1998-2000) inflicted on the people reportedly caused a certain dissent among the top leaders. Paresh Barua, the C-in-C, is leading the hardliners, and is often dubbed a 'dictator'. He is supposedly holding out on the issue of talks with the Government. The recent surrenderees (of 1998, 1999 vintage) have also commented on the wallowing-in-luxury lifestyle of the leaders, which has surely disillusioned the Assamese intelligentsia. And to imagine that four or five top leaders of today were among the youthful, starry-eyed, intellectual group which had met in April 1979 at the 300-year old pavilion of the Ahom Royals, to speak about establishing a "sovereign, socialist Republic of Assam". The details of leadership as known is given here.

What was the identity of members who joined it initially? Several of the founding members of ULFA belonged to the Asom Jatiyatabadi) Yuva Chhatra Parishad (AJYCP), having close links with AASU as well The ULFA leaders actively participated in the anti-foreigners agitation, and the first Chairman of the outfit, Bhadreswar Gohain, was later elected Dy Speaker of Assam Assembly as the AGP nominee.

The AJYCPP roots of ULFA should tell their own story. Formed in March 1978, it quickly made its mark in Assam's public life because of its good organisational network and dedicated workers.

Essentially a secessionist outfit, it termed Indian Constitution as a tool for colonial exploitation of Assam and demanded right to self-determination. All this obviously had informed the thinking and philosophy of the ULFA leadership, whose profile follows.

High Command

1. Arbindo Rajkhowa (Real name, Rajiv Konwar)—Chairman.
2. Paresh Barua (Barua and Chetia hail from the same village)—C-in-C.
3. Anup Chetia alias Golup Barua (In Dhaka Jail since December 1997)—Secretary General.

4. Manoj Hazarika—Vice Chairman (Till 1994).
5. Pradip Gogoi (in Jail since April 1998)—Vice Chairman.
6. Raju Baruah, Dy C-in-C.
7. Sashadhar Choudhury—Foreign Secretary.
8. Raju Baruah alias Hitesh Kalita—Deputy Commander-in-Chief.
9. C. Hazarika—Finance Secretary.

Senior Officers

1. Mithinga Daimary—Publicity Secretary (Relieved of his charge in mid-2000. Paresh Barua personally handling the media.)
2. Ashanta Baghphukan—Organising Secretary.

   (He was ULFA's Senior-most leader in Bhutan who rose to become Organising Secretary in 1999. He took over the post after the arrest of Pradeep Gogoi.)
3. Pranati Deka (in jail since September 1997)—Cultural Secretary.
4. Babul Sarma—Chief Medical Officer, ULFA units in Bhutan.

Middle Level Officers

1. Dhrishti Rajkhowa—Appointment unknown.
2. Tapan Barua—Commander, ULFA's 28th Bn.
3. Capt Lohit Deuri—General Staff Officer, GHQ, ULFA, Bhutan (Surrendered).

It seems equations among the top leaders keep changing. The Chairman, C-in-C and Foreign Secretary decide on all important issues. The trio, known as the Group of Three, constitute the Central Core of ULFA leadership. Rajkhowa is believed to be a moderate, with his C-in-C being a hardliner, who had ordered attacks on the non-Assamese Hindi-speaking people in October 2000. The fourth important man Ashanta Bagh Phukan, is considered a theoretician. Raju Baruah, who is the Operational Commander, issues orders to the lower ranks for specific "acts".

So three of its top leaders are in jail. Pradeep Gogoi, Vice-Chairman, was arrested on 8 April 1998 at Calcutta, third important leader of ULFA to be held in the recent past. Its Cultural Secretary, Pranati Deka, was arrested in Bombay in September 1997. Her arrest gave rise to the Tata Tea-Assam Government controversy. She is wife of C. Hazarika, ULFA's Finance Secretary. Its Secretary General Anup Chetia alias Golup Barua, was arrested in Calcutta on 21 December 1997. Chetia's arrest followed a red corner notice issued by Interpol. Exact circumstances leading to the arrest of Gogoi are still shrouded in mystery. Was it a surrender dramatised as an arrest?

Gogoi, known to be in favour of talks for quite sometime now, "reportedly told his interrogators that ULFA was at the moment not interested in escalating violence. Occasional acts of violence committed by ULFA were only to keep up the morale of its cadres. ULFA leaders arrested earlier told their interrogators that C-in-C Paresh Barua was dictatorial and was trying to take over the entire organisations. Some reports suggested a rift within the outfit between the Ahoms and non-Ahoms. The reported move by Barua, an Ahom, to oust Chairman Rajkhowa, a non-Ahom, acquires credibility in this context.

Gogoi, who is in-charge of recruitment of cadres and their training in Bhutan camps told the police that for the past few months he was thinking of severing his ties with the outfit. He also admitted that the General Secretary of the Association of Voluntary Agencies for Rural Development (AVARD), Sanjoy Ghose, who was abducted by ULFA fron Majuli on 4 July 1997, was killed in captivity.

Foreign Hand

The subject of some neighbours muddying the waters of Indian insurgency has been discussed in some detail in Chapter 2. Here only a few selective facts will be mentioned in brief.

Pakistan, India and Bangladesh have been uneasy neighbours. If Kashmir issue has bedeviled relations between the former two, the in-migrants influx has done the same for Indo-Bangladesh relations. All three carry the load of problems left over by the Partition. Indian rebels have traditionally been given shelter and succour by these two neighbours, who in turn suspect India to be doing the same for their rebels. Given the realities, it is obvious that each country maintains hyper-active Intelligence presence in the other two. But as some would say, history, memory and ideology, however powerful their motivation, by themselves do not constitute facts. Therefore Indians assert that their claims about the involvement of these two nations and their Intelligence agencies, are based upon interrogation reports of captured insurgents and on documents recovered from them as well as during the raids on their camps.

It is certain that some ULFA militants had crossed over into Bangladesh by end-1988. The link and liaison work was possibly mediated initially by the PLA militants whose own links with Bangladesh go back decades.[42] The Dhaka authorities were certainly not unaware of the goings-on. The links with ISI were possibly forged almost immediately after securing access to Bangladesh. A senior ULFA leader claimed credit early 1992[43] for mediating links with the ISI[44]! Indian Intelligence is fairly clear on the broad profile of the movement of scores of ULFA cadres from small towns and villages of Brahmaputra Valley to somewhat similar environs of camps in the rural Sylhet; and then finally to a totally different world of the ISI in Pakistan, and in some cases also to Mujahideen camps in Peshawar and to some Afghan areas under Mujahideen control. Thence, the methods employed to test and break-in the new recruits were exactly the ones laid down in any textbook on classical terrorism and insurgency. A recruit was received by an Intelligence agent, lodged in a Dhaka safe house, given a Muslim name, and after confirming his credentials and suitability for the tough and risky job, found a local job. The initial training also included familiarisation with Islamic rituals and learning of Bengali, Assamese, or Urdu, as demanded by his future employment. A number of them are employed in India's North-East, and the brighter ones and fluent in Urdu are flown to Pakistani.

The first batch of 10 ULFA ultras was taken to Pakistan mid-1991. Subsequently, 5-6 batches of 10 to 15 militants each, were sent annually. By 1996-97, estimated 310 had been trained by the ISI. But subsequently, there were some problems, mainly "because it was difficult for anyone to manipulate ULFA", even if initially, it allowed itself to be used by some foreign agencies.

A photograph in *Sunday Observer* of 22-9-1991 hardly left any doubt about ULFA-Bangladesh linkages showing as it did the top ULFA leaders (Chairman, his Deputy, Manoj Hazarika, and Partha Bora) in a building adjacent to the Parliament in Dhaka. (Sheikh Hasina coming to power later broke the idyll but temporarily.) Paresh Barua possessed a Bangladeshi passport, as did many others who stayed in that country. Rajkhowa and Anup Chetia cultivated links with Islamic fundamentalists in Bangladesh. ULFA set up several profitable companies in Dhaka (covering media consultancies, soft drinks, manufacturing etc.), enabling them to make a lot money for luxurious living as also for sustaining their outfit. When Chetia was arrested on 21 December 1997, he had on him a state-of-art satellite telephone, three passports under different names, and large amounts in foreign currency: $ 65,000, Rs. 28,500 (Indian), 32,500 (Bhutanese) and 2,390 (Pakistani).

ULFA had started income-generating projects in Dhaka (grocery shops, drug stores, etc.), Mymensingh (Poultry farms) and Narsangdi. Chetia was in-charge, as CEO, ULFA Enterprises, Bangladesh before his arrest on 27 December 1997 by Hasina Government. The arms and ammunition (procured from Thailand and Myanmar) purchased with money thus earned was cached in several madrasas and mosques in Sylhet and Cox Bazar areas for subsequent use in India for its anti-India movement.

Its Dhaka connection forced ULFA to forget the very *raison d'etre* of its movement. Having built it up all on an anti-immigrants plank, it changed course mid-way when its leaders sought sanctuary in Bangladesh, and put all its money in Dhaka banks. Obviously, they could not keep all their cash in Bangladesh and still continue to inveigh against it and its nationals for whatever reasons. They were losing their autonomy. Final betrayal came when

ULFA allowed ISI agents to operate its fortnightly magazine Freedom on website. Freedom's 15 June 1999 editorial strongly supported the intrusion of Pak troops and Afghan Mujahideen into Kargil hills. Obviously, ISI was editing Freedom from within Pakistan. "ULFA had sold itself to Pakistan.... I cannot accept its complete surrender to the ISI", was the comment of a disillusioned ULFA supporter on 8 November 1999. He, a former rebel, further added: "...A camp in Bhutan was out of bounds for cadres from other camps. The ISI agents were imparting training to brainwash the specially-selected activists there. Only Rajkhowa, Paresh Barua, Raju Baruah and Munna Mishra could visit that camp." Some instances of the ULFA-ISI-Bangladesh-Pak nexus are cited here:

1. "Pakistan's ISI has now spread its tentacles to Nepal to carry out its anti-India activities in North-East" (Home Minister Inder Jit Gupta in Lok Sabha on 14 May 1997). So ISI had started operating from most of the countries in India's neighbourhood. ULFA, of course, continued issuing its proforma denials.
2. ULFA turned a blind eye to infiltration by Jamaat in the Sylhet-Cachar border areas.
3. "State Ministers and bureaucrats are paying taxes to ULFA which has stashed away Rs. 500 crore abroad" (Tezpur Corps Commander, Lt Gen RK Sawhney, March 1997).
4. "ULFA, which has shifted base from Bangladesh to Bhutan, paid Rs. 50,000 per head for training its cadres in Myanmar" (SULFA leader to Nagaon Police in May 1997).
5. Before Kargil conflict, a 80-100 strong batch was sent to Afghanistan via Bangladesh, thence by air to Karachi on Bangladeshi passports, and finally driven to camps in Afghanistan, for training in hilly terrain. ISI charged substantial sums for this training from ULFA, possibly over a crore. ULFA was also warned that any anti-Pak stance could rupture this link. That should explain ULFA pro-Pak stance during Kargil War, which lost much of public support for ULFA. ULFA even asked Indian Army not to fight the "freedom fighters in Kashmir" (A SULFA leader).
6. "I first went to Pakistan from Bangladesh in September 1990...and later to Afghanistan. ISI offered us money to blow up refinery and rail tracks.... While in Afghanistan, I was getting copies of reports published in Guwahati that very day. There are a large number of agents working for the Pak and Bangladeshi Intelligence, not their nationals but Assamese people who regularly transmit information to these countries from Assam...when we were translating our

> Constitution from Assamese into English, the ISI people said, Give us the Assamese version. We have people who can translate the document'. ...It was all so sad" (An ex-ULFA militant who had made initial contact with the ISI).

Bangladesh was not the first country ULFA established contacts with; that distinction belongs to Burma. It contacted KIA initially in 1986, as also NSCN. The KIA charged heavily for training the ULFA cadres, which initiated it into narco-trade network. It was the time Burma was engaged in CI operations against its own insurgent outfits, numbering over half a dozen. When KIA camps got raided, ULFA came under pressure to shift base. It was then, around 1989, that ULFA contacted ISI and Afghan Mujahideen. It was still later that ULFA made contacts with Field Intelligence of Bangladesh, and less successfully with the LTTE. Later it deepened its cooperation with the LTTE and at a certain stage became recipient of arms from the LTTE's clandestine narco-arms network, though the Naga and Meitei rebels remained its major beneficiaries. When NSCN was training ULFA cadres in its Burmese Naga Hills bases, Indian and Burmese Armies launched a joint operation, code named Golden Bird in 1995, which nearly ended ULFA presence in Burma.

But there is an interesting off-shoot to the active phase of the ULFA-Burmese relations. From their Burmese bases, ULFA had, through the good officers of NSCN(I-M), established a number of safe houses and liaison offices in Thailand, essentially for arms procurement. Senior ULFA leaders frequented Changmai (hottest arms market for illegal arms trade then, and even today) to augment their arsenal from the Khmer Rouge elements operating on the Ranong Coast and Bangkok for rest in the 5-star resorts. They also developed links with ex-drug baron Khun Sa's disbanded Mong Tai Army, both for arms and for a narcotics conduit.

As a result of joint operations and improved economic relations with Myanmar since 2000 (India helped in construction of Tamu-Kalewa-Kalemyo Road), ULFA came under pressure to move out. Hasina Government, coming to power in 1997, put pressure on ULFA to wind up its camps and as a first effective step, it froze its bank accounts. In the latter half of her tenure, even the Hasina Government went soft on ULFA due to the domestic politics. New Delhi kept pressure on Begum Zia also against ULFA. Some reports suggested ULFA shifted its Operations and General Headquarters to the base in thick jungles of Bhutan's border areas around mid-1995. Others say it was by end-1997. But Chairman and C-in-C continued staying in Dhaka, visiting Bhutan periodically; e.g., all senior leaders converged to Bhutanese camps for Raising Day Celebrations in April 2000. From Dhaka, Paresh Barua used to visit Bangkok frequently, but discontinued these peregrinations after the arrest of the NSCN(I-M) leader Muivah in Bangkok. Later reports talk of nearly all leaders shifting to their Bhutan camps. "Bhutan Government have talked to the ULFA leadership to move out, as a result of the Indian insistence, but so far majority of ULFA cadres are ensconced in their Bhutanese sanctuaries". No doubt Thimpu is putting pressure on ULFA and Bodo outfits to vacate their soil. But this is easier said than done. Some observers feel the Royal Bhutanese Army does not have the fire power and the logistics to force the ULFA and NDFB out of their bases in Bhutan. It did not seem keen to seek help from India. It is also possibly true that Thimpu has some genuine difficulties. The economy of many villages in Southern Bhutan revolve around the militant camps at places like Kalikhola and Noglang. Moreover, the ULFA cadres have been good guests, under instruction never to be high-handed towards the locals. Moreover, ULFA has nowhere to go. It seems inevitable that ULFA-Bhutan problem will have to await the solution of ULFA-India problem!

All this notwithstanding, Bhutanese Army finally acted in December 2003 and smashed all the ULFA (NDFB and KLO) camps in three weeks.

It is to be noted that ULFA was not content in ingratiating itself with the immediate neighbours of India. Casting its net far and wide, ULFA wrote to the Secretary General of the UNO, in an effort to influence the international audience. In its letter dated 26 October 1990, it urged him to declare Assam a colony of India (Phanjaubam Tarapot, Insurgency Movement in North-East India, 1993, p. 12.

It is Ethnic Cleansing (October-December 2000)

ULFA giving up its ideological plank and resorting to ruthless killings of non-Assamese Hindi-speaking people have been mentioned earlier. Without giving details of individual incidents, their date-wise victims are given here:

October 2000

22(15), 27(10), 27(3, by NDFB), 31(4)

November 2000

8(8, by NDFB), 17(7), 24(8), 25(4), 26(8), 28(3), 30(19), 30(3, by UPDS).

December 2000

7(28), 28(8, by UPDS),

By September 2000, the situation in violence-ridden Assam had appreciably changed for the better. The SULFA were claiming that three years of CI operations under the Unified Command (set up, mid-1997) had broken the back of ULFA. After all, 1500 of its cadres had surrendered since 1998 (*The Hindu*, 24-11-2000). It was in this circumstance that a re-oriented if not re-vamped ULFA resorted to attention-grabbing killings for short-term gains. The first casualty was DGP, Assam, P.V. Sumant, given marching orders. Harekrishna Deka replaced him.

The most worrying aspect of October 2000 killings was that it was for the first time that ULFA had resorted to targeting unarmed civilians of a particular community. It had followed in the foot-steps of the Kashmiri terrorists who had cleansed the valley of the Kashmir! Pandits. This was the start of the ethnic cleansing in Assam.

It is to be noted that ethnic killings were started in Assam (Karbi-Anglong district) by the UPDS and DHD militants' six months before the ULFA resorted to it in October 2000. In April 2000 in two incidents, UPDS and DHD had killed 11 timber dealers of Bihari origin and 11 Nepali-speaking people on the 9th and 19th respectively. The Hindi-speakers continued to be targeted periodically in the two Hill districts of Assam till September 2000 when unidentified gunmen killed relatives of two senior UPDS militants. "The killings stopped immediately", wrote the Press. But the very next month, ULFA picked up where the UPDS had left, mowing down 15 Biharis in two incidents on 22 October 2000. That is how ULFA launched on a new course. Here are some press comments of the period:

1. The Sadiya massacre, where 28 non-Assamese were killed on 7 December was 8th such incident since 22 October, taking the toll beyond the 100 mark in less than two months. The victims have been Biharis, Marwaris, Nepalis, and Bengalis (*Hindustan Times,* 9-12-2000).
2. Assam never had it so bad, not since 1500 Muslims were massacred at Nellie at the height of Assam Agitation in 1983. In less than two months since 22 October this year, 'a reoriented' ULFA killed over 105 non-Assamese. Most of them were Biharis, a few Marwaris, Nepalis, Oriyas and Bengalis (*Hindustan Times,* 12-12-2000).
3. At least 80 people were killed in seven weeks between 21 October and 7 December 2000 (*The Hindu,* 15-12-2000).
4. Nearly 150 people belonging to non-Assamese and minority communities have become victims of such massacres in Assam this year (*Hindustan Times,* 30-12-2000).

Predictably, the tremors of the killings reached as far away as Rajasthan. In Bihar, some Assamese passengers were roughed up in the trains going to Assam from Delhi. Some Assamese youths pasted notices on shops owned by Biharis and Marwaris, asking them to quit Assam. If the situation had gone out of hands on this front, it would have been what ULFA desired. Luckily, it did not go that far.

A little known outfit, Assam Tiger Force (ATF), claiming to have been raised in January 2000, owned responsibility for these killings. In a statement issued on 30 October 2000, it not only made the claim but also added further:

"All non-Assamese must leave the State. We agree with ULFA's struggle for Assam's sovereignty, but not with the view of AASU and AGP that only Bangladeshis be expelled from Assam.... The attacks against Hindi-speaking people in Dibrugarh and Tinsukia districts, followed by one in the Nalbari were only first acts of violence...." The police said the ATF was a non-existent, fictitious outfit. K. Sarmah, DIG Police, said two of the 159 ULFA militants who surrendered at Dispur on 6 December 2000 (Romen Nath and Suresh Bora) had admitted that they had been sent to Assam from an ULFA camp in Bhutan to execute these communal killings

Various theories were doing the rounds about the real culprits behind these killings. A "Senior Minister" said he had heard it suggested that a Central Intelligence Agency was behind it all, to get the Governor's rule imposed in Assam. The AGP and Congress blamed each other, for being "allies" of ULFA. Mahanta said the Congress was helping and being helped by ULFA to destabilise his Government, aimed at winning the Assembly elections barely 6 months away (these were due in May 2001). Mahanta claimed to have documentary proof, and wanted Congress barred from contesting the elections. BJP blamed both these parties. Shortly after his surrender (He was one among 159 who surrendered at Dispur on 6 December 2000), Romen Nath (mentioned above) said he and two other ULFA leaders Drishtri Rajkhowa and Raju Baruah had been asked by Paresh Baruah about three months earlier in a Bhutan hide-out to make plans for these killings (He had a change of mind and surrendered). ULFA's objective was to have Governor's rule imposed in Assam which would afford a free hand to SULFA whose unchecked excesses would alienate the people. That would give an opportunity to ULFA to try and win back people's faith it had lost over the past few years, especially after its support to Pakistan during the 1999 Kargil War. To beat it all was the strange spectacle of a senior Assam Cabinet Minister Abdul Muhib Mazumdar (Irrigation) sitting in *dharna* near the State Secretarial to protest against the Administration's role as a silent spectator after these killings. He had forgotten the principle of "collective responsibility of the cabinet".[45] Mazumdar, Chairman of UPPA, a constituent of 4-party Ruling Alliance, sat in *dharna* along with leaders of various religious, linguistic and ethnic minority groups like those of Biharis, Nepalis, etc. The *dharna* was organised by the Coordinating Committee for Minorities of Assam (COCMOA) to which were affiliated 9 organisations including UPPA, UMF, linguistic Minorities Forum, and All Assam Nepali Students' Union. All this is sad commentary on the political class, and no comments are deemed necessary.

Speaking in the Lok Sabha on 18 December 2000, Home Minister Advani said, *inter alia:* "....One major impediment in containing insurgency in the North-East is the fact that pursued by SULFA, the militant often slipped into the neighbouring countries like Bhutan, Myanmar and Bangladesh.... Bhutan has already taken decision not to allow insurgents to take refuge in their territory."[46] Taking an overview of the situation in the entire North-East, Advani said: "Of the 8 States in the Region, 4 were largely peaceful. The situation in Assam, Tripura, Manipur and Mizoram has caused some concern. Assam in recent past has taken a turn for the worse."

Revenge Killings of ULFA Kin and Sympathy(?) Wave!

Assam witnessed a string of mystery killings of ULFA kin in the wake of end-2000 communal killings by ULFA (and UPDS) ultras. It led to an ironic situation where on the one hand, militants are engaged in a war with the SF, and the relatives of these militants are forced to seek personal protection from these very SF against the unidentified who seemed to be after their lives, on the other! The police had to post a picket at the house of Paresh Baruah, in Dibrugarh district, after a group of people fired at it early hours of 6 December 2000 (*Frontline,* 5-1-2001).[47]

'Mystery' gunmen continued targeting ULFA activists' kin apparently in retaliation to the communal massacres since 22 October. SULFA was suspected to be the mystery gunmen. The people killed/injured in the deadly ULFA-SULFA combat are listed here.

Lethal Duel: ULFA Versus SULFA

December 2000

- Paresh Barua's ancestral home attacked, his aged parents being the obvious targets. Both escaped unhurt.
- Deepak Choudhury, brother of ULFA's Foreign Secretary, Sasadhar, killed on 8 December at his residence in village Halosa in Nalbari district, a hot bed of ULFA militancy; obviously an act of avengement as Deepak was shot dead hours within ULFA militants butchering 28 people in Tinsukia on 7 December.
- Angry people torched the shop at Borbori in Nalbari, belonging to a relative of Tapan Barua, Commander of ULFA's 28th Bn.
- Houses of two senior ULFA leaders, Babul Sarma (in village Ghoghrapur, Tinsukia district) and Sailen Sarma, fired at on 6 December.
- House of ULFA's Sashi Phukan at Baihata in Kamrup district, blown up on 23 December, with two powerful hand grenades. None injured, as the house lay abandoned at the time. It was the 8th assault on this house.
- ULFA militant shoots at the dreaded SULFA member Monikut Kalita alias Tarzan (and his associate) in Mangaldoi, on 29 December. Kalita had gone to a nursing home to visit his pregnant wife when he came under attack.

January 2001

- SULFA's Avinash Bordoloi alias Sailen Haloi and his two associates (Ridip and Jabrang) were killed on 2 January at their agricultural farm at village Borbhag-Sholmara in Nalbari district. Avinash's two other friends sustained serious injuries. Interestingly, Mahanta and Agriculture Minister Chandramchan Patowari with senior officials, had visited the farm on 28 October 2000 to take stock of the good work done by the former militants led by Bordoloia, a top former ULFA leader, who had quit the outfit on 15 August 2000 to start this farm.
- Dwijen Haloi and Pulin Haloi, Kin of ULFA Dy C-in-C Raju Baruah, killed on 3 January.
- Jyotish Sharrna, brother-in-law of ULFA militant Subhas Sharma abducted from Guwahati and killed on 4 January.

(*Source: Hindustan Times*, 4 and 8 January 2001.)

"Retaliatory killings by unknown assailants have killed at least 6 family members of ULFA leaders", wrote *The Outlook* of 25-12-2000. These retaliatory attacks were a replay of a similar wave of killings witnessed in 1998 when ULFA Chairman Rajkhowa's brother (Umakant Rajkonwar's eldest of the 9 children, Dimba Rajkonwar was killed in August 1998) and the entire family of the outfit's Publicity Chief Mithinga Daimary, were killed.

A surprising, perhaps not all that surprising, aftermath of these so-called mystery killings of the ULFA kin was an anti-SULFA sentiment across the state, and a series of protests against the 'eliminator Government' and SULFA in Nalbari and Guwahati. On 4 January 2001, over 8000 people took out a funeral procession with the bodies of Dwijen and Pulin Haloi, kin of ULFA Dy C-in-C. Their anger was against the Government "blind to the high-handedness of the SULFA activists". On 5 January 2001, protestors joining the cortege of Jyotish Sharma, kin of ULFA militant Subhas Sharma, killed the previous night, initially about 1500 swelled to 5000. Instead of proceeding to the cremation ground, they went to the DC's Court where members of various political parties and AASU joined them and expectedly, made "political speeches". Some protestors even threw stones at the police. In addition, an East Guwahati *bandh* was called in protest and consequently, educational institutions and business establishments in half of the town remained closed. All this should compel one to ponder over several questions. Why this excessive sympathy over the death of the kin of ULFA insurgents? All wanton violence and killings are abhorrent. How was it then that all these protestors remained ensconced within their houses when the innocents were being murdered over the years by the ruthless ULFA ultras? Why did not any of these leaders, who made passionate anti-Government and by extension and implication, anti-SF political speeches on the 5th, muster people for rallies and processions to show sympathy for the relatives of the victims of the long-running ULFA death dance in Assam? Or, coming to the recent past, why did not these politicos bring even a small number of sympathisers to commiserate with the families of the hapless Biharis and Marwaris killed in scores by the ULFA and UPDS during October-December 2000, in the plains and hills of Assam? Were these processions actuated by the genuine sympathy for the slain, or by the fear of ULFA gun? A kind of insurance policy for tomorrow! Or, is AASU still sympathetic towards ULFA, its half-brother, and its objectives? Will Assam's—or, for that matter, India's—political class conduct themselves with national interest in mind, ignoring the sectional, selfish, or party interests? Could the Indians, at least a vast majority of them, think national rather than provincial? Could they rise above their ethnic, linguistic, regional and religious puniness?

The officials had reasons to be apprehensive about these ULFA-SULFA clashes, and the consequent killings. The clashes which left 21 dead during December-January (2001) period alone, could have helped the ULFA to regain some lost ground. The analysts felt the ULFA whose mass base had eroded rapidly over the last half a decade, had every thing to gain from the chain of such mystery killings, particularly so if these were perceived to have been initiated by the police-backed SULFA. If there are certain ULFA-specific gains in the situation, a cynical counter-poser to ULFA leadership could be: Could some calculating, desperate elements, within the outfit, themselves have played some part, directly or indirectly, to foment, or even initiate, these killings?

ULFA on the Decline?

The analysts ascribe the 'success' of ULFA's attention-grabbing end-2000 communal killings spree to a complacency among SF top brass, flowing from the sustained CI operations by the Unified Command since 1997 and large scale surrenders by its cadres during 1998-2000. Bhutan's threat of evicting it from its soil, gradual dwindling of its mass base, and cool response to its recruitment drive to replace the losses through mass surrender were adding to its woes. It was a frustrated leadership that ordered the communal killings, abandoning its ideologically-driven philosophy, for short-term gains. But even that seemed to have back fired. Instead of retrieving some lost ground, these killings further made a dent in its image, particularly losing the support of certain intellectual quarters. ULFA leadership, through these killings, had intended to give its cadres an issue. After all the Biharis were outsiders and Marwari businessmen had long since been identified with exploitation of the locals. But it seemed to have back fired. It is a telling commentary on the morale of the ULFA cadres that even the spate of the killings during October-December 2000 did not staunch the stream of surrenders by its activists. Till 6 December 2000, over 160 of its cadres had surrendered with their arms since these killings began on 22 October 2000. Things had not been well, not only among the ranks but also with the leadership, with rampant dissensions over the years. The divided leadership had not held a joint meeting for several years, as revealed by the Intelligence. Its top leaders, the Chairman and C-in-C frequently changed their hide-outs in Dhaka, Karachi and Bangkok. "With most of its leaders living abroad, the estimated 2500 ULFA cadres, mostly the unemployed youth from the lower middle class, are rudderless and are coming under the influence of the ISI." Adds a confident Intelligence officer: "Despite brave front put up by its leaders, ULFA activists are on the run." *Times of India* of 29 November 2000 wrote: "In the past three years, 863 ULFA cadres have been killed in encounters, 2425 weapons seized, and over 1 crore in cash recovered from the militants."

An important indication of dissensions within the leadership surfaced with the reports that Publicity Chief Mithinga Daimary was stripped of his prestigious charge in December 2000. In a peremptory move, Paresh Barua disbanded the Publicity wing and took over the responsibility himself.[48] Perceptible erosion of ULFA's mass base and large-scale set-backs during 1997-99 period had made Paresh Barua edgy. He held Daimary responsible for these negative developments and deprived him of his charge, though his falling health (liver sclerosis) was given out as the ostensible reasons for the change. Barua personally started ringing up the press offices to pronounce ULFA's positions on various issues. The communal killings were ordered by Barua to regain some lost support, in the face of opposition from Rajkhowa and Choudhury (the two with Barua constituted the Core Group of ULFA leadership, called Group of Three, or Ruling Group), and Baghphukan.

All this and other contemporaneous events showed that all was not well with ULFA, which gave "credence to the reports that it has been sending feelers to the Government for talks but only in some foreign country". It was not a surprise then that even when the ULFA continued on its bloody trajectory, there were good news coming from the countryside which bode ill for the outfit. The villagers had stopped providing succour and shelter to the ULFA militants. "In the past year and a half (1999-2000), there have been at least 30 incidents in which the villagers either lynched the militants to death or handed them over to the SF." Even the local newspapers have stopped giving the rebels the kind of splash they used to do 3-4 years back (say, during the 1993-98 period). All this, and the continued dissensions among its leadership, and large-scale surrenders go to show that all is not well with the outfit. The next logical question can be: Is the ULFA on the decline? Some events and signs, as mentioned above", do seem to point towards it. But it cannot be immediate!

Distraught by large scale surrenders, the disconcerted ULFA leadership launched a recruitment drive in the Lower Assam districts in July 2000. "But to its dismay, the outfit received lukewarm response from the unemployed youth who were no more eager to join it." Thus wrote a well-known local Daily, *The Sentinel* of 26 September 2000. It seemed as if the people of Assam were tired of the mindless violence for the last two decades, including the milder variety of it during the latter part of the AASU Agitation (1979-85). There is a kind of yearning for the peace. Assam Governor highlighted the fact that the ULFA Raising Day on 7 April 2000 witnessed the common people openly joining the peace rallies all over the state for the first time.[49] To its chagrin, even the newspapers carried editorials condemning ULFA's violence. DG, BSF added his bit while speaking at New Delhi on 16 October 2000: "ULFA has finally broken up since people are no longer with it".[50] In October 2000, hundreds of followers of Assam's 15th century saint, Sri Sankaradeva, undertook a peace march from Sadiya in the extreme east, through its heartland, culminating in a rally at Dhubri in its west. The Rally was significant because it was organised by the *Satras* of Assam (numbering over 800), set up by the greatly revered Sankardeva and family members of several ULFA leaders and cadres participated in it. For the first time since its inception in 1979 the ULFA leadership was losing control over its cadres, as indicated by large-scale surrenders. The recent surrenderees, who were members of ULFA over long years, expressed disillusionment with it as "it has become a terrorist organisation devoid of any revolutionary image".

Paresh Barua was in the total grip of the ISI, obeying all its dicta without a murmur; and part of money collected by ULFA was also controlled by the ISI. "The ULFA cadres fighting the Indian Army along with the Pak Army during the Kargil War alienated vast majority of people of Assam."[51] ULFA leaders calling the Kashmir terrorists 'freedom fighters' was not only thoughtless but also anti-national provocation that further angered the ULFA cadres and common Assamese like. ULFA might reject the Indian Constitution and boycott the elections held under it and ask the Assamese not to exercise their franchise, but 70 per cent of them much above the nation average of 59 per cent, defying the call, went to the polling booths and cast their vote, during the 1999 Lok Sabha poll. More hearteningly and surprisingly, in a number of cases, the immediate family members of top ULFA leaders voted in the 1999 Elections, as they did in some earlier ones.

Aware of attenuating mass support and need to dismount the high horse, ULFA dropped two of its original demands and offered to talk to the Centre on the sole issue of sovereignty for Assam, with its C-in-C directly conveying its stance to the PMO. Expectedly the Government rejected it out of hand and refused to invite ULFA for talks—denying them any illusions of respectability. Where does the movement go from here? Will it repeat the vicious, mindless communal killings of end-2000? Will it dish out more of the same: extortions, kidnappings, retributions, killings, et al to add to the people's woes and sufferings? Will it continue to seek for the soft targets to spread terror among the masses in order to 'win' them over to their side? Will it continue to seek meanings in methods and motives other than the ideological and intellectual high-mindedness with which it came to be on 7 April 1979? If that be so, what a great fall it would be for an organisation founded to bring *aikya* (unity), *biplab* (revolution), and *mukti* (deliverance, freedom or sovereignty) to the Assamese! The only other option for ULFA is to open constructive, realistic talks with the Government to restore peace and prosperity to Assam which it desperately needs and deserves by right, and its people fervently hope for. We will have to wait for the coming years.

At the end of it all, where does the outfit stand today *vis-a-vis* the objective realities? To repeat, in the 3-year (1998-2000) period, over 700 of its cadres had been killed in encounters and over 2500 surrendered. During 2000 alone, about 1300 militants, mostly of ULFA, had surrendered. An overview of the militancy-related statistics (1997 to 2000) should be useful to assess the ground realities.

Militancy-related Statistics: 1997-2000

Head	*1997*	*1998*	*1999*	*2000 (Till August)*
Incidents	427	735	447	210
Militants killed	167	180	212	312
Militants arrested	587	742	812	510
Militants surrendered	—	227	970	1186
Arms looted	28	125	168	08
SF killed	85	72	77	56
Civilians killed	285	531	214	179

To be realistic, the preceding should not be read as an obituary notice on ULFA's times and life. It will be an act of naivete to treat all the above adverse and negative development concerning ULFA as anything more than the straws in the wind. The ULFA leaders can still muster resources to strike at the soft targets selectively, even at the SF through the IEDs. All efforts must be made to bring the recalcitrant outfit to the high table, whatever the difficulties and means necessary for the purpose.

Events and Trends: 2001-2002

What follows is a brief look at the events and situation after the end-2000 communal killings.

Violence by ULFA

The ULFA militants killed two AGP leaders in Bongaigaon district on 25 April 2001, and two again in Nalbari district on the 28th. This was during the run upto the Assembly poll, held in May 2001 (*Hindustan Times*, 29-4-2001).

The murder of 6 AGP workers on 3 May 2001 at the Party's office at Bogorihati in Nalbari's Belsor Police Station created strong anti-ULFA sentiment in Nalbari, a district which has contributed maximum cadres to the banned ULFA. "We want justice", "Bury ULFA rebels alive", and "ULFA murdabad". It was possibly the worst shock for ULFA in its stronghold.

People Indifferent to ULFA Deaths

The Frontline of 25 October 2002 has listed 15 cases of individual killings of ULFA militants at the hands of the SF between 13 May and 11 September. How the public sympathy for the banned outfit is gradually drying up is best summed up by the headline assigned to the story by the respected Fortnightly: "Increasingly, public opinion in Assam is much less exercised over the killings of 'suspected militants' than it was a decade ago." Here is telling excerpt from the story:

> "In contrast to what used to be the case a decade ago, there is not even a ripple of reaction to similar incidents now. Public opinion.... Could not care less, it seems."

Groundswell against ULFA seems to be palpable. The people seem to have had enough of the violence. There is an obvious yearning for peace. Does the outfit have its ears to the ground? Will it heed the warning signals? The next incident is even more pregnant with meanings and warnings, for ULFA.

ULFA Insurgents' Kin Sue the Outfit

Families of 202 ULFA cadres filed petitions before the Assam Human Rights Commission (AHRC) at Guwahati on 7 June 2002 against the ULFA C-in-C, Paresh Barua for either forcing or luring their family members into joining him. Among the complainants are the families of the ULFA's Foreign Secretary (Sasha Choudhury), its Cultural and Public Relations Secretaries. The petitioners demanded that Barua return their children to their homes. Sasha's father, Dinabandhu Choudhury, has alleged that Barua forced his son to join ULFA.

Among the petitions received, 80 are from Nalbari district, an ULFA stronghold, 51 from Barpeta, 21 each from Marigaon and Kamrup, 12 from Goalpara, 10 from Bongaigaon, and 5 from Tezpur districts. A Guwahati-based NGO, took the initiative to bring the families before AHRC.[52]

Peace Talks Initiatives

During his 5-day trip to the North-East in April 1998, Defence Minister George Fernandes failed to make contacts with ULFA leaders, though he had offered unconditional talks to them. He had claimed "some private parties were already meeting militants on my behalf". Rajkhowa rejected the proposal same day, 6 April 1998, dubbing India as "terrorist" for occupying "our country". But morale of the cadres seems to be low. The *North-East Daily* says: "Resentment among ULFA cadres currently in Bhutan has been brewing for some time.... Several of them have been writing pessimistic letters to their relatives, lamenting the way they have to live and face hardship."[53]

Nothing was heard on the issue till Rajkhowa made the offer on 27 November 2001, "provided Government of India is ready to accept our pre-conditions". The statement faxed to newspapers in Assam came on the 11th anniversary of the ban on the extremist outfit. Assam's Chief Minister Tarun Gogoi welcomed the offer of political settlement of "Indo-Assam Conflict", made for the first time by ULFA Chairman? The Government has adopted "wait and watch" policy on the offer, as they did before opening talks with NSCN(I-M). ULFA is obviously under pressure from Bhutan as well.[54] New Delhi's move to tighten the vigil along the Indo-Bhutan border "by deploying 10 battalions of BSF"[55] prevented the possibility of ULFA cadres sneaking back into India.

ULFA has not sent any feelers to the Government expressing its willingness for negotiations, Gogoi said on 7 December[56] 2001. He said it was "welcome" that ULFA had expressed publicly its desire for negotiations. He again said on 13 June 2002 that the Centre should initiate talks with the ULFA, as it was doing with the NSCN(I-M).[57]

The opposition AGP on 11 July 2002, asked ULFA to shun violence and come forward for a negotiated settlement. The Legislature Party Secretary, Dilip Kumar Saikia, made this appeal to "brother" Arbindo Rajkhowa in a 3-page open letter.[58] The Press reported (in June 2002) that Governor Sinha deputed a state civil servant to open talks with ULFA's Foreign Secretary Sasha Choudhury at Singapore. He denied the report.[59]

The way Arbindo Rajkhowa's father, undoubtedly a freedom fighter of some eminence, has been treated with respect and extra consideration, also seems to be a part of the Government's plans to facilitate peace talks with ULFA. Umakant Rajkonwar, the oldest freedom fighter of Assam, turned 100 on 11 January 2001. His birth centenary was observed in a big way, with senior ministers participating and planting saplings as a part of ceremonies to honour him. Laudatory references were made to his contributions in the freedom struggle. He was the Chief of the 9th Unit of the Shanti Vahini in Upper Assam during the Quit India Movement of 1942. Arbindo Rajkhowa is the 6th child and youngest son of Umakant. Chief Minister Gogoi released Rs. 30,000 for medical treatment of Umakant Rajkonwar in April 2002.[60]

Ban Extended: 2003-05

"In a setback to peace hopes in Assam, the Centre extended ban 7-2-03 on ULFA (as also on NDFB) under the Unlawful Activities (Prevention) Act, 1967 for two years" (*HT*, 8-2-03). ULFA was first declared an unlawful organisation on 27 Nov. 1996 and the ban has been extended every two years ever since.

With New Delhi engaged in extended talks with NSCN(I-M) over the last 6 years, there were hopes of some such understanding with the ULFA also, especially when it has expressed a desire for such peace talks. But ULFA's preconditions seems to have come in the way.

Sanjoy Ghose Murder Verdict

The murder case came to a close with P.K. Phukan, additional sessions judge, awarding life sentence to accused (Moni Neog and Kania Hazarika). Six others, including C-in-C Barua were declared absconders. They had abducted the social worker on 4-7-97 when he was on his way to village Mekheliga on Majuli, and killed him the same evening.

When Ghose, INLAK scholar, founder of URMUL, Rajasthan, and CHARKHA, New Delhi, and winner of Sanskriti Award, landed at Majuli, his friends and family thought he had gone crazy as the Island was infested with the ultras of ULFA and the latter took him as an Army spy. For the first three months of their stay, Ghose, head of the AVARD-NE and his volunteers stayed at the Islander's houses. Subsequently, his work at the grass-roots level made him so popular with the locals that he became an 'enemy' of the contractors for whom Majuli was a milch cow, where last year's imaginary works could be shown as having been washed away by the current floods of the 'wicked' Brahmaputra. The things became worse when Dweep-Alok, mouth piece of AVARD-NE, started exposure of cases of corruption in the money for development allotted by the centre. When the locals saw the benefits of 'his work' in contrast to the 'work' done by ULFA, the outfit was bound to do to him what it indeed did on 4-7-97, having told him repeatedly in talks to leave the island, the 'advice' obviously falling on the deaf ears. In his short stay, Ghose has shown that "if the youth could be helped to see the path of constructive work and development, much of the problem would end", he had written in his diary, which his wife later published in a book (Exp., 28 Aug. and 2 Sep. 2003).

It was no surprise that his abduction and murder caused widespread resentment. Records show 20 ULFA cadres were lynched over 7 years. There is hope even if there is one Ghose heading a NGO against the ten fraudulent ones in the field only to make a name and money; of ccurse the latter must be tolerated and kept under strict scrutiny.

ULFA: 2002-2005

Now a brief look at the outfit in the first half of the first decade of the 21st century.

ULFA Rebel's Kin Killing: Fresh Probe

Inter-party politics is the bane of the Indian polity. Assam's Congress Government, after rejecting the report of a commission headed by a retired Guwahati High Court Judge, constituted 27-8-05 a new commission headed by a retired Supreme Court Judge (Justice K.N. Saikia) to probe the "secret killings" (mostly relatives of ULFA militants) in Assam, since 1998. All the cases referred to the commission, including five specific ones, took place when Mahanta-led AGP was in power. Critics dubbed it as politics of vendetta.

ULFA: Post-Bhutan Scenario

Two weeks after Bhutanese action against ULFA, its Chairman Rajkhowa addressed a letter to the Chairman of the PRC, seeking "temporary shelter" in view of the Bhutanese offensive. "We will request you to permit our cadres enter your territory extra-legally to save their lives. They have no other option. Your people should extend them minimum temporary hospitality necessary for their survival." The letter was e-mailed to Guwahati newspaper offices 28-12-03 (*Exp.,* 29-12-03).

Meanwhile, NSCN(K)-controlled-Naga Hills of Myanmar became an operating base for ULFA by mid-2004. These Hills "are now home to close to 4,400 ULFA cadres" (*Tribune*, 13-10-04) Spate of attacks on oil installations and civilian targets in upper Assam (Jul-Oct 2004), closer to Myanmar Naga Hills, came from ULFA cadres ensconced there. "Central Command Headquarters of ULFA is now based in Bangladesh."

Paresh Baruah, lodged in a BDR camp at Srimangal "has been actively reorganising ULFA ranks after the Bhutanese offensive. He hosted a meeting of 9 groups like NDFB, PLA, ATTF, ANVC, HNLC, etc. in March 2004 in Gulshan II, a Dhaka locality, in a house belonging to an important Bangladesh politico. His task of re-building ULFA is not easy because of low morale of the cadre after the Bhutanese crackdown, "while the gap between him and Rajkhowa has widened." *The Indian Express* of 27-6-03 had reported "Barua is alive and in Dhaka". He was injured in 27-5-03 shoot out. "In an interview to BBC, Baruah denied any rift with Rajkhowa."

Again, the press had reported a shoot-out when a major meeting of anti-India insurgent groups was taking place at a North Shamoli safe-house under the joint auspices of the DGFI and ISI. "Sources said food for 160 participants was specially catered from the Golf club" (*TOI*, 30-07-04). Besides this safe-house, three other ULFA camps were also attacked that day by gunmen. "Needle of suspicion behind these attacks, that left 21 dead, points to the rival group led by Rajkhowa." Intelligence suspected among the dead at North Shamoli could be Baruah. Among the other dead identified as top ULFA cadres close to Baruah more Paramjit Saikia, Lalit Hazarika and Biju Deka. "The bodies are lying at the Dhaka Medical College mortuary and efforts are on identify the other person killed."

Dhaka denied the incident but the press reported it widely. Bangladesh has consistently maintained that there were no ULFA training camps on its soil. Indians however "point out to the existence of ULFA locations at Mack Towers, Glove Pharma and Asia Hostel, while the DGFI safe-house is located in North Shamoli.

Like on some similar occasions earlier, an e-mail from Baruah a week later showed that he was alike.

In his e-mail statement in Assamese of 16-12-04, Rajkhowa said "Paresh Baruah is seriously ill and shifted to a safe place for an urgent medical operation." He said because of his illness, Baruah would, for now, not maintain his usual regular communication with the *literature* Indira Goswami and other intellectuals, media persons, and other organisations, and requested the latter to forward him their suggestions and advice through the e-mail address: rubybhuyan@yahoo.com.

Meanwhile, the unified command decided 17-12-04 to step up CI operations in the wake of a fresh spurt in violence by the ULFA.

ULFA Violence: Continues

Feb. 2003. Three mortar attacks in 5 months. In all the three attacks, the ultras used 60 mm mortars with 10 tailfins "used by the Chinese and Pak armies". Indian Army 60 mm mortars have 8 tailfins. The last such attack was on the IAF base near Guwahati airport on 23-02-03. The earlier such attacks came in October 2002 when similar mortar bombs landed at the Dispur Secretariat Complex, followed by five more exploding on 25 December near the Bishop House.

March 2003. ULFA blew up a storage tank (containing 5000 KL of motor spirit) of Assam Oil Division, barely a km from the Digboi Oil Refinery on the 7th. Its ultras blew up two pipelines the same day near Duliajan.

2 April 2003. A SULFA leader Nayan Das alias Guli was lynched to death by irate residents in Dibrugarh for his misbehaviour with a woman.

15 August 2004. The IED explosion triggered by ULFA at the Independence Day celebrations venue, Dhemaji College, killed 16 people, including 2 women and 10 children. "It was the worst in the recent months.

The 7-month peace in Assam following Operation Flush out in Bhutan in December 2003, thus proved to be a proverbial lull before the storm." Going overboard, Tarun Gogoi had declared that ULFA's back was broken. Analysts felt certain amount of complacency could also have crept in as Assam Government had possibly ignored several sporadic incidents of militant violence prior to the 15 August blast.

2 October 2004. Gandhi Jayanti was marked by several blasts, in a widespread operation spanning 48 hours. The Government obviously did not learn a lesson even from 15 August blasts, said the critics, "as reports of possible militant strikes on 2 October were taken lightly". ULFA was believed to be regrouping in Bangladesh and Myanmar after its Bhutan discomfiture, and every one seemed to have forgotten NDFB after many of its top leaders including Vice-President Dhiren Boro and Publicity Secretary B. Erakdao were arrested. Obviously biding its time, NDFB decided Gandhi Jayanti was convenient, being a day prior to its 19th Raising Day.

Beyond the capability of a single outfit, ULFA and NDFB were obviously involved as the two are known to have had a strategic alliance and specific areas of operations. They were two of the 9 outfits that had banned Hindi films across the Region from 15 November 2003. The NSCN(I-M) did not figure in the list while the NSCN(K) had later dissociated itself from the ban.

2 Oct. 2004. Twin blast at Dimapur kill 26 persons. "Dimapur, kissing the Assam Nagaland border, has also been a convergence point of other outfits of the Region like ULFA, NDFB and DHD", after essentially being the den of NSCN(I-M). The latter being in peace mode since July 1997 and engaged in serious peace talks with New Delhi cannot be remotely linked to these blasts. "After promptly announcing a reward of Rs. 5 lakh for information leading to the capture of the culprits, the NSCN (I-M) blamed a non-Naga outfit and a Naga ally for the blasts" (Rahul Karmakar, *HT*, 5-1-0-05). The identity of the latter is obvious, NSCN(K), it is the former phrase which draws the ULFA into its ambit, howsoever irrational it might sound. Hence the inclusion of Dimapur blasts in this list. The non-Naga outfit could either the ULFA, NDFB, or DHD. The ULFA has an alliance with the NSCN(K) for a toehold in Arunachal as also in Myanmar, and why would it risk both by purposeless strike at the Naga Civilians? Both NDFB and DHD belong to the Bodo-Kacharis stock, and Dimapur was the capital of the last Kachari Kingdom. And to wit, the DHD had staked claim to the Nagaland town some time back. So the Region "appears poised for a never-before showdown between the NSCN(I-M) and "culprit outfit".

June 2005

After lying low for some period, the banned ULFA sprung into action in June 2005.

20th. Threw a grenade inside the high-security zone of the new Secretariate building complex in Guwahati.

25th. A grenade thrown at a police station at Sibsagar injures 6 persons.

26th. CRPF Group Office at Guwahati comes under grenade attack, injuring 12, including 6 CRPF men.

"Recently invited for talks by New Delhi, ULFA had demanded the release of its 10 jailed leaders", to enable it to take a decision on the talks offer. Flexing its muscles through these June 2005 attacks, ULFA was sending a message to New Delhi against its dilly-dallying on the release of the jailed leaders, some analysts felt.

ULFA Attacks: Run-up to the Big Day (15 August) 2005

It has been the normal practice for these North-Eastern outfits in the (recent) past to unleash an orgy of violence before and on the Independence Day, often acting in concert. It was no different for 15 August 2005.

2nd: CRPF-Police team ambushed in Tinsukia, killing one sepoy and injuring five others.

6th: Grenade explodes in Guwahati, injuring two.

7th: Blast in two pipelines at Sibsagar and Dibrugarh.

8th: (1) Explosion in oil pipeline in Tinsukia. (2) Bombs defused near two schools in Jorhat. (3) Explosion at an ASEB powerhouse.

9th: (1) Gas pipeline explosion at Desaiborha in Sibsagar. (2) Explosion at a steel plant along Assam-Arunachal border. (3) Convoy of trucks carrying food items fired at in the KA district, killing one man. (4) Assam's MOS, Home, Rockybul Hussain told the Assembly 9-8-05 that "the ULFA has exploded 17 bombs and grenades since 6 August".

10th: (1) IED blew up railway tracks near Tihu railway station in Lower Assam, cutting rail links between Assam and the rest of India. (2) A police-station in upper Assam attacked. (3) Assam Government called the Army in aid to civil power.

SOME IMPORTANT EVENTS

ULFA Hits out at its 'Mentor'

In a statement, e-mailed on 7-12-04 by its C-in-C Baruah, ULFA lashed out at the NSCN concept of Nagalim, timing its outburst with the prolonged visit of the (I-M) leaders Swu and Muivah to India for sustained talks with the Central leaders, and asserting that the Nagas never in history had any control over Assam. Its incarcerated Vice-Chairman Pradip Gogoi, presented before the TADA Court at Guwahati 8-12-4 was more direct in attacking the NSCN: "We will not give an inch of Assam to fuel the Greater Nagaland dream of the NSCN."

US puts ULFA on Terrorist List

The US State Department in its "2004 Country Reports on Terrorism" released 28 April 2005, added ULFA to the Other Selected Terrorist Organisations (OSTO) List. The outfits on the OSTO List are the entities that do not target the national security of the US or its citizens.

ULFA Leader Released

A Guwahati Sub-Divisional Judicial Magistrate released 2 June 2005 Ramu Mech on bail.

"Major Player in Real Estate Business"

BSF claimed the ULFA leaders are running seven upmarket hotels (Surma International, Hotel Mohammadia and Hotel Padma International are in Dhaka; Hotel Keya International and Hotel Yamuna in Sylhet; and Hotels Basundhra and Rajking in Chittagong) and some nursing homes in Bangladesh. The MHA reports indicated Barua's business interests in Bangladesh (*Exp.,* 4-6-05).

ULFA Setting up Bases in Nepal

Intelligence culled from various sources disclosed ULFA setting up five camps in Nepal in the areas under the Maoist leader Pushpa Kumar Dahal, likely located in the districts of Bara, Dang, Syaganja Chitwan, Sagarmatha, and even Solok humbu, whose claim to fame is the Mt Everest.

Barua's trusted aide Rana Deuri, from Darrang district, is in-charge of these Nepal Camps, housing about 150 cadres. Deuri is close to the CPI (Maoist), which has for the past few years figured in the ULFA's "Golden Triangle" plan for the movement of the cadres between Bhutan, Bangladesh and Nepal. The ouster of the ULFA set-up in Bhutan following "operation All-Clear" in Dec. 2003 necessitated these camps, which might not be exclusive to ULFA, but possibly shared with the Maoists. In any case, analysts have long suspected an ULFA-Maoist nexus.

The report of ULFA shifting base from other adjoining countries come at a time when some intellectuals are trying to bring ULFA to the negotiations table at New Delhi.

ULFA-Centre Talks: Long in Coming

There were reports of Defence Minister contacting ULFA leaders during his April 1998 visit to the Region. Then for the first time since it was outlawed in 1990, its Chairman offered to talk to New Delhi on 27-11-01 if it accepted his pre-conditions (*Frontline,* 04-01-02). Both proved abortive.

From early 2004, noted Assamese writer and Jnanpith awardee Indira Mamoni Goswami has been active in bringing ULFA and New Delhi to the table. On 15 Nov. 2004, she submitted a 'petition' (nivedan is her choice for the term) to the Prime Minister's Special Advisor, M.K. Narayanan. She met the PM on the 16th. She told the press that PM agreed to her suggestion to initiate the process to open dialogue with ULFA by Jan. 2005. She thought the centre should have no problem talking sovereignty with the ULFA, since the former is in sustained talks with the NSCN (I-M) whose plank once was sovereignty.

7 Dec., Narayanan conveyed to Goswami Centre's willingness for talks with ULFA. Barua says 'No' to PM's offer as his letter made no mention of 'sovereignty'. 9 Feb. 2005, Goswami, who offered her services as mediator, handed over Rajkhowa's letter to Narayanan, pleading for an "agreement with honour and dignity". AASU welcomed the PM's letter, and wanted the Government to declare a unilateral cease-fire.

A MHA official handed over first formal letter to Goswami on 26 May 2005 for Rajkhowa (AA, 29-5-05). It was signed by Narayanan which, Goswami said on 28 May, expressed Centre's preparedness to hold "unconditional talks" to discuss "Assam's sovereignty", described by ULFA as the "core issue", an obvious contradiction in terms. In his telephonic conversation with her on the 28th, Goswami, the "go-between" informed the press at Delhi that Barua told her that some points in the letter such as abjuring the violence prior to talks required clarification.

The Hindu of 3-05-05 says the centre has chalked out a course to enter into a peace dialogue with ULFA, even when the US has put it on their terror list. Security analysts feel the US declaration would put pressure on Bangladesh to curb ULFA "activities at a time when Dhaka itself was being seen as a hub of Islamic radical outfits, which numbered 31 in January 2005. Scenario in Bangladesh is worrying with rising attacks against journalists, left and secular elements in the recent past. All this shows that the extremist groups are gaining ground in Bangladesh. No wonder the extremist fundamentalist groups are seeking, says the leading strategic journal Jane's Intelligence and Insight, formation of a greater Islamic territory, covering some areas in India also.

In a letter handed over to Narayanan on 30-6-05 by Goswami, Rajkhowa says "we can talk if focus is on sovereignty" (*Exp.,* 02-07-05). Four days after Narayanan wrote his 27-05-05 letter to the Chairman and C-in-C, the latter called the newspaper, demanding that the Government release 10 of its top leaders lodged in different jails "before they could discuss the letter".

In the editorial of their mouthpiece, *Freedom* of 15-7-05, Rajkhowa says their quick response to the letter from the PMO has not been reciprocated by the latter.

ULFA threatens 14-09-05 to withdraw from the peace process unless the Army stops its operations inside the Dibru-Saikhowa (National Park) Reserve Forest in Tinsukia district (AA, 15-9-05). Goswami said the ULFA wanted the

Government to mellow down its military operations. The stalemate continues as the Army refused to concede, reasoning that all earlier cessations of operations were utilised by ULFA to re-equip, rest and augment its strength. On the 20th, two ultras were killed inside the Reserve Forest, one of them identified as Achinta Saikia, Financial Controller of the outfit's 28th battalion.

On 21-09-05, a delegation of the People's Consultative Group (PCG) was barred from visiting villages inside the Reserve Forest. The Army stopped them at Bhuijanghat, informing them that the boats to ferry them to their destination were not available as these had been requisitioned by the Army due to operational reasons.

Given the circumstances, it is unlikely that the meeting between the ULFA appointed 11-member PCG and the NSA, M.K. Narayanan, "scheduled for the first fortnight/week of October 2005 will take place" (*Exp.* and *Hindu*, 21 and 22 Sep. 2005).

Talks were held but to no Avail

It must be put on record that the first round of talks between the PCG and the PMO indeed took place in Oct. 2005 and Prime Minister Manmohan Singh put in a brief appearance. Second round too was held at the PMO while the third round was held on 22 Jun. 2006 at the MHA by Home Minister Shivraj Patil. Talks broke down subsequently as ULFA insisted on release of its five senior leaders under detention.

ULF Depradations: No let up

After the failure of talks, the Government annulled cease-fire on 24 Sep. 2006 and resumed counter insurgency operations. The secessionist outfit to continued with its vivious ways. Some of the atrocities committed by ULFA are put on record here.

Editors tell ULFA: "Media gag must go"

Media persons hit out at ULFA on 14 June 2006 for the recent threats issued to four city-based journalists and asked it to withdraw it immediately. The threat was issued by ULFA C-in-C Paresh Barua through an e-mail on 8 June.

Speaking at the meeting organised by the Journalists Union of Assam (JUA) affiliated to the Indian Journalist Union at the Guwahati Press Club, DN Chakravarti, Editor, *Dainik Assam* (the oldest Assamese daily) came down heavily on the outfit and said: "The ULFA has lost its ability to identify friends and foes.... It is pursuing a meaningless philosophy which is proving to be self-destructive as well as harmful to the Assamese society."

5 Jan 2007: ULFA Kill 16 Non-Assamese

Six migrant brick kiln workers – mostly from Bihar and UP – were shot dead by ULFA militants in four separate incidents in Upper Assam's Dibrugarh, Tinsukia, and Sibsagar districts. 5 labourers were killed at Tingri Chariali, 35 km. from Dibrugarh; three killed and five murdered at Borhapjan (Tinsukia); and three killed at Gobindapore brick field at Borhat near Kamrup (Sibsagar).

5 Jan 2007

"95% oppose ULFA's demand for independence". A civil society group, Assam Public Works (APW), claimed that more than 95 per cent of nearly 2.6 million people, interviewed by its 1800 volunteers in nine (Bongaingaon, Goalpara, Guwahati (metro), Dhubri, Darrang, Sonitpur, Lakhimpur, Dhimaji and Nalbari) of Assam's 27 districts, rejected the demand for independence by the outlawed ULFA.

The APW, known for its anti-ULFA stance, claims to have several relatives of the separatist group as its members. Abhijeet Sarma, General Secretary of the APW said only 5 per cent of the people surveyed in the opinion poll to elicit public response to ULFA's demand for independence/sovereignty, supported its demand and the rest thoroughly rejected it.

The opinion poll for the remaining 18 districts "would be taken up soon", he said on 5 Jan 2007.

Army Seizes 43 ULFA Weapons: 10 Jan 2007

Defence sources on 10 Jan 2007 said that "the Army is all set to launch air strikes by helicopters in some of the most inaccessible hideouts of ULFA militants."

The Army, on its first day of counter-insurgency operations, got a major success by seizing 43 weapons including a sophisticated Universal Machine Gun (UMG), besides unearthing an·ULFA militant's plot to ambush the Convoy of GOC, 4 Corps in Upper Assam's Tinsukia district.

The UMG, recovered from an overground ULFA activist, was used in the killing of Bihari labourers in Tinsukia district on 5 Jan 2007, the first day of the 5 day violence (5-9 January) in Upper Assam's three districts that killed 71 non-Assamese migrants in Assam. The UMG has the capacity of firing 1,000 rounds (bullets) in one strike.

The over-ground ULFA activists were also instrumental in providing all necessary logistic support to outfit's militants belonging to its 28th Battalion.

This self-styled (SS) 28th Battalion of the secessionist ULFA was found to be responsible for these (recent) killings of migrant Bihari labourers in Upper Assam. Sources confirmed that "this unit has been entrusted with the responsibility of carrying out insurgent (violent) strikes in Upper Assam. While the 28th is active in the Upper Assam, the ULFA leadership has entrusted the same task of spreading insurgency in the Lower Assam to its 27th Battalion.

It was revealed that the ULFA has also patterned the structure of its fighting units on Indian Army's. "They have similar sepoy and officer ranks for their cadres. Each battalion of theirs has also four companies."

The ULFA's top leadership, known to be leading a life of luxury in their hide-outs in Bangladesh, is coordinating the insurgency strikes and extortion drive of these so-called battalions.

Extortion Drive by ULFA Continues: Jan 2007

Apart from continuing the targeting of innocent civilians, the latest being the record killing of 71 Bihari migrant labourers in 5-day (5-9 Jan 2007) murderous spree in three districts of the Upper Assam, the ULFA has also continued with its old modus operandi of collecting ransom money by writing extortion letters – couched in ideologically appropriate terminology – to representatives of various companies in Assam to raise funds for its operations and other nefarious activities.

One such letter, recently written to the manager of a tea estate in Assam, was recovered by the troops during their operations against ULFA ultras after their early Jan 2007 killings of the non-Assamese labourers in Upper Assam. The extortion letter written by the ULFA's SS Lt Prabal Neog of the 28th Battalion to this manager reads: "Revolutionary Congratulations, we the ULFA, do hereby ask you/your company to contribute Rs. 30 lakh for a just cause and hope that you will comply with our proposal as soon as possible."

Post-Talks Situation: Early 2007

24 Sep. 2006: ULFA Cease Fire is called off in Assam

New Delhi called off 6-week ceasefire and resumed military operations against the ULFA following stepped up attacks and extortions by the rebels. Peoples Consultative Group (PCG), a civil society team appointed by the ULFA to mediate with the Centre on its behalf to get the two on the negotiations table, failed to get a written commitment from the rebels that its leadership would come for talks if their jailed comrades were released. The release of five of their senior leaders was the pre-condition they laid down for the initiation of talks with the Centre. Knowing the ULFA to be on elusive customer as shown by their past experience in dealing with it, the government interlocutors told the PCG that they were willing to consider their demand if rebel would give a written commitment as mentioned above. When ULFA decided against yielding to this demand, the Government expectedly called off the cease-fire. Surprisingly, the PCG feigned surprise at New Delhi's move, which was utterly inexplicable as they had been kept informed of the developments.

Peace talks between ULFA representatives and the Centre formally broke down first week of October after PCG pulled out of the peace process and ironically, blamed the Centre for calling off the truce.

Army steps up Operations: 8 Oct. 2006

Army launches anti-insurgency operations in parts of eastern Assam, close to the Myanmar border, to flush out rebels of the outlawed ULFA, soon after the ceasefire was called off. At least four ULFA rebels were killed and six more captured during this offensive. The cadres of 28th Battalion of ULFA were the main targets as they were active in eastern parts of Assam. The rebels were reportedly holed up in the thick forests of this area.

Movement of troops in these jungles is slow and risky. The best option is to air drop soldiers in specific locations, guided by intelligence inputs. A fleet of helicopters was on stand by for this purpose.

"The ULFA too stepped up its attacks in the past fortnight with a string of grenade explosions and blasts, killing three people and mounding another 33, including 10 soldiers". Intelligence reported a large group of ULFA guerrillas armed with explosives and sophisticated weaponry had sneaked into Assam from bases in Myanmar's North Sagaing Division in the last fortnight.

Analysts aver civil society groups like the PCG are best advised to avoid acting as mouthpiece of rebel outfits like ULFA. A stage comes when they get to be used by these outfits. They cannot hope to affect the thinking or attitude of the ultras, and in due course, start criticising the government for one reason or other. The worst, after a time, they start exerting pressure on the government to accept one demand or other of the rebels. But on the other hand, they can not persuade or pressure the rebels on even a very minor concession.

The PCG got the government to declare a ceasefire to enable it to persuade the ULFA to move to the talks table. One extension after another failed to move the ultras. Even when the government agreed to consider their demand for release of the in jailed leaders, they refused to give a written commitment for joining the talks. After all this, PCG ends up blaming the government for calling off the ceasefire which it had declared unilaterally and in the face of the strong opposition of the Army. Army had reasons to oppose this truce. It is wiser by the earlier experience. The ULFA has always used such truce periods in the past to reorganise, re-equip, re-coup and strengthen itself.

'ULFA used the Talks to Regroup'

The Army was opposed to any cease-fire agreement with ULFA because it is aware of this outfit's tactic of using all such interragrums to re-equip and regroup itself. ULFA has been active for over two decades, and no one knows its history better than the Indian Army. But once the political decision was made, Army simply has to fall in line.

But after the outfits' outrage on 5 November 2006, when it killed/injured 14/53 in two blasts in the heart of Assam's capital, both politicians and civil officials seem to be wiser to the truth told to them by the Army. If Chief Minister Gogoi admitted security failure, Union Home Secretary VK Duggal had somewhat similar message for his political bosses at the centre.

Duggal, accompanied by Joint Secretary, North-East, DGP BSF Mitra and DGP CRPF JK Sinha, visited two blast sites and later met Chief Minister Gogoi. "The meeting concluded on a note that ULFA's senior leaders had bought time on pretext of 'peace talks' with the centre."[61]

"ULFA was completely destroyed. Its senior leaders intiated the peace talks, which we now feel was a *tamasha*. They actually used this time to mobilise themselves to carry out the attacks like this"? Sinha told a daily.[62]

During the meeting, the intelligence inputs revealed that ULFA went on a recruitment drive and also strengthened itself monetarily, while pretending all the time that it was serious about talks.

A day after the ULFA killed 14 in two blasts, the Congress Party, which had been engaging the banned outfit in talks, "ran for cover, drawing plans for peace campaign in Assam's ULFA strongholds", wrote political analyst.[63] The campaign, of course, will not name ULFA. How carefully the political parties safeguard their party interests even in grim situations where national security is threatened. It is difficult to understand, much less appreciate, such squeamishness.

The UPA government and the ULFA have been in contact through a People's Consultative Group (PCG) since September 2005, but the violence continued in the State. Congress policy makers, clearly alarmed by the latest mindless violence perpetrated by ULFA, were inclined to give up the 'peace initiative'. Now they concede that the ULFA's peace overtures were not genuine. Between September 2005 and June 2006, there were 52 blasts and 41 civilian deaths. Now it was realised that the extremist outfit merely used the truce to regroup, recruit, and extort.

Indians are Migrants, Bangladeshis Could Go later: ULFA

Finally, the ULFA has shown its true colours. For the outlawed outfit, it is the migrants from the Indian sub-continent, and not the Bangladeshis who are the "real infiltrators into Assam". They must go first because these "illegal migrants to Assam from the Indian sub-continent have threatened the very existence of the state, created a chaotic situation in the social formation and occupied the political and economic spheres at the expense of the indigenous people.

There views of the outfit have been reflected in the Dec 2006 issue of Freedom, its monthly mouthpiece. It reminded the readers about the beginnings of the Assam Movement led by the AASU in 1979 when the focus was on "outsiders" and not necessarily Bangladeshi infiltrators.

The ULFA might have said so in so many words for the first time by putting its creed in cold print. The terror trail drawn here leaves nothing to imagination. Its main enemies are Indian. In the last few years, especially after its ouster from the jungles of Bhutan, the outfit has repeatedly said that the illegal migrants into Assam/North-East do not include the Bangladeshis. They are obviously paying back the debt they owe to Dhaka for offering them sanctuary and shelter in their post Bhutan second life. Here are the cold statistics.

- Oct 2000. ULFA guns down 15 people in Tinsukia and Dibrugarh districts.
- Dec 2000. 26 non-Assamese massacred in Upper Assam.
- Nov 2003. Over 100 Hindi-speaking people killed in retaliation for rape of a North-Eastern girl in a train in Bihar.
- 9 Jun 2006. 6 killed, 16 injured in a blast at Machkowa, Guwahati.
- 5 Nov 2006. 14 killed, 40 injured in blasts in Guwahati.
- 23 Nov 2006. 3 killed, 9 injured in blast at Guwahati railway station.
- 6 Jan 2007. 48 killed, mostly from Bihar and West Bengal, by ULFA in a 3-hour orgy in Upper Assam, including some places on Arunachal Pradesh border.

Army to take Baton from Police in Guwahati: Dec 2006

The last Assam Police bastion against the ULFA is likely to make way for the Army. Ever since the Operation Bajrang, the full-fledged offensive againist the ULFA in 1990, the Army troops have been handling security almost everywhere in Assam except in Guwahati.

But the outlawed ULFA seems to be "getting too hot to handle by police with limited fire power", offered a police officer by way of on explanation—or perhaps justification. Soldiers in battle fatigues may soon make the men in Khaki play second fiddle.

The threat by ULFA to disrupt the 33rd Natural games, scheduled to be held at Guwahati in Feb. 2007 might have hastened the decision of the police to "cede territory."

The decision to deploy the Army in Assam's capital seems to have been taken on 24 Dec 2006 at the meeting of the Unified Command which, set up in 1997, is a coordination body of the State administration, the Army, the Police, para military forces and the intelligence agencies. Its success in Assam persuaded New Delhi to replicate it in Jammu & Kashmir to combat insurgency.

ULFA's 'B 'Force' in Army's cross-hair: Jan 2007

"B company spells terror in Assam", reads a news headline as the Army and other security forces continue its offensive launched on 9 Jan 2007, in the jungle areas adjoining the Assam-Arunachal border. Army's prime target will be ULFA's elite fighting unit, the 28th Battalion, who are killers of the 69 Hindi-speaking migrants in eastern Assam. They used cell phones to keep in touch. Intelligence disclosed: "Intercepts revealed that the massacre was carried out by the 'Bravo' or the B company of the ULFA's 28th Battalion." It has been trained at camps in Myanmar.

The Battalion, with an estimated strength of 350 plus is reported to have masterminded and executed some of the worst massacres in Upper Assam, including the latest round of serial killings.[64] "The unit also serves as the nerve-centre of ULFA for planning, kidnappings and extortions", said a senior officer of HQ, 2 Mtn Div. He also showed a ransom note for Rs. 30 lac sent to a tea estate manager and signed by 28th battalion commander, self-styled Lt Prabal Neog.

Its headquarters, earlier called 'Camp Kashmir' in Myanmar's Sagaing Division, moves among six locations in the country, two of which it shares with the NSCN(K).

Defence Minister AK Antony, accompanied by Chief of Army Staff Gen JJ Singh and Defence Secretary Shekhar Dutt, visited Dinjan on 10 Jan 2007 to take stock of the situation.

The Army has been targeting the 28th Battalion leadership since the end of the cease fire in Sep 2006. "Nearly 15 top-notch operatives have been eliminated in a string of counter-terror operations by crack teams. But the outfit continues to regroup and re-arm itself."

Car Bombs Arrive in Assam: 4 Feb 2007

The car bomb that exploded outside a police station at Guwahati in Assam on 4 Feb 2007 has understandably rattled the security establishment. The bombing planned and executed by ULFA and first of its kind in Assam, signals the advent of a deadly form of urban terrorism. If the banned ULFA and other terror outfits in the region, assisted, trained and armed by agencies like the Pak ISI, have decided to use car bombs, then it is only a matter of time before suicide bombers are deployed to further the separatists' agenda. Till now, the insurgents would carry explosives on bicycles and plant them in crowded areas, or they would hurl grenades from motor-cycles. The 4 February bombing opens up a fearful possibility of insurgents changing their tactics. This obviously points towards more troublesome days in the North-East.

Forces Strike Back After Outrage by ULFA: Jan 2007

Thousands of Armymen, para military forces and police from Assam and Arunachal Pradesh continued raids for the third day on 11 Jan 2007 on ULFA strongholds and bases in a jungle terrain described as "hostile and thickly wooded in Assam and adjoining border areas of Arunachal Pradesh."

A source put the total strength of the security force about 20,000. The counter-insurgency offensive came after a wave of attacks by ULFA ultras which killed 72 Hindi-speaking migrant-workers (mainly from Bihar and West Bengal) in the state during the last week. These attacks were Assam's worst violence in years and came after New Delhi called off a 6 – week ceasefire in Sep 2006 and resumed military campaign against the militants for stepping up violence and extortions.

Army is backed by the helicopters in its simultaneous operations in two states.

They have not Given up on Talks: Mar 2007

Nine months after the talks between ULFA-appointed People's Consultative Group (PCG) which was headed by Indira Goswami, and the Government of India broke down, there is a fresh move to revive the process. Interestingly, it is Goswami again who is behind the initiative, though this time she is going to press the ULFA to come forward for the direct discussions with New Delhi. Obviously the lady is wiser for her last abortive attempt to bring the devious ULFA on the negotiations table.

Goswami, who along with a group of eminent citizens of Assam recently floated the Citizens Peace Forum (CPF), said on 19 Mar 2007 there was every possibility of re-opening the negotiations especially if the society as a whole wanted it.

Goswami is not the only one working to see the talks between ULFA and New Delhi becoming a reality. There is another 'Curious' group working for the same aim. A platform of ULFA sympathisers, named People's Committee for Peace Initiative (PCPI), has been formed for the purpose.

The PCPI convened a conclave on 22 March, 2007 to revive Assam peace talks, starting a public debate on resolving the issue. Some interesting participants shared their thoughts.

- If Naga Human Rights leaders mooted the idea of a plebiscite to resolve the conflict, other rebel leaders holding ceasefire with New Delhi proposed peace talks without any pre-conditions.
- Political leaders like AGP President Brindawan Goswami and Praful Mahanta also favoured unconditional peace talks, with the former

saying the sovereignty issue should not be a stumbling block in starting these talks.

- The CPI also attended the peace conclave and demanded the suspension of the Army operation. How one wishes the daily[65] should have named this worthy.
- DHD leader Dilip Nonisha, who was among the prominent rebel leaders invited to the conclave reiterated that the agenda for the talks could not be decided without an initial round of direct talks.

ULFA's Condition for Talks: Still Acting Tough

ULFA on 16 Feb 2007 nipped the speculation that time was rife about a "track-II negotiations" with the government in the wake of the insurgent group's decision to call off the boycott of National Games. In the latest internet issue of its mouthpiece, Freedom, ULFA C-in-C Paresh Barua denied having entered into any sort of "track-II negotiations with New Delhi." His only condition was that "restoration of Assam's sovereignty should be on the agenda for talks". He further clarified: "In principle, ULFA is ready for a plebiscite, not referendum, under international supervision."

ULFA chairman Arbindo Rajkhowa on 29 Mar 2007 rejected Assam Chief Minister Tarun Gogoi's offer for unconditional talks and threatened to step up violence by suicide bombers.

In a hardhitting statement, he ruled out the possibility of budgin from their demand of sovereignty.

He also criticised the Congress MP Kirip Chaliha for his remarks against Indira Goswami who played the role of mediator in 2006 peace talks between New Delhi and ULFA, which never took off.

Can ULFA be Trusted? Or, Should it be?

It is a sad saga of murder and mayhem. For nearly three decades, ULFA has proved a tough, and often slippery customer. Should New Delhi call off all attempts at the negotiated settlement and go all out for a military solution? Should another chance be given to the sincere lady, Indira Goswami, to persuade the recalcitrant ULFA leadership to come forward for direct talks with the centre? Should another group of ULFA-friendly citizens, People's Committee for Peace Initiative (PCDI), also be given a chance to try their hand at peace-making? These are all inter-related questions, with no easy answers.

Some aspects of possible talks with ULFA are discussed, with a glance at the past events, with the aim of weighing the future options.

Tarun Gogoi offers Unconditional Talks

He has been criticised for offering talks and another truce to ULFA. Will the politicians, particularly at the state level, ever make an effort to learn from the past experience? Having himself said that "ULFA tock full advantage of the temporary ceasefire in Aug-Sep 2006 to recruit, regroup and initial", how does he offer another truce to that outfit? It is obvious that Gogoi simply refuses to learn! He should have known that the ULFA's appointment of the 11-member People's Consultative Group (PCG) in Sep 2005 was a ploy to save, rather extricate, its leaders holed up in the Dibru-Saikhowa reserve forest. Expectedly, the first action of the PCG was to demand the immediate suspension of the anti-insurgency operations. The centre conceded the request in good faith, in spite of stiff opposition from the Army, as the latter knew better.

The rulers have short memories. A shrewd leader like the late Hiteshwar Saikia regretted the "biggest" mistake of his life when he allowed the pro-talks ULFA leaders to move about freely after Operation Rhino in 1991, hoping that they would persuade their peers in exile to come to the negotiations table. What happened actually? A volte-face and massive ULFA build up in Bhutan.

Whither the current anti-insurgency operation (Jan-Apr 2007) launched after the yet-another abortive (and futile) cease-fire in Aug-Sep 2006 will be taken to its logical conclusion is not certain. The future holds the answer. What is certain is that the most powerful ULFA duo of Rajkhowa-Barua would continue to be elusive. Gogoi must be wiser after two of them administered a snub to him through their internet mouthpiece Freedom. They questioned his authority even to offer talks to ULFA. Yet again, both declared defiantly that the issue of sovereignty must be/have to be on the agenda of talks. More than all this, C-in-C Barua demanded pebiscite under international supervision.

There is no hope of ULFA relenting until India can nab its most powerful leader, Barua, which is unlikely as he is ensconced in a safe, palatial house in Dhaka. But that is possible only if Dhaka cooperates, which again is unlikely, Bangladesh's neutral, transitional Government's tough action against its own terrorists notwithstanding.

Is ULFA Losing Public Sympathy and Support?

There are people who indeed are convinced that the ULFA is losing public sympathy because of its blood-thirst. In continuing to write chapters into its time on violence, it remains blind to this fact. The slide began after the killing of 13 innocent Assamese, mostly women and children, at Dhemaji on Independence Day in 2004. And now, with most sections of the civil society, including the Asom Sahitya Sabha, AASU and even the AGP opposing secession—for them peace is the priority— the ULFA seems to be caught up in the downward spiral of its own making.

What could be the cause or reason for its persistence and stubborn refusal to read the times? Some feel it could be a NGO's recent opinion poll which showed 95 percent Assamese rejecting the ULFA demand for sovereignty. Does it hope to change the trend by its ruthless Jan 2007 murder of 71 Hindi-speaking Biharis? Venting its anger in such an inhuman way is unlikely to constitute the means to what is now a largely unacceptable end. The poll ridiculed Chairman Rajkhowa's oft-repeated claim that sovereignty is not ULFA's demand but people's mandate.

There are some other related aspects of ULFA's tactics that demand attention. As early as in 2005 the official thinking was, and perhaps still is, that it is pointless making overtures to ULFA because its demand for "Swadhin Asom" will die a natural death.[66] It is possibly to counter this thinking that the ULFA adopted the oft-tested tactics of serving notice on the non-Assamese Hindi-speakers to quit Assam. It is obviously aimed at keeping the sagging morale of its cadres high.

At another level, this would amount to openly welcoming migrants from Bangladesh, something not entirely unexpected not only because it has enjoyed the hospitality of that country for years but also because ULFA can hardly afford to antagonise its foreign host that has for all these years been invigorating it. But this open-arms policy for foreign Bangladeshis has implications for its standing with the common Assamese citizens. They had run an intense, passionate and often violent anti-foreigners movement under AASU. It will seriously dent ULFA's much-vaunted 'popularity'. At a more practical level, the ULFA could not be unaware of the fact that if the so-called outsiders stop work even for a day, Assam's entire economy would crumble. But then, is ULFA really concerned with the well-being and prosperity of Assam and its people?

Some opine ULFA alone cannot be blamed for the continuing mayhem. Despite all caution by the security establishment, militants continue to trigger blasts. May be, a more vigorous anti-insurgency campaign is the answer. The Unifiled Command, of course, has launched just that in Jan 2007. But ultimately, political solution is the way out. But that will remain a distant dream till ULFA is forced to sit on the negotiations table.

But what is more worrisome is the blast reported from the Bodo region of Bongaigaon, which is suggestive of agents provocateur It is obvious that the need of the hour is to stand united against the communal virus? Is that a tall order?

Wealthy ULFA Bankrolls Bangla Parties $ 6 m: Feb 2007

The banned ULFA is reported to have pumped in over $ 6 million to fund major political parties (like Bangladesh Nationalist Party, BNP, and the Awami League, AL) in the forthcoming Bangladesh elections, said a leading US think-tank—Strategic Foresight Inc, popularly Stratfor.

The funds have gone to at least 15 candidates belonging to both the BNP and AL. "ULFA is hedging its bet in order to protect its militant and business operations in Bangladesh should either party win." Some other comments and observation from the Stratfor report:

- The ULFA's core leadership is believed to have been living in luxury in Bangladesh for 15 years "under the protection of its political allies in Dhaka. As long as the ULFA can continue funding the appropriate candidates, it can ensure that Bangladesh government will resist caving into Indian demands to crack down on the militant group."
- Observing that $ 6 million was a "handsome contribution coming from an Indian militant outfit, the report said ULFA was no "ordinary organisation". Its chief, Paresh Barua, was "an enormously wealthy racketeer worth approximately $ 110 million" with business operations throughout India, Bangladesh and Persion Gulf. The business interests included hotels consultancy firms, driving schools, tanneries, department stores, textile factories, travel agencies, investment companies, shrimp trawlers and soft drink factories.
- Barua's businesses in Bangladesh is handled by a senior government official in Dhaka.
- The ULFA funded its militant activities "through a sophisticated extortion network". Major tea companies in Assam continuously faced "pay or die" threats but preferred to stay quiet, both out of fear as well as business interests. ULFA has increasingly become more concerned with its financial interests.
- ULFA is aware that New Delhi would not budge in its refusal to give in to the outfit's demands and therefore "is focusing its military operations to bleed the security forces in order to strengthen its negotiating position. That explains "its recent attacks on the migrant workers – mostly from Bihar – in Assam. Besides ULFA, Bangladeshi Islamist groups and Pakistan's ISI are other players having stakes in Bangladesh.

ULFA issue in Assam Assembly: 6 Mar 2007

Assam Assembly was informed by the Government on 6 Mar 2007 that the outlawed ULFA has not as yet responded positively to the efforts of the Centre and State to hold direct talks, while formal talks with the NDFB, holding a ceasefire with security forces, have not started because of the failure of the outfit in submitting its charter of demands.

Speaking on behalf of Chief Minister Tarun Gogoi, Assam's Forest Minister Rockybul Hussain clarified: "Three rounds of talks were hold with the ULFA-appointed People's Consultative Group (PCG) but in the later stages, the militant outfit did not look sincere for talks, and, in fact, taking advantage of the situation it started regrouping itself, besides launching violent attack."

The other points that emerged from the Assembly proceedings are given below:

- Prime Minister Manmohan Singh has made it clear that doors for talks are still open provided the ULFA abjures the path of violence.
- As many as 87 persons, 83 civilians and 4 security personnel, were killed in violence by militant outfits in Assam in the month of January (2007) alone.
- In Jan 2007, ULFA and KLNLF militants triggered 28 explosions in the different parts of the Karbi Anglong district of the State, killing 12 civilians and four security personnel.
- The police, Army and paramilitary forces, operating under a unified command, played a major role in containing acts of violence by the militant outfits.
- Altogether, 459 persons have been killed and nearly 13,530 injured in ULFA related violence since 2001 in the State.

ULFA Threatens to Step up Attacks: 8 Mar 2007

In a statement issued on 8 Mar 2007 in Guwahati, the outlawed outfit has threatend to step up attacks as the Centre and the State are reluctant for a political solution to the decades-old conflict in Assam. "We are compelled to continue our armed struggle to achieve our goal of sovereign Assam," it said. Referring to the initiative of the noted Assamese author Dr. Indira Goswami, ULFA alleged Government was not sincere to resolve the conflict through dialogue.

Ironically, the outfit was brazen enough to reiterate that it believes in political solution to the conflict but government was indulging in harassing the innocent people of the state in the name of counter-insurgency operations.

It also confessed its involvement in 5 March land mine blast in Dhemaji district, meant to target a CRPF vehicle. A local commander of the ULFA told a daily on phone: "It was just the beginning of a fresh round of attacks". The security agencies had already warned of the ULFA offensive in the run-up to "Sainik Divas" it observes every year on 16 March.

One of the main reasons for failure of the Goswami initiative was insistence of ULFA, before the start of the talks, on the release of 5 of its jailed leaders: Bhimkanta Buragohain, Ramu Mech, Mithinga Daimary, Pradip Gogoi and Pranati Deka.

Action Against ULFA: Defence Minister: 20 Mar 2007

Defence Minister AK Antony told the Lok Sabha on 20 Mar 2007 that "during the last two and a half month, the security forces have launched counter-insurgency operation against the outlawed ULFA and as a result 33 of their ultras were killed and 114 injured".[67]

Birthday Musings: 7 Apr 2007

On 7 Apr 1979, five likeminded youngmen met at the historic Rangghar, an amphitheatre of the erstwhile Ahom royalty in Sibsagar district of eastern Assam. After hours of confabulations on the lawn of the two-storeyed oval-shaped pavillion, the five men conceived the idea of "liberating the State from colonial clutches of Indian imperialism" through armed struggle.

Today 28 years down the line, the ULFA is not only dubbed as an outlawed terrorist outfit by New Delhi, the group has also graduated to become one of the most dreaded separatist organisations in India's North-East.

The rest is the history already narrated in some detail in this chapter. The outfit refuses to concede that it has lost much-claimed popularity with the Assamese, who seem to here rejected the idea of sovereignty, the central plank of ULFA's constitutional architecture.

It is only the ego of its leaders, Rajkhowa and Barua, particularly of the latter, that comes in the way of its holding direct talks with New Delhi. The latest offer of unconditional talks came from Assam Chief Minister Tarun Gogoi on 27 Mar 2007. Two days later, ULFA through its Chairman snubbed the Government, declaring in an e-mailed statement: "We are not mad to sit for unconditional talks after having lost 10,000 of our freedom fighters in our struggle for independence. The offer of unconditional talks is not acceptable to us."

Let us end, wishing a better sense to the ULFA leadership than reflected in the e-mailed statement.

NOTES

1. Cited by B.C. Verghese, 1997.
2. Dhekiyal Phukan (1829-89), became Sub-Assistant Commissioner in 1850. A friend and admirer of the Baptist Mission in Assam, he regularly wrote for the first Assamese journal, *Orunodoi*. It was largely due to his efforts that Assamese was restored as the official and Court language of Assam in 1873. He had pleaded this cause in his memorandum to Moffat-Mills in 1853.
3. Guha, 1977.
4. Kanaklal Barua (1872-1940), a law graduate, became an Extra Assistant Commissioner in 1900. Later, elected member of Assam's Legislative Council, he was appointed Minister for Local Government. Actively associated with historical research, he served as a member of the Indian Historical Records Commission.

5. Kamala Kanta Bhattacharyya (1855-1936) was the Editor of Assam Hitashi and actively involved in the National Movement; was known for his radical views.

6. Lakshmikant Bezbarua (1864-1938) belonged to the family of personal physicians to the Ahom Kings. Easily the most prolific and influential Assamese writer (novels, plays, short stories and satirical pieces) of modern period, he is known as *Sahityarthi*. He was determined to establish Assamese language (and literature) in its own right, with a rich literary tradition of its own; and engaged in a long debate with those who thought otherwise. He married the grand-daughter of Devendranath Tagore, Prajnasundari Devi.

7. Chandra Sudhir, *Economic and Political Weekly*, Vol. XVII, No. 32, 7-8-1982.

8. Misra, Udayon, 2000.

9. Ambaikagiri Roy-Choudhury (1885-1967) joined the Anarchist Group in 1904 and was interned at Barpeta. He edited *Chetna* from 1918. He was jailed for a year for his joining the Non-Cooperation Movement. He was a front-ranking writer in Assamese.

10. The Cabinet Mission Plan had provided for the division of British Indian provinces into three Groups A, B and C. Group C was to consist of Bengal and Assam. It was an obvious mismatch between the two constituent provinces when it came to taking decisions by a majority in the Group's Legislature, whose membership configuration is given below:

Group C States

		Members	
	General	*Muslim*	*Total*
Bengal	27	33	60
Assam	7	3	10
Total Members	34	36	70

The table shows clearly that Bengal as a political entity and the Muslims as a religious entity, were in a win-win situation. Hence the fears of the Assamese, a hapless minority on all counts.

11. *Ibid.*

12. Misra, Udayon, 2000.

13. See n. 10.

14. Saiyid Muhammad Saadhullah Khan, in all, headed five ministries in Assam at different times during the April 1937-February 1946 period. An Assamese Muslim, he is seen as largely responsible for the large-scale entry and settlement into Assam of Bengali Muslim immigrants from the then (East) Bengal. His "Grow More Food" plan during the World War II was dubbed by Lord Wavell as "Grow More Muslims" plan, in his Diary. In just one year (1939-40), his Government settled Muslim immigrants on 100,000 bighas of land in the Brahmaputra Valley. He understandably supported the Grouping

Plan of the Cabinet Mission, "which would have handed over Assam to Bengal and erase the borders between the two for an unchecked flow of immigrants".

15. Bhuyan, A.C., ed, Political History of Assam, Vol. III, 1978; cited, Misra, Udayon, 2000.
16. Sanjoy Hazarika, 1994, cited by Dinesh Kotwal of IDSA, in his "Contours of Assam Insurgency" in *Strategic Analysis,* March 2001.
17. It was his failure to keep this promise that compelled ULFA's Publicity Director to publicly ask people to boycott, at the pain of death, 1998 Parliamentary Elections (*The Outlook*, 23-2-98). Was it because of this call that Mahanta's AGP did not get a single seat in this Election as well as the one held in October 1999.
18.. Incidentally, it is the same K.P.S. Gill who was once the bete noire of the AASU agitationists, heading the Assam Police as he did during the Agitation, but by that time had become a national hero for turning Punjab back from the brink. But by that time, Mahanta was past the mid-course of his second tenure and no more a political green horn as he obviously was during his first tenure (1996-2001) as Assam's Chief Minister.
19. Why Mahanta did not emulate the simple and straightforward decision of his counterpart in J and K, Farooq Abdullah, who took over the direct command of a similar unified structure in his State, was not comprehensible to the men in uniform, fighting insurgency in the North-East.
20. From published sources and the SF releases.
21. Union Home Minister Indrajit Gupta supplied the information in Lok Sabha on 14 May 1997.
22. Documents seized from the Bodo militants disclosed this information.
23. Earlier Mcneill and Magor; now owned by the BM Khaitan group.
24. They were S.M. Kidwai, then GM, TTL and his deputy, Hamid Haq.
25. For fuller details, see *India Today* of 20-10-1997, *The Outlook* of 27-10-1997, *Indian Express* of 5-10-1997, *The Frontline* of 28 November 1997 and *Sunday Observer* of 21-9-1997.
26. In a self-serving advertisement in the Press, the Government claimed credit for surrender of 4516 ultras, belonging to ULFA (2781), BdSF (1735) and DNSF, etc. (*Hindustan Times,* 28-10-1995). "The Government sanctioned a total of Rs. 3121 lakh for their rehabilitation under 100 per cent margin money schemes.... 876 jobs have also been provided."
27. There were heart-rending scenes at village Nij-Juluki in Nalbari district. The names of 5-member family of ULFA Publicity Secretary Mithinga Daimary (real name Dipak Das) gunned down by SULFA were: Dipak's brother, Dharnidhar Das, a popular doctor in the locality, his pregnant wife Runjyoti, Dipak's mother Phuleshawari, and his sister Latika. Dipak's father was away at his daughter's house (*The Outlook*] 31-8-1998).
28. There was a precedent of a BSF battalion being raised from the ranks of ex-Naga rebels. It gave an excellent account of itself.

29. *The Hindu*, 3-4-1999.
30. *The Frontline*, 4-6-1999.
31. *The Hindu*, 24-4-1999.
32. *Hindustan Times*, 15-11-1999.
33. Gen Sinha in an interview with *The Frontline* issue dated 27-8-1999.
34. *The Frontline*, 27-8-1999.
35. *Ibid*.
36. Barun Das-Gupta, *Hindustan Times*, 15-8-2000.
37. Mahanta had been invited by the Corps Commander for the surrender ceremony for 51 militants held at Tezpur on 24 July 1998. Choosing to be absent, he sent his senior minister Z.N. Sharma to stand in for him. Pray, who was this Minister? He is the same personage against whom Army had registered a FIR in October 1997. What was Mahanta trying to convey through his absence? Again, why should he detail of all ministers in his cabinet Z.N. Sharma to represent him? Again, perhaps, it is not so subtle a message to the Army!
38. 315 of these have been rehabilitated, Mahanta told the press at Shillong on 23 January 2000 (*The Hindu*, 24-1-2000).
39. This is the BSF figure; cited by Dinesh Kotwal in his IDSA Paper dated 18-11-2000.
40. Barua gave interview to the *Asamiya Pratidin*: cited by Samudra Gupta Kashyap in *Indian Express*, 3-1-2001.
41. *Hindustan Times*, 18-1-2001.
42. The existence of Manipuri settlements in Bangladesh, especially in Sylhet district, had helped to establish these links. Reports indicated that the "hide-outs and training camps of the Manipuri insurgents exist in Srimangal, Bhanugarh and Dhamai areas, close to one another. Interrogation reports of arrested ULFA activists, some of which have been published, confirm these facts.
43. It was around the time (1992) when ULFA Chairman had written to Prime Minister Rao offering talks but carefully prefaced schedule for the talks and an eventual deal got bogged down subsequently
44. *The Frontline*, 11-2-1994.
45. Unable to explain his participating in public protest against his own Government, Mazumdar simply replied: "Governor's speech at Bongaigaon has left me with no other alternative" whatever that might mean!
46. *Times of India* 19-12-2000.
47. Against this report of the respected *Frontline* fortnightly, the so-called national daily, *Hindustan Times*, mentions Paresh Barua's house being in Tinsukia district. This much for the care and attention the 'venerable' press brings to bear on a matter of fact concerning the location of the house of

very important—if not the most important, which perhaps he is—ULFA leader!

48. In this regard, it might be apt to mention here that ULFA had received a big jolt earlier in the year with the arrest of top leader Chitra Dehengia and the busting of its Central Publicity Office in a mid-night swoop on 7-8 January (2000) in Shillong.
49. Gen Sinha's interview to the *Assam Tribune* of 24-4-2000.
50. He was addressing the IAS officers course at the India International Centre, cited by Dinesh Kotwal, in his IDSA Paper dated 18 November 2000.
51. *Assam Tribune*, 8-9-2000.
52. *Hindustan Times*. 8-6-2002.
53. Cited by *The Outlook*, 20-4-1998.
54. Passing through Kolkata on his way to Thimpu on 2 December 2001, Bhutan's Home Minister Lyonpo Thinley Gyamtsho told *Frontline* (4-1-2002) that ULFA alone had 9 camps in Southern Bhutan. ULFA had agreed to close 4 of the camps by December 2001. "At the other 5, they will reduce the s]trength by now and eventually close them as well."
55. *The Frontline*, 4-1-2002.
56. *The Hindu*, 8-12-2001.
57. *The Hindu*, 14-6-2002.
58. *Indian Express*, 12-7-2002.
59. *Hindustan Times*, 5-6-2002.
60. *Indian Express,* 1-4-2002.
61. *Indian Express*, 7.11.2006.
62. *Ibid*.
63. Verghese K. George, *Indian Express,* 7.11.2006.
64. Rahul Singh and Rahul Karmakar (*Dinjan*, Tinsukia/Guwahati), *Hindustan Times*, 12 Jan 2007.
65. Manoj Anand, *Asian Age*, 23 Mar 2007.
66. Editorial, *The Statesman*, 25 Jan 2007.
67. All India Radio, 21 Mar 2007.

5

Bodos : Struggle for Bodoland

"Bodos are presently running one of the oldest ethnic movements in Assam." It has had a chequered history since its very inception: sometimes intense, then rather quiescent, and yet again, occasionally lapsing into horribly violent phase, before returning to a comparatively peaceful mode. But in the recent times, somewhere along the way the Movement has spawned militant outfits to further its cause, which are BdSF, BLT and NDFB. But to the dismay and chagrin of all concerned, the last-mentioned has developed into a virulently secessionist movement. This Chapter traces the history of Bodoland Movement and acts of terrorism by these outfits.

Bodos in History

The Bodo "problem" and subsequent insurgency is of comparatively recent origin. Since the 1970s, sections of this ethnic group have been "trying to regain the old glory when the Bodos ruled the valley unchallenged for centuries".

For a proper perspective on the issue, it is necessary to know the past of the Bodos, and their present economic, social, political, linguistic and cultural condition, compared to other tribal groups in the region.

Belonging to the great Mongoloid stock, the Bodos are often known as Kacharis, particularly among the non-Bodos,. But they themselves prefer the term 'Bodo'. The term 'Bodo' is a genus of large number of ethnic communities like the Boros, Boro-Kacharis, Sonowal-Kacharis, Thangal-Kacharis, Deuries, Rabhas, Tiwas, Misings, Mechs, Dimasas, Hojais, Karbis and the Barmans (of Cachar). But presently the term generally embraces the Bodos, the Boro-Kacharis and the Mechs.

They had once established a prosperous kingdom, centred round Dimapur. Under pressure from the neighbouring rulers, the capital had to be shifted to Maibong (in North Cachar district) and finally to Khaspur (in Cachar district). The historians aver that this kingdom belonged to the Dimasa-

Kacharis, rather than to the Bodos. In the pre-historic times (Mahabharata period, to be specific), the Kacharis are credited to have established two kingdoms in the Brahmaputra Valley, viz, Bana's at Sonitpur and Narakasur's at Pragjyotishpur. The Koch-Rajbongshis, who later demanded a ST status, once had established a kingdom covering Western Assam and Northern Bengal areas, but they refuse to be identified with the Bodo-Kacharis, any more.

It is admitted today that the Bodos once were a prosperous, cultured and distinct identity (nationality). In the past, their language was fairly advanced, with a strong grammatical base. Even up to the 1960s, it was known as dowan (spoken language alone). The strength of Bodo kingdom and their language can be judged by the fact that the Bodo names of the places and rivers survived the influence of the six-century long Ahom rule. The scholars hold that the Aryans and the Bodos (of the Mongoloid stock) have borrowed from each other and enriched each other in the fields of religious beliefs, cultures and languages. So the mythological war of Hari-Hara and the Rig Vedic Sukta 191/10 are indicative of the amalgamation of the two races, some kind of a melting pot phenomenon.

The majority of Bodos is still Hindu. They nurture a feeling of having been exploited and discriminated against by the so-called Assamese society, a justification for their movement for a separate state.

The Bodos and Aryans are not autochthonous communities. But the former claim they are the first comers, and hence entitled to a better share of land and resources.

The supremacy the Bodos enjoyed could not be sustained for the last few centuries. The sociologists ascribe this decline to the family-based rice-liquor consumption, rendering them less energetic, complacent and fatalistic. Consequently, the men-folk lost their work-culture. The ethnic resurgence among them in the recent years is attributed to the realisation that such liquor consumption has been their social enemy. So the youth has been forsaking it. This single point analysis is rather narrowly focused. There are other reasons for the political consciousness, compelling them to seek a place for themselves under the sun, which are summed up below:

1. There has been widespread expansion of educational institutions among them. Census data show that the literacy among the tribals (and the Bodos are their major segment) rose from 18 per cent in 1961 to 49.14 per cent in 1991; and the comparative figures for males were 28.39 per cent and 59.82 per cent, and for females 6.64 per cent and 38.99 per cent. This rate of spread of literacy among them is higher than the state average.

2. The Bodo Sahitya Sabha and Tribal Sangha played an important part to usher in an era of revivalism and self-regeneration, knitting them into a united community.
3. Restoring the Bodo language to a place of pride, and making it medium of education for the Bodo children. It made them conscious of their cultural heritage.
4. Scholarly research restored intrinsic glory to the Bodo history and their past achievements became better known. The British scholars had made great contributions in this field. The discovery and study of the historic fort at Dimapur is a shining example of this contribution.
5. The demographic concentrations of the Bodos in certain parts, spread in the large areas of the State, proved their strength. The population clustering of the Bodos on the north bank of the Brahmaputra could be cited in this connection. The Bodos are seen in all districts of the State, but are essentially concentrated in the area between the rivers Sankosh in Kokrajhar and Dhubri districts and the Orang in the Darrang district. This area is constituted by the districts wholly or partly—of Kokrajhar, Bongaigaon, Barpeta, Nalbari (northern parts), Kamrup (Rangia subdivision), and Darrang (northern parts). There is a total of 23 Development Blocks where the tribal population is more concentrated.[1] Of the total of 2494 villages, with tribal population, there are 300 with 100 per cent tribal population and 821 with predominantly tribal population between 50 and 100 per cent.
6. Starting with the mid-19th century, outsiders started entering Assam. From the early years of the 20th century, tribal lands started coming under pressure of these outsiders, particularly the migrants from the then East Bengal, later East Pakistan, and now Bangladesh. They would occupy vast vacant areas—Khasland, VGR, PGR, or Forest Land in these tracts and settle there. A large number of foreigners were settled on the tribal land under politico-religious considerations, as by Assam's Saadullah Ministry's policy of rehabilitating Bengali agriculturist Muslims there under the garb of Grow More Food campaign during World War II. Obviously, there was resentment at the tribals losing control on their own land. To reassure the tribals, the British had instituted the Inner Line system in the 1870s and in the late 1940s, Assam passed legislation constituting the Tribal Belts and Blocks. All such measures failed to eliminate the threat to the tribal identity as perceived by the Bodos, and their organisations came to the conclusion that Bodo autonomy was the answer to their problems. Hence the Movement.

Having briefly mentioned the environs that generated ethnic and political consciousness among the Bodos to revive their old glory, a look into their distant past should be of interest. They are one of the original settlers of the Brahmaputra Valley, and are reputed to have brought settled agriculture to the Region as also introduced silk weaving to it. They obviously had a glorious past, with a kingdom over the Brahmaputra Valley, down to North Bengal, Cachar Hills, Sylhet and Tripura. They had their colonies near the streams, water (di, being their word for it), hence the Bodo names like Dikhu, Diphu, Dihang, Dibru and also Tista or Dista: Grierson also mentions about Mech rule, in Pragjyotishpur for over 4000 years which began to decline by the 11th century AD. Bodos are most important Indo-Mongoloid people in East India who marked their physical presence over the entire land mass of Assam (barring eastern parts inhabited by Kuki-Chins, and Khasi and Jaintia Hills) and North and East Bengal. Being of Tibeto-Burman origin, they belong to Tibeto-Chinese Linguistic stock. The Indo-Mongoloids were known to the Vedas, Mahabharata, Ramayana, Kalika Purana, and Yogini Tantra and Kirata, who find prominent mention in the Epics.[2]

They came from areas like China, Tibet, Mongolia and Siberia, but Rev Sydney Endle thinks they are the autochthons of Assam. They ruled under different rulers at different points in time, that is, Kiratas, Asuras, Mlech and Danavas. In the comparatively recent historical times, Bodo kingdom was at zenith during the reign of Koch King Nar Narayan (1540-84). It was after the assassination of Raja Govind Chandra in 1832 that the last Bodo kingdom (in Cachar) was extinguished, with its annexation by the British. It was following this 'demise' that the Bodos started feeling marginalized, and were submerged under other hegemonies. So, not only do they have a proud past, the present Bodo Movement for autonomy (and even sovereignty, as by NDFB) has an ancient ancestry. "Militancy among the Bodos has its roots in the paternalistic attitude of the Assamese Caste Hindu elite", was the more recent cause.

Origin of the Bodo 'National' Identity

It was replacement of Assamese with Bengali in schools and courts in 1937 by the British at the 'instigation' of its Bengali officials that really hurt the 'national' pride of the Assamese. It was during the long protest and agitation against this decision that saw the beginning of rise of the Assamese middle class which finally saw their language restored to its rightful place in 1873. The year 1838 saw the establishment of literary society like the Assamiya Bhasa Unnati Sadhani Sabha which later metamorphosed into Assam Sahitya Sabha (ASS), the harbinger and upholder of the Assamese nationalism, that is, Assamiya identity, which remained unchallenged till about 1920s. There were no dissenting voices. It was the educated elite which led the way in this happy harmony. First graduate among the Bodos of Goalpara, Rup Nath

Brahma, was not only a minister in 1938 Assam Ministry but also was to become President of the History Section of ASS in 1956. Obviously, the Bodos were a part of the happy family till a particular point in time, and the issue of separate identity was not central to their educated elite which was rather taken up with social issues. The idea of separate identity gains importance somewhere in the 1930s-1940s period. The birth of Bodo Sahitya Sabha (BSS) was the culmination of the identity issue. The Bodo elite was well aware and deeply conscious of the ethno-consolidating role of Bodo language.

The large-scale import of outsiders to work the tea gardens of Assam—the tea gardens in Upper Assam alone needed 5,27,000 labour in the opening years—has had far-reaching implications in the history of Assam that is plaguing the state till date. The Bodos today are locked in deadly conflict with the descendants of these importees, for preserving their identity. Perhaps it was to establish this identity that the Bodos exhibited their inclination for the Roman script since 1884 when they came in contact with the missionaries; and particularly since the publication of an authentic monograph. The Kacharis, in 1911 by Endle wherein he narrated some Bodo folk tales in Roman script with analogous English translation. And that inclination played a crucial role in fostering and sustaining the Bodo movement in the post-Independence India, based on and informed as it is by the emphasis on their separate identity.

Birth of Brahmaism. The beginning of the 20th century, is significant because of the emergence of the Bodo middle class, though meagre in number, they had certain level of formal education. During the British rule, the middle class grew from the external compulsion of conquest and the need for playing a role, even, if subservient, in the conqueror-conquered relationship at several strategic but still comparatively minor points. But more importantly, there was also an external factor at play. It was the Vedic Movement under the guidance of Kalicharan Brahmachari in 1907. It saw the growth of a small middle class among the adherents of the new faith who adopted the suffix 'Brahma after their name. Born Kalicharan Mech in April 1860 at Kazagaon in Dhubri Sub-division, he was the preceptor and leader of the Brahma Movement, dedicating his life for the upliftment of his backward community The opening of the East Bengal State Railway branch line from Calcutta to Dhubri in 1902 facilitated his frequent trips to Calcutta whence he came in contact with Srimat Param Hansa Sibnarayan Swamy who finally initiated him in 1907. Thus it was that Kalicharan Mech became 'Brahma' and also started preaching the tenets of Brahmaism. He emphasised that education was a must for socio-economic upliftment of Bodos. The establishment of a Bodo hostel at Dhubri was a natural step and expectedly, it became a centre for Bodo intellectuals. In 1919 was formed the Bodo Chhatra Sanmelan.

Finally, the Bodo Mahasanmelan became the main platform for activities of Bodo intellectuals, Jadavchandra Khokhlary being its first President.

Mahasanmelan's third conference adopted certain measures for social reforms: (1) Bride price lowered to Rs. 51. (2) Restrictions on women going to market removed. (3) Marriage by capture banned. More importantly, over 3000 youngmen took the oath to abide by such injunction. People were encouraged to take to trade and business in agricultural produce. Kalicharan organised the Brahma Company. Trade relations were developed with Bengal. The attempt first and last among the Bodos failed.

The position of the areas and tribes declared 'backward' under Section 52(A) of Government of India Act, 1919 was to be examined by the Simon Commission which had called the representatives of the Primitive and Backward Tribes to Shillong on 4 January 1929 for submitting their memoranda on the subject. Bodo leaders' aspirations to be identified as a separate 'nation' were manifest in the memorandum submitted by the Plains Tribals of Assam in 1929, and it is the year some analysts feel the modern Bodo movement may have started from. Here are some important points from the memorandum:

1. "In spite of our glorious past, we are not getting our due. We oppose mixed electorate because of which we have no representatives in the Legislative Council.
2. "In spite of our large numbers, all advantages of reforms are being enjoyed by a Brahmin, a Kshatriya, or a Sudra.
3. "Of the four seats for Assam in Central Legislature, one is earmarked for Muslims and three for non-Muslims; one out of the latter must be reserved for Bodos.
4. "We oppose the merger of Goalpara into Bengal. We Bodos can by no means call ourselves other than the Assamese.[3]
5. "We demand compulsory primary education.
6. "We must get share of political power through representation in the Council as also in local bodies.[4]
7. "Historically and traditionally, the Bodos stood on a very high level and socially, they enjoyed splendid isolation. But educationally and politically, they are backward, having fallen on evil days.
8. "Indians are fit for self-Government. Dyarchy is unworkable.... The provincial autonomy should be granted immediately."

MOVEMENT FOR IDENTITY

Bodo Movement : Phase I : 1930-67

Bodo elite, growing with the post-1919 Act reforms, had developed a political mind during the 1920s but failed to make any tangible gains for some years. In their 1929 Memorandum, they blamed the existing stratification in the Hindu society for their problems. Andrew Clow, Governor of Assam (1942-46), was making the same point, perhaps with some bias: "The Assamese, both caste Hindus and Muslims, professed solicitude for the tribes, but neither had studied the question nor any real sympathy with them. The feeling of deprivation among these communities thus fostered the growth of local organisations, i.e., the Kachari Sanmilan, Koch Rajbongshi Sanmilan, Chutia Sanmilan, Muttock Association, etc. throughout the Province. Initially, they all functioned independently...., but in 1933 joined hands to form All Assam Plains Tribes League (AAPTL, TL for short)."

In 1933, TL held its first session at Nagaon under the Presidentship of Jadav Chandra Khokhlari. Bhimbar (B.B.) Deuri attended the session, first time entering the direct politics. The same year, Deuri community was recognised as one of the Plains Tribes of Assam. The 1935 Act proved the turning point for the Plains Tribals of Assam, as five seats were reserved for them in the State Legislative Assembly under it. B.B. Deuri became a prominent spokesman of the Plains Tribals. By now tribal land was coming under serious onslaught from the immigrants, and also to an extent, from the local non-tribal traders, businessmen, and moneylenders. TL was fighting desperately against this occupation of their land by non-tribals. TL had joined the Saadullah-led Assam United Party Government[5] in 1937, but revolted against his pro-immigrants policies. When consequently, the Congress formed its first Ministry in September 1938 under G.N. Bordoloi after Saadullah's resignation[6], the TL made an agreement with it, as Bordoloi's proposals for protective system for tribal belts, known as Line System, to safeguard the tribal lands against encroachment by the immigrants, earned their approval. But when Bordoloi resigned in the wake of Britain joining World War II, Saadullah again succeeded to win the support of TL leaders on 10 March 1940 and formed his third Government in Assam,[7] agreeing to abide by the Line System. But his pro-immigrants policy and handling of the Line System caused anxiety amongst the tribals. The total rupture came when Saadullah supported the Cabinet Mission Plan of including Assam with Bengal in Group C. Tribals opposed it vehemently: "We are culturally more akin to Assamese than Bengalis." At fifth session of TL at Mangaldoi, they withdrew support from Muslim League. Both Rupnath and Deuri joined the Congress Party in July 1946, under an agreement. The TL stood transformed into Tribal Sangh (TS), a socio-cultural organisation. The well-meaning Assam Land and Regulation (Amendment) Act of 1947 created 33 reserved belts and blocks in Assam to protect the tribal lands against alienation and encroachment by the outsiders. But unfortunately, the Act proved inadequate for the intended purposes. The widening hiatus between the Congress and non-Congress Bodo leaders became glaringly painful when the former nominated Dharnidhar Basumatari for the Lok Sabha seat. It was perhaps first attempt by political parties at dividing the tribals, which was to become a pattern in the later years. Bodo leaders became painfully aware that if their joining hands with the Muslim League and Congress from time to time during pre-1947 India had gained them nothing, the experience was no different in the Independent India. They were convinced that the Congress Party failed to show sufficient urgency to keep its promise of safeguarding the interests of the tribals. They regretted the conversion of the TL into. TS, as the move had frozen the Bodo political activities for two decades till 1967 when they created the Plains Tribal Council of Assam (PTCA). To PTCA goes the credit of being the first Bodo organisation to demand Bodo autonomy, a separate homeland for Bodos, howsoever nebulous the concept at that stage! Side by side stood the Bodo intellectuals, already engaged in raising the community (identity) consciousness among them. They had (already) established a Brahma Boarding School at Dhubri and founded the Bodo Club which proved to be the mother of Bodo Sahitya Sabha (BSS), established in 1952. BSS was to play a vanguard role in awakening and fostering self-respect and identity consciousness among the Bodos in the decades to come.

Bodo Movement: Phase II : 1967-87

In the face of persistent demand for autonomy by various groups, Prime Minister Indira Gandhi offered to reorganise Assam on the basis of a federal structure on 13 January 1967. The Assam students opposed it but the ABSU formed on 15 January 1967 welcomed the move and in fact, wanted a homeland for Bodos in the plains of Assam. It was in fact with active support of ABSU that the PTCA was formed on 27 February under Presidentship Modoram Brahma, to formulate a suitable response to Mrs Gandhi's proposal. Subsequently, PTCA demanded an autonomous region in the shape of a UT, called Udayachal for Plains Tribals of Assam including Bodos. On 19 May 1968, BSS demanded introduction of Bodo as medium of instruction upto Secondary stage. The demand was conceded, effective 23 September 1968. Thus, not only PTCA, mostly led by the Bodos, was the first to seek autonomy in 1967,[8] the Bodos themselves were the first to win the case for their language to be media of instruction in 1968. Here lies the rub and an important fact of political life: The language is a potent weapon in the hands of communities to further their political cause including exclusivity, separatism and even secession. And Bodos had learnt their lesson from the Assamese themselves who had launched a long agitation against the decision of the British to replace Assamese by Bengali in 1837 in courts and administration. 35-year struggle by the Assamese compelled the British Government in Assam to restore Assamese in the Courts in 1872, and in education department a year later. Coerced by the Assam Sahitya Sabha, Assam Government passed the Official Language Bill of 1960, under which Assamese was declared the sole official language of state. Some analysts feel this declaration led to the unraveling of composite Assam, which ended only with the Parliament passing the North-Eastern States (Reorganisation) Bill 1971. With it, the Region stood divided into 5 States and two Union Territories—Assam being just one among the Seven. But this did not stop the PTCA in its tracks. It stood by its demand for the UT status in 1972, and in the same year BSS launched a movement for Roman script for Bodo language. When PTCA held its session at BACinadi on 20 April 1973, the Assamese press and politicians, sensing a threat to Assam's integrity, accused the Plains Tribals of "getting money from CIA". Incensed by the charge, the Bodo leaders were more firmly set on their demand. On 9 October 1973, Assam's Plains and Hill leaders met Mrs Gandhi in Guwahati and pressed their case for UT and Roman script. In April 1975, she offered Devnagri script and it was accepted by the BSS and ABSU. With the language issue out of the way, the movement for Udayachal (as a UT) was intensified.

The Emergency (1975-77) put a freeze on all activity, and when it was lifted, PTCA entered into an alliance with Janata Party on 4 June 1977 to contest forthcoming Parliamentary Elections. The PTCA won only one (Kokrajhar) seat but enough votes otherwise to win recognition from the Election Commission as a regional party. In the 1983 elections for the Sixth Assembly, it won four seats of the nine contested and joined the Golap Borbora Coalition Ministry, with Samar Brahma Choudhury becoming (Cabinet) Minister for Forests. The 1985 Elections saw a set back for PTCA, with only Charan Narzary returning to Assembly and Samar Brahma Choudhury to Lok Sabha. When the latter demanded Autonomous Region for the Plains Tribals, not the UT, ABSU staunchly opposed it, wanting nothing short of UT. PTCA was on a down slide thence on. After 1985 Elections, it got split into PTCA and PTCA-P (Progressive), the latter advocating Mishing Bodoland. This election put AGP, political face of AASU, into power. So then on, ABSU was fighting its battles with its one-time comrades-in-arms of the 1979-85 anti-foreigners movement.

For a while in 1984, there appeared on the horizon United Tribals Nation Liberation Front (UTNLF). Expectedly, it spawned United Bodo National Liberation Front (UBNLF). Both the outfits disappeared gradually as the ABSU became more effective.

Surprisingly, signing of Assam Accord on 15 August 1985 did not bring peace to the State. If the Bodos and Karbis were demanding Bodoland and an autonomous state within Assam (later UT), the ULFA wanted outright Independence. It should be interesting to see what led to the Bodoland demand. It was not the issue of identity crisis to begin with, but the language that stirred the Bodo heart, which in turn was impelled by the State Government's decisions in 1960 (Official Language Bill) and 1972 (Assamese as Medium of Instructions Bill). But the Bodos got what they wanted in 1968 (Bodos as the medium of instruction) and 1975 (Hindi script). But these very successes goaded them to other demands. PTCA had been demanding only UT status, but with its decline post-1985 elections, leadership devolved on the Bodos. The urges and aspirations of the ethnic Bodos were the underlying cause, and the apparent success of the youthful AASU in its Movement, had further fired their immigration. Later, it was a question of upping the ante. If Assam students could, why not the Bodo students?

Bodo Movement : Phase III : 1987-93

Formed in 1967, the ABSU Movement took a new turn with the election of Upendra Nath (Upen) Brahma as its President in 1987. He had impressive academic attainments: Physics Honours graduate, MSc in Physics, and Law student of Guwahati University. Till a certain stage, ABSU was supporter and part of the AASU Agitation and Upen, as a student of Cotton College, Guwahati, had closely seen and studied the AASU leaders in action. He now led ABSU Movement on same lines, becoming its moving force. Bodo elite turned to him. They had observed with dismay the Assamese 'Chauvinism' under their 'caste Hindu leaders'. Within a year, Brahma's ABSU gained near complete hold, kind of 'civil hegemony', over large sections of Bodo society. This obviously alarmed the UTNLF and AGP. With its policies and fiasco in 1985 polls, PTCA had been marginalized. Brahma and his ABSU became the prime movers of the Bodo Movement.

Brahma decided to launch a democratic mass revolution on the Gandhian non-violent ways on 2 March 1987; aimed at a separate State of Bodoland by 1990, dividing Assam on 50:50 basis. It was to be a Bodoland within Indian union, not within Assam. ABSU presented a memorandum to Governor B.N. Singh and Chief Minister Mahanta on 1 April 1987, containing a 92-point charter of demands.[9] They raised a volunteer force under Phukan Ch. Baro as Chairman and Anchula Gwra Bodosa as Convener for this peaceful movement, which did not remain so for long.

On 19 June, ABSU held a huge Bodo rally at the Judges Field, Guwahati its first for a separate state. The returning students were attacked by mobs, when a Sujit Narzari was killed, becoming the first Bodo martyr to the cause. The ABSU had by then got the support of the Mishings, Deuris, Lalungs and Rabhas, convincing them "that the separation would help all of us". This single death put the ABSU on an agitationists path, well and truly, as the following events show:

1. 21 July. Public protest through mass hunger strikes and mass religious prayers; followed by oath-taking sessions.

2. 27 August. 12-hour tribal area banch and 24-hour National Highway blockade at Lailangpara, near Rowta Chirali in Darrang district.
3. During August, large-scale arrests of ABSU activists.
4. 9 September. State-wide ABSU 'band' attracted suppressive measures by AGP Government and AASU.
5. 24-25 September. 36-hour tribal area bandh.

The year 1987 saw 15-phases of ABSU Movement. The same year it also draw some support, even if indirect, from UMF, Congress (I), UTNLF and Lok Dal (B). May be, they all wanted to spite the AGP. The United Reservation Movement's Council, floated by the foursome, launched a padayatra, starting from Dhubri and Sadiya, and the two columns converged on Guwahad to hold a protest rally at the Judges Field.

The year 1988 saw more phases of the agitation. (1) 27 April. 72-hour Assam bandh: 20th Phase: ABSU starts losing faith in democratic ways. (2) 21 May. ABSU holds joint meeting with All Assam Koch-Rajbongshi Kshatriya Sanmilani (AAKRKS) to garner support for their movement. (3) 4 June. 180-hour Rail Roko bandh, accompanied by bomb blasts. Violence was in the air. (4) Mahanta holds talks with Brahma. No results. (5) July. All Cachar-Karimganj Students Union (ACKSU) and All Assam Minorities Students Union (AAMSU) extended support to ABSU, as they too were opposed to the process of Assamisation pursued by AGP Government This show of unity riled the Government and Assamese in general. (6) 28 August. Joint meeting of ABSU, ACKSU and AAMSU. They worked out a common programme of 50-hour Rail Roko in Assam (for September) and further bandhs and Rail Rokos (for October). (7) September-October. All Assam Tribals Students Union (AATSU) and Tribal Students Federation (TSF) also declared their support for ABSU. The Movement was now entering (perhaps, had already entered) a militant phase.

The formation of a new Bodo body, Bodo People's Action Committee (BPAC), was an important landmark of the year 1988, with the aim of mobilizing all people in Bodoland. Actually, it adopted militant practices, viz, armed training for its cadres, and acquisition of arms and ammunition, of which there was plenty, particularly of local manufacture variety. BPAC thus turned out to be an armed wing of ABSU, Brahma Group, its main faction; the other was led by Ramsiary. BPAC adopted terrorist methods not only against the non-tribals living in the mixed population villages of Dhubri, Kokrajhar, Barpeta, Nalbari, Darrang and Sonitpur districts but also against the political rivals like BPTC, which though in decline, still claimed the support of all Plains Tribals, including Bodos.

Thus by 1988, ABSU (Brahma) had emerged as a force to reckon with. An eminent Assamese had put it aptly: "Presently, the ABSU is ruling the roost in the tribal areas as did AASU in Brahmaputra Valley during the Assam Movement, 1979-85."[10]

In March 1988, BPAC and ABSU had started movement for a separate Bodoland on the North Bank, spread from River Sankosh to Sadiya, over an area of 25,478 km^2, with a population of 4.47 million with 51 per cent Bodo majority. They had two additional demands: (1) Creation of two autonomous districts of Neelachal and Lalung on the South Bank. (2) Notification as STs of Bodo-Kachari groups living in Karbi Anglong district. They wanted Bodoland to be created as a UT initially, being elevated to statehood subsequently. When reminded of lack contiguity in the proposed State, they promptly pointed out to the precedent of Goa, Daman and Deo. This detail was essential to follow the contours of the demand and the movement to attain it. The demand[11] touched the ten districts of Assam: Dhubri, Kokrajhar, Bongaigaon, Barpeta, Nalbari, Kamrup, Darrang, Sonitpur, Lakhimpur and Dhemaji; with a total population of 11,238,965 as per 1991 Census, against Assam's total of 22,294,565. Bodoland was sought to be created out of these ten districts.

The 19-22 December Bashbari conference was another landmark of 1988, as ABSU and BPAC had gathered on a public platform for the first time, and also because it was attended by other organisations like the TSF, ACKSU, TUJS, Tripura Sundari Nari Bahini (TSNB) and All Jharkhand Students Union (AJSU). An important decision it took was to suspend 89 demands from the 92-point charter mentioned above, leaving only three political demands; the most important being creation of Bodoland as a full-fledged state. Mahanta categorically ruled out any "further fragmentation of Assam", and Prime Minister Rajiv Gandhi concurred. So fat was in the fire! ABSU charged PTCA[12] and AGP Government of conspiracy to crush 2-year old Bodo Movement.

ABSU had suspended the Movement on 30 October 1988 "to create peaceful atmosphere for discussions". All the tribal organisations of Assam convened a conference on 16-17 January 1989 to analyse political situation, under the chairmanship of Samar Brahma Choudhury. The participants were disturbed over the violence in state. ABSU and UBNLF chose to stay away. Expectedly, ABSU resumed its agitation in February 1989.

Before resuming the chronology of the Movement, a brief mention of some of the memoranda submitted by its protagonists should be of interest:

1. Earliest memorandum dated 20 May 1967 by PTCA was to President Zakir Hussain. It was signed by various PTCA leaders, viz; Biruchan Doley, BSc, LLB, President; Samar Brahma Chaudhury BA, Vice-President; Charan Narzary, MA, LLB, General Secretary, and Praful

Kumar Bhabara, BA (Hons) and Ajit Kumar Basumatari, both Joint Secretaries. They had attached following documents with the memorandum:

(a) Agreement between AAPTL and Assam Congress of 10 September 1939, Shillong.

(b) Agreement between AAPTL and Assam Muslim League, signed with Sir Saadullah, then Prime Minister of Assam.

(c) Memorandum of 20 March 1947, by Assam Tribal League submitted to the Constituent Assembly of India and Supplement submitted to its Minority Advisory Committee.

(*d*) Memorandum by *Assam Tribal Sangh* before U.N. Dhebar, Chairman, Scheduled Areas and STs Commission of India, 1960-61.

2. ABSU leaders presented on 22 January 1987 a number of documents to the Government to justify UT status for the Plains Tribals on North Bank for "all-round security and development of Bodos".

3. The Memorandum dated 23 August 1987 demanding 50:50 division of Assam. It had a list of 53 Questions and Answers, couched in rhetorical flourish!

4. ABSU presented their case in a booklet (perhaps, 'pamphlet', or even 'tract' would be better word to describe it) dated 10-11-1987 to the President, Prime Minister, and Home Minister. All manner of condemnation, and criticism were handed down to the Assamese people for their acts of commission and omission. At the end, it was signed as under:

GWJW NTH WNG[13]

Sincerely Yours
For and on behalf of ABSU
Upender Nath Brahma
President, ABSU
Rabi Ram Brahma
General Secretary

New Delhi
Date 10-11-87

1989

There were two long bandhs: for 120 hours on 16 February and 175 hours on 2 March.

During the year, terrorist activities in Kokrajhar district were on the increase. Meanwhile, the emergence of Congress(I) Ministries in Tripura, Meghalaya, Nagaland, Mizoram, Manipur and Arunachal had changed the political landscape in the North-East. AGP Government itself was tottering due to violent depredations committed by ULFA and BdSF, and the Party was being wracked by internal squabbling. The opposition to the Movement was rising. Abdul Muhib Mojumdar, Dy Leader, Congress Legislature Party, wrote to Rajiy Gandhi on 29 January, asking him to concede to the ABSU in Assam a Darjeeling-type disposition in West Bengal. The Government had held two abortive talks (26 June 1988 and 11 January 1989) with ABSU, the latter being represented by its Shillong-based Vice-President, Pradeep Kumar Daimary.

BdSF Appears on the Scene

Meanwhile, the BdSF had come into prominence. For record, it was constituted on 3 October 1986 at Odal Khasibari village in Darrang district, "to liberate the Mongoloid-dominated Indo-Burma Region. Like ULFA, it was a secessionist outfit, having no use for peaceful means. A year later, failing to get its demands acceded to, the frustrated Bodo leadership started preparing for a bitter battle. It raised Bodo Volunteer Force (BVF) under Prem Singh (P.S.) Brahma, as its military chief. Now there were two Bodo armed outfits, and an internecine conflict was inevitable. The ULFA stepped in to help its rival BdSF under Ranjan Daimary; and it later joined hands with the KIA (in Burma) and the NSCN(I-M). This hostility between the two Bodo outfits was to dog the movement for long, and entailed a heavy human cost.

It is relevant to mention here that the Bodos had been exposed to elements of the guerrilla tactics as far back as 1962 when the Special Security Bureau (SSB), established in the wake of Sino-Indian war, set up training camps at Halflong, Chakrata, etc.[14] Typical of the Indian political ethos, its opponents later accused the Congress of building up the BdSF through Central Intelligence Agencies as a counter to both ULFA and the AGP. And the Forum for Restoration of Civil Liberties, in a letter to the Prime Minister, said so in so many words:

1. "RAW was involved in Bodo agitation, and supplying weapons to them. They were targeting only *Assamese* and *Assam Police*, none others.
2. "SSB was imparting training to the ABSU extremists.
3. "SFF (Special Frontier Force) was directly involved in conducting bomb attacks in different parts of *Northern Assam*.... 'SFF was a secret agency of the Cabinet Secretariat and its most recruits were *Tibetans* and *Khampas*.' They were inducted into Assam to help Bodo extremists, and they resembled them.... *Assam* Police seized large quantities of explosives whose sophisticated variety showed that the source of supply could only be the Government."

The Forum did not disclose the source of such serious allegations, against the State and its agencies and the latter did not react as is the practice in such cases. This is the liberty run riot, indeed! But one wonders if the democracies can afford, or even survive, such unbridled freedom to malign it in the name of freedom of expression and criticism.

The Talks Begin: August 1989

The first round of talks between the Government of India and ABSU was held on 28 August 1989; by this time, ABSU and PTCA were 'enemies'. Ram Vilas Paswan represented New Delhi at the Second Round on 25 October 1989. It decided to set up a Joint Committee representing the Central and State Governments and ABSU.

The ABSU leadership suffered a big blow when its President, Upen Brahma died young on 1 May 1990. He was succeeded by Sanchuma Khunggur (S.K.) Bwiswmauthiary (also spelt 'Bwismutiary').

The 8th round of talks was held on 11 September 1990, extended up to the 13th. The tripartite Meet decided to set up a 3-member expert committee to demarcate the Bodo areas. When Paswan visited Kokrajhar on 21 October, he was invited to address a 20-lakh strong Bodo rally at Debargaon-Balagaon, whence he was presented a memorandum by ABSU.

Now we enter the period when people got tired of the agitation and the tribal economy, because of the bandhs and rasta roko, was coming to be shattered. "The Central Intelligence Agencies found the AGP Government behind the activities of the AGP." By the end of the 1980s frustration was setting in as evidence of intimidation, extortions, kidnappings and killings had generated anti-Movement sentiment. On the other hand, ABSU and BPAC complained of alienation early 1991. By then, political entities in the field were PTCA, PTCA(P) UTNLF, UBNLF, ABSU and BPAC.

The 3-member Experts Committee under Dr. Bhupinder Singh, IAS, was set up on 25 February 1991 when Assam was still under President's Rule. It submitted its report on 30 March 1992, recommending creation of two Autonomous Councils. The larger one was to be on the western central side, with a population of 1.07 million, predominantly Bodo, with some Rabhas and Sonwals, covering Bodo concentrations in the districts of Dhubri, Kokrajhar. Barpeta, Nalbari, Kamrup and Darrang. The second Autonomous Council, after an intervening gap, to be set up on the eastern side, was to cover the districts of Dhemaji, Lakhimpur and Sonitpur, and consists of Mishings (315,000) and Deuris. ABSU and PTCA rejected the Report. About this time, March 1992, BdSF, raised in October 1986, marked its presence on the violence stakes, killing 6 people including a pregnant woman, in mid-March. It signified recrudescence of Bodo violence after a fairly long lull in 1991. Since it is in the nature of extremist movements to breed more militant bodies, the emergence of the more violently inclined BdSF was no surprise, because of the failure of the Government-ABSU/BPAC talks to produce results, and "inordinately long time taken by the Committee to study the population patterns in the Region and suggest the nature of autonomy for the Plains Tribals". The absence of reliable Census data because of the cancellation of the 1981 Census operations under the AASU threat might have rendered Committee's work more difficult and time consuming. Because of the lack of results from the talks and "inordinate delay in Report", it was natural for people to become frustrated and restive, which eroded the influence of ABSU and BPAC among the people, creating conditions conducive for ascendance of more militant outfits like BdSF. The Bodo movement's history had such precedents. An older, milder organisation like the PTCA, which had reigned supreme for two decades (1967-85) had to yield ground after mid-1980s to ABSU, which modeling itself on AASU, had appeared out of the blue to take charge of the Movement. The PTCA was on the downslide ever since, in particular, after the murder of its well-known leader Samar Brahma Choudhury in August 1992.

By the time the Committee submitted its Report (March 1992), the Congress Government under Saikia was in power, after trouncing Mahanta's AGP in the June 1991 Assembly Poll. After the Bodo leaders rejected the Report, Saikia invited them for fresh talks, where they demanded 4443 villages in nine districts. Some more meetings saw them adding another 209 villages with some Bodo population, and 1035 villages which, as per official records, had no Bodo population at all. Many ding-doing battles later, the Bodo Accord was signed on 20 February 1993. The critics commented: "violence was officially rewarded with the signing of the Accord". The Accord did not solve the Bodo problem, in fact it complicated it further. The Bodo leaders insisted that the Memorandum of 10 November 1987, earlier submitted to Government of India, be made a part of the Bodo Accord. Having allowed it to be attached to the Bodo Accord, on the insistence of the 'intelligent' (or 'clever') Bodo leaders, the Assam and Central Governments would not be able to extricate themselves from the ramifications flowing from the contents of the 1987 Memorandum, as would be seen later. It makes an interesting reading, even if its reasoning may not be too plausible on certain aspects, figures in some cases highly exaggerated, and some parts or statements even incomprehensible. The Memorandum is attached as Appendix at the end of this chapter in a condensed version, but without doing any violence to the over-all integrity of its contents or their essential import. The condensed version is in the original language of the Memorandum.

Bodo Movement Phase IV: February 1993 to End-2000

The 1987 Memorandum was signed by S.K. Bwismutiary and Rabi Ram Brahma. The 1993 Accord was also signed by the Chairman of the BPAC, in addition to these two original signatories. For Assam Government, it was signed by the Additional Chief Secretary, 'in the presence of Rajesh Pilot, Union Minister of State for Home and Chief Minister Saikia. It was obviously signed in a hurry, as at that time neither was the Bodo areas delimited nor its boundary delineated. And these lacunae were to prove its undoing.

On 7 March 1993, Bodoland Autonomous Council (BAC) was inaugurated at a public rally in Kokrajhar. 11 Bodo militants, led by Prem Singh (P.S.) Brahma, Chief of Bodo Volunteer Force (BVF), surrendered with their weapons before Saikia and Pilot. About 2000 followed suit in the coming days. On 8 April, BdSF militants abducted Bolin Bordoloi, TTL executive, and demand a ransom of Rs. 15 crore (He was released 11 months later, night 1-2 March 1994). Bodoland Executive Council (BEC) members were sworn-in on 20 May by Assam's Home Secretary, at Kokrajhar; S.K. Bwismutiary as Chief Executive Member (CEM) and P.S. Brahma as Executive Member (EM); the latter was No. 2 in the BEC. There were two other EMs.

BdSF denounced the Bodo Accord in a statement on 25 May. It bode ill for it. On 1 June, Garla Botha Basumatiary was elected President of the ABSU. The new ABSU Executive dissolved the BPAC and BVF Bodoland People's Party (BPP) launched at a convention (2-3 July) in Kokrajhar, with S.K. Bwismutiary as President; it signs an agreement on political understanding with Assamese Congress (I). On 12 July, the Bodoland Legislative Party (BLP) is divided on a decision of Assam Government—entrusting Senior Ministers the responsibility to 'look after' the interests of nine constituencies which had returned the Bodo Movement—supporters in June 1991 Poll. "The wily Saikia is already at work."

5 October 1993. Widespread communal riots in Kokrajhar and Bongaigaon districts, leaving 19 dead, almost all of them Muslim. 30,000 fled their homes, seeking shelter in camps. Was it ethnic cleansing, as the riots came in the midst of the apprehensions on the delimitation of the BAC area? Assam Government announces an All-Party Committee to delineate the BAC area on 14 October 1993. After Saikia survives a no-confidence motion on 15 October, the Committee is dissolved. They were obviously playing games (The BLP had supported the no-confidence motion).

Now came the crunch. On 28 October, Assam Government announces unilaterally that the BAC will include 2570 villages. Bwismutiary denounced the decision. He quits as CEM on 16 November. On 20th P.S. Brahma is appointed CEM of the interim BEC. Elections to a Regular BEC was to be held by 20 November, but was not held. The Bodo leadership was obviously split by Saikia's Congress.

On 10 December, Assam Government issues notification, demarcating boundary of the BAC territory, with an area of 5,186 km^2 and 2570 villages. The BAC area was spread across 29 Assembly Constituencies, but the 10 km wide belt in the north touching the international border with Bhutan was not included in it. It had population of 21,37,445, of "which only 38 per cent were the Plains Tribals. Only 1110 villages of its 2570 total enjoyed the tribal majority. All this was bound to spell trouble, at least in future. The 62 per cent non-Bodos were bound to fear the consequences, and they were not wrong as the later events were to prove. Denouncing the notification, ABSU demanded inclusion of the border belt as also additional 515 villages in the BAC.

On 28 December, State Government reconstituted the interim BEC, further marginalising the Bwismutiary faction including R.R. Brahma, former General Secretary of the ABSU under both Upen Brahma and Bwismutiary and one of the signatories to the 1987 Memorandum and 1993 Accord. Thus ended the year 1993, with the ABSU having scored a kind of victory, but badly split subsequently, perhaps consequently.

At 4-6 March 1994 session at Guwahati, Bodo Sahitya Sabha revives its demand for Roman script for their language. BdSF continues abductions and violence: 8 policemen killed in an ambush in Barpeta district on 10 January; 7 persons from 'one community' shot dead in Bongaigaon district; and a tea estate owner abducted. Majority of BLP supports Saikia Government; two dissidents formed a splinter, New BLP, on 4 April.

This is summary of the happenings and mishappenings in the post-Accord one year. Now some other details, BAC was to be a 40-member body: of which 30 were to be reserved for STs; 35 to be elected, and 5 nominated. BAC Bill was introduced in the Assembly on 5 April 1993. Koch-Rajbongshi Community was against the Accord and wanted 'right of self-determination' (to opt out of BAC) because, as it put it, "BAC's 18 lac will include 12 lac who are Koch-Rajbongshis". Its immediate demand was for ST status for itself.[15] The BAC Act, duly passed by the Assembly, was gazetted on 14 May 1993. Then on, Bodo Accord became a football, with P.S. Brahma assuming pro-Saikia stance and Bwismutiary resigning and leading hardline faction against the Accord and Saikia Government. Subsequently, it was a dance of death and destruction as much between the two Bodo outfits as against the unarmed common citizens. If the BPP, ABSU and Bwismutiary wanted more and more villages/areas to be added to the BAC, their opponents, led by BdSF, set their gaze at secession. Bodo Accord was flawed from the beginning. Its signing was hurried through, more because of the game of one-up-manship between the Union Home Minister (S.B. Chavan) and his Deputy, Minister of State (Pilot), and not because of its intrinsic soundness. Saikia later 'claimed' he had warned Pilot against it as the crucial matter of the BAC area had not been settled; and "Pilot however refused to listen and told me the draft had Prime Minister Rao's blessings".

BdSF was on the violent trajectory, 1994 onwards. In the communal riots in May-July 1994, many villages were razed to ground, forcing 5,400 refugees into 26 camps. One such camp was attacked in Barpeta, leaving 52 dead and 113 injured. Coming in the wake of similar carnage in October 1993, it seemed to be aimed at ethnic cleansing. Muslims were the initial target of the Bodo fury, though in the later years, Hindu settlers of East Bengal origin also came to grief. Alarmed by the wanton violence, Army was called out. It launched Operation Karanti in July 1994 against the BdSF in Barpeta district. Its goal eventually was to free the 2.837 km^2 Manas Wildlife sanctuary from the clutches of the BdSF, which had held sway over its vast jungle for the last 8 years. The insurgents had free run over the sanctuary, were operating from the safety of their camps inside Bhutan. Army could not go all out against the terrorists in the sanctuary not only because of its terrain and thick jungle but because of its proximity to the porous and unmanned 400 km border with Bhutan. When chased, they used the sanctuary as a safe passage to reach the hills of Bhutan, out of Indian Army's reach. Still Army had acted vigorously against the militants who had not only killed over 20 officers and men of the Forest Department over the last few years, but also looted large quantity of ivory stored at the Forest office of Barh Bari in Manas. Moving into the Manas on 26 July, 2 days after the Barpeta massacre, the troops had rounded up over 120 BdSF ultras in Phase 1. In the next phase, another 95 were in the BAC, with large quantity of RDX and IEDs.

Acting unilaterally again, Assam Government added 112 villages more to the BAC area. Their total reached 2682, including 2570 announced initially in October 1993. ABSU resented unilateralism; wanted inclusion of all the 515 villages demanded earlier, as also of the border belt; and announced fresh programme of action November 1995 onwards.

Now the situation was worse for peace in the area, which was the prime objective and reason for signing the Accord in the first place. In February 1993, when it was signed, the Bodo Accord was widely hailed as a model for resolving several ongoing sub-nationalist movements in Assam and elsewhere in the North-East. But by October 1995, less than three years from the initial euphoria, the model was not only frayed at the edges, it also looked like a sure recipe for disaster. While the Bodo insurgents had rejected the Accord out of hand, the moderates too got disillusioned by mid-1995 at its tardy implementation. If the moderate leadership was divided down the line by this time, the fault surely lay with themselves, the protagonists of the Bodoland, for allowing themselves to be manipulated by the crafty politicians and State Government. If the ABSU was threatening to revive its original demand for a separate State on the North Bank in 1995, it was to be understood in terms of competitive radicalism of various Bodo groups. The State Government displayed an element of ad hocism in its handling of the Bodo problem, conceding things in driblets, and unilaterally. As per the mutual understanding the election to the BAC was to be held within 6 months of the formation of the Interim BEC (which was done on 20 May 1993). The deadline, 20 November 1993, came and went, without anybody caring or remembering. It has been described above how S.K. Bwismutiary was marginalized, and P.S. Brahma made the GEM in 1993. When P.S. Brahma threatened to withdraw support from the Saikia Government in 1995, posing a direct threat to its life, the 'wily' Chief Minister lost no time to announce holding of elections to the 40-member BAC for 31 October 1995. And in turn, ABSU's above mentioned threat to resume agitation had something to do with these elections 'announced' by Saikia. Known as "sly politician", he forgot all about 31 October elections once he fortified his position with his customary manipulative skills. But why blame Saikia if the credulous Bodo leaders allow themselves to be taken for a ride, or to use a blunt expression, allow them to be fooled, time and again by such self-serving politicians? Nothing illustrates the ironic twists in the situation better than the 16 October 1995 *Times of India* Editorial:

> "When the Bodo leaders made a demand for a separate State during the AGP regime, it was seen by many as counter-weight to the muscle acquired by the AASU. Such is the irony of politics that the AGP today faces a 'social boycott' by AASU and there is no love lost between the Congress and moderate Bodo leaders. If the AASU leaders have fallen out with the brethren, so have ABSU leaders with the Congress, once their strong supporters. While the implementation of both Assam and Bodo has left much to be desired, Mr Saikia has established a record of sorts by granting autonomy to other ethnic groups like Rabhas Karbis, Lalungs and Mishings."

One may ignore Saikia's wiliness, but he certainly can and must be accused of the original sin of permitting himself, a senior Congress leader and Chief Minister of a State, to be bamboozled and coerced into consenting to an Accord, which he knew, very well, would explode in his face because of its inbuilt flaws and infirmities, by a junior but enthusiastic Central Minister just because "it has the approval of the Prime Minister". If he is (was) credited with near-success with ULFA by enticing large number of its cadres into surrender, he is also blamed for not trying hard enough with BdSF for "some ulterior purposes". But all said and done, he did receive overtures for talks from the BdSF in June 1995. Majority of Bodos are Hindus, only 25-40 per cent being Christians who are better educated. The leadership and cadres are Christians who started exerting themselves after the failure of largely Hindu advance guard leadership to show results."[16] "The BdSF is largely recruited from around Udalguri and any communal polarization could further complicate matters."

BdSF was in mood to resile from its stand. In a statement it issued on its 9th Foundation Day on 3 October 1995, it asserted that "It is still committed to armed struggle to secure right of self-determination for Bodos.... It does not accept the Bodo Accord." Obviously, given such hardline positions, no peace could be espied on the horizon. As if to make the point, 7 Bengalis and 1 Bodo were killed violently on 9 October at Kalaiga on the eve of a public rally by a pro-Congress youth group.

The Year 1996 : Bodo-Santhal Violence

There were violent Bodo-Santhal clashes in May 1996. The Bodos claimed the discovery of bodies of three Bodo girls from "a jungle outside the Adivasi (Santhal) village of Satyapur under Gossaigaon PS in Kokrajhar district on 10 May and "burning of several Bodo houses on the night of 10/11 May" (as alleged by Amrit Lal Basumatari, former MLA and former MP) caused these riots. The District Administration insisted that the clashes began only on 15 May, the day AGP Government was sworn-in,[17] and continued for 5 days. Four members[18] of Adivasi Council of Assam claimed that the attackers were Bodos armed with modern weapons, which should be seized. The Bodoland State Movement Committee (BSMC) leader Pramila Rani Brahma, cited Intelligence reports about some Santhal boys arrested in West Bengal trying to procure arms, after "getting armed training in camps". By July, the riots had spread to Dhubri district from Kokrajhar.[19] It was a worst Bodo-Santhal riots,[20] which spread over 2,500 km^2, devastated 75 villages on both sides, rendered 200,000 people homeless, and left 100 dead. "7,000 Santhals fled to West Bengal".[21]

BLTF blew up RCC bridge at Rakholduli in Bongaigaon district on 27 December, cutting off road link between the Region and rest of the country. They planted IEDs in the Brahmaputra Mail; consequent explosions near Sesapani station in Kokrajhar district destroyed 3 coaches and left over 30 dead.

BdSF[22] claimed 98 lives in 1996. It was reported to be the armed wing of the NDFB. "By mid-1990s, it had redesignated itself as the Bodoland Army."

Towards the end of the 1996, BSMC Chairman, S.K. Bwismutiary, and ABSU Vice-President, Anil Basumatary, appealed for a cease-fire between the

Bodo groups. Curiously, then came ULFA, asking BdSF and newly formed BLTF to stop the fratricidal clashes that would benefit only Indian State machinery".[23]

Bodo militant groups killed 260 persons in 1996.[24]

1997: Bodo Militants Continue the Killings

Some of the important cases of sabotage and killings are listed here: (1) Bodo militants caused 42 deaths between January and 7 May 1997.[25] (2) On 9 June, Chief Minister Mahanta had narrow escape when an IED-caused explosion missed his car by a few yards, near the Kamakhya Hill in Guwahati. He was on his way to the office from airfield. The fact that he had returned from Delhi a day before his scheduled date shows how the state apparatus has been penetrated/compromised. There was greater cause for concern. 300-metre wire connected to the IED was laid over the telegraph poles in part and dug underground the rest of its length. It should have been there for days, if not weeks, before it was actuated by a subversive who had ensconced himself in a hut amongst the rest of the inhabitants of the colony. Neither the wire nor the subversive were ever noticed. (3) Rail track blasts on 1 January and 13 August. (4) On 12 and 15 August, 29 non-tribals, mainly Santhals and Bengalis gunned down. The Bengali Tiger Force (BTF) answered by killing Bodos on the 17th. (5) From 1 to 20 July, 17 Army men killed in attacks and IED explosions, launched by NDFB (experts in IED use), NSCN(I-M) and ULFA. Most daring assault was on a Brigade Headquarters under 57 Mtn Div.[26] (6) During 17 June-23 August, 30 Army men including one Brigadier, one Colonel and one Captain, were killed in 10 ambushes laid by ULFA and NDFB separately.

26 July 1997. ABSU Rally at Guwahati. In a memorandum to Assam Governor, Loknath Mishra, ABSU President, Urkhao Gwra Brahma demanded tripartite talks, because "three-year experiment with BAC has failed". People's Democratic Front (PDF), till then for an Autonomous Council, announced: "It is no more for Council as the Government had failed to finalise BAC before June 1997 and Guwahati High Court has ordered State Government not to include in the BAC villages with less than 50 per cent Bodo population. PDF also join in demand for Bodoland" (*Times of India* 27-7-1997).

21 August 1997. State Cabinet decides to demarcate the BAC boundary and hold BAC elections in December 1998. ABC rejects both the proposals as "the BAC experiment has already failed".

September 1997. The United Front Government at the Centre, convinced that previous Government had acted unwisely in the matter, convened this Tripartite Meet, inviting BSMC, ABSU, PDF, Bodo Sahitya Sabha (BSS) and All Bodo Women's Welfare Federation (ABWWF). Representing the hawkish face of BSMC, its Chairman, one time moderate and former President of ABSU,

S.K. Bwismutiary reverted to demanding a full-fledged state of Bodoland, practically embracing the entire area of present Assam north of the Brahmaputra, and creation of two autonomous districts of Neelachal and Lalung. Hearing the extreme voices, the Government proposed setting up a Joint Working Group (JWG) to renegotiate the entire Bodo Accord. JWG was still-born as the Government and Bodo Groups failed to agree on its terms of reference.

To stop fratricidal killings among the Bodo outfits, which had gone on during 1996 and 1997 in Nalbari, Kamrup, Darrang districts, Peace Committees were set up in several districts, comprising representatives of ABSU, BSMC, PDF and BSS.

1998: Events and Incidents

Tripartite Talks: May (25-26) 1998. 50 Bodo leaders from ABSU, BPAC, BSS, ABWWF, All Bodo Employees Federation, etc. attended the Meet, which ended in a deadlock as Bodos insisted on Bodoland State. The Centre and Assam Government urged them to reduce Bodo-Jharkhandi Santhal tensions, which had claimed 50 lives recently. The situation was becoming explosive as the Santhal youth had raised Bisa Commando Force (BCF) and Adivasi Cobra Militant Force" (ACMF) to counter BLTF and NDFB attacks on the Santhal villages. The Meet failed" to address an important issue about the status of Koch-Rajbongshis, second largest group in BAC area, next only to the Bodos. The community, treated as part of the OBC Conglomerate till then, had been agitating for ST status. Soon after the meet ended, BLTF unleashed an orgy of violence. In a span of 3 days in June (2-4), it blew up four road bridges on NH-31 and a rail bridge between Chautara and Gossaigaon, 250 km from Guwahati. Not aimed at killing civilians, they wanted to cut off the North-East from the mainland. Besides the shift in strategy, violence was also a warning to BLTF rival, NDFB which was inclined to respond to efforts of George Fernandes (an activist Minister in the March 1998-April 1999 Vajpayee Government) to bring it to the negotiations table.

Meanwhile, Surojit Mitra, a lawyer who had been able to get the bail for militants with an unerring regularity, had become an overground link with the Bodo outfit. He was shot dead in Guwahati on 13 June 1998, "soon after he came into limelight for arranging a 45-minute telephonic talks between the secessionist NDFB and Fernandes, during the latter's recent visit to Assam". NDFB reportedly shot the mediator for crowing about his "achievement" publicly.[27]

Tripartite Talks of November 1998. Besides the three parties, the Government also invited non-Bodo groups for the meet on Bodoland, making it a "quadripartite talks". Its opponents said the creation of BAC itself was a mistake because Bodos were not in a majority in the area; and Bodos were divided into two rival groups, one demanding a separate State and other a separate Nation (Adivasi Council of Assam). Another non-Bodo group, Gossaigaon Anchalik Committee, an earlier supporter of Bodoland, told the meet they no longer supported the demand as the Bodos had committed heinous crimes in the BAC area. The BAC, headed by its Interim Chairman, Kaneshwar Narzary, had its own demands: (1) Rs. 25 crore for construction of a capital complex. (2) Army should raise a separate Bodo Regiment. The PDF, having a majority of MLAs in Bodo areas, demanded that the talks for Bodoland (they called it Boro Hadot) be held at the Home Minister's level.

Violence Continue. Between April 1997-March 1998, there were 11 cases of track sabotage and 92 Rail Roko and bandh calls. "The things are no better for the year 1998-99 so far" (*The Outlook,* 13-7-1998).

1999: Events and Incidents

In March 1999, Mahanta added another 259 villages to 2682 (original 2570 plus initial addition of 112) already under the BAC. Total now stood at 2941. The notification dated 2 April 1999 asserted that "2941 villages included now were, close to their original demand of 3031". The practice of conceding; demands in driblets seemed to proving a bane rather than balm for the troubled situation, whetting, rather than quenching the thirst. So fully aware how the State Governments surrendered before their violence at successive stages, all Bodo outfits rejected the notification. ABSU President, U.G. Brahma said: "347 villages included in the 1996 notification excluded now.... Actually, 356 more villages, as also Rupsi Airport in Dhubri district and Bongaigaon Refinery, should have been included. Manas National Park also excluded, dividing BAC area into two.... We will launch Bodoland State agitation." BSMC MP, S.K. Bwismutiary: "Notification is 2 years too late.... Bodoland should, include area from the Sankosh to Sadiya, in addition to 32 Revenue Circles in the south." PDF General Secretary Gangadhar Ramchiary: "We will not compromise on Bodoland."

BAC challenged the 2 April 1999 notification in Supreme Court. The petition admitted on 1 October said "the Assam Government has issued the Notification, unilaterally deleting 347 villages from BAC area without consulting it, as required under the BAC Act.

Violence Continues. (1) One Army major and 7 Bodo ultras killed in an encounter when 11 Sikh raided a NDFB hide-out in jungles of Bishwanath Chariali Reserve Forest, bordering Arunachal Pradesh, in Assam's Sonitput district. (2) PDF President G.B. Basumatari shot at and injured by NDFB ultras in Kokrajhar district.

The leaders of BLTF (Ranjan Daimarv and D.R. Nabla) and NDFB (Hagrama Basumatari) met on 30 May and decided to make peace and put an end to internecine clashes between their outfits. BLTF wants Bodoland within India and NDFB a sovereign Bodo nation.[28]

After April 1999 Notification, there was no initiatives from the Centre, mainly because the Vajpayee Government fell that month and new Government (again under Vajpayee) took over in October only, after passing through the Kargil crisis (May-July) and an extended election process (July-October).

2000 AD: BLTF Comes Round

No tripartite or quadripartite meeting was convened possibly because they had produced no results in the past. But the new Government achieved a major breakthrough by making BLT agree to a cease-fire. The ground rules for suspension of operations between the SF and BLT were framed after a tripartite meeting between representatives of the MHA, Assam Government and BLT (led by its Vice-Chairman Chumang Brahma), and announced on 29 March. Operations were suspended effective 15 March for 6 months. The suspension was renewed for another 6 months in September 2000. Some analysts believed the NDFB would follow suit.

Intra-Bodo Differences and Violence

The BAC petition, admitted by the Supreme Court on 1 April 1999, says "80 lakh Bodos living on the North Bank for centuries were a neglected lot." But the bigger if bitter truth is that they are a divided and fractious lot. The division among them might have existed earlier too, but it became worse after they tasted power with the formation of provisional BAC in 1993.

The BLT cease-fire with the Government in March 2000 might not have brought it any closer to NDFB, but a fragile peace held between the two since the beginning of that year. But it broke down when Bineshwar Brahma, President of the BSS, was killed on 19 August at Guwahati by a suspected NDFB ultra. Brahma, a Senior Manager with the FCI, was arguably the tallest figure among the Bodo writer-intellectuals, fervently advocating reunification of Bodo political formations to achieve his ultimate aim of a separate Bodoland. Two days after his killing, Bodo MLA, Mohini Basumatary was killed, possibly in retaliation, by suspected BLT cadres triggering fears of another round of fratricidal clashes between the rival Bodo factions. The worst BLT-NDFB clash came on 12 December which left 9 BLT militants dead.

Basumatari belonged to the then 4-year old Party called PDF which the Intelligence claimed was the overground face of the banned NDFB. Likewise, BLT is said to be the protege of ABSU. Since 1996, when PDF won 7 seats to the Assembly, the two Bodo factions (PDF, NDFB vs ABSU-BLT) had been at loggerheads. "For the last 6 months, the Bodo social leaders and elders have been engaged in bringing unification between the two opposing groups", wrote *The Outlook* of 4 September 2000. Brahma, a highly respected intellectual and leading the unity move, had made good progress in this direction. This worried the NDFB, and hence his elimination. Brahma after all was an intellectual and a man of ideas—so more dangerous for NDFB than the BLT's bullets.

Not only are the NDFB (demanding sovereign, Bodo state) and BLT (wanting Bodoland within India) are poles apart, their political wings, PDF and ABSU, are also divided on political issues, the main among them being linguistic; viz the choice of script for Bodo language, hanging fire for years. It has undergone several changes in the last three decades. In the early 1960s, Roman was the chosen script. Then Devnagri was adopted. Now, a section of the Bodos mainly Christians and followers of NDFB and its political wing, PDF favour re-introduction of Roman script. Bineshwar Brahma, a leading litterateur and intellectual, was opposed to any more changes, "because the language was suffering due to constant alterations". ABSU, the leading Bodo group, spearheading the Bodoland Movement, is also for Devnagri script. So another reason for the elimination of Brahma could be to silence a strong and well-respected advocate of the Devnagri. Adds BLT Publicity Chief Daimary Mainao: "As far as May 1999, NDFB Chief had threatened to kill Brahma if he failed to accept Roman script for Bodo."

After the twin killings, "Kokrajhar and other Bodo areas have witnessed a string of killings".[29] ABSU President had then issued a warning: "If the Centre does not step in immediately, we may have Kashmir-like situation in Bodo areas.... With fratricidal killings likely to rise."[30]

The BLT-NDFB acrimony got accentuated with the former entering into a cease-fire agreement with the Government in March 2000, and it spelt into the neighbouring Arunachal as they started taking shelter in its border areas. "In December 2000, the Centre has deployed 18 additional companies of the CRPF in 17 districts of Assam and prohibitory order under Section 144 of the CrPC has also been imposed along the states border with Arunachal Pradesh."

The End-2000 Situation

Eight years past the signing of the February 1993 Bodo Accord, the situation was no better. In fact, it was back to the violent pre-Accord days. The moderate Bodos were dissatisfied, demanding addition of many more villages and areas to the jurisdiction of the BAC. The two Bodo armed outfits were engaged in bloody battles. The Bodos were still voicing their oft-repeated grievances; to cite Sansuma Khunggur Bwismutiary, the lone Bodo MP (March 2000): "Considering that the Bodos are indigenous people or Assam, they could have been accorded due status at national or state level.... But even our language is not incorporated in the 8th Schedule.... Though a bill was passed in 1984 to make Bodo an Associate Language (in Assam), it has not been implemented so far."

What is the picture on the other side of the fence? A large number of villages and populations, led by the Koch Rajbongshis, the (second) largest community after the Bodos, were unhappy at their incorporation in the BAC area. They want referendum on the issue, which is totally unacceptable to the Bodos. It is the minority dictating terms, considering that the Bodos constitute 38 per cent of the population in the BAC area. The situation is pregnant with future troubles. To add to the woes of the common people, for the first time, the ethnic Bengalis and Santhals have raised outfits like the BTF etc. to counter the depredations committed by the Bodo militants.

The UMFA President, Golam Osman, submitted a memorandum to the PMO on 12 December 2000, "opposing 100 per cent reservation for the indigenous people in Parliament and State Assembly, declaring it to be violative of the Assam Accord".

In the given scenario, the peace does not seem to have a chance in the Region; at least not in the near future. Not only that elections for the regular BAC have not been held as such in spite of repeated promises, the finalisation of the BAC area itself is subjudice as the Interim BAC has submitted a petition to the Supreme Court in 1999.

TOWARDS BTC

Now a brief look at the situation during the years 2001 and 2002.

Violence Continues

With the BLT observing cease-fire since March 2000, NDFB has continued the blood-letting of innocents, mostly non-Bodos. After lying low for over six months, it killed 31 people (all Bihari and Bengali settlers) in two incidents in latter half of January 2002: 13 on the 15th in two villages (Sikarjhar inside Manas Park, and Doulajhar, under Bijni PS, 35 km away) on the Indo-Bhutan border (Bongaigaon district); and 18 on the 22nd in Jangalbari village under Udalguri PS (Darrang district). In both cases, the ultras crossed over from their hide-outs in Southern Bhutan, and crossed back after carrying out the killings. The NDFB, with at least 15 camps just across the border, "has adopted the hit-and-run tactic in the last 3-4 years" (*The Outlook,* 4-2-2002). Further outrages: (1) 4 injured in an IED blast in Kanchenjunga Express at Alokjhar in Kokrajhar district, on 5 April. (2) A 12-hour *bandh* by ABSU on 14 April to protest the killing of its Education Secretary, Khwamkhawmban Boro, on 12 April. (3) Two NDFB cadres killed in an encounter in Sonitput district on 9 May. (4) Five ultras killed in Darrang and Nalbari districts on 22 and 23 May. (5) Two ultras killed in Satgharia village in Darrang district, on 25 August. (6) On 27 October, NDFB ultra gathered 31 villagers from Patgiri-Hatisar (in Kokrajhar district) on Indo-Bhutan border, in the open area and gunned them down. 21 died on the spot, all non-Bodos (Earlier, NDFB had killed 9 non-Bodos in a relief camp at a forest village near Kokrajhar, on 14 July).[31]

"Perhaps the most horrifying aspect of the gruesome 27 October killing of 21 non-Bodos is that such outrages have become chillingly routine exercise."[32] In a significant coincidence, there was a mortar attack in the high security area of Dispur capital complex in Guwahati on the 27 October evening, within hours of massacre on the Assam-Bhutan border, by suspected ultras of ULFA, which has close links with NDFB; both outfits have bases in Bhutan. The NDFB, around since 1987, is one of the more potent militant outfits in the Region, with considerable striking power. It is the group that has seen the least number of desertions and surrenders among the North-East outfits; so very little intelligence is available on it. It seems to be intent to thwart the formation of the BTC under the Sixth Schedule.

Is BTC the Solution?

March 2000 BLT-Assam Government cease-fire agreement was a landmark in the strife-torn Region. A year after this agreement, Mahanta and Bodo representatives, led by Bodo tribal MP S.K. Bwismutiary, held high level deliberations presided over by Home Minister Advani, on 28-30 March 2001. The idea of an alternative structure to replace the BAC[33] was apparently mooted soon after the cease-fire, and was accepted at this March 2001 Meet. The Autonomous Region under the Sixth Schedule, to be carved out of Assam, was to be called Bodo Territorial Council (BTC). Mahanta, replying to a question on the planned Autonomous Region, said on 29 March 2001: "There are already four autonomous regions existing in the state." The Bodos also demanded liberal financial package spread over the next 10 years for Infrastructural development, inclusion of the Bodo language in the 8th Schedule of the Constitution and setting up of a Central University in the Bodo area. The creation of the new BTC with four co-terminus district was an important feature of the agreement. At least 10 rounds of tripartite talks have preceded the Home Minister's discussions (with Assam Government and BLT). Advani also held separate discussions with Mahanta and Bodo groups. "The pact will be finalized after assembly polls" (due in May 2001).[34] Another long-standing Bodo demand has urged upon the Government to take steps to include the Bodos living in the areas of other autonomous councils in the ST list.

Assam Government gave its nod to the formation of the BTC, in February 2002 and asked the Centre to amend the 6th Schedule for the purpose. This consent provoked more opposition than expected, with several non-Bodo groups threatening to launch agitation against it. Leading the opposition is the Sanmilita Janagoshthiya Sangram Samiti (SJSS), an umbrella body of 18 non-Bodo groups which said "non-Bodo population in the proposed area has been totally marginalized". Samiti convener Phani Medhi said: "...Gogoi's Congress Government has simply ignored the interests of the non-Bodos living in the proposal area; they will have to live under fear.... Several villages with no Bodo population have been included in the proposed BTC area.... Government has succumbed to the pressure from a Bodo armed group (read, BLT), and non-Bodos would also not hesitate from resorting to violence...." On the other hand, BLT Chairman Hagram Basumatari welcomed the move and wanted the Government to prove its sincerity by getting the Constitution suitably amended for an early creation of the BTC.

An All-Party Meeting convened by Assam Government on 20 March 2002, attended by BJP, AGP, CPI, CPI(M) and JD(U), resolved that the boundary of BTC be finalised on the basis of the 1999 Notification on the boundary of the BAC. The ABSU immediately rejected the All-Party recommendation, asserting that in that case there would be no different between the existing BAC and proposed BTC. ABSU President Rabiram Narzary wanted inclusion of 155 more villages in addition to those already notified in 1993 and later in 1999. The Government had included 2570 villages when BAC was initially created in 1993, and added another 112 in 1995. In 1999, AGL Government added 632 villages in the BAC which were located in the 10 km belt on the Assam-Bhutan border, but simultaneously struck off the names of 371 villages located on the southern boundary of the BAC area. With the Centre negotiating the issue with the BLT since early 2001, the Bodo groups favouring a solution under the 6th Schedule of the Constitution, are demanding (mid-2002) the inclusion of these 371 villages, apart from including 155 more beyond the Pachnoi River, which is the eastern boundary of the existing BAC area.

From early 2002, the Bodos started complaining against the delay in setting up BTC. On 23 April, Mishing Brahma, recently elected unopposed to Rajya Sabha as a consensus candidate of four opposition parties (including AGP and BJP), and ABSU Adviser, condemned the delay when the proposal was cleared by the Cabinet Sub-Committee and an All-Party Meeting at the state level in February. He threatened to revert to their earlier demand of statehood. On 16 May, BLT Chairman H. Basumatari threatened "to withdraw from the talks if the issue is not decided within this month". On 16 June, BLT General Secretary Derhachat Basumatari threatened to revive the agitation if the Government continued to delay the creation of BTC.

At the 4 July 2002 tripartite meeting, attended by the representatives of the Centre, State (Chief Minister Tarun Gogoi) and Bodos and presided over by Advani, Assam Government formally agreed to the creation of the BTC. Unlike the BAC, which was set up simply as an "administrative authority within the state of Assam under a scheme", the BTC is to be constituted under the provisions of the 6th Schedule. This will entail an amendment to the 6th Schedule, which was applicable initially to "the hill tribes of Assam", and which today covers only two Hill districts of Assam. The 4 July Meeting also decided to set up an expert committee, comprising officials of Centre and the State, to draft "a modified form" of the 6th Schedule, for the purpose, and which would also safeguard the rights (status and even safety) of the non-Bodos living within the BTC area covering issues of land ownership, inheritance rights, and their role in the BTC polity. Gogoi told the Press after the Meet: "After consulting all parties, State Government had agreed to grant 126 villages in addition to these proposed under the 1999 Notification which carved out the BAC formed in 1993.... But the Bodos were demanding 101 more villages for the BTC area.... There would be 3070 villages falling in the BTC area, where Bodo population would be about 33 per cent.... Bodo would be included in the 8th Schedule and Koch-Rajbongshis would be included in the ST list."

Despite the consensus reached so far, formidable hurdles still remain in the path of creation of the BTC. For NDFB, avowedly committed to a "sovereign Bodoland", any accommodation with BLT is out of question. Its Chairman explicitly rejected the BTC. Then SJSS, comprising 18 non-Bodo groups, dominated by the Koch-Rajbongshis, are opposed to any form of greater political autonomy for the Bodos. There are reports, denied by SJSS leaders, that the combine is closely linked with ULFA. If that is true, ULFA, which has acknowledged links with the NDFB, would also have some kind of links with an outfit whose objectives run contrary to even moderate Bodo nationalist aspirations.

SJSS (Sanmilita Jangosthiya Sangram Samity) alleges that the creation of the BTC would turn the non-Bodo people into "second class citizens, and give the Bodos the opportunity to oppress us". Their fears got worse when the NDFB, BLT,[35] etc. demanded that Bodoland be liberated. The militants raised the slogan "Liberated Bodoland is for Bodos only", and since 1994, they have been drawing up an Action plan to "cleanse" Bodo villages of non-Bodo settlers, including Hindu and Muslim Bengalis from former East Pakistan and Adivasi groups like Santhals, Oraons, Mundas and Rajbansis, to change the ethnic composition of the areas (In fact, Adivasis settled in Assam during the days of the Raj). As the militant groups know that the Bodos in the BAC area do not constitute more than 30 per cent of the total population of about 30 lakh, they need to evacuate non-Bodos in order to dominate the Region. Massacres, arson and land-grabbing by Bodo militants forced thousands of non-Bodos to flee their villages and take shelter in the camps set up by the Government. Currently (mid-2002), over 100,000 non-Bodos were sheltered in 21 camps in Kokrajhar, Goalpara, Bongaigaon and Dhubri. The non-Bodos are painfully conscious of the fate that awaits them when the Bodos get their BTC.

Another complicating factor is the decision of the State Government to concede the demand of two communities to be classified as STs—Koch-Rajbongshis, who belong ethnically to the Bodo-Kachari stock, though they have become 'detribalised', and the Adivasis. "The case of Koch-Rajbongshis is interesting in that the process of de-tribalisation which generations of them have gone through, and re-tribalisation, which some of them are now seeking, are among the unobserved constants in the process of social change in Assam."[36] Rather surprisingly, their demand for ST status is strongly opposed by the Bodo leadership.

Since the Bodo Accord, ethnic tension has been prevailing in the BAC area, covering nearly 2,300 km^2 in Kokrajhar, Bongaigaon, Barpeta, Nalbari, Darrang, Mangaldoi and Sonitpur districts on the Northern Bank. Bodo leaders wanted 515 more villages in the BAC, and later in the proposed BTC, because the area, they claimed, was contiguous. Then the Saikia Government rejected the demand as the Bodos formed less than 2 per cent of their population. The Bodos will not only be a minority in the BTC area, "constituting about 38 per cent of it total population", they will be reduced to a hopeless minority in the predominantly Adivasi areas. The BLT attacks earlier, and by the NDFB presently (early 2000's) on the non-Bodo settlements, especially those of the Adivasis (the preferred nomenclature for those who were once known as Tea Garden Labour and ex-Tea Garden Labour) had racial cleansing as their objective. It was no surprise that All Assam Tea Tribe Students Association called for a 24-hour state-wide Bandh on 11 November 2002 to oppose the inclusion of tea tribal dominated areas in the proposed BTC under the 6th Schedule, and demand security to non-Bodos—in the Bodo dominated areas, besides 60 per cent reservation of Government jobs for tea tribes.

The creation of BTC under 6th Schedule raises other issue that have a bearing on the broader tribal politics of the region. The privileges and benefits enjoyed by the tribes under 6th Schedule are jealously guarded by them. Hence, any move to extend the provisions of the 6th Schedule to the plains tribes (Bodos in this instance) is bound to find resistance from those who are exclusively covered by these provisions. Indeed, one of the three major demands of the Bodoland agitation, the demand for the recognition of the Bodo Kacharis of Karbi Anglong as a ST in that district, in effect their inclusion in the 6th Schedule, was resisted by the leadership of the Autonomous State Demand Committee (ASDC), the dominant political party in that district throughout the Bodoland Agitation. Bodoland Accord does not even refer to this demand, though it refers to the "scheduling and de-scheduling of the SCs and STs residing within the Bodo areas". Ironically, as mentioned above, the BLT is demanding ST status for the Bodos residing in Karbi Anglong, but oppose the demand of the Koch-Rajbongshis in the proposed BTC area for the very same ST status.

If the non-Bodos were apprehensive about their rights and status in the BTC, the Bodos themselves are not buoyant about the future of the BTC, which is yet to be formed. Although the ongoing talks between the BLT and the Centre have made progress, the Bodo people fear that Assam Government would let them down in the creation of BTC. After all, "it was after 14 rounds of talks since March 2000 between the BLT and the Centre that a Sub-Committee was to be formed to prepare the proposals for the formation of the BTC for consideration by the Centre and Assam Government (The Sub-Committee cleared the proposal for formation of BTC in February 2002). "The current mood of the Bodo people and organisations is reminiscent of the situation that prevailed before the signing of Bodo Accord on 20 February 1993 between the Centre and the ABSU. Although the Accord paved the way for the formation of the BAC, it failed to put an end to the Bodo militancy in the State.[37] Some Bodo leaders are skeptical about the fate of the BTC: Will it go the BAC way? Perhaps, excessive pessimism is uncalled for.

APPENDIX

Why Separate Bodo State?

(Memorandum dated 10 November 1987)[38]

Population Pattern of Assam

The population census of 1971 was vague, and far from truth. Correct figures of tribes cannot be determined from this Census. Some tribes or sections of them, who used to speak Assamese or told it as their mother-tongue, were included as Assamese speaking people. Lakhs of tribals were dropped out from their respective tribes through administrative (intentional) manoeuvring but included in the general Assamese people.

On the basis of Linguistic Survey of India and comparative study of 1971 census and also from the local studies in various districts and sub-divisions of Assam, populations in Assam can be estimated as follows in 1986. Of course, correctness cannot be claimed as exact but amounts to approximation.

Population of Assam as in 1986 (Established)

Total	2,25,00,000
Muslims	40,00,000
Bengalis	33,00,000
Tribals	64,00,000
Others	88,00,000

Composition of Others

Tea-garden Workers and Family Members; Santal/Munda etc.

Adibasis	25,00,000
Nepalis	6,00,000
Rajbongshis	5,00,000
Others (General)	52,00,000
Total Non-Tribal Population	1,61,00,000
Percentage of Tribal Population	28.5

Plains Tribals of Assam

1. Barmans of Cachar
2. Boro Kacharis
3. Deoris
4. Hojais
5. Kacharis including Sonowals
6. Lalungs
7. Meches
8. Miris
9. Rabhas

According to 1961 census, total population of these Plains Tribals was 9,56,858, which works out to 9.06 per cent of Assam's population.

Break-up of Tribal Population of Assam

Adibasis	25,00,000
Boro	40,00,000
Miri (Mishing)	6,00,000
Rabha (Koch)	4,00,000
Mikir (Karbi)	6,00,000
Sonowal Kochari	2,00,000
Deori Kachari	1,50,000
Dimasa Kochri	1,50,000
Kuki	15,000
Borman (Kochari)	15,000
Garo	15,000
Naga Tribe	10,000
Khasi Jayantia	10,000
Hwar-man, Hojang and others	35,000
Total Tribal Population in Assam	64,00,000

District-wise Break-up of Boro Population in Assam

Kokrajhar	6,00,000
Dhubri	3,00,000
Goalpara	3,35,000
Barpeta	4,00,000
Nalbari	4,50,000
Kamrup	3,50,000
Pragjyotishpur	10,000
Darrang	5,00,000
Sonitpur	4,00,000
Lakhimpur	4,00,000
Nagaon	1,00,000
Karbi Anglong	1,00,000
Jorhat	50,000
Sibsagar and Dibrugarh	5,000
Total Boro Population in Assam	40,00,000

Population of Linguistic Bodo Group of People of Assam

Boro Kachari	40,00,000
Rabha	4,00,000
Sonowal	2,00,000
Lalung	2,00,000
Deori	1,50,000
Dimasa	1,50,000
Barman	15,000
Garo	15,000
Hajong and Hojai Kachari	20,000

Chutiyas and Moran Kacharis—completely Assamised and as such their figures could not be known.

Total Bodo Groups Population in Assam:—51,50,000.

Here difference between terms Bodo and Boro is obvious. Boro includes mainly the purely Boro-speaking people although some sections of them might have forgotten their Boro language. But the term Bodo refers to all Kachari or Bodo Groups of people such as Boro Rabhas, Koch Mech, Garo Sonowal, Lalung, Deori, Dimasa, Soraniya, Barman, Hojai, Hajong, Tripuri (Tipperah), Chutiya and Moran whose languages are very close to Boro or Bara. That is why languages of those Kachari clans are known as Bodo Group languages and those tribes are known as Bodos as a whole.

Rajbongshis are not included here, as they speak Assamese. Undoubtedly they are Hinduised Bodo Mongoloids. They are also of same stock of Bodo but after adoption of Hinduism, *i.e.* Vaishnavism, they have totally forgotten Bodo language. Now they speak Assamese.

Total Boro and Mech Population: State- and Country-wise

States:	Assam	40,00,000
	West Bengal	40,000
	Meghalaya	30,000
	Nagaland	15,000
	Arunachal	2,000
Countries:	Nepal	10,000
	Bangladesh	5,000
	Bhutan	2,000
	Total Boro and Mech Population	41,04,000

As regard the terms Boro and Mech, there is no difference between the two. Of course, the Boros of Nagaland, Jalpaiguri of West Bengal and that of Northern part of erstwhile Goalpara district of Assam are sometimes known as Mech, but there is no difference in their language. Mech is nothing but bad name given to Bodos by the neighbouring non-Bodos.

Total Population of Linguistically Bodo Group of People: State- and Country-wise

States:	Assam	51,50,000
	Tripura	7,00,000
	Meghalaya	5,00,000
	West Bengal	40,000
	Nagaland	15,000
	Arunachal	2,000
Countries:	Nepal	10,000
	Bangladesh	5,000
	Bhutan	2,000
	Total Bodo Group of Population	64,24,000

Bodos are the largest tribe in the Plains of Assam and their Bodo language is of Tibeto-Burmese Family. From above, it is obvious that the Bodos are the great nationality spread in extensive areas around the world.

Area of Proposed Union Territory

	Present Area (Sq km)	*Area to be included in the Union Territory (Sq km)*	
Districts (9)			
Kokrajhar	4,716.5	4,716.50	
Lakhimpur	5,646.4	5,646.4	
Dhubri	2,745.5	1,372.5	
Goalpara	2,843.5	710.8	
Barpeta	3,307.3	1,653.6	
Nalbari	2,022.8	1,111.4	
Kamrup	4,625.9	1,155.2	
Darrang	3,465.3	2,752.3	
Sonitpur	5,255.2	4,204.2	
Sub-Divisions (2)			
Majuli	1,241.0	1,241.0	
Sodia (Sadiya)	914.0	914.0	
Union Territory	Total	25,478.1	(A)
Assam Total		78,523.0	(B)

1. If Union Territory conceded, Assam's remaining area will be	B-A	53,044.9 sq km (C)
2. Area of two Hill (Karbi Anglong 10,331 km^2 and NC 4,890 km^2) districts		15,222.0 sq km (D)
3. If the Hill Districts too go their own army, Assam's remaining area will still be	C-D	37,822 km^2 (E)
4. Total Tribal Area (Proposed)	A+D	40,700.1 km^2
5. Area of Cachar (Undivided)		6,962.0 km^2 (F)
6. Worst case scenario, if Cachar too gets away, the rump state will still be	E-F	30,860.9 km^2

Assam will still be second largest in North-East, next only to Arunachal Pradesh. Hence no question of impossibility of further division of Assam can arise.

(It goes to the credit of Bodo leaders that they did not leave any one in doubt about their concept of the proposed Bodoland. They seem to have diligently dotted their i's and crossed their t's.)

Union Territory was to be created by joining the entire areas of Kokrajhar and Lakhimpur districts and Majuli and Sadiya sub-divisions and Northern parts of Dhubri, Barpeta, Nalbari, Goalpara, Kamrup. Dartang and Sonitpur districts. Southern boundary will lie near Rupshri, neighbouring parts to the North of Bilasipara, Jogighopa, Barpeta, Howli, Pathsala, Nalbari, Rangia, Barhata Chirali, Mangoldoi, Tezpur, Biswanatha Chirali, while these towns will remain in Assam. In the North, boundary will be Bhutan and Arunachal Pradesh; in the East will be Arunachal Pradesh and Assam; and in the West, will be West Bengal.

The area of proposed Union Territory extends from Sankosh River (near Srirampur) in the West to Mazbat/River Pasnoi (near Sadiya) in the East. It will span 700 km East to West and 36 km average from North to South.

Population of Proposed Union Territory: 1986

1.	Population of Present Assam	2,25,00,000
2.	Population of proposed Union Territory	61,37,914
	Tribal Population in Union Territory	42,96,000
	Non-Tribal Population in Union Territory	18,41,914
	Percentage of Tribal Population	70
	Percentage of non-Tribal Population	30
3.	Remaining Population in Rest of Assam	1,63,61,086
	Area of Rest of Assam	53,044.9 km^2
4.	Density in Rest of Assam	308 per sq km
	Density in Proposed Union Territory	241 per sq km

Tribe-wise Population in Proposed Union Territory

Boros	33,50,000
Mishing	5,00,000
Rabhas	1,41,000
Sonowals	1,00,000
Deoris	1,00,000
Garos	5,000
Karbis	40,000
Lalung	60,000
Total Tribal Population in Union Territory	42,96,000

Memorandum of Settlement
Bodoland Accord

20-2-1993

Sd/- Sd /-

S.K. Bwismutiary K.S. Rao

President, ABSU	Additional Chief Secretary Government of Assam
Sd /-	Sd /-
Rabi Ram Brahma	Subhash Basumatari
General Secretary	Chairman, BPAC

In the Presence of:

Rajesh Pilot, Minister of State, Ministry of Home Affairs, Government of India

Hiteswar Saikia

Chief Minister, Assam

They get the BTC

07 Feb. 2003. Contours of the final shape of the BTC emerged when the senior Bodo leader and Rajya Sabha MP Urkhaw Gwra Brahma told the press *(Exp.,* 8-2-03) that the BLT and Guwahati "have agreed on a 46-seat BTC of which 30 would be reserved for the STs, 5 for non-tribals, 5 open and 6 to be nominated by the Assam Government. Only the last category needs more discussion." BLT spokesman Mainao Daimary assured this formula would safeguard the interests of the non-Bodos in the BTC.

10 Feb. 2003. Ending a decade-long insurgency, Hagrama Basumatary, Chairman of the secessionist BLT, signed a Tripartite Agreement with the Centre (R.C.A. Jain, Secretary, Border Management, MHA) and State Government (Chief Secretary P.K. Dutta), for the creation of the BTC which would abolish the existing Bodo Autonomous Council (BAC) formed as a result of the 20-2-1993 Tripartite Agreement. The Memorandum of Settlement (MOS) was signed in the presence of Deputy PM Advani, Chief Minister Tarun Gogoi, and the two MoS in the MHA—I.D. Swami and Harin Pathak.

The MoS gives the community: (1) A University. (2) Inclusion of Bodo language in the 8th Schedule. (3) Besides Kokrajhar, three new districts of Udalguri, BACsa and Chirang. (4) More autonomy to the proposed Bodoland Territorial Area District (BTAD) under the Sixth Schedule (39 Departments had been transferred to it within a month of its constitution). (5) A Rs. 100-crore annual allocation. (6) BTC to have (said the sources) 3082 villages "beyond the Pasnoi river, Bijni town, areas around Dhaligaon, Shrirampur and Orang and Manas National Parks" *(Frontline* 14-3-03). (7) A centrally funded Central Institute of Technology.

The damper on the celebrations came not only from the fierce opposition to the Accord from the rival Bodo outfit of the NDFB, but also from the SJSS, a conglomeration of 18 non-Bodo groups, who announced a 100-hour bandh in western Assam, starting 14 February.

There are many other contentious issues flowing from or impinging upon the creation of the BTC. An angry mob of the *Koch-Raiboneshis* (KRs) ransacked (4-8-03) the BJP office, Guwahati, demanding ST status for the KRs. After all, they are aware that a Constitution Amendment Bill tabled in the Lok Sabha on 1-8-03 to give more autonomy to the Bodos in the BTC under the 6th Schedule "is likely to be passed smoothly with the support of the BJP and Congress". The KRs have been demanding the ST status for long, and the Bodos are stoutly opposed to it for they know—and are afraid—that once granted this demand, they (the Bodos) would be reduced to a 'helpless' minority—given the past experience in the North-East! Getting ST status by the KRs would only be the first step to demand an ADC for themselves within the BTC, and eventually to a UT, if not a full-fledged state. Hence the Bodo fears, and opposition, even when "the Union Tribal Affairs Minister has already informed Parliament that KRs are not 'eligible' to be enlisted as ST". In the North-East, mere ministerial assertions do not put a full stop to any issue. After all, the Sixth Schedule, exclusively crafted for benefit of the Hill Tribes of Assam, was being bent/extended/stretched "at that very time" to confer its benefits to a Plains Tribe (read 'Bodo') of Assam. It was a question of the ability of a particular group to put 'requisite' pressure—peacefully or otherwise—on the State and the Centre. The KRs apart, there are other problems in implementing the BTC.

The clause 8 of the 10-2-03 BTC MoU says the Centre would "sympathetically" consider the inclusion of Bodo-Kacharis living in the Karbi-Anglong (KA) and North-Cachar Hills Autonomous Council areas as ST-H (Hills), because the Bodos remonstrate that while they are recognised as ST in the Plains, why not in these two Hill districts. But the Karbis and North Cacharis, enjoying this status in the two Hills, have been up against this demand of the Bodos. On 24-7-03, an ASDC delegation led by Jayanta Rongpi, MP, submitted a memorandum to the Dy PM Advani urging him "not to disturb the ST-H list at the time of creating the BTC." The BJP is in a fix. The Congress and the ASDC, arch enemies in the two Hill districts, joined hands not only to oppose clause 8 of the BTC accord but the BTC Bill itself.) Things do not end up here. The Kukis, claiming to be 35,000 strong in the KA district, are demanding, as discussed earlier, a Kuki Autonomous Regional Council there under the Sixth Schedule. Otherwise, loudly proclaim their two representative outfits (The Reorganisation and Confederation of Kukis and its armed wing, KRA): "We will fight till the last drop of our blood." The strong opposition of the non-Bodo communities, led by the SJSS, has been mentioned above. It is obvious there is nothing known as final solution to anything in the North-East!

Now a word on the all-important issue of population mix and the territory of the proposed BTC. It is obvious that the BTC, like the earlier BAC, falls well short of the original demand for a full-fledged separate state of Bodoland, articulated rather provocatively in their March 1987 assertion: "Divide Assam fifty-fifty." The rhetoric notwithstanding, it is worth stating that the Bodo people are one, if not the largest, of the eight Plains Tribal people of the Brahmaputra valley of Assam (nine if we include the Barak Valley districts), let alone the rest of the plains tribal people who themselves are deeply divided on the issue.

The difficulties faced by the authorities in giving practical shape to the Feb. 2003 Accord can be understood by a single fact that it took them 9 months after signing of the MoS to issue Notification for Constitution of the BTC. But it was not surprising as certain things were left unsaid, uncertain, or vague in the MoS. "There is still some lack of clarity about the total area of the BTC, the total number of villages and towns that will come within that area, its total population and more importantly, its ethnic mix" (M.S. Prabhakara, *Frontline,* 05-12-03). Rather broadly, this 'ethnic mix' comprises, apart from the Bodo population, the caste Hindu Assamese who historically belong to the same ethnic block as the Bodos, Adivasis and the immigrant Muslim Communities, each one of which is "apprehensive about the political and economic consequences of a formal acknowledgement of Bodo hegemony in areas which they view, equally, as their home". Such issues left unclarified is bound to impinge upon the functioning of the yet-to-be formed BTC.

As for the territory of the BTC, which will comprise of four new contiguous districts—Kokrajhar, Baksa, Udalguri and Chirang—on the North bank of the Brahmaputra, it is being carved out of the 8 districts of Assam. Dhubri, Kokrajhar, Bongaigaon, Barpeta, Nalbari, Kamrup, Darrang and Sonitpur. The area of these 8 districts is about 27,100 Sq km, 35 per cent of Assam's total area. The area of the BTC works out to 40 per cent of the said 27,100 Sq km area.

Again, there was no finality about the number of villages that were to fall within the territory of the BTC, at the time of signing of the 10-2-03 MoS. Indeed, wrangling over this issue was one of the factors that delayed the issuing of the Notification. As per the MoS, BTC was to comprise 3082 villages. The addition of 55 other villages, demanded by the BLT, was to be discussed further. Consequent to the post-Accord negotiations, a further 13 villages (or a further 25 villages, says another report) would be included in the BTC area, thus bringing the total in the BTC area (as of end 2003) to 3095 (or 3102). Further discussions on the inclusion of the remaining 82 (or 70) villages were to follow the formation of the Interim Territorial Council. Such vagueness and imprecision is understandable.

Some of the important towns to be included in the BTC area are Kokrajhar, the Bodo heartland as it were and the home of the earlier Bodo autonomist/ nationalistic assertion, the major part of Bongaigaon, including the refinery and petro-chemical complex, Bijni, Sidli, Tamalpur and Udalguri—the last another historical seat of Bodo autonomist/nationalistic assertion.

Now for the population of the BTC area, and more critically, its 'population mix' "The MoS wisely, and perhaps unavoidably, remains silent on this crucial question." In the late 1980s, the Bodo leaders claimed that in Assam alone Bodo population was 40 lakhs, an understandable exaggeration. The 1991 Census records the total Bodo population in Assam at 12,67,015 that includes the Bodos living outside the BTC area. The total ST and Bodo populations in the 8 districts relevant to us are indicated in the table below:

District	*Total Population*	*ST Population*	*Bodo Population*
Dhubri	13,32, 475	32,260	22,628
Kokrajhar	8,00, 659	3,29,461	3,18,432
Bongaigaon	8,07, 423	1,41,542	1,33,904
Barpeta	13,85,659	1,10,452	1,03,413
Nalbari	10,16,390	1,79,641	1,47,690
Kamrup	20,00,071	2,14,340	1,12,796
Darrang	12,98,860	224,957	1,89,962
Sonitpur	14,24,287	1,52,498	1,02,369
Total	1,00,65,924	13,85,151	11,39,194

The table shows the total Bodo population in the 8 districts amounts to a little over 11 per cent of their total population. Earlier we have seen that Bodos in the BAC (now BTC) area accounted for about 38 per cent of its total population.

It all started with the BLT, "the most dreaded militant outfit with a 1,000 strong cadre", announcing early 2000 its decision to bid "farewell to arms", and signing a cease-fire agreement with the Centre on 29 Mar. 2000. A day after signing this agreement, the BLT leaders organised a public meeting at Debargaon near Kokrajhar to apprise the public of the cease-fire accord.

BTC Boundary. A contentious issue was resolved 25-6-02 when an All-Party Meeting convened by Tarun Gogoi agreed to extend the eastern boundary of the proposed BTC beyond the Pachnoi River, the existing BAC boundary (*HT* 26-06-02).

BTC Cleared—Longlast

The Assam Government issued a notification authorising the Constitution of the BTC nine months after the signing of the 10-02-03 Accord. The notification was delayed, especially because of the contentious issue of demarcation of the Council's territory. The final hurdle was cleared 31 Oct. 2003 when the Government agreed to include 25 more villages to the BTC territory, taking the total number of the villages to 3,108. The Notification also declared the BTC as covered under the 6th Schedule.

While the ABSU, BLT and other Bodo groups welcomed the development, the SJSS expectedly called for a 100-hour bandh from the day the BTC assumed office.

Protection of Non-Tribals in the BTC Area

The Lok Sabha passes two Constitution Amendment Bills 8-8-03 unanimously. The 99th Amendment Bill protects the rights of the non-tribals in the newly elected BTC in Assam. Dy PM Advani told the House that the decision to establish the BTC was taken after 21 rounds of tripartite talks. He also said "no change will take place in the boundaries of the North-Eastern States despite pressure from certain quarters".

The 94th Amendment Bill empowers the Government to set up a separate National Commission for Scheduled Tribes (NCST) by bifurcating the existing National Commission for Scheduled Castes (NCSC). The minister for Tribal Affairs. Jewel Oram said the proposed NCST would comprise a chairperson and two other members and the "NCSC shall have a chairperson, vice-chairperson, and three other members".

The 99th Amendment would also entitle the Boros and Boro-Kacharis residing in Assam, including in the BATD, the benefits of the ST status.

They Lay Down Arms

6 Dec. 2003. Cheers from the massive crowd rent the air at the Banergaon Mini-Stadium in the Bodo heartland of Kokrajhar as the first 100 BLT cadre waving white flags entered the ground in the five Tata mobile pick-ups. Then came 2,500 rebels in their jungle fatigues, led by their Chief Hagrama Basumatary, who has reverted to his original name Hagrama Mahillary after returning to the ways of peace. He lowered the BLT flag, hoisted the white flag, and then led the rebels in laying down arms "before chief Minister Gogoi in what is the biggest ever surrrender ceremony in the history of the North-East insurgency" (*Week,* 21-12-03). Mahillary also announced the dissolution of the BLT.

BLT Chief Becomes the CEM

7 Dec. 2003. A day after the surrender, a 12-member Interim Executive Council (IEC) of the BTC, headed by Mahillary is sworn in at the Gauhati University Campus. Dy PM Advani, who was the chief guest, said the event was "the happiest in his political career".

The elections to the BTC, under Article 14 of the MoS "are to be held within 6 months of the constitution of the IEC", which under the given conditions, meant before 7 June 2004.

Bodo in the 8th Schedule

Even as the Lok Sabha passed the Constitution Amendment Bill 22-12-03 to include the Bodo language in the 8th Schedule, S.K. Bwismutiary, the sole representative of the newly-raised BTC, stood up and waved (The Government also included Santhali, Maithili and Dogri in the 8th Schedule). Presently, there are 18 languages in the 8th Schedule.

The Convulsions on Way to the BTC Elections

ABSU announced 11-4-05, a month before the elections to the BTC fixed for 13 May, the launch of a new political party including all Bodo socio-political groups, at a convention to be held at Kokrajhar on the 12th. The aim, said Rabiram Narzary, former ABSU President, was to ensure that non-Bodos do not wield power in the BTC. Accordingly, the Bodoland People's Progressive Front (BPPF).

Formed on the 12-4-05, the BPPF stood split by the first week of May 2005, with the former BLT leaders and cadre in one camp and the erstwhile ABSU leaders in the other. The cracks appeared at the Kokrajhar Headquarters of the BTC when several leaders of the disbanded BLT filed nominations against BPPF President Rabiram Narzary and several other official candidates. The quarrel took a serious turn when the present BTC chief Mohillary extended open support to his former comrade-in-arms, Mono Kumar Brahma, the rebel candidate against Narzary in Banargaon Constituency.

Confusion prevailed when the voters saw Narzary and Rajya Sabha MP U.G. Brahma sharing one platform to address election rallies and Mohillary campaigning for the rebel candidates. These leaders had worked together for the Bodo cause till the other day.

"Mohillary and four other official BPPF candidates have already won the election uncontested. The trouble could be traced to the time when Mohillary and two Bodo MPs (Brahma and Bwismutiary) were elected members of the BPPF's policy-making body. The Mohillary group saw in Narzary a potential rival for the top post of the CEM of the BTC. A formal disclaimer from the Narzary that he was not interested in becoming CEM or Dy CEM, was seen as a patch-up effort by the party" (*Hindu,* 7-5-05).

NDFB GRABS THE HEADLINES

The BLT decision to foresake violence and its talks with authorities leading to Feb. 2003 Accord and subsequent issues of creating the BTC and thereafter the elections for the Council had kept the outfit in the news for long years. Now some news about its equally potent rival, the NDFB, and its decision to jump on the centre stage.

Some Incidents Involving NDFB

28-4-03, NDFB demands Rs. 5 lakh annually from the NHPC (National Hydel Power Corporation) on the clear undertaking that it would not disturb its functioning.

Too many leaders in the BAC during Nov. 2002-Apr. 2003. The outlawed outfit suffered another major blow when the Kolkata police arrested two of its cadres including the founder member Sunil Brahma in the city on 29 Apr. 2003. Brahma from Darrang district, is the former Organising Secretary of the outfit and was also in charge of its cadres in North Bengal and Sikkim, as also its bases in Garo Hills in West Meghalaya. It was in Nov. 2002 that its General Secretary Gobinda Basumatary was arrested from a train at Rangiya, while its Vice-President Dhiren Boro was arrested in Gangtok on 1 Jan. 2003. The NDFB, sidelined following the BTC Accord by the BLT and operating primarily from its hide-outs/bases in Bhutan, "is now left with only two top leaders at the decision-making level", Chairman Ranjan Daimary and Publicity Secretary B. Erakdao.

Is it Demoralisation?

The return of senior NDFB leader Bijoy Boro to Guwahati in the end-July 2004 was another blow to the outfit, and the analyst were undecided: was it a surrender or arrest? The incident was seen as a major development on the insurgency front in Assam, after all, NDFB was the only major outfit left in the jungles. "Disillusionment with the struggle and particularly the leadership of Ranjan Damnary led to the arrest or surrender of senior leaders like Gobinda Basumatary, Dhiren Boro, and Finance Secretary Nileshwar Basumatary" (Rajee Sharma, *Tribune,* 17-10-04). With the fate of another senior leader, B. Erakdao, unknown, the sudden appearance of the Chairman's Chief Assistant and NDFB's arms procurer, Bijoy Boro and Benu Boro in Guwahati, had set the tongues wagging: "Are they abandoning the sinking ship one by one?" It was a pertinent query for two reasons: (1) of the three outfits in Bhutan, it suffered the most in terms of casualties and loss of arms. It was nearly wiped out in operation. All-Clear in Dec. 2003, leaving it a moribund and almost defunct. The remaining 200-strong armed cadre was entirely Bangladesh-based, at its Boyalcharri base in Khagracharri district of the CHT. Its only intact formation, 3rd Battalion, too was headquartered there. So, its ability to carry out insurgency-related operations is severely limited. (2) The total support by the Bodos for the BTC signed by the BLT seemed to be the undoing of the morale of its leadership. Some analysts feel it might itself go in for the face saving negotiations with the Government.

Presently, only a handful of senior leaders like Susranga, 'Army Chief', his Deputy Dinthilang, and Maj Rava Gothal, 3rd Battalion Commander, "Cluster around Daimary in Bangladesh (October 2004)". Two houses in Dhaka and the Boyalcharri base provide safe havens for the rump leadership. Given his hopeless situation, Daimary seemed to be in no hurry to initiate dialogue with the Government. His optimism possibly stems from his faith in the continued Dhaka support, and help from the old benefactor ULFA to sail through the choppy waters.

By way of show of force, the NDFB in coordination with ULFA organised violence in Assam during 2-5 Oct. 2004, killing 40 persons and injuring another 106. "They are obviously not a spent force yet."

Still Wanted by Interpol

NDFB chief is still on the "Wanted List" of the Interpol which issued a notice against P.P. Nabla, alias Ranjan Daimary in 1997. Here is Interpol profile of Nabla: "A post-graduate in political science, has undergone rigorous arms training and is also well-versed in guerrilla warfare. He is the man who conspired with the NSCN to mount an armed movement to cede Assam from the Indian Union."

NDFB Chief in Uranium Plot?

Two men in possession of a kilogram of semi-processed Uranium were arrested in Guwahati on 17 Apr. 2005. The seized uranium was suspected to have been stolen/smuggled out of Meghalaya. The police sent it for tests to a laboratory, suspecting the consignment to be of Uranium-235 which can be used for preparing low-grade explosives. The sources stated the processing technology of semi-processed uranium is available only with the state.

The trap was laid after the reports that the two persons were carrying RDX but actual catch turned out to be the Uranium. The Intelligence discovered on the 19th that certain Chinese agencies had assigned two crucial tasks to Ranjan Daimary: (1) To transfer dollar funds to Singapore, (2) Uranium smuggling from Meghalaya *(AA,* 20-4-05).

NDFB Comes on Board

Daimary's (or Nabla's) 30 Sept. 2004 statement offered cease-fire effective 15 October. Talking tough, Gogoi said on 25 October that he would not soften his Government's stand against the outfit. After consulting the MHA, he "has sent a letter to Nabla, now in Bangkok, to let him know the names of his representatives to begin talks for a negotiated settlement". In an equally tough report, through the NDFB spokesperson S. Sanjarang, it accused Assam of derailing peace process, and added: "We would not talk to Assam Government. Centre should not equate BLT with NDFB. We are also against talks on the modalities adopted during the talks with the BLT.... NDFB has nothing to do with the BTC Accord. ABSU must understand that our ceasefire declaration was sincere and honest, aimed at resolving the conflict peacefully and democratically...our talks will be based on our principles and ideology. When we meet Indians, certainly we will talk on our historical and legitimate rights."

The NDFB said on 16 April 2005: "In view of continuation of our talks with New Delhi to formalise the cease-fire and to formulate the modalities of talks, the NDFB has extended the cease-fire for another 6 months? The initial 6-month unilateral cease-fire of the NDFB had lapsed on 15 April *(AA,* 17-4-05).

The formal cease-fire agreement between the NDFB and New Delhi, signed on 24 May 2005 marked the end of 19-year long violent movement by the outfit (The 6-year armed struggle by the BLT had ended with the 10 Feb. 2003 BTC Accord). The MHA sources said the bilateral "Cease-fire would be effective from 1 June. The NDFB has been on a unilateral cease-fire mode since 15 Oct. 2004. The outfit agreed to hand over a list of its cadres as well as its weapons, and also set up a joint cease-fire monitoring group, comprising of equal representation from the Central and State Governments and NDFB.

Formed on 3 October 1986 as BdSF in Odla Khasibari village, off Udalguri town near the foothills of Bhutan, at the initiative of Ransaigra Nabla Daimari alias Ranjan Daimary, it changed its name to NDFB on 18 April 1993 and has a current cadre strength of 700 men. Over 1,000 cadres have surrendered in phases since 1992 while about 300 died in clashes with the SF (Another source put its cadre strength around 2,000). It has bases in Myanmar and Bangladesh, and temporary bases in Arunachal. It is active in Nalbari and Dhubri areas (*Exp.,* 25 and 26 May 2005).

17-06-05. A peace rally was organised by the All-Bodo Peace Forum at Udalguri which was attended by thousands of Bodos in traditional attire who welcomed the cease-fire agreement that came into effect on 1-6-05 for a period of one year and pledged their support to the peace process. Forum chairman Moniram Mochahari wanted support of the masses for meaningful dialogue. The Rally, witnessing an unprecedented gathering of more than 40,000 people, was addressed by leaders of various North-East organisations including Harangse Sangtam, President Naga Hoho, Artrex Shimray, Chief Adviser, NESO (North-East Students Organisation), Kanaksen Deka, Assam Sahitya Sabha and U.G. Brahma, Rajya Sabha MP.

Same day (17-06-05), a 12-member NDFB delegation led by General Secretary Govinda Basumatari (alias B. Swmkhwr) attended the meeting of Cease-fire Monitoring Group, presided over by Rajiv Agarwal, JS, MHA, which discussed the setting up of designated camps for the NDFB cadres and other formalities relating to the implementation of ground rules of the Agreement. The NDFB informed the Centre and Guwahati that it had about 2,000 cadres.

Here is its General Secretary talking to the press at Udalguri, Darrang district, as reported by the *Hindu* of 20-6-05: "NDFB will hold peace talks on the basis of its original demand for a 'sovereign Boroland'.... Our ideology is liberation of Boroland, to have free Boro nation.... We will submit a 'Memorandum of Settlement' to the Centre on the issue. We want to liberate

Boroland, from the Indian expansionism and occupation. If the legitimate demand was turned down by the Centre, the NDFB would have no option but to resume its struggle." The bluster and rhetoric are understandable.

OCTOBER 2005 SITUATION: AN UNEASY CALM

After years of bloodshed, there is a relative calm in Assam's Bodo heartland after the signing of the NDFB cease-fire effective 1 June 2005. After the BLT signed BTC Accord on 10-2-03, its cadres laid down their arms. But the return of the armed youth to the mainstream has disturbed the equilibrium of Bodo politics, and triggered a power struggle between various organisations, representing the state's largest Plain tribe. If the 13 May 2005 elections to the BTC divided the BPPF into two factions led by the former ABSU leaders and former BLT leaders, the analysts are apprehensive of a more serious conflict between the BLT and NDFB rebels in the days to come. Particularly so, when the results of the NDFB dialogue with the Centre and their implications for the existing BTC set-up are not yet clear.

The BTC elections had witnessed group clashes between the two factions, who are ruling the present council in an unhappy cohabitation. The huge turn out at the 17 June Rally persuaded the feuding BPFF leaders to close ranks lest the NDFB wean away their supporters. They are worried that the NDFB will play an important role in the next Assembly poll due in May 2006. They have not forgotten the role played by the now defunct People's Democratic Front (PDF), a political party raised on behest of the NDFB, which secured control of the BAC for the support its MLAs gave to the then ruling AGP. The NDFB could revive the PDF, especially as it has all the time to do so, since the cease-fire is in force. There is also worry on another front: The non-Bodo parties, national and regional, might cause dissensions/splits in the Bodo parties, and thus gain a foothold in the BTC affairs.

For now, all eyes are set on the Assembly polls. And the Bodos could play a major role in deciding the outcome in 12 seats in the BTC area, which in turn could affect the formation of the State Government. This can happen only if they do not allow the outsiders to play any role on their turf for sectional or party gains. While the formal negotiations between the NDFB and the Centre are unlikely to reach a decisive phase before the Assembly polls, the NDFB and its arch rivals, the ABSU, the former BLT and their allied factions are likely to engage in a turf war before the polls to position themselves favourably to gain the support of the Bodo masses for these subsequent polls. It should not be forgotten that all major political parties certainly will woo the Bodo leaders to retain or capture power at Dispur.

WILL THERE BE FRATRICIDAL 'WAR' ONCE AGAIN IN BODO LAND?

Ever since the Bodo Liberation Tigers (BLT) struck a second Bodo Accord with the Centre and Assam Government in 2003 and became ruling entity in

Bodoland Territorial Council (BTC), there was always fears lurking in the minds of the analysts and congnescenti that the rival secessionist outfit, National Democratic Front of Bodoland (NDFB), still fighting for its objective and waiting in the wings, will not find it easy to accept, much less welcome, the development which resulted in its marginalisation among its constituency, the Bodos concentrated in the BTC area. The latest spark that could ignite the conflagration between the cadres of the NDFB and erstwhile BLT now dissolved came on 26 and 31 Mar. 2007. Before going into its details, a bit of history.

The first Bodo Accord was signed by the All Bodo Students Union (ABSU) in 1993 as a result of which the Bodoland Autonomous Council (BAC) came into existence. The agitation, talks and other development leading to its creation has been delineated in detail earlier in this chapter. The BLT was disbanded and its cadres came overground with the signing of the second Bodo Accord and creation of BTC subsequent to the disbandment of the erstwhile BAC. Ever since its formation, former cadres of the BLT are in power in BTC. Meanwhile, the NDFB entered into a ceasefire agreement with the Centre on 24 May 2005.

The agreement came into effect on 1 June of the same year (2005) and some armed NDFB cadres along with some top leaders moved from their hide-outs in jungles into designated camps set up by the Government in BTC areas. The Centre had set a 31 Mar. 2007 deadline for the outfit to submit its charter of demands, but it replied that was no need for such a charter as its demand for a "sovereign Bodoland" was well known to the centre. The deadlock on this issue has persisted, with the talks nowhere on the horizon. The rivalry between the two Bodo groups is understandable as the NDFB wants a share of the pie in BTC—in simple terms, a share of power to rule the Bodoland.

Now to the cause of latest trouble. The question that analysts are asking: Is the Bodo heartland (read, area under BTC) bracing for a fresh bout of fratricidal clashes between the NDFB and the BLT which has disbanded in 1993 but whose former militants rule the BTC. The spark for the latest turf war came from an attack on an NDFB camp at Medaghat in lower Assam's Baksa district on 26 Mar. 2007. Two NDFB militants were killed and three others injured. The NDFB alleged that the attack was launched by the former BLT militants. Refuting the accusation, BTC Chief Executive Member (CEM) and the former BLT Chief Hagrama Mahillary ascribed the incident to the anger among the general public, as it was fed up with the NDFB's extortion drive in violation of the ceasefire agreement.

The Medaghat attack was followed by the killing of a personal security officer (PSO) of a BTC Executive Member (EM) at Kumarikata bazar under Tamilpur police station limits of the same district on 31 March. The unidentified gunman also snatched away the PSO's service pistol. Now the roles stood reversed. Blaming the incident on the NDFB, Mohillary challenged the rival militant group to a gun battle. The NDFB, on the other hand, accused Mohillary's BPPF (Hagrama)—Bodoland People's Progressive Front (Hagrama)—through a pamphlet, of raising a new militant outfit called Bodoland Royal Tiger Force (BRTF). The NDFB charged that arms training was being imparted to the BRTF cadres in remote areas of Baksa, Kokrajhar and Chirang district. It also accused the former BLT rebels of trying to provoke the NDFB into pulling out of the ceasefire and warned "our patience may run out."

The situation in Bodoland is tense as neither of the two groups seems to be interested in reconciliation despite appeals by organisations like the Bodo Sahitya Sabha (BSS). On 1 Apr. 2007, the BPPF (Hagrama) launched a campaign urging businessmen not to buckle under the NDFB's "extortion demands." Not to be outdone, the NDFB too launched peace rallies.

It is obvious that the NDFB is keen to conclude an early peace with New Delhi. It is only after that peace agreement that it can make bid to claim some political space in Bodoland politics at first, and subsequently at Guwahati. It is equally obvious that the former BLT rebels are in no mood to yield any political space to its rival. It is worth remembering that the BPPF (current *avtar* of the disbanded BLT) is not only ruling party in the BTC but is also a partner of the ruling Congress in Guwahati. The recent elections (early 2007) to the State Assembly has only confirmed the importance the BPPF has for the ruling Congress led by Chief Minister Tarun Gogoi. He needs Hagrama's support to continue in the seat of power.

So to put it honestly, the rivalry betweeen the two outfits is being seen as the fallout of the dealy in the talks between the Centre and NDFB. The former BLT rebels are apprehesive of such talks as they can result in an accord that will enable their rivals to claim share of power both at the BTC, and then at the state level! Can the NDFB be blamed if they are convinced that its rival is coming in the way of start of these talks, one way or the other? It may even be seeing the 26 March attack in the same light.

There is another cause for worry for the BPPF. While the talks with New Delhi remain elusive, the NDFB leaders have been moving out of camps and making fervent appeal to the public to support the cause of a "sovereign Bodoland." The BPPF (Hagrama) was not worried so long as the NDFB campaign was confined to the outfit's traditional stronghold in Udalguri. But the NDFB slowly began moving into Kokrajhar, hoping to exploit the rivalry and consequently tug-of-war between the BPPF factions, led by the former BLT leaders and former ABSU President, Rabiram Brahma. This foray by the NDFB into Kokrajhar, considered a bastion of the erstwhile BLT, has obviously worried the present BTC rulers.

To the further consternation of the BPPF (Hagrama), the BPPF (Rabiram) and other Bodo organisations such as the ABSU, Bodo Women's Justice Forum, and the All Bodo Peace Forum have condemned the attack on the NDFB designated camp and rallied behind the outfit (Sushanta Tulukdar, *The Hindu*, 4 Apr. 2007).

The fight for political space in the Bodoland heartland can prove fatal to the much-desired peace there, because the two diametrically opposite forces could relapse into the days of the fratricidal clashes of 1998-2000. The only hope for the ordinary Bodo people seem to be an early intervention by New Delhi and Guwahati. The best way is for the Centre to invite the NDFB for talks. Any further dilly-dallying could result into an unimaginable tragedy for Bodos, and Assam itself.

NOTES

1. Kailash Sharma, *Bodo Insurgency in Assam,* in B. Pakam (ed), *Insurgency in North-East India,* 1997.
2. G.P. Singh (1967) has an interesting detail about Kirata King Naraka of Pragjyotisha. He was a foster child of Raja Janaka of Videha and an ancestor of King Bhagadatta. Naraka reputedly came to Pragjyotisha at 16 as a political adventurer, prior to the commencement of *Kaliyuga,* roughly in 3102 BC in pre-Mahabharata War period.
3. This was in response to the demand by some Bengali-speaking sections of Goalpara for merging it with Bengal (The refrain, of course, is different today: Bodos are not Assamese). Memorandum of the Bodo Community of Goalpara was drafted by Srijut Jadav Chandra Khokhlari of Assam Kachari Jubok Sanmeloni.
4. Local Boards were created in Assam for the purpose of managing affairs of local interest.
5. Rev J.J.M. Nichols-Roy of Progressive Nationalist Party and Rupnath Brahma, a Bodo, were the ministers in the 1937 Ministry.
6. Prior to this resignation, Saadullah had two stints as Muslim League Chief Minister of Assam.
7. Rupnath Brahma, a Bodo, again joined this Government of Saadullah.
8. Some elite groups among the Ahoms espoused separatism with the formation of Ujoni Assam Rajya Parishlid (UARP) in 1967, demanding the Ahom State in Upper Assam, comprising (undivided) districts of Sibsagar, Lakhimpur and Dibrugarh. But the demand petered out by 1978 with the merger of UARP with the Janata Party.
9. ABSU was rather good in presenting memoranda. In 1872-83 period, it had presented a large number to India's Presidents, Prime Minister and Home Ministers.
10. It was B.K. Kakati, former Editor, *Assam Tribune.*
11. Plains Tribals leaders under the banner of AAPTL had played a crucial role during 1937-47 period, voicing the demand for autonomy for all the Plains

Tribals. The AAPTL was converted into a socio-cultural organisation, Tribal Sangh, under the 1947 agreement with the Congress Party, entrusting to its care the political interests of the Plains Tribals of Assam. When they found the Congress not doing anything for their problems, the Plains Tribal leaders regretted the wasted 20 years and decided to revive their own efforts under a new organisation, PTCA, in 1967. But after it faired poorly in 1985 elections, PTCA was edged off the Centre stage, with the ABSU and then BPCA taking over reins for sectarian movements, exclusively for the Bodos, their rhetoric to the contrary, notwithstanding! In the coming years, PTCA was almost marginalised.

12. On PTCA's role in the past, see n. 11 above.
13. It has not been possible to determine the identity of this signature. One wonders if this is the transliteration of the Bodo name.
14. Hazarika, 1994.
15. The community was then represented by Kshatriya Sanmilani, whose President was Sri Phani Medhi.
16. Ahmed, Syed Zuberi, 1995.
17. Was it a macabre coincidence? Five years ago, the day after the Saikia Ministry was sworn-in (1 July 1991), 14 persons, mostly Assam officials and ONGC employees, including a Soviet national, Sergei Gretchenko, working with Coal India were abducted from Marghareta by ULFA. Eight of these were exchanged for captured ULFA insurgents, the fate of the rest being unknown. The body of the Soviet expert was subsequently found in a jungle.
18. Their names: Mathius Tudi, Simon Suren, Latindra Suren and Bodon Hasda.
19. *Times of India,* 15-8-1996.
20. The 1983 riots in Assam Valley, consequent to an ill-fated election that brought Saikia to power for the first time, was a bigger catastrophe. It was a mockery of poll process. Clashes spread across the valley. Over 300 people were killed, many of them immigrant Muslim settlers, especially at Nellie. There were also Bodo-Assamese clashes at Gohpur, Upper Assam, and attacks on Hindu Bengali settlers. ABSU's poll boycott call was too strong. Several polling booths reported no voting Again for record, in the 1994 riots, the Muslim settlers were the main targets.
21. In a sense, these riots also had a political angle. Bodos had asked Santhals to vote for the BSMC candidates in the recent Assembly Poll, but they voted for the AGP candidate, Rajendra Mushahary (who won and was made a Cabinet Minister). The Bodo reaction to the 'defiance' was obviously not long in the coming, concluded some analysts.
22. BdSF, formed on 3 October 1986, had grabbed the headlines when it carried out a major strike in a Tea Club in Dhekiajuli in 1990.
23. NSCN(I-M) had helped and guided Paresh Barua set up ULFA in April 1979.
24. Home Minister Inderjit Gupta informs Rajya Sabha on 14 May 1997.
25. *Ibid.*
26. *The Hindu,* 23-7-1997.
27. For details, *See India Today,* 29-6-1998.
28. *See The Hindu,* 15-6-1999.

29. *The Outlook*, 4-9-2000.
30. Pity of the situation for the common, innocent and unarmed Bodos is that one Bodo outfit does not blench from aiding and abetting a third party to inflict violence on them, just to spite its rival. This is exactly what happened, as described earlier, when to avenge the killings of 29 Bengali and Santhal settlers by the NDFB, the BTF killed 12 Bodos on 17 April 1997, with the tacit support of the BLT! The-tacit understanding between the BTF and BLTF has a history of sorts. The BTF, still in its infancy, came to the notice of Assam Government through newspaper reports in May 1997. Deemed then as "only a gang of extremists having links with the BLTF", the SF were asked to zero in on its Chairman, Rabin Das. The BTF might have surfaced later, but its leaders had come in contacts with the BLTF in their earlier *avataras* in 1994, when the Saikia Government was in power. An organisation called Bodoland Autonomous Council Coordinating Committee (BAC-CC) was floated to represent all communities living in the Bodo-dominated areas, including the Bengalis. Its convener was ABSU leader, Prem Singh Brahma, who later (1996-97) spearheaded the activities of the BLTF. Members of the Bengali Yuba Chhatra Parishad (YCP) who were on the BAC-CC, became close to Brahma. The young leaders of YCP of those earlier days later organised BTF. Having known its leaders since 1994, Brahma took BTF under his wings; equipped them with automatic weapons and explosives; and helped them with donations. This very proximity of BTF to BLTF earned for it the wrath of the latter's underground rival, NDFB, which was suspected to have been responsible for the killings of the Bengalis.
31. *The Frontline* 22-11-2002, *Outlook* 4-2-2002, *Hindu* 22-4-2002, *Hindustan Times* 6-4-2002, *Indian Express* 17 and 23 January, 2 and 5 May 2002.
32. An anguished M.S. Prabhakaran in *The Hindu* 22-11-2002.
33. The Bodoland Accord of 20 February 1993 (which gave birth to the BAC) was supposed to bring to an end the 6-year long agitation that was formally launched in March 1987. The Bodo agitationists' war cry—divide Assam 50:50—and the all-too-evident hostility to and alienation from the larger Assamese Society of which many Bodo people consider themselves a part, encapsulated the Bodo nationalistic aspirations as articulated by the ABSU leadership. Relevant in this context are facts that Mahanta's AGP was ruling Assam when the agitation was launched and Saikia Congress was in power when the Accord was signed. Both the political parties, which held power alternately since the Assembly elections of 1983, have drawn their own inferences and sought to make political capital out of these undeniable pacts.
34. *Hindustan Times* 31-3-2001.
35. BdSF was formed on 3 October 1986, and it later came to be known as NDFB. The BLT split away from NDFB in June 1996. After four years of its own violent activities, BLT concluded a cease-fire with the AGP Government in March 2000.
36. *The Frontline* 2-8-2002.
37. *The Frontline* 24-5-2002 and 22-11-2002.
38. The excerpts from this Memorandum are produced verbatim for their information value and for intrinsic thinking of the Bodo leaders, unvarnished and unpretentious.

6

Bangladeshi Immigrants : Will they Carve One More Pakistan Out of India?

The subject of Bangladeshi migrants have been troubling India for a long time. Because of its implications for the nation's security a detailed examination is called for.

Migrants All

Most of the population groups in the North-East either have their roots outside India or have migrated to the region from different parts of Indian Hinterland. In the pre-British era major population flows were from the east of the region: from south-west China and Upper Burma, and beyond. During and after the colonial rule, there was a large scale influx of Bengali-speaking people, followed by Nepalese and the tribal people from Central India and Bihar. The British administrative structures and economic ventures absorbed Bengali clerks and officials and the Central Indian tribal people and the Bihar labourers were absorbed in the tea gardens and oil fields.[1]

Assam has been receiving in-migration from outside its boundaries since time immemorial.[2] But in the modern times, the problem started with the take-over of Assam in 1826. But what made matters worse was the situation that preceded and existed at the time of take-over. The Moamaria insurrections (1769-75), the subsequent civil wars caused by the princely conspiracies and mutual suspicions, and lastly and worst of it all, the Burmese invasion, conquest and consequent occupation had devastated an already collapsing polity, leaving the land destitute and practically depopulated. It was not only a case of forlorn hope but also of a forlorn landscape, with despoiled villages and wretched society, or whatever was left of it. "When the British took over Assam, there was nothing known as law and order." This should explain why they needed people from outside to run the administration of their newly-acquired territory, the subordinate civil servants from Bengal, familiar with the British revenue and other Governmental systems. Then as the British started restoring economic and political situation in Assam, the manpower was required or imported to restart and develop road and rail communications and inland water-ways. The largest influx was caused for the need to open and work the tea gardens. The decision to develop Assam on the modern lines by launching industrial enterprises like coal mining, oil installations, saw mills, etc. yet again required manpower beyond its borders. "Therefore at progressive stages, the Chinese, Baluchis, Bengalis, Biharis, and tribal labour from middle India was imported or flocked to avail of the new opportunities."[3]

Marwari merchants organized extensive trade network to provide essential supplies and services. Bengali agriculturists, mostly Muslims, Nepalese graziers, Punjabi handimen, ex-servicemen and other settlers added to the throng. Thus a demographic transformation of Assam and to an extent, the entire North-East, had begun. That this huge influx was to cause ethnic, religious, racial and social tensions of the stupendous proportions in course of time could not be foreseen at that stage. But that the disturbing and far-reaching consequences of a Muslim deluge in particular could be foreseen by a British official by 1931,[4] decades before the actual explosion, is a testimony of and a tribute to the foresightedness generally associated with the country he belonged to. The AASU Anti-foreigners agitation of the late 1970s had its origins in these population transfers. The issue is still alive, and as sensitive and emotional even today.[5]

Import of Labour: Its Physical Dimensions

To revert to the situation following the Burmese occupation of Assam, Anglo-Burmese war, and the British take over, there was hardly any cultivation, and complete disruption and chaos were facts of life. To make matters worse, the floods, famines, and diseases like Kala Azar, Cholera and Malaria had added to the devastation of the land and the people. This was the situation that stared the new (British) rulers in their face in 1826. The problems were stupendous. The vast tracts of waste land and jungle needed to be resettled. Assam's upper classes lacked the wherewithals to undertake this task as their *paiks* and slaves had deserted them (The British had banned slavery). The need to import labour was self-obvious. Meanwhile, the Daflas, Miris, Abors, Khamtis and Singphos were pressing on the plains, "taking advantage of the vacuum and absence of an effective civil authority. This added urgency to a desperate situation, compelling the British authorities to offer land grants and incentives to attract settlers from Bengal, essentially Muslim agriculturists.

By mid-19th century, tea plantations had started coming up. They needed mostly unskilled labour. By 1900, more than one million acres of land were committed to the tea gardens, but a mere one-third of this acreage had been planted. This fast expanding tea acreage demanded increasing number of garden labour which the local populace was unwilling or unable to supply. This naturally led to a regular inflow of workers from outside Assam; mainly from Bihar (the Jharkhand areas), and some from Orissa, (the then) CP (Central Provinces), UP and (the then) Madras Presidency (mainly, Andhra areas). Here are two estimates of figures for migrant tea garden labour, set apart by a period of mere 20 years—signifying tripling of the labour force in this short space.

Year	*Labour Force*
1891	4,25,000
1911	13,00,000

Because the transit to Assam by river was slow, Sir Henry Cotton, Governor of Assam ordered "speedy completion of the Assam-Bengal Railway and the Eastern Bengal Railway. That is how large-scale immigration, including that of Muslims, started. What is the situation some of these labour communities face today? About 45 per cent of it, the *adivasis,* whose forefathers were brought by the British in the 19th century from Jharkhand to work in the tea gardens, are considered foreigners! Most tribes oppose their inclusion in the list of STs because of fear that they will compete for the few jobs available to them under the reservation quota.

Muslim Agriculturists: Welcome to begin with?

Some analysts aver that the Bengali migrants, particularly Muslim farmers, made substantive contribution to the agricultural development of Assam. Initially their hard work which improved the agricultural economy of the state, was appreciated but in the subsequent decades when they started affecting the land rights and the livelihood of the indigenous people, the resentment started. The 1911 Census Report described these migrant farmers as "hardy and prolific cultivators, working their way northwards. The people are accustomed to the risk arising from the diluvian and devastating floods which other cultivators are unwilling to face." But when the influx began to undermine the interest of indigenous people, things went sour. The 1931 Census Report contained a perceptive observation by the Census Commissioner, C.S. Mullan: "In the 30 years since the beginning of the Century, millions of migrants from across Assam's border had settled quietly in the Province which would affect the Assamese society more profoundly than did the Muslim invasions of the past...and its consequences would be impacting the Assamese polity for long years to come."[6]

The new entrants created acute economic and social problems since the mid-1930s as they started settling down in the forest land, particularly in the tribal areas. Forcible occupation, purchase, mortgage etc. paved the way for the land alienation of the indigenous population, as also the problem of landlessness. Unplanned clearance of the forest led to the problem of the soil erosion in the hills and consequent floods in the plains. Trade and commerce were monopolised by the more enterprising capital-owning migrants, and the modern professions too were cornered by the better qualified among them. Presence of a large number of migrants shook the foundations of the Assamese social structure and created the sons-of-the-soil solidarity among them. The percentage of the Assamese speaking population considerably declined while the share of the Bengali-speaking populace rose in direct proportion. In certain parts of state, the immigrant population constituted more than 70 per cent of the total population and in the *char* (river islands) area, 90 per cent are immigrants.[7] During the years 1901-1991, in terms of population growth Assam became the fastest growing region in the entire sub-continent. The table on next page shows the growth of the Assamese population against the backdrop of the overall growth of Indian population.

The demographic changes resulted in acute conflicts over language, education and employment policies, leading to the Assamese fear of being overwhelmed demographically, culturally, and economically by the migrants. "Scholars have noted that mass movements in a traditionally insular area invited linguistic, ethnic and religious strife. Settlement of an alien population leads to battle over resources, particularly land."[8] The consequent tension manifested itself in different forms, ranging from political agitation, violent struggle to militant activities and insurgencies. As a result, the AASU agitation (1979-85) against the presence of "foreigners" has fuelled the conflict throughout the region. Insurgents of various hues have cited the unchecked migration as the prime reason for their 'struggle' against the established order. The term 'foreigners' began to strike an emotional chord in the Assamese breast as it evoked the frightening images of the (Muslim) hordes from a neighbouring country (Bangladesh), entering the state and forcibly occupying their lands!

Migrants and National Security

Till the recent years, migration and security were considered distinct subjects for academic studies and political discourse. Analysts and scholars focused generally on defence strategy and power relations between the states. Preserving the territorial integrity of the State and stability of the Government in the face of the external and internal military threats were considered a matter of "high politics", while migration was considered "Low politics". However in the recent years there is a growing recognition that migration does not involve only human and personal security and human rights issues but also has internal and international security implications. Migration has now come to be considered one of the "new security threats" and Myron Weiner has treated population flows as an independent rather than as a dependent variable of his security analysis. He identified five categories of situations where migrants/refugees may be perceived as a security threat.[9] In view of the surge of Islamic fundamentalist violence in various situations and regions, the presence of Bangladeshi Nationals in large numbers in India (Assam and other States) of both legal and illegal variety, is a cause of concern for the Indian security establishment.

Comparative Rates of Population Growth: India and Assam 1901-1991

Year	*Population (1901-1991)*		*Growth Percentage*	
	India *Assam*	*Annual* *India* *Assam*	*Decaded* *India* *Assam*	*Progressive Growth Rate over 1901 (%)*
1901	23,83,96,327	—	—	—
	32,89,680	—	—	—
1911	25,20,93,390	.56	5.75	5.75
	38,48,617	16.99	169.9	16.99
1921	25,13,21,213	-0.03	-0.31	5.42
	46,36,980	20.48	204.8	40.95
1931	27,89,77,238	1.04	11.00	17.02
	55,60,371	19.91	199.1	69.02
1941	31,86,60,580	1.33	14.22	33.67
	66,94,790	20.40	204.0	103.50
1951	36,10,88,090	1.25	13.31	51.47
	80,28,856	19.92	199.2	144.06
1961	43,92,34,771	1.96	21.51	84.85
	1,08,37,329	34.97	349.7	229.43
1971	54,81,59,652	2.20	24.80	129.94
	1,46,25,152	34.95	349.5	344.57
1981*	68,33,29,097	2.22	24.66	186.64
	1,80,41,248	23.35	233.5	448.41
1991**	84,39,30,861	2.11	23.50	254.00
	2,24,14,322	24.23	242.3	581.35

* In 1981, census was not conducted in Assam. Based on 1971 census and 1991 census figures, the population of Assam as on 1 March 1981 has been interpolated.

** The Indian population reached the 1 billion mark on 11 May 2000, according to an official release.

Most states in the North-East are waging wars against their foreigners: viz. Assam against the Muslims from Bangladesh and the non-Assamese outsiders from other parts of India; Arunachal against the Chakmas, Hajongs and Tibetans; Mizoram against the Chakmas from Bangladesh and Chins from Myanmar; Tripura tribals against the immigrant Bengalis; immigrant Manipur against the Chins; and Meghalaya, against the outsiders of all descriptions including the Bangladeshis. The indigenous inhabitants and some scholars have a point when they assert that the economic and security implications of the mass migration into the region have not been adequately addressed as yet. The measures to check infiltration from across the borders have not been successful. The continued flow of the refugees into the region has only compounded the picture. What is even more galling to the states in distress is that the anti-infiltration measures undertaken by them are not only proving inadequate but are also being resented by the very nation that has been the main source of this migration. In December 1988 foreign minister of Bangladesh Abdus Samad Azad declared that his Government was opposed to any Indian move to fence the border, because he said rather ominously, "It is not in the interest of the improvement of bilateral ties between two neighbours."[10] It is curious logic, indeed, the ties will improve only if India continues to allow the migration from his country.

Bengali Dominance: How did it happen?

Here are different perceptions of the Bengali influx. After 1911, large number of Mymensinghia (Muslim) cultivators moved into Assam. C.S. Mullan, Census Superintendent, puts it succinctly in his 1931 Census Report: "where there is waste land, thither flock Mymensinghias.... In a silent invasion, half a million persons had transported themselves from Bengal to Assam over the preceding 30 years." Mullan suggests the flood gates opened about 1906, the year immediately after that landmark event of Bengal Partition of 1905 when Assam was joined with East Bengal to create the province of East Bengal and Assam. If the Bengali nationalists saw the Partition as a British ploy to weaken their struggle for independence, the Assamese saw it as an attempt by the Muslim leaders to push large number of their co-religionist into Assam and occupy the so-called "vacant agricultural lands". But the local British officials had their own perspective on the issue : "these migrants have cultivated land lying uncultivated, and in the process generated a sense of competition among the lethargic local (Assamese) population.... With the increase in the local produce, Assam had favourable balance of trade."

But for the Assamese opinion, it was a facetious reasoning, as the result was not an unmixed blessing. The dividend from tea was repatriated to London; the Marwaris sent money outside the state; and the tea labour sent remittances home. What was the net result?

Men were coming in

Money was going out!

So how did the common Assamese gain?

In fact, besides the doubtful economic gains, the growing immigration was perceived by the Assamese as a threat to their identity and culture. They feared domination of the Assamese life by the ethnic Bengalis. So it was not only a question of Bengali Muslims forcing out the Assamese Hindus from their lands, it was also the fear of the Bengali Hindus edging out the latter from the government, educational, commercial and trading institutions that caused consternation among the Assamese.

These fears had foundations in the very early years of the British take over, when they imported the Bengalis for manning the subordinate services and for running the day-to-day administration on the British pattern that had prevailed in Bengal since 1765. As a result, the Bengalis came to dominate the administration in the Province sooner than later. The worst manifestation of this domination was the decision in 1839 to declare Bengali the official vernacular in Assam, accepting the argument of the Bengali officials and scholars that Assamese was but a dialect of Bengali. Their own language yielding place to a foreign language in their own Province deeply hurt the Assamese pride. (It was only as a result of sustained agitation that Assamese was restored to its rightful place in 1873.) But this was not the only cause for the hurt feelings and perception of injustice to the Assamese. Assamese grievances on in-migration and language were aggravated as a result of political structuring, as Assam on take over was tagged to Bengal Province as a mere division under a commissioner. The mischief was undone only in 1874 when Assam was freed from the apron strings of Bengal in 1874, and created as a separate Chief Commissioner's Province. Even this eclat did not come as an unmixed bliss, because on its creation, the incorporation of Sylhet district with Assam had started a 'war' of valleys, Surma versus Brahmaputra; and this war had Bengali versus Assamese cultural overtones since Sylhet was a predominantly Muslim district. Even this celebration of less than ideal (and flawed) separate identity did not last beyond three decades, as Assam was merged into Eastern part of Bengal to create a United Province in 1905, as mentioned above. An ill-disguised communal divide, the decision was annulled in December 1911, restoring the *status quo ante* effective 1 April 1912. But it did not end the War of Valleys, as the assertive and better off Surma Valley continued competing politically and culturally at every turn with its bigger but not so advanced Brahmaputra rival. And the unceasing immigration continued evoking fears and suspicions in the Assamese mind because the predominantly-Muslim district of Sylhet continued to be part of Assam.

The two decisions mentioned above had done permanent damage to the social, cultural and political fabric of the Assamese society. The transfer of large Bengali population to the so-called *Vacant* forest lands, particularly during the time when Assam was part of the United Province of East Bengal and Assam (1905-12) has been touched upon above. As for the second, putting Bengali-speaking Sylhet district under Assam in 1874 has its own consequences, essentially unhappy and unfortunate for Assam. The 1931 Census indicated that there were only 1,61,000 Assamese speakers in Assam against the huge majority of 4,76,000 speakers of Bengali language. (The linguistic balance must have been even more violently disturbed against the Assamese language when Assam in 1905 was joined with East Bengal to form a United Province, and remained so till 1912.) It should be apt here to mention relevant facts of history which are on record. When the then Congress Premier of Assam, G.N. Bordoloi, met Viceroy Lord Wavell on 1 April 1946, he denounced the theory that there were many large tracts of uncultivated land in his province to be colonized. Even more significantly, he conveyed to Wavell that Assam was prepared to hand over Sylhet to Bengal since it was too much of a political liability, with serious implications for Assam's future.[11]

To revert to the chronology, from 1920 onwards the Assamese interest were sought to be safeguarded by the Line System; but that was often breached through by corruption and connivance. The same fate overtook the parallel efforts to safeguard the tribal lands by demarcating a series of tribal belts and blocks. The colonists, mostly Bengali Muslims, were settling on the Crown waste land. "The Assamese respond was rather timid and ineffective, Assam lost out to a flood of migrants, Bengali and Muslim."

The situation only worsened in 1920s and 1930s because of the Muslim League's communal politics. In the second half of the 1930s, the migration not only continued unabated, it was in fact encouraged by various non-Congress Ministries headed by Mohammad Saadullah Khan,[12] under the official garb of "Grow more food" campaign to boost the war effort.[13] In a moment of candour, the then Viceroy of India, Lord Wavell (1944-47) was constrained to dub this campaign as "Grow more Muslims" campaign.[14] But a British civil servant had seen it coming much earlier. C.S. Mullan, already quoted partly, with an insight rare in his counterparts of today, had made a perceptive observation in the Census Report of 1931.[15]

> "In fact the way they have seized upon the vacant areas in Assam Valley, seems almost uncanny, without tumult, without fuss, without undue trouble to the district revenue staff, a population which must amount to over half a million has transferred itself from Bengal to Assam Valley during the last 25 years, an event which seems likely to alter permanently the whole future of Assam and destroy more fully than did the Burmese invaders of the 1820s, the whole structure of the Assamese culture and civilisation."[16]

So what the Burmese invasions and occupation of the early 19th centuries and the repeated Muslim invasions of the earlier centuries could not do with all the violence inherent in their endeavours, "These silent invaders have done from within and apparently", as Mr Perceptive wrote in 1931, "without any undue trouble" to any one. Not surprisingly, the Assamese are still paying for that influx—or "invasion", as it has been called so often—, and there seems to be no way out either. The AASU movement of the late 1970s that shook Assam (and India) directly flowed from that influx. And to imagine, a British official foresaw it as early as 1931. An Urdu poet puts it all so aptly and eloquently, "history stands testimony to the fact that people suffer for centuries for an error made in a moment".

Bordoloi Saves Assam for India

The Assamese cannot be blamed for being paranoid about the Bengali domination. They have historical reasons to be apprehensive of the dangers, starting with the examples already cited above. Then came the Cabinet Mission Plan of 16 May 1946. Having already seen the machinations of Saadullah and Muslim League in the 1930s, this plan simply convinced the Assamese that the Muslim League was bent upon absorbing Assam within Bengal. It was a foretaste of things to come. The plan placed Assam in Group C with Bengal. The Group's Constituent Assembly was to have 36 Muslim Seats and 34 General Seats, which was obviously reflective of the communal balance in the zone. The majority community would certainly dictate terms with this composition. Some critics have harshly castigated the Congress Party for having been eager to accept this plan, goaded solely by an urge to ascend to power (even at the cost of) sacrificing Assam in the process. It was a valiant fight put up by Bordoloi, with active and unstinted support from Gandhiji that saved the day for Assam, and India, as the Congress ultimately rejected the plan. Had the plan gone through, the Assamese have no doubt that they would have been reduced to a hopeless minority in their own home, "overwhelmed by the torrential flood of Muslims from Bengal". This was not an imaginary fear. Even a known well-meaning Muslim leader, a professed liberal, Mujib-Ur-Rehman, had written in his *East Pakistan: Its People, Determination and Economics,* 1946:

> "Because East Pakistan must have sufficient land for its huge population and Assam will give it full scope for expansion, and because Assam has abundant forest and mineral resources like coal, petroleum, etc. East Pakistan must include Assam to be financially and economically strong."

In view of the above, Assamese fears about the Muslim immigrants are well founded indeed!

In fact, some analysts opine that having failed to have their way with the Cabinet Mission Plan, Bangladeshis are now trying to achieve the same end by exporting Muslim to Assam through all possible means.

Is the situation regarding the exploding numbers in Bangladesh any better today, 57 years after Mujib wanted Assam as a lebensraum for his East Pakistan? Far from it. Not to speak of any possibility of its reaching stabilization levels, the Bangladeshi population is almost spinning out of control. Here is the population growth since 1947:

Bangladesh Population

Year	*Population (Millions)*
1947	42 (at Partition)
1971	75 (at its Independence)
1993	119.80
1998	130.70
2001	135.60

Its density of population at 909 per Sq km is highest in the world, and "there is no effective family planning programme in place, barring some individual efforts which are frowned upon by the clerics". The 1991 Census Report reveals the birth rate at 31.6 per 1000. Out of a total of 2,28,00,000 fertile women 68.18 or 1,50,00,000 refuse to practice any kind of family planning methods. Unchecked growth is leading to a land crises, apparent from the fact that there was only 0.20 acre of land per head in 1992, "and it would be near zero by early decades of 21st century".[17]

1947-Partition-Induced Influx and India's Unilateral Generosity

Assam came into its own in 1947, with the shedding of Bengali (Muslim) dominated Sylhet district, and spanning of the entire North-East, bar Manipur and Tripura Princely states. Not for a moment should one forget that Assam was hobbled at its birth with the unpleasant legacy of large migrant population already within its borders and what was worse, the cataclysmic events of 1947 had only increased the pace and size of the in-migration exponentially. Assam was up against the deluge of migrants. An early amendment of Assam Land Revenue Regulation in 1947 redefined a series of 10 Tribal Belts and 23 Tribal Blocks to protect the plains Tribes (of Assam) from losing more traditional lands and forests "to the continuous onrush of these immigrant hordes".

The Partition itself had generated movement both ways to regulate which the Permit system was introduced in July 1948. The Indo-Pak Passports came into effect from 15 October 1952. An important fact of history needs a mention here. Undoubtedly, there was movement in both directions after the Partition. But in the subsequent period, an asymmetry developed in the overall situation as far as the total number of refugees who remained in India (Assam) and

East Pakistan (East Bengal) were concerned. In the years following the partition a large number of refugees who had gone to East Pakistan returned to Assam to claim their property, taking advantage of the laxity of laws and humane conditions that prevailed there, but no such reverse flow took place as far as the Hindus, who had come into Assam were concerned, as will be seen hereafter.

Articles 5, 6 and 7 of the Indian Constitution were subjected to a wide interpretation to keep the doors open for the people (Muslims] returning to Assam from East Pakistan. The provisions of Article 7 in particular were exploited by unscrupulous elements involved in the business of not only helping the East Pakistanis to return to Assam, but also claiming their properties. The Indian Citizenship Act of 1955 could not help stem the return tide either, as it had provisions for conferring citizenship by registration after due inquiry by the district collectors. The process was well-intentioned but it was subjected to elastic interpretations under allurement or duress.

The whole process was vitiated by an unspoken fiction embodied in the Nehru-Liaquat Pact of 1950, following the communal violence in the eastern parts of the sub-continent, leading to the mass exodus of the minorities both ways. Since the violence had erupted two years after the partition, it was believed the refugees would return to their homes once calm returned. Unlike the western region of India where the exchange of population was deemed final and the abandoned assets were declared evacuee property to be used for payment of compensation to the incoming refugees; the Nehru-Liaquat Pact stipulated that the Eastern Refugees returning home by 31 December 1950[18] would get back their properties (This provision itself was in relaxation of another law as will be seen shortly). This opened a veritable Pandora's box for the harassed Assamese authorities. In the Eastern side, compensation on the western India model was never paid,[19] though refugee relief was doled out for years for various fancy schemes like the Dandakaranya project. In these circumstances, the Citizenship Act, Rules and Registration notwithstanding, it was an absolute conundrum to determine who was a foreigner. India, Assam in particular, was to pay a heavy price for this original sin. And to wit, this came about—or rather, was brought about by doing violation to Article 7 of the Constitution which prescribed a cut-off date not later than 17 July 1948 for migrants from Pakistan, with a very elastic provision for granting citizenship by registration thereafter. The Nehru-Liaquat Pact pushed the datum line back to the end of 1950, as mentioned above. The Indian generosity did not end with this extension.[20] More of it was to follow. The reasons? Some feel it was a case of unrequitted love; others dub it as capitulation before the hard-headed Pakistan blackmail; and his more inveterate critics blame it on his (Nehru's) infatuation with his self-image of a great, liberal world statesman! So, speaking in the Parliament on 27 July 1962, he admitted that "the infiltration from (East) Pakistan has continued but much of it took place in the first five years of Independence when the border was not adequately guarded.... Probably it will be difficult now to deal with the illegal immigrants who came before 1952, we may therefore fix 1952 as the date of our inquiry."[21] As was only to be expected and could have been anticipated with a little study and examination of the patterns of immigration and certain insight, the influx continued, punctuated by a flurry of diplomatic notes.

Indian Parliament passed the Immigrants (Expulsion from Assam) Act in 1950 which implicitly draw a distinction between the Hindu refugees (victims of the anti-Hindu violence in Pakistan) and illicit Muslim migrants (driven by land hunger as hitherto). It was repealed in 1957 because of political compulsions or whatever, and there followed another major relaxation that directly led to the abandonment of Indian, essentially Assam's interest. The Indira-Mujib Pact of 1972 tacitly provided that Bangladesh would not be held responsible for the persons who had illegally migrated to India (read, Assam) before the birth of the new Republic on 25 March 1971.

Some argued that the virtual invitation to the Hindu refugees from East Pakistan to settle and seek jobs in India under the 1950 Act was responsible for the 'alarming' influx of Hindu refugees during 1951-71 period. The critics are only partially right, because the Act stood repealed in 1957.

The Government of India launched a Reversion of Immigrants from Pakistan (RIP) scheme in 1964 and financed a special Assam police force to strengthen the border control. The force was simply allowed to waste away, and Assam Government was accused of not following the West Bengal law regarding official sanction for transfer of immovable property to any foreigner. Though some foreigners were caught and expelled under the Foreigners (Tribunal) Order 1964, but the lenient attitude towards the continuing illegal influx continued both in West Bengal and Assam, particularly in the latter as it was still sparsely populated compared to the former, and hence the favoured destination for the illegal immigrants, rather infiltrators.

The whole issue has wider implications that impinge upon our electoral politics, and hence on the Indian polity? And in a wider context, on India's national security itself. The analysts have alleged corruption at different levels and sinister machinations of vested interest of certain political parties, desirous of building up their vote banks and to promote their electoral fortunes. This indeed was playing havoc with the national security for personal, party, or sectarian gains. To take the process to its logical end, vigorous campaigns were mounted to have the "illegal immigrants" included in the electoral rolls. An honest and impartial scrutiny by the concerned officials in this respect and protests by certain political parties and forces were immediately ascribed to communal bias, and even more reprehensibly, as denial of justice to the minorities (read Muslims). No wonder, the student leader P.K. Mahanta was to later denounce the "inclusion of foreigners in the electoral rolls as a nefarious form of political conversion which emboldened unscrupulous elements to pass off foreigners as minorities and allege communal bias against those seeking their repatriation". What is even more blatantly reprehensible is that any attempt to delete the names of illegal immigrants from the rolls and their subsequent expulsion from India raises ever louder howls in the name of "protection of minorities' rights" and humanitarian grounds. An average Indian is rather amused to see the protagonists using the plural "minorities" when, in fact, they are invariably espousing the cause of only single predominant minority from the erstwhile East Pakistan, now Bangladesh. May be the niceties of political discourse and delicacy of the issue pregnant with implications beyond the national frontiers demand the fine print. But speaking cynically, the employment of less than forthright terminology in such political discourse is outright chicanery and evasion of truth! Perhaps it is only proper that the last word on the issue should rest with the man (P.K. Mahanta 1986) who was in the thick of anti-foreigners agitation in Assam:[22]

> "Indian citizenship has been put in a melting pot in Assam. The effect of Partition, wrong and misplaced notion of national interest, obligations under international treaties, (not even presented in parliament); and above all, a convenient interpretation of humanitarian considerations, in clear derogation of lawful rights of bonafide citizens residing in Assam, and formation of a sub-nationality having a distinct culture and heritage; all those have entered into an unholy alliance to promote the vested interests of groups of persons to subjugate and trample (on) the rights of the people of Assam."[23]

Optimism of a Pakistan Leader

It is pertinent that M.A. Jinnah's Private Secretary Moinal Haque Choudhury told him, "I shall present Assam to you on a platter."

Z.A. Bhutto in his book, *Myths of Independence,* referring to the dispute between India and Pakistan, wrote: "one nearly as important as Kashmir dispute is that of Assam and several districts adjoining East Pakistan... To these East Pakistan has very good claims. Even a Pro-India President of Bangladesh like Sheikh Mujib-ur-Rehman had once said 'East Pakistan must have sufficient land for its huge population and Assam will give it full scope for expansion.' It has also to be noted that next to Kashmir, Assam is the state with the highest percentage of Muslim population in India. It can thus be seen that Assam is a potential flash point in India's relations with her neighbours."

After independence the influx of illegal migrants from East Pakistan and now from Bangladesh has continued unabated.[24] This influx is due primarily to economic reasons. With a 2.2 per cent rate of growth of population, Bangladesh is a Malthusian night-mare. The density of population in Bangladesh is 987 per Sq km as against 289 in Assam. The per capita income of Bangladesh is only Rs. 1,700 per year, which is half the per capita income of Assam.

AASU Movement: Demands, Course and Consequences

The AASU had been protesting the presence of foreigners in Assam and demanding their expulsion, since the mid-1970s. The agitation meant a series of strikes and bandhs, some often turning violent. The publication of electoral rolls for the by-elections to the Mangaldoi Parliamentary Constituency in 1978 proved a flash point, with the AASU concluding that its demand for stemming the tide of foreigners into the state and their exclusion from the rolls had not been taken seriously either by the Central Governments (Indira Gandhi's and post-Emergency Morarji Desai's) or by the Janta Party's at Guwahati. Thus this by-election triggered a demand for weeding out the foreigners from the rolls, which was conceded. Soon after the exercise was started, it became subject of stay order with the rivals claiming large scale detection of foreigners, on the one side, and harassment and victimisation of genuine Indian nationals, on the other. Needless to say, the subject of contention in almost all cases were the Muslims from Bangladesh. Frustrated by the stay order, AASU became even more determined on the issue. When the Lok Sabha was dissolved due to internal dissonance in Janata Party it demanded state-wide revision of the electoral rolls for the 1980 General Elections. Conceding the demand, Chief Election Commissioner ruled that the 1977 Electoral Rolls be treated as the base and deletions and additions be determined through objections and applications, respectively. The Assamese saw the decision as a *volte-face,* even betrayal, as they had wanted an earlier date as base line, and launched a huge agitation. AASU and AAGSP staged massive street demonstrations, more than 3 million people reportedly by courting arrest between 12-17 November 1979. Seeing the situation spinning out of control President's Rule was imposed on the volatile State on 12 December 1979. Before that, of the 400,000 objections filed, 250,000 had been disposed of. The process, if it had continued, would have produced practical result. But alas, it was cut short.

The nation went through the 1980 General Elections. But the agitation aroused such passions in Assam that no polls could be conducted there except in the Bengali dominated Barak Valley (Cachar) area, a fact which only exacerbated the acrimony between the two rival valleys. Consequently the anti-socials targeted the Bengalis in Brahmaputra Valley, which led to the communal violence. The fat was truly in the fire. AASU finding no solution, was on the war path, and launched an oil embargo to stop flow of Assam's oil from Duliajan to Nunmati and Barauni refineries. It created inter-state tensions, and West Bengal and Tripura Governments protested the anti-Bengali character of the agitation. Targeting of Bengalis led Prime Minister Indira Gandhi to dub the Assam movement as a RSS ploy, a usual tactic by then of the non-BJP Parties caught in difficult situations. Politics had vitiated an emotive issue. AASU was invited to Delhi for talks that proved abortive.

Given these developments, the base of movement began to erode by end-1980, with Muslims, Leftists, Bengalis and even tribals beginning to move away. The powerful students organization, AASU split vertically, with the Muslims forming their own All Assam Minority Students Union (AAMSU). For the next two years, there were acts of mindless violence, bomb blasts, and killings, culminating in a determined effort to disrupt the conduct of February-March 1983 Assam Assembly Elections. Over 1600 culverts and bridges were destroyed (Government figures). Arguably the most violent election any where,[25] it climaxed in the Nellie massacre—a macabre saga of inhuman brutality. "The Lalung (Tiwa) tribals were 'instigated' to set upon the immigrant Muslims, who had settled 'stolen' their lands." Over 1200, including women and children, fell to the mob fury. In series of eruptions in Darrang and Lakhimpur districts, the Muslims, Bengali Hindus, and Bodos were principal victims.

The violent anti-foreigners agitation continued two years after Nellie, ending up only with the tripartite 15 August 1985 Assam Accord whose major terms were:

1. The bone of contention in the main was the cut off date for determination and deportation of foreigners. AASU was for 1952 and Government for 1971, compromise being struck on 1961, 1-1-1961 being the base date. Again AASU (and its junior partner AAGSP) had sought disenfranchisement of immigrants who came to India in the 1961-71 period; but it was restricted to 10 years.[26]
2. Early elections to Assam Assembly.
3. The post-1971 immigrants were to be deported.
4. Setting up of third oil refinery.
5. Reopening the sick paper mills.
6. Establishing an IIT and a Central University in the State.

Consequences of this agitation and violence flowing from it are summed up here:

1. It crippled the state administration and its economy. Some aver the agitation and its progeny put the state's economy back by half a century.

2. The turbulence it spawned is not yet over, the thread having been picked up by ULFA, regarded as AASU's even more violent child. Bodos and some others have learnt a lesson or two from the AASU book.
3. It deepened the distrust between different communities of Assam: between Hindus and Muslims; tribals and non-tribals; and Assamese and Bengalis.
4. Some critics blame AASU as the progenitor of electoral violence in Assam.

The students came to power in 1985 Elections. As will be seen shortly their two stints in power failed to solve the problem/issue that had brought them to power. The critics asked cynically: was the AASU agitation meant to merely replace the professional politicians with the Student politicians?

It should also be noted that AASU was not the first to ring the alarm bells against the foreigners, though they were the first to do it violently. Politically-conscious Assamese had formed the Assam Protection Association to safeguard the interest of the indigenous Assamese (Plains people and the Hill men) threatened by the hordes of immigrants. The Assamiya Sanrankshni Sabha had warned Nehru in its 1937 Memorandum: "unless the Congress Party bails out Assam from the danger of extinction of Assamese race, the Assamese intelligentsia will favour secession".

Students in Power

Their first Ministry (1985-90) could depart no more than 900 foreigners. Another analyst says "they could not detect more than 347 foreigners in all the five years they were in power; and what was more mortifying, they could not deport even one of these 347 by June 1990". What was worse, during this period, an armed insurrection under ULFA gained such a menacing strength that the Mahanta Ministry had to be dismissed in November 1990. This exit, in fact an indignity, was caused not only by lack of political experience but also by the infighting for power and pelf, the fell disease generally the politicians are believed to be heir to!

The Assembly Polls, after a stint of President's Rule returned Saikia and Congress to power. During his regime (1991-96), ULFA grew even stronger, in collaboration with the NSCN and the BdSF. But what came as a shock to AGP and the people at large was Saikia's assertion in 1994 "that there is not a single illegal migrant in Assam". This was indeed surprising in view of Prime Minister Narasimha Rao's speech at a public rally in Guwahati in July 1992. The sober and scholarly Rao, recognizing the legitimacy of the students grievances, had declared *inter alia*: "The Center was prepared to amend the IMDT Act.... The illegal migration of foreigners into Assam and their permanent residence here had caused a serious situation in the State." This was a remarkable stand taken by the All-India President of the ruling party in Assam where the Congress was accused of practicing vote bank politics with the help of the immigrant community, and tacitly encouraging its in-migration.

The second AGP Government came to power in May 1996. In its Election manifesto, the "AGP had promised that the Army would be withdrawn, black laws repealed, and people of Assam given the right of self-determination."[27] "When the AGP took over, in a bizarre development, the Chief Secretary and the DGP of Assam deserted their posts and left Assam overnight." Initially the new Government was reluctant to adopt tough measures against the ultras. By August 1997, violence had climbed to its zenith: A brigadier and two colonels had been killed in Guwahati; Mahanta himself had escaped death narrowly: the explosions had occurred in trains, notably the Brahmaputra Mail; the Bodos went on a killing spree to achieve ethnic cleansing; and consequently, after massacre of 700 non-Bodos, over 200,000 (mainly Santhals) had sought safety in refugee camps. It was then that the unified command was set up. Mahanta was reluctant to head it, unlike his counterpart in Kashmir Farooq Abdullah.

Its second stint (1996-2001) in power also did not fair any better. It blamed the opposition and the IMDT Act for its inability to detect and deport foreigners. "The idealist Students have failed the people", seemed to be the verdict after their 10 years in power. The infighting had intensified in the second stint. Allegation's of 'unabated influx', this time from its own parent organization, AASU, continued to be made, despite the construction of border roads and fencing, with watch towers, under the terms of 1985 Accord. Did it point out to the lack of commitment to the cause under exigencies of power?

The most telling comment on the AASU agitation and its success is that the organization accused Mahanta, its one-time and longest-serving President, "of betraying its agitation against the Bangladeshi migrants". He was branded "the greatest traitor the State has ever seen". He took no steps to get the IMDT Act repealed, said Samujjal Bhattacharya on 21 August 2002 *(Indian Express,* 22-08-2002).

AASU Agitation and the STs

Because of its composition, ideology, and causes it was fighting for, the "Silent Coalition" against the Assam Movement included 'old' and 'new' Muslims, and 'yellow' and 'black' tribals, as categorized by Moin-ul-Hussain (1983). He avers the yellow (plains) tribals, autochthons of Brahmaputra Valley, registered a decline in terms of percentage to the total population from 22.5 per cent in 1872 to 10.70 per cent in 1971. Explanation? They were Sanskritised, consequently Assamised, and finally accepted Assamese as the medium of instruction. Of the total ST population of 1.6 million (1971) in

Assam—Bodos, Rabhas, Tiwas, Mishings (Miris), Sonwals (Kacharis) and Deoris, being the most numerous plains tribes, in that order, and the Karbis, Dimasas, and other hill tribes—only 1.1 million were recorded as speakers of Tribal languages in 1971 Census.

The tribal identity and livelihood were always tied to land and forests. A steady erosion of their rights had already taken place due to the encroachment of their land by the immigrants. The tribal belts and blocks were also under attack over the years due to several reasons, including demands of development. All this had caused serious discontent among the tribals. It was not a recent happening either, having started by the early years of 20th century. There was always simmering anger below the impassive tribal exterior. The Nellie massacre, unimaginable in its horror, was an erruption of this anger and grievance, in a manner of speaking.

The tea garden labour, mostly from Jharkhand, was in the category of STs till 1947 when they were de-scheduled by Assam Government, these black tribals became Assamiya, a cultural rather than a territorial category. In 1961 Census, of 1.7 million tea tribals, all but 208,000 had returned Assamese as their language, the figure going up to 384,000 by 1971. Other languages spoken by them were Oriya, Santhali, Munda, Oraon, Telegu, etc.

The plains tribals supported the AASU movement since it espoused the protection of the reserve forests and vacant Government waste lands against encroachment by the foreigners. Later on, some difference cropped up between the two. Particularly after the AGP formed the Government in 1985. Sections of tribal population voiced their fears of being absorbed by the much larger Assamese society, worried about the loss of their ethnic identity, others complained of discrimination in the field of economic development. The grievances ran deep enough to compel the Bodos to demand a separate Bodoland, the reasons for which were embedded no doubt, in the pre-movement days. The 1960 Language Bill perhaps had given birth to the idea.

The IMDT Act and its Politics

The AGP Government ascribed its inability to determine and deport the foreigners to the machinations of the opposition parties, the hurdles put up by the vested interests, and in the main, to the existence of the IMDT Act. The AGP had become aware of it during its first Government (1985-90) and wanted the repeal of the Act. It maintained that stance while in opposition (1991-96). The political observers noticed a shift in its stance when the party returned to power in 1996. Now follows the story depicting the venal politics around this Act, and the games various parties are playing on the question of its repeal. "It is obvious that for their short-term gains, they all are ignoring the nation's security interests."

Prime Minister Rao was the first to promise to amend or repeal this Act at a public rally in Guwahati in July 1992 as it was coming in the way of dealing with the serious issue of foreigners in Assam. During his week long visit to the Region in October 1996, Deva Gowda publicly revealed that independent surveys had detected over 3.75 lakh illegal immigrants in Assam, as against a mere 1400 detected by the tribunals set up under the IMDT Act. He announced that the Act would be repealed as it was loaded in favour of the illegal immigrants. On his return to Delhi, he developed cold feet in the face of opposition from the left and Congress, the two crutches his UF Ministry survived on. "For the Left, illegal immigrants constitute an unassailable vote bank." "The Congress would not antagonize its minority vote bank by supporting the repeal of the Act." Their critics assert these two parties would not countenance even an amendment of the Act, not to speak of its repeal, to safeguard their 'constituencies'. Now read the account of the meeting of the Home Ministry's Consultative committee on 11 November 1996 presided over by the Home Minister and CPI Stalwart, Inderjit Gupta. Congress opposed the move on the ground that it (repeal) would lead to undue harassment of genuine citizens. G.M. Banatwala of IUML, expectedly, criticized the decision and asked Gupta to review it. The Left Parties, serious opponents of the move, did not attend the meeting. Gupta was in an embarrassing position, because the State (Assam) unit of his Party, CPI, was for tough measures against the aliens, while its "national leadership was worried that the repeal would have an adverse impact on the minority community in West Bengal and harm it politically". Acting adroitly, Gupta ended the meeting,[28] leaving it to the Parliament to take the decision on the issue. The farce did not end here. The AGP, a constituent of the ruling UF at the centre, was doing a tight rope dance of its own. On the one hand, Mahanta wanted the Act scrapped, but he could ill afford to alienate the Muslims who formed a large chunk of his vote bank, on the other. Still worse, his own Ministry was propped up by a political party (UPPA) that stoutly espoused the cause of the immigrants.

Given these contrarieties, the UF found itself in a cleft stick over the question of bringing the issue before the Parliament in its winter session 1996. The ensuing debate would only expose its internal fissures. But its worst fears arose from the scenario where it would be opposed by its supporting parties and supported by its confirmed opponent, the BJP—the party was pariah of the Indian politics of the time and no one wanted to touch it even with a barge pole. The UF was mortally scared of the spectacle of being found in the company of the BJP, only Party which openly sought the repeal of the Act. It is a different matter though that the Deva Gowda Ministry fell before they came to crossing this embarrassing bridge.

The hypocrisy of it all was too glaring to be missed at the said meeting. While divergent views were expressed on the IMDT Act,[29] members from all parties expressed serious concern over the continuous infiltration by the foreigners into the North-East. This indeed is the bane of Indian politics—politicians and political parties placing their party, sectarian, and even personal interests above those of the nation's.

AGP's silence and ambivalence on the Act during its second Government was understandable. In the May 1996 Assembly polls, the party had won over two dozen seats in western Assam which has a large concentration of Muslims. But interestingly, and expectedly, the AGP started making appropriately shrill noises against the illicit immigrants as soon as the parliamentary poll was announced in May 1999. It asked the Central Election Commissioner to "ensure the deletion of names of 3.75 lakh illegal immigrants from the Electoral Rolls before the polls".

The fact is that, notwithstanding all the sound and fury, the Act remains on the statute book. Some analysts fear another bout of violence as and when it is repealed. What are the main reasons the proponents of its repeal offer to support their case?

1. Under the Act, a foreigner is defined as the one who entered India (Assam etc.) from across the border after 25 March 1971, exempting all others who entered before that date. Further, the Act which came into force on 15 October 1983 does not cover those who have been identified as foreigners under other Acts like the Passport Act, 1967, Foreigners Act, 1946 and the Immigrants (Expulsion from Assam) Act, 1950.
2. It is applicable to Assam only and overrides all other Acts mentioned above. Thus if a foreigner enters any other part of India, he can be prosecuted under the foreigners Act. But if he enters Assam, he cannot be booked under that Act as the IMDT Act makes it redundant.
3. The process of identification under the IMDT Act is rather cumbersome. Unlike the laws in other countries, including UK, where the onus lies with the accused to prove that he is not a foreigner, this Act charges the complainant with this responsibility.
4. The Complainant/accuser must be living within 3 km of the place where the illegal immigrant is staying. The complaint can be made only on prescribed form that cost Rs. 25 and must be accompanied by a sworn affidavit of two persons.
5. As for the procedures, the Tribunals refer the cases to the investigating Agencies before whom the complainant is called to prove that so-and-so is a foreigner.

It is a complex issue not only because the humans and human emotions are involved in it. There were instances when even in case where expulsion had been ordered, it rarely took place. Though the IMDT Act needs to be repealed, but there are parties who feel replacing it with a tougher one may not be the solution "as that would only open the flood gates for harassment of the innocent Muslims". They suggest the solution lies in Permit System that allows the Bangladeshis to work here for a specific period.

At a tripartite (Centre, Assam Government and AASU) meeting at New Delhi on 1 July 1999, the AASU demanded a discussion on the contentious Citizenship Act. This demand assumes significance in the light of AASU's long-standing plea for the repeal if the IMDT Act, 1983. Having announced its decision to do away with the Act, the Vajpayee Government during its second coming (March 1998) could not push the necessary legislation through Parliament due to an ambiguous stand of the Congress Party on the issue. Incidentally, a Cabinet Note over the repeal of this Act had been awaiting clearance for some months when the Vajpayee Government fell on 17 April 1999.

It is worth noting that the Vajpayee Government could not get the Act repealed even after its third coming (October 1999) though it is running in its fourth year (2003), for the reasons of a divided polity, as mentioned above. In any case, no one—an individual or a political party—seems to be interested in its repeal any more. Interestingly, Mahanta kept repeating his Government's public stand till he was out of power in 2001 Assembly Polls. In a 'live chat' in the *Times of India* on 19-1-2001, he says "The problem remains as it is and we are trying our level best to stop infiltration from Bangladesh.... But the issue now is that the IMDT Act is the main hurdle to detect and deport infiltrators from the state."

One of the example of discrimination by New Delhi cited by the Assamese is the enactment of this very IMDT Act for detecting and deporting foreigners in/from Assam. While the Foreigners Act was deemed adequate for this very purpose for the rest of the country, what was the need and urgency for this special enactment for Assam only, which made it well-nigh impossible to deport any illegal immigrant to his/her country of origin? What was the meaning and implication of the new enactment?

Put simply, it means that a Bangladeshi illegal migrant coming into West Bengal, Bihar or any other State of the union has to be identified and dealt with by the State, but in Assam the onus of identifying an illegal immigrant has been shifted to the shoulders of the common citizen. Why has the Indian State abdicated is elementary responsibility of determining and deporting a foreigner from the sacred soil of India?

In December 2000, a delegation of the United Minority Front of Assam called on Home Minister L.K. Advani and cautioned him against the move to scrap the IMDT Act, saying that, "it would plunge the State into more turmoil".[30]

Speaking at a public meeting at Nagaon 25 February 2001, and referring to the controversial act, Advani said "The BJP is in favour of scraping it."

How the issue has been politicized was clear from the way Prime Minister Vajpayee's statement offering work permit to Bangladeshi migrants, during the election campaign for Assam Assembly in May 2001 was criticized. The Congress said it was meant to garner votes, made as it was three days before the polling. The Communists said it was meant to deny the voting rights to the migrants. The Shiv Sena said it was against the national interest "and was a deviation from the BJP's stand when it had been in opposition" (*Indian Express,* 8-5-2001).

Indigenous Assamese: Meaning, Implications and Controversies

> The 10 April 2000 Centre-AASU representatives meeting in Guwahati evolved this definition of indigenous people of Assam:
>
> "Those whose names figure in the 1951 National Register of Citizens (NRC) and their descendants. And for the seven districts of Assam where the NRC is not available, the Electoral Rolls of 1952 would be taken as the basic documents."

"This once again propelled the murky politics of citizenship in the State to the center stage."[31] The critics were up in arms. The Assam accord already provides March 25, 1971 as the cut-off date for deletion and deportation of illegal foreign migrants. By fixing new cut-off dates of 1951 (NRC) and 1952 (Voter List) in the new definition, the Centre seems to have pushed back the cut-off date by another 20 years. The minorities say it would work against the interests of the post-Partition migrants and the riot-affected people from parts of Assam who had fled to East Pakistan only to return later. To wit, 3,00,000 Muslims from western Assam, who had fled in 1950, returned to Assam under the Nehru-Liaquat Pact signed later that year. They were returning in batches till about 1952, by which time the exercise of preparing the NRC of 1951 as well as the Voters List of 1952 was over. Therefore the names of these absentee Muslims did not figure in these two documents. The definition has further implications.

At the biannual tripartite talks, held alternatively at New Delhi and Guwahati[32] to ensure the implementation of the 1985 Accord, AASU has lately been voicing demand for cent per cent reservation of seat for the "indigenous" people of Assam in the local bodies, assembly and parliament. The press reports suggested in May 2000 that "the demand has already been accepted".[33] The AASU holds that its demand for reservation stems from clause 6 of the 1985 accord.

In the State, with the complex population composition, AASU's demand for 100 per cent reservation for "indigenous" people, not for "Assamese" people, opened a veritable Pandora's box, evoking a sharp reaction from different segments of the people; viz plains tribals, hill tribals, religious and linguistic minorities etc. The new definition of "indigenous" has made matters worse. It seems, the critics aver, the "indigenous" Assamese have learned no lessons from the consequences that followed from the precipitate action of passing the Language Bill of 1960, namely, the vivisection of Assam. AASU must pause and cognitate if they are not creating sense of insecurity among the minority groups and thereby reinforcing the resolve of Bodos, Rabhas, Karbis, Kacharis, etc. for separate states of their own.

In-Migration: Dimension and Implications

After the Indian Independence, it was the Muslim immigration that became the cause of greater concern to the Assamese because of its religious, political and socio-economic ramifications, and it is quite understandable that it caused serious controversy between its supporters and opponents. The former were accused of making political capital out of the immigrant population, using them as vote bank to gain, to retain, and stay in power; and the latter are obviously chauvinistic, out to disrupt the harmony of Assam, supported by the communal forces. The identity of either side is well-known.

There are various views about the extent of illegal migration into Assam. The large increase in Assam's population in the inter census period of 1951-1961 (34.98 per cent against overall Indian average of 21.6 per cent) was cited as proof of the extent of the influx. It is rebutted by the argument that due to 1950 communal riots, Muslims had fled Assam and consequently the 1951 was an undercount. Those who had fled, returned and were counted in 1961—hence the seemingly large increase. The official version views the matter in perspective. The Census of India 1961, Paper No. 1 of 1963 estimated "that the missing persons of 1951 and their progeny would account for 2,75,000 Muslims enumerated in Assam in 1961. The balance 'excess' decadel growth was a result of illicit immigration." This aspect of increase in Muslim population in Assam was also analysed and well documented in another study of comparative demographic patterns in Assam and Tripura on the one hand and East Pakistan on the other, based on the 1961 Census figures of India and Pakistan. "The population deficit of specific East Pakistan districts in relation to national population trends was found to indicate a neat fit with the corresponding excess noticed in the adjacent regions of Assam, West Bengal and Tripura."[34]

Interestingly, in this game of the figures, different sets of the same are bandied about to prove or disprove a position, depending upon the presenter. The number and composition of the 1961-71 influx are even more contentious. The Home Minister informed the AASU delegation in 1980 that 9,67,000 immigrants had entered Assam during 1961-71; 2,14,000 being displaced person (DPs) in the wake of 1965 Indo-Pakistan War and subsequent communal riots. The break down of the remaining 7,53,000 illicit immigrants was given as below:

Hindus	631,000	Christians	30,000
Buddhists	65,000[35]	Muslims	27,000

A sympathetic Muslim academic on the other hand, feels that the Muslims are unduly castigated on the issue. He says, like the Chinese, all of whom were rounded up and dispatched from Upper Assam during the 1962 War, Muslims in Assam also became victims of prejudice and discrimination. He cites Census data showing that the percentage of Muslims in total population of Assam has remained virtually unchanged.

Year	*Percentage of Muslims*
1951	25.68
1961	25.30
1971[36]	24.56

The influx of illicit land-seeking immigrants from East Pakistan (Bangladesh) into Assam had started in 19th century, but assumed serious dimensions since 1947. But matters came to a head in the latter half of the 1970s through a combination of circumstances. Assam had shrunk[37] politically and newly emerging Assamese middle class encountered lack of economic opportunities. Shakdher, CEC, addressing the Chief Electoral Officers of states at Ooty on 4 October 1978 had painted a grim picture of situation caused by the immigration. He expressed concern about large scale inclusion of foreign nationals in the electoral rolls and castigated political parties for demanding that the names of such immigrants be included in the rolls. The result will be some foreign nationals taking part in our electoral processes, which will directly impinge our sovereignty. AASU and AGP estimates of infiltrators in Assam, if accurate, are rather disturbing.

Illegal Infiltrators in Assam

Year	*Number*
1961	10,00,000
1971	23,00,000
1979	35,00,000
1981	50,00,000

Even as sober and senior a journalist as B.G. Verghese wrote in 1980 that 1.80 million foreigners had already been enrolled (by 1980, that is), "representing as much as 20 per cent of the Assamese registered voters. The problem no one doubted was the Bangladeshi Muslims in Assam."

The high percentage of Muslim population in Assam has always worried the Assamese cognoscenti. The Cabinet Mission statement of May 1946 for Assam had 34,42,479 Muslims against 67,62,254 non-Muslims (based on 1941 Census). So Muslims were 33 per cent of Assam's population in 1941. When Muslim majority Sylhet district voted itself out in 1947, this percentage dropped. It was 24.03 per cent in 1971, still high for the concerned Assamese. It climbed to 28 per cent in mid-1990s. It is also a fact that Muslim population as a percentage of India's total has been on the increase, as seen here:

Increasing Trend in the Growth of Muslim Population in India

Sl. No.	*Year*	*Percentage of Muslim Population*
1.	1951	9.9
2.	1971	10.8
3.	1981	11.3
4.	1991	12.12

But more alarming declaration came from the AASU at Dibrugarh in July 1992, that "the ethnic Assamese were only 31.70 per cent in Assam". It set the alarm bells ringing. It was obvious that the ethnic Assamese formed a majority in Brahmaputra Valley only.

Here are official figures from the Census of India Report, released in mid-1995, giving religious break up of the country. It says the Muslim population of Assam had recorded a growth of 77.42 per cent during 1971-91 period. The percentage of the Muslims to the total population of the State ("where the 'indigenous' people are living under constant fear of being outnumbered by the Bangladeshi migrants, both Hindus and Muslims") has gone up from 24.56 per cent in 1971 to 28.47 per cent in 1991. The Hindu population of the State on the other hand, shows a decline from 72.51 per cent of the total population to 67.13 per cent during the same period (*Indian Express,* 25-7-1995). The 'alarming' statistics failed to draw any comments from political parties bar the BJP which saw in the increase a vindication of its claim about unabated influx of Muslims from Bangladesh. The party analyses this continuing influx as a sinister design by Bangladesh, helped by Pakistan ISI, to incorporate Assam "through other means", to create either a greater Bangladesh or a separate Muslim nation in India's North-East! The party and some other critics ascribes the silence of non-BJP parties on the dangers to India's integrity "to their dependence on the illegal immigrant for their hold on power". The latter, in turn, blame the BJP for practicing "communal politics".

The other six States in the Region have also recorded a high growth rate of Muslim population. "Mizoram primarily a Christian State, for instance has shown a massive 105.80 per cent rise, while Nagaland came second with 74.84 per cent increase during 1971-91." Hindus, on the other hand, have registered declining trends of growth within three States Manipur, Meghalaya and Mizoram.

The district-wise figures in Assam are even more telling in this regard. The 1991 Census Report revealed that while the Hindus constituted more than 70 per cent in 12 of the 23 districts, the Muslims were 50 per cent or more in four districts. Yet again, 10 out of 23 districts presently have more than 30 per cent Muslim population. *See* the table below:

Muslim Population (Over 30 per cent) in 10 Districts of Assam (1991 Census Report)

Sl. No.	*District*	*Total Population*	*Muslims Total*	*(%)*
1.	Dhubri	1,325,653	9,38,789	70.46
2.	Barpeta	1,382,715	7,76,974	56.18
3.	Hailakandi	448,506	2,46,016	54.8
4.	Goalpara	661,801	3,32,275	50.18
5.	Karimganj	825,551	4,06,706	49.2
6.	Nagaon	1,892,087	8,93,322	47.19
7.	Marigaon	640,376	2,89,835	45.3
8.	Cachar	1,215,952	4,19,150	34.5
9.	Bongaigaon	806,472	2,64,393	32.74
10.	Darrang	1,286,633	4,15,859	31.01

The AASU asserts it is an unnatural and unusual increase, and expectedly ascribes it to illegal immigration. It is significant that most of these districts are either contiguous to Bangladesh, closer to it, or located in Lower Assam.

The 1991 Census figures for 5 border districts of West Bengal have also shown an unusual increase in the Muslim population (Relevant table is given later under West Bengal heading).

Demographically, Assam has not only seen faster growth against the Indian average, it in fact has been the fastest growing area in the sub-continent. Its population has grown by 676 per cent from 3.3 million in 1901 to 22.3 million in 1991, comparative figures for India being 354 per cent: 238.4 million in 1901 and 843.9 million in 1991. Even when the growth rate was nearly static for all India during 1911-21, it was as high as 20.48 per cent for Assam

(Census Report). Had Assam's population increased at the same rate as the rest of India between 1901 and 1991, that is 354 per cent, then Assam's population would have been 14.9 million rather than 22.3 million, a whopping increase of 7.4 million. Here is what, in the words of Myron Weiner (*sons of the soil, 1978*), the presence of these migrants has done to Assam and the Assamese:

> "It has shaken the foundation of Assamese social structure and created solidarity among the Assamese even while generating cleavages between the indigenous Assamese and the indigenous tribals. It has influenced the educational, social, and economic aspiration of countless Assamese, determined their central political cognizance...(it has) given rise to powerful assimilationist and nativist sentiment and backlash separatist agitation, to massive conflict over languages, education and employment policy."
>
> (The growth rate statistics were as menancing and phenomenal in Tripura too, where the population over the last 100 years has registered 20-fold increase. The cause as in Assam was largely due to a great influx of refugees from Bangladesh. The detail are discussed in Tripura Section.)

This demographic 'aggression' caused disquiet among both the plains and hills, adversely affecting their land and livelihood. The tribals in particular were the worst sufferers, because the expansion of the plough and the increase in the number of Bengali tenants, mainly the Muslims, progressively alienated them from their land. It was the increasing marginalisation of the tribal communities which first gave rise to the militancy in the state, that later crossed into insurgency, ala the Bodo community, and to an extent the Naga tribes. It was this internal dissonance that provided a cause and an opportunity to the intelligence agencies like the ISI to indulge in geopolitical machination in India, posing a serious threat to its security and sovereignty.

Baljit Rai, retired DGP, who served in the area, warns the nation about the perils of illegal immigration, quoting alarming figures/facts, in his book, *Demographic Aggression against India: Muslim Avalanche from Bangladesh.*

> "The 6 districts of West Bengal (24-Parganas, South and North Nadia, Murshidabad, Maldah, and West Dinajpur), 4 districts of Bihar (Purnea, Katihar, Kishanganj and Araria) and 10 districts of Assam (Dhubri, Barpeta, Hailakandi, Goalpara, Karimganj, Nagaon, Marigaon, Cachar, Bongaigaon, Darrang) have become extensions of Bangladesh.
>
> "Hindu presence in Bangladesh has been systematically and assiduously decimated from 28 per cent of population in 1947 to less than 10 per cent in 1991.

> "With a few honourable exceptions, the national media has applied total censorship and failed to highlight the gravity of the problem; with some newspapers going out of their way to support the cause of the infiltrators.
>
> "In contrast, Bangladeshi journalists and intellectuals are far more open, honest, and forthright in staking the claim to Lebensraum in North-East India to unload their excess population. *The Hindu* journalists in India, on the other hand, appear to be supine and strangely inclined to be somnolent. Not many of them have come out of their secular cocoon to contest or refute the irrational territorial claims made by the Bangladeshi intellectuals."

Home Minister Gupta told the Lok Sabha on 3 December 1991 that there were one lakh Bangladeshi nationals in Delhi, with 9,561 Pakistan nationals overstaying. The figure for West Bengal was 5.87 lakh and for Rajasthan, 25,000.

But the figure cited for West Bengal is nowhere near the reality. T.V. Rajeswar, Governor West Bengal (1991-92) and ex-Director, IB, asserts that "not more than 20 per cent of the illegal flow is checked". The figure of 5.87 lakh, on this basis, shoots to 29.35 lakh. The State Government declared "about 28 lakh Bangladeshi nationals entered the State between 1972 and 1988 of whom 5 lakh stayed back". This was till 1988!

Significantly, Government gave no figures for illegal immigrants in Assam/ North East, an issue on which an entire movement was launched. It be noted that Bangladesh asserts "none of its nationals are staying outside its boundaries, certainly not in India". But what the Indians must note with concern is the repeated statements in Bangladesh about India's North-East being its Lebensraum. The popular perception in that country is that at the time of Partition "it was cheated off the whole of India's North-East, in particular, Assam, which has always been viewed as its natural expanding space. The continued migration from Bangladesh to Assam over the years is to be seen and understood" in the context of the "strong hope" expressed in that country that the "historical injustice" done to it would ultimately be corrected. Bhutto and Mujib have already been quoted in this context. Now read an intellectual justification for the same view, by Sadiq Khan who honestly, openly articulated his perception in the 18 October 1991 issue of the Dhaka *Weekly Holiday*:

> "Along the new international order, there should also be a world demographic order, with its globalised manpower market.... There is no reason why regional and international cooperation could not be worked out to plan and execute population movements and settlements to avoid critical demographic pressures in pockets of high concentration.... A natural outflow of population pressure (in Bangladesh) is very much on the cards and will not be retainable by barbed wire or border patrol

measures. The natural trend of population overflow from Bangladesh is towards the sparsely populated lands of the South-East in the Arakan side and to the North-East in the seven sisters side, of the Indian Sub-continent."[38]

The author Khan leaves no one in doubt about the policy and intentions of Bangladesh. Is it any surprise that the Assam leaders have often alleged that despite the 1985 Assam Accord and subsequent construction of border roads and fencing, and 'patrol measures', there has been no effective check on migration from Bangladesh?

A specialist on the subject, Sanjay Hazarika,[39] did an exhaustive Case study, "Bangladesh and India's North-East: factors behind the flow," and after studying the figures he gathered from various sources, including Dhaka-based Institute of Development Studies, came to certain conclusions, summed up here:

> 'Taken in its entirety, the migration from East Pakistan or Bangladesh has resulted in the creation of a Sub-nation with the size of population of Australia.... A population of 10 to 13 million has moved lock, stock and barrel from its roots and set up new homestead in another neighbouring nation. It has moved illegally, without proper visas, passports, or any other documents worth the name. And settled into new nation with ironically, the documents that most nations give to their nationals, *viz* voting rights, ration cards, property deeds."[40]

Their helplessness against the illegal immigrants, and the inability of the Governments at New Delhi and Guwahati to undo the preposterous situation because of venality of Indians who sell themselves for a few coins, have turned large sections of the Assamese and tribals in North-East inveterate anti-outsiders as well. Often it seems the Bengalis in Assam, Marwaris in Dispur, Sylheti Bengalis in Mizoram, Chakmas in Arunachal Pradesh, and non-tribals in Bodo areas are as un-welcome, as are the foreigners. This hopelessness of their situation leads to frustration which results in periodic violence against the outsiders: the violent anti-Bengali agitation in 1960; campaign for deletion of names of foreigners from electoral rolls in February 1983; and Nellie tragedy when "7000 Bengali Muslim settlers were done to death". They fear going the Tripura way where the tribals, who were in majority till 1950, were gradually reduced to a minority in their own home by the Bengali immigrants. Are not their occasional "Chauvinistic" excesses justified, they ask? The Assamese elite often reminds the critics: "Between 1911-41, the Muslim population in Assam nearly quadrupled, during the days of the Raj."

Assam's destiny was intertwined with that of Bengal since the 1826 take over by British due to a variety of reasons, administrative, political and economic till the defining year of 1947. In this period, a major threat to its cultural and political identity came from a kind of demographic invasion, mostly by landless Muslim agriculturists and labour, drawn by prospects of working on uncultivated Government and tribal wasteland as also in tea gardens. C.S. Mullan's remarks in 1931 Census Report about "This migration of half a million population will destroy...the whole structure of Assamese culture and civilisation" has been quoted earlier. The 1947 partition did not seem to make any difference so far as the migration—the silent invasion—was concerned. The Census Commissioner R.B. Vaghai, echoing Mullan, one of his famous predecessors, wrote in the 1951 Census Report: "I have seen hundreds of persons coming in and settling in Assam and their hunger for land was so great that they frequently encroached on government reserves and lands belonging to local people."

A Muslim Nation in the North-East?

To some the fear of a Muslim nation emerging in India's North-East is highly over-blown. Others feel the fear is not entirely unfounded. May be, a discussion of the issue is called for. The concerned Assamese point to the long-standing plan of the Islamic leaders, both religious and political, to grab North-East, at least a major part of it, to convert it into Lebensraum for the burgeoning population of East Pakistan, now Bangladesh. Their plan is simple, as the former see it: "first, swamp the land with the migrant population upsetting the demographic balance in favour of the Muslims. Then up the ante by loudly or vociferously complaining against the injustice and discrimination against them (Muslims), inflaming unrest, and subsequently the secessionist sentiment among the impressionable Muslim youth to act as the vanguard of the Islamic Jehad. The rest of course would follow."

The people who fear the denouement have their own arguments. The study of the border belt of West Bengal yield some telling even disturbing statistics. 20-40 per cent villages in these districts are said to be predominantly Muslims. This trend, concentration of minority community, including Bangladeshi immigrants, in these villages, has resulted in the majority community moving into the urban centres, looking for security. Then comes to one's mind Lin Piao's classic theory of villages surrounding, and then overwhelming the cities.

The border districts of West Bengal mentioned above have a population of 27 million (1991). With one million people of Bihar's Kishanganj, it totals to 28 million—of which 17 million are Muslims—concentrated in this belt. A concerned MOD official chips in: "Proceed through the Siliguri corridor and add western districts of Lower Assam, and a more sensitive area in Asia is difficult to imagine, surrounded as it is by not-so-friendly neighbours." An analyst completes the nightmare: "A few thousand vociferous but misguided civil rights activists protesting this or that decision of the Government, or alternatively, a dozen anti-national subversives, aided and abetted by the ISI and bent upon disrupting peace, can disrupt or paralyse the communication links through this corridor cutting off the entire North-East from rest of the country." The scary scenario pushes into one's "attention what Kissinger wrote in his *The White House Years*, 1971 :

> "The inevitable emergence of Bangladesh which we postulated, presented India with fierce long-term problems. For Bangladesh in fact was East Bengal separated only by religion from India's most fractious and most separatist State, West Bengal. They shared language, tradition, culture, and above all, a volatile national character. Whether it turned nationalist or radical, Bangladesh would over time accentuate India's centrifugal tendencies. It might set a precedence of creation of other Muslim States, carved this time out of India. Once it was independent, its Muslim heritage would eventually lead to rapprochement with Pakistan."

Should not some Indian analysts descry potential threat to India's security on its eastern marches? Some starry-eyed scholars who saw Bangladesh as a nation under perpetual debt of gratitude to India are already wiser by now, seeing the ground realities. India-bashing is a popular sport of opposition parties, and the ruling party cannot even dare to be seen as overtly pro-India even if demanded by its national interest. Bangladesh like Pakistan, has already declared itself as an Islamic Republic. One part of the Kissinger Prophesy, the two drawing closer, is nearly through. It is time the Indians start worrying about the second emergence of a Muslim nation. But the stark reality is that the vote bank politics of various political parties in West Bengal and Assam make them insensitive, even oblivious, to such dangers!

To make matters worse, some recent reports suggest that "six border districts of Assam too have turned into Muslim-majority one". AGP's second spell (1996-2001) in power was truly indicative of the games the parties play to remain in power. Its Ministry survived with the active support of a religious party which vehemently espouses the cause of the immigrants, legal or otherwise. Can one imagine a more preposterous compromise to stick to power? No wonder, his critics accused Mahanta of softening his stance on expulsion of illicit immigrants.

What is the number of Bangladeshi immigrants in India in absolute terms? Unofficial estimates put the figure at 15 million: West Bengal 7 million, Assam 5 million, Bihar 2 million, and the rest in metropolitans like Delhi, Mumbai, etc. The official figures speak of 10 million. Whatever the correct figures, it is high enough to alarm the strategic analysts, as it has geo-political implications for India's internal and external security interests. Well-meaning individuals have periodically made efforts to acquaint the nation with the serious nature of the issue, as described earlier. Some effective measures devised to undo the damage had to be abandoned because of partisan politics. The flawed Nehru-Liaquat Pact, 1950 had enabled large numbers of East Pakistan's nationals to return to Assam and claim Indian citizenship. To undo the mischief, New Delhi enacted the Immigrants (Expulsion from Assam) Act the same year, and "consequently 6 lakh such immigrants were pushed backed into East Pakistan". The Empire struck back. The furore raised by certain political parties and their strident camp followers compelled the Government to repeal the Act in 1957. The MHA, in consultation with Assam and West Bengal, approved in 1963 the Prevention of Infiltration programme, as proposed by B.N Mullick, Director IB. During the next two years, about 150,000 illegal immigrants were repatriated to East Pakistan. This scheme too was given up in 1967 for reasons mentioned above.

The 1971 war pushed 10 million refugees into India. The 1972 Indira-Mujib Pact noted that about 7 million of mem had returned; and of the rest, those who entered India prior to 25 March 1971 were to be allowed to stay in India. It was a case of misplaced generosity. Why should a nation be allowed to wash its hands off its own nationals, just because it has had a regime change?

To determine the dimension of the problem, West Bengal Governor suggested in June 1989 and again in January 1990 to conduct a Census of Immigrants in his State. The same was to follow in Assam and Bihar. Again, politics intervened and the idea was dropped. The political class is simply not serious over this issue which poses a direct threat to our security. Bangladesh itself conducted a Census of Bihari Muslims in March 1992 prior to their planned repatriation to Pakistan. Indians must recognize the seriousness of the issue, remembering how a mere 7 lakh immigrants in East Europe had generated so much consternation there. Why do we forget how bigger and more prosperous nations zealously guard their borders against the aliens: US against Haitians and Chinese boat people; Australia against unfortunate refugees fleeing from China, Vietnam, and of late, Afghanistan, and Bangladesh itself from Rohingyas.

And pray, what price Indian generosity? Bangladesh blatantly denies presence of any of their nationals in India? Worse, some of their scholars (Sadiq Khan quoted above) are brazenly making a case for India's North-East (essentially Assam) providing a Lebensraum for their burgeoning numbers! Their Finance Minister tells the press in Dhaka on 15 April 1993: "If the issue of Ganga water was not solved, it might force their people in future to migrate to India." By citing a set of comparative density of population figures (given below), some analysts almost seem to be offering a sinister suggestion that Assam is the obvious destination for the Bangladeshi immigrants.

State		*Density Per Sq km*
Assam	-	286
West Bengal	-	767 (highest in India)
Bangladesh	-	849 (Perhaps, highest in the World)
India	-	273

The Muslim leaders in Assam seem occasionally intent on adding fuel to the fire. "The BJP and AASU in Barpeta, Lower Assam are up in arms over a speech by a Gogoi Minister," says a story in the *Indian Express* of 3-1-2003. At a Panchayat Election Campaign meeting "last Thursday, Ismail Hussain, Minister of State for Irrigation, had said that the Congress was all for Muslims and Assam would one day become a Muslim land". Was it a Freudian slip or a statement of intent?

If political class has been remiss in this regard, the Census Commissioners and CEC, have done their duty by the nation, warning against the foreigners vitiating the nation's electoral processes, thus not only fringing its sovereignty but also posing a threat to its security. More gratifying is a realistic view of the judiciary on the issue, as will be seen shortly.

West Bengal Situation: Is it any better?

As migration effects West Bengal also, a brief examination of the situation there is called for, even if the ruling CPM-combine continues to claim it to be "a haven of peace and tranquility". The June 1999 blast at New Jalpaiguri Railway station, killing 85 people and injuring many more, shattered the myth of a safe haven. The arrest of two ULFA insurgents next day from Siliguri and subsequent investigations based on the interrogation and intelligence reports disclosed considerable ISI penetration in the state. Earlier the Top Secret May 1999 military intelligence Report on the Internal Security situation in the 28-km wide Siliguri Corridor had disclosed that "Muslim fundamentalist organisations with ISI support are having a field day by encouraging changes in the demographic pattern of the area." India's IB put the increase in Muslim population in or around Siliguri area at an astounding 150 per cent in the past 7 years (1991-98) against 30-40 per cent in other Muslim dominated belts in the State. Far away from the hot zones of Kashmir, Punjab, and even Coimbatore, Siliguri Corridor and area beyond in West Bengal "have today become, starting early 1990s, the newest and most preferred playground of the LSI" (cited in the *Outlook* of 2-8-1999). This is not the first time that the evidence of activities of the ISI muddying India's insurgency waters in the North-East has washed up; it really started with it helping Phizo with a fake passport to travel to England from East Pakistan, in 1956.

But what should cause deep concern to India is ISI's rising presence in West Bengal in the recent years, helped by its 2187 km long porous border with Bangladesh along ten districts. Says Ranbir Samaddar, a political Scientist: "Unchecked infiltration has created an alarming phantasm among the locals' fears of Lebensraum. Free and easy passage of ISI agents, ready to exploit the discontent and sense of insecurity among the sections of the local Muslim population in the post-Babri Masjid demolition scenario." Laments an Intelligence officer: "West Bengal is a sitting duck for the ISI...the border is porous.... It is difficult to identify Bangladeshi nationals; and worse, political parties and administration abet infiltration, and are passive." Here follow some statistics that should worry the Indians, starting with two border districts neighbouring the Siliguri corridor.

Population Trends: Two Border Districts of West Bengal

(Figures in percentage)

S.l. No.	*Item*	*Jalpaiguri*		*Murshidabad*	
		1981	*1991*	*1981*	1991
1.	Total Population	22.14	28.02	36.97	47.40
2.	Hindu Population	87.50	84.42	41.15	38.37
3.	Muslim Population	8.75	10	58.67	61.39

Now some data from the Census and Intelligence Report (cited in *The Outlook* of 2-8-1999):

1. Nearly 10 million Bangladeshis, most of them infiltrators, have entered India and overstayed, with proper papers. Disconcerting pointers have been available for a long time now.
2. The 1981 Census revealed that in the eight border districts of West Bengal the population has grown by 30 per cent during 1971-81 whereas the remaining districts registered growth rate below 20 per cent.
3. During 1981-91, the Muslim population in West Bengal grew by 36.89 per cent as against the national average of 32.76 per cent.
4. Here are revealing figures about the contrasting trends in the percentage of Hindu and Muslim communities in the total population of West Bengal, taken from two enumerations, held 20 years apart.

Percentage of Hindu and Muslim Population in West Bengal

Sl. No.	*Community*	*1971 (Percentage)*	*1991 (Percentage)*
1.	Hindus	78.12	74.71
2.	Muslims	20.46	23.61

5. Infiltrators have mostly settled in the districts of Jalpaiguri, Darjeeling, North and South Dinajpur, Malda, Murshidabad and Nadia. While the over all growth of population in the State during 1971-91 has been 47.9 per cent, it was much higher in the five border districts as shown here:

Growth in 5 Border Districts of West Bengal: 1971-91

Sl. No.	*District/State*	*Growth of Population between 1971-1991 (Percentage)*
1.	Jalpaiguri	53.00
2.	West Dinajpur[41]	57.70
3.	Malda	59.00
4.	Murshidabad	67.00
5.	Nadia	63.24
6.	West Bengal	47.90

Radical Muslim Organisations: A State Home Ministry Top Secret document lists seven such outfits functioning in the State. Five of them are:

1. Jamait-e-Islami-e-Hind (JEI-Hind). A "fanatical Communal organisation", having bases in almost all districts, particularly the border districts, and in the districts of North Bengal, bar Darjeeling.
2. Jamait-Ahle-Hadis. Established in 1906, this fundamentalist outfit is funding the setting up of a Jamia Rahamania (Muslim University) in Dhulian, Murshidabad. It operates from 1 Marcus Street, Kolkata and has strong bases in North 24 Parganas and South Dinajpur districts.
3. Students Islamic Organisation (SIO). Set up in 1981, it supports the self-determination for the Kashmiris, and is run from 14, Alimuddin Street, Kolkata, a few houses away from the ruling CPI(M)'s sprawling headquarters. The SIO is "trying to get closer to the SCs and STs; and has 2000 members."
4. Students Islamic Movement of India (SIMI). Founded April 1997, it is in touch with other Muslim outfits and such ultra Left groups as "students belonging to Santosh Rana group of CPI(ML)". It also has links with the dreaded Islamic Chharra Shibir, the radical students wing of the JEI-Bangladesh and operates out of Kolkata and a dozen other districts.
5. Tablighi Jamat. Drawing ideological guidance from the Mecca-based pan-Islamic organisation Rabita-e-Alam-Islam (world Muslim League),

this outfit is attempting to unite the Muslims to counteract any attack on Islam by the VHP, RSS and other Hindu fundamentalist groups.

What should be more alarming is the plethora of Intelligence reports revealing the illegal border crossings by members of these outfits, networking with the radical Islamic groups in Bangladesh, and the latter pledging them funds and arms. Some examples:

1. A number of people from Islamgarh in North Dinajpur district walked over to Panchagarh in Bangladesh to attend the 2-day Islamic conference convened by the Jamaat-e-Islami (JEI).
2. A JEI meet decided that the trainees in their district units would be provided archery and fire-arms training and *lathikhela* (stick-wielding) "for encountering opponents during riots and for self-defence".
3. In December 1997, Abul Kasham and Abdul Raut, members of the JEI-Hind and residing in the northern outskirts of Kolkata, crossed over to Bangladesh to attend a JEI District conference. There they pledged arms and ammunition from India to the Bangladesh JEI before the local municipal elections and gave a call for removing Hasina's Awami League Government from power.
4. There have been a number of meetings "between JEI functionaries and members of West Bengal-based radical Muslim outfits in the past two years" (1998-99). The state intelligence listed "56 such important meetings" during the year 1996-97 alone.

A Weekly'[42] quoting Home Ministry files and Intelligence reports gives the following information about the dangers ahead:

1. A dozen mosques under construction in the State without any permission.
2. "The ISI is cultivating hostile and hardline Islamic groups in State in the absence of any rebel formations," says a South-Asia Security analyst.
3. Then there are post-Jalpaiguri explosion Intelligence reports worrying the security agencies. The Army has identified villages with "curious" population mix, in and around Siliguri that provide safe haven for the ISI operatives. Chapra is one such village, 55 km from Siliguri, with a population of 25,000, the nerve centre for "illegal border trade and fake currency racket of Saudi *Riyals* and other currencies". There is Islampur, a town 70 km from Siliguri, with a population of 1 lakh, a known "stronghold and hub of ISI functionaries". The town has a skewed demographic mix: some 2,000 Pushto and Baluchi settlers from Afghanistan, engaged in moneylending and ("suspected ISI

activists"); 6,000 Iranians who settled here in the late 1960s, "all of them without any vital documents and involved in narcotics smuggling;" and some Saudis who "indulge in smuggling and other illegal activities".

4. There are ostensibly educational institutions suspected of sheltering ISI activists and agents. Two names:

   (a) Tauhid Education Trust, Mahadabad. The Army intelligence warned about the Trust which is imparting religious education, preserving Islamic, religious scripts, and "maintaining vigil on anti-Islamic activities". Its boy's hostel has 650 students and 500 day scholars, and 60 teachers, including some foreigners. The girls hostel has 500 residents and 25 teachers. "The Trust is funded with financial assistance from various gulf countries." The Trust, geostrategically located near the porous borders of Bangladesh and Nepal, "could encourage subversive acts around the Siliguri Corridor and be used for launching a religious movement". Its chairman, Maulvi Abdul Salafi, is reportedly "a person of doubtful credentials". The Army Intelligence believes the Maulvi and his Trust are instrumental in propagating Muslim fundamentalism in the guise of educational and welfare institutions, by providing shelter to illegal Muslim foreigners who enter India, and thus contributing to Islamisation of the area.

   (b) Al-Jamiatul Rahaman Islamic Viswavidyalaya in Dhulian area of Murshidabad, a shadowy educational institution, is also under suspicion. Since 1987, some 50,000 people "attend a huge religious congregation, held every year, to raise funds for this University", which has received permission under the Foreign Contributions Regulations Act for foreign contribution's amounting to Rs. 1,03,500 from the Islamic Development Bank, Jeddah, Saudi Arabia.

The analysts aver that it is obvious from the foregoing that West Bengal faces as serious a threat from the influx and infiltration of the foreigners as the beleaguered Assam "but the Marxist Parties seem to be least concerned". The obvious question is: Does this veneer of non-challance come from ideological moorings or is it born of the less-exalted reasons of vote bank politics and sectarian interests? The Left Front's management of the ISI threat seems to be abysmal. "The Marxist Parties have abetted infiltration in the border districts openly, arranged food and shelter to bolster their vote bank." An Army intelligence report comments matter-of-factly: "the local administration has apparently turned a blind eye to the problem". Here is the summary of criticism against the Left and its Government:

"No one has ever heard the Communists led by the venerable Joyti Basu ever voicing their concern on the issue of Muslim influx from across the borders. The Left Front has not even discussed the issue within the four constituent parties or the Government. There has been an avalanche of Intelligence reports landing at the table of the state's Home Minister Buddhadev Bhattacharya for the last few years, but it was only recently (June 1999) that he could bring himself to admit during a visit to Murshidabad that 'there are a lot of ISI operatives here'. It is not only that the religion is a holy cow even for the Marxists but the minority community also belongs to the same class; hence the reluctance of the four Left Parties' Ruling Combine to initiate any counter measures to stem the rot even after the admission by a senior Minister and No. 2 in the Government pantheon, Bhattacharya (now Chief Minister), about the threat from the ISI."

Debabrata Bandopadhyay, Director, State Intelligence, wrote the Weekly, was more honest and forthcoming in his assessment: "the threat of ISI is really serious in West Bengal. The Region has become a fertile ground for them." Will the powers-that-be stir themselves to take some positive measures? The answer, going by their track record, could possibly be a resounding 'No'.

Figures of increase in percentage terms in some of the West Bengal Assembly Constituencies bordering Bangladesh between the years 1961 and 1991 are unusually high.

Percentage Growth in Some West Bengal Assembly Constituencies for 1961-91

Sl. No.	*Constituency*	*Percentage Increase 1961-91*
1.	Islampur (in West Dinajpur district)	88.89
2.	Karandighi	113.83
3.	Goalpokhar	96.01
4.	Maldah	115.50
5.	Murshidabad	69.57
6.	Bahrampur	74.62
7.	Kishanganj	79.40
8.	Karimpur	95.85

"The BSF deployed to check infiltration across the border has its hands tied up. The request for personnel is not met adequately and the pressure from local panchayats dominated by the leftist cadres has made the situation worse. The Panchayat head and the cadres, arrange the ration cards for the infiltrators and get their names included in the voters lists. Other benefits too are given to them to build solid and reserve vote banks. This wide scale malpractice is dangerous to the national security."[43]

Equally significant are the 1991 Census figures on the percentage of Muslim population for the five border districts of West Bengal given in the table below:

Muslim Population: Border Districts of West Bengal (1991)

Sl. No.	*District*	*Muslim Population (Percentage)*
1.	24-Parganas (North and South)	56
2.	Nadia	48
3.	Murshidabad	52
4.	Malda	54
5.	Islampur Sub-Division (of West Dinajpur)	60

An English Daily describes the running feud between the Ruling CPM Party and the State Election Department on the eve of the 1999 Parliamentary Poll that shows the attitude of the Party and its Government towards these immigrants:

> "With the Voters Lift being revised in the state, the infiltration issue has revived with an apparently inflated number of new applicants awaiting inclusion in the list.... The differences between the CPM and Election Department have opened up the issue. While the tight-lipped Department did nothing but released the cold figures about the aspiring applicants, CPM has already refused to accept that infiltration could be a factor contributing to the increase.... The Department has already spotted areas in the border districts where the increase is almost 19.67 percent.... It is not that some at least in the CPM are not worried about the increase in the number of voters. For the first time during the Left Front's 22-year rule, when the Party's politburo members met Chief Electoral Officer (CEO), Jahwaar Sircar, they complained about 'Various irregularities' in the process of revision of the Voters List.... The CPM blamed the "communalist and fascist forces for trying to include the bogus and underage voters in the final List. But it ruled out the possibility of the Bangladeshi infiltration.... CEO Sircar said, 'We take this rise very seriously and have to gear up our machinery for inquiry and screening process.... The Final List has to be prepared by 21 July'."[44]

A weekly reported that DGBSF, Parkash Singh, before his retirement, had informed the MHA by a letter that "the infiltration has reached an alarming stage in West Bengal and the North-East States" and warned that if proper measures were not taken "to tackle "the infiltration and insurgency in the North-East, the entire area would very soon, plunge into a Kashmir-like situation". Excerpts from the letter:

> "Compared to other states, the border districts of West Bengal have recorded an alarming rise in Bangladeshi infiltration. From 1983 to 1993, the No. of names in the voters list of these districts has risen from 7 to 14 per cent. When the leftists came to power in 1977, the State Assembly voters totalled 2,60,32,989. The figure reached 4,25,08,579 in 16 years, an increase of 53.28 per cent."[45]

Crescent classroom. Murshidabad district in West Bengal has the 'distinction' of being a part of Pakistan for two days from 15 August to 17 August 1947, when the Radcliff Award which respected demography but not geography was amended bilaterally. The district reverted to India as it is the link between North and South (West) Bengal but its dominant Muslim population (64 per cent in 2001) makes it a socio-cultural island of sorts. The neighbouring Malda district too has a large Muslim population "but Murshidabad is more of a fanatic oddity in a State not much given to stand off along communal lines". Barua Rahamani Education Society (BRES) is spearheading a drive to purity education as the syllabi of the Government run *Madrasas* lack Koranic contents and Arabic literature. BRES, an organisation of Islamic leaders with strong Saudi Arabian ties and founded in 1993, has already opened 109 madrasas in the State (including 35 in Murshidabad, 22 in Malda and 10 each in Birbhum, north Dinajpur and Nadia. Over 40,000 attend the BRES classes and the number is growing. It is not the number that is worrying but the BRES's almost totally communal syllabus. A book on economics tells the students that the chief sources of national income is the divine act of "expropriating the property of the vanquished enemy". A history text justifies the destruction of the Somnath Temple because: "The Pandits and Brahmins of Gujarat began a conspiracy and turned the Temple into the Centre of political activities." BRES is flush with Arab funds. "In West Bengal now, as in Afghanistan in 1980s, fundamentalism gets a boost when Marxists are out to prove their secular credential" (*India Today*, 25-6-2001; *Crescent Classroom* by Sumit Mitra).

Government Wakes up to the Danger: Long Last

CPM-dominated Government of West Bengal has shown awareness about the seriousness of immigration problem for the first time in its quarter-of-a-century rule in the State. Excerpts from the *Indian Express* of 17-6-2002:

> "The Central Agencies (including BSF) on vigil along the 1,150 km. border with Bangladesh in Southern West Bengal are planning a demographic mapping of the five districts to investigate the profiles of Bangladeshi settlers.... Writers Building is now more vocal than ever on the 'new menace of infiltration by fundamentalist-cum-terrorists from Bangladesh.... State's hardening stand on infiltration.... Besides the mapping, the Agencies may propose an investigation into Bangladeshis' overstaying their visas in nine districts and Kolkata. The Agencies set up after the

recent spurt in population in South Dinajpur, Nadia. Murshidabad and North 24 Parganas districts, that did not match the state's population growth rate.... A census report suggests the average growth rate in these districts is a little over 4.27 per cent unlike the rest of the state.... For example, in south Dinajpur and Malda, the figures are 22 per cent and 25 per cent compared with the state's 18 per cent."

Consequences of Unchecked Migration

Do the following seven tables reflect the consequences of continued, unchecked, un-interrupted (or is it politically-connived at) influx of the foreigners on the three States of India?

Percentage Growth of Population between 1991 and 2001 in Assam Districts Bordering Bangladesh

District	*Muslims*	*Non-Muslims*	*Total*
Dhubri	29.5	7.1	22.9
Goalpara	31.7	14.4	23.0
Hailakandi	27.2	13.3	20.9
Karimganj	29.4	14.5	21.9
Cachar	24.6	16.0	18.9

Percentage Growth of Population between 1991 and 2001 in Four other Districts of Assam

District	*Muslims*	*Non-Muslims*	*Total*
Barpeta	25.8	10.0	18. 9
Nagaon	32.1	11.3	22.2
Marigaon	27.2	16.3	21.2
Darrang	28.9	9.5	15.8

Percentage Growth of Population between 1991 and 2001 in Districts of West Bengal

District	*Muslims*	*Non-Muslims*	*Total*
South 24 Parganas	34.2	11.5	20.8
North 24 Parganas	23.0	22.6	22.7
Nadia	21.9	18. 8	19.5
Murshidabad	28.4	16.4	23. 8
Malda	30.7	19.4	24.7
Kolkata	19.0	0.7	3.9
South & North Dinajpur	31.9	22.7	26.1
Jalpaiguri	31.3	20.4	21.5
Cooch Behar	18.5	12.8	14.2
Total West Bengal	25.9	15.3	17.8

Muslims as Percentage of Population in Districts of Assam

	1991	*2001*
Districts bordering Bangladesh		
Dhubri	70.4	74.3
Goalpara	50.2	53.6
Hailakandi	54.8	57.6
Karimganj	49.2	52.3
Cachar	34.5	38.1
Four other Districts		
Barpeta	56.1	59.4
Nagaon	47.2	51.0
Marigaon	46.0	47.6
Darrang	32.0	35.6
Total Assam	28.4	30.9

Muslims as a Percentage of Total Population in Districts of West Bengal

District	*1991*	*2001*
South 24 Parganas	29.9	33.2
North 24 Parganas	24.2	24.2
Nadia	24.9	25.4
Murshidabad	61.4	63.7
Malda	47.5	49.7
Kolkata	17.7	20.3
South & North Dinajpur	36.8	38.4
Jalpaiguri	10.0	10.8
Cooch Behar	23.4	24.2
Total West Bengal	23.6	25.2

Percentage Growth of Population between 1991 and 2001 in Districts of Bihar

District	*Muslims*	*Non-Muslims*	*Total*
Kishanganj	35.2	25.0	31.71
Araria	36.1	32.4	34.0
Purnea	44.1	30.8	35.4
Katihar	39.7	25.4	31.1

Muslims as Percentage of Population in Districts of Bihar

District	*1991*	*2001*
Kishanganj	65.8	67.6
Araria	40.5	41.2
Purnea	34.5	36.7
Katihar	39.9	42.5

Source for these 7 tables: Arun Shourie, *Ind. Exp.* of 09-10-04.

The *TOI* of 22 May 2005 is making no revelation when it says the demography of some of the border districts of West Bengal is changing because of the illegal immigration from across the Bangla border. In some places, like Malda and Murshidabad, the border is demarcated by rivers and the fencing is not yet complete, making it near impossible to control the immigration.

A common complaint against the immigrants is that they come in search of jobs and get ration cards easily with the help of the politicians. Friends in villages near the border provide shelter. It is easy to identify a Bangladeshi in the North-East but not so in West Bengal because of the common language. Here is data from three districts from the 2001 Census.

Districts	*2001 Population (Percentage)*	
	Hindus	*Muslims*
Malda	49	49
North Dinajpur	52	47
Murshidabad	36	64

Floating Migrants in Tripura

Sharing an 856 km border with Bangladesh, Tripura has a different type of infiltration problem: A large floating Bangladeshi population crosses the border at daybreak for work and returns home at sunset. Sources say Agartala has 5000 Bangladeshis located just 2 km from the border (Can they be called the NRIs, rather, [NRTs], non-resident Tripuris?). They go for 'work' each morning—men are mostly rickshaw-pullers; women, maids; and even the children as rag-pickers—and return the evening. Says Arunaday Saha of Tripura University matter-of-factly: "Cheap labour ignores all boundaries. I do not see any human-face in this cross border movement, I see only the economics." The cheap labour makes them an acceptable, even welcome, commodity!

Illegal Bangladeshis: Detailed Distribution

The MHA has estimated the state-wise distribution of these immigrants as on 31 Dec. 2002 (*The Week,* 16-2-03). *See* table here:

Illegal Bangladeshis in India: Distribution

State	*Number*	*State*	*Number*
Arunachal Pradesh	1,080	Mizoram	39
Assam	67,00,300	Nagaland	79,800
Bihar	6,41,390	Orissa	41,670
Gujarat	150	Punjab	345
Haryana	800	Rajasthan	3,390
Himachal Pradesh	25	Tripura	4,44,867
J&K	480	Uttar Pradesh	34,867
Karnataka	15	West Bengal	76,80,122
Madhya Pradesh	950	Andaman and Nicobar	4,050
Maharashtra	28,089	Delhi	5,02,345
Meghalaya	40,510	Total	1,62,05,284

National Commission for Minorities (NCM) Raises Alarm

15 Feb. 2005. The NCM said there was an "abnormally high" growth of Christian population in the North-East and this could be due to illegal Bangladeshi Muslim migrants reporting themselves as Christians. Its Chairman Trilochan Singh told reporters while the population of Christians had remained the same at 2.3 per cent for 1991 and 2001 but scientific analysis of the 2001 Census data showed its "abnormally high" growth particularly so in the districts bordering Bangladesh. Nagaland, Mizoram and Meghalaya "have the highest percentage of Christians at 90 percent, 87 per cent, and 70.3 per cent respectively", Singh said (*HT, TOI*, 15-2-05).

8 June 2005. The NCM is worried that unchecked influx of Bangladeshis into the North-East could upstage the dominance of tribal communities and lead to their losing reservations in legislatures and Parliament. In his letter to Chairman, Delimitation Commission, Justice Kuldip Singh, Trilochan Singh asked the commission to devise 'special provisions' to ensure continued political representation to the tribal communities. He also points out that such an influx has affected the life and culture of tribals who are a majority in the Region.

The reason—or, is it provocation—behind the consternation of the NCM that impelled it to write this letter is the recent analysis conducted by Prof Ashish Bose, Chairman of the NCM's Experts Committee, on the Census 2001 data on the religions (*Express* 9-6-05).

Panic in Upper Assam: April-May 2005

"On 12 April 2005 when Assam was celebrating the Rongali Bihu festival, youths at Bihutoli in Chiring (Siring), Chapori (Saproi) locality of Dibrugarh town were busy planning an economic blockade of Bangladeshis" (*TOI*, 22-05-05). These youths set up the Siring Sapori Yuva Mancha (SSYM) and launched a campaign on 24 April, asking locals not to employ Bangladeshis or give them shelter. Gathering storm, the campaign spread to other parts of Upper Assam, taking on Communal Colours. It triggered alarm bells from Guwahati to Delhi. The Assembly poll due in less than a year, the issue took a political hue, all the three major players, Congress, BJP and AGP, exploiting it for partisan ends.

The SSYM had a 4-point agenda: do not employ illegal migrants for household work; do not travel in vehicles driven by them; do no business with them; and do not rent out houses to them. Said an activitst: "We saw a massive increase in the number of illegal Bangladeshi labourers in Dibrugarh in the last one year." By mid-May many Bangladeshis left, and the movement had spread to three other Upper Assam districts of Sibsagar, Jorhat and Golaghat. The SSYM circulated leaflets and sent SMS. Panic stricken, the immigrants working as rickshaw-pullers, domestic help, and brick-kiln labour fled these districts to the safety of the five immigrant-dominated districts of Dhubri, Goalpara, Kokrajhar, Marigaon and Nagaon.

That a little-known group could generate so much insecurity shows how fragile the peace is. Only 500 people had left, said the Dibrugarh DC, H.N. Borah. But the Intelligence put the figure at 6,000 though the local sources claimed 15,000 had fled. Mindful of the polls in 2006, Gogoi ordered the probe into the exodus.

Deportation of Foreigners: Problems

What is the record of both the Congres; and AGP Governments? Here is a set of figures from the national dailies. During the 1986-93 period, the Police picked up 2,87,000 as suspected foreigners and referred them to the Screening Committees, composed of the Deputy Commissioners and Superintendents of Police of the districts concerned. As required under the IMDT Act, these Committees were required to refer these cases to the Tribunals, constituted for the purpose. "These Tribunals are pathetically short of staff and Government of India are reluctant to make up the shortages", an official laments. Consequently the Tribunals could identify only 9,000 of the 2,87,000 suspects as foreigners. Of these 9,000 only 876 could be deported! And most of the deportees, in any case, re-entered India (Assam), and then, it was business as usual, say the analysts.

If the long-winded procedures both administrative and judicial hamper the deportation of illegal migrants, the party politics muddies the waters further, as the whole issue gets enmeshed in the political 'minority versus majority' polemic.

The issue was in focus at the Chief Ministers' conference of the North-Eastern States in Delhi on September 28, 1992. At the 1995 Dhaka SAARC meet the Prime Ministers of India and Bangladesh agreed to sort out the issue. But there has been no movement since.

Now a brief account of what came out of Maharashtra Government's (BJP-Shiv Sena) efforts in 1997-98 to deport the illegal immigrants from Mumbai. The issue generated immense hear between Mumbai and Kolkata, not surprising for those "well acquainted with the tactics and political character of the CPM and Leftists of all hues". The West Bengal Government was accused of "disrupting the deportation by evoking the Bengali sentiments and by adopting the 'unfederal' behaviour; thus not only stopping the process but also enhancing the morale of the illegal immigrants". It was the Right verses the Left. As during the AASU Movement, the Communists dubbed the BJP-Sena Government not only as Anti-Muslim but also as Anti-Bengali. The latter saw it as a deliberate move to defame it as communal and accused the CPM-Conumnunist of reinforcing their support base among the illicit migrants staying in West Bengal. "They have secured their vote bank, even if in the process, they have served the cause of Bangladesh." One cannot blame Dhaka if it sees in this Sena-CPM polemics an endorsement of their official stance that there is not a single Bangladeshi in India.

Most astounding statements on the issue reportedly came from Chief Minister Basu: "What is the point in deporting when they are sure to return to India sooner rather than later!" The critics have called it a surrender ro vested and sectarian interests. Now examine a defiant statement by Feroze Sheikh, born to Bangladeshi parents in Mumbai: send me back and I will return with 10 more!" (Asian records 22-1-1999). The valid question that cries for an answer is: "Is this defiance the cause of Basu's postulation— rather, an outcry of despair—or its effect?"

The problem of Bangladeshi nationals staying illegally in Delhi is of long vintage. "It assumed serious proportions of late as they have become key players in the Capital's soaring crime graph" (*Times of India,* 9-6-2000). The police was asked to identify them and initiate proceedings for their deportation. A police officer laments: "It is a highly challenging task as they look no different from Indians and speak the same language. Most of them have 'proper' ration cards. If the identification is difficult, deportation is even more so, as the issue becomes play-thing in the hands of the political parties for electoral considerations. Police sources assert the number of illegal immigrants run into "several lakhs".

In the wake of happenings in Kashmir and ISI activities in various parts of India, these foreigners have become a security risk; particularly so after terror struck the Indian Parliament and the US Twin Towers.

As for Home Minister's statement about one lakh Bangladeshi nationals in Delhi, the news weekly "Dhaka Courier" in its issue of 6-12 September 1991 carried an account with names and photographs of "more than 1,50,000 Bangladeshis who have found a home in Delhi".[46]

Now a set of official figures to see the difficulties involved in deportation. Till 1993, expulsion notices were served on a total 5018 illegal migrants, of whom 1186 were extradited. However, during the same period 16,334 fresh immigrants, including the 908 're-infiltrators'; were discovered. How difficult, even frustrating, is the task for the agencies involved in executing it?

Here is an economist (1991) re-emphasizing the point made above: "Influx will always remain a fact here. Assam's population density is 287 per km^2 as compared to Bangladesh's 800 and people keep crossing into India."

But long last the nation does not seem to be accepting, this counsel of despair. Home Minister Advani announced on January 7, 2003 that "orders have been issued to the States to identify and deport 15 million illegal Bangladeshi immigrants and 11,500 Pakistanis who have overstayed illegally". The issue has assumed seriousness because these illicit immigrants pose a threat to Indian security. The MHA has decided to issue to the Indian citizens (in the 13 States, in the first instance) the Multi-Purpose National Identity Card (MNIC) to provide credible individual identification system, as also to act as a deterrent against future illegal immigration (*Times of India,* 8-1-2003). The issue of MNIC to all Indians would cost Rs. 5000 crore (*Indian Express,* 13-1-2003). Will it succeed, is yet to be seen?

Advani's directive of "throwing out" the illegal foreigners (essentially, 15 million Bangladeshis and 15,000 Pakistanis) will not be easy to execute. It is easy to see "why" in the official record of Assam, the State probably worst affected in the country because of the Bangladeshi influx. It has been able to expel only a 1501 since the signing of the Assam Accord in 1985. Number who may have crept in during the same period? Records show that in those 17 years, Assam has pushed back over 22,500 Bangladeshis as they attempted to cross over. Infiltration has been a problems for long, but more serious since Independence. Over 2,00,000 people were deported from Assam under the provisions of the Foreigners Act between 1952 and 1984, till the Assam Accord was signed. The deportees number over 1,74,000 during the 1952-66; 69,000 during 1967-73; and 5,148 during 1973-84. Interestingly, after the State Congress Government (with Centre too under it) enacted the controversial IMDT Act in 1983, the number of Bangladeshis detected and deported from Assam started coming down. Enters AGP President Brindaban Goswami. "This in itself is enough to prove that the IMDT Act was specifically passed by the Congress to safeguard the interest of the Bangladeshi infiltrators...we have been demanding the repeal of the same." The BJP too has been demanding the same and its President M. Venkaiah Naidu urged Prime Minister Vajpayee on January 11, 2003 to have the Act scrapped. He said: "Illegal and large scale of Bangladeshis into India is not a Hindu-Muslim question, but one that is directly linked to our national unity, security and economy." But the Congress regime in Assarn is opposed to the scrapping of the Act, as it feels the Act safeguards Muslims against discrimination and harassment in the name of deporting Bangladeshi immigrants. "It is also a fact well-known by now that illegal Bangladeshi migrants are in a commanding position in as many as 36 assembly constituencies of Assam apart from being in a majority in four of the States' 23 districts" (Samudra Gupta Kashyap in *Indian Express,* 14-1-2003).

Assam Governor, Lt Gen (Retd) S.K. Sinha, had blown the whistle in his November 1997 Report to the Union President about the dangers posed to the Nation's integrity by these immigrants, expressing the fears this "majority" population (in bordering areas would soon demand merger of these areas with Bangladesh. Some excerpts from the 42-page Report:

> "....Unless the border fencing in the North-East, especially Assam, is done seriously, country's security is in danger. As important as the Kashmir issue is, the one involving the influx of the Bangladeshis, for this might first lead to a demand for merger of the North-Eastern border areas with Bangladesh, and ultimately lead to a situation when Dhaka would cut off the Region from the rest of the country.... The demographic pattern in the Region has already changed, reducing the indigenous population to a minority.... The Muslim population of Assam rose by 77.42 per cent during 1971-91, compared to 41.89 per cent for the Hindus; the All-India increase in Muslim population for that period being only 55.04 per cent...(We are aware of) How Pakistan leaders and pro-Pakistan leaders of pre-Independence days made consistent efforts to include Assam and adjoining areas in Pakistan, and same efforts are being carried out by Bangladesh in later years. The political parties are guilty of indirectly encouraging infiltration to build up their solid vote bank, an allegation constantly voiced by AASU since 1979.... C.S. Mullan wrote in 1931 that within 30 years, Sibsagar would remain the only district in the State where 'the Assamese will remain a majority'. This prophecy is well on its way to becoming true as reflected by the present demographic pattern of Assam. The IMDT Act, 1983 must be repealed immediately as instead of curbing influx, it was only helping infiltrators. That only 9,955 persons have been identified under this Act proved how ineffective it has been" (cited by Samudra Gupta Kashyap in *Indian Express,* 17-12-1998).

There is no doubt that illegal migration has adversely affected not only the political situation in the State, to the detriment of India's national security, but also the livelihood of the common Assamese. Writes M.K. Shukla (from Lanka in Nagaon district) in *Hindustan Times* of 28 September 1999: "The indigenous tribals of the villages in the south-eastern parts of Nagaon Parliamentary Constituency have lost out even the limited labour market to Bangladeshi infiltrators." He was only confirming a minor specificity of the larger reality, Governor Sinha had sketched in his report; *viz,* Nagaon had acquired the 'distinction' of being a Bangladeshi majority district, similar to the far away districts of Dhubri, Goalpara, Karimganj and Hailakandi.

" Governor Sinha told *The Hindu* (17-7-2000): "The people felt enraged over illegal migration and at losing their identities.... I have sent a report on it.... The centre is evolving its response to some of the points...." If Advani's 'directive' of 7 January 2003 to expel foreigners from the country is the response, it should be welcome, even if belated by five years!

As for expulsion from metropolitans like Mumbai, Delhi, etc. the situation is very serious. Instead of decrease in immigration the numbers are adding up. "Silently, without local authorities noticing, the population of Bangladeshis in Mumbai's Golibar enclave has swelled, by some estimates, to about 20,000 in just two years (2000-02)", says J. Dey in *Indian Express,* 14 January 2003. Expulsion is an uphill task, indeed.

Is Deportation Impossible—nearly?

"Taking a U-turn on its resolve to deport at least 3,000 Bangladeshi migrants every month, India is likely to tone down the exercise very soon", the *Indian Express* of 28-4-05 informs us. "Earlier this week", the MHA decided a rethink on this policy, as it felt the deportation exercise was "un-implementable". Some realisation this, about a serious security issue that has plagued the nation since its very birth 50 years ago!

The decision will have a serious impact on the states like Assam, Nagaland, Maharashtra and West Bengal whose Chief Ministers had voiced serious concern over the free run the illegal migrants were having in their states, at the recent Chief Ministers conference in New Delhi presided over by Prime Minister Manmohan Singh. West Bengal Chief Minister Buddhadev Bhattacharya had even sought Central intervention, alleging that the Pak ISI was making use of the porous border.

What is the reason behind this give-up, though the MHA would like to term it as 'rethink', even if in reality it is 'surrender' to an unreasonable, blustering, and overbearing neighbour. One of the key reasons that forced a rethink, the MHA officials would like us to believe, was BDR's persistent denial to take back the Bangladeshi migrants. "Once the BDR denies to accept the illegal migrants, there is very little India can do", a senior officer tells the *Express.* Assuming superior airs of morality and humanism, he further pontificates: "Though the BSF can be asked to push back the illegal migrants, the Ministry feels it is an 'inhuman practice' and will not be encouraged under any circumstances." So India will accept all comers. Even mighty USA and powerful European nations do not follow such a "liberal" and "humane" policy towards migrants from smaller nations, forget about a nation of 180 million people and still adding to its numbers. Will some one ask this MHA worthy what happens to over 320 million Indians who are still living below the poverty line? More importantly, is India governed by bureaucracy? Where, pray, is the political leadership? Or, may be, the latter is speaking through the former. As an analyst says, the Ministry, in line with the Congress-led UPA Government stand, is now treating the issue of illegal migrants as a "human problem". "Sources indicated that the parameters of the new policy will be sketched out later this month" (April 2005). "Well, we are waiting."

Tripura Fencing: Revisited

Fencing on Tripura border has its own share of problems. At the 3 May 2005 high level meeting at the MHA, the NSA, M.K. Narayanan had advocated the need to go ahead with the fencing between the Zero Line and 150 yards on Tripura-Bangladesh border, even though strongly opposed by Dhaka. The BDR is against fencing in this particular area of about 200 km, claiming that some of the 938 villages in this region are in their territory. Even though India rejects this claim, there is some dispute on the issue.

Inadequacies of Anti-Infiltration Measures

How effectual have been the administrative and political measures against the influx of the foreigners, illegal or otherwise, so far? Can physical measure really deter a determined infiltrator from entering a neighbouring country? The *charlands,* the islands formed between different channels of the Brahmaputra, get submerged when the mighty river is in spate during monsoons. This is worst of the times for population who inhabit these islands as they move from *one charland* to another in country boats. Their thatched houses are washed away by the turbulent waters. The river has no respect for the international boundaries nor do the people in the rainy season. It is the most opportune time for the infiltration and smuggling as the distributaries of the rivers increase manifold and the goods can be carried to remote villages in boats on either side of the border. But more worrisome is the smuggling of human beings.

The BSF men charged with the duty of guarding these borders shift to the boats and establish floating outposts in the heart of the river when the border outpost are submerged. Of the 126 km Assam-Bangladesh border, that the two BSF Battalions are required to guard, about (25 + 46) 71 km is riverine, for which they have a water Wing.[47]

Equally difficult is the task of protecting the sanctity of the land border on the North-Eastern Frontier because of thick vegetation in the submontane terrain. "It is the continuous infiltration of the Bangladeshis over the past 5 decades which is of immense concern. Political persecution of the minorities in that country and the economic compulsion of the majority have forced thousands to sneak into India."[48] Checking such infiltration is a near impossible task without active support from the local population. Since the populations on either side of the border have same socio-economic and religio-ethnic composition, information is rarely offered voluntarily to the BSF, laments an officer of the force. Lack of communication and an open border make the task even more difficult. It was because of these problems that the Assam Accord of 1985 had provisions for construction of border fencing and roads. But the implementation has been slow. "It took all of 7 years after the Accord to complete a mere 30 km of fencing and 52 km of road against a total of 72 km of road and fencing proposed under it."

The situation was even worse in Meghajaya, where out of 168 km of road and fencing proposed to be laid, only 50 km and 33 km of these two respectively were completed till 1992.

In December 1988, Bangladesh Foreign Minister Abdus Samad Azad declared that his Government was opposed to any Indian move to fence the borders and added rather ominously: "It is not in the interest of the improvement of the biliteral ties between the two neighbours. It is not a good omen for bilateral ties and also not conducive to present initiatives on the creation of a South Asia Free Trade Area."[49] It is rather a curious logic, the Foreign Minister telling India that unless it continues to allow the migration from the very country which is its major source, the relations between the two neighbours would deteriorate!

The progress on construction of road-cum-fencing project, launched in 1987 as an anti-infiltration measure under the 1985 Assam Accord, has been rather halting and tardy. While India shares 4096-km-long border with Bangladesh, only 852 km of fencing has been completed so far (2002), at the cost of Rs. 139.79 crore. The worst hit is the Assam portion, 262 km long, of which only 149 km has been fenced so far in a period of 15 years. The work on construction of roads too is progressing at a snail's pace, with only 2539 km against a total border length of 4096 km having been completed in these 15 years. The government's ambitious project to fence the Indo-Bangladesh international border to halt illegal infiltration will take another 5 years to be realized. "The border fence project has entered phase 2 with the Government estimating a sum of Rs. 847 crore for the 2,429.5 km, the date for completion being fixed at 2007."[50]

The fencing work again hit a road block in May-July 2005 with Bangladesh stoutly opposing any construction within 150 yds of the zero line. BDR are known to firing and shelling the BSF-led construction parties engaged in the task. Taking a U-turn on its decision to continue border fencing despite protests from Bangladesh, "the MHA has suspended fencing 3 May 2005 along 212 patches where villages on the Indian side stretch upto the international boundary". Home Minister Patil, explaining the change in stance, sources said, wanted the CCS, the MEA, and the PM to take a view on the issue as the consequences of fencing this 4,000 km border were not limited to his Ministry only. Patil issued the suspension orders even as the BSF and section of officials urged that fencing be continued.

The BSF and BDR have an informal agreement on not having defensive structures within 150 yds of the *"Zero* Line". Adhering to this would mean leaving out 254 Indian villages, with a population of 65,000, outside the fence. The MHA made a power-point presentation to Patil in the presence of M.K. Narayjm, N.S.A., Neelam Deo, JS (Bangladesh), MEA; Home Secretary, V.K. Duggal; and the DGBSF. This meeting assumed great significance coming as it did a day after the MOD released its Annual Report, slamming Bangladesh for being "insensitive and unresponsive" to India's Security concerns.

There was contention in July 2005 with India demanding that it must erect the fence closer to the Zero Line where topography compels it to do so and Bangladesh insisting "No fencing within 150 yds of this Line". The problem becomes acute where the two differ on the demarcation of the boundary. Thus is the fencing work "has hit a road-block at two points in Tripura and one in West Bengal".

The MHA is determined to complete the fencing by 2006 (as Patil announced recently), "as the detection and deportation of the infiltrators has failed to address the problem". The infiltration is going on unabated along the porous Bangla border. The areas from where bids are made include 24 Parganas, Nadia, Murshidabad, Malda, and Dakshin West Bengal; Dubri in Assam; and Gokul Nagar and Udaipur in Tripura. "The BDR is supporting infiltration."

K. Natwar Singh, during his 2-day Aug. (6-7) 2005 visit to Dhaka, told the press: "A strong fence was useful for both sides to achieve their common objectives of ensuring peace and tranquilty and facilitating interaction between two friendly people while doing their utmost to prevent illegal cross border activity." He was obviously alluding to a sharp increase in cross-border criminal activity, including illegal trade in arms and explosives, counterfeit currency, trafficking in narcotics, women and children (*Tribune, AA* of 3 and 4 May, 1 and 8 Aug., all 2005).

Census 2001: Portentous Fall-out for Ethnic Assamese

As the February 2001 Census got underway the perennial fears of the Assamese and other ethnic communities being swamped by religious and linguistic aliens loomed large in Assam. During the month-long operations the focus was on the Muslims in Assam, most of whom had migrated from Bangladesh along with many Bengali Hindus. The fears that the Census 2001 would show a drop in the Assamese populations are not unfounded. Assamese comprised 60.89 per cent of the State's populations in 1971 Census. But 20 years later, in 1991 Census, this percentage fall to 57.29, while that of the Bengalis rose by almost 4 per cent to 21.5 per cent.

Besides the continuing influx of the Bangladeshis other reasons, given by the demographers for this fall in the Assamese population during the 1971-91 period, are:

1. Movement for a separate Bodoland state had peaked by 1991 and ABSU had advocated against Bodo-speaking population enlisting themselves as Assamese.
2. But a major factor was the decision of many neo-Assamese to revert to this original Bengali Language following an anti-minorities wave in the 1980, marked by the Nellie massacre.

Maulana Abdul Haq, President of Jamiat-Ulema-e-Hind (Assam), said before the census 2001, "There is no reason why the settlers should not call themselves Assamese as they have been doing since 1981." Bengali Hindu organisation like the All Assam Bengali Yuva Chhatra Federation also wanted the Bengali-speaking residents of the State to mark them as Assamese. Whether these exhortations would change the situation for better for the Assamese can be seen after the results of 2001 Census are published, but under the given circumstances, it seems unlikely. The Rabhas are likely to follow the lead given by the Bodos, as the too are demanding a self-ruled territory.

ISI and Extremist Outfits: Nexus in Assam

The ISI with its tentacles spread all over the North-East, is creating disaffection in the Region with the help of extremist elements among the foreigners. It is sponsoring and funding several militant or terrorists outfits to foster anti-India sentiment in the area. Muslim Liberation Tigers of Assam (MLTA) is the leading Muslim extremist outfit which threatened (1995) to create a separate Islamic state in Assam. "Propped up and funded by Iran and some West Asian countries," some of the extremist outfits are listed here:

1. Muslim Voluntary Force (MVF)
2. Students Islamic Movement of India (SIMI)
3. Islamic Revolutionary Force (IRF)
4. Islamic United Liberation Army (1ULA)
5. Assam Minorities Liberation Army (AMLA)

6. Minorities United Liberation Front of Assam (MULFA)
7. Muslim Liberation Front of Assam (MLFA)
8. Special United Reform Army of Assam (SURAA)
9. Islamic Revolutionary Army (IRA)
10. Saddam Bahini (SB)
11. Islamic Sevak Sangh (1SS)
12. Minority Liberation Tigers of Assam (MLTA)
13. Muslim Liberation Tigers of Assam (MULTA)[51]
14. Islamic Liberation Army of Assam (ILAA)

With the help and guidance of the ISI, these outfits are smuggling into Assam arms not only from Bangladesh, but also through Burma from countries beyond it. Ostensibly, they claim to safeguard the interests of the Muslims in Assam, the long-term aim is to destabilise Assam, North-East, and then India in that order. The ISI's nexus with NSCN(I-M) is a given, and the latter's tie up with outfits like ULFA, PLA and Bangladesh Security Forces provides it a safe corridor to Cox Bazar port centre for global narco-terrorist combine. As several Islamic countries reportedly give grants to them, these outfits are never short of funds.

This Pan-Islamic slant to the foreigners issue in Assam gives it a more sinister dimension, which gets flagrantly dangerous for India's security because of the flip-flop attitude of certain political formations towards these infiltrators. "It should be a cause of concern that in 56 out of 126 Assembly constituencies in Assam, the Muslim migrants and their sympathizers had become decisive actors by 1995." Intelligence reported in 1995-96 that "all the 17 JEI MPs of Bangladesh hailing from its borders districts are playing subtle if sinister role in this dangerous anti-India plan". Besides the 14 outfits mentioned above, there are 24 others operating clandestinely. "There are plans to bring all of them under one umbrella organisation, ala 32 separatist groups functioning under the rubric of the APHC in Kashmir.

The MVF, the largest militant group with 500 cadres derives its sustenance from a powerful Agar lobby of Hojjai. MVF and other groups like IRF, MULFA, MLTA, etc., keep adding to their cadres through dubious means, as also from outfits like the SIMI and certain district units of JEI Hind.[52] ISI was using the *Pasban,* a front of the JEI, and Jamaat-ul-Fuqra, as conduit for funds etc. to the Muslim groups in Assam.

Another view holds that the *modus operandi* of these militant outfits is reminiscent of the Muslim League plan of 1947, mooted at Dhaka, "to lay siege of Assam through means devious, violent or otherwise, and to grab it for Pakistan". After all one should not forget that in 1946 the Cabinet Mission had placed Assam and Bengal in group C.

Even Bangladesh made some ostensibly helpful noises occasionally. In November 1998, India and Bangladesh agreed to enforce the 1991 Agreement on illegal immigrants, with the latter pledging that no one would be allowed to use its soil for anti-India activities. But there was little to show in practical terms for such statements pregnant with pious intent.[53]

The Issue Reaches Supreme Court

Whatever be the shenanigans of the political class on the emotive issue that simultaneously impinges on the national security, the nation's highest Court was more pragmatic, when it ruled in March 1993 that possession of a ration card and figuring in the Voters List did not confer any privilege on a suspected foreigner. Seeing the inaction of various Governments since Independence on the issue, it reached the Supreme Court through Public Interest Litigation (PIL) route. On 20 September 1999, its 3-Judge bench admitted a public interest petition from the All India Lawyers Forum, seeking repatriation of the Bangladeshi migrants illegally staying in India. The Petitioner, P.P. Saxena, Forum's President, alleged that about 1 crore Bangladeshis had illegally infiltrated four North-Eastern States—Assam, Tripura, Meghalaya and Manipur—and West Bengal, causing severe constraints on the limited resources of these States. He sought directions to the authorities for their repatriation.[54]

The Court granted 8 weeks time to the Centre to file a comprehensive affidavit dealing with the issue relating to the illegal Bangladeshi migrants in these five States. The court observed that this was a serious matter and the Central Government should take steps to stop this illegal infiltration as it was threatening to change the demography of these States.

The Assam Government in its affidavit, had stated that a total of 4,05,267 illegal migrants were detected in the region between 1952 and 1999, of which 3,47,689 were deported. "In the recent past, there appeared to be a close nexus between the illegal migrants and the fundamentalist organisations on the one hand, and between fundamentalist organisations and Pakistan's ISI, on the other. The State suggested repeal of the IMDT Act, 1983 in view of the impediments in detection and deportation of migrants. "It also suggested intensification of BSF patrolling in border areas by reducing the distance between the border posts, high-tech communication facilities using satellites and issuance of multipurpose photo identity cards in the border villages."

The Tripura Government informed the Court it had pushed back 1,43,188 illegal migrants since 1971. The migration from Bangladesh had a devastating effect, virtually engulfing the indigenous tribal communities who were previously enjoying majority.

The West Bengal stated that it had suggested to the Centre to introduce changes in the Foreigners Act to strengthen the power of the enforcing agencies and to streamline the procedure for deporting Bangladeshis.

The Supreme Court's concern about the unabated migration of Bangladeshis and asking the Government to make "honest" and "serious" attempt to stop the influx assume importance since they posed a threat to India's security.

Proving the point that political and sectarian consideration takes precedence over national interest, three months after coming into power in Assam, the Saikia Government of the Congress party, has sought the Supreme Court's permission to withdraw the former (AGP) Government's affidavit favouring repeal of the IMDT Act. Even though the Congress Government's fresh affidavit said the "Act is not aimed at protecting the interests of Bangladeshis as perceived by the former AGP Regime," the data adduced by it proved the contrary:

> "16 Tribunals constituted under the Act, are dealing with the cases from 23 districts. Tribunals have initiated inquiries on the basis of 3,29,905 complaints, but they could only declare 10,353 persons as illegal migrants. However, only 1494 persons (among these 10,353) could be deported from the State."[55]

Even after being declared illegal migrants under the Act, their actual deportation was not possible, the fresh affidavit said, because the Bangladesh Government refused to accept them without verifying their Bangladeshi nationality.

Supreme Court Hands out a Tough Verdict

12 July 2005. The Supreme Court struck down as unconstitutional the IMDT Act, 1983. The 3-Judge (CJ R.C. Lahoti, JJ G.P. Mathur and P.K. Balasubramanyan) Bench, declaring the 1983 Act and the Rules framed thereunder in 1984 as *ultra vires* of the Constitution, directed that all tribunals constituted under the IMDT Act adjudicating the cases for identification of illegal migrants from Bangladesh cease to function with immediate effect, and these cases would stand transferred to tribunals under the Foreigners Act. The petition filed by the AGP M.P. Sarbananda Sonowal, and now allowed by the Court, had said the Act was only encouraging vote bank politics without addressing the mammoth problem of illegal migrants. The reaction to the judgement was on expected lines: AGP, ASSU rejoice; BJP, Shiv Sena welcomed it; Congress, Left, and the minorities dismayed."

The Court verdict says, *inter alia:* "Local people reduced to minority status, face external pressure.... Bangladeshis took Assam land.... The Act encouraged infiltration in Assam.... It boosted Assam Muslim population.... Assam facing aggression...." It pans Centre on the IMDT Act....

Mamta Banerji alleged "the CPM has packed 8 border districts of West Bengal with illegal migrants. These districts have collectively gained 18 Assembly seats". The Leader of Opposition Advani, speaking in the Lok Sabha, said: "The illegal immigration was the 'biggest disaster' and the 'biggest threat to national security'. The Government must gracefully accept the verdict. Why did it appoint the Group of Ministers (GOM)?"

If Gogoi rushed to New Delhi, the Centre appointed a GOM to study the verdict. The critics alleged its aim was to nullify the verdict (*Hindu, Exp., TOI, HT*—13 and 14 July 2005).

Are the Illegal Immigrants Vitiating India's Electoral Processes?

It is an unfortunate situation where a nation does not seem to be concerned about non-Indians, and that too illegal immigrants from a neighbouring country, participating in its electoral process and consequently dictating the results in not-too-insignificant number of constituencies. Mamta Banerji may not be altogether off the mark when she alleges that the CPM has packed 8 border districts in her state with illegal migrants. The Chief Election Comrnissioners (CEC) in the past did warn the nation against the foreigners vitiating our national elections. L.K. Advani's warning about the "Illegal immigration being biggest threat to our security" is too self-obvious to need further comment. The then CEC B.B. Tandon certainly seemed to be exercised on this count.

Tandon said 14 December 2005 that "almost 1.5 lakh voters on the (Assam) State's electoral rolls are of 'doubtful' nature". This is after the 'D' category figures have come down in the past few years. "The inclusion of the names of the Bangladeshi infiltrators in the State's electoral rolls has remained a major issue for more than three decades now and the Election Commission had in the early 1990s directed the state election officials in Assam to mark as 'D' (D for doubtful) as many as 3.75 lakh voters on the ground that the citizenship status of these voters was doubtful, and suspected to be Bangladeshi infiltrators" (*Express* 15-15-05). The Foreigners Tribunals have, over the years, examined several such names and made revisions. The 1.5 lakh is obviously the latest revised figure in 'D' category as mentioned by the CEC, and he made it clear that these people whose names figure in the State's electoral rolls would not be allowed to cast votes in the forthcoming (2006) State Assembly elections.

Assam has been vociferous about deportation of these Bangladeshis for long decades. They had launched a strident Anti-Foreigners Agitation (1979-85) on the issue. West Bengal has only recently, perhaps after the change in the chief ministership, raised alarm about the illegal immigrants in the state.

Non-Left spectrum of the political parties are demanding the CEC conduct "free and fair" poll in the West Bengal in 2006 a la the 2005 Bihar Assembly Elections.

Supreme Court Admits Another Petition on the Issue

10 Dec. 2004, a 3-Judge Bench (CJ R.C. Lahoti, JJ G.P. Mathur and P.P. Naolekar) admitted a PIL petition by Image India Foundation, expressing concern over the alarming growth of Bangladeshi immigrants in the country, especially in West Bengal and five North-Eastern states. It alleged that the Government of India was ignoring several reliable reports by the Army and others, that if effective measures were not taken to stem the tide, the demography of the Region would change, leading to the possibility of a demand for 'Brihad (Greater) Bangladesh' in the future (*AA,* 11-12-04).

The IMDT Act: Impregnable till Highest Court Acted

The Act came into force in 1983 when Anti-Foreigners agitation was at its peak. The 1985 Accord mentions certain difficulties in implementing the provisions of the 1983 Act as brought out by the AASU.

20 Sep. 1990. The AASU for the first time demands the repeal of the Act. March 1992, the AGP repeats the demand. Now a brief chronology of events to show how this important issue was dealt by all concerned:

1. *11 Aug. 1997.* The Centre accept that the results achieved under the Act have been very poor. The AASU President stated at the meeting that the former Prime Minister during his visit to Assam had informed the AASU that the decision to repeal the Act had already been taken.
2. *6 Apr. 1998.* At a tripartite meeting, the MHA officials inform that the AASU request for the repeal of the Act would be put up to the new Government for decision.
3. *23 Sep. 1998.* At this meeting, the AASU was informed that the repeal of the Act was "under the active consideration of the Government".
4. *Feb.* 1999. In his address to Parliament, the President says the repeal of Act "was under active consideration of the Government".
5. *18 Mar. 1999.* Tripartite meet again. The MHA repeats the "under active consideration" assurance.
6. *1 July 1999.* The AASU urged that an ordinance be issued to repeal the Act.
7. *Mar. 2000.* Sarbananda, erstwhile President of AASU filed a writ petition in the Supreme Court. Avoiding details of how the colours of the Governments kept changing at Guwahati (AGP to Congress) and New Delhi (NDA to UPA), and with the stand and stance on the question of repeal of the IMDT Act, suffice it to say that the course of the Sarbananda petition went through tortuous turns and twists before the Supreme Court delivered its judgement on 12-07-05.

Are Only Some Governors Patriotic?

"The (Assam) Congress Government is in crisis over the Report sent by the Governor, Mr (Lt Gen) Ajai Singh to the MHA regarding the huge and unchecked infiltration across the border", says *HT* 14-4-05. The report comes at a time when Chief Minister Gogoi was yet to come out of the open threat hurled at him by Jamiat-Ulema-e-Hind President Maulana Asad Madani when he was attending the Jamiat's rally at Guwahati on 3 Apr. 2005. The threat: "The Jamiat will overthrow his Government if its demands like the job reservation for Muslims and seats in the Lok Sabha and the Assembly were not met within 6 months."

The Report says Assam's border with Bangladesh was one of the world's most fluid borders "with 6,000 Bangladeshis daily crossing it and a large number of them illegally settling here, thus threatening the demographic character of Assam". Such a huge influx could lead to setting up of bases of the Pak ISI and international terrorist outfit's like the Al Qaida.

An analyst avers that Madani's threat, and now the Governor's Report "are certainly going to help the BJP and the AGP to charge Gogoi of appeasing the Muslims". The Congress is the only major party opposed to the repeal of the IMDT Act, only applicable in Assam, which others feel comes in the way of deporting illegal migrants to Bangladesh.

The Report is seen as the vindication of the stand of the political parties like the BJP, Shiv Sena, AGP, etc. and organisations like the AASU, All India Lawyers Forum for Civil Liberties, and individuals like Sarbananda—some of whom had petitioned the Supreme Court for striking down the IMDT Act on the ground that it has failed in its aim of checking illegal immigration, and instead, it proved a shield for 20 lakh Bangladeshis, settled in the border districts. Governor Ajai Singh is not the first to paint a grim picture on this issue, as a former Governor, Lt Gen SK Sinha, presently Governor of J & K, had also sent a similar report to the President, saying how the influx has turned Lower Assam into a Muslim majority area. Sinha had also said the settlement of huge proportion of foreigners in the border districts, posed a grave threat to the security and integrity of the nation. As is their wont, the Congress and the Communists had accused Sinha of raking up communal passions but Ajai Singh's Report "has also said that the demographic changes due to illegal migration are eroding the social and religious fabric" of Assamese Society (*Tribune,* 4-5-05). The sanctuaries of the Bangladeshi population, "mushrooming in the border districts of Assam will provide trans-border support for the secessionist and separatist insurgency movements in our state". Sinha too had voiced the same fears, though worded differently. Interestingly, the Governments at the Centre and Guwahati had taken different stands, depending on the party in power there. Is it indicative of the typical

Indian 'condition' (or syndrome) where the party interests comes before the demands of national security'?

These are not the only Governors who chose to be the whistle blowers when the nation's security is relegated to second position. Two more come to mind: (1) Lt Gen VK Nayar who resigned as Manipur Governor when his report to the President that his Chief Minister was colluding with the insurgents was ignored. (2) T.V. Rajeshwar, West Bengal Governor, too had warned the Centre about the threat posed to the nation by this unchecked influx. It may be a mere coincidence that the three are Armymen and the fourth a Policeman. In contrast, another set of Three Governors in the very recent past (of Jharkhand, Goa and Bihar) come to mind who are generally believed to have failed to defend the Constitution they are sworn to do. So, there are Governors and Governors! Why are only some Governors patriotic enough to do their duty by the Indian Constitution?

Current Situation : Post-Jul 2005 Supreme Court Verdict

Some Important Related Issues

The Supreme Court on 12 Jul 2005 striking down as unconstitutional the IMDT Act 1983 was a seminal judgement; for some, may be historic. The Bench declared the 1983 Act and the Rules framed there under in 1984 as *ultra vires* of the constitution and directed that all tribunals constituted under the IMDT Act adjudicating the cases for identification of illegal migrants from Bengladesh cease to function with immediate effect, and these cases would stand transferred to the tribunals under the Foreigners Act.

Some of the events/decisions starting with this judgement itself are noted hereafter.

- 12 Jul. 2005. Supreme Court strikes down the IMDT Act 1983 as unconstitutional.
- The Supreme Court had directed that "all cases pending before the tribunals under the IMDT Act shall stand transferred to the tribunals constituted under the Foreigners (Tribunals) Order, 1964, and shall be decided in the manner provided in the Foreigners Act. The very first thing the MHA did after the declaration of the Court's judgement was to issue two notification.
- Notification One : Called the Foreigners (Tribunals) Amendment Order, 2006, under which the Foreigners (Tribunals) order, 1964, was made applicable to the whole of India except Assam.
- Notification Two : Called the Foreigners (Tribunals for Assam) Order, 2006, under which a new set of laws was created exclusively for Assam.
- Under the Foreigners (Tribunals) Amendment order, 2006, as well as the Foreigners (Tribunals) order, 1964, the onus of proving citizenship was on the suspected 'foreigner'. But under the Foreigners (Tribunals

for Assam) Order, 2006, the onus of proof was on the complainant, as under the struck down MDT Act, 1983. Opponents of the order issued under Notification Two argued that all the objectionable provisions of the IMDT Act 1983 struck down by the Supreme Court were brought back by the Executive.

- 5 Dec. 2006. As was to be expected, the Supreme Court scrapped the Foreigners (Tribunals for Assam) Order 2006, which was brought through a gazette notification after the Supreme Court struck down controversial I MDT Act, 1983 on 12 Jul 2005. The Bench declared the impugned order of 2006 as "unreasonable and issued in an arbitrary exercise of power". It also directed the centre to constitute within four months a sufficient number of tribunals under the 1964 Order to effectively deal with foreigners who have illegally come from Bangladesh or are residing in Assam.
- 30 Jan 2007 : "Halt the delimitation process" An all-party delegation from Assam, led by Assam Assembly speaker Tanka Bahadur Rai met Home Minister Patil and demanded that the delimitation process should immediately be stopped in the State until the National Register of Citizens is completed. Other members of the delegation were : Prithibi Majhi and Sarat Borkotoky (both Congress), Chandra Mohan Patowary (AGP); Parimal Shukla Baidya (BJP); Drupad Borgohain (CPI); and Parameshwar Brahma (BPPF).

The Delimitation Commission is now demarcating boundaries of parliamentary constituencies in the State based on the 2001 Census figures.

Many political parties feel that for detection of foreigners in Assam, the update of the NRC on the basis of 1971 voter list is important.

Reactions to Supreme Court Rulings of Jul 2005 and Dec 2006

The Supreme Court order of Dec. 2006, quashing the Foreigners (Tribunals for Assam) Order, 2006 issued by the ruling UPA has expectedly evoked mixed reactions in Assam More importantly, it has brought centre stage the politics of migration.

The judgement has been hailed by the influential AASU and the major Opposition parties, the AGP and the BJP. The AGP felicitated its MP from Dibrugarh, Sarbananda Sonowal, who was one of the petitioners who had challenged the impured 2006 Order, along with Charan Deka a BJP leader. Incidentally, Sonowal had also filed a petition challenging the erstwhile IMDT Act 1983, which was struck down by the Supreme Court in July 2005.

It may be of interest to know that the Bench imposed an examplary cost of Rs. 25,000 to be paid to the petitioners, Sarbananda and Charan Deka, who challenged the controversial 2006 Order.

Minority (Muslim) bodies on the other hand expressed fears that in the absence of adequate legal protection, genuine Indian citizens may be harassed by the police. All Assam Minority Students Union (AAMSU) called for a State-wide 12 hour bandh, which was marred by incidents of stone-throwing by bandh supporters in some pockets of northern Assam. After the Supreme Court had struck down the IMDT Act, 1983, Muslims had demanded an amendment to the Foreigners Act 1964; they also wanted the amended law to be applicable throughout the country. These demands became vociforous after Dec. 2006 ruling.

What is the main striking point? While under the IMDT Act 1983, the onus lay on the complainant to prove that the accured person was not an Indian citizen, under the Foreigners Act the onus is on the person who faces the complaint to prove that he or she is an Indian citizen and not a foreigner. The AASU, AGP and BJP objected to the Foreigners (Tribunals in Assam) Order, because it shifted the onus of proof back to the complainant and thus came in the way of detecting and deporting "foreigners". The three parties also contend that there cannot be two laws on the same subject : one for Assam and the other for the rest of the country.

After the latest (Dec. 2006) ruling, Congress led coalition government of Assam rushed to pacify the Muslim Community with Chief Minister Tarun Gogoi promising measures to ensure no one was harassed or made to feel insecure. But the Assam United Democratic Front (AUDF) was cynical, accusing the State Government of "deceiving the minorities" in the name of protecting them. The AUDF was formed after the IMDT Act was struck down in Jul 2005 and it represented itself as a replacement for the Congress as the protector of the minority interests. The latest ruling has provided it more fuel to attack the Congress, accusing it of deliberately leaving some legal loop-holes while issuing the two notifications, one for Assam and the other for rest of the country, with the ulterior motive of winning the support of minorities in the Assembly polls.

The AUDF criticism was also echoed by the Char Chapori Sahitya Parishad (CCSP), Assam. Its President Hafiz Ahmad repeats allegations of the AUDF that Congress had intentionally left the loopholes to pose as saviours of Muslims once the 2006 Order is struck down. The CCSP says the Foreigners Act gives the police enormous powers, which are often abused. It cites figures to prove their point. Before the promulgation of the IMDT Act, 210,446 Muslims were driven out of Assam between 1952 and 1971 without trial and without any opportunity to defend their status. It again says that 192,339 people mere deported from the State between 1972 and 1983 in a similar manner.

Obviously, there is a wide chasm between the stands taken by the Muslim bodies/political parties and the parties like the AASI, AGP and BJP. But all of them agreed that once the National Register of Indian Citizens (NRIC) in Assam is updated on the basis of the electoral rolls of 1971 and photo identity cards are issued, the problem may be solved once for all. At a tripartite meeting on 5 May 2005 which was attended by Prime Minister Manmohan Singh, Home Minister Shivraj Patil and Chief Minister Gogoi, it was decided that the NRIC would be updated with the names of all persons who had settled in Assam before 25 Mar 1971, and their dependents.

While the issue of detection and deportation of foreigners in Assam has been mired in legal battles the entire affair has taken a heavy toll on the State exchequer. The Assam Government spent Rs. 400 crore on detection and deportation of foreigners in the past 21 years after the signing of the Assam Accord in 1985. And what did all this achieve? During all these years, only 2,221 illegal Bangladeshi immigrants have been expelled. The State Minister, Implementation of the (1985) Assam Accord, Dr. Bhumidhar Barman disclosed these figures in the Assembly on 12 Dec. 2006. The opponents of the IMDT Act claim that these meagre figures only prove their point that this Act came in the may of Assam expelling the illegal migrants to the country they came from. It will be of interest to know how many "illegal foreigners" are expelled will be expelled now that the impuned Act is out of the way.

Barman also informed the Assembly the same day that the Government did not have the exact number of illegal immigrants living in Assam at present.

Influx Continues in Different Form : BSF Confirms : Nov. 2006

It is difficult to put a number to the immigrants who cross over from Bangladesh to India every day.

On 28 Nov 2006, BSF, DG AK Mitra, however, came up with a tally of Bangladeshi nationals who entered India with valid documents during the past five years through the integrated check-posts and never returned. The figure for such Bangladeshis, officially shown "missing" in records, amounts to a whopping 1.5 lakh.

Mitra believes, like so many other analysts, Indian and foreign, that it is the eastern region, and not Jammu and Kashmir, which could become a problem area in the future. "No one knows where they (1.5 lakh Bangladeshis) went!"

Intelligence agencies had sounded an alert when a dozen Pakistani nationals walked through the Wagah border in 2005 to watch cricket matches and disappeared. It prompted security agencies to slash the cricket visas during the recent (2006) matches, and scaled up the survillance.

Mitra, who ordered increased vigil along the India-Bangladesh border in view of the political development (during the days of the care-taker government) in Dhaka and the impending polls, suspects that some of those who entered India legally would have been involved in anti-India activity.

"They must have come for something." He admitted that his force could not stop illegal cross-overs from Bangladesh.

Mitra's serious concern was that every terror attack trail led to Bangladesh. Initially, it was economic migration, but of late investigation into various terror strikes in the hinterland has revealed that the Bangladesh border was freely being used by militants to enter India. That makes the illegal migration problem a little more serious. He was briefing the media at New Delhi ahead of the Raising Day of the BSF on 1 December (Alok Tikku, *Hindustan Times,* 29 Nov 2006).

Analysts find a pattern in the infiltration by terrorist and insurgent groups from the eastern border. Insurgents from the North-East entered India through North Bengal; those using Bangladesh as an entry point into Jammu and Kashmir or other parts usually took the South Bengal route.

When asked if the Khaleda Zia Government supported the anti-India outfits, his reply : "It is 'safe presumption' to make as the BNP has been in alliance with the JEI and the Islamic Oikya Jote, both rabidly anti-India."

BANGLADESHIS IN INDIA : A POTENT THREAT TO NATIONAL SECURITY

Bangladeshi migrants/entrants/infiltrators are a serious threat to India's strategic interests and national security and unfortunately the subject has not received the attention it deserves in informed circles and security community, not to speak of the political and academic establishment. Only a few commentators have dilated upon the subject in the past, and some of them only in passing. 'Political correctness' is the main reasons for the journalists, academics and strategic analysts shying away from the 'sensitive' issue. In India, any subject impinging upon its "minority community" in any way is rather 'no go' area.

The author distinctly remembers a senior journalist (and son of an eminent journalist of the yore) waxing eloquent on the danger posed to India's security and integrity by the Bangladeshi immigrants in India—mostly illegal—who are already a majority in more than a dozen districts bordering the international frontier (with Bangladesh) in the states of Assam and West Bengal. This was at the India International Centre, New Delhi sometimes in 1990s. Listening intently to his passionate concerns for nation's security and integrity because of this continuing ingress—some call it silent invasion—the author addressed an innocuous, even innocent, question to this senior journalist : "I can clearly see your concerns on the issue, but I have never seen any article by you on the subject in any newspaper. Why have not you written one?" His reply stunned me : "I can't even think of doing so. I shall straight-way be called a (Hindu) communalist!"

The issue of Bangladeshi (and earlier East Pakistani, and still earlier East Bengali) infiltration has been discussed above in some detail from its inception in mid-19th century till end of the 20th century. What follows are the events of the last decade or so, relevant to the subject, preceded by a brief summary to put the issues in perspective.

The influx of illegal migrants has continued unabated for decades by now, and as a result the security scenario in India's North-East has registered a palpable change for the worse with an estimated 12 million Bangladeshis having infiltrated since 1971. The situation has reached such as alarming stage that Bangladeshi migrants are in a position to influence results of elections in about 32 percent of constituencies[56] in Assam. The IB estimates put the number of illegal immigrants way back in 1998 at 1.1 crore with the largest concentration in Assam and West Bengal

It must be recognised that the impact of this huge illegal immigration into Assam has been far-reaching, and profound. If from 1891 till Independence (1947), its population grew at around 20 per cent per decade, the corresponding figure is presently pegged at a harrowing 53 per cent.

The Bangladeshi politicians and academics alike are brazen enough to deny any illegal immigration into India, essentially Assam and West Bengal. One of its Prime Minister smugly announced on the Indian soil during an official visit that there is not a single illegal Bangladeshi in India!" But the data compiled by demographers at the Bangladesh Institute of Development Studies reveal that nearly 3.5 million people disappeared from East Pakistan between 1951 and 1961 probably as a result of partition while another 1.5 million may have have entered India between 1961 and 1974.

That is not all. There is more to come. Astonishingly, a quarter of the 10 million refugees who came to India to escape the killings and hardships during[57] the war of Liberation never returned. Inexplicably, we Indians are indeed keen to keep the horrible fact under wraps. It is obvious that the Indian policy makers are yet to decipher the threat to Indian security from this massive illegal foreign population entrenched in the North-East. The growth of multiple Islamist organisations in the North-East and their metastatis are only making India's security concerns even more acute, assest the analysts.

It is a matter of grave concern that even after the Group of Ministers' comprehensive report on reforming the National Security System viewed seriously the large scale illegal migration and its serious implications for the internal security in the eastern theatre during the NDA regime, the nation is yet to see through the problem that is assuming an alarming proportion every passing day.

Bangladesh Terrorists Eye Border Areas of Assam

There are reports of Jamiat-ul-Mujahideen Bangladesh (JMB) regrouping itself since mid-2006. It adopted a new name for itself Kital Fi Sabilillah (KFS)

which translates into "establishment of Islamic rule." It appears to be working in a more scientific way—concentrating into areas where it has strength. It has divided this area into five commands with established leadership hierarchy, ideological indoctrination and arms training camps.

The Indo-Bangladesh border remains highly porous even after parts of it has been fenced, and it is a haven for smugglers from both sides. Not only illegal infiltration continues having started in 1820s with the British take-over of Assam, a large quantities of illegal arms and ammunition too enters India most of which are for criminal activities but considerable quantities supplement the arsenals of radical Indian terrorists for a 'right' price.

JMB Chief Sheikh Abdur Rahman confessed that first JMB foreign unit was set up in Murshidabad district of West Bengal in 2001. Presently it is under re-vamp to prepare it to provide strategic depth for terrorist activities of the JMB during 2007 elections. Murshidabad is a strategic centre for the activities of SIMI and Jamat-ul-Islam-e-Hind and is a traditional conservative Muslim stronghold—making it attractive for JMB across the border.

JMB is eyeing border area of Assam to consign it a role similar to the one for Murshidabad, namely, to provide strategic depth to the terrorist activities during the 2007 Bangladesh poll. It is emboldened by the reports that the MULTA in Assam's bordering area is increasingly linking up with the JMB in Sylhet.

Assam's border areas would yield more fertile ground to the JMB since its six Muslim-majority border districts have already put forward a demand that these be constituted into a separate state.

Regrouping of the JMB and its plans for the 2007 elections period are portentrous development for India at geo-strategic level, and for Assam at local level as it immediately threatens its integrity.

So, as far as India is concerned, these developments portend a hot winter in Bangladesh. India cannot remain complacent and unruffled if Bangladesh sinks into turmoil in the course of the 2007 elections. Assam will face crisis situation if the JMB violence forces large-scale exodus of Bangladeshis into border areas of Assam, where, by then, JMB would have already pushed enough activists of its own to make further trouble. Assam is already facing threat of disintegration consequent to demand for a separate Bodoland and for UT status by two Hill Districts. The Muslim-majority districts, abetted by the Muslim extremists and JMB activists, will be third entity vociferously voicing for further vivisection of Assam.

NOTES

1. Sabri Bandopadhyay and Debesh Chakraborty, *Migration to the North-Eastern Region and Problems of Security* in Sanjukta Bhattacharya and Rochana Das (ed), *Perspectives on India's North-East,* 1998.

2. See Chapter 1.
3. Verghese, 1997.
4. *See* notes 6 and 15 below.
5. As soon as the General Election to Indian Parliament were announced by the Election Commission in June of that year, AASU demanded the deletion of nearly 5 lakh foreigners from the Electoral Rolls of the State, terming them as "illegal immigrants".
6. This profound and far-sighted observation by C.S. Mullan has been quoted appreciatively as often as it has been deprecated as a mischievous British ploy to divide the Hindus and Muslims, depending upon the identity and proclivity of the analyst.
7. Goswami, A. and Gogoi, T.K., "Immigration and Demographic Transformation of Assam, 1901-71", in B.L. Adbi (ed), *North-East Region: Problems and Prospects of Development* (Chandigarh CRRID), 1984, cited by Sri Radha Datta in *Strategic Analysis,* March 2000, monthly publication of the IDSA.
8. Sanjay Hazarika, "Insurgency in North-East India" in B. Pakem (ed), *Insurgency in North-East India,* 1997.
9. Weiner, Myron, *Security, Stability and International Migration, in International Security,* Volume 17, No. 3, Winter 1992-93, pp. 91-126.
10. Assam Recorder, 21-1-1999, p. 27856.
11. Luckily for it, Sylhet went out of Assam, minus its Karimganj Subdivision, on 15 August 1947.
12. Saadullah led three Ministries in Assam consequent to the elections held in 1937, under the provisions of Government of India Act, 1935.
13. Guha, Amalendu, 1977.
14. Wavell, *Viceroy's Journal.*
15. Excerpts from the 1931 Census Report, cited by Guha, Amalendu, 1977.
16. An ultra liberal, leftist academic, who has found nothing right with any post Narasimha Rao (1991-96) Governments in power since 1996 and would go to any lengths to liberate them, and support any anti-India resolutions on the nuclear issue at the UN or any other international fora which condemns the NDA Government's Nuclear Policy, recently dubbed Mullan's insightful 1931 observations as "mischievous" without explaining why in a 1998 article in an equally BJP-phobic fortnightly, published from the South.
17. The data cited here is from a Bangladesh Family Planning Department booklet of November 1994.
18. Critics of Nehru accused him and Indian officialdom of not learning from the history of unchecked influx of immigrants into Assam for the last 50 years and more. This provision should never have been written into the Pact. It left the door ajar for the subsequent mischief. Not only large number of people returned to Assam but Pakistan made use of the provision for propaganda purposes. To make matter worse, and as should have been anticipated, there was hardly any reverse flow out of Assam.
19. It should be a subject of an interesting and rewarding inquiry by a scholar or an eminent judge to determine the reason for such a decision in the East. Because of a proper decision in the west, the refugees from the West Pakistan

were able to stort afresh from scratch and made a success of it generally, many even rising to the very top in the fields of their chosen endeavour. On the other hand, why the refugees in the East were kept on doles and for years, rendering them mendicants, is beyond comprehension. Most remained refugees for years on end, fewer ever rising to positions of eminence in any sphere of life. Given equal chances, they should have fared as well, if not better, than their brethren in the west. Or, does the whole thing have to do with the different character traits of the Punjabis and the Assamese or Bengalis? One does not know the answer.

20. It is easy to see that the Indian generosity in this provision and in subsequent relaxations is informed by the humanitarian considerations but is bereft of the hard-nosed realities of political calculus. Not only was it never reciprocated by Pakistan, but it was also made a butt of wild and unsubstantiated accusations by that country. The price of all this generosity of Delhi was, of course, paid by the already hard-pressed Assam.
21. Cited by Verghese 1996.
22. Cited by Verghese 1996.
23. This is Mahanta, enjoying the first flush of power, after taking over in (end) 1985, and obviously, the idealism and sincerity of his convictions are still to desert him. But he certainly could not be comfortable with such thoughts today, having failed to have achieved his goals during his two stints as Chief Minister. The issue, detection and expulsion of foreigners, on which they had mounted a 7 years agitation, remains where it was before he assumed the reins of power in 1985: UNRESOLEVED and SIMMERING! The foreigners expelled by him during his 10-year stint in power, did not cross three figures. During his second stint, the chair mattered more than the mission!
24. Lt Gen (Retd) SK Sinha, PVSM, Governor of Assam, Insurgency in Assam, the *USI* Journal, July-September 1998.
25. These elections, boycotted and actively or violently opposed by AASU and AAGSP, were an unmitigated disaster. It left 3-5,000 people dead.
26. A serious charge the critics laid at their door was the students' agreeing to 1971 as the cut-off date (with minor concessions), the very formula offered to them by Indira Gandhi five-year back which they had haughtily spurned. The unsaid but clearly implied accusation was they had unnecessarily plunged Assam into five years of violence, destruction and disruption.
27. Lt Gen (Retd) SK Sinha, Governor Assam, in his lecture at the USI, New Delhi on 29 July 1998, excerpted in the *USI* Journal, July-September 1998.
28. For details of this meeting, see *Times of India* of 13-11-1996. Other related information is culled from its issue dated 2-2-1997.
29. It was reported that it was UPPA's Abdul Mohib Majumdar who had conceptualized the IMDT Act of 1983 in the first place, and had got it later incorporated in the 1985 Assam Accord.
30. *Times of India* 13-12-2000.
31. *Hindu* of 24-4-2000; Wasbir Hussain, *Of Natives and Aliens.*
32. September 1998 and September 1999 talks were held at Guwahati; and the March 1999 and May 2000 rounds were at New Delhi.
33. Barun Das Gupta, *The Hindu,* 28-5-2000.

34. Verghese, B.C., et al., 1980; Hussain, M., 1993.
35. They are the unfortunate Chakmas displaced by the Kaptai Dam in the Chittagong Hills Tract.
36. No Census was taken in Assam in 1981, and the 1991 Census omitted all denominational figures for states.
37. Nagaland had become a separate state in 1963. In January 1972, Meghalaya (with Manipur and Tripura) achieved statehood and Mizoram and Arunachal Pradesh got UT status. Assam had "lost" all these territories in less than a decade.
38. Cited in *Times of India* 5-12-1991
39. Sanjay Hazarika worked for the *New York Times* in the first half of the 1990s and carried out this study for the American Academy of Art and Science, Toronto University.
40. This speaks volumes for the value system of some Indians and their sense of and regard for nation's interests. They provide all these documents to the illicit immigrants for a consideration, enabling them to get Indian Citizenship overnight. It is a crying shame. The counterparts and partners-in-crime of these anti-national Indians are the political parties and other entities who vehemently espouse the cause of there illicit immigrants (turned "Indian nationals") and thwart all efforts at their deportation.
41. The West Dinajpur district was divided into two districts of North and South Dinajpur, effective 1 April 1992.
42. *The Outlook,* 2-8-1999.
43. Saikat Neogi, "Bangladesh Infiltration into West Bengal," in the *Organizer Weekly,* 14-4-1994.
44. The story headed, *List revision rakes up infiltration issue,* datelined Calcutta is by Santanu Bannerjee, *Indian Express,* 2-6-1999.
45. Cited by Saikat Neogi, in his, "Bangladeshi Infiltration into West Bengal," *The Organiser Weekly,* 14-4-1994.
46. Cited in *Times of India,* 5-12-1991.
47. Surinder Awasthi, *Times of India,* 23-1-1992.
48. An official cited by Awasthi, n. 47.
49. Asian Records, 22-1-1999, p. 27856.
50. Samudra Gupta Kashyap, "Indo-Bangla Border still a free-way for all," *Indian Express* 5-6-2002.
51. Some intelligence Reports suggest that the outfits at sers 12(MLTA) and 13 (MULTA) are different names of the same outfit.
52. A report in *Assam Daily* of 5-2-1995.
53. *Times of India,* 23-11-1998.
54. *The Hindu,* 21-9-1999.
55. Syed Liaquat Ali, *Hindustan Times,* 10-8-2001.
56. Seema Sangupta, *The Pioneer,* 19 Jan. 2007.
57. *Ibid.*

TERRORISM IN INDIA'S NORTH-EAST A GATHERING STORM

TERRORISM IN INDIA'S NORTH-EAST
A Gathering Storm
(In 3 Volumes)
(Volume-2)

Col. Ved Prakash

PUBLICATIONS

KALPAZ PUBLICATIONS

DELHI-110052

Terrorism in India's North-East
A Gathering Storm

Rs. 2500 (Set)

ISBN: 81-7835-660-0 (Set)
ISBN: 81-7835-661-9 (Vol. 1)

Published in 2008 in India by
Kalpaz Publications
C-30, Satyawati Nagar,
Delhi-110052
E-mail: kalpaz@hotmail.com
Phone : 9212729499

Laser Type Setting by: Quick Media, Delhi
Printed at : Singhal Print Media, Delhi

DEDICATED TO

My grandson, Aryan Sharma,
with
a fervent plea to the present generation to
render his generation the world over
safe from the scourge of terrorism

Contents

7

Terrorist/Insurgent Groups in Assam

This chapter deals with the terrorist and insurgent outfits operating in Assam, ending up with a timeline of incidents where available. The information is from the open sources, including the internet and has been duly acknowledged.

TERRORIST/INSURGENT GROUPS OF ASSAM

Proscribed Terrorist/Insurgent Groups

- National Democratic Front of Bodoland (NDFB)
- United Liberation Front of Asom (ULFA)

Active Terrorist/Insurgent Groups

- Adivasi Cobra Force (ACF)
- Dima Halim Daogah (DHD)
- Hmar People's Convention-Democracy (HPC-D)
- Kamtapur Liberation Organisation (KLO)
- Muslim United Liberation Tigers of Assam (MULTA)
- United People's Democratic Solidarity (UPDS)

Inactive Terrorist/Insurgent Groups

- Adam Sena (AS)
- Adivasi Security Force (ASF)
- All Assam Adivasi Suraksha Samiti (AAASS)
- Barak Valley Youth Liberation Front (BVYLF)
- Bodo Liberation Tigers (BLT)
- Gorkha Tiger Force (GTF)
- Harkat-ul- Jehad (HUJ)
- Harkat-ul-Mujahideen (HUM)

- Islamic Liberation Army of Assam (ILAA)
- Islamic Sevak Sangh (ISS)
- Islamic United Reformation Protest of India (IURPI)
- Karbi National Volunteers (KNV)
- Karbi People's Front (KPF)
- Koch-Rajbongshi Liberation Organisation (KRLO)
- Muslim Liberation Army (MLA)
- Muslim Security Council of Assam (MSCA)
- Muslim Security Force (MSF)
- Muslim Tiger Force (MTF)
- Muslim United Liberation Front of Assam (MULFA)
- Muslim Volunteer Force (MVF)
- People's United Liberation Front (PULF)
- Rabha National Security Force (RNSF)
- Revolutionary Muslim Commandos (RMC)
- Tiwa National Revolutionary Force (TNRF)
- United Liberation Front of Barak Valley (ULFBV)
- United Liberation Militia of Assam (ULMA)
- United Muslim Liberation Front of Assam (UMLFA)

NATIONAL DEMOCRATIC FRONT OF BODOLAND (NDFB)—TERRORIST GROUP OF ASSAM

Formation

The National Democratic Front of Bodoland (NDFB) was formed on October 3, 1986. The outfit was originally established as the Bodo Security Force (BdSF) under the leadership of Ranjan Daimary. On November 25, 1994, the BdSF rechristened itself as the NDFB.

The outfit is currently observing a cease-fire agreement with the Government.

Objectives

The NDFB was formed with the purported objective of securing a 'Sovereign Bodoland' in the areas north of the river Brahmaputra.

According to the 'constitution' of the outfit, which was adopted on March 10, 1998, nearly twelve years after its formation, the objectives of the outfit are the following.

- Liberate Bodoland from the Indian expansionism and occupation;

- Free the Bodo nation from the colonialist exploitation, oppression and domination;
- Establish a Democratic Socialist Society to promote Liberty, Equality and Fraternity; and
- Uphold the integrity and sovereignty of Bodoland.

Another significant demand of the NDFB concerns the script of the Bodo language. Currently, the Bodo language is written in Devnagri script; NDFB, whose members are mostly Christians and prefer to use the Roman script.

Leadership

The NDFB is headed by its 'chairman', Ranjan Daimary alias D R Nabla. However, in recent times, most of the outfit's top leadership have either been arrested or have surrendered.

The 'Vice President' Dhiren Boro was arrested in Gangtok, Sikkim's capital, on January 1, 2003. Its 'general secretary', B Swmkhwr alias Govinda Basumatary was arrested earlier, on November 25, 2002.

On June 5, 2004, Bhutan handed over the head of the NDFB's 'central headquarters', Lt. B Udang alias Udang K R Brahma to the Indian authorities.

Finance secretary, Niteswar Basumatary alias B J Jabda surrendered to the Assam Police authorities in Guwahati on March 17, 2004.

NDFB's deputy commander-in-chief, Bijoy Boro, was arrested in Bangkok during July 2004 and was subsequently deported to India. At present he is under the custody of the Assam Police.

The 'publicity secretary', 'Lieutenant' B Irakdao is reported to be missing following the Bhutanese military operations in December 2003.

Areas of Operation

The areas in the north and north-west of the river Brahmaputra in Assam form the main expanse of operation of the outfit. The NDFB is traditionally active in the Bongaigaon, Kokrajhar, Darrang, Barpeta, Dhubri, Nalbari and Sonitpur districts. It is also known to be active in the Garo Hills region of Meghalaya, close to the Assam-Meghalaya border.

In the year 2004, the outfit's activities have been reported from Nalbari, Barpeta, Dhubri, Sonitpur, Kokrajhar, Bongaigaon, Chirang and Karbi Anglong districts.

Cadre Strength

Prior to the Bhutan operations, the strength of Bodoland Army, the armed wing of the NDFB, was estimated to be around 3500. Most of its cadres were based in the 12 camps located in southern Bhutan. However, a large number of cadres either surrendered or were arrested during and after the operations. The strength of the outfit, at present according to sources, is not expected to be more than 2000. Most of these cadres are based in the outfit's camps in Myanmar and Bangladesh. Additionally, there are several temporary camps in different locations of Arunachal Pradesh and in the Garo Hills region of Meghalaya.

Arms and Ammunition

The NDFB cadres have access to sophisticated arms and ammunition. They have been found to be using AK Series rifles, light machine guns, M-16 rifles, rocket propelled grenades, mortars and Chinese-make grenades. Cadres are trained in making and planting improvised explosive devices.

Linkages

The NDFB acts in collaboration with the ULFA. In addition, the NDFB shares a close relationship with the other outfits like the Kamatapur Liberation Organisation (KLO), the Achik National Volunteers Council (ANVC) and the National Socialist Council of Nagaland-Khaplang (NSCN-K). Unconfirmed reports also suggest linkages between the Maoists of Nepal and the NDFB.

According to a list submitted by the Indian authorities to their counterparts in Bangladesh, the NDFB maintains at least two camps in the Khagrachari and Tangail districts of that country.

Prior to its dislodgment from Bhutan, the outfit was reported to have established working relationship with certain elements in Bhutan. Several Bhutanese officials were reported to have visited the training camps located inside Bhutan and have been alleged to openly aiding the NDFB cadres.

NDFB, along with the ULFA, on various occasions was found to be allegedly channelling its funds through the "Bhutanese diplomatic bag" to their leaders based in Southeast Asian capitals.

The Chin National Liberation Army (CNLA), a militant outfit of Myanmar, has also supplied arms and ammunition to the NDFB in the past.

Negotiations for Peace

The NDFB, on October 8, 2004, announced a six-month long unilateral cease-fire with effect from October 15. The move was not reciprocated by the Government and security force operations continued against the outfit, amidst threats of a pull out by the outfit. At the end of the ceasefire period, the outfit further extended the truce on April 15. Meanwhile, the Assam Government released Govinda Basumatary, the arrested general secretary, to open a channel of communication with the outfit's top leadership reportedly based in Bangladesh. Several parleys between the outfit's leadership and representatives of the Union Government and Government of Assam were held in different parts of the State and New Delhi. It resulted in the signing of a tripartite cease-fire agreement on May 25, 2005, at New Delhi.

UNITED LIBERATION FRONT OF ASOM (ULFA)— TERRORIST GROUP OF ASSAM

Formation

United Liberation Front of Asom (ULFA) was formed on April 7, 1979 by Bhimakanta Buragohain, Rajiv Rajkonwar alias Arabinda Rajkhowa, Golap Baruah alias Anup Chetia, Samiran Gogoi alias Pradip Gogoi, Bhadreshwar Gohain and Paresh Baruah at the Rang Ghar in Sibsagar to establish a "sovereign socialist Assam" through an armed struggle.

Leadership

Arabinda Rajkhowa is the 'Chairman' of ULFA. 'Vice Chairman' Pradip Gogoi was arrested on April 8, 1998, and is currently in judicial custody at Guwahati. 'General Secretary' Anup Chetia is under detention in the Bangladeshi Dhaka after being arrested on December 21, 1997. The outfit's founding member and ideologue Bhimakanta Buragohain, 'Publicity Secretary' Mithinga Daimary and 'Assistant Secretary' Bolin Das were arrested during the military operations in Bhutan in December 2003. Earlier, 'Cultural Secretary' Pranati Deka was arrested at Phulbari in the West Garo Hills district of Meghalaya.

The ULFA has a clearly partitioned political and military wing. Paresh Barua heads the military wing as the outfit's 'commander-in-chief.

Following the military operations in Bhutan in December 2003, most of its top leadership reportedly operates from unspecified locations in Bangladesh. According to reports, ULFA is in the process of relocating its camps in Myanmar, Mon district of Nagaland, Garo Hills of Meghalaya and Tirap and Changlang districts of Arunachal Pradesh.

Areas of Activity and Influence

The ULFA's organisational structure is divided into four zones. The zones and their areas of influence are enumerated below :

East Districts	*West Districts*	*Central Districts*	*South Districts*
(Purb Mandal)	(Paschim Mandal)	(Madhya Mandal)	(Dakshin Mandal)
Lakhimpur	Dhubri	Darrang	Hailakandi
Jorhat	Kokrajhar	Karbi Anglong	NC Hills
Sibsagar	Bongaigaon	Nagaon	Cachar Hills
Tinsukia	Goalpara	Morigaon	Karimganj
Dibrugarh	Barpeta	Dhemaji	
Bokajan div. of Karbi Anglong	Nalbari	Part of Sonitpur	
Golaghat	South Kamrup	North Kamrup	
Part of Sonitpur			

A military wing of the ULFA, the Sanjukta Mukti Fouj (SMF) was formed on March 16, 1996. SMF has three full-fledged battalions (Bn): the 7th, 28th and 709th. The remaining battalions exist only on paper—at best they have strengths of a company or so. Their allocated spheres of operation are as follows:

- 7th Bn (HQ- Sukhni). Responsible for defence of GHQ
- 8th Bn Nagaon, Morigaon, Karbi Anglong
- 9th Bn Golaghat, Jorhat, Sibsagar
- 11* Bn Kamrup, Nalbari
- 27th Bn Barpeta, Bongaigaon, Kokrajhar
- 28th Bn Tinsukia, Dibrugarh
- 709th Bn Kalikhola

Links

The ULFA sought shelter in the forests on the Indo-Bhutan border from the early 1990s and established several camps in the forest areas of southern Bhutan. Over the years, it reportedly developed linkages with several officers and personnel of the Royal Bhutan Army (RBA) and Police—which ensured, among other things, a steady flow of rations, logistical support as well as aid and contacts for money laundering. The ULFA's Bhutan set-up had a reported strength of around 2000 cadres spread across the outfit's 'General Head Quarters', it's 'Council Head Quarters', a 'Security-cum-Training Camp' and a well-concealed 'Enigma Base'. Numbering around 30 in all, the major camps of the ULFA in Bhutan included:

1. Mithundra
2. Gobarkunda
3. Panbang
4. Diyajima
5. Pemagatsel Complex

   (*i*) Khar (*ii*) Shumar (*iii*) Nakar
6. Chaibari
7. Marthong
8. Gerowa
9. Sukhni (Merungphu): 'General HQ'
10. Melange
11. Phukaptong: 'Council HQ'

12. Dalim-Koipani (Orang)
13. Neoli Debarli

Most camps and other establishment of the ULFA were in Sandrup Jongkhar, a district in southern Bhutan that borders Assam's Nalbari district. The RBA is reported to have destroyed all the outfit's camps and observation posts during the military operations launched in December 2003.

In 1986, ULFA first established contacts with the then unified National Socialist Council of Nagaland (NSCN) and the Kachin Independence Army (KIA) of Myanmar for training and arms. ULFA linked up with the Kachins through the 'good offices' of the Naga rebels. It learnt the rudiments of insurgent tactics from the Kachins (who reportedly charged Rupees 100,000 per trainee).

Subsequently, links were established with Pakistan's Inter Services Intelligence (ISI) and the Afghan Mujahideen. Reports indicate that at least 200 ULFA activists received training in Pakistan and Afghanistan. Seized documents and interrogation of some arrested activists revealed that the Defense Forces Intelligence (DFI) of Bangladesh had also trained ULFA cadres in the Sylhet district.

ULFA also has a number of camps in Bangladesh. The ISI and the Directorate General of Field Intelligence (DGFI) of Bangladesh are agencies which reportedly facilitate the ULFA's presence and operations. Several details of ULFA's Bangladesh connection were exposed when the Bangladeshi authorities arrested its leader Anup Chetia on December 21, 1997. He is currently under detention at the high-security Dhaka Central Jail. The main charges against Chetia include illegal entry into Bangladesh, possession of two forged Bangladeshi passports, possession of an unauthorised satellite telephone and illegal possession of foreign currency of countries as diverse as the US, UK, Switzerland, Thailand, Philippines, Spain, Nepal, Bhutan, Belgium, Singapore and others. Two other accomplices, identified as Babul Sharma and Laxmi Prasad, were also arrested along with Chetia.

Apart from running training camps, ULFA launched several income generating projects in Bangladesh. It has set up a number of firms in Dhaka, including media consultancies and soft drink manufacturing units. Besides it is reported to own three hotels, a private clinic, and two motor driving schools in Dhaka. Paresh Barua is reported to personally own or has controlling interests in several businesses in Bangladesh, including a tannery, a chain of departmental stores, garment factories, travel agencies, shrimp trawlers and transport and investment companies.

ULFA's camps in Bangladesh have been functioning since 1989, at which time there were 13 to 14 such camps. Commencing initially with using Bangladesh as a safe haven and training location, ULFA gradually expanded its network to include operational control of activities and the receipt and shipment of arms in transit before they finally entered India. The Muslim United Liberation Tigers of Assam (MULTA) and Muslim United Liberation Front of Assam (MULFA) are the chief suppliers of arms for the ULFA through Bangladesh. Owing to greater vigil along the known routes of ULFA arms flow, the group has, in recent times, been making attempts to set up bases in Meghalaya, especially in the West Garo Hills to coordinate the transit of arms coming through Bangladesh.

ULFA has for long maintained close linkages with the Pakistan's ISI which procured several passports for Paresh Baruah and other ULFA cadres. Several ULFA cadres have also received arms training from the ISI at various training centres in Pakistan, close to the Afghanistan border. The top ULFA leadership was also in close touch with certain officers of the Pakistani High Commission in Bangladesh, who have arranged for their passport in various names and travel to Karachi, from where they have been taken to the terrorist training centres run by the ISI and its affiliates. ULFA had also announced its support for Pakistan during the Kargil War. They described the Pakistani intruders—primarily Pakistani Army regulars and Afghan mercenaries—as 'freedom fighters'. Some children of top ULFA leaders are reportedly studying in the USA and Canada under ISI protection. Reports indicate that the ULFA's mouthpiece, ULFA's website newsletter Swadhinata also known as 'Freedom', receives editorial support from ISI agents inside Pakistan. It was in 'Freedom' that the ULFA first supported the Pakistanis during the Kargil War. The ISI has provided ULFA cadres with arms training, safe havens, funds, arms and ammunition. Training has been given at camps in Pakistan, Bangladesh and Bhutan. At least 300 ULFA cadres were also trained at Rawalpindi and other locations in Pakistan. The training included courses in the use of rocket launchers, explosives and assault weapons. Paresh Baruah has been regularly visiting Karachi since 1992-93. He is also reported to have met Osama bin Laden in 1996 during a visit to Karachi. The ULFA leader was reportedly taken to a camp on the Pakistan-Afghanistan border, where he not only received assurance of military help in the form of arms and ammunition, but also assurances of co-operation and logistical support of all international organisations owing allegiance to bin Laden, including the International Jehad Council, the Tehrik-ul-Jehad, Harkat-ul-Jehadi-e-lslami (HuJI), apart from the Al Qaeda.

The ISI has also trained ULFA terrorists in counter intelligence, disinformation and use of sophisticated weapons and explosives. Pakistan has facilitated the visits of Paresh Baruah and other ULFA leaders to Singapore, Thailand and other countries, and a channel for the transfer of funds and arms has been created. Several *Madrassas* (seminaries) and mosques sponsored by the ISI in the Sylhet and Cox's Bazaar areas are being used to hoard and transfer arms procured by the ULFA from Thailand and Myanmar. The ISI largesse enabled ULFA to buy arms in Cambodia, paying for these in hard currency routed through Nepal. The ISI also 'introduced' ULFA to LTTE transporters who, for a fee, undertook to transport arms from Southeast Asia into Myanmar. In April 1996, Bangladesh seized more than 500 AK-47 rifles, 80 machineguns, 50 rocket launchers and 2,000 grenades from two ships off Cox's Bazaar. Four Tamils were among those arrested.

Co-operation between various terrorist organisations in India's north-east and foreign groups was formalised with the formation of the Indo-Burmese Revolutionary Front (IBRF) in 1989. The IBRF was made up initially of the NSCN-K, ULFA, United Liberation Front of Bodoland, Kuki National Front (KNF) (all from India) and Chin National Front {Myanmar). Paresh Baruah is reported to have paid a substantial sum of money to the Kachins for the first large consignment of weapons from Thailand. Manerplaw in lower Myanmar on the border with Thailand is the stronghold of the rebel Karen National Union which, in 1993, is reported to have delivered, from the Cambodian arms market, AK-56 rifles, machine guns, rocket-propelled guns and anti-tank rifles to the ULFA. The organisation's cadres have identified an arms dealer, an ethnic Kachin and wife of an assassinated Manipuri rebel Themba Song. The Communist Party of Burma is known to have gifted some weapons, mainly Chinese-made M10 rifles, to ULFA and Naga terrorist organisations.

Arrested ULFA cadres have claimed that Baruah used to smuggle heroin, procured in Myanmar, into Assam as part of "a personal operation". According to surrendered ULFA cadres, the ULFA terrorists had also crossed over into China via Bhutan and established contact with the Chinese Army. The group, on the basis of these contacts, had a rendezvous with a Chinese ship on the high seas in March 1995 during which a weapons' consignment was transferred to them. A further consignment ultimately landed up in Bhutan in 1999, though it was actually acquired in 1997. ULFA also runs profitable narcotics business in Myanmar and Thailand. A close nexus between ULFA and the Liberation Tigers of Tamil Eelam (LTTE) had also been reported. The LTTE is reported to have trained various ULFA cadres in explosives handling.

(*Source* : http://www.satp.org/satporgtp/countries/india/states/assam/terrorist_outfits/ulfa.htm)

INCIDENTS INVOLVING UNITED LIBERATION FRONT OF ASOM (ULFA)

2006

- December 31: Two unidentified ULFA militants are killed and four others, Arun Thapa, Jagu Dorji, Veer Bahadur and Samuty Chakma, are arrested during a counter-insurgency operation at Mendo in the Lohit district of Arunachal Pradesh. A cache of arms and explosives, including one 7.65 mm Italian automatic pistol, two local-muzzle loaded rifles, one magazine, two rounds of cartridges, two fired cases, along with a radio set, a sony MP4 recorder, and a mobile phone, is recovered from the incident site. The arrested ULFA cadres confess during interrogation that they were planning to target security forces on the eve of New Year in Lohit as well as in the Tinsukia district of Assam.

- December 30: A huge cache of arms and explosives, including several gelatine sticks, nine detonators and small arms, 90 pieces of assorted explosives weighing nearly two kilograms, was recovered from two arms suppliers, Pradeep Basumatary and Bangal Mushahary, who were arrested from an unspecified place near Runikhata in the Chirang district. They confess to having procured arms and explosives from a company based in Hyderabad and later supplied the same to the Assam and Meghalaya-based outfits, including the ULFA and NDFB.

  Three persons, Kishore Deka, Pankaj Kalita and Nayan Thakuria, are arrested from Betkuchi under Gorchuk police outpost in Guwahati city, for serving an extortion note worth INR 50,000 on a fake ULFA letter pad to a trader at Fancy Bazaar.

- December 28: A search operation is carried out at Mariani in the Jorhat district along the Assam-Nagaland border. One person is arrested. However, Assam Police neither confirm nor deny the report. According to police sources, both the Adivasi Nationalist Liberation Army and ULFA cadres are making a quick getaway by crossing the border to Nagaland, which has become a safe haven for various militant factions.

- December 27: A police constable is seriously injured when the ULFA militants opened fire on police personnel who were searching for Mantu Saikia alias Bijoy Das, a cadre of the outfit, at Bhatiapar Rupahimukh in the Sibsagar district

  One kilogram of brown sugar worth INR 1.30 crore is recovered from six militants of the ULFA and NDFB, who are arrested from a hotel at Gossaigaon town in the Kokrajhar district. While three ULFA cadres are identified as Sumi Ram Rava, Budhadev Rava and Rupa Rava, three suspected cadres of the NDFB are identified as Monu Basumatari, Sagar Basumatari and Sintu Musahari.

  Assam Police confirms that Chief Minister Tarun Gogoi is at the top of ULFA's hit list. The recent arrest of ULFA cadres in Dibrugarh and Sibsagar districts in Upper Assam and their subsequent interrogation revealed that the ULFA was "planning something big to attract the Centre's attention towards its demands."

- December 26: A self-styled woman 'corporal of the 28 battalion' of the ULFA, Karabi Phukan alias Bandita Phukan, was arrested by security force personnel during a counter-insurgency operation at Teokghat under Sonari police station in the Sibsagar district.
- December 25: A cadre of the Bravo company of the ULFA, Biswajit Bora alias Raktim Suraj Gogoi, is reported to have surrendered at Maibela in the Sibsagar district. He deposited some Chinese-make grenades, three gelatin sticks, eight fuse wires and 15 rounds of AK-47 ammunition.

  Assam Government confirms that three ULFA militants, Samiran Baruah, Numal Chetia and Bonti Gogoi, who were arrested in Sibsagar district on December 23, gave Dibrugarh police a list of the names and addresses of the ULFA militants operating in the capital city.
- December 24: A school teacher, Narayan Sapkota, was arrested from Guwahati and is later remanded by a city court to police custody for five days, for helping ULFA militants in their extortion drive in Assam's capital.

  The Army recovers 6,700 copies of an ULFA propaganda bulletin from a vehicle near Sonari town in the Sibsagar district.

  The ULFA-backed PCG rejects Prime Minister Manmohan Singh's offer of "safe passage" to top ULFA leaders as a 'political gimmick'.
- December 23: A woman cadre of the ULFA, identified as Bobby Chetry alias Manisha Sarma, is arrested by the city police during a search operation at an unspecified place near the Guwahati Medical College Hospital.

  A court remands Samiran Baruah, the mastermind of the recent blasts triggered by ULFA in Guwahati, along with two of his accomplices, Numal Chetia and Bonti Gogoi, for three days. They were arrested at Abhaypur near Sonari town in the Sibsagar district. According to their confession, the '28th battalion' of ULFA was planning bigger terror attacks than those triggered recently in the Guwahati city.

  A grenade was hurled by suspected ULFA militants at a shop at Maharipara Bazar Chowk under Goreswar police station in the Baska district. However, the grenade fails to explode. The owner of the shop, Chita Pandit, earlier served an extortion note, failed to pay the ransom amount.
- December 22: The Central intelligence agencies revel, following the arrest of a ULFA militant, Prabal Saikia, from Shillong on December 19, that the ULFA is trying to use Shillong-Cherrapunjee and Shillong-Pynursla routes and other parts of Jaintia Hills in Meghalaya for trans-

shiftment of arms from Bangladesh and exfiltration of its cadres to Bangladesh.

Prime Minister Manmohan Singh reportedly told Assam Chief Minister Tarun Gogoi that the Union Government would offer safe passage to top ULFA leaders if they come forward for direct peace talks with the Government.

- December 21: A trader, Pawan Newar, is shot dead by ULFA militants at Beltola area in Guwahati city.

  An improvised explosive device, planted on a bicycle, is triggered by suspected ULFA militants in the Athgaon area of Guwahati city, injuring at least 20 persons. "The ULFA was behind the blast," says Avinash Joshi, Kamrup District (Metro) Deputy Commissioner.

  A grenade is exploded by the ULFA injuring two persons including a trader, Babulal Agarwalla, in Gaurisagar area of Sibsagar district. Earlier, Babulal had received an extortion note from the ULFA.

  A ULFA militant, Bodhiya Bhumij, and a linkman of the outfit belonging to Bangladesh, Dildar Hussain, are arrested at Ticklipam under Namsai police station in the Lohit district of Arunachal Pradesh.

- December 19: A 'commander' of the ULFA '27th Battalion', 'captain' Pallav Saikia alias Ananta Kakati, is arrested along with his wife Moromi at an unspecified place of Meghalaya. Moromi, earlier arrested by the Royal Bhutan Army during the operation to flush out the ULFA militants from Bhutanese territory, rejoined the ULFA after she was released by Indian authorities.

  A factional clash among the ULFA militants occurs leaving three militants, including 'commander' of the 28th battalion, Prabal Neog alias Benu Bora, dead at unspecified places inside the Manabhum Reserve Forest in the Lohit district of Arunachal Pradesh.

- December 17: The ULFA threatens to mobilise public resistance against the Oil India Limited's (OIL) attempt to carry out seismic survey on Brahmaputra river bed to search for hydrocarbon.

- December 15: A person belonging to the Adi tribe, identified as Biru Tayeng, and a ULFA linkman, Keshab Bora, are arrested by security force personnel during a search operation at Sarkholia Chapori along the Assam-Arunachal Pradesh border. A single-barrel gun, explosives and some ULFA-related literature are recovered from Tayeng's possession.

  Assam Legislative Assembly appeals to the ULFA to withdraw its call for a boycott of the 33rd National Games scheduled from February 9 to 18, 2007.

- December 13: At least four Army personnel are injured as a bomb, planted inside a pressure cooker by the ULFA militants, explodes at Kakotibari in the Sibsagar district.
- December 12: Two ULFA militants, identified as Kolia Moran alias Swapna Moran and Menua, surrender to the 2 Bihar Regiment at Tinsukia. They also deposited three hand grenades, 10 mines, a pistol and explosive materials to the authorities.

  Hundreds of people blocked the Dibrugarh-Lahowal-Tengakhat-Duliajan road in the Dibrugarh for more than three hours demanding the release of suspected ULFA link-man Bhaimon Hazarika, who was reportedly arrested on charges of providing logistical support to the militants involved in the explosion on December 8 that killed at least five persons. State Government asks top ULFA leaders like 'chairman' Arabinda Rajkhowa and 'commander-in-chief, Paresh Barua to take part in the peace talks with the Centre.

  Chief Minister Tarun Gogoi stated that the Assam Government is not opposed to the PCG initiatives for facilitating the talks between the militant outfit and the Centre. However, he clarifies that his Government does not think the PCG to be the representative of the people of Assam.
- December 11: Forest and Environment Minister Rockybul Hussain informed the State Legislative Assembly that at least 1,051 cadres of various militant outfits, including the ULFA, were killed in encounters with the security forces since May 2001.

  A civil society organization, Dhubri Zilla Nagarik Manch (Dhubri District Citizen Forum), calls for a 12-hour general strike in the Dhubri district demanding the arrest of Abu Taher Bepari, the Legislator of Golokganj Assembly constituency, for his alleged links with the ULFA.
- December 10: Assam Police identifies Madhurjya Gohain, a cadre of '28 battalion' of the ULFA, as the mastermind of the December 8-IED explosion killing four police personnel and one civilian at Suraj Nagar under Tengakhat police station in the Dibrugarh district "Gohain is an expert in handling explosives," says an unnamed police officer.
- December 8: An IED planted by the ULFA blows up a requisitioned police convoy at Suraj Nagar under Tengakhat police station in the Dibrugarh district, killing four police personnel and the civilian driver. The ULFA claimed responsibility for the blast and said that the explosion was executed to avenge the killing of three of its members, including middle-rank leader Charan Majhi, by the police on November 3.
- December 6: Assam Government appeals to the ULFA to withdraw its call for sportspersons to stay away from the forthcoming National Games.

- December 5: A ULFA militant, Jiten Munda, is shot dead by security force personnel at village Torani under Pengeri police station in the Tinsukia district.
- December 4: A link-woman of the ULFA, identified as Namita Kalita, is arrested from Guwahati in the Kamrup district. "Namita was acting as a very important liaison person between the underground ULFA cadres and those who are in various jails, besides channeling funds for the rebel outfit," says Rajen Singh, the additional police chief of Guwahati city.

  Another woman cadre of the ULFA, Chayanika Bora alias Maini Bora, who was arrested from Gowal village under Teok police station on December 2-night, was remanded to police custody for seven days after she was produced in a court in the Jorhat district.
- December 2: A woman cadre of the ULFA, Chayanika Bora alias Maini Bora, is arrested during a search operation at Gowal village under Teok police station in the Jorhat district. Two more persons are also arrested for providing shelter to the ULFA cadre.

  The ULFA asks the Union Government to give a written commitment that the issue of Assam's 'sovereignty' will be discussed in the negotiations.
- December 1: An encounter between the security forces and suspected ULFA militants is reported from Dighaliagaon under Naharkatia police station in the Dibrugarh district.
- November 30: A SULFA cadre, Nripen Mohon, is shot dead by ULFA militants at Mohmora village in the Sibsagar district.
- November 30: Assam Police say that the ULFA has established links with the Liberation Tigers of Tamil Eelam (LTTE) of Sri Lanka. "The ULFA leadership has established diplomatic relations with the LTTE and there is evidence in that regard," informed an official of the Assam Police. "The ISI (Inter-Services Intelligence of Pakistan) introduced LTTE's arms suppliers to ULFA leaders and two Tamils were arrested in Cox's Bazaar in Bangladesh when a huge quantity of ammunition meant for the ULFA was seized," said the official, adding, that arms were also supplied to ULFA through Cambodia, for which the group paid "hard currency routed through Nepal." Reports added that the ISI had facilitated recent visits by top ULFA leaders, including its 'commander-in-chief, Paresh Baruah, to Singapore, Thailand and other countries.

  The Inspector General of Border Security Force of Assam, Meghalaya, Manipur and Nagaland Frontier, Jyoti Prakash Sinha, said that both the ISI and Bangladesh Nationalist Party (BNP) threatened' ULFA to dissuade itself from peace talks with the Government of India. He mentioned that on September 3, 2006, a meeting between the ULFA, ISI and BNP leaders was arranged at Hotel Agrabad in Dhaka, capital of Bangladesh. The meeting was attended by ULFA chief Paresh Barua, the ISI Brigadier T. K. Bax and BNP leader Tarique Rehman Zia, who is the son of former Bangladesh Prime Minister Khaleda Zia.

- November 29: Suspected ULFA militants trigger an IED blast blowing off a security convoy, killing one Army personnel, N. Yella Reddy, and injuring four Army personnel and two civilians at Asomiagaon under Joypore police station in the Dibrugarh district.

  A surrendered ULFA cadre, Bhaskar Saikia alias Mission Sonowal, is shot dead by unidentified gunmen at his residence in the Lengrai village of Tinsukia district.

  The Union Ministry of Home Affairs said that the ULFA has been recruiting unemployed youths and set up training camps in deep forests. The Union Minister of State for Home Affairs, S. Reghupathy, informed the Rajya Sabha (Upper House of Parliament) that the possibility of ULFA recruiting their cadres from neighbouring countries can not be ruled out.

  The Government is aware that the insurgent groups from Northeast have set up camps in the neighbouring countries, he added.

- November 28: Prime Minister Manmohan Singh said that the ULFA is under the grip of Pakistan's ISI. He told a 12-party delegation from Assam, led by former Assam Chief Minister Prafulla Mahanta, which met him in New Delhi that he was ready to restart talks with the ULFA but the group would first have to shake off the ISI yoke guiding its actions.

  The delegation had urged Dr. Singh to resume "unconditional" talks with the ULFA. Mahanta said after the meeting, "The PM said Centre is ready for talks (with ULFA) as and when they come out of the clutches of ISI."

  A ULFA militant, Lalit Moran, is shot dead by SF personnel in an encounter at Liton Hatigarh in Watiat village under Pengeri police station in the Tinsukia district. Suspected ULFA militants attacked Rangapara police station in the Sonitpur district with a grenade.

- November 27: A ULFA cadre, Joneshwar Sonowal, is arrested from Tengapathar under Talap police station in the Tinsukia district.

- November 24: A person, Madhu Debnath, who was injured in the November 23-explosion triggered by the ULFA at the railway station in Guwahati, succumbs to his injuries increasing the number of fatalities to four.

Army accuses Pakistan's external intelligence agency, the ISI, of planting "sleeper agents" among the immigrant population of Assam. The General Officer Commanding in Chief of the 4 Corps, Lt. General R. K. Chhabra, said: "The ISI that is backing ULFA in cooperation with the Directorate General of Forces Intelligence (DGFI) in Bangladesh has sleeper agents among migrants on river isles. ULFA leadership is in Bangladesh, thanks to ISI and DGFI. Jihadi groups from Bangladesh are providing arms and finance to ULFA.

The jihadi elements have taken root. They are not into terrorism in a big way, but involved in gun-running, fake currency rackets and drugs. They went to Bangladesh for training and are now lying low as sleeping agents of the ISI."

- November 23: Three persons, including a woman and a child, are killed and 11 others are injured when an explosion was triggered by suspected ULFA militants at the railway station in Guwahati.

  The victims are identified as Vinay Chauhan, a rickshaw-puller, his wife Reena Chauhan and their child Uday. The Cyclotrimethylenelrinitramine (RDX) planted in a cycle-rickshaw was reportedly detonated by the programmable timed delayed device.

  Sibsagar district police stated that only 40 per cent of the huge ransom extorted in the name of ULFA goes to the outfit, with the rest 60 per cent being invested in business by persons who are never suspected to be ULFA activists. This was revealed from the confession of two ULFA agents, Anupam Ojah and Anil Dutta, arrested earlier.

- November 22: An IED is exploded by suspected ULFA militants targeting a security convoy at an unspecified place near Naguapara village in the West Garo Hills district of Meghalaya.

- November 21: Assam Police confirm that elephants have destroyed several makeshift camps of the ULFA at chaporis (sandbank) along the River Neamati in the Jorhat district. "We had information about the rebels setting up camps on these small islands and were planning to take action. But the elephants did the job for us," said a senior police officer.

  Ranjit Das, a boat operator who was arrested earlier from the island of Majuli for helping ULFA militants going across the river, confesses to the Police that elephants had also forced the militants to change their travel plans.

  Militants prefer to cross the river by night but no boatman wants to take the risk now for fear of running into wild elephants on the sandbanks, said Ranjit.

- November 20: Paresh Deka, a constable arrested for his alleged links with the ULFA, is remanded to police custody. Ranjit Das, a boat operator, is arrested from the island of Majuli for helping ULFA militants going across the river Neamati in the Jorhat district.
- November 19: The 7th Battalion' of the ULFA has established camps at Kawaimari near Deothang in Bhutan. "With the intensified counter insurgency operations in Upper Asom districts, the 7th battalion of the militants had set up the camp in Kawaimari," informs the Special Branch of Assam Police, adding, "We are aware of their movement. Operations are on and the security forces had gunned down the commander of the 1st camp of the 7th battalion Dipak Deka on Friday night."
- November 17: An extortion note bearing signatures of two ULFA-backed PCG members, Lachit Bordoloi and Dilip Patgiri, is recovered from two persons, Rebot Bora and Pankaj Sarma, arrested during a search operation near the Guwahati Commerce College.

  The extortion note citing amount worth INR 20,000 was meant for D. Hojai, the Director of Health Services. Troops recover an IED planted by the ULFA under a culvert at Sengelimora village in the Sibsagar district.
- November 16: The ULFA-backed PCG member Indira Goswami announces her withdrawal from the peace process. "I am hurt by the lack of transparency," said Goswami, adding: "I am not a politician. And as such I feel hurt because of the delay in the peace talks process... I am primarily an author and would like to concentrate fully on creative work. I think I have fulfilled my role as peace facilitator and have succeeded in bringing the government and ULFA closer through the People's Consultative Group."
- November 15: At least eight ULFA militants, including a 'lance corporal of 27 battalion' Shankar Bora, are arrested from Bokolia under Howraghat police station. One Chinese grenade, an AK-47 magazine and INR 1.27 lakh are recovered from their possession.

  A ULFA militant Ashis Gohain, is arrested by police personnel in a search operation at the Assam State Transport Corporation bus terminus in Nagaon. An M-20 pistol is recovered from his possession. The ULFA demands protection of the rights of non-Bodo people in the Bodoland Territorial Council administered areas.

  The outfit refers to allegations about "a certain section" of the people extorting money from "non-Bodo indigenous people" residing in the Bodoland areas.

- November 14: The ULFA triggers an IED blast damaging crude oil pipeline of the Oil India Limited at Dishangpani in the Sibsagar district. The crude oil caught fire immediately after the explosion. However, the authorities managed to control the blaze before it caused more damage. At least seven kilograms of Cyclotrimethylenetrinitramine (also known as RDX), concealed in a pressure cooker by the ULFA, are recovered from a road at Sarupathar near Sapekhati in the Sibsagar district and later defused by SF personnel. Two detonators fixed with the RDX and some wires are also recovered from the incident site.

  An ULFA cadre, Bhaimon Gogoi alias Bidyut Chetia, arrested at Kokilamukh area in the Jorhat district, confesses to his interrogators that the outfit during its latest extortion drives in Majuli subdivision, extracted ransom worth INR 5,00,000 in two months.

  Bhutan's Ambassador in India, Dago Tshering, said: "We have no report whatsoever of the ULFA setting up any new camp inside Bhutan or operating from anywhere in the country. On our side, the Royal Bhutan Police (RBP) has been deployed to check or keep vigil over any militant influx, and on your side, we are aware of the SSB deployment for the same purpose."

- November 13: An ULFA link man, Monoranjan Sen, is arrested by SF personnel during a search operation at Golokganj Senparawas near Agomoni in the Dhubri district.

  A surrendered ULFA cadre, Basanta Kalita, is shot dead by unidentified gunmen at Luitpathar near Sualkuchi in the Kamrup district.

  A police personnel and two civilians are injured when suspected ULFA militants lobb a grenade at Superintendent of Police (Operations) Jitmal Doley's official residence at Panbazaar in Guwahati city.

  A suspected ULFA cadre, Monoranjan Sen alias Dinesh Sen, was arrested from Shernagar village under Golokganj police station in the Dhubri district. The Bharat Sanchar Nigam Limited Assam Telecom Circle receives from Assam Police a list of at least 97 mobile phone numbers suspected to have been used by ULFA militants in the Tinsukia district for verification. The Union Government conveys to the ULFA-backed People's Consultative Group members that counter-insurgency operations against the banned outfit will be stopped only after it gives a written commitment for holding direct talks with the Government. "The Centre has asked for a written commitment from ULFA about the date of holding talks," said Indira Goswami after an hour-long meeting with the National Security Advisor ML K. Narayanan.

- November 11: A ULFA militant, Thulonto Borgohan, is shot dead in an encounter with SF personnel at No. 1 Labour Enclave in the

Hukunpukhuri Tea Estate along Jaigyakhowa-Barekuri Road in Tinsukia district.

An ULFA cadre, Bhaimon Gogoi, is arrested at Nahatia area near Kokilamukh in the Jorhat district. A pistol, ammunition and three mobile SIM cards are also recovered from his possession. Gogoi confess during interrogation about a linkman harbouring ULFA cadres and helping them in extortion drives.

- November 12: Suspected ULFA militants trigger an explosion targeting an oil pipeline of the Oil India Limited at Habeda Tea Estate under Bordubi police station in the Tinsukia district. Another explosion is triggered at Ketujan in the same locality.

  A 'corporal' of the ULFA, Bhaikon Gogoi alias Mintu, is arrested by SF personnel following a brief encounter at Sasoni Ambari under Naharkotia police station in the Dibrugarh district. While another militant, Ram Gogoi, manages to escape from the encounter site, two radio sets and a couple of mobile phones are recovered from possession of the arrested militant.

- November 11 : Suspected ULFA militants trigger a bomb blast in a gas pipeline of the Oil India Limited at Dhekulajan under Tengakhat police station in the Tinsukia district.

- November 10: Two CRPF personnel, Bansi Lal and Khagen Chetia, are killed and eight others were injured in an ULFA-triggered IED explosion targeting two security convoys near Sadiya police station in the Tinsukia district.

  A grenade is hurled by ULFA militants at the residence of Nagaon district Superintendent of Police Krishna Das, injuring police personnel guarding the house.

  A bomb specialist of the ULFA, Monoranjan Borphukan alias Manab Baruah, surrenders before the District Magistrate of Dibrugarh, Ashutosh Agnihotri. Monoranjan deposits two hand grenades, 90 rounds Self Loaded Rifles cartridges, four grenade fuses and two detonators.

- November 9: The Union Government extends the proscription on the ULFA.

  An ULFA linkman, Biswajit Rai, is arrested in a search operation at Kachokhana area under Golokganj police station in the Dhubri district. Extortion notes, pads, a diary and incriminating documents are recovered from his possession.

  A 'corporal' of the '28th battalion' of the ULFA, Amal Hazarika alias Mrinal Barua alias Dipak, surrenders before the Jorhat District administration. Two grenades, 10 rounds of ammunition and the magazine of an M-16 rifle are deposited by him. Another ULFA cadre, Gopul Lonfoi, surrenders before Morigaon District Collector at the Army's Red Horns Division camp near Jagiroad in the Jorhat district.

- November 8: A child, Debojit Moran, is shot dead and his sister, Dipanjali Moran, is wounded in a cross fire between Army personnel and the ULFA militants at Mohong village under Pengeree police station in the Tinsukia district.

  Two bicycle-borne ULFA militants open fire with AK-47 rifles killing a grocery shop employee, Ghanashyam Das, at Kulhati Chatrashal under Hajo police station in the Kamrup district.

- November 7: Assam Governor, Lt. Gen. Ajai Singh, confirms involvement of the ULFA in the November 5 twin blasts at the Fancy Bazaar and Noonmati areas in Guwahati. Sections of the Hindi-speaking community, who settle in Guwahati, desert Assam following the November 5 bomb blasts triggered by the ULFA.

- November 6: An unidentified ULFA militant is killed in an encounter with the Police at Santinagar under Noonmati police station in the Guwahati city. Explosives, including 13 grenades, nine electric detonators and some wires are recovered from his possession.

  The Union Home Ministry convenes a meeting of senior army officials and central forces in New Delhi to review the security scenario in Assam. Home Secretary V. K. Duggal, while chairing the meeting, says that the involvement of the ULFA is suspected in the blasts. Duggal claims that the situation is under control and adequate security personnel are deployed in the State.

  The ULFA 'Charlie company commander', Jiten Dutta, claims that a "third force" has engineered the blasts in Guwahati to defame the outfit. Dutta claims that ULFA was in no way involved in the twin explosions.

- November 5: At least 14 persons are killed and more than 52 others sustained injuries in two separate bomb blasts triggered by suspected ULFA militants at Fancy Bazaar and Noonmati area in Guwahati. Seven persons, including three identified as Paban Shah, Monsun Rai and Puranmal Choudhury, are killed and several others wounded in a bomb explosion at a tea stall in the Jai Narayan Road of Fancy Bazaar. Further, four persons, Majid Ali, Mustan Ali, Manuara Begum and Manoj Das, are killed and seven others wounded in another explosion at Patharquarry area in Noonmati near installations of two Public Sector Undertakings, the Indian Oil Corporation and Oil India Limited.

- November 3: Three ULFA militants are killed by SF personnel in a counter-insurgency operation at Kardoiguri under Moran police station in the Dibrugarh district. Two out of three slain militants are identified as 'area commander' Charan Majhi and a corporal in the 'C' Company of the '28 Battalion' Anup Dehingia. According to police sources, a huge cache of arms and explosives, including one AK-56 rifle, one Spanish M-20 pistol, 73 rounds of live ammunition, one mobile phone, 100 grams of suspected RDX, two packets of explosives, 32 detonators, one safety fuse, one programmable timer explosive device, a packet of splinters, along with camping materials like polythene sheets and ground sheets and some documents is recovered from the encounter site.

- November 2: Assam Director General of Police, D.N. Dutt, says that the ULFA is "using certain stretches of the Bhutan for taking shelter." Earlier, S. K. Sarkar, Additional Director General of Police (Intelligence) of West Bengal, had said that the ULFA and the KLO were establishing camps in Bhutan and Nepal and are being helped by the Maoists of Nepal. Bhutanese embassy in New Delhi denies the presence of ULFA or any other militant group in the country. Jigme Tenzin, third secretary in the press division of the embassy, says, "I would like to state for the record, that since the removal of all 13 camps of the ULFA from Bhutan during the military operations conducted by the royal Bhutan army in 2003, there has been no presence of the ULFA or any other group inside Bhutan." Tinsukia District Police arrested a person, Nirmal Singh Gurung, for distributing Subscriber Identity Module (SIM) cards of the Bharat Sanchar Nigam Limited to suspected ULFA cadres.
- November 1: ULFA threatens to strongly resist attempts by a Public Sector Undertaking, Oil India Ltd, to explore petroleum oil in the Brahmaputra basin.
- October 30: ULFA explodes three IEDs simultaneously in upper Assam's Tinsukia district soon after troops crossed the area. However, no casualties were reported.
- October 29. One ULFA cadre identified as, Kanak Rava, was arrested by the security force personnel during a search operation near Dadan police outpost in the Goalpara district. A Chinese-made hand grenade was recovered from his possession.
- October 28: Two children were killed and several others sustained injuries in the ULFA triggered twin bomb explosions at Guwahati on the banks of the river Brahmaputra during Chhath Puja (an annual Hindu festival dedicated to the worship of the sun).
- October 27: At least three civilians were killed and 22 persons, including one woman, a child and two Central Reserve Police Force personnel, sustain injuries when an improvised explosive device planted on a bi-

cycle parked in front of Paramount Restaurant is triggered at Dhekiajuli town (140 km north of Guwahati) in the Sonitpur district.

An ULFA militant, Milan Saikia alias Bhaskar Sonowal, surrenders before the Dibrugarh District Administration.

- October 26: A trader, Jayanta Dey, is shot dead by the ULFA militants at Doomdooma in the Tinsukia district, for his failure to respond to the extortion notice served on him by the outfit.
- October 23: An unidentified ULFA cadre is killed and another wounded, when a grenade targeting SF personnel explodes at village Narayanpur in the Lakhimpur district. "The grenade exploded in the militant's hand before it could hit the target.

  One of the bombers died on the spot and another was seriously injured," said Assam Police (Intelligence) Chief, Khagen Shamna.
- October 23: A senior police official posted in a Bodoland Territorial Council-administered district says that the ULFA militants were spotted in areas just across the border with Bhutan. "I will not say that they (ULFA) have established major camps in the jungles of Bhutan as yet, but their presence there has certainly been noticed," says the police official.

  The ULFA-backed People's Consultative Group member, Indira Goswami, appeals to the union Government to restart the peace process with the group.
- October 21: A ULFA cadre, Mahendra Gogoi alias Manaspratim Gogoi, is arrested from Magarahat village in the Sibsagar district.

  The '28th battalion' of the ULFA reportedly announces a ceasefire on its own without waiting for the formal 'directive' from its high command and the outcome of the ongoing negotiations between the Union Government and the ULFA-backed People's Consultative Group.
- October 19: At least four ULFA cadres, Rantu Medhi, Dhanen Ray, Munawar Hussain and Shahjahan Ali, are arrested from Bongaljura area in the Goalpara district.

  Two ULFA cadres, Aftab Ali alias Rantu Medhi and Dhanen Ray alias Appu Saikia, and a linkman, Munawar Hussain, are arrested in a search operation at Bangaljihar in the Goalpara district, for their involvement in the recruitment of new cadres for the outfit.
- October 18: A surrendered ULFA cadre, Kamal Hazarika, is shot dead by suspected ULFA militants at Borabhayapuri under Tengakhat police station in the Dibrugarh district. All the major political parties in Assam condemn the ULFA for carrying out explosions, other subversive activities, and bringing in children and students into militancy.

- October 17: Two ULFA linkmen, Kabindra Sonowal and Arup Bora, are arrested from Jokhai area in the outskirts of Dibrugarh town.

  ULFA militants kill a civilian, Dilip Barua, whose dead body is recovered from Meseki forest under Pengri police station in the Tinsukia district.

- October 16: SFs foil a plan by the ULFA to plant IEDs and blow up oil and gas pipelines at Duliajan under Lankasi police station in the Tinsukia district. Digging tools and wires are recovered from the incident site.

- October 15: A trader, Omprakash Agarwalla, is shot dead by ULFA cadres at his grocery shop under Mom police station in the Sibsagar district. He was earlier served extortion note by the outfit, according to police sources.

  One ULFA cadre, Gautom Kalita, is killed in an explosion of a crude bomb that he was manufacturing at his rented accommodation at Kahilipara in Guwahati.

  The ULFA-backed People's Consultative Group seeks a communique from the Assam Government on the stalled peace process with the outfit.

- October 14: The ULFA kills a trader's son, Ghanashyam Maheswari, at Machkhowa in the Dhemaji district for his refusal to pay ransom to the outfit.

- October 12: The Union Ministry of Home Affairs submits to Myanmar's Government a list of 15 militant camps run on its soil by the outfits, including ULFA.

- October 11: The ULFA triggers an IED explosion blowing up a security convoy and injuring security force personnel at an unspecified place near Dasaijan village in the Tinsukia district.

- October 9: A bicycle borne ULFA militant hurls a grenade injuring one person at a crowded shopping place at Digboi in the Tinsukia district.

- October 8: Two motorcycle-borne ULFA militants, Simanta Bora and Baikuntha Gogoi, hurl a hand grenade at the Amguri police station in the Sibsagar district.

  A civilian, Lakhi Das, was injured and the building of the police station was partially damaged. The duo were arrested in the subsequent search operation.

- October 8: An ULFA cadre, Keshab Saikia alias Kachu, is injured in an encounter with security force personnel at Hillcidhari village in the Dibrugarh district. An electronic detonator, 500 gm of TNT explosives and incriminating documents were seized from the injured militant. However, the two militants managed to escape from the encounter site.

- October 7: An IED is exploded by the ULFA at Borhat Sibsagar district. However, no casualty was reported in the incident.

  A grenade is hurled at Tengakhat police station in the Dibrugarh district. However, no one is injured in the incident. Later, two persons, Diganta Sonowal and Bhupen Sonowal, were arrested from the nearby Langri Borhulla village in connection with the grenade attack.

- October 6: A ULFA 'corporal', identified as Debojit, is killed by SF personnel in a counter-insurgency operation at an unspecified place in the Sibsagar district.

- October 5: Four civilians and three police constables are injured in a grenade blast triggered by two motorcyde-borne ULFA militants targeting a security convoy in front of the Doomdooma police station in the Tinsukia district.

- October 5: Two other motorcyde-borne ULFA militants hurl a hand grenade at Namrup police station in the Dibrugarh district in a simultaneous attack. The compound wall of the police station was partially damaged.

  The Central Intelligence Wing submits to the Army a list of at least 25 ULFA cadres, who have taken shelter at various places of upper Assam, most of them belonging to the '28th battalion' of the outfit, and all of them are equipped with sophisticated arms and explosives, including assault rifles of AK-56, AK-57, AK-47, along with other communication gadgets. The list includes Jiban Moran, Jiten Dutta, Probal Neog, Bijoy Chinese, Ujjal Gohain, Poresh Majhi, Jun Bhuyan, Rubul Sarma, Pranjal Saikia, Dibakar Moran and Aagan Barua.

- October 4: Two ULFA collaborators, Ghanakanta Hazarika and Sashidhar Hazarika, are arrested by the North Lakhimpur police from Badhakara area.

- October 4: Across Assam, wine shops remain open throughout the day, defying a 'directive' of the ULFA to open liquor outlets only after 7 pm on weekdays. "For all practical purposes, we are running the business on behalf of the government, which has given us licence to do so. We cannot open or close as we like. If we do so, our licences can get cancelled," said Alok Datta, the general secretary of the All Assam India-made Foreign Liquor Retailers' Association.

- October 1: The ULFA triggers a hand grenade blast targeting police personnel at Nalanipalam in the Dhemaji district. While the grenade attack fails to hit its intended target, a male child, Debabrata Dhingia, is kilted, and at least 20 persons are wounded.

- September 29: Suspected ULFA militants trigger a grenade explosion injuring eight persons at a shopping place, the Central Plaza market complex, in the Tinsukia city. Two vehicles are also damaged in the blast.

- September 29: Suspected ULFA militants use a powerful bomb to blow up a portion of the Oil India Limited (OIL) pipeline at Salbari under Tingkhong police station in the Dibrugarh district. OIL spokesperson Phanindra Dev Choudhury said, "It was a 10-inch gas distribution pipeline and our workers were on the job throughout the night to repair the damaged facility. The extent of the damage is yet to ascertained."
- September 29: Police recover and defuse a powerful bomb planted by the ULFA in a dustbin on the busy Plaza-Assam trunk road in Tinsukia town.
- September 28: At least six persons, induding two SF personnel, are wounded in an IED explosion triggered by the ULFA at a shopping place at Digboi in the Tinsukia district.
- September 27: Suspected ULFA cadres trigger a grenade explosion targeting SF personnel at Kundil in the Tinsukia district.
- September 27: An encounter between Army and ULFA militants is reported from an unspecified area in the Tinsukia district.
- September 27: The ULFA-backed PCG pulls out from the peace talks with the Union Government. The PCG spokesperson, Aroop Borbora, said: "we feel that due to the attitude of the Government, which made a complete summersault on the assurances given earlier, holding of further parleys with the Government would not serve any purpose."
- September 27: A decomposed dead body of a suspected ULFA cadre was recovered from a drain at Bordumsa in the Changlang district of Arunachal Pradesh.
- September 25: A ULFA cadre, Mohipal Moran, is killed and five soldiers wounded during an encounter at Borpathar under Pengeri police station limits in the Tinsukia district. A 9 mm Chinese pistol, five rounds of 9mm ammunition, seven rounds of AK-47 ammunition, a hand grenade and cash worth INR 50,000 are recovered from the slain militant. Two ULFA cadres are arrested following the incident.
- September 25: The ULFA 'chairman' Arabinda Rajkhowa has stated that his outfit is not bothered about the breakdown of the cease-fire. "We don't want a truce and instead committed to ending the war. The Government of India's ceasefire announcement in August was nothing but a drama enacted by them," Rajkhowa stated.
- September 25: Chief Minister Tarun Gogoi offers the ULFA leadership one more chance to meet their jailed leaders. "I can allow the ULFA leadership, if they want to consult the jailed leaders on the peace

process. I have no problems if it leads to bringing peace in the state," he says.

- September 25: The ULFA 'commander-in-chief' Paresh Barua warns all 'Indians living in the North-east' to pay taxes to the outfit and also appeals to the local inhabitants to contribute according to their means to the outfit's coffers.
- September 24: The Union Government declares resumption of counter-insurgency operations against the ULFA in Assam, after the deadline for suspension of operation against the outfit expires on September 20. A statement issued by the Union Ministry of Home Affairs (MHA) says that the 'suspension of operations' against the outfit is called off 'with effect from today'. The statement adds, "Operations had been suspended some time back because of the possibility of direct talks with ULFA towards (the) peace process. However, efforts for pursuing the peace process by the government will continue."
- September 24: A 'corporal' of the ULFA, Diganta Baruah alias Bitupan Baruah, is killed in an encounter with SF personnel at Mazmamoroni near Lekhapant under Digboi police station in the Tinsukia district. However, another injured militant manages to escape from the encounter site. Further, nine Army personnel and a civilian, Dwipen Baruah, are also injured in the encounter.
- September 23: The ULFA kills a tea estate manager in Assam. Police said four ULFA cadres shot dead Haren Das, a manager of the Hailanga tea estate in front of his residence, in Digboi town. The attack comes a day after the Union Government indicated that military operations against the outfit could resume.
- September 22: ULFA militants kill police personnel, Ranjit Sonowal, at Than Gaon village under Barbaruah police station in the Dibrugarh district. The militants opened fire on police personnel, who were searching for an extortionist belonging to the outfit identified as Debu Dutta.
- September 22: National Security Advisor M. K. Narayanan conveys to the ULFA-backed PCG member Indira Goswami that the Union Government will not extend the suspension of counter-insurgency operations against the outfit in Assam without receiving a written commitment from it on holding direct peace talks.
- September 20: Assam Chief Minister Tarun Gogoi states that the ULFA is yet to refrain from carrying out its extortion activities.
- September 17: According to Intelligence Bureau (IB) sources, at least four training camps are run along the India-Bhutan border where ULFA cadres are getting trained by the LTTE in carrying out suicide attacks.

- September 16: At least INR 16,00,000 is recovered from the possession of two suspected ULFA cadres, identified as Ramzan Ali and Bablu Deka alias Niberan Deka, who were arrested from Mawiong in the East Khasi Hills district of Meghalaya.
- September 12: The ULFA seeks time till September 20 to respond to the Union Government's demand for a formal letter before carrying forward the negotiations.
- September 7: Army officials state that the ULFA cadres are involved in extortion, despite the suspension of counter-insurgency operations against the outfit.
- September 5: The suspension of counter-insurgency operations against the ULFA is extended till September 15. The extension is announced by the Union Home Secretary, V. K. Duggal, following a meeting with the ULFA-backed People's Consultative Group (PCG) members, Indira Goswami and Rebati Phukan, in New Delhi.
- September 5: The National Security Adviser M. K. Narayanan denies any step on part of the Union Government to unilaterally release five arrested ULFA leaders. Before holding a meeting with the ULFA-backed PCG members, Narayanan says, "Let them come for talks first."
- September 3: The Union Government decides to convene an inter-ministerial meeting to discuss the peace process in Assam, following the ULFA's refusal to give a written commitment on direct talks with the Government.
- September 3: Assam Chief Minister, Tarun Gogoi, while making a case for a direct communication between the Government and the outfit, says that more civilians than militants are killed in the State since the ULFA constituted the PCG to negotiate on its behalf.
- August 31: The ULFA in a communique assures the Union Government that five of its jailed leaders will not abscond, once they are released. A letter written by ULFA 'commander-in-chief' Paresh Barua is delivered to Union Home Secretary V.K. Duggal by mediator Indira Goswami.
- August 30: Union Home Secretary V. K. Duggal says that the Union Government is expecting a response from the ULFA, before the suspension of counter-insurgency operation expires on September 5. "They have time until September 5 and we expect a response before that," said Duggal.
- August 28: The Border Security Force demands deportation of ULFA 'general secretary' Anup Chetia, and other leaders from Bangladesh at the bi-annual meeting with the Bangladesh Rifles in Shillong, the capital of Meghalaya.

- August 24: Meghalaya DGP, W. R. Marbaniang, says that counter-insurgency operations against the ULFA will continue in the State, despite the suspension of Army operations by the Union Government in Assam. "We have taken care of ourselves and the army is only assisting us in (counter-insurgency operations). In 99 per cent cases, the state police are doing the job," says the DGP.
- August 24: The Union Government seeks a written assurance from the ULFA to come for peace talks as a condition for the release of its five arrested leaders. The Government asks the outfit to announce its team for negotiations and to specify a timeframe to start direct talks. However, the outfit rejects such conditions set by the Government.
- August 23: The Union Government decides to extend the suspension of counter-insurgency operations against the ULFA by 15 days. A decision to this effect is taken at the meeting between the Government and the ULFA-backed PCG to decide modalities for direct negotiation with the outfit. While the National Security Adviser M. K. Narayanan and officials from the Union Ministry of Home Affairs represent the Government, the PCG is represented by Indira Goswami and Rebati Phukan. "As of now, we have decided to extend the suspension of the army operations against ULFA for 15 days," says the Union Home Secretary V. K. Duggal.
- August 21 : The Union Government asks the ULFA backed-PCG members to stand for personal guarantee for the release of five arrested leaders of the ULFA.
- August 19: The ULFA denies that it had declared a unilateral cease-fire. The outfit's 'chairman' Arabinda Rajkhowa says that the ULFA will exercise 'restraint' in response to the Union Government's suspension of security operations against its cadres. Rajkhowa says, "We will exercise restraint in response to the government's announcement to suspend operation and we will try our best to maintain our restraint." He also urges all concerned "not to create confusion by quoting statements not made by the ULFA on serious issues concerning the people."
- August 15: The ULFA along with KLO, MPLF, NLFT and TPDF, in a joint statement, calls upon the people of the North East region to boycott the Independence Day celebration and also calls a 12-hour general strike.
- August 14: Three persons, including a woman and her son, are killed and seven others sustain injuries when suspected ULFA militants trigger a grenade explosion targeting security convoys near Lifecare Nursing Home at Duliajan town in the Dibrugarh district.

- August 14: A grenade explosion is triggered at Makum Petrol Depot in the Tinsukia district.
- August 14: Assam Chief Minister Tarun Gogoi, while asking the ULFA to abjure violence and extremism, says that difficult issues can be resolved only through dialogue and negotiations. He mentions that the Union Government is doing its best to create an atmosphere where direct talks can be held with the outfit "Peace and progress is the need of the hour, without which commerce, industry or trade can never take root in the State. Terror and violence must be removed if problems like lack of development and unemployment are to be resolved," says the Chief Minister.
- August 13: The Union Government decides to halt all operations by security forces against the ULFA for a few days. Union Home Secretary V. K. Duggal says, "We have advised army and other security forces in Assam to suspend their operations against ULFA for a few days." He further says, "However, this does not mean that if they resort to any misadventure that will not be replied back. Appropriate action will be taken." The decision comes days ahead of a crucial meeting between the representatives of the Union Government and mediators appointed by the outfit in New Delhi to discuss modalities for initiation of direct peace talks.
- August 13: The ULFA has set up three camps in the Sandrup Jhongkar district of Bhutan, after its cadres were driven out by a counter-insurgency operation in December 2003. According to the report, Hira Sarania, a top leader believed to be close to the outfit's 'commander-in-chief Paresh Barua, is heading the cadres operating from these camps.
- August 12: A woman, Jongti Devi, is killed and eight persons wounded in a grenade explosion, suspected to have been triggered by the ULFA, at Bamunimaidan locality in Guwahati. Additional Superintendent of Police, Rajen Singh, says that the blast occurred around 7.20 p.m. in the Bamunimaidan railway colony area. The blast occurs amidst heightened security measures in the city with police and para-military forces intensifying patrolling to foil sabotage attempts by the ULFA militants, who have called for a boycott of the Independence Day celebrations on August 15.
- August 11: Six police personnel are killed after suspected ULFA militants ambush a police convoy at Ratanipathar under Pengeri police station in the Tinsukia district.

  While five personnel are killed at the incident site, another succumbs to injuries in the Assam Medical College Hospital.
- August 10: The ULFA along with KLO, MPLF, NLFT, TPDF in a joint statement call upon the people of the North East region to boycott

the Independence Day celebration and also jointly call a 12-hour general strike for August 15.

According to official sources, there has been some movement of ULFA cadres in Garo Hills since the last few months.

The outfit's cadres cross into Bangladesh from West Garo Hills plain belt areas and enter into Assam from the Tikrikilla, Rongsai, Bajengdoba and Mendipather areas.

- August 8: At least four new training camps of the ULFA were reportedly found along the India-Bhutan border in the Nalbari district.

  Arunachal Pradesh Police arrest five persons, Nuney Tayang, Nakul Chai, Dwarika Meso, Surendra Singh and Makhan Hazarika, from Lohit district for helping the ULFA.

  While four of them are office bearers of the State Congress, another one is a relative of a leader of the party.

- August 7: An unidentified person is killed and 15 others, including four Central Reserve Police Force personnel and a child, are injured when ULFA militants explode a grenade at Digboi Chariali in the Tinsukia district.

- August 6: Two unidentified ULFA militants are killed when a grenade, they were carrying, explodes at Mission Chariali near Defence Theater in the Tezpur district. Several persons are also wounded in the explosion.

  Eight paramilitary force personnel are wounded when suspected ULFA militants hurl a grenade at a Central Reserve Police Force patrol party near Bhojo railway station under Charaideo subdivision in the Sibsagar district. A hardware shop owner, Sanjay Agarwal, is shot at and wounded by suspected ULFA militants at Gaurisagar Tiniali in the Sibsagar district.

  A ULFA militant, Sundar Chetia, who is arrested from Tinsukia district, confesses during interrogation that he has been extorting money ranging from Rupees 50,000 to Rupees 1,00,000 annually for the past three years and sending them to Ujjwal Gohain, 'finance controller of the 28 battalion' of the outfit.

- August 5: At least 15 persons are injured when suspected ULFA militants trigger a grenade blast at Jonai in Dhemaji district.

- August 4: A grenade is triggered by ULFA cadres, targeting a security convoy, killing one SF personnel, Manoj Kumar, and injuring two others at Dhelakhat in the Tinsukia district.

- August 3: The National Security Adviser M. K. Narayanan informs the peace interlocutor Indira Goswami that the Union Government is seeking a formal letter from the outlawed ULFA for the release of its five arrested leaders as well as for direct peace talks.

"The government wants a formal letter from the ULFA seeking the release of the five jailed leaders and giving consent to sit for direct talks," says Goswami in New Delhi.

- August 1: A hardcore United Liberation Front of Asom (ULFA) cadre, 'sergeant major' Rajen Dutta, is killed during an encounter with the SF personnel at Tamulbari in the Dibrugarh district. An AK-47 rifle, a mobile phone, three SIM cards and cash worth INR 1,000 are recovered from the incident site.
- July 31 : Four ULFA cadres are shot dead in two separate encounters with SF personnel in the Nalbari district. While, two militants, Bhupen Lahkar and Hemanta Deka, are killed at Arora village, two others, including one identified as Jyotirmoy Bhattacharya alias Kaushik Sarma, are shot dead at Dhaniagog village on the bank of the river Pagladia.
- July 31 : An ULFA cadre is arrested following the encounter at Arora village. A cache of arms and explosives, including one 9 mm pistol, 3 Chinese grenades, and 3 rounds of live ammunition, is also recovered from the two encounter sites.
- July 31: An ULFA leader, Mridul Hazarika alias Bhaskar Barua, who was a prime accused in the Sanjoy Ghosh murder case of 1997, is shot dead by police personnel in an encounter at Khanakrishnapur village under Gogamukh police station in the Dhemaji district. While two other militants, Anil Basumatari alias Gadapani and Bhaben Sonowal alias Biplab Kachari, surrender, a cache of arms and explosives is recovered from the encounter site. Sanjoy Ghosh, who worked with the NGO Avard-NE, was abducted and subsequently killed by the ULFA in July 1997.
- July 29: The ULFA communicates to the Union Home Ministry that its precondition for direct peace talks with the Union Government is release of the five leaders—all members of the Central Committee, ULFA's highest decision-making body—jailed at Guwahati in Assam. The communication to the Home Secretary Vinod Kumar Duggal is sent through the peace interlocutor Indira Goswami, who belongs to the ULFA-backed People's Consultative Group (PCG).
- July 28: An unidentified civilian is killed by ULFA militants at Sadiya in the North Lakimpur district, while a cadre of the outfit is shot dead in an encounter with SF personnel inside a hotel at Margherita town in the Tinsukia district.
- July 26: The peace interlocutor belonging to the People's Consultative Group (PCG), Indira Goswami, conveys to the Union Home Secretary, V. K. Duggal, refusal of ULFA to name its representatives for direct

peace talks with the Union Government unless its five arrested leaders are released ahead of the talks.

- July 25: The Union Minister of State for Home Affairs, S. Raghupathy, informs the Lower House of the Parliament that available reports and confession of arrested ULFA cadres indicate links of the outfit with the Inter-Services Intelligence (ISI), the external intelligence agency of Pakistan.
- July 24: A group of women cadres of the ULFA manage to escape following an encounter with SF personnel at Khowji village in the Lohit district of Arunachal Pradesh.
- July 19: The Union Government asks the ULFA to establish direct contact with the government without which, it says, there will be no scope for the proposed peace process to move forward. "The ULFA must communicate their demands, including release of jailed leaders, in black and white directly to the Centre for the peace process to proceed further," the Union Home Secretary V.K. Duggal tells interlocutor Mamoni Raisom Goswami. Goswami says from New Delhi that the Union Home Secretary informs her that ULFA must make direct contact with the Government and place their demands instead of communicating through intermediaries. Only then can their demands be considered.
- July 18: Troops of the Red Horn Division stationed at Dhubri neutralise a fake currency racket besides arresting two ULFA linkmen and recover one pistol and some live ammunition from Dingdinga village under Tamarhat police station limits in the Kokrajhar district.
- July 16: A ULFA cadre, Pradip Das, is arrested from Hatigaon area in Guwahati city. Several incriminating documents and six batteries used in Improvised Explosive Devices (lEDs) are recovered from his possession. Assam's Director General of Police, Deepak Dutta, informs that while the ULFA is planning a major attack in any of the four lower Assam districts in 'retaliation' to the killing of its cadres, the Lashkar-e-Toiba (LeT), intends to attack the Guwahati railway station soon. "The ULFA is planning a major attack in retaliation to the killing of its six cadres in any of the districts of Kamrup, Baska, Nalbari and Barpeta," says the Director General of Police.
- July 13: Meghalaya Police suspects that the ULFA leader Rubul Ali, who was killed in the July 11 encounter in Garo Hills, is a linkman of the Pakistani ISI. "The ULFA-ISI nexus has been going on for quite long time and it is suspected that the ISI has been providing assistance to the ULFA in term of arms, training and funds," said police sources.
- July 12:Two kilograms of ivory worth over INR 100,000 are recovered from a ULFA linkman, Bolin Dutta, who was arrested by the Army

Intelligence personnel at unspecified place under Dhola police station in the Tinsukia district. According to official sources, besides aiding the activities of the outfit, Dutta was also involved in smuggling forest produce from Paglam in Arunachal Pradesh. The ULFA-backed People's Consultative Group threatens to pull out of the peace process with the Union Government, following the July 11 killing of six ULFA cadres in Assam and Meghalaya.

- July 11: Four ULFA cadres, identified as Rubul Ali, Prabal Dutta, Rudra Barua and Dulu Kalita, are killed by the troops during an encounter at Tinfa village under Mendipathar police station in the East Garo Hills district of Meghalaya. While three ULFA cadres were arrested, a cache of arms and explosives, including one AK rifle, four grenades, pistol, several rounds of ammunition, along with INR 40,000 were recovered from the incident site. Two ULFA cadres, Pradip Rajbangshi and Mrinal Rajbangshi, are killed in an encounter with the SFs at Baglamari village in the Nalbari district. Two 9 mm pistols, three Chinese grenades, 8 rounds of live ammunition, a radio set and cash worth INR 30,000 were recovered from their possession.
- July 7: Police arrests two militants of the ULFA and a linkman of the outfit from Birubari locality of the Guwahati city in connection with the outfit's extortion demand of INR 15 Lakhs on the Reserve Bank of India regional director Amarendra Sahu. The arrested militants were identified as Mantu Bezbarua and Gautam Sarania alias Rahul Deka. Police also recovered a grenade from their possession.
- July 3: The ULFA 'serves' an extortion note of Rupees 150 milion to the Regional Director of the Reserve Bank of India in Guwahati. The letter is signed, on June 25, by an ULFA 'commander', Hira Sarania, who is allegedly involved in several extortion acts in the past.
- July 1 : The ULFA expresses its willingness to hold 'direct talks' with the Union Government at the earliest.
- June 26: Two ULFA cadres, Paban Gayan and Manaj Baruah, are arrested from Deopani under Bokajan police station.
- June 23: A student of the Guwahati University, Rinku Basumatary, wounded in the June 9 ULFA triggered explosion at Machkhowa in Guwahati city, succumbs to his injuries.
- June 16: The Union Ministry of Home Affairs objects to the ULFA's plea for releasing its five leaders. The Cabinet Committee on Security, while discussing the issue at New Delhi, is of the view that the outfit should give up violence, surrender arms and should adopt an honest approach to peace before such a step can be taken.

A frontal organization of the ULFA, Assam Watch, is operating in the United Kingdom. Mukul Hazarika, is the co-ordinator of the Assam Watch. Intelligence sources say that Assam Watch sponsored ULFA's chairman, Arabinda Rajkhowa and general secretary, Anup Chetia, to attend a meeting of the United Nations Sub-Commission's Working Group on Indigenous People at Geneva in July 1997, while Interpol had issued a Red Corner Alert notice against the top leadership of the outfit for its involvement in the abduction and killing of Sanjoy Ghose of the Association of Voluntary Agencies for Rural Development- North East (AVARD-North East).

- June 15: Four ULFA cadres, identified as Bijoy Kalita, Rudra Barua, Hemanta Kalita and Kamal Ahmed, in a letter sent to local media persons, say that they are planning to float a new outfit to continue their "revolution" under the leadership of one self-styled 'captain' of the outfit. They, quoting a letter reportedly written by the ULFA 'chairman' Arabinda Rajkhowa, say the outfit's chief is planning to liquidate them. They further said several ULFA leaders, including Bening Rava, Abhijit Deka and Nilu Chakravarty, who the outfit claims have gone missing following the Army's counter insurgency operations in Bhutan, were killed on Rajkhowa's orders.

  Assam Police says that following the formation of the ULFA - backed People's Consultative Group on September 8 in 2005, the ULFA militants have triggered off as many as 52 blasts, majority of those were in late January and early part of February and again from June 8 to 12 in 2006. The reports further said that at least 41 civilians are killed and 135 are injured in ULFA's violence since September 8, 2005. During the same period, the outfit attacked the security force personnel on 15 occasions in which six are killed, while 41 are injured. During the same period, the security forces are engaged in encounters with the ULFA cadres on 20 occasions, in which 21 militants are killed and 48 are arrested. The sources further pointed out that in the first five and half months of 2006, as many as 29 civilians are killed, as compared to the death of 20 civilians and injury of 78 in 2005. The fatality figure among the security personnel in ULFA's violence in 2005 is six.

- June 14: A civilian, Monoj Gogoi, who was wounded in the June 12 blast triggered by the ULFA at Digboi town in the Tinsukia district, succumbs to his injuries.

  Two ULFA extortionists, Paresh Das and Moinul alias Islam, are arrested by the Guwahati city police during separate search operations from Basistha and Garigaon areas in the Kamrup district.

- June 13: A ULFA cadre, identified as Phulen Nath alias Kamal Barman alias Pintu Das, is killed in an encounter with the police at Kamalnagar atop Narakasur Hill under Dispur police station in the Kamrup district. While two other militants manage to escape from the incident site, the owner of the residence, Bhaben Rabha, is arrested on charges of harbouring ULFA cadres. A cache of arms and explosives, including one unexploded grenade, 24 detonators, fuse wires, one 7.62-bore Pakistani-made pistol and four rounds of ammunition, are recovered from the encounter site. According to police sources, the slain militant is involved in the June-9 blast at Machkhowa in the Guwahati city in which five persons died.

Assam's Director General of Police D. N. Dutt confirms that the ULFA is involved in all the recent blasts in the State, following the denial of the outfit of its involvement. He says, "All the inputs we have point to the fact that the militants belonging to the ULFA were behind the recent blasts. For a very long time, we had the inputs that the ULFA was planning to explode a series of bombs from June 9 to 11 and they started a day ahead."

- June 11 : A security force personnel, identified as Bircharan Singh, who is among the three injured in the ULFA's grenade attack on a patrolling vehicle at Makum in the Tinsukia district, succumbs to his injuries.

  Suspected ULFA cadres blow up a railway track between Borhat and Baruahnagar railway stations in the Sibsagar district. Rail links between Upper Assam and the rest of the country are snapped for several hours following the blast.

- June 10: Suspected ULFA militants trigger two more blasts in the Guwahati city killing one person and injuring 19 others. Inspector-General of Police (Special Branch) Khagen Sharma informs that suspected ULFA militants lobbed a grenade targeting a police post at Bamunimaidam area in which two police personnel are injured. Another blast occurred under the Ganeshguri flyover close to the Dispur capital complex killing one person and wounding 17 others.

  The ULFA denies its hand in the six bomb blasts in which civilians are injured, but owns up three blasts on the oil and gas pipelines at Naharkatia, Digboi and Chabua. In a statement, ULFA chief Paresh Baruah claims the blasts in Guwahati, Dhubri, Mangaldoi, Haibargaon, Golokganj and Doomdooma are "masterminded by Inspector-General of Police (Special Branch) Khagen Sharma and the forces opposed to peace talks between the Centre and the outfit." Baruah says the attacks on the pipelines are carried out in protest against the tightening of security around oil installations, which is to "facilitate the plundering of Assam's natural resources."

- June 9: At least five persons, including a 10-year-old boy and a woman, are killed and 16 persons wounded in a powerful explosion triggered by the ULFA at Machkowa vegetable market in the Guwahati city of Kamrup district. Senior Superintendent of Police Nitul Gogoi said that the bombs, believed to have been planted in a vegetable basket, have exploded at 4.20 pm at the wholesale vegetable market when it was at its busiest moment.
- June 8:The ULFA triggers a series of grenade explosions at various parts of the State leaving at least 25 persons wounded. While six persons are injured in a blast at Haiborgaon in the Nagaon district, another is injured when militants trigger a blast at Islampur Chowk in the Mangaldoi district.
- June 5: A civilian, Dilip Das, is shot dead by the ULFA cadres at Sonapur Chowk under Kamalpur police station in the Kamrup (rural) district. The militants were targeting a SULFA cadre, Narayan Das, in the incident.
- May 23: A clandestine meeting of the ULFA leaders is held somewhere near Alipurduar in the Jaipalguri district of West Bengal at the end of May. Intelligence Bureau officials indicated that many ULFA cadres have reportedly landed at Siliguri.
- May 21: Two ULFA militants, senior leader Bijay Kalita and linkman Subrata Paul, are arrested from Siliguri in the Jalpaiguri district of West Bengal.
- May 20: A senior engineer of the state-owned OIL is released after being abducted by unidentified terrorists a day earlier. An OIL spokesman said K. Mohan Rao, a drilling engineer, was abducted while he was going from the company headquarters at Duliajan to a remote installation.
- May 18: The Union Government confirms that the outlawed ULFA has sent to the Oil and Natural Gas Corporation a demand note of Rupees Five billion. The Union Minister of State for Petroleum and Natural Gas, Dinsha Patel, said in the Parliament that there have been four disruptive incidents by the ULFA resulting in minor damage to the property of ONGC in the recent past.

  An unidentified ULFA cadre was arrested from Siliguri in the Jalpaiguri district of West Bengal.
- May 17: Four ULFA cadres, including 'commanding officer' Mrinal Hazarika, Jagat Barua, Mahesh Gupta and Pradip, are arrested at Siliguri in the Jalpaiguri district of West Bengal. Inspector-General of Police

(North Bengal) K. L. Meena says that several documents, an active satellite telephone, two mobile phones with Assam Telecom Circle numbers, an improvised pistol with a few bullets, Rupees 20,370 in Indian currency and Rupees 13 in Nepali currency were seized from their possession.

- May 14: An ULFA cadre, 'corporal' Puspa Borah alias Sanchar Chetia, who had surrendered along with a pistol, two magazines, 16 rounds of ammunition and a Chinese hand grenade, before the Superintendent of Police of the Udalguri district on May 13, is found dead inside the lock-up of the district police station. According to police sources, Puspa Borah committed suicide.
- May 10: Five ULFA cadres, 'sergeant major' Jagadish Mahanta alias Rajesh Sarma, 'corporal' Ameer Hussain alias Raj Ahmed, Pradeep K. Barman alias Control, Dinesh Sarkar alias Mithun and Purno Roy alias Pumi, surrender before Colonel M.K. Das and Additional Superintendent of Police Umar Ali at Dhubri district. They deposited an AK-47 rifle, three 9 mm revolvers and 45 rounds of ammunition.
- May 9: Two SF personnel, Rubul Ali and Dhruba Borsaikia, are killed in an ambush by the ULFA at a place near the Borahibari railway station in Sibsagar district. Five persons including the former State Transport Minister and senior AGP leader Pradip Hazarika are wounded in the attack. Hazarika has figured in ULFA's list of 'conspirators' in the 'secret killings', the outfit recently claims, that has taken place during the AGP regime. Twenty five empty shells of AK-47 ammunition are recovered from the incident site.
- May 8: Unidentified militants shot at and wounded a SULFA cadre, Jayanta Maran, at his residence in Nalani in the Tinsukia district.
- May 2: An unidentified 'leader' of the ULFA along with two Delhi-based sex workers, who were arrested from Guwahati in the Kamrup district, are remanded to ten days of police custody by a local court. Additional Police Chief of Guwahati Rajen Singh, while describing the use of sex workers by the ULFA as baits to extort and abduct businessmen in the State, said, "This is the latest modus operandi of the ULFA - luring businessmen with the help of call girls and then extorting money from them."
- April 24: The Public Works Department chief engineer, Suren Das, who was abducted and later released by the ULFA, is in a state of coma due to cerebral malaria. Das has started suffering from cerebral malaria while in captivity.
- April 21: Unidentified assailants kill two surrendered ULFA militants, Lolit Moran and his wife Momi Moran, at Gotong village under

Doomdooma police station in the Tinsukia district. Both the low-rung ULFA cadres had surrendered to the army in 2004. Police sources said that a group of ULFA militants led by Tedho Moran alias Rocket, who are active in the area, are suspected to be responsible for the killing.

- April 8: Security forces arrest a linkman of the ULFA, Pradip Doley, from his house at Madhya Lakhipur under Jonai police station in the Dhemaji district. An AK-56 Rifle, 160 rounds of ammunition, two magazines and a motorcycle are recovered from his residence. Two of his accomplices, however, manage to escape.
- April 4: An ULFA militant, Bhubaneswar Haloi, surrenders before the army personnel near Bihuguri in the Sonitpur district.
- April 1: Prime Minister Manmohan Singh said that the process initiated by the Union Government to restore peace in Assam will be expedited, but rules out talks with the ULFA on the "sovereignty" issue. Dr. Singh, who arrived in Assam on a two-day election campaign, told a press conference in Guwahati that negotiations would be held within the constitutional framework. "The ULFA may raise the issue during talks but that does not mean all issues are open to negotiation," he says. "Doors will be open to all those who shun violence. Two rounds of talks have been held with certain groups [the discussion with the ULFA-formed People's Consultative Group] and we will accelerate the peace process," he added.
- March 31: Three ULFA cadres along with one KLNLF activist surrendered before the army at Diphu in the Karbi Anglong district. ULFA cadres, Indra Prasad Barua, Lakhi Prashad Nath alias Raj Deka and Parag Hazarika, also deposited an AK 47 rifle, two magazines, 67 rounds of cartridges and four hand grenades.
- March 31: The ULFA chief, Arabinda Rajkhowa, in an electronic message calls on the people of Assam not to vote for any party that has not made any commitment on resolving the "Asom-India political conflict". He said, "The people should only vote for politics that would ensure sovereignty for Asom."
- March 29: The police recover four grenades, an AK series rifle, 30 rounds of live ammunition, a magazine, a 9-V battery, some electronic gadgets and incriminating documents following an encounter with suspected ULFA militants at Satakona under Dudhnoi police station in the Goalpara district. The militants, however, managed to escape and police subsequently arrested two linkmen of the outfit, Sanjit Barsund and Lokesh Sangma.
- March 28: Suspected ULFA cadres abduct Abhisek Agarwal, the 25-year-old son of a biscuit factory-owner, in the Tinsukia district after

the businessman failed to meet a deadline for payment of extortion money. The outfit has reportedly launched a massive extortion drive in Upper Assam, primarily in the Tinsukia and Dibrugarh districts, targeting businessman and Government employees.

- March 18: A woman, identified as S. Begum, is killed and 10 persons are injured in a ULFA triggered bomb blast near the railway track at the Bamunimaidan rail yard in Guwahati.
- March 17: A SULFA cadre, identified as Binod Baishya alias Jit Kalita, is shot dead by suspected ULFA militants at Ghograpar in the Nalbari district.
- March 9: The Guwahati city police put several businessmen in the city under their scanner accusing them of contributing large amounts to the ULFA. Police sources say that the businessmen are paying the outfit via electronic money transfer facility. A senior police official says that "During police questioning, the businessmen admitted they had transferred money to towns such as Hissar in Haryana and Anand in Gujarat after the ULFA issued them instructions." The official also says the ULFA has stepped up their extortion drive in the city after the peace process between the Centre and the PCG begins in 2005. The outfit has collected at least Rupees 30 lakh from the Dispur police division area alone. He further says, "The amount will be much higher if the figures of all the four police divisions are added up."
- March 7: Mediator Indira Goswami said that the third round of talks between the ULFA-constituted PCG and Union Government will be held only after the Legislative Assembly elections in Assam stated for April 3 and 10.
- February 28. Suspected ULFA cadres trigger a blast at the BG Yard near Bamunimaidan in Guwahati city killing one civilian and injuring five others, including a woman.
- February 25: A joint army-police team arrests a ULFA cadre, Uday Bharali, from Taranigaon under Sadiya police station in the Tinsukia district. A modified AK-47 rifle, 65 live ammunitions, a radio set and incriminating documents are recovered from his possession.
- February 21: Armed ULFA militants assault four villagers and abduct an AGP activist, Brikudhar Doley, from his residence at Kemi-Jelom village under Poba Reserve Forest in the Dhemaji district recently.
- February 13: Normal life is affected in the State following a 12-hour general strike called by the ULFA to protest against the killing of nine persons in police firing and death of Ajit Mahanta during Army custody at Kakopathar in the Tinsukia district. There are, however, no reports of any untoward incident from any part of the State.

- February 10: Police arrest five hardcore ULFA militants from different parts of the Guwahati city for their alleged involvement in a series of grenade attacks in the run-up to the Republic Day celebrations on January 26. One M-20 pistol, an Austria-made grenade, 13 rounds of ammunition and two magazines are recovered from the arrested who were identified as Bubul Deka alias Gajen Deka alias Mansur Ali, Chandan Baishya alias Prabin Thakuria, Mohammad Piyar Hussain, Abdul Salam alias Hamid and Ratan Sarkar.
- February 10: Eight civilians and a SF are killed during clashes between the villagers and SFs following the alleged custodial death of a suspected United ULFA militant at Kakopathar in Upper Assam's Tinsukia district. The ULFA cadre, whom the villagers describe as a civilian, was detained by the army on February 6 and his dead body was subsequently recovered.
- February 7: The Union Government and the PCG agree, during a meeting at New Delhi, on a series of CBMs to bring the ULFA to the negotiation table. A joint statement said that the Government of India has agreed to examine and initiate a series of CBMs with regard to human rights violations and to examine the release of detained ULFA leaders in consultation with the State Government.
- February 7: Two ULFA militants, Swapan Roy and Sabed Ali alias Hasinur, surrender before the BSF authorities at Azadnagar in the Coochbehar district of West Bengal. The duo, hailing from Rupasi village under Golakganj police station in Assam's Dhubri district, deposit two improvised explosive devices.
- February 1: Counter insurgency targeting ULFA is called off by Army in the outfit's chief Paresh Baruah's native village, Jeraigaon, in the Dibrugarh district following demands by the villagers. However, army authorities maintain that the operation is "routine in nature" and is called off only because "the security think tank felt it had served its purpose".
- February 1: Surrendered ULFA cadre, Raju Chakraborty, is injured when a group of unidentified assailants shoot at him at Salkocha under Chapar police station in the Dhubri district.
- January 24: A suspected ULFA militant is killed and three others are injured in an explosion in the Ganeshguri locality of Guwahati city. Police sources said that the ULFA militant, Munin Das hailing from Ghograpar in the Nalbari district, was carrying the explosive and traveling on foot to avoid the intensified checking of vehicles by the security forces.
- January 24: An IED is detonated by suspected ULFA cadres at Chhaygaon circle office precincts causing no casualty.

An ULFA cadre, Bhogeswar alias Debojit Bora, was arrested from Nagabat Tinali under Borholla police station in the Jorhat district. Bora is identified as a 'lance corporal' in the '28th battalion' of the outfit.

- January 23: ULFA militants exploded a grenade near the nail factory at Bengenakhowa in the Golaghat district.
- January 23: ULFA militants exploded a hand grenade at Mayong police station in the Morigaon district.
- January 22: ULFA cadres lobbed a grenade targeting SF personnel near Gauhati Commerce College in the Guwahati city injuring five SF personnel.
- January 22: ULFA activists hurled a grenade in front of the Assam Police Reserve at AT Road in the Guwahati city killing a civilian.
- January 22: ULFA militants detonated an improvised explosive device (IED), planted in a requisitioned bus, injuring three police personnel in Guwahati city.
- January 22: One police personnel is killed and five others sustain injuries in an encounter with ULFA cadres at Ewarlangtha Gorgaon along the Assam-Nagaland border in the Golaghat district.
- January 22: ULFA triggers a blast in the precincts of the Assam State Transport Corporation building in Jorhat injuring a civilian.
- January 22: Gas pipelines at Chetiapathar under Chabua police station and Bokulia Chariali under Duliajan police station are blown up by the ULFA.
- January 22: A gas pipeline, running through Lengri tea estate under Tengakhat police station in the Dibrugarh district, is blown up by the ULFA.
- January 22: ULFA cadres shot dead a petrol pump owner at Sadiya township in the Tinsukia district.
- January 22: ULFA militants lobbed a grenade at a police patrol team on the Sessa bridge in the Dibrugarh district injuring four police personnel.
- January 22: ULFA cadres blew up a gas pipeline near Bherbheri under Bordubi police station.
- January 22: Guwahati city police arrests seven ULFA cadres from the outskirts of the city and also recovered a Chinese grenade from their possession.
- January 21 : ULFA militants blew up a power tower of the North Eastern Electric Power Corporation at Bhoju in the Sibsagar district.

- January 21 : ULFA militants blew up a transformer at Konwar Gaon near Lakhimpur.
- January 21 : Three SF personnel are wounded when ULFA cadres blew up a power transformer at Hindugaon Tiniali.
- January 21 : A gas pipeline is blown up by the ULFA at Mahmora Silgrant under Namrup police station in the Dibrugarh district.
- January 21 : ULFA cadres shot dead a trader, Iswar Chand Jain, at Sonari in the Sibsagar district.
- January 21 : ULFA cadres triggered a blast on pipelines of the Oil India Ltd inside Rangali Reserve Forest under Kakatibari police station in the Sibsagar district.
- January 20: Ten persons, including eight personnel of the Central Industrial Security Force (CISF), are injured in a grenade attack by the ULFA at the entrance of the Guwahati Refinery at Noonmati in Guwahati city.
- January 16: A ULFA militant is failed in an encounter with the police at Santipur in the Tinsukia district.
- January 15: OH and Natural Gas Commission (ONGC) intimates the Assam Government of an extortion letter served by the '28th battalion' of the ULFA on its corporate office at Nazira in the Sibsagar district demanding Rupees 5000 million.
- January 12: Suspected ULFA militants attack a Royal Bhutanese Army patrol and kill an army guide near village Gerwa in the southern district of Samdrup Jongkhar of Bhutan bordering Assam.
- January 2: ULFA 'chairman', Arabinda Rajkhowa, in the outfit's mouthpiece Freedom reacting to Chief Minister Tarun Gogoi's announcement of a safe passage for the outfit's cadres during the Bihu festivities said that the Union Government is playing a 'dangerous game' by "talking of peace and unleashing the armed forces on its unsuspecting cadre at the same time."
- January 1: Arabinda Rajkhowa rules out holding direct peace talks with New Delhi unless the Government released some of their senior jailed leaders.

2005

- December 30: SULFA cadre, Biren Neog, is killed in police firing at Digboi in the Tinsukia district.
- December 27. Officer-in-charge of the Nelli outpost and a ULFA cadre are killed in an encounter at Durapani under Jagiroad police station in the Morigaon district.

- December 22: Police dismantles a bomb-making factory of the ULFA at Pushpawan village under Merapani police station in the Golaghat district.
- December 16: SULFA cadre Manikut Kalita is killed by the ULFA at Dipila Chowk, about 18 kilometers away from Mangaldoi town.
- November 18: Two ULFA cadres are killed in an encounter with the Army at Medhipara village under Bilasipara police station in Dhubri district.
- November 18: A SULFA cadre, Parikhit Hazarika, abducted earlier by an unidentified group on November 17, is found with stab injuries at the Digboi-Pengeri road in the Tinsukia district. Hazarika succumbs to his injuries at the district civil hospital.
- November 6: Three suspected ULFA cadres, Buten Gogoi, Pradip Gohain and Divyajyoti Gohain, are arrested from Rojabari under Chabua police station in the Dibrugarh district.
- November 4: Two unidentified ULFA militants are killed by the Army at Tekelipathar under Pengeri police station in the Tinsukia district.
- November 1: The ULFA, in its fortnightly newsletter Freedom, greets the People's Consultative Group for starting the peace process with the Centre and raising the matter of sovereignty in the meeting.
- October 27: A ULFA cadre, 'Lance corporal' Meena Bokolial alias Meena Gogoi of the outfit's '28th battalion' and three other women cadres, Binita- Hazarika, Monalisa Moran and Khyanmanti Moran, are arrested by the Army at Dighalipathar in the Philobari area of Tinsukia district.
- October 26: A round of negotiations between the Union Government and the ULFA-backed People's Consultative Group (PCG) is held in New Delhi.
- October 25: Two ULFA terrorists, Chand Barman alias Ritesh Saud and Surat Deka alias Rupjyoti, are killed by the police at Mowamari Chapori in the Darrang district.
- October 25: Security forces arrest Nripen Sarma, chairperson of a women's organisation Lovita, along with two other members from the organization's office at Chayygaon in the Kamrup district on charges of having a nexus with the ULFA.
- October 24: Suspected ULFA terrorists kill a hotel employee, Pramode Singh, at Khowang in the Dibrugarh district for nonpayment of extortion money.

- October 7: A ULFA cadre, Dulu Sonowal, is shot dead during an encounter with the SFs at Jokai Sohikota Tepuguri village in the Dibrugarh district.
- October 1: ULFA, in its mouthpiece Freedom, says that it would not start any negotiations with the Government till the time Army operations against the outfit are completely stopped.
- September 29: The ULFA sends a formal letter informing the Prime Minister's Office of the formation of the People's Consultative Group.
- September 26: Two ULFA terrorists, Nilim Kumar and Hiren Dohotia, are killed by the Army at Dibru-Saikhowa in the Tinsukia district.
- September 23: A ULFA cadre, identified as Azad Barua alias Swadhin Ray, is arrested from a flat in the South 24 Parganas district of West Bengal.
- September 20: The Army, during its ongoing operations in the Dibru-Saikhowa reserve forest, kills a ULFA "battalion commander", Achintya Saikia, and one of his woman associates in an encounter near Ajuka village.
- September 19: Biju Chakravarti alias Shailen Sharma, a senior ULFA cadre, is arrested along with his wife from a locality near Amber Fort in Jaipur, capital city of Rajasthan.
- September 14: ULFA chairman Arabinda Rajkhowa, in a press statement, says 12 of the outfit's cadres have been killed in the army operations in the Dibru-Saikhowa forests. Army authorities, however, deny this.
- September 8: ULFA calls for a dawn-to-dusk general strike in protest against "Government's negligence towards the treatment of ULFA leader Robin Handique leading to his death."
- September 8: ULFA announces a 10-member people's consultative group headed by mediator Indira Goswami to enter into a dialogue with the Union Government.
- August 31 : Robin Handique, 'Political Advisor' of the ULFA, dies at Kanaklata Civil Hospital following kidney failure.
- August 30: Two ULFA terrorists shoot dead a school-teacher, Sukleswar Medhi, in front of the Balitara High School in Nalbari district. A ULFA terrorist is killed in the subsequent army operation in the same area.
- August 30: Army launches an anti-insurgency operation in the Dibru-Saikhowa reserve forest in Tinsukia district in search of ULFA terrorists, Prabal Neog, Jiten Dutta and A. Saikia of the '28th battalion'.

- August 27: One person is killed and 14 others sustain injuries when ULFA cadres hurled two grenades at a police party on the national highway at Changsari in the Kamrup district.
- August 22: C. Bora, a doctor, and two nurses are arrested from Rupaisiding in the Tinsukia district for alleged nexus with the ULFA. The doctor confesses of having treated several ULFA cadres.
- August 16: ULFA militants shot dead a civilian at Khamti Mohang village under the Bordumsa Police Station limits.
- August 11: Six ULFA collaborators are arrested from the Charigaon and Koronga areas of Jorhat district.
- August 9: An activist of the human rights organisation, Manab Adhikar Sangram Samiti, Benudhar Hazarika, is arrested from Abhayapuri village under Borholla police station in the Jorhat district for nexus with the ULFA.
- August 7: Four persons are killed and 12 others sustain injuries in an explosion triggered by the ULFA at a bus stand at Boko in the Kamrup district.
- August 7: ULFA carries out a series of explosions targeting army installations, oil and gas pipelines, electric and telephone exchanges in the Nalbari, Sibsagar, Dibrugarh, Jorhat, Tinsukia and Lakhimpur districts.
- July 31: ULFA asks politicians from New Delhi to keep away from campaigning in the Legislative Assembly elections in early 2006. The outfit's chairman, Arabinda Rajkhowa, in an e-mail to the local media says, "The practice of inviting leaders of national parties to the state, as if they were leaders from Assam, and listening to their speeches must be stopped immediately."
- July 27: A ULFA terrorist and one Army personnel are killed in an encounter at the 12-Mile area inside Tinkupani reserve forest under Lekhapani police station in the Tinsukia district.
- July 26: Three ULFA cadres are killed and another sustains injuries in an encounter with the Army personnel between Jagun and Jairampur in the Sibsagar district.
- July 18: Guwahati city police arrests four ULFA linkmen from various parts of the city.
- July 14: Suspected ULFA terrorists trigger an explosion targeting a security forces' vehicle inside the Duramara Reserve Forest area under Pengeri Police Station in Tinsukia district.
- July 11: ULFA 'Commander-in-chief' Paresh Baruah, in a letter to the Prime Minister, threatens to 'reconsider' the option of negotiating with

the Government if the dialogue process does not focus on sovereignty for the State. The outfit further says that any dialogue process could begin only after the release of 10 of its leaders currently held in various jails in India, Bangladesh and Bhutan.

- June 26: Twelve persons, including six CRPF personnel, are injured in an IED explosion triggered by suspected ULFA terrorists in the Nine Mile area of Guwahati city. Two persons succumb to their injuries subsequently.
- June 24: A police officer, Puna Gogoi, is killed by the ULFA at Talap Bazaar in the Tinsukia district.
- June 22: Mojammel Haque, a ULFA 'commander', is arrested from a hideout at Baxirhat in the Coochbehar district of West Bengal.
- June 22: Two unidentified ULFA cadres are killed in an encounter with the police at Jonai in the Dhemaji district.
- June 20: Suspected ULFA terrorists trigger a powerful explosion at the State Secretariat complex in the capital Dispur.
- June 19: Four ULFA terrorists and one soldier are killed during two encounters in the Nalbari district.
- June 16: Four ULFA terrorists, including three woman cadres, are killed in an encounter with the police at Doloni village under Khowang Police Station in the Dibrugarh district.
- June 16: Ten ULFA cadres, including 'sergeant major' Amit Chandra Mandal, surrender before the Army in Dhubri along with some arms and ammunition.
- June 9: An hotelier in Guwahati city, Hemendra Dutta Choudhury, is arrested for alleged nexus with the ULFA.
- June 7: Fourteen terrorists belonging to different militant outfits, including the ULFA, surrender before authorities at the Misa Army camp.
- June 5: Arms and ammunition belonging to the ULFA's '109 battalion' are recovered from the Bamundanga area of Goalpara district.
- June 6: A woman, identified as Suchitra Rai, is arrested from Basugaon in the Kokrajhar district for alleged links with the ULFA.
- June 5: Two ULFA terrorists belonging to the outfit's '28th battalion', identified as Apurba Barua and Pawan Moran, are killed during an encounter with the army personnel at Jokaichowkgaon under Doomdooma police station in the Tinsukia district.

- June 5: Police in Guwahati arrest Tapan Deka, a junior engineer of the Northeast Frontier Railway, and his daughter from the Jalukbari locality for suspected links with the ULFA.
- June 4: Suspected ULFA terrorists explode a bomb beneath a microwave tower at Gutanagar.
- June 1: Three ULFA terrorists surrender before the Army authorities at Panbari in the Dhubri district.
- May 30: ULFA 'commander-in-chief' Paresh Baruah asks for the release of four of the outfit's leaders before commencement of talks with the Union Government.
- May 27: An IED explosion by the ULFA damages the wooden bridge at Maithong on the National Highway No. 52, connecting the eastern parts of Assam and Arunachal Pradesh.
- May 26: ULFA triggers IED explosions in the Choto Dirak and Dirak Chariaii areas near Kakopathar in Tinsukia district damaging the electric transformers.
- May 26: Suspected ULFA cadres kill a leader of the Congress party, Amrit Dutta, at the Dhekorgorah Block office under Pulibor police station in Jorhat district.
- May 26: Three security force (SF) personnel are wounded in an explosion triggered by the ULFA targeting an army vehicle at Digboi-Pengeri road in the Dibrugarh district.
- May 25: A hardcore ULFA cadre, Ashanta Rajguru alias Raj Baishya, is arrested from an unspecified location on the Assam-Meghalaya border.
- May 24: A civilian is killed by suspected ULFA terrorists at Dirakmukh under Dhofa police station in the Tinsukia district.
- May 24: Four ULFA collaborators are arrested from the Noonmati police station area in Guwahati and Rongjuli police station area in Goalpara.
- May 23: Three persons, including one SF personnel, are injured as suspected ULFA terrorists trigger an IED explosion in the Noonmati locality of Guwahati city.
- May 21 : A college teacher and a freelance journalist are arrested from Bilastpara in the Dubri district and Panbazaar in Kamrup district respectively for alleged links with the ULFA and involvement in several explosions in Guwahati.
- May 20: Four ULFA terrorists are arrested along with a unspecified number of IEDs from Kumarikata in the Baska district.
- May 20: Suspected ULFA cadres trigger an IED explosion partially damaging a bridge at Sadiya in the Dibrugarh district.

- May 20: One Indo-Ttbetan Border Police (ITBP) personnel is killed and four others sustain injuries during an ambush by the ULFA at Borhat under Sonari subdivision in the Sibsagar district.
- May 14: Two ULFA cadres, Debajit Amche and Palesh Malang, are arrested from the Rangfang gaon area in Karbi Anglong district.
- May 14: Police recover two universal machine guns, three magazines and 60 rounds from an ULFA hideout at Masuk in the West Garo Hills district of Meghalaya.
- May 9: Three ULFA terrorists are killed during an encounter with the Army at Kothalguri in the Dibrugarh district.
- May 8: Army personnel kill two ULFA cadres, identified as Ugra Barman and Uddipta Bharali, at Dhanbil in the Nalbari district.
- April 27: Two ULFA terrorists are arrested from Baruabamungaon in the Golaghat district.
- April 24: Six ULFA cadres, including a woman 'sergeant major', are arrested at Sesupani in the Tinsukia district.
- April 18: Four ULFA terrorists are arrested during two separate operations at Baichara village and Jail Road area in the Nalbari district.
- April 12: Sixteen ULFA cadres surrender before the General Officer Commanding of the 2 Mountain Division at Laipuli in the Tinsukia district.
- April 2: A ULFA cadre is killed by the Guwahati City Police during an encounter at Panjabari-Bagharbori Napara area under Dispur police station limits.
- April 1 : Two ULFA terrorists are killed in an explosion at Kharbilpar village under Barama police station in the Baska district.
- April 1 : ULFA carries out several explosions in Guwahati, Dhemaji and Tinsukia targeting security forces and oil pipelines and injure more than 15 persons.
- March 27: Four ULFA terrorists, including hardcore cadre Khagen Boruah alias Rana Gohatn, surrender before the Sibsagar district police.
- March 24: Police arrests three ULFA terrorists from the residence of an advocate near the Assam Engineering College in Guwahati.
- March 16: A suspected ULFA terrorist is killed in an encounter with the security forces at Misa Hatkhola under Khairabari police station limits in the Darrang district.
- March 16: Diganta Baruah alias Kesar Jyoti Saikia, 'second commander' of the ULFA's 'Enigma group' and a bodyguard of Paresh Baruah, are

killed during an encounter at Nikhira village under Khairabari police station in the Udalguri district.

- March 15: Six people are injured during an explosion suspected to have been triggered by the ULFA at Bihpuria in the Lakhimpur district.
- March 14: Hiten Thakuria, a ULFA terrorist, is killed in an encounter with the Army at Ghasbari village in the Dhubri district.
- March 12: Suspected ULFA terrorist, Parag Das, is killed during an encounter with the police in the Lokhra area of Guwahati city.
- March 11 : One person is killed and nine others are wounded as ULFA terrorists lob a grenade targeting a police vehicle in front of the headquarters of the Congress party in Guwahati city.
- March 11 : ULFA terrorists trigger an explosion in front of a hotel near the Sibsagar police station injuring 11 people.
- March 9: One police personnel is killed and seven others sustain injuries as suspected ULFA terrorists trigger several bomb explosions across the Bongaigaon, Kamrup, Dhubri and Sibsagar districts.
- March 2: Two ULFA terrorists, Biren Gogoi and Naren Gogoi, are arrested from Lengeri Bamunbari No. 2 village in Dibrugarh district.
- February 28: Two ULFA terrorists, including Suman Barua alias Ruby Bhuyan, editor of the outfit's mouthpiece *Freedom,* and Chandan Borah, a bomb expert believed to be trained in Pakistan, surrender before the Assam Police in Guwahati.
- February 26: Three ULFA terrorists, identified as 'lance corporal of Sivasagar' Amar Mili, Pallav Kakoti alias Ban Moran and Nasang Rangpi, are killed in an encounter with Army personnel at Kheroni Hatimura under Bordumsa police station on the Assam-Arunachal Pradesh border.
- February 20, 2005: Suspected ULFA cadres hurl a grenade at a grocery shop located at Kakopathar Tiniali under Kakopathar police station in Tinsukia district injuring the owner and four persons.
- February 10: A ULFA terrorist is killed in an encounter with the Army personnel at Khalenapara under Barama police station in the Baska district.
- February 8: ULFA terrorists explode a bomb at Kardaiguri village in the Tinsukia District targeting the Army personnel on patrol. However, no loss of life or injury is reported.
- February 7: A ULFA cadre is killed during an encounter with the Army personnel at Jagun Meo under Lekhapani police station in the Tinsukia District.

- February 7: ULFA terrorists explode a grenade targeting a shop at Rupai Chaiding under Doomdooma police station in the Tinsukia district.
- January 26: A ULFA cadre is killed during an encounter with the Army at Amguri under Lakhpur police station in Goalpara district.
- January 26: Two persons are seriously injured as ULFA terrorists trigger an explosion near Bamunimaidan in Guwahati City.
- January 26: ULFA cadres explode a bomb under a culvert at Bongaigaon.
- January 26: ULFA cadres explode two bombs near the Judges' field in Guwahati City targeting the Republic Day celebrations. Three persons, including a police officer, are injured in the second explosion.
- January 25: ULFA terrorists lob a grenade near Railway Gate No.3 at Maligaon in Guwahati City.
- January 24: Suspected ULFA terrorists trigger a grenade blast at Ganesguri in the capital Guwahati injuring seven persons.
- January 23: ULFA activists hurla grenade targeting the outer barricade of Golaghat Jail in Golaghat district.
- January 20: ULFA terrorists explode a bomb targeting a portion of a gas pipe line at Sarupathar Bengaligaon under Chabua police station in Dibrugarh district.
- January 19: ULFA cadres hurl a bomb at Mangaldoi police station compound in the Darrang district resulting in injuries to a police personnel.
- January 19: ULFA terrorists hurl a grenade at Jonai police station in the Dhemaji district.
- January 19: An Electric Tower located at Toklai tea estate in the Jorhat district is damaged due to an explosion triggered by the ULFA.
- January 19: One person is killed and six others sustain injuries during a bomb blast triggered by suspected ULFA terrorists at Boxirhat under Golokganj police station in the Dhubri district.
- January 15: An ULFA terrorist, Ajit Deka, is killed in an encounter at Gandhibari village under Tamulpur Police Station in the Nalbari district.
- January 11 : Fourteen civilians, including a nine-year-old girl and four women, are injured when suspected ULFA terrorists trigger an explosion at the Marwaripatty area of Jorhat town.
- January 8: A surrendered ULFA (SULFA) cadre, Ashok Das, is killed by suspected ULFA terrorists in the Barama town of Nalbari district.

2004

- December 30: Security forces' arrest two ULFA terrorists, Jayanta Gaon and Arup Dutta, suspected to have been involved in the improvised explosive device blast at the Jalukonibari police outpost on December 24, from an unspecified place in Jorhat district.

- December 28: ULFA terrorist, Dipak Das, is killed during an encounter with the Army at Aagsia village in the Kamrup district.
- December 27: Two ULFA cadres, Narak Rabha and Dipak Rabha, surrender before the police at Goalpara.
- December 26: Three ULFA terrorists are killed following an encounter with the police at Mornoi Garchouk along the Assam-Nagaland border in the Jorhat district.
- December 24: Unidentified ULFA terrorists hurt a grenade targeting the Janukoni police outpost under Titabor police station in the Jorhat district.
- December 22: Assam Police kill a ULFA cadre, Ujjal Roy alias Aliul Islam, at Bhaibazar in the Dhubri district.
- December 18: Six persons are injured as suspected ULFA terrorists lob a grenade targeting a vehicle in the Noonmati area of Guwahati city.
- December 17: In an e-mail message, 'Chairman' of the ULFA, Arabinda Rajkhowa, states that the outfit's 'commander-in-chief', Paresh Baruah, has fallen ill and is being shifted to a safe location for surgery.
- December 16: Medhi, a 'sergeant major', of the ULFA surrenders before the troops at Panbari in the Dhubri district.
- December 16: One person is killed and 12 others sustain injuries when suspected ULFA terrorists lob a grenade in the Paltan Bazaar area of Guwahati city.
- December 15: ULFA terrorists hurl a grenade targeting a police team and injure nine persons at Silapathar in the Dhemaji district.
- December 15: ULFA terrorists lob a grenade at a CRPF patrol party at Sadiya Bazaar in the Tinsukia district.
- December 14: Two persons are killed and 26 others sustain injuries when a timer explosive device, planted by ULFA terrorists, explodes at Maya *Bazaar* in Morigaon town.
- December 14: A timer device explodes opposite the Haiborgaon police station in Nagaon town killing one person and injuring 17 others.
- December 14: A CRPF personnel and a civilian are injured when unidentified ULFA terrorists lob a grenade near a cinema hall in Guwahati city.
- December 14: Two army personnel are wounded in a bomb blast by ULFA terrorists near the Guwahati railway station.
- December 14: ULFA detonates a bomb blast targeting a rural telephone exchange at Kakojan in the Tinsukia district.

- December 13: Two police personnel are killed and eight others sustain injuries in two explosions engineered by the ULFA in front of the Hatigaon police outpost in Guwahati city.
- December 10: Two hardcore ULFA terrorists, Raju Gogoi, an explosive expert and 'major' Jyotish Nath, surrender at Panbari in the Dhubri district and the district headquarters of Sibsagar district.
- December 9: An unidentified ULFA terrorist is killed during an encounter with the Army at Merkuchi village in the Nalbari district.
- December 9: ULFA rejects the invitation from the Prime Minister's Office (PMO) for peace talks. Talking to media houses in Guwahati over telephone, the ULFA 'commander-in-chief', Paresh Barua states that the PMO letter sent through noted writer Mamoni Raisom Goswami was 'self-contradictory and confusing'.
- December 8: The Nazira Police arrest Bijuli Devi, wife of ULFA 'second lieutenant' Sujrt Mohan, commander of 'B' camp at Myanmar with her two-year-old child from an unspecified place in the Sibsagar district.
- December 5: Two hardcore ULFA terrorists, 'second lieutenant' of the outfit's '109 Battalion', Rubul AH and 'lieutenant' of the same battalion, Subhash Sharma, are killed in an encounter with the army at Kumarbari in the Kamrup district.
- December 5: Two ULFA terrorists killed in an encounter with the army personnel at Kumarbari under Palashbari police station in Kamrup district.
- December 4: Three militants belonging to the ULFA including a woman cadre surrender to the army authorities in Dibrugarh.
- December 3: The Sentinel quoting police sources reports that ULFA is planning a major offensive in Dhemaji district and 20 hardcore cadres of the outfit trained in the Kachin area of Myanmar are trying to sneak into the district.
- November 29: Suspected ULFA terrorists trigger an explosion at an unspecified place in Tinsukia district damaging two electric poles.
- November 29: ULFA 'commander-in-chief', Paresh Barua claims that at least 150 ULFA cadres have been working in various security force establishments in the country. In an interview to the Sentinel Baruah says, "As the Indian security forces have sneaked in their members into our organisation, we are also adopting a similar policy."
- November 27: Three ULFA terrorists including a woman cadre and a doctor working for the outfit are arrested from Tengapukhuri under Mathurapur police station limits in Sibsagar district.

- November 27: ULFA 'chairman' Arabinda Rajkhowa, in a press statement, demands a plebiscite on the issue of sovereignty of Assam. He assures that the outfit would follow the verdict of the plebiscite and urged the Government of India to do the same.
- November 26: Three ULFA terrorists surrender before the Tinsukia district administration at Tinsukia.
- November 25: ULFA terrorist Nomal Gogoi is killed and another terrorist is arrested following an encounter at Dhingchapari near Sadia in Dibrugarh district.
- November 25: ULFA, on the eve of the 'protest day', triggers a series of explosions in different parts of the State injuring six persons.
- November 23: A ULFA terrorist, Biswajit Bora and three of his aides are arrested by the security forces following an encounter at Maskhowa under Deberapar police station in Jorhat district.
- November 22: Two ULFA terrorists, Praneshware Rabha and Bokul Rajkhowa, are killed in an encounter with the army at an unspecified place along the Assam-Meghalaya border in Goalpara district.
- November 21 : Two ULFA terrorists, a 'general secretary' of the Dhubri district unit, Atul Baruah alias Arabinda Nath and Sushen Bepari, a 'lieutenant' in the outfit's 'central communication', surrender before the Dhubri Superintendent of Police at Dhubri.
- November 19: Three ULFA terrorists, belonging to its 'Enigma-B group' including a woman cadre surrender before the army and police authorities at Tamulpur in Nalbari district.
- November 18: In an e-mail message to the local media, ULFA's 'chairman', Arabinda Rajkhowa, expresses willingness to begin a peace dialogue with the Government of India, provided the outfit is formally invited. He reiterates that no discussion would be possible without the outfit's demand for sovereignty on the agenda and described the issue as "a right of the people of Assam" and not a "mere demand by his organization".
- November 16: Talking to The Sentinel over the phone, the ULFA's 'commander-in-chief', Paresh Barua make it clear that any talks with the Central government must have 'sovereignty' as the core issue to make it a meaningful exercise.
- November 15: A ULFA terrorist, Jayanto Moran alias Jotin surrender before the army authorities in Tinsukia on November 15.
- November 15: ULFA terrorist Amal Barua alias Jiban Sarma killed in an encounter at Milanpur village in Golaghat district.

- November 14: ULFA terrorist, Prakash Boro alias Mukti Kachari arrested subsequent to an encounter at Jagiroad in Morigaon district.
- November 10: Six ULFA cadres surrender before the Army at Missa in Nagaon district.
- November 9: ULFA 'second lieutenant', Tulu Bora killed following a gun battle with the troops of Red Horns Division at Chiramoga in Goalpara district.
- November 8: An ULFA terrorist Manas Das alias Mridul killed near Nalbari town.
- November 4: Self-styled 'second lieutenant' of the '28th battalion' of the ULFA, Simanta Saikia alias Simanta Chinese along with his associate, Nijut Chetia surrender at the Laipuli Army camp in Tinsukia district along with an AK-56 rifle and ammunition.
- November 1: An army personnel is killed following an encounter with the ULFA terrorists at Lakhrakhan under Sepakhati police station in Sibsagar district.
- October 30: ULFA threatens to target Congress ministers, ML As and other district and local-level leaders of the party to avenge the killing of five cadres of the outfit in Lakhimpur district on October 29 by the security forces.
- October 29: Five ULFA terrorists, members of the outfit's 'Action Group', are killed in an encounter with the security forces at Kasojuli village under Laluk police station limits in Lakhimpur district.
- October 29: 13 ULFA terrorists, including a women cadre surrender before the police at Dibrugarh along with an AK-56 rifle, a .56 pistol, a wireless set and several rounds of ammunition.
- October 27: Eight ULFA cadres surrender before the district administration at Sibsagar along with an AK-56 rifle, one hand grenade, one gun, magazines, live cartridges and a wireless set.
- October 19: Troops of the Army's Red Horn division arrests the 'commander' of the ULFA's Bongaigaon unit, Pulak Bharali, alias Uday Das from Utamar village in Dhubri district.
- October 12: Suspected ULFA terrorists kill two civilians at Mridongpara in Tinsukia district.
- October 3: Two persons including a six-year-old boy were injured as ULFA terrorists open fire at a weekly market at Gossaigaon in the Kokrajhar district.
- October 3: ULFA terrorists blow up a gas pipeline near Borhat Tea Estate in the Sibsagar district disrupting supply of gas to several tea factories of Upper Assam.

- October 3: Seven army personnel were injured in a grenade attack by ULFA terrorists at a bus carrying them at Medongpara Dhola Road under Doomdooma police station in the Tinsukia district.
- October 2: Suspected NDFB and ULFA terrorists trigger a series of bomb blasts and open indiscriminate firing at various places in lower Assam killing at least 24 people and wounding over 40.
- September 30: Assam police arrests two ULFA terrorists including a "bomb expert" identified as Mihir Chetia, from Halwating Tea Estate along the Assam-Nagaland border in the Sibsagar district.
- September 29: ULFA terrorist Lohit Chandra Roy alias Akon Hazong, killed in an encounter with the Assam Police at Bidyapur Rabhapara in Bongaigaon district.
- September 23: Two ULFA terrorists are killed in an encounter with the troops at Nayapara under Krishna police station in Goalpara district.
- September 22: Two ULFA terrorists are killed in an encounter with the army personnel at Singimari under Palasbari police station in Kamrup district.
- September 21: ULFA terrorists kill a civilian at Rashigaon in Bongaigaon district.
- September 15: Two ULFA terrorists are killed in an encounter with the security forces at Khitakimari village under Golokganj police station in Dhubri district.
- September 12: Two ULFA terrorists, including a self-styled lieutenant, Rakta Cheleng, are killed in an encounter at Mulong Pahar under Ledo police station in Tinsukia district.
- September 7: Two ULFA terrorists are killed in an encounter at Balatarigaon in Barpeta district.
- August 29: Two army personnel are killed in an IED explosion by suspected ULFA terrorists at Shantipara-Sakumari in Kamrup district.
- August 27: 47 ULFA cadres surrender at the Assam Rifles camp at Chardwar in Sonitpur district.
- August 26: ULFA terrorists trigger a series of bomb blasts in different districts of Assam, killing six persons and injuring 80 others.
- August 25: One person is killed and 10 others, including two police personnel, are injured in a grenade attack by ULFA terrorists in front of a movie theatre at Dibrugarh town.
- August 25: Assam Police arrests self-styled 'lieutenant' of the ULFA's '28th Battalion', Anju Saikia alas Dalimi Dutta, from Puthinadi in the Jorhat district.

- August 19: ULFA 'Commander-in-Chief', Paresh Baruah, in a statement to the media denies his outfit's involvement in the August 15-explosion at Dhemaji.
- August 15: Seventeen persons, including 16 school children, were killed as ULFA detonates explosives at the venue of Independence Day celebrations at Dhemaji town.

  A separate explosion by the ULFA, at the venue of Independence Day celebrations at Dhakuakhana in Dhemaji district, results in no casualty.
- August 14: One civilian is killed and 18 others are injured as suspected ULFA terrorists trigger a grenade blast inside a cinema hall at Gauripur in Dhubri district.
- August 10: Two ULFA terrorists, a SULFA cadre and a police personnel are killed in an encounter at Jorabat in the Kamrup district.
- August 8: ULFA explodes five powerful improvised explosive devices targeting two transmission towers of the Power Grid Corporation of India Limited and Assam State Electricity Board at Trtabor in the Jorhat district.
- August 7: A security force personnel is killed as suspected ULFA terrorists lob a grenade on a vehicle of the Border Security Force (BSF) at the Machkhowa locality in Guwahati city.
- August 3: A Block Development Officer of Manikpur in Bongaigaon district killed by suspected ULFA cadres in front of his office.
- August 2: The Assam Police arrests Simanta Phukan alias Bastav Deodhai Phukan, chief of ULFA's 'Enigma unit' and commander of the outfit's '28th battalion' along with his associate Dulal Baruah, from Napam Wising village under Gaurisagar police station in Sibsagar district.
- July 23: Two ULFA cadres, identified as Ratiul Barua and Dhaniram Barua, are killed in an encounter at Sundardheki in the Lakhimpur district.
- July 22: ULFA 'district commander' of Bongaigaon, Hitesh Rai, is killed during an encounter at Majigaon.
- July 21: ULFA terrorists kill two activists of the Congress and Bharatiya Janata Party at Jagun in the Tinsukia district.
- July 17: Media reports indicate that 25 northeastern militants including several ULFA cadres have been killed in separate attacks by unidentified assailants in various localities of Dhaka city. Bangladesh Government denies the occurrence of any such incident.
- July 17: Suspected ULFA terrorists kill a trader at Kabaitari market in the Bongaigaon district for non-payment of extortion money.

- July 16: Unidentified militants fire at the residences of three ULFA cadres in Sibsagar city.
- July 16: ULFA terrorists trigger a blast targeting a telephone exchange at Chabua in the Dibrugarh district, causing extensive damage to the exchange.
- July 15. Six persons, including three Assam Police personnel, are wounded when suspected ULFA terrorists hurled a hand grenade near the Bongaigaon civil hospital in the Bongaigaon district.
- July 15: Suspected ULFA terrorists blow up an oil pipeline belonging to the Oil India Limited at a village near Tengakhat in the Dibrugarh district.
- July 15: ULFA terrorists blow up a gas pipeline of the Assam Gas Company at Bismile in the Dibrugarh district.
- July 14: ULFA terrorists kill a SULFA cadre, identified as Monul Haque, at Hajo in the Kamrup district.
- July 10 : Twelve persons are injured during a grenade explosion in a cinema hall at Nagaon by suspected ULFA terrorists.
- July 9: ULFA terrorists shoot dead two local leaders of the Congress party, identified as Debajit Haloi and Bipul Talukdar, at Santipur Milan Chowk under Barama police station limits in Nalbari district.
- July 2: Assam police arrest a man, identified as Nirmal Das, for allegedly harbouring ULFA terrorists from the Basistha locality of Guwahati city.
- June 29: A suspected ULFA woman cadre, namely Mamoni Devi alias Bibha Hazarika, is arrested from Sarupathar in the Golaghat district.
- June 29: Seventeen terrorists belonging to the ULFA, NDFB and Tiwa Liberation Tiger Force surrender at Misa in the Nagaon district.
- June 28: Union Minister of State for Defence, B K Handique, speaking to the press in Guwahati rules out the possibility of the Union Government announcing any unilateral cease-fire with the ULFA.
- June 28: Thirty-nine terrorists, including four women cadres of the ULFA and Bodo Tiger Force (BTF), surrender at North Lakhimpur along with 10 assorted weapons.
- June 24: Seven bus passengers are killed and fifteen others sustain injuries as suspected ULFA terrorists detonate a bomb inside a passenger bus at Majgaon under Mathurapur police station limits in the Sibsagar district.
- June 21 : ULFA triggers a bomb blast in the premises of the Telephone Exchange cum Post Office of the Bharat Sanchar Nigam Limited (BSNL) at Tengakhat in Dibrugarh district. The explosion partially damages the office although no casualty is reported.

- June 20: Assam Chief Minister Tarun Gogoi in an interview to *The Telegraph* says that the Union Government is keen to have negotiations with the ULFA and the NDFB on the lines of the dialogue with the NSCN-IM.
- June 19: Seventeen people are wounded as suspected ULFA terrorists trigger an explosion at Chamber Road in the Tinsukia town. One person later succumbs to his injuries.
- June 19: Suspected ULFA terrorists trigger an IED and blow up a coal-laden goods train at Ultapur railway station between Digboi and Margherita in the Tinsukia district derailing eight bogies. A driver of the train was injured in the incident.
- June 18: ULFA serves an extortion demand amounting to Rupees 25 lakh on a business establishment, SRI Company, in the Mangaldoi town.
- June 17: Three ULFA cadres are arrested from Bordubi in the Tinsukia district.
- June 17: One ULFA terrorist is killed during an encounter with the Army at Lokrapara village in Goalpara district.
- June 16: Assam Chief Minister Tarun Gogoi, in an interview to the *Press Trust of India* in Guwahati, says that the ULFA has shown the 'first signs' of coming to the negotiation table to solve the insurgency problem.
- June 16: ULFA 'commander-in-chief' Paresh Barua, in a telephonic conversation with the Guwahati-based vernacular daily *Pratidin,* rejects the Chief Minister's statement as baseless.
- June 14: ULFA terrorist Rohit Mardi alias Hopna Mazda of Bharaguri village in Kokrajhar district killed in an encounter with Army at Pachim Mannatari village under Tihu PS in Nalbari district. An AK-56 rifle with two magazines, 24 rounds of AK-56 live ammunition etc are recovered from him.
- June 11 : Chief Minister Tarun Gogoi states in Guwahati that, "The recent understanding between the ULFA and the NSCN-IM is a threat to the State."
- June 9: Twenty-three people are wounded when suspected ULFA cadres explode a grenade inside a cinema hall at Tinsukia. One of the injured dies a day later.
- June 4: A surrendered ULFA (SULFA) cadre is killed by suspected ULFA terrorists at Chakchaka Bazaar under Sarbhog police station limits in Barpeta district.
- June 4: Suspected ULFA terrorists blow up an oil pipeline of the Oil India Limited at Geetapathar in the Tinsukia district.

- June 3: Self-styled district commander of the ULFA in Nagaon, Siba Rajbongsi alias Rajen Gohain, is arrested by the Army from Diphu in the Karbi Anglong district.
- June 3: Three ULFA terrorists are killed in an encounter at Bhalukdabi village in the Goalpara district.
- May 31 : Six surrendered ULFA and NDFB terrorists are arrested while extorting money from a private hospital at Udalguri.
- May 29: ULFA 'foreign secretary', Sashadhar Choudhury, in a statement, demands the release of seven of the outfit's leaders, missing during the Bhutan Military operations in December 2003, in exchange for the release of the Assam State Minister G C Langthasa's son whom it had earlier abducted.
- May 22: Twenty ULFA terrorists surrender to the Army authorities at Tamulpur in the Nalbari district.
- May 10: A school teacher of Kukurmara village is killed by two ULFA terrorists at Tan Tan High School in the Kamrup district.
- May 5: Hardcore ULFA terrorist, Rudrajit Deodhai Phukan of Deoraja Mantania village in Sibsagar district, is killed during an encounter with the Army at Na-Kathalguri village in Tinsukia district.
- April 30: One ULFA terrorist is killed in an encounter with the Army at Bordoloinagar under Tinsukia police station in Tinsukia District.
- April 27: Security forces recover seven kilograms of RDX planted by suspected ULFA terrorists underneath the railway tracks at Kurshakati in the Kokrajhar district.
- April 26: Two ULFA terrorists are killed during an encounter with the Army at Lakhopur village in the Nalbari district.
- April 24: Two ULFA terrorists are killed in a bomb explosion inside a building under construction at Bishnu Nagar in Tinsukia District.
- April 14: Two persons, including a child, are killed when suspected ULFA terrorists hurled a grenade targeting a group of security force personnel at Ganeshguri in Guwahati city.
- April 10: Three ULFA cadres are killed during an encounter with the troops near Hahim in Kamrup district along the Assam-Meghalaya border.
- April 6: Nine police personnel are injured in a bomb blast, suspected to be carried out by the ULFA, at Ghuguha in the Dhemaji district.
- April 4: Two ULFA terrorists, identified as Bhaba Gogoi and Navajyoti Gogoi, are killed in an encounter with the police at Changpur in Golaghat district.

- April 3: Twenty people are wounded in a bomb explosion triggered by suspected ULFA terrorists inside a movie hall at Simaluguri in the Sibsagar district.
- March 31 : Speaking to the media in Dhaka, Bangladesh Foreign Minister Morshed Khan rules out the possibility of handing over ULFA leader Anup Chetia, who is now in jail, to Indian authorities.
- March 29: Two ULFA terrorists are killed during an encounter with the Army's Red Horn Division at Aranga Nala in Kamrup district.
- March 24: ULFA terrorist Biki Chutia alias Rakesh Chutia of Purana Matapung is killed in an encounter with Army at Daimali Tea Estate under Doomdooma police station limits in Tinsukia District.
- March 20: Suspected ULFA terrorists detonate explosives targeting the underground oil pipeline at Ratnapuria Chetiapathar in Sibsagar district.
- March 7: A goods train coming from Ledo to Guwahati is derailed when suspected ULFA terrorists explode an Improvised Explosive Device on the railway track at a place between Bhojo and Sufrai railway stations under Sonari police station in the Sibsagar district.
- March 4: Two security force personnel and a ULFA terrorist are killed in an encounter at Doholapara village in the Barpeta district.
- March 3: Eight ULFA and one NDFB cadre surrender at the Udalguri army camp of the 62 Field Artillery Regiment in Darrang district.
- March 3: Assam Police recover a huge cache of arms and ammunition, kept buried by ULFA terrorists in Bishondoi village in the Dhubri district. 12 AK-56 rifles, one US carbine, one rocket launcher, 28 rounds of AK-56 ammunition, seven universal machine guns magazines, one camera, some wireless sets, six rocket launcher cells and documents relating to arms training are recovered.
- March 3: Four ULFA terrorists are killed in an encounter with troops of the Red Horns Division of the Army at Tepkilobana in the Kamrup district.
- February 25: Assam Government extends the period of 'general amnesty' to cadres of the terrorist organizations- ULFA, NDFB, anti-talks faction of the UPDS and anti-talks faction of the Dima Halim Daoga (DHD) - till March 31 to enable them to surrender.
- February 24: Two unidentified ULFA terrorists and a SULFA cadre are killed in an encounter at Samotiapara village in Nalbari district.
- February 19: Atul Barooah, 'Finance Secretary (Western Zone)' of the ULFA, is killed during an encounter at Bhagadoli village in Dhubri district.

- February 12: Three suspected ULFA terrorists are killed near the Assam-Meghalaya border under Boko police station jurisdiction in Kamrup district.
- February 9: Eleven ULFA cadres, hailing from the Nalbari and Nagaon districts, surrender before the authorities after fleeing from their Bhutan camps following the Royal Bhutan Army (RBA) operations in December 2003.
- February 6: Five ULFA terrorists, including two women cadres, are arrested from a Nagaland-bound private vehicle near Borhola in the Jorhat district.
- January 31: Fifty-three ULFA cadres surrender at Tamulpur in the Nalbari district along with 56 assorted weapons.
- January 30: Three ULFA cadres surrender at Barpeta Road camp in the Barpeta district.
- January 28: Four ULFA terrorists trying to enter Assam from Bhutan are killed during an encounter at Paharbasti under Tamulpur police station jurisdiction in the Nalbari district.
- January 23: Twenty-six ULFA cadres surrender at Udalguri in the Darrang district.
- January 19: ULFA terrorists explode an IED targeting a crude oil pipeline of the Oil India Ltd (OIL), embedded seven feet under the ground, at Na Pathar village in the Sibsagar district.
- January 16: ULFA terrorists kill a civilian at Maj Mamorani village under Digboi police station jurisdiction in Tinsukia District.
- January 15: ULFA terrorists explode bombs on gas pipeline at two locations in the Tinsukia district.
- January 10: Suspected ULFA terrorists trigger an explosion targeting an over-ground crude oil pipeline of the Oil and Natural Gas Commission (ONGC) at Fakumharmoti in the Sibsagar district.
- January 8: Ten security force personnel are injured in twin ULFA strikes near Krishna! in the Goalpara district and Ghilabari in Kamrup district.
- January 5: North East Peoples' Forum (NEPF), a conglomeration of 16 political parties in the region, urges the ULFA to hold talks with the Union Government.
- January 5: Six ULFA and two Muslim United Liberation Front of Assam (MULFA) terrorists surrender to the Army along with small arms and ammunition at Laipuli under Tingkhong police station limits in the Dibrugarh district.

- January 4: ULFA 'chairman' Arabinda Rajkhowa reacting to the Bhutanese Prime Minister Lyonpo Jigmi Thinley's speech at the South Asian Association for Regional Cooperation (SAARC) Summit in Islamabad, Pakistan, in a press statement, labels him as 'a liar dictated by New Delhi'. He claims that there was absolutely no truth in the Bhutanese Premier's assertion that the Kingdom "suffered from the presence of three armed extremist outfits of northeast."
- January 3: Six ULFA cadres surrender at Laipuli in Tinsukia and Bengtol in the Kokrajhar district.

2003

- December 31: Sixteen ULFA terrorists surrender at Jorhat.
- December 29: Two ULFA terrorists are killed in an encounter at Sargapur village in the Nalbari District.
- December 27: Two unidentified ULFA terrorists are killed in an encounter with the Army at Batiagaon under Sarthebari police station limits in Barpeta District.
- December 26: ULFA 'commander-in-chief' Paresh Baruah, in an interview to a Guwahati based newspaper, offers conditional dialogue with the Union Government on the issue of Assam's sovereignty through a neutral third party mediator.
- December 26: ULFA's ideologue and founder member Bhimakanta Buragohain alias Mama surrenders along with three other ULFA leaders before the Indian Army at Tezpur in Sonitpur district.
- December 25: Five ULFA terrorists are killed while attempting to enter Assam from Bhutan at Baltinadi area under Tamulpur police station limits in the Nalbari district.
- December 23: Three ULFA terrorists are killed in separate encounters along the India-Bhutan border at Kumarikata and Tamulpur in the Nalbari district.
- December 22: ULFA 'Chairman' Arabinda Rajkhowa in a letter to the Chinese authorities asks for safe passage for its fleeing cadres from Bhutan.
- December 20: ULFA 'publicity secretary', Mithinga Daimary is arrested during military operations in Bhutan and later handed over to the Indian Army.
- December 20: Seven ULFA terrorists surrender in the Darrang district after escaping from their camp in Bhutan.
- December 20: ULFA along with the NDFB and the KLO calls for a 48-hour shutdown in 'Assam, Bodoland and Kamatapur' in protest against the military operations in Bhutan.

- December 19: Three ULFA terrorists are killed as they enter Indian Territory from Bhutan in the Manas Reserve Forest area of Barpeta district.
- December 18: Three ULFA terrorists are killed during an ambush laid by the Army in Panbari Reserve Forest under Bijni police station in Bongaigaon district.
- December 16: 63 ULFA cadres surrender at the 4 Corps headquarters in Tezpur.
- December 15: Royal Bhutan Army (RBA) launches military operations against the ULFA, NDFB and KLO terrorists holed up in 30 camps in southern Bhutan.
- December 8: Three persons are killed and six others sustain injuries as a time bomb planted by suspected ULFA terrorists explodes in front of a hardware store at Makum market in the Tinsukia district.
- November 29: ULFA terrorists kill three persons, including two police personnel, and injure four others in an ambush at Mejeragaon village under Silapathar police station limits in Dhemaji district.
- November 27: Three ULFA terrorists are killed in an encounter at Ghopapara Basti in the Nalapara Nala village of Darrang district.
- November 24: ULFA kills two civilians at Khanhkholobari under Udalguri police station limits in the Darrang district.
- November 22: ULFA terrorists kill 11 labourers of two brick kilns and injured seven others in the Bordubi area of Tinsukia district.
- November 19: Two ULFA terrorists are killed in an encounter at Gaikhowa village under Golokganj police station jurisdiction in Dhubri district.
- November 19: ULFA cadres kill four Hindi speaking persons in Nalbari town.
- November 19: Four women are killed and seven others sustain injuries as ULFA terrorists open fire at Gangquarter in the Bongaigaon district.
- November 18: Five truck drivers are killed and seven others are injured as ULFA terrorists open fire at Basirhat in Dhubri district.
- November 16: ULFA kills two persons at Nakerbari village in the Nalbari district.
- November 15: Suspected ULFA terrorists kill two businessmen at the Golakganj market in Dhubri district.
- November 10: Two ULFA cadres are killed in an encounter at Urangnala Guabari village near the Indo- Bhutan border in Nalbari district.

- October 28: One ULFA terrorist and a police personnel are killed during an encounter at Borkhuiha village in Nalbari district.
- October 27: Two ULFA terrorists are killed in an encounter at Betagaon in the Kamrup district.
- October 24: Pranati Deka, 'cultural secretary' of ULFA, is arrested along with another ULFA cadre at Phulbari in the West Garo Hills district of Meghalaya.
- October11 : Five persons are killed while another is injured in an attack by the ULFA near Dighal Tarrang Tea Estate in Tinsukia district.
- October 6: Two ULFA terrorists are killed during an encounter at Khalingduar reserve forest in the Darrang district.
- October 2: ULFA terrorists kill Deben Saikia, a village chief, at Kailash under Pengari police station limits in the Tinsukia district.
- September 27: Two ULFA terrorists are killed during an encounter at Ballamjora village under Gossaigaon police station jurisdiction in Kokrajhar district.
- September 14: Five persons, including two army personnel, are killed in an ambush by ULFA terrorists at Mukongpathar under Pengeri police station jurisdiction in Tinsukia district.
- September B: Police confirms that ULFA was behind the blast that occurred at the Athgaon area of Guwahati in Assam on September 7, 13 persons had been injured in the incident and one of them succumbed to injuries later.
- September 4: Six ULFA terrorists, including the Kolong-Kopilt Anchalik Parishad 'area commander' Manoj Bora alias Bhim, surrender before the Nagaon district police chief.
- September 2: Former Army personnel suspected to have links with the ULFA is killed at Tankibasti village under Paneri police station limits in the Darrang district.
- August 28: Two ULFA terrorists are killed in an encounter near Barpathar village under Bijni police station limits in Bongaigaon.
- August 27: A Court in Assam's Kamrup district sentences to life two ULFA terrorists convicting them in the Sanjoy Ghosh abduction and murder case. Ghosh, a social worker had been abducted on July 4, 1997, from Majuli and was subsequently killed.
- August 25: ULFA terrorists blow up a goods train causing extensive damage to the 200-metre rail track between Lakwah and Safrai railway stations in the Charaideo sub-division of Sibsagar district.

- August 24: ULFA terrorists kill a woman and her son at Basugaon in Kokrajhar district.
- August 23: Court in Dhaka pronounces that ULFA general secretary Anup Chetia would remain in Kashimpur Jail for six months more than the stipulated term awarded for various offenses under Bangladeshi laws, as he had failed to pay the fine of Taka 10,000.
- August 23: Two ULFA terrorists and a member of the Village Defence Committee are killed during an encounter at Sakapara village under Lakhipur police station limits in Goalpara district.
- August 20: Five ULFA cadres surrender before the Nagaon district police chief.
- August 19: ULFA terrorists abduct a tea planter from the Tokopathar area under Pangeri police station limits in Tinsukia district.
- August 18: Five ULFA terrorists are killed at Ghopabasti under Paneri police station limits in the Darrang district and separately two more in the Sessapani area of Kokrajhar district.
- August 16: One ULFA terrorist is killed at an unnamed place under Bijni police station limits in Bongaigaon district.

  Reports indicate that ULFA has set up a camp in the Changpang area of Nagaland that has some Government-controlled oil installations.
- August 16: Two ULFA terrorists are killed in an encounter under the Khoirabari police station-limits, Darrang district.
- August 10: Two ULFA terrorists are killed in an encounter in the Solmara area of Nalbari district.

  Approximately 40 unidentified gunmen attack a ULFA hideout at Tiluka in Bhutan killing four ULFA cadres and injuring five more.
- August 7: ULFA women's wing secretary Bhomtta Talukdar alias Deepali is arrested from the Jangrinpara village of Barpeta district.
- August 6: Three ULFA cadres are killed during an encounter at Srirampur in Kokrajhar district.
- August 4: A media report indicates that unidentified gunmen attacked two ULFA hideouts at Kinzo and Babang in Samdrup Jongkhar district and killed three ULFA cadres. Four attackers were also killed in the incident.

  Asom Public Works ULFA Parial Committee (APWUPC), an organisation of the ULFA kin, starts a signature campaign in protest against the ULFA's demand of *Swodhin Asom* (independent Assam).
- August 3: ULFA terrorists kill a tea estate-owner and his two sons at Diasajan in Tinsukia district.

- August 2: Three ULFA terrorists are killed and two police personnel injured during an encounter in the Dakshin Haldibari area of Jalpaiguri district in the State of West Bengal. Two ULFA terrorists are killed in Nalbari district.
- July 23: Two ULFA terrorists are killed in an encounter in the Koksaguri area of Kokrajhar district.

  Media reports say that the 81st National Assembly of Bhutan adopted a resolution for 'the last attempt' to persuade ULFA, NDFB and the KLO to close down their camps within this year 'peacefully' failing which terrorists would face 'military action'.
- July 20: ULFA terrorist is killed in an encounter at Shimu Kapur, Kokrajhar district.
- July 17: Three ULFA terrorists are killed during an encounter inside the Chariduar reserve forest of Sonitpur district. ULFA terrorist killed during an encounter in Nalbari district.
- July 11 : Media reports from Bhutan indicate that Bhutan National Assembly was unable to reach a consensus over the issue of the way to tackle NDFB, ULFA and the KLO.
- July 11 : ULFA terrorist is killed during an encounter at Machakolgre village in the East Garo Hills district of Meghalaya. A joint hideout of ULFA and the Meghalaya-based Achik National Volunteer Council (ANVC) is destroyed in East Garo Hills district of Meghalaya.
- July 10: ULFA terrorist is killed and two personnel of the Central Reserve Police Force (CRPF) are injured during an encounter at Sonpoirabari under Barpeta police station limits. A woman is also killed in the crossfire.
- July 7: Two ULFA terrorists are killed in an encounter in the Rangjuli area of Goalpara district.
- July 2: The Nine-day Army cordon laid in search of ULFA terrorists suspected to be hiding inside the forest areas of Lakhipathar in Tinsukia district is lifted.
- June 29: ULFA 'assistant finance secretary' Rustom Choudhury alias Harimohan Roy is killed during an encounter at Kumargram in the Jalpaiguri district of West Bengal.

  Report indicates that ULFA and NDFB have formed a new outfit named Gorkha Bhutan Liberation Front (GBLF) with 300 Nepalese Gorkha youths from Bhutan.

  ULFA woman cadre killed during an encounter at Bitukana in Meghalaya and two more ULFA cadres, including a woman are subsequently arrested.

- June 27: Reports indicate that heavy monsoon rains and an outbreak of malaria forced an unspecified number of ULFA terrorists to abandon their jungle bases in Bhutan and seek safe places in the North-Eastern States. 19 United ULFA and 11 NDFB terrorists surrender before the General Officer Commanding (GOC) IV corps Lt. Gen. Mohinder Singh at Tamulpur in Nalbari district.
- June 26: Suspected ULFA terrorists kill the Personal Assistant (PA) of a Member of Assam Legislative Assembly (MLA) representing Bhawanipur, Sarbananda Choudhury, at Betbari, under Patacharkuchi police station limits in Barpeta district.
- June 25: Counter-insurgency operations against the ULFA initiated in the forest areas of Lakhipathar in Tinsukia district.
- June 23: ULFA terrorists ambush an Army convoy at Juriapool in Assam's Tinsukia district and killed a civilian and injured 10 troops.

  Report says that ULFA 'commander-in-chief' Paresh Baruah in an interview to the *British Broadcasting Corporation's (BBC's) Kolkata correspondent* on June 21 admits that he was indeed attacked by unidentified gunmen in Dhaka on May 27.
- June 22: Inspector General of Police (Special Branch), Khagen Sarma says that while the '28th battalion' of the ULFA was responsible for the attack on an oil storage facility in Tinsukia district on June 20, a 22-member ULFA 'hit-squad' was involved in the attack on a Central Reserve Police Force (CRPF) camp in Dhubri district on June 21.
- June 21 : A ULFA terrorist is killed and two security force personnel are injured during an encounter at Panbari, Dhubri district, following an attack by ULFA terrorists at a Central Reserve Police Force camp.

  Reports indicate that ULFA, the Manipur People's Liberation Front (MPLF), a conglomerate of three terrorist groups-United National Liberation Front (UNLF), People's Liberation Army (PLA) and People's Revolutionary Party of Kangleipak (PREPAK)- active in Manipur, and the Tripura People's Democratic Front (TPDF), a front outfit of the All Tripura Tiger Force (ATTF), operating in Tripura under a common platform have launched a "Coordinated Regional Military Offensive for liberation of the Region from Indian colonial occupation," code named "Operation Freedom". The reports further said that attacks under the 'operation' started on June 17.
- June 20: State Government issues directives to the Deputy Commissioners and district police chiefs to remain vigilant following intelligence reports that some ULFA terrorists would sneak into the State to find safer places due to heavy rains. The report further indicates

that ULFA cadres in small groups have already entered Lakhimpur, Darrang, Nalbari, Barpeta, Bongaigaon, Dhubri, Goalpara, Jorhat, Tinsukia, Sibsagar, Dibrugarh and Karbi Anglong districts.

ULFA terrorist and two personnel of the Central Industrial Security Force (CISF) are killed in an encounter at Nagajan in Tinsukia district. The terrorists also blow up an empty crude oil tank with a rocket launcher.

- June 19: Security forces arrest three ULFA terrorists from a hideout following an encounter at Bikonggiri in the Phulbari area of West Garo Hills district in Meghalaya. The Dibrugarh police arrest a woman home guard personnel, Junali Gogoi for her alleged links with the ULFA.

  Report indicates that Bangladesh Director General of Field Intelligence (DGFI) is probing into the reported attack on ULFA 'chief Paresh Baruah on the outskirts of Dhaka on May 27, 2003.

- June 17: In Darrang district, three hardcore ULFA terrorists and an Army Major are killed in an encounter, and a woman also receives bullet injuries in the crossfire at Neogpara village under Kalaigaon police station limits.

- June 16: ULFA terrorist is killed in an encounter at Lotkapara, under Golokganj police post limits, in the Dhubri district.

- June 13: Police increase surveillance on the border areas of Assam following reports that the ULFA terrorists are compelled to move out of their hideouts in the mountainous regions of Bhutan, Myanmar and Garo Hills area in Meghalaya and also from the regions in upper Assam due to heavy rains.

  Report says following recovery of a letter from a slain terrorist a three-month over-ground organisation of the ULFA the Asom Yuva Chatra Parishad (AYCP) is unearthed. The organization is said to be in operation in 18 of the State's 24 districts.

- June 12: ULFA terrorist Akon Gogoi alias Pranjal Gogoi alias Chabua Moran is arrested from his residence at Bhadhara village under Chabua police station, in Dibrugarh district. Subsequently, on the basis of the information provided by the arrested terrorist, ULFA 'communication centre' is unearthed at Kakopathar in No 2 Dirak village, Tinsukia district and an ULFA conduit Prafulla Hazarika is also arrested by a joint police team of Dibrugarh and Tinsukia districts.

  ULFA terrorists kill a local trader near the Hemlai Tea Estate under Teok police station limits in Jorhat district for not paying an extortion amount of Rupees 200,000 demanded by the outfit earlier.

- June 11: One ULFA terrorist is killed in an encounter at Sarthebari, Nalbari district.

- June 10: Paresh Baruah, ULFA 'commander-in-chief' in a telephonic interview with a vernacular daily in Guwahati, *Asamiya Pratidin,* dismisses claims of attack (May 27) on him by unidentified assailants in Bangladesh.
- June 10: ULFA terrorist Bipul Bora alias Cobra who acted as a bodyguard of the ULFA 'deputy commander' Raju Baruah surrenders at the Army Headquarters in Tezpur, Sonitpur district
- June 8: Woman ULFA cadre and two members of the human rights organisation, Manab Adhikar Sangram Samiti (MASS), which allegedly acts as a front of the ULFA are arrested from Ananda Nagar locality in Guwahati city.

  Police in Nalbari district recover a huge cache of arms induding eight anti-tank explosives allegedly belonging to the ULFA from Barkhanajan village.
- June 7: Four persons sustain injuries in a grenade attack in Dhemaji town allegedly carried out by the ULFA.
- June 6: One ULFA terrorist is killed in an encounter at Sikorajan in the Fitobari area of Tinsukia district.
- June 4: Assam Public Works ULFA Partya! Committee (APWUPC) submits petition before the Assam Human Rights Commission (AHRC) to issue summons to the ULFA 'commander-in-chief' Paresh Barua for forcibly confining their kin for arms training in the jungles of Bhutan.
- June 3: Reports indicate that ULFA agreed to share the proceeds it would extort from the Tirap, Lohit and Changlang districts in Arunachal Pradesh with the National Socialist Council of Nagaland-Isak Muivah (NSCN-IM).
- June 2: Three NDFB terrorists and two ULFA terrorists, including a 'sergeant major' of letter's women's wing, surrender at Thakurbari in the Sonitpur district.
- May 31: An ULFA conduit is killed by his colleagues at Barbheta in Goalpara district.
- May 30: Two ULFA terrorists 'sergeant major' Soru Hajo alias Bhupen Kalita and Aswini Sarma alias Ramesh Sarma- are killed in an encounter at Katpuha village in Nalbari district.
- May 29: ULFA terrorist Clever Momin surrenders before the Meghalaya police in the East Garo Hills district.
- May 28: Railway Protection Force identifies four insurgency prone sectors in the Northeast and says that the ULFA is active in the Guwahati-Rangiya-Srirampur and the Rangiya-Rangapara sector.

- May 27: ULFA 'commander-in-chief' Paresh Baruah escapes unhurt in an attack by four unidentified assailants while he was leaving his transport agency, 'Challenger' at Uttara town in the Bangladeshi capital Dhaka.
- May 26: Police in Sonitpur destroy an ULFA hideout near the Assam-Arunachal Pradesh border at Jarubari hillock under Sootea police station and arrest a front ranking terrorist, involved in the killing of officer-in-charge (OC) of Gohpur police station corporal Bibek Hazarika alias Prasanta Barpatra Mudoi.
- May 24: Two ULFA terrorists are killed in separate encounters in the Kumar Kali reserve forests near Lakhipur in Cachar district and in the Puntan reserve forest of south Kamrup district, ULFA terrorists kill their former colleague (Surrendered ULFA) at Basugaon, in Kokrajhar district.
- May 23: Report indicates that the ULFA has asked its cadres to prepare to leave their camps in Bhutan following Bhutan Government's warning to ULFA, NDFB and KLO to vacate its territory by June 30, 2003.
- May 21. Security forces repulse ULFA attack at Borjhora in Assam's Dhubri district. No injuries on the either side are reported.
- May 16: In its fortnightly mouthpiece *Freedom,* ULFA warns the Government not to adopt the Mizo model to tackle the demands made by it.
- May 18: Reports indicate that the Tripura-based ATTF has acquired rocket launchers and Rocket-Propelled Grenades through ULFA.
- May 17: Police personnel from Assam arrest ULFA 'Enigma group' commander identified as Lal Singh alias Amar Singh alias Alman Singh from Tura, district headquarters of West Garo Hills district in Meghalaya. His two female associates are also arrested.

  Bhutanese King Jigme Singhye Wangchuk calls upon the people to volunteer for formation of a 'militia force' to counter Indian insurgent groups-ULFA, NDFB and the KLO on its soil.
- May 15: Report indicates that ULFA has floated an 'overground wing' under the name of Asom Jatiya Parishad.
- May 14: Two ULFA terrorists killed in an encounter at an unnamed place in Assam's Darrang district.
- May 14: ULFA 'sergeant' is arrested at a local bus stand at Adabari in Guwahati.
- May 12: ULFA terrorist killed in encounter at Nimaitola, Bongaigaon district.
- May 9: ULFA terrorist killed in an encounter at Andhargaon village in Bongaigaon district

- May 6: Unidentified assailants attack ancestral house of ULFA 'commander-in-chief' Paresh Baruah at Jeraigaon, Chabua police station limits in Dibrugarh district.
- April 29: Meghalaya Police Chief L. Sailo says that a joint operation with Assam would be carried out in the Garo Hills area of Meghalaya where ULFA and NDFB have intensified their activities.
- April 23: ULFA terrorist killed and three police personnel injured in encounter at Borpathar village, under Bijni police station limits, Kokrajhar district.
- April 23: ULFA terrorist killed in an encounter at an unnamed place under Baithalangshu police station-limits, Karbi cells.
- April 18: ULFA terrorist killed in encounter at Bograguri village, Nalbari district.
- April 16: Report indicates that the Meghalaya-based Achik National Volunteer Council (ANVC) has reached an understanding with ULFA and NDFB to operate together in the Garo Hills area of Meghalaya.
- April 10: Police in Meghalaya seize among other things, 11 big shoulder-borne rockets, an AK 56 rifle, several thousands of medium machine gun-ammunition and two communication sets from an ULFA hideout at Rongdupara, in West Garo Hills district.
- April 7: ULFA cadres reportedly gather for the 24th 'raising day' at Talli village, Golokganj police station-limits, Dhubri district.
- April 5: Four ULFA terrorists killed in an encounter at Silkhaguri, Bongaigaon district.
- April 3: Suspected ULFA terrorists fire rocket-propelled grenade at a petroleum gas bottling plant in Palasbari, Kamrup district.
- April 1 : ULFA terrorist killed at Jurigaon, in Assam's Goalpara district.
- March 30: ULFA terrorist killed in encounter at Jatiabangra in Tamulpur area, Nalbari district.
- March 21 : ULFA 'sergeant major' Manoj Deka killed in encounter in the Nalanga Pahar area, Kokrajhar district.
- March 21: ULFA 'sergeant major' identified as Manoj Deka killed in encounter in the Nalanga Pahar area, Kokrajhar district.
- March 18: ULFA terrorist identified as Jitu Konwar alias Nitu Gogoi alias Ritu Sarma arrested in Sibsagar district.
- March 16: Six civilians are killed and 55 more injured in an Improvised Explosive Device (IED) blast set-off by ULFA terrorists under a passenger bus, on National Highway No. 7, Bamunghopha, Goalpara district.

- March 13: ULFA 'commander' of a Bhutan-based camp, identified as 'Captain' Kamal Gogoi, surrenders to General Officer Commanding (GOC), IV Corps, Lt Gen Mohinder Singh at the corps-headquarters in Tezpur, Sonitpur district.
- March 12: Two motorcycle-borne ULFA terrorists attack Bongaigaon police station, injuring four policemen and three civilians.
- March 10: Reports indicate that ULFA terrorists are planning to abduct a group of Russian engineers of the Moscow-based company LARGE, engaged by the state-run Oil India Limited. Speaking in Delhi Deputy Premier Advani rules out immediate negotiations with ULFA terrorists.
- March 9: Assam Chief Minister Tarun Gogoi says ULFA is desperate and that the March 8-attack on an oil refinery in Tinsukia was just to maintain its visibility.

  Assam Public Works ULFA Parial Committee, an organisation of ULFA kin criticises ULFA 'commander-in-chief' Paresh Baruah for attacks on innocent persons and important installations like oil pipelines.
- March 8: ULFA terrorists set-off an explosion at a five million-litre petrol reservoir at Digboi Refinery, in Tinsukia district, causing a huge loss of approximately Rs 200 million to the Indian Oil Corporation (IOC), a public sector enterprise. In another attack, they damage a gas pipeline facility at Kathalguri, in the same district, in a blast.

  A group of ULFA terrorists attack and partially damage the Darrangiri police outpost in Goalpara district. While none police personnel are injured in the attack, the fleeing terrorists kill two persons and injure six more at a nearby migrant-settlement.
- March 7: ULFA terrorists fire rocket-propelled grenades at a police commando barrack in Bongaigaon district town. No one is injured in attack.
- March 4: ULFA cadres alleged to be planning attacks on oil pipelines are arrested from Teok area in Jorhat district.

  ULFA terrorists flee following a clash with a joint team of police and Central Reserve Police Force (CRPF) personnel at Baruathan in Dhemaji district.
- March 3: At a meeting in Guwahati, the Unified Command's strategy group recommends the formation of a 'crack police team' for Guwahati to counter ULFA-attacks.
- February 25: ULFA attacks a local petrol pump at Chagolia, Dhubri district, injuring a person.
- February 18: Three ULFA terrorists are killed in an encounter at Borrangajuli village, Darrang district.

- February 18: A couple affiliated to the ULFA is arrested from Koligaon bus station, Mangaldoi police station-limits in Darrang district.
- February 19: ULFA kills a personnel of Assam Police's Commando Battalion in an ambush at Nongardon Nepalibasti, Baithalangshu police station-limits, Karbi Anglong district.
- February 15: The ULFA's mouthpiece, *Freedom* says that a solution to its problems' is ID be sought outside the Indian constitution.
- February 12: ULFA 'sergeant' Nipul Bora surrenders to the Sonitpur district police chief.

  Union Minister of State for Home I.D. Swami while speaking in Dimapur, Nagaland, says the ULFA should come forward for talks without any preconditions.
- February 11 : Four persons sustain injuries in a grenade blast triggered by ULFA terrorists inside the Prem Chandra Champalal complex, in Bara Bazar (local market) area of Assam's Goalpara district.
- February 3: ULFA terrorists abduct businessman from Jagiroad in Morigaon district.
- February 3: Former Assam Chief Minister Chief Minister Prafulla Kumar Mahanta appeals to Union Government to start peace process with ULFA at the earliest with an 'open mind'. He also says that government should go ahead with peace process even if the ULFA wants to discuss 'sovereignty' of Assam.
- February 2: ULFA calls differences over geographical boundaries in Northeast to be an 'internal matter' and appeals for resolution without the involvement of Union Government.

  ULFA claims responsibility for blast at an underground oil pipeline in Upper Mamoroni area of Tinsukia.
- February 1 : Two ULFA terrorists killed in encounter at Nanoi reserve forest of Darrang district.
- January 30: ULFA 'political trainer' Bandana Das alias Babita Kalita arrested by police in Kamrup district.
- January 24: ULFA kills one SF personnel at Bhuyanpara inside the Manas National Park in Barpeta.
- January 22: 10 Northeast-based terrorist outfits, including ULFA, give Republic Day (January 26) 'boycott call'.
- January 21: ULFA terrorist killed in encounter at Rangchali in Dibrugarh district.
- January 20: Two ULFA terrorists killed in encounter at Rangsali, Tinsukia district.
- January 14: ULFA terrorist killed in encounter at Patkijuli village, Nalbari district.

- January 13: ULFA reported to be planning major offensive against some 'controversial' public personalities in Assam, including Ministers, ruling Congress Party's Legislators and bureaucrats.
- January 5: Assam government decides against granting safe passage to ULFA leaders and cadres during festive season of *Magh Bihu.*

2002

- December 25: Suspected ULFA terrorists throw five mortar bombs in quick succession in Kalibari and Ambri areas of Guwahati killing two civilians, including a five-year-old child. 16 more are injured in these incidents.
- December 24: An ULFA terrorist is killed in an encounter in Bagicha Chuba, Kalaigaon, Darrang district. Two ULFA terrorists are killed near Nakati forest, in Kokrajhar district.
- December 23: All Assam Students' Union (AASU) president Prabin Boro volunteers to broker peace with ULFA.
- December 22: Three ULFA terrorists are arrested from Kaimari village, Golakganj police station -limits, in Assam's Dhubri district.
- December 17: Reports say the ULFA, in its fortnightly *Freedom,* alleged that security forces in Assam killed at least 500 ULFA and National Democratic Front of Bodoland (NDFB) terrorists in various encounters during the past 18 months.
- December 16: The Sanjoy Ghosh abduction-cum-murder-case trial indicting ULFA begins in Guwahati.
- December 11 : ULFA terrorist Manoranjan Doley alias Mangal Singh is arrested in a search operation in Assam's Golaghat district at No. 3 Tarani Gaon, Merapani police station-limits.
- December 9: Police in Assam's Lakhimpur district arrest ULFA terrorist Rabin Deuri from Bhogpur, Bihpuria circle.
- December 7: Two ULFA women cadre surrender to the 181st Mountain Brigade in Assam's Tinsukia district.
- December 5: Two ULFA terrorists, Pranjal Borah and Jayanta Ray, are killed in an encounter in Putani village, Samaguri police station-limits, in Assam's Nagaon district.
- December 4: Reports quote ULFA 'chairman' Arbinda Rajkhowa as saying the outfit would continue its 'armed struggle'.
- December 2: Assam Chief Minister Tarun Gogoi in a memorandum to Prime Minister Vajpayee alleges that Bhutan was 'cleverly relocating' ULFA camps to evade pressure from the Indian government.

  Self-styled ULFA 'corporal' Meghnath is killed in an encounter in Maomari, Dudhnoi police station-limits, Goalpara district, Assam.

- November 27: Four persons are injured in a grenade attack by suspected ULFA terrorists near Chilarai Bridge, Golokganj police station-limits, in Assam's Dhubri district.
- November 21 : Assam Police chief (Director General) H K Deka says, in Guwahati, top-ULFA leaders have lost control over the rank and file and the latter indulge in extortion independent of their leaders.
- November 18: A report indicates that ULFA 'commander-in-chief' Paresh Baruah has directed his cadres to target the tea industry in Assam for extortion.
- November 17: ULFA mouthpiece *Swadhinata* reiterates preconditions for peace talks.
- November 13: ULFA terrorists set free local contractor Alimuddin Ahmed abducted on September 2.
- November 12: Two ULFA terrorists, including a woman cadre are arrested from Dimow, in Assam's Sibsagar district.
- November 6: A group of villagers, in Assam's Bongaigaon district, lynch two ULFA terrorists. Two ULFA terrorists are killed in an encounter in Tinsukia district.
- November 6: Reports indicate of ULFA's extortion drive in Barpeta and Bongaigaon districts of Upper Assam. Reports also indicate of ULFA-National Socialist Council of Nagaland- Khaplang (NSCN-K) tie up for extortion.
- November 5: Reports say a joint police team from Tingkhong and Borbam has nabbed ULFA terrorist Pankaj Gogoi in Assam's Dibrugarh district.
- November 3: In a joint operation with the Central Reserve Police Force (CRPF), Assam police destroy a training camp situated at the foothills of Molapahar, in Tinsukia district, being jointly used by ULFA and NSCN-K.
- October 31: Five ULFA terrorists led by 'corporal' Himan Deori of the outfit's *Enigma-A* group and seven NDFB terrorists surrender at the Tamulpur Army camp, in Assam's Nalbari district.
- October 30: Two top terrorists of ULFA's *Enigma Group* are killed in an encounter in Ajanta Path area, Guwahati, Assam.
- October 21 : ULFA terrorist identified as Dipu Gogoi is arrested in Moranhat, Dibrugarh district, Assam.
- October 15: ULFA, through its mouthpiece *Freedom*, reiterates the demand for a 'plebiscite' in Assam.

- October 12: An ULFA terrorist and his wife, also an ULFA cadre, are nabbed from a bus at Haloating Chariali, near Amguri, in Assam's Sibsagar district.
- October 6: An ULFA terrorist is killed in an encounter in the Jamduar Reserve Forest, Gossaigaon police station-limits, Kokrajhar district.
- October 5: Police sources suspect ULFA might have been behind a bomb blast that occurred in Assam's Nagaon district, killing a civilian and injuring three others. A school teacher from Garumara is arrested in Jorhat district for alleged links with ULFA.
- October 2: An ULFA terrorist is killed in an encounter in Bihjia village, in Assam's Nalbari district.
- October 1: ULFA women 'sergeant' Tulsi Rabha and another woman cadre, Malti Santoshi, are arrested from Somphong Par, near Balda village, Goalpara district.

  ULFA, in its mouthpiece *Freedom*, terms the government's effort of furthering development in Assam as 'mischievous' and a ploy to intensify counter-measures against the outfit.
- September 30: ULFA 'cultural secretary' Pallavi Phukan alias Kunjalata Deuri is arrested in Baluguri village, Tinsukia district, Assam.
- September 26: Media reports indicate, Assam is vigilant against any threat that might emanate from the suspected nexus between the ULFA and Nepal's Maoists.
- September 24: A court in the Bangladeshi capital Dhaka sentences ULFA 'general secretary' Anup Chetia and his two accomplices to seven years imprisonment for 'illegal possession' of a satellite phone.

  Sibsagar Chief Judicial Magistrate remands ULFA 'east zone commander' Ramu Mech and his body guard to seven days in police custody.

  Reports indicate ULFA has shifted two of its training camps from their current, unspecified location in Bhutan to Narphung, also in Bhutan.
- September 23: ULFA terrorists abduct a civilian from his residence in Kheremiagaon, Mariani police station jurisdiction, Jorhat district.
- September 22: Prabin Konwar alias Ramu Mech, the ULFA 'east zone commander', and another ULFA terrorist identified as Ranjit Rajkhowa alias Jyoti Chaliha are arrested from a private nursing home in Dibrugarh district of Assam.
- September 20: ULFA terrorists kill a security force personnel in an ambush near Orang River at Gowabari in Assam's Darrang district.

- September 19: Two ULFA terrorists are killed in an encounter the security forces near the Nanoi river embankment in Assam's Darrang district.
- September 18: The General Officer Commanding (GOC) of the 'Red Horn Division' of the Army, stationed in Assam, Major General Gaganjit Singh claims that terrorists from two ULFA camps in Myanmar are ready to surrender, but are, however, being restrained by their leaders.
- September 15: In its mouthpiece Freedom, ULFA denies its suspected involvement in the Howrah-New Delhi Rajdhani Express derailment on September 9, in Bihar State. Approximately 119 persons had been killed in the accident.
- September 14: ULFA terrorists and a security force personnel are killed in an encounter following a raid on a terrorist hideout at Uttarkuchi village in Nalbari district of Assam.
- September 12: Report says, a court in Dhaka would pronounce its verdict on detained United ULFA 'general secretary' Anup Chetia, on September 24. ULFA terrorist nabbed from a place under Bilasipara police station limits, Dhubri district, Assam.
- September 10: ULFA terrorist killed in an encounter in Bhebladongpar, Patacharkuchi police station limits, Barpeta district of Assam. ULFA terrorists kill a Surrendered ULFA (SULFA) cadre at the local club-cum-library in Balajan in Dhubri district, Assam.
- September 6: ULFA self-styled 'lieutenant' Lakhyajit Gogoi alias Bhaimon Gogoi and another ULFA terrorist, Arvinda Konwar alias Devanand Chetia, arrested by Assam Rifles in Nagaland's Mon district. Assam Governor Sinha says ULFA's 'preconceived mindset is impeding negotiations.
- September 1: Five ULFA terrorists arrested from Bhekulajan village, Duliajan police station limits, in Assam's Dibrugarh district.
- August 31: Three ULFA terrorists killed following an encounter in Bamunkuchigaon, Patacharkuchi police station limits, Barpeta district.
- August 30: Two ULFA terrorists killed in an encounter in Suktaguri village, Darrang district.
- August 29: Report says an ULFA 'sergeant' and a female cadre surrendered to security force (SF) personnel in Assam's Dibrugarh district. A report indicates that oil companies in Assam have paid extortion money to ULFA.
- August 28: Five ULFA terrorists killed in an encounter in Kachkuripathar, Sarthebari police station limits, Barpeta district.
- August 22: Government confirms that South Abhayapuri (Bongaigaon district) Legislator Chandan Barker's son, abducted on March 2, 2002

from Falakata in West Bengal, is in ULFA's captivity. Alert people apprehend three pseudo ULFA cadres while trying to extort money from a local businessman, at a place under Kokrajhar police station limits.

- August 19: Reports indicate that intelligence sources suspect ULFA's hand, besides that of the Kamatapur Liberation Organisations (KLO), in the August 17-Jalpaiguri (West Bengal) killings in which five Communist Party of India- Marxist (CPI-M) activists had been killed.
- August 18: Reports claim ULFA is trying to unite with the Manipur-based United National Liberation Front (UNLF).

  Reports state that ULFA is trying to take advantage of the differences between Bodo and non-Bodo groups over the formation of the Bodoland Territorial Council with the aim of creating disturbances in the Assam.
- August 14: Four ULFA terrorists killed in separate encounters— two near Suklapara in Kamrup district and two more near Dudhnoi in Goalpara district.
- August 13: ULFA conduit arrested from Gauripara area in Guwahati.
- August 12: ULFA terrorist killed in an encounter near Darrangamela, Nalbari district. Suspected ULFA conduit arrested from Aarikusi, Nalbari district, Assam.
- August 10: ULFA issues a press release refuting allegations of its involvement in the abduction of seven BLT cadres.
- August 6: Sanmilita Janagosthiya Sangram Samiti (SJSS), a platform of various non-Bodo organisatons, hails the 'moral support' extended by ULFA to its opposition to forming the Bodoland Territorial Council (BTC).
- August 4: ULFA terrorist killed in an encounter in Khoirabari, Kamrup district. Two ULFA terrorists arrested at a place under Hatssinghirnari police station jurisdiction, Dhubri district.
- August 3: Basanta Gogoi alias Dipen Bora, a 'corporal' in ULFA's 28th battalion, killed in an encounter in Chamguri village, Dibrugarh district.
- August 2: Two ULFA terrorists killed in an encounter in Umananda, Darrang district.
- August 1: The ULFA, in its mouthpiece *Freedom*, says Bodoland Territorial Council (BTC) would create political chaos.
- July 29: Four ULFA terrorists, including a self-styled 'lieutenant' and a woman cadre, killed near Ghaghrapar in Assam's Nalbari district.

- July 25: Reports say a nine-member ULFA team led by Ashanta Phookan entered Golaghat district to sabotage Independence day (August 15) celebrations.
- July 24: ULFA terrorist killed in Kukapar village, Barpeta district.
- July 20: Media report indicates security force personnel apprehend strikes by ULFA on Independence Day-eve in Assam.
- July 19: ULFA alleges that increased presence of Indian security forces on Assam's border with Bhutan is a hurdle in withdrawing from bases in Bhutan.
- July 17: Manipur-based United National Liberation Front (UNLF) while claiming responsibility for the July 16 killing of three security force personnel near Jirighat in Assam's Cachar district in a statement, indicates that attacks were carried out at ULFA's behest. Reports say, ULFA terrorists vacated two camps in Bhutan.
- July 16: Six ULFA terrorists, on their way to a training camp in Myanmar arrested by Assam Rilfes (AR) personnel in Mon district of Nagaland.
- July 14: Two ULFA terrorists killed in an encounter at Dighali village, Nalbari district.

  Intelligence reports caution authorities in Assam about the presence of a 70-member-strong ULFA gang in Sibsagar district, allegedly led by 'operation commandant' Dristi Rajkhowa," and warn that the group might sabotage Independence Day celebrations.

  Media report indicates that ULFA and NDFB terrorists based in camps in Bhutan may approach hospitals in West Bengal for treatment, following shrinking of medical facilities in Bhutan.

  Three ULFA terrorists arrested from Netabari village while on an extortion bid.
- July 10: Three ULFA terrorists arrested from Pallel Bazar, in Manipur's Thoubal district.
- July 8: Two ULFA terrorists killed in an encounter in the Barpathar area of Golaghat district.

  Sidharthamani Bora, the self-styled finance secretary of ULFA's Sowansiri Anchalik Parishad surrenders in Jorhat.
- July 6: Major General Gaganjit Singh, General Officer in Command (GoC), 21st Mountain Division rules out presence of a women suicide squad of the ULFA.
- July 5: A senior police official says ULFA has trained women in 'intelligence gathering'.

- July 3: Report claims 20 ULFA terrorists, including women cadres, infiltrated Assam to extort money and recruit cadres.
- July 1 : ULFA in its mouthpiece *Freedom* asks Assamese students to launch anti-Hindi campaign, say reports.
- June 26: ULFA terrorist killed in an encounter at Kardoiguri village in Tinsukia district. A report says ULFA involved is in fake currency circulation in Assam.
- June 25: Three ULFA terrorists killed in an encounter at Nanoipara, under Paneri police station limits.

  Civilian killed and 28 more, including three SF personnel, injured in a grenade attack by suspected ULFA terrorists near Mayapuri cinema in Bongaigaon.
- June 23: Two ULFA terrorists, one SF personnel killed in Subansiri-encounter, Nalbari district.
- June 21 : A report says, ULFA is continuing with its recruitment drive in Upper Assam.
- June 20: Police in Dibrugarh arrest two ULFA terrorists from Khowang and Moran areas in separate raids.
- June 19: Two ULFA terrorists, one security force personnel killed in an encounter near Achabam Tea Estate, Dibrugarh district. Assam Public Works (APW), a Guwahati-based Non-Governmental Organisation (NGO) refutes ULFA's charges that it had, at the behest of the government, mobilised people to file complaints with Assam Human Rights Commission against ULFA Commander-in-Chief Paresh Baruah.
- June 18: Six ULFA terrorists killed in separate encounters-two at Vishnupur, Ulubari, another two at Lakhimpur, and two more at the Dumni Tea Estate, Nalbari district. One SF personnel also killed in the last encounter. ULFA terrorist arrested from Bisondoi village of Assam's Dhubri district.

  Reports hold, ULFA and NDFB procure arms from a Manipur-based terrorist outfit, the United National Liberation Front (UNLF).
- June 12 : Arpan Saikia, believed to be ULFA's 'operation commander' for Rangpur Anchalik Parishad, arrested in Pathalibum village in Dibrugarh district.
- May 29: ULFA terrorist arrested from Thekeraguri village, under Tingkhong police station limits.
- May 28: ULFA terrorist arrested from Ratanpur near Tingkhong in Dibrugarh district.
- May 26: Inter Services Intelligence (ISI) may use ULFA's 'commander-in-chief' Paresh Barua to target its chairman, Arabinda Rajkhowa, claim reports.

- May 25: Two ULFA terrorists killed in an encounter near Sukhanjali village in Nalbari district.
- May 22: Four ULFA terrorists arrested following a joint operation launched by troops of the 2nd Mountain Division and personnel of Assam and Nagaland police at Lahurijan village, under Bokajan police station limits.
- May 20: Self-styled ULFA commander Tapan Baruah alias Madan Das killed in an encounter at Talpathar Majhgaon in Tinsukia district.
- May 19: ULFA's 28th battalion's 'sergeant major' identified as Diganta Dihingia killed in encounter at Chetia Handique village in Sibsagar district. Assam police arrest ULFA terrorist from a house under Simaluguri police station limits.
- May 18: 10 ULFA terrorists, including a woman cadre, surrender in Nalbari district.
- May 16: Reports say ULFA mouthpiece *Freedom (Swadhinata)* leveled allegations against the Indian government of carrying out 'reconnaissance surveys' over its camps in Bhutan for a possible military offensive.
- May 14: Nine persons injured in various attacks carried out by ULFA terrorists, allegedly, jointly with NDFB terrorists at Gauripur in Dhubri district.
- May 12: ULFA terrorist killed in an encounter at Dalanghat village in Darrang district.
- May 10: ULFA terrorist killed in an encounter at the Pachim Kamarkuchi village under the Nalbari police station limits.
- May 9: ULFA conduit arrested from Nij Bihuguri village, under Tezpur police station limits. ULFA has renewed its attempt to escalate its terrorist acts in parts of Assam, claim reports.
- May 8: Two ULFA terrorists killed in separate encounters in Nalbari district—in Elangidal and Dahali villages respectively.
- May 6: ULFA terrorist killed in an encounter in Umananda village, under Goreshwar police station limits.
- May 5: ULFA terrorist killed in an encounter near Kekankuchi in Nalbari district.
- May 1: Encounter between Jorhat police and ULFA terrorists reported at Panijangaon under Mathura East police station limits. There were, however, no casualties.
- April 25: ULFA terrorist Bulbul Bora, self-styled 'corporal and weapon training instructor', killed in an encounter in Mahakhuli, Nagaon.

- April 22 ULFA terrorist killed in an encounter with security forces in Nalbari district Kokrajhar police recover the dead body of a girl from Hatimatha.
- April 20: Seven ULFA terrorists surrender at Laipuli in Tinsukia. One more terrorist surrenders at Barhampur camp, Nagaon.
- April 19: Two United Liberation Front of Asom ULFA terrorists killed in an encounter at Barandhara under the Ghagrapaar police station limits of Nalbari.
- April 18: A ULFA terrorist identified as Bikash Das killed in an encounter at Dahkaunia under the Nalbari police station limits. A suspected ULFA conduit identified as Deepak Roy arrested in Gossaigaon Natabari village under the Tamarhat police station limits of Kokrajhar district.
- April 17: One unidentified ULFA terrorist killed in an encounter at Pipla village under Patacharkuchi police station limits in Nalbari.
- April 15: Bagaribari police personnel arrest two Muslim Revolutionary Democratic Front (MRDF) terrorists from the Sonkosh.
- April 13: Two ULFA terrorists injured in an encounter at the North Bishnupur area, Nalbari.
- April 12: Jorhat police arrest one ULFA 'acting district commander' Jagat Phukan of Dhansiri Anchalik Parishad.
- April 8: One ULFA terrorist killed by near Hathigor in Darrang.
- April 7: Two ULFA terrorists killed in an encounter at Balilessa Soondartala in Nalbari district. ULFA observes its 'raising day'.
- April 4: ULFA chairman, Arabinda Rajkhowa, rejects the safe-passage offer by the Assam government.
- April 3: One ULFA terrorist surrenders at Barhampur camp, Nagaon.
- March 30: One ULFA terrorist killed in an encounter at Dalledela village under Phulbari police station limits in West Garo Hills district of Meghalaya.
- March 29: ULFA terrorist killed in an encounter at Bihira village near Nalbari, Assam.
- March 24: ULFA reiterates preconditions - venue for talks should be a third country, should be under United Nations (UN) supervision; and 'sovereignty' should also be discussed, for talks, indicate reports. A self-styled 'sergeant major' Dilip Saloi alias Bhaiti Adhikary killed in Kamrup encounter, Assam.

  Separately, A self-styled commander of 'B' Group, Arantu Hazarika alias Dwipen Talukdar killed in an encounter at Arikuchi Balagaon in Nalbari district on March 22.

- March 22: Two ULFA terrorists, including a woman cadre, killed in an encounter in a reserve forest under the Patacharkuchi police station limits of Barpeta district, Assam.
- March 20: ULFA terrorist surrenders before the Nagaon district police chief in Assam.
- March 19: Seven ULFA terrorists - four at Akhara, 70 kilometres west of Guwahati and three in Dhubri killed in separate encounters in Assam. Separately one ULFA terrorist killed in Kamrup and another arrested in Nalbari.
- March 18: Suspected ULFA terrorists kill a trader at Bhatipara village under Boko police station limits, Kamrup in Assam.
- March 17: Five ULFA terrorists - three from Balipara village and one each from Shanristipur in Nalbari and Nagaon arrested in Assam.
- March 16: One ULFA terrorist killed near No. 2 Bongaon under the Tihu police station limits, Assam.
- March 7: Two ULFA terrorists killed in the Ripu Reserve Forest area, near Gossaigaon, Assam.
- March 5: One ULFA terrorist killed in Niljulki village, Nalbari district, Assam.
- March 3: Two ULFA terrorists killed in an encounter in Nemukur Konwargaon, near Bokota, in Sibasagar district, Assam.
- February 27: ULFA terrorist killed in encounter at Gugoloni under Naharkotia police station limits in Assam.
- February 24: Four ULFA terrorists killed at Boragaon in Tinsukia district in Assam.
- February 22: One ULFA terrorist killed at Dhantola in Nalbari, Assam.
- February 20: One ULFA terrorist killed in the Dirok reserved forest area, Tinsukia in Assam.
- February 19: ULFA terrorist killed near Guwahati.

  Suspected ULFA terrorists kill two youths at Bistupur in Nalbari, Assam.
- February 14: Five ULFA terrorists killed near the Assam border with Arunachal Pradesh.
- February 10: Two Surrendered ULFA (SULFA) terrorists killed at Naharbari Kopili Xatra near Mangaldai.
- February 3: ULFA terrorist killed in an encounter near Birubari Nizorapar in Guwahati, Assam.
- January 31 : Three ULFA terrorists killed near Boko in Kamrup district, Assam.

- January 29: A ULFA terrorist killed in an encounter at the Dibru-Saikhowa reserved forest near Doomdooma, Assam.
- January 27: ULFA terrorists kill two security force (SF) personnel in Kamrup district, Assam. Ten others injured in a separate attack in Golaghat.
- January 22: A ULFA terrorist killed in an encounter in the Raimana Reserve Forest area near Gosssaigoan.
- January 20: Four ULFA terrorists killed in an encounter at Toji village near Agomani on the Assam-Bangladesh border.
- January 9: Two ULFA terrorists killed in Kokrajhar, Assam.
- January 1 : United Liberation Front of Asom (ULFA) offered a 30-day safe passage by the Assam government.

2001

- December 30: Suspected ULFA terrorists kill a Congress (I) activist near Bejkuchi village, under Nalbari police station limits.

  A ULFA terrorist killed under the Duni police station limits, Darrang district.
- December 28: Suspected ULFA terrorist killed under the Kalaigaon police station limits in Assam.
- December 23: Two ULFA terrorists killed in an encounter in Nijkhusla, Kamrup district in Assam.
- December 21 : Six Surrendered ULFA (SULFA) activists arrested in Shantinagar, near Guwahati in Assam.
- December 20: Three ULFA terrorists killed in an encounter near Suwagpur, Darrang district, Assam.
- December 18: Five ULFA terrorists-three in Nalbari and two in Sadiya along the Assam-Arunachal Pradesh border, killed in Assam.
- December 15: Three ULFA terrorists arrested from the Motapam village near Dholaghat in Tinsukia district.
- December 9: One ULFA terrorist killed in encounter and two others arrested in Khoirabari and Darrang districts respectively.
- December 6: One ULFA terrorist killed in an encounter near Kumsung in Tinsukia district, Assam.
- December 2: Reports indicate ULFA likely to 'close' camps in Bhutan.
- November 27: ULFA declares as a 'protest day'. Its Arabinda Rajkhowa appeals for a political settlement.
- November 23: Three ULFA terrorists killed in an encounter near Bolajhar in Darrang.

- November 21: ULFA terrorist killed in an encounter in the Dangori Reserve Forest area. Two ULFA terrorists arrested separately in Guwahati.
- November 18: Suspected ULFA terrorists kill Asom Gana Parishad (AGP) leader in Rangajan village, Tinsukia in Assam.
- November 10: 'Chief of ULFA platoon division arrested in Siliguri, West Bengal.
- November 5: Two ULFA terrorists arrested in Dhubri.
- October 22: Three ULFA terrorists killed in Bholpur under Tamulpur police station limits in Nalbari, Assam. Five ULFA terrorists surrender in Nalbari.
- October 21 : ULFA terrorist killed in encounter at Donjargaon in Nalbari, Assam.
- October 20: Two ULFA terrorists killed in encounter near the Dikcham Tea Estate, Rajgarh, in Dibrugarh district, Assam.
- October 18: Two ULFA terrorists lynched by the locals in Bijupara, Kamrup district in Assam. Security forces kill one ULFA terrorist in Darrang.
- October 17: Two ULFA terrorists arrested at Balikuchi village under the Nalbari police station jurisdiction.
- October 15: ULFA 'publicity secretary' along with 10 others surrender in Lajpuli, Tinsukia.
- October 11 : Four ULFA terrorists surrender in Golaghat.

  Kamrup ULFA 'area commander' killed at Patharkmhah in Ri Bhoi, Meghalaya.
- October 8: Two ULFA terrorists surrender in Jorhat.
- October 6: Central Bureau of Investigation (CBI) personnel arrest five ULFA terrorists in connection with Tinsukia district police chief murder in May 1996.
- September 27: Two ULFA terrorists and one Army personnel killed in encounter at Kumarigaon in Mahadevpur area along the Assam-Nagaland border.
- September 21 : Two Army personnel killed in an ULFA-triggered bomb-blast near Kakapathar Kumchang Tea Estate. Another succumbs to injuries later.
- August 17: The ULFA reiterates its earlier pre-conditions for a peace process to be initiated. These are: (1) Talks would have to be held at a mutually decided venue outside India. (2) Talks would have to be held under the supervision of the United Nations. (3) The main issue to be discussed is 'sovereignty' for Assam.

- August 5: Three ULFA terrorists killed and five security force personnel injured in an encounter at Nalapara village along the Indo-Bhutan border in Darrang district.
- July 29: Two CRPF security force personnel and a driver of the vehicle they were travelling in killed and five more security force personnel injured in an Improvised Explosive Device (IED) explosion caused by suspected ULFA terrorists at Bhalukjuli in Goalpara district.
- July 27: ULFA Chairman Arabinda Rajkhowa, addressing the outfits Martyr Day celebrations, calls for a referendum in the State to decide the issue of sovereignty for which the outfit is fighting. He adds that his organisation wants a 'political solution' to the 'Indo-Assam conflict.'
- July 17: ULFA, in its mouthpiece *Freedom*, calls upon the NSCN-IM to review its stand on an extended Nagalim to 'avoid being projected as a chauvinistic outfit'.
- July 6: Media reports suggest that the ULFA 'commander-in-chief' Paresh Baruah has been injured in an explosion at the residence of a political activist of the Jatiya Samajtantrik Dal in Bangladesh, Mir Kasim Ali.
- June 13: Three ULFA terrorists killed in an encounter at Lainagar Dimrohala in Dibrugarh district.
- June 6: 12 security force personnel injured in a pre-dawn rocket attack by suspected ULFA terrorists on a Central Reserve Police Force (CRPF) camp at Dhupdhara in Goalpara district.
- June 4: Three ULFA terrorists killed and five police personnel injured in an encounter at Dhalajan Fatagaon in Jorhat district.
- May 3: Six AGP activists killed and 16 civilians injured in separate attacks by suspected ULFA terrorists in Nalbari and Goalpara districts.
- May 2: An AGP office holder and another AGP activist killed in an attack by suspected ULFA terrorists at Raniganj in Bilasipara.
- May 1: The general secretary of the State unit of the Bharatiya Janata Party (BJP), and also the party's candidate from Dibrugarh constituency, Jayanta Dutta and four other persons were killed and nine others injured in separate ULFA attacks in Dibrugarh town.
- April 29: Twelve AGP activists were injured as suspected ULFA terrorists exploded a grenade near 'Janata Bhawan', the official residence of the Chief Minister in Guwahati.
- April 25: The then Chief Minister Prafulla Kumar Mahanta, addressing a press conference in Guwahati, alleges that ULFA terrorists in connivance with the Congress Party were targeting the AGP candidates.

- April 24: Two AGP activists were killed by ULFA terrorists at Diwanpara and Chakihali Bazar of Bongaigaon district.
- April 15: Three security force personnel were killed in an attack by ULFA terrorists near the Paneri police station in Darrang district.
- March 30: Five ULFA terrorists killed in two separate encounters in the Tengi village of Tinsukia district and Kalakuchi village of Nalbari district.
- March 17: Three youths, suspected to be police informers, were first abducted and later killed by ULFA terrorists at Burinagar village in Nalbari district.
- March 15: Six ULFA terrorists belonging to the outfit's 'Enigma Unit' killed in an encounter in a forest area under Krishnai police station in Goalpara district. On the same day, six ULFA terrorists, led by the outfit's Kamrup district 'operation commander' Raju Ahmed surrender at Baihata Chariali in Kamrup district.
- February 24: ULFA's Kamrup 'district commander' shot dead. On the same day, eight ULFA terrorists are arrested.
- February 23: Six ULFA terrorists killed and three more injured in an encounter with security forces in Meghalaya, at Garobadha in the West Garo Hills district, on the Assam-Meghalaya border.
- February 12: ULFA threatens wildlife campaigner Vivek Menon for campaigning against poaching of elephants and rhinos in the State.
- February 2: Three ULFA terrorists were killed in an encounter in the Mazgaon area, Bongaigaon district. On the same day, 13 ULFA terrorists, including the outfit's 'foreign liaison officer', 'communication officer' and 'medical-in-charge', surrender at the Misa Army camp near Nagaon.
- January 31 : Four ULFA terrorists were killed in two separate encounters at Khangbari and Soneswar village.
- January 26: 123 ULFA terrorists surrendered in Guwahati.
- January 2: Three Surrendered ULFA (SULFA) men, including former ULFA leader Abinash Bordoloi, were killed by suspected ULFA terrorists in Nalbari district.

2000

- December 17: Army sources claim that the ULFA chief, Paresh Baruah has been injured and his deputy, Raju Baruah killed in an internecine clash in the Chittagong Hill Tracts of Bangladesh. However, Paresh Baruah later contacted news agencies and contradicted these reports.
- December 13: I D Swami, Union Minister of State for Home Affairs, speaking in the Parliament, confirms the reports that ULFA has been procuring arms from the Chinese Army.

- December 8: Brother of Sasha Choudhury, 'foreign secretary' of ULFA killed by unidentified assailants in Nalbari district.
- December 7: 28 Hindi-speaking traders and farm workers from Bihar were killed by suspected ULFA terrorists near Sadiya.
- December 6: 153 ULFA terrorists surrendered in Dispur. House of Paresh Baruah, ULFA chief, in Dhubri district attacked by unidentified miscreants.
- November 28: Three non-Assamese, Biharis, were killed by ULFA terrorists in Tinsukia district.
- November 26: Four non-Assamese, 'Biharis' were killed by ULFA terrorists.
- October 27: ULFA terrorists massacred nine persons and injured 12 others in the Nalbari district.
- October 23: 15 persons were killed by suspected ULFA terrorists killed in two separate incidents in Tinsukia and Dibrugarh districts.
- September 18: A news report stated that in a special joint operation conducted over a period of two weeks, eighteen ULFA terrorists were killed in Bhutan.
- September 16: Two hundred ULFA terrorists operating in central Assam's Nagaon and Morigaon districts surrendered with their 'commander' Pranab Bora alias Swapnil Deka Raja.
- September 10: An ULFA terrorist, who was the main accused in the killing of Sanjoy Ghosh, General Secretary of an NGO, AVARD-NE, killed in an encounter in Jorhat.
- August 18: Four hardcore ULFA terrorists killed in an encounter with army in Tinsukia.
- August 15: Three hundred ULFA terrorists including one of its top leaders Lohit Deuri surrendered before Assam's Chief Minister. A 'commander' of ULFA, Anil Bora alias Basant Phukan killed in an encounter with police in Dibrugarh.
- August 12: Four ULFA terrorists killed in an encounter with army in Tinsukia.
- May 27: ULFA's 'Assistant Publicity Secretary' who was also a Central Committee leader and the editor of *Freedom,* Swadhinata Phukan, alias Kabiranjan Saikia, killed in an encounter with security forces at Gendheli, Jorhat district.
- March 14: Chief Minister Mahanta alleges that Pakistan's High Commissioner in Bangladesh is playing an active role in sending ULFA terrorists to Pakistan for arms training.

- March 5: The then State Veterinary Minister Hiranya Konwar escaped an assassination attempt by ULFA terrorists near Moran, Sibsagar district.
- February 27: ULFA terrorists killed the then State PWD and Forest Minister, Nagen Sharma. Four others were also killed in the attack, in Nalbari district.

1999

- October 2: ULFA attacks Assam Revenue Minister, Or. Zoii Nath Sharma's convoy. Sharma escapes unhurt while three Asom Gana Parishad (AGP) activists and a security guard are killed.
- September 24: ULFA kills Dr. Pannalal Oswal, the BJP candidate for the Dhubri Lok Sabha (Parliamentary) seat, ahead of the polls.
- May 11 : Seven security force personnel were killed and two others injured in an ambush laid by ULFA terrorists in Nagaon district.
- February 4: ULFA and three other Northeast insurgent groups launch websites (http://www.geocitJes.com/CapitolHill/Congress/7434/ulfa.htm).

1998

- December 20: Six security force personnel and four civilians killed in an ambush laid by ULFA terrorists in Dhubri district.
- September 28: Seven security force personnel killed in an ambush laid by ULFA terrorists in Goalpara district.
- August 24: Three people killed in a massive bomb blast at Guwahati railway station. ULFA claims responsibility for the incident.
- July 24: 51 ULFA terrorists surrender.
- May 15: ULFA warns the Naga terrorist outfit, National Socialist Council of Nagaland Isak-Muivah (NSCN-IM) about encroaching on Assamese territory. The warning follows reported killing of a family member of a ULFA leader by the NSCN-IM.

1997

- July 4: Prominent social activist Sanjoy Ghosh killed by suspected ULFA terrorists.
- June 8: Assam Chief Minister Prafuila Kumar Mahanta escapes a bid on his life when ULFA terrorists attack his convoy in Guwahati.

1996

- August 19: ULFA terrorists kill 13 security force personnel in three separate attacks.
- May 18: ULFA terrorists gun down Ravi Kant Singh, Superintendent of Police (SP), Tinsukia district.

- April 28: Lt. Col. Devendra Tyagi shot dead by ULFA terrorists in the Kamakhya temple, Guwahati.
- April 25: ULFA terrorists kill a local Congress (I) leader and four others near Margherita town, Tinsukia district.

1995

- November 23: Five security force personnel and their civilian driver killed in a ambush laid jointly by ULFA and Bodo Security Force (BdSF) terrorists.
- August 3: ULFA terrorists kill eight security force personnel in an ambush in Kamrup district.

1994

- November 20: Central government extends ban on ULFA.
- June 29: Security forces arrest Pradip Gogoi, the Vice-chairman of ULFA.

1992

- April 11 : ULFA terrorists gun down ten security force personnel.
- January 14: State government suspends Operation Rhino; ULFA agrees to participate in a political dialogue with the government.

1991

- July 1: ULFA resumes terrorist activities, abducts 14 people, including an engineer, a national of (the erstwhile) Soviet Union.

1990

- November 28: Central Government imposes President's Rule in Assam as terrorist activities unleashed by ULFA reach unprecedented heights. The entire State of Assam is declared a "disturbed area"; ULFA banned under the Unlawful Activities (Prevention) Act, 1967; army launches Operation Bajrang.
- May 9: ULFA terrorists kill Surendra Paul, a leading tea planter, causing many tea estate managers to flee the State.

1979

- April 7: United Liberation Front of Asom (ULFA) founded under the leadership of Paresh Barua.

(*Source :* http://www/sat/org/satporgtp/countries/india/states/assam/terrorist-outfits/ULFA-tl.htm)

ADIVASI COBRA FORCE (ACF)

Formation

Adivasi Cobra Force (ACF), also known as the Adivasi Cobra Militant Force (ACMF) was formed in the second half of the 1990s.

Objectives

The ACF was formed with the purported objective of protecting the Adivasi (tribal) people of Lower Assam through an armed revolution.

Leadership and Area of Operation

Its commander Durga Minz leads the outfit. The other senior members are Xabrias Khakha and Kandu Murmu. The outfit has an estimated strength of 100 terrorists.

Initially formed in the Kokrajhar district, it subsequently widened its activities to the Bongaigaon and Dhubri districts. Since then, it has indulged in sporadic acts of killing and extortion in the area primarily targeting the tea gardens in the three districts.

Linkages and Activities

Even though the outfit is in its nascent stage, a recruitment drive is currently on to expand its strength. According to media reports, in the month of May and June 2001, the outfit managed to extort a huge ransom amount from the people in the Kokrajhar, Bongaigaon and Dhubri districts to continue its training programme in Bhutan. The ACF is reported to maintain links with the Kamatapur Liberation Organisation (KLO), a terrorist outfit based in certain districts of Assam and North Bengal. KLO has also reportedly assisted the ACF in setting up camps along the Bhutanese border. According to intelligence sources, it has also been trying to establish links with a particular militant group in Bihar to procure arms and ammunition. Furthermore, the outfit maintains few camps in the Kokrajhar district of Assam. In the year 2000, security forces destroyed a camp belonging to the outfit along the border of Kokrajhar district.

On September 19, the ACF declared a unilateral cease-fire till January 2002 and urged the government to initiate a dialogue with it. Subsequently, on October 4, 2001 , an ACF delegation met the Chief Minister in Guwahati. Since then, there has been no further dialogue with the outfit. Media reports, however, suggest that the outfit has resumed its terrorist activities.

DIMA HALIM DAOGAH (DHD)—TERRORIST GROUP OF ASSAM

Formation

Dima Halim Daogah (DHD) is an offshoot of the erstwhile Dimasa National Security Force (DNSF), which had surrendered en masse in 1995, except for its self-styled Commander-in-Chief Jewel Garlossa, who subsequently launched the DHD. The outfit is currently observing 'ceasefire' with the government.

Objective

It's declared objective is to create a separate State of 'Dimaraji' for the Dimasa ('sons of the great river') tribe, comprising Dimasa dominated areas of the North Cachar Hills and Karbi Anglong districts of Assam and parts of Dimapur district in Nagaland.

Leadership

The outfit is led by its President Pranab Nunisa and Chairman Dilip Nunisa. Kanta Langthasa functions as the home secretary of the outfit whereas, Yathong Dimasa is the additional commander-in-chief. Rongsling Dimasa is its organising secretary.

On June 24, 2004, Pranab Nunisa, the former commander-in-chief of the outfit and the head of the outfit's armed wing, the Dima National Army, took over the command of DHD by ousting its President Jewel Garlossa on charges of anti-DHD activity. Nunisa, in a press statement, said that Garlossa has already formed a separate outfit on March 31, 2003, named 'The Black Widows', which also has a private army.

Area of Operation

The outfit's mostly operates in Cachar, N C Hills, Karbi Anglong and Nagaon districts of Assam. It also has a strong presence in the Dimasa dominated Dhansiri area of Karbi Anglong district.

Funding

Extortion constitutes a major source of funding for the outfit. Even after entering into the ceasefire agreement, the outfit continues its extortion activities in the Cachar district. It especially targets the tea gardens located in the area. The villages most affected by the outfit's activities in Cachar district are Thaligram, Tikolpar, Khaspur, Bagherkona, Madhuranagar, Amranagar, Chandighat, Pangram, Arunabond and Salganga.

Similarly, DHD's extortion activities have been reported from Diphu, Hamren and Bokajan sub-divisions of Karbi Anglong district and the Hojai sub-division of adjoining Nagaon district.

Linkages

The DHD has reportedly forged links with the Inter Services Intelligence (ISI), Pakistan's external intelligence agency. The nexus came to light after security forces commenced investigating the diversion of public funds into the coffers of the militant outfit in April 2000.

The DHD is also reported to have linkages with the National Socialist Council of Nagaland-Isak-Muivah (NSCN-IM) and the National Democratic Front of Bodoland (NDFB).

Peace Negotiations

A ceasefire agreement was signed between the DHD leadership and the Union Government on January 1, 2003 and the agreement has been periodically extended. On January 1 , 2004, the ceasefire was extended for a period of one year, till December 31, 2004. On September 23, 2004 a six-member DHD delegation led by 'chairman' Dilip Nunisa met Union Home Minister Shivraj Patil in New Delhi and submitted a memorandum demanding a separate homeland for the Dimasa tribals. However, the tardy progress of the negotiation process has disappointed the DHD leadership, whose Chief Dilip Nunisa on December 4 termed the delay as "intentional procrastination".

Incidents

2006

- December 13: A DHD leader, Amol Ponglu, is killed and two cadres are injured when militants of the Black Widow, the anti-talks' faction of the outfit led by Jewel Garlossa, attacked them at Umrangshu in the North Cachar Hills district. A junior engineer of the North Eastern Electric Power Corporation, Manilal Thousen, is also killed during the dash.

  The beheaded body of a DHD militant, Jaulal Raijung, is recovered from Langting under Maibong police station in the North Cachar Hills district. According to police sources, Raijung may have been killed by suspected cadres of his outfit.

- December 2: A DHD leader belonging to the Dilip Nunisa faction, 'lieutenant' Mazran Dimasa, is wounded when he is attacked by the rival anti-talks faction led by Jewel Gorlosa at Maibong town in the North Cachar Hills district. Mazran's wife, Riya Maibongsa, and a civilian, Ananta Langthasa, are also wounded in the attack.
- December 1: Two DHD cadres, Formet Nunisa and Ramen Hagjer, are arrested from Diphu in the Karbi Anglong district.
- November 16: Assam Government is working on a "special" economic package for the twin hill districts of Karbi Anglong and North Cachar Hills to convince groups such as the UPDS and DHD to give up their demand for statehood and involve themselves in planning and development of the backward districts. "We are planning the package in such a way that it could be close to the budgets of certain states whose territories are smaller than the two districts combined. If we draw up an annual budget that is more than that of these states or at least on a par, we see no reason for its rejection by the militant leadership. The package could be worth around Rs 500 crore," said an unnamed official.

- October 30: Suspected DHD militants abduct Samdes Ardau, a revenue officer in the North Cachar Hills Autonomous Council, from his Haflong residence.
- October 23: The NDFB, DHD and UPDS are reportedly involved in extortion activities, despite the fact that all these outfits are under ceasefire agreement with the Union Government.
- October 22: A CPI-ML leader, Lantuk Phangcho, is abducted by the militants from Umrangshu in the North Cachar Hills. Involvement of the Jewel Gorlosa faction of the DHD is also suspected in the abduction.

  At least 12 DHD cadres along with a civilian driver are arrested, while traveling in two vehicles, near Umrangsu in the North Cachar Hills district. A huge cache of arms and explosives, including five Russian AK-47 assault rifles, four Chinese AK series rifles, 15 magazines with 16 rounds of ammunition, an M-16 rifle with 105 rounds of ammunition, a rocket launcher, five hand grenades, two detonator hand grenades, an improvised flame grenade thrower, three pieces of dagger, two vehicles, along with INR 36,135, a set of combat uniform and four mobile cell sets, is recovered from their possession.
- October 18: The dead body of a DHD cadre is recovered from Khinmung Basti under Mahur police station in the North Cachar Hills district.
- October 7: Two civilians are killed and three others injured in crossfire during an encounter between security forces (SFs) and cadres of the Black Widow faction of DHD at Mujam village under Kherni police station in the Karbi Anglong district. The SF personnel were carrying out a combing operation in the area following the October 6 attack on the Railway Protection Force in the adjoining North Cachar Hills district. Tools used for making arms, military fatigues and incriminating documents were found in a temporary camp of the Black Widow near the incident site.
- October 6: At least 13 Railway Protection Force personnel are killed by in an ambush by the DHD militants belonging to the Black Widow faction in the North Cachar Hills district.
- September 18: A DHD cadre belonging to its Black Widow faction, Ajit Hagjer, is arrested from Hotel Geetanjali at Panbazaar in the Guwahati city.
- September 10: DHD cadres belonging to the anti-talks faction headed by Jewel Garlossa set ablaze two labour camps at different construction sites of the Northeast Frontier Railway's broad gauge project in the

North Cachar Hills, as the companies involved in the project fail to pay ransom to the militants. Additional Superintendent of Police Bidyut Buragohain confirmed that two labour sheds at Asong Haju and Saron Basti under Mahur police station were set ablaze by at least 12 cadres of the outfit.

- September 6: DHD militants belonging to the Jewel Garlossa faction shot dead two cadres of the rival Dilip Nunisa faction at Langting under Maibong police station in the North Cachar Hills. One of the slain militants was identified as 'lance corporal' Lampthou Dimasa.
- September 1: An anti-talks faction of the DHD, Black Widow, which is operating in the hill districts of the State, destroys an excavator worth INR 6000,000 used in a railway project to terrorize the contractors to meet the demand for ransom amount. The NSCN-IM is suspected to be conniving with the Black Widow to maintain its influence in the North Cachar Hills district. The railway construction work between Lumding and Silchar through North Cachar Hills is affected, as contractors decide to suspend construction work due to extortion threat by militant outfits.
- August 20: An internecine clash among DHD cadres belonging to the Jewel Garlossa faction occurs at Lanfer village under Kheroni police station in the Hamren sub-division of Karbi Anglong district, following the escape of five cadres of the outfit from its camp in North Cachar Hills.
- August 7: Four persons are wounded in a grenade blast triggered by suspected militants belonging to the anti-talks Jewel faction of the DHD at Mahur market in the North Cachar Hills district.
- July 30: Two DHD cadres, V. Dimasa and Ithang Dimasa, are arrested from Silchar town in the Cachar district. According to police sources, the arrested militants confess to have come from their camp in North Cachar Hills district to Silchar for medical treatment.
- July 26: An unidentified DHD cadre belonging to the Jewel Garlossa faction triggers a grenade explosion, targeting CRPF personnel, killing three civilians, including one female child, and injuring three others at a railway station in Maibong of North Cachar Hills district.
- July 3: A trader, Jagannath Prasad, is killed, and at least 18 persons are wounded in a grenade explosion triggered at a market place in Haflong town of North Cachar Hills district. Subsequently, a caller, identifying himself as the 'area commander' of the Jewel Garlossa faction of the DHD claims responsibility for the grenade attack reportedly intended 'to teach a lesson' to the shop owner.

- June 20:The Zemi Students Union, Asom (ZSU-A) accuses and condemns the Dilip Nunisa faction of the DHD for its involvement in the May 8 abduction and subsequent killing of three Zemi Naga youths in the North Cachar Hills district.
- June 18: The dead bodies of three unidentified persons, belonging to Zemi Naga tribe, who were abducted by the suspected DHD cadres on May 8 from Fiding village under Mahur police station in the North Cachar Hills district, are recovered after a month at an unspecified place near a rail track.
- June 12: Three cadres of the anti-talks Black Widow faction of the DHD, Shishuranjan *Bar,* Chandrakanta Naiding and Peikhuk Rangkhol, are arrested from a hotel at Bhangagarh in the Guwahati city of Kamrup district. Incriminating documents and Rupees 5,00,000 are seized from the arrested militants.
- June 4: A DHD cadre, Shyamal Langthasa, of the Gortosa faction is reported to have deserted a designated camp in the North Cachar Hills district on an unspecified date in May.
- April 28: The 'deputy commander-in-chief' of the DHD, identified as Naizing Daulagapu, is shot at and wounded by suspected militants belonging to the breakaway faction of the outfit led by Jewel Garlossa at Upper Dibbarai under Haflong police station in the North Cachar Hills district.
- March 30: DHD militants belonging to the Jewel Garlossa faction kill a worker engaged by a railway contractor and injure another at Retzole in the North Cachar Hills district. Seven rounds of empty cartridges of AK-47 assault rifles were recovered from the incident site.
- March 28: The North Cachar Hills district police recover three rocket launcher shells, two pistols, nine magazines, one revolver and an unspecified amount of ammunition from a husband and wife, identified as Afhringdaw and Dipali Warisa. They were traveling from Guwahati to Umrangso and are allegedly linked to the Jewel Garlossa faction of the DHD.
- February 23: A school-teacher is killed in an exchange of fire between cadres of the HPC-D and DHD in the North Cachar Hills district. DHD chief Dilip Nunisa said that the vehicle in which his deputy Yathon Dimasa, the public relations officer of the outfit Samir Dimasa and their bodyguard were traveling was ambushed by the HPC-D at Mahadev Tilla. In the exchange of fire, the school teacher who was passing by is also killed.

- January 21: DHD chief Dilip Nunisa said that Ministry of Home Affairs officials have confirmed January 31 as the date for another round of dialogue between the Union Government and the outfit to be held in New Delhi. The previous round of dialogue between a DHD delegation and Union Home Minister Shivraj Patil was held in New Delhi during June 2005.

2005

- December 14: Union Minister of State for Home Affairs, S. Reghupathy, while speaking in the Rajya Sabha (Upper House of Parliament), said that cease-fire was currently on with the DHD along with other militant outfits of the North East.
- December 13: DHD announces cease-fire with the UPDS in the Karbi Anglong and North Cachar Hills districts during Christmas festivities.
- December 6: Two unidentified militants of DHD's Jewel Garlossa faction are killed at Retzol near Haflong in the NC Hills district.
- December 3: 379 houses are set ablaze by the DHD in six villages of Mohendijua and Lunhnit areas in the Karbi Anglong district.
- December 2: Suspected DHD militants, armed with grenade launchers and AK rifles, open indiscriminate fire at Sirkangnep village in the Karbi Anglong district killing four persons, including a two-month-old infant.
- October 23: Security forces arrest five armed *DHD* cadres from Umrangshu Bazaar in the North Cachar Hills district.
- October 21: Suspected DHD militants kill nine UPDS cadres at Tamulbari under Diphu police station in the Karbi Anglong district.
- October 17: Suspected DHD militants waylay two passenger buses traveling from Ziriktnding at Charchim under Kheroni police station in Karbi Anglong district and kill *23* persons, including nine women, belonging to the Karbi tribe.
- June *23.* DHD chairman Dilip Nunisa says that the outfit is ready to compromise on its demand of the integration of Dimasa-inhabited areas of Assam and Nagaland "if Delhi accedes to the call for Dimaraji statehood."
- May 19: DHD cadres serve extortion notes targeting the non-Dimasa population in and around Harinagar under Jaipur police station limits in the Cachar district.
- May 10: Three Dima Halim Daogah cadres were reported to have been killed during an encounter with the Meghalaya Police personnel at Pendung village in the Jaintia Hills district of Meghalaya.
- April 27: Superintendent of Police in Karbi Anglong district says that the DHD has been using conduits from various tribal communities to

carry out illegal activities in the districts of Karbi Anglong and North Cachar Hills.

- April 22: The DHD chairman, Dilip Nunisa, in an interview, accuses the Union and State Governments of promoting a rival faction, the Blaek Widow, to weaken the DHD's struggle for a separate state.
- April 21: Suspected terrorists belonging to the anti-talks faction of the DHD kill a villager after setting fire to two houses in the Lanku Garu Basti area under Umrangshu police station of the North Cachar Hills district.
- April 11: Black Widow, a splinter group of the DHD, abducts Lakhyajoti Langthasa, an executive member of the North Cachar Hills Autonomous District Council.
- January 20: DHD leaders meet the Union Government representatives and say that no solution short of a separate 'Dimaraji' State would be acceptable to the outfit.
- January 2: Four suspected DHD cadres are arrested while extorting money from Kalain in the Cachar district.
- January 1: Cachar district police arrests a suspected DHD cadre from an unspecified place in the district.

2004

December 28: Cease-fire agreement between the Government of India and the DHD is extended till December 31, 2005, following a tripartite meeting between the group, the State Government and the Centre held in Guwahati.

- December 4: The DHD Chief Dilip Nunisa, expresses disappointment over the delay in holding negotiations with the government and terms the delay as "intentional procrastination".
- November 25: Three DHD cadres arrested from an unspecified place in the Cachar district along with five AK-47 rifles, one SLR and a huge quantity of ammunition.
- October 30: DHD and NDFB cadres open fire on a Dimapur bound truck at Sat Mile.
- October 17: DHD calls for a 48-hour general strike in the North Cachar Hills district to protest against the alleged 'atrocities' by the army personnel on its cadres.
- October 13: Assam Police arrests three DHD cadres from an unspecified place along the Assam-Mizoram border.
- September 23: A DHD delegation meets Union Home Minister Shivraj Patil in New Delhi and submits a memorandum demanding a separate homeland for the Dimasa tribals.

- July 29: Suspected DHD terrorists kill a teacher, namely Altaf Hossain Barbhuyan, at Karkat Basti in the Cachar district.
- June 28: Jewel Garlossa, the ousted DHD 'Chief' in an interview with Sentinel terms the 'takeover' of the outfit by the 'military wing' chief Pranab Nunisa as a 'gross violation of the ceasefire agreement.'
- June 24: Pranab Nunisa becomes the president of the DHD. He ousts the former president, Jewel Garlossa for anti-DHD activities.
- May 19: DHD releases a trader, whom the outfit had abducted on May 16 from Tumpreng under Hojai subdivision in Nagaon district.
- May 16: DHD cadres abduct a trader from Tumpreng under Hojai subdivision in Nagaon district.
- April 11: A civilian working as an employee in a fuel pump killed during a grenade attack by DHD terrorists at Sukanjan under Bokajan police station in Karbi Anglong district.
- March 18: DHD terrorists shoot at and injure a couple at Singaribasti near Hojai town in Nagaon district, following an unsuccessful attempt to abduct their son.
- March 15: Three DHD cadres arrested by the Army for their alleged involvement in extortion activities in Pailapool area under Lakhipur police station in the Cachar district.
- January 1: Ceasefire with the DHD extended upto December 31, 2004.

2003

- December 29: Cease-fire between the DHD and Union Government is extended by one year from January 1, 2004.
- December 27: Jewel Garlossa, President of DHD, in a press statement, appeals to insurgent outfits in the northeastern region to come forward for negotiations.
- November 26: A trader is injured in an attack by a group of DHD terrorists for having refused to pay extortion amount to the outfit in the Diphu town of Karbi Anglong district.
- August 28: Report indicates that the DHD would discuss the issue of Statehood for the Dimasa tribe in the Northeast during a meeting with representatives of the Union Government slated to be held in September 2003.
- August 7: Suspected DHD terrorists abduct a civilian from the Lumding area in the North Cachar Hills district.
- August 4: DHD terrorist is lynched while allegedly attempting to extort money from a local businessman at Lamsakhang bazaar in the Karbi Anglong district.

- July 17: Media reports indicate formation of Hmar Hunam Santo (HHS) with links to the HPC-D as counter outfit of the DHD in Assam.
- July 7: DHD 'commanding officer' Yaohang Dimasa threatens to carry out counter attacks against the HPC-D alleging the latter of attacking Dimasa villages in Cachar and North Cachar Hills district of Assam.
- July 6: DHD terrorists kill an employee of Lengrijan Tea Estate under Khatkhati police outpost in Karbi Anglong district.
- June 30: DHD threatens to target HPC-D cadres under code name "King Cobra" in the North Cachar Hills and Cachar districts of Assam.
- June 27: Cease-fire with DHD in operation since January 1, 2003 extended for another six months, beyond June 30.
- June 17: Reports indicate that the Union Government is likely to extend the cease-fire with the DHD for another term, beginning July 1. The earlier cease-fire agreement, which was in force for six months, ends on June 30.
- June 15: DHD terrorists kill a tribal youth of Hmar community at Haflong, district headquarters of North Cachar Hills.
- June 13: The North Cachar Autonomous District Council submits a memorandum to the visiting Cabinet team urging, among others, to start the proposed dialogue with the DHD early.

  DHD 'vice-chairman' Dilip Nunisa warns that the outfit would conduct 'raids' on alleged HPC-D hideouts in the neighbouring States of Mizoram and Manipur.
- June 12: DHD says that its cadres were not involved in the Mahur incident that occurred on June 10.
- June 10: DHD terrorists set ablaze 60 Hmar dwellings in two villages of Garden Basti and Saron in the North Cachar Hills district.
- June 1: Report indicates that the DHD is yet to decide over extension of its six-month cease-fire with the Union Government that came into effect on December 31, 2002. The DHD 'vice-president' Dilip Nunisa alleges that while the security forces act "provocatively" against its cadres, Hmars terrorists target the members of the Dimasa tribe.
- May 29: DHD alleges that cadres of the Hmar People's Convention-Democracy (HPCD) are involved in the killing of a Dimasa youth at Haflong, district headquarters of the North Cachar Hills district on May 28.
- May 28: Railway Protection Force identifies four insurgency prone sectors in the Northeast and says that the DHD is active in the Lumding-Halflong sector.

- May 27: DHD 'vice-president' Dilip Nunisa complains against the alleged detention of his team by an Army officer at Lumding Tin-Ali in North Cachar Hills district.
- May 15: DHD says it would not carry out retaliatory attacks to avenge the killing of State Veterinary Minister G.C. Langthasa's son, on May 12.
- May 7: Suspected Hmar terrorists kill two DHD cadres at Redzol, near Halflong, North Cachar Hills district.
- May 2: 15 DHD cadres arrested on April 29 are provided 'safe passage' to their hideouts in North Cachar Hills district.
- May 1: DHD threatens to call off cease-fire, in operation since December 31, 2002 over the arrest of its 15 cadres on April 29.
- April 30: DHD denies that its 15 cadres arrested on April 29 had violated the ground rules of the cease-fire and demands their release.
- April 29: Security forces arrest 15 DHD cadres from Thaba Basti, North Cachar Hills district, on charges of violating cease-fire ground rules.
- April 16: Security forces arrest nine DHD terrorists under Lakhipur subdivision (administrative unit), Cachar district.
- April 10: Hmar Peoples' Convention-Democrat (HPC-D) denies involvement in the massacre of 23 Dimasa tribals following their abduction in Cachar district on March 31.
- April 9: A group of approximately 40 armed DHD terrorists attack Hmar settlements and set ablaze 25 dwellings at Radzol, Harangajao police station-limits, North Cachar Hills district.
- April 2: DHD 'Vice-president' Dilip Nunisa threatens to call-off the cease-fire following an alleged attack by the Hmar People's Conference (HPC) on a Dimasa (a tribe) settlement in Cachar district.
- April 1: Bodies of 23 Hmars recovered near Mastul hill area, 15 km from Sonai, in Cachar district.
- March 31: Hmar People's Convention-Democrats (HPC-D) terrorists abduct 23 Dimasa tribals from Chekarcham and Meghnathal villages, Sonai police station limits in Cachar district and later kill them. Approximately 450 dwellings were also torched and some 500 persons were rendered homeless.
- March 26: DHD cadres attack Hmar villages and ask Hmars to leave the North Cachar Hills area or to face dire consequences.
- March 5: DHD cadres attack two Hmar villages—Balmul and Multhajao in North Cachar Hills district forcing nearly 800 Hmars to desert their

homes and flee to Hmar-dominated village of Hmarkhawlien in Lakhipur subdivision of adjoining Cachar district and Kolasib town in north Mizoram.

- February 3: DHD 'president' Jowel Garlossa reiterates demand for *Dimaraji* (separate Dimasa State).
- January 7: DHD 'commander-in-chief' Pranab Nunisa says idea of autonomy is irrelevant for people of Karbi Anglong and North Cachar Hills districts.
- January 2: Report indicates that process of ground rules of cease-fire agreement between government and DHD are being finalised with Assam government.
- January 1 : Various Dimasa civil society groups welcome cease-fire agreement between Dima Halim Daogah (DHD) and Assam government.

2002

- December 30: DHD announces unilateral 'suspension' of activities and 'cessation of hostilities' with security forces (SFs) with effect from December 31, for a period of six months.
- December 19: A group of DHD terrorists attack the Dilai police outpost of Bokajan police station, in Assam's Karbi Anglong district.
- December 12: A security force (SF) personnel is killed and nine more troops are injured in an ambush laid by suspected DHD terrorists at the eight mile point between Umrangshu and Doyangmukh, North Cachar Hills district, Assam.

  North Cachar Hills district Additional Superintendent of Police (ASP) N R Seal succumbs to his injuries at Silchar Medical College Hospital. DHD terrorists had ambushed his office in Haflong, on December 9.
- December 9: DHD terrorists lay an ambush and injure two railway policemen and a railway engineer, at Langting, in Assam's North Cachar Hills district.

  DHD terrorists attack North Cachar Hills district Additional Superintendent of Police (ASP) N R Seal, while he is in his office. His Personal Security Officer (PSO) is killed in the attack.
- November 22: DHD terrorists shoot at and injure a nine-year-old boy at Babunala Borbasti, under Lumding police station-limits, in Assam's Nagaon district.
- November 13: Reports indicate DHD terrorists have intensified their extortion drive in North Cachar (NC) Hills district of Assam.
- November 4: Police arrest a DHD terrorist following an encounter at a place under Bokajan police station-limits, Karbi Anglong district.

- November 3: DHD terrorists attack the bungalow of Pathemara Tea Estate manager in Assam's Cachar district and kill a private security guard and injure two others.
- September 20: DHD terrorists abduct a teacher of Lumding Hindi High School in Assam's Nagaon district.
- September 13: A DHD self-styled 'sergeant', Krbrte Nunisa killed in an encounter near Maibong in North Cachar Hills district, Assam.
- September 1: DHD terrorists set ablaze 27 vehicles at a quarry in Madhuraghat, Udarbond police station limits, in Assam's Cachar district, as the vehicle-owners refuse to meet with the extortion demand.
- August 23: Police arrest two DHD terrorists near Haflong Railway Station, North Cachar Hills district, Assam.
- August 22: The abducted daughter of the assistant manager of Kalain Tea Estate, Cachar district, returns home after 77 days in captivity. Reports say DHD terrorists facilitated her rescue in order to falsify suspicion of their role.
- August 6: The driver of a Dimapur-bound bus is killed in arson committed by suspected DHD terrorists in Kokrajhar district, who had set the bus afire.
- July 22: Reports say DHD terrorists have served extortion notices on tea planters in southern Assam, demanding huge sums as 'protection money'.
- July 18: Seven security force (SF) personnel killed in an ambush allegedly laid by DHD terrorists near Diyungmukh, a local market in North Cachar Hills district.
- July 14: DHD terrorist killed in an encounter near Bara Langpher village in Karbi Anglong district.
- July 3: Police seize 72 rounds of live cartridges and a walkie-talkie at Dhansiri in Karbi Anglong district, after an encounter with DHD terrorists.
- June 24: Eight Oil and Natural Gas Commission (ONGC) employees killed, six more injuried at Dawafi, in Karbi Anglong district.
- May 28: DHD terrorist killed in an encounter at Hojaipur Basti in Karbi Anglong district.
- May 18: Santosh Mohan Deb, a local Member of Parliament (MP) demands Army operations against DHD.
- A report says DHD set up camps in a jungle enclave near Khagrachheri in the Chittagong Hills Tracts, southeast Bangladesh.
- May 8: Report alleges DHD of targeting railway employees and contractors, engaged in Lumding-Sitchar gauge conversion.

- May 5: Report indicates DHD allegedly forged "strategic alliance" with the NDFB in the North Cachar Hills district of Assam.
- May 1: Report says DHD served extortion notices to the Bengali residents of Thaligram, Nagadoom, Chalrtacherra, Bagerkona, Pathimara and Guabari villages under Khaspur in Cachar district.
- March 24: Three DHD terrorists surrender in Haflang, North Cachar Hills district.

2001

- November 3: DHD terrorists kill two persons, including a police personnel near Diphu in Karbi Anglong district. Two others were also injured in the incident.
- September 30: DHD terrorists abduct two employees of a private firm from Dhansiri railway station in Diphu, Karbi Anglong district.
- September 21: Two DHD terrorists killed in an encounter at Haflong in North Cachar Hills district.
- September 3: Suspected DHD terrorists abduct two Northern Frontier Railway (NFR) employees from the Mandaradisha station, North Cachar (NC) Hills.
- August 3: DHD along with 11 other terrorist outfit calls for the boycott of Independence Day celebrations.
- July 18: DHD terrorist killed at Odali Tiniali, in Nagaon.
- July 14: Two DHD terrorists arrested at Umrangsho.
- April 14: Kanta Langthasa, 'Home Minister' of Dima Halim Daoga (DHD) was arrested by the Guwahati police.
- February 8: Nine police personnel were killed and three more injured in an ambush laid by DHD terrorists near Dehangi in North Cachar hills district.

2000

June 30: Three security force personnel killed and two others injured in an ambush laid by DHD terrorists in North Cachar Hills district.

May 18: Six persons, including an Executive Magistrate, killed in an ambush laid by DHD terrorists near Haflong, North Cachar Hills district.

KAMTAPUR LIBERATION ORGANISATION (KLO)

Origin

The origin of the Kamtapur Liberation Organisation (KLO) can be traced to the attempts of certain members of the Rajbongshi community belonging to the All Kamtapur Students' Union (AKSU) to organise an armed struggle for a separate Kamtapur State. For this purpose, they approached the United Liberation Front of Asom (ULFA). ULFA reportedly agreed to train them in order to gain foothold outside Assam, in the other geographically contiguous Indian States, to use them as transit routes. ULFA's line of thinking was that, it would not only facilitate the movement of its cadres to their base camps in Bhutan but also provide a safe haven for the injured or sick cadres.

The KLO came into existence on December 28, 1995. At the time of its formation, its cadre strength was an estimated 60. However, subsequently, it is said to be operating with approximately 300 'active cadres'.

Objectives

The objective of the KLO is to carve out a separate Kamtapur State comprising six districts—Cooch Behar, Darjeeling, Jalpaiguri, North and South Dinajpur and Malda—of West Bengal and four contiguous districts of Assam—Kokrajhar, Bongaigaon, Dhubri and Goalpara. At its inception, the KLO was an over-ground organisation and was formed to address problems such as large-scale unemployment, land alienation, perceived neglect of Kamtapuri language and identity, and grievances of economic deprivation. Soon, its strategy transformed into waging armed struggle.

Leadership and Organisation

Tamir Das alias Jibon Singha is the chairman of the KLO. He was arrested in October 1999. However, he regained control over the outfit after he was released by the Assam Police in a bid to make the other KLO cadres surrender.

Milton Burman alias Mihir Das is the second in command of the outfit. Tom Adhikary alias Joydeb Roy is the outfit's 'crack squad' chief. Both of them were arrested by the RBA during the December 2003 operations.

Bharati Das, Chairperson of the Women's Wing, was arrested from Jalpaiguri district in West Bengal on August 7, 2002. The outfit's operations chief, Suresh Roy, surrendered on January 24, 2002.

Some of the other prominent KLO insurgents who could be in positions of decision-making are Hiten Roy, Ravi Rajbongshi, Rahul Roy and Kajal Roy.

Area of Operation

The KLO is active in following areas of West Bengal and Assam

West Bengal—six districts of North Bengal

- South Dinajpur
- North Dinajpur
- Coochbehar
- Jalpaiguri
- Malda
- Darjeeling

Assam—four districts of lower Assam

- Kokrajhar
- Bongaigaon
- Dhubri
- Goalpara

However, the outfit is most active in Alipurduar in Jalpaiguri and the Siliguri sub-division of Darjeeling.

The KLO maintains a string of camps in Bhutan. Several of its camps are located across the Wangchu river, close to Chuka district in Bhutan. According to Lyonpo Thinley Gyamtsho, the Bhutanese Home Minister, two of its camps are in the Bhangtar and Lhamoizingkha areas of Bhutan.

Linkages

The KLO is alleged to be the armed underground wing of Kamtapur People's Party (KPP). Available evidence suggests that it maintains close linkages with the ULFA. Soon after its formation, its members were imparted arms training during 1996-97 in Samdrup Jhankar in Bhutan, and also subsequently at Gelengphu and Kalaikhola. The KLO's headquarters is situated near that of ULFA's at Samdrup Jhankar. Reports even suggest that the KLO is the brainchild of Raju Baruah, ULFA's 'deputy commander'.

As mentioned already, the ULFA wants to use West Bengal as a transit point to cross over to Bhutan, and then into Bangladesh. Also, this area provides a safe haven for injured and battle-weary ULFA cadres.

The outfit is also reportedly linked to the National Democratic Front of Bodoland (NDFB). Media reports suggest that the KLO, ULFA and the NDFB have formed an umbrella organisation to coordinate their activities. Moreover, the KLO is also said to have linkages with the Maoist insurgents of Nepal. An August 2001 report indicated that, a meeting of NDFB, KLO, ULFA and the Maoists was held at Birganj, near the Indo-Nepal border, to discuss a joint strategy to carry out subversive activities against India.

Besides these linkages, the Tiwa National Revolutionary Front (TNRF), an insurgent outfit based in the Nagaon district of Assam, also has a working relationship with the KLO. In addition, the National Socialist Council of Nagaland-Isak-Muivah (NSCN-IM), too, reportedly maintains links with the KLO.

Reports also suggest that Pakistan's Inter Services Intelligence (ISI) is assisting terrorist groups, including the KLO, to commit subversion along the Siliguri Corridor of West Bengal.

Major incidents 2006

- December 25: A KLO militant, Swapan Rai alias Rahul Rai, arrested from Tarchuk village by the Gouripur police, is remanded to seven days police custody by the judicial magistrate in Dhubri district.

- November 21 : Forensic experts and Police suspect the involvement of the KLO along with ULFA in the November 20-bomb blasts.

  Central intelligence agencies say that the Jama'atul Mujahideen Bangladesh (JMB) used the KLO to trigger the November 20-bomb blast.

- November 20: At least 10 persons are killed and 50 injured in a bomb blast inside a compartment of the Haldibari-Siliguri Passenger train at Belacoba station in West Bengal's Jalpaiguri district. The KLO's involvement is suspected in the blast.
- September 27: A KLO cadre, Ajit Adhikary, is arrested by police from the Bhandijelas village in the Cooch Behar district of West Bengal. The arrested militant was trained under outfit's chief, Jeevan Singha, in Bangladesh.
- September 21: A new outfit, Darjeeling Gorkha Maobadi Sangthan, has an operational alliance with the KLO, which is fighting for a homeland for the Koch and Rajbongshi communities in North Bengal.
- August 10: The KLO along with MPLF, NLFT, TPDF and ULFA in a joint statement call upon the people of the North East region to boycott the Independence Day celebration and also jointly call a 12-hour general strike.
- May 29: Three KLO cadres, Nataraj, Dilip and Manoj, are arrested from their hideout at Kharibari near Siliguri in the Jalpaiguri district of West Bengal. According to police sources, the three were arrested following the confession of a ULFA cadre who was detained from the same locality on May 18.
- May 24: Six KLO cadres are arrested from different places in the Malda district of West Bengal.

  According to police sources, one of the three, arrested from Kanturka village under Habibpur police station, was involved in the murder of a CPI-M leader about four months ago.

- January 31: The six-month cease-fire agreement earlier concluded between the Army authorities and eight militant outfits, including the KLO, expires.
- January 25: A hardcore KLO cadre, Bhabesh Roy, is arrested along with seven linkmen of the outfit from Shamukhtala in West Bengal's Jalpaiguri district. Inspector General of Police (North Bengal), Kishanlal Meena, said that Bhabesh was trained in a militant training camp in Bangladesh's Chattagram area and was attached to the All Tripura Tiger Force (ATTF). The seven arrested linkmen were allegedly working for the outfit in different areas of North Bengal.
- January 20: KLO calls for a general strike on Republic Day (January 26) in the Northeastern States.

2005

- December 21 : Home Minister says that there is a nexus between the Nepalese Maoists and the ULFA and KLO. He however says that there has been no exchange of weapons between them, though there are reports of training of each other's cadres. There are also reports of some people being taken for training to Nepal and vice versa.
- April 29: A front-ranking KLO leader, Pulasta Burman, is arrested from Changrabandha near the Bangladesh border in the Coochbehar district of West Bengal. The Inspector-General of Police (North Bengal), K. L. Meena, says that Burman was arrested when he crossed over to Changrabandha village in the Mekhliganj sub-division area. Burman, one of the founder-members of the outlawed KLO, is also a close associate of the group's chief, Jiban Singha. Burman had been evading arrest for the last few years after having managed to flee the Bhutan army's operation against KLO camps in the country's jungles during December 2003 to Bangladesh.
- March 9: Union Home Minister, Shivraj Patil, speaking in the Upper House of Indian Parliament (Rajya Sabha) says that ULFA and KLO have forged links with the Maoist insurgents of Nepal.
- January 20: ULFA, TPDF, KLO and MPLF jointly appeal to the people of the North-east to boycott the Republic Day celebrations on January 26 and call for a general strike on that day.

2004

- November 19: Three KLO linkmen are arrested in connection with the killing of a driver from Siliguri in the Jalpaiguri district.
- October 28: Two KLO militants, Parimal Basunia alias Pramod Das and Pahar Singh alias Batrish Das, are arrested from Jalpaiguri district of North Bengal and in Guwahati in Assam.
- September 5: West Bengal Police arrests seven KLO militants from Mathabhanga in the Coochbehar district. They also recover two kilograms of RDX, four AK-56 rifles, 12 magazines, 496 rounds of ammunition of AK-56, two M-20 pistols, 21 rounds of M-20 ammunition from their possession.
- August 9: At least eight persons suspected to have links with the KLO are arrested from different parts of the Coochbehar district in West Bengal.
- August 8: Security forces kill a KLO cadre in an encounter at Boxirhat in the Dhubri district of Assam.
- August 8: Border Security Force (BSF) sources say that KLO has recruited 20 youths, mostly from the Rajbanshi-dominated parts of Jalpaiguri district in North Bengal. BSF Inspector General Sukhjinder

Singh Sandhu was says that these youths were being trained at an unknown location in Bangladesh.

- August 6: Two suspected KLO cadres, Goutam Shil alias Bibek Barman and Nimai Dutta alias Bimal Barman, are beaten to death by villagers at Bazitchatra in the Cooch Behar district.
- March 13: KLO militants open indiscriminate firing and kill two traders at Ranglajhar market under Moinagaon police station in the Jalpaiguri district along the Assam-Bengal border. Three others are injured in the firing.
- February 24: A KLO cadre, Bhyamal Barman alias Akshy Das, is arrested from Natabari village in the Coochbehar district of West Bengal. He is reported to be a close associate of KLO leader Tom Adhikari.
- February 8: Two suspected KLO cadres are arrested following raids at the Changimari and Pukari areas of Kumaragram village in the Jalpaiguri district of West Bengal. Four AK-56 rifles and 170 rounds of 7.62 mm ammunition are recovered from them.
- January 18: Cooch Behar Police arrest three KLO linkmen from Buxirhat police station area on the charge of sheltering terrorists.
- January 18: North Bengal police intelligence sources report that the fugitive KLO 'commander-in-chief Jibon Singha, now in Dhaka, is scheduled to meet the functionaries of Pakistan's external intelligence agency, ISI, in Bangladesh to seek their help.
- January 18: A KLO militant, identified as Helatu Das, surrenders at the Kumargram police station in the Jalpaiguri district of West Bengal.
- January 17: West Bengal police arrests eight linkmen (five from Falakata, two from Dhupguri and one from Mainaguri) of the KLO in the Jalpaiguri district.
- January 16: A relative of the West Bengal Forest Minister Jogesh Burman, identified as Shyamal Roy, is arrested at Jharbeltoli under Falakata Police Station in the Jalpaiguri district for his alleged close links with the KLO. Police sources say that Roy had given shelter to KLO cadres on several occasions and has links with the outfit's senior leaders like Tom Adhikary, Milton Burman and Anirban Rava.
- January 14: Suspected KLO militants kill four civilians and injure several others in an attack on a video parlour in West Bengal's Cooch Behar district.
- January 11: A KLO linkman, Meghnath Roy, is arrested from Shidhabari under Alipurduar police station limits in the Jalpaiguri district.
- January 2: A KLO militant is shot dead during an encounter with the police in the Jalpaiguri district.

2003

- December 29: Royal Bhutanese Army (RBA) hands over 12 KLO cadres to the Indian Army. Jalpaiguri Divisional Commissioner Balbir Ram says that the RBA handed over the cadres at Binaguri cantonment in the Jalpaiguri district.
- December 22: KLO in a press statement released in the name of its 'chairman' Jibon Singha terms the military offensive in Bhutan as unjustified. The statement says, "Bhutan has inscribed the history of monumental betrayal by arresting and extraditing our Central Committee members to India when they went to negotiate with the authority of Bhutan in response to their invitation."
- December 20: Top KLO leaders Tom Adhikari and Milton Barman confess to the abduction and subsequent murder of timber merchant Naresh Das from Kumargram in the Jalpaiguri district of West Bengal in year 1998 in collaboration with the ULFA.
- December 20: The 48-hour bandh (shutdown) called by the KLO, ULFA and NDFB evokes a mixed response and partially affects life in Assam. It was called in protest against the crackdown launched by the RBA on their camps in Bhutan.
- December 18: Reports suggest that KLO chief Jibon Singha has been killed in the anti-insurgency operations in Bhutan.
- December 17: KLO senior leaders, Milton Burman and Tom Adhikary, are arrested by the Royal Bhutan Army (RBA) during operations against Indian terrorists based in Bhutanese territory.
- December 3: Security forces recover the body of a surrendered KLO cadre from Balapasa near the Assam-Bengal border.
- November 1 : The Jalpaiguri district police in North Bengal kill two suspected KLO terrorists inside the Buxa Tiger Reserve near the Indo-Bhutan border. Two AK-56 rifles and 59 rounds of ammunition are recovered from the incident site.
- August 6: Northeast terrorist groups including ULFA, NDFB, NLFT and KLO call for the boycott of Independence Day (August 15) celebrations,
- July 23: Media reports say that the 81st National Assembly of Bhutan adopted a resolution for the last attempt' to persuade ULFA, NDFB and the KLO to close down their camps within this year 'peacefully' failing which terrorists would face 'military action'.
- July 11 : Media reports from Bhutan indicate that Bhutan National Assembly was unable to reach a consensus over the issue of the way to tackle NDFB, ULFA and the KLO.

- May 17: Bhutanese King Jigme Singhye Wangchuk calls upon the people to volunteer for the formation of a 'militia force' to counter Indian insurgent groups - ULFA, NDFB and the KLO on its soil.
- May 9: Chief of the Indian Army, General N C Vij discusses the activities of ULFA, NDFB and KLO with the Bhutanese authorities.
- May 3: Report indicates that the Bhutanese Government has asked Indian terrorist groups, including NDFB and ULFA and the Kamtapur Liberation Organisation (KLO), operating in parts of Assam and West Bengal to leave by June 15.
- February 15: Two KLO terrorists are killed in an encounter at Kherabari, Gossaigaon police station limits, Kokrajhar district.

2002

- December 5: A KLO terrorist is arrested in Siliguri, West Bengal, while returning to India from Nepal.
- November 18: Two KLO terrorists are arrested from a place under Bakshirhat police station-limits, Cooch Behar district of West Bengal.
- October 11 : Terrorists of the KLO kill a leader of the Democratic Youth Federation of India (DYFI) in Bankachumari, Haat, Jalpaiguri district.
- October 9: Two terrorists of the KLO and a security force personnel are killed in an encounter at Punki village, Jalpaiguri district, West Bengal.
- October 1: A KLO terrorist, who had received arms training in Bhutan, is arrested from Baxirhat, Cooch Behar district, in West Bengal.
- August 31: Two KLO terrorists are killed in an encounter at Beltoli village, Cooch Behar district, West Bengal.

  West Bengal police arrest a timber dealer in Takura forests of Haldibari, Cooch Behar district, for allegedly supplying arms to KLO terrorists.
- August 29: A KLO terrorist is arrested from his Nazijote hideout in West Bengal's Siliguri district.
- August 28: A front-ranking terrorist of the KLO, Rohini Adhikari, allegedly involved in the August 17-Dhupguri massacre, is killed in an encounter in Hamuktala, Jalpaiguri district, West Bengal
- August 26: Six persons, including an employee of the Cooch Behar district collectorate, is arrested in the district for alleged links with the KLO.
- August 24: Inspector General of Police (IGP) (North Bengal) Bhupinder Singh says terrorists belonging to the ULFA and KLO have jointly carried out the August 17-terrorist attack in Dhupguri.

- August 17: Terrorists of the KLO kill five activists of the Communist Party of India—Marxist [CPI-M] and injure 14 others at its local office in Dhupguri town, Jalpaiguri district in West Bengal.
- August 5: Three KLO terrorists, including its women's wing chief Bharati Das, are arrested from Shaltali village, Jalpaiguri district in West Bengal.
- May 26: Six Central Reserve Police Force (CRPF) personnel are injured in a landmine blast triggered by terrorists of the KLO at Kajulibasti, near the India-Bhutan border, Jalpaiguri district in West Bengal.
- May 24: Two KLO terrorists are killed and a police personnel injured in an encounter in Dhumpara forests, Jalpaiguri district in West Bengal.
- May 14: A KLO terrorist is killed in an encounter near Siliguri in West Bengal. Two more terrorists manage to escape.
- January 31: Speaking at the Assam State conference of the CPI-M in Guwahati, West Bengal Chief Minister Buddhadeb Bhattacharya accuses the Inter Services Intelligence (ISI) of Pakistan of backing terrorist outfits like the KLO to engage in subversive activities in the region.

2001

- October 22: Terrorists of the KLO kill a leader of the Revolutionary Socialist Party (RSP) in Madhya Haldibari village, Jalpaiguri district in West Bengal.
- October 4: Union Ministry of Home Affairs convenes a joint meeting of officials from Assam and West Bengal to review threats emanating from the increasing nexus between the ULFA and the KLO.
- July 22: Bomb explosion is reported at the Jalpaiguri railway station.
- July 19: Speaking in the West Bengal State Legislative Assembly, Chief Minister Buddhadev Bhattacharjee says the KLO is receiving arms training from the ULFA, and if they join with the Maoists in Nepal, a deadly situation could arise in North Bengal.
- July 15: Buddhadeb Bhattacharya says the State government is prepared to talk on development issues in North Bengal with the KPP if it leaves the path of militancy and gives up its links with the KLO. He criticises the KLO for extorting money in North Bengal for use by the KPP and for its linkages with the ULFA.

2000

- October: A joint team of KLO and ULFA terrorists abduct a tea garden owner.

- August 7: KLO terrorists kill a local leader of the CPI-M in Jalpaiguri.
- May 4: Terrorists of the KLO kill a local leader of the CPI-M at Ghogsapara, near the Assam-West Bengal border.

1999

- November: KLO and ULFA terrorists loot a railway cash counter near Siliguri.
- July 1999: In the first reported KLO-ULFA joint-armed operation, a tea garden owner is abducted from the Latabari tea estate, Dooars region, North Bengal. Also, it is the first time that militants in North Bengal have used sophisticated arms like AK-47s.

1995

- December 28 : KLO is founded.

MUSLIM UNITED LIBERATION TIGERS OF ASSAM (MULTA)

Formation

The Muslim United Liberation Tigers of Assam (MULTA) was founded sometime in the year 1996. MULTA is one among the approximately 14 Islamist terrorist outfits reportedly operating in the State of Assam. MULTA and the Muslim United Liberation Front of Assam (MULFA) are also said to be part of the All Muslim United Liberation Forum of Assam (AMULFA). AMULFA was reportedly founded to coordinate the subversive activities of Islamist terrorist elements in the Northeast region of India. Though its time of founding is not known, AMULFA is believed to have taken shape at the behest of the Inter Services Intelligence (ISI), the external intelligence agency of Pakistan. The then Chief Minister (CM) of Assam, Prafulla Kumar Mahanta, in his statement on the floor of the Assam Legislative Assembly on ISI activities in the State, on April 6, 2000, said MULTA and MULFA were being guided by the ISI. Mahanta further claimed that the ISI had drafted a plan to cause subversion in the State by appealing to the religious sentiments of vulnerable sections in the society, in Assam.

Leadership and Cadre Strength

Available reports have, thus far, not been able to home in on the names of the leadership of MULTA. Similarly, the cadre strength of the outfit is yet not known. However, security forces have arrested many MULTA cadres and several more have also surrendered to the authorities in the State. A majority of MULTA cadres, reports indicate, are drawn from the poorer sections of the Muslim population in the State and have no more than minimal formal education.

Aims and Objectives

Reportedly, MULTA, as is allegedly the case with the other Islamist terrorist outfits in the State, seeks to mobilise the Muslim youth in Assam to 'fight' for the 'cause' of Muslims. Reports have also indicated that the outfit has as its objective the waging of *jehad* against India, to eventually set up a 'greater independent Islamistan' for the Muslims of Assam. MULTA cadres, in fact, reports suggest, are attempting to emulate the terrorist outfits operating in the Indian State of Jammu and Kashmir, and claiming that they are waging *jehad* against the Indian state.

Linkages

The outfit has established both intra and inter-regional linkages. Reports suggest it has linkages with the National Socialist Council of Nagland -Isak Muivah (NSCN-IM). NSCN-IM operates primarily in Nagaland. The NSCN-IM has allegedly provided training to MULTA cadres in the Jiribam jungles. Some reports even indicated that cadres of other Assam-based terrorist outfits championing the Islamic cause in Assam, too, had trained with the NSCN-IM.

MULTA is also said to be a constituent of the United Reformation Protest of India (URPI), another organisation that claims to be a platform for various Islamic terrorist outfits operating in the Northeast. A MULTA cadre arrested on July 9, 2002, in Bilasipara, Dhubri district, Assam, disclosed this. Besides, reports of June 21 , 2002 have expressed the apprehension that the Al Qaeda might spread its network across the State. Fleeing Al Qaeda terrorists are looking for safe houses after the US campaign against them started in Afghanistan in the aftermath of the 9/11 attacks on the US. These cadres, reports indicate, might turn to the Islamist terrorist outfits in the State to secure safe houses.

According to intelligence sources, the ISI had backed the formation of the AMULFA, of which MULTA and MULFA are members. The sources also claim that the ISI is even providing training to these two outfits in the Sylhet district of Bangladesh under the command of one Rustom Ali, who is said to be a former Pakistani Army officer. Sources further claim that the AMULFA would finally be linked with the United Liberation Front of Seven Sisters (ULFSS), in ISI's larger plan to destabilise the Northeast region.

There have also been reports indicating that MULTA has been receiving help from the Jamat-e-Islami (JeI) of Bangladesh, a fundamentalist group that is a member of the ruling coalition in that country.

Dhubri district of Assam has witnessed the maximum number of incidents involving MULTA terrorists. A MULTA cadre whose arrest was reported in the media on July 4, 2002 confessed to the police that the passage along the International Border in the Golokganj area of Dhubri district is used as a route to infiltrate into the State from Bangladesh. Nagaon and Morigaon districts of Assam have also witnessed MULTA activities. A few of its cadres have been arrested in Darrang district, too. Moreover MULTA allegedly maintains base in Jiribam sub-division of Manipur.

Extortion from the local population in the areas it operates, abductions for ransom and the illegal arms manufacture and trade in them have been identified as the main activities of the outfit. The outfit's cadres have also been involved in committing murders. For instance, a MULTA terrorist killed son of the Deputy Chief of Dhubri city police on April 14, 2002. Besides, the outfit, allegedly at the behest of the ISI, has also plans to create communal disturbances in Assam. This was stated in media reports on August 30, 2002, quoting Assam Inspector General of Police Siba Brata Kakati. Further, an unnamed intelligence official was quoted in the same report as saying that approximately 30 MULTA terrorists were waiting to cross into Assam after having completed training in Bangladesh.

Finance

Reportedly extortion is a major source for its finances. The sale of illegal weapons is another source to finance its activities. In fact, several MULTA terrorists were arrested on the charges of illegal arms manufacture and their sale.

Incidents

2006

- December 25: A MULTA cadre, Nishan Ali, is arrested from Demdema village in the Dhubri district. A bomb is recovered from his possession.
- December 24: The Army and the Special Branch of Assam Police arrest Matibur Rahman, a cadre of Black Widow, anti-talk faction of the DHD led by the Jewel Garlossa, from Pailang village in the Cachar district. Rahman reportedly confessed to have been recruited by the Black Widow for maintaining link with Manipur-based PULF, Pakistan's Inter-Services Intelligence (ISI) and LeT. The report adds that PULF had tied up with the MULTA and MULFA, and extended its operation to Barak Valley.
- December 6: A MULTA cadre, Nabab Ali, is arrested by security force personnel during a search operation at Bokola village under Jamuguri police station in the Sonitpur district.
- November 30: Two suspected MULTA militants, Inamul Hussain and Zamila Begum, are arrested from Tinghoriadoom Gaon under Tinghoria police outpost in the Tinsukia district. Four detonators are recovered from their possession. Based on their confession, six persons were arrested subsequently for interrogation.
- November 29: The Inspector General of BSF for the Assam, Meghalaya, Manipur and Nagaland frontiers, Jyoti Prakash Sinha, said that at least 14 cadres belonging to the MULTA and MULFA were sent to Bangladesh to study religion. But they received arms training there and came back to the Northeast. He also mentions that Pakistan's ISI

is clandestinely working in Bangladesh to bring all Northeast-based insurgent outfits and Jihadi elements to work under one umbrella.

- November 1: A suspected MULTA cadre, Matiur Rahman, is arrested by security force personnel during a search operation at Jhaskal Drtiya Khanda village under Golokganj police station in the Dhubri district. A huge cache of live cartridges of AK-47 rifle is recovered from his possession.
- July 21: The four MULTA militants, including the self-styled 'commander' Nur Islam alias Limbu, who were arrested by Assam Police on July 18, are reported to have confessed that at least 20 cadres of their outfit used Shillong and Lad Rymbai in Jaintia Hills of Meghalaya as their routes to escape to Bangladesh in recent past.
- July 18: Guwahati City Police arrests a self-styled 'commander' of the MULTA, Nur Islam alias Lambu, from the Ambari area. Reports said that at least 20 MULTA cadres have gone from Assam to Bangladesh passing though Meghalaya for training.
- March 29: Army personnel, following a MULTA cadre Quasim Ali, recover four bombs from a house in the Goalpara district.
- January 22: Three suspected MULTA cadres are arrested from the Dhubri and Golokganj police station areas along the India-Bangladesh border of Dhubri district. One .38 revolver, one handmade pistol, three rounds of live cartridges and a demand note of Rupees 26,000 are recovered from two MULTA cadres, Mohibul Hoque and Shohidul Hoque of Hoverpara village. Five grenades weighing one kilogram each and some incriminating documents are recovered from the third, identified as Aminul Hoque of Darbarpara village.

2005

- November 27: Three ULFA cadres, identified as Sirajul Haq, Bogen Neog and Ritu Sarma, and a MULTA cadre, Moinul Haq, surrender before the Superintendent of Police in the Dhubri district.
- July 31 : Acting on a tip off, the Dhubri district police arrest two suspected MULTA cadres from a hide out in Chagolia along the Assam-West Bengal border. The arrested militants, identified as Ashraful Hussain and Baschu Mian, hail from Nakkati Nagar in the Cooch Behar district of West Bengal.
- July 21: A MULTA cadre, Abuwal Hussain, is arrested from Bidyardabri Part V village in the Dhubri district.
- July 20: A MULTA cadre, Moinul Haque alias Laden, is arrested at Sindurai under Golokganj police station in the Dhubri district.
- March 14: Assam Home Minister, Rockybul Hussain, speaking in the Legislative Assembly, discloses that 4,768 terrorists have surrendered

in the State between January 2001 and February 2005. He says that the surrendered include 1168 ULFA, 776 NDFB, 2548 BLT, 48 MULTA and 4 NSCN cadres.

- February 5: Lumding police arrest two MULTA cadres, belonging to the Naukhuti village of Nagaon district. A pistol, a revolver, a sten gun and a rifle are recovered from their possession.

2004

- September 22: A MULTA cadre, Dadul Ali, is arrested from the Urimghat area of Golaghat district along with a SBBL gun and a pistol.
- September 19: Assam Police arrests a MULTA cadre from Hatsinghimari in the Dhubri district and recover a pistol and 25 rounds of ammunition from him.
- September 7: A MULTA cadre, Mohammed Abdul Laskar, is arrested at Lanka in the Nagaon district recently. A 9 mm pistol is recovered from his possession.
- September 5: A girl student, who is abducted two months ago by Wajid Ahmed, brother of Sayed Sabir Ahmed, 'commander-in-chief' of the MULTA, is rescued by the Assam Police from New Delhi and brought back to the Nagaon district.
- September 1 : Security forces recover at least 50 high-velocity electronic detonators from a private residence at Baghahat under Sonai block in the Cachar district. A person, identified as Mohammed Ibomcha, suspected to have links with either the PLA of Manipur or the MULTA was arrested in this connection.
- August 30: A MULTA cadre, Nur Hussain, surrenders before the Army at the Bashbari camp in Dhubri district.
- August 28: Cachar district is put on maximum alert amidst reports that the ULFA is collaborating with the MULTA and PULF to carry out subversive activities in the district.
- August 27: At least 70 terrorists, including 47 ULFA, 11 NDFB, 8 BTF and 4 MULTA cadres, surrender at the 5 Assam Rifles camp at Chardwar in the Sonitpur district. They also deposit arms and ammunitions, including AK 47 rifles, 9 mm pistols, revolver and 264 live ammunitions.
- July 30: Nagaon 'district commander' of the MULTA, Sayed Sabi Ahmed, is arrested from Dimaruguri on charges of extortion.
- May 22: At least forty-seven terrorists, including 20 ULFA, 25 NDFB and 2 MULTA cadres, surrender along with 42 assorted weapons to the Army authorities at Tamulpur in the Nalbari district of Assam.

- April 12: Lohit Nath, a student of Class IX of Kokrajhar Higher Secondary School, who is abducted by suspected MULTA cadres on March 18, 2004, is released after 25 days at Latapara under Bilasipara subdivision.
- April 6: Army personnel arrest a MULTA cadre, Abdul Khalek, from Khalihamari village in the Nagaon district.
- March 29: A MULTA cadre surrenders along with arms and ammunition before Lt Gen. Anup S. Jamawal, General-Officer-Commanding of the Army's Gajraj Corps at Tezpur.
- March 18: Suspected MULTA cadres abduct Lohit Nath, a student of Class IX of Kokrajhar Higher Secondary School.
- February 24: A MULTA cadre, identified as Sakimuddin Haque alias Ilias Bhutto, is arrested by the Army at Paglahat Bazaar under Golokganj police station in the Dhubri district. He is reported to have close links with the ULFA.
- January 31: At least 156 terrorists including 53 ULFA, 91 NDFB, 4 BTF and 4 MULTA cadres surrender at Tamulpur in the Nalbari district.
- January 28: Thirteen cadres belonging to the ULFA, NDFB and MULTA surrender before security force personnel.
- January 3: Two MULTA cadres surrender to the army at Laipuli in the Tinsukia district.

2003

- December 31 : One MULTA terrorist surrenders in Jorhat.
- November 26: One MULTA terrorist is arrested in the Cooch Behar district of North Bengal.
- October 30: A MULTA terrorist, identified as Mohammad Ali Jinnah, is arrested from Bogulamari village in the Dhubri district of Assam.
- October 10: A MULTA terrorist, identified as Nurul Haque, who was allegedly involved in illegal arms smuggling from Bangladesh to Assam, is arrested on an unspecified date from Geelaldah in the Cooch Behar district of West Bengal.
- August 17: MULTA cadre surrenders with two AK-47 rifles and an unspecified quantity of ammunition before the police in Dhubri district.
- June 19: Media reports indicate that terrorist outfits, including the ULFA, the NDFB and the MULTA, among others, are currently active in Dhubri district.
- June 14: MULTA terrorist Abdul Ali is arrested from the outfit's hideout at Larkuchi under Mukalmua police station limits in Nalbari district.

- June 5: Reports indicates that MULTA terrorists under the leadership of Najimullah have intensified their activities among the minority community in Dhubri district along the India-Bangladesh border.
- June 2: Police in the Kokrajhar district destroy a MULTA camp at Bengtol in the Indo-Myanmar border area.
- May 21 : Report indicates that a group of 28 MULTA terrorists led by a 'second lieutenant' Abdul Jalil have infiltrated into Assam from Bangladesh.
- May 20: Reports indicate that MULTA has 'purchased' 55 houses in the Sylhet district of Bangladesh in 2003 to shelter recruits and some leaders of the outfit from Assam.
- May 2: Two MULTA terrorists surrender to the police in Dhubri district with a pistol and 36 grenades.
- March 26: MULTA 'sergeant' arrested from an unnamed place in Nagaon district.
- March 8: Three MULTA terrorists are arrested in Lalkura village, Golokganj police station-limits, Dhubri district, while on an extortion bid.
- January 19: Three MULTA terrorists arrested from Hatigaon area in Guwahati.

2002

- December 3: Muslim United Liberation Tigers of Assam (MULTA) extremist Manowar Hussain alias Yearuddin is arrested from a place under Bogribari police station-limits
- September 24: Police arrest MULTA Dhubri 'district commander' Md Abdur Rahman from Uchita village, Golokganj police station-limits, Assam.
- September 18: Two MULTA terrorists make an unsuccessful bid to abduct a local businessman from Panikhaiti area, Nagaon police station-limits.
- August 30: Reports say police sources indicated that MULTA, along with other terrorist outfits, is championing the 'Islamic cause' and might spread communal hatred in Assam.
- August 19: Police arrest two MULTA terrorists—Jamaluddin Sheikh and Abdus Salam—from Jhulan mela, an annual traditional fair held in Dhubri district, Assam, for their alleged involvement in illegal arms trade.
- July 22: Six MULTA terrorists surrender in Dhubri district.
- July 9: MULTA terrorist arrested for allegedly running an illegal gun-making factory in Boyjer Alga Char area, Bilasipara, Dhubri district.

- July 8: Security forces arrest one MULTA cadre each from Nagaon and Golaghat districts, following the interrogation of another a cadre arrested earlier at Panbari, Dhubri district.
- July 4: Intelligence sources say MULTA is receiving help from the Jamat-e-lslami (JeI), a fundamentalist political party of Bangladesh and a member of the ruling coalition.
- June 26: Report says two arrested MULTA terrorists revealed during interrogation that the son of Dhubri district police deputy chief was killed by a MULTA terrorist, on April 14, at Belguri village, Golokganj police station limits, Dhubri district.
- January 11 : Report says a MULTA terrorist was among the 34 terrorists killed in various incidents in Kamrup in the year 2001.

2001

- September 23: Five MULTA cadres arrested by security forces in Assam's Darrang district.
- 26 January: Four MULTA, besides 134 from various outfits, surrender to Assam Governor Lt. Gen. (Retd.) S.K. Sinha at the Republic Day function in Guwahati.

2000

- October 24: 10 MULTA terrorists, besides 53 from various other outfits, surrender to Assam Governor Sinha and Chief Minister Prafulla Kumar Mahanta at Bilasipara, Dhubri district.
- March 31: Abdul Jalil Ragbi, Assam Jamiat Ulama vice-president denies, in Guwahati, the presence of MULTA or MULFA in Assam.
- January 25: Security forces arrest four MULTA terrorists from Nalbari and one more from Jorang Pathar village in Nagaon district, Assam.

1996

- MULTA founded sometime in the year.

UNITED PEOPLE'S DEMOCRATIC SOLIDARITY (UPDS)

Formation

The United People's Democratic Solidarity (UPDS) was formed in March 1999 with the merger of two terrorist outfits in Assam's Karbi Anglong district, the Karbi National Volunteers (KNV) and Karbi People's Front (KPF).

The outfit signed a cease-fire agreement for one year with the Union Government on May 23, 2002. However, this led to a split in the UPDS with one faction deciding to continue with its subversive activities while the other commenced negotiations with the Government. Currently, there are two factions: pro-talks and anti-talks. On May 16, 2004, the UPDS (Anti-Talks) rechristened itself as the Karbi Longri North Cachar Hills Liberation Front (KLNLF) and its armed wing as the Karbi Longri North Cachar Hills Resistance Force (KNPR). Subsquently, it became Karbi Longri National Liberation Front (KLNLF).

Leadership

Kiri Rongphar was the founder 'chairman' of the outfit. Horen Singh was its 'supreme commander'. Both were arrested on October 22, 1999. On August 22, 2002, UPDS 'commander-in-chief' Long Kumar Kiling died of injuries sustained during a feline attack in the forests of Karbi Anglong district.

At present, two factions of the outfit operate under a different set of leadership

Office bearers	*Pro-Talks Faction*	*Anti-Talks faction*
Chairman	Longder Singner alias H E Kathar	Pradip Terang alias Pongbi Dilli
General Secretary	Haren Sing Bey	Har Sing Timung
Commander-in-Chief	Thong Teron	Men Sing Takbi alias Willingson Timung
Deputy Commander-in-Chief	Lengba Engleng	
Vice-president	Ke-up Jisso alias Moniram Ronghang	
Defence Secretary	Nandu Terang alias Ananda Terang	
Publicity Secretary	Wajaru Mukrang	Laden Ronghang
I/C Central Publicity Cell		Thong Teron alias Rupsing Teron
Foreign Secretary	Mohan Engti	
Assistant Foreign Secretary/ Revenue/ Finance/Taxation		Biren Lekthe alias Risso Tokbi
Finance Secretary	Dhon Sing Rongpi	

The total cadre strength of the UPDS is estimated to be a little more than 150 (including both factions), out of which at least 50 are believed to be armed with sophisticated weapons.

Areas of Operation

The outfit's main area of operations is in the Karbi Anglong district, with a relatively minor presence in the North Cachar Hills district.

Linkages

The outfit is known to have grown with the active assistance of the National Socialist Council of Nagaland-Isak-Muivah (NSCN-IM). It is reported to have procured arms and ammunition from Bhutan and Bangladesh. The NSCN-IM is alleged to be still providing arms training to UPDS cadres. On May 11, 2004, 31 UPDS cadres (anti-talks faction) along with five NSCN-IM militants were arrested from a bus on the Paren-Ghaspani Road on their way to Dimapur. These cadres had undergone training at a NSCN-IM camp and were reportedly part of the recent batch that passed out from there.

The UPDS also shares a 'working relationship' with the National Democratic Front of Bodoland (NDFB) and the United Liberation Front of Asom (ULFA).

Funds

Abductions for ransom and extortion are the main sources of income for the UPDS. Even the pro-talks faction is known to have indulged in several cases of extortion. According to official sources, the anti-talks faction generates a considerable amount of revenue by targeting the ginger producing Kukis in the Singhason Hills area. The non-Karbi traders are also targeted for extortion.

Incidents

2006

- December 29: One UPDS militant, Augustin Kramsa alias Longki Rongpi, is arrested by the Nagaland Police in Dimapur. He along with three of his accomplices abducted Robin, a trader and a civil society activist, from Mentila village in the Karbi Anglong district on March 5, and later killed him on the same day at Nahorjan. The abductors also demanded a ransom worth INR one million for the release of Robin from his wife, Amphu Brahma, before he was killed. One 7.65 US made pistol, two live bullets and one vehicle were recovered from Augustin's possession.
- November 27: An encounter between UPDS cadres and security forces occurs at Deohari village under Hamren sub-division in the Karbi Anglong district.
- November 26: A suspected UPDS militant, Rajib Tisso, is arrested from the Lahorijan area under Khatkhati police station in the Karbi Anglong district. One AK-47 assault rifle, one magazine and 30 live cartridges are recovered from his possession.
- November 16: Assam Government is working on a "special" economic package for the twin hill districts of Karbi Anglong and North Cachar Hills to convince groups such as the UPDS and DHD to give up their demand for statehood and involve themselves in planning and

development of the backward districts. "We are planning the package in such a way that it could be close to the budgets of certain states whose territories are smaller than the two districts combined. If we draw up an annual budget that is more than that of these states or at least on a par, we see no reason for its rejection by the militant leadership. The package could be worth around Rs 500 crore," said an unnamed official.

- November 13: At least seven suspected UPDS militants are arrested by security force personnel during a counter-insurgency operation at Kaniya Bey village near Diphu in the Karbi Anglong district, for violating cease-fire rules. Six AK 56 rifles, 16 magazines, one 9 mm pistol, one revolver, a single-barrel gun and 650 rounds of ammunition are recovered from their possession
- October 24: The Khasi farmers at Block-II areas in the Ri-Bhoi district allege that they are being extorted by the KNV militants. According to these farmers, each of them has to pay a "tax of INR 100 for each item (agricultural produce) sold at Umlaper and Umwang market, while INR 50 and above has to be paid for owning cultivable land in Block-II area." They say, "We are fed up of continued harassment. We are helpless as there is no one to provide security and we have no other place to go," by adding that such illegal collection "goes on throughout the year and aggravates during the harvesting season." The Khasi farmers further mention, "One who expresses his inability to pay the tax, the KNV militants threaten to take away the cultivable land or the crops."
- October 23: The NDFB, DHD and UPDS are involved in extortion activities, despite the fact that all these outfits are under ceasefire agreement with the Union Government, indicates media reports.
- October 22: A CPI-ML leader, Lantuk Phangcho, is abducted by the UPDS from Umrangshu in the North Cachar Hills.
- October 18: A civilian, Brarlil Lawai, is assaulted by the KNV militants at Pampret village near Sabuda under Block I in the Ri-Bhoi district along the Assam-Meghalaya border.
- September 27: Two Karbi Longri North Cachar Hills Liberation Front (KLNLF) militants, 'sergeant major' Mangal Kiling and Hemmere Tiso, are arrested from a hideout at Kishanganj village under Howraghat police station in the Karbi Anglong district. A cache of arms and explosives, including two AK 47 rifles, hand-grenade, rocket launcher, one 9mm French-made pistol and 40 rounds of ammunition, along with INR 5,000 is recovered from the incident site.
- September 26: Three employees of a manufacturing enterprise, Vinay Cements Ltd, including its senior manager, Ravi Shankar Thakur, are abducted by cadres belonging to the Karbi Longri North Cachar Hills

Liberation Front (KLNLF) from a mining site near Umrangsu in the North Cachar Hills district. Two junior employees, Prabir Kumar Das and Nahor Singh, are subsequently released. However, involvement of Kuki militants in the abduction incident is also suspected.

- September 11: The UPDS announces its suspension of peace talks with the Union Government. However, the outfit says it will continue with the cease-fire.
- September 7: A bus driver, Pradip Boro, is shot dead and another, Babujan Hazarika, is abducted by militants of the Karbi Longri North Cachar Hills Liberation Front (KLNLF) at Langthang under Samaguri police station in the Nagaon district. According to police sources, two drivers were waiting near their buses at Langthang Bazaar, when three cadres of the outfit demanded ransom from them, and later attacked them on their refusal to pay.
- September 6: Suspected KLNLF militants abduct a tea grower, Rajendra Singh, from Bogijan in the Golaghat district.
- August 5: Two Karbi Longri National Liberation Front (KLNLF) cadres are arrested from Silputa under Bakulia police station in the Karbi Anglong district. They are identified as William Kathar and Ranjit Teron. Several incriminating documents, a diary and some arms and ammunition are recovered from their possession.
- July 5: Meghalaya Chief Minister J.D. Rymbai accuses the UPDS, of violating the cease-fire rules by indulging in unlawful activities along Assam-Meghalaya border. The outfit had signed a cease-fire agreement with the Union Government on May 23, 2002.
- July 1: Several farmers of Mawlasnai area in the Ri-Bhoi district, having their cultivable lands in the Madan Umwang and Khlieh Umwang areas, are served with demand notes by the UPDS cadres to pay ransom. The farmers were later asked by the militants to attend a meeting at Madan Umwang, and are threatened of dire consequences in case of failing to attend the meeting.
- June 28: Several civil society organisations and chiefs of traditional local self-governance institutions, Rangbah Shnongs, urge the Meghalaya Government to create some more police outposts and deploy more police personnel to prevent the UPDS militants from harassing Khasi-Pnar families in the Block-I and II areas of Jaintia Hills district in Meghalaya.
- June 27: Suspected UPDS cadres attack a police outpost at Khanduli in the Jaintia Hills district of Meghalaya. While no casualty of police personnel is reported in the incident, a civilian is wounded by the militants.

- June 25: Meghalaya Home Minister R. G. Lyngdoh, while expressing concern in the State Legislative Assembly over the reported threat of the UPDS in Jaintia Hills, says that the Assam and Meghalaya Governments are committed to ensuring safety and security of the people in the border area. "People living in the border areas in Jaintia Hills have been meted out harassment by the cadres of certain militant organizations," says the Home Minister.
- June 23: The villagers of Moolaber, Skap, Deinler, Saba, Myntang, Psiar, Lum Moojem, Khatkhasla,

  Mooshrot, Mukroh and other adjoining villages near Labang-Nongphyllut in the Jaintia Hills district are extorted Rupees 200 each by the UPDS cadres. The villagers are asked by the militants to stop cultivation and farming in the area which, the militants claim, falls under 'Karbi land'. "The UPDS militants have recently called meetings in each and every village of the area and asked the local residents to pay a tax of Rs 200 for each household. Each village in the area has a minimum of 140 households and thus the militants must have mopped up at Rs 30,000 from each village," said LD Lakiang, the president of a civil society organization, Joint Action Committee of Jaintia Hills.
- June 21: Three unidentified UPDS cadres are killed in an encounter with the police at Umkhyrmi in the Block I area of Jaintia Hills district along the Meghalaya-Assam border. One AK 56 rifle, two hand grenades, 68 rounds ammunition and one camera were recovered from the encounter site.
- June 19: A huge cache of arms and explosives is seized by the Jaintia Hills district police following an encounter with atleast ten suspected UPDS militants and Karbi National Volunteers at Umkhyrmi along the Assam-Meghalaya border. The cache include one AK-47 rifle, one Chinese rifle, two Chinese hand grenades, three magazines of AK-47 rifle, 68 rounds of live ammunition and one camera. According to police sources, while all the militants managed to escape from the encounter site, three of them sustained injuries.
- June 15: The Bokajan police recover the dead body of a Karbi KLNLF cadre, Mirjeng Teron alias Bhupen Teron, from an interior village in the Karbi Anglong district. According to the Additional Superintendent of Police (headquarters) Atul Gogoi, at least six UPDS militants abducted Mirjeng Teron from his residence at Japarajan and later buried his body in the village after killing him.
- June 10: At least 20 suspected UPDS and Karbi National Volunteers militants enter a village and assault two persons, Kedrik Phawa and Damon Lamare, near Wanpung under Block I in the Ri-Bhoi district of Meghalaya.

- May 10: Two KLNLF cadres, 'corporal' Kolam Sing Engti and Babu Ram Teron, surrender at Diphu, headquarters of the Karbi Anglong district. They also deposit two 9 mm pistols and four rounds of ammunition. According to sources, the KLNLF, which has been set up in 1999 following the split in UPDS, has as many as 60 cadres currently.

  At least 20 suspected UPDS and Karbi National Volunteers militants enter a village and assault two persons, Kedrik Phawa and Damon Lamare, near Wanpung under Block I in the Ri-Bhoi district of Meghalaya.
- May 3: A combined team of the Assam Police and the Nagaland Police arrests the 'joint secretary (home)' of the UPDS, Dhonsing Teron, from an unspecified location in Dimapur town. Two vehicles are recovered from his possession.
- April 29: A pharmacist, Abdul Salem, is abducted by militants from Tinglijan medical sub-centre under Bokajan police station in the Karbi Anglong district. District Superintendent of Police Anurag Tankha informs, "Yesterday, we interrogated an autonomous council member and arrested an UPDS (United People's Democratic Solidarity) activist with the help of Dimapur police. The findings of a preliminary investigation suggest the UPDS involvement in the kidnapping, but we are not ruling out the hand of the Karbi Longri North Cachar Hills Liberation Front either."
- April 10: The UPDS 'defence secretary', Thong Teron, is killed at Satgaon under the Dongkamokam police outpost in the Karbi Anglong district by the security personnel of Sing Teron, an executive member of the Karbi Anglong Autonomous Council, during an exchange of fire. Subsequently, the UPDS militants killed two persons in retaliation in the Tongkory area of the district.
- March 31: A KLNLF cadre, Rongpi, who surrendered along with three ULFA cadres before the army at Diphu in the Karbi Anglong district, deposits one country-made revolver, a grenade and some detonators.
- January 25: UPDS 'Publicity Secretary' Tong-Eeh-Nongloda says that the outfit is hopeful of a fruitful outcome from its fifth round of talks with the Union and the State Government in New Delhi on January 31. Nongloda also blames the State Government's lackadaisical attitude in fulfilling its demand and says, "Therefore, the talks may not yield any good results."
- January 17: UPDS, active in the Karbi Anglong district of Assam, decides to drop its main demand for an autonomous state and instead settles for additional powers to the existing autonomous council. The outfit's

'general secretary', Saiding Eh, says that the new set of proposals, which include granting of special financial, legal and political powers to the existing district council, will be placed before the Union Government during the next round of talks tentatively slated for the end of January 2006. "We want more powers for the council," Eh says. He also says that the outfit will also seek direct funding from all the ministries instead of the money being routed through Assam Government and an end to all interference of the State Government in the council's activities.

- January 9: Karbi Anglong district police releases the UPDS 'publicity secretary', Tongeeh Nongloda, and two other cadres who are arrested on charges of cease-fire violation. However, the personal security officer for Nongloda, Langroiso Terang, is still under detention.
- January 9: Police arrests UPDS 'publicity secretary', Tongeeh Nongloda, from Dilai in the Karbi Anglong District for reportedly carrying a 9mm pistol. Nongloda is detained at the Bokajan police station. Commenting on the arrest, the outfit's 'joint secretary' Ozaru Mukrang said that 20 members of the outfit are allowed to carry arms after the cease-fire. "Later, we requested the government to issue the order to four more cadres and the Special Branch Headquarters gave the green signal for it, although the licenses have not been issued as yet" Mukrang claims. He further added that Nongloda is among the four persons "permitted" by the authorities to carry arms.

2005

- December 26: UPDS asks the villagers of Madan Umwang and other adjoining areas under Block-II near Sabuda in the Ri-Bhoi district, not to harvest rice without paying 'annual tax' to the outfit.
- December 23: UPDS denies carrying out any extortion drive in Khasi villages in the bordering areas of Ri-Bhoi district of Meghalaya and Karbi Anglong district in Assam. The outfit's 'publicity secretary', Tungeh Nongloda, claimed, "Our senior cadres went to the villages to carry out an investigation regarding the matter and found that none of our cadres were resorted to extortion as reported." Nongloda, however, disclosed that the outfit collects Rupees 100 as "annual collection" from each house in Karbi Anglong district. "Besides, we collect donation from ginger planters and traders, but we don't coerce anybody", he added.
- December 21 : UPDS says that the outfit will not attend the Joint Monitoring Group meeting unless the nine arrested UPDS cadres are released from police custody. The 'publicity secretary' of the outfit

Tong-Ehh Nongloda said, "Government is adopting an irrational policy which will stymie the peace process."

- December 13: DHD announces a cease-fire with the UPDS in the Karbi Anglong and North Cachar Hills districts of Assam during Christmas festivities. DHD's military wing chief Pranab Nunisa in an interview says that the outfit has extended a hand of friendship to the Karbi outfit in view of the forthcoming festive season. He further claims that his outfit is not involved in the recent violent activities in the two districts.
- December 6: UPDS militants issue threats to villagers in Mawlasnai and surrounding areas in Block-II bordering the Ri-Bhoi district. In a letter issued to a villager, the outfit asks a farmer to vacate his plot of land as it does not belong to him.
- December 4: Unidentified militants set ablaze 300 houses in different villages in and around Diphu in the Karbi Anglong district. The State Government, meanwhile, deploys army personnel in the district instructing them to "mount an offensive on militant groups indulging in violence as well as to enforce the ground rules of ceasefire." Chief Secretary S. Kabilan says that operations under the Unified Command have already started and shoot-at-sight orders have been issued against any person, other than security force personnel, found wearing army uniform and carrying arms. The UPDS and DHD cadres are asked to remain within their designated camps, he added.
- December 1 : Police arrests six cadres of the Black Widow group led by Jewel Garlossa along with UPDS militants from a place near Bokolia under Howraghat police station in the Karbi Anglong district. Currency notes amounting to Rupees 61,450 are recovered from their possession.
- October 21: In the continuing ethnic clashes between Karbi and Dimasa tribals in Assam's Karbi Anglong district, suspected DHD militants kill nine UPDS cadres at Tamuibari under Diphu police station. A group of 12 UPDS militants is reported to have set 12 houses ablaze in the Kakubasti and seven houses in the Kishibam village. Subsequently, during their attempt to enter Tamuibari village, DHD militants ambush the group and nine UPDS cadres are killed on the spot.
- October 19: Assam Government says that in the ethnic violence between the Karbis and Dimasas in Karbi Anglong district, a total of 72 persons, including 60 Karbis, nine Dimasas and two Nepalis have died and 1014 houses set ablaze since September 26. Government spokesperson Ripun Bora says that 50 relief camps have been set up sheltering 22,469 people displaced from 43 villages.

- October 10: UPDS asks the Assam Government to shift the designated DHD camp in the Dhansiri subdivision of Karbi Anglong district, to North Cachar Hills.
- October 9: Six persons from the Bura Fanchu and Longsing Engti villages are killed and hundreds of houses are torched by unidentified terrorists in separate incidents on under Diphu and Bokajan police stations in the Karbi Anglong district. The other affected villages are identified as Monsing Ingti, Bura Terang, Kangthar Kro, Norik Teron, Diliram Terang and Longso. N. N. Goswami, Additional Superintendent of Police in Karbi Anglong district, said the killings are a result of the clash of interests between the UPDS and DHD.
- August 17: UPDS alleges that the KLNLF is trying to stall the peace process between the Government and the outfit. Accusing the KLNLF of involvement in the recent attacks in Karbi Anglong district, the outfit's 'publicity secretary' Tungeh Nongloda says that, "It was a handiwork of the KLNLF which cares little about the life and welfare of the innocent people".
- July 20: The cease-fire between the Union Government and UPDS is extended for a year, up to July 31, 2006. An agreement to this effect is signed at the BSF sector headquarters at Patgaon in Guwahati by representatives of the UPDS, the Union and Assam Governments.
- July 12: UPDS opposes the setting up of a designated camp for NDFB cadres in the Karbi Anglong district. The outfit's joint secretary Mukharng says: "We are not opposed to any movement, but setting up of a designated camp in Karbi Anglong will only pave a way for other NDFB cadres from Nagaland and Meghalaya to take shelter in our areas."
- May 24: UPDS denies its involvement in the killing of KLNLF 'general secretary', H S Timung. The UPDS 'publicity secretary' Tung-eh-Nongloda claims: "The accusations by the KLNLF against us for the killing of Timung and his family members are baseless and malicious and figment of their imagination."
- May 4: Three UPDS cadres are captured by the residents of Kordoiguri village under Bokajan subdivision in the Karbi Anglong district recently.
- April 4: Assam Government announces the extension of the general amnesty offer to the cadres of the ULFA, NDFB, UPDS and the DHD up to April 30 to "enable them to surrender and join the mainstream."
- March 30: UPDS revokes its threat to call off the cease-fire with the Government from April 1, citing "outpouring of public sentiment on the peace process." Following the appeal by three Karbi organisations,

the UPDS 'publicity secretary', Tong eh-Nongloda, says in Diphu, "They offered moral support to our demand and promised to stand by us on the issue of political negotiations. That is why we have decided to withdraw the March 31 deadline."

- March 23: The pro-talks faction of the UPDS reportedly threatens to take up arms again if the ongoing talks between the UPDS and the Government failed to yield any result. Observing the sixth 'foundation day' in the forest area under Hamren subdivision in the Karbi Anglong district of Assam, the UPDS leadership blames the State Government's apathetic attitude towards the problems of the UPDS for the failure of the talks. Reiterating its demand for a separate State with Karbi Anglong and NC Hills districts, the UPDS leadership alleges that though the Central Government and the Union Home Ministry have asked the State Government to submit the charter of demands of the UPDS, it is yet to submit it till date.
- March 10: UPDS and KNV militants attack and injure four persons in the Lamalong market at Mawhati in Ri-Bhoi district.
- March 5: Suspected cadres of the UPDS and KNV indulge in looting at Moolber in the Block-I area of Jaintia Hills district of Meghalaya. They also reportedly decamp with a rifle of a police personnel posted in the area.
- February 1: A joint team of the Karbi Anglong Police and Army arrests a UPDS cadre, identified as Elwin Rongphar, from Hatigarh near Bokajan in the Karbi Anglong district of Assam. One .9 mm pistol along with five rounds of live cartridges and Rupees 2,20,250 are recovered from his possession.
- January 19: The third round of tripartite talks held between a five-member delegation of the UPDS, the officials of MHA and Assam Government in New Delhi remains inconclusive, in the wake of Assam Government seeking three months' time to table the report of the State Cabinet Sub-Committee.
- January 1 8: Security force personnel arrest two UPDS cadres belonging to its anti-talks faction from Heidipi under Bokajan police station limits in the Karbi Anglong district recently. Two SBBL guns, two AK-47 live rounds, two 7.65 mm live rounds and two fired SBBL cartridges, along with incriminating documents are recovered from the duo.
- January 6: Police arrests four ULFA and three UPDS cadres from an unspecified place in Assam.

2004

- December 31: The Assam Police recover bodies of two persons, identified as Umesh Mahato and Babul Biswas, suspected to have been shot dead by UPDS terrorists for defying its ban on cutting bamboo from Silvetta in the Karbi Anglong district.

- December 31: KLNLF cadre, Arch Phangso, surrenders before the Army authorities at Manja in the Karbi Anglong district.
- December 30: Suspected UPDS terrorists kill two persons and injure four others for alleged defiance of the outfit's ban on cutting bamboo near Rangmongvey in the Karbi Anglong district.
- December 27: The pro-talks faction of the UPDS threatens armed operations against the bamboo traders who violate its ban on bamboo felling.
- December 24: Briefing newsmen at Diphu in the Karbi Anglong district, the 'general secretary' of the pro-talks faction of the UPDS, Saiding-Eh, threatens to 'drive out' illegal Bangladeshi migrants who had come to the twin districts of Karbi Anglong and North Cachar Hills after being evicted from neighbouring Nagaland.
- December 12: The security forces' arrest a KLNLF cadre along with a rifle and some ammunition from Kuwani in the Jorhat district.
- December 12: The UPDS imposes a ban on bamboo trade in the twin districts of Karbi Anglong and North Cachar Hills districts with effect from December 12, cutting off the supply of raw materials to Hindustan Paper Corporation Ltd's (HPCL) Jagiroad mill in Morigaon district. The outfit in a statement said that the HPCL would be permitted to use the bamboo gloves in the twin hill districts again after two years provided the company makes an effort to rejuvenate the green cover within the period.
- December 8: The security forces' arrest two KLNLF cadres and recover an unspecified quantity of arms and ammunition after raiding one of its hideout at No. 2 Chakihola in the Bhomizgaon area of Jorhat district.
- December 9: The UPDS accuses Union Government of violating the cease-fire ground rules and threatens to take up arms. Its 'publicity secretary', Tong-Eh-Nongloda, alleged that the security forces' are still carrying on counter insurgency operations against its cadres despite the cease-fire agreement.
- November 30: The KLNLF announces a week-long campaign against the controversial pact that was signed between Holiram Terang led faction of the Autonomous State Demand Committee (ASDC) and the Kuki National Assembly (KNA) that promises a separate 'homeland' to the minority Kuki tribe within the Karbi Anglong district on December 4, 2000.
- November 30: The KLNLF announces a week-long campaign against the controversial December 4, 2000 pact, signed between Holiram

Terang led faction of the Autonomous State Demand Committee (ASDC) and the Kuki National Assembly (KNA) that promises a separate 'homeland' to the minority Kuki tribe within the Karbi Anglong district.

- November 11 : One person is killed and four others injured in a grenade attack by the KLNLF terrorists in Umrangsho in North Cachar Hills district.
- November 11: One person is killed and four other injured in a grenade attack by KLNLF terrorists in Umrangsho in North Cachar Hills district.
- November 7: UPDS threatens to launch an 'all-out operation' to 'root out' KLNLF from the twin districts of Karbi Anglong and NC Hills.
- November 5: A clash between KLNLF and UPDS terrorists is reported from Tokopahar under Bokajan police station in Karbi Anglong district.
- September 24: Suspected KLNLF terrorists kill one person and injure two others at the Dalamara Tea Estate in Karbi Anglong district allegedly for their refusal to pay extortion money.
- August 13: UPDS terrorist, Deori Phangcho and his accomplice, Bimal Phangcho, are lynched to death by a mob at Bhaksong in Karbi Anglong district.
- August 11: The UPDS (pro-talks faction) threatens to take up arms if the Government fails to protect the Karbi people from Kuki militants.
- August 3: Six cadres of the KLNLF, including a 'commander', surrender before Army authorities at Mariani in Jorhat district.
- July 30: The Union Government extends its cease-fire with the UPDS for another year up to July 31, 2005.
- July 6: UPDS (pro-talks faction), in a press release, warns its breakaway faction to "return to its fold or face its military strength."
- July 4: Suspected cadres of the KLNLF kill a tribal youth and injure four other members of his family at Doigrung village under Bokajan police station limits in Karbi Anglong district.
- June 26: The KLNLF militants open fire on an ambulance at Silbheta under Howraghat police station in Karbi Anglong district. However, no casualty has been reported.
- June 5: Normal life in Karbi Anglong district is paralysed as a result of a 72-hour general strike called by the pro-talks faction of the UPDS in protest against the killing of three of its cadres on May 30 by the army personnel.
- April 25: Six people, including a former MLA, injured in a grenade attack by suspected militants of the UPDS-anti-talk faction at a crowd at Diphu in the Karbi Anglong district.

- March 29: One UPDS cadre is killed in an encounter with the security forces at Ramtokbigaon under Howraghat police station in Karbi Anglong district.
- March 19: UPDS cadres kill four Kukis including a woman and a child at remote Thengbong village atop Singhason Hills in the Karbi Anglong district.
- March 3: Security forces arrest three women cadres of the UPDS-anti-talk faction at Khomen Ingti Gaon under Howraghat police station in the Karbi Anglong district.
- February 27: The anti-talk faction of the UPDS in a statement issued by its general secretary, H E Kathar agrees to initiate a dialogue with KRA if NSCN-IM 'acts as the mediator and guarantor'.
- February 21 : Suspected UPDS cadres abduct two tea executives from a private tea garden located within the Bokajan police station limit of the Karbi Anglong district.
- January 21 : Security personnel recover dead bodies of two persons belonging to the Kuki tribe, suspected to be killed by the militants of the anti-talks faction of the UPDS at Kanjan, in Karbi Anglong district.
- January 20: Two villagers are injured in an attack by UPDS terrorists at the Singhasan hill area in Karbi Anglong district.
- January 17: The anti-talk faction of the UPDS kill four woodcutters and injure another at the Rangadubi reserve forest in the Karbi Anglong district.
- January 5: Suspected UPDS cadres attack a ginger laden truck at Phuding in the Karbi Anglong district, killing a Kuki tribal on the spot and injured another two.

2003

- December 24: UPDS (anti-talks faction) welcomes the offer of peace talks proposed by the KRA.
- December 12: UPDS (anti-talks faction) rejects KRA's peace proposal.
- December 2: UPDS (anti-talks faction) declares a movement against the Kukis in Karbi Anglong and North Kachar districts of Assam.
- November 17: UPDS (anti-talks faction), in a press release, asks the KRA to release eight abducted Karbi youths by December 1 and threatens to launch 'Operation Search' if the outfit fails to meet the deadline.
- November 14: UPDS (pro-talks faction), in a press release, demands the KRA to immediately hand over 13 Karbi hostages. It also urges the anti-talks faction to hand over three abducted Kukis from the Singhasan Hills area.

- November 16: Karbi Anglong district police recovers nine bullet-ridden bodies of Kuki tribals, suspected to have been killed by UPDS terrorists in the Singhasan Hills area.
- November 14: UPDS (anti-talks faction) terrorists kill nine Kuki civilians and set ablaze 70 houses in Gangjam village in Singhasan hills area of Karbi Anglong district.
- November 12: UPDS (anti-talks faction) terrorists set ablaze five Kuki houses killing three children at Lenmol village in the Diphu district.
- November 11 : Suspected UPDS (anti-talks faction) terrorists abduct and kill four Kuki students from Hidim Teron village near Manja in the Karbi Anglong district.
- November 11 : Suspected UPDS (anti-talks faction) terrorists kill six Kuki civilians and set ablaze 70 houses at Gangjam village in the Singhasan hills area of Karbi Anglong district.
- November 9: UPDS and KNV terrorists kill a Khasi civilian at Deinler village in Block I area along the Meghalaya-Assam boundary.
- November 4: UPDS and KNV terrorists killed a Khasi civilian at Psiar village in Block I area along the Meghalaya-Assam boundary.
- October 8: Suspected UPDS (pro-talks faction) terrorists rape three schoolgirls, abduct five persons of the Bodo tribe during a raid on two villages—Daldali and Kathalbari near Diphu in Karbi Anglong district.
- October 6: Police arrest five pseudo UPDS terrorists from the Hidipt Bazaar area in Karbi Anglong district.
- September 14: Suspected UPDS terrorists rape three women in the Gandhipur area of Bokajan subdivision in Karbi Anglong district.
- August 22: Police in Karbi Anglong district arrest four persons in connection with the killing of five civilians by UPDS terrorists on August 21.
- August 21: UPDS terrorists kill five persons, including four women of the family of a migrant, at Manja village in the Karbi Anglong district.
- August 2: UPDS' anti-talks faction releases an engineer of the Government's Public Welfare Department (PWD) near Kaziranga National Park in Assam's Nagaon district. The terrorists had abducted the three engineers on July 8 from Dokmoka.
- July 26: Anti-talks faction of the UPDS asks 'aliens' to quit Karbi Anglong and North Cachar Hills districts.

  Media reports indicate that the Karbi Anglong North Cachar Hills Peoples' Resistance (KNPR), armed wing of the UPDS, planned strikes under 'Operation Longri' (homeland safeguard) against security forces.

- July 24: UPDS terrorist killed in an encounter at Longkiranghang in Karbi Anglong district.
- July 12: UPDS terrorist is killed in an encounter at Langlakso, under Howraghat police station limits in Karbi Anglong district.
- July 9: Six persons are injured when suspected UPDS terrorists throw a hand grenade near a Cinema hall in Diphu, the headquarters of Karbi Anglong district.
- June 30: UPDS's anti-talks faction drafts a manifesto and a map of its proposed "Karbi Anglong and North Cachar Hills self-rule territory". UPDS' camp destroyed and five cadres arrested at Denkek Langso in Karbi Anglong district.
- June 27: One UPDS terrorist of the anti-talks faction is killed during an encounter at 19 Kilo, near Umrangchu in Assam's Karbi Anglong district.
- June 24: Leader of the UPDS' anti-talks faction HE Kathar offers to mediate between the Dimasas and Hmars in Cachar and North Cachar Hills district of Assam.
- June 14: UPDS terrorists kill three persons and injure three more at village Langki Ranghang Bihari Basti in Karbi Anglong district. Death toll later rises to four.
- June 9: Police in Bokajan, Karbi Anglong district recover dead body of a trader from the forest area of Bhetagaon killed allegedly by UPDS terrorists for not paying the extortion sum demanded by them.
- June 3: Report says that the UPDS has issued death threats to the residents of Mukroh and Saba villages in Meghalaya's Jaintia Hills district over the payment of a ransom of Rupees 500,000.
- April 27: UPDS terrorists open fire on a Guwahati-bound moving train near Diphu in the Karbi Anglong district injuring two passengers.
- April 25: UPDS begins its rail-road blockade in Karbi Anglong and North Cachar Hills districts.
- March 13: A report indicates that the UPDS has served extortion notices on the teaching staff of a local school at Bokajan, Karbi Anglong district.
- March 7: A report indicates that the UPDS has renewed its demand for the 'self-determination' of the *Karbis* (a tribe) and other 'indigenous people' living in Karbi Anglong district of Assam.
- February 18: A UPDS terrorist surrenders in Bokakhat, Jorhat district.
- February 6: UPDS terrorists kill civilian near Kramsagaon, Karbi Anglong.

- January 25: Four persons, including a woman of a migrant family, killed by UPDS at Diphu, Karbi Anglong.
- January 20: Suspected UPDS terrorists trigger bomb blast derailing Howrah-bound Kamrup Express train at Diphu, Karbi Anglong.
- January 7: Karbi Anglong North Cachar Hills People's Resistance (KNPR), armed wing of UPDS, calls for boycott of Republic Day celebrations.
- January 6: UPDS sets free three abducted government employees in Karbi Anglong district.
- January 5: UPDS calls for seven-day economic blockade commencing January 12 in certain areas of Karbi Anglong and North Cachar Hill districts to protest alleged destruction of forests by ginger cultivators.

2002

- December 19: UPDS terrorists abduct three employees of the Agricultural Engineering Department at Katrijangaon, under Diphu police station-limits in Assam's Karbi Anglong district.
- November 3: Five UPDS terrorists are arrested from Silanijan, Borpathar police station-limits in Assam's Karbi Anglong district, while trying to extort money from a local businessman.
- October 28: Reports say two UPDS terrorists are arrested by the security forces at a place under Bokajan police station-limits, Karbi Anglong district, Assam.
- September 25: UPDS might clash with an unidentified group of approximately 70 Kuki terrorists in Karbi Anglong, a media report from Assam indicates.
- August 22: UPDS 'commander-in-chief' Long Kumar Kiting dies of injuries following a feline attack in the forests of Karbi Anglong district, Assam.
- August 6: UPDS's Haren Bay faction holds consultations with Union Home Ministry officials in New Delhi to formulate the ground rules for a proposed cease-fire agreement.
- July 28: UPDS general secretary Haren Singh says terms of cease-fire agreement with the Union Government would possibly come into force on August 1.
- July 3: UPDS is a threat to the Tiwa community, allege various Tiwa organisations in a memorandum to the Union Government.
- June 23: Three UPDS terrorists killed in an encounter on Silanijan-Sokihola Road, under Bokajan police station limits.
- May 28: UPDS chairman denies allegations of extortion in Taradubi village, Baithalangso police station limits.

- May 23: UPDS general secretary Horensing Bey signs 'cease hostilities' agreement with the Union Government, for a period of one year, that is till year 2003.
- May 20: Suspected UPDS terrorists kill four members of a non-Assamese family, including a 26-day old child, at Matikhola village, Karbi Anglong district, and set ablaze five houses in the vicinity.
- April 10: Suspected UPDS terrorists abduct two Public Welfare Department (PWD) assistant engineers in Umpanai, Karbi Anglong.
- March 24: Two UPDS terrorists lynched by local residents in Tardubi village, West Karbi Anglong.
- March 19: UPDS terrorist killed in an encounter at Ronghoghar village under Diphu police station limits, Karbi Anglong.
- February: UPDS terrorist's dead body found in Barpathar, Karbi Anglong.
- January 31 : Reports indicate that UPDS plans joint attacks on security force personnel with the United Liberation Front of Asom (UUFA) terrorist outfit.
- January 27: Suspected UPDS terrorists injure 12 persons in a grenade attack at Diphu.
- January 23 : Unidentified terrorists kill the vice-chairman, Gandhiram Terang of the UPDS at Gandhiram Terang in Karbi Anglong district.
- January 12: UPDS terrorists kill a person at Ram Chorang village, under Bokajan police station limits.
- January 4: Two UPDS terrorists surrender to Nagaland governor Shyamlal Datta at Kigwema near Kohima.

2001

- December 23: Suspected UPDS terrorists kill a Parbattya Chattagram Jana Sanghati Samity (PCJSS) leader at his residence in Rangmati.
- December 3: UPDS terrorists kill nine persons, including six polling officials by triggering an Improvised Explosive Device (IED) explosion at Lamelangsnu in Karbi Anglong. Five others were also injured in the attack.
- November 24: UPDS camp at Chakihula Charikhuti in Karbi Anglong destroyed by the security forces.
- September 21 : Suspected UPDS terrorist killed at Howraghat in Karbi Anglong.
- September 3: Two United People's Democratic Solidarity UPDS terrorists killed in an encounter at Upper Deopani in Karbi Anglong.
- August 25: Suspected UPDS terrorists kill four persons by blowing up a truck at Bhuligaon, near Bokajan in Karbi Anglong district.

- July 30: The UPDS in a press release, calls for a boycott of the Independence Day celebrations on August 15.
- July 18: Three civilians including a woman killed by suspected UPDS terrorists at Barmatikhola of Hamren subdivision in Karbi Anglong district.
- May 10: Three security force personnel killed in an ambush laid by suspected UPDS terrorists at Dewhah Chakihota in Karbi Anglong district.
- January 7: Four non-tribal settlers killed and four injured by suspected UPDS terrorists at Diphu.

2000

- December 31 : Four Hind-speaking persons killed by suspected UPDS terrorists at Disobai forest in Karbi Anglong district.
- December 28: Eight persons from the Hindi-speaking community killed by suspected UPDS terrorists at Ranganagar village in Karbi Anglong district.
- September 14: Suspected terrorists of NSCN-IM and UPDS kill eleven people including ten policemen in an ambush near Diphu.
- July 15: UPDS terrorists massacre 10 persons, including two women and four children, in Langparpang, Karbi Anglong district.
- April 19: UPDS terrorists kill 11 persons in two separate incidents in Karbi Anglong district.
- April 9: Terrorists of the UPDS massacre 11 persons in Karbi Anglong district.

ASSAM : NETWORKING AND LINKAGES

Terrorist Outfits in Assam : Good at Networking

The security scenario in Assam is presently tinged with uncertainty, with a number of events criss-crossing and overlapping the template that governs its conduct. Even the United Liberation Front of Asom (ULFA) phenomenon begins to witness a complicated game. Organisations such as National Democratic Front of Bodoland (NDFB) and United People's Democratic solidarity (UPDS) that have entered into ceasefire agreement with the governments are showing signs of belligerence over the delay in dialogue process. The group such as Dima Halam Daogah (Garlosa) (DHD(G)) which continues to stick to their anti-dialogue position, are engineering alliances with organisations such as NSCN(IM), with ramifications for not only the area in which it operates, but also with implications for the Indian Government and Naga leaders' dialogue. The most critical aspect that is going to impact conflict in Assam in the future will be the 'new interest groups' that has emerged with the proclamation of *global Salafi movement*, and one which is entering the country from India's neighbours particularly Bangladesh.

The ethnic cauldron that grips Assam has ascertained that almost every ethnic group in the state are asserting their identity[2] by either taking up arms or by demanding separation from Assam. Although ethnic assertion is a reality and has its roots in history, the fact of the matter is that the fault lines have become pronounced as a result of the neglect that the ethnic minorities are heir to. In the hill Assam, conflict flared up between UPDS and DHD in North Cachar Hills and Karbi Anglong as a result of a jostle for space. The Dimasas are pitted against each other on anti and pro talk lines[3]? Around 800 members of pro-talk DHD (Nunisa) faction is billeted in four camps spread across NC Hills and Karbi Anglong districts since the declaration of cease-fire with the Government of India in 2003. Factional clashes and frustration have crept in as a result of delay in the dialogue process.

NSCN (IM) is aiding the anti-talk DHD (Garlossa) group, popularly called the Black Widow Group. The Jewel Garlossa of the anti-talk DHD faction has entered into a 'Hebron Agreement'[4] with NSCN (IM) on August 14, 2006. According to the agreement, NSCN (IM) would aid Garlossa's group to strengthen itself in NC Hills and in return DHD(G) would help NCSN(IM) to annex part of NC Hills and Karbi Anglong into the latter's dreamland, Greater Nagalim[5] NSCN(IM) is already sheltering about 300 cadres of Garlossa group in its camps in Nagaland. On the other hand, the critical aspect that is poised to engulf Assam is "New Interest Group". The urgency with which this conglomeration is seeking to enter the region, coupled with the continuing illegal migration from Bangladesh, is fraught with serious national security implication. This is specially so because allegiance of Bangladeshi migrant continues to be informed by experiences from across the border. The ground situation is a witness to this, contrary to what certain intellectuals seem to argue about the creation of a Neo-Assamese social formation, or about the Assamysation of illegal migrant. The mere fact that Assamese is being maligned as the mother tongue in certain areas, which are occupied by the illegal migrants, and the fact that more and more illegal migrants [especially in the post IM(DT) ACT era] are taking on working Assamese[6]. Recent developments have indicated that process of instituting *Nizam-e-Mustafa* in the region and of *Brihotor Bangladesh* has been expedited. The development has perhaps a result of not only the 'transformative movement'[7] that Islam is passing presently through but also because of the political climate in Bangladesh. In fact, the real motivation for such a progression is more political than religious. Indeed, even the intelligence organisations such as ISI and DGFI are in reality quite modern and are driven by politics and not religion some analysts aver.

Important aspect that must be kept in mind is that one can no longer talk in terms of separate *tanzeems*, when the new interest group is being referred to. The entire movement is now perhaps being guided by Al Qaeda, in a unique modular manner, with each 'sleeper cells' working independently of one another. The novelty of the movement is that no conventional command and control exists presently, and each tanzeem/module/cell is to simply follow a set of general ideology motivation, and not instructions, which would necessitate a communication network. This is precisely why the coordination system between the groups is not revealed to any of the anti-terrorist squads/ intelligence agencies to un-earth the links. It may appear to be absurd in the present day but, gradually the linkages and networking is in progress through Muslim United Liberation Tigers of Assam (MULTA). There are no longer strict compartments from which puritans operate. Only the methods are different which explains perhaps the reasons for law enforcers facing dead ends. There is no pattern of discovery, apart from a decisively anti-India agenda.

Bangladesh continues to be the main abetter of the new interest group. It indeed is a section of intelligentsia of Bangladesh backed by the politics of Bangladesh that seeks annexation of Assam to Greater Bangladesh. Sadeq Khan[8] and Abdul Momin[9] had propagated the theory of Lebensraum and later proponents gave it a religious colour as this region and its location makes it most viable to achieve such a goal. It must however be understood that almost all illegal migration from Bangladesh into Assam and other parts of India are for economic purposes. The objective of Nizam-e-Mustafa is the new interest group's techniques of exploiting Islam in order to consolidate the annexation that is happening as a result. Today, Bangladesh has emerged as the crucial "mid-point" between the troubled spots of South East Asia and South Asia for the new interest group. For instance, was Jemaah Islamiah to carry out a bombing, say in Bali, Bangladesh would be the after action "pull-out" area. This is true for puritans who are perpetrating violence in India : trigger off explosions in the country and return to safe haven of Ukhiya in Bangladesh. Jama'atul Mujahideen Bangladesh (JMB) and Jagrata Muslim Janata Bangladesh (JMJB) etc are demanding Islamic rule in Bangladesh. But an important reason is the pullout factor and Bangladesh's emergence as the most important anti-India base for inimical foreign agencies. Moreover, state's patronage for such groups exists despite cosmetic action against the Islamists. Therefore, even as Dhaka is seen to be acting against home grown puritans like "Bangla Bhai", foreign ones like Ikram-ur-Zaman of the "Revival of Islamic Heritage Society", which is a Kuwait based Islamic group, are released immediately after his arrest. This was mainly to avoid his interrogation by the United States.

The Directorate General of Field Intelligence (DGFI) along with the Pakistani Inter Services Intelligence (ISI), of which it is a virtual surrogate, is spearheading the activities of the new interest group in Assam. A clear indication of this aspect has come to the fore recently with Brig Azam Mir[10] joining as Deputy Director General of the organisation.[11] According to information, Mir has been tasked with the job of modernising DGFI on the lines of the American Central Intelligence Agency (CIA). One of his first decisions has been to set up a separate North East India cell. One of the important operations that has been undertaken recently is to legitimise the puritanical groups that have been cosmetically banned in Bangladesh. Therefore, Harkat-ul-Jihad-al-Islami-Bangladesh (HUJI-B) has formed an ovet-ground party by the name of Sachetan Islami Janata.[12]

Now we examine the ULFA factor, which is turning out to be a complicated issue. ULFA phenomenon offers a complicated challenge which the Indian government has to deal with. Moreover the organisation has successfully created "Operation Confusion". It is worth our while to have a look at the ULFA background. American author Shelby Tucker writes about having met ULFA 'chairman' Arabinda Rajkhowa at the headquarters of the Kachin Independence Organization (KIO), political wing of the KIA, at Pajau Bum, during his trek across Myanmar around 1989[13]. Former ULFA cadres say the group's 'commander-in-chief', Paresh Baruah, too, was in Myanmar's Kachin hills around that time.

Such trips were among the first attempts by rebels from Assam to strengthen strategic alliances with militant groups located in India's South Asian neighbours like Myanmar. In 1985 itself, the ULFA opened shop in Bangladesh, setting up safe houses at Damai village in the Moulvi Bazaar district, bordering the North-eastern Indian State of Meghalaya[14]. In 1990, the ULFA had its Pakistani contacts in place, and leaders like Munin Nobis (since surrendered) were instrumental in establishing the links. Nobis told an Indian analyst during extensive interviews in October 2002 that the Pakistanis facilitated the crossover of a number of ULFA leaders, including Paresh Baruh, into Afghanistan through Pakistan's North West Frontier Province. These visitors, assisted by the Pakistani Inter-Services Intelligence (ISI), met Gulbuddin Hekmatyar, a top Afghan Mujahideen leader of the time. Not surprisingly, ULFA cadres, who surrendered in the wake of the Bhutanese military assault on their camps in December 2003, talked of the presence of an Afghan-trained artillery expert in their Bhutan bases[15]. By the end of 1990 and early 1991, the ULFA had set up well-entrenched bases inside Southern Bhutan, mainly in the district of Samdrup Jhongkar, bordering western Assam's Nalbari district.

Dhaka rejected the observations made in the Canadian Security Intelligence Service (CSIS) report and has been consistently denying that it had become the latest hub of Islamist terror groups, including the Al Qaeda. The fact remains, however, that a local terrorist group, the Harkat-ul-Jehad-al-Islami Bangladesh (HuJI-BD), led by Shauqat Osman, with the avowed objective of establishing 'Islamic rule' in Bangladesh, is indeed active in the country. Western media reports suggest this group has an estimated 15,000 cadres.[16]

It is in this context that some western media reports of the ULFA sending its representatives to attend a meeting of radical Islamist outfits, organized by the HUJI-BD, at a secret rendezvous in Bangladesh in the summer of 2002, arouse curiosity. On May 9, 2002, 63 representatives of nine Islamist groups, including Rohingya forces, the Islamic Oikya Jote and the ULFA, met in Ukhiya and formed the Bangladesh Islamic Manch, a United Council under the HuJi's leadership[17]. The ULFA is not an Islamist outfit and is rather secular in the sense that its cadres are drawn from diverse groups and communities, cutting across religions. But what cannot be ignored is the possibility that ULFA would have to arrange for sanctuary for some of these Islamist militant leaders or cadres as a *quid pro quo* for its continued stay in Bangladesh, should the pressure against terror is to be upped by Dhaka.

Both the Indian and Bhutanese security establishments were stung by the news of the launching of the Bhutan Communist Party (Marxist-Leninist-Maoist) on April 22, 2003, the 133rd birth anniversary of Lenin[18]. Pamphlets widely circulated by this new group in the Bhutanese refugee camps in Nepal and in areas inside Bhutan itself, revealed that the new party's objective was to 'smash the monarchy' and establish a 'true and new democracy' in Bhutan[19]. Both New Delhi and Thimphu were quick to put the KLO under the scanner. Security agencies soon came to the conclusion the KLO was active and had pockets of influence in the strategic North Bengal areas of West Bengal and could act as a bridge between the Maoists insurgents in Nepal and the newly emerging Maoist force in Bhutan. Besides, Indian intelligence agencies were aware of the fact that the KLO had provided sanctuary to fleeing Maoist cadres from Nepal, that the outfit had acted as a link between the Maoists and the radical left-wing activists in Bihar, and that it received help from the Maoists in setting up a number of explosive manufacturing units in North Bengal. These speculations were proved to be correct as KLO has joined hands with not only Nepal Maoists but also with Communist Party of India (Maoists). Through KLO, ULFA has established its contacts with Nepal Maoists. ULFA's commander of 28th Battalion had visited Nepal sometime early 2006.

During the offensive in Bhutan, in a dramatic move, ULFA 'chairman', Arabinda Rajkhowa, appealed to the Chinese leadership on December 25, 2003[20], to provide safe passage to the insurgents from Bhutan for temporary shelter in China. Rajkhowa in his fax communication to the Chinese leadership said: "We have come under massive attack of Indo-Bhutan joint forces and our combatants have been forced to retreat up to the Sino-Bhutan border due to all out air and artillery campaigns[21]. Beijing was quick to turn down the ULFA plea and cautioned that it had alerted its frontier forces to prevent any intrusion of Indian militants. A Chinese Embassy spokesperson in New Delhi said the Chinese Frontier Forces were quite capable of preventing the entry of Indian insurgents into their country and that they were closely monitoring the development of the situation. It is not that China or sources in China have always maintained a distance from Indian separatists. Indian insurgents had not only visited China in the past for help, but had received assistance from sources within the country.[22]

ULFA continues on a course of action that belies its sincerity for peaceful solution. It continues to indulge in extortion[23], recruitment and more importantly, Paresh Baruah was issuing statements that were clearly indicative of his belligerence. In an interview to the *Assam Tribune*, Paresh Baruah was not only not appreciative of the gesture the government and the army have shown, but in response to a question about the ongoing peace process, he stated, "so far, any process of peace talks with Indian government has not resolved any conflict satisfactorily. Unilateral suspension of operations by Indian forces is a tactic to divert attention from the main issue." The reason for initial show of interest for a negotiated solution and indeed the constitution of the People's Consultative Group (PCG) could have been a part of the foresaid Operation Confusion the Paresh Baruah is perpetrating. ULFA wanted extension in the suspension of army operations in order to utilise the period for a mode of functioning inside Assam that was conducive to it without instituting formal ceasefire. However anti-India forces guiding ULFA were possibly using the process to test the distance to which the Government of India would go in the peace process.

Even UNLF is a Serious Threat to Assam

The United National Liberation Front of Manipur, one of the older and powerful armed anti-government forces in the North-East, besides posing serious threat to Manipur, its area of operations, is also to be perceived, of late, a threat to Assam. The UNLF has been trying to garner support in the Manipuri-dominated areas of South Assam, particularly in Lakhipur, Jirighat, Fulertal and Banskhandi in Cachar district.

This is a passage which they often treat as a corridor during an emergency, especially when Army operations are on. Passing through the Barak Valley, the fugitives reach Guwahati often to escape arrest, or even for medical treatment, since they are not easily recognised by the Assam police. SS Sgt Maj Jadumoni Singh alias Angacha, 32, was arrested on 4 Nov. 2006 by an Army team from a Coffee shop, near the Down Town Hospital in Guwahati. He was wanted by Lakhipur police, and after his arrest, it turned out that at one time he was a computer student. The insurgent groups in the region, like their counter parts elsewhere have stepped into cyber space to do their anti-India chores. The Army seized a desk-top computer, a printer, Rs. 40,000 in cash and some documents.

His interrogation revealed a distinct pattern of UNLF's functioning. In operational terms, the UNLF has three formations.

- Mariel Task Forces (MTF). Active in Churachandpur area of Manipur.
- Wang Brel Task Force (WTF). Active in Manipur Chandel district.
- 2nd Battalion. Based in Myanmar but operates in the Nagaland. Myanmar border areas, adjacent to Nagaland's Mon town.

Sources disclosed that some activists of the UNLF operates from the Guwahati city, and have a nexus with some other outfits like ULFA. Thus, the involvement of the UNLF in the recent upsurge of terrorist activities in Guwahati, essentially because of its alliance with ULFA.

The reports credit UNLF with more than 2,000 hardcore cadres operating in Manipur. They are trained on rocket launchers, AK-rifles and some other weapons and explosives.

U. Meghen, the mastermind and chief of the outfit is presently enjoying sanctuary in Bangladesh's Sylhet district.

Most of the training of the NLFT cadres is conducted in the Myanmar Camp, located near Truilo. Cadres from some other outfits like the ULFA, PLA etc. are also trained there, perhaps collectively, sources disclosed. The cadres are assigned new names during this training. It is a tough regime of training from dawn till dusk. It seems no meals are served at night (Bishway Chamak Goswami, *The Statesman*, 4 Dec. 2006).

The jungle route starts from Tizit, in Nagaland, passing through the NSCN(K) area, where the outfit provides guides till Truilo, near the 2nd Battalion Base Camp of the insurgents in Myanmar.

The extremists are known to earn handsomely by selling drugs and small arms from the infamous Golden Triangle. The route from Myanmar traverses through Moreh on the Manipur-Myanmar border; thence through Silchar and Lakhipur to Meghalaya-Assam border near Jorhat and down to Guwahati. The next stop is Siliguri in West Bengal before moving through Bihar and the mainland.

A final ward on ULFA's threat to Assam. It must be understood that the state, having lost large swaths of its areas to four states after 1947 till 1987, is still a fragile entity. Not only because it could be swamped by Bangladeshi influx, but also because the only two hill districts in its folds are facing serious militant agitations for grant of UT status, possibly a penultimate goal before full-fledged statehood. Worse still, the North Bengal's KLO agitating for an independent Kamtapur wants to add adjoining districts of Western Assam to their pet homeland project. On the top of it all, the UNLF eyeing parts of Southern Assam cannot be, and should not be, viewed lightly. It indeed is a serious threat to Assam's integrity posed by a secessionist outfit operating in a neighbouring state.

NOTES

1. Khaled Abou el Fadl, *'The Great Theft: Wresting Islam from the Extremists'*; Harper Collins, New Delhi, 2006, p. 76.
2. Chauvinism in mainstream Assamese society is manifest in the manner in which Nagaland, Meghalaya and Mizoram broke away from Assam in the past. As also in the cry for separate homelands by different ethnic groups inside Assam today.
3. A lesser known reason for division between DHD(N) and DHD(G) is purely geographical. Whereas DHD(N) members are from Karbi Anglong, Nagoan and Nagaland, the DHD (G) are predominantly from NC Hills. Also there is a clan formation in this issure, with DHD(N) members hailing from the Nunisa Clan.
4. Camp Hebron is the general headquarter, and designated camp of NSCN(IM) located in Intanki Reserve Forest near Nagaland's Manglamukh near Dimapur.
5. Garlossa foidor NSCN or buja-buji: uttar Cachar ekanxo eri dibo Nagalandok (Garlossa faction's agreement with NSCN: a part of NC Hills will be given to Nagaland). Asomiya Pratidin, Guwahati, September 15, 2006.
6. As brought out by Jaideep Saikia during 'Peace and Development in North East India' seminar at Shillong on September 26th, 2006.
7. Abou el Fadl has argued that there is sufficient drift between the belief system of the reformed moderates and the more conservative and strict puritans. He compares the transformative movement (which Islam is at present passing through) as no less dramatic than the Reformation movement that swept through Europe at one time and led to long and bloody religious wars; El Fadle, *op cit.*
8. Sadiq Khan : Editor and publisher of *"Holiday"* and former diplomat of Bangladesh.
9. Abdul Momin : Former Bangladesh Foreign Secretary and country's first ambassador to China.
10. BSF sources.
11. Maj Gen Sadeqh Hussain Rumy continues to be the Director General.
12. HUJI link suspected in attack on UK envoy; *"Daily Star, Dhaka"*; September 5th, 2006.
13. Shelby Tucker, *Among Insurgents, Walking Through Burma,* Delhi: Penguin Books, 2000, pp. 82-83.
14. Wasbir Hussain, *"Cross Border Links and Strategic Alliances"* Faultlines, February 2006, p. 108.

15. Surrendered ULFA 'lieutenant', Domeshwar Rabha, said Afghanistan-trained rebel Satabda Kumar was the chief instructor of the ULFA's artillery squad inside Bhutan. Kumar, he said, was also 'commander' of the group's 'General Headquarters' in Bhutan that was neutralized during the Bhutanese military assault in December 2003. See Hussain, "We picked up our AKs and fled," *Sentinel*, December 24, 2003.
16. South Asia Terrorism Portal, www.satp.org.
17. Wasbir Hussain, *"Cross Border Links and Strategic Alliances"* Fault lines, February 2006, p. 115.
18. *'Maoists form unit in Bhutan,'' Times of India,* Delhi, May 18, 2003.
19. *Ibid.*
20. *"Arabinda SOS to China for safe passage, shelter" Sentinel,* December 28, 2003.
21. *Ibid.*
22. *'China turns down ULFA plea for safe passage,''Assam Tribune,* January 1, 2004.
23. The latest case of which was the extortion note sent by ULFA's Hira Sarania, Commandant of 709 Battalion to Nagrujuli Tea Estate for Rs. 1 crore.
24. R. Dutta Choudhuri, *"Center Should be Sincere: ULFA C-in-C", The Assam Tribune,* Guwahati, September 20, 2006.

8

Arunachal Pradesh : Evil Winds Disturbing the Idyll

Terrorism has Penetrated this State Too

This has the distinction of being the largest state area-wise! This has been the only state untouched by the terrorism bug, but alas no more so! There are ripples in the idyll.

Key Statistics : Arunachal Pradesh

Date of formation		
Union Territory	21 Jan., 1972	
State of the Union	20 Feb., 1987	
Area	83,743 sq. km.	
Population	1,097,968	
Capital	Itanagar	
Major Religions	Buddhism	
	Hinduism	
	Christianity	
Chief Languages	Monpa	Adi
	Muji	Digaru
	Aka	Mishmi
	Sherdukpen	Idu-Mishmi
	Nyishi	Khamti
	Apatani	Miju-Mishmi
	Tagin	Nocte
	Hill Miri	Wancho
		Nepali
		Bengali

Any first time visitor to Arunachal Pradesh will most likely end up saying: "Thank God, this state is haven of peace, unlike most other states in the

North-East, which are in the grip of insurgency/militancy related violence." Arunachal is an island of peace and stability—almost. Given its diversity, it is microcosmic representation of larger reality called 'India'. The state embraces within its fold 25 major tribes and 111 minor and sub-tribal ethnic groups. (As a matter of minor detail, the Arunachal tribes-systems. The first group, professing Buddhism, comprises Monpas, Sherdukpens, Membas, Khamptis, Khambas and Singphos. The second group practising a religion which may be defined as magico-religious beliefs and practices, included Akas, Khowas, Mijis, Bangnis, Sulungs, Nishis, Apatanis, Tangins, Hill Miris, Adis, Mishmis, and Tangsas/Tanghshas. The third group believed in "sort of animist religion and practised head-hunting" and included Wanchos and Noctes.) "In all, there are 82 languages and dialects, most of which have been preserved through tales and legends.[1]" Like the Nagas, Mizos and Khasis, various ethnic groups in Arunachal, too, are deeply rooted in their tradition and socio-economic mores. But no one has raised chauvinistic slogans like "Khasi by blood, Indian by accident", as some have done in Meghalaya.[2]

What is written above was strictly true till the early 1990s, so to say. It is largely true even today but for some ripples in the idyll, discernible for the last few years. Decidedly, the ripples are faint for the moment, but demographic dissonance could assume serious dimensions if some issues troubling the Arunachalis, like the presence of Chakma and other communities, are not attended to urgently.

Some of the issues and problems causing the tensions, or the ripples, speaking metaphorically, are discussed in this chapter.

Chakmas, Hojangs, Tibetans and other Outsiders

'Foreigners' and 'outsiders' have often been used as a grist to their political mill by the local ethnic leaders of various states in the Region. They seem to come handy when they want to make political gains against their rivals.[3] The tribal ire against outsiders in the North-East once again reared its head in the early 1990s. It seemed the chauvinists were emboldened by the reluctance of the State Government to 'discipline' the agitationists. In fact in some states like Arunachal, the Chief Ministers are supporting the anti-foreigners agitations. The Centre itself have been hamstrung, it would seem, since its action against such agitations would be conceived as an infringement of the State's autonomy guaranteed by the Constitution. The Centre's inaction in such situations, particularly in sensitive states afflicted by the insurgent violence, is bound to embolden forces inimical to India to muddy the waters further. The NSCN(I-M) is exactly doing that in large parts of Changlang and Tirap districts of Arunachal, bordering as they are the state of Nagaland. "The Christian missionaries are also quite active in Arunachal, emphasising the ethnic and cultural exclusiveness of its people from the rest of the country."

The Chakma issue has become volatile in the recent years, touching raw emotions of the people of the State, essentially under the instigation of the political class. The All Arunachal Pradesh Students Union (AAPSU) had from time to time been demanding the settlement of the Chakmas elsewhere in the country, and the "Quit Notices" issued by it on the Chakmas, Hajongs, Tibetans, Bangladeshis and others in mid-1994 precipitated the matters. While some observers feel the "Quit Notices" were politically-inspired,—in any case, all such moves by a party are so dubbed in our country by its political opponents and some scholars—to others, the immediate provocation for the students was the letter dated 7 July 1994 of P.M. Sayeed, Minister of State for Home, addressed to Nyodak Yonggam, a Rajya Sabha MP from Arunachal. The letter conveyed the Centre's decision to consider citizenship rights for Chakma, Hajong, Tibetan and Yobin refugees, who came to India before 25 March 1971.

Before proceeding any further, a word on the inception of the problem. It is one of the ironic contradictions and a serious miscarriage of justice that the Chittagong Hills Tract (CHT), with its 97 per cent Buddhist population, was allotted to Pakistan in 1947 under the Radcliffe Award. The luckless Chakmas were destined to suffer—and have indeed been suffering—from that very day of the horrendous decision. In their first exodus from (the East) Pakistan, they had fled to Tripura, seeking safe haven for themselves from the repression/persecution in their CHT home. Over 60,000 of the Chakma refugees from their Tripura Camps were sent to Arunachal (then NEFA) in 1964. They had fled their ancestral abode because of religious persecution, alienation of their land to Bangladeshi (Muslim) intruders, and displacement caused by a dam (Kaptai) built in their territory. Despite the serious population pressures in the rest of the country and the vast land available in Arunachal, the Indian Government did not allow any sections of Indian people to migrate to this State. The Chakmas were allowed to migrate there perhaps because of the fact of their being Buddhists, whose presence there would not create any ethnic dissonance presumably since there were many Buddhist tribes in Arunachal. But all such hopes were belied because the Arunachal people see in the shelter given to the Chakmas as an effort to cause encroachment on their land. They felt they were under no obligation to accommodate the Chakmas midst them because they were victims of persecution at home and could not even hope to return because of this very reason

It is not that no effort was made to enable the refugees to return to the CHT where they had started a violent insurgent movement against the persecution and against the Government policy of settling outsiders on the tribals lands in CHT. India and Bangladesh (under Sheikh Hasina) signed an agreement in December 1997 to end the 22-year long insurgency in the CHT (divided in three hill districts of Khagrachari, Rangamati and Bandarban), and to enable the Chakmas from their refugee camps to return home. To be brief, the Agreement did not work, essentially because of the virulent opposition mounted by the fundamentalist BNP, then in opposition. After the unhappy experience of initial batches of refugees, the majority of them decided to stay back in their camps/villages in India, mainly in Tripura (just across from the CHT), Mizoram (the eastern neighbour of the CHT), and Arunachal. The condition of the Chakmas staying in the CHT is nearly impossible because of the settlement of the Muslim agriculturists from the over-populated plains of East Pakistan/Bangladesh in planned manner, the State-orchestrated persecution and repression, abductions, rape, conversions, arson, and forced eviction from their traditional habitat. The nightmarish existence often forces them "to flee the hill". India simply seems to be unable to bring the recalcitrant Bangladesh to see reason and create conducive conditions for the refugees to return home, by abiding by the December 1997 Agreement provisions. Bangladesh is in a win-win situation here. Not only is its Hindu population unable to return home (to CHT), even its (Muslim) nationals—the illegal migrants in various states of India (Assam, West Bengal, Delhi, and Maharashtra, mainly Mumbai)—are determined to stay put there.

The continued stay of the Chakma refugees is causing political, economic and social tensions in the States concerned; viz Arunachal, Mizoram and Tripura—the last one not violent or, even serious yet. But what has set the alarm bells ringing is the rapid increase in Chakma population in Arunachal in the last three decades. Some estimates put the figure over 1,10,000—a huge increase from 60,000 in 1964. Originally they had been settled in compact areas. However, over the years they seem to have encroached upon the surrounding forest areas. The then chief minister Gegong Apang accused in 1994 that "Chakmas have denuded our forests, killed village headman in many places, and are even arranging arms training for the Chakma Youth."[4]

The Chakmas have their own version of the situation. Seeing an economic angle to it, they say their relative prosperity is being grudged by others. The vested interests are being accused of trying to grab the fertile land owned by Chakmas. They have lost right to jobs, to conduct business, and are no longer covered by the Public Distribution System, since the early 1990s. Some Chakma leaders claimed in mid-1994 that "more than 500 Chakmas have recently died of malaria because of the refusal of Government hospitals to treat them"[5]. Thus the Chakmas and Hajongs are under serious threat of deportation since 1994. The two successive Chief Ministers (Apang and Mithi) have met the prime minister and made formal requests to move these hapless refugees from their state. Although a Parliamentary Committee had recommended grant of citizenship to the Chakmas, the issue is still hanging fire because of agitation by the AAPSU and stiff opposition from all political parties of the State, who held their first joint meeting on the Chakma issue in September 1995.

The AAPSU renewed its deport-the-Chakmas agitation in 1996. The Apang Ministry was a willing ally: "We will resign if Chakma problem is not solved." Thus Chakmas are living on borrowed times. They are under same serious threat in Mizoram. "With threatened disenfranchisement as of 1 September 1996; they feared being refugees once again." Tripura then seemed the only State in the Region willing to accommodate them, "but the refugee camps there are death traps where malnutrition, disease and death stalk the inmates." In this situation of all-round gloom, the nation's Judiciary seemed to be their only saviour, as the Supreme Court ruled in January 1996 that they could not be evicted/deported forcibly.

The Arunachal Government got another chance to express its strong feelings against the Chakma settlers when it filed an affidavit[6] in the Supreme Court, giving its views on a Public Interest Litigation seeking the Court's intervention in detecting the foreign nationals living in the country. The points made in its affidavit are summed up here:

> "Arunachal fears it may soon become the next destination for Bangladeshi influx in the North-East. It is the only State in the North-East which has not witnessed tribal insurgency and influx of foreigners so far.... The State fears that the Chakmas and Hajongs who arrived here from East Pakistan in the mid-1960s are potential harbourers of Bangladeshi infiltrators, who can obtain fake PRCs (Permanent Resident Certificates) from other North-Eastern States and enter Arunachal.... The State has witnessed a number of agitations against resettlement of over 60,000 Chakma refugees of former East Pakistan. The Centre had given them settlements without realising the adverse impact on the economy and identity of the State's indigenous people."

Arunachal's affidavit, interestingly, denied "there is any separatist outfit operating in the State", but the then Chief Minister (Apang) had stated in his January 1999 letter to the Governor, recommending dissolution of the Assembly, that Ministers and MLAs hailing from Tirap and Changlang districts, which border Nagaland, had resigned under threat from underground militant organisations.[7]

The Chakma refugees continue to be an unhappy, hapless lot whose future could be as dark as their past was in the CHT! One instance should suffice to show their plight. In February 1999, 40 armed Nishis entered the Chakma village of Kokila on the Assam Arunachal border and 90 km from Tezpur; and warned the villagers to vacate within 3 days or be prepared for arson and massacre. A massacre had taken place in the same village in 1995. The Nishis had then taken away the property of the Chakmas. They have been residing in the State for the past three decades, and were granted refugee status in the State under an agreement signed by the late Indira Gandhi and Mujib-ur-Rahman. The matter was brought to the notice of Home Minister L.K. Advani, and the Human Rights Commission *(The Hindu,* 16-2-99). In any case, they can never forget the ominous slogans raised during the 1994, 1996, and subsequently, by AAPSU-led crowds: "Go back Chakmas, we do not want you any more.... Do not make Arunachal a dumping ground for refugees." The politicians could inflame the passions at any time of their choice to draw political mileage.

Chakmas and Hajongs: Brethren in Adversity

The two groups seem to be at the receiving ends in Arunachal. The Chakmas, one of the two largest ethnic groups among a dozen indigenous hill tribes, generally known as Jumma people, are original inhabitants of the CHT, with an area of 5,093 square miles, 10 per cent of Bangladesh's area (CHT was annexed by the British in 1860s). Jumma leader and ex-MP Upendera Chakma cited 3 important events that completely devastated Jumma tribes, setting off a long period of their suffering: (1) Abolition of the CHT Regulation, 1900 by Ayub Khan in 1960. (2) Adoption of long-term policy of resettling of the plains people in CHT to outnumber the Hill tribes. (3) Construction of 153 ft high Kaptai Dam on the Karnaphulli in 1962. It submerged 40 per cent of the arable land of the Jumma tribes and uprooted over 100,000 people.

Between 1947 and mid-1960s Chakmas and other tribes moved to Assam, Meghalaya, Mizoram and Tripura. Hajongs, a hill tribal minority in Mymensingh district also moved out during the same period. By July 1964, 140,000 Chakma and Hajong refugees had moved to these states. There were three category of Chakma, Hajong refugees:

(1) 1947-March 1971. They got citizenship rights and ST status in Assam, Meghalaya, Mizoram and Tripura.

(2) Chakmas in south-west Mizoram which runs along the CHT enjoy district level autonomy to plan and implement their own development schemes.

(3) Unfortunately those Chakmas and Hajongs who entered India at the same time and were settled in Arunachal are still "foreigners".

This is the background of these luckless people. Their situation has been discussed above. In January 1996, the Supreme Court ordered against any coercion against these "refugees" of Arunachal. They are the third numerically major ethnic group in the state, and as such the indigenous population see them as a potential political force. Hence their demand that they either quit or stay minus ST status and without any rights to contest in 60 ST Assembly seats. All this flows from the fact that the three dominant tribes of the State (Nishis, Adis and Mishmis) see a design in the Chakmas' exponential growth and fear that their political dominance in the State would be eroded. It is for this season that these three tribes have been at the forefront of the campaign to drive out the Chakmas out of Arunachal.

Political considerations are making the situation curious and curiouser. The MHA team, comprising of Additional Secretary P.D. Shenoy and Joint Secretary G.K. Pillai, visited the State in March 1999 and reportedly recommended that 3 additional seats be created in the State Assembly to accommodate the Chakmas (H. Khogen Singh; *HT,* 9-3-04). This would dispel the fears of the indigene's of losing their political dominance as they would continue to have the current 60 seats for themselves. It would at the same time bring the migrants into the political mainstream, they have been yearning for since long. The Centre has not acted on it. On the other hand, the State Government has been defying the Supreme Court order of 1996 ruling that under Section 3(1)A of the Indian Citizenship Act, 1955 every person born in India on or after 26-1-50 and before 1-7-87 is a citizen of India. Under this ruling, about 35,000 Chakmas born in India after 1964 are citizen by birth. But the "intransigent Arunachal Government has not granted them citizenship". The State has also not paid any heed to the 1997 Judgement of the Delhi High Court that the Chakmas be registered as voters. The State continues to block the Election Commission's (EC) efforts to revise the election rolls in order to include the Chakmas in the voter list. In a letter to the PMO early February 2004, the EC warned the Centre that the Chakma issue could snow ball into a volatile political issue and requested that problem be solved amicably and expeditiously" (*Times of India,,* 26-2-04). In spite of the above cited directions of the Supreme and High Courts, the Arunachal Cabinet passed a resolution on 14-05-03 not permitting the enrolment of Chakmas in the voters list. The EC directed the State vide its Letter of 2-01-04 that the Chakmas of four constituencies—Doimukh, Chowkham, Bordumsa-Diyum and Miao, all in Miao Sub-Division of Changlang district, where nearly 60,000 Chakmas live—be enrolled in the voters' list. The EC feels the State Government exceeded its jurisdiction by interfering with its constitutional responsibility by not revising the rolls as directed by it. The EC in its letter to PMO stressed that action would be taken against the Electoral Registration Officers (ERO) as they were not abiding by its direction to include Chakmas in the rolls. The EC made it clear that "it shall not be able to conduct any elections in these four constituencies unless the State authorities comply with its direction". *The HT* (26-2-04) said "in what will probably make electoral history, voters at least in 4 Assembly segments in Arunachal may not be able to cast their votes in the coming (April-May) Lok Sabha polls". On 3 March

2004, the EC ordered the inclusion of 1,497 people from among those 60,000 Chakmas in the voters' list for these polls. The rights conferred on these lucky 1,497 voters represent a major victory for the Chakmas and Hajongs, who have been fighting for this right for the last 40 years (AJ. Philip, *Tribune,* 28-3-04). "Sources say the EC has sent to the Centre copies of representation from various North-East organisations demanding the inclusion of Chakmas in the electoral rolls" *(HT,* 26-2-04).

It bears repetition that unlike the Tripura Chakmas, who are recent migrants, the Chakmas of Arunachal have been living there since 1964 when they were displaced from their CHT home due to the construction of the Kaptai Dam and entered India possessing documents given to them by Indian Government and were settled by it in that State. Thus they are neither illegal immigrants nor are they squatters. Surely they deserve a better deal. Some analysts feel the Chakmas deserve and must get sympathy from Arunachal, a State with least population density figure—a mere 13 people to a Sq km—) in the country, with Delhi being the most dense, 9,294, against all-India figure of 324.

Political rhetoric has become the bane of this issue. In the mid 1990s, when L.K. Advani was in opposition, he wrote numerous letters to the then Home Minister (S.B. Chavan) to grant citizenship to the Chakmas, and often raised the issue vehemently in Parliament. "Today (9 March 04), as Home Minister, the same Advani is sitting over the 40,000 applications for citizenship by the Chakmas for last 7 years." While intent on bringing down the 19-year Apang Ministry, Mithi said in 1998 that there was no insurgency in Changlang and Tirap districts, the area was up against Apang for having been neglected by him, the same Mithi soon after ascending to power, enacts a tough anti-insurgency APROCA to fight insurgency! The Union Minister of State of Home (Chinmayananda) criticized State Government (11 July 2003) headed by the Congressman Mithi for launching of "Operation Hurricane" against the Naga insurgents when the Centre was trying to bring peace to the Region by holding talks with the two factions of the NSCN. Yet again, going by the semiotics, NSCN(K) backs Mithi and the Congress (as it does in Nagaland) but the NSCN(I-M) is closer to Chief Minister Apang and the NDA (*Ind. Exp.,* 14-8-03). It is politics again that in 2002 the State granted citizenship to over 90 Tibetan families in Tawang district, because, this small migrant group (which numbered a mere 3,050 in 1976) did not threaten the dominance of the entrenched political class, but it would not do the same for the too numerous Chakmas—the third largest community in Arunachal—as that would threaten the political fortunes of the three dominant tribes of the State, reflecting the internal dynamics of the state, against the strident stance of the three major tribes, other minor tribes are not so paranoid about the presence of the Chakmas. "In fact, some like the Singphos, Tangshas and Khamptis have even sympathized with the Chakmas and helped them in their hour of need."!

A Majestic Voter in a Battle Won

"Manjulika Chakma has reason to feel special. The EC has setup an exclusive polling booth for her in Dharampur. And, Presiding officer T.B. Singh, carrying two EVMs and accompanied by 15 armed guards, has started a 6-hour trek on 6-10-04 just to ensure that she gets to cast her vote on the 7th (Rahul Karmakar, *Ind. Exp.*, 7-10-05). Dharampur, home to 2,000 Chakma settlers, created electoral history by becoming a single voter station during the Lok Sabha polls in May 2004. Manjulika is the only one who was enrolled in the voter list because none of the other villagers could prove that they were born in India, a prerequisite as per court order. In face of the stiff opposition from the indigenous tribes, the EC decided to set up a polling booth in each of the Chakma settlement, even if there was a single voter as in the case of Dharampur.

Miao ADC A.K. Sharma was doubtful about Singh making it to Dharampur since it was near-impossible to cross the swollen Noa-Dehing in such a turbulent weather.

But Singh's task is far easier than that of S. Kumar who left Miao 7 days back on foot with three sets of material for polling stations in Bijaynagar, Gandhigram and Ramnagar. To wit, Bijaynagar is 148 km from Miao and one has to cross the angry Noa-Dehing thrice and at least six other mountain rivers en route. Sharma said the copter service in his area in this weather was simply not possible. Arunachal's Chief Electoral Officer (CEO) M.K. Parida had, indeed, sought IAF Chopper service for 51 far-flung areas. With only 20 materialising, the CEO was forced to send polling staff on long, arduous marches, many armed with salt and sticks to confront leeches and snakes on the way.

It is the Indian democracy at its best. It is not easy to work but India has done it ever since 1947, with a measure of success in the face of the dire forebodings of the doubting Thomases, particularly of the west! The Chakmas indeed must be happy and thankful, having won a battle under it, overcoming all the hurdles.

An Ominous Naga Shadow over Arunachal

The then NEFA, on recommendations of the States' Reorganisation Commission, lost its Tuensang Frontier Division in mid-1950s to the Nagas of the Assam's Naga Hills District. The Two entities were joined to create NHTA which became full-fledged State of Nagaland on 1 December 1963. The Naga affairs continue to cast a gloomy spell over the political situation of Arunachal ever since, and particularly over its two south-eastern districts of

Tirap and Changlang, bordering Nagaland and Myanmar respectively. Arunachal has been free from the militancy-related violence, excepting its Tirap and Changlang districts which because of their geographical proximity with Assam, Nagaland and Myanmar, have been used by the insurgent groups, operating in the area, for transit between Nagaland and Myanmar. There is some Naga population in the two districts which facilitates the process.

Even on so serious a matter as the presence of insurgents in the parts of Arunachal, politics plays a part. Apang in January 1999 had categorically talked about the presence of insurgents in the districts of Tirap and Changlang. His successor, Mithi, within four months of taking over in January 1999, denied any Naga activity in Tirap and Changlang. He told a daily on 2 May 1999: "Since the two districts border Nagaland and Myanmar, some parts of population have attachment with the Nagas in terms of language and culture. May be, in the process, some local youth from Nocte and Wangchuk tribes joined the Naga rebels led by Khaplang because of the neglect of area by the Apang Government. Six months ago, there were incidents of extortion. No more. A series of meetings between the local people and the underground has brought about a big change in the situation there."[8] The same Mithi takes a U-turn in September 2002, admitting the presence of insurgents in the two districts—though not of NSCN(K) but of the NSCN(I-M): "The NSCN(I-M) is targeting ministers from Tirap and Changlang districts because they are insecure with the new Arunachal Pradesh Control of Organised Crime (APCOC) Bill, 2002." He justified the introduction of the new Crime Bill, saying it was essential in view of deteriorating law and order situation in the State and the escalating gang warfare between the NSCN(I-M) and NSCN(K) in the two districts.[9]

The events to follow were to prove Chief Minister Mithi wrong on a major count: It was NSCN(I-M) which was active in the two districts, not its rival, NSCN(K). A senior Minister (Tingpong Wangham) and a veteran Congress MLA (T.L. Rajkumar) of the ruling Congress Party were arrested at Itanagar on 30 May 2003 under the Arunachal Pradesh Control of Organised Crime Act (APCOCA). The police accused them of having links with the NSCN(I-M) militants and extending them monetary help. An other former Minister and sitting MLA (Congress) T. Wanglat, also wanted by the police under the provisions of APCOCA has been absconding. All the three hail from Tirap, the district that borders Nagaland and is one of the two Arunachal districts that have a veritable NSCN(I-M) presence. The names of the three were reportedly found mentioned in the diaries of two top NSCN(I-M) cadres who were arrested last year. The three were also mentioned for giving money to the militants. Sources disclosed that the police wanted to arrest the three several months ago, but the Congress had apparently been resisting any such move in the interest of the party and Government's image.

There is a near consensus in the State that if the Chakma issue is not resolved in the near future, Arunachal could be in for an Assam-type situation. It is worth remembering that two State Chief Ministers—Apang and his successor Mukut Mithi—have openly come out in support of the students' demand. The situation could be frightening, knowing that the Chakmas themselves conducted an insurgency movement, which claimed over 25,000 lives till December 1997 Agreement with Dhaka, against the armed forces of Bangladesh for 22 long years.

U.T. Status for Tirap and Changlang Districts?

It seem these two districts are destined to remain in limelight. The two have been believed to be providing shelter and succour to the Naga rebels, as also facilitating their transit between Indian and Myanmarese areas.

One does not understand a Nationalist Congress Party (NCP) member Wangki Lowang's motive in moving a resolution in Arunachal Assembly on 30 March 2000, demanding UT status for the two districts. Surprisingly, all 12 members from the two districts, including several members of the Mithi Cabinet, supported the private members' resolution, stating that it was based on "Popular Public demand". They said both the districts were the "most neglected areas of the State and had been deprived by the previous Government". Chief Minister Mithi was not forceful enough; "...Although the demand was genuine, the State Assembly had nothing to do with it.... I see no reason for a separate UT status in view of the concern shown by the present Government for the economic development of the area." Perhaps they were all playing games to do down the Apang Government. Finally, the Assembly rejected the resolution by voice vote. Unless handled carefully, the demand could gather further support in course of time, and vested political interests could then fan the embers. The seeds sown even casually sprout in due time.

The Spill-over Insurgency

Strategically, Arunachal is possibly the most important State of the Region, sharing international border with three countries. Generally, it has been a peaceful State but disturbed conditions and serious insurgency related violence in the neighbouring States of Assam and Nagaland cast its shadow on it, particularly the border areas. Some instances should suffice.

In well-planned move to divide the Assamese Society, ULFA ultras killed nearly 90 Hindi-speaking (Biharis and Marwaris) people between October and mid-December 2000.[10] In the worst of such incidents, ULFA militants gunned down 28 Bihari labourers who were returning from the weekly market at Sonpur near Tezu in Arunachal, on a hilly road in Tinsukia district near the Arunachal-Assam border, on 27 December 2000. As a result, panic gripped Arunachal, which sounded a State-wide alert Combing operations were launched by the SF in Tirap and Changlang districts. "Insurgents have been making hit-and-run raids from their bases in these areas. Night curfew will continue in the outer periphery of Assam."[11] Chief Minister Mithi admitted that after being chased out of Bhutan, ULFA had set up some hide-outs inside Arunachal territory, in which they moved frequently.

The ULFA Cadres carried out three IED explosions between 12 AM and 2.30 AM on 27-5-05, disrupting road communications in the Lohit and Anjaw districts. The blasts occurred at Bordirak and Sorudirak, both hamlets in Kakopathar area in Tinsukia district, damaging a power transformer and snapping HT lines. Power supply was disrupted in Kakopathar and Namsai areas; the third was under a Bailey bridge (popularly Maithong bridge) on the Kakopathar Chowkham (Lohit district) Road.

The NDFB, with its bases in thick forests near the Arunachal-Bhutan border, also sought safe havens in the nearby areas of Arunachal when under pressure by the Bhutanese Army.

The Intelligence reports that "the NSCN(K) is of recent years active in Arunachal's Tirap and Changlang districts touching international border of Myanmar; the Bodo ultras are active in the districts of West Kameng, East Kameng and Tawang; and ULFA frequently use thick forests of Arunachal along its border with Assam". The following are some of the militant outfits that came to the notice of the Intelligence:

UPVA United People's Volunteers of Arunachal.

ULMA United Liberation Movement of Arunachal.

PRAA Patriotic Revolutionary Army of Arunachal.

LTA Liberation Tigers of Arunachal.

ADF Arunachal Dragon Federation.

All these outfits must essentially be in their nascent state, and some of these may be nothing more than a collection of a few individuals mainly interested in extortions, but even then, unless handled carefully, they could spread their popular base among some discontent section of Arunachalis and threaten the peace of this largely peaceful State at some future date.

'Monpas up in Arms Against Tibetan Refugees'

This is the caption of a story in *The Hindu* of 15 March 1997. The Monpa Preservation Committee (MPC) in Tawang district had strongly objected to the issuance of ST certificates to Tibetans, particularly in Tawang district, alleging that "it is jeopardising the opportunity extended to the Monpa tribes in the area". The MPC Memorandum to Chief Minister Apang stated that the Tibetans who migrated from Tibet after the 1959 upheavals, "are recognised as refugees and have not even been accepted as Indian citizens". The

Memorandum alleged that a State Government circular recently directed the Deputy Commissioner of Tawang district to issue ST certificates to the inhabitants of Shyo village, thus recognising them as bona fide Indian citizens. The other area of State where the Tibetan refugees (they numbered 3,000 in 1976) were settled are Kurangling (Changling district) and Dhargayling (Tezu).

The MPC claimed that the villagers of Shyo were none but the Tibetan refugees and that many of them possessed refugee cards thus enjoying facilities extended by the Tibetan Government in Exile and also from the Government of India. They further claimed even the State cabinet had not as yet considered the question of recognising these Tibetans as bona fide Indian citizens and urged the Government to stop issuance of ST certificates to the Tibetan refugees in the interests of the genuine STs of the area.

That the Monpas are Buddhist like the Tibetans only goes to show that the issues of bread and butter takes precedence over religious affinities. And such cleavages could disturb the peace of the idyllic State.

Rising Hopes and Aspirations: Explosion of

Some analysts suggest the real danger in Arunachal could be entirely different. Education is throwing up a crop of young men and women, who are not so deeply rooted in their tribal traditions and ethos, and who aspire to power and success without waiting too long. The State has not been able to generate enough jobs to absorb them. They belong to "get rich quickly" category—impatient of administrative and constitutional processes. Frustrated aspirations could lead them into improper, even illegal, ways. They could do anything—any thing—to achieve their goals. This essentially economic problem could turn into political one—chaotic, explosive, and unmanageable at certain stage. Arunachal may not need the presence of Chakma refugees to descend into the chaos depicted above. But if the local youth sees the Chakmas responsible for their 'plight', the chaotic condition will be reached faster.

Inequality and Iniquitous Developments: Sharing Prosperity

Democratic disequilibrium and process of acculturation could soon disrupt the traditional matrix of relationship between land and people. The growing disparity between various tribal groups has also heightened the cleavages in the inter- and intra-tribal relations. Likewise, the economic development must be evenly and equally spread, otherwise the less-developed would nurture sense of injustice. In the same way, the larger tribe must not only get their due share of the political cake, but must ensure that the smaller tribes get theirs.

The 19-year rule of Arunachal's longest-serving Chief Minister Apang, and country's second (after Jyoti Basu) ended[12] when seven ministers belonging to the Nyishi (earlier Nishi or Nissi) Community resigned on 9 January 1999 at the behest of the Nyishi Elite Society and all Nyishi Students' Union, organisations representing the community's intellectuals and youth. They accused him of having failed to fulfil the hopes and aspirations of the people in general and the Nyishi tribe in particular, as also of unequal regional development; and as a result, some pocket of the State have seen much development while some other regions have been deliberately kept backward. Right or wrong, these were politically correct accusations. It is for note that the Nyishi tribe is the second largest in Arunachal, next only to the Adi.

It is not only unequal regional development within Arunachal that can disturb inter-tribal and inter-regional tranquility, the faster development and greater prosperity across the border could pose even a bigger threat to the state's fragile peace. As China pours resources into the south-eastern corner of Tibet to build new infrastructure, Arunachal just south of the Nyingchi Prefecture faces a new threat—a widening development gap across the contested border. Called the "Green Pearl" of the Tibet-Qwghai plateau, the Nyingchi Prefecture is blossoming as Beijing is intent on developing Tibet's border region in particular. While Tibet itself has developed 12 per cent per year over the last decade, "The Nyingchi Prefecture has grown at 17 per cent" and is one of the richest parts of Tibet claimed the local officials. The per capita income of the Prefecture now stands at 13,000 Yuan (one yuan is a little over Rs. 5), which is more than four times those in Arunachal. It is in India's interest to provide greater resources to Arunachal to reduce this "unhealthy" gap (C. Raja Mohan, *Ind. Exp.,* 16-6-05). Chinese ambassador Sun Yuxi threw a pebble in the pool on 1-4-05 ahead of the visit by Chinese Premier Wen Jiabao by claiming that the State of Arunachal was still "a disputed area" between the two nations. Reacting sharply to Sun's claim, Arunachal Home Minister Jarbom Gamlin termed it "erroneous" and said the State was an integral part of India and "we have lodged a strong protest with the MEA" *(Asian Age,* 6-4-05).

Another apt example of smaller tribes clamouring for a share in the pie is a 24-hour State-wide bandh, called by the All Nishing Students Union (ANSU) on 21 October 1998, to demand, among other things, setting up of the Western Divisional Headquarters and the office of the DIG of Police at Yachuli in Lower Subansiri district.[13] The *bandh* evoked good response in Nishing-dominated districts of Arunachal, including Itanagar where all business establishments remained closed. Private vehicles were off the road. Educational institutions did not function. Attendance in all State and Central Government offices was thin; and so was it in banking and postal services. Barring a few stray incidents of stone-throwing at vehicles including that of the State Home Minister and detention of some 30 bandh supporters, the bandh was generally peaceful.

Ripples versus Storm-waves

The leaders of Arunachal will have to display a plenty of human wisdom and astuteness and political savvy to ensure that the "ripples" mentioned above do not transform into turbulent storm-waves in the future.

Nexus : Arunachal Pradesh

Arunachal Pradesh is affording a transit route from Myanmar for ULFA, NSCN(K), UNLF and PLA. Its neighbouring districts with Nagaland provide hiding places for NSCN and ULFA.

NOTES

1. Roy, Ash Narain, *Hindustan Times,* 18-11-94.
2. *Ibid.*
3. To be fair to them, politicians in the rest of India are no different when it is question of 'protecting' their indigenous flock against the so-called outsiders; e.g., Bal Thackrey against the non-Maharashtrians in Mumbai and the Punjabi (Akali) politicians against the Bihari labourers and wage earners in agricultural areas of that state.
4. *Hindustan Times,* 18-11-94.
5. *Ibid.*
6. Syed Liaquat AH, *Hindustan Times,* 4-10-99.
7. Kalyan Chaudhury, *Frontline,* 12-2-99.
8. Gurmukh Singh, *Times of India,* 3-5-99.
9. *The Week,* 22-9-02.
10. An emergency meeting was convened by the Home Minister Advani on 8 December 2000 to assess the Assam situation created by the communal carnage perpetrated by the ULFA ultras. Attended by Governor S.K. Sinha and P.K. Mahanta of Assam, Army Chief Gen S Padmanabhan, and Union Home Secretary Kamal Pande, the meeting decided to give the Army a free hand to put down the insurgents and send an additional 27 companies of Central Security Forces to Assam to help the 127 companies of Paramilitary and Army units already engaged in anti-insurgency operations there.
11. *The Frontline,* 5-1-01.
12. Gegong Apang was back again as Chief Minister in the 2003 Assembly polls.
13. *The Hindu,* 23-10-98.

9

Chakmas are Facing Hostility in Arunachal Will they Resort to Terrorism in India also?

Chakmas are luckless people who suffered in British India till 1947, are still suffering in their CHT home under Bangladesh Government and continue to do so in Free India also. Presently they are under attack in three states of the Indian Union—Arunachal Pradesh, Mizoram and Tripura, in that order. Instead of discussing their plight and issues involved in a piecemeal manner, the Chakmas are discussed here in entirety.

Chakmas resorted to violence in defence of their rights and to preserve their land and heritage in Chittagong Hills Tract (CHT) against the East Pakistan authorities and subsequently, post-1971, Bangladesh Government. Will they be forced to take up the arms in India too?

Chakmas : A Historical Perspective

Broadly speaking, the Chakmas are believed to be scattered throughout the North-East barring perhaps Manipur, Nagaland and Meghalaya, and throughout the eastern part of Bangladesh, but mainly in the Chittagong Hills Tract (CHT). In India, they are presently found in Mizoram, settled on the eastern side of its border with CHT; in Tripura, as refugees; and in Arunachal, as 'foreigners'.

Origin and People

The Chakmas are a distinct tribe, localised in the southwestern part of Mizoram. In racial terms, the tribe belongs to the Eastern Group of the Indo-Aryan family, whose dialect is Chakma, a corrupted form of Bengali language written in corrupt Burmese script. Risley, a former noted Census Commissioner, classified them in the group of Mongolian racial type. Lewin (1870) was the first to suggest that they migrated from Arakan and then moved into CHT in the last quarter of the 19th century. This is the view of the wesern scholars. The foremost Indian authority on the subject, Suniti K. Chatterjee, has established that the tribal/racial groups in India's North-East did not come from the east only; they also came from the west, that is, various areas in

India like Bengal, Bihar, and from as far as Punjab. The Chakmas themselves claim they originally came from a country called Champango or Champanagar—some placing it near Malacca and assigning them Malayan origin. But predominant view places Champanagar in "the North-western provinces of Hindustan". S.C. Dutta (*The Wild Tribes of India*), confirming their western origin, holds that they are a branch of Lushai-Chin-Thadou Group of tribes. But A.M. Hutchinson (*An Account of the CHT*), agreeing with Chatterjee, says the tribe "belongs to the Eastern Group of the Indian Aryan Family". Digging deeper, he traces their "origin to the Arracanese and the tribes of Bihar dating somewhere about 1630 AD" but dismisses as a myth the claim of their connection with the Kshatriyas of Champanagar. More specifically, he traces their origin to the union between the soldiers of Nawab Shaista Khan, Governor of Lower Bengal under Aurangzeb and the hill women about 1670 AD. He goes further, interestingly: "They were Buddhist by birth but evidently had a leaning to the religion of their fathers, as the Mohammedan names of their chiefs testify. The tendency toward Hinduism becomes strongly apparent during the time of Kalindee Rani (1832-74), the period when the worship of Goddess Kali and Lord Shiva was introduced."

But the Chakmas dismiss Hutchinson theories—particularly of any Muslim blood—out of hand. But presently two theories hold field. One, they belonged to Assam and were subsequently driven out by the Ahoms. The other, mentioned above, holds they belonged to Burma and were driven out by their own tribal cousins, Thadou Lushai-Chin Group of tribes. The Chakmas accept the latter theory which the predominant opinion holds to be more accurate, considering their features, way of life, and cultural identity which are closer to this group's as also to their present neighbours.

They are called *Tui Tekh* by the Burmese people.

The Chakmas claim they lived a settled life like the Lushais. But the Mizo authors, of late, hold that by the time Thangluah Sailo and Zedeng Lal's (=Chiefs) extended their power to the Chittagong Hills, there was not a single Chakma in the (south or south-west) Lushai Hills, barring some who had been captured and brought as slaves by the raiding Lushai tribes. The raid of Chengri Valley in 1889 by Lianpunga was also the result of the Chakma intrusion in the hunting reserves of the Lushai Hills.

The Kharbari of Dinlibagh, Jaiswadar, holds that the Chakmas entered Mizoram with Zakhupa, a Tlagau Lal (=Chief) who moved westward to the present-day Mizoram. He ruled over Ngharun and Mullianpui. Initially his Chakma followers settled within his lands, subsequently migrating to Tipperah and Borapansui. By 1916, some Chamas lived in Marapara under Chief Pu K. Ziang. By 1925, some were found settled in Aivapui and Mualvaum under Fuldengsui Lal. During World War II, the British organised Chakma Transport

Corps, and large number among them stayed back in the then Lushai Hills, not returning to Chittagong. The official records show that 175 Chakma families emigrated from CHT into the Lushai Hills in 1949. This is essentially Mizo view of the issue, because the Chakmas themselves claim much older settlement in south and south-western Mizoram.

The scholars believe that as a result of their long interaction with other races, especially Bengalis, the Chakmas have lost many of their original ethnic traits and speak a dialect (Chakma) which is nearly same as the one of south-eastern Bengal. But in spite of this all, they claim to have retained and preserved a distinct cultural and ethnic identity.

Their habitation has a geo-political significance as they are found in three countries—India, Burma and Bangladesh (home to the vast majority, concentrated in CHT).

Anthropological Picture

An average Chakma is of medium stature, thick build, with a well developed chest. Their daily work involves a lot of hard manual labour for both men and women, which result in muscular legs, arms and chest. They have Mongoloid features, slanting eyes and flat nose. The average nasal index works out to 77.7 and average cephalic index 79.9. The hair is straight and normally rarely grey. A Chakma is rarely seen with a moustache or beard.

It needs a mention that Chakma Jatiya Parishad in a 1991 letter submitted to Prime Minister V.P. Singh and signed by its President, B. Chakma and S.K. Chakma, ex-MLA, claimed the Chakma population of Mizoram to be 70,000.

Religion

The Chakmas are predominantly Buddhists. But one can discern an obvious influence of Hinduism and Pre-Buddhism animistic faiths. Thus while practising Buddhist rites and ceremonies, they also worship Hindu gods and goddesses like Shiva, Kali, Durga, Laxmi (Lakkhi, as they call her), the effect of the Bengali neighbours, and observe animistic rituals like propitiating evil spirits through animal sacrifices. This is one major tribe which has been largely successful in thwarting all attempts at their conversion first by the Christians and later by the Islamic preachers.

Each Chakma village has a Buddhist temple *khyang,* and a monk. The temple has the image of Buddha before which all Chakmas bow their head in reverence. The monk chants the Buddhist hymns like *Pancha-Ashta,* and *Dasha-Shila,* and Mangalasutra, besides explaining the scriptures like *Binay, Abhidharma* and *Sutra.* The Buddhist priest, called oza, is summoned for the purpose. They also worship Hindu gods at home for which they summon the services of a Brahmin priest.

Population

Chakma Population Growth in Mizoram (1901-91)

Census Year	*Chakma Population*	*Decadel Growth (Per cent)*
1901	198	—
1911	302	52.10
1921	680	125.10
1931	836	22.94
1941	5,088	508.60
1951	15,297	200.64
1961	19,337	26.41
1971	22,393	15.80
1981	39,905	78.20
1991	54,194	35.80

Source : Census Reports.

Economy

Though they profess Buddhism, the Chakmas eat the flesh of animals like goat, cow, fowl, pig, buffalo, besides fish, frog and reptiles. Their normal diet includes rice-bread *(pitha),* milk, pulses, leafy vegetables, radish, pumpkin, yams, chillies, brinjals, cauliflowers, tomatoes, peas, and fruits like bananas, jack fruit, oranges, guavas, berries, etc. They are fond of local drink, prepared from rice and a local root, *mali.* Depending upon its alcoholic contents, there are three varieties of Chakma rice beer: Jagara, Kanji and Davini. Interestingly, the drinking was limited to the male of the species, as was essentially the case with the early Hindu and Bengali societies. Both sexes are fond of chewing the betel leaf, though in addition, the men are also fond of smoking *hookah.*

The Chakma women are expert weavers, spinning yarn from the short staple cotton on a *taklee* (charkha) made of bamboo. They weave on tension looms. They dye their clothes in bright colours like red, yellow, green, indigo, dark pink, black and orange. The vegetable dyes are obtained from *Kalra,* turmeric and indigo leaves and barks of mango and *kale-gab* trees, besides the root of a particular local wild tree, *Rang ganch* (=dye tree). But the aged women prefer the lighter colours like cream and grey. They are known for their handicrafts, in particular of cane and ubiquitous bamboo. They manufacture baskets, big bins, musical instruments, drinking cups, receptacles for storing oil, spears, bow and arrows, from the bamboo. The bamboo pipes are used for fetching water from long distances, and storage at home; as also for carrying water to the fields from its source. They also fashion rafts out of the bamboo. Obviously, they are good at carpentry and wood-carving.

The Chakmas: Struggle for Survival and Autonomy

Historically speaking, the worst-affected, as result of 1937 separation of Burma from India, were the people of the CHT which fell to the administration of the British Bengal; and consequent to the Partition of India 10 years later, became part of (East) Pakistan. The Region belongs to the Southern Burma-Mizo Hills-Arakan complex and should have become part of Assam in 1937. But it would have been an administrative inconvenience to govern it from Shillong, given its location and underdeveloped state of Southern Assam areas then, and so the British considered it prudent to tag it with Bengal. Even then, if the Sylhet area of Assam was given an option to join (East) Pakistan in 1947 being predominantly non-Muslim, the CHT area of Bengal, being predominantly non-Muslim, should have been given an analogous option to join India. But Radcliff awarded this area, predominantly inhabited by the Buddhist population, to Pakistan. Thousands of Chakmas fled to India in 1947 as a result of the Partition and subsequent oppression unleashed by Dhaka and its policy of settling the Muslim farmers in the area. So the Chakmas have suffered in Pakistan/Bangladesh since 1947 and they have complained of being discriminated against in India (Mizoram, Tripura and Arunachal Pradesh) since the 1980s.

PLIGHT OF CHAkmAS IN BANGLADESH

Chakmas, non-Bengali and Buddhist, lived in peace and with dignity, sans much prosperity, like any other tribes of British India. Their travails began during 1946-47 when negotiations began over the partition of India, and the CHT went to Pakistan on 15 August 1947. CHT had a non-Muslim majority—overwhelmingly Chakmas—of 97 per cent. Once Pakistan was created, the Muslim Bengalis from the Plains of East Pakistan started pouring in and there has been no let-up since then. Now it is the Chakma vs (Bengali) Muslim problem. The woes of Chakmas began from there. British colonial rulers had provided CHT with a protective legislation in 1900, ensuring them unhindered possession of their land, distinct way of life and institutions. This was their (British) way of preserving the identity of a small ethnic group. At Partition, they had openly pleaded for accession to India for demographic and historical reasons. Post-1947, they were systematically persecuted for their express desire to join India. So as the Plains Muslim settlers were brought into CHT, Non-Muslims were uprooted, and their lands snatched away by brute force. Muslim colonisation and the consequent population displacement was accompanied by arson, forcible conversion, abduction, rape and mass killings. Then Pakistan Government decided to help the Muslim in-migration to CHT in more systematic manner.

In the 1956 Constitution of Pakistan, the status of "Excluded Area" was retained. "Once the authorities felt confident of eliminating the *Kafirs,* and that primarily because of India's passivity to sacrifice every Hindu-Buddhist interest if it clashed with Islam, CHT was deprived of its special status as an 'Excluded Area' under the Pakistan Constitutional amendment Act, 1963[1]." The Regulation became effective in 1964. With the rapid increase in the number of immigrant Muslim settlers from the Plains and their high-handed methods, obviously acquiesced, sanctioned, and even encouraged by the official agencies, the local tribals felt increasingly insecure and started moving out to India. By the end of 1964, the CHT was closed to the foreigners. Obviously, Dhaka wanted to hide the unpleasant. Construction of Karnafuli (popularly, Kaptai) Hydro-Electric Dam (the same year) submerged about 40 per cent of the District's arable area, uprooting about 1,800 families, involving 10,000 people. "The process of rehabilitation was tardy and half-hearted, and more so, when the displaced persons were the despicable *kaftrs.*" This was among the earlier cases of "development" projects causing forced displacement in the subcontinent. Another author says, "they were not even given compensation"[2]. The Project devastated the agricultural economy of the local people. The exit/'eviction' of Chakmas was not unexpected; after all Pakistan was only being true to its traditions, only the world outside, especially India, seemed to be oblivious of the inevitable. When pushed to the wall in the post-1971 war and Independence of Bangladesh, a section of Chakmas decided to take to the arms. It gave birth to the Shanti Bahini, which will be dealt with later.

One section of opinion has seen the Chakma problem primarily as of "economic and social rights of a community," and amenable to a solution if handled sympathetically—even if this 'if' is too much to expect from Bangladesh. Others however, seeing it through a nationalist prism, argue that the issue is essentially of "a struggle for self-determination". Having been independent during pre-colonial period, Chakma autonomy was preserved during the British rule. Seen this way, the Chakma demands, including UN intervention, particularly after 1971 events, cannot be dismissed merely as a socio-economic agenda.

A word on physical and ethnic dimensions of CHT located in the south-eastern part of Bangladesh, bordering India on the east and Myanmar on its south-east. Covering a land area of 13,231 km[3], CHT today comprises of three districts; Khagrachari, Bandarban, and Rangamati. Both by geography and administrative divisions, CHT is distinct and separate from the Chittagong Port and the surrounding Chittagong Plains. At the Partition, these three parts—Chittagong Port, Plains and Hill Tracts (CHT)—were clubbed together and awarded to Pakistan, as mentioned earlier.[4] The differences between CHT and rest of East Pakistan/Bangladesh also spill over into demography: while Bengali Muslims inhabit the Chittagong Plains, the CHT has been predominantly Buddhist. The Buddhists, Chakmas, "are a dominant group, and CHT has a number of other non-Chakma tribes like Buddhist tribe of Marmas, Hindu tribes like Hajong, and the smaller Christian tribes of Panknua, Bawn and Mru."[5] Moreover, unlike the rest of Bangladesh, the population of CHT is of Sino-Tibetan origin.

The Chakmas started moving out of CHT after 1947. Over the years, this demographic shift has worked against the Chakmas. On the one hand, the Bengali Muslim migrants moved into the CHT, consequently the Chakmas fled to India, on the other. This in-migration of Muslims and out-migration of Chakmas proved detrimental to the interests—political, social and economic—of the latter community. The population shift, starting in 1947, accelerated during the construction of the Kaptai Dam in CHT, and intensified following the formation of Bangladesh—the secular image and credentials of Banga Bandhu, notwithstanding. One analyst adds: "Even the secular Sheikh Mujib as Prime Minister did nothing to stop the Muslim colonization of CHT."[6] The usurpation of their land by the settlers and oppressive Government policies caused the depletion of the Chakma population in CHT. In 1951 (Census), the non-Chakmas were just 9 per cent of CHT population, but in 1991, their share had climbed to 49 per cent—all Muslims. This further aggravated the Chakma-Muslim tension, which often led to further influx of Chakmas into India. In 1991, if the Hindus constituted 10.5 per cent of the total population of Bangladesh, the Chakma population of Bangladesh at 623,300 represents just under 0.59 per cent of the national population. However, their numbers in CHT, their traditional homeland, constitute only 51.43 per cent of its 974,445 population. Obviously there has been almost continual outflow from the CHT.

Here are figures to show the depletion of Chakma population in CHT. A scholar says that historically, "the terrorization of Hindus and Buddhists began with one-sided Noakhali massacre of 1946." As for the CHT, Chakmas and other Hindu tribes constituted 98 per cent of its population then, against 2 per cent Muslims. By 1995, the respective figures stood at 54 and 46.

The first influx of refugees took place shortly after partition when 400 families (totalling 25,000) fled to India. India has absorbed a huge post-1947 refugee influx and Chakmas too were housed and absorbed the same way. Their small number, widespread dispersal in the sparsely populated North-East, and their ethnic proximity largely softened any potential opposition from the indigenous population. Moreover, absorption was feasible partly because ethnic consciousness in the Region was still in its infancy. The second wave of Chakma exodus was fuelled by construction of Kaptai Dam[7] which submerged 54,000 acres of arable land used by Chakmas for plough cultivation and displaced 100,000 Chakmas of which 40,000 fled to India.

Unlike the past, India took this influx rather seriously, though circumstances and humanitarian considerations persuaded her to accept these refugees and rehabilitate them in Tripura and Mizoram. If the 1965 India-Pakistan war prevented their repatriation to CHT, the onset of insurgency in Mizoram created problems for their continued presence in Mizoram and Tripura. Consequently, the Chakmas were rehabilitated in the then NEFA (presently Arunachal Pradesh), largely because it was sparsely populated, and also because its population was Buddhist in the area chosen for their settlement which would provide a cultural environment for rehabilitation and subsequent absorption. The post-1962 strategic calculation *vis-a-vis* China also played a part in the decision. Thus between 1964-69, about 15,000 Chakmas and Hajongs were settled in NEFA. Meanwhile, the Indira-Mujib Agreement of 1972 redefined the status of Chakma refugees in India and those who had come before 1971 were declared non-Bangladeshis, which meant almost all the migrants who were in India till then. It was a huge concessions to Mujib at the altar of Indo-Bangladesh friendship; of course demanded by the then prevailing political ambience. It left New Delhi saddled with the problem of rehabilitating the Chakmas in the North-East.

But the process of settling Chakma refugees in India was not smooth; in fact after initial acceptance al be it reluctantly, the problem has assumed unpleasant configuration, even hostile opposition in all the three states—Mizoram, Arunachal Pradesh, particularly since its elevation to statehood, and Tripura. But the problem in these three States are to be solved by India domestically. However, the Chakma problem as it is presently referred to pertains to the Third Wave of Chakmas who fled to India in late 1970s following serious political and social tensions and upheaval in CHT.

Unlike the previous occasions, this influx was sporadic, not confined to any specific period, nor linked to any specific development in Bangladesh. Since 1977, small groups of Chakmas began to cross over into Tripura but the trend took a definite turn by June 1984. By 1987, the number of refugees swelled to 50,000, rising to 70,000 in 1991—most of them housed in various camps in Tripura. The continuous flow of refugees, coupled with India's inability to repatriate them, snowballed into major crisis for India.

The influx this time was a reflection of general deterioration of the conditions of minorities in Bangladesh. Since Partition, Pakistan Government undermined the local autonomy of the Chakmas by disbanding the indigenous *Jumma* police force. Gen Ayub Khan in 1963 deprived CHT of its "Excluded Area" status, paving the way for outside interference in their affairs. Consequently, the non-*Jumma* population virtually took over the administration of CHT. As a result, Chakma leader Manabendra Narayan Larma fought 1970 Parliamentary Elections, demanding *inter alia* "autonomy with its own legislature for CHT".

Within days of formation of Bangladesh, which heightened their hopes and aspirations, a group of Jumma leaders led by Larma met Mujib and demanded a 4-point Charter: (1) Autonomy for CHT, with its own legislation. (2) Retention of Regulation 1900 in Bangladesh's constitution and its inviolability. (3) Restoring the offices of Jumma Chiefs. (4) Ban on the influx of non-tribals into CHT. Rejecting their demands outrightly, Mujib urged the Chakmas to merge with Bengali nationalism. Being non-Bengalis ethnically and linguistically, their political aspirations were always suspect. However, the 1972 Bangladeshi Constitution maintained their British Era special status.

With a view to exerting (political) pressure, in March 1972 Larma formed first Chakma political party PCJSS (Parbatiya Chattagram Jana Sanghati Samiti = United People's Party of CHT). Electoral compulsions during the first Parliamentary Elections in 1973 made Mujib espouse Bengali chauvinism, and he declared that Bengali is the only identity in Bangladesh and the Jumma community must embrace it. This was his riposte to Larma's demands for (1) Expulsion of Bengali immigrants settled in CHT after 1972. (2) Compensation for Jumma Kaptai Dam evacuees. (3) Fixation of water level in the Dam at 90 ft. The assassination of Mujib in 1975 made things uncertain for the Chakmas. Going underground, Larma organised militant Gana Mukti Fouz (=People's Liberation Army), popularly Shanti Bahini, which regularly confronted the Government troops. The Zia Government tried to set up a pliable, Chakma leadership but failed; consequently even its development activities in the CHT became suspicious.

Nuanced changes in Bangladeshi national identities further aggravated Chakma apprehensions. Bengali nationalism, instrumental in creation of Bangladesh, ran its course and the ethno-linguistic identity was replaced by religious-Islamic identity. This shifting national identity was not sudden. The 1972 constitution had explicitly underlined the centrality of Bengali nationalism—a clear message to Chakmas. Zia sought to consolidate his position by underscoring the *Bangladeshi* identity. In 1978, he changed the nomenclature of citizenship from *Bengali* to *Bangladeshi.* A Chakma scholar read ominous signals: "The State began a concerted effort to invent the citizen in communally defined ways: Muslim as opposed to Hindu and Bangladeshi as opposed to Bengali (coded to mean Hindu Bengali) or non-Bengali (ethnic minorities, tribals, and Biharis[8])." This transmogrification of national identity created new problems for the Chakmas. They always remained outside the pale of national mainstream. Under Pakistan they were singled out as non-Bengalis in the days of rampant Bengali nationalism, and as the Islamisation process accompanied the post-1971 Bangladeshi nationalism, they were still left out as they were non-Muslims! Did they have a hope of a reconciliation with the majority?

The real problem was the demographic change in CHT, encouraged and promoted by Dhaka. During 1979-83, over 400,000 Bengali Muslims were settled in CHT, lured by a settlement policy underpinned by a host of financial incentives and long-term political implications. It irrevocably impaired the ethno-social fabric of the area.[9] Some argue the settlement policy was motivated by economic and demographic reasons. One-tenth the area of Bangladesh, CHT has one per cent of its population. Endowed with rich resources, it is the single largest reserve forest in Bangladesh. When the influx ruptured the socio-cultural fabric and economic condition of the indigenous people, trouble was bound to follow—and it did. Besides general Chakma unrest, the hopelessness gave birth to the Shanti Bahini. Consequently, the Government adopted repressive measures *vis-a-vis* the Chakmas and the CHT was brought under the Jackboots. The 1972 Constitution had repealed their exclusive status and introduced a land distribution policy unfavourable to the natives, who practised Jhum method. The official policy of settled cultivation was considered an interference in their traditional lifestyle. At times, the settlers, joining hands with the military, an occupation force, perpetrated massacres, which drew widespread attention and condemnation. The Chakmas suffered large scale killings and oppression. It were these developments, namely prolonged neglect of Chakma demands, Islamisation of Bangladesh, forced settlement of outsiders, onset of Chakma militancy, and military/punitive campaigns against them, which led to the third wave of Chakma exodus into India.

It was this wave which produced intractable problem for India. Most Chakmas of second influx were settled in NEFA "which refused to absorb them. In a firm departure from the past, India refused to accept the third wave Chakmas, insisting upon their eventual return/repatriation to their homes in CHT. India had no option, having faced strident opposition over the absorption and rehabilitation of the Chakmas who came to India in the past, especially during the Kaptai dam phase. The proximity of the Region to India's 'turbulent' North-East bred fears that CHT could become a safe haven for some of India's extremist outfits. Hence India's reluctance to accept any further influx of Chakmas and determination to eventually repatriate them to Bangladesh. These refugees were accommodated in camps at Takumbari, Panchrampara, Karbook, Lebachara, Shilachari and Kathalchari— all in the CHT-Tripura border areas. A sustained series of talks led to Indo-Bangladesh Accord on Chakmas, but before that a word on Shanti Bahini.

During the Mujib regime, the two nations had cordial ties. After his assassination in 1975, things turned sour as Bangladesh became friendly with anti-India insurgencies. "India reciprocated by taking Shanti Bahini under its wings", in its fight for autonomy. Once the outfit got Indian help, the movement became more vigorous, also more violent. Bahini leaders like Sudatto Priya Chakma (alias Maj Roxio) confirmed that the Indians trained at least three batches of its leaders, and seven batches of its cadres. The first batch of 22 leaders was trained at Chakrata, and they later became sector and sub-sector commanders for the Shanti Bahini. They gave the nascent Bangladesh Army harrowing times. Bahini leaders also confirmed that India supplied almost its entire weaponry—mostly Chinese small arms captured from the Pak troops in 1971.

The RAW was reportedly pressurising the Bahini during the 1970s to accept an autonomy package offered by Dhaka, its sources asserting that India was funding it just enough to ensure its bare survival. Others suggested that at the peak of guerrilla war in CHT India had promised to train and arm upto 20,000 cadres within 6 months. But its founder leader Manabendra Larma was reluctant to accept the offer lest he might become a play thing into India's hands. But just before Bahini's political arm, the PCJSS, called a meeting of its Central Executive Council, Mrs Gandhi lost the 1977 Elections. Her successor, Morarji Desai, a man of strong principles, discontinued the Indian support to Shanti Bahini and Kaderia Bahini (an outfit of pro-Mujib fighters led by Kader Siddiqui, 1971 war hero), based in Meghalaya.

The Accord

The uncertainties following Mujib's assassination forced India to tread carefully. There was a need to strike a balance between India's desire to seek friendlier ties with Dhaka and her determination to repatriate refugees to CHT. While Dhaka did not declare the Chakmas to be non-Bangladeshis; it denied the presence of its nationals, including Chakmas in India, hence there was no question of their returning to Bangladesh.[10] India's persistence paid and Dhaka initially agreed to accept 6,500 refugees, and the Ershad Government raised the number to 24,000. A formal agreement was reached in December 1986, to go into force on 15 January 1987."[11] On the eve of the deadline, Shanti Bahini cadres attacked a Bangladeshi border post, leading to renewed violence in CHT. It not only halted repatriation process but also resulted in a further exodus.[12] In August 1987, following Foreign Minister P.V. Narasimha Rao's visit, Dhaka agreed to the repatriation of 29,000 Chakmas, though there were over 50,000 refugees in the Tripura Camps. But this agreement led nowhere because Bangladesh Government failed to create conditions which would persuade the refugees to return. Then followed six rounds of talks in 1993 under Khalida Zia but they failed as both sides disagreed on terms, conditions, and size of repatriation. Things changed for better when Sheikh Hasina took over in June 1996. Following seven rounds of talks, the CHT Accord was signed on 2 December 1997 between Dhaka and PCJSS.

The December 1997 Accord was facilitated by India's initiatives. India withdrew its erstwhile support for Shanti Bahini and urged Chakmas to seek political solution to their problems. It was a crucial shift because the Bahini had enjoyed political and logistical support from India since the mid-1970s.

Things began to change in the mid-1980s, especially after Rajiv Gandhi took over in 1984. Desiring a political settlement of ethnic movements in North-East, he reversed the erstwhile policy and ceased India's support to Bahini from March 1985. The reevaluation of this policy was "further impelled by internal divisions within the Bahini and PCJSS. The United Front Ministry's Gujral Doctrine and signing of the December 1996 Ganga Water Accord, favourable to Bangladesh, facilitated the December 1997 CHT Accord.

The Peace Accord formally ended nearly two decade-long tribal insurgency in the three hill districts of the CHT, adjoining India and Bangladesh. The official records say over 9,000 rebels, SF, and civilians were killed and 65,000 tribals displaced in the prolonged insurgency."[13]

Conceding the long-standing demand for autonomy, Dhaka agreed to set up a Regional Council (=Parishad) to govern the Region—CHTRC. Headed by a Jumma leader, CHTRC would be consulted whenever the Government enacted a law concerning CHT. Bangladesh Government would have a ministry headed again by a Jumma leader. The existing local councils of three districts would exercise greater control over land, a major complaint of the Chakmas. Dhaka did not yield on two demands of PCJSS: (1) On troop withdrawal, it did not go beyond closure of temporary camps. (2) It did not agree on eviction of the Bengali settlers. Although, international pressures did play a role in nudging Dhaka towards the Accord, it was opposed to any outside participation in the implementation phase, and outrightly rejected the Chakma demand for a role for the UNHCR or ICRC.[14]

The Opposition Party, BNP, staunchly opposed the Accord and launched a series of nation-wide protests. It blamed Hasina Government and Awami League of (1) "Surrendering one-tenth of country's territory and sovereignty."[15] (2) Forfeiting the fundamental rights of the Bengalis in CHT—thus reducing the non-tribal Bangladeshis residing in CHT to second-class citizens. (3) A sellout to India. The BNP made its intentions clear by refusing to participate in the parliamentary debate when the Accord was ratified in 1998. At one time, it even vowed to cancel the Accord if voted to power, and in tune with this stand, its 2001 Manifesto pledged to "reach an acceptable solution to the problem". And Awami League lost the 2001 Poll.

The implementation of the Accord was not a smooth affair. Sheikh Hasina appointed Kaplaranjan Chakma as Minister for CHT Affairs but she took more than a year to install (on 30 May 1999) the Interim CHTRC of 21 members, headed by its Chairman, Chief Negotiator, and former guerrilla commander Jyotirindra Bodhipriya Larma, better known as Shantu Larma and younger brother of the late M.N. Larma, father of the tribal insurgency who was gunned down by rivals. J.B. Larma, who enjoyed the rank of a State Minister, at the colourful installation ceremony, reiterated his appeal to the Government for 'quick and proper' implementation of the Accord, including withdrawal of army camps except the six cantonments in the 45,000 sq mile rugged region, in line with the Accord.[16] Since early 1998, about 12,000 families numbering 70,000 Chakma refugees have returned to their homes in CHT. In March 1998, about 2,000 cadres of Shanti Bahini surrendered their weapons. But rehabilitation of these refugees has been far from smooth and complete. Presently, over 20,000 Chakmas are designated as "internally displaced returnees", simply because "their land has been grabbed by the settlers". And this when a Land Commission headed by retired judge Anwar-ul-Huq was constituted, though it has since become non-operational following his death. Since land has been the main cause of contention, a popular discontent continues among the Chakmas as the settlers continue to occupy the tribal lands. The continued demographic balance in favour of the Bengali settlers has come under severe criticism even from the international community.[17] If a section of CHT tribals are resentful of the settlers occupying 'their' lands, a sense of unease prevails among the latter.

It needs to be noted that even setting up of interim CHTRC faced many hiccups. In October 1998, PCJSS led by Shantu Larma 'rejected' the formation of the council, alleging that "the Hasina Government did not keep its promise to nominate three Bengali settlers selected by PCJSS to the council".[18]

Fresh unrest has been brewing in CHT in the recent years. The things came to such a pass in November 2000 that J.B. Larma, Chairman of CHTRC and Chief of PCJSS, threatened to go back to bush war because of "failure of the Government" to implement the Peace Accord. It was a sign of the dissensions within the tribal camp that his statement was dubbed "irresponsible" not only by Kalaparanjan Chakma, Minister for CHT Affairs, but also by other top tribal leaders, including Bir Bahadur, MP. Meanwhile, a report by CHT Ministry said that 98 per cent of the Accord has been implemented. The crux of the CHT problem even after signing of the landmark Agreement has not been removed. Charu Bikash Chakma, close friend of M.N. Larma, founding leader of tribal insurgency, explains: "The tribals are still worried about their cultural identity and exclusive rights in the hills while Bengali settlers, majority of whom were brought to the region by military rulers, are worried about their right to reside and earn their livelihood in the region."[19] Tribals, erstwhile predominant majority now reduced to a little more than half of the 1 million CHT population, feel they are original inhabitants of the hills and Bengalis had always ruled the CHT region only under special arrangements, by granting autonomy and exclusive rights to the 13 tribes in the area.

In May 2002, J.B. Larma said the BNP-led Government must take immediate steps to implement the 1997 Peace Accord. He held non-implementation as the main cause of the deteriorating law and order situation. He was speaking "against a backdrop of fresh violence in the hills that claimed at least eleven people in April, leaving scores of others injured".[20] The new wave of violence, which led to many fleeing their homes, was due to clashes between two tribal organisation—one that supports the Accord, viz PCJSS, and other, the anti-Accord United Peoples Democratic Front, UPDF, a front of Pahari Chatro Parishad (PCP), led by hardliners who had opposed the 1997 Accord itself. Larma spoke of his recent good discussions with Premier Khalida Zia but alleged "that the Army is still running the CHT affairs".

The situation in hills was on the boil again in the late 2003, mainly because of clashes between the two tribal armed factions, PCJSS and UPDF, vying for dominance. The SF exchanged heavy gunfire with the armed outfit on 24 December. Larma again demanded withdrawal of the Army, saying there was no civilian rule in CHT. Meanwhile, leaders of Parbatya Garo Parishad (PGP), ruling alliance backed organisation, demanded cancellation of 1997 Accord, and stressed on equal rights for both tribals and Bengalis for establishing peace in the area. The PGP also called for launching of combing operations against the Terrorists operating in the hilly region (Haroon Habib, *Hindu,* 3-1-04). The series of abductions and counter-abductions by the two groups have added a new dimension. So it is two groups fighting each others and the Army combating the terrorists!

The hardliner UPDF had stridently opposed the Peace Accord. Its leader Sanjay Chakma and his colleagues were arrested on 12-1-01. On 16 February 2001, its cadres abducted 3 foreigners, 2 Danes and 1 Briton, when they were conducting a survey for a road project in Rangamati district. The hostages were freed on 17 March when the kidnappers fled after a brief gun battle with the Army commandos who raided their hide-out at Nakshachhara, 35 km off Rangamati Hill town, in deep forests (*Hindu* and *HT*, 18-3-01).

Post-1947, their land and their cultural identity have been major concerns of the Chakmas. Nirupam Chakma, Mizoram Minister and leader of Chakmas of the state alleged in a memorandum to Prime Minister Rao on 2 August 1991 (HT) that the voting process at the time of election to the three District Councils was often manipulated. Bangladesh had constituted the Three District Councils in June 1989 to enable the CHT Tribals to manage the hill affairs themselves. Drawing Mr Rao's attention to the acts of repression and economic exploitation, he recalled that CHT commission on Human Rights had in November 1990 observed: "There is constant denigration of the economic, social and cultural characteristics of the hill people."

East Pakistan/Bangladesh Population: Religious Communities (By Percentages)

Census Year	*Muslim*	*Hindu*	*Remarks*
1901	66.1	33	Minor Groups
1911	67.2	31.5	Buddhist-0.6
1921	68.1	30.6	(1991)
1931	69.5	29.4	Christians-0.3
1941	70.3	28	(1951)
1951	76.9	22	Others-0.3
1961	80.4	18.5	(1991)
1971	85.4	13.5	
1981	86.7	12.1	
1991	88.3	10.5	

Source: Bangladesh Government Websites.

Minority Seats in 315-Member Parliament

Year	*Minority Members*	*Year*	*Minority Members*
1954	72	1988	4
1970	11	1991	11
1973	12	1996	14
1979	8	2001	4
1986	7	—	—

Representation in Army and Police and Banks

	Number of officers: 2/Lt to Maj-Gen		
	Total		*Minority*
Army	3,807		68
	Number of ASP/Asst Com to IG		
	Total		*Minority*
Police	870		53
	Posts	*Total*	*Minority*
Banks	GM	39	1
	Directors	7	0
	Governors	37	3

Source: Amalendu De, *Prasanga Anupprabesh,* Essays on Indo-Bangladesh Demographic Scenario and Influx from Bangladesh, pp. 18 and 19.[21]

There were large numbers of communal (read anti-Hindu) violence before and after the 2001 Poll; and several Hindus were killed, raped and abducted in these incidents—even and especially after Khalida Zia took over. The condition of minority in many aspects has been an unhappy one, as the preceding tables show:

CHAkmAS: TRAVAILS WITHIN INDIA

The luckless Chakmas have been fleeing to India from CHT, ever since India's partition. They have variously been branded as "refugees", "Foreigners" and "Trespassers" (=Takam; an object to be strangulated or butchered). The Chakma question in the North-East remains hopelessly tangled. Presently there are three major Chakma populations concentrated in Tripura, Arunachal and Mizoram, and all are under pressure to leave. They do not seem to be welcome anywhere, not even in Mizoram which they have inhabited even before Partition.

Arunachal Pradesh Chakmas

The community faces the prospect of eviction as "foreigners" after growing roots over four decades. 65,000 Buddhist Chakmas and Hindu Hajongs—the latter 10 per cent of the settlers—had come to India when their villages were inundated by the waters of the Kaptai Dam in 1964—flooding the best farmland and devastating the economy of the Region. Subsequently, they were settled in sparsely-populated NEFA. But things became difficult for these Chakmas in 1995-96 when all political parties lined behind the students who wanted these "foreigners" to be moved out of the State. All Arunachal Pradesh Students Union (AAPSU) issued them a "quit notice" to leave by 30 September 1995. The second notice set the deadline for 31 December 1995. All the 60 MLAs of the State, including Chief Minister Apang and his Ministers, announced that they would resign from their parties as also from Assembly unless the Centre decided by 31 December to deport the Chakmas from the state. Apang seemed to be having his way when the Union Government appointed a high-power committee on 26 December under Prime Minister Rao, which included some other Ministers and Apang to book into the matter. The objective was to stall the 31 December ultimatum.

The Chakmas received hope and relief from another quarter. Acting on a petition filed by the NHRC, the Supreme Court passed an interim order on 2 November 1995 against evictions under coercion or force. The real shot in the arm came when Court delivered final Judgement on 10 January 1996, upholding the right of the Chakmas to apply for the Indian Citizenship, and directed the State Government to register their citizenship. "It is beginning of a victory for us", said Subimal Bikash Chakma, President of Committee for Citizenship Rights of the Chakmas (CCRC) of Arunachal. Itanagar was ordered to use force to thwart any forcible evictions.

In September-October 1995, there were attacks on Chakma settlements, and over 2,000 Chakmas fled to Assam. But they were made to cross back into Arunachal. Guwahati was seldom helpful. On 13 September 1994, Chief

Minister Saikia had asked Tinsukia District administration to issue shoot-at-sight orders to prevent Chakmas from Arunachal entering Assam.[22]

The Court ruled that the citizenship will now be processed by the Centre, through the District Collectors. It castigated the State for refusing to forward their applications, thus denying the Chakmas the right, Constitutional and statutory, to be considered for registration as citizens of India. In 1992, Home Minister (State) M.M. Jacob had told Parliament that "there was no question of deporting these refugees from Arunachal", adding that there were no reports of their involvement in anti-national activities. Arunachal officials have been speaking about these refugees indulging in criminal and anti-national activities, expressing concern about the Central Government accepting their demand for citizenship.[23]

Between August 1994 and December 1995, the CCRC repeatedly complained to NHRC about the AAPSU issuing threats and ultimatums to Chakmas. Accepting the evidence given by NHRC that economic blockades called by AAPSU after 30 October 1994 had affected the supply of the rations and medical and other essential supplies, the Court noted that "there exists a clear and present danger to the lives and personal liberties of Chakmas". Denied basic education in the three districts of Changlang, Lohit, and Papumpara, they had faced the worst economic blockades since September 1994. Subimal explained their plight (January 1996): "We are not allowed to buy or sell in the market.... AAPSU activists beat shopkeepers who transact with Chakmas. Fields of ginger, our main produce, lie rotting. Our ration cards and Public Distribution System facilities were withdrawn (1991) on the ground that agricultural items produced by us are sufficient to meet out demands." The litany of woes goes on. The only middle school in Changlang was closed down in 1994. The Miao HS School where Subimal studied does not admit Chakmas. In Lohit district, the lone Primary School was wound up in 1995. At least 37 *anganwadi* centres in Changlang and Lohit districts have been shut down" (*The Frontline,* 9-2-96).

The demand for their eviction will possibly strengthen the Chakma demand for UT Status in Arunachal, as their counterparts have already done in Mizoram.

Though the Chakmas have managed to stay on in the State, they have suffered immensely. The process of Chakma dispossession started long ago. Employment opportunities in the State Government, open to them until 1980, were closed that year. The issue of trade licences was stopped and those given till 1975 were cancelled. Not only ration was denied to them but even the ration cards issued to them were confiscated to prevent the holders from claiming voting rights.

Citizenship could have ended their helplessness. The Centre is all for it. But if the centre has hung back, it is because the State Government and AAPSU are irreconciliably opposed to the communities. It being a sensitive state abutting China and facing threatening noises from its leaders, New Delhi perhaps felt it wise to let sleeping dogs lie.

Arunachal (had) attracted the greatest attention among the three states, mainly for two reasons. Here, attempts were made to brand the entire community as foreigners and evict it en bloc though it is not made up of illegal immigrants—it was settled here by the Centre four decades ago when it was NEFA and part of Assam.

Tripura Chakmas

58,000 refugees (1996 figure) who fled CHT in the wake of military crack down against Shanti Bahini in the late 1980s, continue to live in camps/ settlements on Bangladesh/Tripura border. The stalemate continues because the refugees have spurned offers from Dhaka to take them back, saying the conditions in CHT, which had been their home, were not yet conducive.

More than a lakh of Chakma and other non-Muslim tribals, living in various refugee camps in India, majority in Tripura, are being sought to be sent to their original home in CHT—being an economic and social burden on India's limited resources, and also resented by the locals. In early July 1995, following the talks between PCJSS leader, J.B. Larma and Bangladesh Workers Party Chief, Rashid Khan, at Duduk Onhari in Khagra-Chhari district of CHT, cease-fire between Bangladesh SF and Shanti Bahini, due to lapse by the end of that month, was extended till the end of September. Under an agreement between New Delhi and Dhaka for the return of the refugees the much-awaited third phase of repatriation in June 1995 did not materialise. It was a shock to many. A fact-finding Indian team found sense of insecurity and uncertainty prevailing there. The first two batches of Chakma refugees were never rehabilitated as per the Agreement, because the land, primary means of livelihood, and which had been stolen by the Muslim settlers from the plains was never allotted to them. That was the minimum expectations of the returning Chakmas, leave aside the threat to the honour, dignity, and the all-pervading sense of terror. Again the SF had continued to occupy the houses abandoned by the fleeing Chakmas. Upendra Lal Chakma, President of Jumma Refugees Welfare Association, saw little chance of rehabilitation in Bangladesh until certain conditions, like the involvement of UNHCR and IRC in their rehabilitation process, are met. And this demand has always been rejected out of hand.

That temporary cessation of hostilities in 1995 was of no help to Chakmas who have been struggling for a fair deal ever since 1947 but received only harassment and humiliation. Victims of religious bigotry in an Islamic State, they have been fleeing to India for shelter and succour. They had a glimmer of hope in the 1997 Peace Treaty. But no substantial gains—by way of their return to their homes—came their way as the BNP was deadly opposed to the Treaty from day one. Whatever little hope they had banished when that Party won the 2001 Poll. They are continuing to live in the camps. They have not forgotten the days when, at one time, 30,000 Bangladeshi troops were trampling their land and their honour under their feet. They are wary of returning to that nightmare.

Mizoram Chakmas

In Mizoram too, the community faced hostility in the mid-1990s. They are living along the State's western border with CHT, in its southern part. Here too, two opposition parties, the MNF and Brig Sailo's People's Conference (PC) now Mizoram Janata Dal (MJD) as well as the powerful students organisation, Mizo Zirlai Pawi (MZP) had asked all Chakmas who came after 26 January 1950, to leave the State by 31 December 1995. The State Government issued a notification asking all foreigners to leave voluntarily by 24 December 1995.[24] And this when the Chakmas have political identity of their own in the shape of an (Chakma) Autonomous District Council (CADC) in Mizoram's Chhimtuipui district. Many of them are Indians but sharp rise in their numbers, "from 39,000 in 1981 to an estimated 80,000 in 1994 in State's population of 700,000,"[25] alarmed the Mizos— People and Government. The astounding rise, (over 100 per cent), in a decade led to the beginning of a political movement seeking their ouster.

The MZP is spearheading the "oust-Chakma movement". In late 1995, its activists fanned out into Chakma villages to "help" prevent Chakmas from registering themselves on the electoral rolls. "In places, the Chakmas were assaulted and their houses burnt down." To most Mizos, "foreigners" and Chakma migrants are synonymous. Ironically they do not regard the Chins of Burma—many of them live in Aizawl, and work in the handloom industry, forests and in homes as well as on construction sites across the State—as "foreigners". Indeed, the Mizos and Chins are kin: looking alike, speaking the same language, and having relatives on either side of the border. Seasonal movement of the Chins into and out of Mizoram are accepted as normal, even if few Mizos migrate to Burma, where economic condition are less inviting.

MZP wants to throw the "foreign" Chakmas out as most of them are outsiders. The latter claim that they are in the area even before the Mizos entered it though it is acknowledged that 'some' did come in illegally. Yet, there is no part of the North-East which does not host illegal migrants (mostly Muslims) from Bangladesh and none has been able to deport them (The worst sufferers in this regard have been Assam and Tripura).

The Mizos who got UT status in 1972 (and then full-fledged State in 1987) did not like the idea of the centre granting District Council to the Chakmas the same year. "The result was a simmering rage that is finding expression in the current (1995-96) campaign against the Chakmas." There was a talk in Aizawl in 1995 about the opposition moving a resolution in the Assembly for derecognition of Chakma District Council. That showed the level of distrust between the two communities.

Given the situation, it was no surprise that the Chakmas started demanding, a 'homeland' for themselves in Mizoram, viz a Union Territory (UT). Leaders of three Chakma organisations—Young Men's Buddhist Association, Young Buddhist Welfare Association, and Young Chakma Association—in a memorandum to Prime Minister Rao in October 1995 argued for a UT consisting of Chakma-inhabited areas of southern and south-western Mizoram. There are 25,000 Chakmas in Chhimtuipui district, covered by CADC (Chakma Autonomous District Council). 25-30,000 live in other two districts of Lunglei and Aizwal, sans any autonomous unit. The demand for UT was spurred by a shrill anti-foreigners agitation that focussed so sharply on Chakmas that others such as Nepalis, Myanmarese, and ethnic Bengalis from Bangladesh seemed to have been forgotten. The MNF, MJD and MZP have created a popular belief in a "large-scale Chakma influx". Leaders of MNF, MJD and MZP, and others including Chief Minister Lalthanhawla of the Congress (I), in a memorandum to the CEC in 1995 claimed that the 1991 Census figures showed an abnormal increase in the population of Chakma and other minority communities since 1981. 3,327 names of Chakmas were struck off the roll during the revision that year. The revision was challenged because the disenfranchised claimed they were the genuine voters. If all the Chakmas who came after 26 January 1950 are to be disenfranchised, an extremist stance espoused by MZP (and also by the MNF-affiliated Mizo National Defender, MND), that would mean only 3.3 per cent Chakmas are entitled to be citizens.

That the Congress Government was not willing to side with extremist stand was evident when the 15 June 1995 deadline set by MZP for foreigners to quit passed without much effect. In the Assembly, an MNF sponsored resolution for eviction was defeated by the Congress (I) on the ground that the Chakmas were not the only foreigners in the state.

The Chakma Autonomous District Council (CADC) functioning since 1972 has not been able to improve the socio-economic conditions of the tribe, the third largest after Pawi and Lakher and least developed among the three—mainly because of isolation and poor communications in their areas. The CADC stretches over only 1,500 km^2 and covered only 25,623 Chakmas (in 1992). More Chakmas are residing outside the CADC area. Here is a picture of their underdeveloped state:

1. Kamlanagar is headquarters of CADC. "The shortest road linking Kamlanagar is a 3-day journey on foot from the nearest point on the Lunglei-Demagiri metalled road."
2. Most areas in CADC are without electricity and health care.
3. First Primary, ME and High School in their area were opened in 1959, 1972 and 1979 respectively. By 1991, there were 42 Primary and 2 High Schools, and no college in the CADC area. There were only 12 graduates, 18 PUs and 138 matriculates in the "60,000 Chakma population of Mizoram".

The Chakmas do not seem to be getting a fair deal from rhe Government either. Saiha, Headquarters of Chhimtuipui district, lies in the Lakher ADC area. The district-level officers/departments are concentrated there. So the fruits of all technical departments are enjoyed mostly by the Pawis and Lakhers-Saiha being far away from Chakma area. 60 and 30 per cent of the district grants are utilised by the Lakhers and Pawis respectively, leaving a paltry 10 per cent for the Chakmas. If they nurture sense of grievances against the State Government, they have their reasons. Again, of the 5 Chhimtuipui district seats in Mizoram Assembly, 2 each are allotted to Pawis and Lakhers, leaving one for the Chakmas. Feeling discriminated against, they want consolidation of Chakma-inhabited areas of Lunglei and Aizawl districts in another ADC. Hence the demand for a UT of their own. They have another grievance. The Chakma-dominated area of Demagiri was once a part of CHT. In 1893, when the two districts of south and north Lushai Hills were merged to constitute the Lushai Hills district, a strip on the eastern end of the CHT, including Demagiri, with a population of 1,500 was transferred to it for administrative reasons. So they feel this area should have been included in the CADC jurisdiction.

NON-MIZO TRIBES UNDER SIXTH SCHEDULE

The main idea behind the framing of the Sixth Schedule was to provide simple and inexpensive administrative machinery in the tribal districts of Assam to enable them to protect their customary laws, traditional institutions, forests, law of inheritance, and their mode of administration of justice. It also provided them political autonomy within the Union.

Based on the provisions enshrined in the Sixth Schedule, the Government of Assam enacted Autonomous District (Constitution of the District Council) Act in 1951. Consequently, the Lushai Hills District Council (later, Mizo District Council) came into being, with 24 members, on 23 April 1952 and the Pawi-Lakher Regional Council, with 12-member, on 23 April 1953.

Mizo District Council

Created in 1952, it functioned for 20 years till 1972 when it ceased to exist as the Mizo District was elevated to the status of a UT. It enacted some useful laws and functioned well for initial few years. It often failed to implement rules framed by itself, e.g. the Council was never summoned thrice a year.[26] The heavy expenditure over establishment became a burden on the State Exchequer, even if it was not an exception in this respect, when compared to other District Councils under the Sixth Schedule. It was also criticised for not tapping its resources optimally. Out of 6919 m^2 of land, only 70 m^2 had been assessed. Others hold it did not have sufficient power and authority to take effective part in the development schemes.

Regional Councils

To grant a measure of autonomy, smaller tribes were provided with the Regional Councils. Thus Pawi-Lakher Regional Council (PL-RC) was constituted on 23 April 1953 to safeguard to ethnic interests of Pawi and Lakher tribes, as also of the Chakmas, generally settled in their areas. Its functioning was marred from the day one due to the linguistic incompatibility of the two tribes.

Functioning of PL-RC started stumbling soon after its constitution. The first problem was of language which could work as lingua franca for three communities. The first meeting of the PL-RC was held, reportedly, without understanding each other's language. Because Mizo was used to transact Council business, the Lakhers and Chakmas could hardly follow the language, and for that reason if became virtually impossible to hold any meeting together. Ultimately, in 1958 the Lakhers decided to keep off the PLRC meetings, leading to a stalemate in the functioning of the PLRC. So, around 1970-71, the Union Home Ministry was seriously engaged in the idea of granting separate Regional Councils (RCs) to the three communities. A Lakher Chief told the Union Minister of State for Home Affairs that there would be bloodshed if the Pawis and Lakhers are grouped together under the roof a single District Council again.[27]

In late 1971, the Centre decided to disband PL-RC and establish three Regional Councils, one each for the Pawis, Lakhers and Chakmas. When Mizoram was granted UT status in 1972, the three RCs,were upgraded to the status of District Councils (DC)— Pawi DC, Lakher DC, and Chakma DC.

Why were Chakmas initially not granted their own RC or DC under Sixth Schedule? It is a story of misfortune that bears retelling, al be it briefly. In their 1000-year old journey, which started from Arakan, they moved towards further north and west—meeting in the CHT and its adjoining areas and then spreading upto the Bay of Bengal, until it was trammelled by the emergence of Bangladesh and the 1971 reorganisation of India's North-East. Early history of their settlement on the banks of River Karnafulee, and around the confluence of Karnafulee, Tuichawng and Thega, can be traced to the year 1763 when the East India Company by a Proclamation demarcated the Chakma territory as spreading over "all the hills from Pheni River to the Sangoo and from Nizampur Road in Chittagong to the Hills of Kooki Raja" (possibly meaning the South Lushai Hills).[28] It has already been described how the Rutton Puiyas villages including Demagiri (Its very name suggests that it has been inhabited by the people of ancient Indian origin) became part of South Lushai on 1 April 1898, earlier having been part of the CHT. So obviously, Chakmas were a distinct tribe from the Lushais. But a researcher says: "The tribes occupying the territory from the North Patkoi to the south of the Chin Hills of Burma formed a single ethnic unit, closely knit in race and culture.... These tribes (the Kukis, Chins, Lushais, Hill Tipperahs, Chakmas and Mughs)[29] despite being mutually estranged due to exigencies, political or otherwise, must have, at the same time, influenced one another in diverse ways and at different times, through innumerable points of contact."[30] One opinion says Demagiri originally belonged to the Lushai Chief Rutton Puiya who later gave it up to the British—and not other way around. "Rutton Puiya had strong economic ties with the Chakmas; many of whom lived in and around Demagiri."[31] It seems that the ethnic group inhabiting this region as original settlers comprised Chakmas as well. So when Demagiri area was transferred to South Lushai Hills from CHT, as a result, the Chakma Raja "had to forego some of his land and subjects who had been inhabiting beyond River Thegakhal".[32] In due course, the Chakmas inhabiting the eastern banks of rivers Thegakhal, Tuichawng, Mar, and their tributaries started being reckoned as the inhabitants of the Lushai Hills. An MLA (F. Lalchhawna) once dilated upon the history of the Chakmas in southern Mizoram: "During British period, I had the experience of working among the Chakmas as circle interpreter under SDO Lunglei. The Chakmas then were allowed to settle in Landhoka Lokicherry. Their grievances were not officially taken up by the court unless they had a badge of Peace Camp. Their land was vast but sparsely populated."[33]

A word on the plight of Chakmas in later years. They were the predominant inhabitants of CHT—97.18 per cent of its population in 1872. In 1881, not much before the transfer of Demagiri area to South Lushamills, they made 72.13 per cent of the CHT population. Subsequent to India's Partition, due to persistent persecution and atrocities on them, the Chakmas from CHT crossed over to the Lushai Hills across the Thegakhal, *i.e.* River Kawrpui. They became the Pakistani, and later Bangladeshi (Chakma) refugees in India. F. Lalramliana. MLA, avers: "Right from the British days, the land lying between the Chawng and Kawrpui Rivers, was occupied by the Chakmas... (Later), the Chakmas had come in from Bangladesh towards the areas occupied by the Tuikuk, Pang, Tlanglam, Pawi (tribes) etc. and settled down in the unoccupied areas."[34] This influx seems to have alarmed, if not antagonised the Lushais against the Chakmas. So when it was time for the Constituent

Assembly and Bordoloi Committee to discuss the question of granting District Council to the Lushais and Regional Councils to the minorities like Pawi, Lakher and Chakma, several negative factors worked against the latter, particularly the Chakmas inhabiting the western part of South Mizoram. One, barring two co-opted members from Lushai tribe, all the minority tribes went unrepresented in this committee. The report of this Committee was so lop-sided that its Para 2(b) said: "The Lushai Hills district except for an inappreciable number of Lakhers in the extreme south contain a uniform population."[35] So, if the Pawis failed to merit recognition as one of the larger STs of erstwhile Lushai Hills, at the hands of the Committee, and consequently, the Constituent Assembly, what hope could the Chakmas nurture for themselves—of having a Regional Council of "their own? So whatever attention and consideration the Committee bestowed on the Pawis and Lakhers was the result of "some deal between its Chairman and the Mizo Union".[36] Two, all such deliberations were based on the 1941 Census which was doubted even by certain members of the Constituent Assembly. Three, many of the Chakma villages were under Lushai/non-Chakma Chiefs. A senior political leader from South Mizoram (then MLA and later MP), Hiphei, explains: "The Lushai and Lakher...seemed to be the first recognised STs, since there was a clerk each from their ranks, but none from others. There was no politician from the area presently represented by Chhimtuipui district, so the Chiefs took up all political matters. Besides, they, being on good terms with the British, were given the choice about creating institutions under Sixth Schedule.... So Mizo district was created for the majority tribe, and Pawis and Lakhers, being similar tribes, were made to share the PLRC. There were reasons for Chakmas being ignored. The chieftainship of Pu Thangchhukheia, not having been born to a chief, had been derecognized by the British; so the area inhabited by the Chakmas then had no chief. Consequently, since they did not belong to the Lushai clan, and had no specific area of their own, the Chakmas were placed under the PL-RC."[37]

That is how the Chakmas, the third largest non-Lushai ST after Pawi and Lakher in the then Lushai Hills district during 1941-51, were denied a RC and placed under the PL-RC. Suhas Chatterjee has also another reason for Chakmas being in disfavour; "The English officers like Raben, Lewin, Murray, etc. took the help of the Chakmas to subdue South Lushai. Later, the Lushais and others got converted to Christianity and adopted English as 'medium of instruction' and thus became favourite of the British. The Chakmas, refusing to convert, were neglected.[38] Lack of education even at the high school level, and consequent absence of political awareness, can also be ascribed to their failure to get a RC of their own. The opposite view is that as there were so many minority tribes[39] vying for attention, the larger two among them were granted a RC, viz Pawi and Lakher. Interestingly, even the naming of the PL-RC posed problems—should the term Pawi be written first, or otherwise.

Two Chakmas were elected to the first 10-member PL-RC in 1953—confirming their position as one of the larger minority tribes of Mizoram. For the same reason, one Chakma was nominated as a member to the Mizo District Council in 1952. The functioning of the PL-RC and its subsequent disbandment have already been a covered above.

NOTES

1. Saradindu Mukherji, *HT,* 10-8-95.
2. Sanjoy Hazarika, *HT,* 1-1-96.
3. *Seen* n 1.
4. Indeed, the fate of CHT remained undecided at the time of Partition. It was resolved only on 16 August 1947, a day after the Indian Independence, when it was awarded to Pakistan (Sabyasachi Basu Ray-Chaudhury and Ashis K. Biswas, A *Diaspora is made: The Jummas in North-East India*; Subir Bhaumik et al. (ed), *Living on the edge: Essays on the CHT* (Calcutta: South Asia Forum for Human Rights, Calcutta Research Group), p. 139.
5. Sreeradha Datta, Scholar, IDSA, New Delhi; her Paper *The Minorities in Bangladesh: Study of Hindus and Chakmas,* 2-8-03.
6. *See* n 1.
7. The Chakmas pleaded with Dhaka for decreasing the height of the Dam, arguing that lower reservoir level would submerge for less area, especially the Island settlement. But as the navigation in the Chittagong sea-port depends upon the water level in the Karnafuli river, this fact dictated the control and flow of water from the reservoir.
8. Lamia Karim, *Pushed to the Margins: Adviasi Peoples in Bangladesh and the case of Kalpana Chakma,* in Contemporary South Asia, Vol. 7, No. 3, p. 308.
9. *Report of the International Working Group for Indigenous Affairs— Human Rights in CHT*. Bangladesh, submitted to the SEC, of the UN, Geneva, 12-6-91, cited Sreeradha Datta, n 5.
10. Statement of Bangladeshi Foreign office spokesman of 30-10-80.
11. *Asian Recorder,* Jan. 29-Feb. 4, 1987, p. 19291.
12. *Asian Recorder,* July 2-8, 1987, p. 19531.
13. Haroon Habib, *The Hindu,* 1-6-99.
14. Chaudhury and Biswas, n 4, pp. 164-65.
15. *Asian Recorder,* 8-14 January, 1998, p. 27004.
16. Habib, n 13.
17. *See* www. derechos. org/nizkor/europe/palamento/bengalae. htm for the text of the resolution of the European Parliament which also discussed the settler question.

18. Haroon Habib, *The Hindu,* 31-10-98.
19. *Hindu,* 17-11-2000.
20. *Hindu,* 9-5-2002.
21. *See n.* 5.
22. T.K. Rajalakshmi, *Frontline,* 9-2-96.
23. P.M. Sayeed. MOS Home, said in July 1994 that "the Chakma/Hajong refugees, who entered India before 25 March 1971, would be considered for grant of Indian citizenship". New Delhi reaffirmed its intention on the issue in November 1994 (*Frontline,* 9-2-96).
24. Tapas Ray, *Frontline,* 12-1-96.
25. Sanjoy Hazarika, *HT,* 1-1-96.
26. Collection of Mizo District Council Acts and Rules, p. 130.
27. Proceedings of Mizoram Legislative Assembly: 5th Session of the Fourth Mizoram Legislative Assembly; published by the Assembly Secretariat, Aizawl, pp. 111-36.
28. R.H. Hutchison, *Chittagong Hills Tracts,* p. 24.
29. B.S. Guha, 1911 (1951).
30. Sarin (1980), p. 177.
31. Suhas Chatterjee, *Mizoram Encyclopaedia,* 1970, Vol. I, pp. 155-60.
32. S.P. Talukdar, *The Chakmas: Life and Struggle.*
33. *See* n 27.
34. *See* n 27.
35. B. Shiva Rao (ed), *The Framing of India's Constitution: Select Documents,* Vol. III.
36. Sarin (1980), p. 204.
37. *See* n 27.
38. *See* n 31.
39. The minority tribes were Chakma, Pang, Tuikuk, Tlanglau, etc.

10

Manipur : Some select Terrorist Outfits

Manipur has the dubious distinction of having largest number of militant/ insurgent outfits operating within its boundaries—about 50 at one time. Some of these have been mentioned in chapter 1. Here follows a somewhat detailed look at some of the terrorist outfits. List of terrorist groups of Manipur appears on the next page.

The terrorist outfits' detailed descriptions end up with time line of incidents over the last few years.

Kangleipak Communist Party (KCP)

Formation

The Kangleipak Communist Party (KCP) was formed on April 13, 1980, under the leadership of Y. Ibohanbi. Although the group is ostensibly Communist, named after the historical name of Manipur, i.e. Kangleipak, the KCP is more concerned with the preservation of Meitei culture and demands secession of Manipur from India.

Founder of the KCP, Y. Ibohanbi, was killed during a security force operation in 1995. Subsequently, the KCP split into several factions such as the ones headed by City Meitei (KCP- City Meitei), Prithvi (KCP-P), Mangang (KCP-M) and Noyon (KCP-N). On May 30, 2005, four front-ranking KCP cadres, including Moirangthem Boicha alias Prithvi, chief of the KCP-P, and his wife Ibemcha Devi were killed during an encounter with the security forces (SFs) at Nongada Makha Leikai in the Imphal East district.

Following a decision taken during a five-day central committee meeting held during May 4-8, 2006, the KCP factions are reported to have merged together.

Objectives

The main objective of KCP is to restore the independence of the erstwhile Manipur kingdom and to bring about an egalitarian society, which is to be achieved by uniting all ethnic-Mongoloid groups belonging to South-East of Himalayan region, liberating Manipur from the Indian rule, building up the strength of the working class and reviving the indigenous culture.

Terrorist/Insurgent Groups - Manipur

Proscribed Terrorist/ Insurgent Groups	*Active Terrorist/Insurgent Groups*	*Inactive Terrorist/ Insurgent Groups*
• **Kangleipak Communist Party (KCP)**	• **Hmar People's Convention-Democracy (HPC-D)**	• Chin Kuki Revolutionary Front (CKRF)
• Kanglei Yawol Kanna Lup (KYKL)	• Kuki Liberation Army (KLA)	• Hmar People's Convention (HPC)
• Manipur People's Liberation Front (MPLF)	• Kuki National Army (KNA)	• Hmar Revolutionary Front (HRF)
• People's Liberation Army (PLA)	• Kuki National Front (KNF)	• Indigenous People's
• **People's Revolutionary Party of Kangleipak (PREPAK)**	• Kuki Revolutionary Army (KRA)	• Revolutionary Alliance (IRPA)
• United National Liberation Front (UNLF)	• National Socialist Council of Nagaland–Isak-Muivah (NSCN-IM)	• Iripak Kanba Lup (IKL)
	• People's United Liberation Front (PULF)	• Islamic Revolutionary Front (IRF)
	• United Kuki Liberation Front (UKLF)	• Islamic National Front (INF)
	• **Zomi Revolutionary Army (ZRA)**	• Kangleipak Kanba Kanglup (KKK)
		• Kangleipak Liberation Organisation (KLO)
		• Kom Rem People's Convention (KRPC)
		• Kuki Defence Force (KDF)
		• Kuki Independent Army (KIA)
		• Kuki International Force (KIF)
		• Kuki Liberation Front (KLF)
		• Kuki National Organisation (KNO)
		• Kuki National Volunteers (KNV)
		• Kuki Revotionary Front (KRF)
		• Kuki Security Force (KSF)

Proscribed Terrorist/ Insurgent Groups	*Active Terrorist/Insurgent Groups*	*Inactive Terrorist/ Insurgent Groups*
		• Manipur Liberation Tiger Army (MLTA) • North East Minority Front (NEMF) • People's Republican Army (PRA) • Revolutionary Joint Committee (RJC) • United Islamic Liberation Army (UILA) • United Islamic Revolutionary Army (UIRA) • Zomi Revolutionary Volunteers (ZRV)

The KCP has, in the past passed decrees with an objective of widening its level of social acceptability. In February 2005, it banned Government doctors in Manipur from working in private clinics. In April 2005, the KCP pressed for the introduction of the Manipuri script, Meetei Mayek, in educational institutions in the State. In September 2005, the outfit banned shooting and exhibition of digital movies and music albums for a year.

Leadership

The KCP held its 'second national convention' on October 20-23, 2006, at an undisclosed location in Manipur and reconstituted the Party Central Committee. The party hierarchy consists of:

1. President - Senggoi Meetei
2. Vice President - K. K. Mangang
3. General Secretary - K. K. Nganba
4. Information and Publicity - H Poirei
5. Organisation Secretary - Sh. Pakhangba

The KCP started with a small number of cadres. However, its strength has grown over the years and presently, it is known to have about 100 cadres. Half of its active cadres are known to possess an array of weapons ranging from AK series rifles, US carbine, Chinese-made grenades and mortars.

Areas of Operation

The KCP is mostly active in the valley areas of Manipur, though it has also been found to be engaged in extortion and other activities in the hill districts, such as Churchandpur.

Funding

Like most other insurgent groups in the northeast, the KCP funds its activities through extortion of local villagers and businessmen.

Linkages

The KCP has a close working relationship with most of the outfits operating in the valley districts of Manipur. Even though, the UNLF had imposed a ban on the City Meitei faction of the KCP in the beginning of 2006, the ban was reportedly revoked to pave way for the unification of various factions. In October 2005, the KYKL too had banned the KCP-P.

In the past, the KCP maintained operational linkages with the National Socialist Council of Nagaland-Khaplang (NSCN-K) and the United Liberation Front of Asom (ULFA).

Incidents involving Kangleipak Communist Party : 2006

December 25: Security force personnel arrested a Kangleipak Communist Party (KCP) militant, Khumanthem Sunil Singh alias Nanao alias Tomnao, at Awang Khunou in the Imphal East district.

December 24: Two suspected KCP militants identified as S/S Captain Tombi and S/S Lt. Rajesh were shot dead by security force personnel during a counter insurgency operation at Gova-jang village under Moreh police station in the Chandel district along India-Myanmar border.

December 18: A KCP militant, Longjam Bidyananda alias Abung alias Ingba, was arrested by the SFs.

December 3: Two Kangleipak Communist Party cadres are shot dead by the SF personnel in a counter-insurgency operation at Khonaithong village in the Thoubal district. An SLR and one AK-56 rifle along with ammunition were recovered from their possession.

December 1: A youth, Gurumayum Sunil, was shot at and injured and subsequently paraded before the media by the UNLF cadres at an unspecified place in the Imphal East district, for his alleged involvement in extortion at Soibam Leikai. The UNLF claimed that Sunil was a former KCP cadre.

November 22: During a search operation, police arrested four KCP cadres from unspecified locations in the capital Imphal.

One KCP cadre, Laishram Ranjit Singh alias Manaoi, was arrested by SFs at Patsoi.

November 21: SFs arrested one KCP militant, 'corporal' G.B. Thoiba, from Keibi in the Imphal East district.

October 30: The security forces shot dead a cadre of the Kangleipak Communist Party, 'private' Suranjoy Singh, at Laipham Khunou Mayai Leikai under Heingang Police station in the Imphal East District. One nine mm pistol along with a magazine containing three live rounds was recovered from the slain militant.

October 19: The 'general secretary' of the KCP, identified as Ksh Noyon alias Laba, who was arrested from Khudengtabi near Moreh in the Chandel district, is later remanded to police custody for seven days by the Chief Judicial Magistrate in Imphal.

Kanglei Yawol Kanna Lup (KYKL)

Formation

Kanglei Yawol Kanna Lup (KYKL), meaning "the Organisation to save the revolutionary movement in Manipur" is a Meitei terrorist group formed in January 1994 following merger of the Oken faction of the United National Liberation Front (UNLF), the Meiraba faction of People's Revolutionary Party of Kangleipak (PREPAK) and the Ibo Pishak faction of the Kangleipak Communist Party (KCP).

The outfit suffered a major setback after its inception when two of its top leaders—'chairman' N, Oken and 'commander-in-chief' N. Thouba Singh, were reportedly arrested on an unspecified date. Earlier during 1995-96, a large number of its lower-ranking cadres either deserted the outfit or surrendered before the security forces. Further in 1996, the outfit split into—the KYKL (O), led by Namoijam Oken and KYKL (T) led by Achou Toijamba. However, after five years of inter-group rivalry, the Oken and Toijamba factions decided to reunite sometime in mid-February 2002. Reports indicated that the move was prompted by the purported objective of unity among various terrorist outfits in the region.

Objective

The purported objective of the KYKL is to 'rebuild' the Manipuri society by clearing it of all vices like immoral activities, drug trade and corruption. According to the KYKL 'Public Relations Officer' S.K. Loya, the group stands for 'nationalism' of the entire Northeastern region to be based on the principle of "all for one and one for all". Towards the end of 2001, the outfit launched 'Operation New Kangleipak' (ONK), an 'anti-corruption' campaign to 'clean up' the educational system in Manipur. While the outfit continues its activities under the ONK, it has also pledged open support to other terrorist groups who reportedly work against the narcotics trade, drug addiction, immoral activities and corruption in the society.

Leadership

Following reunification in 2002, the outfit has formed an ad hoc 'central executive committee', with Achou Toijamba as 'chairman' and Keisham Yaima as the 'general secretary'. It has also formed a 'military commission' known as Meeyamgi Yawol Lanmee (MYL), which is jointly headed by Namoijam Oken and Toijam Ibochou. Keirungba Khuman is the 'deputy finance secretary' in whose name extortion notes to the general public are reportedly issued.

Areas of Operation

The outfit primarily operates in the four valley districts of Imphal East, Bishenpur, Thoubal and Imphal West in Manipur.

Source of Funding

KYKL funds its activities primarily through extortion that it collects jointly with the Nagaland-based National Socialist Council of Nagaland-Isak Muivah (NSCN-IM). For instance, media reports had indicated that an unidentified faction of the KYKL had aimed to extort between Rupees 20 million to 30 million during the February 2002 Legislative Assembly elections in Manipur.

Linkages

The outfit has close linkages with the Nagaland-based NSCN-IM. Further, indications of a re-grouping of terrorist outfits in the region was visible towards the later part of the year 2002 with the nexus between the Zomi Revolutionary Army (ZRA), Kanglei Yawol Kanna Lup (KYKL) and the NSCN-IM. Besides, the KYKL has also developed 'working arrangements' with the Meghalaya-based Achik National Volunteer Council (ANVC). Reports have also indicated that KYKL maintains links with the Khaplang faction of the NSCN (NSCN-K) with the latter providing training and shelter to KYKL cadres at its bases in Myanmar.

Incidents

2006

- December 16: SF personnel arrest a Kanglei Yawol Kanna Lup (KYKL) militant, identified as Haorokcham Premkumar alias Sanayaima, from Konthoujam Mayai Leikai in the Imphal West district.
- December 15: One KYKL militant, Y. Nabachandra alias Naba, is arrest by security force personnel during a search operation at Maidangpok Awang Leikai in the Imphal West district.
- December 12: SF personnel arrested a Kanglei Yawoi Kanna Lup (KYKL) militant, identified as Oinam Birjit Singh, from Kakching Khunou in the Thoubal district.
- December 10: SF personnel arrested a KYKL cadre, Takhellambam Shanta, during a search operation in the capital Imphal. Two letters detailing the expenditure of the outfit were recovered from his possession.
- November 21: Six KYKL militants, Kiomeiton Singh, Inaobi Singh, Aprameshwar Singh, Somorjit Singh and Maipak Singh, were arrested

during a search operation at Phungreitang in the Ukhrul district. Chinese 9 mm pistol with two live rounds, two live rounds of 7.62 mm and extortion letters are recover from their possession.

- November 4: Kanglei Yawol Kanna Lup (KYKL) captured and later shot at and wounded two persons, Seram Angou-sana and Sapam Jonjon alias Sanayamba, for allegedly extorting money in guise of cadres of the outfit. The duo is later paraded before media at two unspecified places in the Imphal East district.
- October 30: Two Kanglei Yawol Kanna Lup (KYKL) cadres including a woman are arrest from Indira Park Imphal.The woman cadre was identified as Kshetrimayum Tamphashana alias Bina Devi while the other cadre was identified as Khangembam Premjit alias Prem alias Basanta.
- October 28: The security forces (SFs) arrested a KYKL cadre identified as Khulem Bidur Singh of Luker in the Imphal West district.
- October 26: Kanglei Yawol Kanna Lup (KYKL) warned an officer of the State Education Department, S Geeta, of 'capital punishment' in case of her failure to 'surrender' to the outfit within seven days, S Geeta along with another official, S. Shamu President of AMESTA, are allegedly involved in siphoning off huge amount of funds meant for mid-day meal scheme.
- October 30: Two KYKL cadres, including a woman, were arrested from Indira Park Imphal.
- October 28: The security forces arrested a KYKL cadre, identified as Khulem Bidur Singh of Luker, in the Imphal West district.
- October 26: Kanglei Yawol Kanna Lup warned an officer of the State Education Department, S Geeta, of 'capital punishment' in case of her failure to 'surrender' to the outfit within seven days, S Geeta along with another official, S.Shamu President of AMESTA, was allegedly involved in siphoning off huee amount of funds meant for mid-day meal scheme.
- October 12: The KYKL threatens a senior Manipur School Education Department official, S. Geeta Devi, with 'capital punishment' in case of her failure to take voluntary retirement from service within 10 days, for her alleged involvement in misuse of funds meant for the midday meal scheme.
- Ajyusi 20: A KYKL cadre, Chongtham Ratan Meitei, is arrested from Nongren Mayai Leikai, in the Imphal East district.
- August 7: KYKL bans all open debates and meetings on the controversies relating to Meitei script, contending that such arguments

would derail the move to replace the existing Bengali script with the Meitei script. The ban will remain in force for the next 10 years. The outfit also warns death penalty to anyone who violates its diktat.

- June 29: Manipur Police arrests two KYKL cadres, Ayekpam Bijen Singh and Laishram Chitreshwor Singh alias Ibungomacha Singh, from BT Road in the capital Imphal. 26 live rounds of AK-47 ammunition are recovered from their possession.
- June 23: A KYKL cadre, Angom Rabi, is arrested from Sekmai in the Imphal West district.
- June 15: SFs arrested a KYKL, Maibam Sapaba, during a search operation at Takyel near Imphal city.
- June 11: SFs arrested two KYKL cadres, U. Manglem and M, Jiten from Sekmaijin under Kakching police station limits in the Thoubal district.
- June 10: A KYKL cadre, Girdhar Sharma is arrested from Nungoi in the Imphal West district.
- June 7: Two KYKL cadres, N. Samananda Meitei alias Nanao and Tekcham Mani Meitei alias Amar, are arrested from Heirok and Wangjing respectively in the Thoubal district.

  Two more KYKL cadres, Charoibam Boynao Singh alias Wangba and Lokhai, are arrested from the Larnphei Sanakeithel and Moirangpurel areas in the Imphal city.
- May 24: Three KYKL cadres, Laishram Ibungo Singh, Ningombam Sur alias Angom Singh and Naoroibam Singhajit alias Ibomcha Singh, are arrested from a spot near Johnstone Higher Secondary School in the capital Imphal. Two mobile phones are recovered from their possession.
- May 9: A 19-year-old girl, Chuireingawon Sithengtha, is killed, while a 20 year-old boy, Thokchom Ramananda, sustained injuries in a crossfire between security force personnel and suspected KYKL cadres at Toubul in the Bishnupur district.
- May 8: Two KYKL cadres, Ningthoujam Shyamkahai and Khundrakpam Ranjit, are killed in an encounter with the security force personnel at Zouveng Meitei Leikai in the Churachandpur district. Two 9mm pistol along with four magazines are recovered from the site of the incident.
- May 7: A 'project officer' of the KYKL, Huidrom Pakpa alias Santosh Meitei, is arrested from Khagempalli Huidrom Leikai in the Imphal city.
- April 23: SFs neutralize a KYKL camp at Chalong in the Chandel district. A cache of arms and ammunition, including 17 lethode bombs,

magazines, Indian and Chinese hand grenades, two radio and other electronic gadgets, are recovered from the camp.

- April 21: A KYKL cadre, Lairenjam Nandakishore, is arrested from an unspecified place in the Imphal West district.
- April 10: Two KYKL cadres, Moirangthem Ibungochouba Singh alias Sangai and Saikhong Anand Singh, are arrested from Kakching in the Thoubal district. One hand grenade, four rounds of AK ammunition and incriminating documents are recovered from the arrested militants.
- April 9: Two KYKL cadres, Moirangthem Ibungochouba Singh alias Sangai and Saikhong Anand Singh, are arrested from Kakching in the Imphal East district. One hand grenade, four rounds of AK ammunition and incriminating documents were reportedly recovered from their possession.
- March 28: The Imphal East district police arrested a KYKL cadre, Khumanthem Shyam Singh alias Rohen, in a search operation at palace gate.
- March 18: A former KYKL cadre, 'Sgt' Mayanglambam Bijen alias Bicky, is shot dead by militants at Chirang Ching in the Chandel district, for his alleged 'unauthorized quitting of the outfit and acting as an agent of the security forces'.
- February 27: A KYKL cadre, Th. Manihar Singh, is arrested from Mayang Imphal area in the Imphal West district. Based on information provided by him, another cadre of the outfit, W. Suranjoy Singh, is arrested from Maning Khunou.
- February 27: The KYKL imposes certain restrictions in connection with the Class XII and HSLC examinations commencing on March 1 and 2 respectively. The outfit bans the use of unfair means in these examinations, and asks all concerned officials to perform their duties effectively and responsibly. It also promises appropriate action against anyone interfering with examination officials in the proper performance of their duty, in a statement, the KYKL also asks all sections not to call any form of general strikes, or blockades in the period from March 1 till April 1, when the examinations will conclude.
- February 26: KYKL cadres assault office bearers of the All Manipur Taekwondo Association for their alleged 'failure to keep an agreement reached with the outfit's Special Task Force way back in January 2005'. However, taekwondo officials allege that the outfit is interfering in the affairs of the association on behalf of its former general secretary, identified as Kongkham Indubhushan.

- February 19: Three KYKL cadres are arrested by a combined counter-insurgency squad of Assam Rifles personnel and Thoubal district police at Kakching Khunou.
- February 13: KYKL asks the KCP to 'produce within a week, a white paper on the charges leveled against' the journalist Ratan Luwangcha, who is attacked and wounded by cadres of the KCP on February 8.
- February 6: Two youths KC Singh and NH Singh shot at and wounded by three suspected cadres of the proscribed KYKL for allegedly taking drugs at Kakching Kakyai Mayai Leikai under Kakching police station in the Thoubal district.
- February 6: A suspected woman symphathiser of the KYKL, Thangjam Shileima Devi, is arrested by the Imphal west police from her home at Sagolband Tera Khuraijam Leikai under Lamphei police station.
- January 30: A suspected KYKL cadre is shot dead at Thambalkhong Sabal Leikai under Porompat police station in the Imphal East district. One Chinese hand grenade is recovered from the possession of the slain militant. Another cadre of the outfit, however, manages to escape.
- January 30: A suspected KYKL cadre is shot dead at Thambalkhong Sabal Leikai under Porompat police station in the Imphal East district. One Chinese hand grenade is recovered from the possession of the slain militant. Another cadre of the outfit, however, manages to escape.
- January 29: In a reshuffle of KYKL cadres, Ongthon Mangang has 'replaced' Thanil Mangang as 'deputy secretary of finance' of the outfit and 'Lt.' Thoiba Manang 'replaced' 'Capt.' Ahanjao Manang as 'commander' of Operation New Kangleipak.
- January 28: A KYKL cadre, Athokpam Dolendro Meitei alias Amarjit, is arrested from Top Khunou under Porompat police station in the Imphal East district.
- January 14: KYKL announces that if Th. Chaoba, the ex-state Bharatiya Janata Party (BJP) unit president, "is not expelled after the January *M* elections, all those elected should resign from BJP."
- January 10: KYKL rejects the appeal issued by the 28 BJP candidates contesting the civic elections to lift ban on them. Manipur Unit President of the party and the former Union Minister for Sports, Chaoba Singh, resigns from the party post, subsequent to the outfit's threat to target its leaders, workers and candidates campaigning for local body elections to be held on January 17.
- January 8: The proscribed KYKL prohibits the participation of any BJP candidate in the forthcoming civic bodies' elections. The outfit's

'deputy secretary, publicity and research' says that no electioneering activity by the BJP candidates will henceforth be allowed.

2005

- December 29: Four children are injured in a KYKL triggered Improvised Explosive Device (IED) blast at Ngariyan community hall on the Old Cachar road connecting the Bishnupur and Tamenglong districts.
- December 23: Deputy Inspector in the Education Department of Imphal East district, Sanasam Biren Singh, is paraded and shot at his left calf as 'punishment for alleged corruption' by the KYKL under its anti-corruption programme Operation New Kangleipak.
- December 20: Two KYKL cadres, Laishram Basanta Singh and Urikhaibam Manglen Singh, are arrested from Keirak under Kakching police station in the Thoubal district.
- December 11: A former KYKL cadre, Laiphrakpam Dilip Singh, is killed by unidentified militants at Leishoi Leikai under Moirang police station in the Bishnupur district.
- December 9: Four cadres of the KYKL, identified as Lukram Romen Singh, Konthoujam Kuber Singh, Huidrom Setha Meitei and Maibam Khumai Meitei, are arrested from the Shikhong area in the Thoubal district.
- November 30: A KYKL cadre, Sharungbam Surjeet Singh, is arrested along with a UNLF cadre, Sanabam Apik Singh, from Yambem village in the Thoubal district.
- November 10: KYKL claims responsibility for the November 8 bomb explosion in the Imphal city and says that a particular shop has been targeted as it has refused the outfit's demand of 'tax'. Another youth, Chongtham ibomcha, injured in the explosion, succumbs to his injuries, increasing the number of dead to two.
- November 3: Cabinet Committee on Security (CCS) extends the ban on four militant outfits, including the KYKL operating in Manipur, for two years. Addressing press persons after the CCS meeting chaired by Prime Minister, Dr Manmohan Singh, Defence Minister Pranab Mukherjee says that the Union Government has decided to extend the ban on UNLF, PLA, KCP and KYKL. He also informs that the ban is extended as the outfits still continue to indulge in unlawful activities in India's North East.
- November 2: KYKL has imposed a ban on Melas (local fairs) saying, "these Melas have become a bed rock of immorality, obscenity and drug abuse." The outfit's 'Deputy Secretary Publicity & Research',

Apabi Mangang, claims that Melas "help in a big way in the larger strategy of the Government of India to corrupt the people of the State morally, economically and politically."

- October 29: Two KYKL cadres, Salam Joychandra alias Abong and Oinam Naocha, are arrested from Chandapur Meitei Leikai under Kumbi police station in the Bishnupur district.
- October 16: Three youths are shot on their calves by suspected KYKL cadres for their alleged 'addiction to Spasmo Proxyvon', at Turen Wangma under Kakching police station in the Thoubal district.
- October 1: The KYKL imposes a ban on the activities of the KCP-P. The outfit says that KCP-P cadres will be "awarded capital punishment if they continue with their activities".
- September 29: Two KYKL cadres, Wahengbam Manglem alias Rajen and Phairenbam Chandrakumar Singh alias Kumar, are arrested from the Moirang Lamphai area in the Churachandpur district.
- September 26: A KYKL cadre, Konsam Romen alias Somen alias Sikteen, is arrested from Kumbi Setapur Mayai Leikai in the Bishnupur district.
- September 25: A KYKL cadre, Thounaojam Basanta alias Tily alias Sanathoi Singh, is arrested from Waheng Khuman Mayai Leikai in the Thoubal district.
- September 19: Eleven security force (SF) personnel are killed in a KYKL attack at Upper Ngariyan village in the Tamenglong district.
- September 18: A temporary camp of 30 KYKL cadres is neutralized at Kharan hills under Yairipok police station in the Senapati district.
- September 4: Two KYKL cadres, 'lance corporal' Thounaojam Jiten Meitei alias Ibungo and 'lance corporal' Thongam Hemanta Meitei alias Premjit, are arrested from Leikinthabi area in the Imphal East district.
- September 1: The headmaster and an assistant teacher of Abdul AN High Madrassa (seminary), Mohammed Sikander Ali and Mohammed Abdul Halim, are assaulted and paraded before the media by KYKL cadres for allegedly mis-utilising the funds of the school, tampering with their service books to extend their service, and selling off the rice meant for mid-day meal scheme. Ali has been asked to return the salary he earns after his retirement date.
- August 11: A KYKL cadre, Waikhom Inao Meitei alias Rupachandra, is arrested from the Tera Bazaar area of Imphal West district.

- August 10: Four civilians are killed and two others wounded in crossfire between SFs and KYKL cadres at Umathel under Waikhong police station in the Thoubal district. While the militants have managed to escape, three magazines of AK 47 rifles with 70 to 80 fired cases along with fired cases of lathode bombs and RPG rockets are seized from the incident site.
- August 3: A KYKL cadre, Laiphrakpam Dillip, allegedly involved in extortion activities, is arrested from Moirang Bazaar area in the Bishnupur district.
- August 2: A KYKL cadre, Khwairakpam Inao Singh allias Ramakanta, is arrested from his residence at Lamshang Mayai Leikai locality in the Imphal West district.
- July 7: A KYKL cadre, Chirom Hemanta alias Erei, of Waikhong *Bazaar,* is arrested from Tumukhong in the Imphal East district.
- July 3: A civilian, earlier abducted by the KYKL for ransom, is rescued from Pandon area in the Imphal West district.
- June 27: A senior accountant and an official of the Manipur education department are kneecapped by the KYKL at an unspecified place. Both the persons have earlier been 'charged of siphoning Rupees 20 lakhs each from the departmental funds and are 'set free' by the outfit after shooting them on their legs.

  A KYKL cadre, Salam Punshiba Meitei alias Punshi is arrested from Khabeisoi in the Imphal East district.
- June 21: KYKL has 'banned' civilians from attending or taking part in civic action programmes taken up by the paramilitary forces and Indian Army. The outfit threatens to execute people who attend such programmes.
- June 18: Two KYKL cadres, Ningthoujam Ojit and Leitanthem Ibomcha, are arrested from Tera Sapam Leirak and Langthabal Phuramakhong areas of the Imphal West district.
- June 18: A KYKL cadre, MSanta alias Ibungo alias Jet, is arrested from Kiyam Siphai Babu Bazaar area in the Imphal city.
- June 12: A KYKL cadre, Ngangbam Mangal Singh alias Ibungo, is arrested from Khuman Lampak bus terminus area in the Imphal West district.
- June 9: A KYKL cadre, Loktongbam Bedanta, is arrested at Sagolband in the Thoubal district. One 9 mm Norinco pistol along with magazine containing six rounds and Rs 15000 are recovered from his possession.
- May 24: A suspected KYKL cadre, Thiyam Chaoba, is killed at Kasom Khullen in the Ukhrul district. A Chinese pistol with magazine, five

rounds of ammunition and incriminating documents are recovered from the incident site.

- May 24: A KYKL cadre, Thoudam Biramani, is arrested at Achanbigei Awang Leikai in the Imphal East district.
- May 22: Two KYKL cadres are arrested from Sekmaijin in the Imphal West district.
- May 19: Three Education Department officials are kneecapped by the outlawed KYKL cadres at an unspecified place in the Churachandpur district accusing them of corruption of Manipur. According to reports, the three officials who had surrendered to the outfit earlier were paraded before a media team and then shot in their legs. Further, 49 teachers, allegedly appointed through corrupt means, were also paraded by the outfit and asked not to serve in the Education Department in future.
- May 18: Four militants, including a KYKL cadre, are arrested from Chingjao area in the Thoubal district. One carbine machine gun manufactured in Myanmar is recovered from their possession.
- May 17: A KYKL cadre, Naorem Sandeep Singh, is arrested from the Keishampat Churachandpur parking area in the Imphal West district.
- May 15: Three KYKL cadres are arrested from Ngangkhalawai in the Bishnupur district and another is arrested from Pungdongbam village in the Imphal East district.
- May 6: A KYKL cadre is killed during an encounter with the police at Dharamsala in the Imphal West district. Two extortion notes are recovered from his possession.
- April 27: Three KYKL cadres, including the outfit's 'deputy finance secretary', are arrested subsequent to a search operation at Phungreitang in the Ukhrul district. A communication device, 22 rounds of AK ammunition, fuse wire, mobile phone, currency notes worth Rupees 1,27,586 and incriminating documents are recovered from them.
- April 26: KYKL says, "We have awarded capital punishment to the five youths for their crimes against the revolutionary movement as well as the mothers of Manipuri youths, since they were responsible for drug abuse by a large number of youths of the state."
- April 25: KYKL announces its 'new tax policy' under which the outfit will stop serving 'donation letters for huge amounts' and will collect extensive tax from the people. The outfit, however, says that 'money in bulk' will continue to be collected from the corrupt officials, outsiders and from those who earn their money through dubious means. It adds that the policy will remain valid till April 2006.

- April 24: KYKL says said that all drug sellers will be killed without any warning while all drug abusers will be punished with a bullet on the leg.
- April 22: KYKL claims to have killed five persons at Kshetrigaon for their involvement in drug trade.
- April 15: A KYKL militant is arrested subsequent to a search operation at Thoubal Okraro in the Thoubal district.
- April 15: The proscribed KYKL asks Phanjoubam Tarapot, Imphal correspondent for the Press Trust of India, to issue a public apology by April 17 for what the outfit terms as misreporting of its stand on the ongoing agitation for the introduction of the indigenous Meitei Mayek script in the State replacing the Bengali script. The outfit says that failure to do so will invite 'stern punishment'.
- April 13: A KYKL cadre, Laishram Chand alias Tompok of Ngangkha Lawai Awang Leikai, is arrested from the Bishnupur district.
- March 30: A KYKL cadre is arrested subsequent to an exchange of fire at Keibul Lamjao area in the Imphal East district.
- March 24: Two KYKL cadres, identified as Irom Oken alias Meghajit and RK Naocha alias Sushilkumar alias Rocky, are arrested respectively from Moirang Khunou in the Bishnupur district and from Khurai Chingangbam Leikai area in the Imphal East district.
- March 8: 16 transport agency proprietors are arrested by the Imphal West district police for having not paid a sum of Rs 95 lakhs to the department with KYKL's help.
- March 8: The outfit has asked six teachers, including the Principal of Thambal Marik College at Oinam in Senapati district, to resign from their respective posts within 20 days on charges of 'encouraging the students to use unfair means' in the ongoing Class XII examination.
- March 3: Two KYKL cadres are arrested from Narnbol Balram Khul in Bishnupur district. Separately, a youth is shot in his leg by unidentified militants for drinking alcohol at Haipi under Kangpokpi police station in the Imphal West district.
- March 2: The KYKL shot at and injured the owner of a restaurant for violating its diktat of shutting down all cabin restaurants.
- March 2: KYKL imposes a 'curfew' within 300 meters of all examination centers for the Class XII examination scheduled to start from March 3. The outfit warns to fire upon anybody violating the orders.
- February 28: KYKL imposes a 'ban' on the functioning of cabin restaurants in the State with effect from March 1 and has asked people

to stop visiting such places. A statement issued by the outfit says that such restaurants are a "major factor in the moral degeneration of our society".

- February 27: KYKL has paraded two zonal education officers, Athokpam Shamu and Moirangthem Sanatombi Singh, before the media and pronounced them 'guilty of corruption'. Both are asked by the outfit to resign from their posts.
- February 26: The KYKL 'Deputy Secretary', Apabi Mangang, warns contractors engaged in construction work of the Education Department to maintain quality and not to make profits.
- February 24: Six militant camps, including one of the KYKL, are neutralized at Keibul Lamjao in the Bishnupur district. A huge cache of arms and explosives including one M-16 rifle, one carbine, two pistols, 18 lethode bombs, one RPG, six hand grenades and a large assortment of ammunition, are recovered.
- February 17: Five SF personnel are killed and two others wounded in an attack by the KYKL at Kumbi in the Bishnupur district.
- February 14: A suspected KYKL cadre is killed during an encounter with the police at Pechiching in the Thoubal district.
- January 24: Two KYKL sympathisers are arrested from the Imphal East district and two vehicles along with two demand letters of the outfit are seized from them.
- January 18: KYKL claims responsibility for torching two trucks between Ningthoubung and Hengbung villages in the Senapati district.
- January 11: A KYKL cadre, Mutum Abung alias Naobi, is arrested from Khurai Lamlong Bazaar in the capital Imphal.
- January 6: The outlawed KYKL, intensifying its Operation New Kangleipak, asks the heads of educational institutions in Imphal to impose the eeyongphi phanek (traditional local dress) as uniform for girl students of classes IX and X from the forthcoming academic session, beginning in February.

2004

- December 28: KYKL has reportedly taken hostage a retired school principal and a school cashier for 'misappropriation of school funds amounting to Rs. 2 lakhs'.
- December 17: N Bijoy Singh and R K Ranjan, Vice-Chancellor and Registrar of the Manipur University, are released by the KYKL after being shot in their legs. According to a KYKL statement, both are 'punished' for flouting rules in the appointment of the Director of the Audio Visual Research Centre in Manipur University.

- December 13: KYKL abducts the Vice Chancellor of Manipur University, Dr N Bijoy Singh, and Registrar, Dr RK Ranjan Singh, from the campus.
- December 13: Two KYKL terrorists, Thongbam Shantikumar and Kwairakpam Rabin Singh, are arrested from the Thana and Ithina areas of Bishnupur district.
- December 7: Four KYKL terrorists are arrested from unspecified places in the Imphal West district.
- November 27: Security force personnel destroy a camp of the KYKL located in the southeast region of Behiang in Churachandpur district.
- November *25:* The Yairipok police recovers the dead body of a man allegedly killed by the KYKL from Laiching area in Thoubal district.
- November 24: The KYKL shoots six examination investigators in their legs at an undisclosed location in Imphal city for having encouraged students to indulge in malpractices in a school-level examination.
- November 13: KYKL terrorist Longjam Ojit arrested from Paobitek under Wangoi police station in Thoubal district.
- October 12: Security forces arrest KYKL terrorist Bindursing alias Arunbalemba from Patsoi in Imphal West district.
- September 11: A CRPF personnel and a KYKL terrorist are killed during an encounter at Wangoo Laipham under Kumbi police station in Bishnupur district.
- June 10: A KYKL terrorist killed at Tezpur Lamkhai under Waikhong police station jurisdiction in Thoubal district in an encounter with Assam Rifles personnel.
- May 28: KYKL claims responsibility for the killing of two 'imposters', Thokchom Abung on May *25* at Lamboiching and Maibam Pheijao on May 12 in the Imphal West district, accusing that they were members of a gang of extortionists, which had been misusing the KYKL's name.
- April 24: The former Director General of Police of Manipur, Y. Jugeshwor Singh shot dead by KYKL terrorists at his residence in the capital Imphal.
- April 14: KYKL kills one of the alleged drug traffickers, identified as Sorokhaibam Shanti. Police recovered the deadbody from Moirang Khunou in the Bishnupur district.
- April 4: The Bharatiya Janata Party (BJP) vice president in Manipur, N. Tombi, and one of the general secretaries, Sarath Singh, resign from the party in view of the 'ban' on campaigning imposed by the KYKL.

- March 24: Imphal East district police arrest one KYKL terrorist, identified as Sagolsem Rome Singh, from Lamlai Mayai Laikai in the Imphal East district.
- March 12: KYKL imposes 'prohibitions' around examination centers' as part of its 'Operation New Kangleipak' programme for 'smooth conduct' of the Class 12 examinations in Manipur.
- February 12: KYKL sets February 15 as deadline for Bharatiya Janata Party (BJP) Manipur Pradesh president Chaoba Singh to quit the party and also put its army units under Lalhaba Tengol led by its chief of army staff, 'colonel' K.Koireng on alert for any eventuality.
- January 6: Three KYKL terrorists are killed during an encounter that occurred between the Heirok Part III Litan Makhong and Enganglok areas of Thoubal district.

2003

- December 14: Security forces kill two KYKL terrorists in an encounter at Larong in the Chandel district and recover two 9 mm pistols with two live rounds, 25 live rounds of AK 47, two hand grenades, among other things from the encounter site.
- November 18: KYKL kills one cadre for deserting the outfit to join UNLF in Manipur.
- November 8: At least eighteen armed KYKL cadres reportedly desert the outfit to join the Manipur People's Army (MPA), armed wing of United National Liberation Front (UNLF) in Manipur.
- November 03: KYKL decides to 'execute' seven-drug traffickers under its custody in Manipur and issues a deadline to all drug traffickers and abusers to 'surrender' before November 7.
- October 13: KYKL releases the abducted Principal of LMS Law College, Kiran Chand Singh, from captivity at an undisclosed place in Thoubal district. He was abducted from his residence on September 28, 2003.
- October 3: Seven KYKL terrorists are arrested by a combined team of Thoubal police, personnel of 3rd Indian Reserve Battalion (IRB) and the Imphal West district police from different places in Manipur.
- September 7: KYKL sets free I L Laishram, the abducted bureaucrat, at Sugnu near Imphal after a week in captivity.
- August 21: A combined team of the Thoubal district police commandos and 3rd Indian Reserve Battalion personnel kill a suspected KYKL terrorist during an encounter at Nongbalkhong hillock near Ikoppat village in the Thoubal district.

- August 11: KYKL issues a diktat to ban cabin restaurants and similar food joints to stop 'immoral activities' with immediate effect.
- July 11 : A suspected KYKL terrorist is killed during an encounter at Charangching Khunou in the Chandel district.
- June 27: KYKL issues 'ban' notices for three branches of the State Council for Educational Research and Training while accusing them of inactivity and indulging in corruption.
- June 18: Security forces destroy a KYKL hideout located at Ngariyan hills in the Bishenpur district and kill one of its cadres in the ensuing encounter.
- June 08: Manipur police destroy an abandoned camp of the KYKL at Longumpat in Bishenpur district.
- June 2, 3: Four KYKL terrorists are arrested from various places in the State.
- May 30: Women's groups, including the All Manipur Nupi Marup and All Manipur Keithel Nupi Lup, announce a social boycott of the KYKL following reports of the outfit's involvement in the abduction and subsequent killing of an Imphal-based trader.
- May 29: A KYKL 'lance corporal' is killed in an encounter with the security forces in Thoubal district.
- May 28: Eight KYKL terrorists are arrested in separate raids in Bishenpur district in connection with the April-19 abduction and subsequent killing of a trader.

  SFs destroy a training camp of the KYKL at Khangbung village, located on the higher ridges of Khoupum valley, Tamenglong district.
- May 4: KYKL announces a 'ban' on *bandhs* (general strikes) in Manipur from May 15 onwards.
- April 13: KYKL declares support to the proscribed Revolutionary People's Front (RPF) over a ban imposed by the latter on selling and consuming tobacco products in Manipur.
- March 16: Two former KYKL terrorists are killed in an encounter at Awang Khunou, under Patsoi police station-limits, in Imphal West district.
- March 11: Four KYKL terrorists and one SF personnel are killed during an encounter in Oksu village, Imphal East district.
- March 10: KYKL terrorists attack and injure S.K. Women's College principal N. Shamungou Singh in Nambol, Bishnupur district, for allegedly failing to curb malpractice during the school examinations.

- March 3: KYKL terrorists 'expels' three students for 'examination malpractices' reportedly with the approval of Council of Higher Secondary Education, Manipur (CHSEM) during the examinations at Pole Star College, Wabagai. The outfit also rebukes two invigilators for 'negligence' during the examinations.
- February 10: Five Border Security Force (BSF) personnel are killed in a KYKL laid ambush near Leingangtabi along the Imphal-Moreh road.
- January 12: KYKL claims responsibility for killing a lecturer at an unknown place in Manipur on January 6.

2002

- December 31: KYKL sets free five persons, it had abducted earlier, unharmed at an undisclosed location in the Thoubal district. Earlier, the outfit had issued 'capital punishment' to all the five for alleged involvement in 'corruption' in the Education Department.
- November 2: KYKL denies involvement in looting of an Oil Pump depot in Manipur, where some six armed-men looted Rupees 30,000 in cash and other valuables on an unspecified date.
- October 25: Imphal West police arrests a KYKL cadre from the Lamshang police station area.
- September 1: Border Security Force personnel arrest a KYKL terrorist, identified as Nongthombam Deepak, from the Rengkai Road area in Imphal.
- September 21: KYKL terrorists attack Nameirakpam Nodiachand, a former State Legislator at Uripok.
- August 6: Border Security Force personnel arrest three KYKL terrorists from various hideouts in the State.
- August 24: KYKL (Oken) terrorist, identified as Wangkhem Manisana, surrenders at a special surrender ceremony held at Chief Minister Okram Ibobi Singh's residence in Imphal.
- August 17: KYKL announces imposing dress code in Manipur and sets September 20 as the deadline for the implementation under what it calls, 'Operation New Kangleipak'.
- May 23: KYKL releases abducted Manipur Council for Higher Secondary Education (MCHSE) Secretary K. Joychandra Singh held captive since May 16 at the Loijeng Chingkhong area under Lamlai police station limits after injuring him.
- March 21: Suspected KYKL terrorists kill an examination invigilator and injure six others in separate incidents a various places, on the first day of annual examinations of the Board of Secondary Education.

- April 26: KYKL claims responsibility for the killing of a civilian at Yaralpat on Tinsid Road alleging him of indulging in extortion in the name of the KYKL.
- April 17: KYKL issues 'appeal' for a free and fair election to the Manipur University Students Union (MUSU), to be held on April 27.
- April 14: Unidentified assailants kill a surrendered KYKL terrorist at Thanga village in Bishnupur district.
- February 17: Toijamba and Oken factions of the KYKL decide to merge.
- February 14: Two security force personnel are killed and five others injured in a KYKL-Oken laid ambush along the Itham Moirang Purel road.
- February 7: A group of approximately ten suspected KYKL terrorists shoot at an activist of the Manipur State Congress Party at Nambol.
- January 19: Suspected KYKL terrorists attack two State Government officials at CI College road in Bishnupur alleging them to be indulging in corruption.
- January 7: Suspected KYKL (Oken) terrorists trigger Improvised Explosive Device (IED) blast killing four India Reserve Battalion (IRB) personnel in Mundum Mahadeva Lamkhai, Thoubal district.

2001

- September 12: Manipur police kills two suspected KYKL-O terrorists during an encounter in the Keibul Sambram area of Bishnupur district.
- August 29: A media report indicates that KYKL has issued a warning that women not wearing the traditional dress - PMneks or Sarongs - could face death penalty.
- August 24: Seven terrorists, including a woman cadre of the KYKL-O, are arrested after SFs unearth an underground camp of the NSCN-IM and KYKL-O combine at Ngariyan in Bishnupur district.
- June 12: United National Liberation Front (UNLF) and KYKL-O agree to stop internecine hostilities.
- May 10: An unidentified KYKL 'area commander' is killed at an unnamed place in the State.
- February 3: A suspected KYKL -T terrorist is killed during an encounter at Bashikhong Kongba Irong.
- January 22: KYKL-Oken faction claims responsibility for the January 17-assassination attempt on the All Manipur Students' Union (AMSU) President, Gourashyam, at an unknown place.

2000

- August 23: SF personnel arrest a KYKL terrorist from Athokpam Bazar in Thoubal district.
- August 21: Three KYKL terrorists are arrested in Imphal West district.
- August 7: A KYKL terrorist surrenders at an unknown place.
- July 4: Eighteen terrorists, including an unspecified number of KYKL terrorists, surrender in the presence of Manipur Chief Minister Nipamacha Singh in Imphal.

People's Liberation Army

Formation

The People's Liberation Army (PLA) was established under the leadership of N. Bisheswar Singh on September 25, 1978.

Objectives

The PLA aims to organise a revolutionary front covering the entire Northeast and unite all ethnic groups, including the Meiteis, Nagas and Kukis, to liberate Manipur. PLA, though a Meiti outfit, claims itself to be a trans-tribal organisation seeking to lead the non-Meiteis as well.

Leadership and Structure

In 1989, the PLA formed a political body called the Revolutionary People's Front (RPF). RPF runs a government-in-exile in Bangladesh. Irengbam Chaoren is the 'President' of the RPF. It has a Vice-president, a General Secretary, Secretaries in charge of Home, Finance, Foreign Affairs, Publicity and Communication, Social Welfare, Health and Education.

As part of its revitalisation efforts, the PLA was reorganised on the lines of a disciplined army. The militant wing now comprises four divisions—Sadar Hill West areas of the Valley of Manipur, Sadar Hill areas in the eastern Valley, the entire hill areas in Manipur and the entire Imphal area. Each division has a commander, lieutenants, sergeant and lance corporals in its ranks. PLA activists are equipped with sophisticated arms. The group has also been reportedly involved in widespread extortion operation.

Linkages

PLA recruits were trained in guerrilla warfare by the then united National Socialist Council of Nagaland (NSCN) at its headquarters in Challam, beyond the Somrah Tract, in north Myanmar during the eighties. PLA is also reported to have contacts with Pakistan's Inter Services Intelligence (ISI). The ISI's nexus with the PLA came to notice through a document recovered in January 1991 from Biren Singh, the Finance Secretary of the RPF.

It has a government-in-exile in Bangladesh where the PLA has set up a number of bases in the Sylhet district. Two camps in Myanmar and five camps in Bangladesh are currently known to exist, where about 1,000 recruits have received arms training.

Incidents 2006

- December 31: Security force personnel arrests two People's Liberation Army (PLA) militants, identified as L. Hemojit Singh alias Sena and T.Jacky Singh alias Arun, during a search operation at Wanjing Khunou in the Thoubal district. Three live rounds of 9 mm and two rounds of an unknown calibre were recovered from their possession.
- December 27: Two suspected PLA militants, Yaiphaba and Dinokumar, are killed when an Improvised Explosive Device they were handling exploded accidentally at Umathel Kakching Khunou Lamkhai under Waikhong police station in the Thoubal district. One damaged mobile handset and some wires were recovered from their possession.
- December 15: PLA militants shot dead two civilians, Mohammed Ahamad Ali and Amirjan, at an unspecified place in the Thoubal district. In a statement issued by the communication and publicity in-charge of the outfit, N Wangba, the duo were awarded 'capital punishment' for being informers of the security forces.
- December 12: A suspected PLA militant is shot dead by security force (SF) personnel during a counter-insurgency operation at Arong Nongmaikhong in the Imphal West district. One M-20 pistol and two live rounds were recovered from the slain militant.
- December 9: An encounter between SF personnel and suspected PLA cadres occurred at Nongpok Keithelmanbi under Yairipok police station in the Imphal West district. However, there was no casualty.
- November 30: Suspected People's Liberation Army militants attacked security force personnel who retaliated at Kumbi Setapur under Kumbi police station in the Bishnupur district. However, no casualties are reported.

  A PLA cadre, Sanasam Angouba alias Inglemba alias Ingocha alias Tiken, is arrested from Lilong Arapti area in the Imphal East district.
- November 20: At least six Central Reserve Police Force personnel, including an Assistant Sub-Inspector, are injured when militants ambushed their convoy at Nambol Sabal Leikai in the Bishnupur district. The militants reportedly escaped after the ambush. In a subsequent search operation, several empty cases and a bomb were recovered from a vehicle abandoned by the militants. The PLA claimed responsibility for the ambush.
- November 7: Police arrested two 'Corporals' of the PLA, Konsam Iboyaima alias Jamini and Yumlembam Bungo alias Malemnganba,

during a search operation at Bishnupur and Nachou in the Bishnupur district.

- November 1: A PLA cadre, identified as a 'sergeant major' Khingba, was shot dead by security force personnel in a counter-insurgency operation at Kakching Khunou under Waikhong police station in the Thoubal district. Another cadre of the outfit, Leimapokpam Gautam, was arrested. A 9 mm pistol along with a magazine having four live rounds of ammunition was also recovered from the possession of the militants.
- October 27: One PLA cadre, Thoudam Inao Singh alias Dinesh, was arrested from Sekmaijin under Mayang Irnphai Police Station.
- October 22: A People's Liberation Army cadre, Chongtham Naocha alias Ratan, was arrested at Kiyam under Patsoi police station in the Imphal West district.

  The PLA captures three persons, Miabam Sanjay alias Naobi, Angom Sureh alias Nongbal and Heiningsungbarn Amitkumar, for their involvement in the extortion under the guise of the cadres' outfit. They were later paraded before the media at an unspecified place in the Bishnupur district.
- October 21: A PLA cadre, Inao Singh alias Sana, is arrested by SF personnel during a search operation at Khurkhul under Sekmai police station in the Imphal West district.
- October 15: One PLA militant, 'corporal' Khongbrai-latpam Govin Sharma alias Washington, is arrested from Samaram in the Thoubal district.
- October 11: A PLA cadre is arrested by security force personnel in a search operation from Imphal city.
- August 20: Manipur Police arrest a PLA cadre, Angomjambam Lokhon Meitei alias Amarjit, during a search operation at Lairenkabi Mamang Leikai in the Imphal East district.
- August 11: Two PLA cadres, Loitongbam Sunil alias Abungo and Bogen, are killed during an encounter with a team of Manipur Police at Takhel Mamang Leikai under Lamlai police station jurisdiction in the Imphal East district.
- July 30: PLA kill one of its former colleagues, Kangabam Romio alias Bobby, at Okram Chuthek under Irilbung police station limits in the Imphal East district.
- July 27: A PLA cadre, Thoudam Khambaton alias Umakanta Singh, is arrested from Khurai Thoudam Leikai in the Imphal East district.

- July 22: A nine-year-old boy, Haobijam Surjakanta, is killed in crossfire between PLA and a team of Manipur Police personnel at Wangjing in the Thoubal district.
- July 21: Manipur Police arrests a PLA cadre, Maibam Anand alias Ibomcha, from Ukgongshang Mayai Leikai in the Thoubal district.
- July 19: A PLA cadre, Kangbam Naoba alias Sadat, is arrested from New *Bazaar* in the Churachandpur town.
- July 15: SFs arrest two PLA cadres from Lungbam Awang Leikai in the Imphal West district.
- July 14: Assam Rifles kill a PLA cadre at Thiyam village under Irilbung police station limits in the Imphal East district.
- July 13: Manipur Police arrests a PLA cadre, Moirangthem leo alias Ibomcha, from Khurai Thoidingjam Leikai in the Imphal East district.
- July 12: A PLA cadre, Mohendro Singh, is arrested from Keithelmanbi Bazar in the Imphal East district.
- July 12: SFs arrest three PLA cadres, Elangbam Lokendro Singh, Mayengbam Mangal and Huirongbam Ingocha Singh, from North AOC area of Imphal city.
- July 10: SF personnel arrest a PLA cadre, Athokpam Kangla alias Sumi Meitei, from the New Bazaar area of Churachandpur town.
- July 9: SFs arrest a PLA cadre, Sukham Khing Singh, during a search operation at Kakching Khunou in the Thoubal district.
- July 2: SFs arrest a PLA cadre, Kh. Sangilcharan, from a spot under Kakwa police station limits in the Imphal West district.
- June 28: PLA cadres kill a civilian, Takhellambam Menaka, at Wangoo Lupa Marup in the Thoubal district.
- June 28: The dead body of a police personnel, Nongthombam Kumar, who was abducted by PLA from the Imphal area on March 16, is recovered from Heingangching under Heingang police station limits in the Imphal East district.
- June 24: One PLA cadre, Joy, is arrested from Moirangpurel in the Imphal city.
- June 21: A PLA cadre, R.K. Sanayaima, is arrested from Thiyam under Nambol police station limits in the Bishnupur district.
- June 19: Two PLA militants are killed in an encounter with the SFs at Samurou Maning Leikai under Wangoi police station limits in the Imphal West district. Another PLA cadre, Nabakumar, is arrested from Iroishemba Chingol near Imphal city.

- June 14: Three PLA militants are killed and four others wounded in an ambush laid by the SFs at Wakshu under Tengnoupal police station limits in the Chandel district. Three AK-47 rifles along with a huge cache of ammunition and incriminating documents are recovered from the incident site.
- June 11: A PLA cadre, Athokpam Ngub alias Nanda is arrested from Athokpam in the Thoubal district.
- June 10: A PLA cadre, Naobi is arrested from Nungoi in the Imphal West district along with 14 rounds of AK rifle.
- June 9: One PLA cadre, SS lance corporal Jotin Kumar, is killed in an encounter with the security force personnel at Lamlong under Tengnoupai police station limits in the Chandel district. One 9 mm pistol, and a Kenwood radio set are recovered from the slain cadre.
- June 7: A PLA cadre, Yaima Singh alias Megha is arrested from Khekman in the Thoubal district.
- June 1: A PLA cadre, Hakujam Nanaw, is arrested from Marignthei under Tengnoupai police station limits in the Chandel district.
- May 22: A security force personal and a PLA cadre are wounded in an exchange of fire at Yongkhul under Tengnoupai police station limits in the Chandel district.
- May 20: A PLA cadre, Lieutenant Feroz Ahmed is killed in an encounter with the SFs on the MantripukhrhAhallup road under Heingang police station limits in the Imphal East district. One 9 mm pistol is recovered from the incident site.

  Two PLA cadres, Manglen Singh alias Kaka and Lemba Singh alias Ranjit are arrested from Yainqbi under Mayang Imphal police station limits in the Imphal West district.
- April 29: SFs Kill Nongmeikapam Punshiba, a senior leader of the PLA, at Laphupat Tera of Imphal West district. H Gnim pistol with five rounds of ammunition is recovered from the killed militant.

  A PLA cadre, Punshiba alias Makak, is arrested from the Pulem Pat area along with one 9 mm pistol and a magazine containing 10 live rounds.
- April 27: A PLA cadre, Longjambore alias Sanathoiba, is arrested along with one 9 mm Chinese pistol from the Chandel town.
- April 22: A PLA cadre is arrested from Salam village in the Imphal West district.

  Another PLA cadre is arrested along with one M-20 pistol and three live rounds of M-20 ammunition from the DM College Campus in Imphal city.

- April 20: A PLA cadre, Lt. Th. Inaoton alias Chinglen, is arrested from Phaknung in the Imphal East district.
- April 14: A PLA cadre, Ph. Premananda Sharma alias Ibungosana, is killed in an encounter with the security forces at Lupa Marup under Sugnu police station limits in the Thoubal district. One .9 mm pistol along with four live rounds is recovered from his possession.
- April 13: A PLA militant is killed in an exchange of fire between the troops of 33 Assam Rifles and the outfit's cadres at Kakching Khunou under Waikhong police station limits in the Thoubal district. One M-20 pistol and six live rounds of AK-47 ammunition are recovered from the site of the encounter.
- April 10 : People of Keinou area in the Bishnupur district capture two persons, Mohammed Hasan alias Tomba and Mohammed Azad Khan, while they are extorting money in the guise of PLA cadres and hand them over to police personnel.

  Two PLA cadres, 'SS L/CpP Kh Robinchandra Singh alias Krishna and 'SS Pvt' T Brogen Singh, are arrested during separate search operations from Lamsang Awang Leikai in the Imphal West district.
- April 6: Two persons, Mohammed Fazul Hague and Mohammed Munik, are killed and two others, including a woman, are wounded by suspected PLA cadres at Pangong Makhong Chingthak under Porompat police station in the Imphal East district.
- April 5: A PLA cadre, 'sergeant major' Baari alias Mayengbam imbakgcha Singh, is arrested at Arapati Maning Leikai under Lilong police station in the Thoubal district.
- April 3: Two militants, including a PLA cadre, are killed by security force personnel in an encounter at Saiton Khunou under Moirang police station in the Bishnupur district. Police sources said that one M-20 pistol with two live rounds, two hand grenades, and two live rounds of AK-47 ammunition are recovered from the encounter site. However, two militants, including another PLA cadre, managed to escape from the incident site.
- March 29: A PLA cadre, Mohammed Bov, was found dead at his residence in the Sora Langthabal area of Thoubal district. A 9 mm pistol is recovered from the incident site. The exact cause for his death is yet to be ascertained since unconfirmed reports mention that he may have committed suicide.
- March 29: A person, Akham Satischandra, is caught while extorting money from an educational institution posing as a cadre of the RPF,

political wing of the PLA, and is later paraded before the media by volunteers of the All Manipur Students' Union at a place in the Imphal East district. A pistol is recovered from his possession.

- March 27: A former militant, Konjengbam Abung alias Gulapi Singh, is shot dead by four unidentified militants at Phumiou Leikai under Lamshang police station in the Imphal West district. The slain person was a PLA cadre and later joined the KCP before giving up arms and eschewing violence.
- March 21: A PLA cadre, Kanta alias Manjana, is arrested by the Thoubal district police from Heirok. 200 grams of IED material, one detonator, three live rounds of 7.62 mm and gun powder are recovered from the arrested PLA cadre who was allegedly involved in the March 13-ambush on slain police inspector N. Lokhon Singh and firing on the BSF post at Heirok.
- March 21: Three PLA cadres, Keisham Binakumar alias Joykumar, his wife Keisham Rina Devi, and Huidrom Bijen alias Naoba, are arrested during a search operation at Ngaikhong. Another PLA cadre jumps into the river and is drowned while being chased by the troops at Arong Nongmaikhong in the Imphal West district.
- March 21: According to the 2005 Annual Report of the Manipur Police, 23 militants, including four PLA cadres, surrendered during the year.
- March 16: The residence of a CPI Legislator, Dr. M Nara, is attacked by suspected PLA cadres at Thoubal Tentha.
- March 13: Nine cadres of six militant outfits, including two PLA cadres, surrender along with a large cache of arms and ammunition before the Commander of 3 Corps, Lt. Gen. Z.U. Shah, at the Headquarters of Inspector General of Assam Rifles (South) at Mantripukhri in the Imphal city. The surrendered PLA cadres deposit one AK 47 rifle, one hand grenade, RS Kenwwod, one 9 mm pistol and a huge amount of ammunition.
- March 11: Four unidentified PLA cadres and a woman, Maikham Singlai, are killed and a two-year old child is wounded in an encounter between the SF personnel and militants near Chingkhan yonyei village under Tengnoupal police station in the Chandel district. Three AK-47 rifles and one AK-LMG are recovered from the slain militants.
- February 24: A PLA cadre, identified as M. Joykumar alias Kangleipak, is shot dead by security force personnel in an encounter at Katang village under Tousem sub-division in the Tamenglang district.
- February 23: Troops neutralise a PLA hideout and kill a cadre of the outfit, N Kangleipak Meitei, at Katyang village under Tousem sub-division in the Tamenglong district. An AK-47 rifle, an automatic

grenade launcher with 17 live grenades, a SLR, an US carbine, four 12 bore rifles, two radio sets, a radio set interceptor, generator set, 12 rifle magazines along with incriminating documents, large number of uniforms of the outfit and large quantity of ration and medicines are recovered from the hideout.

- February 20: PLA 'arrests' a person, Moi-rangthem Sanjoy Meitei, from the Imphal East district for his alleged involvement in the collection of a huge amount of money from the people on the promise of providing them contract works on behalf of the outfit.
- February 20: Four police personnel are killed by the PLA at Thoubal *Bazaar* and in the retaliatory firing, one militant is killed. However, two others manage to escape from the incident site. One 9 mm pistol and two hand grenades are recovered from the incident site.
- February 7: Two PLA cadres, identified as 'Pvt' Lohim alias James and 'Pvt' Logjemba, are killed by the SFs in an encounter at a place along Ngarian hillock road under Irilbung police station in the Imphal East district. One 9 mm pistol and ten rounds of ammunition are recovered from the incident site.
- January 28: A PLA cadre, Laiphrakpam Boy alias Boynao, is arrested during a search operation at Moirangkampu Makha Leikai in the Imphal West district.
- January 26: Chingkai village headman, Kamkhohe alias Kampu, is arrested from the Lamphel area of Imphal West district in connection with the murder of Inspector General of Police (Intelligence), T. Thangthuam, by the PLA on December 31, 2005.
- January 25: Two PLA 'bomb experts', Nandeibam Nandakishore alias Bung and Maibam Dhamendra Singh, are arrested by the Imphal West district police from Imphal Palace Gate.
- January 23: Four suspected PLA cadres are killed in an encounter with the security forces (SFs) at Sandankhong in the Bishnupur district. Apart from a vehicle, one motorcycle, three AK 47 rifles, one lethod bomb, three magazines, 24 bullets and six bombs were recovered from the incident site.
- January 15: The PLA 'arrests' four persons, Bharatiya Janata Party leader Thoudam Naba-chandra, Sahomburg Moirangthem Ibungo, the lecturer of Education Department of Biramangol College, Meisnam Lokendro and Khangenbam Sanahal, for allegedly collecting Rupees Two lakhs from people in different places of the Churachandpur district on behalf of the outfit.

- January 14: A PLA cadre, M. Basanta alias Koba, reportedly an Improvised Explosive Device (IED) specialist, is arrested from the Koirou village under Singjamei police station in the Imphal West district.
- January 14: Two SF personnel, Ananda Mani and Sukadev Singh, and one unidentified PLA cadre are killed during search operations at the Khoibu Maring village in the Chandel district.
- January 8: A suspected PLA cadre is shot dead in an encounter with the police inside the DM College campus at Thangmeiband in the Imphal West district. Three of his accomplices, however, manage to escape. A 9 mm pistol with three live rounds, and a Kinetic Activa-brand scooter are recovered from the incident site.
- January 4: Two PLA cadres, Salam Premjit alias Naoton and I. Rome, are arrested during separate search operations from Moirangpurel Khunou Makha Leikai in the Imphal East district and from Sapam Leikai in the Thoubal district respectively. Four AK-47 rifles are recovered from the latter.
- January 4: An unidentified PLA cadre is arrested in a search operation, subsequent to a militant ambush on the Thoubal district police personnel, at Nongbram under Yairipok police station.

2005

- December 31: The Manipur Inspector General of Police (Intelligence), Tunglut Thangthaum, is killed along with a Constable and two police personnel are injured in a suspected PLA ambush at Oinam area in the Bishnupur district.
- December 4: Three PLA cadres, including a woman, are arrested from the Thoubal district. About 300 blank permits are reportedly recovered from the woman.
- November 26: Police commandos of Imphal West district arrest a PLA cadre, Maibam Bor Singh, from the Awang Sekmai Koujeng Leima area.
- November 3: The Cabinet Committee on Security (CCS) extends the ban on four militant outfits, including the PLA operating in Manipur, for two years. Addressing the press after a CCS meeting chaired by Prime Minister, Dr Manmohan Singh, in New Delhi, the Defence Minister Pranab Mukherjee said that the Union Government has decided to extend the ban on UNLF, PLA, KCP and KYKL. He also informs that the ban is extended as the outfits still continue to indulge in unlawful activities in India's North East.
- November 1: A Civilian Nandeibam Navy alias Ratan, is shot at and wounded by PLA cadres somewhere in the Imphal East district. The

victim is shot for allegedly 'extorting money' from Kongba Makha Chongbi bazaar in the name of the outfit.

- October 19: The Chandel district police arrests three PLA cadres, Khuraijam Manao alias Nilamani, Nongthongbam Abung alias Tisan and Khudam Shyam, from Japhou Bazaar.
- October 13: A combined team of Bishnupur police commandos and Gorkha Rifles arrests two militants belonging to the PLA and PREPAK from Thanga Chingning. While the PLA cadre has been identified as Tongbram Babuchand Meitei from Chandrapur Merabam Leirak, the PREPAK cadre is identified as Ningthoujam Nabachandra alias Deven from Keibul Heikha Leikai.
- October 11: Two militants, one each belonging to the UNLF and PLA, are killed in an internecine clash at Kam Ranga village under Jiribam police station in the Imphal West district. While the police have recovered the body of UNLF cadre, identified as Ningombam Sanathoi alias Umbiien, PLA cadres have managed to take away the body of their slain colleague.
- October 10: The Imphal West district police arrests a PLA cadre, Moirangthem Rameshwor alias Maninganba Singh, from Keishampat Churchandpur bus parking on Tidim road.
- October 10: SF personnel kill a PLA cadre in a counter insurgency operation at Chassad in the Ukhrul district on. An AK-47 rifle, three magazines, one hand grenade and one radio set are recovered from his possession.
- October 8: Three PLA cadres are killed in an encounter with the SFs at Thanga Tangkhul village under Kamjong Chasad sub-division in the Ukhrul district. Three AK-47 rifles, one M-16 rifle, nine magazines, one radio set, three hand grenades and a huge quantity of ammunition are recovered from the incident site.
- October 3: A PLA cadre, belonging to the 'finance department' of the outfit, identified as Thangjam Romesh, is arrested from Lamding Ngam Leikai in the Thoubal district.
- September 30: Two PLA cadres, identified as Thokchom Bungcha and Oinam Kunjabi, are arrested from Moirang Thana Leikai area and Chandapur bus stand in the Bishnupur district.
- September 26: Troops of the 33 Assam Rifles in a joint operation with the police arrest a PLA cadre, Sanajit alias Sana, from New Chakan bazaar. A scooter, a typewriter, two sets of WLL telephones, 9 mm rounds, one kilogram of gelatin, Rupees 20,000 and incriminating documents are recovered from him.

- September 25: A hardcore PLA cadre, Th. Sana alias Max, is arrested from by a combined team of Thoubal district commandos and 33 Assam Rifles personnel from Kakching Chumnak Leikai under Kakching police station. Currency worth Rupees 20,000, twenty half kilogram packs of gelatin, one typewriter, two live rounds of 9 mm pistol, two sets of WLL telephone and one scooter are recovered from his possession.
- September 21: Two Border Security Force (BSF) personnel are killed in a PLA ambush at Kumbi Khodrak road in the Bishnupur district.
- September 19: One SF personnel is killed in a PLA triggered IED explosion near Jiribam in the Imphal East district.
- September 16: A PLA cadre, Boby of Keibul Sangram, is arrested during a search operation at an unspecified place in the Bishnupur district.
- September 13: PLA releases the Manipur Students' Union leader, Kh. Ashok Kumar, after a week in captivity. He is handed over to his family members in the presence of some mediators at an undisclosed location.
- September 11 : Six PLA cadres are arrested during a search operation in front of the Bishnupur police station. The arrested militants are identified as Ahongshangbam Chittaranjan, Longjam Thakur alias Romesh, Mutum Ngongo alias NG, Aribam Sanatomba Luwang alias Tomboy, Oinam Sunil alias Nanao, Yumnam Robert alias Bobo alias Malemnganba alias Meiraba.
- September 10: The Imphal West district police arrest four PLA cadres, Sorokhaibam Premchand Singh, Soibam Lalngam Meitei, Mohammed Jane Khan and Ningombam Bibhas Singh, from Lalambung Makhong.
- September 10: Three PLA cadres are arrested from Uripok area in the capital Imphal. Two of the arrested are directly involved in the September 6-abduction of Manipur University Students' Union president, Ashok Kumar Singh.
- September 6: Unidentified militants, who claim to be members of the RPF, political wing of the PLA, assault and later abduct the president of the Manipur University Students' Union, Ashok Kumar Singh.

  PLA cadres trigger an explosion targeting a road opening party of the BSF near Laikoi Ching under Lamlai Police Station in the Chandel district. No casualty is reported in the incident.
- September 3: A suspected PLA cadre, Oinam Naoba alias Nanao, is arrested near Machu Cinema hall in the Imphal West district. A demand letter of the outfit is recovered from him.
- August 27: A PLA cadre, R. K. Meiraba alias Romeo, is killed in a counter insurgency operation at Sekmajin in the Thoubal district.

- August 14: A PLA cadre, R. K. Kanta alias Ibungo, is arrested at Haobam Marak Chingtham Leikai in the Imphal West district.
- July 31 : A PLA cadre, Okram Tomba, is arrested in a search operation at Ningthoukhong in the Bishnupur district.
- July 30: The Imphal East district police arrests a PLA cadre, Lonongoai Dikam Singh, from Singjamei Oinam Thingel locality during a search operation.
- July 27: Three PLA cadres along with a UNLF cadre are arrested during search operations at Kakching Khunou and its surrounding area in the Thoubal district. One 9 mm pistol and three live rounds of ammunition and incriminating documents are recovered from their possession.
- July 26: A PLA cadre, Thingujam Jiten alias Vinod, is arrested from Waikhong Bazar Maning Leikai in the Thoubal district.
- July 15: A suspected PLA cadre, Nanao, is arrested during a raid at Yairipok Keithelmanbi Maning Leikai locality in the Thoubal district.
- July 11: The RPF, political wing of PLA, claims responsibility for the July 10 bomb attack on the Assam Rifles patrol at Waithou in the Thoubal district. The outfit's 'communication and publicity assistant secretary' Lily Leima says that PLA cadres have returned to their hideout safely after the incident.
- July 10: Three SF personnel are killed and seven persons, including two civilians, are wounded in a PLA triggered bomb explosion and subsequent ambush on a SF patrol at Waithou Area in the Thoubal district.
- July 10: A former PLA cadre, Aheibam Herojit, missing from his residence reportedly since July 7, is killed by unidentified militants at Nungchappi in the Imphal East district.
- July 6: The Imphal West police arrests a PLA 'corporal', identified as Khundrakpam Shanta alias Paikhomba of Heirok part-II, from the RIMS main gate.
- June 30: Five SF personnel and four suspected PLA cadres are killed and three others injured in an encounter at Thangjng Ching in the Churachandpur district. Four AK-47 rifles, one lethode launcher, one pistol, one radio set, one grenade and incriminating documents are recovered from the incident site.
- May 29: A PLA cadre, Dolendro Singh, is arrested along with some incriminating documents at Sawombung area under Lamlai police station in the Imphal East district.
- May 26: A trader is killed by suspected PLA cadres at Ningthoukhong *Bazaar* in the Bishnupur district.

- May 25: A civilian, Arun Thakur, is shot at and wounded by unidentified militants at Uripok locality of the capital Imphal. The victim had reportedly defied the 'ban' on using tobacco products 'imposed' by the PLA and KCP.
- May 22: Two PLA cadres, Ramesh Hijam and Tomba Meitei, are arrested at Kamengsabal under Lamsang police station in the Imphal West district.
- May 13: The Imphal West district police arrests a PLA cadre, Sorokhaibam Iboton Singh, from the Lamshang Bazaar area.
- May 12: The Imphal East district police arrests a PLA cadre, Mutum Sanathoi, from the Kongba area.
- May 11: A PLA 'sergeant', Nongthombam Ingo, is arrested from the Khurai Sajor Leikai Babu Hotel area of the Imphal East district. One Sub Machine Carbine and one magazine along with six live rounds of 9 mm ammunition are recovered from his possession.
- May 9: The Imphal East district police arrests a PLA cadre, Yaikhom Rohen, from Phaknung village.
- April 15: A PLA cadre is arrested from Heitup Pokpi Heirok part-I locality in the Thoubal district.
- April 5: A civilian and one police personnel are injured in an exchange of fire between the SFs and suspected PLA cadres at Baruni Chingkhong under Lamlai police station in the Imphal East district. Meanwhile, two cadres of the outfit are arrested from Khuga Tampak area in Churachandpur district. One AK-47 rifle along with five live rounds of ammunition is recovered from their possession.
- March 24: At least six women cadres of the PLA are arrested during two separate raids carried out in the Bishnupur district.
- March 4: A PLA cadre is arrested during search operations at Wahengbam Leikai area in the Bishnupur district.
- January 31: The Imphal West District police arrests a PLA cadre, Moirangthem Romesh Singh, from the Yaiskul area.
- January 25: A 'town commander' of the PLA, Mahendro Singh alias John, is arrested along with some live ammunition from Churachandpur town.
- January 20: The Thoubal district police commandos arrests a 'second lieutenant' of the PLA, Nonthombam Sudeshkumar, along with his wife during a raid at Khoidum Pat, and SF personnel arrest two other PLA cadres, Boycha and Romeo, during a separate raid at Sagolmang in the Imphal East district. One Chinese made pistol, one magazine and a few rounds of ammunition were recovered from their possession.

- January 16: A PLA hideout is neutralized at Theogtang Zoukanou in the Churachandpur district, and a huge cache of arms and ammunition, including 76 AK-47 and AK-56 rifles, 20 SLRs and other small arms along with a large quantity of ammunition, are recovered.
- January 9: The Imphal East district police arrests a PLA woman cadre, Pebam Sophia alias Sanathoi, during a raid at Khurai Ningthoubung Leikai in the capital Imphal. Based on her confession, security forces conduct a similar raid at Singjamei Kshetri Leikai, in which another PLA cadre, Laishram Mocha alias Nanao, is arrested. A computer along with 27 compact discs is recovered from the latter.

2004

- December 20: The Imphal East District police arrest two PLA terrorists, Asem Yaima and Asem Shyam, from the Mantripukhri area of Imphal on charges of extortion from an oil pump at Sekmai
- December 13: A PLA terrorist is killed during an encounter with the police at Singjamei Maibam Leikai in the Imphal East district.
- December 12: The Imphal East district police arrests a PLA terrorist, Mohammed Firoz Shaha, from the Palace Gate area of Imphal.
- December 10: Manipur Police personnel kill a PLA terrorist during an encounter at Lalambung Makhong in Imphal city.
- December 9: A PLA terrorist, Tolen, is arrested from an unspecified location in Imphal.
- December 5: The Imphal West district police arrests a PLA cadre, Kabrabam Inaobi Singh, from the Uripok area of Imphal city.
- November 18: The RPF and the PLA call for a boycott of Prime Minister Manmohan Singh's schedule visit to the state on November 20 and 21, saying that there is no reason to celebrate the visit of the Prime Minister of a country that has 'forcibly annexed' Manipur.
- November 15: Two PLA terrorists, Halngam and Angkholet arrested from L Khabal village in Churachandpur district.
- October 12: PLA terrorist Dinamani alias Dina arrested from Patsoi in Imphal West district.
- October 9: Six PLA terrorists and a security force personnel are killed in an encounter at Khonkai in Churachandpur district.
- October 1: A CRPF personnel is killed and fifteen persons injured in a PLA ambush on a CRPF patrol party at Geliana in Churachandpur district.
- October 1: PLA terrorist Hamom Dumdumba arrested from the Sanjenthong area of Imphal city.
- September 26: Suspected PLA terrorists detonate explosives targeting the official residence of Dr. S Budhichandra, candidate of the Congress

party for the Konthoujam bye-elections to the State Legislative Assembly, located at Lamphel Sanakeithel area of Imphal city.

- September 18: Two PLA terrorists, Laishram Boston alias Binoy alias Ajit Singh and Khundrakpam Persun Singh alias Ronaldo, are arrested from Maibam Leikai Bokul Makhong and RIMS crossing area in Imphal West district.
- September 16: Two PLA terrorists, including a'lance corporal' identified as Nongthonbam Ibomcha alias Chandrakumar, are arrested from the Keibi Loushangkhong area of Imphal East district during a cordon and search operation.
- September 15: Security forces arrest two PLA terrorists from Wangjing-Salungbam in Thoubal district.
- September 3: The RPF and its armed wing, the PLA, call for a general strike on September 5, boycotting the visit of Union Minister for Home, Shivraj Patil, to Imphal.
- July 10: A suspected PLA woman cadre is killed during an encounter with the Assam Rifles personnel at Yaiphalok Maring village in Imphal East district.
- June 2: Assam Rifles personnel kill a suspected PLA terrorist at Kakching Khunou under Waikhong police station jurisdiction.
- May 24: Security forces kill a PLA terrorist in an encounter at Sanjenbam Lamkhai in Imphal West district.
- April 23: Suspected PLA terrorists attack the private residences of three Congress ministers, Family Welfare Minister Bijoy Koijam, Minister of State for Fisheries Maniruddin Sheikh and Minister of State for Public Health Engineering Mohammad Allauddin, in different parts of Manipur.
- April 4: Security force personnel belonging to the 12th Assam Rifles (AR) kill a PLA terrorist identified as Konjengbam Sanjoy near Keibi Loushangkhong village in Imphal East district.
- March 26: Two Assam Rifles personnel are killed during an encounter with suspected PLA terrorists at Thanga Heisnam Leikai in the Bishnupur district.
- March 24: Security force personnel arrest three PLA terrorists in separate incidents in the Imphal East District.
- March 18: Two PLA terrorists are arrested from the Imphal West district along with a 9 mm Mauser pistol, one magazine, three live bullets and four live bullets of 9 mm pistol.

- March 15: Security force personnel kill a suspected PLA terrorist, identified as Khumanthem Naoba, at Khurkhui in the Imphal West district.
- March 7: Report indicates that PLA's 'Operation Red Star' launched against the security forces from June 25, 2003, to February 25, 2004, has ended.
- March 2: Assam Rifles personnel kill a suspected PLA terrorist, identified as Irengbam Shyamananda, during an encounter at Awang Sanjenbam in the Imphal East district.
- February 27: Imphal East District police arrest two PLA cadres from Uripok Bachaspati Leikai.
- February 17: Two Central Reserve Police Force (CRPF) personnel are killed during an ambush laid by suspected PLA terrorists at Moirang Khunou in the Bishnupur district.
- January 29: Two PLA terrorists are killed in an encounter at Sanjembam village near Imphal.

2003

- December 23: A Revolutionary People's Front (RPF) terrorist is arrested from Leimapokpam Khunpham Mayai Leikai in the Imphal West district.
- December 17: Two PLA terrorists are killed during an encounter with the security forces at Loitang Khunou under Sekmai police station jurisdiction in the Imphal West district of Manipur.
- December 13: PLA terrorists attack the 28th Battalion of Central Reserve Police Force (CRPF) at Kwakta in the Bishenpur district of Manipur.
- November 30: Tripura Police arrests four PLA terrorists from Kadamtala in the North Tripura district.
- November 29: Two PLA terrorists are killed in an encounter with the security forces in the Yairipok area of Thoubal district.
- October 15: Security force personnel kill three PLA terrorists during an encounter at Singda village in the Imphal West district of Manipur and recover an AK-47 rifle with magazine, one 9 mm pistol with magazine, a radio set, 200 grams of explosive materials, two detonators, 15 rounds of AK-47 ammunition and two live rounds of 9 mm ammunition from the encounter site.
- September 2: Assam Rifles personnel kill a PLA terrorist during an operation at Okshu Ngakhasi Chingjin, under Lamlai police station limits in the Imphal East district.

- August 26: At least three suspected PLA terrorists, including a woman cadre, are killed when a bomb exploded accidentally near the Sekmai police station in Imphal West district.
- August 20: Security force personnel arrest at least six PLA terrorists from the Iroisemba Chingjin area in the Imphal West district.
- August 6: Manipur Police kill one suspected PLA terrorist during an encounter in the Wabagai Keirak area of Thoubal district.
- July 27: Manipur Chief Minister Okram Ibobi Singh and Irrigation Minister W. Brajabidhu Singh escape unhurt when PLA terrorists attack their convoy at Wangjing area, about 35 kilometers from the State capital Imphal. Two of their security guards are killed and seven others injured during the subsequent encounter with the terrorists.
- July 23: Three PLA terrorists are arrested from the Keishamthong Hodam Leirak area in Imphal.
- July 8: Dead body of Revolutionary People's Front (RPF) 'publicity chief', Ningthoujam Mangoljao alias Sanjit, is recovered from the Nambul River near Irom Meijrao in Imphal West district. RPF is the political wing of People's Liberation Army.
- July 4: At least five terrorists, including three PLA cadres, are arrested from various places in the Imphal West and East districts.
- June 25: At least four RPF terrorists, including a 'corporal', are arrested from the Imphal East district.
- June 14; 'Central committee' chief of PLA identified as Khomdram Lalaba alias Jayentakumar is killed during an encounter with the Manipur Police at Nandeibam Uku, under Singjamei police station limits in Imphal East district.
- June 12: A Woman cadre of the PLA identified as Angom Romita alias Nanao succumbs to her injuries at a local hospital in Imphal.
- June 9: Security forces during a search in the vicinity of the Ukhongsang village in Thoubal district arrest a PLA terrorist along with one sympathizer.
- June 3: Imphal West district police arrest a PLA terrorist from the Loitang Mamang Leikai area.
- May 30: Assam Police arrest a suspected conduit of the PLA from the Christian Basti area in Guwahati after securing specific information from a PLA terrorist, Bimal Singh, arrested earlier on May 28.
- April 29: Security forces arrest three persons, including a hardcore PLA terrorist, identified as Wahengbam Dhanajeet, on charges of extortion from local engineers in the Sawombung Kabui Khunou.

- April 13: Proscribed Revolutionary People's Front (RPF), political wing of the PLA, observes 'martyrs' day' and urges the general public to pay 'homage' to its slain cadres at the memorial in Cheiraoching, Manipur.
- March 19: Police arrests four PLA terrorists during separate raids across the State.
- February 20: Army personnel operating in Jiribam subdivision, Manipur, destroy a terrorist hideout jointly used by PLA and the Kuki National Front (KNF) in the Sonapur area of Imphal East district.
- February 17: A PLA suspect is arrested in connection with the murder of Manipur Electronic Media Journalists Union vice president and Vision North East chief correspondent Yumnam Meghajit Singh.
- February 8: Tripura Police arrests three PLA terrorists from the Deorachara area in North Tripura district.
- January 21: PLA demands Rupees one million for the release of abducted Food Corporation of India (FCI), Dimapur District Manager, R Sadashiban.
- January 5: Four PLA cadres are arrested from Hiracherra, under Kailasahar police station limits, in North Tripura district while crossing over to India from Bangladesh following their training in that country.

2002

- December 30: Manipur police arrest two PLA terrorists from Waithou village, Thoubal district, Manipur and recover a wireless set, some incriminating documents and some live rounds of AK-47 rifle.
- December 12: Four PLA terrorists are arrested from Nongpok Sekmai, Thoubal district. They are identified as Th. Jiten Singh, H. Somorendro Singh, S. Nande Singh and A. Basanta Singh.
- December 1: Imphal West district police shoot dead a PLA terrorist in an encounter in Tharoijam Mayai Leikai, Manipur. A revolver, some live ammunition rounds and some live ammunition rounds and some incriminating documents are recovered.

  Imphal West district police arrest two suspected PLA terrorists, identified as Khumanthem Amujao and Leihoutabam Dinesh Sharma, along three other suspects.
- November 20: A PLA terrorist is killed in an encounter with police in Kiyamgei Mamang Leikai, under Singjamei police station-limits, Manipur.

  Manipur police arrest three terrorists of the PLA, identified as corporal Laishram Ojit, Leishungbam Rajen and sergeant Nongthonbam ingo, in Bamon Kampu, Imphal East. They also and recover a Spanish Lama pistol, three magazines, 27 9 mm bullets, a Chinese-made grenade, a Kenwood communication set, a foreign-made cordless mother telephone with antenna, among other things.

- September 10: Police chargesheet two PLA terrorists, arrested in Delhi, on March 15, 2002, under the Prevention of Terrorism Act (POTA), They are also chargesheeted under the Indian Penal Code, Arms Act, Unlawful Activities (Prevention) Act and Passport Act.
- July 08: Three suspected PLA terrorists and a sympathizer are arrested from Sapermeina in Senapati district. Two 9 mm pistols and a stolen car are seized from their possession.
- June 12: Manipur Police commandos shoot dead a PLA terrorist and arrest another in Khurai, and seize a 9 mm pistol and a Chinese made hand grenade from them.
- June 7: A suspected PLA terrorist is arrested from a hotel at Laitumkhrah in Shillong, Meghalaya.
- May 14: The Thoubal district police arrest a woman PLA terrorist in Thoubal Wangban. She hails from Langathel Khumanthem Leikai village and is believed to have had trained outside India.
- May 3: Security forces in Manipur shoot two PLA terrorists dead in separate incidents and recover a 9 mm pistol with some live ammunition rounds.
- April 23: Two terrorists of the Peoples Liberation Army (PLA) are caught by residents of Uripok Lamboikhongnangkong village for extortion and repeated theft of vehicles.
- April 22: Two terrorists and three civilians are killed following clashes between the PLA and the Border Security Force (BSF) between Sugnu and Sangaikot.
- April 10: PLA claims responsibility for killing four security force personnel at Pangei, on April 9 and for the April 2-killing of a security force personnel.
- March 27: PLA announces it had, on March 23, shot dead two of its cadres, whose bodies were recovered in Iroisemba Loukon, situated between Tangjeng and Gwaltabi villages, for alleged links with security forces.

2001

- September 18: Army personnel kill five PLA terrorists during encounter at Khoupum valley near Mamong village in Tamenglong district.
- May 3: Three PLA cadres arrested in Tripura.
- February 20: Four People's Liberation Army (PLA) terrorists gunned down at Naorem in Bishnupur district.

2000

- December 20: Three PLA cadres killed in Chandel and Thoubal district.

People's Revolutionary Party of Kangleipak (PREPAK)

Formation

The People's Revolutionary Party of Kangleipak (PREPAK) was formed under the leadership of R.K. Tulachandra on October 9, 1977.

Objective

Claiming to be the "most genuine revolutionary groups" in Manipur, the PREPAK's main demand is the expulsion of 'outsiders' from the State.

Leadership and Structure

PREPAK became dormant after its leader Tulachandra was killed in an encounter with the security forces in 1986. Following his death, S. Wanglen became the Commander-in-Chief (C-in-C) of PREPAK. The organisation's General Secretary, Lumbeban Masunga was killed on May 19, 1993. At present, Achamba is the Chairman and Tajila is the C-in-C of PREPAK. The group has a strength of approximately 200 insurgents. It is primarily trained by the National Socialist Council of Nagaland-Isak Muivah (NSCN-IM). The PREPAK is also part of Manipur People's Liberation Front (MPLF), along with United National Liberation Front (UNLF) and the People's Liberation Army (PLA).

Areas of Operation

It is largely confined to the valley in Manipur. PREPAK is also reported to carry out attacks in certain areas of Mizoram and in North Tripura. One of its camps is in Sajik Tampak in the Chandel district in Manipur. It also operates in Tizit in Nagaland's Mon district.

Linkages

PREPAK is reported to have received weapons and training in exchange for hard cash from the Kachin Independent Army (KIA) of Myanmar. It is also reported to have training camps in Bangladesh.

Incidents

2006

- December 23: SF personnel arrested a People's Revolutionary Party of Kangleipak (PREPAK) militant, identified as Bunty Gangpam, during a search operation at Sangaiprou in the Imphal East district.

  A PREPAK cadre, Bunty Gangpam, is arrested from Sangaiprou area under Singjamei police station in the Imphal West district.

- December 18: SF personnel arrest two PREPAK militants, Thoudam Iboyaima alias Boyai and Takhellambam Hemanta alias Ibomcha, during a search operation in the Imphal West district.

- December 12: An unidentified militant hurled a bomb and subsequently opened fire at the residence of the Director of Agriculture, Athokpam Ibouchouba Singh, at Top Makha Leikai in the Imphal East district. However, no casualty was reported. Reports added that earlier the state agriculture office at Sanjenthong was locked by suspected PREPAK militants due to nonpayment of extortion amount.
- December 5: A civilian, Nongthombam Awangba, is shot at and wounded by PREPAK militants at an unspecified place in Imphal, for his alleged involvement in the rape of two women at Sekmaijin on November 19.
- December 3: Two PREPAK militants, 'lieutenant' Wairokpam ibotombi alias Herojit alias Toni and Khumu-kcham Joykumar alias Luwang, are shot dead by security force personnel in a counter-insurgency operation at Koinai-Tang in the Chandel district.
- November 27: Two unidentified PREPAK militants locked up the main office building of the Manipur State Agriculture Directorate at Sanjenthong in the Imphal East district. Refusal to pay ransom was suspected to be the main reason behind this act.
- November 26: A People's Revolutionary Party of Kangleipak militant, Thokchom Bobo alias Wangba, was arrested from Kongba in the Imphal East district.
- November 23: People's Revolutionary Party of Kangleipak militants shot dead their own cadre, identified as Laishram Herojit, at Sekmaijin in the Imphal West district for his alleged involvement in the rape of a woman a day earlier.
- November 22: Two suspected PREPAK cadres reportedly issued a threat letter containing a live bullet to the executive engineer of the Public Works Department of Thoubal division, R.K. Mobisana, at Singjamei Okram Leikai in the Imphal West district. One PREPAK cadre, would-be mother-in-law, when the girl reportedly eloped with her boyfriend, Subir Ahmed alias Boycha, at Sekmaijin in the Imphal West district. One PREPAK cadre, Laishram Herojit and four unidentified youths raped a girl identified as Wahida Bibi and her would-be mother-in-law, when the girl reportedly eloped with her boy friend, Subir Ahmed alias Boycha, at Sekmaijin in the Imphal West district.
- November 21: A civilian, identified as Dijayangliu, was killed and four others, G Golmei, Ahen-ma Rongmei, Ganthoidai, Tailungkho, sustained injuries when a vehicle in which they are traveling slipped over the greasy oil spilled on the road by suspected general strike supporters

near Oriental College Gate along National Highway 53 in the Imphal West district. Police sources said that the general strike was called against the alleged killing of a PREPAK militant after he was released from the prison

- November 19: Three bombs exploded inside the campus of the Border Security Force post at Tronglaobi in the Bishnupur district. Similarly, another bomb exploded at Keirenpat near the Jammu and Kashmir 15 Light Infantry camp. Manipur Police suspected the involvement of People's Revolutionary Party of Kangleipak in the explosions.
- November 18: A cadre of the PREPAK, identified as Mairembam Open alias Premkumar alias Prem, was arrest by security force personnel in a search operation at Toubul Mamang Leikai in the Bishnupur district.
- November 16: PREPAK claimed responsibility for the hand grenade explosion inside the Chief Minister's residence at Babupara in the Imphal West district.
- November 15: A PREPAK cadre, Ningthoujam Binoy alias Khaiba, was shot dead by unidentified gunmen at Khurai in the Imphal West district.
- November 13: People's Revolutionary Party of Kangleipak claimed to have killed at least five security force personnel and wounded 20 others in militant attacks on the Assam Rifles' post at Kakching Lamkhai in the Thoubal district.
- November 10: SF personnel recovered one AK-56 rifle, a magazine along with 20 live rounds, one electronic detonator, two lethode bombs and a bulb allegedly used as explosive device accessory from the residence of a person, Th Mong-yamba. The seizure was made following the confession made by the PREPAK militants arrested two days ago at Porompat police station in the Imphal East district.
- November 8: Two PREPAK militants, Puyam Mongjaba alias Biren alias Sunil and Pangambam Laxmi alias Neha alias Ibe, were arrested at Khurai Sajor Leikai in the Imphal East district. One 9 mm pistol made in Taiwan along with two live rounds of 9 mm ammunition, one Directorate of Information and Public Relation identity card, a driving license and some incriminating documents were reportedly recovered from their possession.
- October 9: The PREPAK, in a statement issued on its 29th 'foundation day', asks the indigenous tribes of Manipur not to practice birth control to combat the influx of migrants by increasing their own population.
- October 7: The PREPAK warns the All Manipur Muslims Coordinating Committee of dire consequences, if they go ahead with their proposed

Thoubal district bandh on October 9 that coincides with the 29th 'rising day' of the outfit.

- August 16: A PREPAK cadre, Ranjit Singh, is arrested from Arapti Mamang Leikai in the Thoubal district.
- August 13: A PREPAK cadre, Kangujam Rajesh alias Naobi, is arrested from Bashikhong area under Iribung police station jurisdiction in the Imphal East district.
- August 3: A group of PREPAK cadres attack a security patrol party at New *Bazaar* area of Churachandpur town in which one Border Security Force personnel is killed.
- July 21: SFs arrest a PREPAK cadre, Waikhom Romen Meitei alias Tomba, from Lamlongei Makha Leikai in the Imphal West district.
- July 20: A PREPAK cadre, Langpoklakpam Sanatomba, is arrested from Langthabal area of Imphal city.
- July 18: Manipur Police personnel arrest two PREPAK cadres, Aheibam Oken Meitei alias Papulal and Lairenmayum Romesh Sharma, from Takyel Kolom Leikai in the Imphal West district.
- June 15: A PREPAK cadre, Mutum Thakur Singh alias Deva, is arrested from Lamdeng under Lamshang police station limits in the Imphal West district.
- June 14: SFs arrested two PREPAK cadres, Gopal Singh and Thokchom Dogendro from Chingarel Tejpur and Canchipur near Imphal city.
- June 5: A PREPAK cadre, Salam Kameni Meitei, is arrested from Takyelpat in the Imphal West district.
- May 31: PREPAK parades two persons, Maibam Binoychand and Koijam Iboyaima Singh, before the media persons at a unspecified place in the Imphal West district, for allegedly trying to garner supply orders for printing and stationery items in the Family Welfare Department, Government of Manipur, in the name of one of its cadre, Lemba. They were later released unharmed after a warning.
- May 25: Two PREPAK cadres, S Momon alias Bony and Mohammad Taslimuddin, are arrested from the Singjamei area of Imphal city.
- May 24: A PREPAK cadre, Okhen Meitei, is arrested from Takyel in the Imphal West district.
- May 22: Suspected PREPAK cadres kill one of their former colleagues, Ningombam Momo, while his associate, Shougrakpam Mocha is shot at for extorting money in the name of the outfit at Kwakeithel Laishram Leikai under Singjamei police station limits in the Imphal West district.
- April 30: A PREPAK cadre, Haobijam Nabakanta alias Nika, is arrested from the Keishampat area of Imphal city.

- April 27: A PREPAK cadre, H. Surjitpa, is arrested from Maring Hanabok in Manipur.
- April 21: A PREPAK cadre is arrested from Gwaltabi Bazaar in the Imphal East district.
- April 15: A PREPAK cadre, Moirangthem Arun Singh alias Konu, is arrested from the Khurai area of Imphal city.
- March 23: A school head master, Thokchom MR alias Ibungochouba Meitei, is dragged away from his residence and subsequently shot dead by unidentified militants at Tera Sayang Kurabu Makhong under Lamphel police station in the Imphal West district. Three empty cases of 9 mm are recovered from the incident site. Thokchom, reportedly a former PREPAK cadre, had been served an extortion notice amounting to Rupees 3000, which he has refused to pay.
- March 21: An army personnel, P. N. Hazarika, is wounded during an ambush on a security convoy at Moirang Khunou in the Bishnupur district by the PREPAK.
- March 21: According to the 2005 Annual Report of the Manipur Police, 23 militants, including eight PREPAK cadres, surrendered during the year.
- March 13: Nine cadres of six militant outfits, including a PREPAK cadre, surrender along with a large cache of arms and ammunition before the Commander of 3 Corps, Lt. Gen. Z.U. Shah, at the Headquarters of Inspector General of Assam Rifles (South) at Mantripukhri in the Imphal city. The surrendered PREPAK cadre deposits a US made cabine and a magazine.
- March 9: The PREPAK announces its decision to stop taking up contract or supply work henceforth. The outfit has reportedly undertaken contract or supply work to raise funds for its 'armed struggle'.
- February 27: A PREPAK cadre, K. Ngougo Sana Singh alias Nganthoi, is arrested from Sugnu in the Thoubal district.
- February 21: Security force personnel arrest a PREPAK cadre, Wahengbam Rajesh Singh, from Utlou in the Bishnupur district. Demand letters and 9 mm pistol ammunitions are recovered from his possession.
- February 15: The Imphal West police arrest a suspected PREPAK cadre, identified as Takhelambam Kunjaraj alias Ibomcha Singh, from Hiyangthang near Nando Brick Field.
- February 6: Two PREPAK cadres, including a woman sympathiser, are arrested by the SF personnel from an unspecified place in Manipur.

- January 19: A suspected PREPAK cadre, Chandam Jiten alias Malemnganba, is shot dead by the security force (SF) personnel in an encounter at Konsam Leikai in the Imphal East district. One 9 mm pistol along with ammunition is recovered from the incident site.
- January 16: The 'finance secretary' and 'SS lance corporal' of the PREPAK, Ningthoujam Chaoba, allotted the 'group number 12460' and responsible for extortion and 'tax collection' in the general area of Moreh, is arrested from the Moreh bazaar in Chandel district.
- January 14: A 'retired' UNLF cadre, Oinam Pahari Singh, is killed by suspected cadres of the PREPAK at Kumbi Awang Leikai under Kumbi police station in the Bishnupur district.
- January 12: A PREPAK cadre is killed and one 9 mm pistol with some live rounds is recovered from Yurenjam in the Imphal West district.
- January 4: Two factions of the PREPAK, led by M. Biren Singh and Nongdren Khomba, have announced their merger, reportedly for lending an international look to their 'struggle'.

2005

- December 25: Two extortionists are attacked and injured by PREPAK cadres for allegedly collecting money in the name of a militant outfit at Naorem Leikai under Singjarnei police station in the Imphal West district.
- December 9: Four PREPAK cadres, Lukram Romen Singh, Konthoujam Kuber Singh, Huidrom Setha Meitei and Maibam Khumai Meitei, are arrested from the Shikhong area.
- December 4: Two PREPAK cadres are arrested from the Imphal West district.
- December 1: Two PREPAK cadres are arrested from Khongman Bashikhong area.
- November 15: A PREPAK cadre, Oinam Loken alias Leishemba, suspected to be involved in the firing on the residence of the Revenue Commissioner, Sharatchandra, about a month back, is arrested near the Moirang College in the Bishnupur district.
- November 11: Three to four hideouts of suspected PREPAK cadres are neutralized at Thanga Lawai in the Bishnupur district. One self-loading rifle, one magazine with 30 live rounds, one magazine post, water bottle and daily necessities are recovered from the hide-out.
- November 6: A self styled chairman of the PREPAK, Meishnam Biren alias Achanba, is arrested from Haobam Marak Irom Leikai in the Imphal West district.
- October 24: A PREPAK cadre, Kshetrimayum Ajit Singh alias Boby, is arrested from the Kawakeithel market area of Imphal West district.

- October 21: The residence of Arambam Binodini, Joint Director of Department of Tribal Development and Other Backward Classes, is attacked by PREPAK at Sagolband Moirang Leirak under Imphal police station, for her failure to meet the deadline for payment of extortion money issued by the outfit.
- October 16: Two PREPAK cadres, Ningthoujam Kishan alias Inaomacha alias Prem alias Iboba and Thounacjam Ibomcha Meitei alias Chamba alias Tachouba, are arrested from Loktak Project area and Bashikhong Loumanbi in the Bishnupur district.
- October 13: Two PREPAK cadres are arrested by the Imphal police from Pishumthong and Haobam Marak. One 9 mm pistol along with 8 live rounds is recovered from their possession.
- October 13: A PREPAK cadre, Ningthoujam Nabachandra alias Deven, is arrested from Keibul Heikha Leikai in the Bishnupur district.
- October 4: A PREPAK cadre, Salam Boinao, is arrested from Nachou Mayai Leikai in the Bishnupur district, while collecting items earlier demanded by the outfit from a civilian's house.
- September 30: A PREPAK cadre, Laishram Tamubi Singh alias Naocha, is arrested from Thinungei Makha Leikai in the Imphal West district.
- September 29: Two 'recruitment agents' of the PREPAK, Sunder Singh alias Khonjaba and S. Subon Singh, are arrested from Haukha Heinou Makhong in the Thoubal district.
- September 26: A PREPAK cadre, Amakcham Naocha alias Raju, is arrested from Pangal Leirak along Ayangpalli Road.
- September 16: A former PREPAK cadre, Konthoujam Dhamen, is shot dead by unidentified militnts at Mutum Phibou Mayai Leikai under Wangoi police station in the Imphal West district
- September 16: A PREPAK militant, Oinam Sanayaima alias Yaima, is arrested from Moirang Khunou in the Bishnupur district.
- September 10: A suspected PREPAK cadre, Robindro alias Thoithoiba of Moirang Okshabung, is killed and an Assam Rifles personnel sustains injuries during an encounter at Kumbi Tera Kha Sandam Leikai in the Bishnupur district. One AK-47 rifle, three magazines with 151 live rounds of AK-47 ammunition, one purse and one water bottle are recovered from the slain militant.
- September 9: A PREPAK cadre, Kongrailakpam Samsan Sharma, is arrested from the Sagolband Bijoy Govinda bridge area in Imphal West district. According to police sources, he is also an arms supplier for militant outfits operating in Manipur.

- September 5: A former PREPAK cadre, Thounaojam Gojen, is killed by unidentified militants at his residence located at Haokha Mamang Leikai in the Thoubal district.
- September 3: Two PREPAK militants, W Chriba alias Bideshwar and Suraj alias Bocha, are arrested from Tamenglong.
- August 18: A PREPAK cadre, Thounoujam Boro alias Thonglen, is arrested from the Mayai Koibi area of Imphal West district.
- August 8: A senior cadre of the PREPAK, Kangjam Menjor Singh alias Irei, is arrested from the Imphal West district. Official sources said that Irei was 'commander' of the Imphal West and Bishnupur districts and in-charge of the home, organisation and finance departments of the outfit.
- July 13: A PREPAK cadre, Wangkhem Samananda Singh, is arrested at Singjamei in the Imphal East district. He had allegedly collected an extortion amount of Rupees 1.7 lakhs from the steel and cement shops located between Canchipur and Moirangkhom areas.
- July 12: A PREPAK cadre, Sagolsem Gambhir Meitei alias Nongpokngakpa, is arrested from the Moirangkhom area in Imphal West district.
- July 7: Four PREPAK cadres are arrested from the Langthabal area of Imphal West district, while another is arrested from Uripok Bachaspati Leikai. According to a statement issued by the Superintendent of Police, they had planned to abduct a forest department official to force the department to yield to their demand for deducting two per cent of the total annual budget allocation for the department.
- July 5: A woman cadre of the PREPAK, Kangujam Sanajaobi Devi, is arrested from her residence in the Kwakeithel Heinou Khongnembi Lamdong area in the Imphal West district. One 9 mm pistol with six live rounds, one magazine, currency notes worth Rupees 20,000 and one motorcycle are recovered from her residence.
- June 29: A PREPAK cadre, Langpoklakpam Binoy alias Lakpa, belonging to the outfit's General Secretary faction, is arrested along with some incriminating documents at Hiyangthang Maning Leikai in the Imphal West district.
- June 27: PREPAK cadres shot one of their colleagues, Gurumayum Umakanta Sharma, in his leg for allegedly taking drugs.
- June 20: Eight terrorists belonging to the UNLF and PREPAK are killed in an encounter with the police near Phoipi in the Hengiep area of Churachandpur district. A cache of weapons, including six AK-47 rifles, one RPG with four rockets, one M-16 rifles, one G-3 rifle, a shot-gun

and a lethode launcher, were recovered from the incident site. Two army personnel are also injured in the encounter

- June 15: Two suspected cadres of the General Secretary faction of PREPAK are killed at Hengkok village under Hengiep police station of Churachandpur district.
- June 7: A PREPAK cadre, Langoijam Dhanachandra Singh, is arrested from Thangapat in the Imphal East district.
- June 6: A suspected female cadre of the PREPAK, Sartorji Kom, is arrested along with a mobile phone from Wangthrok Phungzayung Village under Moirang Police Station in Bishnupur district.
- June 5: A PREPAK terrorist, Heisnam Manisana, is arrested in the Lamphel Super Market area of Imphal West district.
- May 20: Two PREPAK terrorists, Oinam Charlie and Phanjabam Nelson Singh, are arrested from Kakching Khunou area in the Thoubal district and from the State Guest House area in Imphal city respectively.
- April 30: Two persons are killed and another injured in separate attacks by the PREPAK at Nongpok Sekmai and Nungba under Yairipok police station in the Thoubal district. All the three persons are parents of PREPAK cadres who have surrendered on April 23. A PREPAK spokesperson has told local media that the action was necessary to warn those cadres who wanted to surrender and disclose party secrets to the Government.
- April 29: Four cadres belonging to the 'Vice-chairman' group of the PREPAK along with a huge cache of arms and ammunition, including AK-series rifles and one lethode launcher, surrender before the Chief Minister Ibobi Singh at an official ceremony in Imphal.
- March 10: A PREPAK cadre, Ningthoujam Kenedy, surrenders before the Manipur Chief Minister Ibodi Singh.
- March 6: A PREPAK cadre is arrested along with one AK 56 rifle, one lethode launcher, 125 rounds of live ammunition and three magazines at Lamlong village in the Imphal East district.
- March 7: Five PREPAK cadres are arrested along with eight Lethod bombs, 24 live ammunitions of M-16 rifles, one US-made Carbine and 10 rounds of live ammunition in separate search operations from Singjamei Makha Oinam Leikai and Singjamei Mayengbam Leikai areas of the Imphal East district and from Wabagai Makha Leikai area in Thoubal district.
- March 14: A former PREPAK cadre is killed in the Thiyam Konjin Umbilok area of capital Imphal.
- March 5: A PREPAK cadre is arrested along with one US-made carbine with 10 live rounds of ammunition from Thoubal district.

- February 24: Two camps of the PREPAK are raided and a cache of arms and ammunition are recovered by a combined team of the Manipur Police and Army from Keibul Lamjao in the Bishnupur district.
- January 31: A PREPAK cadre, Huirem Boby, is arrested from the Naoremthong area of capital Imphal.
- January 23: Four PREPAK cadres are arrested from Oinam Thingel Aheibam Leikai and Samurou Awang Leikai localities in the Imphal West district.
- January 20: Six PREPAK cadres, Elangbam Bobo, Elangbam Rabichandra, Soraisam Tamnubi, Ahongshangbam Aruna, Thongram Raju alias Anand and Lisham Inao alias James, are arrested during two separate search operations at Hiyanglam-Wabagai in the Thoubal district and at the Thangal Bazaar area of capital Imphal.
- January 9: Five terrorists are killed in a factional clash between cadres of the hitherto unknown group, PRK, and PREPAK at Khordak in the Bishnupur district.
- January 7: PREPAK claims responsibility for shooting one Elangbam Tomba at Keisamthong in the capital Imphal on January 6, allegedly for sheltering PRK cadres.
- January 7: PREPAK claims responsibility for shooting one Elangbam Tomba at Keisamthong in the capital Imphal on January 6, allegedly for sheltering PRK cadres.

2004

- December 28: The PREPAK claims responsibility for the shooting of a civilian, Laishram Churasingh, at Kwakeithel in the capital Imphal on December 26 for his 'anti-PREPAK activity'.
- December 21: A PREPAK cadre, Wahengbam Hemanta Singh, is arrested by the residents of Uripok in the capital Imphal, while he is trying to extort money from the private residence of State Health Minister, Nandakumar Singh.
- December 13: The Imphal West police commandos arrest a PREPAK terrorist, identified as Langpoklakpam Lohel, from Paona bazaar in Imphal city.
- December 7: Security force personnel arrest three PREPAK terrorists from Paona Bazar in the Imphal city.
- November 26: Two PREPAK terrorists, Md Sanayaima and Sarangthem Nanao, surrender before the police at Thoubal along with one AK-56 rifle along with two magazines, an SLR with three magazines and 339 rounds of ammunition.
- November 26: Imphal city police arrest one PREPAK terrorist, Laishram Ratan Singh, from Thangal Bazaar.

- November 20: A PREPAK terrorist, Khundongbam Kiran, is killed during an encounter with the police at Heirok Bazar in the Thoubal district.
- November 21: Two PREPAK women cadres, identified as Wahengbam Memthiobi Dev and Laishram Ranibala, are arrested from Bishnupur Bazar.
- November 16: The Imphal West district commandos arrest two PREPAK terrorists Irom Chaoba and Leisangthem Sophiya from Paona *bazaar* in the heart of the Imphal city.
- November 11: Two PREPAK terrorists including a woman cadre arrested in separate incidents from Khuningthel Salam Mamang Leikai in Imphal West and Ningthoukhong in Bishnupur district.
- October 25: Security forces arrested three PREPAK terrorists from Naoremthong Bazar, Moirangkhom and Langol Games Village areas of Imphal West district.
- October 26: Two PREPAK terrorists arrested from Lamdeng village of the Imphal West district.
- October 20: Two PREPAK terrorists arrested from Lamdeng Makha Leikai in the Imphal West district.
- August 23: Two PREPAK terrorists arrested from Bamon Leikai in the Imphal East district and Pishum Thongkhong in the Imphal West district.
- August 22: PREPAK terrorist Tharoijam Herojit alias Mangal arrested from Takyel in Imphal East district.
- August 18: PREPAK terrorist Adhikarimayum Kiran Sharma alias Tombi arrested from Phubala in Bishnupur district.
- August 17: Three PREPAK terrorists arrested from Nachou in Bishnupur district.
- July 1: A security force personnel is killed and two others injured in an attack by suspected PREPAK terrorists on a SF patrol party at the Tiddim Road-Lailamveng junction in Churachandpur district.
- June 19: PREPAK cadre Lourembam Robindro killed by the police at Kwakhethel in Imphal West district.
- June 7: The 'Red Army' wing of PREPAK ambush an Army post at Khonmunliyan Kuki village in Chandel district.
- April 5: 'Red Army' cadres of the PREPAK launch an armed attack at the post of the 17th Assam Rifles located at Kangla fort in Imphal.
- March 9: Assam Rifles personnel kill two PREPAK terrorists in separate incidents at Heirok in the Thoubal district and near the NG Mani College under Lamlai police station in Imphal East district.

2003

- December 9: The PREPAK claims in a press release to have 'sorted' out its internal differences, which had led to the killing of 11 cadres in November 2003 in Manipur.
- December 6: PREPAK revokes 'military operation' against its factions after an 'amicable settlement' before the expiry of the December 6 midnight deadline.
- November 17: At least eleven PREPAK terrorists are killed during a clash with cadres of an unnamed terrorist outfit in the Setpur hills area of Bishenpur district.
- October 23: PREPAK sets free the General Secretary of Manipur Amateur Boxing Association, Khoibi Salam, along with two other members of the association after five days of captivity, near an undisclosed place in Bishenpur district.
- October 9: PREPAK commemorates its 26th 'foundation day at the Imphal East and Thoubal districts.
- October 7: Assam Rifles personnel kill two suspected PREPAK terrorists at an unspecified place in the Thoubal district of Manipur.
- September 21: PREPAK claims responsibility for the September 20-terrorist attack on the Central Reserve Police Force (CRPF) at Sugnu in the Thoubal district. Six civilians and one CRPF personnel were killed during the ensuing encounter.
- September 20: At least six civilians and one security force personnel are killed during an encounter between security forces and PREPAK terrorists in the Sugnu area of Thoubal district in Manipur.
- September 18: Police arrest at least four terrorists, including two PREPAK cadres, along with some incriminating documents from different places in the Imphal East district.
- August 30: Assam Rifles personnel kill one suspected PREPAK terrorist at Leipharok Maring village under Irilbung police station limits in Imphal East district.
- June 17: The Imphal West district police arrest a PREPAK terrorist, Takhellambam Sitam of Langthabal Awang Leikai, at Canchipur near Imphal.
- June 14: During Statewide search operations, Manipur Police arrests six terrorists, including two PREPAK cadres.
- June 1: PREPAK's 'Red Army' cadres attack a Central Reserve Police Force (CRPF) post at Tuinem, situated on the boundary between the Churachandpur and Bishnupur districts of Manipur.
- May 29: Security forces arrest 14 terrorists affiliated to various terrorist outfits, including the Kangleipak Communist Party (KCP), People's

Liberation Army (PLA), Kanglei Yawol Kanna Lup (KYKL) and PREPAK from various places in Manipur.

- May 21: Security forces arrest five PREPAK terrorists during a search operation in the Sekmaijin area following an attack on a CRPF camp at Moirang Khunou, under Moirang police station limits.
- May 12: Seven terrorists, including five PREPAK cadres, are arrested from the outskirts of Imphal.
- May 6: PREPAK's 'Red Army' attacks a Border Security Force (BSF) camp in Moirang, Bishnupur district.
- February 17: Security force personnel arrest three PREPAK terrorists from two different places - Charangpat in Thoubal district and Uchiwa in Imphal East district.
- January 10: Three terrorists affiliated to the MPLF, which consists of three outfits including the PREPAK, killed in a prolonged encounter at Sajik Tampak area in Chandel district, bordering Myanmar.
- January 1: Manipur People's Liberation Front (MPLF), in which PREAPK is a constituent, asks all outfits in the region to put an end to extortion in the name of armed movement, commencing January 15, 2003.

2002

- December 24: Two PREPAK terrorists identified as Kshetrimayum Gose and Ananthem Sachikanta are killed in an encounter with State police commandos in Khwairamband Bazar, Imphal.
- November 12: PREPAK observes black day in memory of slain leaders killed in two encounters-on November 12 in 1978 and in 1985.
- November 4: Inaocha, an ex-cadre of the PREPAK recruited into the security forces, is killed in a shot out with colleagues at a camp of the Manipur Rifles in Leikun village, Chandel district, Manipur.
- October 7: Two PREPAK terrorists are killed and two more manage to escape during an encounter in Tharoijam Awang Leikai, under Patsoi police station-limits, (West Imphal district), Manipur. A Chinese-made revolver and a hand grenade are seized from the slain terrorists.
- August 10: A combined team of the 1st and 2nd Divisions of India Reserve Battalion (IRB) and Imphal East and West police arrest two terrorists of the PREPAK.
- July 3: Tourangbam Brojeshwar, a self-styled home secretary and a top PREPAK leader, is arrested with incriminating documents following a raid in the Uripok area near Imphal.
- June 4: In a statement, PREPAK blames ZRA (Zomi Revolutionary Army) for internecine killings in Manipur and holds ZRA responsible for the killings of six of its members on June 1, near Aina village, Churachandpur.

2001

- October 11: Manipur police commandos arrest a PREPAK terrorist from Sagolband Moirang Hanuba Leirak, near Tera police outpost.
- October 8: The Central Committee of the PREPAK urges the people of Manipur to extend support to the outfit and to carry out a united armed struggle.
- August 3: Three terrorists from different outfits, including PREPAK, surrender in Loktak in Bishnupur district, Manipur, with an AK-56 rifle, an M-22 rifle, a .303 rifle and a huge quantities of ammunition.
- July 27: Urrikhinbam Sarat alias Meiraba, a senior leader of PREPAK, killed in an encounter at Nungou Ching in Thoubal district. He had been a leading member of the permanent committee of the Manipur People's Liberation Front (MPLF), an umbrella organization of UNLF, PLA and PREPAK.
- March 1: The organisation rejects the then Manipur Chief Minister Radhabinod Koijam's ceasefire offer.

2000

- December 31: Two persons, including a police personnel were injured when suspected PREPAK terrorists attacked a Mizoram police outpost at Vatin, a hamlet on the border between the two states.
- February 8: Suspected PREPAK terrorists hurl a powerful grenade at the private residence of Manipur Chief Minister, W. Nipamacha Singh, in Wangboi, Imphal district.

1999

- April 6: Two security force personnel were killed and six others injured when a PREPAK terrorist snatched a rifle from a jawan in the Bagbassa camp of the Assam Rifles in North Tripura and fired indiscriminately.

United National Liberation Front (UNLF)

Formation

The United National Liberation Front (UNLF), the oldest Meitei insurgent group in the State was formed under the leadership of Areambam Samrendra Singh on November 24, 1964 to achieve independence and a socialist society. A pan-Manipuri Youth League was formed in December 1968, which functioned as an overground body for the UNLF. Later, differences within the outfit surfaced over the issue of strategies to be adopted. While Samrendra Singh sought to spread ideological consciousness before launching an armed struggle, the more radical leader Oinam Sudhir Kumar established a Revolutionary Government of Manipur (RGM). Samarendra Singh was killed by unidentified terrorists in Imphal on June 10, 2001. In the seventies and eighties, the UNLF concentrated mainly on mobilisation and recruitment. In 1990, it decided to launch an armed struggle for the 'liberation' of Manipur from India. In the same year, it formed an armed wing called Manipur People's Army (MPA).

Objective

The UNLF aims to establish an independent socialist Manipur.

Leadership

Rajkumar Meghen alias Sana Yaima is the current Chairman of UNLF. Other important leaders include 'General Secretary' Th Sanachou; 'Secretary of Defence' A. Wangpa; 'Secretary of Organisation' M. Nongyai; and 'Secretary of Publicity' N. Thabal. The Women's wing Chief is Nganbi Devi; Deputy Women's wing Chief: Banti Devi. The then UNLF Chairman, Namuizum Okendra was arrested on May 19, 1993.

Structure

The outfit's armed wing is called the MPA (Manipur People's Army). It also maintains a communication and publicity cell.

Area of Operation

The outfit operates in the Jiribam valley and Cachar district of Assam.

Linkages

Soon after its formation, the UNLF leaders established a political relationship with the authority of the then East Pakistan, and underwent military training in that country in 1969. They also supported the Pakistani army during the 1971 Bangladesh liberation war. Later, the group also developed a relationship with China even while continuing its relations with Pakistan. On June 14, 1975, UNLF leader N. Bisheswar Singh and 16 other Meitei rebels proceeded to Lhasa to seek Chinese assistance. The group has links with Naga and Mizo terrorist outfits as well. On May 22, 1990, the UNLF, along with other insurgent groups operating in the Northeast — the National Socialist Council of Nagaland - Khaplang (NSCN-K), the United Liberation Front of Asom (ULFA), and the Kuki National Army (KNA) — floated a pan-Mongoloid coalition called the Indo-Burma Revolutionary Front (IBRF) to wage a "united struggle for the independence of Indo-Burma". The UNLF has training camps in Myanmar and Bangladesh. It also maintains close association with the NSCN-K.

Incidents

2006

- December 29: UNLF militants attack, using mortar shells, the Border Security Force post at Aijang near Sajik Tampak in the Chandel district. However, no casualty is reported.

- December 22: A former UNLF cadre, Laishram Surchandra alias Ngouba, is shot dead by unidentified gunmen at unspecified place between Maryland and Salungpham in the Thoubal district.

  One security force personnel is killed and five others sustain injuries in an attack by the UNLF at Khenjoi-Dingpi range in the Chandel district.
- December 18: Security force (SF) personnel shot dead a suspected United National Liberation Front militant in a retaliatory fire, when the militant riding a bicycle reportedly opened fire towards the SF personnel on foot patrol at Moirang Khunou under Moirang police station in the Bishnupur district. One 9 mm pistol, five live rounds, one empty case, a bicycle and INR 45 were recovered from his possession.
- December 15: A UNLF militant, Aheibam Boy alias Raju alias Nathuba, is arrested by SF personnel at Awang Khunou.
- December 13: SF personnel refuted the allegation of displacement of villagers of Khengjoi due to SF operations, made by the UNLF on December 12, as baseless and malicious. SF authorities added that the valley-based militants have laid a large number of improvised Explosive Devices in the area, more than 19 of which have been recovered and defused by the troops.
- December 9: An encounter between SF personnel and UNLF cadres was reported at Wailou range in the Chandel district.
- December 8: The Assam Rifles has described the claims of the United National Liberation Front of killing two security force personnel at Khenjoi in the Chandel district on December 6 as false and baseless.
- December 6: The UNLF claimed to have killed at least two security force personnel besides injuring some others in an encounter at an unspecified place between Phaijol and Khengjoi ranges in the Chandel district.
- December 4: A United National Liberation Front cadre, Kh. Kiran alias Nganu, is arrested at Soagolband in the Imphal West district.
- December 2: A United National Liberation Front cadre, Kiran alias Dak, was arrested from Patsoi in the Imphal West district. One 9 mm pistol with a magazine containing four live rounds was reportedly recovered from his possession
- December 1: A youth, Gurumayum Sunil, was shot at and injured and subsequently paraded before the media by the UNLF cadres at an unspecified place in the Imphal East district, for his alleged involvement in extortion at Soibam Leikai. The UNLF claimed that Sunil was a former Kangleipak Communist Party cadre.

- November 30: The UNLF cadres are reportedly trying to garner support in areas of south Assam, particularly Lakhipur, Jirighat, Fulertal, Banskandi in the Cachar district.

  Three UNLF cadres, Ngasepam Chitrakumar alias Thoiba alias P. Ngamba, Irengbam Raghumani Singh and Nong-thombam Thoi alias James Jit Singh, were arrested from the Imphal East district on an unspecified date. One 0.38 automatic pistol loaded with 8 rounds of 0.38 live ammunition in magazine were recovered from their possession.

- November 24: The Imphal Police arrested eight UNLF cadres during a search operation at Khalok Kom village in the Churachandpur district. However, a leader of the outfit, '2nd Lt.' Yumlembam Tomba Singh, managed to escape from the incident site.

- November 23: SF personnel arrested a United National Liberation Front cadre, 'corporal' Tombisana, during a search operation at Moreh in the Chandel district.

- November 14: Two persons, Sham alias Anthony and H. Dibheshwor, were arrested for their suspected links with the UNLF from Zoveng in the Churachandpur district.

- November 11: A cadre of the United National Liberation Front, 'sergeant major' Y Ratan Singh alias Khamba, was arrested at Khurai Chingabam Leikai in the Imphal West district.

- November 10: A civilian, identified as Nameirakpam Ibomcha, along with his wife Kunjeshori were reportedly extorted by suspected UNLF militants at Soibam Leikai Khamlabung Leirak in the Imphal East district.

- November 8: UNLF militants captured a youth, Mayengbam Surjit, for allegedly disguising himself as the cadre of the outfit at Mantripukhri in Imphal East district.

- November 6: Three UNLF cadres, Lairenjam Thanil alias Tomba, Soibam Basanta alias Ibungo and Khangenbam Janendra, were arrested at Wangoi Laiphrakpam in the Imphal East district.

- November, 1: Manipur Police brought back four UNLF cadres, arrested earlier in October by the Meghalaya Police and later remanded by a magistrate to police custody. Two UNLF cadres, Tongbram Inao Singh alias Tiken and Laishangthem Naoba alias Pari, were arrested from the Patsoi area in Imphal West district.

  Polices sources said that, one motor cycle was recovered from the possession of the arrested militant.

- October 28: Three UNLF cadres, Khulem Maniton Singh, Khumu-kacham Dabal Singh alias Jeevan and Konthoujam Megha Chandra Singh were arrested from the Patsoi area.

- October 17: Two UNLF cadres, Kiran Ngamba and Amit Kumar alias Nungthing Choba, are arrested from Ashang Khullen in the Ukhrul district.
- October 13: Two UNLF leaders, Jayanta Kumar Singh alias M. Milan Singh and Phanjoubam Ghanshyam Singh alias R.K. Romeo Singh, who were arrested from the Indira Gandhi International Airport in New Delhi on their way to Kathmandu on October 4, confess during interrogation that their outfit is in the process of coordinating with the PREPAK and PLA to unite all the Meitei outfits.
- October 11: At least six UNLF cadres are arrested by security force personnel in separate search operations in Imphal city.
- August 20: One UNLF cadre, Konthoujam Sanjoy alias Longthone, is arrested from a spot between Angtha and Wangkhem in the Thoubal district.
- August 16: One UNLF cadre, Laishrarn Ibungo Meitei alias James, is arrested from Singjamei Kainahanbi in the Imphal West district.
- August 13: SFs kill two UNLF cadres during an encounter at Laibi under Tengnoupal police station jurisdiction in the Chandel district. One AK-47 rifle along with magazine, a .303 rifle along with magazine and a Motorola radio set are recovered from the incident site.
- August 11: Three UNLF cadres are killed while two others sustain injuries following an exchange of fire with the SF personnel at Semol in the Chandel district. Two AK-47 rifles along with a huge cache of arms and ammunition and incriminating documents are recovered from the incident site.
- August 10: SFs arrested two UNLF cadres, S Jagat Singh and Ph Ashokumar alias Amju, from an undisclosed location in the Thoubal district. Also, an exchange of fire between the Assam Rifles and UNLF cadres takes place at Khenjoi in the Chandel district.
- August 9: A Junior Commissioned Officer of the Assam Rifles, Ajit Sangma, is killed when UNLF cadres detonate an improvised explosive device near Y.K. College in Wangjing in the Thoubal district.
- August 8: A UNLF cadre, Sapam Shantikumar alias Manaoton, is arrested from Lamlong in the Imphal East district.
- August 4: Manipur Police arrest a UNLF cadre, Yurembam Ibomcha Singh alias Robin, during a cordon and search operation at Mahabali Mamang Leikai in the Imphal East district.
- August 3: One UNLF cadre, Yanglem Birla Singh alias Thoibi, is arrested from Patsoi in the Imphal West district.

- July 22: SFs arrest a UNLF cadre, Jallo Laishram, during a search operation at Moreh Ward No. 7 in the Chandel district. One Chinese make hand-grenade is recovered from his possession.
- July 19: Four civilians are wounded when UNLF cadres fired several lethod bombs and 2-inch mortars from across the international border at a security post at the border town of Moreh in the Chandel district.
- July 16: SFs arrest five UNLF cadres, N. Boinao Meitei, O. Hemanta Singh, T. Brojen, Th. Priyokumar and M. Premkumar, during a search operation from Moreh in the Chandel district.
- July 11: SFs arrest one UNLF cadre, Thingujam Somorjit, from Kongpal Chanam Leikai in the Imphal East district.
- July 13: UNLF kills a Junior Commissioned Officer of the Assam Rifles, T.B. Pun, at Moreh town in the Chandel district. The militants also injured a woman in the firing.
- July 12: Two UNLF cadres, Zila Meitei and Upendro, are killed during an encounter with the SFs at Mantripukhri under Heingang police station limits in the Imphal East district.
- June 29: One UNLF cadre, Yelam Ratan alias Khamba Singh, is arrested at Paomei colony in Imphal.
- June 28: UNLF kills a civilian, Salam Chandramohon, at Uchathol in the Imphal East district accusing him to be a collaborator of the security forces.
- June 27: One UNLF cadre, T. Naobi, is arrested from Tera Amudon Leikai in the Imphal city.
- June 23: Unidentified gunmen kill one UNLF cadre, Houbijam Inaocha alias Areiba, at Tronlaobi Maning Gelmoun Kuki village under Moirang police station limits in the Bishnupur district.
- June 16: A fierce encounter between the Assam Rifles personnel and cadres of the UNLF occurs at Khengjoi Range in the Chandel district.
- June 15: One UNLF, Khumanthem Babu, is arrested during a search operation at Takyel near Imphal city. While, an encounter is reported between the SFs and UNLF cadres at Khenjoi in the Chandel district.
- June 12: One UNLF cadre, Arangbam Satrajit alias Naopet, is arrested from Khurai Nandeibam Leikai in the Imphal city.
- June 1: UNLF shot at and wounded three youths, Thangjam Anand, Ningthoujam Bidyasagar and Salam Borchandra Singh, at two different places in the Imphal East and West districts as 'punishment' for their alleged involvement in extorting money in the name of the outfit.
- May 28: UNLF kills a youth, Khuamnam Lanthoingamba alias Boby alias Loken, at Meitei Leikai in the Churachandpur town for his 'anti-party' activities.

Two UNLF cadres, Ramesh Singh and Basanta Singh, are arrested from a spot near Khangbarol in the Chandel district. One hand grenade, ten rounds of AK-47 Rifles, five rounds of 7.62 mm SL Rifles and incriminating documents are recovered from their possession.

- May 25: One UNLF cadre, M Rishikanta alias Meiraba is arrested from Thangal Bazaar in the Imphal city.
- May 15: A UNLF cadre, Inaocha Singh alias Kanglo is arrested from Kakching Khunou in the Thoubal district.
- May 12: UNLF kills a man, Pukhrambam Momcha, allegedly as a punishment for raping a 10-year-old girl about two years back at an unspecified place in the Imphal East district.
- May 5: An encounter takes place between the security force personnel and cadres of the UNLF at Tingkhai Khunou in the Bishnupur district.
- May 1: One UNLF cadre, Yurembam Tombi alias Yuhenba, is arrested from Keirao Lairembi Lampak under Irilbung police station limits in the Imphal East district.
- April 26: UNLF militants kill a youth, Ngangom Sanathoi, at Sadokpam under Lamlai Police Station limits in the Imphal West district.
- April 12: An 'area commander' of the UNLF, identified as Takheliambam Badal alias Apabi is arrested from Jiribam Higher Secondary School campus in the Imphal East district. One 9 mm pistol is recovered from his possession.
- April 4: A UNLF cadre, Laishram Lukhoi, is arrested from Kakwa Huidrom Leikai in the Imphal West district.
- March 21 : According to the 2005 Annual Report of the Manipur Police, 23 militants including three UNLF cadres, surrendered during the year.
- March 18: The Churachandpur district-based Hmar Inpui, apex body of the Hmar community, gives its full support to the allegations that a number of Hmar women were criminally assaulted by cadres of the UNLF and KCP in the Tipaimukh subdivision on January 16, 2006. Chief Minister Ibobi Singh disclosed in the Legislative Assembly that a judicial inquiry headed by a former Judge of West Bengal High Court will investigate the issue.
- March 14: A youth, identified as Ibohanbi alias Ramesh, is shot at and wounded and later paraded before the media at an unspecified place in the Bishnupur district by the UNLF cadres for his alleged 'promiscuous behaviour and misuse of the outfit's name for personal benefit'.

- March 13: Nine cadres of six militant outfits, including three UNLF cadres, surrender along with a huge cache of arms and ammunition before the Commander of 3 Corps, Lt. Gen. Z.U. Shah, at the Headquarters of Inspector General of Assam Rifles (South) at Mantripukhri in the Imphal city.
- March 13: HPC-D refutes the accusation of its involvement in the displacement of Hmar people from Manipur made by the UNLF.
- March 11: A woman, Hoinu Haokip, is killed and three persons, including two women, are injured in a UNLF triggered bomb blast at Hollenjang village in the Chandel district.
- March 11 : The HPC-D accuses the KCP of its involvement along with the UNLF in the assault on Hmar women and extortion of money from Hmar civilians in the Churachandpur district.
- March 10: Chief Minister O. Ibobi Singh, while responding to a debate in the Legislative Assembly, assures to find out the facts regarding the issue of alleged criminal assault on Hmar women by non-tribal militant outfits, including the UNLF, in the Parbung and Tipairnukh areas of Churachandpur district in January 2006. "The government will endorse the unanimous decision of the House to find out the facts," the Chief Minister said.
- March 8: On the occasion of International Women's Day, a large public rally of at least 10,000 people is organized by a conglomerate of four women's organizations, the Joint Women's Organisation, in the streets of Churachandpur district in protest against the alleged assault on Hmar women by non-tribal militant outfits, including the UNLF, on January 16-night at Lungthulien village in the Tipairnukh subdivision.
- March 1: A UNLF cadre is arrested by Assam Rifles personnel from an unspecified place. Explosives are reportedly recovered from the arrested militant.
- February 28: An IED expert belonging to the UNLF, identified as 'SS' Pvt Premjit, is arrested from Ahalup in the Ukhrul district. IED material and explosives are recovered from the possession of the militant who is suspected to be involved in a number of bomb blasts in and around Imphal.
- February 24: Manipur Government sends relief material for Hmar refugees, who are presently living in the neighbouring State of Mizoram after being reportedly driven away by the UNLF from Churachandpur district.
- February 22: UNLF kills a person, Ningthoujam Kennedy alias Jiten, at an unidentified place as 'punishment' for his alleged connivance

with the security force personnel and 'involvement in extortion from the people on behalf of the outfit'.

- February 18: A militant belonging to the MPA, armed wing of the UNLF, is killed and four others, including three SF personnel, are injured in an encounter at Eigyang village in the Chandel district.
- February 16: A UNLF militant, L. Nganba alias Khagemba, is killed and four Assam Rifles personnel are wounded in two separate encounters between SFs and cadres of the MPA, armed wing of the UNLF, at Eigyang near Sajik Tampak under Chakpikarong police station in the Chandel district.
- February 15: A UNLF cadre, Elangbam Boinao, is shot dead by personnel of the Assam Rifles in an encounter at a place near Kakching Khunou under Waikhong police station in the Thoubal district. An AK-47 rifle with magazine and seven live rounds of AK-47 ammunition are recovered from the possession of the slain militant. Another militant managed to escape.
- February 15: Five Army personnel are wounded in a UNLF triggered IED explosion along the National Highway-39 near Tasar Farm at Sangakpham in the Imphal East district.
- February 15: UNLF asks KCP to 'produce a white paper on the charges leveled against' the journalist Ratan Luwangcha within a week. The journalist was attacked and wounded by KCP cadres on February 8.
- February 10: A security force personnel, who was wounded on January 8 in a UNLF triggered blast at Ningthoukhong in the Bishnupur district, succumbs to his injuries.
- February 6: A UNLF cadre is arrested from Sekmai in the Thoubal district.
- February 5: A soldier is wounded in an ambush by MPA, the armed wing of UNLF, at Sugnu in the Thoubal district.
- February 2: One militant is killed, while three others are wounded and an equal number of them abducted during an internecine clash between suspected cadres of the UNLF and NSCN -IM at a place under Kasom Khullen police station in the Ukhrui district. All the casualties are NSCN-IM cadres.
- January 27: HPC-D's 'information and publicity secretary' R. Palate rejects UNLF's 'accusation' that his outfit is responsible for the 'torture' of villagers of Parbung and Tipaimukh subdivisions in the Churachandpur district. He says that the Barak river region has been the main source of income and means of livelihood for the people of Tipaimukh, "but since UNLF's 'occupation' of the region, heavy 'taxes'

on all items/commodities pertaining to the Hmars without the 'consent' of the HPC-D had paved way for the deteriorating relationship between the UNLF and the Hmar outfit."

- January 24: The HSA accuses UNLF at Aizawl for harassing the Hmar community in south Manipur.
- January 23: The HAS claims at the Shillong Press Club in Shillong that 81 people are killed in landmine blasts and booby traps planted by Manipur-based militants, including MPLF and UNLF, at Tipaimukh in the Churachandpur district in the past two years.
- January 22: Two UNLF cadres and one security force (SF) are killed in the counter insurgency Dragnet in the Parbung and Thanlon sub-divisions of Churachandpur district. So far in this operation, nine UNLF cadres and two SF personnel, including an Army officer, have been killed, according to General Officer Commanding of the Army's 57 Mountain Division, Major General G. G. Dwivedi.
- January 20: A Lieutenant Colonel of the Indian Army, Rajiv Bakshi, is killed by militants in an ambush at Parbuna area under Tioaimukh sub-division in the Churachandpur district, and four UNLF cadres are also killed in SFs' retaliatory firing following the ambush. Four AK-47 rifles along with a huge cache of ammunition, explosives and Improvised Explosive Devices (IED) are recovered from the incident site.
- January 14: A 'retired' cadre of the UNLF, Oinam Pahari Singh, is killed by suspected PREPAK cadres at Kumbi Awang Leikai under Kumbi police station in the Bishnupur district.
- January 11: Two women, Tochil and Lunpur are injured in a clash between cadres of the UNLF and HPC-D at Lunthilien village under Parbung police station in the Churachandpur district.
- January 10: A UNLF cadre, Sansenba, is killed in an encounter with the SF personnel at Khoubuk village under Sugnu police station in Chandel district. One 9 mm US-made pistol with two live rounds, AK-47 ammunition, one combat shirt and a paper with photographs of UNLF cadres are recovered from the incident site.
- January 7: Two suspected HPC-D cadres are killed in an encounter with UNLF militants at Damdei under Parbung police station in the Churachandpur district.
- January 3: Three SF personnel are killed and five others wounded during an encounter with the UNLF cadres at Longpi village under Nungba police station in the Tamenglong district.
- January 2: One SF personnel is killed in an IED explosion triggered by suspected UNLF cadres at Munlian Ghat village under the Jiribam police station in the Tamenglong district.

2005

- December 27: Four UNLF cadres and one SF personnel are killed in an encounter at Ningthoukhong Mamang Pat near Loktak Lake in the Bishnupur district. One AK-56 rifle and a magazine with 30 live rounds are recovered from the incident site.
- December 26: Two UNLF cadres, Ratikanta Pukhrambam alias Babocha and L. Brajamani, reportedly involved in recruiting local youth, are arrested at Awang Jiri Mayai Leikai in the Imphal West district. Demand notes of the outfit are recovered from their possession.
- December 16: Three UNLF militants, identified as 'SS' pvf Elangbam Hemanta, 'SS' Ningombam Bomen and Koijam Tomba, are arrested respectively from the Uyemok Mamang Leikai, Keibi Awang Leikai and Kameng localities.
- December 11: A 'private' of the UNLF, Samadram Benerjit alias Najban, is arrested and four rounds of ammunition are recovered from his possession.
- December 11: A UNLF militant, 'corporal' Morieo, is killed in an encounter in the Chakpikarong subdivision of Chandel district. His body was however taken away by his colleagues. One AK-47 rifle, one magazine, 31 rounds of ammunition and incriminating documents are recovered from the encounter site.
- December 6: A Border Security Force BSF personnel is killed and two others injured in a UNLF triggered IED explosion at Yairipok Bamon Leikai Mang in the Thoubal district.
- November 30: A UNLF cadre, Sanabam Apik Singh, along with a KYKL cadre is arrested from Yambem village in the Thoubal district.
- November 19: One SF personnel and four civilians are killed during an exchange of fire between the SF personnel and a combined team of NSCN-K and UNLF militants at Longmai part-III village under Longmai police station in the Tamenglong district.
- November 14: UNLF claims responsibility for the November 12 ambush on the CRPF foot patrol. The outfit says that the attack is a reply to the "tall talks of Lt General Arvind Sharma, GOC 3 Corps of the Indian Army". It further adds that it "can strike at the Indian forces anytime and anywhere at will".
- November 9: A UNLF cadre, Thongam Gandhi alias Prithibi, is arrested from his residence at Khurai Kongpai Thongam Leikai in the Imphal East district.
- November 7: UNLF has refuted the claim by GOC 3 Corps, Maj. Gen. A.K. Samantaray, that several militant outfits active in the Imphal

valley, including the UNLF and PLA, are in contact with the army and are contemplating surrender. In a statement, Ksh. Yoiheiba, 'senior publicity officer' of the outfit, describes the claim as "lies and rubbish" which are "intended to create confusion among the rank and file of the UNLF."

- November 5: A UNLF cadre, Yahounganba alias Khumai Nanao, is arrested from Waikhong in the Thoubal district. Following his confession, another cadre of the outfit, Kiran Leishangthem, was also arrested from the Thoubal Leishangthem area. One pistol and three live rounds are recovered from him.
- November 3: The Cabinet Committee on Security (CCS) has extended the ban on four militant outfits, including the UNLF operating in Manipur, for two years. Addressing press persons after a CCS meeting chaired by Prime Minister, Dr Manmohan Singh, Defence Minister Pranab Mukherjee says that the Union Government has decided to extend the ban on UNLF, PLA, KCP and KYKL. He also informs that the ban is extended as the outfits still continue to indulge in unlawful activities in India's North East.
- November 1: UNLF is requested, by 'chief commander' of the mobile task force belonging to City Meitei faction of the KCP, N. City Meitei, to reconsider its decision to impose a ban on his outfit. N City Meitei says that his outfit does not indulge in abduction for ransom and does not create terror for the public unreasonably.
- October 20: A UNLF cadre, Tekcham Romenkanta alias Ibungo alias Puya alias Malem, is arrested at Palace Gate in the Imphal city.
- October 18: Two KCP cadres are killed by suspected UNLF militants at Tentha in the Thoubal district, while another cadre manages to escape. UNLF had earlier imposed a ban on all the three factions of the KCP 'accusing' them of indulging in extortion in the name of revolution. The two slain militants have been identified as Khumukcham ibungo and Yengkokpam Amu alias Rojen belonging to the Prithvi and Emoinu factions respectively.
- October 17: UNLF claims to have taken into custody three KCP cadres during 'special drives' carried out by the outfit against KCP cadres involved in extortion activities.
- October 11: Two militants, one each belonging to the UNLF and PLA, are killed in an internecine clash at Kam Ranga village under Jiribam police station in the Imphal West district. The slain militant of the UNLF is identified as Ningombam Sanathoi alias Umbilen.
- October 9: Four SF personnel are killed by the UNLF at Zoupi under Chakpikarong police station in the Chandel district.

- October 3: A UNLF 'lance corporal', Salam James alias Lantemba alias Alberson alias Santosh, is arrested from Moirang Lamkhai in the Bishnupur district.
- October 1: UNLF declares a ban on the activities of the KCP-P. A statement by the outfit says that the KCP-P "has gone against the wishes and aspirations of the people and has been leaving a bad impression on revolutionary movements launched by other underground organizations".
- September 28: Two UNLF cadres, Chingangbam Naobi alias Chand and Moirangthem Bimolchand alias Roshan alias Melei, are arrested respectively from JN Hospital Campus at Porompat in the Imphal East District and from Ningthoukhong in the Bishnupur district. A .38 pistol along with one magazine and six round of ammunition are seized from the latter's possession.
- September 18: A UNLF cadre and an eight-year old girl are killed during an encounter between the army personnel and militants at Pamzal village in the Churachandpur district.
- September 16: A UNLF cadre, Kh. Diamond, is arrested from an unspecified place in the Bishnupur district.
- September 13: A UNLF cadre, Philem Manaobi, is arrested from Moirang Lamkhai in the Bishnupur district.
- September 12: A UNLF cadre, Samurailatpam Bamkinchandra Sharma alias Malem Khaiba, is arrested from Kakwa Asem Leikai in the Imphal West district.
- September 4: A UNLF cadre, Ningthoujam Inao alias Basanta alias Momo, is arrested from Thangal Bazaar in the Imphal West district.
- August 22: UNLF claims to have carried out two attacks on Army personnel in the Henglep area of Churachandpur district injuring seven soldiers.
- August 9: Two suspected UNLF cadres are killed near Thoubal River under Yairipok police station. One AK 47 rifle, one pistol, a large quantity of assorted ammunition and explosives are recovered from the incident site.
- July 31: UNLF cadres shot the *pradhan* (chief) of the Mantrikhong Naorem Leikai Gram Panchayat in his thigh for alleged fraudulent withdrawal of public money misusing the outfit's name. The pradhan, Sagolsem Surendrakumar, is paraded before journalists at an unspecified place in the Ukhrul district where he has reportedly confessed his 'misconduct'.
- July 27: One UNLF cadre along with three of the PLA is arrested from Kakching Khunou and its surrounding area in the Thoubal district.

One 9 mm pistol, three live rounds of ammunition and incriminating documents are recovered from their possession.

- July 15: A UNLF cadre, Sanasam Loken Singh, is arrested from the Khagempalli Nganappi Thong area in the Imphal West district. Three of his accomplices, however, have managed to escape. Acting upon information provided by him, police personnel subsequently arrested another cadre of the outfit, Sanasam Rabi Singh alias Lan-puba, from the Kwakeithel Nganappi Thong area.
- July 15: Manipur's Legislative Assembly unanimously adopts a resolution urging the Union Government to hold peace talks with militant outfits operating in the State. During discussion on the resolution, Chief Minister Okram ibobi Singh rules out the UNLF's demand for a plebiscite under the aegis of the UN on question of Manipur's sovereignty. He says, "The response (of the UNLF) to the appeal for peace talks is positive. But holding a plebiscite and involving a third party in resolving the problem is not practicable. The negotiations should be under the Constitution. It is an internal matter."
- July 6: Two UNLF cadres are killed and three SF personnel wounded in an encounter at Asnang Tangkhul village along the Myanmar border in the Ukhrul district. The outfit claims that the incident occurred when the SFs tried to over run one of its camps. However, it denies having suffered any casualty.
- June 30: UNLF claims to have injured two soldiers stationed at Pukhao in a bomb attack targeting a security convoy.
- June 26: A heavy exchange of fire has been reported between UNLF cadres and SFs at the border town of Bhutankhal near Jiribam in the Imphal East district. The outfit's claim of killing four SFs in the encounter is denied by the troops.
- June 20: Eight militants, including six UNLF cadres, are killed near Phoipi in Henglep area of the Churachandpur district. A cache of weapons, including six AK-47 rifles, one RPG with four rockets, one M-16 rifle, one G-3 rifle, a shot gun and a lethode launcher are recovered from the encounter site.
- June 14: Three UNLF cadres, including a woman, are arrested in the Sekmaijin, Laphupat Tera and Arong Nongmaikhong areas of the Imphal West district. Their interrogation subsequently leads to the recovery of arms and ammunition from an abandoned camp of the outfit in the Arong Nongmaikhong locality. The cache includes an AK-56 bayonet, four magazines, 100 live bullets, one 9 mm pistol along with four live ammunition, two communication devices and some incriminating documents.

- June 11: A UNLF cadre, Mayengbam Khoilencha alias Open, is arrested from the Lamphel area of the Imphal city.
- June 9: A UNLF cadre, Laishram Chaoba alias Tonjao, is arrested from Takyel Khongban in the Imphal West district.
- June 6: A UNLF cadre, A. Romesh, is injured in an explosion triggered by unidentified militants at Keiphundai area in the Tamenglong district.
- May 25: A UNLF militant, identified as 'lance corporal' Pukhrambam Manao, is arrested from Sagolband Moirang Hanuba Leirak in the Imphal West district.
- May 22: A UNLF militant, Elangbam Hemba alias Ningthouren Singh, is arrested from the Laphupat Tera area in the Imphal West district.
- May 16: A former UNLF cadre, Mandengbam Ton, is killed by unidentified militants in front of SAI Museum at Takyelpat in the Imphal West district.
- May 15: A UNLF cadre is arrested from Lamboikhongnangkhong in the Imphal West district.
- May 12: A UNLF militant is killed and two SF personnel along with two civilians are wounded during an encounter near Bhutankhal Makha Leikai under Jiribam police station in the Imphal East district. One UMG, one IED and a radio set are recovered from the slain militant. The outfit, however, claims to have killed two soldiers and injured three others.
- April 25: Two Assam Rifles (AR) personnel are killed and four others are wounded by the UNLF at Sonaour under Jiribam police station in the Imphal East district. UNLF, however, claims that six AR personnel are killed in the ambush.
- April 20: UNLF claims responsibility for the April 17 incident of abducting and killing of a civilian at the Khabam Maning Leikai area in the Bishnupur district. The outfit has reportedly 'accused' the civilian for his involvement in killing one of its cadres in 2000.
- April 3: A former UNLF cadre is killed by unidentified terrorists near Heirok part II Litan Makhong in the Thoubal district.
- April 1: A huge cache of arms and ammunition are recovered from the militants belonging to the UNLF and KNF at Khongsai Veng under Porompat police station in the Imphal East district. The cache has included 74 electronic detonators, 75 ordinary detonators, a 38 pistol with one magazine, 16 rounds of .38 ammunition, two 30 mm anti-aircraft shells, 169 rounds of .303 rifles, communication devices, nametags and badges of the outfits. Three terrorists of these two outfits are also arrested subsequent to the recovery.

- March 25: Two NSCN-IM militants are killed and another injured in an internecine clash with the UNLF and another unidentified Kuki outfit at Yangnom in the Ukhrul district.
- March 21: Manipur Chief Minister Okram Ibobi Singh informs the Legislative Assembly that his Government will send feelers to the outlawed UNLF to initiate peace talks, but rules cut the possibility of involving a third party in the process.
- March 9: An 'administrative camp' of the proscribed UNLF is neutralized near Khoirentak in the Bishnupur district and a large quantity of ration is recovered.
- March 5: A UNLF militant is arrested from the Imphal East district.
- March 4: Two UNLF terrorists are killed at Laphupattera in the Bishnupur district. Four AK-56 rifles, six magazines, 66 bullets, two Chinese made hand grenades and a communication device are recovered from the incident site.
- March 3: A girl, suspected to be a UNLF informer, is arrested from Tuilaphai village in the Churachandpur district along with six rounds of ammunition and seven empty cases.
- February 26: UNLF reiterates its demand for involving the United Nations to achieve a solution to Manipur's armed conflict. The outfit had earlier issued a four-point proposal in this connection.
- February 24: Six militant camps, including two of the UNLF, are neutralized and a huge cache of arms and ammunition recovered at Keibul Lamjao in the Bishnupur district.
- February 23. Three UNLF terrorists are arrested from the Kekrupat Bus Parking area in Imphal West district.
- February 20: Three UNLF terrorists are shot dead by the BSF personnel at the Kamalpur border area of Dhalai district in Tripura. One civilian sustained injuries and one UNLF cadre is arrested. One AK-47 rifle, one pistol along with magazines and a mobile set are recovered from the incident site. The encounter is reported to have started, after the entry of an armed group of UNLF cadres into Bagaicherri village from their Bangladesh hideout and abduction of a person, who has reportedly sustained injuries in the crossfire. This is the first incident of killing of a Manipuri outfit's cadres in an encounter with the SFs in Tripura.
- February 16: In an attack by NSCN-IM cadres on a UNLF camp near Aven village of Tousem subdivision, one cadre each of the two outfits are killed, according to a spokesperson of the former.

- February 16: One UNLF cadre is killed and four persons are injured at Mandu village.
- February 15: Two UNLF cadres are killed in the Tamenglong district.
- February 8: Three hardcore UNLF cadres, including an 'area commander for the Imphal West district, are arrested by the Imphal West district police from various places. They are identified as Soubam Somen alias Nungaidaba, Moirangthem Rajesh alias Tomcha and Huirom Romen alias Makulong, who are actively involved in several cases of extortion from Government departments, according to the Imphal West district SP, S. Ibocha.
- February 5: One SF personnel is killed and two others are injured in an attack by suspected UNLF cadres on an army post at Gothol in the Churachandpur district.
- February 2: Responding to Manipur Governor S.S. Sidhu's appeal to militant groups to come to the negotiation table, the UNLF 'chairman', Sana Yaima, in a press statement in Imphal, has come up with a four-point proposal to "end the conflict satisfactorily once and for all." The four proposals are: a 'plebiscite' under the supervision of the UN, deployment of a UN peacekeeping force, surrender of all weapons to the peacekeepers and transfer of political power in accordance with the outcome of the plebiscite.
- January 31: Two SF personnel are wounded in a UNLF-triggered bomb attack at Yairipok in the Thoubal district.
- January 29: The UNLF has cautioned the NSCN-IM leadership over the latter's raising once again the Naga integration issue, terming it as a dangerously myopic policy that has the potential to plunge the whole region into endless conflict and chaos. The outfit, in a statement issued by its 'department of publicity', has also taken the view that the NSCN-IM, in seeking an exclusive solution to the 'Indo-Naga political process' through the creation of a 'Nagalim', is indulging in illusion.
- January 28: A UNLF cadre, Maibam Robert Singh, is arrested along with a .38 pistol at Khurai Thangjam Leikai in the capital Imphal.
- January 27: Two civilians are wounded in an IED explosion triggered by suspected UNLF terrorists at Sehao Kuki in the Chandel district.
- January 26: Seven persons, including two SF personnel, are injured in an UNLF-triggered explosion targeting a SF vehicle at Chandrapur village in the Imphal East district.
- January 24: UNLF admits that two of its cadres are killed in a shoot out with the security forces' near Singmui Lamkhai in the

Churachandpur district on January 23. The outfit adds that it has 'lost' one AK 56 rifle, one M-18 and one 9 mm pistol during the incident.

- January 23: Two suspected cadres of the MPA, armed wing of the UNLF, are killed in the Shingmun area of Churachandpur district. Two automatic rifles, one grenade launcher and one pistol are also recovered from the incident site. Army sources further claim to have unearthed a cache of ammunition, mines, explosives, radio sets and ration belonging to terrorists in the Singhat subdivision.
- January 19: A UNLF terrorist, Ningombam Bipin, is arrested along with several extortion notes from Lamphel Super Market area of capital Imphal.
- January 17: A UNLF terrorist, Sougrapam Surjit Singh, is arrested from Thangal Bazar in the heart of capital Imphal.
- January 17: UNLF claims that ten Army personnel are killed and another ten wounded in an attack, carried out by its MPA cadres at a newly set up Army camp at Tuilaphai in Churachandpur district. However, the Army denies the UNLF claim.
- January 16: Two army personnel are killed in an encounter between SFs and UNLF cadres at a location between Tuilaphai and Sijon villages in the Churachandpur district.
- January 15: An UNLF terrorist, Khangernbam Angousana, is arrested by the Imphal West District police from North AOC area of capital Imphal.
- January 10: Three UNLF cadres, identified as Saikhom Shamungou, Sanasan Ngongo Singh and Thiyam Sunder Singh, are killed at Bunghol Khullen village under Yairipok police station limits in the Thoubal district. An AK-47 rifle, two Chinese-make hand-grenades and some ammunition are recovered from the incident site.
- January 9: A lance corporal' of the UNLF, Dolen Singh alias Kebru, is arrested from Heingang in the Imphal East district.
- January 4: A UNLF terrorist, Lamabam David alias Sonaba, is arrested from Takyel Khongban in the capital Imphal.

2004

- December 21: The UNLF in a statement condemns the 'punishment' meted out to the Vice Chancellor and Registrar of Manipur University by the KYKL.
- December 12: About 200 civilians from Manipur flee to Tamu in Myanmar following heavy exchange of fire between the security forces and cadres of the UNLF in the interior areas of Somtal, Chejang and Tuitong in Chandel district.

- December 9: A security force personnel and two UNLF terrorists are killed in a series of encounters in the vicinity of Phoibi Ching in the Churachandpur district.
- December 9: The MPA, armed wing of the UNLF, claims to have killed three Army personnel during an attack between Phoibi Ching and Seneyan Khul in the Churachandpur district.
- December 8: The UNLF claims to have killed at least four Army personnel in an attack carried out by its armed wing, the MPA, at Tangshang village in Churachandpur district.
- December 3: The UNLF claims to have killed three security force personnel following an encounter at a place between New Somtal and S Pungjoi villages in the Chandel district.
- November 29: UNLF cadre, Naorem Manimohan Singh alias Kaoba, is arrested from Haoreibi in the Thoubal district.
- November 24: A security force personnel and a minor girl are killed during an explosion triggered by the UNLF between Molcham and Tuileng villages in the Chandel district.
- November 17: UNLF terrorist Md Rafi alias Akbar arrested from Kwakta in Bishnupur district.
- November 13: Two security force personnel are killed and another injured in an encounter with UNLF terrorists in Songtal area in Churachandpur district.
- November 13: UNLF terrorists detonate explosives at a place near the Sapermeina police station along the NH-39.
- November 1: A UNLF terrorist is arrested from a place between Thinungei and Phubala in Bishnupur district.
- November 2: Security forces arrest a suspected UNLF cadre from Heingang-Ahalup area in Imphal East district.
- October 30: One Jammu and Kashmir Rifles personnel is killed and several others injured in an encounter with UNLF terrorists at Alu Shingtam in Churachandpur district.
- October 27: UNLF's self-styled 'sergeant major' Sanabam Prabin alias Prem killed in an encounter with the security forces at an area between Koirengei Akham Leirak and Achanbigei under Heingang Police station in Imphal East district.
- October 18: Six UNLF militants and a security force personnel are killed in an encounter at Borobekra village of Jiribam-sub-division in Imphal East district. One AK-56 rifle, three magazines, ninety live rounds, one rocket launcher and a photo album are recovered from the site of the encounter.

- October 18: UNLF 'captain' Maimom Gyaneshore alias Chaoba arrested from Thoubal parking area of the Imphal city.
- October 16: Security forces arrested a UNLF terrorist from Lamphelpat near New Reserve Line in Imphal West district.
- October 11: Security forces arrest UNLF terrorist RK Kanta alias Kodompokpi from Koirengei in Imphal West district.
- October 8: Security forces arrest two UNLF terrorists including a female cadre, identified as Kangujam Singhajit Singh and Heikrujam Ibemcha Devi from Khongman in Imphal East district.
- September 14: Security forces arrest UNLF terrorist Angom Sarat alias Ibungo, from the Panglian village of Churachandpur district.
- September 4: A UNLF terrorist arrested from the Porompat Pangal Leirak road crossing in Imphal East district.
- July 28: Three security force personnel are killed in an ambush by the Manipur People's Army (MPA) terrorists, armed wing of the UNLF, in the Namthilok area of Ukhrul district.
- July 16: A CRPF personnel is killed and nine others are injured in an attack by UNLF terrorists at Tuibong in Churachandpur district.
- April 25: Three UNLF terrorists are killed during an encounter with the police at Yairipok in Thoubal district.
- April 18: The UNLF calls for a 17-hour general strike starting midnight of April 19 to boycott of the first phase of Lok Sabha (Lower House of Parliament) polling for the Outer Manipur Parliamentary constituency.
- April 9: UNLF terrorist Haobijam Premkumar arrested from Khoirenthak Upper Village in Bishnupur district.
- February 15: UNLF cadres lob a grenade at the official residence of Food and Civil Supplies Minister Ph. Parijat Singh at Kanglapat road near the capital Imphal.
- January 6: UNLF hands over one of the killers of Lungnila Elizabeth, the minor daughter of a Manipur legislator who was kidnapped and killed in November 2003, to women activists at an undisclosed location in the Imphal East district.
- January 5: Suspected terrorists of Manipur People's Army (MPA), armed wing of the UNLF, kill one Central Reserve Police Force (CRPF) personnel at Khumoi village in the Churachandpur district.

2003

- December 18: The Imphal West district police arrests one UNLF terrorist identified as Yumnam Kiran from Kiyamgei Mamang Leikai.

- November 24: UNLF calls for a 'united struggle' by all terrorist outfits in the Northeast on its 39th 'raising day commemoration'.
- November 8: At least eighteen armed KYKL cadres reportedly desert the outfit to join the Manipur People's Army (MPA), armed wing of UNLF, in Manipur.
- November 5: Two soldiers are killed and three others sustain injuries in a bomb explosion triggered by suspected UNLF terrorists in the Moreh area of Chandel district.
- October 23: Ten ULF terrorists are killed in separate encounters with the security forces in the Bishenpur and Imphal West districts. One mortar launcher, two AK-56 rifles, two carbine machine guns and one 9 mm pistol, besides a large cache of ammunition are recovered from the slain terrorists.
- October 13: Three UNLF terrorists are arrested at Kakching Khunou in the Thoubal district.
- September 18: UNLF terrorists kill one of their former comrades after abducting him on September 15 from the Langol area in the Imphal East district of Manipur.
- August 24: One UNLF terrorist is killed during an encounter at Nongangkhong in the Thoubal district.
- August 23: A combined team of Bishnupur police commandos and Central Reserve Police Force personnel kill one suspected UNLF terrorist during an encounter in the Thoubul area. Separately, two UNLF terrorists are abducted and later killed by some unidentified gunmen in the Imphal East district near a High School at Thambalkhong Sabal Leikai.
- July 21: Security force personnel kill at least seven UNLF terrorists in an encounter at Moreh in Chandel district.
- June 30: Assam Rifles personnel kill two terrorists, including a 'district secretary' affiliated to UNLF, during an encounter at Nepal Pali, under Lamlai police post limits, in Imphal East district, Manipur, and recover an AK 56 rifle with 19 live rounds and a US carbine with 24 rounds of ammunition.
- June 28: Assam Rifles personnel kill two UNLF terrorists, including a 'district commander', in an encounter at Mayang Imphal in the Imphal West district.
- June 27: UNLF 'finance wing' member Narengbam Loken is arrested from the house of a local resident at Tera Loukrakpam Leikai in the Imphal West District. Cash worth Rupees 130,000 and some incriminating documents are also recovered from his possession.

- June 19: Two surrendered UNLF cadres employed in the 2nd Indian Reserve Battalion (IRB) are killed by unidentified gunmen inside the campus of a local college in Imphal.
- June 14: Manipur police arrests one UNLF cadre along with six unidentified terrorists in separate Statewide search operations.
- June 12: Rival terrorist outfits of Manipur - UNLF and the United Kuki Liberation Front (UKLF) - agree to end hostilities between themselves and also decide to work towards resettling villagers displaced as a result of their conflict.
- April 26: Security force personnel kill one UNLF terrorist during an encounter in Thoubal district and recover a US-marked nine mm pistol, three detonators with wire, 55 rounds of AK-47 ammunition and materials for making Improvised Explosive Devices (IED) from the encounter site.
- April 6: UNLF terrorists kill one of their colleagues at Komlaching, under Yairipok police station limits in Thoubal district for indulging in extortion without 'prior permission' of the outfit.
- March14: The wangbral task force (WTF) committee of the UNLF expels four cadres for misappropriating Rupees 7,74.525 and for violating party rules and regulations in November 2002.
- February 14: Security forces arrest one self-styled sergeant major and publicity secretary of the UNLF during a combing operation at Uripok.
- January 22: UNLF among at least ten other Northeast-based terrorist outfits to call for a 'boycott' of Republic Day (January 26) celebrations.
- January 20: Security forces arrest four UNLF terrorists from a temple in Jaipur village, Cachar district of Assam.
- January 10: Three terrorists affiliated to the MPLF, which consists of three groups including the UNLF, are killed in a prolonged encounter at Sajik Tampak in the Chandel district.
- January 1: Manipur People's Liberation Front (MPLF), which includes the UNLF, asks all outfits in the Northeast to put an end to extortion in the name of armed movement, commencing January 15, 2003.

2002

- December 8: Ukhrul Superintendent of Police S Manglemjao escapes a UNLF ambush. However, four other policemen are killed in the incident.
- October 15: UNLF, a member of the MPLF conglomerate comprising of three terrorist outfits, protests the merger of Manipur with the Indian

Union, on the anniversary of the merger. Normal life in Manipur is been paralyzed following a seventeen-and-a-half-hour statewide general strike called by the umbrella organization.

- October 12: A joint team of police commandos arrests two UNLF cadres, identified as Salam Jibarn Singh alias Ichingakpa and Khumukcham Premjit Singh.
- September 25: MPLF, of which UNLF is a member, calls for people's support to strengthen traditional brotherhood among peoples and to forge revolutionary solidarity to fight the common enemy.
- August 10: Red Horns Division of the Army kills an unidentified UNLF terrorist in an encounter in Dooni, under Borbori police station-limits, in Nalbari district of Assam.
- August 9: Imphal West police arrests UNLF terrorist from Keibul Sangram village.
- August 6: Border Security Force personnel arrest four UNLF terrorists from a hideout and seize several UNLF combat fatigues and many incriminating documents.
- July 17: UNLF claims responsibility for the July 16-attack on the 14 Jat Regiment near Jirighat, in Cachar district, Assam. The UNLF claims in statement that 10 troops had been killed in the ambush, laid by its armed wing—the Manipur Peoples Army (MPA).
- July 18: In a statement, the United National Liberation Front (UNLF) claims responsibility for the July 16-attack on the 14th Jat Regiment near Jirighat and admits that it has linkages with the Assam based United Liberation Front of Asom (ULFA) terrorists.

  A media report quoting official sources accuse UNLF of supplying arms and ammunition to various terrorist outfits in the Northeast with the active connivance of Myanmar's security forces.
- July 14: UNLF terrorists attack personnel of the Army's Jat Regiment from atop the hills of Jujam near Jirighat, in Cachar district, Assam, killing three, including an officer and seriously injuring six others.
- June 2: Border Security Force (BSF) personnel arrest nine terrorists belonging to the UNLF and the People's Revolutionary Party of Kangleipak (PREPAK), including two women, from the Thamnapokpi area of Manipur.
- May 25: UNLF terrorists lift the 'ban' they imposed on two vernacular dailies *Poknapham* and *Kangia Pao,* on May 22, for inaccurate reporting of a factional fight between the terrorist groups.

- May 22: UNLF imposes a ban on the publication of Poknapham and Kangia Pao newspapers accusing them of publishing incorrect reports without verification.
- April 5: Two terrorists of the UNLF and the National Socialist Council of Nagaland - Isak Muivah (NSCN-IM) are killed in an internecine clash in Sotobekra, Hengchumpunji and Saikhulphai areas, south of Jiribam.
- March 27: Two suspected UNLF terrorists are killed in an encounter in Mayang Langjing, on the Khurkhul-Larnsang road.
- February 21: UNLF terrorists kill four Assam Rifles personnel, including a Captain, and injure three others in an ambush near Yairipok Top Chingtha.
- February 14: All the 192 terrorists of Manipur arrested in December 2001 by the Myanmar Army are set free. The release took place in four batches beginning January 3.
- January 27: The Armed wing of the UNLF, Manipur People's Army (MPA), attacks an Assam Rifles camp in Yairipok in Thoubal district.
- January 16: A UNLF press statement says the outfit would not participate in the forthcoming State Assembly elections, due in February 2002.

2001

- December: The Myanmar Army arrests 192 United National Liberation Front (UNLF) terrorists from Tamu and Kalamayeo areas following a series of raids on their hideouts. The arrested men include UNLF chairman R.K. Meghen.
- November 24: The UNLF's Manipur People's Army attacks a BSF camp at the Phubala area in Bishenpur district in Manipur with rocket launchers.

  UNLF observes 37th foundation day anniversary.

  UNLF says that the idea of a joint 'liberation struggle' initiated by the United Liberation Font of Asom (ULFA), National Socialist Council of Nagaland - Khaplang (NSCN-K) and UNLF with the formation of the Indo-Burma Revolutionary Front (IBRF) in 1990 is slowly but definitely becoming a reality.
- November 25: ULFA claims that the Myanmar Army has seized a huge cache of arms and ammunition from UNLF hideouts during the first week of November. The seizures included 1,500 AK series rifles and SLRs.
- November 17: Police in Hmarkhawlien, Cachar district, arrest two UNLF terrorists fleeing from Jiribam following a clash with the NSCN-IM.

- November 16: UNLF terrorists attack a Border Security Force (BSF) patrol returning from Morian Bazar in Bishenpur district and trigger two Improvised Explosive Device (IED) explosions. Four BSF personnel sustain serious injuries.
- November 16: Two UNLF cadres were arrested in Cachar district.
- Nov 2-8: Conflicting media reports suggested the arrest of nearly 200 UNLF cadres and leaders in raids conducted by the Myanmarese army.
- October 14: Three security force personnel were killed by MPA cadres at Kwakta in Bishenpur district.
- October 4: UNLF killed two security force personnel and injured four others in an ambush in Chandel district.
- February 13: United National Liberation Front (UNLF) Chief Sanayaima alias Meghen, speaking at the 36th anniversary of the outfit, appreciates Union government's willingness to hold talks with insurgent groups of Northeast. He, however, says issues such as independence of Manipur, right to self-determination and demilitarization must be brought under the ambit of the negotiations.

2000

- November 23: UNLF, on its 36th Foundation Day, reiterates demand for the liberation of the oppressed people from the Indian Union.
- June 10: A. Samarendra Singh - UNLF founder who was also a Manipuri playright and social worker, shot dead by terrorists in Imphal.
- May 8: Eight Manipur People's Army (MPA) terrorists- cadres of the armed wing of United National Liberation Front (UNLF), killed in an encounter in Wangoo Laipham, Thoubal district.

1999

- February 15: UNLF militants kill nine security force personnel in Churachandpur district.

Kuki National Front (KNF)

Formation

Kuki National Front (KNF) was formed under the leadership of Ranco Thangboi Kuki on May 18, 1988 primarily to counter the National Socialist Council of Nagaland-Isak-Muivah (NSCN-IM) hegemony in the Kuki-inhabited areas.

Objective

The primary objective is to secure a separate State or Union Territory for the Kuki community and the unification of all scattered Kukis in the new homeland, 'Kukiland'.

Leadership

The KNF split in 1995, with one unit identifying itself as the "presidential faction" and the other as the "military council". The former again split into KNF (Samuel faction) and KNF (Zougam faction).

KNF (Presidential faction) remains the most powerful of all the factions and has claimed to be the 'real KNF'. Thangboi Kipgen is the 'President' while L.H. Stephen is the 'Information and Publicity Secretary'. Its 'defense secretary' Hengkhotinmong alias Mangboi Kipgen was killed in an encounter with the Manipur Police at Kangchup in the Imphal West district on December 21. 2005.

The total cadre strength of the outfit (inclusive of all factions) is estimated to be between 400 and 500.

Areas of Operations

KNF operates extensively in the Churachandpur district. It also operates in other Kuki inhibited areas of the Chandel, Tamenglong and Senapati districts.

Source of Funding

The KNF funds its activities primarily through extortion and collection of 'protection fees' from the civilians in its areas of operation. 'Sergeant' Max Kuki reportedly heads its financial-related matters in the Sadar Hills areas of Manipur that comes under Division I, while Division II concerning Moreh and surrounding areas of the Chandel district is under the purview of 'Sergeant' Galngam. Division III covering Imphal and surrounding areas is under the charge of one Romel Kuki.

Linkages with other Groups

Besides having links with several Kuki militant groups, the outfit maintains close ties with several valley-based outfits like the United National Liberation Front (UNLF) and People's Liberation Army (PLA). It is also said to have links with the Khaplang faction of the National Socialist Council of Nagaland (NSCN-K). Unspecified reports state that about 300 KNF recruits had undergone training in Kachin Independence Army (KIA) camps in Myanmar.

Major incidents

2006

- November 30: The 'public relation officer' of the Samuel faction of the Kuki National Front, 'captain' Namjapao, is shot dead and another cadre, Henjapao, sustained injuries when they were attacked by the rival Kuki National Army cadres at Bijang in the Churachandpur district.

- November 16: Security force personnel arrested a Kuki National Front (KNF) militant, Lunkim Thangkhomang Khongsai alias Mangboi, from Chingmeirong in the Imphal East district. Two letters of extortion, signed by T S Roneg of the outfit, was recovered from his possession.
- April 1: Four staff members of a private recording studio belonging to the Hmar community are abducted by KNF cadres belonging to its Zougam faction from Tuibong for their refusal to pay extortion amount of Rupees 200,000.

2005

- December 21: The 'defense secretary' of KNF, Mangoi, is killed during an encounter with the police in the Imphal West district.
- December 15: Four militants are killed in a clash between the KNA and KNF-P at the Koubru Hill Range under Gamnom Sapermeina police station in Senapati district.
- August 28: The KNF opposes any handing over of 'Kuki territories' to the NSCN-IM without prior consent and mandate of the Kuki tribals. Claiming that Nagas are the 'non owner of the land', the outfit says that it is keeping a close tab on the Union Government's negotiations with the NSCN-IM.
- May 11: Suspected KNF cadres abduct Paokai Haokip, a former Member of Parliament, and four village chiefs from Saitu in the Senapati district, accusing them of "a nexus with the security force personnel."

  Assam Rifles personnel neutralise a KNF camp located near K Sajal village of Sadar Hills.
- April 4: Three KNF (Samuel faction) cadres are killed during an internecine clash with the rival Military Council faction (KNF-MC) at Molcham village in the Churachandpur district.
- March 30: KNF cadres shoot at and injure five wine vendors in the Kalapahar area under Kangpokpi police station in Imphal East district.
- March 10: A KNF (Zougam faction) cadre, identified as Alex Khaute, surrenders before the Chief Minister Ibobi Singh.
- February 23: Three KNF (Military Council faction) cadres are arrested from the Lamlong area in Imphal East district.

2004

- October 25: Three KNF terrorists are killed in an encounter at a place between KR Lane and Golapati in the Imphal East district.
- October 24: Security forces kill a KNF-P cadre, identified as Nekhogin Kipgen, at Kalapahar under Kangpokpi police station limit in the Senapati district.

- September 21: Security forces arrest a cadre belonging to the KNF-MC faction during cordon and search operations at New Checkon in the Imphal East district.
- February 28: Three senior KNF-Z cadres are killed by the rival KNF-S in a factional gunfight at Hengjang near Patlian village in the Churachandpur district.

2003

- September 13: Assam Rifles personnel kill at least 10 KNF-MC cadres during an encounter at Sangtun village in the Senapati district.
- July 31: KNF issues a diktat to the National Hydroelectric Power Corporation and its contractors, who are executing the Loktak project, to restrict movement of their vehicles along the Leimatak route in Bishnupur district.
- July 13: Three suspected KNF cadres are killed during an encounter with the police at Gelbung village under the Saparmeina police station limits in the Sadar Hills area.
- April 05: KNF-MC claims responsibility for the grenade explosion at the Eastern Motors Ltd in Chingmeirong in which four persons, including two security force personnel, were injured on April 3.
- February 20: Army personnel in Jiribam subdivision unearth a PLA-KNF hideout in Sonapur area of Imphal East district and recover a Universal Machine Gun, a large quantity of ammunition and some incriminating documents.

2002

- July 25: Both the factions - the Military Council and Zougam - of the KNF decide to reunite through an agreement. The outfits agree to 'bury internal differences' to continue the joint-fight for 'Kukiland'.
- March 14: A KNF-MC cadre is killed in an encounter with the security forces near Bungmual village.

2001

- August 27: Three militants are killed in an internecine conflict between suspected cadres of the Zomi Revolutionary Army (ZRA) and KNF-UNLF combine at Tokvum village, south of Churachandpur police station.

2000

- November 28: Two KNF cadres are arrested from the official residence of the State Transport Minister in Lamphel.

1998

- December 6: Sixteen KNF cadres are arrested from Yangnoi and Keitheimanbi in the Senapati district.

- May 29: The KNF enforces closure of St. Xavier's School at Moirang in the Bishnupur district for a year as the school authorities refuse to pay a sum of Rupees 20,000 as demanded by the outfit.
- January 17: Seven KNF cadres are arrested from different parts of Manipur.
- February 26: Eight KNF cadres are arrested from different parts of Manipur.
- February 20: One KNF cadre is arrested from Porompat in the Imphal East.

1997

- June 24: Four KNF cadres are killed during an encounter with the Army at Haipi under Kangpokpi police station jurisdiction in the Senapati district.
- May 12: Nine KNF cadres, including a woman, are killed at Thinganagphai Kuki village in the Churachandpur district during a raid by the security forces.
- April 30: Eight Manipur Rifles personnel and a civilian are killed and 16 persons are injured as the KNF cadres ambush a security party escorting passenger buses at Saparmaina on the National Highway-39, thirty-five kilometers from the State capital Imphal.

1996

- October 29: Suspected KNF cadres attack a police party killing two police personnel, including a Deputy Superintendent of Police, and injure six others at Mata village in the Churachandpur district.

1995

- August 14: KNF calls for a 48-hour Manipur bandh (strike) to press for the demand of a separate Kukiland to be carved out of the Kuki-inhabited areas in Manipur.

Kuki Revolutionary Army (KRA)

Formation

The Kuki Revolutionary Army (KRA) was formed in December 1999, allegedly with the support of the Isak-Muivah faction of the National Socialist Council of Nagaland (NSCN-IM).

Leadership and Cadre Strength

Its top leaders include: Chairman—Thangkeng Hangshing, Publicity Secretary—Zet Kuki and Information Secretary—D.T. Haokip.

It is believed to have about 450 cadres of which about 180 of them are based in the Karbi Anglong district of Assam.

Aims and Objectives

Its primary objective is to secure a "separate State" for the Kuki tribe within the Indian union and the unification of all scattered Kukis in the new homeland. In Assam, its declared objective is the creation of the "Kuki National Council", an autonomous administrative council for the Kukis in the Karbi Anglong district.

The population of Kukis in Manipur was recorded at 2,69,522 (Census 2001). They are mainly concentrated in the Churachandpur and Senapati districts and have a presence in the Moreh town of Chandel district.

In Assam's Karbi Anglong district, the Kuki population is approximately 35,000. (Total population of the district was recorded at 8,12,320 according to the Census 2001).

Areas of Operation

Its area of operation includes parts of the Churachandpur, Chandel and Senapati districts in Manipur, and also the Kuki-inhabited areas of the Karbi Anglong district in Assam.

Linkages

The outfit maintains linkages with several militant outfits of the Northeast that includes: United Kuki Liberation Front (UKLF), Kuki National Front - Military Council (KNF-MC), NSCN-IM, National Democratic Front of Bodoland (NDFB) and Dima Halim Daogah (DHD).

Incidents

2005

- September 14, 2005: Eight Karbi civilians are killed and several others sustain injuries as suspected KRA militants open indiscriminate fire at Thekerajan village in the Karbi Anglong district of Assam.
- January 12, 2005: A combined team of the UKLF and KRA cadres kill the 'chief of the Kuki National Army (KNA)', Vipin Haokip, during an internecine clash at Diyang in the Churachandpur district of Manipur.

2004

- May 4, 2004: At least seven KRA cadres are killed during an encounter with the troops near Moinam village in the Ukhrul district of Manipur.
- March 24, 2004: KRA militants kill at least 33 Karbi villagers at three separate places in the Karbi Anglong district.
- March 16, 2004: Three members of a family are killed by suspected KRA cadres at Thailung village in the Karbi Anglong district.
- February 12, 2004: Three KRA cadres are killed during an encounter with the security force (SF) personnel at Saijang village in the Karbi Anglong district.

2003

- December 3, 2003: KRA cadres kill three Karbi villagers at Mansing Teron village under Manja police outpost in the Karbi Anglong district.

  Two KRA cadres are killed in an encounter with the SFs at Julium under Manja police station limits in the Karbi Anglong district.
- December 2, 2003: Three Karbis are killed and twenty-nine houses are set ablaze by the KRA at Mentarang village under Diphu police station limits in the Karbi Anglong district.
- December 1, 2003: KRA cadres kill five Karbi villagers in an attack on a church at Zero Point under Bokajan police station jurisdiction in the Karbi Anglong district.
- November 29, 2003: KRA militants kill seven Karbi villagers and set 250 ablaze dwelling huts at the Paksangso, Rongkini, Zilangso, Bey Gaon, Napak Terang and Ringhang villages under Bokajan police station limits in the Karbi Anglong district.
- September 14, 2003: SF personnel kill three KRA cadres during an encounter near Senaikathel in the Ukhrul district.
- August 9, 2003: SFs rescue the former Commissioner of Education, Hangsing, from the hideout of NSCN-IM and KRA near Thumion Khullen village in the Senapati district.

People's United Liberation Front (PULF)

Formation

A communal clash between the dominant Meiteis and the Pangals (Muslims) on May 3, 1993 over monetary transaction in the Lilong Bazaar area of Thoubal district led to approximately 150 deaths in the Thoubal and Imphal districts. Subsequently, discontented members of the minority Muslim community formed a number of Islamist militant outfits. People's United Liberation Front (PULF), founded in 1993, was one of them.

Objective

Besides seeking to safeguard the interests of the minority Muslim community in Manipur, PULF's purported objective is to secure an Islamic country in India's northeast through an armed struggle in collaboration with other Islamist fundamentalist groups.

The outfit also envisions a society based on 'Islamist values' and to this end, has 'acted' against the prevalence of substance abuse and alcoholism among Muslims in the State. It has also passed diktats on the dress code for Muslim girls in the State.

Leadership and Cadre

Bashir Laskar is the 'commander in chief' of the outfit. Mustaffa functions as the 'deputy finance secretary' and Seikh Sahid Ahmed its 'publicity secretary'.

Apart from drawing its cadres from the Muslim community in Manipur, PULF also has recruits from the Muslim community in Assam. For instance, on July 22, 1999, the Assam Police in Barpeta district arrested four PULF militants, Mohammed Saifu Islam, Mohammed Akbar Ali, Zehirul Islam and Hazarat Ali, belonging to the Howly area of Barpeta district. They had reportedly joined the outfit in 1997. Their interrogation revealed that the outfit also has cadres from the Nagaon and Lakhimpur districts of Assam.

Total cadre strength of the outfit is known to be less than 100.

Areas of Operation

PULF currently operates in several areas of the valley districts and Moreh in the hill district of Chandel in Manipur. Lilong in the Thoubal district is reportedly its stronghold.

Till 1999, it reportedly maintained units in three districts of Assam: Barpeta, Nagaon and Lakhimpur. Incidents involving the outfit have also been reported from the Barak valley area of Assam.

Arms and Training

PULF was in possession of rusty and locally-made weapons in its formative years. However, the Isak-Muivah faction of the National Socialist Council of Nagaland (NSCN-IM), which trained its cadres mostly in the Ukhrul district and also in Myanmar, is reported to have provided the outfit with sophisticated weapons. The outfit now possesses an unspecified number of AK-series rifles, stenguns, carbines, though most of its attacks involve the use of explosives, hand grenades and gelatin sticks.

Funding

Extortion targeting the civilian population and traders in its areas of operation constitute the major source of funding for the PULF. Further, the outfit is known to have indulged in the smuggling of arms and explosives for money. For instance, on April 21, 2005, four Mizo youths were arrested at Behara railway station in Cachar district of Assam along with packets of detonators, eight packets of gelatine sticks and 400 packets of the explosive rolls. The youths were being used by the PULF as carriers. On April 18, 2005, another Mizo youth was arrested along with 294 gelatin sticks from the Cachar Express train near Silchar in Assam.

Linkages

PULF maintained close links with the NSCN-IM for arms and training in its formative years. The extent of its linkages with the outfit at present is not known.

According to official sources, the PULF is known to have linkages with the Inter-Services Intelligence (ISI) of Pakistan as well as other Islamist outfits operating in India's Northeast.

Incidents

2006

- December 29: A suspected People's United Liberation Front (PULF) militant shot at and wounded a civilian, Moirangthem Meghachandra, at an unspecified place in the Imphal West district over his refusal to hand over a bike to the militant.
- December 20: The three Lashkar-e-Toiba (LeT) militants, who were arrested by the Delhi Police on December 19 near the Red Fort in the national capital, came from Manipur. The police claimed to have recovered two kilograms of RDX, a hand grenade and two detonators from the arrested persons, who were allegedly planning to carry out bomb blasts at crowded market places in Delhi. The Joint Commissioner of Delhi Police (Special Cell), Karnal Singh, informed that this is the first time that the LeT has been found to have links in Manipur. He also said that a lead into the activities of the module was provided by two Bangladeshi nationals, who were arrested in the Capital on October 16, 2004 with plastic explosives. During interrogation, one of the three arrested militants, Salman Khurshid Kori, said that he was sent to Pakistan occupied Kashmir for training in 2001 and had recruited few persons for the purpose. He also claimed to have mediated between the Manipur-based Islamist outfit, the People's United Liberation Front (PULF), and LeT militants based in Bangladesh.
- December 15: SF personnel seized the vehicle of Rural Development Minister, Mohammed Allauddin, in which the PULF cadres transported blankets and store items from the minister's house on December 14. Though the minister denied the charge, one of the arrested militants, Habibur Rahman, reportedly told the SF personnel that the blankets were lifted from the minister's house.
- December 14: Security force personnel arrested six PULF militants along with 20 blankets and other store items at Thoubal. The report added that the blanket and store items were brought from the house of an unidentified minister in the capital Imphal.
- December 11: A civilian, Mohammed Belal alias Abdul Gani, was shot at and wounded on charges of peddling drugs by the PULF cadres in Imphal. Six persons, alleged to be involved in drug trade were also asked by the outfit to surrender. The outfit threatened to award 'capital punishment' in case its orders are not complied with.
- December 10: PULF, in a statement, accused a civilian, Mohammed Mangi alias Tamijur, of being a police informer and claimed to have opened fire targeting his house at Keikhu Mayai Leikai in the Imphal East district. The statement further said that Mangi would be awarded 'capital punishment' if he continues with his activities.

- November 22: Security forces (SFs) arrest a 'sergeant Major' of the People's United Liberation Front, Mohammed Apikpa alias Apik alias Sajitkhan, near the office gate of Family Welfare Department at Lamphel in the Imphal West district.
- November 13: SF personnel recover a RPG and a 303 rifle during a search operation near a lake at Kyamgei Pal Ahanbi in the Imphal West district. The seizure was made following the confession of two PULF militants arrested from Tulihal Airport on November 10.
- November 10: Two cadres of the PULF, 'lieutenant' Mohammed Waris Khan alias Wagi, the 'deputy finance secretary' and '2nd lieutenant' Mohammed Illiaz Khan, were arrested at Tulihal Airport in the Imphal West district.
- November 4: A political activist belonging to the Nationalist Congress Party, Md. Amutombi Gogimayum, was shot dead by suspected PULF militants at Mayang Imphal in the Imphal West district. One motorcycle and three live rounds of .32 ammunitions were recovered from the incident site.
- October 9: A former cadre of the PULF, Mohammed Azad Khan, is shot dead by some unidentified gunmen at Koijam village under Kakching police station in the Imphal East district.
- August 11: PULF cadres kill a 35-year old man, identified as Adin, at Urup Kangthak in the Thoubal district allegedly for misusing the name of the outfit.
- July 19: A PULF cadre, Mohammad Abo alias Sarifkhan, is arrested from New Checkon in the Imphal city.
- July 16: SFs arrest three PULF cadres, Mohammad Majiboor Rehaman, Mohammad Aktar Khan and Mohammad Ziao Rehaman, from Masjid Road in Imphal city.
- July 8: A PULF cadre, Mohammad Amu alias Tayeb Ali, is arrested during a search operation at Keirao Mayai Leikai in the Imphal East district.
- June 23: Two PULF cadres are killed in an encounter with the Manipur Police at Lilong Chingkham under Lilong police station limits in the Thoubal district. Three AK series rifles, five magazines and some quantity of ammunition are recovered from the incident site.
- June 21: Two PULF cadres, Mohammad Tomba and Mohammad Abdul Kadir, are arrested from Hatta and Paona Bazaar respectively in the Imphal city.
- June 17: Internal feud among the cadres of the PULF claim the lives of two of its cadres, Mohammad Ekramudin alias Boy and Mohammad Iqbal, at Abeng village in the Tamenglong district.

- June 5: One PULF cadre, Mohammad Rajauddin alias Ningthoubi alias Ayub, is arrested from Keirao Mayai Leikai in the Imphal East district.
- May 20: A PULF cadre, Mohammad Apikcha alias Bony is arrested along with one Italy made 9 mm pistol from Kiyamgei area in the capital Imphal.
- May 14: A PULF cadre, Mohammad Ithemcha is arrested from Soura Awang Leikai in the Thoubal district along with five live rounds of 7.62 mm LMG.
- May 11: Assam Rifles personnel kill the PULF 'Commander-in-Chief' Bashir Lashkar alias Muthi alias Moti along with his 'deputy home secretary' Mohammad Shafi alias Rami in an encounter at Kakmayai under Yairipok police station limits in the Thoubal district. Two 9 mm pistol with 12 live rounds one Chinese head gear, two mobile phones, one calculator, some incriminating documents along with extortion notes, Rupees 6,500 in cash and one vehicle used by the duo are recovered from the incident site.
- May 8: A combined team of the Manipur Police and Assam Rifles kill two suspected PULF cadres in an encounter at Sora Mamangching under Kakching police station limits in the Thoubal district. One AK-56 rifles, one M-16 rifles and two pistols along with live ammunitions are recovered from the incident site.
- May 7: Suspected PULF militants attack the private residence of the Manipur Legislative Assembly Speaker, Maniruddin Sheikh, at Lilong under Lilong police station limits in the Thoubal district. However, there are no reports of casualty.
- April 27: Two PULF cadres, Maulan Mujibar Rahman and Sharif Khan alias Abo, are arrested from Soura in the Thoubal district.
- March 11: Two PULF cadres, including its main 'finance collector' disguising himself as a rickshaw puller and the other identified as Mohammed Hassan, were killed while extorting money from civilians by the Imphal East district police personnel at Hatta Golapati under Porompat police station.
- January 2: Two civilians were killed by suspected PULF cadres at Ukhongsang and Yairipok Malom under Yairipok police station in the Thoubal district.

2005

- September 20: PULF claimed responsibility for killing a youth, identified as Najib AN, near Wangkhem Junior High School under Yairipok police station in the Thoubal district, for selling drugs.
- September 20: PULF claimed responsibility for killing 29 year old Mohammad Habibur near his Singda Makha Leikai residence under Yairipok police station in Thoubal district, for allegedly working for the army.

- June 23: Three PULF cadres belonging to the 'finance section' of the outfit were arrested during a cordon and search operation by the security forces at Langol Khunjao and Khunnou villages of the Thoubal district.
- June 7: Three PULF cadres, identified as Mohammed Aziz Khan, Mohammed Akbar Khan and Mohammed Abdul Gafar, were arrested from different places in the Thoubal district.
- April 10: Suspected PULF cadres threw a hand grenade at the residence of Mohammed Soleiman, an inspector with the vehicle department, at Thoubal Moijing.
- March 16: PULF terrorists carried out two bomb attacks on two houses in the Imna Makha Leikai area of Imphal city.
- March 9: PULF asked five teachers and staff working in the DI Office Lilong in Thoubal district to 'surrender' to the outfit within 20 days or be ready to face the consequences on charges of corruption.
- February 28: PULF, in a statement, claimed that two drug peddlers have surrendered to the outfit.
- February 25: PULF terrorists attacked a passenger bus at Sora for having 'violated' the outfit's orders of suspending vehicular movement along the Imphal-Moreh route. Consequently, transporters suspend services along the route in protest against the attack.
- January 15: Two suspected terrorists of the PULF were killed during an encounter with the police at Keirao Makting Ingkhol Leirak in the Imphal East district.

2004

- December 12: Cadres of the PULF killed an auditor of the Auditor General office-Imphal branch at Kyamgei Oinam Loukol in the capital Imphal for his refusal to pay up Rupees 5 lakhs.
- December 10: The PULF 'banned' the consumption of alcohol among Muslims in Manipur.

2003

- May 5: Three hostages, abducted on April 26 by PULF terrorists from the Pallel area of Chandel district, escape from captivity.

2001

- June 7: Five persons, including four Bihari traders, are killed by the PULF at Kakching in the Thoubal district.

1999

- July 22: Four PULF militants, Mohammed Saifu Islam, Mohammed Akbar Ali, Zehirul Islam and Hazarat Ali, belonging to the Howly area of Barpeta district in Assam were arrested by Assam Police in Barpeta district.

1998

- February 14: Three PULF cadres were arrested from different parts of Manipur.

United Kuki Liberation Front (UKLF)

Formation

The United Kuki Liberation Front (UKLF) is one of the several small militant groups fighting for an ethnic Kuki state, Kukiland. The outfit was formed on March 29, 2000.

Objective

The purported objective of the UKLF is to uphold the interests of the Kuki community and form a separate Kuki state called 'Kukiland'.

Leadership

S.S. Haokip is the 'Commander-in-Chief', while N.C. Brollint Baite is the 'Information and Publicity Secretary'.

The exact cadre strength of the UKLF is not known although reports indicate that it is a small outfit.

Areas of Operation

The outfit is active primarily in the Churachandpur district of Manipur. However, their presence has also been noticed in the Kuki-inhabited areas of the Chandel and Senapati districts.

Source of Funding

The UKLF funds its activities primarily through extortion and collection of 'protection fees' from the civilians in its areas of operation.

Linkages with Other Groups

It reportedly has close financial and military links with the Isak Muivah faction of the National Socialist Council of Nagaland (NSCN-IM).

Major Incidents

2006

- February 9: UKLF claims to have killed a civilian, Jangthong Khongsai, for his alleged 'anti-people and anti-party activities, including extortion and harassment of innocent people, at Sugnu in the Thoubal district.

2005

- January 12: A combined team of cadres from the UKLF and Kuki Revolutionary Army (KRA) kill the 'chief of Kuki National Army (KNA) during an internecine clash at Diyang in the Churachandpur district.

2004

- July 7: Three suspected UKLF cadres, including the Imphai 'town commander' and the '2nd lieutenant' in its 'finance department', are killed by the police during an encounter in the Langol reserve forest area near Lainingkhui village in Imphai West district.

2003

- February 16: Unidentified assailants kill three UKLF cadres at New Lamka in the Churachandpur district.
- July 11: Two UKLF cadres, including a 'sergeant', surrender before the Manipur Chief Minister, Okram Ibobi Singh, in Imphal along with a M-16 rifle, two magazines and 203 rounds of ammunition.

2002

- September 22: Three UKLF cadres are killed in an internecine clash with cadres, of the KNA at an unspecified place in the Churachandpur district.

Zomi Revolutionary Organisation/ Zomi Revolutionary Army (ZRO/ZRA)

Formation

The Zomi Revolutionary Organization (ZRO) was formed in 1993 and its armed wing, the Zomi Revolutionary Army (ZRA), was formed in 1997 following an escalation of ethnic violence between the Kukis and Paites in the Churachandpur district of Manipur.

Objective

The purported objective of the ZRO/ZRA is to protect the interests of the Paite community from the 'onslaught of any community or group'. It further attempts to bring all the Zomi people, divided by artificial State boundaries in various countries, specifically in Myanmar (Chin State), India (Manipur and Mizoram) and Bangladesh (Chittagong Hills Tracts), together under one administrative unit—'Zogam', which means 'land of the Zomi' under the Indian Union.

Leadership and Cadres

Thanzlianpau Guite, reportedly a former Member of Parliament in Myanmar, is the 'President' of ZRO and Judgeson, the 'Defence Director'. K. Marx Vaiphei functions as the 'Information and Public Relations Secretary' of the ZRO.

Phanzlianpau Guite is the 'President' of the ZRA. D Kamsuanthang is the outfit's 'General Secretary' and Jimmy Suanpu is its 'Information and Publicity Secretary'.

Its cadres are mostly from the Paite community.

Areas of Operation

The outfit primarily operates in the Paite-dominated areas of Churachandpur district in Manipur, especially the Singnat sub-divisional headquarter bordering Myanmar. Its activities have also been noticed in the bordering areas in Mizoram and Manipur.

Source of Funding

The ZRA funds its activities primarily through extortion and collection of 'protection fees' from the civilians in its areas of operation. According to a June 2004 *Frontline* report, ZRA cadres, in return for a small toll fee, ensures that travellers are not looted, abducted or shot at by other armed groups.

The ZRA, according to media reports, in June 2004 alleged that some of its cadres were paid only partially by the Mizo National Front (MNF) Government in Mizoram for having campaigned for its candidates in Champhai constituency bordering Manipur. Opposition leader in Mizoram, Lal Thanhawla, alleged on June 12, 2004, that the MNF 'owed money' to the ZRO from "services rendered" and since a part of the money is yet to be paid, ZRO activists had resorted to collecting money from the people of Mizoram.

Linkages

The ZRA maintains close links with Kanglei Yawol Kanna Lup (KYKL), a valley-based outfit of Manipur, and the National Socialist Council of Nagaland-lsak Muivah (NSCN-IM). The ZRO also has maintained fraternal ties with the Kuki Liberation Organisation (KLO), each providing the other "full cooperation in all spheres with the objective of strengthening the blood ties among the Kuki-Chin-Mizo-Zomi people." A 'memorandum of understanding' was signed between the two outfits on December 17, 2002.

Similarly, the ZRA ended its hostilities with the Hmar outfit, the Hmar People's Convention-Democracy (HPC-D), by signing a peace agreement on April 8, 2004, at Lailam Veng, Lamka in Churachandpur district. According to terms of the agreement, both outfits agreed to work closely "in the spirit of mutual understanding and cooperation for the welfare of the people and for achieving their shared objectives."

Peace Negotiations

A statement by the ZRO on August 9, 2005 said that the outfit has reached a cease-fire understanding with the security forces for a period of six months, beginning August 1. The statement said that the outfit "viewed the steps taken by the Indian government in this regard as a positive approach towards better understanding of our unique history and realisation of the need for permanent solution to the longstanding aspirations of the Zo people."

However, the ZRA, in spite of the announcement, continues to indulge in terrorist activities in the targeted areas.

Incidents

2006

- August 20: Two civilians are killed, while four others sustained injuries when a group of ZRA cadres opened fire towards a crowded church targeting a patrol party of the Assam Rifles at Vengnuam in the Churachandpur district.

- July 12: An exchange of fire between rival cadres of ZRA and United Socialist Revolutionary Army (USRA) take place at Lamka in the Churachandpur district.
- July 10: An exchange of fire takes-place between the rival cadres of ZRA and USRA at a spot between Phailen and New Lamka in the Churachandpur district.
- June 29: ZRA kills a youth, Ginpithang Kipgen, at a place between Nengthal and Ngathan in the Churachandpur district.
- June 27: One UNLF cadre, T. Naobi, is arrested from Tera Amudon Leikai in the Imphal city.
- June 23: A ZRA cadre, Pauminlun, is killed during an encounter with the security forces at Lailam Veng in the Churachandpur district. One AK-47 rifle with nine live rounds of ammunition is recovered from the encounter site.
- February 19: United Socialist Revolutionary Army accuses ZRA of showing disregard and contempt to the Vaiphei tribe and reportedly asks them not to take part in the coming Zomi Namni celebration. The outfit says: "As our tribe identity has been challenged, USRA believes the Vaipheis need not submerge themselves in the so called community Zomi."
- January 31: The six-month cease-fire agreement earlier concluded between the Army authorities and eight militant outfits, including the KNO, KNA, KNF-Z, KNF-MC, KLO, KLA, ZRA and ZRO expires.

2005

- September 19: One ZRA and six ZRF cadres are killed in an internecine clash at Loibual village in the Churachandpur district. A girl suffered a stray bullet injury in the clash. The ZRA cadres also decamped with the weapons of the deceased ZRF cadres.
- September 1: Central Reserve Police Force claims that a vehicle recovered from the ZRA cadres at IB Road in the Churachandpur district on August 29 belongs to a son of the chairman of the Manipur Assembly's hill areas committee, identified as Songchinkhup, who has admitted that the vehicle belongs to his son Tual Minthang and has been taken away at gunpoint by some militants a few days ago.
- August 29: Six ZRA cadres were arrested along with a consignment of arms and ammunition by a Central Reserve Police Force patrol party at IB Road in Churachandpur. A vehicle belonging to the son of a

Congress party leader in the State, in which they were travelling, was also seized.

- August 20: Suspected ZRA cadres kill a civilian identified as Khaikholien at Runani village under Thanlon police station in the Churachandpur district.
- August 9: ZRA announces a six-month long cease-fire with the security forces with effect from August 1.
- June 9: A civilian is killed and three others sustain injuries after being caught in the crossfire during a clash between ZRA and Zomi Revolutionary Force cadres in the Sumtuh and Mualpheng areas of Churachandpur district.
- June 9: The police arrest a ZRA female sympathiser, identified as Niyangmuan Kirn, from Lamka in the Churachandpur district. 62 live bullets of AK-47 rifles, six receipt books of the outfit along with a sum of Rupees 72,900 was recovered from her possession.
- April 19: Suspected ZRA cadres kill Jamkhothang alias Thang-boi alias Joy Vaiphei, 'operational commander' of the United Socialist Revolutionary Army, a breakaway faction of the ZRA, at Rengkai in the Chandel district.
- January 13: ZRA cadres kill two of their former colleagues who had deserted the outfit at an undisclosed place in Manipur.

2004

- December 26: ZRA terrorists kill a civilian at Ngathal village in the Churachandpur district for alleged 'anti-ZRA activities'.
- December 16: ZRA cadres kill a former president of the All Tribal Students Union-Manipur, identified as E. Vungkholian Paite, and another person at Lamphelpat in the Imphal city for "conspiring against the outfit".
- July 1: The ZRA, in a statement issued by its 'commandant 201 battalion' T. Romeo, denies involvement in extortion in Mizoram's Champhai town near Myanmar border. Further, it alleged that the extortionists were from 'Zothon faction' "a bunch of gangsters having their base in Champhai who have come together without the knowledge of ZRO."
- June 1: Bishnupur police commandos arrest nine ZRA insurgents, including the outfit's 'town commander', from Bengnom New Lamka in the Churachandpur district.
- June 1: Three ZRA cadres are arrested from a passenger bus at Kha Potshangbam in the Bishenpur district.

- May 29: Security personnel belonging to 19 Garhwal Rifles arrest one ZRA cadre, identified as Tulianthang Baite of Bungmual village, from his residence in the Churachandpur district.
- May 9: Security force personnel kill a ZRA cadre identified as Liankhosin at New Bazaar in the Churachandpur district.
- April 8: The ZRA and Hmar People's Convention-Democratic (HPC-D) terrorists sign a 'peace truce' during a meeting held at the residence of L B Sona, 'chairman' Zomi Council, to settle the misunderstanding between the two groups.
- March 31: ZRA militants kill two HPC-D cadres and a civilian at Rengkai village in the Churachandpur district.
- March 28: Three ZRA cadres are killed in a fresh spurt of internecine killings with Hmar People's Convention-Democracy (HPC-D) group at Rengkai village in the Churachandpur district.

2003

- November 14: Eight armed ZRA cadres are arrested from the Mizoram-Myanmar border town of Champhai. One 9 mm pistol, one US made M-16 assault rifle and 40 rounds of ammunition were recovered from their possession.
- June 13: The ZRA claims that a Government vehicle bearing registration number MN-01-G-0068, belonging to the electricity department, had been provided by Power Minister T Phungzathang, hailing from Churachandpur, along with a sum of Rs. 2.6 lakhs, to a 'captain' of the ZRA without the knowledge of the organisation.
- February 16: ZRA cadres shot at and wounded a person, namely Thangkhanlian Paite, in the New Lamka area. Reports claimed it was in retaliation to extortion of money from the public in the name of the outfit.
- January 5: Boder Security Force personnel arrest two ZRA terrorists from Churachandpur district. One 9 mm pistol, six live rounds of cartridges and one magazine are recovered from their possession.

2002

- December 17: ZRO and Kuki Liberation Organisation (KLO) sign a 'Memorandum of Understanding' for providing full co-operation between these two groups in all spheres with the objective of strengthening the blood ties and as a step towards unification and confederation of all Kuki-Chin-Mizo-Zomi group of people in South Asia.

- September 7: A ZRA cadre, hailing from Lalhenkha village of Jiribam sub-division of Imphal East district, surrenders to the Border Security Force (BSF) at Kwakta in the Bishnupur district of Manipur.
- June 1: ZRA terrorists kill six People's Revolutionary Party of Kangleipak (PREPAK) cadres during a shootout at Kaimunnon village in the Churachandpur district.
- March 13: Four ZRA terrorists are killed in an encounter with the Assam Rifles personnel at Thanlon village in the Churachandpur district.

2001

- August 27: Three terrorists were killed in an encounter between two rival groups at Tokvum village in the Churachandpur district. One group suspected to be the ZRA attempted to intercept another consisting of Kuki National Front (KNF) and United National Liberation Front (UNLF). While the first two are reported to belong to ZRA. the third deceased was a member of the KNF.

Kuki National Army (KNA)

Formation

The Kuki National Organisation (KNO) and its Armed Wing, Kuki National Army (KNA), were formed in 1988. The first batch of the cadres, under the command of Thangkholun Haokip, was trained by the Kachin Independent Army (KIA) in Myanmar.

Objectives

The main objectives of the KNA is to bring together all the Kuki-inhabited areas separated by artificial boundary created in 1935, specifically in the Kabaw valley of Myanmar and the Kuki inhabited areas in the hill districts of Manipur under one administrative unit called 'Zalengam' (Land of freedom). In case of the eventuality of such integration not materializing, the KNA aims at the creation of two Kuki states: one within Burma i.e. 'Eastern Zalengam' and the other within India, 'Western Zalengam'.

The KNA's relationship with other Kuki and Zomi militant outfits, however, remained hostile. On December 29, 2005, three Kuki militant outfits, the Kuki Revolutionary Army (KRA), United Kuki Liberation Front (UKLF) and the Kuki National Front-Samuel (KNF-S), merged under the banner of the Kuki National Council (KNC) to carry out operations against the KNA. A decision to this effect was announced by the 'commanding officer' of the KRA, Maj Max, at Sadar Hills area in Manipur.

In Myanmar, the Kuki National Army waged guerrilla warfare against the Military Junta between 1991 and 1999, mainly targeting patrol parties and also Steamers along the Chindwin River.

Leadership

P. S. Haokip is the 'president' of the KNO and 'supreme commander' of the KNA. Anton Kuki is the 'Home Secretary'. The other senior members are Khaikholun, vice-president for Eastern Zalen-gam, Lalminthang Vaiphei, vice-president for Western Zalengam, S. N, G. Haokip, Public Relations Secretary, Amitabh T. S. Haokip, Defence Secretary, Zalen Kuki, Foreign Secretary, Joshua Haokip, Education and Development Secretary, T. H. German Haokip, Intelligence and Analysis Secretary, Benjamin Paite, Trade and Commerce Secretary, Kamkhenpao Zou, Art and Culture Secretary, Thangboi Karong, Forest and Environment Secretary and Thangsang Hmar, Medical Secretary.

The KNA has an estimated strength of 600 cadres armed with an array of weapons like AK-Series, G-series, M-series and 60 mm mortar.

Areas of Operation

KNO/KNA operates in the hill districts of Manipur and adjoining areas in Assam. It also has marginal presence in the Kabaw valley in the Northwest of Myanmar.

Finances

The KNA primarily depends on extortion for financing its activities.

Linkages

The KNO/KNA maintains strategic linkages with the Kachin Independent Organisation/ Kachin Independent Army, the Democratic Alliance of Burma, an alliance of pro-democracy exile organizations and ethnic insurgent organizations in Myanmar and the Federation of Ethnic Nationalities of Burma. It is also known to have close working relationship with the National Socialist Council of Nagaland-Khaplang (NSCN-K). Earlier, it maintained links with outfits such as the United National Liberation Front (UNLF) and Assam-based United Liberation Front of Asom (ULFA). However, such linkages have weakened over the years. KNA is also an affiliate of the Indo-Burma Revolutionary Front, an umbrella organization of several militant outfits, including the ULFA, UNLF and the NSCN-K.

Negotiations

KNA has avoided confrontation with the security forces and have made appeals and sent petitions to the Union Government and other high-level officials in New Delhi for fulfilling their objectives. Memoranda submitted to the Government of India since 1995 include:

1. October 2, 1995: Memorandum to P. V. Narasimha Rao, Prime Minister.
2. October 4, 1995: Memorandum to A. B. Vajpayee, Leader of the Opposition.
3. June 17, 1996: Memorandum to H. D. Deve Gowda, Prime Minister.

4. January 27, 1997: Memorandum to K. R. Narayanan, President of India.
5. July 30, 2004: Memorandum to Dr. Manmohan Singh, Prime Minister.

On September 22, 2005, the Union Defence Minister Pranab Mukherjee informed in the Manipur capital Imphal that at least eight militant outfits (including the KNA) in Manipur have declared informal ceasefires' with the Union Government. However, on January 31, 2006, the agreement expired.

Incidents

2006

- December 23: The Kuki National Organisation (KNO), the political wing of Kuki National Army (KNA), asked the UNLF and its armed wing, Manipur People's Army (MPA), to stop operating in Kuki areas, stating their presence and activities have caused serious harm to the Kuki communities.
- December 4: A civilian, Hoichong Haokip, is killed in crossfire between security force personnel and the Kuki National Army cadres at Sipiyang village in the Senapati district Police sources said one M-16 rifle, two magazines, several live rounds, eight number of letter heads, photographs, dresses, magazine pouch and shoulder badges bearing KNA logo were recovered from the incident site.
- November 30: The 'public relation officer' of the Samuel faction of the Kuki National Front, 'captain' Namjapao, was shot dead and another cadre, Henjapao, sustained injuries when they were attacked by the rival Kuki National Army cadres at Bijang in the Churachandpur district.
- November 21: A civilian, identified as Hatneo, was injured in a crossfire that followed the attack on a camp of the KNA by a rival unidentified outfit at Muolvailup village in the Ukhrul district.
- November 9: The Kuki National Army militants reportedly seized seven grams of heroin No. 4 from at least 15 alleged drug traffickers at various places in Tuibuong and Hmar Veng areas of Churachandpur district.
- November 7: Suspected KNA militants shot dead a woman, Nemkhohoi alias Hoineu, at Tuibuong Hmarveng area in the Churachandpur district. District police recovered the dead body and also recovered a few grams of heroin from her possession.
- October 21: Three suspected KNA cadres are killed in an attack by militants belonging to the KRA at Ekou under Saikul police station in the Senapati district.
- September 21: Three ZRA cadres are beaten to death after being abducted by rival cadres of the KNA at Sielmat in the Churachandpur district.

- August 2: KNA kills a civilian, R.K. Pratap, at Saparmeina *Bazaar* in the Senapati district.

2005

- September 22: Union Defence Minister Pranab Mukherjee informs in Imphal that at least eight militant outfits (including the KNA) in Manipur have declared informal ceasefires' with the Union Government.
- March 6: A KNA cadre is killed at Kanglatombi in the Imphal West district
- January 20: KNA cadres abduct Additional Chief Engineer of Irrigation and Flood Control Department from Khumanom village in the Churachandpur district.
- January 12: A combined team of the United Kuki Liberation Front (UKLF) and Kuki Revolutionary Army (KRA) militants kill the chief of Kuki National Army (KNA), Vipin Haokip, during an internecine clash at Bijang in the Churachandpur district.
- January 12: Security force personnel kill a suspected KNA militant, identified as Zangkhopao Kuki, during an encounter between Panshang and Molnom villages in the Ukhrul district.
- January 7: KNA cadres kill a student, identified as Tongthang Khongsai, at Molnom Kuki village in the Ukhrul district.

2004

- November 16: The Imphal East district police during a search operation arrested a KNA cadre, identified as Hegin Lupho alias Paogin, from Mahabali Kabui village in the Imphal East district.
- September 21: Security forces arrest two militants belonging to the Kuki National Front-Military Council (KNF-MC) and the KNA during cordon and search operations at New Checkon in the Imphal East district.

2003

- January 20: KNA militant abducts the Additional Chief Engineer of Irrigation and Flood Control Department from Khumanom village in the Churachandpur district.

2002

- September 1: Manipur Police arrest two KNA militants at Pureilomba in the Imphal East district. They had allegedly come to collect an extortion amount of INR 2.7 lakh from a local businessman.
- April 8: The KNA declares a cease-fire with the NSCN-IM.

1997

- June 13: Fifteen Myanmar security force personnel and 10 civilians are killed as the KNA ambushes an Army truck at Thenjen village of Myanmar bordering the Chandel district of Manipur.

1994

- October 23: Chief of KNA, Hanglen, in a press statement, 'vows to establish' a 'Kuki State' within Burma (Myanmar).

1993

- April 15: KNA militants kill four Naga militants and set ablaze their houses in the Parouland and Kutal Khunthak villages of Chandel district.

Source: South Asia Terrorism Portal (SATP).

Manipur Terrorists : Their Linkages

The UNLF, formed on November 24, 1964, under the leadership of Arambam Samarendra Singh to establish an independent socialist Manipur, has a rather frightening history, in so far as its one-time allies are concerned. At its inception, the outfit shared a close 'political relationship' with the then East Pakistani regime, and in 1969 underwent military training in that country. The group is also said to have backed the Pakistani Army during the Bangladesh liberation war in 1971. Not just depending on Pakistan, the UNLF moved closer to China with a team headed by N. Bisheswar Singh proceeding to Lhasa in 1975 to ask for Beijing's assistance. Now headed by Rajkumar Meghen alias Sana Yaima, the UNLF is also close to the NSCN-K and has training camps in Myanmar and Bangladesh.[1]

Events on the insurgency front in India's Northeast have shown that rebel groups have often succeeded in neutralizing the reverses faced by them by entering into deals with other insurgent groups, and these alliances act as force multipliers. Insurgent politics in the region registered a very important development in year 2000—the signing of a deal for joint operations by the ULFA and United National Liberation Front (UNLF), a Manipuri insurgent group whose primary area of operation was Manipur's Jiribam Valley and neighbouring Assam's Cachar district. A UNLF statement on July 29, 2000, disclosed the agreement between that group and the ULFA for the first time. Significantly, the statement came less than a fortnight after the UNLF claimed responsibility for the July 16, 2000, killing of three soldiers in the Cachar district of Assam. Given the admission about the agreement, the ULFA could well have provided logistic support to the UNLF in carrying out that ambush.

It is linkages such as these and the potential for immense trans-border movement by cadres of these groups that has made the ULFA-UNLF pact so significant. The ULFA would like to describe the agreement as a 'fraternal bond sealed to fulfil certain tactical goals.' It may not have been a purely bilateral pact, but could have emanated from the loose pan-Mongoloid coalition called the Indo-Burma Revolutionary Front (IBRF) forged in May 1990, of which both the ULFA and UNLF were a part. Formed to wage a 'united struggle for the independence of Indo-Burma', the IBRF itself was a failure, primarily because it was too much of a problem for its leaders to hold on to a coalition of insurgent outfits that claimed to represent diverse tribes and communities.

What then was the need for the ULFA to tie up with the UNLF in 2000 or vice-versa? The ULFA's main fighting machine, until the Bhutanese crackdown in December 2003, was located in Bhutan. For several years before the crackdown, the ULFA had been under pressure from Thimphu to pull out of the Kingdom.[2]

Under the circumstances, the ULFA perhaps was eyeing the UNLF's bases and training facilities in Myanmar and Bangladesh. A denial from Dhaka notwithstanding, it is a fact that Bangladesh has been a favourite hiding place for the ULFA leaders. The ULFA knew that, in the event of a possible assault on its camps inside Bhutan, the group would have to have an alternative destination to head for and that would obviously be either Bangladesh or Myanmar, or both. The pact with the UNLF was, therefore, an absolute must for the ULFA, as 'hiding places'. Besides that some concrete training bases in Bangladesh and Myanmar would also be necessary.

At one stage, some of the ULFA arms consignments were even traced to the Khmer Rouge in Cambodia, a deal brokered in 1993 by General Bo Mya's Karen National Union (KNU), an anti-Yangon guerrilla group[3]. That deal was apparently clinched by ULFA's self-styled foreign secretary, Shasha Choudhury, who visited the KNU base at Manerplaw on the Thailand-Myanmar border. As surveillance increased, rendering weapons smuggling more difficult, the ULFA might then have pinned its hopes on the UNLF to serve as a conduit for shipment of military hardware from Myanmar rebels. The UNLFs equations with the Junta in Myanmar also appears to have been extraordinary, at least around year 2000, a fact which the ULFA may have taken note of while forging a deal with it. In December 2001, as many as 192 UNLF cadres, including some top leaders, were 'arrested' by the Myanmarese Army. Interestingly, all of them were set free by February 14, 2002, in four phases.

The People's Liberation Army (PLA) has bases in Bangladesh as well as in Myanmar, opposite general area Beheng and Kabaw Valley. They have linkages with NSCN(IM) only for purchase of weapons. PLA has links with PREPAK militant group of Manipur.

People's United Liberation Front (PULF), a Meitei Muslim militant group, has bases in Bangladesh opposite Karimganj' South Assam. Till 2001, this group only had few old vintage weapons and did not have enough funds to buy new weapons. After it established its links with DGFI of Bangladesh during 2002, it was funded and armed by the intelligence agency of Bangladesh. The main task assigned to this group by the DGFI is to establish a safe corridor through Karimganj for the agents of ISI and Bangladesh. It has also been given a task to spread Islamism in Manipur and surrounding areas.[4] PULF trained and armed by NSCN(IM) at its time of creation, is considered to be a potentially dangerous outfit. The other groups like: Islamic National Liberation Front, Northeast Minority People's Front and Islamic National Front have an objective of establishing an independent Islamic state to be carved out of Manipur, but remain unnoticed. Perhaps they have linkages with ISI in Bangladesh.

The smaller groups appeared to have followed a carefully structured policy of keeping their activities localised. Thus the Zomi Revolutionary Army (ZRA) operates in Paite dominated areas of Churachandpur district, the Chin Revolutionary Army (CRA) operates in Churachandpur, Mizoram and Myanmar. These groups simply sustain themselves through extortion, drug trade and criminal activities. They have avoided killings both of civilians and security forces.[5]

The recent operation being carried out and pressure being exerted by Myanmar security forces on the camps of Indian insurgent groups based in Myanmar, especially on UNLF and NSCN(K), have made these groups to establish their links in other places also. The arrest of four UNLF leaders on October 1, 2006 near Dhoki on Indo-Bangladesh border,-shows they were trying to cross over to Bangladesh. Later on October 4, 2006 arrest of its three leaders including *two* self-styled Lt. Colonel, (one of them handles finances of the group) confirms this hypothesis. The leaders arrested at Delhi Airport were on their way to attend meeting with UNLF chairman R K Meghem at Kathmandu. This indicates that UNLF is trying to establish its contacts in Nepal perhaps with Nepal Maoists. The group may also be planning to shift from Myanmar to Nepal and to also strengthen its bases in Bangladesh.

NOTES

1. Wasbir Hussain, *'Northeast Rebels: Strategic Alliances and Open Borders,''* Paper presented at seminar on 'Dynamics of Border Managemnt, Past, Present and Future,' organized by the Border Security Force at the Police Officers' Mess, Shillong, October 7-8, 2002.
2. Wasbir Hussain, *''Cross Border Links and Strategic Alliances'' Faultlines,* Februaryy 2006, p. 123.
3. Wasbir Hussain, *''ULFA gets new weapons from Khmer Rouge,'' Asian Age,* August 14, 1995.
4. BSF and Assam Rifles sources.
5. Bibhu Prasad Routray, *'Small Wars of the Northeast'',* SAIR, Vol. 3, no. 21, December 6, 2004.

11

Manipur : Too Many Insurgencies Death and Destruction Unlimited

Manipur : Essential Information

Date of Formation	21 January 1972
Population (2001)	23,88,068
Area State	22,327 sq km
Valley	2,239 sq km
Hills	20,088 sq km
Capital	Imphal
Principal Languages	Manipur
	Thado
	Tangkhul

Manipur Backgrounder

Manipur is known for its ethnic and cultural diversity. But the State has been plagued by internecine conflicts among different ethnic groups and tribes. The State is home to the Meiteis - the major ethnic group in the State - who embraced Hinduism in the seventeenth century. There are about 30 different tribes inhabiting Manipur. Some of the larger tribes include Nagas, Kukis, Paites, Thadous, Simtes, Vaipheis, Raltes, Gangtes and Hmars. Unlike the Meiteis, who occupy the Imphal Valley, the other tribes inhabit the surrounding hill districts. The Meiteis constitute more than 50 per cent of the population but occupy only one-tenths of the State's area.

The Meiteis do not belong to the Scheduled Tribe (ST)-category while the hill tribes enjoy certain privileges like job reservation, protection of their lands from settlement and ownership by non-STs even if they are Manipuris. This has been strongly resented by the Meiteis who perceive that the hill tribes are garnering benefits disproportionate to their population.

Manipur was merged fully with the Indian Union on October 15, 1949, but it became a full-fledged State more than two decades later, in 1972. This delay in granting statehood caused discontent among the Meiteis who felt that their identification with 'Hindu India' brought them no political or economic benefits. This gave rise to secessionist tendencies among a section of the Meiteis and a number of separatist groups emerged thereafter. On November 24, 1964, Samarendra Singh founded the United National Liberation Front (UNLF) to achieve independence and establish a socialist society. In December 1968, a breakaway group of the UNLF, led by Oinam Sudhir Kumar, established a government-in-exile called Revolutionary Government of Manipur (RGM) with headquarters in Shylhet, in the then East Pakistan. The RGM was backed by Pakistan. The primary objective of the RGM was to 'liberate' Manipur through an armed struggle. The RGM maintained an elaborate underground organisation. Its administrative and civil set-up included a home minister, a finance minister, a foreign minister and an army chief of staff with Sudhir Kumar as General Secretary.

However, the Meitei secessionist movement received a serious jolt when most of its leaders were arrested during the Bangladesh liberation war in 1971. The movement gradually fizzled out with rest of the leaders accepting the amnesty offered by the then Chief Minister of the State, R.K. Dorendro Singh.

Some of the Meitei rebels, including N. Bisheswar Singh, were detained in Tripura jails in the company of Naxalites-leftwing extremists. Bisheswar Singh and his associates were indoctrinated there into Maoist- thought. After his release from jail, Bisheswar, along with a team of 16 other Meitei rebels, left for Lhasa in Tibet, on June 14, 1975, to seek Chinese assistance. The team returned to Manipur in 1976 after receiving extensive training in guerrilla warfare. On September 25,1978, Bisheswar formed the People's Liberation Army (PLA) to achieve independence through armed struggle.

Apart from the formation of the PLA, Manipur witnessed the growth of a number of Meitei underground organisations with similar objectives in the late seventies and early eighties: People's Revolutionary Party of Kangleipak (PREPAK) led by R.K. Tulachandra in 1977 and Kangleipak Communist Party (KCP) in 1980. Some lesser known insurgent groups such as Poirei Liberation Front (1979), Meitei State Committee and United People's Revolutionary Socialist Party also sprang up.

Meitei insurgents stepped up their activities during 1979-81. They unleashed a violent campaign looting banks and treasuries and killing many security force personnel. The number of persons killed in acts of violence went up from two in 1978 to 14 in 1979, 36 in 1980, and 51 in 1981. In order to tackle the situation, the entire Imphal Valley was declared a disturbed area and the Armed Forces (Special Powers) Act, 1958, was imposed on the Valley in September 1980. Subsequently, security forces arrested Tulachandra, the leader of PREPAK, while the leader of the rival PREPAK faction, Maipak Sharma, surrendered in the same year. Security forces also succeeded in destroying several bases of the Meitei insurgent groups. Security forces, while raiding a PLA camp in Tekcham, Thoubal district, killed nearly its entire top-leadership and arrested Bisheswar on July 6, 1981. On October 26, 1981, the PLA, PREPAK and the KCP were notified as unlawful organisations. Counter-insurgency operations continued and on April 13, 1982, the new PLA leader, Thoundam Kunjabehari and eight other activists were killed in an encounter in Kadampokpi, near Imphal.

Following these setbacks, the PLA failed to keep up the momentum, though sporadic low-level terrorist activities continued. But two other Meitei insurgent groups - PREPAK and the KCP found it difficult to recover from the losses suffered during counter-insurgency operations.

By the end of the eighties, Manipur was once again engulfed in insurgency. Meitei extremists groups, particularly the PLA, stepped up their activities. PLA militants killed Vandana Mallick, an Indian Police Service (IPS) officer in an ambush near Imphal on April 8, 1989. Importantly, the PLA reorganised itself and formed a political wing called the Revolutionary People's Front (RPF) in the same year. The RPF seeks the secession of Manipur from India. The RPF established a government-in-exile in Bangladesh's Shylhet district, with Irengbam Bhorot Singh as the president. The RPF had a vice-president, a general secretary, secretaries in charge of various departments: home, finance, foreign affairs, publicity and communications, social welfare, health and education. The armed wing of the RPF - the PLA - was similarly reorganised on the lines of a disciplined army. The PLA had set up two camps in Myanmar and five in Bangladesh. Reports indicate that about a thousand PLA recruits received arms training in these camps. The PLA also formed a united front of Meite extremists called the Revolutionary Joint Committee (RJC) along with PREPAK and KCP. In its bid to enlist the support of the people, the PLA launched an armed campaign against social evils. It took to enforcing total prohibition and gunning down rapists, besides launching a vigorous drive against drug peddlers, in the early nineties.

Moreover, Meitei insurgent groups sought to project a pan-Mongoloid identity. They rejected the Bengali script, which they believed suppressed their language and culture. To assert their separate identity, they revived the practices of old Meitei religion - *Senamahi*.

The insurgents also began to raise their voice against the *Mayangs* (outsiders) settled in Manipur. They perceived that domination by outsiders was largely responsible for their economic and social backwardness. The *Pangals* or Manipuri Muslims who constitute over seven per cent of the population had been considered as *Mayangs.* In May, 1993, more than 90 people, including women and children, were killed in a series of clashes between the Meiteis and *Pangals,* in Thoubal and Imphal districts. Reports indicate that the People's Republican Army (PRA) that was set up in the early nineties instigated the communal clashes. Reports also suggest that a section of the *Pangals* established links in Bangladesh and with Pakistan's Inter Services Intelligence (ISI) for weapons and other assistance. Besides, a number of new outfits such as People's United Liberation Front (PULF), North East Minority Front (NEMF), Islamic National Front, Islamic Revolutionary Front (IRF) and United Islamic Liberation Army (UILA) had been formed in order to protect their community.

While Meitei outfits remained active in the Imphal Valley, the major Naga insurgent goup - National Socialist Council of Nagaland-lsak-Muivah (NSCN-IM), unleashed a reign of terror in the Naga-inhabited areas in four of Manipur's five hill districts, namely, Ukhrul, Senapati, Tamenglong and Chandel. The NSCN-IM used Ukhrul district particularly (where its leader Muivah was born) as a base for collecting funds and recruiting cadres. The NSCN-IM carried out several terrorist acts in Manipur in the nineties. On June 29, 1993, NSCN-IM militants killed 26 security force personnel and eight civilians in an ambush on National Highway No. 39. During May-September 1993, NSCN-IM militants killed as many as 120 security force personnel. On July 31, 1995, they attacked a Manipur Rifles post, in Kangohud, Senapati district, and looted 22 weapons and 3,784 rounds of ammunition. Again in August 1995, NSCN-IM militants made a vain attempt on the life of the Deputy Chief Minister, Chaoba Singh.

The ethnic conflict between the Nagas and the Kukis - a major tribal group in Manipur, constituted another problem of the State. Clashes between the two groups are now not heard of. A number of Kuki outfits like Kuki National Army (KNA), Kuki National Front (KNF) and many others had been struggling for a separate State within the Indian Union since the late eighties. The ethnic conflict had an added dimension as a result of a bitter struggle to control drug trafficking and smuggling of contraband through the border town of Moreh. The NSCN-IM controlled this illegal commerce till Kuki-Naga clashes erupted in 1992. The Kukis captured it from the Nagas, but the NSCN-IM remained determined to drive its rival out of Moreh, as well as out of Kuki settlements in the Naga dominated hill districts. The conflict had resulted in the death of nearly a thousand people and an enormous loss of property. Over 2,000 houses were burnt and hundreds of villages were affected.

The entire State's polity remained polarised along ethnic lines. In addition to Meitei, Kuki and Naga rebel groups, several other tribes, such as the Paite, Vaiphei and Hmars had also launched their own terrorist groups in recent years. There had also been frequent internecine conflicts, particularly between the Kukis and the Paites. Violence between the Kukis and the Paites had peaked in 1997-98, when clashes claimed over 1,000 lives with 4,600 houses torched and hundreds of thousands of rupees-worth of property destroyed. However, there were no violent incidents between these two tribes since the signing of an agreement between their leaders in October 1998.

Introductory

It is a tragedy of the horrendous proportions that a tiny 22,327 Sq km State of great scenic beauty has been subjected to wrack and ruin by nine ethnic underground movements, demanding dismemberment of this polity, heir to 2000-year old written history, to carve out a number of miniscule entities, they call 'homelands'. Simultaneously, there are at least four known insurgent outfits who are wreaking even greater havoc on the idyllic State in terms of killings and destruction, in the name of an 'Independent Manipur' for over the last three decades, claiming that Manipur was 'forcibly' merged with the Union in October 1949. The figures for civilian killings during the last six years are enough to show the scale of tragedy:

1997	205	1999	1122	2001	140
1998	127	2000	127	2002	189

Besides the twin dangers staring the Manipuris in their face, viz, secessionism and disintegration, they are also victims of internecine inter-tribal violence convulsing the State. The Naga-Kuki and Kuki-Paite strifes are two of their worst manifestations. But it is instructive to note that Manipur had no such tribe as 'Naga' or 'Kuki', and there were 29 tribes listed by their names like Kabui, Maring, Thadou, Paite, Hmar, etc. The generic terms like 'Naga' and 'Kuki' were introduced only after the advent of the British (in 1826), less than two centuries ago, to identify different tribes in the hills for their own 'convenience'. Some scholars have seen ulterior motives behind this British ploy.

It again needs noting that it is not only domestic outfits like the NSCN who are working for dismemberment of the State, there are external forces also at work. The Myanmar-based underground KNA also wants to form an independent sovereign Kuki state by carving out certain Kuki-populated areas of Myanmar and joining them with certain similar areas of Thoubal, Ukhrul and Chandel districts of Manipur. Two other Kuki outfits, viz KNF-P (Presidium) and KNF-MC (Military Council) are separately demanding 'Kuki land' or 'Kuki Homeland' comprised of all the Kuki-settled areas of Manipur, to have their own administration, economic rights, justice system, and civil and social laws according to the Kuki traditions, customs and usages. KNA, active in Chandel district, is obviously getting support from the Indian (Manipuri) Kukis.

Then there are lesser-known outfits with much more ambitious aims. The Zomi Revolutionary Army (ZRA) wants to unite all Zomis (Paites, Simptes, Vaipheis etc.) scattered in different parts of India (mostly in Churachandpur district of Manipur), Bangladesh and Myanmar. The KLA is fighting for liberation of Kuki areas of India's North-East (mainly in Manipur, Assam and Tripura), Bangladesh and Myanmar. United Kuki Liberation Front (UKLF) demands a separate Kuki Homeland comprising of Kuki areas in India (essentially in Manipur) and Myanmar. What is worse than inter-tribal killings is intra-tribal violence. The UKLF, having forged links with NSCN(I-M) is locked in hostilities with KNA, armed wing of KNO. The HPC-D (Democratic) wants a Hmar ADC to be formed by carving out Hmar areas of Manipur (mainly in Churachandpur district), Mizoram, Assam.

These outfits may be fighting for their individual goals, but collective consequence, if their demands are met/realised will be tearing apart all the five hill districts, totalling 20,089 Sq km, from Manipur, 22,327 Sq km. It will mean an emaciated Manipur, comprising four valley districts, which measure a mere 2,238 Sq km—10 per cent of its present size. And to remember that Manipur had once extended its boundaries upto River Chindwin in Burma, present Cachar in Assam and Doyena/Dhunsiri in the then Naga Hills (now Nagaland).[1] This is a broad-brush picture. Details will follow.

ROOTS OF INSURGENCY

Some scholars trace the inception of insurgency to the Maharaja's signing of merger agreement while on a visit to Shillong for "Consultations" with Assam Governor, Shri Prakash. He had arrived on the 17th and the merger agreement was signed on 21 September 1949, under which Manipur was merged with the Union on 15 October 1949. Some people like to believe that he was cajoled, persuaded, pressurized, coerced, or browbeaten into signing the merger. There were even rumours/loose talk that "the Maharaja had been placed under house arrest till he signed the Agreement". It is also true that Manipur was one of the last three States (Junagarh and Benaras being other two) to merge with the Union. But it is even more true that there was no popular dissatisfaction in the valley after the signing of the Agreement.

A word on the political scene in the State. Manipur was the first State in Free India to hold elections in June 1948, under a Constitution promulgated by the Maharaja earlier in the year. The Manipur Krishak Sabha (of Hijam Irabot, who was then underground) formed a coalition government, and the Maharaja appointed his younger brother, Priya Brata Singh as Chief Minister of this government. The Communist leader Irabot was the only one to react sharply and oppose the merger of Manipur with India, questioning the authority of Maharaja to do so without reference to the Manipur Assembly functioning since June 1948. But the Communists had a vested interest to take this line as the Independent India would thwart their designs of waging a class war in the North-East to bring a revolution in the Region to establish a proletariat heaven there. Born on 30 September 1896, he rose to head the first political party, Nikhil Manipuri Mahasabha, in 1938—thus becoming the first political, 'nationalist' leader of the valley people. But later he veered round to Marxism. Consequently, the Communist ideology made strong inroads into Manipur, with Irabot having developed a strong kinship with the Communist leaders of Bengal and Assam during his stint in Sylhet Jail (1940-43). On the eve of India's Independence, he was concealing his true colours by vaguely suggesting Manipur's relations with India on the lines of the State's position in the Soviet Union. Imbued with Marxist philosophy, he started advocating armed revolution preached by Mao. When Chief Minister Brata Singh issued arrest warrant against him in late 1948, Irabot went underground. During this period, the Communists under him "wanted to liberate Manipur from feudalism of Manipur kings and semi-colonial rule of Indian State". When the Centre mounted a drive against the Communists and the police was hot on his heels, he fled to Burma in September 1949. There he signed an agreement with the United Front, composed of People's Comrade Party, Burmese Communist Party and Communist Party of Burma; and the three agreed to give him some "occupied territory", including Kabaw valley and Angoching. He set up an outfit, expectedly named Manipur Red Guards, to fight for the "Independent Socialist Republic of Manipur". But it was all over with his premature death at his Headquarters at Tangbo village on 25 September 1951 (one source says Irabot turned down Sardar Patel's "proposal for 'Purbanchal' to include Manipur, Cachar, Lushai Pahar part of present Mizoram and Tripura."[2]

Were his Red Guards Manipur's first secessionist outfit. It seems his legacy survived in Manipur, providing a fertile soil whence sprouted a crop of rebellious movements, some of which were outright secessionist.

Meitei-Tribal Relations

In the long past, the Kingdom of Manipur was not a territorially defined entity. The borders of the State expanded or contracted, depending upon the character and strength of the Raja at any given time. They not only fought wars with the Burmese kings, but also used force to subdue and control the turbulent tribals in the hills around the valley. They were required to pay tribute to the Rajas, and their refusal could invite punitive action. The Rajas also made use of inter-tribal hostilities to settle scores with the offending tribes. The land has always been precious possession to the tribes and was often the cause of conflict between them. The Rajas' attacks on the hill tribes invited inroads from the latter into the plains of the valley. The cultural differences between the plainsmen and tribesmen was also the cause of conflict.

The conflict between the Nagas of Manipur and the Kukis is also centred round the claim to the land. The Nagas, the older inhabitants, resent the Kuki immigrants occupying the hills and enlarging their foothold on the hills of Manipur in the North. The bloody fight continues till date, having taken thousands of lives over the last two centuries.

The commerce and trade that unite the people also failed to achieve that end in Manipur. The tribals produced very little in their hills, and thus even the barter between the hills and plains was rather limited. The head-hunting proclivities of the Nagas came in the way of expanding their intercourse with the plains people.

During the 1917 rebellion against the British, the Kukis had also attacked the Naga villages, angered because they had not helped the Kukis against the British. When the Nagas started the Zeliangrong Movement (1930s) against the British, they retributed by avenging the Kuki excesses against them thirteen years ago. Such historical hostility has never subsided in this land, with its horrendous consequences.

After annexation of Manipur, the British introduced a new revenue system and implanted a *Lamboo* in each village for its effective implementation. His job was simply to convey Government orders. But being the representative of the British, he, though a mere peon, came to be looked upon as a bossy presence, deeply resented by the village headmen who were the administrative chiefs and religious heads of their respective tribes. It only added to the hostility of the tribesmen towards the Manipur government and Meiteis.

On annexation, the British took over the direct control of the administration of the hill areas—widening the hiatus between the tribals and the Meiteis. On the eve of India's Independence, the Nagas opposed the merger of their lands with India and wanted the British to declare the Naga hills as a directly British-controlled territory. To make the matters worse, some analysts claimed that even the Free India did not do enough for the tribals. So, the British had placed the Hills and Hill people under the direct control of its Political Agent since the 1830s. Maharaja Churachand (1908-41) had repeatedly tried to get these Hills under his control but was overruled by the British. The hiatus had thus remained between the Meiteis and Hill tribes for these long years. It was only when India got her Independence that the Manipur Hill People's (Administration) Regulation, 1947 was promulgated which reverted the administration of the Hills to Maharaja's control—after more than a hundred years. But after the Indian Constitution came into force in 1950, the Hill people of Manipur, like their counterparts in other States of the North-East, came to be governed under provisions of the Autonomous District Councils with which the State Governments had little to do. The result of this separate governance of the Hills and plains is there for all to see; the strife and dissonance between the two.

The adoption of Hinduism by the Meiteis also seemed to have created some differences in the community. In the 1930s, sections of Meiteis raised their strong voice in favour of revivalism— severely criticising Hinduism for disorienting their traditional faith. It needs to be said that in the olden days, both the Meiteis and hill tribals had practised animism. The Hinduism was widely embraced by the Meiteis, but did not spread to the hills. This also widened the chasm between the two peoples.

Revivalist Movement

The conduct of Hindu rituals and ceremonies involved some expenses which some Manipur families could not afford. Unfortunately, some Hindu priests also resorted to exploitative practices. All this caused certain resentment and hostility towards the Brahmins. The discontent continued to simmer, and nearly three centuries after its introduction in Manipur, the opposition grew strong enough for certain sections of the Meities to demand reversion back to their old animistic beliefs. Post-Independence, the revivalist movement even generated anti-India feelings. The movement for revival of the ancient Meitei faith was initially started in Cachar by Naoria Phullo, who founded a society called 'Apokpa Marup' in 1930. It found support in Manipur also. In 1945, another revivalist society, 'Meitei Marup', was founded under the Presidentship of Pukhrambam Surachand. This movement was known as 'Sanamahi Movement'. Initially aimed against the over-enthusiastic Brahmins "for atrocious imposition of the Hindu precepts; its anti-Brahmin plank expanded into anti-Bengali one. Progressively, the Movement swerved into anti-Hinduism, and in the recent years it has assumed an anti-Indian form, essentially because of political reasons."

The leaders of Sanamahi Movement are determined to popularise the ancient Meitei script and are sincerely given to discover its ancient manuscripts. They worship deities of Pakhangba, Leimaren, Sanamahi and Umangalais. The point to note is that these traditional Meitei deities are also worshipped by the Hindu Meiteis. That way, there are hardly any ground to believe that the activists of the Sanamahi Movement are anti-Hindu. Still if some sections indulge in anti-Hindu, even anti-Indian stance, it is for political reasons.

But the Meiteis have embraced the Hinduism so widely that reversing the trend is not easy. Still, it must be accepted that a part of the Meiteis are creating dissensions within the community under the garb of revivalism.

Post-Independence Situation

After merger of Manipur with the Indian Union, subterranean dissatisfaction among sections of Manipuris on the subject of the religion and Manipuri script surfaced as an emotive issue. Some political parties projected the merger of Manipur as illegal and unconstitutional, brought about by pressurising the Maharaja into it during his visit to Shillong in September 1948. These parties used the emotive issues of religion and language to mobilise the people for political gains. The militant outfits of the Meitei community are playing the same game. They blame the adoption of Hinduism by the Meiteis for the ethnic divide and strife within it. The argument goes that with conversion the Meiteis lost their pristine faith and tradition. The anti-Hinduism campaign started by certain groups might not have created any serious divisions within the Manipuri community, but it did succeed in creating a wave of resentment against the Government of India in particular, and the people in the rest of the country in general.

The prominent voice for 'independence' of Manipur was that of Hijam Irabot, an underground Communist leader who had fled to Burma. With his death in 1951, the movement weakened, but did not die. It was revived when his followers formed the UNLF (United National Liberation Front) to seek independence from India. The UNLF not only antagonised the Meiteis with its extremist demand, it failed to win other hill people, the Nagas and Kukis to their side. But the contagion caught on.

Like majority of people in the North-East, the Manipuris too did not take part in India's Freedom Movement on large scale. Even when the Japanese and INA forces occupied Manipur and reached right upto Kohima, the people of Manipur remained passive spectators, indifferent and disinterested. However, on the eve of departure of the British, some political elements did start mouthing independence demand. In subsequent years, a number of outfits launched on a militant course, later graduating into the secessionist movements.

Manipur presents a rather complex picture of ethnic division of its people. The tiny State has been carved into ethnic domains of different communities, living a sequestered life in communicado. Meiteis, over 60 per cent of its total population, are occupying a mere 8 per cent of its total area, essentially the valley. The Raja had full control over the valley, but only a nominal one on the hills. As the kings always came from the Meitei ranks, the community is deeply/emotionally attached to the State, and its integrity. Occupying a limited area, theirs cannot be a decisive voice in the affairs of Manipur.

The Nagas of Manipur hills who are politically and emotionally attached to their brethren of the Naga Hills, are least interested in preserving the integrity of Manipur; and are in fact clamouring to be a part of the Greater Nagaland. The other main tribal groups are of Chin-Kuki origin, who have shown no proclivity for a separate identity or independence for Manipur. Occupying as they are the foothills of Manipur in the Naga-dominated areas, they are primarily concerned with the protection and safety of their people. This has necessitated a constant conflict with the Nagas.

ORGANISATIONS: SECESSIONIST AND MILITANT/TERRORIST

By 2001, there were "over 50 militant groups operating in the North-East; Manipur alone has 17".[3] At this time, there were over 19,590 insurgents/extremists operating in the Valley and the Hills. The break down was 9,070 in the valley and 11,510 in the Hills. Of the arms total of 11,635, there were 4,975 in the valley and 6,660 in the Hills, including Nagaland and Cachar Hills. The Intelligence places the overground workers/sympathisers of all these outfits at 78,360-97,950 in the Region. The figures include those of the NSCN.

UNLF (United National Liberation Front)

It was born on 24 November 1964 under a young leader, Arambam Somorendra, joined mainly by the Meitei youth. Aimed at achieving independence for Manipur, it also intended to liberate the Kabaw valley, once held by Manipur through conquest but later restored to the Burmese by the British in 1834.

The 1965 war had exacerbated relations between India and Pakistan. Finding the time opportune, the UNLF sent a group of activists under Sudhir Oinam to explore the possibility of seeking help from East Pakistan to achieve its aim. They established their base at Sylhet, which had large community of the Meiteis settled there—migrating there for safety during the Burmese invasion of 1819. While Oinam was still finding his feet, another larger group of Meiteis landed at Sylhet from Manipur, transiting through Meghalaya for training in the guerrilla warfare. The latter group was arrested, kept in jail, and later handed over to the Indian Army at Tripura border. They were lodged in the Dharmapur jail till their release after 1971 Indo-Pak war. The Pakistani authorities had arrested them in 1967-68 for two reasons: (1) They were not as yet prepared to get involved by training such anti-Indian groups on their soil; (2) They were also not convinced of the potential and capabilities of the UNLF, which had yet to secure a popular support in Manipur.

The Meiteis' group, including senior members like Oinam, Biseswar, Sanojaoba etc., failed to get any support from Dhaka. Some of them had slipped from the hands of the Pakistani officials and remained in Dhaka, narrowly escaping expulsion. Due to dissensions, Oinam was expelled from UNLF. He, having stayed back at Sylhet, founded his own outfit, Revolutionary Government of Manipur (RGM) there. After persistent effort, he succeeded in gaining confidence and support of Pakistani authorities at Dhaka. He and his cadres got weapon and guerrilla training from Pak officers. They even helped the Pak Army during the 1965 war. After the birth of Pro-Indian Bangladesh after 1971 war, all hopes of the Meitei rebels getting any further help in Dhaka disappeared. They were either arrested or slipped back into Manipur. After an unhappy experience in Dhaka, the UNLF leaders were divided on future course of action. One group, led by the hot-headed youth, wanted to resort to an immediate armed action. The other, more pragmatic, wanted to hasten slowly. Both groups realised that to run such a mass movement, a lot of funds and arms were needed. Thus started the race for fund collection through extortions, looting the bus passengers, etc. The militancy in Manipur had entered its violent phase.

Having failed to woo Dhaka, the Meitei rebels decided to approach the Chinese. During their stay in East Pakistan, the rebels had learnt from the Chinese agents that they could get the necessary training from the Chinese in Lhasa. After various hardships, Biseswar and some others reached Lhasa via Nepal in 1975. They received training in weapons, guerrilla tactics and lessons on the Communist ideology for about two years. They returned to Manipur, ready to change the world. In 1978, they formed a new underground militant organisation, People's Liberation Army (PLA) under the Chairmanship of Nameirakpam Biseswar, and started recruiting Meitei youth, easily available because of prevailing unemployment in the State.

It was about this first batch that someone wrote recently: "Nearly 15 years after the death of Irabot, about 200 Meitei youths set out for East Pakistan for guerrilla warfare training, meant to facilitate the birth of an independent Manipur.... Most of them died of disease, or were killed. And their founder leader, Somorendra, later gave up the underground life, and became a noted playwright, poet, social worker, and theatre personality. He had got several national literary awards. He was finally felled by the bullets of two assassins on 16 June 2000 while attending a social function at Salanthong, near Imphal."

The present chairman of UNLF is Rajkumar Meghen alias Sanayaima. Its General Secretary is Khundongbam Tomba alias Sunil or Pambei. The Intelligence places its cadre strength at 2,500 (2001). It has links with RPF, PREPAK, ULFA, NSCN(K), KNF(P), KYKL (T-Toijamba Group) and TPDF. On 9 February 1987, it renamed its armed wing, PLA, as Manipur People's Army (MPA), to distinguish it from Biseshwar's PLA.

The UNLF continues to aim at freeing of Manipur from the "shackles of Indian imperialism".

In 1990, UNLF joined the IBRF formed by the ULFA and NSCN(K). For record, it condemned the Nine-eleven terrorist attacks on the US Mainland.

PLA

People's Liberation Army (PLA) was founded by Biseswar Singh and his acolytes in 1978 after their return from Lhasa where they had gone to receive guerrilla warfare training from the Chinese. Biseswar was the first Chairman. PLA's main objective was to organise the people's support and wage an armed struggle for liberation of Manipur from India and establish an egalitarian state based on socialism. The PLA aimed at creating a revolutionary front covering Nagaland, Manipur, Tripura, Meghalaya, Mizoram, Assam and Arunachal Pradesh. It was an ambitious political overreach for which they undertook guerrilla warfare, political assassination, robbery, kidnappings and killing of ihe security force personnel.

The next couple of years (1978-81) saw a spate of violent activities, including the attacks on SF, mainly aimed at snatching their weapons, so sorely needed by the rebels. They had, meanwhile, set up their camps in the neighbouring Burmese jungles. Initial attacks and ambushes against the SF succeeded, as the terrain helped the rebels and the former failed to get any intelligence on the rebels from the locals. The Lhasa trained cadres mostly led the attacks. The PLA also sent its cadres for training to Burma under the KIA (Kachin Independent Army). There were serious differences at the leadership level, dividing the cadres in several groups. There were inter-group clashes, in which senior leaders like Sudhir Oinam and Sanojaoba were killed; such losses hampered the movement.

The Army raided a PLA camp at Choro, a border village in Chandel district in October 1980. The camp was destroyed and several senior cadres killed. The increased violent activities by the PLA during 1979-80 period forced the Government to requisition additional Army and para-military forces units to conduct counter-insurgency operations. The government also declared the Manipur valley as 'Disturbed Area'. The Manipur hills had already been declared so. With this declaration, the Armed Forces (Assam and Manipur) Special Powers Act, 1958 stood automatically promulgated in the entire State. In October 1981, the Government of India declared certain Meitei militant outfits as 'unlawful Associations' under the provisions of the Unlawful Activities (Prevention) Act, 1967. Such organisations included PLA, PREPAK, KCP. All this and increased action by the SF scattered the militant network and shattered their morale—forcing them into their hide-outs and on the backfoot. The PLA suffered their worst loss on 6th July 1981 when the SF smashed their super-secret hide-out in Takcham area of the Thoubal district. Many senior leaders were killed and the chairman, Biseswar was captured alive. The SF had acted on an information. Interestingly, it was after quite sometime that the raiding party under 2/Lt Cyrus Pitawala learnt that they had netted the big fish, PLA chief Biseswar and officer was awarded Ashok Chakra for the success. After long and acrimonious discussions over the succession issue, Kunjabehari became the new chairman of PLA. Still, internal bickering continued.

Under the relentless pressure from the SF, the PLA could not regroup its cadres, and were on the run for safety. They suffered another jolt on 13th

April 1982 when the Army raided their camp in the Kudampokpi area, near Imphal, and after an encounter lasting seven hours, the new Chairman Kunjabehari and 8 other senior leaders were killed, and many captured. Such onslaughts broke its back, and the PLA stood disintegrated, and in tatters. Their cadres went into hiding, many crossing over into Burma where they had links with the Burmese insurgent outfits. Even in this dire situation, infighting over leadership continued, claiming several lives. The cadres remained underground for over four years, emerging in valley in 1987 only to pick up the pieces once again and to start the fight with same zeal and vigour. PLA formed a political wing, Revolutionary People's Front (RPF), and again came to be known for its ruthlessness. While the PLA continued with its armed revolution, its parent outfit, the UNLF, engaged itself with social work and in eradication of social evils, to win over the people to their side. It was mainly aiming at spreading anti-India sentiments. It opened its door to non-Meiteis, but it failed to woo the hill tribes into its parlour.

The leaders of UNLF made several attempts to unite the insurgent outfits of Manipur and other states in the North-East, and even some across the border. One tangible success was the formation in 1990 of the Indo-Burma Revolutionary Front (IBRF), embracing NSCN(K), ULFA and UNLF. The Grouping was to work unitedly for independence of the Indo-Burmese border regions. They branded the Government of India as their common enemy. The General Secretary of UNLF, Sana Yaima alias Raj Kumar, the great grandson of Manipur's legendary hero Tikendrajit, was the moving force in forging the IBRF. But it remained a rag-tag combine, sans any achievements to its credit.

UNLF, formed in 1964 to counter the influence of the NNC, has succeeded in securing the valley against any inroads by the hill tribes, none of whom ever tried to dominate the Meiteis of the valley. It is a different matter though that it is nowhere near its aim of achieving independence for Manipur. In 1991, the UNLF leadership decided to activate its cadres to launch an armed action in the valley. It has been at it since then: targeting SF personnel deployed in remote areas and snatching their arms; and gaining high-profile publicity as bonus. Due to high rate of unemployment, getting educated youth to fill its ranks has not been a problem. Such educated youth can be easily motivated to fight for an emotive cause like independence. Besides the easy money, the prospects of quick recognition and halo of heroism around their head have pulled many a well educated youth to the militant outfits like the UNLF and PLA.

The UNLF is mother outfit, which has spawned several offsprings. One group of rebels broke away from it in 1969 under Sudhir Oinam to form Revolutionary Government of Manipur (RGM). Infighting claimed the lives of Oinam and his companions. Later in 1978, Biseswar formed PLA, Eastern Region, as stated above. Some members of this outfit separated again to form

People's Revolutionary Party of Kangleipak (PREPAK). Another group emerged as Kangleipak Communist Party (KCP). Later, after 1990, numerous militant groups belonging to different ethnic entities mushroomed in Manipur, each functioning independently, essentially devoted to protect its people at the community or local level. Presently (2005), 23 outfits are active in Manipur.

On 24 November 1993, on the occasion of its 29th anniversary, the Central Committee of UNLF issued an interesting statement. While acknowledging the existence of ethnic contradictions in the State, it stated that "a solution has to be found whereby all ethnic groups can co-exist together. We urge all ethnic groups to join hands and fight India together for a bright independent future. A new brotherhood and unity will emerge in an independent country (Manipur) where all will share the fruits equally". Whom is the UNLF trying to fool with such statements? Certainly, not the Nagas!

The history of PLA is thus far intertwined with that of UNLF, its parent body. The two suffered another major blow in November 2001 when the Burmese Army bust three camps of Manipur insurgents in Tamu and surrounding areas. The recoveries were beyond expectations, in fact, stunning: more than Rs. 2 crore in cash, 2 boxes of gold biscuits, and 1400 sophisticated weapons. It was a severest blow for UNLF and PLA.

Incidentally, UNLF was among the few outfits to condemn nine-eleven.

First established under the chairmanship of the late Nameirakpam Bisheswar Singh on 25 September 1978 at Koubru Hill in north-west of Imphal, present chairman of the PLA is Irengbam Bhorot alias Chaoren. Manohar Mayum Pravin Kumar alias Ngouba is vice-chairman. Its cadre is 3,000 strong. It has links with KCP, NSCN(K), ULFA, TPDF and PREPAK, and aims "to regain lost territories of Manipur and to unify people of Mongolian origin of South-middle Asia".

The RPF is the political wing of the PLA.

The PLA had ambitious plans of creating a revolutionary front covering Nagaland, Manipur, Tripura, Meghalaya, Mizoram, Assam and Arunachal; clearly an overreach, which they wanted to realise through guerrilla actions, political assassinations, robbery, kidnapping and killing of the SF personnel. It suffered a major setback in 1981 when the founder started negotiations with the Government and subsequently joined the national mainstream.

The reach of the PLA should be judged from the fact that two of its ultras (Capt K Brojan Singh, Chief of RPF's External Affairs Department and his associate (Ibotombi Sopam) were arrested from their hide-out in South Delhi on 15 March 2002. The police had information that they had planned disruptive activities in the capital. They also had plans to motivate Manipuri students to join the outfit. The Police recovered a .38 Colt revolver, 61 live cartridges, a laptop, and Rs. 30,000 in cash (*The Hindu* and *Hindustan Times,* 17-3-02).

After his capture on 6 July 1981, Biseswar had fought 1985 elections from behind bars and won as an independent. Out of prison, he had denounced violence and criticized leaders of the valley-based insurgent outfits. He had become a local legend and continued to be revered by many. But he met a violent end. The 48-year founder of the PLA was kidnapped from his home on 8 August 1994, and on the night of the 10th, he was shot dead near the Thongkak Lairembi temple, Imphal. His assassination meant that the Government and the people had no reason to think the insurgents would accept non-violence or forgive 'traitors'. But there seemed another side to his personality; he had been arrested in connection with the Hindu-Muslim riots, unprecedented in Manipur, near Imphal in May 1994, a few months before his gruesome murder.

PREPAK

The People's Revolutionary Party of Kanglepak is a valley-based Meitei insurgent group fighting for an independent Manipur. Most of its top leaders have either been killed or arrested during the CI Operation, considerably weakening the outfit. Its first General Secretary was I. Sellung Singh. Some of the Senior PREPAK members were former PLA cadres who had parted company with the latter because of differences with its leadership. It espoused collective farming, nationalisation of all trade and businesses, and establishment of People's Courts. On the political side, it aimed at creating pan-Mongoloid movement on ethnic lines and an independent State, geographically embracing all North-Eastern states barring western area of Assam and a part of Tripura. They aimed at independence for Manipur; and the armed revolution was the weapon to achieve it. They targeted outsiders living in Manipur through use of coercive methods and pressure tactics. Like the PLA, the PREPAK also suffered heavily in the counter-insurgency operations conducted by the SF. The surviving cadres fled Manipur to take shelter in Myanmar. Of late, it seems to have revived itself and is active again. PREPAK was set up on 9 October 1977 at Koubru hill in north-west of Imphal (PLA too was raised there). Its founder was R.K. Tulachandra Singh. The present cadre strength is 1,500. Its Chairman is Achamba Singh alias Subhash and Palliba Singh, General Secretary.

The three outfits (UNLF, PLA and PREPAK) fighting for 'liberation' of Manipur for over three decade, formed a united front, known as Manipur People's Liberation Front (MPLF) on 1 March 1999. Sanayaima of the UNLF is the convener of the MPLF, and Sanasam Gunen alias Phalguni, the Gen. Sec., RPF, is the Publicity Chief.

KYKL (Kanglei Yawol Kann Lup)

KYKL was formed by the break-away groups of the UNLF, PREPAK, KCP, etc. at PREPAK HQ in Bangladesh, on 25 May 1994. A year later, it broke into two factions (1995) led by Mutum Ibopishak Singh/Namoijaim Oken Singh, KYKL(O) and by Achou Toijamba Singh, KYKL(T). Each faction has a cadre strength of 500. KYKL(O) had links with NSCN(I-M) and ZRA, and KYKL(O) with UNLF, RPF and PREPAK. The two factions reportedly merged into one around 2001, and it is KYKL once again.

For some recent years, KYKL has taken over the role of moral police. For years, examinations have been reduced to a farce in Manipur. Most students resort to mass copying, and even those who pass in first division do not get admission in other States. In the Higher Secondary Examination in March 2002, the outlawed KYKL rounded up 3 teachers and 8 youths, as in defiance of the "Curfew" imposed by the outfit, they had passed on answers and torn pages of books to some examinees. They were "Kneecapped" (shot through their knees) for the "crime". Some time earlier, the KYKL ultras had "Kneecapped" some professors of Manipur University, for they had taken money for special favours at the time of admissions and for tampering with the marks. On 30 August 2003, KYKL issued a pledge that it would "clean up the State Education Department," and kidnapped an IAS officer I.S. Laishram, former Education Commissioner, accusing him of accepting bribes from teachers promising them promotions and increments. On 7 September, the KYKL released the Official, and ordered him to seek voluntary retirement. It is a piquant situation for Laishram: The KYKL threatened that he would be tried in their court if he did not retire by 30 September; and the State Government suspended him for surrendering to the KYKL. The hapless official "disappeared" after his release. The police launched a massive search to track him down (*The Hindu,* 31-3-2002; *Indian Express,* 4-9-2003).

In a further bid to enhance their social relevance and pro-people image, the KYKL (one of the 20-odd underground armed outfits of Manipur) asked the teachers on 21 April 2003 to stop taking tuitions from 1 May. The statement also said that it "will also monitor regular holding of classes in the schools and colleges".

KCP (Kangleipak Communist Party)

It was established on 15 May 1990 under the late S. Maipak Sharma, a former PREPAK leader. Its present chairman is Leibakmacha Singh, and Ksh. Laba alias Noyon is the General Secrerary.

KNA (Kuki National Army)

Its political wing is KNO (Kuki National Organisation). They aim at establishing 'Independent Sovereign Kuki State', by joining the Kuki areas of Burma and India (Parts of Manipur districts of Thoubal, Ukhrul and

Chandel). Established in May 1998 at Moloni in Burma, it is primarily based in Burmese border areas. It was supported by some important Kuki leaders from Manipur. Its founder Chairman is Thongkholum Haokip. With a cadre strength of 600, it is operating in some interior hill districts of Chandel, Ukhrel and Churachandpur.

KNF (Kuki National Front)

It was formed on 18 May 1988. Later, a faction marched out to set up KNF (P-Presidium) under Semtinthang Kipgen as Supreme Commander. The remaining outfit came to be called KNF (MC). KNF (MC), strength 500, has links with PLA, ZRA and ZRO. KNF (P), 200 strong, has no links as yet. Both the factions are fighting for Kukiland a separate State to be carved out of Manipur districts and Burmese area on western side of Chindwin River. They are operating in Churachandpur, Senapati and Thoubal.

The Intelligence reports their strongholds in the areas astride the Indo-Burma border where thousands of Kukis are settled.

Early 1990, they had threatened to launch an offensive against those extremists who extorted money from Kuki villages. Ironically, almost around the same period, they themselves launched a massive fund collection drive in certain villages in Manipur, Halflong in Assam, and Molnoi in North-West Burma.

According to the Intelligence, while the KNF Chairman Nokhulum Kipgen and KNF C-in-C Sol Hulmum are from Burma, the KNF vice-chairman Henkholum Kipgen and Gen. Sec. Hemkhohang Haskip are from Manipur.

ZRA (Zomi Revolutionary Army)

The Zomis (which include Paite, Simte, Vaiphei and Tiddim Chin tribes) established ZRA on 7 May 1993 at Phapjam, Burma. Its declared aim is to foster distinct Zomi identity of these tribes and to unite all the Zomis scattered in different parts of India, Bangladesh and Burma.

Its President is Thanglianpao Paite of Pangmol village in Burma and Kamsuanthang Paite of village Pearsonmum in Churachandpur district is Gen. Sec. With 500 cadres, it mainly operates, in Churachandpur town and Thanlon subdivision of this district, Barak valley and Cachar in Assam; and Chimnuai and Laitui areas in Chin State of Burma. It has links with NSCN(I-M) and KNF (MC).

Hill-based Minor Groups

These groups are HRA, HPC (D), KLA and UKLF.

1. *HRA (Hmar Revolutionary Army)*

Military arm of Hmar Re-unification Front (HRF), HRA aims to protect Hmars from the aggressive Kukis, Mizos and other larger ethnic communities.

2. *HPC (D) (Hmar Peoples Convention, Democratic)*

Splinter group of HPC, it opposed the HPC's 27 July 1994 Accord with Mizoram Government. It is fighting for a Hmar ADC to be carved out of Hmar areas of Mizoram, Manipur and Cachar district.

3. *KLA (Kuki Liberation Army)*

Established 22 July 1992 under Hemlal Gangte alias H. John of village Molhoi Gangte of Bishnupur district, it is fighting for creation of Kukiland by joining the Kuki areas of Manipur, Nagaland, Assam, Tripura, Bangladesh and Myanmar. With a cadre strength of 50, it operates in parts of Senapati, Ukhrul and Thoubal districts of Manipur. It maintains links with UNLF and Chin National Front of Burma.

The KLA kidnapped a German, Heinrich Wolfgang on 23 March 2003, for an alleged ransom of Rs. 1 Crore. On the 29th, Malsawm Vaiphei, Director of Publicity and Information, KLA, told the reporters that the German was kidnapped for interrogation "about the NGO he was working for". This incidentally is the first time in Manipur, and second time in the North-East, that a foreigner has been taken captive by ultras. Earlier, the ULFA had abducted Sergei Gritchenko, an Engineer working for Coal India Ltd., in June 1991 from Margherita in Tinsukia district. He was, however, killed while trying to escape.

Some of the recent abductions by the KLA are listed here, with the ransom amount demanded:

(*i*) 8 December 2002, Victor Keishing, son of former Chief Minister and sitting MP (RS), Rishang Keishing; Rs. 10 lakhs.

(*ii*) January 2003, Konjenbam Ibotombi, Additional Chief Engineer, Irrigation and Flood Control Department; Rs. 30 lakh.

(*iii*) 18 March 2003, Dy GM, BSNL, J. Lunkim; Rs. 30 lakhs.

(*iv*) They have been ambushing policemen off and on in Ukhrul and Thoubal districts.

4. *UKLF (United Kuki Liberation Front)*

Established early 2000 under U. Nelson Kuki alias M. Thongkholum Kuki as chief of Army, it aims to form a Kuki Homeland from Kuki areas of India and Burma. Reports also say it is for "abolishing" KNA and KNO from Manipur, whatever it may mean. 50 strong, it operates in Chandel district of Manipur and Tamu area of Burma. It has alliance with NSCN(I-M). The UKLF kidnapped two journalists from village Sinam in Chandel district on 8 October 2002 to protest the "poor coverage" of its activities by the Press, as their Commander told them during detention. They were let off with a warning on 10 October at Palel, 45 km from Imphal *(The Hindu,* 11-10-02).

5. *MRNP: only for Record*

An underground group, Manipur Revolutionary Nationalist Party (MRNP), had surfaced in 1953, demanding "restoration of independent status of Manipur". Possibly floated by the Irabot Communists/acolytes, it soon died out because of mass arrests of its leaders and tightening of the security measures in the State.

Some of these 'minor' groups grew to be major ones in subsequent years as will be seen in the following pages.

PROBLEMS OF FIGHTING THE INSURGENTS

Domestic Nexus

Through coercion or persuasion, most militant outfits have established unholy nexus with Government and Police officials. This makes the anti-insurgency operations of the SF that much difficult. Then the militants collect considerable amount called 'protection money' from the traders, professionals, rich people, even ordinary citizens by assuring them personal safety if they paid the fixed amount. Any reluctance to pay it could cost them their lives. It is an open blackmail, but the people concerned have no choice because the Government SF cannot protect them all the time from these ultras.

Then, some of the outfits have formed front organisations which maintain close contacts with intellectual, politicians, social workers, media, and bureaucrats to create alternate channels to further their cause, lending it a veneer of respectability. These fronts help these outfits to pose as pro-people, genuinely interested in improving the lot of the poor.

Most of the militant outfits have setup political and social frontal organisations to gain the public support through the welfare-related activities as also to use them to achieve their own ends. They are used to protest against the 'excesses' committed by the SF against the 'innocent' civilians and lead the mass agitations against the human rights violations committed by the SF. These organisations also come handy to file legal cases against the members of the SF for their acts of commission and omission in the courts of law and in the NHRC. They fight on several fronts to malign and denigrate the SF, often on frivolous charges. The press—English and especially the vernacular—is used to project themselves as milky-white innocents and brave warriors fighting for the cause of all Manipuris, and simultaneously painting the SF as the villains of the peace.

They have intelligently refrained from attacking policemen, mostly Meitei. The militant outfits have unilaterally declared onesided cease-fire against the Manipuri Police. Killing a local Policeman raises public hue and cry, generating public anger against the militants. In a small 1800 Sq km valley such opposition can cost the rebels heavily, and they would lose the grass-root support of the people for whom they are waging the battles against the mighty India. However, the rebels do issue diktats to the police force to refrain from initiating any action against them, including the criminal investigations. They are also advised not to accompany the central police and security forces during their counter-insurgency operations to avoid an inadvertant casualty. All this has reduced police pressure on these outfits. This is possibly one of the reasons that explains low success rate in the counter-insurgency operations launched by the SF—implying that they do not get necessary intelligence outputs from the police, a *sine qua non* for success in such operations.

Nexus with Foreign Outfits

The prominent militant outfits like NSCN(I-M), PLA, UNLF, KNF, PREPAK and KCP have established professional links with the Myanmarese insurgent outfits. They use their facilities and expertise to train their own recruits in guerrilla warfare and procurement of arms and ammunition from the illegal arms market, operating in South-East Asia. Their camps are used as safe havens by the Indian ultras and their leaders. These services are provided for agreed considerations; often hard cash, or an agreement to ensure safe trafficking of narco drugs through Manipur for various destinations.

Narco Menace

The geo-strategic setting of the North-East impacts each State in the Region. The narcotic drugs, particularly the high quality heroin, have been smuggled into Manipur from the Golden Triangle, "where the dreaded 'Number Four' is abundantly manufactured". Official calculations have it that a minimum of 6-7 Kg of heroin was being smuggled into Manipur on daily basis from the Triangle through Myanmar. While half of it was smuggled out of Manipur, the remainder was for consumption within. Its dangerous consequences should be clear if it is stressed that "the use of this drug was unknown in Manipur until early 1983". The addicts fell victim to some of its other sinister accompaniments as well. By February 1972, 1428 youth tested HIV Positive.

New Delhi initiated moves for joint operations against the insurgents in co-ordination with neighbouring countries. In this connection, it is important to mention the May 1986 visit of Gen Sundarjl to Myanmar—the first by an Indian Army Chief to that nation. During the visit, the General stressed upon the military leadership the importance of dealing firmly with the NSCN and other insurgent groups operating from its soil against India. It should be recorded that the Burmese authorities/military have extended all cooperation to India's anti-insurgency operations (*See* Chapter 2).

Vested Interests Breed Corruption

As for the corruption and venality fostered by the insurgency and the vested interests wanting its continuance, an analyst writes (1995):

> "Nagaland and Manipur...have the highest per capita development expenditure allocated to them. The annual budgets of these two States amount to Rs. 1000 crore. With such outlay and nothing to show by way of development, it is clear that more of the funds have been going into the pockets of political and administrative leadership of these States. In fact, it will not be an exaggeration to say that several political leaders of Manipur and Nagaland have (developed) a vested interest in perpetuating the ethnic strife in this region."

Manipuri Governor, Lt Gen (Retd) VK Nayar, accusing the State Chief Minister, Rishang Keishing of being in nexus with the Naga rebels is too recent an event to need a narration here (*see* Chapter 2). He wrote a detailed letter to the President on the subject. The upright General put in his papers in December 1994 when he was telephonically asked by a "certain Home Minister" to take a particular line of action, which he thought was an utter constitutional impropriety.

Recruitment: Militant Outfits

Militants pick up educated youth after careful recruitment for induction in their cadres. They are put through medical examination before being dispatched to their assigned jungle camps, located in remote inaccessible areas of Manipur, or even across the border in Burma. The subjects covered during the recruit training are drill square parade, weapon training, use of explosives, field craft, guerrilla tactics, jungle survival under scarcity conditions, and living off the land. Some outfits even include ideological lessons in their syllabi.

Inculcation of strict discipline is an essential part of life of the cadres. The militants maintain insulated layers among their cadres. The lower rungs of their cadres have limited access to information, not even knowing the real names of their senior leaders, who are generally known by their code names only. Even when the SF captures the former, they fail to get any actionable intelligence from them.

Arms Influx via Manipur

"The recent return of the Rohingya (Muslim) community to Myanmar after some years stay in Bangladesh has enhanced the possibility of the influx of the ISI-supplied arms and ammunition for the militant groups in the North-East through the Manipur border", the Intelligence reported on 30 August 2002. This is because the ISI operatives had infiltrated the Rohingyas ranks. That creates the avenues for exploitation of the Rohingyas by the ISI operatives and their handlers to ensure the movement of arms and narcotics to the insurgents in the North-East from the South-East Asian arms bazaars. The Rohingyas still in Bangladesh are being used to forward "goods" to their kin in Myanmar for onward dispatch to Manipur.

The Army informed New Delhi that the PLA was creating political space through RPF which in turn is strongly propagating the cause of the minority community in the valley. A disturbing trend becoming evident is that the local youth belonging to these outfits and working for the ISI had got involved not only in arms and narcotic smuggling but also in the—espionage activities, far removed from the original charter of the separatist groups. The Army feared that a large number of youth reported to the ISI during the Indo-Pak stand off during 2001-02.

Question of Morale

600 men of the 7 Manipur Rifles refused to move from Khabeisoi near Imphal to Tahou in Senapati district, NSCN(I-M) stronghold, on the ridiculous plea that they did not want to be separated from their families. They not only took up arms but also demolished a wooden bridge, the only means of access to their campus, to deny entry to their DGP. It took the officer 5 hours to cajole the 'mutinous' men to let him in. Fighting insurgency tells on the morale of men, especially with raw nerves among them.

Inter-Ethnic Fighting

Various underground outfits are engaged in factional fights. Two major groups, UNLF and NSCN(I-M) have been gunning for each other, as are the (I-M) and (K) factions of NSCN. Likewise, the cadres of UNLF and KYKL(O) had been killing each other for six years till the PREPAK brought a truce between the two on 12 June 2001. While the cause for factional fights generally is over the leadership issues or differences among the senior leaders, the strife between the UNLF and NSCN(I-M) originated on the Iatter's demand for division of Manipur. Again the clash between NSCN (I-M) and KNA can be traced to the Iatter's demand for creation of Kukiland by joining some Kuki areas of Myanmar and some parts of Manipur inhabited both by the Kukis and Nagas.

It is a matter of concern that thousands of villagers had become either displaced or homeless persons due to ethnic feuds in Manipur during the 1990s, and it is still continuing. Hundreds of women/children have been widowed/orphaned. Two inter-ethnic feuds deserve attention: Kuki-Naga Conflict and Sadar Hills issue.

Kuki-Naga Conflict

The lucrative Moreh is not the only cause of this conflict. The 'war' between the Kukis and Nagas goes back in history, essentially because the two were 'neighbours' and both practised the sport of head-hunting. The terms 'Kuki' and 'Naga' were unknown in those days, they fought their battles under their clan/

village names. "Being the first to manufacture/use the gun among the tribals of the region, the Kukis committed more crimes than the Nagas." Taking advantage of these feuds, the British used Kukis against the Nagas. But the Kuki rebellion of 1917-19 forced the British to befriend the Nagas. The second-phase of Jadonang's Zeliangrong movement had both anti-British and anti-Kuki overtones.[4] The 'divide and rule' policy of colonial India created this 'we' and 'they' syndrome. The unity moves by some leaders (Lunneh of Motbung and Shri Largo) in 1947 proved abortive. Their 1956 armed revolt was seen as an opportunity by the Naga leaders to avenge their historical grudge against the Kukis. "During 1956-64, the Naga devastated nearly 60 Kuki villages in Tamenglong and Ukhrul districts."[5] The two tables below show the categorisation of the tribes in Manipur and their strengths.

Manipur Tribes: Categorisation

Naga group	*Chin-Kuki group*		*Non-categorized group*
1. Angami	1. Aimol	7. Koirao	1. Maring
2. Mao-Maram	2. Anal	8. Koireng	2. Moyon
3. Sema	3. Chiru	9. Lusei	3. Monsang
4. Tangkhul	4. Chothe	10. Sukte	
5. Kabui	5. Gangte	11. Vaiphei	
6. Kacha Naga	6. Hmar	12. Zou	

Manipur Tribal Groups: Population

Group	*1971*	*1981*
Naga	1,49,125	1,96,195
Chin-Kuki	1,70,107	2,24,171
Non-categorised	13,807	18,366

Source: The 69th Anniversary of Kuki Rebellion, 1917-19 Souvenir; Published by Kuki Independence War Memorial Committee, Imphal, 19-12-1985.

The smaller tribes anthropologically known as the 'old Kukis' became cause of trouble between the Kukis and Nagas. Some analysts feel their classification into the 'old Kukis' and 'new Kukis' by the earlier writers was responsible for the disunity among the Kukis. The erroneous classification has resulted in the identity crisis for the smaller tribes in the hills of Manipur till date. Consequently, the old Kukis are socially, linguistically and culturally Kukis; domestically Meiteis because of their long inhabitance in their vicinity, and politically Naga under coercion or convenience. Some of the old Kuki tribes participated in the Kuki festivals as Kukis also participated in the Naga festivals. Some of them even do not know whether they will be Kuki or an old Kuki or absorbed as Naga. Both Nagas and Kukis claim these smaller tribes as part of their respective families. It is, therefore, no surprise that those tribes have suffered heavily in the Naga-Kuki strife. These smaller tribes are coerced/influenced into the Naga ethnic label by the Nagas, especially the Tangkhuls. The old Kuki tribes, mainly Anal, Chothe, Lamkang, Chiru, Maring, Moyon, Monsang now align themselves with the Nagas, though there is hardly any historical or cultural evidence to support the fact. Again, "Marings were motivated to call themselves Naga more by the Church leaders than any other agency."[6] It is because of this frenetic rush to claim such tribes that Churachandpur became the main battlefield for the Nagas and Kukis—both claiming this district for themselves.

Sadar Hills Issue

It is the issue that divides the Nagas and Kukis. There was hardly any administration in the hills prior to the 1917-19 Kuki rebellion. The British had divided the hills into the NE and NW sub-division, with respective HQ at Ukhrul and Tamenglong. For administrative convenience, they created Sadar sub-division in 1933 with Kongpokpi as its HQ. In 1949, when State merged with India and the districts were re-organised, the Sadar sub-division was put under the newly-created North-district, later renamed Senapati district. The Kukis have persistently demanded elevation of Sadar sub-division to a district, first time voiced in the Kuki Chiefs *Zonal* Council Meeting on 3 September 1970. But the Nagas are opposed to this demand. The 1974 Nayal Commission not only recommended creation of such a district but even proposed inclusion of some villages from Senapati and Ukhrul districts into it. The 1982 Cabinet decision approved creation of three new districts: Bishnupur and Thoubal by bifurcating the Imphal district and Sadar, by elevating the sub-division. The former two came into existence but not Sadar—"even though the invitation cards had been printed to the effect". The Naga opposition won the day, second time.

Ethnic Landholding

District	*Percentage of landholdings*	
	Kukis	*Nagas*
Churachandpur	98	2
Chandel	75	25
Senapati	50	50
Ukhrul	30	70
Tamenglong	30	70

Source: Memorandum of Kuki Students Organisation, Delhi Branch, to the PM, 27-6-2001.

Kukis Killed by the Nagas

Manipur	750
Nagaland	130
Assam	18

Kuki Village Burnt/uprooted by the Nagas

Manipur		***Assam***	
Chandel	69	NC Hills	92
Churachandpur	18	***Nagaland***	
Senapati	64	Kohima	16
Tamenglong	92		
Ukhrul	82		
Total	325		

Source: Memorandum to the PM, by Kuki Innpi, Imphal, 1996.

A look back in history should be revealing on the antiquity of this rivalry. Once the British took over Manipur, administration of the hills came under the British—Maharaja being reduced to a nominal head. The trouble really began with the British settling the Kukis at the exposed frontier of the State. The 'smart' idea was to interpose a war-like tribe between the Nagas of the Hills and Meiteis of the Plains/valley. The buffer would check the depredations of the Nagas, thus ensuring peace in the valley. But the decision got the Kukis locked in a deadly feud with the Nagas, not only because they thwarted their occasional inroads into the valley but also because they had 'usurped' their lands. In a major raid, the Nagas (Kabuis) destroyed a Kuki settlement in 1918. The Kukis retaliated by burning 20 Kabui villages, taking 20 heads. The Kukis from Burma too attacked the Nagas across the borders. Having superior arms, the Kukis claimed more than 200 Naga heads during 1917-19. This was during the period when the British had used the Nagas against the Kukis when the latter rebelled against the British demand of recruiting their kin to serve as Labour Corps in the European theatre.

Kukis: Some Tacit Support ?

The KNO and KNA, its armed wing, were born in August 1987. While the KNO demanded an autonomous State in Sagaing Division of Burma, it espoused the cause of the Kuki-inhabited areas of Ukhrul and Senapati districts, Imphal valley (including Imphal and Bishnupur towns), Assam and Nagaland. The Kuki militants allegedly got moral support from Imphal and New Delhi, "for they openly claimed to be collecting material and personnel to 'fight and finish' the NSCN."

The Kuki-Naga clashes renewed in May 1992 on the Indo-Burmese border in the Moreh area "because of the Kuki refusal to share the underground illegal cross-border commerce and narco-trade booty with the Nagas". In retaliation for killing of a Kuki in January 1993, the KNA served a "quit notice" on the Nagas. The result was a long period of recurring, intermittent bloody feud.

On 18 November 1995, the Kuki ultras pulled out four Nagas out of a bus in Manipur and shot them dead. On the 19th, 7 Kukis were dead in a shoot-out with the SF. Ethnic strife has continued to simmer in the State's hills after peaking in August-September 1993 when 87 Kukis were hacked in a single incident. By September 1995, some 600 lives had been lost—most of them Kuki villagers, victims of 'Nagaland Guard' volunteers, apparently backed by the NSCN(I-M), though it denied involvement.

Though the Naga-Kuki hostility is rooted in history, these clashes were sparked by a dispute over control of smuggling at Moreh, a town on Burma border in Chandel district, peopled by some 40,000 Kukis, Nagas, Meiteis, Tamils, Keralites, Sikhs, etc. "Electronic goods, cameras, and high-grade 'number four' heroin produced in South-East Asia's Golden Triangle are/were the main contraband items, with the trade estimated between 3-700 crores of rupees a year. But the violence spread over large parts of the State, indicating deeper causes were at work" *(The Frontline,* 15-12-95). The Nagas were against the Kuki's demand for Kukiland because the Kukis were late settlers, and hence 'foreigners' in a land where the Nagas had settled long before them. Some viewed the violence as the NSCN(I-M)'s attempt to trigger an exodus of Kukis considered loyal to Indian Forces, and thus clear a safe corridor between its bases in Burma and Bangladesh. "After all the NSCN's ultimate aim is to create an independent Nagalim comprising the present Nagaland and Naga inhabited areas of Manipur, Assam, Arunachal and Burma", they argue. The Naga separatists have a name—Southern Nagaland—for the part of Manipur they want to annex. This worries Kukis, since they live in this area in large numbers, and the Meities who see this as a conspiracy to yank the highlands (90 per cent of Manipur's 22,327 km^2 area) out of their State to create Nagalim. The cause of the serious apprehension was the Kamson Plan (discussed later).

The situation was serious and Chief Minister Keishing's slanging match with the Army did not help matters (Keishing had accused the Army and his own Deputy Chief Minister of plotting against him. When the Army announced it had launched "Operation Sunny Vale" in August 1995 at the State Government behest, Keishing said publicly that he learnt the name itself from the press reports). But Keishing admitted that situation was serious: "Extortion by insurgents is rampant. By mid-September 1995, 109 civilians were killed in the Valley and 28 in the Hills during the year, besides 46 SF men." The violence went on till the end of year, and occasionally during the following years. Kuki-Naga violence had claimed over 600 lives in the Hills till 1995 itself.

The revenge seems to be the leitmotif. On 1 June 1999, the KNF militants shot dead 9 Naga tribals after forcing them out of a bus going to Imphal from Nongdam. It was the revenge for the killing of one KNF cadre by the NSCN(I-M) earlier. The KNF had alleged that the NSCN (I-M) insurgents were killing people taking advantage of the cease-fire.

A historical perspective on the Kuki-Naga rivalries is offered in the Appendix hereafter.

Appendix

Kuki-Naga Rivalries (Historical Perspective)

"It is worth noting that the tribes belonging to these two groups and commonly classed together as Naga and Kuki tribes in the context of Manipur State, occupy definite areas in these Hills", wrote Hodson (1911) "A line drawn across the map following the Kubo (Kabaw, today) Valley Road via Aimole and joined to the Cachar Road which traverses the western Hills from Bishnupur in Manipur to Jirighat on the western boundary of the State, separates the Naga (North) Area from the Kuki (South) Area, without excluding more than a few small Kabui (Naga) villages which lie to the south of Nongba (Nungha). North of that line we find Naga villages and to the south of it, Kuki settlements, though for various reasons, economic and political, the Kuki settlements exist not only in the British District of the Naga Hills in the vicinity of Henema but also far away on the north-east of the Manipur State, in the neighbourhood of Melome and Lapvome where the Frontier has been delimited and ascertained only within the last few years" (Hodson, 1911).

As for the Kukis, they indeed are, to an extent, found everywhere in Manipur. "We are like the birds of the air, who make our nests here this year and who knows where we shall build next year, a Kuki told Hodson. It is noteworthy that the Kuki's racial affinities are with the tribes of the Lushai Hills (Mizos) and not with their geographical neighbours—the Naga tribes to the north and Meiteis to the south.

An interesting feature about the growth of ethnic groups in Manipur is the spread of medley of tribes in its Hills. Major Naga groups—Kabui, Mao, Tangkhul, etc.—settled in the northern Hills fairly early in the history. In the past, they enjoyed autonomy within their territorial boundaries. Subsequently, a little later, a large number of separate ethnic groups, mostly tribal, during an influx from Burma, came to Manipur, and they were liberally grouped under the rubric of 'Kukis'. South and south-eastern Hills areas of Manipur were mostly settled by these Kukis. Some analysts suggest that settling of these

Kuki groups in the areas between the plains of Meiteis and Burma as buffer communities was the result of the policy of the Meitei kings.

That the Nagas deemed these late-comers as intruders in 'their Hills' from the Day One is no secret, and that explains the Naga-Kuki animosities with their roots going back to those early days. It was not only because of this Naga-Kuki animosities that 29 tribes, granted constitutional recognition as STs of Manipur consequent to the modification of the list of STs of Manipur in 1956, were recognised as STs under their individual tribal names, sans the generic rubric of 'Naga' and 'Kuki'; but also because grouping them under these two appellations would strengthen the two consequent collectivities in their dealings with the State government—and the two could flaunt their bargaining powers to brow beat the latter. That the device has not worked is obvious from the tacit support all Naga Tribes of Manipur are giving to the demand of Greater Naga land espoused for long by the NSCN, and one day they all could openly demand the merger of 'their Hills' with the existing State of Nagaland. The possible disintegration of their State does not look far-fetched to the Meiteis of the Valley. It was no surprise that they reacted so violently—burning and destroying important buildings and movable government properties—when New Delhi extended the Cease-fire Agreement with the NSCN(I-M) to their State (and Assam and Arunachal) in June 2001. The Kuki tribes too are acting in unison. They are demanding the creation of a Kuki majority district.

The Centre's talks with the NSCN(I-M) Duo (July 2003) is dead-locked over the issue of Nagalim (=Greater Nagaland). And the Meiteis are waiting the denouement with trepidation.

Now a specificity in the Naga-Kuki animosities. Nagas and Chin-Kukis have also been fighting each other around Moreh, mainly over the profits from the contraband trade and narco-money. It is essentially the Tangkhul Nagas (Muiva's tribe), dominant in the Ukhrul district in Manipur's north-east, who are fighting the Kukis; and it is also the tribe known to have provided maximum strength to the insurgent ranks.

The Manipuri anxieties over their Naga population is not without any basis. The Naga rebels boycotted the February 1998 Parliamentary polls in Manipur and Nagaland. All Nagas in the Northern Hills of Manipur abided by this diktat willingly. But the Kukis in southern Hills of Ukhrul district under Litan PS fully participated in the polling In spite of this, there was not a single clash between the two communities. "This is mainly because the peace has prevailed since the cease-fire with the NSCN(I-M) in 1997"; may be partly, the quiet is also due to the presence of the SF. Otherwise, the two hostile groups have divided the areas between themselves! The Kukis dare not saunter into the Naga dominated territory, and *vice versa*.

Tribal Populations: Trends

Going back a few decades, it should be noted that tribal population in Manipur showed a decennial decline of 1.3 per cent in 1941 over that of 1931.

However, 1951 Census recorded an abnormal decennial growth of 26.8 per cent, which could be ascribed to a large scale influx of the Burmese into the Hills of the neighbouring Manipur as a result of disturbed conditions caused by World War II. The Table below indicates the growth rate in case of various tribes of Manipur between the Census year 1961 and 1971.

Manipur Tribes: Growth Rate between 1961 and 1971

Tribe	*Population*			*Decennial Growth*
	1961		*1971*	*Rate (Per cent)*
Aimol	108		836	674.0
Anal	4,868		6,670	37.0
Angami[N]	632		70	- 802.8
Chiru[N]	1,809		2,785	53.9
Chothe	1,035		1,905	84.1
Gangte	4,856		6,307	29.9
Hmar	15,365	(6)	23,312	51.7
Kabui[N]	29,218	(3)	40,257	37. 8
Kachcha Naga[N]	9,734		13,026	33.8
Koirao	406		1,620	299.0
Koireng[N]	531		458	-15.9
Kom	5,477		6,550	19.5
Lamgang	1,866		2,622	40.5
Mao[N]	28,810	(4)	33,379	15.8
Maram[N]	4,928		4,539	-8.6
Maring[N]	7,745		9,825	26.8
Mizo	2,746		7,483	172.8
Monsang	1,342		930	-44.3
Moyon	647		1,360	110.2
Paite	17,026	(5)	24,758	45.4
Purum	82		–	–
Ralte	80		154	92.2
Sahte	–		3	–
Sema	4		3	-33.3
Simte	2,818		4,177	42.8
Tangkhul[N]	43,943	(2)	57,851	31.6
Tarao 'C'	NA		NA	NA
Thandou	47,994	(1)	59,955	24.9
Vaiphei	8,215		12,347	50.3
Zou	6,761		10,060	48.8

A. Naga tribes are marked by [N].

B. The figures in brackets under column 2 indicate the ranking of the tribes in Manipur, population-wise.

C. The Taraos enumerated 472 in 1981.

The figure above show an irregular trend in growth among the different tribes in Manipur during 1961-1971. "Higher decadel increase/decrease is often found among the less populous tribal communities than among the more populous ones. This phenomenon is indicative of the erratic changes in the ethnic identification of the less populous tribes on the one hand and affiliation of a few unscheduled tribes to this or that ST on the other."

Kuki-Paite Pact

The Kuki-Naga conflict led to a spin-off conflict between the Thadou-speaking and the Paite-speaking groups. The latter is a family feud and not ethnic conflict as reported in the media. There is no particular history of conflict between the two communities. Though they divide themselves into the most diverse ways, yet the fact is that Chin-Kuki-Mizo are historically and culturally one people. Paite sources ascribe the misunderstanding over issue of nomenclature as the cause of conflict. The Kukis on the other hand state that during the height of Kuki-Naga conflict, the Paites instead of supporting them, maintained closer relations with the Nagas, both at the underground and overground levels. The real cause however appears to be the apprehensions of the Paites that the Kukis displaced as a result of the Kuki-Naga conflict would dominate/subjugate them in various ways. But signing of Peace Accord between Zomis and Kukis for restoration of peace in Churachandpur district on 1 October 1998, restored harmony between the two. The parties agreed that the nomenclatures Kuki and Zomi shall be mutually respected by all. The two seem to have come closer than ever before. The formation of Indigenous People's Revolutionary Front (IPRF) by the Kuki and Zomi militants show they are from same group, indeed blood brothers.

District-wise Distribution: Paite and Thadou Tribes (1981 Census)

Manipur

Tribe	*North (Senapati)*	*West (Tameug-long)*	*South (Chura-chandpur)*	*Central (Imphal East & West)*	*East (Ukhrul)*	*Teng-noupal (Chandel)*	*Total*
Paite	201	17	29,156	1045	109	432	30,960
Thadou	23,061	4,359	17,196	1,502	5,116	5,233	56,467

Source: R.K. Birendra Singh, Census of India, Series 13, Manipur, Pt IX, Delhi, Controller of Publications, 1988, pp. 386-451.

Number of Persons Displaced in Kuki-Paite Conflict (Estimates, till 1998)

Tribe	*Killed (Number)*	*Displaced (Number)*	*Village Burnt/Uprooted (Number)*
Kuki	200	7,500	40-50
Paite	290	15,700	50-55

For record, the two sides had signed four accords before the one in October 1998 which has held so far. The fourth was signed on 20 April 1998, which lasted a couple of months. Their ethnic war broke out in June 1997, when the Paite neutrality in the Kuki-Naga feud was perceived by the Kukis as hostility. "By mid-1998, over 800 tribals and SF personnel had been killed; 60,000 tribals fled to Mizoram and over 40,000 houses, granaries, schools, etc. burnt." In addition, thousands of other tribals migrated to other parts of Manipur.

July 1997 saw one of the worst bouts of Kuki-Paite violence. In less than a month, nearly 100 people were killed, 300 houses burnt down, and 10,000 rendered homeless in the District of Churachandpur. During the period, the truce signed at 1.00 PM on 7 July 1997 by T. Samuel Haokip, Defence Secretary of KNF and J.K. Reuben of the ZRA, representing the Paites, under the aegis of a goodwill mission from Mizoram, lasted exactly 3 hours. Around 4.00 PM Kuki rebels gunned down 20 Paites in Singhat village.

The Paites have their own suspicions about the Kuki intentions as the latter's Kukiland includes many Paite villages. So it goes on and on, though peace has held since October 1998.

NAGA-INSURGENCY AND MANIPUR

The Nagas formed their first wide-based political organisation, Naga National Council, NNC, in 1946. To everyone's consternation, the NNC declared Naga Independence unilaterally a day before India was to become independent (15 August 1947). The declaration was a signal that Naga insurgency was on. Phizo, the Chief protagonist of the move, was arrested in July 1948 for anti-Indian activities but was released shortly thereafter. He became President of the NNC in 1950 and steadfastly led the Naga secessionist battle for long years. He conducted a referendum in Naga Hills where the Nagas supposedly voted for independence in overwhelming numbers.

The Nagas again proved their solidarity in the NNC leadership under Phizo by boycotting Indian General Elections 1952, as also the elections to the Autonomous District Council the same year.

The Government of India outrightly rejected the demand for independence, and offered maximum autonomy to the Nagas under the Indian Constitution, which of course was rejected out of hand by Phizo. The NNC mounted a violent campaign for independence early 1950s. Some moderate Naga leaders like T. Sakhrie were opposed to the mindless violence unleashed by the NNC under Phizo. The former was Phizo's one-time ardent supporter and a close confidante. In 1956, Phizo declared Naga independence and formed an underground government, Naga Federal Government (NFG). The same year, Sakhrie, the dynamic and revolutionary Angami Naga leader was mercilessly butchered by the Phizo loyalists at Chichama village where he had taken shelter after threats pronounced by Phizo. Now Phizo was under physical danger because of the counter-insurgency operations launched by the Indian Army and from the Sakhrie loyalists baying for his blood. Shrewd as he was, Phizo fled Naga Hills for East Pakistan and subsequently made it to England where he stayed (and led the secessionist movement) till his death.

Early 1960s, Phizo selected a young and dynamic Thuenglang . Muivah, known for his organisational skills and dexterity in diplomatic negotiations, to obtain support and help from rebel leaders in Burma and Communists in China to further the cause of the Naga independence. That Muivah's selection for an important assignment was to cast long shadows on the Manipuri polity will be seen shortly—he being a Tangkhul Naga from the Manipur hills. The Nagas had their Hills elevated to a full-fledged state of the Union on 1 December 1963. The 1964 elections to the Nagaland Assembly resulted in the first popularly elected Government under the Chief Ministership of P. Shilu Ao. But the militants continued the violence. The Naga rebels signed the 11 November 1975 Shillong Accord with the Government of India, agreeing to accept the Constitution of India. It brought the dissensions to the surface. Phizo neither approved nor condemned the Accord. The Accord split the movement, leading to the birth of new outfit NSCN, which again got split in two factions, viz NSCN(I-M) and NSCN(K), in 1988. The moderate Nagas who were for a peaceful solution have been ruling the state ever since 1963. But the rebels have sustained the violent movement.

All this while, the people in Manipur were viewing the Naga revolt with alarm and fear, because the Nagas of Manipur hills were supporting the Naga rebellion and provided a safe haven to the rebels whenever they were under pressure from the SF. Their fears got aggravated when Muivah, a Tangkhul from the Manipur hills, became a leading figure in the rebel leadership. The Manipuri Nagas had been supplying not only funds to the rebels but also volunteers for the rebel ranks. Consequently, not only the Meiteis of the valley felt threatened, even the Kukis came under threat since the Nagas of Manipur had considered them outsiders and "land grabbers".

The Meiteis were the first to react to this threat, asking their ranks to wake up as their very self-respect and even survival was at stake. In 1964, the UNLF was raised under the leadership of Arambam Somorendra. It was an underground movement devoted to unite the people and fight for their honour which they thought lay in the independence of Manipur. The Naga revolt gave them a *raison d'etre* to strengthen the demand for independence which had existed in an inchoate form ever since Manipur's merger with India.

The fear of the Naga dominance caused by the rise in the strength of the Naga rebellion helped the UNLF to win grass-roots support of the Meiteis. Having ruled the Hill Tribes for centuries, the Meiteis could not accept the dominance of the former in the Manipur polity.

The Kuki tribesmen also strove to strengthen themselves to contain the dominating influence of the Naga rebels in the Naga Hills and Manipur Hills. They reviewed and re-established links with the Kuki insurgents in Burma, where a demand for a separate Kukiland was gaining momentum. The Burmese Kukis had named their militants outfits as Kuki National Organisation (KNO) and Kuki National Army (KNA), and they were dominating Burmese Chin Hills. Significantly, the Manipur Kukis also designated their outfits as KNO and KNA.

The integrity of Manipur state stood threatened when Muivah became an important Naga leader of the underground, then formed his own NSCN post-Shillong Accord; and this outfit split in 1988 into NSCN(I-M) and NSCN(K). The forebodings of the Manipur people came true when the Naga rebels made demand for the Greater Nagaland (=Nagalim) by including the Naga-dominated hills of Manipur in it. The demand was made public in 1988. The same year, the Burmese Kukis demanded Kukiland in Burma and Manipuri Kukis demanded a Kuki district (Sadar hills) in Manipur to include Kuki areas of Tamenglong, Senapati and Ukhrul districts of Manipur. The Nagas are dead set against any such demand which will favour the Kukis in the Naga areas.

It may be fair to say that the Meitei militancy rose as a counter to the Naga insurgency. If the nucleus of NSCN was formed in 1978, as a result of post-1975 Accord split of the NNC, the same year the Meitei rebels formed their first underground outfit, PLA. Prior to the birth of PLA, the Meitei rebels had sent their cadres to East Pakistan and later to China for weapons and training. Though the Meitei and Naga ultras have never fought each other, some analysts suggest that the former have acted as a deterrent against the depredations of the latter, who have never challenged the Meiteis in the valley.

It is pertinent to observe that the ways and methods adopted by the Meitei and Kuki rebels are similar to those of the Naga rebels of Nagaland; viz, the style of propagation, methods of tax collection and extortion, attacking SF for snatching their weapons, use of social and even educational organisations and media to spread their cause, procurement of weapons, use of narco money to augment their funds, training their cadres in India and abroad, and dressing them in military uniforms.

The Kukis were the worst sufferers as a result of the Naga uprisings. The Nagas attacked them viciously to force them out of the Manipur hills, till the latter organised themselves. The Paites were with the Kukis in this fight till the early 1990s. They were reputedly from the same larger tribal family.

Later, it is claimed, the Nagas succeeded in drawing a wedge between the two; and mid-1990s the Paites started claiming an identity of their own, different from that of the Kukis. Subsequently, the Kuki-Paite hostility became so intense that the two fought bloody battles during 1997 and 1998. Hundred were killed on either side, and large number of villages burnt and razed to the ground—in blind revenge. The fratricidal feud ended—thankfully with the signing of Peace Accord between the two on 1 October 1998.

It is not only through the violence unleashed by their insurgent outfits that the Nagas have tried to see the fulfilment of their Greater Nagaland dream by 'grabbing' the Naga areas of Manipur; they have also tried constitutional stratagem for the purpose.

Mid-1995, Meijinbing Kamson, the Naga MP from Manipur and Minister of State for Home (Rajesh Pilot's successor) placed a proposal before a Parliamentary Committee that the entire highlands—five Hill districts of the then 8 districts of Manipur—be brought under a single ADC under the Sixth Schedule, which guarantees a high degree of autonomy. Chief Minister Rishang Keishing, also a Naga, endorsed the proposal. It brought back unpleasant memories of September 1995 when the Nagaland Assembly had unanimously passed a private member's resolution, moved by former Chief Minister P. Vamuzo of the NPC, to the effect that all Naga inhabited areas of Nagaland and Manipur be brought under a single administrative unit. It was an apparent call for Greater Nagaland. In a memorandum to the then Prime Minister Narasimha Rao, former Manipur Minister O. Joy Singh of Manipur People's Party (MPP) had pointed out that the Nagaland Congress (I) had supported the resolution. People also recalled that the Naga Students' Organisation had advocated in a booklet a "United Nagalim" (=United Naga Homeland) which included four of Manipur's Hill districts and a part of Myanmar. Joy Singh had also mentioned that Chief Minister Keishing was leader of the United Naga Integration Council (UNIC) until it merged with the Congress (I) in 1972. The merger agreement had stated that the Congress had nothing against the Naga integration movement and that no disciplinary action would be taken against any member for being associated with it. What Joy Singh did not mention in his memorandum but was widely known and talked about was the fact that Keishing had been accused by Governors among others, of maintaining links with the Naga insurgents.

So the Kamson proposal was a ploy and a step in the subsequent disintegration of Manipur. The five Hill districts at the centre of the controversy—Senapati, Tamenglong, Churachandpur, Chandel and Ukhrul—already had 6 ADCs. While Churachandpur had two—Sadar Hills and North District—the remaining four one each, formed under the Manipur Autonomous District Councils Act, 1971. Kamson's proposal is not new. The State's Hill Area Committee, which has constitutional sanction and comprises of MLAs elected from the Hills, have passed resolutions to this effect since 1978. But to bring the Hills under the Sixth Schedule, the Constitution had to be amended because only Tripura, Meghalaya and Mizoram were listed in the schedule. The Kukis and Meiteis are opposed to the Kamson-Keishing proposal. Though inclusion in the Sixth Schedule is welcome since it ensures speedy development of the highlands, there is consensus in favour of continuing with the six existing ADCs and clearly against consolidating them into a single ADC, which will be a State within a state. The Assembly has 60 members, and the single ADC too was supposed to have 60 members. This would be too much like a parallel structure. "It will take away 90 per cent of state's area out of the control of its government—a penultimate stage for final denouement of creation of Nagalim, or Southern Nagaland, at the very least, said a concerned Meitei.

The single ADC would lead to domination of minor tribes by the major ones. Among the ADCs incidentally, only two—Sadar Hills (of Churachandpur) and Senapati—are dominated by the Kukis; the rest are dominated by the Nagas. Of the state's nearly 8,00,000 (1995) hill tribal population, the majority are Nagas. Kukis, Hmars, Paites, etc. make up a little less than half. "The Hmar's loyalties are however not clear; they often sided with the Nagas in the past. The Kukis are thus opposed to any such move. But most concerned and pained are the Meiteis; not only because it would spell disintegration of their State but also because of shrinking space available to them. These non-tribals, numbering 1.2 million (1995) in the State's total population of about 2 million, have been feeling concerned over the years. Existing laws do not allow them to buy land in the tribal-inhabited highlands, covering 90 per cent of State's area, but the tribals are free to buy land and settle—as many have done—in the four valley districts, which cover's only 10 per cent of state's area. The 1993-95 Kuki-Naga violence, and the occasional clashes since then, led many Kukis and even some Nagas to take shelter in the safe areas of valley, increasing the squeeze on the land and urban facilities. During 1994, (and on occasions subsequently) the Valley, surrounded by Hills, went without essential commodities for a long time and prices skyrocketed as Naga insurgents in the Hills suddenly raised their 'taxes' on buses and goods vehicles plying on the highway. The Meiteis cannot be blamed if they see the single ADC move as a conspiracy to carve southern Nagaland out of their State.[7]

Needless to say, the Kuki Inpi Manipur (KIM), the apex body of Kuki organisations, expressed staunch opposition to the Kamson plan.

Manipur-based United Naga Council (UNC) asked Naga MLAs to sign declaration by 25 October 2003 (*Ind. Exp.,* 25-10-2003), confirming that they support the peace process initiated by the Centre-NSCN(I-M) talks, its early completion, and the political integration of Nagas by removing 'arbitrary boundaries' (read, "joining of Manipur Hills with Nagaland"). Keeping in mind the undertaking given by them to the UNC on 7-2-02, it asked the MLAs, to declare their stand on the Peace Talks. On the other hand, Chief Minister Ibobi is under pressure to procure signatures of Naga MLAs promising that they would not break up Manipur.

'Manipur was on Fire'

Ever since the 1 August 1997 Cease-Fire Agreement, and its subsequent yearly extensions, there were lingering suspicions and simmering anger against the Government of India's latent understanding with NSCN(IM). It was widely rumoured/believed that the Naga rebel duo of Issac and Muivah had been given 'certain assurance' on their demand for Greater Nagaland/Nagalim.

Since 1995, three Prime Ministers—P.V. Narasimha Rao, H.D. Deve Gowda, and A.B. Vajpayee—had met the rebel leaders abroad. In 1997, within a week of cease-fire pact, the government had to dispatch its interlocutors to explain to the NSCN how "cease-fire extension to Manipur and Assam would take a little while more".[8] A year later, Swaraj Kaushal repeated the promise. The Centre dragged its feet and Kaushal resigned. Kargil followed, with its attendant Indo-Pak tensions. By May 2001, the NSCN had enough of dilatory tactics and threatened to bury the cease-fire and retreat to the jungles. What happened subsequently is too recent a history to need detailed narrative. Some bare facts should suffice. The 14 June 2001 announcement by the Centre extended the Ceasefire Agreement, till then applicable (limited) to Nagaland, to areas beyond it, by adding three crucial words, "without territorial limits", to the text. The long nurtured fears of Manipur came true and the State went up in flames. The Meiteis, who count 18 lakh in State's population of 23 lakh, were up in arms (The Nagas count 2.5 lakh). The rampaging masses torched the Assemhly Building, the Chief Minister's office, the Assembly Speaker's residence, and the legislator's bungalows in Imphal. Finally, bowing to the wrath of the agitationists on 27 July the Prime Minister announced at a meeting of the Chief Ministers of seven North-Eastern States that the Bangkok agreement to enforce the cease-fire in areas beyond Nagaland had been revoked. New Delhi should have foreseen the shape of things to come. In September 2000, 8,00,000 people had gathered in Imphal and declared their total opposition to any move to extend the cease-fire to neighbouring states. And they had their reasons. In terms of area, the four districts of Ukhrul, Tamenglong, Senapati and Chandel will take away 15,519 km^2 out of Manipur's present area of 22,327 km^2.

Now it was Nagas turn to react. The NSCN duo totally opposed the unilateral revocation of 14 June agreement. "The Centre is going to trigger a civil war in Manipur between the Nagas and Meiteis..., with this unilateral decision", announced a meeting of the Naga organisations of Manipur at Senapati, which observed a total *bandh* against the 27 July decision. The local Naga students bodies launched an 'economic' blockade on National Highways 39 and 53, the lifelines of Manipur. The UNC President, K.S. Paul Leo said, "Historically, Nagas have been wanting to live as one people under one political roof." The UNC said four hill district of Manipur be merged with Nagaland, along with the 26 villages of Churachandpur district. It resolved that the Nagas in Manipur would sever ties with the State after the June 2001 violence which had displaced more than 50,000 Nagas from the Imphal Valley.

New Delhi must tread warily and display all the sensitivity while dealing with the NSCN(IM), which with a cadre strength of 4,000 and 3,500 modern weapons, is the strongest insurgent movement in South-East Asia, after the LITE. Until the cease-fire, it was running training camps for the ultras of UNLF, HPC, Paite National Convention, and ATTF, among others for a fee-of Rs. 1 lakh per head. That is why if the dialogue collapses, the North-East may again plunge into violence in mayhem, which may last for decades.

It was a direct threat to the State's integrity when all Naga organisations decided to vest the apex United Naga Council (UNC) with powers to administer the Naga-inhabited areas of Manipur by 'snapping all ties' with the State government. On 8 August 2001, they decided against paying taxes to the State Government and issued quit notices on all civil officials and SF serving in four Hill districts *(Hindustan Times,* 10-8-01).

The suspected NSCN(I-M) ultras warned Meiteis (24 November 2001) in the Imphal valley not to travel along the National Highways, particularly NH53, Imphal Jiribam-Silchar route "from today". They stopped several buses at Agaro Mile area in Tamenglong district and warned the Kukis not to travel on this route in future. Reports said the militants also threatened to prevent the Meiteis from travelling along NH39 (Imphal-Dimapur-Guwahati). The Imphal valley, dominated by the Meiteis, is surrounded by the hills inhabited by 29 tribes, including Nagas.

It was no surprise that the United Committee of Manipur (UCM) asked the centre to guard the NH39 and 53 — the very lifelines of their Valley. It accused that the NSCN(I-M) ultras and others had been collecting huge amount of money as 'taxes' from the truck drivers plying on these Highways, and also carrying out "kidnapping, rape, molestation, extortion and snatching of valuables of people using these roads".

Depradations Continue

Despite the fact that the Bodos and Nagas having chosen the path of negotiations, and even the ULFA showing some inclinations for the same, the Manipur insurgents have refused to tread this road even after invitations from New Delhi, including the November 2003 call from the Deputy Prime Minister.

On 23 March 2003, the KLA ultras abducted a German, Heinrich Wolfgang, from a place 25 km from Imphal, when he was going to inspect some development projects, undertaken by his German NGO. Denying that it had demanded a ransom of Rs. 1 crore, it claimed the German was wanted for interrogation. But they had abducted Victor Keishing, son of Rishang Keishing, former Chief Minister, in Dec. 2002 and demanded Rs. 10 lakh ransom.

For the first time, two PLA ultras, including self-styled capt K Brojen Singh, Chief of its External Affairs Department were captured from their hide-out in Delhi in March 2002. The Police recovered from these terrorists a .38 Colt revolver, six live rounds, a laptop, and Rs. 30,000 in cash. So, even Delhi is within reach (*The Hindu* and *Hindustan Times,* 17-3-02). Had the police not acted in time, they could have caused a serious, headlines grabbing terrorist incident.

Manipur is 'Disturbed Area'

The Raj Bhavan notification of 9 June 2000 says: "The Manipur Government has declared the entire State as 'disturbed area' under the provisions of the Armed Force (Special Power) Act, 1958 to deal with the insurgency problem. The Act came into force from 1 June, and shall continue for two years." It was subsequently, extended for another two 2-year terms.

They Run a Paralleled Government in Manipur

"Their Lordship, Chief Justice ot Tangkhul Naga; from Terror Tax to self-styled Court: How Manipur is held hostage." This is the attention-grabbing headline of the *Indian Express* story by Rahul Pathak, date lined Ukhrul, 13 August 2004. It speaks of parallel Government set up by Naga rebels in parts of Manipur. "Ukhrul is Naga territory, home to NSCN(I-M) leader Th. Muivah, and one of the districts that he wants included in Greater Nagaland. While Meitei insurgents in the Valley take protection money to fund their operations, the NSCN(I-M) here collects a 2 per cent tax to run the district." Says local supremo Ramthing Hungyo, the dapper President of *Tangkhul Naga Long* [the Tangkhul tribe dominates the NSCN(I-M) leadership], "We have our own judicial system." He shows Pathak the Court room, where notices have been pasted outside, listing two cases in what the type-written words read: "The Court of the Chief Justice of Tangkhul Naga Long." Ramthing explains this is the "High Court". Below it are five "area Courts", while 350 village Courts function as lower judiciary. Indian rules do not apply here. But how are the criminals punished? "We have our own jail, even our own police," says he matter-of-factly. There is enough evidence to suggest that what we are witnessing is a Parallel Government, more than a surreptitious underground

(UG) movement. Life has been peaceful in the four Naga-dominated districts (Tamenglong, Senapati, Ukhrul and Chandel) since the 1997 cease-fire. This also means that Chief Minister Ibobi's writ hardly runs in 4 of the 9 districts of Manipur.

The Centre has been unable to broker peace with the spectrum of Meitei insurgents—PLA driven by leftist ideology; UNLF, PREPAK and KYKL, the Meitei nationalists who still refuse to accept Manipur as part of India; and some smaller outfits (including KNF) pure extortionists. So pervasive is the terror that it has paralysed all of Manipur. Streets are eerily empty after 5 PM. No one imports things into the State without paying the insurgents. This has gone on for 3 decades. Why don't they kill the civilians? They don't need to, as they just do not disobey them. So mostly the soldiers are targeted. Is the Indian State withering? Here at least, it seems so. It is time New Delhi acts.

Even before Pathak wrote his piece, the Indians in the know were aware of the "fact" of the UG outfits running a parallel administration, forming "liberated zones" in Tamenglong, Churachandpur, Chandel, and of course, Ukhrui, we have just *seen* above. Manipur Government employees, scared by the spate of kidnapping for ransom and exorbitant, rampant extortions, had fled to relatively secure Imphal. This allowed the said insurgent outfits and big brother NSCN(I-M) to rule the interiors (Shishir Gupta, *Exp.,* 16-6-04). When the UPA Government moved 44 Mountain (Mtn) Brigade (Bde) into Chandel area, one of its intended aims was to instill confidence among these Government employees to work in the interior areas of Manipur. "Instruction to return to work have already been issued to them."

But the larger objectives of relocating this Bde—some 3,000 troops—lay somewhere else. New Delhi had been reviewing, after the UPA took over, the Centre's dialogue with the NSCN(I-M) duo, deadlocked over the issue of Greater Nagaland. New Delhi's emissaries (Kaushak and Padmanabhaiah) and Director IB have been talking to Swu and Muivah for six years by now. Some analysts feel their outfit has utilised this interregnum not only to reorganise, refit and strengthen itself, but also to extend its geographical reach beyond Nagaland. This has serious implications for the Region, particularly for Manipur, and to an extent for Arunachal. The Indian officials have watched with concern the shrinking base/influence of the NSCN(Khaplang), once seen a powerful rival to the I-M group. Analysts see these developments as the reason for compelling New Delhi to relocate 44 Mtn Bde engaged in CI role—Operation Orchid—at Dimapur to Manipur, with Headquarters at Chandel, as part of 57 Mtn Div, already engaged there in CI tasks—Operation Hifazat. Another view is that by moving troops close to the Myanmar border, the Government may be waiting (and expecting) for that nation to do a Bhutan: Crack down on North-East insurgents ensconced in the camps across the border and operating in Indian territories from the Myanmarese territory. The Headquarter 44 Mtn Bde was reported to be established at Chandel by end-May 2004. Not far from Moreh-Tamu crossing on the India-Myanmar border, this Bde would not only check infiltration of insurgent from across the border but also keep a keen eye on their activities there. It is for this aim in view that the 44 Mtn Bde commander would be on hotline with his Myanmar counterpart to obtain not only real time information on the movements of these insurgents but also about their activities in the fields of gun-running and narco-trade. Finally, this Bde will be handy to launch joint operations against the insurgents of both the countries operating in their border areas—as and when such a decision is taken by New Delhi and Yangon.

Important Events : 2003–04

Row over Arrest of NSCN(I-M) Cadres

The Manipur Police detained 13 NSCN cadres, including its Home Secretary A.K. Lungalang, Deputy Publicity Secretary K. Chawang, and senior member David Pere, on 6 October 2003 at Tulibari in Senapati district, on Tamenglong-Imphal Road while they were on their way to attend a meeting scheduled for the 8th. They had arms (an AK-56 and a M-20 rifles) and ammunition with them. After talking to Dy PM Advani 5 times on the 7th, Chief Minister Okram Ibobi Singh decided to hand them over to the Cease Fire Monitoring Committee. V.S. Atem, Convener, NSCN(I-M) Steering Committee, demanded the immediate release of the cadres, and condemned the arrest as violation of the ceasefire agreement. On the other hand, the United Club of Manipur (UCM), All Manipur Students' Union (AMSU), and other Manipur groups announced one day *bandh* for 8-10-03 as protest against the Government decision to let the NSCN(I-M) cadres go scot-free and demanded that they be tried for illegal possession of arms, apart from flouting the cease-fire ground rules. The incident is indicative of pressures and counter-pressures the Government is subjected to in such situations *(Indian Exp.,* 8-10-03).

Lok Sabha (LS) Elections: April-May 2004

The residents of Hundung village in Ukhrul district—home to NSCN(I-M) General Secretary Muivah and other top rung leaders of this outfit—bordering Burma keenly voted in the 20 April election to the outer Manipur constituency. They could not vote in 1998 and 1999 polls owing to the boycott call by the NSCN(I-M) (*Hindu,* 7-4-04; *HT,* 28-4-04).

On 2 February 2004, the KYKL issued a call against the BJP contesting the poll, and "banned" it from holding meetings, workshops, and other poll-related activities. It set 15 February as the deadline for resignation of Th. Chaoba Singh, President Manipur BJP, from the Party. Chaoba sought "forgiveness" and asked the outfit on the 27th to "excuse him for the past mistakes that he had committed". But V. Satish, in-charge of BJP affairs in the North-East, said the Party would field its own candidates for both the LS seats from the State. The RPF "banned" Congress from the LS polls *(Hindu,* 8-3-04; *Exp.,* 7-3-04).

Cl "Operation All Clear": September 2004

The Indian Army launched a major strike against rebels (of PLA, MPA, armed wing of the UNLF, and other smaller outfits) in September 2004 in Manipur's Bishenpur (Bishnupur), Chandel, and Churachandpur districts, bordering Burma, in which "25 rebels have been killed and over 40 detained," with the help of Burma, which has sealed its border. Army sources said these are not joint operations. Details of operations came to light even as India and Myanmar have begun preparations to launch joint military operations against various insurgent groups which have operated with impunity from camps in Burmese territory on the western flank of the Arakan Ranges in the north-western region (Mahendra Ved, *TOI*, 9-11-04; *Tribune/PTI,* 25-12-04).

The Operations had begun even as the Centre offered to talk to Manipur groups, including Apunba Lup, amalgam of 32 agitating organisations, and consider replacing/changing (and some say even withdrawing) the Armed Forces Special Powers Act (AFSPA). The Lup leaders met Prime Minister Manmohan on 1 November.

"Some 7,500 SF have surrounded 50-70 rebel camps, with around 1,500 guerrilla fighters therein." Intelligence has identified about 100 camps in the jungles of Manipur, harbouring 2-3,000 rebels. "Army claims to have destroyed most of these camps." Myanmar promised to cooperate in the battle against insurgents when the country's military ruler, Senior General Than Shwe visited New Delhi in October 2004. "Yangon has since moved hundred of soldiers to parts of Myanmar", says Kughalo Mulatonu, No. 3 leader of the NSCN; led by S.S. Khaplang.

Terrorist Violence

Some of the more important incidents are recorded here:

- Heavily armed militants attacked the private house of Chief Minister Ibobi with grenades late on 2 March 2004 night at Athokpam area in Thoubal district. Earlier, the ultras had opened fire at his house on 11 February.
- 3 October 2004: The CBI team would investigate the kidnapping and murder of 8-year-old Lungnila Elizabeth, a Std VIII student and daughter of Manipur Education Minister Francis Ngajokpa on 3 November 2003. The team would meet two State Ministers and Assembly Speaker whose name had been mentioned by two persons allegedly involved in the killing. The kidnappers had demanded a

ransom of Rs. 8 lakh, of which more than Rs. 4 lakh had reportedly been paid (*Exp.*, 4-10-04).

- Manipur Police confirmed on 15 December 2004 that Manipur University Vice-Chancellor Ngairangbam Bijoy Singh and Registrar R.K. Ranjan were abducted on the 12th. The outfit behind the crime was not named.
- Five police commandos were killed by the ultras in an ambush at Napetpalli area in Imphal East district on 25 December 2004. The identity of ultras was not disclosed though the area was infested mainly by the PLA and KYKL cadres.

2004 Storm over the Armed Forces (Special Powers) Act (AFSPA), 1958

It is an ironic situation that Manipur was on the boil in 2004. The cause of all the turbulence was an Act, AFSPA, actually meant to bring peace to the troubled State! It all started with the alleged custodial death of Thangjam Manorama on 11 July 2004. The widespread, spontaneous, popular protests spurred by the alleged rape, torture, and murder" of the 32-year-old activist, took the appearance of a near mass-uprising within a month. The Director-General Assam Rifles (DGAR), Lt Gen Bhupinder Singh dismissed allegations of excesses on Manorama and reiterated the Army's claim that she was an active cadre of the banned militant outfit PLA, and was killed while trying to flee from SF custody. Initially, the women took the lead, culminating in the dramatic and visceral intervention on the 15 July morning when "a group of them appeared naked in front of the Kangla Fort, Headquarters of the Assam Rifles in Manipur, holding up banners ("Assam Rifles, Get out"; "Indian army Rape us"), shaming the authorities and indeed the Indian State, without some manifestation of strident protest and resistance". Subsequently, the protests/ demonstrations became a more generalised phenomenon, with the leadership being provided by 'Apunba Lup', a loose alliance of some 32 socio-cultural and political organisations. The death on the Independence Day by immolation of a student leader Pebam Chittaranjan, adviser of the Bishenpur unit of the Manipur Students' Federation, voyeuristically filmed by a TV channel and continuously broadcast, and the cremation of his body (which his family refused to receive) by the authorities, further inflamed the passion. By the end of August, the State was up in arms. The violence may not have been of the scale of June 2001, "when Manipur was on fire". But it was as widespread.

Some quarters firmly believed that the whole agitation, sustained over a period of three months, was entirely orchestrated by militant outfits of the valley. Specific sections of the civil society were nominated in turn, who would "obediently" carry out the diktats of the militants by staging loud demonstrations or enforcing a *bandh*.

The immediate focus of the unrest was the AFSPA. "The irreducible demand is withdrawal of the Act; nothing more, nothing less. We do not have a long list of demands. Where is the need for talks?" This was the response of Jagar Thoudam, spokesman of the Lup, on 20 August, to the Union Government's offer to 'hold talks'.

The AFSPA has its origin in an ordinance promulgated by Lord Linlithgow in 1942 to firmly deal with the anti-war stance of the National Congress Party. It has been in force in Manipur since September 1980. The Army swears by the Act in a State like Manipur where 23 Militant outfits kill, kidnap and extort for a variety of causes. Chief Minister Ibobi is only too aware of the Government's handicaps without the AFSPA shield. But he has his political compulsions. The Army argues that the Act was the cornerstone of its functioning in terrorist-hit areas, and that fighting low-intensity war without it was near impossible. The human rights groups, in turn, insisted the Act offered a licence to kill and rape. Its opponents give empirical data: "It has been in force for 46 years and Naga insurgency is still far from over. In fact there are many more insurgencies. While in 1958, only the Nagas had picked up arms, Government figures now speak of about 80 militant outfits in the North-East." "There were only a couple of militant groups in Manipur when the AFSPA was enforced 24 years back. Today there are 23," says Yambem Laba, ex-chairman of Manipur Human Rights Commission. Some security experts feel the Act is not essential to curb insurgency. The only provision of the Act that gives the SF any significant advantage is the power to arrest and raid without warrant. "An alternate methodology can be found outside the Act, which should simply be annulled for all the trouble it has created."

The opponents say if New Delhi could repeal POTA, even when that draconian low, benignity personified when compared to AFSPA, had only a few weeks to run before it became defunct, why was it so stubbornly refusing to do anything about the demand to do away with this Act? Their conclusion is simple: New Delhi is not sensitive to the sentiments of the people of the North-East.

But did the imposition of the Act help in the first place. What do the figures say?

The Toll in Manipur

Year	*Civilians*	SF *Men*	*Terrorists*	*Kill Ratio*
2000	93	51	102	1:2
2001	70	25	161	1:6.4
2002	36	53	101	1:1.9
2003	27	23	148	1:1.64

Source: SATP

The desirable kill ratio in such a situation is 1:5, or even lower. The conclusion, they feel, is obvious: the act is not necessary to fight the insurgency. Hence its continuance cannot be justified.

Handling of the situation by the Centre left much to desire. The Home Minister Shivraj Patil could visit Imphal only in first week of September, and Prime Minister not for another 6 weeks. Then two central ministers made contradictory statements on an important issue. A day after the Defence Minister Mukherjee denied that the Centre was planning to replace Assam Rifles (AR) with the BSF, Patil said he was open to the idea of withdrawing Assam Rifles from Manipur which has 12 AR battalions presently deployed in CI role. No one seemed to have talked to the Army Chief Gen NC Vij who said he simply had no troops to replace the AR units.

Several organisations in Manipur had for long been alleging excesses on innocent people by SF engaged in CI operations and demanding withdrawal of the AFSPA. The UPA Government—and the NDA combine earlier—were warily circumspect as not to commit them even to review the Act, as they deemed it necessary for the Army to carry out CI operations. A young Manipuri woman Irom Sharmila went on "fast unto death" in November 2000, demanding the withdrawal of the Act from Manipur. For 3 years and a month, the Centre and Imphal remained indifferent to the indefinite fast by 33-year-old Sharmila who, under judicial detention, continues to be forcibly nose-fed at Jawahar Lal Nehru Hospital in Imphal for refusing to end her ordeal until the withdrawal of the act from the whole of Manipur, as it has already been withdrawn from Imphal, under political compulsion. The naked protest by a dozen Manipuri women had brought the issue in sharp focus, and enraged the entire population of the State. But even this partial withdrawal had come after certain amount of political drama and administrative convulsions!

In the days following the 15 July naked protest, pressure mounted on the Ibobi Government to repeal the Act. Patil's offer—which in any case had been rejected by Mukherjee, his senior in the Cabinet—did not amuse political leaders, student leaders and social activists as they all asserted that it was the Act and not any specific armed force (Assam Rifles, in this case) that was at the root of the problem. Though the steering committee of the three-party ruling Secular Progressive Front (SPF) had already recommended that the Act be withdrawn, the CPI, one of the three partners, threatening to quit if nothing happened by 13 August, Ibobi Singh wasted more than 8 hours on the 10th in an attempt to call a meeting of his cabinet to endorse this recommendation of the SPF. The reason why the meeting did not start till 7 PM when all the ministers had gathered at the CM's residence by 10 AM was the 'missing' Cabinet Secretary—not usual happening in the given situation. It was rumoured that the 'missing' act had been planned in advance.

It was a political ploy. Because when the Cabinet passed the resolution for repeal of the Act, there were simply two possibilities: The Centre would impose the President's Rule or the Congress High Command would dismiss Ibobi and replace him with Th. Debendra Singh, who enjoyed the confidence of two Central Ministers, Mukherjee and Santosh Mohan Deb. Moreover, Ibobi was aware of New Delhi resolve not to repeal the Act in a hurry. The CPI, with 5 MLAs in the 39 strong SPF in a house of 59, said on the 10th that "Patil has not been briefed thoroughly on the issue despite the fact that situation has gone from bad to worse during the past one month". Surprisingly, even as the organisations spearheading the anti-Act agitation did not stage any demonstration on the 10th, Dr N. Bijoy Singh, Vice Chancellor, Manipur University staged an 8-hour sit-in *dharna* on its campus in Imphal, demanding withdrawal of the Act. Finally, Ibobi saved his Government and offered a bait to the strident Lup when the Cabinet after an hour-long meeting on the 12th withdrew the "disturbed area" status of 20 km^2 area falling in seven Assembly segments in Imphal Municipal limits, rendering the AFSPA ineffective there. But this much-delayed decision, expressly against the wishes of the UPA Government at the Centre, did not assuage the Public anger, nor mollify the 32-Member Lup, which continued to vociferously demand the repeal of the Act. "We have rejected the partial withdrawal of the AFSPA. It has to go in totality as the entire Valley districts as also the hills are affected by it", said Jagat Thoudam, President, All Manipur United Clubs Organisation, one of the main agitating bodies. To make the matters worse, the 4 Hill districts observed a dawn-to-dusk *bandh* on the 12th to demand the withdrawal of the Act from entire Manipur, echoing the demand of the Lup, and for same reasons—any valley specific decision on the Act would be viewed as partisan.

Finally, the issue reached the highest court of the people, as it must, for its final resolution. The trouble-torn State started limping back to normal after a 4-month impasse, when the Prime Minister assured a delegation of the LUP on 1 November that he would consider replacing the AFSPA with "a more humane law that will address both the concerns of national security and the rights of citizens". The Centre's decision defused the explosive situation created by the alleged rape and killing of Manorama on 11 July and the naked protest by a dozen women on the 15th, which snowballed into a widespread agitation against the Act. Manmohan Singh agreed to a suggestion by LUP that an expert group look into the legal, constitutional and "moral" aspects of the AFSPA. As a goodwill gesture and to create a congenial atmosphere, LUP suspended its agitation programme, including that against the teaching of Hindi. The PM's assurance came nearly 3 weeks before his scheduled visit to Manipur, and was preceded by the UPA Government's announcement of a Rs. 250 crore package for the State for development projects in education, health, power, transport and communication. The package was finalised when the Chief Minister met the Union Minister for Development, North-Eastern Region, P.R. Kyndia, on 26 October.

Prof Arambam Lokendra, leader of the LUP delegation told the press after the meeting that it had only pressed the demand for the withdrawal of the Act. The LUP had agreed to send the delegation after much prodding by Manipur Governor S.S. Sidhu, and after three rounds of discussions with him. Lokendra said, "'Since Sidhu took over (in early September), he has been reaching over to different sections of people and trying to get a fix on their concerns." Another person who helped in the dialogue process is Falguni Raj Kumar, whose appointment as Special Advisor-designate in the Home Ministry, was announced on 21 October. The appointment of a local Meitei officer as the pointmen on Manipur helped hasten matters. Ex-CM Keishing also held several meetings with the LUP, after being requested by Patil to act as the facilitator.

The PM, who arrived Imphal on 20 November 2004 for a 2-day visit, was greeted by a city shut down by a *bandh* call given by the banned RPF. The day was marked by the handing over otofhe presence of the PM. The moment of 'de-militarisation' of the historic Fort touched the heart of every Manipuri, "as it has been the symbol of Meitei pride, an embodiment of the myths, philosophy, culture, arts and literature". Historian Bimala Devi says: "The Manipur kings ruled from the 236.62 acre Kangla Fort for 2000 years." People believe there are 108 sacred sites inside the complex. The Fort, in the heart of Imphal, has been the focal point of social unrest in Manipur ever since the British occupied it in April 1891, and post-1947, was taken over by the Indian Army—Assam Rifles to be exact. In 1976, four years after Manipur achieved statehood, the Government took a decision that the Assam Rifles (AR) should vacate Kangla. The AR had their own problems moving to Maha Koireng, 20 km from Imphal, as ordered. The Centre fixed July 2000 for them to move out completely—which happened only on 20 November 2004. The PM told the LUP delegation that met him on the 20th that the Review Committee, set up on the 5th as agreed during the 1 November meeting, would submit its report within 6 months. The committee is headed by the ex-Supreme Court Judge and ex-Chairperson Law Commission, Justice (Retd) B.P. Jeevan Reddy. Its other members are S.B. Nakade, an academician; P.P. Shrivastava, ex-bureaucrat; Lt Gen (Retd) VR Raghavan; and Sanjoy Hazarika, journalist (*FL* 10 Sep., 3 Dec.; *Exp.* 10 Aug., 21 Oct., 5 and 21 Nov.; *HT* 12 and 22 Aug., 21 Nov.; and TO/ 3 Nov.—all of 2004; and *Hindu* 21-1-05).

Repealing the AFSP Act : An Unfortunate Debate : 2006

The nation has witnessed some passionate debate for sometime consequent to the demand by some human rights activists that the Armed

Forces Special Powers Act be repealed. A goodly lady, Irom Sharmila, under misplaced beliefs and misconceived notions about the provisions of the AFSPA, has been fasting in Manipur—presently in Delhi—for the last six years.

The AFSPA is an enabling legislature that enables the soldiers engaged in counter insurgency operations, to deal effectively and without too much loss of time, the insurgents and terrorists who are out to kill the innocents for no faults of their.

The activists vociferously demanding its repeal seem to be generally uninformed about the powers this Act gives the soldiers in insurgency-afflicted areas. It does not protect the soldiers against any breach of law like the rape, undue or unduly-long detention, extortionist demands etc. All it does is to grant powers to troops to arrest or open fire under certain situations. Such power is not granted to all soldiers, only to the officers, Junior Commissioned Officers (JCOs) and Non-Commissioned Officers (NCOs). In peace time, the Armymen can not open fire or arrest a person without the written permission of a judicial officers. As such (judicial) officers can not accompany soldiers engaged in fighting terrorists in remote, hilly, jungle, or inaccessible areas, so the Parliament after due deliberation had given such powers to Army under this Act, passed in 1958.

The most 'cogent and powerful' argument given in favour of repealing the Act by its opponents is : As the Act has failed to eradicate terrorism/insurgency in the nearly 50-year period it has been in operation/force, it is useless Act and should be repealed. At one level, it is too innocent an argument to deserve the dignity of a reply. At another level, it is a facile, facetious and frivolous logic which can be dealt with a quick reply. If a mere enactment of law could eliminate crime, this world should have been peopled by angels by the end of the 18th century—if not earlier.

Another equally innocent argument, in fact a cliche by now, is that force of arms can not eliminate terrorism or insurgency. Nothing could be more fallacious. Until the terror merchants are convinced that their violent ways would not pay, they will continue to use more and more violence against the innocent. It is only the force of arms, used effectively by the troops, that would convience the ultras to foresake their violent addiction and come to the negotiating table. The Army's role ends there, and then it is over to political leaders. It can be emphatically stated that it is combination of arms and political acumen that will solve the problem of terrorism and insurgency. Either of them by itself would prove ineffective and impotent to deal with the scourge.

A Vinoba or JP could persuade the hardened dacoits to come out of their jungle hideouts because they were by then tired of the harshness and starkness of their existence. A Gandhi could effectively win over the British might because they were decent human beings and civilised nation. But none of them—the Gandhis, the Vinobas, or the JPs—can succeed against the terrorists blinded by hatred, inhumanity, and beyond-the-logic religious extremism blinded by the indoctrinated religious fundamentalists.

That Indian debate on the Act is generally uninformed has been stated above. An analyst puts it differently if more effectively : "Prime Minister Manmohan Singh has again stirred the pot—without adding substance to its contents—on the emotionally charged but intellectually deficient debate on the AFSPA, promising amendments to make it 'more humane'."(Ajai Sahni, Executive Director, Institute for Conflict Management; *Times of India,* 10.12.06.) Significantly, the PM virtually repeats himself after two years, as he had promised in November 2004 a review of the Act in the light of the 'humanitarian values'. Meanwhile, a number of ministers and senior officials have rejected any dilution of the Act.Pranab Mukherjee has rightly argued that "it is not possible for the armed forces to function" in the absence of the enabling provisions of the AFSPA.

In the 'heated' debate, the human rights organisations have blamed the Act for all kinds of real or imaginary 'excesses' by the security forces. In the polarized debate there is little reference to specific clauses of the law, and even more, to any empirical links between the provisions and identifiable excesses.

In counter-terrorist operations, a few acts of excess by some soldiers is unavoidable. To state this is not to justify the indefensible. It is merely to stress that the soldiers, at least some of them could react emotionally in an extraordinary situation of extreme provocation or of enormity of the crime committed by the terrorists—all their training, notwithstanding. A soldier, after all is a human being, heir to all the pain and feelings a man is amenable to. In July 1956, Naga insurgents in a hilly area wiped out an entire platoon of 32 men of an infantry battalion, in an ambush. In March 1977, Mizo insurgents, from a distant hill top, shot dead a JCO who was to proceed on pension the very next day. These are just two instances of extremely painful situations where some soldiers could lose balance and be guilty of committing a degree of excess.

Soldiers are under extreme mental and psychological pressure while combating terrorists. In a crowded market—say, of Srinagar, Kohima, or Baramulla—a terrorist standing in a crowd could shoot and kill a soldier in the spur of a moments. In the recent months, dozens of soldiers and junior officers have killed their colleagues or committed suicide in Jammu and Kashmir.

Combating terrorists is not an easy job, when they might happen to be your own countrymen. Fighting the enemy is simple and straightforward for a soldier : Either you kill him or get killed by him. On the other hand, a terrorist is may be a brother led astray. Fighting him is an unequal battle.

The preceding three paragraphs are meant neither to justify excesses by soldiers, nor to condome them. It is a plea for the civil society to appreciate the problems a soldier faces while functioning in insurgency environment. Let it be put on record that the Indian Army has acted responsibly while combating terrorism and insurgency and nation should be proud of it.

Coming back to the AFSPA, it needs to be emphasised that its constitutionality and of its various provisions have been up-held by the Supreme Court in the Naga People's Movement of Human Rights Vs Union of India, 1997. Most of the misconceptions related to the Act were addressed by the judgement. *Inter alia,* as regards the 'draconian' powers of 'arrest without warrant', this "is not very different from the power which has been conferred on a police officer", with the additional provision that the person detained must be handed over to the police "with the least possible delay."

The Act confers no immunity against prosecution, only demanding government sanction for such prosecution, as is the case for any public servant.

The reality of human rights violation to a certain extent—as mentioned above—in insurgency afflicted areas cannot be escaped. The case of Thangjam Manorama was tragic and indefensible. There can be no two opinions on that. However, no excess by troops enjoys even the slightest protection under/of this Act.

It needs to be said that empirically the presence of the Act has little to do with human rights' abuses. National Human Rights Commission data for 2001-02 indicates that the highest number of custodial deaths occurred in UP (186), Maharashtra (146), and Bihar (144), and none of these states were under the AFSP Act. On the other hand, Manipur which has this Act in force witnessed no custodial death in that year (2001-02).

It needs to be understood that the Act is an enabling legislation that confers minimal powers on the Army to operate in a situation of widespread internal disorder. If the Act or comparable legislation is absent or denied to them, the security forces cannot carryout counter-insurgency tasks under law.

The choice before the policy makers is not whether to apply the Act to situations of insurgency or terrorism, but whether the Army is to be deployed in a particular state under a serious situation of this nature.

Insurgency is not a law and order situation amenable to be handled by the police. It is an extraordinary situation that needs extraordinary instruments to handle it. The AFSP Act is only one—and in the given Indian situation, possibly the last—such instrument. Let vociferous human rights not play with the nation's security and safety of its citizens. There is no place for populist emotions in a serious situation that insurgency/terrorism poses before the nation. The existing laws cannot deal with extroadinary situations. Indians should examine the laws and measures instituted by the US to combat the menance after one single incident of 9/11. Indians have suffered and experienced hundreds of 9/11's since the very dawn of their Independence—nay, even before that defining event.

In fact, India has come to be seen as a soft state as far as countering/combating terrorism is concerned. If her External Affairs Minister personally chaperoning notorious terrorists (convicted and undergoing prison terms in Indian jails) in an aircraft on 31 December 2000 to be handed over to the Taliban regime to secure the release of Indians abroad an airliners, was an unseemly sight, indicative of the weak-kneed policy of the BJP-led NDA government, the rescinding of the POTA by the Congress-led and Communist-supported UPA government was seen as an act of obeisance at the altar of 'vote bank' politics and an act of naked 'minority appeasement', by some political analysts.

It was ironic that the Congress-led UPA rescinded the POTA, which was meant to fight the terrorist depredations against the innocent, hapless victims, Congress government of Maharashtra has in place MOCOCA, an equally 'harsh' Act meant to fight the hardened criminals. This is ludicrous situation, to put it mildly.

India is possibly—no, certainly—the worst victim of terrorism, and most of it externally (first China, and now Pakistan) inspired and sponsored, and one can't be proud of the fact that it has no clear-cut, declaratory policy on terrorism. That it has become an object of party politics should be a matter of deep concern for all thinking Indians. The only way out is that the two opposite poles of the Indian polity—the Congress and the BJP—must join hands to forge a no-nonsence counter-terrorism policy. This may seem near-impossible today, but it must come about sooner rather than later if India is to come out a winner against this worst threat the world is facing presently.

This is also a plea to the civil society not to ask its security forces to fight the determined terrorists—all primed into willing suicide bombers by the religious fundamentalist and ideologues—with their both hands tied behind their back. They can never save the nation if they are compelled to fight this way.

State can force-feed an activist, says Court : 21 Jan 2007

New Delhi : Giving the State the right to "force-feed" persons accused of attempt to suicide, in case they refuse to take food, the Delhi Court has said that Ram Manohar Lohia hospital authorities here were well within their rights to secure and maintain the health of the 35-year old Irom Chanu

Sharmila, who has been on a hunger strike since 2000 to press for a repeal of the Armed Forces Special Powers Act (AFSPA), which allegedly gives sweeping powers to the Army in Manipur.

Joint Strategy against the AFSPA Planned : 9 December 2006

A conclave of anti-APSPA organisations headed by the Apunba Lup of Manipur which has been spearheading the movement against the Act, vowed to intensity struggle to get rid of the Act that has "brutalised life in the region", since it provides sweeping powers to the security forces deployed in the insurgency-hit states of the region. The All Assam Students Union (AASU) headed the conclave which was organised at Guwahati by the Apunba Lup.

The convention resolved to reject the Prime Minister's promise made recenty in Imphal to amend certain provisions of the Act and declared nothing short of complete repeal of the Act was acceptable.

The AASU advisor and the Chairman of the North-East Students Organisation (NESO), Dr Samujjal Bhattacharrya informed the conclave that an effective strategy would be evolved to facilitate a region-wise movement demanding the annulment of the Act.

"Repeal the AFSP Act," demand the MPs : 12 December 2006

A strong plea for repealing the Armed Forces Special Powers Act was made by NCP member PA Sangma and several others in the Lok Sabha which also appealed to Irom Chanu Sharmila, who has been on a hunger strike for the last six years, to end her fast. Sangma dubbed the Act a "symbol of domination and repression" and demanded its immediate repeal, saying it had failed to curb insurgency and several new groups had mushroomed.

Such a reasoning coming from a seasoned politician like Sangma, who has not only been the first tribal to hold an exalted position of a cabinet minister at the Centre and has handled more than one ministry with aplomb and distinction but has also adorned the chain of Lok Sabha's speaker, is totally unexpected, to put it mildly. Going by his argument, India and other governments in the world should repeal all the anti-smuggling, anti-crime/ homicide, and anti-social laws from the statute books which are there for centuries and have not only failed to prevent these crimes but actually have helped in increasing their frequency and stridence.

Manipur Assembly Polls Feb 2007 : AFSPA Unites all

Two key dilemmas, or more accurately, life and death issues, dominated the skyline during these elections. One is the AFSPA and the other is the question of the State's territorial integrity. It is rather ironical that while the former is a unifying issue across the entire political spectrum, the one on the territorial integrity is perceived to be a dividing factor between clearly defined communities.

The AFSPA was enacted by the Centre 49 years ago as a measure to empower its armed forces to quell the Naga insurrection in the region. There was some opposition to the Act as special powers conferred on the soldiers were seen to have been misused.

In 1997, the Supreme Court of India heard a 1982 PIL (Public Interest Litigation) field by the Naga peoples movement for the Human Rights, and People's Union for Democratic Rights, challenging the constitutional validity of the Act. A 5-judge Bench headed by Chief Justice JS Verma upheld the validity of the Act.

For years, there has been an intense agitation, as detailed above, for the repeal of this Act on the grounds that "it is anti-people, discriminatory and one that violates the very basic fundamentals of the right to life." Under extreme and volatile public pressure, during his 2006 visit to Manipur Prime Minister Manmohan Singh announced the appointment of a committee headed by Justice (Retd) BP Jeeva Reddy to examine the Act and its various 'objectionable' provisions as demanded by the agitationists. The committee has submitted its report but it has not been made public so far.

It must be put on record that Irome Sharmila who is on a fast unto-death for years took her protest to Delhi in 2006. She was arrested and the authorities continued with her force-feeding. Subsequently, she was transferred back to Manipur where she continues to be under medical care as of date (12 April 2007).

Current Scene : 2005 and Onwards

Script Issue Hots up

The 3-month old agitation led by MEELAL (Meitei Erel Eyek Loinasilon Apunba Lup) turned violent, 13-4-05, when its activists set on fire the Manipur Central Library in Imphal, demanding change of script from Bengali to Meitei Mayek. It was seen as a fight for ethnic identity, which was damaged by King Pamheiba when he embraced Vaishnavism under the influence of missionaries from Bengal and issued order to replace the 29-letter Mayek with the Bengali script. The blaze destroyed books worth Rs 10 crore. The outlawed KCP also had called for a 5-day (10-14-4-05) general strike in support of the demand.

The Ibobi Government gave in, and approved (16-5-05) the introduction of the Meitei script in class I and II from the next academic session and subsequently till the university level in the next one decade (*HT,* 13, 14, 16-4-05; *AA,* 17-5-05; and *Exp.,* 17-5-05).

Blockade 2005: Nagas Flex their Muscles

When Ibobi Singh declared 18 June as State Integrity Day and Public Holiday, the idea was to honour 18 martyrs who died in 2001 in an uprising against extension of the Centre's cease-fire with the NSCN(-IM), to Manipur. In a multi-ethnic State where its three major communities (Meiteis, Nagas and Kuki-Chins) are political rivals, what is cheese for one can be chalk for the other. The Integrity Day gesture was seen by the Nagas as a challenge and impediment to their demand/dream of Greater Nagaland. The declaration of annual commemoration day triggered a blockade of Manipur by ANSAM (All Naga Students' Association of Manipur), effective 20 June. "No transport is allowed for the last 6 weeks on NH-39 (Dimapur-Kohima-Imphal) and NH-53 (Silchar-Jiribam-Imphal), the two life lines of Manipur" *(Exp.,* 5-8-05). The Nagas are all backing the NSCN(I-M) idea of Nagalim. The blockade has put paid to the movement of 400 trucks that daily carried the essential supplies (foodstuff, fuel, life-saving medicines, etc.) between Assam and Manipur. With agitators on NH-39 and NH-53 refusing to budge, "Manipur is depending on Myanmar for fuels and edibles" (Sudhir Ranjan Sen, *Exp.,* 18-07-05). Early August, the situation was so critical that the MOD arranged airlift of essential items for Manipur, with the IAF airlifting the first consignment from Guwahati to Imphal on 6 August *(Hindu,* 7-8-05). By the end of July, a litre of petrol was selling at Rs. 81 and a gas cylinder at Rs. 750. Adding to the blockade, Imphal based transport agencies called a strike on 17-7-05 to protest extortion by militants.

The UCM blamed the Centre for not developing NH-53 as an alternate route for Imphal, and appealed to ANSAM to settle the issue through talks. Democratic Students Association of Manipur (DSAM) also made similar appeal. 15 July, the MHA sought the Army's help for clearing a 200 km stretch of NH-53, of the Meitei insurgent groups "which controlled most of it right now". The Army, which had been actively engaged in CI operations for last two months, opened the NH-53 through large-scale deployment of troops, on 18 July. But it had to be closed within 24 hours as the NSCN(I-M) ultras blew up the bridge on Irang some 120 km from Imphal (It was restored by 26 July). Irang, in Tamenglong district, incidentally is symbolic of the mental divide between the Hills and the Valley. The NSCN(I-M) blew it up to add teeth to the Naga imposed economic blockade. This Para alone should suffice to show what a tangled ethnic skein Manipur is, and unravelling it would require a super-human sincerity and perseverence. In fact the things were becoming messier. Ibobi Singh invited ANSAM for talks, and requested his Nagaland counterpart, Neiphiu Rio, 4-8-05, to help end the blockade, but to no avail, even when the former had talked of a civil war in Manipur.

A scuffle with Security personnel at a liquor joint in Senapati district on the 9th, resulting in injury to two protesters, led to the "angry" Naga youth setting ablaze 10 buildings/offices, including that of the District Magistrate, on 10-7-05, in Tamenglong, Ukhrul and Chandel districts. "It .was obviously an attempt to assert their presence and support to the proposed Nagalim of the NSCN(I-M)", wrote *Asian Age,* 11-7-05 (Manoj Anand). 10 July, NSCN(I-M) condemned use of force and bullets against the peaceful Naga peoples" involvement for "their legitimate aspirations of living in an integrated homeland. The Naga Students Union of Delhi took out a peace rally, on 18 July to support these aspirations. The ANSAM asked "all Naga tribal MPs and MLAs of Manipur to resign as the Naga identity and dignity cannot be safeguarded in the prevailing' circumstances in the State" (*Hindu,* 15-7-05). In support of the ANSAM blockade, the Nagaland-based Naga Students' Federation (NSF) had been blocking all Manipur-bound vehicles on NH-39 and NH-53. A stage came, 21-7-05, when all educational institutions in Manipur were closed indefinitely as buses and vans transporting students suspended services for want of fuel supply.

After hectic parleys, the blockade was lifted "for the time being" on 10-8-05.

Cl Operations: 2005

The Army gained a major success on 19-6-05 when the troops, after a long march and a few skirmishes en route, cleared the insurgency affected Henglep Sub-division (Churachandpur) of insurgent groups. A number ol hide-outs were also smashed. Earlier, in another major operation, the NH-53 upto Kaiphundai had been cleared of insurgents.

The Army stepped Lup its drive in June-July to "exterminate" insurgent strongholds in the so-called "liberated zones" along the India-Myanmar border. "Over a dozen militants have been killed in just the last one week" (*TOI*, 23-7-05). Following the success of Joint India-Bhutan operations in December 2003 against outfits like ULFA, NDFB and KLO, the Indian Army has by now achieved "certain level of coordination with the Myanmarese Army in its fight against the militants in the North-East.

On 20-2-05, three NLFT ultras were killed and one injured in an encounter with the BSF men from the Belchera camp. After kidnapping a jeep driver, the insurgents were fleeing towards Bangladesh when they were challenged by the BSF. The encounter re-established the suspicion that the North-East militants, specially the Manipuris are using Tripura as a corridor to maintain links with their hide-outs/bases in the Sylhet district of Bangladesh. The BSF recovered some arms and nearly Rs. 15 lakh Indian currency from them (*Hindu,* 21-2-05).

One of the two KYKL militants was killed in an encounter with the police commandos at Dharamsala area of Imphal West district on 7-5-05 *(AA,* 8-5-05).

Army Clears Manipur's last militant stronghold : Dec. 2006

An hour of sunlight remained as soldiers of 10 JAK L1 combed the dense undergrowth for the IEDs on 19 Dec 2006. They had already discovered and neutralised 44. In the large clearing below, the huts of Kuki village of Khengjoi are dark and silent. This relatively large settlement of Khengjoi had been vacated before the troops arrived.

Earlier in the year (2006), Army's counter-insurgency operation had cleared the Churachandpur district of militant camps. Presently the troops are engaged in similar mission in Samtal area of Chandel district, last stronghold of militants in Manipur.

Not to be left behind in its propaganda war, the UNLF said on 18 Dec 2006 that many villagers from Khengjoi and Dingpi areas were taking shelter with them at Molcham village.[9]

Army spokesman declared "the New and Old Samtal area along the International Border with Myanmar is the last stronghold of militants in Manipur". This area was under Army's focus ever since the earlier clearing of the militants camps in South Manipur.

Heavy Exchange of fire in district Senapati : 12 February 2007

Heavy exchange of fire took place between Assam Rifles soldiers and Kuki militants from the village of North Boljang in Manipur's Senapati district on 12 Feb. 2007.

The troops had surrounded the village the previous day after getting reports that the militants were roaming about in the village. As they started combing operations, the ultras belonging to the Kuki National Front (Military Council) opened fire. Subsequently, they fled into the nearby thick jungles.

Militants Kill 15 Police Commandos : 24 Feb. 2007

In a major strike, separatists ambushed and killed 15 police commandos and wounded four more on 24 Feb 2007. Heavily armed militants attacked a convoy of the India Reserve Battalion (IRB), a specially raised anti-insurgency commando force by the Manipur Government, near village Zoujangtek in Bishenpur district, 45 km south-west of Imphal. The IRB commandos were on a routine patrol when they came under intense firing from atop a hill.

The security forces launched a massive hunt to track down the separatists. No one claimed the responsibility but the area is a stronghold of the PLA, UNLF and KYKL.

This was the biggest such strike in Manipur during the past five years.

"There are some 19 odd rebel groups, active in Manipur area contiguous to the Myanmar international border, with demands ranging from secession to antonomy and the right to self-determination."[10]

During the past decades, more than 10,000 people have lost their lives to insurgency in Manipur, bordering Myanmar.

Manipur Assembly Polls Feb. 2007 : Political divide Intensified

If the polls united the rival parties across the entire political spectrum, the question of the State's territorial integrity split them vertically betweem the Naga and non-Naga communities.

Nagas want the unification of the Naga-majority hill districts in Manipur. Meities, Kukis and others oppose any such move, because they consider this move as a first step to take all the Naga-inhabited areas out of Manipur for final merger with Nagaland to realise their dream of Greater Nagaland. May be, Nagas have a case.

Nagas feel injustice has been done to them by the authorities, both pre-1947 and post-1947, drawing boundaries arbitrarily, ignoring the realities on the ground. They feel organic people-land relationship has and continues to define the dialectical parameters of what constitutes the Naga understanding of their dignified existence. The Naga experience is however riddled with instances where their contiguous land has been fragmented with state boundaries which are not of their making. "The most well-known example is the one of Lungwa village, which is divided into two by the Indo-Myanmar international border."[11] Similarly, Nagas and their lands are also in the states neighbouring the state of Nagaland. This indeed is a long-standing grouse Nagas have nurtured over the decades.

In 1947, NNC Secretary T Sakhrie requested Sri Akbar Hydari that the territories inhabited by the Nagas be united at once. Today, 60 years later, the same question is bedevelling the NSCN(1M) Centre-negotiations, last round held in March 2007.

Undoubtedly, the Nagas have a case. But equally well, there is counter point also. Can the Union of India arbitrarily undo the centuries-old boundaries of some states just to meet Naga aspirations. Then, the Nagas are not the only community or state in India unhappy on this score. Just to cite two examples : The Mizos in the North-East want a Greater Mizoram, and across the breadth of the country, Maharashtra is demanding certain areas from the contiguous State of Karnataka. All concerned must pause and think coolly : where will this conundrum of demands and counter-demands lead India to? Can force be the answer? A democratic way must be found out to craft a common, transparent approach to this vexed issue. An all-party concensus is the only solution.

15 Securitymen Killed : 24 Feb 2007

The terror struck a day after the three-phase assembly poll ended peacefully in Manipur on 23 Feb 2007. 15 security men of India Reserve

Battalion (IRB) were killed and four others injured. A convoy of 70 personnel led by IRB 6 Battalion Commandant Dhiren Singh, returning after completing their election duty at Khoupum in Tamenglong district, was ambushed by the militants near the small village of Ngarijan Laimaton on Old Cachar Road, at 10 AM on 24 February.

The ultras attacked the leading truck with automatic rifles and rocket launchers from a hill top near Khoirok Chiru Lamkhai. Empty cases of M-16 and AK-series of rifles and some bombs were recovered from the site.

Tribal Kuki Leader Killed : March 2007

Suspected Kuki militants of either the Kuki National Army (KNA) or Kuki Revolutionary Army (KRA) gunned down on 9 March 2007 a Kuki tribal leader, Yamthang Haokip, near his house. He was the President, Kuki Impi, the apex Kuki civil organisation, at Siakul in Imphal district. No outfit claimed responsibility subsequently.

In the recent times, Kuki militants have gunned down Kuki tribal leaders in several districts.[12]

PLA Militants Dispense Quick Justice : March 2007

Imphal Valley-based insurgent groups are as much feared as they are admired. When friends like them are around to administer free justice and do social service, few may complain.[13]

The PLA executed a youngman on 13 March 2007 for murdering a 7-year-old boy for gold ear rings he was wearing to buy his "fix". Perhaps justifiably, writes a daily, because the PLA has for years been fighting the drug menace which has plagued Manipuri society. Five years ago an estimate suggested "Manipur has more than 12,800 HIV/AID cases," the most in the country.

Before he was executed, the culprit was produced before the media where he reportedly confessed his crime. Some years ago, the UNLF, the oldest militant group, shot dead the culprit in an identical case, killing a boy for his ear rings. When an infant son of a sub-inspector was kidnapped, not only was the child restored to the parents, the culprit was caught and executed. But what stands out most distinctly and tellingly is the execution of a contractor and the Chief PWD Engineer in 1996 holding them responsible for the collapse of a hockey stadium while under construction at the Khuman Lampak sports complex for the National Games.

In one way, this fast-track justice is a sad reflection of the police's drained credibility. At least one Union official has admitted "that the Manipur Government's writ does not run beyond certain limits." How many times must the police be modernised to function effectively and efficiently?

Incidentally, above details are from an editorial in a daily, titled, "Rebels in charge : Good or bad Manipuris to judge."[14]

Kukis Demonstrate at Delhi to Seek Safety : March 2007

On 23 March 2007, about 800 Kukis, Hmars, Chins, Mizos and some Naga youths demonstrated in New Delhi to vent their anger against the Imphal Valley-based UNLF, Manipur Chief Minister Ibobi Singh and his Government. This was second time within this month they condemned the alleged abduction and "deportation" of 400 Kukis on 13 March 2007 by the UNLF and the Myanmarese Army, and is seen as a revenge for the 5 March demonstration on Delhi by about 300 Kuki students, students there to draw the Centre's attention to their people's plight in Manipur's Churachandpur and Chandel districts.

They were shouting "UNLF, down down!", "UNLF–get out" etc. They wanted an immediate Army operation against the UNLF and demanded that land mines be deactivated, and their victims rehabilitated.[15]

When they were prevented from going to Prime Minister's house to present a memorandum, they burnt an effigy of Ibobi Singh.

4 PREPAK Ultras held from Manipur and Kolkata : April 2007

A joint police-military operation resulted in the arrest of four senior cadres of the people's Revolutionary Party of Kangleipak (PREPAK). These militants were arrested from the Imphal airport and a Kolkata hotel on 7 April 2007.

These arrests are the result of an operation which spanned several months and involved Manipur police, Kolkata CID, a unit of the Manipur-based 57 Military Div and Kolkata-based Military Intelligence unit.

PREPAK Finance Secretary Y Sanjay Singh and political Secretary L. Ibobi Singh were arrested on 7 April outside Imphal airport. Rakesh, SS Capt and 'fighting' Group Commander, and RK Dinesh, Chief of Organisation Committee were picked up from a Kolkata hotel same day.

The duo arrested at Imphal airport had just disembarked from a Kolkata-Imphal Indian Airlines flight. A large amount of foreign currency including US, Chinese, Myanmarese, Thai and Indian, six credit cards and two PCs were seized from the Kolkata flats. Eastern Command CPRO Wing Cdr RK Das briefed the media in Kolkata.

The arrested cadres are members of one of the three factions of the PREPAK headed by former Finance Secretary Shanti. The militants had reportedly decamped with about Rs. 80 lakh of party funds following a three-way split of the PREPAK some years back.

Sources said seven senior cadres, including Shanti, were staying in several flats in Kolkata with their families. They were under surveillance since Sep. 2006 following a tip off.[16]

Two of the arrested militants were arrested from a flat in the Bagha Jatin area, following a raid by the Army and the CID The two had been residing there for six months, posing as Jadavpur University students. Shanti did frequent this house, but presently he is in Bangkok. The PREPAK faction made a base in Kolkata for a safe hideout. This base proved handy for fund-raising and recruitment of college students. Of late, the South Kolkata area surrounding Jadavpur University has been transformed into a safe haven for the militants from the North-East.

NOTES

1. Mackenzie, 1884.
2. One Manipuri author has called Irabot a true "nationalist"—whatever it may mean! But an incident that shows the nationalistic fervour of the Manipuri kings needs a mention here. When the Simon Commission was discussing the separation of Burma from the British India in 1930, the then Maharaja, Churachand, was given the option of joining Burma. He refused the offer, citing close social and cultural ties the Manipuris had with India. His son displayed another trait of the Manipur kings when the British advised him to shift to a safer haven when the Japanese forces had besieged Imphal in 1942 during the World War II. To his credit, Bodh Chandra stayed put, choosing to share the travails and tribulations of his people.
3. *India Today,* 2-7-01. Some major ones are NSCN(I-M), ULFA, DHD, NDFB, PLA, UNLF, PREPAK, NSCN(K), ATTF, HNLC, ANVC and KNA.
4. Singh, K.S. (ed.), *Tribal Movements in India,* Vol. I, 1982, p. 56.
5. Goswami, B.B., *The Mizo Unrest,* 1979, pp. 68-70.
6. Das, R.K., *The Manipur Tribal Scene,* 1985, p. 18.
7. *The Frontline,* 15-12-95.
8. *India Today,* 23-7-01.
9. Kartyk Venkatraman, *Indian Express,* 20 Dec. 2006.
10. Syed Zarir Hussain (Guwahati), *The Pioneer,* 25 February 2007.
11. Akum Longchari, *The Tehelka,* 24 February 2007.
12. Iboyaima Laithangham, *The Hindu,* 11 March 2007.
13. These are the opening lines from a togue-in-cheek editorial in *The Statesman,* 17 March 2007.
14. *Ibid.*
15. Anil Bhatt, *The Statesman,* 2 April 2007.
16. Kartyk Venkatraman and Ravik Bhattacharya, *Indian Express,* 10 April 2007.

TERRORISM IN INDIA'S NORTH-EAST A GATHERING STORM

TERRORISM IN INDIA'S NORTH-EAST
A Gathering Storm
(In 3 Volumes)

(Volume - III)

Col. Ved Prakash

KALPAZ PUBLICATIONS
DELHI-110052

Terrorism in India's North-East
A Gathering Storm

Rs. 2500 (Set)

ISBN: 81-7835-660-0 (Set)
ISBN: 9788178356631

Published in 2016 in India by
Kalpaz Publications
C-30, Satyawati Nagar,
Delhi-110052
E-mail: kalpaz@hotmail.com
Phone : 9811692060

Laser Type Setting by: Quick Media, Delhi
Printed at : Singhal Print Media, Delhi

DEDICATED TO

My grandson, Aryan Sharma,
with
a fervent plea to the present generation to
render his generation the world over
safe from the scourge of terrorism

Contents

12

Racial Tensions in Meghalaya Consequence : A Demand for Garoland

Essential Information : Meghalaya

Date of Formation	21 Jan 1972
State within Assam	2 April 1970
Area	22,429 sq km
Population	23,18,822
Capital	Shillong
Chief Language	Khasi
	Garo
	English
	Bengali
	Assamese
Major Religions	Christianty
	Hinduism

Political Evolution and Early Disenchantment

After a long, sustained struggle, the Khasis, Jaintias and Garos achieved a 'State within Assam' on 2 April 1970 and subsequently graduated to full-fledged statehood on 21 January 1972. The state had hardly completed three decades of statehood when the Garos started demanding a separate Garoland, with obvious implications for the integrity of the State.

Here is the 1973 breakdown of the tribal population of Meghalaya :

Tribe	*Population*	*Pecentage*
Khasi	3,84,006	38
Jaintia	82,493	8
Garo	4,11,532	41
Hajong	23,938	2.39

A Historical Perspective

Wedged between Bangladesh and the residual Assam, the Meghalaya people had very little contact with the rest of the country till the 19th century when the area was annexed piece-meal with British India: Khasi States in 1829-33; adjoining Jaintia Raj in 1834; and Garo Hills, created a district in 1856 and made a part of the then Assam. The wave of Aryan migration and Muslim invasions did not have much impact in this area. The contacts with the plains people during the pre-British period were essentially for the purposes of petty trade, which they, mainly the Khasis, carried out with the adjoining area of Sylhet. The exports from the Khasi Hills on the eve of British take-over consisted of limestone (17,00,000 maunds), Coal (45,000 maunds), smelted iron (45,000 maunds)[1], besides oranges, betel-nuts, leaves, etc.[2] If Meghalaya is home to the rainiest place on earth, it has to be flush with nature's bounty in the shape of flora and fauna. It boasts of nearly 700 rare species of medicinal herbs and 300 orchids. And to know that of the 17,000 species of orchild the world is home to, India has over 1,200 of them; and one fourth of the latter figure are claimed by the geographically small State of Meghalaya. Again of over 1,400 butterfly species found in India, more than 500 are indigenous to Meghalaya, some with impressive names like Quaiser-e-Hind and Rajah.

Khasis and Jaintias are essentially the same people, and the Garos have little in common with them.

It is predominantly inhabited by the Garo, Khasi and Jaintia + tribal communities, in that order. Two main diasporas of Meghalaya are mentioned below:

1. *Garo Diaspora:* Two lakh of them inhabit Assam and a little less than one lakh are in Bangladesh, earlier East Pakistan.
2. *War Jaintia Diaspora.* The *War* Jaintias of Dawki border had moved into various districts of Meghalaya and even outside the State to Manipur, Mikir Hills, Cachar, Mizoram and East Pakistan. Sale of betel leaves in Bangladesh cultivated by these Meghalayans (*war* Jaintias and Myllat of East Khasi Hills) had boosted the economy of Bangladesh to such an extent that the "government there virtually gives them a free hand". Their number is placed between 10-20,000. It was about then that a study on Displaced people says: "There are tens of thousands" (an obviously exaggerated number) of Meghalayans (Khasi people of *war* Jaintia) who has already made part of Sylhet district of the present Bangladesh as their habitat even before Independence. They have their own villages, run by their own administration, away from the interference of Dhaka. They vote in election of both Bangladesh and India. What do we call them, then? Illegal aliens of Bangladesh, or Internally Displaced People (IDP) of

the Meghalaya? Their number in the North-East, beyond the confines of Meghalaya, is about 10,000, scattered in areas where *pan* leaf and betel-nuts can be cultivated.

Racial Tensions and Ethnic Militancy

Meghalaya may have been a 'peaceful' state on the surface but there are, of late, rumblings of racial tensions and incipient insurgency just below it. The atmosphere is vitiated not only by tribal-non-tribal tensions and Garo-Khasi distrust, but also by some nascent militant (and insurgent?) outfits encouraged and nurtured by outside insurgency movements like ULFA and NSCN.

The year 1977 saw the inception of inter-communal troubles in Meghalaya in the shape of violence against the outsiders. After the initial eruptions, the state was generally able to bring the situation under control, not letting it to assume serious dimensions. But the situation proved more volatile in the subsequent years. But there was major rioting in 1979 between tribals and *dkhars* (outsiders). But luckily, there were no fatalities.

But in 1992, at the end of the rioting, 31 lay dead in Shillong—30 of them outsiders and one tribal who fell to police bullets. Shillong, with a population of over 350,000, in East Khasi Hills district, has 60 per cent tribals, majority being Khasis. There are some Garos and Jaintias but they are not nearly as vocal as a certain section of Khasis, "who would like their community to dominate affairs in every sphere". Among the 40 per cent non-tribals are Central Government employees on temporary posting and settlers from outside the state, of which two largest groups speak Bengali and Nepali—the rest being Assamese, Biharis, Punjabis, and Marwaris in substantial numbers. The trouble started in August when activists of two militant "son of the soil" organisations—Khasi Students' Union (KSU) and Federation of Khasi, Jaintia and Garo People (FKJGP) —forced non-tribal traders to close down on the pretext that they did not possess valid "trading licences" issued by Khasi Hills District Council (DC). It did not subside even if they knew that these traders had applied since long for these licences and the DC had been sitting over them. Just as the Government's effort to restore peace seemed to be succeeding, violence became widespread in October 1992 when the FKJGP announced a road blockade on the day of Durga Puja, sacred and special to the settlers, and young men from the latter took to the streets in defiance. What followed was rioting, fifth since 1979. The toll was heavy, for obvious reasons, for the outsiders as mentioned above.

A year and a half after this rioting, tension again gripped Shillong in April 1994. This time the issue was more serious: the right of the "outsiders" (people from other states) to live and vote freely in Meghalaya. In March 1994, Chief Electoral Officer announced that state's 10,47,000 voters would be issued photo identity cards by 18 June as directed by CEC T.N. Seshan. But the KSU announced it would allow this only after the names of "foreigners" had been deleted from the electoral rolls with 1951 as the cut off year with respect to the migrants from Bangladesh. But KSU President Paul Lyngdoh clarified[3] that the "foreigners" also meant the Indians who had settled after 1951 (it may be noted that in Assam, 1971 has been accepted as the cut off year in view of the influx from Bangladesh). The process of photographing voters in the state's 60 constituencies, scheduled to get under way on 2 April, was nearly a non-starter in East Khasi Hills, especially Shillong, with the KSU bringing life to a standstill on the identity card issue through *bandhs*, picketing, people's curfew, and drum-beating (throughout Shillong) on 25, 26, 27 April and 13 May. All this created an atmosphere of panic in the non-tribal community. Incidents of assault had added to the fear psychosis. There were riots when some youngsters from "outsiders" decided to hit back. The most serious so far—which would have resulted in bloodshed but for the downpour which sent the men scurrying indoors—was on 19 May at Loban after the tribal *dorbar* pronounced excommunication on a non-tribal karate exponent with a reputation for toughness. The people felt the *dorbar* had no jurisdiction on a non-tribal, and the offence, if any, should have been handled by the police. The rains saved the situation, though the authorities had sought 10 companies of Central Paramilitary forces.

The *dorbar's* action was clearly a provocation at a time when the area was already in the grip of tension over the issue of electoral rolls. They did not seem to be shy of lighting the fires. The FKJGP raked up the issue of trade licences, which had proved explosive in 1992, on 18 May 1994, the day before the Loban incident, when its activists forced the closure of a number of shops belonging to non-tribals in Lower Mawprem area of Shillong. KSU's Lyngdoh. denied its involvement even though he defended the action. But in the past, such as in 1992, the KSU and FKJGP were reported to have worked together on such missions.

Some observers believe the KSU and FKJGP are not overly keen to avoid violence. The KSU had scrawled "we prefer violence to cowardice" on Shillong's walls in 1994. Neither were all the outsiders ready to take it lying down. They had their grievances. The Loban area of Shillong had almost exclusively been Bengali-inhabited till 1994 but was no more so. An educated settler laments (1994): "Since 1979 about one fourth of Shillong has been 'cleansed' of non-tribals. Only 15 percent of State Government jobs are open to us, and even here, we are tricked out of these.... Government contracts, too, are almost entirely out of our reach. 50 of the 60 Assembly seats are reserved for the tribes. There are now only two non-tribal MLAs, though our population would call for about a dozen.... For the first time this year, many of us found our names struck off the rolls for the District Council election.

Now they want to disenfranchise us even in the Assembly and to throw us out lock, stock and barrel."

The KSU-FKJGP 'intransigence' and non-tribal frustration is a highly inflammable mixture in itself. The proclivity of certain politicians to use these organisations to better their career interests further vitiates the climate. S.C. Marak, Chief Minister in 1994, had stated this openly, without identifying the individuals. Did he mean P.P. Lapang, the then PCC (1) President, who was Chief Minister during October 1992 riots and lost. Did he want Lapang discredited? He was believed to have taken a 'softer line' towards the rioters? B.B. Lyngdoh of the Hill Peoples Union, too would have liked to see Marak in trouble "because his bid to pull down the Government a few months ago had ended in failure".[4] Lik Mawlong, General Secretary of Meghalaya Federation of Regional Parties (MFRP), who fought the Congress in the 1993 Assembly Poll, was openly supportive to the KSU. He told a Fortnightly, "The KSU is a catalytic agent for furthering the cause of the people.[5]

Politics is the Villain of the Piece

In a manner of speaking, it was a *de ja vu* for the observers on the scene. During the 1992 riots, it was an open secret in Shillong that certain people close to the Congress (l)'s P.R. Kyndiah, then Speaker of the Assembly (and later Governor of Mizoram, 1994-95) had stirred up trouble. Kyndiah had his reasons for being sore with Lapang, the then Chief Minister. The former felt tricked out of the Chief Ministership to which he thought he was entitled because of the crucial role he had played as speaker pulling down B.B. Lyngdoh's Government.

The populist attitude of all such self-serving political parties seemed to help the KSU-FKJGP combine. But still, the going was not easy in 1994. Taking a tough line, Marak not only rejected the KSU demand for fixing 1951 as cut-off year, he even refused to discuss the issue with its leaders, advising them to meet the members of a Cabinet Sub-Committee set up for the purpose. The then Finance Minister, John Deng Pohrmen, was equally harsh: "They are immature youngsters who do not know the difference between a 'foreigner' and an 'outsider'. They only want to imitate AASU."

The change in job reservation policy was another issue the KSU was not having its way with, in early 1990s. Since the creation of Meghalaya in 1972, the Khasi and Jaintia communities have together enjoyed a reservation of 40 per cent, the Garos also 40 per cent, other tribes and OBCs 5 per cent, and the remaining 15 per cent are unreserved. The KSU wants this replaced by a combined 90 per cent reservation for Khasis (and Jaintias) and Garos together. The Garos saw through this demand—a ploy by the more educated and also more assertive Khasis to corner the larger share of jobs. This greatly angered them and the fall-out seemed to be the demand for a separate Garo

State espoused by an outfit called Garo National Council (GNC), which had been a part of a faction of the Hill People's Union (HPU) until 1993. There was litigation, too, by the Garos against the Meghalaya Public Service Commission for favouring the Khasi and Jaintia tribes in matters of employment. The Jaintias too felt aggrieved, on similar grounds: some feeling that the Khasis were cornering too many jobs. They feared their identity might be lost in the dominant Khasi milieu.

Garos Resent Khasi Domination

It was obvious that the earlier tribal-non-tribal divide was now narrowing down to an intra tribal divide, al be it on different issues. The Khasi domination was being resented by the other two ethnic groups of the State, Jaintia and Garo, all because of too aggressive (some thought, even clever) attitude of the KSU. Worse for the KSU was division within the Khasi society on the issue of electoral rolls. The Synjuk Ki Rangbah Shnong an association of Headmen, expressed support for making 1971 the cut-off year. It was a blow from an unexpected quarter. The headmen enjoy great prestige in Khasi society. Obviously, they resented the KSU's diktats as an attempt to usurp their traditional authority.

If KSU's such moves created divisions within the tribal groups, and even within the Khasi tribe, its demand for 90 per cent reservation of seats in the high schools and colleges of Shillong—the academic capital of the entire North-East—for Khasis, angered tribal students' unions from other states of the Region. Sensing this anger, the KSU agreed (1994) to settle for a first-preference system instead (This incidentally, was more than enough for Khasi students, since their number was for smaller than that of seats available in Shillong).

It was perhaps this isolation within Meghalaya, and beyond, which explained its lurch towards the militancy during the period, mid-1990s. One KSU slogan on a wall next to the State Assembly, then read: "Long live Khasi militants." The militants they had in mind belonged to HALC. The outfit is known to have received training and arms from NSCN(I-M). The official sources believe the HALC's aims are not secessionist, that it works for "rooting out evils from Khasi society and building up the Khasi nation"—whatever it might mean. It was obvious to the analysts that given KSU's veneration for the HALC the outfit was bound to play a major role in any future confrontation between the tribals and non-tribals. Even more interestingly, as we would see a little later, HALC was to play a role for the Khasis (in the 1998 Assembly Poll), within the tribal society—against the Garos and Jaintias—just as the NSCN(I-M) was accused of aiding Naga "village guards" in their war on Kukis in Manipur, Nagaland and Assam. The KSU had started warning the centre from 1994 against "treating Meghalaya as its colony".

Khasi Liberation Army Surfaces

Another little known outfit came to light in 1994 when action was initiated against a Khasi language paper, *Mawphor,* for publishing a lengthy 'hit list' of corrupt politicians, officials and businessmen drawn up by till then unknown 'extremist outfit', called the Khasi Liberation Army.

Political instability also seems to be generating social tensions and ethnic hiatus. February 1998 Assembly poll should be as good an indicator as any—without going into too many details, or more accurately, plots and sub-plots. S.C. Marak's Congress got 25 seats in 60-member Assembly; B.B. Lyngdoh's United Democratic Party (UDP) 20 seats; BJP, 3; Hill State People's Democratic Party (HSDP), which fought elections on the plank of working for the creation of a separate Khasi State, 3; People's Democratic Movement (PDM), 3; and Independents, 6. Marak was sworn in Chief Minister (he had held the post from 1993 to 1998 also) on 28 February, but resigned on 10 March when his candidate for speakership lost by a single vote. UDP's Lyngdoh formed the Ministry with the help of the regional parties on 12 March, as leader of the United Parliamentary Forum.

Political analysts were perturbed over the blatant divide among the parties along tribal lines. The Congress is seen as a party of Garos—Marak is a Garo; so was P.A. Sangma earlier—whereas the regional parties hold sway in the Khasi and Jaintia Hills. In fact, Congress got wiped out in Jaintia Hills in this election. During the 26 years since 1972 birth of Meghalaya, it has been ruled by a Garo Chief Minister for 20 years. The Khasi's Lyngdoh belongs to this tribe—who regard themselves as more advanced than the Garos, who resent this. The Khasi-Garo ethnic divide has come into play in a big way this time, and this does not augur well for the state, already wracked by tribal-non-tribal tensions during the last decade. The new cleavage between Meghalaya's two major ethnic groups could only aggravate the situation, the analyst feared.

Given the political culture of Meghalaya, the Lyngdoh Ministry too faced rough weather after about five months. On 27 July 1998, he resigned in the morning, and was sworn-in again as the head of the JUDP and Congress Ministry—the two sworn enemies conjugating to form the Meghalaya Parliamentary Forum (MPF), which had a combined strength of 49. D.D. Lapang of Congress was Deputy Chief Minister. The top job was to be split; Lyngdoh was to hold office till 16 November 2000, and then hand it over to Lapang.

As for the longevity of the Ministry, it should be noted that although Meghalaya had five assemblies from 1972 to 1998, there were 12 Governments. Party loyalties were obviously not long lasting, it seemed. Ethnic factors complicated things even further. As will be seen, the ministers were accused of colluding with the insurgents. The shape of things to come could be seen in the February poll itself. The Congress had formed a government in 1993 under Marak that lasted five years (till 1998), with just 24 MLAs, one less than its tally in 1998. But in 1998, it could not succeed in alluring even independents who had been ministers in the 1993-98 Ministry. This was largely because of the emergence of a "Third force" in Meghalaya politics. Hynniewtrep National Liberation Council (HNLC), a small Khasi insurgent group operating in the state. It also harped on the fact that Khasis (including Jaintias) though majority in the state had their Chief Minister for less than five years since 1972, primarily because they lacked unity. So the HNLC had warned wayward elements in the UPF of dire consequences should they cross over to the Congress. The threat had worked—at least for that time.[6]

Racial violence, on the upswing on the heels of Lyngdoh forming a coalition early August 1998 with the Congress led by Lapang had claimed 15 lives till the 23rd, all non-tribals. They were victims of over-zealous 'vigilante' groups formed, ironically, to curb violence. It was to check the thefts and burglaries that the Dorbar Shnongs decided to set up locality-wise vigilante groups for night patrol. The groups started checking the credentials of residents returning home at night or loitering about. But these groups primarily formed of Khasi youth reportedly began to target non-tribals with whom they had decade-long rivalry over land, trade and employment. Lyngdoh Government was unable—perhaps unwilling—to control the vigilante groups, resulting in the killing of so many non-tribals. In contrast, Marak (1993-98) had been able to control the racial violence Meghalaya had witnessed for 15 years before he took over.

Are the Foreigners usurping Jobs?

But it must be conceded that communal violence in one form or another is endemic to the North-East, resentful of the "Indians", Bangladeshis, Nepalis and Tibetans residing in the region "and usurping the jobs rightfully belonging to the local tribals". All insurgent groups in the Region have made a major issue about "infiltration" not only from Bangladesh but also from other parts of India.[7]

The job opportunities are limited and local outfits like the KSU fan the flames in a difficult situation. Even Chief Minister like Marak (1993-98), who had a credible record of maintaining peace and order, had the need to appease the KSU. It was for this reason that he reportedly wrote to Union Home Minister S.B. Chavan in 1995, requesting him to find ways and means to check the uncontrolled entry of Nepali immigrants to the state—reasoning that the Bangladeshis could be detected since they have to carry passports and visas, unlike the Nepalis who under the 1950 Indo-Nepal Treaty are free to enter India without any such documents. But Marak himself was not clear as to how the Centre could do it in view of this treaty. By singling out the Nepalis, Marak had verily made them the target of wanton attack by both the student and insurgent organisations whose manifest aim, analysts believe, "is to expiate the ills afflicting the tribal societies by exterminating non-tribal businessmen or non-tribals *per se*". The KSU has been consistently demanding detection of all 'foreigners', be they of Bangladeshi or Nepal origin, and even outsiders, like the Bengalis, Biharis, Punjabis, and sweepers—the last having been brought here by the British. Ignoring the fundamental right enshrined in the Constitution, Marak even endorsed the totalitarian view of introducing a work permit system in the state in lieu of the equally obnoxious inner line permit (ILP) regulation, which is applicable in Arunachal, Mizoram and Nagaland but not in Meghalaya.

Marak's claim that the influx of Nepalis had increased after lifting of the Restricted Areas Permit (RAP) System by the Centre smacks of Centre-baiting. So he too joined other Chief Ministers of the predominantly tribal states, making influx of the 'foreigners' a potent issue to lash the Centre with. Ironically, the Chief Ministers including Marak, had held the view earlier that lifting of the RAP would facilitate development of tourism in these areas and the foreigner influx would not pose a serious threat.

But Marak is unable to prove how the lifting of RAP would increase the influx of Nepalis when they do not need visas to enter India in the first place. But worse, Marak had sought to club Indian citizens also with 'Nepali foreigners', on the issue of work permit.

In 1996, Khasi society seemed to have particularly been convulsed by xenophobia. An analyst wrote: "Khasis were determined to keep out the Bangladeshi migrants flooding the state. At the street level, this degenerated into attacks on even those Bengalis living there for generations and the KSU assumed inquisitorial powers: It banned mixed marriages for Khasi women. Durga Puja leads to communal tensions and the non-Khasi traders have to pay protection money to militants. Murder was not unknown when they can't meet exorbitant demands." The consequences are there for all to see: This led to a capital flight, forced migration, and was destroying the multi-cultural, -lingual, -religious state, so far living in harmony with its diversity. "There is even a talk of work permits for other Indians."

Was It Start of the Militancy?

Now for the militancy/insurgency situation in Meghalaya. The formation of the Meghalaya United Movement (MUM) in 1989 was indicative of a rudimentary militancy in Meghalaya. Its main objective was all-round development of the Khasi society, and subsequently, in due course, secession from India when the idea became acceptable to the society at large. The MUM had secured some small arms and an understanding with ULFA for facilitating the passage of their volunteers to and from Bangladesh. The outfit did not make much headway, as very few volunteers joined its ranks.

In 1991, A'chik Liberation Matgrik Army (ALMA) came into being with the main objective of creation of a separate Garoland comprising of Garo inhabited areas of Meghalaya, Assam and Bangladesh. It also wanted eradication of corruption and expulsion of foreign nationals. Its strength was estimated over 50. Its arms included AK-47, carbines, M-20 pistols, country-made revolvers, grenades and detonators. The outfit had working relations with the ULFA and NSCN. Its 3-year existence ended with its surrender on 25 October 1994.

There was in existence for a short while in early 1990s an outfit with a grand name ot Meghalaya United Liberation Army (MULA).

In 1992, another insurgent group came into existence; namely, Hynniewtrep Voluntary Council (HVC). Its main objective was eradication of social evils afflicting the Khasi society, especially the youth. It also struck an understanding with the ULFA for passage to and from Bangladesh in the manner of the MUM. The HVC had carbines, revolvers, crude guns and .22 rifles. The Press reported that the SFs recovered/captured all its weapons, except some revolvers. The estimated strength of the Council's cadre was between 15 and 20.

The year 1992 also saw the birth of the Hynniewtrep A'chik Council (HALC) to foster secessionism among the youth. It framed a 21-point charter of demands. The HALC advocates an armed revolution for full separation from India. Its cadres possess carbines, revolvers, country-made weapons, and a few rifles. Barring the rifles, all other arms have been seized by the SFs. The HALC has working arrangements with the NSCN. The pamphlets issued by the HALC on the fifth death anniversary of Wickliffe, ex-Deputy Syiem of Nongstoin (21 October 1993) speak of secession from India. The theme was re-iterated through two booklets published on his sixth anniversary (21 October 1994). Yet again, its press release of 23-1-1995 called for non-cooperation on every Republic Day on 3-3-1995, through another press release, the HALC demanded "traditional governance for the people".

It is to be noted that the reports of the Intelligence Agencies have mentioned that secessionist outfits like the NSCN and ULFA, specially the former, help raise some minor groups for furthering their own ends. The latter get willingly used, without ever coming to know the real intention of the former, and the reasons for help extended to them. Outfits like HVC, HALC, etc., might belong to this category.

The above is the situation on the militancy front till mid-1990s. Towards the second half of the decade, two outfits—HNLC and ANVC—claimed the militancy stakes. It bears repetition that militant Naga leaders have been using

Shillong as a sanctuary since the 1950s. NSCN(I-M) have been playing big brother in the North-East, including Meghalaya. SS 2 Lt Mumba Mao of NSCN(I-M), who had been functioning as the area commander of Shillong was arrested in September 2000 from Jingkieng area of the City.[8] NSCN(I-M) was instrumental in the formation of HALC in 1992. The outfit was rechristened subsequently as HNLC when the Garo youth in its ranks launched a separate movement, viz A'chik National Volunteers' Council (ANVC).

Towards the end of the 1990s, when the action squads of the HNLC suddenly stepped up their operations, Meghalava once again found itself in the grip of violence. The Intelligence reports that HNLC is an umbrella organisation of various smaller groups that are active in Assam and Nagaland. Fighting for Khasiland, it relies on these small groups to raise funds through extortion and to acquire arms and ammunition. The *modus operandi* of the HNLC became known after the arrest of 5 members of the North-East Red Army (NERA), including its SS C-in-C Ching Thang Khiew, in Shillong on 27 August 2000. Founded in the latter half of 1999 and with its operational base at Nongpoh in Ri Bhoi district of Meghalaya, the NERA has close links with HNLC and helps it in collecting money. It was involved in several cases of extortion, abduction and looting. NERA's members were reportedly behind the then recent kidnapping of the Shillong-based businessman, Rajesh Sethia.[9]

Intelligence sources said that the HNLC must have learnt the art of the playing big brother from the NSCN(I-M), to which it pays tribute. In turn, the banned NSCN(I-M) has extended consultancy services to the HNLC for nearly a decade, that is almost since its birth. It also helped the Khasi youth to 'fine tune' their skills in guerrilla warfare. Interrogation also revealed that the HNLC modelled its operational structure on that of the NSCN(I-M). It operates through three commands: Eastern, covering Jaintia Hills district; Central, Shillong, and surrounding areas; and Western, West Khasi Hills district. NSCN(I-M), HNLC and ANVC had given a boycott call for Independence Day celebrations. The latter two had also given separate calls for a 36-hour *bandh* on 14 August 2000 to frustrate Government plans for these celebrations. They had their reasons for the boycott call: ANVC, with its stronghold in the Garo Hills, said that the Garos continued to be deprived of their rights, both political and economic "for 53 years since Independence" and the HNLC's protest was against the colonial rule of New Delhi. On the night of 15 August, gun battles raged in Shillong between SF and HNLC militants, leaving a CRPF Havildar dead. The ultras of HNLC helped by the NSCN(I-M), carried out simultaneous attacks on police patrols between 9 PM and 1 AM at 11 places.

Both these outfits demand separate ethnic state of their own— Khasiland and Garoland. Besides these two, press reported the existence of another outfit in the state, *viz* People's Liberation Front of Meghalaya (PLFM).[10] Three other minor outfits are known to exist: (1) Hynniewtrep Liberation Army (HLA). (2) All Meghalaya Tribal Force (AMTF). (3) Khasi Liberation Army. But not much is known about them—but for their nomenclatures.

ULFA and NDFB Export Terrorism to Meghalaya

The militant outfits obtaining external help is always a matter of concern to the authorities. The ISI activities in the North-East, and its help to the militants is no secret any longer. F.A. Khonglam, Meghalaya Chief Minister, discussed the issue with the Union Home Minister at New Delhi in July 2002 and sought additional CRPF units for counter-insurgency purposes. ISI is already actively helping the Indian insurgents ensconed in the camps in Bangladesh; they mostly are from ULFA, NSCN and NDFB. Early 1991, Indian insurgents, particularly of ULFA and NDFB, coming under Army pressure in Assam, started shifting base to jungles in South Bhutan. By 1995, there were 30 camps in the area. From 2000 onwards, they were under pressure to leave Bhutan and therefore early 2002 they started eyeing the Garo Hills of western Meghalaya to build their camps. ULFA joined hands with ANVC which already had several hide-outs in the East Garo Hills district, adjoining Assam's Goalpara district. ULFA militants had started trickling out of Bhutan to Garo Hills through Barpeta district of Lower Assam, avoiding attention of the Indian Army in the area. It seems the Garo Hills will be a temporary shelter before the ULFA settles in Bangladesh to their south.

The ULFA cadres are believed to be taking the riverine route on the Brahmaputra to sneak into Bangladesh in small numbers. In mid-January 2002, 6 ULFA cadres were killed by SF at Angami, Golokganj PS, Dhubri district and inside Raimona RF in Kokrajhar district—both bordering Bangladesh. The 243 km Meghalaya-Bangladesh border continues to remain mostly porous, as only 120 km of this border is fenced, and it is a source of concern to Meghalaya, because of ULFA ultras using it as a transit to cross over to Bangladesh. Chief Minister Lapang urged the Centre in December 2003 "to introduce identity cards as well as work permits to check the influx of Bangladeshi migration which is threatening to change the demography of the State."[11]

The Deputy Commissioner of West Garo Hills district promulgated prohibitory orders within one km stretch of the international border to thwart the movement of the armed militants. The BSF had submitted a list of 79 militant camps in Bangladesh to the Bangladesh Rifles (BDR) officers during a meeting at Shillong on 22 October 2003. The BSF at Bangladesh border has been having unfortunate (almost humiliating) experience at the hands of Bangladesh Rifles (BDR). Its men were caught off guard when the Bangladesh Rifles (BDR)-backed infiltrators occupied the small village of Pyrdiwah in the East Khasi Hills district on 16 April 2001. The BSF again suffered extreme humiliation when BDR personnel butchered as many as 16 of its men at Boraibari, mere two days later on the 18th.[12]

The state has witnessed periodic cases of extremist violence. The ANVC cadres abducted a doctor in December 2001. Khonglam-led NCP coalition government, taking a tough stand, refused to either negotiate with the ANVC, or to pay it a Rs. 20 lakh ransom. To mount pressure on the government, Meghalaya Medical Service Association held a 3-day strike in January 2002. But citing the 'safe rescue' of an abducted doctor from Jaintia Hills recently, the DGP was hopeful of a repeat in this case also. In early 2003, six persons were shot dead by suspected Karbi National Volunteers at Mukhroh village in Jaintia Hills district. Police ascribed the ghastly depradation to the extortion bid by the ultras.

Meghalaya may not be on the boil, but it certainly is not a 'peaceful' state either. An official put it this way: "Meghalaya has been afflicted by extremist violence, but it is no longer a major threat." But the Government should not underestimate the threat they still can face. The internal dissonance—tribal versus non-tribal, and ethnic conflict between the Khasi and Garo tribes, fuelled by their respective militants outfits—can be aggravated by the external factors. It should be remembered that the militants from all the four disturbed states—Assam, Manipur, Nagaland and Tripura—use the State, particularly its capital, Shillong, for rest and recreation and occasionally for mutual consultations and coordination of their anti-national activities. And as stated above, outfits like the NSCN(I-M) and ULFA have successfully fished in the troubled waters helping raising the small local outfits and using them to further their own ends. The State must remain ever alert and watch out these baneful external influences, besides striving for ethnic and racial peace and harmony within.

Politics indeed is interesting, at the very least. A former Minister in Khonglam Ministry was arrested on 27 June 2003 for his alleged links with the proscribed ANVC. He was charged under the Unlawful Activities Act for allegedly allowing his official vehicle to be used for carrying the militants. Police grilled two ANVC members to confirm if Marak had links with their outfit. A police officer said: "We have a dossier on him which gives his criminal background. He has been involved in criminal activities right from his childhood..., has committed robberies even before he became a legislator (PTI, 28-6-2003). A new twist was given to the case, involving the politician-militant nexus, when Marak released a letter reportedly written by Mizoram Chief Minister Zoramthanga, who is himself playing an important mediatory role in New Delhi-NSCN(I-M) talks presently underway, to say that Marak was detailed for a 'peace mission' (*Hindustan Times,* 30-6-03).

HNLC, banned by India, is also carrying anti-India cyber war of its own. *Indian Express,* 4 October 2003 reported that "an obscure Internet newsgroup of 171 members that has seen 33 posted messages in the last year has threatened the free flow of information across India's information superhighway, pitting the Indian Government against Yahoo, one of the world's most popular search engines. Last week, India decided to ban the newsgroup of the separatist HNLC, called Kynhun Lu Bri "Hanniewtrip (groups.yahoo.com/group/kynhun 1), because it carried reports India considers anti-national". When India asked US-based Yahoo to block the newsgroup, the company declined, saying it was not possible as the act (of blocking) may be illegal under US laws.

A border dispute with Assam has bedeviled Meghalaya's relations ever since its creation in 1972. For a long time, Meghalaya has been laying claim on large chunks of Assam territory. The Chief Ministers of the two States have been meeting periodically to solve the dispute, but without any result till date. Tarun Gogoi and F.A. Khonglam met on 18 June 2002, but concluded the discussions by deciding to maintain the *status quo* on the border. Khonglam said there were 12 disputed villages in different areas of the border between the two states. Gogoi told the press that they had agreed not to set up any police post in these areas on either side but keeping in mind the insurgency scenario, police of both the states should maintain closer liaison and coordination. Another meeting between the two Chief Ministers, this time Gogoi and Lapang, in May 2003 could also not go beyond agreeing to maintain the *status quo,* failing to fix a deadline to end the row once and for all.

Occasionally, the issue has become a football between the politicians. Meghalaya Power Minister Martle Mukhim resigned on 31 October 2001, blaming Chief Minister Mawlong of not keeping his promise of solving the border issue within six months of taking over as Chief Minister, "whereas he has been in power for a year and a half".[13]

Gender War

Now for revisiting the realities of matrilineal Khasi society. An acute observer of the scene says the electoral politics in Meghalaya has distorted the relations between the sexes. Ethnographers and feminists alike celebrate the matrilineal society of the Khasis. However, the greater visibility and mobilizing power required by modern politics has meant that the leading Khasi *netas,* are all men.[14]

Modernity seemed to have finally caught up with Meghalaya's Khasi tribals. With many educated girls marrying outsiders or non-tribals, the KSU demanded a law to check these dangerous-liaisons and introduction of an ILP to restrict entry of outsiders even as women activists decided to oppose any change tooth and nail. At the root of the problem is the Khasi tradition of the youngest daughter inheriting the property of her parents. A Khasi student leader fulminates: "The prospect of acquiring property and wealth on marriage to a Khasi girl is very tempting. That is why these outsiders are always trying to hoodwink our girls." The KSU President Paul Lyngdoh, more forthrightly, calls them 'marriages of conveniences', and adds: "As per law, an outsider cannot buy land or get business licence here. So he marries a Khasi girl to get round these hurdles. They then use our girls as a cover to do business here. Many of them sell off our girls' property and vanish. Who will take care of these deserted women and their children? Go to Jaintia Hills and see the plight of these women abandoned by Biharis, Bangladeshis and Nepalis!" In 1995, KSU passed a resolution seeking forteiture of a woman's right to her parents' property on her marriage to an outsider. Though the KSU has been pressurizing the Government to change the law, but no political party wants to alienate the women. CM Marak says tampering with personal laws will spell trouble "and more over how can we stop any one marrying some one of her choice?" (*Times of India,* 15-12-96). "But our fight will continue", says Paul Lyngdoh.

An organisation like Syngkhong Rympei Thymmi, SRT (=Association for Reformation of the Family Structure) has been demanding the present system be changed to patrilineal, since its inception in 1994. The KSU only joined the bandwagon subsequently. It was the logic of misuse of the custom which had brought SRT to the battle between genders. The present system believes in *'long jaid na ka kynthci* (It is the woman from whom family springs). This belief has destroyed the social fabric of our tribal community, says the leader of the SRT. After marriage, the groom who leaves to stay in his parents-in-law's house, is often referred to as *bhun ki briew* (=someone else's son). Women's organisation, *Synjuk ki Seng Samba Sbnob* (SKSSS) also joined the debate, though it has maintained a low profile and has always sought negotiated settlement of the issue. While this debate has been going on, Khasi Hills Autonomous District Council (KHADC) passed the Khasi Social Custom of Lineage Bill 1997, adding fuel to the fire. The 1997 Bill proposes to make the existing custom a law and codify it. The KHADC argues: "We are trying to preserve the system and make the terms very specific so that tribal custom is not misused by unscrupulous people.... The Bill was framed after a lot of discussion, it is in fact, a consensus. It has been enacted to pacify those people who are asking for change in the custom so as to protect the tribal society from the abuse by non-tribals and outsiders." The major reason for opposing the matrilineal system is to stop the marriages between Khasis and non-Khasis. The main clauses of the Bill have in fact, placed elaborate restrictions over what agitated student leaders call "sham marriages". It is towards this end that the Bill has laid down stringent conditions on the issue of marriage between a Khasi girl and a non-Khasi boy. The Bill was passed unanimously by the KHADC, and then forwarded to the Governor for approval. But such elaborate arrangement has not satisfied the men who have, in a memorandum, requested the Governor not to give his assent to the Bill. The main demand of the men's brigade is to enact a law which mandates that any Khasi girl marrying a non-Khasi will be deprived of all her rights and privileges. But KHADC, comprising of tribal chiefs, senior citizens and scholars, enjoys tremendous power. The issue has been hanging fire, and the Bill is still with the Governor, for over five years.

The whole trouble can be ascribed to the fact that the modern Khasi male is no longer willing to play a second fiddle. For the last 12 years (1990-2002), the SRT is waging a crusade to change the Khasi society. Says the SRT President, Keith Pariat: "The Khasi man is sinking morally and intellectually since he has no authority in the family. Khasi women are no longer interested in marrying the Khasi men. Inter ethnic marriages have increased. The survival of the Khasi society is at stake. We are trying to avoid just that." The need to change the system has been felt more acutely ever since outsiders—both from other parts of India and the neighbouring countries of Nepal and Bangladesh—entered the State in large numbers and "took to marrying the Khasi women to take easier road to fortune". To their credit, most women feel that men should be given some property. Says Patricia Lyngdoh, Principal of a College and a social thinker: "I feel the basic structure of matrilineal system should remain but the society should take the changes into consideration and adopt the best of both traditions."

The Bill, still (2003) pending with the Governor, has generated furious debate over the years. The last word on it is still to be heard. But the churning is surely on in the barely half-a-million strong Khasi society. The matriarchal lineage system has given the Khasi women a special status which their counterparts in many advanced communities can only aspire to. Whether it will survive the present onslaught and thrive or find a place in the pages of history books only time will tell.

The last word on the issue has hopefully been heard. After 8 long years, the Governor approved the Bill into law in March 2005. The SRT had demanded that the Governor send back the Bill to the KHADC as it contained many controversial clauses. The Act as passed does address some of the concerns of the SRT but certainly not all. Among the Khasis, a family without a daughter is considered a "dying clan", so the Bill proposed that such a family could follow the *Rap ling* custom—adopt a female child. The SRT felt the son's status was ignored, so the amended Act now permits adoption of a male child too. The SRT, which wants Khasis to replace matrilineal system with the patrilineal, is still unhappy because their main demand—that children be allowed to take the name to their father—has been totally ignored. The debate goes on!

Foreigners and Outsiders

The Bangladesh Government has sought New Delhi's permission (*Exp.*, 4-5-03) to set tip a visa office in Shillong which would give a major boost to trans-border trade. Meghalaya has several transit points to Bangladesh through which coal, timber, cement and oranges are exported.

The state has been very sensitive to the issue of the in-flow of migrants. During the 1979-80, the Bengalis were the "foreign" nationals targeted the most. So was the case during the 1987 agitation. "The State Government detected 12,000 Nepali foreigners of which over 10,000 were expelled in February-March 1987."

The FKJGP activists picked up (on 1-9-04) 31 Nepalis who had arrived at Shillong and were on their way to Jaintia Hills to work in the coal mines. They were later handed over to the police which said the FKJGP's act was illegal as the RAP system was done away within the State in May 1995 and the Indo-Nepal Friendship Treaty, 1950, allows Nepalese nationals to move freely in India and *vice versa.*

Chief Minister Lapang urged the Centre (4-9-04) again to introduce multi-purpose identity cards to check the influx of foreign nationals into the State. In a memorandum to Home Minister Shivraj Patil, Lapang pointed out that the Conference of Chief Ministers on internal security on 17-11-2001 had endorsed the issuance of work permits for the foreigners and decided that the citizens' identity card system should be introduced to check illegal migration *(Hindu,* 6-9-04).

Prohibitory orders were clamped in the districts of East Khasi Hills and Ri Bhoi on 13-9-04 ahead of 20-hour *bandh* on the 14th called by the KSU to protest the Government's failure to fulfil its demands like review of reservation policy, tackling foreigner's influx, and issue of uranium mining in certain areas.

Insurgency : Ceasefire with ANVC

The row over the issue of negotiators for talks between the Centre and the ANVC notwithstanding, "Senior leader P.A. Sangma continues to act as 'facilitator' for the peace dialogue *(HT,* 30-6-03). In May 2003, the Congress-led Meghalaya Democratic Alliance Government embarrassed Sangma by denouncing his claim about having been authorised by Dy PM Advani to open talks with the ANVC. The MHA sources, while confirming that no negotiator had been appointed, admitted that Sangma did indeed get the go-ahead from Advani to contact the ANVC.

On 23 July 2004, the tripartite Peace Pact was signed, suspending the armed operations for six months, and the signatories were A.K. Rastogi, Secretary (Border Management), MHA; P.J. Bazely, Chief Secretary, Meghalaya; and W.K. Marak General Secretary, ANVC. Under the Pact, the outfit deposited 70 weapons with the SF and its 250 cadres would be confined to two Army camps. A Joint Monitoring Group would be set up. The Government hoped that the cease-fire would effectively check the cross-border movement of the Cadres of ULFA and other insurgent outfits to Bangladesh.

Some of the insurgency-related issues/incidents are mentioned below:

1. The state banned a series of one-dayers planned by the ANVC, the Garo outfit that signed a cease-fire on 23-7-04. The State Home ministry was yorked by the Garo militants organising public events beyond the boundary of their designated camps: (1) Chakpot in South Garo Hills district. (2) Williamnagar in East Garo Hills district. The officials feared the militants could be using cricket to brainwash young boys with their ideology—a separate Garo Homeland. The ANVC's Publicity Secretary A.S.N. Sangma thought the Government was unduly suspicious (*HT*, 5-12-04).
2. The Intelligence reported that the ISI was active in the North-East, subverting the Indian nationals. One Lance Naik of the Assam Rifles was arrested (*Hindu*, 13-7-02) who was being paid Rs. 1,00,000 every month for passing on information to an ISI agent attached to the Pak embassy in Kathmandu. Some incriminating document were recovered from his house.
3. After 26-day of captivity, two abducted State officials were released by the ANVC on 26-4-03.
4. Slogan raised by some 'mischievous' elements: "Khasi by blood, Indian by accident."
5. Late night, 24-10-04, a Major and two ULFA cadres were killed in an encounter in West Garo Hills district.
6. The Kolkata police have uncovered links between the extremist outfits active in the North-East (like ULFA and ANVC) with the Jamaat-ul-Mujahideen, a Kashmiri militant outfit (*Hindu,* 3-1-04). This strengthens the suspicions about the Pak ISI being active in different parts of the country.

Is Meghalaya Disintegrating?

If Meghalaya was fruition of a sustained struggle by the Khasi Jaintia, and Garo people led by Capt Williamson Sangma (who became its first Chief Minister in January 1972) and other leaders, presently another Garo, P.A. Sangma, the NCP leader and former Speaker of the Lok Sabha, is mobilizing the Garos for creation of separate Garoland out of Meghalaya, aided by the Khasis under the KSU, who demand bifurcation of the State to create Khasiland for their own reasons. Earlier, the Khasis cited injustice being done to them as the state has been ruled by Garo Chief Minister for long years (as earlier discussed) compared to the Khasi ones, now an innocuous, apolitical issue like education has incited passions for its bifurcation (Manjula Bhattacharyya, *Tribune,* 27-6-05 and 4-7-05).

It all started recently over the failure in the distribution of the mathematics paper in time by the Tura (Garo Hills) based Meghalaya Board of Secondary Education (MBOSE), for the students from Shillong in the Khasi-dominated areas. The enraged KSU demanded bifurcation of the MBOSE, with one secretary each at Tura and Shillong, with a full-fledged Chairman, and called a 3-day *bandh* 23-25 June, in support. The KSU activists torched some Government vehicles and properties. The resignation by the Sports Minister Paul Lyngdoh, a former KSU President and a Khasi in support of the demand, forced D.D. Lapang, the CM and Khasi himself, and heading the Meghalaya Democratic Alliance Ministry, to declare a secretary each for Tura and Shillong, amounting to effective bifurcation of MBOSE. But soon after Lapang announced this decision, the Garo Students Union (GSU) and Garo Citizens Forum (GCF) called a 2-day *bandh*, 24-25 June, in Garo Hills to protest the decision. This prompted the Congress-led MDA to convene a Cabinet meeting (that lasted for 6 hours on 25-6-05) which decided to expand the Expert Committee on Education headed by the Chief Secretary to review the CM's decision and submit a report within two months. The CM was forced to retreat for the time being because of a strong protest by Deputy CM Mukul Sangma, who represents the Garos, contributing 24 of the 60 Assembly seats.

The movement is fast taking the shape for separate states to be carved out of Meghalaya, for the Khasis and Garos. The GCF has already adopted a resolution demanding creation of Garoland. The NCP is mobilising support for an October Rally to officially make the demand for Garoland. P.A. Sangma had flown in from Delhi soon after the 25th theatre, to fish in the troubled waters by demanding that Tura be declared the winter capital of Meghalaya. In fact, reports suggest P.A. Sangma is in touch with Congress leader and Dy CM Sangma and both the Sangmas are moving in the same direction—creation of Garoland.

Ironically, the Garos and Khasis (Jaintias are with them) who waged a long struggle to carve out Meghalaya out of the then composite Assam, are presently fighting each other for the bifurcation of the same Meghalaya into Garoland and Khasiland!

Following the somewhat detailed discussion of inter–and intra-tribal dissonance, political skullduggry, and birth of militancy, an overview of the situation, in the form of a backgrounder, should be of interest.

MEGHALAYA BACKGROUNDER

Meghalaya emerged as an autonomous State on April 2, 1970, and was declared a State of the Indian Union on January 1, 1972. Prior to April 1970, Meghalaya was a part of the composite State of Assam. Following a decade-long peaceful constitutional agitation for a separate Hill State, the Indian Parliament passed the Assam Reorganization (Meghalaya) Act, 1969, constituting the Autonomous State. The Parliament later passed the North Eastern Areas Reorganization Act, 1971, which conferred full Statehood on the autonomous State of Meghalaya.

Homeland to a number of tribes, Meghalaya (Abode of the Clouds) is also known as the 'Scotland of the East' for its scenic magnificence. The Garos dominate western Meghalaya; the Khasis, central Meghalaya; and the Jaintias, eastern Meghalaya. The 'Hynniewtrep' people, a collective name of the Khasi, Jaintia, Bhoi and War tribes belonging to the Proto Austroloid Monkhmer race, primarily dominate Eastern Meghalaya. The Garos or Achiks as they call themselves, belong to the Tibeto-Burman race and predominantly inhabit the Garo Hills.

The State has been plagued with the problem of insurgency since the latter part of the 1980s. Meghalaya has three terrorist outfits operating on its soil: the Hynniewtrep National Liberation Council (HNLC); the Achik National Volunteer Council (ANVC); and the People's Liberation Front of Meghalaya (PLF-M). The first two are currently more active than the last, which is relatively dormant. The HNLC is a product of a 1992 split in the Hynniewtrep Achik Liberation Council (HALC), the first militant tribal organization in Meghalaya, and aims at creating a sovereign State for the Khasis. The ANVC, formed in December 1995, aims to carve out a homeland called 'Achik Land' in the area of the Garo Hills under the provisions of the Indian Constitution. On November 16, 2000, the Union Government declared both the organizations as unlawful associations under the provisions of the Unlawful Activities (Prevention) Act, 1967.

Roots of Discord

The reasons of discord in Meghalaya are manifold. The divide among tribal residents of the State and the non-tribal settlers (mostly Bangladeshis) has been a prime factor for the growing discontent. Commencing with the divide that persisted through the nineteen seventies and eighties, events took a perilous direction in August 1992, when the Khasi Students' Union (KSU) and the Federation of Khasis, Jaintia and Garo Peoples (FKJGP) started issuing threat orders to non-tribal traders, compelling them to shut down their businesses in Meghalaya for not possessing valid trading licences. A riot (widely considered the fifth major riot against the so-called outsiders) followed, claiming 31 lives. In 1994, another round of trouble ensued over the Election Commission's orders for preparing photo-identity cards for all voters, which was resisted by the KSU. The KSU insisted that no photography for the cards would be permitted before the electoral rolls were revised with a 1951 cut-off date with regard to immigrants from Bangladesh.

In addition to the continuing divide between the locals and non-locals, issues of identity, growing corruption and perceived injustice in the Garo hills are considered to be reasons for the violence in Meghalaya. However, the Sharma Commission appointed by the State Government to investigate the various dimensions of the growing ethnic conflict in the State, observed in its report in 1995 that the primary cause of such disturbances has been economic, such as the increasing unemployment rate in the State.

Fatality Index

Between 1994 and 2002, 92 civilians, 68 security force personnel and 44 terrorist fatalities have been recorded in Meghalaya. The general trend had been an increasing civilian and security force casualty rate as compared to the terrorist fatalities. Signs of escalation in the overall death rate are evident in official data: a total of 20 deaths were reported in 1998, 22 in 1999, 36 in 2000, 40 in 2001, and 64 in 2002. Starting from 1997 to 2001, 225 terrorist related incidents took place in Meghalaya. According to Annual reports of the Union Ministry of Home Affairs, in 1997 there were 14 terrorist related incidents, but the following years witnessed a vertical increase— 16 in 1998, 52 in 1999, 73 in 2000, 70 in 2001 and 84 in 2002.

Active Groups

The HALC was a radical organization and could be considered to be the first terrorist outfit in the State. In 1992, following a split in the HALC over inter-tribal antagonisms, the group was renamed and has functioned under the banner of Hynniewtrep National Liberation Council (HNLC) since May 1996. According to the HNLC's 19-point manifesto, the organization stands for the 'national existence and self-determination of our people without subordination under the yoke of foreign powers.' Its objectives include the transformation of Meghalaya into a 'Khasi State' and freedom from the domination of the Garo tribes. *"To* realize its objectives, the outfit calls for the 'unshackling of the motherland and people from the bonds of Indian colonialism, imperialism and chauvinism.' Further, it also aims at fighting 'outsiders', as the group sees Khasi youth as a deprived lot in their own land. The HNLC is active in the Khasi Hills of the State.

The HNLC is understood to have close links with the National Socialist Council of Nagaland-Isak-Muivah (NSCN-IM) faction. Its activities include, among others, fake currency circulation in the State, as well as extortion and other forms of underground activities, primarily for monetary gains. It is believed that the Inter Services Intelligence (ISI), Pakistan's external intelligence agency, has assisted the HNLC in the acquisition and circulation of fake currency.

The second splinter group of the HALC was named the A'chik Liberation Matgrik Army (ALMA), a Garo outfit. The ALMA could not continue the armed struggle and surrendered on October 25, 1994, at Tura. As the State Government dithered over the issue of rehabilitation of the surrendered cadres, in August 1995, a group of Garo militants along with some NSCN-IM cadres made a successful jailbreak attempt from the Shillong District Jail. Among the Garo cadres was Jerome Momin, who went on to form the A'chick National Volunteer Council (ANVC) in December 1995. The ANVC demands a homeland for the Achiks (Garos) comprising the Garo Hill District of Meghalaya, the Garo dominated Nongkhlaw area in the Khasi Hills, and the Garo-inhabited Goalpara and Kamrup districts of Assam, Following the jailbreak, the outfit is understood to have grown with the active assistance of the NSCN-IM. Over the years, the ANVC has come to establish a working relationship with the National Democratic Front of Bodoland (NDFB), and the United Liberation Front of Asom (ULFA), especially after the latter wound up some of its camps in Bhutan and is in the process of relocating them in the Garo Hills. Though media reports suggest a worsening of ties between the ANVC and the NDFB, both groups continue to assist each other in several operations. The ANVC has also established an 'extortion empire' of sorts in the Garo Hills and parts of the West Khasi Hills. According to a list submitted by India to Bangladesh, the ANVC maintains three camps in that country.

The People's Liberation Front of Meghalaya (PLFM) is a relatively new group operating in the Garo Hills of Meghalaya. Reports suggest that the outfit had been re-christened as the Achik National Council (ANC) on August 2001. The PLFM is an offshoot of the Achik Liberation Matgrik Army (ALMA). While most of ALMA terrorists surrendered in 1994, a few formed the ANVC in 1995. The PLFM consists of some of these "surrendered rebels" of the erstwhile ALMA who returned underground after their rehabilitation scheme failed. The primary objective of the PLFM is economic development as well as better educational opportunities for the Garo tribes in Meghalaya. Like the ANVC, one of its claimed objectives is the demand for a separate Garo State. The group is primarily active in Dainadubi and Williamnagar in East Garo Hills, and Dalu in West Garo Hills.

Peace Initiatives

After the terrorist groups refused to heed the State Government's repeated appeals for a negotiated settlement, the Church was seen as a potential mediator in the ongoing conflict. The Church leaders, under the banner of Shinong Khasi Jaintia Church Leaders' Forum (SKJCL), had offered their services to the State Government to initiate talks with terrorist groups, especially the HNLC. However, there has been little response from the insurgents of this group, who have accused the political establishment of a 'lack of sincerity' towards solving contentious issues.

Peace efforts with the ANVC, on the other hand, have been more successful, as the outfit has been open to the possibility of a negotiated settlement with the Government. In fact, it started a dialogue with the Mizoram Chief Minister, Zoramthanga, and the Intelligence Bureau Director, K.P. Singh, in Bangkok in January 2003. However, no further dialogue has taken place since. On September 5, 2003, Chief Minister D.D. Lapang handed over a letter to the President of the Garo Baptist Convention (GBC), Grover C.R. Marak, authorizing him to negotiate with the ANVC. The ANVC has, however, continued to maintain that talks would have to centre on the issue of the creation of a separate Garoland (Land of the Garo tribes).

Political instability in the State has also been a prime factor in the failure to resolve the insurgency problem. Successive Governments have their own approaches, with each new phase being abandoned once power changes hands. In December 2001, the then State Chief Minister, F. A. Khonglam, promised to set up a Cabinet sub-committee to help the Government bring ANVC and HNLC to the negotiating table. With Khonglam's departure from the seat of power, the proposal lapsed into political oblivion.

NOTES

1. One maund = 82.28 pounds.
2. The figures are from Mackenzie (1884).
3. Paul Lyngdoh's interview, *Frontline,* 17-6-94.
4. *The Frontline,* 17-6-94.
5. *Ibid.*
6. Lyngdoh resigned on 6 March 2000, and Ek Mawlong, the erstwhile Speaker, took over as Chief Minister on the 8th, heading a 30-member Coalition Ministry.
7. *HT,* 24-8-98 and *India Today*, 28-9-98.
8. *Frontline,* 13-10-2000.
9. *Ibid.*
10. *Frontline,* 13-4-01.
11. *Exp.,* 14-12-03.
12. *HT,* 25-10-03.
13. *Exp.* of 1-11-02 and 4-5-03 and *The Hindu* of 19-6-02.
14. Ram Chandra Guha : *TOI*, 23-11-99.

13

Meghalaya : Terrorist Outfits and Present Situation

Terrorism may not be as rampant in Meghalaya as, say in Manipur, even then the intelligence agencies insist that the state needs careful attention as it shares the border with Bangladesh. Besides, a number of terrorist scap leaders and senior cadres converge to Shillong for consultations and rest and recuperation. For this reason, Meghalaya has developed into a transit state for militants of several hues for quite some years.

Here is a table indicating terrorist groups operating in Meghalaya, followed by available information about them and their activities.

Terrorist/Insurgent Groups—Meghalaya

Active Terrorist/ Insurgent Groups	Inactive Terrorist/Insurgent Groups
• Achik National Volunteer Council (ANVC) • Hynniewtrep National Liberation Council (HNLC) • People's Liberation Front of Meghalaya (PLF-M)	• Hajong United Liberation Army (HULA)

ACHIK NATIONAL VOLUNTEER COUNCIL (ANVC)

Formation

The Achik National Volunteer Council (ANVC) was formed in December 1995. It was proscribed on November 16, 2000.

Objectives

The ANVC aims to carve out a homeland called 'Achik Land' in the areas of Garo Hills. The proposed 'Achik Land' comprises the present districts of Garo Hills in Meghalaya and a large chunk of Kamrup and Goalpara district of Assam. The 'Garo majority' in these areas is used as the argument for this demand. The ANVC differs from the other Garo separatist organisation, Garo National Council (GNC), which aims for a Garo State comprising only the three districts of the Garo hills.

Leadership

Dilash R. Marak is the 'Chairman' of the ANVC. The outfit's 'Commander-in-Chief' is Jerome Momin. Among the other leaders are 'General Secretary', Wanding R. Marak, 'Publicity Secretary', Artist Sengsrang Sangma, 'Joint Secretary', Janggam Momin, and 'Finance Secretary' Rickie Sangma.

The outfit divides its area of operation into several zones and each zone is headed by a 'commander'. The cadres who function as commanders of different zones are: Chenang Marak (Eastern Zone), Goran Sangma (Southern Zone), Batjang Shera (Western Zone), Ranggam Marak (West Khasi Hills).

Area commanders function below the zonal commanders in the operational hierarchy. Sohan D. Shira functions as the 'Area Commander' of Williamnagar.

The leadership maintains strict vigil on the activities of its cadres. This was manifest in the threats it issued in the year 2000 to its surrendering cadres, who were doing so under the rehabilitation package announced by the Union Government in the year 1998-99, and their family members. The outfit also warned them not to join any other outfit.

Area of Operation

The ANVC is active in the Garo Hills and in certain parts of the West Khasi Hills. It maintains its headquarters at Cheram in the Garo hills area. Among its activities are extortion from the business community in the name of 'fund collection'. Besides that, the outfit also pumps fake currency into circulation.

Linkages

The outfit was reportedly formed with the assistance of the National Socialist Council of Nagaland - Issak Muivah (NSCN-IM). However, it has severed its entire links with the Naga outfit as well as with the National Democratic Front of Bodoland (NDFB). The outfit now maintains links with the United Liberation Front of Asom (ULFA), especially after the latter wound up some of its camps in Bhutan and is in the process of relocating them in the Garo Hills. The ANVC has some of its camps in Bangladesh. It is also involved in fake currency circulation initiated by the Inter Services Intelligence (ISI), Pakistan's external intelligence agency. In Meghalaya, ANVC, along with the other prominent outfit, HNLC, abets this infusion of fake currency and in turn receives considerable operating funds. Extortion remains the major source of funding for the ANVC. Incidents of abduction are frequent in the state. Money is regularly collected from the trading community of the area in the name of 'fund collection'.

Peace Process

On July 23, 2004 a cease-fire agreement was signed between the Government of India and the ANVC for a period of six months. A seven member ANVC team, with the notable absence of Chairman Dilash Marak and Commander-in-Chief Jerome Momin signed the agreement in New Delhi. A ceasefire-monitoring cell has been set up at the Coal India Complex at Araimile in Tura. Two designated camps for housing the surrendered militants are being set up in the Garo Hills region.

Incidents

2006

- November 9: The Union Government extends the proscription on ANVC.
- October 25: The ANVC fails to respond to the appeal made by Meghalya Chief Minister, J. D. Rymbai, and Home Minister, R. G. Lyngdoh, to lay down arms, before the State Government could convince the Union Government to lift the ban imposed on the outfit, indicates report.
- September 28: The ANVC decides to discuss with the Meghalaya Government the conditions of disarmament for lifting the ban on the outfit. "We will have to discuss the matter before taking any decision in this regard," said 'publicity secretary' Arist Sangma.
- September 11: The newly formed Garo outfit, Achik National Liberation Front Army (ANLFA), allegedly accuse the Meghalaya Government of being soft on the ANVC, which is currently under a cease-fire with the Union and State Governments. The ANLFA alleges that the State Government is turning a blind eye to the 'atrocities' committed by the ANVC cadres in Garo Hills.
- August 31: The self-styled 'chairman' of the ANVC, Dilash Marak, figures in the list of wanted militants, residing in Bangladesh, handed over by the Border Security Force (BSF) to the Bangladesh Rifles (BDR) during their meeting in Shillong.
- August 31: Two political parties, the Hill State People's Democratic Party from Khasi Hills and Garo National Council from Garo Hills, at a joint statement demand the creation of separate provinces for the two major tribes of the State. Both the parties are opposed to the idea of 'Greater Garoland' demanded by the ANVC. However, the ANVC criticizes the joint proclamation of the two parties as a "political propaganda".
- August 28: The ANVC states that it has discussed the issue of Garo Hills with the Union Government in New Delhi in July 2006. The 'publicity secretary' of the outfit, Arist Sangma, said, "We submitted our memorandum and said separate Garoland was our demand."

- August 8: Meghalaya Government starts the Disaster Awareness and Search & Rescue Training programme for ANVC cadres at Tura in the West Garo Hills district.
- July 11: The cease-fire agreement between the Government and ANVC is extended by one more year. An agreement to this effect is reached during the Joint Monitoring Group held in New Delhi on an unspecified day. The ANVC entered into a tripartite cease-fire agreement on July 23, 2004.
- May 30: Meghalaya Home Minister H. Donkupar R Lyngdoh, while responding negatively on the request of the ANVC to the Union Government to lift the ban imposed on it, says, "Let people be satisfied with their non-violence and peaceful existence." "No doubt, the illegal activities of the ANVC has reduced to a great extent; but until people are satisfied, the ban should continue," adds the Home Minister.
- May 28: The ANVC asks the Union Government to withdraw its ban on the outfit to facilitate peace talks.
- May 10: The ANVC, while criticizing other Garo outfits such as the ANLF and United UANF, terms them as "group of extortionists and dacoits who have no ideology or principle." "Both UANF and ANLF are only after money and they are not fighting for the cause of the people of Garo Hills," said ANVC 'publicity secretary' Arist Sengsrang Sangma. "We are fighting for a separate state and our demand is very much within the framework of the Indian Constitution while the so called UANF has claimed that the organisation is fighting for independence which is not at all acceptable both to the Government of India and the Garos as well," he added.
- May 1: Chief Minister D. D. Lapang, while expressing the State Government's willingness to hold talks with the militant outfits, says, "But we have no say on the issues, which are totally depended on the initiative of the Union Home Ministry." He further adds, "We have to patiently wait and see things to happen because whatever steps that have been followed with the ANVC, the same thing will be done with HNLC."
- April 7: An ANVC cadre is killed by three of his colleagues at Tura in the West Garo Hills district.
- April 5: The JMG meeting held at the BSF premises in Guwahati decides to conduct a joint survey for setting up a designated camp for the ANVC cadres in the South Garo Hills of Meghalaya by the end of April 2006. The existing camp at Jetra in the Ri Bhoi district will be dismantled following complaints from paramilitary forces.

- March 27: Meghalaya Chief Minister D.D. Lapang, while responding to the issue of negotiations with militant outfits, informs the Legislative Assembly that a "Joint Monitoring Group (JMG) has been formed to monitor the cease-fire with the ANVC. The next JMG meeting will be held on April 5 in Guwahati, said, while adding that, "We are thinking of adopting similar pattern as the first step to initiate dialogue with HNLC."
- March 24: The ANVC calls for the formation of a separate state known as the 'Garoland State' for the Garos in Meghalaya. The 'publicity secretary' of the outfit, Arist Sengsrang Sangma, says that it is high time for all Garos to come under one umbrella and demand a separate state.

2005

- December 14: Union Minister of State for Home Affairs, S. Reghupathy, while speaking in the Rajya Sabha (Upper House of Parliament), says that cease fire and suspension of operations is on with ANVC along with certain other militant outfits of the North East.
- November 16: Police kills Tiko Areng, a militant belonging to the ANLF, a splinter faction of the ANVC at Dongranggre near Shallang in the West Khasi Hills district. One 9 mm pistol and a grenade are recovered from the incident site.
- November 9: ANVC 'publicity secretary', Arist Sengsrang Sangma, says, "We have told the cadres that those who are willing to leave can do so without deserting or running away from the camps." Commenting on reports that some former ANVC cadres have formed a new outfit, the ANLF, he says, "We will try to neutralise ANLF with the police, otherwise there will be law and order problem in Garo Hills." He further says that the relation between the police and the ANVC has improved considerably over the past few months.
- November 6: Two ANVC cadres, M. Marak and N. Momin, who have escaped from the Chokpot cease-fire camp, are killed by a joint team of Meghalaya Police and the army near Thapha in the East Garo Hills district. Three Chinese-made hand grenades and three rounds of AK-47 ammunition, besides documents such as extortion notes and money receipts are recovered from the incident site.
- November 4: Meghalaya Police kills two hardcore ANVC cadres, Rarik Sangma and Rabi Marak, and arrests two others at Bangsiminol under Mendipather police station in the Garo Hills district. Police sources informed that the slain militants are part of a group of nine ANVC cadres who have deserted the outfit's camp at Samanda in East Garo

Hills and Chokpot in South Garo Hills and have made attempts to form a new outfit, the AN LF. Police also recover an AK-56 rifle with 20 rounds of ammunition, three hand grenades and an SLR with 17 rounds of live ammunition from the incident site.

- September 4: ANVC threatens to call off the cease-fire agreement with the State Government protesting against the latter's constant allegation of truce violation by the outfit. The outfit's 'Publicity Secretary' Arist Sangma said, "We express concern over the state government's often repeated statement that the ANVC is engaged in extortions... If the government continues with its wild allegations, we will be forced to go back to the jungle."
- July 18: The cease-fire between ANVC and the Union Government is extended for a year with effect from July 23, 2005. The decision is taken following a meeting between the ANVC leaders and MHA officials at Patgaon in the Guwahati city of Assam. The ANVC is asked to submit names of its cadres taking shelter in the two designated camps in East and South Garo Hills to the Union Government and also keep its arms and ammunition in safe custody.
- July 6: Meghalaya Government sends a note to the Union Government detailing the acts of cease-fire violation by the ANVC. Chief Secretary P. J. Bazeley said that the State Government would agree to extend the cease-fire agreement beyond July 23 provided the truce ground rules are framed and strictly adhered to. He says, "We have told the Centre that we will not be a party to the cease-fire with the ANVC if there are no proper ground rules."
- May 11: Two ANVC cadres, Ganesh Sangma and Nicholas Sangma, and one of their associates are arrested from Borsora in the West Khasi Hills district of Meghalaya.
- April 19: Meghalaya Chief Minister, D D Lapang, while addressing a press conference in Shillong, said the ANVC is violating the cease-fire agreement.
- April 14: Meghalaya Home Minister, Mukul Sangma, says that failure to settle issues relating to the cease-fire ground rules have led to the delay in starting the peace process with the proscribed ANVC.
- March 30: A tribunal makes recommendations for the extension of the proscription on the HNLC and ANVC for another year.
- March 8: Meghalaya Home Minister, Mukul Sangma, says that the State Government will begin peace talks with the ANVC only after the outfit adheres to the principles of the cease-fire.
- January 17: The ceasefire agreement between the Government and the ANVC is extended by six months. The agreement is reached

during the JMG meeting held at Tura in the West Garo Hills district. The duration of the present ceasefire is set to expire on January 23.

2004

- December 23: As a first step towards fulfilling the cease-fire ground rules, the ANVC submits a list of 100 of its cadres to the State Government. Informing this in Shillong, the State Home Minister, H.D.R. Lyngdoh, says that these cadres will be accommodated in the two designated camps. However, the outfit is yet to submit the list of arms and ammunition, adds Lyngdoh.
- December 22: Union Government extends the ban on two militant outfits of Meghalaya, the ANVC and HNLC. In an official notification in Shillong, the MHA cites the reasons for extension stating that although the ANVC agrees to abjure violence and expresses willingness for talks within the framework of Constitution, it continues "collection of funds and extortion, acquisition of sophisticated weapons and recruitment of new cadre."
- December 10: Meghalaya Government asks the ANVC chairman Dilash Marak and 'commander-in-chief' Jerome Momin to confine themselves to the Garo Hills area.
- December 9: The JMG meeting between the banned ANVC and the representatives of the MHA and the Meghalaya Government takes place in New Delhi to discuss the 'ground rules'. Following the second round of the tripartite talks of JMG, the ANVC agrees to submit the full list of its cadres to the State Government by December 20 to facilitate the implementation of cease-fire ground rules. The cadres will stay in two designated camps in the Garo Hills region.
- July 23: ANVC signs a tripartite agreement with the Union and Meghalaya Governments for immediate suspension of hostilities. The agreement is signed by the Secretary, Border Management in the MHA, A.K.Rastogi, Chief Secretary of Meghalaya, P.J. Bazely, and representatives of the ANVC led by its 'General Secretary' Wanding K Marak.
- July 2: The abducted Indian Forest Service official, D Sathyen, is released unharmed in the South Garo Hills district of Meghalaya after about a fortnight amidst claims by the State Government that no ransom was paid to the abductors.
- June 24: ANVC denies any links to the abduction of D. Sathyean, Indian Forest Service officer posted at the Balpakram National Park. The outfit's 'publicity secretary', Arist Sengsrang Sangma, says that the outfit does not have any connection with the incident.

- June 22: ANVC demands Rupees 15 lakh as ransom for the release of abducted D. Satyan.
- June 18: Suspected ANVC terrorists abduct Forest Officer, D. Satyan, from his house at Baghmara in South Garo Hills district.
- June 1: Suspected ANVC terrorists shot dead a trader from Tura in Meghalaya for failing to pay extortion money demanded by them.
- June 1: Suspected ANVC terrorists kill a trader from Tura in the West Garo Hill district.
- May 10: Suspected ANVC cadres kill a schoolteacher at Kukurmara in the Kamrup district of Assam.
- May 6: Meghalaya Police arrests an ANVC terrorist, involved in truck burning incidents at Borsora on April 28, from Nonghyllam in the West Khasi Hills district.
- March 16: One ANVC terrorist is killed in an encounter with the security forces at Kajinagar in the West Garo Hills district.
- February 20: Suspected ANVC cadres release Borsora Land Custom Station Superintendent, L.H. Faihrem, from captivity at Tila Basti in the East Khasi Hills district. He was abducted on October 9, 2003.
- January 19: One police personnel is killed and four others are injured when an Improvised Explosive Device (IED), allegedly planted by ANVC terrorists went off at Tapadarengchi in the East Garo Hills district.
- February 13: Four ANVC terrorists are kilted by SFs in an encounter near Phulbari in the West Garo Hills district.
- February 10: Meghalaya Police arrests an ANVC terrorist, identified as Jubi R Marak, from an unspecified location in the State.
- February 6: Meghalaya Chief Minister, D D Lapang, accuses former Lok Sabha Speaker and Nationalist Congress Party (NCP) leader P A Sangma of conniving with the proscribed ANVC to remain in State politics.
- January 7: Two ANVC 'sympathizers' are arrested for distributing extortion notes bearing the signature of R Marak of the ANVC 'finance wing' at Mendipathar in the East Garo Hills district.

2003

- December 15: A woman ANVC cadre, identified as Tresy Sangma, wife of the Mendipather 'area commander' of the outfit, is arrested near Mendipather in the East Garo Hills district.

- November 16: Meghalaya Police arrest a self-styled corporal of the ANVC, identified as Havel Sangma, from Bologgitok village in the West Garo Hills district and recover a Japanese wireless hand-set and a tape recorder from his possession.
- November 10: Suspected ANVC terrorists kill three civilians at Rajapal in the East Garo Hills district.
- October 28: ANVC 'commander-in-chief' Jerome Momin indicates that the outfit "would continue its struggle for a greater Garoland and not give in to any moves initiated by the government towards a reconciliation."
- October 1: Two Achik National Volunteer Council (ANVC) terrorists surrender before the police in Shillong, and at Baghmara in South Garo Hills respectively.
- September 30: ANVC decides not to participate in the Meghalaya Government backed peace talks with the Garo Baptist Convention (GPC) after the September 26 incident.
- September 26: Security force personnel kill eight ANVC terrorists in two separate encounters in the West Garo Hills district and recover one AK-56. rifle with twelve rounds of live ammunition, one Pakistan-made .32 pistol with seven rounds of ammunition, two Chinese hand grenades and some incriminating documents from the encounter site.
- September 24: Meghalaya Chief Minister Lapang offers truce to the ANVC and HNLC.
- September 10: ANVC terrorists in Meghalaya release abducted Bajengdoba SBI Branch Manager after nine days of captivity.
- August 7: An ANVC sympathizer alleged to be involved in supplying arms to the outfit is killed during an encounter at Rewak in the South Garo Hills district.
- July 16: Two ANVC terrorists, including a 'commander', are killed during an encounter at Bikonggre village in the West Garo Hills district while three others escape from the incident site.
- June 27: Meghalaya Police arrests former State Minister and senior Nationalist Congress Party (NCP) leader Adolf Lu Hitler Marak at Laban in Shillong for his alleged links with the ANVC.
- June 24: ANVC terrorists ambush a police patrol party near Borsora in the West Khasi Hills district killing two police personnel and injuring three others.
- June 19: Two women ANVC cadres surrender before the State Home Minister R G Lyngdoh at Shillong.

- May 20: At least five ANVC terrorists are arrested from Ampati in the West Garo Hills district.
- May 15: Four ANVC terrorists are arrested from a hideout at Ampati in the West Garo Hills district.
- May 4: Meghalaya Police unearths an ANVC 'finance cell' at Asimggre village in West Garo Hills district and seizes incriminating documents indicating to an extortion racket being run by the outfit in the area.
- May 01 : Suspected ANVC cadres abduct two persons from Balachand, West Garo Hills district.
- April 29: Three ANVC terrorists, including an 'area commander', surrender before the State police at Sonapahar village in West Khasi Hills district with two AK-56 rifles, two wireless sets, four grenades and 216 rounds of AK-47 ammunition.
- April 28: ANVC 'area command headquarters' in the Garo Hills area is reportedly dissolved and brought under the single command of 'commander-in-chief' Jerome Momin.
- April 26: Suspected ANVC terrorists release two abducted Meghalaya Government officials after 26 days of captivity near Willamnagar, East Garo Hills district. ANVC abducts a State Government official from Dadenggri in West Garo Hills district.
- April 23: Reports indicate that 'preliminary talks' were held between the Union Government and the ANVC on an unspecified date in Bangkok, Thailand.
- April 15: Suspected ANVC terrorists abduct a local businessman from Jhanjhani market, Mancachar police station-limits, in Assam's Dhubri district.
- April 13: ANVC releases three of the five Assam-based businessmen abducted on April 7, near Phulbari in West Garo Hills district.
- April 7: Meghalaya police arrest two ANVC terrorists at Weiloi village, East Khasi Hills district, from the vehicle of a former Legislator Adolf L. Hitler Marak.
- April 2: Four suspected ANVC terrorists, including a woman cadre, abduct a businessman at Ampati, West Garo Hills district.
- March 31: The Assam-based NDFB releases Customs officer Dipak Mahanta near Williamnagar in South Garo Hills district. Terrorists had abducted him on February 28, 2003.
- March 24: NDFB sets free the four remaining coal exporters, following the escape of two other exporters from its unidentified

hideout in Meghalaya. ANVC and NDFB terrorists abducted the six coal exporters and a customs official Dipak Mahanta from Gasupara in South Garo Hills district on February 28.

- March 6: ANVC terrorists ambush a vehicle of the Border Road Organisation killing three persons on the spot in the East Garo Hills district. They also loot Rupees seven million and two self-loading rifles before escaping.

  A group of six ANVC terrorists abduct two teachers of a local school at Katuligaon near Ampati in the West Garo Hills district.

- February 28: ANVC and NDFB terrorists abduct six coal exporters and a customs official from Customs station at Ghasuapara in South Garo Hills district.

- February 26: Security forces rescue four abducted persons, including the Subsidiary Intelligence Bureau Assistant Director Deben Singh Rana at Damalgiri, Garobada police post limits in Tura, West Garo Hills district.

- February 13: Union Minister of State for Home Affairs, I D Swami, says peace initiative with ANVC is in progress.

  ANVC terrorists abduct a Government official at Bajengdoba in East Garo Hills district.

- February 2: ANVC terrorists kill Santhosh Hajong, a retired Meghalaya Police Battalion personnel at Ampati, West Garo Hills district.

- January 22: ANVC terrorists abduct a Government official from his residence at Bajendoba, East Garo Hills district.

- January 14: Suspected ANVC terrorists kill three persons in Songsak, near Williamnagar, East Garo Hills district, for allegedly using the outfit's name to extort money from local residents.

- January 3: The Union Home Ministry extends ban under the Unlawful Activities (Prevention) Act of 1967 on the ANVC and the Hynniewtrep National Liberation Council (HNLC) in Meghalaya.

2002

- December 31: ANVC demands Rs two million as ransom for medical practitioner P. Bezbaruah's release

- December 19: ANVC terrorists abduct medical practitioner P. Bezbaruah in Williamnagar, East Garo Hills district.

- December 12: A businessman abducted from Nidhanpur, Assam, flees from an ANVC hideout despite being hit by bullet in the leg.

- December 9: Union Ministry of Home Affairs (MHA) establishes contact with ANVC and confirms the possibility of peace talks in the future, most likely in Delhi in the year 2003.
- December 1: Terrorist-attack on a passenger bus in West Garo Hills, Meghalaya, injures two passengers. The ANVC's hand is suspected in the attack.
- November 12: ANVC relates the 1996-Wakabua raid to the rise of terrorism in Garo Hills. At the same time, the outfit's southern command in-charge and publicity-wing head Sohan D Shira says the September 9, 2002-killings of Deputy Superintendent of Police Paichon Sangma and five others, near Chokpot, was in retaliation to the Wakabua camp raid.
- October 05: Meghalaya Chief Minister F A Khonglam discloses he is in possession of certain evidence against three Ministers from the Garo Hills region having nexus with the proscribed ANVC terrorist outfit. He says they all belong to the Congress and the Nationalist Congress Party (NCP).
- September 24: An ANVC terrorist is killed and another arrested by security forces (SF) in Dobu, East Garo Kills district, following a prolonged gun-battle between group of five terrorists and a joint team of Police and Central Reserve Police Force (CRPF) personnel. Three more terrorists escape. A 9 mm carbine, 11 rounds of ammunition and a US-made carbine are recovered from the clash-site.
- September 9: Six Meghalaya police personnel, including a Deputy Superintendent of Police (DSP), are killed in an ambush laid by ANVC terrorists at Chocpot, in the Garo Hills of Meghalaya.
- July 1 : An ANVC terrorist is killed in an encounter with police near Dudhnoi in Assam. Five ANVC terrorists surrender at the Mendipather police station in the presence of Church leaders, in East Garo Hills.
- June 30: Meghalaya Forest Minister Monindra Rava's son, Devajyoti Rava, and four others are killed by unidentified, armed-men at a place between Belguri and Abhiram Para near Tikrikilla. Police suspect the ANVC's hand in the attack.
- June 11: Two ANVC terrorists are killed in an encounter at Amarsang village, near Kulung, under Borsora police station limits, West Khasi Hills district. Two AK-47 rifles, a Self-Loading Rifle (SLR), a Chinese rifle, two 12-bore guns and a large quantities of ammunition are recovered from the site of the encounter.

  ANVC terrorists injured in an encounter in South Garo Hills. Police recovered Rs 1,54,000 in cash from the clash-site.

- May 12: Three Nepalese settlers are, and seven more injured in an attack by the ANVC terrorist outfit at the Tinali settlement near Phulbari in the West Garo Hills district of Meghalaya.
- April 1 : ANVC terrorist killed in encounter near Rangagre village under Tura police station limits.
- March 14: Suspected ANVC terrorists kill eight persons, including four policemen in West Garo Hills.
- March 1 : ANVC terrorists abduct a leading businessman and a manager of a construction company from Chibinang, West Garo Hills.
- February 16: An ANVC terrorist attempting to cross over to Bangladesh killed in an encounter by security forces at Chadogre village in West Garo Hills.
- January 31 : ANVC terrorist and two Border Security Force (BSF) personnel killed in an encounter at Phanda in South Garo Hills district.
- January 22: ANVC conducts a joint attack with National Democratic Front of Boroland (NDFB) terrorists on a security forces camp using rocket-propelled grenades (RPGs) at Tikrikilla in South Garo Hills.

2001

- December 26: ANVC terrorist escapes from the Williamnagar district Jail, East Garo Hills district.
- November 25: ANVC terrorist arrested from a dwelling at Sonatala near Ranikota.
- November 22: ANVC terrorist surrenders to the South Garo Hills District police.
- November 20: ANVC terrorists abduct a Sub-Divisional Officer from Waribok, near Rongrang, in West Garo Hills.
- October 20: Three ANVC terrorists arrested from Doldegre area in West Garo Hills district by a joint team of Meghalaya police and Central Reserve Police Force (CRPF).
- October 9: Two ANVC cadres injured in an encounter on the outskirts of Williamnagar.

1999

August: Two policemen killed when suspected ANVC terrorists blow up two jeeps at Aniaga village in the East Garo Hills.

1998

October: Five security force personnel killed and over Rs. 100,000 looted during an attack in East Garo Hills.

February: Two police personnel killed and Rs. 800,000 looted in an ambush laid by ANVC terrorists, the East Garo Hills.

HYNNIEWTREP NATIONAL LIBERATION COUNCIL (HNLC)

Formation

The Hynniewtrep National Liberation Council (HNLC) is a product of a 1992 split in the Hynniewtrep Achik Liberation Council (HALC), the first militant tribal outfit in Meghalaya. The HALC split due to inter-tribal antagonisms leading to the formation of the HNLC and the Achik Matgrik Liberation Army (AMLA). In the erstwhile HALC, the Hynniewtreps (Khasis who trace their origin to seven celestial families) represented the Khasi and Jaintia tribes and the Achiks represented the Garos in the common fight against the Dkhars or 'outsiders'. The HNLC was proscribed on November 16, 2000.

Objectives

An important objective of the HNLC is to transform Meghalaya as a province exclusively for the Khasi tribe and free it from 'domination' by the Garo tribe. Another objective is to fight against the presence of 'outsiders', as the HNLC feels that Khasi youth are deprived of the fruits of development in the state.

Leadership

Julius K Dorphang is the 'Chairman' of the HNLC. Cheristerfield Thangkhiew functions as its 'General Secretary'. Among the other leaders are 'Publicity Secretary' M. Diengdoh, 'Commander-in-chief Bobby Marwein. HNLC 'Area Commander' Balajied Dkhar was killed in an encounter on August 23, 2000. The HNLC 'Operations group' consists of Khraw Bian, Shining Star Synkhli, Shynshar Nongbri, Bantei Kharkongor, Raju Blah and Kynteilang Kharkongor.

Area of Operation

The HNLC primarily operates in the Khasi Hills of Meghalaya.

Linkages

The HNLC is closely linked with the National Socialist Council of Nagaland-Issak Muivah (NSCN-IM). It also has a front organisation called the HSDF (Hynniewtrep State Democratic Front), whose 'Commander-in-Chief Dominic Kharpuli and three other cadres were arrested on October 20, 2001. The outfit is also reportedly maintaining some of its camps in Bangladesh. It also promotes the circulation of fake currency in the State, which was started at the behest of Inter Services Intelligence (ISI), Pakistan's external intelligence agency, reports hold.

Incidents

2006

- December 25: An extortionist, Asuk Amyrsong, is arrested from Kharkhana village in the Jaintia Hills district along the India-Bangladesh border. However, two others manage to escape. They reportedly served extortion notes of INR 25,000 to a lady, Mala Pohlong, in the guise of HNLC cadres.
- December 20: One HNLC cadre, Aimos Khonglaban, surrenders at Pynursla police station in the East Khasi Hills district.
- November 27: A HNLC cadre, Tensing Khonglah, surrenders before the Superintendent of Police of Shillong City. According to police sources, Khonglah was operating from Sanatula near Silchar in the Cachar district of Assam.
- November 20: Responding to the offer made by the HNLC for peace talks with the Union Government, the Meghalaya Home Minister, Robert G. Lyngdoh, stated that the State Government should be involved in the peace talks "so that it won't be held responsible for any failure in the process." "We are ready to hold talks at any moment and our door for negotiation is always open. But the talks should be a tripartite one like what was done with the ANVC," he added.
- November 9: The Union Government extends the proscription on HNLC.
- October 31 : HNLC has started setting up camps at Block I in the Karbi Anlong district of Assam. Reports added that five hardcore cadres belonging to the "Action Group (Army Wing)" of the outfit set up a camp in Assam.
- October 4: A senior HNLC cadre, Mon Pohrmen, who was the 'commander' of the camp at Panai in Bangladesh, surrenders before Meghalaya Police at Jowai in the Jaintia Hills district. He deposits some sample demand notes before the police.
- September 28: A HNLC cadre, Dap Singh Ritshong alias Syrpai, surrenders before the Meghalaya Police at an unspecified place.
- September 25: Meghalaya Police recover dead bodies of two former HNLC cadres, Philio Hashah and his brother Anthony Hashah, from Wan Khri near Mairang in the West Khasi Hills district. They were killed en route to appear in the district court for a pending case relating to their earlier linkages with the HNLC.

- September 25: Meghalaya Police arrests a HNLC cadre, Tom Jones Rynjah, from Mawlai Syllaikriah in the capital Shillong, and seizes some incriminating documents from his possession.
- September 20: A HNLC cadre, Krinding Lyngdoh, surrenders before the Meghalaya Police at an unspecified location. According to police sources, the surrendered militant, who confessed to having recently returned from Bangladesh, did not deposit any arms.
- September 20: Meghalaya Police kills a HNLC cadre, Bankit Khonjee, and arrests another during an encounter at Umkrem in the East Khasi Hills district. A modified sten gun of 9 mm caliber, one 9 mm carbine, 40 rounds of ammunition and eight empty cases of assorted ammunition are recovered from the incident site. Following the incident, one surrendered HNLC cadre is also arrested for sheltering the HNLC cadres.
- September 10: The Union Government authorises the Meghalaya Government to directly negotiate with the HNLC. Meanwhile, State Chief Minister J. D. Rymbai and Home Minister R. G. Lyngdoh ask the cadres of the outfit to give up arms and return to the mainstream.
- August 30: Disillusioned women cadres of the HNLC, who are in an isolated camp in Bangladesh and are desperate to leave the outfit to join the mainstream, are reportedly being prevented from deserting the militant camp. At least eight women cadres, including six from Shiltong and West Khasi Hills and two from Pynursla in East Khasi Hills, have remained in Bangladesh, according to police sources. "But they are prevented by their top leaders," police say.
- July 15: A HNLC cadre, Diam Salon, surrenders at Jowai police station in the Jaintia Hills district. The surrendered militant escaped from his camp in Bangladesh.
- July 6: At least 435 HNLC cadres were killed, surrendered or arrested by the police personnel so far, says Inspector General of Police, B. L. Buam. Out of the total, 289 were arrested, 27 died in encounters, while 119 surrendered.
- June 29: At least three HNLC militants, including one of their leaders identified as Khrawbor Lartang alias Kordor, Lumbor Nongneng alias Pdit and Precious Star Lamare alias Kos, surrender before the East Khasi Hills district police in Shillong, the State capital.
- June 25: At least ten HNLC cadres, who surrender in the North Tripura district of Tripura on June 21, are brought back and remanded to ten-day police custody at Shillong, the State capital.

- June 23: Two unidentified HNLC cadres are shot dead in an encounter with the police at Nonghyllam near Nongjri village in the West Khasi Hills district. While another militant manages to escape, one carbine, one pistol and few rounds of ammunitions are recovered from the encounter site. According to intelligence reports, the HNLC militants infiltrated into the Indian territory from Bangladesh.
- June 21: At least ten HNLC cadres, including a senior leader, surrender before the Border Security Force personnel at an unspecified place in the North Tripura district of Tripura. The surrendered militants, who desert their camp in Bangladesh, were identified as West Syngkli, Bamut-lang Chyne, Coverland Lar-tang, Oswald Nengnong, Erest Wanshnong, George Tang-sang, Peter Kharmawphlang, Fullmoon Nongsiej, Shemphang Syiem-iong and Larsemson Jala.
- June 19: Two suspected HNLC cadres, Minot and Tensing, are arrested at an unspecified place under Halidayganj police station in the Dhubri district along the India-Bangladesh border, while infiltrating.
- June 15: Two HNLC cadres, Minot Lang and Tensing Khngla, are arrested by the BSF personnel near Makamtilla under Patherkandi block in the Karimganj district while crossing the India-Bangladesh border. Both reportedly were trying to reach the Khasi Hills of Meghalaya through the adjoining Cachar district. They reveal during interrogation that most militant outfits with camps in Bangladesh are planning to push in more cadres to the Indian territory through the border during the monsoon.
- June 2: A HNLC cadre, Tibor Dkhar alias Ban, who left his hideout at Puthisara in Bangladesh, surrenders at Shillong before the Superintendent of Police of the East Khasi Hills district. An AK 47 rifle, suspected to be abandoned by the HNLC cadres, is recovered from the forest area of the North-Eastern Hill University near Mawlai.
- May 31: The HNLC threatens against persons participating in the forthcoming Municipal elections at Shillong, the State capital. The outfit also expresses 'concern' about ongoing influx into the Jaintia Hills.
- May 24: The MHA asks for the estimation of assets of the top leaders of the Hynniewtrep HNLC including its 'chairman' Julius K Dorphang, 'general secretary' Cherishsterfield Thangkhiew and self-styled 'Commander-in-Chief' Bobby Marwein. Official sources say that the MHA is also assessing the activities of the outfit to ensure that it does not indulge in extortion from the businessmen.

- May 1 : Chief Minister D. D. Lapang says that the proposal for peace talks with the HNLC is a better option than seeing the outfit members surrendering. Lapang, while expressing the State Government's willingness to hold talks with the militant outfits, said, "There is nothing to hide and it is true that I had a telephonic conservation with HNLC Chairman Julius Dorphang on the issues related to peace talks."
- April 30 : The Meghalaya Home Department says that insincerity of the 'commander-in-chief' of the HNLC is the main reason for the State Government delaying the peace process. According to Home Department sources, "We have no doubt about the sincerity of the outfit's chairman Julius K Dorphang; but we have got some doubts about Bobby Marwein, who often indulges in illegal activities despite making the initial move for peace process." The sources add that the Union and State Governments are keen to have a cease-fire with the banned outfit, but given the present situation, "both are of the view that the process should be re-examined before arriving at any decision".
- April 27: The Chief Executive Member of the Khasi Hills Autonomous District Council, H. S. Shylla, criticizes the threat of the HNLC to pull out of the proposed peace talks with the Meghalaya Government in protest against the letter's permission for Uranium mining at Domiasiat in the West Khasi Hills district.
- March 27: Meghalaya Chief Minister D.D. Lapang, while responding to the issue of negotiations with militant outfits, informs the Legislative Assembly that a "Joint Monitoring Group (JMG) has been formed to monitor the cease-fire with the ANVC. The next JMG meeting will be held on April 5 in Guwahati, said, while adding that, "We are thinking of adopting similar pattern as the first step to initiate dialogue with HNLC."
- March 27: A former HNLC cadre, Aibor Marwein, is shot at and wounded at Mawlai Nongkwar Block III in the Shillong city. Marwein was arrested in 2002 while being an active HNLC cadre.
- March 24: The Union Home Minister Shivraj Patil, while responding at Shillong to the issue of the reported willingness of the proscribed HNLC to negotiate with the Government, says, "Doors are open for dialogue with any militant group."
- March 21: An HNLC cadre, Khrawkupar Shytla alias Khro, is arrested from Mawlai Nongk-war in the East Khasi Hills district. He confesses about the involvement of HNLC in arms smuggling in Meghalaya.

- March 17: Meghalaya Director General Police, W.R. Marbaniang, says that an unspecified number of misguided youths from West Khasi Hills and other areas have joined the banned HNLC.
- February 21: The Jaintia Hills district police arrest three HNLC cadres, Arwat Kharumnuid alias Jo Swer, Robert Jiteng alias Bah Bah and Khlainbor Pakyntein alias Heprrt, from a camp of coal miners at Jaliaphet. However, two of them subsequently escaped from police custody.
- February 21 : The Church leader, Rev. Basaiawmoit, who was appointed by the State Government to broker peace with the HNLC, establishes contacts with the top leaders of the proscribed outfit and intimates about the Government's desire to have a dialogue with them. He says, "Today (Tuesday) evening, I conveyed the HNLC leadership the outcome of my meeting with the Chief Minister and the State Home Minister."
- February 18: A HNLC cadre, Pynshngaifilang Lyngdoh Mairang, surrenders before Mairang Police in the West Khasi Hills district.
- February 3: A suspected HNLC cadre, who is arrested from Jowai in the Jaintia Hills district, manages to escape during an accident involving the security convoy carrying him near Mawryngkneng.
- January 30: Hardcore HNLC militants take shelter in the Block-l areas along the Assam-Meghalaya border for raising funds for the outfit. The militants have reportedly sneaked into the State from Bangladesh for revitalising the outfit. A militant, Hopeborn Shangpliang, who has surrendered during the second week of January, confesses to have regrouped the militants in the Jaintia Hills district for extortion from the coal traders. A senior police officer says, "The HNLC militants chose Block-l as their area of operation so that the Meghalaya police would not be able to know about their movements."
- January 20: A HNLC militant, Hopeborn Shangpliang, surrenders before police personnel at Jowai in the Jaintia Hills district. He deposits a 9 mm pistol and 10 rounds of live ammunition. Police sources say that the militant, a self-style sergeant of the outfit, had joined the HNLC in 1999. He left the outfit's camp in Bangladesh in 2005 and since then has been operating from Psiar in Block I area of the Jaintia Hills district.
- January 16: The 'publicity secretary' of the HNLC, Sainkupar Nongtraw, expresses doubts over the seriousness of the Meghalaya Government in dealing with the issue of illegal migrants. Nongtraw

claims that the action of the State police in flushing out illegal immigrants as published in newspapers is "an eyewash" and a "fashion show". He further says: "If the State and the Central governments had the responsibility to flush out immigrants who have illegally entered the State, why they took 34 years to initiate measures. May be it is the government which has provided them with land, houses, jobs and at the same time recognised them as the legal immigrants settled in Umpling, Pynthor, Mawprem and other localities of Shillong".

January 8: A senior HNLC cadre, Bashembha Pathaw, is arrested from Psiar village on the Meghalaya-Assam border in the Jaintia Hills district. Ten AK-47 ammunition are recovered from his possession.

2005

- December 23: Meghalaya Police arrests 'vice-chairman' of the HNLC, Teilang Thangkhiew, from a hideout at Pohkseh in the capital Shillong. Police sources say that Thangkhiew returned from Bangladesh a few days back to revitalise the outfit following the arrest and surrender of more than hundred cadres during the recent years.
- December 2: Church leader, Rev. Basaiawmoit, says that the proscribed HNLC is awaiting an official response either from the Prime Minister's Office or the Union Home Ministry to initiate peace talks.

  "After proper consultation with the Home Ministry officials I created a channel through which the HNLC was immediately contacted with the hope of ending the decade-long insurgency problem and bring peace and normalcy back to the Khasi-Jaintia Hills and the State as a whole. I have communicated HNLC's views to the Centre but the latter is yet to respond to it", he says.
- November 3: HNLC is reported to be involved in extortion activities targeting coal traders of the Jaintia Hills district. The police arrest two persons, president of the Meghalaya Transporters and Suppliers Union, Jamrist Rymbai, and his colleague, Chamik Nongpluh, from Lad Rymbai for their connivance with the outfit's extortion activities. Police sources say that the arrested persons have served an extortion note of Rupees 16 lakh (INR) on a coal merchant on behalf of the outfit.
- November 1: The proscribed HNLC, in an e-mail to the local media in Meghalaya's capital Shillong, refutes reports that speculate the surrender of the outfit's 'commander-in-chief' Bobby Marwein and some other cadres. The 'publicity secretary' of the outfit, Sainkupar Nongkhlaw, says, "There are forces who want to create cracks in

our organization and the reports are at their instance... Reports about our c-in-c's surrender is part of the propaganda waged by the forces against the council."

- September 27: Julius K Dorphang, 'chairman' of the HNLC, expresses his keenness for peace talks with the Union Government. The surrendered 'publicity secretary' of the outfit, Mihsalan Kynjing, says that HNLC has made some attempts in the past to initiate peace talks and some members of the group have reportedly met officials of the Union Home Ministry in 2004.
- July 27: The surrendered 'finance secretary' of the HNLC, Yitjanai Sunn alias Iainehskhem Shylla, reports that 200 HNLC cadres, including 10 women, presently camping in Bangladesh, are in a state of disarray. He also claims that the outfit is going through a major financial crisis and at present it has only Rupees 20 lakh in its coffers. He also says that 20 cadres have become victims of fratricidal clashes in Bangladesh and five to six of them died due to malaria. He also confirms that there is a tie-up between the HNLC and NDFB.
- July 25: Six HNLC cadres, including the outfit's Finance Secretary Yit Sun alias Iaineh Skhem Shylla, surrender before the police in Shillong. The others are identified as Donald Wann alias Lumlang from Jaiaw Mawbynna, Elvin alias Treng Saw from Mawlai Syllaikariah, Kohbah from Mawlai Mawtawar, Hamar Ropmay alias Hep Tatoo from Mawlai Nongpdeng and Phyrnai Nongrum alias Bahlieh from Mawlai Umjaiur. The HNLC, however, in a statement issued by 'Information Secretary' Mangkara Dkhar claims that the six have "deserted" its temporary camp. It also charges them with indulging in misuse of power, stealing of official property and violating the principles of the outfit.
- July 22: The police arrest a surrendered cadre of the HNLC, James Sylliang, from Mawlai in the capital Shillong. According to police sources, Sylliang is arrested after complaints are lodged against him for involvement in criminal activities, including extortion.
- July 12: Meghalaya Police says that HNLC leaders are living safely in Bangladesh and are also involved in business activities in that country. The East Khasi Hills district Superintendent of Police, A. S. Rynjah, says, "They (leaders of the banned Hynniewtrep National Liberation Council (HNLC) militant outfit), are living in safe rented houses in Dhaka, Maulavi Bazar and Panai areas." Citing intelligence inputs, he further said that insurgent leaders are also engaged in

business activities by acquiring farms of betel nuts, betel and arecanut in the border villages.

- July 11: Meghalaya Police rescues a trader, Mainak Dey, who was abducted two days earlier from Lawbah village in the East Khasi Hills district. Official sources said that subsequent to an encounter with HNLC cadres, he was rescued. An unidentified HNLC cadre is killed in the encounter and another is arrested while four others manage to escape. One rifle, one shotgun, one country-made pistol, one hand grenade and some incriminating documents are recovered from the incident site.
- June 29: Unknown assailants kill a surrendered HNLC militant, Oli Syiemlieh, near Mawsynram in the East Khasi Hills district. The victim was missing since June 27 and his body with several injuries was recovered from a forest area in Nongtrai.
- June 21: A hardcore HNLC cadre, Forekest Hahshah, surrenders before the Superintendent of Police of West Khasi Hills district at Nongstoin. According to official sources, Hahshah has fled from his camp in Bangladesh recently.
- June 11: A group of unidentified gunmen kill a surrendered HNLC cadre, identified as Pyngtngenlang Tariang alias Bah Bah Panai, near Umkrem village in the East Khasi Hills district. The dead body of Tariang is recovered on the next day.
- June 3: Meghalaya Chief Minister, D. D. Lapang, assures all possible help to Church leader P. B. M. Basiawmoit in his efforts to bring the HNLC to the negotiating table. The Chief Minister says, "We appreciate and admire the move of Mr Basiawmoit and the government will extend all possible helps for him." Lapang further indicates that he has requested the Union Government to speed up the process with the HNLC.
- May 25: Suspected HNLC and NDFB cadres abduct a trader from Moosyiem village in the Jaintia Hills district. They also shot at and injured the trader's brother before escaping.
- April 27: A HNLC cadre belonging to the 'finance wing' of the outfit, identified as Teiskhem Sun, is arrested from the Mawlai area. Subsequent to information provided by Sun, police recover an AK-47 rifle along with 30 rounds of ammunition from a forest area near Umsning in the Ri-Bhoi district.
- April 26: Two HNLC cadres belonging to the finance wing' of the outfit, identified as David Mylliem Umlong and Golden Pathaw, are arrested from the Lewduh and Mawlai Umjaipur areas respectively.

- March 30: HNLC approaches the Union Government for peace talks and in this regard, sends four cadres of the outfit to New Delhi to initiate the peace process. Confirming this, State Home Minister, Mukul Sangma says, "We are expecting some positive outcome regarding the latest development. Details will be made available at the right time."
- March 30: A tribunal makes recommendations for the extension of the proscription on the HNLC and ANVC for another year.
- March 28: Bangla Dhar alias Bang, a senior HNLC cadre, allegedly involved in extortion activities in Dawki and other border areas, surrenders before the Superintendent of Police of East Khasi Hills district.
- March 25: Suspected HNLC cadres abduct Man Bahadur Pradhan, manager of a coal export firm of Sutnga in the Jaintia Hills district.
- February 16: An unidentified 'area commander' of the HNLC is lynched by villagers of Sohkymphor in the Jaintia Hills district. He was allegedly involved in extortion activities in the area.
- January 30: A suspected HNLC cadre is arrested at Jowai in the Jaintia Hills district.
- January 24: An eight-member group suspected to be linked to the HNLC loot Rupees 93 lakh from the Meghalaya Co-operative Apex Bank branch at Khliehriat in Jaintia Hills district. The Meghalaya Director-General of Police, L. Sailo, confirming the link between the group and the HNLC says, "They owe allegiance to the HNLC in some form or the other."
- January 14: Meghalaya Police arrests a HNLC militant, Kobarlan Snaitang, from Pyndensohsaw near Mawsynram in the East Khasi Hills district.
- January 7: Seven HNLC cadres, who surrendered before the Border Security Force authorities at an unspecified place in the State of Mizoram, are likely to be brought back to Shillong on January 8.

2004

- December 22: The Union Government extends the ban on two militant outfits of Meghalaya, the ANVC and HNLC. In an official notification in Shillong, the Union Home Ministry cites the reasons for extension stating that although the ANVC agrees to abjure violence and expresses willingness for talks within the framework of Constitution, it continues "collection of funds and extortion, acquisition of sophisticated weapons and recruitment of new cadre."

For HNLC, the notification says, it openly declares its "secessionist" objective, engaged in armed means to achieve the objective, indulged in intimidation, extortion and looting of civilians for collection of funds for the organisation. Both the outfits, according to the notification, maintain links with other insurgent groups of the North-east region for collecting weapons, carrying out violence, extortion, intimidation and looting besides having camps in some neighbouring countries for "sanctuary, training and clandestine procurement of arms and ammunition."

- December 19: Two surrendered HNLC cadres, Barlin Kharnoir and Firestar Rapsang, are arrested on charges of car-lifting from the Bara Bazaar area of capital Shillong.
- December 15: A HNLC cadre, Spurfield Suting alias Phlex, surrenders before the police at Borsora in the West Khasi Hills district.
- December 13: A hardcore HNLC cadre, Deningstar Rapsang, surrenders before the Meghalaya Home Minister, H.D.R Lyngdoh. He deposits one AK-56 rifle along with three magazines, one M-20 pistol and another 73 rounds of live ammunition. According to police sources, the outfit's 'commander-in-chief, Bobby Marwein, deputed Rapsang to raise extortion money from the capital Shillong.
- December 10: HNLC blames its surrendered cadres for the killing of five HNLC activists in its Bangladesh camps. A statement issued by its 'secretary of information and communication', Mangkara Dkhar, said: "Such policy by the authorities would lead to problems in bringing peace in the State."
- November 17: Meghalaya Police arrests a senior HNLC cadre from Pyndensohsaw near Mawsynram in the East Khasi Hills district.
- November 4: Four extortionists with alleged links with HNLC arrested in the capital city of Shillong.
- October 15: A security guard of the HNLC 'General Secretary' C Thangkhiew surrenders before the police at Pynursla outpost in East Khasi Hills district along with two hand grenades and one SBBL gun.
- October 1: HNLC terrorists shot at a taxi driver at Cheruphi in Jaintia Hilfs district.
- September 29: Police arrest three suspected HNLC cadres, who claimed to be members of the newly formed Hynniewtrep National Youth Front Tiger Force, from Ladthalaboh in Jaintia Hills district.
- September 16: Security forces arrest an HNLC cadre, Shanbor Warjri, from the Mawlai Mawdatbaki area in the capital city of Shillong.

- September 3: A HNLC cadre surrenders to the police at Jowai in the Jaintia Hills district.
- August 30: Police recovers 10 rounds of AK ammunition from the house of a HNLC cadre at Mawlai Motsyiar in the capital city of Shillong.
- August 30: A HNLC cadre, identified as Khlainbor Pakyntein, is arrested from Mawlai Motsyiar in the East Khasi Hills district.
- August 29: Unknown miscreants damage the vehicle of a surrendered HNLC cadre at Jaiaw Langsning in Shillong.
- August 24: A HNLC terrorist, identified as Sadelbert Thongni, surrenders before the police at Nongstoin in the West Khasi Hills district.
- August 3: Twenty-eight HNLC militants surrender before Chief Minister D. D. Lapang in Shillong.
- June 28: Meghalaya Police arrests three HNLC terrorists who crossed over to Meghalaya from the West Khasi Hills border of Bangladesh to extort money from coal exporters of the Borosora area in the State.
- May 18: Five HNLC cadres surrender in Mizoram before the Border Security Force.
- May 3: Reports indicate that the HNLC charges its surrendered cadres for extorting money from the people in the name of the outfit in collusion with the State police.
- March 31 : A surrendered HNLC terrorist, identified as Ibor Marwein, is arrested from the Khasi Hills Autonomous District Council office in Shillong along with one 9 mm pistol and some ammunition.
- April 30: At least eleven HNLC cadres surrender at a Border Security Force camp in Mizoram, bordering Bangladesh.
- March 16: 28 HNLC terrorists, including two women cadres, lay down arms before Meghalaya Chief. Minister D D Lapang at the Meghalaya Police Training Center at Mawiong in the East Khasi Hills district.
- January 30: Eight HNLC cadres, including top leaders Armstrong Lyngdoh and Kitdor, surrender before the Home Minister RG Lyngodh.
- January 14: Fourteen HNLC cadres surrender before the Meghalaya Chief Minister D.D. Lapang in Shillong.

2003

- December 30: Two HNLC terrorists are arrested near the Bangladesh-Tripura border while on their way to Meghalaya via Tripura.

- November 3: Meghalaya Police arrest two office bearers of the Archery Sports Association (ASA) in the capital Shillong for reportedly contributing money to the proscribed HNLC after collecting funds illegally.
- November 2: A hardcore HNLC terrorist is arrested from the Mawlai Syllaikariah area near capital Shillong.
- October 17: Meghalaya Police arrests one HNLC terrorist during raid in the premises of North Eastern Hill University (NEHU) at Shillong.
- October 15: HNLC 'publicity wing' chief, Edward Charles Synrier, is arrested, from a cyber cafe capital Shillong.
- October 1: Meghalaya Police arrests three HNLC terrorist from a hideout near Unium River in the East Khasi Hills district.
- September 27: HNLC 'commander-in-chief' (Western Command), Delphinus Myrthong alias Khraw is killed during an encounter near Nongstoin in the West Khasi Hills district.
- September 24: Meghalaya Chief Minister Lapang offers truce to the ANVC and HNLC.
- September 22: Union Government blocks an HNLC discussion group on the Internet through which the outfit was circulating its newsletter, *The Voice.*
- August 20: Meghalaya Police arrests Mardor Bamon, 'political secretary' of the HNLC from Mawlai.
- August 16: Suspected HNLC terrorists attack police training school at Golf Links, Shillong, with hand grenade.
- July 29: HNLC 'chairman' Julius Dorphang refutes Government's claim over surrender of top cadres and asks the police to reveal the identity of its cadres who have either surrendered or are arrested.
- July 9: Police file FIR under the Unlawful Activities Act for funding the proscribed Hynniewtrep National Liberation Council (HNLC) against 79 businessmen in Meghalaya.
- June 14: Meghalaya Police arrests Paul Lyngdoh, second in command in the finance wing of HNLC from a hideout near Nongthymmai in Shillong.
- June 7: Meghalaya Police arrests two HNLC terrorists, including the 'general secretary' of HNLC's finance wing, at the Nongrim Hills locality, responsible for spreading the extortion network in the Khasi hills and Ri Bhoi districts.
- May 22: Security force personnel arrest a woman HNLC cadre identified as Blister Mary Kurban from Mawngap in the East Khasi Hills district.

- May 14: HNLC 'assistant finance secretary' Heston Bohphang is arrested from his residence at Umpling in the capital Shillong.
- April 19: Two HNLC suspects are killed and three more arrested following an encounter at Maw-pud-village, East Garo Hills district.
- April 23: Security forces apprehend two unidentified HNLC terrorists near Williamnagar, East Garo Hills district.
- March 17: Media reports indicate that HNLC has resumed its extortion drive in the Garo Hills area after maintaining a low profile for approximately a year.
- March 22: Security forces arrest two HNLC terrorists at Mawlai, East Khasi Hills district, and recover three AK 47 rifles, 24 rounds of live cartridges and five magazines.
- March 24: The Shitlong Khasi-Jaintia Church Leaders' Forum (SKJCLF) Chairman Bishop Purely. Lyngdoh announces that the forum is likely to discuss, among others, a peace initiative with the HNLC during a meeting on March 27.
- March 4: HNLC suspects kill a police personnel at Wahthapabru, near Mission compound area Shillong, in East Khasi Hills district.
- February 12: Police unearth a HNLC arms dump, including a carbine, a stengun, 48 bullets of M-16 rifle, 48 rounds of AK series and 103 rounds of hunting rifles, among others, near Wahingdoh, Shillong, East Khasi Hills district.
- February 5: A HNLC arms dump is unearthed near Wahumkhrah River in Shillong. Two AK 56 rifles, an AK 47 rifle, three carbines and unspecified quantity of ammunition are seized from the dump.
- January 29: Police recover arms and ammunition, including an M-16 rifle, a semi-automatic rifle, 41 rounds of M-16 ammunition, 15 rounds of 7.62 ammunition and some incriminating documents among others, from a HNLC terrorist at Distar Marbaniang, in Washingdoh, Shillong, East Khasi district.
- January 18: Reports indicate that 15 HNLC terrorists have sneaked into Meghalaya from Bangladesh to carry out terrorist strikes ahead of the Republic Day on January 26.
- January 10: The SKJCLF urges both the Government and HNLC to hold unconditional talks.
- January 4: In a New Year message, the HNLC reiterates its aim to achieve freedom' for the Hynniewtrep people.
- January 3: Union Home Ministry extends ban under Unlawful Activities (Prevention) Act of 1967 on the ANVC and HNLC in Meghalaya.

2002

- December 23: One HNLC terrorist is killed during an encounter at Qualapatty, East Khasi Hills district.
- December 9: Some 20 HNLC terrorists sneak into Meghalaya, armed with sophisticated weapons, through the porous Indo-Bangladesh border in West Khasi Hills to carry out subversive activities in the region.
- December 7: Meghalaya police arrest four HNLC terrorists from Jaiaw and Mawlai areas and recover a Sten gun and 20 rounds of live ammunition from one of the hideouts of the outfit at Jaiaw.
- December 3: Police arrest Welcome Nongkynrih, a trusted associate of HNLC area commander James, in Mawlai Umjaiur, Meghalaya.
- November 27: A Special Operations Team of Meghalaya police arrests two Hynniewtrep National Liberation Council terrorists identified as Roland Syiemlieh and Banwansuk Nongkseh in Lower Lachumiere area, and recovers a huge cache of arms and ammunition after raiding a hideout, in Mawlai Nongpdeng. The catch includes 591 rounds of M-16 ammunition, two Chinese made hand grenades, a .32 pistol, 5 rounds of SLR ammunition and an AK-47 magazine.
- November 4: HNLC warns the Nationalist Congress Party (NCP)-led government in Meghalaya against counter-terrorism measures and police excesses.
- November 1 : HNLC suffers setback following the largest arms seizure by Meghalaya police. State police unearth a hideout at Khlaw Roman, in Mawlai Nongpdeng, Shillong, and seize 663 ammunition rounds of various makes. The seizure includes 460 rounds of M-16 and 169 rounds of AK-47 ammunition, two Chinese-made high-explosive grenades, a round of SLR 7.62 (self loading rifles), .27 bore cartridges and three rounds of .303 ammunition.
- October 11: Five HNLC terrorists armed with AK-47 rifles kill Kilas Momin, a police personnel in Mawlai Nonglum, Shillong.
- August 27: An HNLC terrorist is seriously injured in an encounter in Mawkriah village, near Shillong while another arrested.
- August 24: Two HNLC terrorists are arrested by the State police in Nongthymmai, near Shillong. The dead body of a suspected HNLC terrorist is found in Shillong.
- August 15: Security arrangements throughout Meghalaya are tightened to ensure the smooth celebration of Independence Day, following a 24-hour *bandh* (general strike) call given by the HNLC and the People's Liberation Front. Chief Minister F A Khonglam

renews his invitation, on the occasion of Independence day, to terrorists groups in the State "to come to the negotiation table and sort out differences in a peaceful manner."

- August 6: Security forces in Meghalaya arrest eight HNLC terrorists from Mawlai, Shillong. The East Khasi Hills district police chief says those arrested are mostly teenagers and add that it confirms that the HNLC is recruiting teenagers into its fold.
- July 1: Meghalaya police arrest an HNLC terrorist from the 3rd milestone, Upper Shillong. An AK 47 rifle, a Smooth Bore Breech Loading (SBBL) gun, a country made revolver, ammunition and incriminating documents are recovered from him.
- June 3: Two HNLC terrorists are arrested in Shillong and another suspected HNLC terrorist in Nongthyllep village, near Mairang, West Khasi Hills.
- May 13: Meghalaya Director General of Police (DGP) L Sailo claims that the HNLC stood marginalised in the state.
- May 8: HNLC terrorists warn all outsiders doing business in Meghalaya to pay 'fixed taxes' and threaten them with 'severe punishment', leading to 'imprisonment and being driven out of the Hynniewtrep land' in case of resistance. The terrorist group also promises to negotiate with those businessmen who found it difficult to pay the 'taxes'.
- April 2: Meghalaya Deputy Chief Minister D D Lapang says the government is unable to spell the terms and conditions for talks with the Hynniewtrep National Liberation Council (HNLC) terrorist outfit as the latter failed to give any positive indication to the government's proposal.
- March 27: Eight HNLC terrorists, on their way to Bangladesh for arms training, arrested from Siatbakon Road.
- March 18: HNLC terrorist Mardor Eamon arrested by Shillong Police and the Special Operations Team (SOT) of Lum Jingshai in Shillong.
- March 16: HNLC terrorist arrested following a raid at Mawlai Umjaiw in Shillong.
- March 6: HNLC terrorists attack the East Khasi Hills district police chiefs office.
- February 16: Three HNLC cadres killed in an encounter at Smrt, East Khasi Hills.
- January 23: HNLC terrorist killed in an encounter and three others arrested at Riatmidi, bordering Mawiai Nangodeng and Mawlai Motsyiar.

- January 10: HNLC terrorist escapes from Lumdiengjri Police Station.
- January 9: Suspected HNLC terrorist killed in retaliatory firing by the police at Lumshai, Shillong.
- January 5: Four HNLC terrorists, including a local 'commander', arrested after an encounter at Shangpung in Jaintia Hills district. Three HNLC terrorists arrested after another encounter at Umsing in Ribhoi district.

2001

- December 21 : HNLC terrorist arrested in Shillong.
- November 12: Two HNLC terrorists arrested by the Shillong Special Operation Team (SOT) at the seventh mile stone in Shillong.
- November 11 : Suspected HNLC terrorists kill one of their own cadres at Panaliar, Jaintia Hills district.
- October 23: HNLC Chairman Julius K. Dorphang discloses that Ching Thangkhiew, the 'Commander-in-Chief of the North East Red Army (NERA), now a defunct outfit, had been "eliminated" because he was assisting the security forces and the RSS against the interests of the HNLC.
- March 28: Two police personnel killed in an encounter with HNLC terrorists near Jaiaw Longsuing, in Shillong.
- March 4: Seng Khasi leader Rijoy Khongshah, was abducted earlier on March 1, 2001, killed by HNLC terrorists.
- February 19: The outfit, in a statement, opposes Census operations in the State and threatens to eliminate enumerators participating in the process.
- January 19: HNLC terrorists attack a police outpost in Shillong and kill two police personnel.
- January 9: Two security guards of a nationalised bank killed in an attack by HNLC terrorists at Mawsynram village.
- January *5:* Five civilians killed and four others injured in an attack by HNLC terrorists on a business establishment in Shillong.

2000

- August 15: Police personnel killed and another injured when fleeing HNLC terrorists fire at security forces.
- August 14: Three CRPF personnel injured as HNLC cadres fire around 600 rounds into the air and also in the direction of the CRPF camp in the State capital Shillong.

PEOPLE'S LIBERATION FRONT OF MEGHALAYA (PLF-M)

Formation

People's Liberation Front of Meghalaya (PLF-M) is a relatively new terrorist group operating in the Garo Hills of Meghalaya. Reports suggest that the outfit has been re-christened as the Achik National Council (ANC). When the Hynniewtrep Achik Liberation Council (HALC) split in 1992, it resulted in the formation of the Hynniewtrep National Liberation Council (HNLC), which represents the Khasis in Meghalaya, and the Achik Liberation Matgrik Army (ALMA), which wanted a separate Garoland State for the Garos. The PLF-M is an offshoot of this Achik Liberation Matgrik Army (ALMA). Most of the ALMA terrorists surrendered in 1994, but a few formed the Achik National Volunteers' Council (ANVC) in 1995. The PLF-M consists of some of these "surrendered rebels" of the erstwhile ALMA who returned underground after their rehabilitation scheme failed. The exact strength of the outfit is not known.

Objectives

The claimed objective of the PLF-M is economic development of the Garo Hills, as well as better educational opportunities for the Garo tribes in Meghalaya. It also demands a separate state for the Garos. In this regard, Chengku Momin, the 'minister for information and publicity' of the PLF-M had warned all the non-Garos, in March 2001, not to contest the State Assembly and district council elections slated for 2003.

Leadership

The chairman of the outfit is Vincent Sangma and Nimush Marak is the 'Commander in Chief'. Besides that L K Sangma is one of the 'area commanders'.

Area of Operation

The outfit is primarily active in Dainadubi, Williamnagar, in East Garo Hills, and Dalu in West Garo Hills. Among its activities include extortion of money to generate funds for its activities. In July 2000, the PLF-M had slapped extortion notices even on some Member of Legislative Assemblies (MLAs) and including two ministers, from the Garo Hills.

Linkages

The PLF-M reportedly maintains close connections with the Achik National Volunteer Council (ANVC).

What follows is a look at Meghalaya terrorism picture is 2006 :

- Meghalaya Assessment—Year 2006
- Meghalaya Timeline—2006.

MEGHALAYA ASSESSMENT—YEAR 2006

Year 2006 has seen a continuation in the trend of decreasing militant violence in Meghalaya, a trend discernible since 2002. A total of 20 persons have died in the year (till September 17), including five civilians and 15 militants. Seven militants were arrested and 20 of them have surrendered till September 15, 2006.

Fatalities in Terrorist Violence - 2006

	Civilians	*Security Force Personnel*	*Terrorist*	*Total*
January	0	0	0	0
February	2	0	0	2
March	1	0	1	2
April	0	0	1	1
May	0	0	1	1
June	0	0	8	8
July	0	0	4	4
August	2	0	0	2
September*	0	0	0	0
Total	5	0	15	20

*Data till September 17, 2006

Source: Institute for Conflict Management database.

Following are some of the militancy-related incidents in Meghalaya in 2006:

January 21: Two traders, Ramashanker Sahu and Nepal Saha, were abducted by unidentified armed militants while returning from a weekly market at Dalu in the Garo Hills district.

February 5: A businessman, P. Saha, is shot dead after being dragged out of a passenger bus coming from Tura to Baghmara and the driver is wounded by Achik National Liberation Front (ANLF) cadres at a place near Sibbari in the South Garo Hills district.

February 13: The Superintendent of Bholaganj Land Custom Station, identified as J. Das, was abducted and later killed by suspected militants. His dead body was recovered from Bholaganj along the India-Bangladesh border fencing area in the East Khasi Hills district.

May 14: A woman was abducted by the ANLF militants from Rangran in the West Khasi Hills district. The South Garo Hills district police rescued her later on May 16 following an encounter killing a cadre of the outfit. A Self-Loading Rifle with a magazine and two live ammunition shells were recovered from the encounter site.

April 26: Two senior State customs officials, Superintendent D. Bora and Inspector Mrinal Sharma, were abducted by suspected United Achik National Front (UANF) cadres from Baburambeel border area in the West Garo Hills district, and were kept hostage in Bangladesh. A day after, an extortion note demanding INR 15 million was received from militants across the India-Bangladesh border by officials of the Gasuapara Customs Land Station for release of the two abducted officials. Following the intervention of the Union Ministry of Home Affairs, they were rescued and handed over by the Bangladesh Rifes to the Government of India on May 14.

May 28: Suspected UANF cadres abduct a nine-year old boy, Vaibhav Singh, from the Fancy Valley locality of Tura, headquarters of the West Garo Hills District.

May 29: A person, Hari Das, was abducted by suspected militants from Beldarpara under Tura police station in the West Garo Hills district.

June 21: Two Achik National Liberation Front cadres, identified as Amelush Momin and Arben Sangma, are shot dead in an encounter with police personnel at Nangalbibra in the South Garo Hills district.

The Achik National Volunteer Council (ANVC), under a cease-fire agreement with the Union Government since July 23, 2004, reportedly reiterated its demand for the formation of a separate state known as 'Garoland State' for the Garos in Meghalaya. The 'publicity secretary' of the outfit, Arist Sengsrang Sangma, said that it is high time for all Garos to come under one umbrella and demand a separate state.

Meanwhile, Chief Minister D. D. Lapang, on March 27, declared, "A Joint Monitoring Group (JMG) has been framed to monitor the cease-fire with ANVC. The next JMG meeting will be held on April 5 in Guwahati. We are thinking of adopting similar pattern as the first step to initiate dialogue with HNLC." Accordingly, the JMG meeting was held in Guwahati where it was decided to conduct a joint survey for setting up a designated camp for the ANVC cadres in the South Garo Hills of Meghalaya by the end of April 2006. The existing camp at Jetra in the Ri Bhoi district was decided to be dismantled following complaints from paramilitary forces. The three-member ANVC delegation led by its 'general secretary' Wanding K. Marak reportedly demanded revocation of the ban imposed on it by the Union Government and initiation of a political dialogue by claiming substantial improvement in the law and order situation in Garo Hills. The request for lifting the ban was later negatively responded by Meghalaya Home Minister H. Donkupar R Lyngdoh, who said, "Let people be satisfied with their non-violence and peaceful existence... No doubt, the illegal activity of the ANVC has reduced to a great extent; but until people are satisfied, the ban should continue."

Prospects for peace with the Hynniewtrep National Liberation Council (HNLC), however, have remained bleak in spite of efforts by the State Government and the Church. In the last week of April 2006, the HNLC chairman Julius K Dorphang requested Chief Minister D. D. Lapang to urge the Centre to expedite the peace process. However, due to reported reservations expressed by the Meghalaya Police to start a dialogue process with a beleaguered outfit, the Union Ministry of Home Affairs has not responded to the offer. The outfit, earlier, had threatened to pull out of the proposed peace talks in protest against permission received by the public sector undertaking, the Uranium Corporation of India Ltd, from the State Government as well as the Khasi Hills Autonomous District Council for uranium mining at Domiasiat in the West Khasi Hills district. The State Home Department said that insincerity of the 'commander-in-chief of the HNLC is the main reason for the State Government delaying the peace process. Meanwhile, Chief Minister Lapang said that the proposal for peace talks with the HNLC is a better option than its cadres surrendering. Lapang, while expressing the State Government's willingness to hold talks with the militant outfits, said, "But we have no say on the issues, which are totally depended on the initiative of the Union Home Ministry." He also said, "We have to patiently wait and see things to happen because whatever steps that have been followed with the ANVC, the same thing will be done with HNLC."

Earlier, year 2005 witnessed a continuation of the decline in militant violence in Meghalaya. In 2005, a total of 29 fatalities, including 26 militants, were reported from the State.

Fatalities of Terrorist Violence - 2006

	Civilians	*Security Forces Personnel*	*Terrorists*	*Total*
January	0	0	4	4
February	0	0	1	1
March	0	0	0	0
April	0	0	0	0
May	0	1	7	8
June	2	0	0	2
July	0	0	2	2
August	0	0	1	1
September	0	0	1	1
October	0	0	5	5
November	0	0	5	5
December	0	0	0	0
Total	2	1	26	29

Source: Institute for Conflict Management database.

Comparative Levels of Violence, 2002-2005 : Fatalities

Year	*Civilians*	*Security Forces*	*Militants*	*Total*
2005	2	1	26	29
2004	7	5	23	35
2003	28	5	27	58
2002	29	18	17	64

Source: Institute for Conflict Management database.

A total of 29 militants were arrested in 2005. Among them was the HNLC 'vice-chairman', Teilang Thangkhiew, who was arrested from Pohkseh in the capital Shillong on December 23. In addition, a total of six militants (all from the HNLC), including HNLC 'Finance Secretary' Yit Su alias Iaineh Skhem Shylla, surrendered during 2005.

The cease-fire agreement between the Union Government and ANVC was extended by six months on January 17, 2005. However, this truce extension was followed by the March 30 judgement of a tribunal recommending for the extension of the proscription on the HNLC and ANVC for another year.

Following the cease-fire agreement between the Government and ANVC and the subsequent confinement of the ANVC cadres in the designated camps, the Garo Hills in Meghalaya has been peaceful. Barring few incidents when small breakaway factions have attempted to create disorder, the Garo militancy is gradually fading. However, following the cease-fire with the ANVC, a number of outfits were formed especially in the Garo hills area to fill the vacuum left behind by the ANVC. Prominent among them are the Retrieval Indigenous Unified Front, UANF, UALF, ANLF, Hajong United Liberation Army, etc. Similarly, the Hynniewtrep National Special Red Army started operations in the Khasi Hills area. Though most of these groups have been neutralised through security force actions, activities of the UANF are still discernible. While commenting on the outfit's plan to form an armed wing, the Meghalaya Director-General of Police, W. L. Marbaniang, said April 5, 2006, "It's a criminal gang without having any ideology." The Meghalaya Police also rejected the outfit's claim of having set up an "underground government" as "an attempt by a group of robbers to terrorise people."

Counter-insurgency operations by Meghalaya Police have marginalized the HNLC to a great extent. The outfit's chairman Julius K Dorphang is reportedly holed up in Bangladesh and commands only a small batch of cadres. According to a statement by the State police department in August 2006, "Disillusioned women cadres of the HNLC, who are in an isolated camp in Bangladesh and are desperate to leave the outfit to join the mainstream, are being prevented from deserting the militant camp. At least eight women cadres, including six from Shillong and West Khasi Hills and two from Pynursla in East Khasi Hills, have remained in Bangladesh."

Meghalaya, which shares a 443 kilometers border with Bangladesh, has served as a traditional route for Bangladesh-based militants operating in India's Northeast. All of Meghalaya's districts (West Garo Hills, South Garo Hills, West Khasi Hills, East Khasi Hills and Jaintia Hills), barring two, East Garo Hills and Ri Bhoi, share borders with Bangladesh. Strategic alliances between home grown militant groups such as the ANVC and the outfits operating in the neighbouring States, such as the United Liberation Front of Asom (ULFA) and the National Democratic Front of Bodoland (NDFB), compound Meghalaya's problems. The ANVC, before it entered into a ceasefire with the Government, assisted such outfits in exploiting the ruggedness of the Garo Hills to play host to militants in transit, and to transport and store arms and explosives.

In May 2005, an explosives supply network backed by Pakistan's external intelligence agency, the Inter-Services Intelligence (ISI), was unearthed in Lad Rymbai and Khliehriat areas of Jaintia Hills District. The operation came to light following the arrest of Mohammad Hasifuddin from Minkrie village under Khliehriat Police Station on May 15. Over 400 gelatine sticks were recovered from his possession. Hasifuddin had reportedly supplied explosives to ULFA to carry out the blast at Dhemaji on August 15, 2004. Ham Bahadur Thapa, a contractor in the coal mines at Khliehriat was also arrested. Police sources indicate that most of the explosives recovered during the raid had been ferried from across the Bangladesh border.

The Garo Hills have also provided significant routes for drugs and arms smuggling. Little, however, is known about the scale of infiltration of Bangladeshis into the State. According to one estimate, illegal migrants, outnumber locals in the Jaintia coal belt. It further mentioned that most of the foreign nationals entering the State from Assam have spread into the Jaintia Hills coal belt such as Lad Rymbai, Khliehriat and Bapung, while others mingled with the people in mixed populated areas of Shillong. Available data indicates that the State Government's efforts at containing the ongoing infiltration have been handicapped by poor detection and an even poorer record of prosecutions and convictions. According to one report, out of the 14,726 foreigners detected since 2001 till March 3, 2006, only 206 have reportedly been prosecuted under the Foreigners Act, 1946. Meanwhile, Meghalaya Home Minister, H. Donkupar R. Lyngdoh, while responding to a supplementary question raised by a Congress party legislator, Robert Garnett Lyngdoh, on March 21, 2006, informed the State Legislative Assembly that 3,094 infiltrators were detained in 2001 out of which just 54 were prosecuted. In 2002, a total of 2,537 persons were detained on suspicion and 42 of them were convicted. In the 2003, the number of detentions was 2,157 and the conviction figure was 72. The detention figure in 2004 was 1,596 with just 18 convictions. Till March 2006, 1,463 persons had been detected as foreigners and 14 convicted. The Central Forces haven't fared any better. According to a status report submitted by the Border Security Force (BSF) before the Delhi High Court on May 22, 2006, just 31 Bangladeshi nationals were deported from the State between January and April 2006.

Source : http://www.satp.org/satporgtp/countries/india/states/Meghalaya/terrorist-outfits/hnlc.htm

Meghalaya Timeline - 2006

Date	*Incident*
1	*2*
January 2	Two hard-core Achik National Liberation Front (ANLF) militants are arrested by the Army personnel at Chialmari in the East Garo Hills district.
January 8	Senior HNLC cadre, Bashembha Pathaw, is arrested along with ten AK-47 ammunitions from Psiar village on the Meghalaya-Assam border in the Jaintia Hills district.
January 16	HNLC's 'publicity secretary', Sainkupar Nongtraw in a statement says that the State police action of flushing out illegal immigrants in "an eyewash" and a "fashion show".
January 21	Two traders, Ramashanker Sahu and Nepal Saha, are abducted by unidentified armed militants while returning from a weekly market at Dalu in the Garo Hills district.
February 5	A businessman, P. Saha, is shot dead after being dragged out of a passenger bus coming from Tura to Baghmara and the driver is wounded by ANLF cadres at a place near Sibbari in the South Garo Hills district. A civilian, Poritosh Saha, is killed by the UANF cadres in collaboration with cadres of the NDFB at Baghmara in the South Garo Hills district. The militants reportedly stopped a bus coming from Tura to Baghmara and opened fire at the vehicle killing the owner, Poritosh, and later escape to Bangladesh.
February 10	The Union Government brings Meghalaya and Arunachal Pradesh under the Surrender and Rehabilitation Reimbursement scheme apart from the States of Assam, Manipur, Nagaland and Tripura. The scheme, which will be retrospectively effective from April 2005, will provide a stipend of Rupees 2000 per month for three years to each surrendered militant and an immediate grant of Rupees 1.5 lakh.

1	2
February 21	The dead body of the Superintendent of Bholaganj Land Custom Station of Meghalaya, identified as J. Das, was recovered from Bholaganj along the Bangladesh border fencing area in the East Khasi Hills district. According to Press Trust of India, the custom official, who was reportedly missing from February 13, was suspected to be abducted and killed in Bangladesh, and his dead body was later dumped in Meghalaya. The Jaintia Hills district police arrest three HNLC cadres, Arwat Kharumnuid alias Jo Swer, Robert Jiteng alias Bah Bah and Khlainbor Pakyntein alias Heprit, from a camp of coal miners at Jaliaphet. However, two of the arrested militants subsequently escape from police custody.
February 22	Meghalaya Government is to continue its ongoing counter-insurgency operations against the proscribed HNLC in the Khasi and Jaintia Hills area, despite its offer for peace talks. "We do not have any information regarding HNLC's offer to come for talks with the Centre and the State Government," says a senior police official. He adds that as of now it is only a proposal and the outfit is yet to sign a truce agreement with the Government.
February 24	A UALF cadre, identified as Tengsal Sangma alias Joseph Sangma, surrenders before Meghalaya Home Minister H. D. R. Lyngdoh at Shillong. The surrendered militant, hailing from Tura, joined the outfit in 2005 and was trained at the outfit's Durgapur camp in Bangladesh.
March 2	A Hindi teacher, identified as Sohizol Haque, is shot dead by suspected United Achik National Front (UANF) cadres at Ringramgri under Dalu police station in the West Garo Hills district.
March 6	Villagers from Nongjri-Umnuih-Nongshken area along the India-Bangladesh border in the East Khasi Hills district announce the slogan 'Gun down a Bangladeshi criminal and collect Rupees 3000' in protest against the alleged killing of people and looting of agriculture produce by Bangladeshi infiltrators.
March 8	A UALF cadre is shot dead by police personnel while rescuing a businessman held captive at a hideout at Salmanpara in the West Garo Hills district. However, three other militants manage to escape from the incident site.

1	*2*
March 14	Meghalaya Government orders the Jaintia Hills district authorities to suspend fencing work along the India-Bangladesh border in areas where locals have complained that their lands will be falling on the side of Bangladesh territory. Meghalaya Chief Minister D. D. Lapang says it does not mean that the work on fencing will be stopped throughout the border as smuggling of cattle and paddy and infiltration from across are rampant.
March 17	Meghalaya Governor, M.M. Jacob, informs the Legislative Assembly that only 195 km (especially in Garo Hills) of the entire 423 km Meghalaya border with Bangladesh are fenced.
March 21	An HNLC cadre, Khrawkupar Shylla alias Khro, who is arrested from Mawlai Nongk-war in the East Khasi Hills district, confesses about the involvement of the outfit in arms smuggling in Meghalaya.
March 24	The ANVC calls for the formation of a separate state known as 'Garoland State' for the Garos in Meghalaya. The 'publicity secretary' of the outfit, Arist Sengsrang Sangma, said that it is high time for all Garos to come under one umbrella and demand a separate state.
March 27	Chief Minister D. D. Lapang, while responding to the issue of negotiations with the militant outfits, says, " A Joint Monitoring Group (JMG) has been framed to monitor the ceasefire with ANVC. The next JMG meeting will be held on April 5 in Guwahati. We are thinking of adopting similar pattern as the first step to initiate dialogue with HNLC."
April 5	The JMG meeting held at the BSF premises in Guwahati decides to conduct a joint survey for setting up a designated camp for the ANVC cadres in the South Garo Hills of Meghalaya by the end of April 2006. The existing camp at Jetra in the Ri Bhoi district will be dismantled following complaints from paramilitary forces.
	The three-member ANVC delegation led by its 'general secretary' Wanding K. Marak demands a revocation of the ban imposed on it by the Union Government and initiation of a political dialogue by claiming substantial improvement in the law and order situation in Garo Hills.
	Meghalaya Director General of Police, W. L. Marbaniang, while commenting on the involvement of the UANF in

1	2
	extortion activities, says, "It's a criminal gang without having any ideology." The Meghalaya Police also rejected the outfit's claim of having set up an "underground government" as "an attempt by a group of robbers to terrorise people."
April 7	An ANVC cadre is killed by three of his colleagues at Tura in the West Garo Hills district.
April 9	A Bangladeshi infiltrator is killed by local villagers in the West Garo Hills area.
April 10	A Bangladeshi infiltrator is shot dead by the Border Security Force personnel in the West Garo Hills area.
April 16	The eastern zone unit of the KSU 'captures' at least 20 Bangladeshi labourers at Umtrew in the Ri Bhoi district. According to KSU sources, a person, identified as Anthony Pamshong, had brought these labourers from Bangladesh with the advice of an engineer working with the North Eastern Indira Gandhi Regional Institute of Health and Medical Sciences in Shillong.
April 26	Suspected UANF cadres abduct two senior customs officials, Superintendent D. Bora and Inspector Mrinal Sharma, at Baburambeei border area in the West Garo Hills district. The militants drag the two officers out of their vehicle and take them towards the international border with Bangladesh.
April 27	Officials of the Gasuapara Customs Land Station receive an extortion note demanding Rupees 1.5 crores from suspected UANF militants across the India-Bangladesh border for releasing two abducted officials.
	The Chief Executive Member of the Khasi Hills Autonomous District Council, H. S. Shylla, criticizes the threat of the HNLC to pull out of the proposed peace talks with the Meghalaya Government in protest against the letter's permission for Uranium mining at Domiasiat in the West Khasi Hills district.
April 30	Out of the 14,726 foreigners detected since 2001 till March 3, 2006, only 206 have reportedly been prosecuted under the Foreigners Act, 1946. A report said that most of the foreign nationals entering the State from Assam have spread into the Jaintia Hills coal belt such as Lad Rymbai, Khliehriat and Bapung, while others mingled with the people in mixed populated areas of Shillong.

1	*2*
	The Meghalaya Home Department says that insincerity of the 'commander-in-chief of the HNLC is the main reason for the State Government delaying the peace process.
May 1	The Meghalaya Government decides to approach the Union Government for the safe release of two custom officials, Dharani Bora and Mrinal Sharma, who were abducted by the UANF and kept in captivity at Mymensingh in Bangladesh.
	Chief Minister D. D. Lapang says that the proposal for peace talks with the HNLC is a better option than seeing the outfit members surrendering. Lapang, while expressing the State Government's willingness to hold talks with the militant outfits, said, "But we have no say on the issues, which are totally depended on the initiative of the Union Home Ministry." He also said, "We have to patiently wait and see things to happen because whatever steps that have been followed with the ANVC, the same thing will be done with HNLC."
May 2	Union Home Minister Shivraj Patil asks for detailed reports from Meghalaya Chief Minister D. D. Lapang following the letter's approach to the Union Government for the safe release of the State custom officials, D Borah and Mrinal Sharma, who were abducted on April 26 and are currently being held hostage by the United Achik National Front in Bangladesh.
May 8	The Central Customs and Excise Employees Welfare Association threatens to launch an agitation to exert pressure on the Union Government to secure the release of the two Meghalaya customs officials, who were abducted from West Garo Hills district on April 26.
May 14	Two Meghalaya customs officials, Superintendent D. Bora and Inspector Mrinal Sharma, are handed over by the Bangladesh Riffles personnel to the Union Government following the raising of the issue by the Union Home Minister Shivraj Patil with his counterpart Lutfozzaman Babar during the recently concluded meeting of the Home Ministers of the South Asian Association for Regional Cooperation countries at Dhaka. The duo were abducted by the UANF cadres from the West Garo Hills district on April 26 and held hostage at Mymensing in Bangladesh.

1	2
May 16	The South Garo Hills district police rescue a woman abducted by the ANLF militants from Rangran in the West Khasi Hills district on May 14 and in the ensuing encounter kill a cadre of the outfit. A Self-Loading Rifle with a magazine and two live ammunition shells are recovered from the incident site.
May 22	12 UANF cadres surrender before the Deputy Inspector General of Police (Western Range), F. D. Sangma, at Tura, headquarters of the West Garo Hills district.
	A status report submitted by the Border Security Force before the Delhi High Court says that at least 31 Bangladeshi nationals were deported from Meghalaya between January and April 2006.
May 23	Seven UANF cadres surrender before Sub-Divisional Officer (civil) at Ampati in the West Garo Hills district.
May 24	The Union Ministry of Home Affairs asks for the estimation of assets of the top HNLC leaders, including its 'chairman' Julius K Dorphang, 'general secretary' Cherishsterfield Thangkhiew and self-styled 'Commander-in-Chief Bobby Marwein.
May 27	The deadline set by an civil society organisation Khasi Students Union for the illegal migrants from Bangladesh to leave coal belt areas in the State, expires.
May 28	The ANVC asks the Union Government to withdraw its ban on the outfit to facilitate peace talks.
	Suspected UANF cadres abduct a nine-year old boy, Vaibhav Singh, from the Fancy Valley locality of Tura, headquarters of the West Garo Hills District.
May 29	A person, Hari Das, is abducted by suspected militants from Beldarpara under Tura police station in the West Garo Hills district.
May 30	Meghalaya Home Minister H. Donkupar R Lyngdoh, while responding negatively on the request of the ANVC to the Union Government to lift the ban imposed on it, says, "Let people be satisfied with their non-violence and peaceful existence." "No doubt, the illegal activities of the ANVC has reduced to a great extent; but until people are satisfied, the ban should continue," adds the Home Minister.

1	*2*
May 31	The HNLC threatens against persons participating in the forthcoming Municipal elections at Shillong, the State capital. The outfit also expresses 'concern' about ongoing influx into the Jaintia Hills.
June 1	Meghalaya Home Minister H. Donkupar R. Lyngdoh, while responding to threat issued by the HNLC against participation in the forthcoming Municipal election at Shillong, accuses the outfit of lacking sincerity on the issue of peace talks.
June 2	A HNLC cadre, Tibor Dkhar alias Ban, who left his hideout at Puthisara in Bangladesh, surrenders at Shillong before the Superintendent of Police of the East Khasi Hills district. An AK 47 rifle, suspected to be abandoned by the HNLC cadres, is recovered from the forest area of the North-Eastern Hill University near Mawlai.
June 6	Two cadres of a little known Garo outfit, Liberation Achik Elite Force, are arrested from Williamnagar in the East Garo Hills district. The arrested militants are identified as Xavier P. Marak and Sylseng Marak, from whom incriminating documents are recovered.
	Three HNLC cadres, Syrpai Rishong, Paul Nongbri and Canly Dkhar, are arrested by the BSF personnel at an unspecified place along India-Bangladesh border, while crossing over to the Indian territory from Bangladesh.
June 10	At least 20 suspected UPDS and Karbi National Volunteers militants enter a village and assault two persons, Kedrik Phawa and Damon Lamare, near Wanpung under Block 1 in the Ri-Bhoi district of Meghalaya.
June 13	The Garo Hills police conduct a raid at the residence of the leader of a little known Garo outfit, Liberation Achik Elite Front, identified as Peter R Marak, at Songsak in the East Garo Hills district and recover one Chinese hand grenade along with some incriminating documents, including demand notes. However, Peter manages to escape from the incident site.
June 16	An unidentified UANF cadre is killed in an encounter at a border village near Mahendarganj in the West Garo Hills district. Another militant manages to escape from the encounter site.

1	*2*
June 19	A huge cache of arms and explosives is seized by the Jaintia Hills district police following an encounter with at lest ten suspected militants belonging to the UPDS and Karbi National Volunteers at Umkhyrmi along the Assam-Meghalaya border.
June 20	Two ANLF cadres, Sonath Sangma and Zobin Marak, are arrested following a brief encounter with security force (SF) personnel at Dugul Ariga near Rongjeng in the East Garo Hills district.
June 21	Meghalaya's Home Minister R. G. Lyngdoh says the State Government is sincere to initiate peace talks with the HNLC so that peace can prevail in the State. "Peace is the priority of the new government and we will go whole length to achieve this goal," says the Home Minister. However, he also warns, "If they engage in criminal activities, they will be considered as criminals and the law will deal with them firmly."
	The State Government says that the Union Government's intervention is necessary to tackle the Meghalaya-Assam border dispute.
	Two Achik National Liberation Front cadres, identified as Amelush Momin and Arben Sangma, are shot dead in an encounter with police personnel at Nangalbibra in the South Garo Hills district. A cache of arms and explosives, including one country-made carbine, pistol, SBBL guns, Chinese-made grenade, and few rounds of live ammunitions, is recovered from the possession of the slain militants.
	Three unidentified UPDS cadres are killed in an encounter with police personnel at Umkhyrmi in the Block I area of Jaintia Hills district along the Meghalaya-Assam border. One AK 56 rifle, two hand grenades, 68 rounds ammunitions and one camera are recovered from the encounter site.
June 22	Meghalaya Government confirms the death of the United Achik National Front's 'chief, Nimush Marak, in the June 12 encounter at Rangamati hideout in Bangladesh bordering Gasuapara village of South Garo Hills district.
June 23	Two unidentified HNLC cadres are shot dead in an encounter with the police at Nonghyllam near Nongjri village in the West Khasi Hills district. One carbine, one pistol and few rounds of ammunitions are recovered from the encounter site.

1	*2*
June 24	The villagers of Moolaber, Skap, Deinler, Saba, Myntang, Psiar, Lum Moojem, Khatkhasla, Mooshrot, Mukroh and other adjoining villages near Labang-Nongphylut in the Jaintia Hills distict are extorted Rupees 200 each by the UPDS cadres.
June 25	A cache of arms and explosives, including one AK-47 rifle, three magazines, one Chinese rifle, two hand grenades, 68 rounds of ammunitions and one camera, are recovered following an encounter between police personnel and unidentified militants at Umkhyrmi bordering the Karbi Anglong district of Assam.
	At least ten HNLC cadres, who surrender in the North Tripura district of Tripura on June 21, are brought back and later remanded to ten-day police custody at Shillong, the State capital.
	Meghalaya Home Minister R. G. Lyngdoh, while expressing concern in the State Legislative Assembly over the reported threat of the UPDS in Jaintia Hills, says that the Assam and Meghalaya Governments are committed to ensuring safety and security of the people in the border area. "People living in the border areas in Jaintia Hills have been meted out harassment by the cadres of certain militant organizations," says the Home Minister.
	A civil society organisation, North East Students Organisation, expresses concern over the unabated influx of foreign nationals into Meghalaya. The NESO demands scrapping of the India-Nepal Treaty of Friendship, which, it claims, is only helping the illegal immigrants.
June 27	Suspected UPDS cadres attack a police outpost at Khanduli in the Jaintia Hills district, A civilian is wounded by militants in the incident.
June 28	Several civil society organisations and chiefs of traditional local self-governance institutions, Rangbah Shnongs, urge the Meghalaya Government to create some more police outposts and deploy more police personnel to prevent the UPDS militants from harassing Khasi-Pnar families in the Block-1 and II areas of Jaintia Hills district.
June 29	At least three HNLC militants, including one of their leaders identified as Khrawbor Lartang alias Kordor, Lumber

1	*2*
	Nongneng alias Pdit and Precious Star Lamare alias Kos, surrender before the East Khasi Hills district police in Shillong, the State capital.
Julyl	Several farmers of Mawlasnai area in the Ri-Bhoi district, having their cultivable lands in the Madan Umwang and Khlieh Umwang areas, are served demand notes by the UPDS cadres to pay ransom. The farmers are later asked by the militants to attend a meeting at Madan Umwang, and are threatened of dire consequences in case of failing to attend the meeting.
July 5	Meghalaya Chief Minister J.D. Rymbai accuses the UPDS of violating the ceasefire rules by indulging in unlawful activities along Assam-Meghalaya border. The outfit had signed a cease-fire agreement with the Union Government on May 23, 2002.
July 6	At least 435 HNLC cadres were killed, surrendered or arrested by the police personnel so far, says Inspector General of Police, B. L. Buam. Out of the total, 289 were arrested, 27 died in encounters, while 119 surrendered.
July 7	A HNLC cadre, Kampher Franky Syiem, is arrested from a hotel at Police Bazaar in Shillong, the State capital. Four demand notes are recovered from the possession of the arrested militant. According to police sources, Syiem serves demand notes varying from Rupees 5000 to Rupees 20,000, and also extracts some amount of ransom.
July 11	The cease-fire agreement between the Government and the ANVC is extended by one more year. The agreement to this effect is reached during the Joint Monitoring Group held in New Delhi on an unspecified day. The ANVC entered into a tripartite cease-fire agreement on July 23, 2004.
	Four ULFA cadres, identified as Rubul Ali, Prabal Dutta, Rudra Barua and Dulu Kalita, are killed by the SF personnel in an encounter at Tinfa village under Mendipathar police station in the East Garo Hills district. While three ULFA cadres are arrested, a cache of arms and explosives, including one AK rifle, four grenades, pistol, several rounds of ammunition, along with INR 40,000 are recovered from the incident site.

1	2
July 13	Meghalaya Police suspects that the ULFA leader Rubul Ali, who is killed in the July 11 encounter in Garo Hills, is a linkman of the Inter-Services Intelligence (ISI), the external intelligence agency of Pakistan.
	Meghalaya Government decides to continue counter intergency operation in its territory, irrespective of the outfit involved and the status of the peace process it might be engaged in. "The government cannot look the other way if there are any antisocial activities. When someone is behaving like a dacoit or if any group carries arms illegally, the law will take its own course," said State Home Minister R.G. Lyngdoh.
July 15	A HNLC cadre, Diam Salon, surrenders at Jowai police station in the Jaintia Hills district. The surrendered militant escaped from his camp in Bangladesh.
July 16	Meghalaya Police arrests at least 650 Bangladeshi nationals, for their suspected links with the Students Islamic Movement of India (SIMI), from the Fourth Furlong area at Polo in Shillong city. However, most of them are later released after interrogation at Sadar police station.
July 18	At least 27 Bangladeshi nationals are arrested at infiltration check posts in Khliehrait and Lad Rymbai of Jaintia Hills district. However, they were later sent to Assam, since they claimed to have hailed from the neighbouring State.
July 27	At least 35 foreign nationals are arrested at an infiltration check post in Byrnihat of Ri-Bhoi district. While ten infiltrators are from Nepal, the rest are reportedly Bangladeshi nationals.
August 8	Meghalaya Government starts the Disaster Awareness and Search & Rescue Traning programme for ANVC cadres at Tura in the West Garo Hills district.
August 9	A suspected Achik National Liberation Front (ANLF) cadre, Mesh Marak, is arrested for his involvement in a highway robbery case from Ginjal under Tura police station in the West Garo Hills district.
August 10	According to official sources, there has been some movement of ULFA cadres in Garo Hills since the last few months. The outfit's cadres cross into Bangladesh from West Garo Hills plain belt areas and enter into Assam from the Tikrikilla, Rongsai, Bajengdoba and Mendipather areas.

1	2
August 13	Meghalaya Chief Minister, J.D. Rymbai, asks militant outfits for peace talks to facilitate the overall development of the State. "The government would reiterate its appeal to militant organizations to shun violence and come to the negotiating table for peace talks", said the Chief Minister.
August 14	The Director General of Police (DGP) of Meghalaya, W.R. Marbaniang, says that there are perceived threats from Islamist terrorist outfits, including Al Qaeda, LeT and JeM, along India-Bangladesh border.
August 17	Meghalaya Home Minister, R.G. Lyngdoh, while expressing the State Government's inability to do much for the progress of peace talks with the ANVC, says, "The Central government will decide as to which demand of the outfit should be considered." "The State government is not in the driver's seat," mentions the Home Minister.
August 24	Meghalaya DGP, W. R. Marbaniang, says that counter-insurgency operations against the ULFA will continue in the State, despite the suspension of Army operations by the Union Government in the State of Assam. "We have taken care of ourselves and the army is only assisting us in (counter-insurgency operations). In 99 per cent cases, the state police are doing the job," says the DGP.
August 28	The ANVC states that it has discussed the issue of Garo Hills with the Union Government in New Delhi in July 2006. The 'publicity secretary' of the outfit, Arist Sangma, said, "We submitted our memorandum and said separate Garoland was our demand."
	Meghalaya Police arrest at least 78 illegal settlers and detect 33 among them to be suspected Bangladeshi nationals at Lad Rymbai and Khlieriat in the Jaintia Hills district. However, reports added that the detected persons will be sent to Assam, since they claim to belong to the neighbouring State.
August 30	Two unidentified persons, whose dead bodies are recovered from Nangapa village near Dagal in the East Garo Hills district, has their hands tied from back, blindfolded, and later shot dead by suspected Garo militants. Reports add that the militants left behind an AK-47 style fake gun carved out of wood with the name of the Achik National Liberation Front

1	*2*
	Army (ANLFA) 'chief, Nobin Marak alias The Scorpion, inscribed on it, which indicates the involvement of a rival outfit. "They were probably dacoits involved in robbery and other crimes and must have had some connection with the ANLFA group hence the mention of Nobin Marak," said a police officer.
August 31	The self-styled 'chairman' of the ANVC, Dilash Marak, figures in the list of wanted militants, residing in Bangladesh, handed over by the Border Security Force (BSF) to the Bangladesh Rifles (BDR) during their meeting in Shillong. The names of an unspecified number militants belonging to the UANF also figure in the list.
	Two political parties, the Hill State People's Democratic Party from Khasi Hills and Garo National Council from Garo Hills, at a joint statement demand the creation of separate provinces for the two major tribes of the State. Both the parties are opposed to the idea of 'Greater Garoland' demanded by the ANVC. However, the ANVC criticizes the joint proclamation of the two parties as a "political propaganda".
September 5	Speaking at the Chief Ministers' Conference on Internal Security in New Delhi, Meghalaya Chief Minister, J. D. Rymbai, while claiming return of peace and harmony to the State, expresses concern about cross-border terrorism supported by Bangladesh as well as unsettled boundary dispute with the neighbouring State of Assam. "Unless the Centre intervenes both by diplomatic and domestic means, the achieved peace in the State would be negated," says Rymbai.
September 10	The Union Government authorises the Meghalaya Government to directly negotiate with the HNLC. Meanwhile, State Chief Minister J. D. Rymbai and Home Minister R. G. Lyngdoh ask the cadres of the outfit to give up arms and return to the mainstream.
September 11	The Khasi Students Union (KSU) decides to intensify its 'direct action' against the illegal Bangladeshi immigrants in case of failure of the Meghalaya Government to implement the three-tier identity-card system. Following the eviction drive at Mawlai and North East Hill University campus in Shillong, the KSU assistant general secretary, Remington

1	2
	Lyngdoh, and its Mawlai Circle president, Joe Marbaniang, say at least 60 suspected foreign nationals engaged in a building construction at Mawlai Mawdatbaki in Pata were initially detained, and were subsequently handed over to the Mawlai Police for verification of their identity.
September 12	The newly formed Garo outfit, Achik National Liberation Front Army (ANLFA), allegedly accuses the Meghalaya Government of being soft on the ANVC, which is currently under a cease-fire with the Union and State Governments. The ANLFA alleges that the State Government is turning a blind eye to the 'atrocities' committed by the ANVC cadres in Garo Hills.
September 12	The Khasi Students Union (KSU) president Samuel B. Jyrwa, while speaking about the KSU's ongoing eviction drive against Bangladeshi nationals in the State, says "There is no holding back since we have been informed by the AASU leadership about more and more Bangladeshis leaving Asom for Meghalaya to evade detection and deportation after the scrapping of IMDT". Jyrwa informed that at least 1,500 suspected immigrants were detected in Meghalaya in the second week of September.
September 13	Meghalaya Government decides to introduce a work permit system to regulate the inflow of labourers as well as to curb the influx of foreign nationals, following the warning issued by the Khasi Students Union (KSU) for 'direct action' against the illegal Bangladeshi immigrants in the State. The KSU president, Samuel B. Jyrwa, says that the students' body will not honour the labour license issued by the Khasi Hills Autonomous District Council during its ongoing checking and eviction drive against the illegal immigrants.
September 16	At least INR 1600,000 is recovered from the possession of two suspected cadres of the Assam-based ULFA, identified as Ramzan Ali and Bablu Deka alias Niberan Deka, who are arrested from Mawiong in the East Khasi Hills district.
September 20	Meghalaya Police kills a HNLC cadre, Bankit Khonjee, and arrests another during an encounter at Umkrem in the East Khasi Hills district. A modified sten gun of 9 mm caliber, one 9 mm carbine, 40 rounds of ammunition and eight empty cases

1	*2*
	of assorted ammunition are recovered from the incident site. Following the incident, one surrendered HNLC cadre is also arrested for sheltering the HNLC cadres.
	A HNLC cadre, Krinding Lyngdoh, surrenders before the Meghalaya Police at an unspecified place. According to police sources, the surrendered militant, who confessed to having recently returned from Bangladesh, did not deposit any arms.
September 25	Meghalaya Police recovers the dead bodies of two former HNLC cadres, Philio Hashah and his brother Anthony Hashah, from Wah Khri near Mairang in the West Khasi Hills district. They were killed en route to appear in the district court for a pending case relating to their earlier linkages with the HNLC.
	Meghalaya Police arrests a HNLC cadre, Tom Jones Rynjah, from Mawlai Syllaikriah in the capital Shillong, and seizes some incriminating documents from his possession.
September 26	The Union Government warns of terrorist attacks to be sponsored by outfits such as the LeT and JeM in Meghalaya. Union Home Secretary V. K. Duggal in communique to the State Chief Secretary underlines that the terrorists' *modus-operandi* will be to attack soft targets, places of national importance, places of worship and economic and vital infrastructure besides creating a communal divide in the country.
	The KSU general secretary, Hamlet Dohling, while speaking about the implementation of a proposed Work Permit system in Meghalaya, says, "We want to urge the government through the Chief Minister to speed up the process since the problems related to influx, especially illegal entry of foreign nationals are alarming."
September 27	At least four unidentified militants are arrested shopping place at Khyndai Lad in Shillong.
	Meghalaya Police arrests four cadres belonging to the Manipur-based outfit, UNLF, identified as Manoj Singh, Prasanjit Singh, Somen Singh and Tomba Singh, while neutralizing a hideout of the outfit's finance wing at Police Bazaar in the capital Shillong.
September 28	A HNLC cadre, Dap Singh Ritshong alias surrenders before the Meghalaya Police at an unspecified place.

1	2
	The ANVC decides to discuss with the Meghalaya Government the conditions of disarmament for lifting the ban on the outfit. "We will have to discuss the matter before taking any decision in this regard," said 'publicity secretary' Arist Sangma.
October 4	A senior HNLC cadre, Mon Pohrmen, who was the 'commander' of the camp at Panai in Bangladesh, surrenders before Meghalaya Police at Jowai in the Jaintia Hills district. He deposits some sample demand notes before the police.
October 18	A civilian, Brariil Lawai, is assaulted by the Assam-based KNV militants at Pampret village near Sabuda under Block I in the Ri-Bhoi district along the Assam-Meghalaya border.
October 24	The Khasi farmers at Block-II areas in the Ri-Bhoi district allege that they are being extorted by the KNV militants. According to these farmers, each of them has to pay a "tax of INR 100 for each item (agricultural produce) sold at Umlaper and Umwang market, while INR 50 and above has to be paid for owning cultivable land in Block-II area." They say, "We are fed up of continued harassment. We are helpless as there is no one to provide security and we have no other place to go," by adding that such illegal collection "goes on throughout the year and aggravates during the harvesting season." The Khasi farmers further mention, "One who expresses his inability to pay the tax, the KNV militants threaten to take away the cultivable land or the crops."
October 25	The ANVC fails to respond to the appeal made by Meghalya Chief Minister, J. D. Rymbai, and Home Minister, R.G. Lyngdoh, to lay down arms, before the State Government could convince the Union Government to lift the ban imposed on the outfit, indicates report.
November 9	The Union Government extends the proscription on ANVC and HNLC.
November 20	Responding to the offer made by the HNLC for peace talks with the Union Government, the Meghalaya Home Minister, Robert G. Lyngdoh, stated that the State Government should be involved in the peace talks "so that it won't be held responsible for any failure in the process." "We are ready to hold talks at any moment and our door for negotiation is always open. But the talks should be a tripartite one like what was done with the ANVC," he added.

1	*2*
November 22	An IED is exploded by suspected ULFA militants targeting a security convoy at an unspecified place near Naguapara village in the West Garo Hills district. Another IED is also recovered from a hillock in the same locality, and is later defused.
November 27	A HNLC cadre, Tensing Khonglah, surrenders before the Superintendent of Police of Shillong City.
November 29	A truck driver, identified as Dhruva Narayan Rabha, is shot dead by suspected Garo militants at Ampang-Dangre village in the outskirts of Williamnagar in the East Garo Hills district.
December 12	The on-going agitation programme of the Garo Students' Union, which is spearheading the demand for holding of the Winter Session of the State Legislative Assembly in Tura, has faced opposition from the Liberation of Achik Elite Force (LAEF), a Garo militant outfit. The LAEF has warned the student body against disturbing the festive season. The outfit's 'Convenor cum Publicity Secretary', Chingkam Marak, said although the LAEF supported the demand for the session at Tura, yet, it should not be at the expense of the Garo people's wellbeing.
December 19	A 'commander' of the ULFA '27th Battalion', 'captain' Pallav Saikia alias Ananta Kakati, is arrested along with his wife Moromi at an unspecified place. Moromi, earlier arrested by the Royal Bhutan Army during the operation to flush out the ULFA militants from Bhutanese territory, rejoined the ULFA after she was released by Indian authorities.
December 20	One HNLC cadre, Aimos Khonglaban, surrenders at Pynursla police station in the East Khasi Hills district.
December 22	The Central intelligence agencies revel, following the arrest of a ULFA militant, Prabal Saikia, from Shillong on December 19, that the ULFA is trying to use the Shillong-Cherrapunjee and Shillong-Pynursla routes and other parts of Jaintia Hills for trans-shiftment of arms from Bangladesh and exfiltration of its cadres to Bangladesh.
December 25	An extortionist, Asuk Amyrsong, is arrested from Kharkhana village in the Jaintia Hills district along the India-Bangladesh border. However, two others manage to escape. They reportedly served extortion notes of INR 25,000 to a lady, Mala Pohlong, in the guise of HNLC cadres.

1	*2*
December 29	The BSF reportedly arrested 776 Bangladeshi infiltrators along the Assam-Meghalaya border in 2006 (till November). 754 are handed over to police and 22 to the *BDR*. According to BSF sources, most of the 754 Bangladeshi nationals handed over to the police are deported to the neighbouring country after talks during the BSF-BDR flag meetings. The report adds that smuggled goods worth over INR 8.5 crore, including forest produce valued at INR 2.4 crore, narcotics worth INR 70.9 lakh and cattle valued at INR 1.9 crore, are recovered from the Indo-Bangladesh border. The seizure includes fake Indian currency worth INR 33,000, which are being pumped into the country from Bangladesh. Two UANF militants, 'general secretary' Bromit A. Sangma and Treson M Sangma, surrenders before the West Garo Hills Police at Tura. They deposit two Chinese made grenades, a wireless set and some documents.

Meghalaya Terrorist Oufits : Nexus and Networks

Meghalaya affords a transit route from Bangladesh for NSCN (IM), which has bases in Garo Hills. Most of the leading insurgent groups have some presence in and around Shillong. Khun Henniewtrep National Awa Kening Movement (KHNAKM) is using its close nexus with NSCN(IM) and NDFB to regroup in Bangladesh. Anchic National Voluntary Council (ANVC) has provided sanctuary and safe passage to ULFA and NDFB cadres in the East Garo hills region.

CURRENT SCENE : 2006 AND ONWARDS

Meghalaya : A review of the Current (Early 2007) Trends

Year 2006 saw a consolidation of the trend discernible since 2002, of decreasing military—related violence in Meghalaya. Till 7 Dec., 2006, 25 people had been killed, including eight civilians and 17 militants[1]. Fatalities during the previous four years were :

2005	29
2004	35
2003	58
2002	64

The Garo Hills, comprised of three districts (East-, South-, and West Garo Hills), as in the previous years, witnessed the largest proportion of fatalities,

15 of the 25 in 2006. District-wise break down of the fatalities in the year 2006 are given here.

District	*Fatalities*		
	Civilians	*Militants*	*Total*
East Garo Hills	4	5	9
West Garo Hills	4	—	4
South Garo Hills	—	3	3
Garo Hills area	8	8	16
Jaintia Hills	—	3	3
West Khasi Hills	—	5	5
East Khasi Hills	—	1	1
Total	8	17	25

Of the 17 militants killed in Meghalaya in 2006, eight belonged to the Assam-based ULFA and UPDS. Of the remaining 9, 5 were claimed by the newly formed smaller Garo outfits, who also claimed 5 of the 8 civilian fatalities.

Prominent among these smaller/minor groups, formed especially in the Garo Hills to fill the vacuum created by the surrender of the Achik National Volunter Council (ANVC) are :

1. United Achik National Front UANF
2. Liberation Achik Elite Force LAEF
3. United Achik Liberation Front UALF
4. Achik National Liberation Front ANLF
5. Hajong United Liberation Army HULA
6. Retrival Indigenous Unified Front RIUF

Similarly, the Hynniewtrap National Special Red Army (HNSRA) is active in the Khasi Hills area.

Apart from killings, the cross-border networks in the North-East, also engage in abductions and extortions targeting villages and government officials. UNAF Chief Numush Marak was killed on 12 Jan. 2006 in an encounter with the BDR at Rangamati hideouts in Bangladesh bordering the Gasuapara village of South Garo Hills district.

While the security forces claim to have successfully neutralised these smaller outfits, the ULFA and NDFB have crafted tactical alliances with these amorphous groups to replace their arrangement with the ANVC to facilitate their cross-border movements.[2]

The Jaintia Hills and its adjoining Ri-Bhoi district witnessed an extensive extortion drive by the Karbi militants (UPDS) from the neighbouring Assam's hill district. On 24 June 2006, several villagers of Moolaber, Skap, Deinber, Saba, Myntang, Psiar, Lum Moojen, Khat Khasla, Mooshrot, Mukroh and other adjoining villages near Labang—Nongphyllut were forced to pay Rs. 200 each by UPDS cadres. On 1 July again, several farmers of Mawlasnai area in the Ri-Bhoi district, with their cultivable lands in the Madan Umwang and Khlieh Umwang areas were served demand notices by the UPDS to pay levies. They were later asked by the militants to attend a meeting at Madan Umwang, and were threatened with dire consequences of their demands were not met.

On 28 June, several civil society groups and chiefs of local self-governance institutions, Rangbah Shnongs, urged the government to create more police outposts and deploy additional police personnal to prevent the UPDS from harassing Khasi-Pnar families in Block I and II areas of the Jaintia Hills. The (then) Meghalaya Chief Minister JD Rymbai on 5 July accused the UPDS of violating rules of the cease fire agreement of 23 May 2002 with the centre, by indulging in unlawful activities along the Assam-Meghalaya border. It is not known if there has been augmentation security forces at the ground level.

Assam-based terrorist groups were involved in 13 incident during 2006 (till 8 December) in Meghalaya. While smaller outfits from Assam have targeted Meghalaya for extortion, but for larger and dominant groups like the ULFA, the state has served as a cruicial transit route to and from Bangladesh. In more specific terms, significant levels of movements have been reported from the Garo Hills.

Prospects of peace with the HNLC have continued to remain dismal despite efforts by the State Government and church. Former Chief Minister DD Lapang feels that proposals for peace talks with the HNLC should be preferred to any call for its surrender. The HNLC top leadership, safely ensconced in Bangladesh, has spurned several attempts by New Delhi and the Church to start a peace process.

In the last week of April 2006, however, HNLC Chairman Julius K Dorphang requested the Chief Minister to urge the Centre to "expedite" the peace process. On 10 Sep. 2006, the Union Government authorised the Meghalaya Government to initiate negotiatious with the HNLC.

Meanwhile, sporadic activity by the outfit continues in the Khasi Hills region. Two of its cadres were shot dead in an encounter with the police at Nonghyllam in the West Khasi Hills district on 23 June. Meghalaya police killed another HNLC cadre, Bankit Konjee, during an encounter at Umkrem in the East Khasi Hills district on 20 September. On the 25th, police recovered the dead bodies of two former HNLC cadres, Philio Hashah and his brother Anthony Hashah, from Wah Khari in the West Khari Hills district.

Now coming to the illegal infiltration from Bangladesh across its 443 km-long international border, Meghalaya has recorded a very poor rate of detection, prosecution, conviction and deportation of foreign nationals. Fencing, an effective deterrout to infiltration has remained unimplemented. Fencing has been found to be damaged along the 198-km-long stretch already fenced in the Garo Hills while the fencing work in the Khasi and Jaintia Hills area has remained paralysed by the protests from the local people. Ironically, on the other hand, official inaction in containing the infiltration is provoking locals to adopt vigilante measures.

On 6 March, villagers from Nongri-Umnuih-Nongshaken area in East Khasi Hills district announced a programme under the call, "Gun down a Bangladeshi criminal and collect Rs. 3,000", in protest against the alleged killing of people and looting of agricultural produce by Bangladeshi infiltrators. Such incidents can further escalate violence in a State that has long been simmering in the absence of adequate and effective policies to neutralise its internal insurgencies and to contain the overflow of troubles from Assam.

With so many militant outfits active in the State and its Government and Centre not showing sufficient awareness to control the situation, Meghalaya could be witnessing more turbulent times in not too distant a future.

Anti Non-tribal Explosion in Shillong? 2 Jan. 2007

Miscreants lobbed a crude explosive device—popular parlance of today calls it IED—at the shop of a non-tribal in Police Bazar, Shillong on 2 January, which injured the owner and three others. It may not—possibly, is not an isolated incident as the police complacence wants us to believe. Some vested interests are possibly trying to rekindle communal fires, which are not unknown to the residents of the beautiful hill station, the capital of Meghalaya.

Shillong by and large may have remained fairly peaceful, but Meghalaya does have a history of torching non-tribal traders : In the most communal holocaust of 1992 as many as 22 lost their lives. Tensions usually during the Puja but this/latest incident could well have been a deliberate attempt to knock non-tribal sentiments. As has happened in the past in similar situations, it is hoped the State Government this time would not delay calling out the Army for helping civil administration.

It is no secret that the contentious issue that has often created communal disharmony in Shillong in the past concerns trade licences for non-tribals in the main Lew duh market (Burra bazar). It is regrettable that this sore should be allowed to fester for so long. Coming to the specifics, the State Government is rather helpless to correct the situation as "the issuance and renewal of the trade licences vest with the Khasi Hills (Autonomous) District Council and the Durbar of the Syiem of Mylliem.[3]"

It is imperative that some sort of understanding if not a comprehensive agreement, is reached between the two side because Shillong has never been the same since the militant Federation of Khasi Jaintia and Garo People served in 1992 notices on 1,500 non-tribal shop-owners to close their establishments. It needs to be said that most of them have been doing business there since generations.

Shillong has been a cosmopolitan town for more than 130 years and most settlers there have identified themselves with the locals. Reciprocation should be the logical response if progress and development of this state are the rewards sought.

It is ironic, if not opportunistic, to see that the three regions of Meghalaya have united against the non-tribal residents, knowing that very recently the Garos mere seriously agitating for a separate Garoland, citing Khasi domination of the state's administration.

Garo Hills are 'Peaceful' : Jan., 2007

After visiting Tura, district headquarters of Garo, an analyst[4] with special interest in the North-East, writes:

> "It is quiet and pleasant, and quite safe. There is hardly any violence and the sole major armed group, the Achik National Liberation Front (ANLF), occupies the Youth Hostel above the cricket stadium. It has a cease fire with the Government of India.
>
> "They collect 'donations' or taxes from every trade in the town, although I am told by the officials that the figure is dropping.
>
> "Republic Day celebrations at the Chandmani grounds were a fun-full affair. The place wore a festive look and there was a palpable ease in the air. Two years ago, there would have been tension and unease as it prevails in Guwahati presently on this day. But less than two years of peace is transforming the area. The cycle changes, the wheel turns."

NOTES

1. Sandipani Dash, *The Pioneer*, 20 Dec. 2006.
2. *Ibid.*
3. Editorial, "Between the lines", *The Statesman*, 5 Jan. 2007.
4. Sanjoy Hazarika, *The Statesman,* 29 Jan. 2007.

14

Mizoram : A Democratic Success Story Original Rebellion and its Resolution

Nagas and Mizos were first to rise in revolt against 'India' though in different decades : the former in 1950s and the latter in 1960s. But there is one major difference : Mizo Accord is a success story, the Nagas are yet to write the last chapter to theirs.

Key Statistics : Mozoram

Date of Formation	
Union Territory	21 Jan., 1970
State of the Union	20 Feb., 1987
Area	21,081 sq. km
Population	8,88,573
Capital	Aizawl
Major Religion	Christianity
Main languages	Lushai/Mizo
	English
	Bengali
	Lakher

Mizoram is a perfect example of the erstwhile rebels seeing the opponent's point of view and giving up rebellion against the State which was willing to accept and accommodate their ethnic diversities and political aspirations. Not only did the chief rebel, the legendary Laldenga, rule the state as its Chief Minister, and then lost power in the successive democratic election, his political creation (the MNF) is ruling Mizoram presently. The interesting, in fact amazing, story of the insurrection and terrorism in Mizoram, is detailed in two chapters :

- Chapter 14 : The original rebellion and its resolution.
- Chapter 15 : How the former rebels turned politicians (are facing the new 'rebels' from the smaller tribes.

From Insurrection to Constitutionalism

It is strength of the Indian democracy that *even* the problem of secessionism is dealt patiently within the framework of the country's Constitution and yesterday's insurrection leaders become today's lawfully elected chief ministers of the states. Mizoram's is the best example of a people pulling back from the brink and becoming happy members of a national family—as varied as India's. What follows surveys the course of MNF's quest for independence, the trauma of the people involved, and the happy end to a painful chapter.

Causes of Insurgency

No single cause can be fixed for the insurgency in Mizoram, but its genesis lay in the colonial rule. It is generally agreed that there was occasionally a concerted effort to keep the Mizos—like other tribals—out of the Indian fold, not forgetting the official, sustained machinations towards this end till the Lushais got their own ADC.

The British, kept the tribals of the North-East as 'museum pieces', hold some scholars, by building an 'exotic barb' around them through the promulgation of various Rules and Regulations. The British subjects (read non-tribals and Indians from the neighbouring plains) were not allowed to go beyond the 'Inner Line' without a permit from the district authority. Whatever their aim or purpose, as a result, the tribals lost their contact with the plains people—creating a cleavage between the two.

Based on the recommendations of the Bordoloi Sub-Committee, Indian Constitution incorporated the provision in the Sixth Schedule for the social and economic development of the tribals in the North-East; it was a direct descendant from "Excluded" and "Partially Excluded" area concept in 1919 and 1935 Acts. A word on the setting up of the Bordolai Sub-Committee. The Cabinet Mission 1946 had suggested an Advisory Committee on the rights of the citizens, minorities and tribals of Excluded Areas. Mission's Chairman Stafford Cripps suggested that a proper and powerful committee should be set up to make proposals for the administration of tribal areas. Accordingly, the Constituent Assembly set up; an Advisory Committee,[1] as per terms of reference of the Cabinet Mission Plan, on 24 January 1947. This Committee appointed three sub-committees. The North-Eastern Frontier (Assam) Tribal and Excluded Area Sub-Committee with G.N. Bordoloi (Premier of Assam) as Chairman[2] was one of the three.

When the Independence was almost an accomplished fact, a section of Lushais under the patronage of British was keen to secede from India and join the Chin Hills of Burma. With this in mind, Macdonald, the Superintendent of Lushai Hills, called a conference of leaders of commoners and representatives of Chiefs and formulated a scheme named after him. The new State shall have legislature and judiciary of its own. The defence, external affairs, etc. would be transferred to Government of India. Macdonald's ulterior motives were seen through and the Scheme, unwarranted and unworkable, was not acceptable to a majority of the Mizos. L.L. Peter, the last British superintendent, took initiative and formed a Committee of Chiefs and Commoners in. 1947 which resolved that the Lushai Hills would join India for 10 years after which they would decide their political future. Mizo Union Party opposed this idea. In the meantime, the Bordoloi Sub-Committee visited Aizawl, met cross-sections of people, and the rest as they say, is history.

It seems too many British officials and scholars were concerned with the future of the Hill people of Assam. J.P. Mills, a British officer was in favour of exclusion of all hill districts of Assam from the reforms scheme and constituting them into a Hill "State under the direct control of His Majesty's Government. But the most sinister of such plans came from a British scholar and constitutional expert R. Coupland. Known after his name as Coupland plan, it was an enlarged version of the Macdonald Plan. It envisaged carving out hill (tribal) areas of India's North-East and Burma's North-West and merging them to create a Crown Colony to be directly placed under the White Hall. The Plan was favoured by R. Reid, Governor of Assam and L.L. Peters. Coupland wanted this Colony for the tribals of Mongoloid stock inhabiting these tracts, "who were consciously neither Indian nor Burmese and they innocently belonged to the Indian or Burman nation". So the Tribals (Lushais) were not Indians in any sense of the word,[3] neither in origin nor in languages or appearance or in habit, or outlook. It was a mere a historical accident that they were tagged to an Indian province.[4] Luckily for India, the Plan was not accepted by the British Parliament.

Despite such shades of opinion—to ensure that the Hills remain a separate entity—the security of the British India was and remained of paramount importance, with China abutting it on the long northern border. Thus it was no surprise that Andrew Clow, Governor of Assam (1945) suggested the merger of the Hill areas with Assam on the condition that the tribal customs and institutions be given due recognition and respect. Still, this did not stop the Mills and Couplands of the British world from offering and promoting plans to keep these areas out of India's fold till its very Partition in 1947—as described above.

The traditional institution of chieftainship was abolished in 1952. The discontented Chiefs joined United Mizo Freedom Organisation (UMFO) to help the Lushai Hills to try and secede from India and join Burma. This was bound to aggravate the crisis in the Hills. The uprising in 1966 was strengthened when the disgruntled Chiefs lent their tacit support to the malcontent elements.[5]

The analysts have partly blamed the Assam Government for the troubles India faced in Mizoram. The Assam Government wooed the MNF in initial stages to run down the Mizo Union (MU) which had blamed the Chaliha Government for neglecting the Lushai Hills for economic development. The MU, in power in Mizo ADC, again blamed the State Government for not allotting adequate resources to fight the 1959 famine, which had provided a cause on a platter to the MNF to spread anti-India sentiment. The 1960 Language Bill generated anti-Assam sentiment among all its ethnic/linguistic minorities. It was also worst case of an intelligence failure, the State being caught utterly unaware when the insurgency erupted. Laldenga, Lalmunawia, and Sainghaka, arrested by security guards while returning from the then East Pakistan, were let off even after a damaging disclosure that they had gone there to enlist Pakistani support for their insurgency bid. It was poor assessment of the ground realities. Chaliha later took the blame for these events. The distances, location, size, shape, terrain, climate, vegetation (jungles), and broken territory helped the insurgents, and thwarted the counter-insurgency operations.

5,000 Mizo recruits had joined the Army and Para-Military Forces during the World War II, and this exposure, along with the greater political and economic opportunities post-1947, had radically transformed the action-space of the Mizos. The Post-1945 retrenchment/demobilisation of the Armed Forces and disbandment of an Assam Rifles battalion made it easy for the insurgent leaders to draw cadres for the MNF. The arms/ammunition dumps left in the area after the War also came handy to them. Some other "usual" factors that helped the cause of insurgency were: the economic backwardness; unemployment; neglect of periphery (North-East) by the dominant "core area" (Mainstream India); exploitation of religious sentiments (Hindu India bent upon absorbing a Christian Land); a neighbour (East Pakistan), unfriendly to India, encouraged the Naga and Mizo rebels by providing them with arms, training, money and shelter for their secessionist/subversive activities; and existing distrust between the Plains People and Hill Tribes, created by the Inner Line Regulation, fostered the sense of separatism. All this was inflammable mixture, which some feel, became explosive with the introduction of political freedom, extension of education, Missionary activities (which brought awareness to tribal community), and money economy. This fertile situation was eagerly seized by a shrewd Laldenga—a retired NCO, an extremely intelligent man, and a slippery customer, at his best—to build a secessionist movement which proved to be a biggest headache, next only to the Naga uprising for the Nation.

Tracing the Course—Briefly

Embers of the insurgency smoulding below the surface erupted ominously at midnight 28 February/1 March 1966. The rebels first cut off the telephone lines, disrupted road communications, and disarmed the State police at Aizawl and other places. The Intelligence should have seen through the things at the conference of political parties at Churachandpur in January 1965, convened to sort out differences between the MU and MNF—the latter bent upon declaring independence of the Mizo Hills and the MU trying to pull it back-from the brink. Laldenga remained unbent. During the 1965 India-Pak War, he recruited 8,000 volunteers to widen his base at grass-root level. He started full-speed clandestine mobilisation and setting up his base in each village.

The insurgency started at 10.30 PM, 28 February 1956 named *Operation Jericho.* The Silchar-Aizawl road was blocked by blowing up culverts/bridges, wireless transmitters smashed, Aizawl Treasury was ransacked, yielding Rs. 64,000 worth of booty. Similar disturbances were simultaneously caused at Vairengte, Kolashib. Champhai, Lunglei, Demagiri, Khawzawl, and Chawngte. The "armed revolt spread like wild fire, even if the majority of the population did not fully support it." Its quick success was attributable to the area's distant location in the isolated North-East, difficult and limited access to it because of the terrain on its internal boundaries, and 70 per cent of its boundaries forming the international borders with Pakistan and Burma. Chaos prevailed in the District, and MNF cadres spread to all corners. It seems the MNF already had a command set up in place, as also a shadow Government, "Mizoram Sawrkar", with legislative, executive and judicial wings, delineated below:

Mizoram Sawrkar

South Division (Run) Hrangchunga	Western Division (Dumpa) PB Rosanga	Eastern Division (Lurh) Ngurchhina (Brother of Laldenga)
Sub Areas (under Deputy Commissioners)		

MNF Defence Wing

(Mizo National Volunteers-MNV)

MNV

At the time of Operation Jericho)

Northern Command	Southern Command	Central Command	Eastern Command	Western Command
27 Division	1 Division	Aizawl Town	31 Division	21 Division

Source: Press reports and Nibedan (1980), p. 62.

Composition of MNF (Presidential) Government

President	Laldenga
Vice-President	Lalmunawia
Finance Secretary	Lalkhawliana
Defence Secretary	Zamawia
Home Secretary	Sainghaka
Chief Justice	John F. Manliana
Foreign Secretary	Lalhminlhanga

Laldenga, being the President, was also the Supreme Commander of the Armed Force. Maj Gen (SS) Vanalhururia was C-in-C Army before the uprising. The recruitment in the MNF Army was made from the students, farmers, and even ex-servicemen, whose response heartened the leadership. Laldenga had been calling for peaceful methods in public, but simultaneously preparing his cadres for an armed uprising. He was practising double standards, like Phizo, the Naga leader. The planning and organising for the final blow had teen proceeding simultaneously. By 30 October 1965 they were ready to take on the world. In a memorandum to the Prime Minister that day, MNF President Laldenga and its General Secretary S. Lianzuala defiantly asked for independence. The Mizo National Army (MNA) was being trained for guerrilla warfare in both Pakistan and China. It had placed its cadres at vulnerable areas in the District for blowing up vital installations. They had been collecting funds from the employees, traders and contractors—through coercion or persuasion.

So the fat was in fire on 1 March 1966. The MNF declared independence. In a bid to internationalise issue, he wrote letters to the world leaders, including Sukarno, Indonesian President.[6] He also claimed the British had assured the Mizos independence after World War II; and consequent to this assurance, the Lushai Brigade and Lushai Scouts had fought for the British on the Burmese front. But there is no evidence of this assurance.

The MNF achieved conspicuous successes to begin with. They had blown up Silchar-Aizawl road at several places to thwart the reinforcement of the SF camps at Aizawl, or at interior places like Champhai and Demagiri. Even the Turial Airstrip was not safe for the Indian Army. On 1 March, (1.30 AM) the MNF volunteers took away a jeep and some explosives from SDO (PWD) at Vairengte. On 2 March, the Government of Assam declared the District as disturbed area. The troops were dispatched by air and road on the 3rd. The Armed Police was placed under the operational control of the Army. But the Army could not reach Aizawl till the 5/6 night. By then, the rebels had done considerable damage. On the 3rd, the Assam Rifles Patrol was ambushed near the Government High School, Aizawl and the same day its Headquarters attacked at Aizawl but they held out till the 5th. The hostiles made an abortive bid to capture their Chinluang post on the very first night of insurgency, but later gave up, as they realised reinforcement was on the way.[7]

1 Assam Rifles was the only unit in the district at that time. The MNF fighters attacked its post (and also of the BSF) at Lungleh and captured it after heavy firing. Their arms and ammunition fell into rebel hands. R.V. Pillai, SDO (Civil) Lunglei and some other officials were kidnapped, and taken to East Pakistan.[8] The MNF flag flew at the SDO's residence. At Champhai, the Assam Rifles Wing Headquarters with two platoons fell to the rebels, and the post was destroyed. At Chawngte, the post fell after stiff fighting and heavy casualties on both sides. Thus, but for its headquarters at Aizwal all other posts of 1 Assam Rifles fell to the rebels. It took more than a month for the Army to regain these posts—and control of administration. But for the 1 Assam Rifles Headquarters, the District Headquarters was under the rebel control for nearly 6 days.

Starting by road and air (helicopters) from Silchar on the 3rd March, Army reached Aizawl on the 5th evening, after clearing all hurdles en route. The rebels started leaving the town, melting into the interior. Then the troops moved on way to Lunglei which was under MNF control. The Army column threatened to bomb the town. On the 9th, two Baptist leaders reached Aizawl and requested the Army against bombing, as that would harm the innocent lives. After some resistance, on the 13th the rebels gave up, taking away some arms, explosives and vehicles from the BRTF.[9] Champhai was retrieved on the 17th. On the 25th, the Union Home Minister informed the Parliament (Lok Sabha) that "all important town and posts have been freed from the MNF control" and the rebels were fleeing to Pakistan or Burma, or hiding in jungles.

But the rebels were far from vanquished.[10] The mopping up operations were to continue. MNF adopted a multi-pronged strategy : full scale insurrection; equilibrium operations in selective places; resort to extortions, coercion and terrorism; intimidation of officers; and politicisation of the common Mizo through propaganda. Certain strategically insignificant places like Tuipang were left alone, but important ones like Demagiri (located on main supply routes from Chittagong) were made targets of attack. They ambushed in mountainous areas and difficult trails. They ambushed the supply convoy at Zawlawn village, on 6 May, killing some soldiers and looting supplies. The army retaliated. Coming under pressure, the MNF kept shifting its Headquarter—Aizawl to the caves of Reick, east of Aizawl. Laldenga escaped to East Pakistan. Even after the Chief Minister appealed for peace at Aizawl on 10 May, the MNF continued their operations: attack at Bunghmun on 16 May, where Laizama and Chhunkhuma were killed; ambush at Bilkhawthlir on 23 May with rebels killing 12 soldiers, and making away with 12 rifles, 2 stenguns and one LMG. This operation was named "Operation Humnalhma" by the rebels. They attacked Army post at Sialsuk on 14 June, and several places on 16 June, under "Operation Monsoon", and kidnapped some local officers. Later, they resorted to "hit and run" tactics, abandoning ambushing and attacks on the posts. The primary aim of rebels was to create disorder, disrupt lines of communications, hinder counter-insurgency drive of the SF, and demoralise their rank and file.

The rebels were getting help from Pakistan and China—aimed at destabilising India. Laldenga, living in Dhaka, returned to attend a MNF meeting at Sialbak on 6 November 1966. They drafted MNF Constitution. He wanted to meet Indian leaders as equals, being President of a "Country", and reiterated his demand for independence. At this meeting, several civilian leaders, including Pastor Zirema, requested him to abjure violence—but to no avail. He wanted MNF to move on two tracks: aiming for independence and seeking negotiations. The 10 December MNF cabinet meeting at Sialsir (near Serchhip) was cancelled due to SF operations in the area. In a serious Army-MNF encounter on 16 December, near Kawlkulh on Seiling-Champhai Road, 7 soldiers were killed.

In June 1967, the rebels launched "Operation Crusade", aimed at consolidating their forces in the Mizo areas of Manipur under command of their Lion Brigade.[11] The rebel units were planning "Operation Monsoon" (=Furthlipui, in Mizo). Meanwhile, MNF launched several attacks at various places including Aizawl to kidnap officials. On 27 December, six soldiers were killed in an ambush near Ghawngre near Pak border. This year (1967), the MNA Headquarter moved from Ralvawng Range (near Baite) to Chin Hills.

The hostiles led by Li (SS) Lianhnuna attacked 6 Maratha troops (Operation Refinement) on 3 March 1968, killing their company commander. "A fortnight later, in a gun fight with the ultras, the SF lost 20 men"[12]; the MNF fired at Borapansuri Outpost (South of Demagiri) in January 1969, from across the border; and two days later, they attacked CRP Post at Tuipuibari (North: Tripura). By end of 1969, 200 Mizo rebels had entered Mizo Hills from CHT. They had an encounter with the SF on 16 February 1970, near Marapara, on Mizo Hills-CHT border.

Driven out of Mizoram MNF cadres had set up camps and bases in East Pakistan (CHT)—monitoring traffic across the border, a difficult job, given the topography.[13] The MNF had "to depend on the charity of the imperialists—getting arms/ammunition from the area around Chittagong port, the centre of international smuggling—who were keen to help the Mizo rebels for their global strategy."[14] After the birth of Bangladesh, MNF shifted its camps to Arakan—near the trijunction of Arakan-Bangladesh-India—to be welcomed by the Arakanese insurgents.[15] MNF was busy establishing contacts with other outfit in Burma and China. Its Intelligence Chief travelled north along the Chindwin to meet KIA leaders. Bualhvanga, a Laldenga confidante, was traversing Southern Burma—both convincing Mizos to join their cause. Lalmunmawia went south to meet the President of Arakan NLF (ANLF), whose leaders— Krahlalung and General Secretary Tunhlsaung—had arranged security and sanctuary for the cadres of MNF, which promised arms to ANLF as a *quid pro quo.* The MNF established contact with China too, through Somra Tracts corridor, east of Manipur, with the Naga Underground acting as go-between. The pro-Peking BCP also gave them sanctuary in Arakan and Chin Hills. But the MNF preferred training in CHT than in China's Yunnan province, due to ideological and religious reasons. But the emergence of Bangladesh did create some problems, as did the dissent within. In 1974, the hardcore regrouped their forces to launch incursions from Arakan, but the dissenters wanted talks. Malsawma Colony reached Aizawl and held one-month long talks which failed. He returned to Arakan. The hardcore attacked and wounded Governor SP Mukherjee on 10 March 1974 during his journey on Silchar-Aizawl Road. In another daring attack, three rebels entered a meeting of senior police officers at their Headquarters at Aizawl on 30 January 1975, and killed three of them, including the IG. The event sent shock waves across the nation.

While the MNF cadres were creating mayhem in Mizoram, cracks developed within the outfit. Shrewd judge of men and matters, Laldenga concluded the famous July 1976 Agreement with New Delhi, bringing life to near normal in the territory. May be because of change of mind he did not like the term "surrender" of arms by his men, and revived the struggle for sovereignty, mass circulating his tape-recorded speech to this effect. When despite his opposition, May 1979 mid-term Assembly poll was held, bringing Sailo's Peoples Conference to power, an irritated Laldenga directed M.C. Lalrimthanga to restart the violence. The MNFs June 1979 'quit notice' to non-Mizos (=vais) to leave Mizoram by 31 July created panic. In the subsequent violence, the house of Agriculture Minister, P.B. Rosanga, was burnt down and SDO (PWD), R.C. Chouchury, was murdered. "All this was planned to incite an anti-Mizo backlash in Silchar and block supply line to Aizawl, to serve the MNF propaganda". But to its chagrin, that not happen.

But the violence was all over Mizoram in 1979. On 2 July, Transmission Centre of AIR and Sivaji Tilla Police Complex, Aizawl were attacked by MNF; so was Serchhip Police Post; and an attempt on the life of IGP (Ved Marwah) and DIG (R.S. Chopra) was made. "Pro-Laldenga group from Parwa" was infiltrating Mizoram to boil the pot again *(The Statesman,* 4-7-79). The combing up operations were re-intensified. Earlier, the rebels had killed SDO (PWD) at Saitual (13-6-79) and attacked SDO, Kolashib. Later, SBI Aizawl was fired upon. Taking a serious view of it all, the MNF was declared an unlawful organisation. But violence continued. In broad day light on 7 August 1979, seven civilians were killed when the truck carrying them was attacked, near Aizawl. The aim was to launch attacks on Government employees, and military and para-military personnel during their journey by small gangs of MNF cadres. In January-February 1980, the rebels attacked several Assam Rifles vehicles—killing some soldiers proceeding on leave. They ransacked a BRTF camp near Thenzol on 21 March 1980, and burnt down an Administrative Block at Bungmun near Champhai. Consequently, curfew was clamped in Aizawl and some other towns. The sporadic incidents of violence by the insurgents continued, and so did the counter-insurgency operations by the SF.

The 1984 Assembly Poll brought the Congress (I), led by Lalthanhawla, to power. The Governments at Centre and Aizawl made sincere efforts to usher peace and harmony in the territory. The result was signing of the Peace Treaty on 30 June 1986—long last.

Flighting Insurgency : A Brief Account

The terrain, topography, weather, isolation, friendly neighbours and ethnically allied tribes across the borders helped the MNF to defy the national writ for quite some time. The State had to institute certain measures to counter the situation effectively. The Assam Government declared the Mizo Hills district as disturbed area under the Armed Forces (Assam and Manipur) Special Powers Act, 1958, which empowered die SF personnel (a JCO or above) to open fire, to destroy arms dump, and to enter and search any place without warrant. The Assam Government also declared the area disturbed within 16 km of both sides of Silchar-Aizawl Road, under sub-rule (I) of Rule 80 of DIR 1962. The Deputy Commissioner of Mizo Hills district promulgated Rule 80 of the DIR, which prohibited the possession of, carrying, use, and sale of arms and ammunition in the district. The Army and BSF were deployed in the district. Gen Manekshaw, Army Chief, suggested (1970) that the Government hand over the administration of the district to the Army, but the latter rejected the suggestion. "During the operations, some villages—Knowngbawk, Pangzawl, Pukpui, etc. were burnt down by the troops."

Unable to face the SF, the rebels fled to jungle hide-outs, and met their requirements of food articles, medicines, cash, etc. through extortions from the villages in the interior. Later, when better organised, they resorted to levying "taxes" on all and sundry.

Grouping of the Villages

It was essential to isolate the rebels and cut off their supplies from the civil population. For this purpose, Army resorted to grouping of the villages, bringing them into protected parameters, and out of reach of the ultras and their coercion. "The scheme was based on the text of Robert Thompson."

The first stage of grouping started on 4 January 1967 under the orders of the Central Government Liaison Officer for Mizo Hills district in accordance with DIR 1962.[16] 50,000 people from 106 villages were resettled in 19 Centres along Silchar-Aizawl-Lunglei Road, starting from Vairengte villages and extending 400 km. These 19 Centres were called Progressive and Protected Villages (PPV). Each PPV was under an Administrative Officer. It was protected by a company strength, under a Captain/Major. Another 63 villages with a population of 40,000 were reorganised into 17 PPVs along the sensitive borders with Burma and Manipur. But the Pawi Lakher Regions (minus Chakma areas) with headquarters at Lawngtlai and Saiha were left out as these were not being used for shelter or succour by the hostiles. Again, there was no grouping along 96 km Aizawl-Thanzol Road, as the habitation in these areas was mostly by the road side. Cut off from their erstwhile supply chain, the rebels perforce had to seek refuge in Pakistan.

The second category of grouping—New Group Centre (NGC)— started immediately after completion of PPVs in 1969. 55,000 population was grouped into 40 NGCs, divided into 6 Sectors on the three borders of the district: (1) Tripura Border, (2) East Pakistan Border, (3) Lunglei-Demagiri Road, (4) Luglei-Lawngtlai Road, (5) Seiling-Champhai Road, (6) Darlawn-Khawbung, North Vanlaiphai-Serchhip Road.

The third category of grouping—Voluntary Group. Centres (VGCs)— started in 1970, under which 110 villages were grouped into 26 VGCs on voluntary basis.

Under 4th Category—Extended Loop Area (ELAs)—40,000 people from 63 villages, along the border of Manipur in the north and Burma in the east, were grouped into 17 ELAs. The grouping was completed by the end of 1969 and the Army handed over the area to the civil authorities in the mid-1970. This grouping along the eastern border facilitated subsequent operations in the Manipur Sector.

The shifting of villages and their regrouping was a gigantic operation which was executed by the Army and Civil Authorities with commendable efficiency, under trying conditions. The total effort is clear from the table below:

Abstract of Population Involved in the Grouping in 1970

Sl. No.	*Group Centres*	*Original*	*Shifted*	*Total*
1.	19 PPVs	16,534	30,241	46,775
2.	40 NGCs	34,450	34,465	88,915
3.	17 EL As	15,919	18,276	34,195
4.	26 VGCs	23,721	23,435	47,156

Source: S.N. Singh, *Mizoram* (1995), p. 222.

There was some opposition to the grouping scheme. It was seen as a political move to divide and rule—"it certainly divided a well-knit Community". It did not fully achieve the aim of isolating the insurgents from the common Mizos, because the tradition of *Tlawn rangai hna* persuaded them to help their fellow beings in an hour of distress, even if they were insurgents. It did cause alienation and frustration among the people affected by regrouping. The rural economy suffered a major setback. The tight security measures, including cordon and search operations, an unavoidable necessity in an insurgency situation, caused certain hardship for the common peace-loving Mizos. Brig Sailo, a retired Army man himself, went to the extent of saying: "The SF, instead of winning the heart, antagonised them during *Operation Security.*"[17] It was an obvious exaggeration, impelled by political considerations, even if one must accept it could never be a painless operation. But there can never be any doubt about its necessity, and consequent help/advantages in its achieving of the goal.

Regrouping started yielding results, aided of course by the vigorous counter-insurgency operations by the SF. Some rebels wanted to rejoin the mainstream. The Government offered an amnesty on 28 January 1967. Encouraged by the response, it offered second amnesty on 21 November 1967. The Government also announced 'Pardon' for the rebels who surrendered with serviceable arms, and even offered cash awards for them at the following rates:

Sl. No.	*Weapon*	*Cash Amount (Rs.)*
1.	LMG	4,000
2.	2" Mor/Rocket Launcher	600
3.	SLR	500
4.	303 Rifle/Stengun	300
5.	Revolver/Pistol	250

Talks and Accord

There were surrenders but the hardcore continued the violence. Counter-insurgency is not the easiest of operations. The intelligence is not easy to come by as the common people have certain kinship and sympathy for the rebels, being their "brothers". Even those inclined to help are diffident for fear of reprisals. It was a long haul, and the SF and the Government finally succeed in the process.

Rev Zirema met Laldenga at Sabual, 62 km south of Aizawl, on 1 November 1966 and asked him to abjure violence as it was contrary to the Christian teachings. When Laldenga insisted upon independence and recognition of his "Government", the talks failed.[18] A senior Raw official, B.P. Singhal, met Laldenga in Pakistan in the guise of a Muslim, named Hasanwalia and brought him to Geneva in clandestine operation for talks. In his letter dated 20 August 1975 from Geneva, he told the Prime Minister that Mizo sovereignty would not be pressed upon.[19] Laldenga returned to India for negotiations, which led to the 1 July 1976 Agreement. It was widely cheered by all section of the Mizos and the Government of Mizoram observed 7 July 1976 as a thanksgiving day. Laldenga had agreed to abjure violence, give up his demand for sovereignty and settle all issues within the framework of Indian Constitution. But the Agreement collapsed when he asked his cadres not to surrender arms.

The MNF again returned to the jungle and violence. But the urge for settling the issue persisted. In July 1980, another meeting was arranged between him and the Prime Minister. He again agreed to suspend all operations and acknowledged Mizoram to be an integral part of India.[20] But this agreement also proved short-lived and MNF again resumed violence. Another initiative came from Yashpal Kapoor (man Friday of Indira Gandhi), who offered a package deal, including the Christmas Gift of Statehood for Mizoram, to the MNF leaders, on the condition of surrender of all arms and cessation of hostilities. Not only the MNF insisted on their demand for a free zone in the Chhimtuipui district, but also on rehabilitation of the cadres and dismissal of the Sailo Ministry under Article 356. As he wanted to consult his colleagues, he made a trip to Parva on 9 March 1981. On his return, he presented a 26-point[21] Charter to New Delhi, which included: (1) Mizoram State with safeguards on the Kashmir pattern, (2) Greater Mizoram, (3) Membership of UNO for Mizoram, (4) Separate Flag, (5) Abolition of Provisions of Sixth Schedule in case of Mizoram, (6) Dissolution of Mizoram Assembly. It was a tall order and talks ended in a failure on 12 January 1982. The MNF and MNA were banned. However, they continued with their activities like intimidation and forcible collection of funds, and harassment of non-Mizos. The MNF was rigid in its demands. Laldenga said MNF's is Political movement and its goal is not a war to defeat the Indian Army.[22] He was keen for political settlement, but some senior colleagues were opposed to negotiated settlement. On the other hand his hosts, Bangladesh Government too wanted him to continue his struggle—offering all help for his success.

Keen on a political settlement, he held a series of talks with the officials and finally met Prime Minister Rajiv Gandhi. The talks continued and an agreement was signed on 23 December 1985 between Arjun Singh—Vice President of AICC (I)—and Laldenga The latter gave up his insistence on sovereignty. "Present Government was to be dissolved, and a coalition Government headed by Laldenga as CM and Lalthanhawla as Deputy CM would be installed." The new Ministry was to be shared by MNF and Congress (I) in the ratio of 4:5. Besides other stipulations, the MNF agreed to end its links with the TNV of Tripura and PLA of Manipur. The Centre agreed to rehabilitate its cadres coming overground. The new State could under the provisions of Part XVII of the Constitution adopt any one or more of languages for official purposes of the state and establish a separate University and a High Court. The rights of Minorities would be preserved as envisaged under the Constitution. But two elements of potential friction still survived:

one, the MNF demand for Greater Mizoram; two, the question of Chakmas. While the Centre wanted autonomy of Chakmas in the shape of Chakma ADC, to continue, both Laldenga and Sailo were opposed to it—on the ground that it would encourage further influx from the CHT.[23] Then came the 30 June 1986 Agreement which was signed by Laldenga for the MNF, Union Home Secretary, R.D. Pradhan for Government of India, and Lalkhuma, Chief Secretary, Mizoram, for Government of Mizoram.

This is one, and perhaps the only one, of several agreements signed by the Centre with a variety of the insurgent/extremist/militant groups of the North-East, that has stood the test of time.

NOTES

1. Para 20 of the Cabinet Mission Statement, 16 May 1946.
2. Other member of this Committee were Rupnath Brahma (Plains Tribal leader of Assam), A.V. Thakkar. Rev Nichols-Roy (Khasi leader), B.N. Rao (Constitutional Advisor of the Constituents Assembly. Two co-opted member from the Lushai Hills were Saprawnga and Khawtinkhuma, both members of Mizo Union Party.
3. R. Coupland (1944), *The Constitutional Problem of India,* Pt III, p. 164.
4. R. Coupland (1944), *Assam Journal of the Royal Society of Arts,* Vol. XC, 11 April 1944, p. 247.
5. S. Barkakati (1969), *Tribes of Assam,* p. 14.
6. The letter was recovered by the SF, and does not seem to have been posted.
7. Palit (1984), *Sentinels of the North-East,* p. 262.
8. B.B. Goswami, *Mizo Unrest,* p. 55.
9. Prasad (1987), p. 185.
10. *Lok Sabha Debate,* 25-3-66, Vol. L, 11, Column 7893-94.
11. Nibedan (1980), p. 110.
12. S.N. Singh, *Mizoram* (1994), p. 212.
13. *See* n 11.
14. *Amrita Bazar Patrika*, 4-7-70.
15. H.K. Sarin (1980), *Insurgency in North-East,* p. 74.
16. Order No. CLDI/1/67 dated Silchar, 2 January 1967.
17. Brig T Sailo (Retd), *Village Regrouping—A misguided concept* (A Pamphlet), p. 2.
18. *See* n 11.
19. *Ibid.*
20. *The Statesman,* 31-7-1981.
21. *The Sunday,* 28-2-82.
22. *Ibid.*
23. *Exp.,* 23-8-86.

15

Mizoram : Smaller Tribes Up in Arms How are the Original Rebels-turned-Rulers Dealing with the New Rebels?

Ironic, it definitely is! Some of the smaller tribes, which had joined the majority Mizos (earlier, Lushais) in their struggle to achieve state of their own, latter rose against them. They accused the Mizos of insensitivity towards their political aspirations, and posing serious threat to their ethnic identities. Incidentally, this was the very accusation the Mizos – and some other tribes like the Nagas—had hurled at the brutal majority of Indians destroying their ethnic identity. So, the chickens have come home to roost!

Before we take up the issue of the 'rebellion' by smaller tribes and how the erstwhile rebels-turned-rulers are dealing with the former who are tracing their well-known footsteps of the yore, it is essential to understand the background of the Mizo struggle (Mizoram Backgrounder) and somewhat detailed information on the terrorist outfits of the state.

Mizoram Backgrounder

The Mizo National Front (MNF)-led terror campaign came to an end in the Northeast Indian State of Mizoram in 1986. The MNF transformed itself into a regional political party subsequent to the signing of a Memorandum of Understanding (MoU) with the Government of India on June 30, 1986. It also formed the government, winning in the State Legislative Assembly elections, following the formal declaration of Mizoram as a State in 1987. Since then, no State-based terrorist outfit has risen to an extent that would seriously disrupt the overall peaceful environment prevailing in the State.

Intermittent incidents, nevertheless, do occur. These involve terrorist outfits whose primary area of operation is outside the State of Mizoram, but have a presence in the State. These include the Bru National Liberation Front (BNLF), Chin National Army (CNA) and the United National Liberation Front (UNLF), among others. The BNLF, which occasionally operates in the Mamit and Lunglei districts of Mizoram, is Tripura-based where approximately 32,000 Brus (Reangs) have been camping in the Kanchanpur sub-division of North

Tripura district. The BNLF's proclaimed objective is to secure a homeland for these 'refugees', and is currently engaged in negotiations with the State Government. The UNLF is Manipur-based, whereas the CNA has its base in Myanmar.

The current situation in Mizoram appears near totally peaceful if seen, especially, in the background of the insurgency that lasted for two decades, between 1966-86. There were no terrorism-related casualties in the year 2001. However, a few incidents of abductions and attacks committed by terrorist outfits operating from across the State's border were reported. The UNLF attacked the New Vervek police outpost (Aizwal) on March 2, 2001. Reports on December 27 said the Vaitin police post (Aizwal) was attacked again by the UNLF. However, the attacks were repulsed and the security forces did not incur any loss. Two Power Grid Corporation of India employees and two of the State Public Welfare Department (PWD) were abducted by Manipur-based Hmar People's Convention—Democrats (HPC-D) terrorists, on April 11, 2001. They were later released, on June 24, 2001.

The year 2000, however, was not so as peaceful. On June 30, 2000 suspected BNLF terrorists killed seven members of the anti-terrorist Hunter Force of Mizoram police and injured four others in an ambush laid along the India-Bangladesh border in the Mamit district. Barring this lone incident, no major terrorist activity was reported in Mizoram. 13 terrorism-related incidents occurred in the State between December 1998 and March 2000. These included the killing of five police personnel by suspected Manipur-based People's Liberation Army (PLA) cadres, at the Vaitin foothills, near Sakerdawi in Aizawl district, on March 24, 1999. This incident again occurred in the border areas of Mizoram.

Seen retrospectively, a perceived sense of loss of identity to Assamese domination was one of the basic factors that worked continuously to the dissatisfaction of a section of the Mizos. Mizoram was previously the Hill District Council of Assam State. Alleged discrimination against the Mizo people in various fields, including incommensurate representation at various levels of governance was another contributing factor. Finally, the alleged neglect of the sufferings of the Mizos during the 1959-famine by the Assam and Union governments, among others, worked as the immediate cause that led to the launching of the insurgency in Mizoram.

The Mizo insurgency, and its termination, is concurrent with the activities of the MNF. Insurgency in the State was at a peak when the MNF perpetrated violent acts against state structures and civilians. With the signing of the Mizo Accord on June 30, 1986, and the transformation of the MNF into a regional political party, the group has remained a part of the active political process in the State. Initially, the group was known as the Mizo National Famine Front (MNFF). It was later renamed Mizo National Front (MNF) on October 22, 1961, with Pu Laldenga as its chairman. The organisation's proclaimed objective was the attainment of a 'sovereign independent greater

Mizoram'. However, it was on February 28, 1966 that the 'movement' turned violent. Government installations at various places, including in Aizawl, Lunglei and Champhai, were simultaneously attacked, under *Operation Jericho.* By March 5, 1966, the Mizo National Army (MNA), the armed wing of MNF, had taken over these districts.

Security forces (SF) secured these places in approximately 10 days during the subsequent counter-insurgency operations conducted in those parts. 95 MNA cadres were killed and another 558 arrested during those operations. 59 SF personnel lost their lives fighting the insurgents. By end-March 1966, MNF leaders, including its president and the top-leadership—the 'high command', were compelled to seek refuge in the Chittagong Hill Tracts (CHT), in the then East Pakistan (now Bangladesh). The MNF was outlawed the year next, in 1967.

The Mizo insurgency entered a new phase of intensity with the MNF adopting guerilla tactics. Counter-insurgency operations, therefore, became more difficult as MNF cadres mixed themselves up with the local civilian population. The SFs suggested resettlement of villages as a counter-strategy. Named *'Operation Accomplishment',* it was launched in January 1967, after the Union Home Ministry gave its consent. Accordingly, 109 villages were relocated into 18 group centres of what was called Protected and Progressive Villages (PPVs), closer to either side of the Vairengte -Aizwal-Lunglei main road. In the ensuing counter-terrorism operations, 36 MNF cadres were killed. 75 security force personnel also lost their lives between January 4 and February 15, 1967. The SFs also arrested 100 MNF cadres. Phase II of *Operation Accomplishment was* launched in 1968-69. During the operation, approximately 240,000 persons constituting some 80 per cent of the total population in the Mizo Hills were organised into 102 groups by the year 1972. The idea was to isolate the terrorists from the civilian population. The terrorists, this way, would head to the nearby jungles. Security operations would be, consequently, directed against the insurgents and civilian deaths could be minimised.

Operation Accomplishment was supplemented by *Operation Blanket* during the later half of 1960s. Self-contained groups of 10 to 15 SF personnel would station in a particular location for a prolonged period of 15 to 20 days under this strategy. This was to give a feeling that their presence was not for a short duration and they were there to stay for the safety of the local population. The villagers would thus feel secured in the presence of the SFs. This was also done to encourage the local population to associate themselves with counter-insurgency operations, and to win their confidence. Also, information about the MNF would come through, it was felt, in the wake of diminishing fear of reprisal by the latter.

The following period saw intensified military action against the MNF. The Bangladesh War and its subsequent liberation from Pakistan in 1971 also led to erosion in the MNF's support and strength. The Union government, after securing a military advantage over the insurgents, offered a surrender package to the MNF. In August 1968, the Union government offered the first amnesty package to the Mizo insurgents. This included pardon to surrendered terrorists for waging war against India, and compensatory money for depositing the arms they possessed. 1,464 unarmed and 64-armed terrorists surrendered under the scheme.

The demand for a separate State also gained momentum during the period. A Mizo District Council delegation met the then Prime Minister Indira Gandhi in May 1971, and put forth the demand. The Union government's offer of conferring Union Territory status on the area was accepted with the condition that Statehood would be granted in the near future. Mizoram, thus, became a Union Territory on January 21, 1972.

Simultaneously, the government also kept the option of talks with the MNF open. Laldenga was invited to Delhi for talks and he held talks with Indira Gandhi in 1980. Although the talks failed, contacts were maintained between the Union Government and the MNF leadership. Eventually, an Accord was signed when Rajiv Gandhi was the Premier in June 1986. Laldenga was appointed as the Mizoram's Chief Minister during the same year. Mizoram also became a full-fledged State on February 20, 1987. Thus, the MNF-led two decades of insurgency came to an end, during which period the State witnessed killings of 350 civilians by the MNF in two phases -1968 and 1973-74.

The continued prevalence of peaceful environment has allowed Mizoram to endeavour on the path of development. With a literacy rate of 88.49 per cent, as per the provisional data of 2001 Census of India, the State continues to be the second most-literate Indian State. In 1998, it was reported to have over taken Kerala; as nation's most literate state. Some achievement this as a cynic put it, for an erstwhile rebellion-infested state! But since the 1990s, the Hmars and Brus have been violently agitating for greater autonomy, including ADC.

Mizoram: Essential Information

Date of Formation	20 Feb 1987
Area	21,081 sq km
Population	8,88,573
Capital	Aizwal
Principal Languages	Lushai/Mizo
	Bengali
	Lakher
	English
Major Religion	Christianity

TERRORIST/INSURGENT GROUPS OF MIZORAM

Active Terrorist/Insurgent Groups

- Bru National Liberation Front (BNLF)
- Hmar People's Convention-Democracy (HPC-D)

Now, some account of smaller tribes of Mizoram and their struggle for recognition of their ethnic identities and preservation of their distinct cultures, languages, political aspirations et al.

LAKHER (MARA) TRIBE GETS ADC

Name, Origin and People

The Lakher is a good example of the tribes who get overshadowed—even dominated—by their better-known, and at times, more powerful neighbours. No other tribes had spotlight on them, as the political space was occupied by the Mizos, not only before 1947, but also after that defining year. During their fight for autonomy, almost all other tribes joined hand with the Mizos for the "Common aim". The non-Mizo tribes became progressively conscious of their own separate identities only when the Mizos got their District Council (1952), UT (1972) and Statehood (1987). So in 1972, the Pawis, Lakhers and Chakmas got their own District Councils. Unhappy with the Mizoram State's reluctance to grant them adequate autonomous space within its boundaries, the three started clamouring for greater cultural and linguistic freedom; and the Chakmas went to the extent of agitating for a UT of their own. Since the early 1990s, the Hmars too have been waging a violent struggle for UT.

What do they think about each other ? An educated Mizo said of the Lakhers, even if not in so direct a manner: "The Lakhers are one of the laziest of tribes, who are rather averse to hard work!" A Lakher was equally prompt to return the compliment: "we are a good natured and a gentle tribe, being exploited by the Lushais."[1]

The Lakhers inhabited south-eastern corner of the Lushai Hills district and south of Haka Sub-Division of the Chin district of Burma, and north of Arakan Hill Tract. In geographical terms, the tribe was located west of Kolodyne River[2] and south of the Blue Mountain. Majority of the Lakher villages were located in the large bend of the Kolodyne ('Chhimtuipui' to the Mizos).

The principal Mara tribal groups were Tlongsai, Howthai, Zeuhnanh, Lialai, Sabeau and Heima (Shendus embraced Pawi as well as Lakher tribes). The Lakhers were surrounded by the Fanais and Lushais in west. Chins in the east and north, and the Khumis, Matus, and Khyengs in the south. The Lakhers were the branch of the 'Lai' tribe of Chin and spoke a language/dialect similar to 'Lai' (Lewin, 1869).

The Lakhers' own name for their tribe is 'Mara', the 'Lakher' being assigned to them by the Lushais when they first saw a woman plucking cotton (La=cotton; kher=to pluck).

Hutton avers that the Lakhers must be, at any period, in so far as their language and material culture are concerned, classed with the Kuki-Chin-Thadou-Lushai Group who have migrated in almost historical times down the Valley of the Chindwin from its source to the Bay of Bengal, continuously throwing off branches of their races westward into the hills, while the vanguard, having turned north again up the same valley and ranges, is still involved in a slow drift back again like their own fabled river, "which runs down to a rock in the ocean and thence flows upwards to its sources".

Here is an early anthropologist, if amateur, on the tribe: "The Lakhers are not remarkable for their beauty, but they are however of good physique, well built and strong. Average height of a male is 167/168 cms. They are taller than the Mizos, and their physical fitness compares favourably with that of their neighbours to the west in the villages situated on the lower hills between the Kolodyne and Lungleh, where inhabitants are not that healthy. The men are far more manly in appearance than the Lushais and have none of that effeminate airs which makes it so easy to mistake many Lushai men for girls. The Lakher women too are rather taller than the Lushai-Kuki women, and are of very good physique. Both sexes are of light brown complexion, with broad noses, high cheek bones, and slightly oblique Mongoloid eyes." He goes on, "In character, the Lakhers are reserved and rather dour on the surface, but when one knows them, they drop their reserve, open up, and are friendly enough. The Lushai is bound by his code of "Talawmnghai," which expects him to be kindly, hospitable and unselfish. In the absence of such a code, the Lakhers, as a community, are unsympathetic, hard, and are entirely lacking in spontaneous charm of manner and genuine kindliness like the Lushais." May be, to soften the harsh edge, he adds a contradictory rider as an afterthought: "However, as individuals, Lakhers are kindly and hospitable...but not so as a race."

MARAS: YEARNINGS FOR AUTONOMY

The Mara tribal group inhabits the south-eastern corner of Mizoram, south of the Chin Hills, and the extreme north of the Arakan Hill Tracts (AHT) of Burma. They are believed to be occupying their present habitat for over two centuries. Never a unified tribe, each Mara village was ruled by an independent, autocratic chief. A chief attacked the neighbouring village to assert supremacy, till the latter subdued and killed him and his subjects in a counter move. The Mara practice of raiding and slaughtering (head-hunting) may be dubbed as barbaric, but some thought that was the only way of ensuring peace and security even if for a short while.

Maras under the British

Once the British took over the CHT and lower AHT, they came in contact with the Maras, Lushais and Lais—the latter three being the only threat to their new acquisitions. They took considerable time to gain control over these tribes. Some of the Mara tribes in Arakan had been under the British rule in the second half of the 19th century. The Chiefs of Saiha, Serkawr and Chapui followed suite in the later part of the 19th and early years of 20th century. In 1931-32, the Zawngling area, till then under loose control of Chin Hills district of Burma, was incorporated into the Lushai Hills district[3] while the adjoining areas continued under the Burmese Government. Thus it was that all the Mara areas come under the British rule but divided under the British Indian and British Burmese administrative control. Earlier, at the Conference of Chin-Lushai Hills held at Calcutta on 29-1-1882 and at the Conference of the Superintendents of three Tracts— Northern Lushai Hills, Southern Lushai Hills, and Chin Hills—held at Lungleh, 14-18 January 1896, the Northern AHT and South Lushai Hills, respectively, were brought under the administrative control of the Chief Commissioner of Assam. Then the Eastern Bengal and Assam Government decided to fix the boundary of the district on the south of Serkawr Region and proposals to this end, made by Col Loch and modified by Maj Cole, Superintendent of the Lushai Hills, were approved by Government vide their Letter No. 423 dated 21-6-1911[4] Keokralong on the CHT border was taken as the western starting point and the line ran fairly straight east across the Kolodvne—past Kaisi to the Sulla and then northeast past Laki, and keeping north of Zawngling, unfortunately for the Maras, as they were separated between India and Burma for administrative convenience and historical reasons.

Like the rest of Indians, the Maras under the British did enjoy certain—if minimum—constitutional rights when the Lushai Hills came under the British. The Government of Assam recommended the exclusion of the Lushai Hills from the Reforms envisaged under the 1919 Act. The fear was that the Hill people may be exploited by the Plains people. Again, under the 1935 Act, the Lushai Hills became the Excluded Area. And wisely, the Constituent Assembly placed the Lushai Hills under the Sixth Schedule.

Dawn of Political Consciousness

In 1938, McCall, Superintendent of Lushai Hills, reported that the Maras, after less than a decade of administration, had realised "that the British control had brought them the safety and prosperity". His successor L.L. Peters, mooted the idea of having a collective body of the Chiefs in Lushai Hills to aid and advise him. Consequently, in 1939 a chiefs' conference was formed, of which Chhohmo, Chief of Serkawr, was a member. It was later re-named as Lushai Chiefs' Council. In 1941, McCall created a District Chiefs Durbar in which chiefs of each administrative circle sent a representative on the basis of election.

Under Hlychho, founder President of Mara Freedom Party and son of Chhohmo, the Maras became politically conscious in early 1940s. During his visit in 1944, Capt AI Bowman, Additional Superintendent, took note of this awakening and advised Chhohmo, Chief of Serkawr, to demand better status for Maras. So, a Mara chiefs conference was convened at Serkawr on 4-1-1945, which was attended by 23 Chiefs, including those of Serkawr, Zawngling, Laki, Chapui, Tongkalong, Vahai, Saiha, Tuippang, Mualbu, Tuithumhnar, and Bungtlang. The resolution dated 4-1-1945 demanded that the Lakhers, divided in three sections, be united and a separate Lakher district be created for them. Its area would work out about 150 miles from north to south, and 130 miles from east to west. As the War was still on, no action was taken on their memorandum. The Chiefs again sent a memorandum in December 1945, repeating the demand for a Lakher Hills district. They wanted to be under either Burma Government or the Crown Colony, but not under the Lushai Hills district. This was the nascent Lakher-Lushai rivalry—if not antipathy—60 years ago! Chhohmo (L) Chief of Serkawr submitted another representation to the Governor of Assam on 7-7-1947, on behalf of the Mara Chiefs, repeating the earlier demands viz the three Lakher areas be united in one district, or "We and our country be given over to Burma.... We have no design to join in with the Mizo Union nor do we wish to be under the rule of the Lushais."

In 1946, the Superintendent, A.R. MacDonold had ordered a fresh election to the durbar, allowing commoners also to elect their representatives, along with the Chiefs who would elect their own representatives separately. In January 1946, the Mara Assembly, presided over by D.A. Penn, SDO, Lungleh, elected Laithuma as their representative. This meeting also passed a resolution for introduction of Lushai as medium of instruction in Schools in Mara area, which proved detrimental to the Lakher interests, educationally and socially.

On 17 April 1947, the Bordoloi Committee[5] visited Lushai Hills and heard varying demands: (1) A section under R. Vanlawma demanded "self rule". (2) The Mizo Union under Ch Saprawnga demanded ADC within Indian Union. (3) Another section demanded self-determination under Burma. Finally, the Committee recommended the Regional Council (RC). A new political Party, United Mizo Freedom Organisation (IJMFQ) was formed on 15 July 1947, which demanded union with Burma. But it could not go far. The Mizo District Council was set up early 1952. The Pawi-Lakher Regional Council (PL-RC) was inaugurated on 23 April 1953, which granted the two minority tribes of Mizoram a fair amount of autonomy to govern themselves.

The working of the PL-RC was marred by inter-tribal quarrels and the Lais were the gainers as they, being educationally advanced, got better jobs and posts. Finally, the Maras convened a General Assembly at Saiha in April

1953 and resolved to set up a new regional party and called it Mara Freedom Party (MFP). The MFP demanded Mara ADC, Mara dialect as its official language, and an opportunity to develop the area according to their own genius. Meanwhile came the election to the third PL-RC, which was boycotted by the Maras. So only the Lais and Chakmas were elected to the RC. The fifth General Assembly of the Maras held at Serkawr on 5 February 1965 resolved to create the Mara ADC. All the Mara staff resigned from the PL-RC and started working for the Mara ADC without any pay. Nothing came out of this futile exercise and the Maras decided to contest elections to the fourth PL-RC in 1966. But due to inter- and intra-tribal bickering, worsened by the toppling game, the RC could not function. It was a tower of Babel, as the members spoke in their own tongue, not understood by others. The Lais too joined, finally, in demanding their own A DC. The leaders of the PL-RC went to Delhi in 1970 to demand ADC for their respective tribe. When under the North-East Areas (Reorganisation) Act, 1971, Mizoram became a Union Territory in 1972, the PL-RC was abolished and in its place, three District Councils were established, named after their own tribes. Thus the MFP claimed success in having their own (Lakher) ADC in 1972.

PAWI (LAI OR CHIN) TRIBE

Pawis in Mizoram

Numbering over 30,000, the Pawis form a small tribe, mostly confined to Chhimtuipui district (Sangau and Lawngtlai Blocks) of Mizoram.[6] To counter the regional policies of the Lakhers and Lushais, and to unite the Pawis living in different pockets of "Mizoram and in the neighbouring areas of Burma, the Pawi elite, led by L. Chinzah, formed Chin National Front (CNF), a clan-based party, in 1965. Indicative of a nationalist spirit, and political vision, they criticised the MNF activities in the Pawi area. They also disapproved of the Lushais acting as a big brother in Mizoram politics and particularly their interference in the PL-RC area.[7] In fact, L. Chinzah wrote in 1967 that "MNF was earning only hatred in Pawi-Lakher region".[8] It is easily conceded that they are not advanced, educationally and politically, like the Lushais and its ruling clan, the Sailos; but they are very proud of their culture, language and traditions. Very conscious of their distinct identity, they are keen to promote their language and culture to preserve it. Like the Lakhers, the Pawis resent being called/identified as Mizos, even though they may not flaunt their identity loudly in the bazars/offices of Aizawl. Given their small number, they nurture psychological fear of being dominated if not swamped by the predominant Mizos. The feeling that they are looked down upon by the Mizos, have generated a sense of dislike for the latter. This political discomfort has been gradually reinforced in the State and reached openly above the surface because all the levers of power are controlled by the Mizos and all financial resources are also diverted to their benefits.

Pawis *(Pois)* Outside Mizoram

Like many other tribes, the *Pois* are also found scattered outside Mizoram. There is a sizeable population of *Pois* (larger designation, Kuki) in Bangladesh's CHT, claimed to be motherland of the Lais *(Pois)* since the historical times. The 1947 Partition ruptured the ethnic unity of the Pawi family—splitting it into three areas of concentration in India, Pakistan/ Bangladesh and Burma. There has always been a strong yearning amongst them to be untied within a compact geographical 'Unit'. To promote this idea and sentiment, the Pawi leader L. Damngama submitted a memorandum to Prime Minister Rajiv Gandhi on 11 February 1988, 'claiming that the tribal King Vanhnuaitlirha of Rengtlang had collected land tax from the people inhabiting the region between Satikang River near Chittagong and Cox Bazar, that is Bay of Bengal. After Vanhnuaitlirha, his son and successor Liankung, ruling from Bandarban, also collected the land tax from this area. After Liankung's death, We (CHT tribals) paid their taxes to Zohan, the king of Lawngtlai upto February 1947. After 1947, *We* (Pawis) found themselves divided into the Indian and Pakistani Pawis—a part of their compatriots already having been apportioned to Burma in 1935.

Pawi leaders claimed they were given assurances during their *Liberation Struggle* by the Bangladesh leaders, particularly Mujib-ur-Rahman that CHT inhabitants could opt for either Bangladesh or India. "The promises not kept, the Pawis of CHT had to live there as slaves." There are some other minor tribes there (Bawm, Brun, Moa-Maria, etc.), who also shared the travails of the Pawis. These people are ardent in their desire to live in India and to regain their lost shore-line between Satikang River and Cox Bazar Port, by liberating their motherland. They have formed a party, the Seawind, with the aim of liberating the 'Pawi Land' under Bangladesh. "A national volunteer force—Hill Tract Pawi Liberation Organisation (HTPLO)—has also been raised."[9]

They are persisting with their struggle. The leaders of the predominant Lai tribe (Pawi) of Mizoram submitted a memorandum to Prime Minister Deve Gowda in December 1996 demanding *Lairam,* a UT to be created in Mizoram exclusively for their ethnic minority community. The Prime Minister assured the delegation led by F. Manghnuna, President, Lai People's Party (LPP), of sympathetic consideration of the demand.[10] They claimed that the Lais who had historically been a distinct tribe, separate from the Mizos and acknowledged as such by the Constitution, were now facing the danger of being swamped by the Mizos, and a UT was the only way to preserve their culture and identity. LPP Vice President L. Chinzah says the aspirations of his tribe have been neglected by the Centre. Another Lai leader, B. Thanchunga claims the Lais have played a significant and peaceful role in the insurgency-torn North-East by abjuring violence and secessionist path.

The Pawis did get their own ADC in 1972, but they do not seem to be content with it, as the above account shows. They have set their eyes on a UT status for their area.

HMAR TRIBE: The Defiant one

The Hmars are one of the smaller tribes of Mizoram.

Name, Origin and People

Certain tribes had migrated/settled in the then Lushai Hills before the main one—Lushai (Mizo). There were constant jostling for space between the two. Repeated Lushai head-hunting expeditions and successive waves of Lushai migration pushed some earlier tribes to the north-eastern part of Lushai Hills, viz, the Hmar and Thado. Are the Hmars part of the Mizo group of tribes? The answer yesterday might have been 'yes' but today it is definite 'no'. Lt Col HWG Gole, the then Superintendent of the District wrote: "The Hmars are only a clan of the Lushais". During the Mizo struggle for autonomy during the 1960s-70s the smaller tribes of the area had submerged their identities into the overarching Mizo identity. Once Mizos got their UT (and later State), the smaller tribes became conscious of their ethnic identity and threat to it from the overbearing Mizo majority. When the Pawi, Lakher and Chakma got their respective ADC, the others like the Hmars, Paites, Riangs, Raltes, Thados, etc. felt ignored, isolated. and discriminated against. So they also started clamouring for ADCs for themselves to preserve their culture and traditions.

The Hmars claim to belong to the Kuki-Chin ethnic group. Even in the SC and ST Lists (Modification) Order, 1936, issued by the Government of India, MHA vide their Modification No. SRO 2477-A dated 29-10-56, the Hmars are regarded as a separate tribe, independent of the Kukis or the Lushais.

The term 'Hmar' itself means 'north'; meaning the people living in the north of Lushai Hills. The term was used by the Mizos in general and the Lushais in particular. Besides their habitat in Mizoram (northern blocks of Aizawl district), they are also settled in the contiguous areas of the following states and Burma:

1. Churachandpur district of Manipur.
2. Cachar and Northern Cachar Hills districts of Assam.
3. Northern and North-eastern parts of Tripura.
4. North-western parts of Burma across the border.

As for their origin and migration, there are several conflicting theories, even if the majority believes they came to India from the Chin Hills of Burma. They seem to have been the first to settle in the Lushai Hills who (Rangkhel and Beite communities of the Hmars) then were driven out to areas mentioned above, first by the Kukis (mainly the Thados and Changsens) and then by the Lushais. Their tradition and folklore have reference to the Sinlung civilisation of the Hmar people. Thus Sinlung.[11] somewhere in the Central Asia, may be inferred to be the original abode of the Hmars. Theory has it that they also emerged out of a cave, and after a time the God closed its exit with a stone, shutting them off from their original home. The stone they talk about is possibly the Great Wall of China which blocked their path back to Sinlung. On their way to the Lushai Hills, the Hmars moved along the Himalayas, came to the Mishmi land and then reached the Irrawaddy, and moving along its course, entered Shan State. Thence crossing the Indo-Burmese border, they reach Lushai Hills. The story of their further feuds fes and pushing around by the Kukis and Mizos has been mentioned above, and the latter two also called the Hmars as 'Khawthlang' (=westerners).

Population: Hmar

Here is some interesting if confusing data on Hmar population from various Census Reports:

1901	–	10,411	1971	–	4,524
1961	–	3,108	1981	–	13,102

If we are to accept the 1901 census figures, the Hmar population today within Mizoram ought to have crossed 1 lakh mark. One fact is clear: The Hmars were often grouped under 'Mizo' head during the subsequent census operations. Presently, the Hmars claim their tribe counts at 1.5 lakhs.

The Hmars are good blacksmiths, carpenters, brass workers turning out all their daily-use items. The Hmar women are good at pottery-making. The availability of good clay for making pots is one of the criteria for choosing a village site. They execute the whole process, from start to finish, manually as they know not the use of wheel.

Let this part end with a lament from a local author: "unfortunately, the Hmar's skill described above is gradually decaying due to corroding effect of western wind that is blowing the Hmar land below the shadow of the cross."[12]

HMAR: STRUGGLE FOR AUTONOMY

Inter-tribal feuds, often leading to head-hunting incidents, were common since the days of early migration of various Mizo tribes. This led to these early migrants settling in the eastern parts of the present Mizoram—contiguous with Burmese territory. The successive waves of migrants (Lusei) pushed the earlier settlers, viz Hmars and Thadous, out of their abode into northern and northeastern end of Mizoram and beyond *i.e.* to the contiguous districts of Assam (Cachar and North Cachar Hills, etc.) and Manipur (Churachandpur etc.). So Hmars and Thadous belonging to Kuki Chin ethnic group and presently occupying these areas—the bordering fringes of these three States—were in regular contact with the plains people of Cachar and Manipur.

The Hmars in northern Mizoram—essentially in the northern Blocks of Aizawl district—enumerated 13,102 in 1981 Census, but merely 3,108 in 1961 and 4,524 in 1971. That only means that the Hmars were included in and counted as part of the large Mizo tribe! For record, they counted 10,411 in 1901. "1.5 lakh Hmars are settled in contiguous areas of Manipur, Assam and Tripura, beyond Mizoram's State boundaries, and in North-Western Burma, beyond its international boundaries."[13]

The Hmar played a vital role in the early political movements of the erstwhile Lushai Hills district. Being in contact with the educated people of the Plains districts, they were rather politically conscious. It was no surprise that H.K. Bawichhuaka, a Hmar, was elected Secretary of the Mizo Union (MU) in 1946. Again, it was another Hmar, Pachhunga, who played an important role in organising public meetings of the MU and in its consolidation. "Both were the destiny makers of Mizoram before the Independence."[14] Things changed after 1947, particularly after Mizoram became a UT in 1972, because the Hmars felt cheated out of the political and economic gains that accrued from these two events. Political power went mostly to the Lusei and smaller tribes like Pawi and Lakher—generating ill-feeling among the Hmars over their deprivation. What was worse, subsequent to its elevation to the Statehood, clan-based politics raised its ugly head, vitiating the hitherto healthy atmosphere. This inter-tribe tug-of-the-war posed a threat to the Mizo society and state. The Hmar battle for preserving its ethnic identity is the most important development in the recent political history of Mizoram. Because of their location near Mizoram's international borders, their struggle has wider, geostrategic implication for integrity of Mizoram and security of India. If not handled carefully, the ethnic tension could spin out of control.

Growing feeling of frustration and not seeing any hope for their community generated a sense of being discriminated against among the Hmar youth. Consequently, they have developed separatist tendencies. The next to follow logically was the raising of militant outfits like the Hmar People's Convention (HPC) and Hmar Volunteer Cell (HVC). The HPC demanded in 1988 an autonomous region, comprising Hmar-inhabited areas of Mizoram, Manipur, Assam (Cachar[15]). They got an enthusiastic response from the Hmar youth, and were able to train 50 HPC cadres in late 1989 in physical and ideological training, at New Vervek, a Mizo village adjoining Cachar.[16] To begin with, the HPC is demanding an autonomous homeland for the Hmars in North Mizoram. The HPC and HVC, resorting to active agitational approach, observed a 120-hour Bandh in the first week of 1990 in support of their demand. Chasing the volunteers, Mizoram Police easily succeeded in locating their not-so-well-planned hide-outs in the south-western Manipur in Churachandpur area. That they had some plans for subversive action was clear from the secret documents found on the person of a young Hmar leader, Leichhung Hmar.[17] Desirous of establishing a distinct identity, they continued their agitation for grant of an Autonomous District Council (ADC) under Sixth Schedule in the Hmar area of North Mizoram, threatening a 'civil war' on the issue. When Hmar volunteer Vanlalliana died in custody on 14 March 1990, S. Khuma, Publicity Secretary of HPC, held the police responsible for his death, though the latter called it a case of suicide.[18]

The armed struggle for an ADC, starting in 1988, had till mid-1991 resulted in the killing of 6 Policemen, one Home Guard and two civilian officers, besides extortions. Some of their subversive activities are mentioned here. The HPC called for a 10-day blockade of Silchar-Aizawl NH54 in July 1989. That the Hmar militants, trained for the guerrilla warfare in the camps located in the wooded areas around the Manipur-Mizoram-Assam trijunction, were in a position to establish a nexus with the NSCN, worried Guwahati. The deep, inaccessible jungle of Cachar afforded a safe passage to the militants for assault in Mizoram and retreat into Manipur. On 13 September 1989, the Assam Police and Village Defence Party in a joint raid arrested five HPC volunteers at Lalpani on Cachar-Manipur border. Their interrogation disclosed that the militants were receiving training under a retired Army major, Zuala. HPC cadres had to shift from Mankachar village under Darilawn PS of Mizoram.

During 1989-91, HPC and State Government had held two rounds of official-level talks, but without any results since the latter was set against any more ADCs as the three already existing had proved a headache for it. It was also wary of setting a precedent, as the Paite Tribe in Aizawl district had by then started clamouring for an ADC of their own. Incidentally, from early days, the Hmars have been demanding tripartite talks, though both New Delhi and Aizawl want the State Government alone to tackle the issue with the Hmars. In April 1988, a HPC delegation had visited Delhi to press their demand for an ADC with the Centre:[19] Hrangkhal, a Hmar MLA from Tapaimukh, Hmar dominated area of south-west Manipur, was the man behind this delegation. Many HPC leaders and over 200 cadres had found sanctuary in Hmar dominated Manipur area of Tapaimukh and nearby Thenlon *(Telegraph,* 8-4-88).

6,000 Hmars of Fulertal, a foothill village, 40 km from Silchar felt aggrieved over the Assam Government's dithering in implementing an order issued by its Chief Secretary on 24 December 1982, giving the ST status to the Hmars in Cachar. L.T. Buhril, a member of Silchar Mohakuma Parishad from Fulertal, accused the Government of depriving the Hmars of economic, educational, and employment benefits due to the STs *(Telegraph,* 1-9-88). The HPC was reportedly encouraged by Thanglein Khuma, a Hmar leader close to Laldenga, former Chief Minister and MNF leader. There were reports that the HPC President J.H. Thanzam, then (1988-89) in Manipur and known as a moderate leader of Churachandpur district, had been organising the Hmars for armed struggle with Mizoram. On 28 June 1989, the Hmar National Union (HNU), an association of over 20,000 Hmars of Barak Valley and North Cachar, held a meeting at Fulertal under the Presidentship of Buhril and expressed solidarity with the cause of HPC. It was also attended by Hmar leaders from Cachar. Karimganj and Manipur. Chief Minister Lalthanhawla rejected their demand (September 1989) for an ADC but expressed willingness to address all their genuine problems. He also said that but for one village, the Hmars had no majority in northern part of Mizoram. Contesting this assertion, Thanzam claimed the State Government had rigged the Census figures to manipulate Lushai majority in the north Mizoram in order to deny the Hmars an ADC covering 5 Blocks, comprising 13 villages like Ratu, Dailawn, Swadgputlawn, etc. in that area. The Hmar Students Union (HSU) is also mobilizing students for the Hmar issue. "The issue of identity of over 1 lakh Hmars and their agitation for its preservation may fuel similar agitations among the minority tribes." This can be seen as a potential danger to the integrity of this sensitive border state. Earlier in June 1989, Thanzam had reiterated that HPC was spearheading a movement for creation of a Hmar ADC, comprising area of northern Mizoram and adjoining areas of Manipur (Churachandpur) and Assam (southern Cachar) having a population of over 80,000 *(Sunday Weekly,* 3-6-89).

Mid-1991, the HPU had sent feelers to Chief Minister Lalthanhawla for a political level bipartite talks on its demand, but nothing more was heard on it.

The Hmar autonomy demand is most important political development but is potentially dangerous for security of Mizoram, and even India as located they are on the international borders, and the movement has geo-political significance. Convinced that fruits of participatory democracy are being enjoyed by others, the Hmars are suffering from sense of deprivation. The Hmars of Churachandpur district are educationally and economically advanced, which has a 'demonstration effect' on their brethren in the adjoining areas of Cachar and Mizoram; and the latter want to be united with the former to develop according to their own genius.

The Hmars who struggled for autonomy, demanding a UT, or the ADC at the very least, later settled with the State Government with an Accord in 1994. Earlier they had been active in the North Cachar Hills, and were—and could be in future too—a potential allies of the NSCN(I-M). But the things have been quiet on the Hmar front since the 1994 Accord.

Aftermath of the Accord: A discord

Consequent to the nine rounds of talks with the Mizoram Government, the parent body, HPC, signed an Accord with it on 27 July 1994. This MoS established the 'Sinlung Development Council', and subsequently, 308 HPC militants surrendered along with their arms. But dissatisfied with the implementation process, a section of the cadres parted ways with the overground HPC and formed the HPC (D) in 1995. As its terrorist violence shows under the relevant time line, it has been now heading the 'war' for an independent Hmar State (Hmar ram) consisting of the Hmar inhabited areas of Mizoram, Manipur and Assam.

It seems to be history repeating itself. When the Naga leader Phizo signed peace poet with New Delhi, the I-M duo rebelled and carried on with the insurgency till date. There is a lesson in all this: When the authorities (the states or the Centre) sign a MoU or MoS with the rebels they must involve second line of leadership with it. Interestingly, second round of talks of the present (2007) series were held at New Delhi with the NSCN (I-M) on 29 Mar 2007, and who were keenly awaiting the outcome from the sidelines? None else than rebels of 'K' faction. What happens when they up the ante?

Reverting to the HPC (D), there seems to be no light at the end of the tunnel!

HMAR PEOPLE'S CONVENTION-DEMOCRACY (HPC-D)

Formation

Hmar People's Convention-Democracy (HPC-D) is an offshoot of the Hmar People's Convention (HPC), which came into existence in 1986, as a political party spearheading a movement for self-government in the north and northeast of Mizoram. The Hmars, who according to the 1991 census, were 12,535 in number in Mizoram, were disappointed with the contents of the MIZO Peace Accord of 1986, which failed to address their demand of a 'Greater Mizoram' integrating all areas inhabited by Hmars in Mizoram, Assam and Manipur under a single administrative unit. Since April 1987, the HPC waged an armed struggle for autonomy, which touched extreme levels of violence towards 1991. Hmar cadres abducted tea executives and triggered off a spate of extortions in the Hmar inhabited areas of the States of Mizoram, Assam and Manipur.

In 1992, HPC representatives and the Government of Mizoram mutually agreed to hold ministerial level talks. Consequent to nine rounds of such talks, a Memorandum of Settlement (MoS) was signed at the Mizoram capital Aizawl on July 27, 1994, for establishing the 'Sinlung Development Council' and subsequently, 308 HPC militants surrendered along with their arms.

However, dissatisfied with the implementation process, a section of the cadres parted ways with the over ground HPC and formed the HPC-D in 1995.

Objective

The purported objective of the outfit over the years has changed from an autonomous district covering the north and northeast Mizoram to an independent Hmar State (Hmar ram) consisting of the Hmar inhabited areas of Mizoram, Manipur and Assam.

Leadership

The outfit's 'commander-in-chief' is Lalrupui. Its military wing is headed by Laltuolien Hmar. While Lalbieknunga functions as its 'deputy commander-in-chief', Lalrawngbawl Pulamte is the 'information and publicity secretary' of the outfit. The cadre strength of the outfit is estimated to be between 100 and 150. In July 2003 during the Hmar-Dimasa conflict in the North Cachar (NC) Hills district of Assam, the HPC-D formed an armed wing, the Hnam Santu (Hmar Protection Cell), under the leadership of chief commander Laltuolien Hmar, to protect the interests of the Hmars from the alleged onslaught of the DHD. The outfit conducted a successful recruitment drive and inducted several young Hmar boys and girls from across the NC Hills and Cachar district into the newly formed cell.

Areas of Operation

The outfit is active primarily in Mizoram; the Hmar inhabited areas of Churachandpur district in Manipur, and the Cachar (with base camps in the Bhuban hill range) and North Cachar Hills districts of Assam.

Often, the outfit has used the Bhuban hill range in Cachar district and the Jinam valley area of the North Cachar hills located at the intersection of Manipur, Nagaland and Assam to set up base camps and plan operations.

Source of Funding

The outfit collects 'protection fees' from the timber mafia in the Cachar district of Assam. Substantial funds are also reportedly generated in foreign countries, notably in the United States, by protagonists of the struggle in the name of protecting Hmar Christians.

There are also reports that the outfit collects protection money from the Hmar tribals.

Arms and Explosives

Over the years, the HPC-D militants have gained access to sophisticated arms like rifles of the AK series, assault rifles of the G3 series and explosives.

However, access to such sophisticated arms is still limited and majority of the outfit's cadres use SBBL single barrel guns, and ordinary country made rifles and pistols.

Linkages with Other Groups

HPC-D, since its formation, has aligned with several insurgent groups active in India's northeast. In its formative years, it maintained a cordial relationship with the National Socialist Council of Nagaland (NSCN), which allegedly provided it with arms and training. It has also carried out attacks with the support of the Manipur-based outfit, the People's Liberation Army (PLA).

In May 2001, the HPC-D joined the Indigenous People's Revolutionary Alliance (IPRA) - a platform of the five Zo ethnic militant groups: the Zomi Reunification Organisation (ZRO), two factions of the Kuki National Front, the KNF-P and KNF-MC, the Kuki National Army (KNA) and the HPC-D. However, at least two incidents of internecine clashes were reported between the HPC-D and the ZRA, the armed wing of the ZRO, during 2004 in the Churachandpur district of Manipur. This finally led to the signing of a truce agreement between both these outfits on April 7, 2004, at an unspecified location in Manipur.

Over the years, the HPC-D has also maintained links with other Hmar militant outfits. In July 1998, the HPC-D joined hands with the Hmar Revolutionary Force (HRF).

The outfit is also believed to have maintained strategic links with the Bru National Liberation Front (BNLF), a Mizoram-based group.

In Assam, the HPC-D is known to have some linkages with certain Islamist terrorist outfits.

MAJOR INCIDENTS INVOLVING HPC-D

2006

- March 13: The HPC-D refutes the accusation made by the UNLF of its involvement in the displacement of Hmar people from Manipur.
- March 11: The HPC-D accuses the KCP of its involvement along with the UNLF in the assault on Hmar women and extortion of money from the Hmar civilians in Churachandpur district of Manipur.
- February 2: Hmar and Paite tribesmen, who were forced out by militants along the Assam-Mizoram border, are reported to have returned to their homes at Thanlon and Parbung in the Churachandpur district. Nearly 1,000 villagers had reportedly fled their homes following a clash between the UNLF and HPC-D in January 2006.
- January 27: The 'information and publicity secretary' of HPC-D, R. Pulamte, while rejecting the 'accusation' of UNLF that his outfit is responsible for the 'torture' of villagers of Parbung and Tipaimukh subdivisions in the Churachandpur district, says that the Barak river region has been the main source of income and

means of livelihood for the people of Tipaimukh, "but since UNLF's 'occupation' of the region, heavy taxes' on all items/ commodities pertaining to the Hmars without the 'consent' of the HPC-D had paved way for the deteriorating relationship between the UNLF and the Hmar outfit."

- January 23: UNLF 'accuses' the HPC-D, of 'conniving' with the SFs and 'harassing' the villagers of Parbung and Tipaimukh sub-divisions in Churachandpur district, forcing them to flee to the neighbouring State of Mizoram.
- January 7: Two suspected HPC-D cadres are killed in an encounter with UNLF militants at Damdei under Parbung police station in the Churachandpur district.

2005

- November 4: HPC-D serves extortion notes on several persons in Mizoram's Vairangte village demanding a portion of their salaries. The notes, written in Hmar dialect, say that five per cent of the salary for October is to be paid to the outfit by November 15.
- March 2: A HPC-D cadre is killed by security force personnel during a counter insurgency operation in the Churachandpur district of Manipur.

2004

- July 26: Suspected HPC-D militants attack a security outpost at Sonai block in the Cachar district of Assam.
- June 12: Six persons including officials, employees and two guards of a cement manufacturing company, are abducted by a group of suspected HPC-D cadres in the North Cachar Hills district.
- April 7: The HPC-D and the Zomi Revolutionary Army (ZRA) sign a 'truce agreement' during a meeting held at the residence of L B Sona, chairman of the Zomi Council, at an unspecified location in Manipur.
- March 31: Two HPC-D cadres are killed during an internecine clash between the HPC-D and ZRA at Rengkai village in the Churachandpur district of Manipur.
- March 28: A HPC-D militant is killed in an internecine clash with ZRA militants at Renki in the Churachandpur district of Manipur.
- January 16: An unidentified terrorist is killed during an encounter between the Army and suspected HPC-D and Naga terrorists at Moulin in the North Cachar Hills district of Assam.

2003

- November 21: HPC-D in a press release refutes news reports regarding its involvement in the abduction of three candidates for the State Legislative Assembly Elections from Suangpuilawn constituency in Mizoram.
- October 14: Two suspected HPC-D cadres are arrested from the Hmarculin area in Cachar district of Assam.
- September 8: Four HPC-D terrorists are killed and another is injured during an encounter in the Jinam Valley area of North Cachar Hills district of Assam.
- August 6: Remaining two officials of the Government's Public Welfare Department (PWD), held captive by the anti-talks faction of the UPDS since July 8 are set free.
- August 5: Alleged plot of the HPC-D to set up a training camp in the jungles near Nagadum village in Cachar district unearthed.
- August 2: Suspected HPC-D terrorists blow up a bus that was being used in the Khuga dam project at Senveg village in Manipur's Churachandpur district by triggering an Improvised Explosive Device (IED).
- July 17: Media reports indicate formation of Hmar Hunam Santo (HHS) with links to the HPC-D as counter outfit of the DHD in Assam.
- July 4: A girl is killed and a school and 25 *Dimasa* (tribe) dwellings are set ablaze by suspected HPC-D terrorists in Berelang village, North Cachar Hills district.
- July 1: Assam Government appoints Justice P C Phukan of the Guwahati High Court to probe into the inter-tribal clashes between Hmars and the Dimasas in the North Cachar Hills and Cachar districts.
- June 29: Four HPC-D terrorists are arrested from the Marshakhal Punji area in Cachar district of Assam.
- June 20: Six HPC-D terrorists are killed in an encounter with the security forces at Phyleh village in Cachar district.
- June 18: Suspected HPC-D terrorists fire a Rocket Propelled Grenade (RPG) on a clubhouse at Kumocheera under Lakhipur police station limits in Cachar district where some members of the Dimasa community had gathered for a meeting.

- June 17: Dimasa Students' Community at Guwahati demands that the Government should flush out HPC-D terrorists from the State who are alleged to be operating from the neighbouring States of Manipur and Mizoram.
- June 16: An estimated 70 HPC-D cadres set ablaze 50 houses in Dipucherra Dimasa village in Cachar district. In an ensuing encounter with the police, one militant is killed.
- June 12: Police recover 10 pipe-guns and two kilograms of gunpowder from a house in Maiserpunji, a Hmar village in Cachar district, following an attack on Dihankru, a Dimasa village in North Cachar Hills district, by suspected HPC-D terrorists who set ablaze approximately 40 houses. Visiting Ministerial team led by State Health Minister Bhumidhar Barman recommends an immediate operation to flush out the HPC-D terrorists from the North Cachar Hills district. HPC-D terrorists set ablaze approximately 15 Dimasa dwellings in the Daudung and Duiyungkhro villages in North Cachar hills district.
- June 10: Five persons are killed and three others injured in a clash between suspected HPC-D militants and security forces near Mahur in the North Cachar Hills district.
- June 9: Ten HPC-D militants are arrested from Bitheipunji in the Cachar district for their involvement in the killing of Dimasa tribals.
- June 8: Two women are killed and a dozen others injured in an attack by HPC-D militants in Kalinagar village of Cachar district.
- June 6: HPC-D terrorists attack Lodi Basti, a Dimasa populated village, which straddles Cachar and North Cachar Hills districts and kill three tribals, including two women. The terrorists also set ablaze approximately 50 dwellings. Three Dimasa youths are killed by suspected Hmar militants in the North Cachar Hills district.
- May 31: Suspected HPC-D terrorists attack a village of the Dimasa tribes, Longreng under Haflong police station limits in Assam's North Cachar Hills district, and kill two of them. Ten tribal dwellings are also set ablaze.
- May 7: Two Dima Halim Daogah (DHD) terrorists are killed in an encounter with HPC-D cadres at Retzol in the Haflong town of North Cachar Hills district.
- April 11: Six HPC-D militants are arrested from the Sonai police station area in Cachar district.
- April 7: An army personnel is killed in an encounter with suspected HPC-D militants at Didkokcherra in the North Cachar Hills district.

- March 31: 26 Dimasa villagers are killed by suspected HPC-D militants in Chekerchand village of Cachar district.
- February 24: Three DHD cadres are abducted by HPC-D militants in the Cachar district.

1999

- August 21: HPC-D militants abduct four milk vendors near Bishnupur village in Cachar district. They are reportedly released after payment of a ransom of Rupees one Lakh.
- March-April: Seven people are killed during an ambush by HPC-D militants in an Hmar-dominated area in Mizoram.

1998

November: Three HPC-D militants are arrested along with some arms in the North Cachar hills district.

Reang (Bru) Tribe: The Violent one

The Reang tribals have a good presence in Mizoram and is the second largest group in Tripura. Also known as Bru (Reang's own name for themselves), the Mizos call them Tuikuks (Tui in Mizo = water) as their settlements were invariably by a river or spring. According to an unsubstantiated version, the total Reang population in Mizoram is about 85,000, scattered in 120 villages in Mamit district where most of the Reang villages are located. The State Government finds such claims hyperinflated and asserts that the total population of the Reangs, Mizos and Chakmas in the district is 64,572 and the Reangs are in a minority.

The Reangs are mostly in the north-west part of Mizoram along the Tripura border.

The Reangs strongly resent Mizo attitude towards their tribe. The latter, according to one version, tend to treat them as a bunch of lazy people who would not learn to follow a civilised pattern of life *(Hindu,* 27-5-98). "The mild-tempered tribe is generally looked down upon by the more forward looking and financially well off Mizos, who call them a semi-nomadic tribe" *(Sunday Observer,* 5-11th April 98). The Reangs mostly live on the Jhum or shifting cultivation of Mizo farms. "The Mizo Christians had imparted formal education and tried to pin them down to one place through various social welfare programmes." But the Reangs continue to live like nomads. It appears that the feeling of deprivation has driven many Reangs to adopt Mizo names. Even the Government officials agree that they might have felt they were treated as aliens and wanted to carve out a future for themselves in a separate homeland.

"The Reangs of Mizoram have been at the receiving end of a schizophrenic violence since October 1997", wrote Nitin A. Gokhale *(The*

Outlook, 11-5-98). Says M.S. John, Information and Publicity Secretary of the Mizoram Reang Refugee Committee (MRRC): "Towards the end of September 1997, we had assembled at Saipuilui village to discuss our autonomy demand when a band of Mizo youth under the banner of the Joint Action Committee (JAC) and aided by several personnel of the Mizoram Armed Police (MAP) attacked the meeting. They charged us with trying to divide Mizoram. After that day, the looting, killing and raping spree began. We had no alternative but to flee for our lives." Soon the trickle became an exodus. By 1 October 1997, over 12,000 Reang refugees were sheltered in 22 camps in North Tripura. By April 1998, 27,000 refugees had arrived in Tripura, alleging persecution at the hands of the majority Mizos Most of the camps were located at/around Kanchanpur, a small market town on Tripura-Mizoram border, and around Gachirampara, 30 km away. "These refugees had been flocking there since October 1997, hounded out of their homes in Mizoram by marauding bands of Mizo youth who burnt down their villages, raped their women, and killed about 50 of them" (Ashis Chakrabarti, *Express,* 7-4-98). While most of them had crossed over to Tripura, others took shelter in Assam's Hailakandi area and forests of the adjoining CHT in Bangladesh. "But the Assam Government refused to help, forcing the refugees to flock to the Tripura camps."

Barely had the Tripura Government got over the repatriation of 50,000 Chakma (who were in that State from 1980s till late 1990s) back to Bangladesh when a fresh crisis was on its hands—26,000 Reang refugees by April 1998. Consequently, the Tripura Government came under financial and social strain. It had spent about Rs. 2 crore on the upkeep of the refugee camps during the first six months itself. Even then Chief Minister Manik Sarkar ruled out the use of force to repatriate the refugees.

But the unhygienic conditions in the camps and malnutrition—each refugee got 450 gms of rice per person per day—took their toll on the refugees: 260 deaths between November 1997 to March 1998 in the main camp at Gachirampara.

Are the Reangs heading towards Insurgency?

One of the reasons for the Mizos to get provoked has been the demand raised by Reangs for an Autonomous District Council (ADC) within Mizoram. It was raised by the Bru National Union (BNU), political outfit formed in September 1997. Mizo Chief Minister Lalthanhawla attributes the exodus to violence incited by the Reang militants of the Bru National Liberation Front (BNLE), military arm of the BNU. The BNLF was allegedly provoking Mizos, and thwarting the return of refugees to their homes in Mizoram to mount pressure on the State to concede an ADC to them. The refugees were demanding the restoration of peace and conducive atmosphere in their villages in Mizoram before they return home.

The Mizoram and Tripura Governments, over serious negotiations, had decided on the refugees' return in November 1997 but an incident in October worsened the situation. A Mizo forester of the Dempa Wild Life Sanctuary was killed on 2 October. Blaming the BNLF for the murder, the Mizos retaliated by burning down 70 Reang villages. About 3,000 refugees who had retraced their steps homeward had to flee Mizoram once again. In 1998, the refugees were assured by Mizo officials of congenial situation back home, but they refused to return. By mid-1998, Upendra Reang, the only post-graduate degree holder among the Reangs, claimed "there are about 51,000 Reangs staying in different camps spread across Assam, Tripura, and even Bangladesh and Burma" *(Outlook,* 11-5-98).

Some charged the Mizoram Government with provoking the Mizos to commit atrocities on Reangs, force them to become Christians, and delete their names from electoral rolls (*Express,* 27-5-98). They moved Human Rights Commission, alleging that organisations like Mizo Zirlai Pawl (MZP), Young Mizo Association (YMA) and Mizoram Police were "involved in a number of rapes, 35 murders, destruction of 2721 Bru temples." The Church countered these allegations as untrue—after all over 90 per cent in Mizoram were Christians; as were 60 per cent of Brus there. Lalthanhawla claimed some vested interests were bent upon creating distrust between the Mizos and Brus to achieve their ultimate objective: formation of a separate State, Reangland, made up of portions lopped off Mizoram, Tripura and Assam. To start with, "they want a slice of northern part of the Zampui Hills which has a fairly large Reang population".

The Government is wary of conceding an ADC to the Reangs as three already exist in the State. The Reangs feel they can fortify their case by getting their brethren from the neighbouring states to clamour for a homeland. The Government is uneasy because of the reluctance of the Reang refugees in Tripura to return to their native villages. Also causing concern to it is the discovery of links between BNLF and NLFT of Tripura. The Bru activists have set up a training camp on the banks of the Sesih river near Nabak village in Bangladesh bordering Mizoram. The camp is located 2 km west of Thangnang village, Bangladesh, in the trijunction of Mizoram, Tripura and Bangladesh.

As-is well-known, the NLFT has a number of Reangs among its ranks. What makes the link between the BNLF and NLFT important—and potentially dangerous—is the latter's close relationship with the other major insurgent outfits in the North-East, such as the NSCN(I-M), PLA of Manipur, and ULFA of Assam.

Two rounds of tripartite official-level inconclusive talks (between New Delhi, Aizawl and Agartala) on Bru repatriation were held at Aizawl and Agartala in June and July 2001 respectively. While the Centre and Agartala wanted Aizawl to take back all Bru refugees, numbering over 30,000, the latter insisted it would accept only genuine ones, which numbered only 11,000. Mizoram also laid down condition that the BNLF militants should first lay down their arms and come overground to ensure that peace was maintained in the State.

The situation on the Bru front does not seem to be normal as yet. Three persons were killed and several policemen went missing when some Reang tribals attacked the Gootgooti outpost along the Assam-Mizoram border in Hailakandi district on 14 April 2002.

The plight of the Bru refugees remain unchanged 7 years after it all stated. "Life has been tough grind for the 33,000 displaced Brus from Mizoram, living in 6 relief camps on either side of the Jampui Hills in the Kanchanpura Sub-Division of Mamit district without enough food and basic amenities..., enduring sub-zero temperatures in winter, with tattered blankets" *(Week,* 7-3-04). Not surprisingly, they fall easy prey to malaria, diarrhoea, dysentery, skin infection and malnutrition. "The mortality rate is high and there is at least one sick person each in the 5,623 displaced families." Yet, no doctor has visited the camps since June 2003 "and they don't remember the last time they saw medicines." Tired by the authorities inaction, the refugees set up a school all by themselves in 1998. "If some of them turn antisocial, and even join the rebels, who are to be blamed?", is the worrying question posed by Bruno Maha, President of the Mizoram Bru Displaced People's Forum (MBDPF), headquartered at the Naisingpara camp on the eastern side of the Jampui Hills, where 3,052 families live. "We are the fifth largest ethnic group in the state. In 1972, the Mizos got their UT, and the Lais, Maras and Chakmas got their ADCs, we were left with nothing", loudly protests A. Swaibunga, Gen Sec of MBDPF.

To unite all the 12 sects of the Bru community, the Reang Democratic Party was formed in 1990 which was later replaced by BRU. People are losing their patience and many refugee youth have joined BNLF which some day "would emerge as an outfit capable of destabilising the only stable state (Mizoram) in the North-East", warns an Intelligence officer.

One analyst worked out the Bru population (2004) as given below:

Total	85,000	In Myanmar	1,500
In Tripura	33,482	In Bangladesh	2,500

In Mizoram (and surrounding area) 18,550.

April 2005 Accord: At last

An Accord signed at Aizawl on 25-4-05 between the Mizoram Government and BNLF brought to an end the 8-year armed rebellion following the October 1997 ethnic-cleansing drive which forced thousands of Brus out of the state. As per the Accord, all the refugees (35,000) living in six camps in North Tripura will return to their ancestral home and will be rehabilitated by the state while the BNLF has agreed to lay down arms. The signing of the Accord was delayed due to the dispute over the number of refugees, as Aizawl was refusing to recognise that all camp inmates were from Mizoram—claiming that a large number among them were residents of Tripura. The 25th Agreement became possible after Aizawl agreed to take a lenient view over the issue.

BNLF President Surjamoni Reang said on 30-4-05 in the presence of his General Secretary S.P. Ushoy that "the BNLF will surrender within next two months" *(HT,* 27-4-05 and *A A,* 28-4-05 and 2-5-05).

The latter half of the year 2005 was spent on arguments and counter-arguments between the BNLF and Aizawl. But the leadership did surrender and some weapons too were handed in. There were some 'incidents' on 14 Feb and 17 Mar 2006 involving BNLF cadres.

Then came the story about the surrender of 809 BLFM cadres. The details follow.

Bru militants surrender evinces suspicion: Oct 2006

The Mizo government seems to the handling the surrender of Bru militants with kid gloves, feel some analysts. Some others feel "it is more interested in the surrender of insurgents than in solving the problems that lead to civil strife". Are the journalist seeing to much in the surrendering, and indulging in an act or cavilling? There may be some merit in the criticism. A detailed examination of the surrender and circumstances attending it may clarify the issues.

809 militants of Bru Liberation Front of Mizoram (BLFM) surrendered on 23 Oct 2006 at the Naisingpara relief camp in Kanchanpur sub-division in the north Tripura district. On the 26th, amid great fanfare and certain elation these cardes of BLFM were formally received at Tuipuibari in Mizoram by Mizoram Home Minister Tawnluia, Chief Secretary Haukhum Hauzel, Home Secretary C Ropianga, DGP Lalnghata Sailo and some Assam Rifles (AR) officials. May be, some thought this reception with ceremony and circumstance was an avoidable drama. This was nothing more than "photo op" for Mizoram Home Minister and officials, as the cadres have made a formal surrender at Naisingpara before Tripura authorities. How can same set of Bru militants surrender twice within the short space of three days?

Now the reasons that form the basis of doubting this entire stage managed show. The surrender of BLFM cadres on 23 October was considered by Mizoram government as epochal as the one by some 150 cadres of Bru National Liberation Front (BNLF) on 26 Apr 2005. The latter surrender was the result of a MoU signed by the State Government with the BNLF on 26 Apr 2005 when 150 of its cadres laid down arms. But it also needs to be said the main provisions of the Apr 2005 treaty remains unfulfilled till date.

Now some critical analysis and review of the Oct 2006 surrender. It needs to be understood that the BLFM was nothing more than a break-away faction of the dominant BNLF. Some may feel that knowing the BNLF engagement in talks with the government, the break away might have been a clever ploy! Then the surrender to Tripura authorities seem to have been managed/ arranged by the AR Battalion in Kanchanpur, and Mizoram had nothing to do with it. The other fact that created doubts about the surrender was the highly-inflated number of BLFM cadres that surrendered.

After all, Mizoram government had refused "until recently to enter into talks with the BLFM" which was considered only of "Minor nuisance value". The State intelligence estimates in Nov 2005 had put the strength of the BLFM cadre about 100 and only a fraction of its foot soldiers were known to possess arms. More interestingly, its entire top leadership had already been arrested in April. Even if some reports indicating a measure of increased sophistication in BLFM ranks and weaponry are/may be partly credible, the 8-fold increase in its cadre strength in less than a year is simply beyond belief—even beyond imagination.

In May 2006, a circular distributed by BLFM among the refugee youths housed in the camps in Tripura had provided an indication of its impending surrender. The circular said two of the outfit's former cadres—Toisarai and Lalrinkima Molsoi—were in charge of "recruiting" members solely for the purpose of making them surrender before the government to get the benefits of the rehabilitation package. It was an act of arrogance—may be, the outfit had talked the matter over with the concerned officials of two state governments—that the circular not only demanded a "contribution" of Rs. 3,000 each for such recruitment and in addition an entry fee of Rs. 200, but also promised an amount of Rs. 90,000 as rehabilitation for each recruit. So it is obvious that the circular succeeded in fulfilling its intended purpose. So many youths rushed to join the outfit to gain the financial windfall. But this circular should not explain the huge accretion in the ranks of this outfit. There could be other reasons/causes. One the intelligence estimates could be inaccurate—perhaps purposely suppressed. Two, some might indeed have joined for pecuniary hopes. Rs. 3,200 for promised Rs. 90,000 is too good on offer to ignore. Three, an understanding even tacit, with the officials: could have attracted the youth.

This second treaty came to be deemed as a major achievement till the seniormost policeman of Tripura, the State that has hosted the Bru refugees since October 1997, made sensational revelation on 4 Nov 2006, in less than a fortnight of their surrender in Tripura. The DGP disclosed that this surrender was a stagemanaged drama enacted jointly by "some Mizoram officials and section of AR officers who picked up some Bru youth from the relief camps. AR Battalion was responsible for the surrender drama".

The story should not rest here. The DGP owes some explaining. How dare he speak against an act of his own government? Why did he speak only after second 'surrender' before Mizoram authorities? Did he feel his force's role and his own as diluted with the second 'surrender'? Had his government gone amiss, 'not giving appropriate recognition to his force' and to himself personally? Is he on the verge of retirement, and thought nothing of committing this act of indiscretion—nay, of outright indiscipline—as he did not get expected rewards? Or, may be, he was miffed by the fact that the Assam Rifles hogged the entire credit and the headlines—at the cost of his force.

Reverting to the main issue, Mizoram did not disappoint, not to speak of failing, the BLFM and its surrenderees. Tawnluia announced a great of Rs. 40,000 to each of the surrendered militants, besides the free rations for one year in the transit camps at Dumbarengpui and Tuipuibari. He also pledged to ensure place in Mizoram.

At another level, the DGP was only repeating his own political boss, Tawnluia. On 29 Mar 2006, the latter, speaking in the Assembly, had blamed the AR Battalion, posted in north Tripura, "of helping the BLFM militants." It all becomes so ridiculous. Was the DGP, GM Srivastava, speaking for his Minister? Yet again, having cast the AR unit as a villain, why did the Minister agree for a 'second' surrender—acknowledging the role of the same AR unit? The whole thing seem so absurd.

Now some statements on strength of the surrendered. On 26 Oct 2006, SP (CID) Lal Dhina disclosed, "Initially there was a list of 757 BLFM militants who were willing to shun the path of violence, but finally the number rose to 802." Ropiange said on 1 Nov 2006: "Earlier, we had thought BLFM to be 100-member group, but it turned out to be 800-plus."

The so-called drama by the Mizoram government is seen by some analysts as a deliberate move by it to soften the wide-spread opposition of the Mizos to the repatriation of 40,000 Bru refugees presently lodged in the six relief camps in north Tripura. This may be seen as delayed implementation of the Apr 2005 accord with the BNLF under which the repatriation of these 40,000 Bru refugees to Mizoram was agreed upon. If the "public welcome" of 802 BLFM cadres—instead of a mere 100—could be managed, it could be seen as a small opening for the 40,000 Bru refugees waiting impatiently in their camps since the Oct 1997 upheaval.

But such an happenstance does not seen to be credible/likely—anytime soon at least! Certain signs are already in the air which indicate that even this limited move of accepting the 802 BLFM cadres has provoked some opposition in some influential political circles of Mizoram. Post-Oct 2006 surrender, the two influential Mizo organisations—Young Mizo Association

(YMA) and Mizo Zirlai Pawi (MZP)—passed resolutions on 15 November that said, unless the credentials of the members of the BLFM were verified both these organisations would not accept them as bonafide citizens of Mizoram. It seems unlikely, if not impossible, that the State government will be able to proceed any further with its deal with the BLFM, until it finds a way to satisfy—rather, placate—YMA and MZP.

As for the MHA, it seems happy with any surrender by any of the militant groups in the North-East as it sees it as a step forward in the direction of ultimate peace in the region. It does not feel overly concerned if the latest surrender has been seen as a 'fraud' by some political observers.

BRU NATIONAL LIBERATION FRONT

Formation

The Bru National Liberation Front (BNLF) is an armed outfit of the Reangs and is currently engaged in negotiations with Mizoram government.

It was formed in 1996 following violent clashes between ethnic Mizos and Reang tribesmen in the Mamith sub-division of Mizoram State. The immediate cause of the conflict was the demand for an Autonomous District Council (ADC) by the Bru National Union (BNU), a political organisation of Reangs that was formed in year 1994. The BNU anchored its demand in the presence of a majority of Reangs in the sub-division, and declared that their rights—political, economic and cultural among others—were not justifiably protected under the prevailing political arrangement.

The Reang Democratic Convention Party (RDCP), another Reang organisation, passed a resolution in this regard. This reportedly provoked Mizo organisations like Mizo Zirlai Pawl (MZP) and Young Mizo Association (YMA)—fearing geographical division of Mizoram—to organise violent attacks, in October 1997, on Reang settlements. As a result, approximately 32,000 Reangs were displaced in the conflict and have since been staying in refugee camps in the Kanchanpur sub-division of the neighbouring Tripura State. The outfit's cadre strength is estimated to be a little over 100.

Aims and Objectives

The outfit proclaims its primary objective as the protection of rights and dignity of Reangs. The demands put forth by BNLF and its pattern of behaviour exhibit its other aims and objectives as well.

BNLF also endeavours to protect the religious identity of Reangs, which it claims to be Hinduism. This is manifested in its vehement opposition to the alleged imposition of Christianity on Reangs. It has also demanded a separate Reang homeland in Mizoram. Subsequently, it transformed its stand and aimed to achieve a separate ADC, and reservation in the Mizoram Legislative Assembly for the community. Besides, it has also taken up with the Mizoram government the issue of repatriation of Reang refugees who had been displaced during the October 1997 ethnic clashes. Only recently, it has agreed to tone down its demand for an ADC and settle for a regional council.

Leadership

Surajmani Reang and Hmunsiama are 'president' and 'deputy commander' respectively of the outfit. Both had managed to escape from the clutches of National Liberation Front of Tripura (NLFT) terrorists, who were holding them captive, in January 2001. Thang Masha is another important leader of the outfit. Other leaders of the outfit include A Joseph, 'advisor'. 'Solomon Prophul, 'general secretary' and S. Bru, the 'organising secretary'.

The BNLF suffered its worst reverse when the then 'general secretary', Hambai Molshoy, and the then army chief, Sheing Molshoy, were killed in an internecine clash with the NLFT on July 9, 2000, at a camp in Bangladesh.

Area of Operation and Strategy

Areas in which BNLF cadres are active include parts of Mizoram, Tripura and Assam. The area where the outfit has carried out major attacks include the Mamit and Lunglei districts of Mizoram, the Hailakandi district of Assam and Kanchanpur sub-division of North Tripura district. The BNLF is also known to be operating in the dense forests along the Mizoram-Tripura border. Besides, its hideouts are located in the Bhuban Hills of Cachar district in Assam.

The outfit is involved in selective abduction for ransom, which is a major source of finance for the terrorist group. In this, non-Reangs and Mizo Christians are the primary targets. Besides, the BNLF is also involved in violent attacks not only against non-Reangs, but also against security force personnel. The outfit was also engaged in internecine clashes with other terrorist outfits in the Northeast, like the National Liberation Front of Tripura (NLFT). Furthermore, its cadres carry out attacks with modern weapons like AK series assault rifles, grenades and bombs, and are well trained.

The BNLF uses both conventional and guerrilla tactics in its attacks.

Linkages

BNLF has both inter-organisational as well as external linkages, which it uses to procure arms and train cadres. Among its external linkages, Bangladesh is prominent. Its cadres reportedly run camp and use Bangladeshi soil, particularly the jungles along the international border with India, to house hideouts. This was indicated by Church leaders, who mediated with top BNLF leaders at the: hideouts in May 2000 for the release of two Mizoram government employees. The same was stated as early as in 1998 by the then Mizoram Chief Minister, Lalthanhawla. BNLF cadres who had survived the

July 2000 internecine clashes with NLFT also confessed that they had hideouts in the Chittagong Hill Tracts (CHT).

In the sphere of establishing and maintaining linkages with other terrorist outfits operating in the Northeast, the BNLF had very close links with the NLFT. It had even signed a 'Memorandum of Understanding' (MoU), which stipulated, *inter alia,* that the NLFT would provide arms, ammunition and every logistic support to the BNLF. Thus, the NLFT helped BNLF grow and gain in strength. This linkage was soured because of the BNLF's alleged pro-India tilt, its contacts with Indian security forces and for abducting and killing Christian employees and police personnel of Mizoram. Eventually, it culminated in a bloody conflict in which approximately 75 BNLF cadres were killed by NLFT terrorists in a raid on a BNLF camp in Bangladesh. The then president and general secretary of BNLF were also taken hostage, but have now escaped from their captors and have since then surrendered to Indian security forces, as already mentioned. Another bloody conflict occurred between the two outfits on September 3, 2000. 14 BNLF and 10 NLFT cadres were reportedly killed at a Bangladeshi hideout of the NLFT where it had invited BNLF to negotiate the release of their president and general secretary. Following these incidents, the BNLF-NLFT connection ended.

After its NLFT linkage turned sour, the BNLF came into contact with the National Socialist Council of Nagaland-Isak Muivah (NSCN-IM), which obliged the outfit by providing an unspecified number of AK 47 rifles and ammunition. Besides, the BNLF has also maintained contacts with the United Liberation Front of Asom (ULFA). This had also been revealed by then Chief Minister of Mizoram, Lalthanhawla, in 1998.

Current Situation

Since September 7, 2001, the BNLF has been engaged in a series of negotiations with the Mizoram Government. However, a solution has not been arrived at even after 11 rounds of negotiations. The 12th round talks, which were to be held in the capital Aizawl on April 29, 2004, were postponed by the State Government citing an 'unhealthy political atmosphere' prevailing in Mizoram. In fact, various political parties and community-based organisations have put up a stiff opposition to any sort of arrangement with the BNLF. The points of difference between the two sides relate to determining the number of refugees who would be repatriated from Tripura and the structure and nature of the political arrangement that should to be put in place after the returning refugees are rehabilitated.

While the BNLF contends that the number of Reangs awaiting repatriation is more than 32,000, the Mizoram Government holds that it is no more than a little over 10,000. On the kind of political arrangement that should follow, the BNLF has toned down its demand for an autonomous district council and is willing to negotiate for something less, a regional council. The Mizoram Government has refused to grant thus far any separate autonomous governing body for the Reangs. Moreover, it is also not ready to accept the BNLF's demand that the Union Government should be involved in the ongoing peace talks. The State Government has also demanded that the BNLF cadres should surrender if a lasting solution were to be found and peace restored in the region.

On May 17, 2004, Home Minister, Twanluia, informed the State Legislative Assembly that an accord between the Mizoram Government and BNLF is to be signed in June. Subsequently, on May 26, State Chief Secretary, H. V. Lalringa, informed that the Mizoram Government has endorsed the draft proposals for laying down of arms by the BNLF cadres and repatriation of Bru refugees lodged in the Tripura relief camps. However, there has been no subsequent progress in this front.

Incidents

Beginning its inception, it has led several violent attacks against ethnic Mizos as well as security force personnel.

2006

- March 17: Police personnel kill a hardcore militant of the BNLF, Jaingba Reang, in an encounter at Dhalaicherra in the Mizoram-Tripura border area. However, four other militants managed to escape from the encounter site.
- February 14: Three truck drivers from Assam's Cachar district and a sub-contractor from the Kolasib district of Mizoram are abducted by suspected BNLF cadres in two separate incidents.

2005

- August 23: The 'general secretary' of the BNLF, Solomon Prophul Ushoy, claims that Bru tribals at refugee camps in Tripura. Who are awaiting repatriation to Mizoram, receive extortion threats from the BLFM. He says, "We are worried about our family. On August 4, we had received an extortion letter from the BLFM demanding Rupees Five lakh. Since we have no money to give to them, we are afraid these people would take action against our family members most of whom are still in Tripura in refugee camps." Ushoy says that the Government should segregate family members of the BNLF and BLFM while repatriating the refugees in order to isolate the BLFM cadres. He also asks the State Government to expedite the repatriation of their family members from the Tripura camps.

- July 26: The BNLF asks for more aid for the Bru community pointing out that they form one of the most backward tribal communities, with a literacy rate of approximately 10 per cent, BNLF chief Surjyamoni Reang said at the Tuipuibari transit camp, where the outfit laid down its arms, he was hopeful that aspirations of the Brus would be respected and also that the Mizoram and Union Governments would provide them adequate development.
- July 25: At least 195 BNLF militants, including the outfit's president Surjyamoni Reang and general secretary Solomon Prophul Ushoy, surrender before the Mizoram Home Minister Tawnluia at the Sidan transit camp in West Tuipuibari. Apart from 195 militants, 62 of their family members also surrender. The arms deposited include two self-loading rifles, two AK-56 UMG, two Chinese rifles, one AK-47 rifle, one US made M 16 rifle and two .303 rifles. Additionally, the militants also hand over a binocular, one radio set and 661 rounds of ammunition.
- July 18: BLFM demands separate talks with the Mizoram Government and threatens not to surrender arms. The outfit expresses its unwillingness to lay down arms with the BNLF, which has recently signed a cease-fire agreement with the Government. Mizoram Government, however, denies possibility of holding another round of peace talks.
- May 3: BNLF 'commander-in-chief', Surajmoni Reang, says that he has already submitted the list of arms and ammunition to the Mizoram home department.
- April 26: BNLF, which signs a Memorandum of Understanding (MoU) with the Mizoram Government, promises to lay down all arms and ammunition within the next two months.
- April 26: Mizoram Government and BNLF sign a MoU. The MoU is expected to facilitate the repatriation of Bru refugees staying in six relief camps in the neighbouring North Tripura district. According to provisions of the MoU, the BNLF cadres will surrender along with arms and come over-ground.
- April 26: The Mizoram Government and BNLF, at the conclusion of the 13th round of talks, agree to sign a peace agreement. Apart from the BNLF, another outfit, the BLFM has also participated in the negotiations.
- April 3: The student body MZP announces that it will boycott the negotiation process between the BNLF and the Mizoram Government in protest against the outfit's kidnapping a student

ahead of the crucial round of negotiations later this month. A MZP statement says that, Lalrinawma, a student of the Kanhmun High School, is kidnapped by the BNLF on March 29. The kidnappers, who claim to be members of a faction of the NSCN, reportedly release the student in return for a ransom amount of Rupees 25,000 on March 30. The BNLF leader Bruto Meshka, however, denies his outfit's involvement in the kidnapping.

- March 29: Mizoram Government and BNLF are scheduled to sign a Memorandum of Understanding on April 6, following 12 rounds of peace talks. The outfit's chief, Surjyamani Reang, says: "We are ready to sign the accord, but need definite assurances on crucial points to pave the way for surrender of arms and ammunition by the rank and file of our outfit." He also says that the Bru refugees from camps in North Tripura district need to be accommodated in resettlement centers for their safety and security with one-year ration provision for each family.
- March 11: The 12th round of negotiations between the Mizoram Government and BNLF is concluded. According to official sources, both sides were able to finalise a draft agreement for the repatriation of the Bru refugees to be signed in April.
- March 5: BNLF enters into an agreement with the NLFT to carry out joint attacks during elections to the Tripura Tribal Area Autonomous District Council.

2004

- November 28: A tribal girl is killed in crossfire between security forces and BNLF militants near Tharma village in North Tripura district of Tripura.
- October 24: Mizoram Government finalises a peace agreement with the BNLF, following the 11th round of peace talks last week. A senior government official said, "The peace formula covers repatriation of the refugees as well as proper rehabilitation or both refugees and BNLF-cadres." A formal peace agreement in this effect will be reportedly signed by both the parties once the Union Government sanctions the funds required to implement the peace package.
- September 19: Eighteen BNLF militants are arrested from Satkarakhal Punji under Dholai police station limits in the Cachar district of Assam.
- August 31: Three contractors and an engineer, abducted on August 23 by the BNLF, from Kulicherra hamlet in the Cachar

district of Assam are released at an unspecified place following the payment of a ransom amount ranging between Rupees 14 lakh and Rupees 18 lakh.

- August 23: Four persons, including three contractors, are abducted by suspected BNLF cadres from the Cachar district in Assam.
- March 5: Six BNLF terrorists, including a 'sergeant' and a 'corporal', surrender before the Mizoram Police at Tuipuibari in the Mamit district.
- January 17: Five BNLF terrorists are arrested from a relief camp for the Bru tribals at Gachhirampara under Kanchanpur subdivision in the North Tripura district.

2003

- July 11: Eighth round of peace talks between the Mizoram Government and the BNLF ends inconclusively in Aizawl.
- July 7: Mizoram Government alleges that funds provided by the Union Government to Tripura for basic amenities to Bru refugees staying in six camps in North Tripura district were being stashed away to the BNLF.
- June 9: BNLF terrorists release three persons, whom they had abducted earlier on June 6 from the Mualthuam area of Mamit district reportedly after a ransom of Rupees 3,000 was paid to them.
- June 9: BNLF terrorists release three persons, whom they had abducted earlier on June 6 from the Mualthuam area of Mamit district, reportedly after a ransom of Rupees 3000 was paid to them.
- May 1: Mizoram Government alleges that Tripura is supporting the Bru National Liberation Front (BNLF).

2002

- November 21: BNLF spokesperson Chandramani Molsoy says the outfit is unwilling to participate in the 8th round of talks with the government, scheduled for December 2002.
- November 20: Mizoram Home Minister Tawnluia says in the State Legislative Assembly, in Aizwal, there is no deadlock in the talks with the BNLF
- October 17: Seventh round of BNLF-Mizoram government talks in Aizawl remains inconclusive.
- September 26: The seventh round of Mizoram-Bru National Liberation Front (BNLF) talks are deferred.
- September 22: Two BNLF terrorists are killed in an encounter in the Ratabari block (administrative unit) of Karimganj district, Assam.

- August 23: BNLF drops the demand for Autonomous Regional Council at the sixth round of talks, in Aizwal, with the Mizoram government, and asks for a Development Council, instead.
- May 23: Fifth round of talks held between Bru National Liberation Front (BNLF) and Mizoram government to resolve Reang issue. The talks end inconclusively.
- April 30: Thang Masha, BNLF president, declares through a memorandum that the outfit is ready to negotiate for a regional council, instead of an Autonomous District Council (ADC).
- March 1: Talks between the government and the BNLF resume. No agreement could be reached at the end of the talks.
- February 28: BNLF and Mizoram government resume talks in Aizwal. The same to be continued on March 1.
- January 17: BNLF declares that its cadres would surrender if government concedes to its demand and includes rehabilitation of Reang refugees.

2001

- September 8: First round of talks starts between BNLF delegation and State government.
- August 11: BNLF terrorist killed in raid by security forces on its hideout in Bhuban Hills in Cachar district in Assam.
- July 15: Mizoram government declares that talks with the BNLF would be bilateral.
- March 12: Mizoram Home Minister states that the government was ready for peace talks with BNLF.
- February 18: Reports say Surjo Moni and Hmunsiama, the president and 'deputy commander' respectively of BNLF, taken hostage by NLFT on July 9, 2000 escapes from their captivity.
- February 16: BNLF terrorists asked to surrender by Mizoram government.

2000

- November 19: BNLF's hand suspected in the Borahaldi carnage that claimed 14 lives.
- September 3: 14 BNLF terrorists killed in an internecine clash with the NLFT at the latter's Thangnan base camp in the Chittagong Hill. Tracts, Bangladesh. BNLF also kills 10 NLFT terrorists in retaliation.
- July 12: Three BNLF terrorists arrested along the Mizoram-Assam border.

- July 9: 75 BNLF cadres massacred by National Liberation Front of Tripura (NLFT) terrorists at one of their hideouts in Bangladesh. The NLFT also takes hostage Surjo Moni and Hmunsiama, the president and 'deputy commander' respectively of the BNLF.
- June 30: Suspected BNLF terrorists kill seven members of the anti-terrorist Hunter Force of Mizoram Police and injure four others in an ambush along the India-Bangladesh border in Mamit district.
- May 16: BNLF sets free two employees abducted on April 15.
- April 19: Suspected BNLF terrorists abduct school teacher near a village along the Mizoram-Tripura Border.
- April 15: BNLF terrorists abduct two Mizoram State government employees from Saithah village.

1999

- September 23: Suspected BNLF terrorists set off a bomb blast near Zawlpui hamlet in Lunglei district. No one was injured in the attack that was possibly meant to target a moving jeep carrying government personnel proceeding on election duty.

1997

- October 21: BNLF kills a wildlife game watcher of the Mizoram government near Persang village.
- BNLF founded.

SMALLER TRIBES IN MIZORAM

What follows is a brief account of some smaller tribes of Mizoram.

Paite

Paites belong to the Old Kuki Group. The term means 'goers'. In Mizorarn, they are mainly confined to the area between the rivers Tyao and Run, in its north-eastern part. The Paites inhabiting Central part of Mizoram have lost their language but those living in Manipur (Churachandpur area) and Mizoram (north-eastern part) have been successful in preserving their traditional values and ethnic traits.

Ralte

The Raltes belong to Kuki group who came from the north. They were subjugated by the Duliens who migrated from Chin Hills. They had distinct social customs and had noticeable difference in the dialects. They were allotted a separate portion of village land. They were predominantly settled in western Lushai villages in Lenkhunga, Kalkhom and Lalrhima. The Ralte Sub-group accepted the dominance of the Duliens but continued to maintain their traditional customs and language. Among the Duliens, the Ralte language is understood and the Sailo chiefs habitually use the Ralte language [Grierson, G.A., *LAI*, 1976 (New Edn), Vol. III, Pt 1, p. 55].

The Raltes have four clans: Khelte, Siakeng, Relhchhun, Kawthi.

Rankhol and Thado

About the middle of the 16th century, the Rankhol settled down in the area, near the Cachar border, but were subsequently pushed northwards by the Thado tribe. The Thados had established settlements in the Lushai and Chin Hills, after dislodging the Rankhol and Bete tribes. But the Thados, in turn, were pushed out by the advancing waves of the Lushai tribes, who pushed northwards by 1810 AD, and as a result the Thados were pushed further north into Cachar between 1840 and 1850. The Thados of the Chin Hills were similarly conquered by the Sokte and were driven towards north into Manipur, where they settled in the southern regions of that State [Soppitt, C.A., (1976) *A Short Account of the Kuki Lushai Tribes,* Aizawl, p. 7].

Shendus

The Shendu tribe includes all the Haka-Chin tribes including the Lakhers (Klangkhanga) and also other Chin tribes such as Maras (Carey and Tuck, *The Chin Hills,* pp. 4-6). The British called them Shendus. Lt Phayrs *(Accounts of Arakan,* p. 2) refers to the Tseindus and gives a list of 13 Tseindu clans, some of which can be identified with Mara clan, and others with Pois. The Shendus, according to Mackenzie *(The North-East Frontier of Bengal,* 1884) were a formidable nation living to the North-East of Blue Mountain. These tribes appeared to be more numerous as a people than any other Indo-Chinese Hill race who extended over a large part of the country. The Lakhers as a separate tribe, were first mentioned in 1852. Capt Tickell refers to the tribe as Heuma or Shendu. Heuma is the name of the Lakher village in North Arakan known to the Lushais as Vaki.

Pangs, Bawms and Tlanglau

They are smaller, even miniscule communities in southern and south-eastern parts of Mizoram, mostly settled in the Pawi and Chakma areas.

These smaller tribes have been decidedly mentioned al be it briefly because unless handled with sensitivity by the ruling Mizo classes, they can be a source of trouble in future. They have seen medium-sized tribes like the Hmar and Bru struggling for and fulfilling their political aspirations. Some among the former can have some such "dangerous" ideas in their heads. At the very least. These tribes can be instigated and/or exploited by more vigorous and troublesome tribes for their own motives.

It is in the interest of the State that its Government displays understanding and sensitivity towards the yearnings of these smaller tribes. They must be kept content with their present status and situation.

TERRORIST OUTFITS IN MIZORAM: THEIR NETWORKING

Mizoram is affording safe passage from Chittagong/Cox's Bazars of Bangladesh to the NSCN (IM) for bringing in the weapons purchased from South East Asia.

DO THE REANGS HAVE A FUTURE IN MIZORAM? APR 2007

This might sound or read like a rhetorical question but even then, the question must be asked, and then coldly analysed in view of the uncertainty that shrouds the fate and future of thousands of the Reang refugees languishing in less-than-healthy camps in Tripura.

The Reang refugee problem is becoming intractable by the each passing day with the Mizoram Government often going back on its promises, under one pretext or the other! Aizawl and the BNLF, a militant outfit, had signed an accord in the State capital on 26 Apr 2005 after prolonged negotiations and it included the provision of Mizoram Government allowing the safe return of 35,000 Reang refugees lodged temporarily in camps in Tripura to their homes. But even after two years of that accord, there is no knowing when these luckless Reangs living in makeshift camps in Tripura's Kanchanpur sub-division bordering Mizoram, will realise their hopes.

The centre has spent more than Rs. 90 crore for their upkeep. Much to the concern of the Tripura authorities, there had been frequent deaths of children and old inmates from diseases in the absence of adequate healthcare facilities.

The influx began in Oct 1997 following ethnic strife in the fringeline dominated villages of western Mizoram along Tripura's fringeline. Reang leaders complained that several of their houses were destroyed in ante-Reang riots, perceived to be a backlash provoked by the Reang minority group's demand for regional autonomy in Mizoram. The number of refugees in camps at one point was 55,000.[20] Where did the 20,000 who left the camps go? Some of them have obviously gone back to their village on their own, and some crossed over to the CHT in Bangladesh in search of the jhum land, the traditional source for their livelihood. Still some other might have mingled with Tripura's local tribal population, belonging to their fold.

It needs to be clarified that the Reangs in Mizoram are now called/ known as Brus to distinguish them from their community in other states, say Tripura.

What could be the Real cause of Bru's troubles in Mizoram? One opinion blames Mizo's chauvinistic attitude. Identified with their sense of an ethnic exclusiveness, Mizo are proud of their chivalrous part. This may possibly be undermining interests of minority tribal groups in the Mizo Hills. None can deny the atmosphere of intolerance and mutual mistrust among the tribal groups in picturesque Mizoram. Reang leaders obviously have a point when they claim to have been reduced to the status of "second-class citizens", stripped off as they have been of their constitutional rights. Mizoram has consistently, perhaps stubbornly, has ignored pleas from different quarters to enable the return of the Reang refugees to their homes. "Despite the Supreme Court directive and National Human Rights Commission's efforts—Aizawl has delayed the resettlement on various pretext."[21]

Mizoram persists with its claim that only about 15,000 of the 35,000 camp inmates are "genuine citizens" of Mizoram. It asserts it is not responsible for "aleins" who have been given shelter in the camps. It has declared that it would initiate the process of taking them back only after all militants have surrendered. Only 38 BNLF militants came over ground after the signing of the Apr 2005 Accord. Some underground ultras decided to continue with the struggle and formed a splinter of the BNLF called "Bru Liberation Front of Mizoram" (BLFM). Hereby hangs another tale, or perhaps, a ploy by the Mizoram Government.

Some analysts aver that Aizawl wants to lure innocent Reang youth into the so-called underground, and officials, civil and police, have been visiting the camps for the purpose. They were told they would be entitled to cash and other rehabilitation benefits if they were ready to wear rebel uniform and surrender. "Trucks were sent to the camps in Kanchanpur from Mizoram to transport them. But all said and done, it is not easy to comprehend the motive behind this Mizoram move! But then something happened on the ground on 23 Oct 2006 which only deepened the suspicions. One simply cannot ignore the fact of 805 BLFM cadres surrendering that day before the Mizoram authorities, and in rebel fatigues indeed!

New Mizoram Governor Lt Gen (Retd) Madan Mohan Lakhera made reference to the surrender in Nov 2006 of 800 BNLF militants but was silent on the repatriation of 33,000 Reang refugees languishing in Tripura camps after fleeing Mizoram in Oct 1997 following (anti-Reang) ethnic violence, wrote a daily on 1 Feb 2007.[22]

Mutual understanding between Aizawl and the BNLF was that the surrender would follow the repatriation of the refugees, but there has been no report to this effect (about the fact of repatriation) so far. This has lent credence to Agartala's suspicion that surrender was, indeed, stage-managed. There is need to determined whether before the surrender, Assam Rifles and Mizoram police allegedly provided some refugee youths with militant uniforms. The figure of 800 is quite considerable knowing Aizawl's earlier claim that only a handful of militants was trying to create trouble.

The Supreme Court directive to Mizoram Government as early as in Jan 2005 should have prompted Aizawl to expedite the process but it still seems firm that all refugees are not its citizens and it will take back only those with valid documents of citizenship.

Like some others, the opposition Congress alleges that the Mizo National Front Government—which incidentally had itself signed the 1986 Mizo Accord with New Delhi that ushered the peace – is breeding militancy by offering an attractive rehabilitation package (Rs. 80,000) to each individual that surrenders. Reports suggest that some refugee "ringleaders" have set up a new outfit in Tripura to fight for a separate homeland there. There have also been reports of smaller militant outfits mushrooming. If their activities are not nipped in the bud, Mizoram may cease to remain one of the most peaceful states in the North-East.

Not only the 23 Oct 2006 surrender by 805 BLFM cadres seems to have been stage-managed, it has implication for Tripura's integrity, and hence that state's deeper suspicions on the subject. It is generally acknowledge by most that the entire show had been arranged without consulting the Tripura authorities, the fact that further fueled its suspicious not only about this "drama about surrender", but more significantly its suspicions about the intentions of the Mizoram Government.

So, it is quite understandable that Agartala lost no time in lodging a protest with Government of India (MHA). Tripura strongly suggested that the Mizoram Government had planned this massive surrender to justify/prove its allegation that refugee camps in north Tripura were safe hide- outs for BLFM cadres.

Of late, tension has been mounting along Tripura's border with Mizoram. Mizoram police and Mizo youth have frequently been raiding the evacuee camps with the ostensible aim of picking up Reang insurgents. To make the situation even more offending to the Tripura and Reang refugees themselves eking out an existence in the camps in Tripura, a senior Mizo official "said in Aizawl recently that the plan for providing rehabilitation to Reang youth had been shelved as the Centre was unwilling to mobilise funds. Even if the Joint Secretary MHA, Naveen Verma, visited the camps in Jan 2007 to assure the refugees of prompt initiative, the prospect of (early) repatriation does not seem bright. On the other hand, such a long stay of Mizoram tribals (citizens) in camps (in Tripura) is creating problems with ominous implications, especially for Tripura, and at wider level, for peace and prosperity of the region as a whole.

There are reasons to believe that Tripura's suspicions, about this Oct 2006 surrender by 805 BLFM militants being a stage-managed show seem to be well-founded. There is, in fact, every reason to question this bloated figure because Aizawl had itself admitted earlier that the strength of the BLFM militants was not more than 100 or so!

Tripura Government may not have said it in so many words, but some analysts see a sinister design behind 'accepting' the surrender of 805 BLFM militants with such a fanfare by the Mizo authorities. Will these fighters be trained in guerrilla warfare and then pushed across the border into Tripura to escalate the support for Reang Homeland in Tripura, which has already been voiced by some small but obscure militant outfits! Mizoram Government may find it an effective way not only to divert attention of the parties concerned away from its promise of accepting the Reang refugees from the camps in Tripura last also shift its 'Reang problem' into its neighbour's court.

There is a reason to state clearly that Mizoram cannot smugly afford to ignore the consequences of procrastinating over the issue of the repatriation of nearly 33,000 Reang refugees from Tripura. If the Government abdicates its responsibility to resettle them, this will merely leave the field open to more militant groups to take up their cause. The situation would not have come to such a pass had the previous Congress government of Lalthan hawla—during whose tenure the exodus started—made serious attempts to take the refugees into confidence.

NOTES

1. These remarks were made by these two gentlemen during their conversation with the author during his tenure (1974-78) in Mizoram.
2. The Kolodyne (spelt 'Kaladan' till and during World War II) is an important River, which forms a part of the boundary between India and Burma in southeastern Mizoram. Its source lies in the hills near Haka from which it flows in a southwardly direction. It turns sharply north from the village Sabawngte in the south—and from there to the point where it joins the Tuipui River (coming from the north) near Mulianpui village, it forms the India-Burma boundary. From this junction, it turns north-west, collects the waters of Tuichang River, and turns south. Another 20 km, it collects the waters of the Mat River, continues flowing south, and finally leaves Mizoram (District Chhimtuipui) to enter Burmese territory, and finally joins the Bay of Bengal.
3. Foreign and Political Department, Government of India, Letter No. F. 185/*x*/28 dated 17-1-1930.
4. R.T. Zachono, *The Maras Towards Autonomy,* in *The Autonomy Movement in Mizoram.*
5. It consisted of Rupnath Brahma, A.V. Thakkar, B.N. Rau, Constitutional Advisor to the Constituent Assembly, and Rev J.J.M. Nichols-Roy, the Khasi leader, Minister of Assam and Member of Constituent Assembly (Aliba Imti, a Naga leader, visited Lushai Hills on 18 April 1947 to study the Mizo situation). The Committee coopted two Mizo leaders: Ch. Saprawnga and Khawtin Khuma.
6. Population Survey conducted by the Pawi District Council, 1983.
7. R.N. Prasad (1973), "Evolution of Party Politics in Mizoram," in *Political Science Review,* Rajasthan, Vol. 12 (No. 3,4), 1973, pp. 204-05.
8. S.K. Choube (1973), *Hill Politics in North-East India,* p. 167.

9. The Sea Wind Party Memorandum dated 11-2-89; cited in *The Sunday Weekly* of 3-6-89.
10. *Times of India,* 5-12-96.
11. A certain "Chhinlung" finds a mention in the story on the origin of the Mizos too. Thus, all their claims of being a distinct ethnic identity not withstanding, the Hmars were originally a part of the larger Mizo tribe and lived side by side for long periods in history, which they either shared or borrowed from each other's folk lore.
12. The author is being harsh on the "west wind...and cross" for decay in skills of the Hmars. The 'decay' is more the result of moderrisation and literacy. A similar thing has happened in as advanced and prosperous a state as Punjab.
13. R. Pudaite (1963), *The Education of the Hmar People,* Imphal, p. 19; cited S.N. Singh, *Mizoram* 1994.
14. S.K. Choube (1973), *Hill Politics in North-East India,* Calcutta, p. 170.
15. *Telegraph,* 8-9-88.
16. *Telegraph,* 4-1-90.
17. *Ibid.*
18. *Telegraph,* 8-4-90.
19. *The Sentinel* of Guwahati, 1-9-89, says the delegation met the National Front (Government) leaders at Delhi.
20. Satyabrata Chakraborti, *The Statesman*, 19 Feb 2007.
21. *Ibid.*
22. Editorial, *The Statesman,* 1 Feb 2007.

16

Nagas : Secessionism to Statehood Last Chapter Yet to be Written

It indeed is ironic that the Nagas who rose in revolt a day before India achieved its Independence, are yet to make the final settlement with the later. In fact, the last round of the long-running talks between them and New Delhi was held in March 2007.

Key Statistics : Nagaland

Date of Formation (Has the distinction of being the first ethnic state to be created in India's North-East)	1 Dec., 1963	
Area	16,579 sq. km.	
Population	1,990,036	
Capital	Kohima	
Major Religions	Christianity, Hinduism	
Main Languages	Angami	Sema
	Ao	Chakhesang
	Chang	
	Konyak	English
	Lotha	
	Songtam	

The Naga insurgency is the oldest in the country, the best organised, with proven sustainability. Presently, it is poised at a critical point of its long journey—peace interregnum with Government of India since 1st August 1997. First a look at its long journey.

Defining the term Secessionism

First its definition. Galula defined it as a protracted struggle conducted methodically, step by step, in order to attain specific intermediate objectives leading finally to the overthrow of the existing order.[1] In today's world, insurgency spans a full spectrum of conflicts ranging from terrorist violence/ subversion to guerrilla warfare and convergence of guerrilla bands into regular units to confront the Government forces in a conventional way. The developing/underdeveloped nations, essentially in the grip of socio-economic inequity, have been afflicted by the scourge. Varieties of injustice, some real and other imaginary, are cited to incite the 'masses' against the Government.

Some Indian scholars and historians are convinced that the British went out of their way to ensure that the plains people and hillmen are kept away from each other, administratively and politically. Even a casual study of the 1919 Act and 1935 Act will show how the tribes, were treated differently, through the mechanism of "Backward Tracts" and "Excluded Areas". Till the very eve of Independence, the British officials were busy designing the infamous Coupland Plan[2] to ensure that the tribal areas of India's North-East and Burma's north-west were grouped into a Crown Colony to be directly ruled by the White Hall, London. The momentum given to the Independence struggle by the 1942 Quit India Movement and the mass upsurge of 1946 left little time for the Plan to fructify, and the British Parliament 'wisely' rejected it.

It was in their History

But seed of the post-1947 Naga trouble lay in their history, and their "independent if wild" ways. One author described each Naga village a Sovereign Republic, and each individual, often, a law unto himself. In one word, they are independent minded! The reckless and defiant Naga spirit is symbolised by the Angamis—the Nagas par excellence! They showed it by deeds. The British had to invest a lot in energy, men and material to tame them! After launching ten punitive expeditions during the period 1837 to 1851, they thought a was prudent to completely pull out of their area for the time being. If the Angamis represent the Naga spirit and defiance, Khonomans can be said to represent the Angamis at their defiant best. For its reckless challenge to them, the British had to destroy Khonoma twice within a span of less than thirty (in 1851 and 1879) years to make it listen to them. Given its "proud" history, is it any surprise that the man who promised independence to his people came from Khonoma, with a telling name of Angami Zapo Phizo!

But it is not that the Nagas had no reasons to feel strongly on the treatment meted out to them by the British! They grew suspicious of the way the British drew the Inner Line, and then kept pushing it out under one pretext or other: one day, it was to subdue a defiant and violent village by bringing it under the administration; another day, it was done to accommodate the newer tea gardens! After all, these were "their" lands being usurped by the foreigners. Simultaneously, the British were handing over the administration of certain reserve forests to the plains districts of Assam for their better management. That was not all. The British not only sought help of the neighbouring states like Manipur and Cachar to control the Naga raids but also encouraged them to occupy some bordering Naga areas! Col Johnstone, Political Agent in Manipur in 1870s, testifies (in his 1896 Book) the boundary being drawn in favour of Manipur. The unkindest cut came when Manipur (under its British Political Officer, Col McCulloch) and Government of Bengal, when Assam was its Division, found it expedient to 'plant' Kuki settlements on the exposed frontiers to act as a shield for their own people against the Naga raids.

On the other hand, the critics aver that post-1947 claims of some Naga leaders of the Nagas being one people fly in the face of facts—far from the ground realities.[3] It is known that Naga tribes were at war with each other. Inter-village/tribe feuds were common and head-hunting was an egregious tradition. There was no paramount power and each village was a State by itself. If occasionally several villages used to unite together to attack another or defend themselves, that was a kind of confederacy, and by no means a political union, or even an attempt at unification. If the Nagas had confined themselves to their villages, and not carried out raids on the plains, the history of Nagaland would have been different—a blissful, isolated existence, each community sequestered to its own village; in one word, they would have continued at the stage of village states.

It were their raids on the plains that invited the attention of powerful 'empires' beyond their hills; the Ahoms first, and then their successors, the British. The British had to move into the Hills to protect the Queen's subjects from their (Naga's) depredations. That was the British claim. Through a process of excursions, promenades, punitive expeditions, and war, spanning over a period of 80 years, 1832 to 1913, the ordered administrations was more or less settled in the Naga Hills, even if some expeditions were found necessary. By the time of World War I (1914-19), it is fair to say that the environs and climate in the Naga Hills were peaceful, and things had settled down. It was under these conditions that an organisation called Naga Club was born. But before proceeding any further, it is apt to recall an oft-repeated charge: Behind the instrumentality of the Inner Line, 1873, the British allowed the missionaries to spread Christianity and education among the tribes. Both led to their isolation from the Indian mainstream, and Indian Freedom Movement. However, the same two factors are believed to have brought a gradual change in the outlook of these people, and infused a sense of nationality among them. The inference is that it was this consciousness about their being a nation which fueled the 'freedom struggle' by their leaders.

The Naga Club was set-up in 1918 at Kohima and Mokokchung.[4] Its members were Government officials and leading Naga Chiefs. The club received wide patronage of the Government and it used to discuss social and administrative problems. It provided a common platform for leaders of different tribes of Nagas. In the absence of any other organisation, the Naga Club, Kohima emerged as an effective political forum for the Naga tribes.

The psychological phase of the Naga insurgency can be said to have formally begun at this point.[5] The Freedom Movement getting momentum under Gandhiji's leadership early 1920s and formation of the national level Swarajya Party were the event that caused concern in London, and the British Government set up a Commission in 1927 under Sir John Simon, with Clement Attlee and E. Cadogan as its members, to suggest constitutional changes for India (in this sense, it was a successor of Mont-Ford and Minto-Morley schemes). When the commission visited Kohima, the Naga Club submitted a memorandum to it on 10 January 1929, signed by 20 persons styling themselves as representatives of various tribes.[6] The Nagas demanded that their Hills be excluded from the proposed reforms and kept under the direct British rule. Was it a precursor to the Coupland Plan of the 1940s, and indicative of shape of things to come? The discerning Indians must have noted the sentiment as an early warning. A mischievous statement by Cadogan in the House of Commons in May 1935 that the Nagas had "a "very shrewd suspicion that something is being done to take away from them their immemorial rights and customs" could have only aggravated their fears, nurtured insidiously by the British officials, and some felt by the church leaders.[7]

Becoming aware of the things, they decided to organise themselves into socio-political units. First off the block, Lothas formed Lotha Tribal Council in 1923. It existed till 1953 when the fight had started. Followed Aos with Ao Tribal Council in 1928, which was dissolved in 1930, and re-raised in 1939. Other tribes had formed their Councils by mid-1940s. 2000 Nagas had done duty in Europe during First World War, and during the Second, fought in their own land, when they saw vast Armies moving as also some guerrilla action (The dumps of arms and ammunition left by the retreating Jap forces were to come handy to the Naga rebels to fight the Security Forces later). The War perhaps wrought in a greater sense of unity among the Naga tribes. The last British Deputy Commissioner, Pawsey (1937-47), therefore had no difficulty in forming the Naga Hills District Tribal Council in April 1945 to help the relief and rehabilitation work. It was converted into Naga National Council (NNC) in April 1946. It at Wokha at a conference of tribal Chief. Thus emerged the first political organisation of Nagas, charged with the task of social and political upliftment of their people. Significantly, it was the first time that the term *national* was used in the Naga phraseology. Was it indicative of the intensity of their feelings?

NNC

The NNC had 29 members, representing different tribes, on the basis of proportional representation. It had no membership fee or any pledge of loyalty. Each house was expected to contribute one rupee each year towards its funds. To begin with, the political objective of the NNC was solidarity of all Nagas, including those of the unadministered areas and the inclusion of their hills within the province of Assam in a free India, with local autonomy and adequate safeguards for the interest of the Nagas assured. Then came the time when there was a lot of kite flying about tribal areas to be directly governed by the White Hall. But nothing came out of it. The Naga demand for autonomy was well received by the Indian National Congress. Its President, Pt Nehru, wrote a letter on 1st August 1946 to T. Sakhrie, Secretary of the NNC, welcoming the NNC aims, and also expressing himself on ideas about tribal policy of free India.[8]

Gradually, there was a discernible change in the mood of NNC. The return to India from Burma of Phizo gave a fillip to certain pro-independence orientations of NNC's stance. Within a year of his return, the June 1947 declaration of the NNC came as a bombshell to the Indians: "The Naga Hills would cease to be a part of India with the departure of the British."[9] The group demanding independence from India was not in majority, but being more assertive carried the day. To accommodate different viewpoints within the NNC, it was resolved that when India gets her independence, the British and the Indian Governments together would act as the Guardian Powers over Naga Hills for a period of 10 years, after which the Nagas were free to decide their future. The proposal was sent to Mountbatten who gave no reply but Nagas were informally advised to put their views before the relevant Committee of India's Constituent Assembly. In its 20 May meeting with the Bordoloi Sub-Committee at Kohima, the NNC outrightly rejected the autonomy offered by the 6th Schedule. Soon after this came Sir Akbar Hydari, Governor of Assam, to Kohima and sew up a 9-point memorandum with the NNC, known as the Hydari Agreement. It got embroiled in a controversy over the interpretation of its clause IX, which offered a review of the Agreement after 10 years, which the NNC thought gave them an option of walking out of the Union. It was rejected by the Government of India.

On 19 July 1947, a Naga delegation led by Phizo met Gandhiji at Delhi in Bhangi colony. They claimed he promised them independence if they did not want to join India.

No person close to Gandhiji confirmed this promise, including Pyare Lal, his Secretary. Nehru dubbed this demand as 'absurd', as "this demand would ruin them". The Nagas reacted by a declaration of Independence unilaterally signed by nine members of the NNC on 14 August 1947, a day before India's.

Phizo was moving fast on the extremist trajectory. Indulging in anti-India activities, he was arrested on 9 July 1948 when found carrying some incriminating documents, and put behind the bars at the Presidency Jail, Calcutta. In December, he was released on short parol to accompany his seriously injured wife to Shillong. There, during his meeting with Nari Rustomji, Advisor to the Assam Governor, he told him that he was misunderstood on preconceived notions, and even volunteered to retire from the politics. Rustomji believed his smooth talk, and he was released unconditionally. Phizo of course returned to his old ways![10]

11 December 1950, Phizo was unanimously elected President of the NNC which then on, took secessionist stance. He conducted a referendum on 16 May 1951. The plebiscite result, expectedly, favoured independence by an overwhelming majority of 99.9 per cent. The people had been simply asked to put their thumb impressions in favour of independence. NNC rejected the Indian constitution when it came into being on 26 January 1950. They also boycotted the First General Elections held in 1951-52. The Prime Minister of India and Burma, Nehru and Thakim U Nu, visited Kohima on 30 March 1953. Learning about Nehru's refusal to receive any memorandum from the NNC, its leaders and even some Nagas left the venue of public meeting just before the Leaders' arrival. The same year, 9 police outposts were opened in Naga Hills. By early 1953, every Naga household had reportedly collected sufficient quantity of salt to run over several years because they thought the *dhawai* (=war) with India was imminent![11] In 1952, there was resentment in the Naga Hills when its entire free (unadministered) Naga areas—consisting of the present Mon and Tuensang districts and part of Zuhneboto district, presently Aghunato and Kiphere Sub-Divisions—were transferred to the NEFA, as its 6th Frontier Division (Naga Hoho, document, 2001).

1953, the action against the NNC members was intensified. Different Acts, including the Assam Disturbed Areas Act, 1955 were imposed to enable the Armed Forces to handle the ultras expeditiously. By 1956, the strength of the underground Nagas had considerably increased and situation was serious. This year, the Army units were deployed in major town like Kohima and Mokokchung. On 22 March 1956, the NCC set up its own Government, the Federal Government of Nagaland (FGN), and hoisted the Republic's flag.[12] "Gen Kaito formed the Naga Home Guards (NHG) with Headquarters at Hoshepur village under Aghunato Sub-Division in Tuensang district. He collected arms from Kohima district left behind by the Allied and Japanese forces during the World War II. A fierce battle was fought between the Indian Armed Forces and NHG...."[13] They also formed an underground Tatar Hoho (=Parliament). Soon large scale violence erupted throughout the Naga Hills, then in Assam.

The Naga Hoho Document of 2001 says Gen KS Thimayya met Kughato at Ghukiye village on 16 October 1956. But more surprisingly, it reports a heated argument between the General and Prime Minister Nehru, when the former suggested a political solution to Naga problem. Nehru banged the table, saying "What a General you are...." General too banged the table and.... There is no way to confirm the authenticity of this story.

The intense difference within the NNC led to polarisation between the extremists led by Phizo and the moderates. The extremists were in minority but they asserted their supremacy, speaking through their guns. The resignation of the moderate leaders like T. Sakhrie and J.D. Jasasokie, General Secretary and Public Secretary of the NNC respectively, angered the extremists so much that they decided on their elimination. Sakhrie (Phizo's brother-in-law) was captured on 18 January 1956 from a house in Chaechama, 30 km north of Kohima, where he had gone on a personal visit, taken to jungle, and brutally murdered there. Soon after this murder, the NNC formed FGN, also called Naga Federal Government (NFG). The extremists continued killing people whose loyalty came under minimum suspicion. As a result, all over the Naga Hills, many villagers, Gaon Burahs (GBs), and Government servants were done to death on the slightest suspicion of helping the Government against the NNC. Besides these killings, the villagers were forced to work for them on chores such as construction of shelters in inaccessible jungle, carrying food and other necessities there as well as forced contribution in kind or cash to their kitty.

There was accretion to their strength. To augment it further, people were enticed into joining the underground by giving a rank generally not below a captain to almost all new entrants. Simultaneously, they started attacking police posts, blocking roads, hijacking the civil buses, all for looting and extortion. Thus reached a stage when the Centre ordered Army into Naga Hills. The Army Chief advised his men that while dealing with the rebels, they must be mindful that they were brother Indians gone astray.

In September-October 1956, some moderate leaders met Nehru in Delhi and Shillong, who promised them maximum possible autonomy to the Nagas within the Union. More and more moderate came forward to demand peaceful, political solution. Meanwhile, the church leaders too came forward for peace, and decided to hold a convention to work out a solution. Accordingly, a Naga Peoples Convention (NPC) was held at Kohima[14] during 22-26 August 1957.

It was attended by 1760 delegates and over 2000 visitors from all the tribes of the Naga Hills and Tuensang area. The rebels, though invited, did not attend. The NPC under the leadership of Dr Imkongliba Ao as President and J.B. Jasokie as Secretary declared their opposition to violence and decided to settle the political issue through negotiations with the Government of India. As an interim measure, they proposed merger of Tuensang Frontier Division back into the Naga Hills district to form a Union Territory, directly under the Government of India. A 9-member delegation of the NPC under Imkongliba met the Governor at Shillong, and Nehru at Delhi. Nehru accepted their proposal, and the NHTA came into being on 1 December 1957, by a Presidential Promulgation. It was placed under the Ministry of External Affairs, and was to be administered by the Governor of Assam as the Agent of the President of the Union.[15]

After the NHTA was formed, the NPC-II was held in May 1958 at Ungma, the largest Ao village in Mokokchung district. It formed a Liaison Committee to contact the rebels, and also formed a Drafting Committee to draft and finalise a 16-Point Memorandum for creation of a state to be called Nagaland within the Indian Union. The third session of the NPC was held at Mokokchung from 22 to 26 October 1959. Some rebels attended as observers. The NPC-III passed the 16-Point Draft after full deliberations over 5 days. It claimed support of at least 75 per cent of the people and was in strong position to put forward the Draft Memorandum, its main points being: (1) Formation of the State Nagaland, within India, and under Ministry of External Affairs. (2) Re-transfer of the forest areas to Nagaland. (3) Consolidation of contiguous Naga areas.[16]

A NPC delegation led by Imkongliba discussed the Draft with the Governor of Assam at Shillong in April 1960. Another delegation, with 15 members and 4 consultants, led by Imkongliba discussed their demands with Prime Minister Nehru in July. The demands were accepted with some changes. Nehru announced the terms of Agreement in the Lok Sabha on 1st August 1960.

In the meantime, Phizo had escaped to London, from where he rejected the Delhi agreement, worked out with the support of majority of Nagas. Under his orders, the rebels launched a recruitment drive and started smuggling arms with active help from East Pakistan and China. The peace for which the NPC had worked so hard became elusive.

Under the provisions of the Nagaland (Transitional Provisional) Regulation, 1961 (Act No. 2 of 1961), an Interim Body of 42 members with an Executive Council of five came into being on 18 February 1961. P. Shilu Ao became the Chief Executive Councillor and Imkongliba Ao, the chairman of the Interim Body— the two posts being equivalent of a Chief Minister and Speaker. As stipulated in the draft, the Government of India declared general amnesty to the rebels but no one came overground from their hide-outs.

The rebels did not pardon the moderates for their exertions to usher peace in Nagaland. The indefatigable Imkongliba Ao was shot dead at his home town of Mokokchung soon after his election as the Chairman. T.N. Angami replaced him as the new Chairman.

Under the provision of the Nagaland Act (Act No. 73 of 1962), Nagaland was inaugurated at Kohima as the 16th State of the Indian Union on 31 December 1963 by President Radhakrishnan. The same day, a 5-member Ministry headed by P. Shilu Ao was sworn in by Vishnu Sahai, Governor of Assam and Nagaland. Shilu Ao declared the occasion "a day of rejoicing" and "the day to redeem our pledge". But the rebels continued the violence, having rejected the new settlement.

Peace Mission

The Naga Baptist Church Council (NBCC) took the initiative to convene the third conference of the church leaders at Wokha on 24 February 1964, which resolved to form a Peace Mission consisting of Jayaprakash (JP) Narayan, Bimalprasad Chaliha and Rev Michael Scott—his nomination was reluctantly approved by New Delhi. After several meetings with the underground, the terms of peace was signed at Sakrabama on 24 May 1964 by three members of Peace Mission and six members for the FGN. The Peace Mission held a preliminary conference on 23 September with India's Foreign Secretary Y.D. Gundevia and Chief Minister Shilu Ao. Formal 3-party talks were held at Chedema near Kohima on 12-13 October, and later on 10-14 November 1964. The talks bore no fruit as the rebels brought in new points not acceptable to the Government. The Peace Mission then prepared a lengthy proposal, though short in substance and submitted it to two parties. There were a total of 6 rounds of talks between Prime Minister Indira Gandhi and Underground Nagas from 18 February 1966 to 5 October 1967 but without any tangible results. But a lot of things happened during this period. JP resigned in February 1966. When Scott was found to be indulging in anti-India activities, he was ordered out of India on 4 May 1966. Meanwhile Chief Minister Chaliha too had resigned. Explaining his reasons on 4 May 1966, he said he had definite evidence to show that the train explosions at Lumding (20-4-1966) and Diphu (23-4-1966), which had left over 100 dead and many more injured, had taken place under direction of the head of the Armed Wing of the rebel Nagas.[17] So, by May 1966, it was all over as far as the Peace Mission was concerned. Even then, the talks had continued till October 1967.

On his return from the last round of abortive talks, Kughato Sukhai was severely criticised. Meanwhile, in a coup which he led, Kaito Sema (Kughato's brother) ransacked the rebel headquarter and captured a huge quantity of arms, ammunition and wireless sets. Kughato was accused of involvement in the coup, and Mhiasiu became the leader of the rebels. Kaito Sema who wanted to have peaceful settlement with New Delhi against the wishes of the pro-Phizo group, was shot dead at Kohima bazar on 3 August 1968.

Though the Peace Mission had been wound up, its place was occupied by the Peace Council consisting of church leaders of the NBCC, which was also the force behind the Peace Mission. The Peace Council was active but it could not bring the rebel leaders into peace process.

Back to Violence

That Nagas had actively participated in the elections to the State Assembly went to show their desire for peace for their land. But the NNC continued on the violent path. In 1972, Chief Minister Hokishe Sema was attacked by the rebels but he had a miraculous escape although several people were killed and his daughter seriously injured. Consequently, the suspension of operations, which was being renewed on monthly basis since 6 September 1964 under the agreement worked out by the Peace Mission, was stopped from 1 September 1972, and simultaneously with it, the "illegal NNC, FGN and its army were declared unlawful associations under the Unlawful Activities (Prevention) Act, 1967. Thus ended one chapter of untiring efforts by Government of India to achieve a peaceful solution of the Naga Problem. Earlier on 11 April 1962, the President of India had issued the Nagaland Security Regulation, 1962, for suppression of subversive activities, maintenance of essential supplies and services, and control of military requirements.

The NNC was kept under pressure, and luckily there was no serious law and order problem. Some of the rebels crossed over to Burma. Towards the end of 1975, the hardcore of rebels surrendered and on 11 November 1975, four top ranking underground leaders signed with the Governor of Assam what has come to be known as Shillong Accord, under which the FGN agreed to accept solution of the Naga problem within the framework of Indian Constitution, abjure violence, bring out the armed men to surrender their weapons, and resolve the residual issues through discussions.[18] For the first time, the Government of India refused to relax the ongoing operations, but it permitted the NNC to become a legal outfit by not extending the Unlawful Activities (Prevention) Act. This decision brought to life an organisation that had been the harbinger of terrorism, death and destruction.

Subsequently, the signatories of the Accord were blamed by the hard-core for conceding too much. They were accused of signing the Accord without consulting Phizo, the President of the NNC and other senior leaders like Isaac Chishi Swu and the then General Secretary Thuingalong Muivah, both camping at that time in the Eastern Naga Hills, Upper Burma. Surrenders at the expected scales did not materialise. While Phizo did not lend support, several underground Naga members led by Swu and Muivah formed the "National Socialist Council of Nagaland" (NSCN) on 31 January 1980.[19]

When Prime Minister Morarji Desai was in London in June 1978 to attend Commonwealth Prime Ministers Meeting, he met Phizo. It proved abortive because Phizo talked of independence and Desai would not like to hear that term. Phizo continued to live in UK as a British citizen, a distant figure far removed from the Naga realities. He practically became a nobody when NSCN was formed to continue the Naga struggle.

For record, the UDF Ministry under Vizol was voted out in March 1975, after just a year in office. J.B. Jasokie of the NNO took over from Vizol but his ministry lasted a mere 10 days. So the President's rule was imposed on 22 March 1975 which continued for 32 months till the 4th Assembly Poll in November 1977.

NSCN Bursts on the Scene

The NSCN was formed on 31 March 1980 in the thick jungles of the eastern Naga Hills in Upper Burma, with Swu as the Chairman; S.S. Khaplang, a Hemis Naga of Upper Burma, as Vice-Chairman; and Muivah, a Tangkhul Naga of Manipur's Ukhrul district, as the General Secretary. It has been waging an armed struggle since then to end the "Indian Occupation of the Naga Nation", and then establish a People's Republic of Nagaland, based on Mao's ideology.[20] The manifesto of the NSCN is based on the principles of socialism for economic solution and a spiritual outlook—"Nagaland for Christ".[21]

The initial strength of 150 cadres rose to 3000, mostly Konyaks and Tangkhuls. The Semas, Kukis, Yimchungers and Maos contributed small numbers. It was able to secure a large array of sophisticated weaponry procured from the KIA and international arms market. They supplemented their supply through robberies, snatchings and smuggling, soon becoming the most powerful outfit in the North-East. Having developed close relations with the KIA at an early stage, it was able to withstand attacks on its camps by the much older FGN. The outfit spread its tentacles beyond the confines of the Nagaland, viz Manipur, border areas of Assam, and even Arunachal. For operational purposes, the areas were divided into different regions and placed under a senior underground members. Again at the Headquarters, several cabinet posts were created and kilonsers (ministers) appointed to them.

Intelligence contacts were established with the senior NSCN leaders and efforts made to persuade them to come to the negotiations table. This created certain internal dissonance and mutual suspicions among the senior figures. On 30 April 1988, an attempt to assassinate Muivah and his Tangkhul supporters was made, in which a large number of rebel cadres were killed. It was the bloodiest internal clash in the 3-decade old Naga insurgency. Muivah escaped. Khaplang was suspected behind the savage plan, because he believed that the Isaac-Muivah duo was initiating moves for secret parleys with New Delhi. (He may not have been wide of the mark because the Duo did conclude a cease-fire agreement with the Government in 1997! More of it later.) With this bloody clash, the outfit got split into two factions—NSCN(I-M) and NSCN(K). The older outfit, NNC, earlier weakened by dissents, dissensions, and splits, again suffered a split after the death of Phizo in 1990, with rival factions rallying round his daughter, Adino, and an old associate, Youthan. But even the split of NSCN has not affected its strength as both factions are effectively operating in their respective areas, NSCN (I-M) being stronger of the two. In the period between 1980 and 1997, the NSCN(I-M) moved from strength to strength, added modern weapons to its armoury, and came to dominate other outfits in Nagaland and parts of Assam through assertive and aggressive postures. It proved itself as a path-setter for other outfits in the North-East, not only by being an inspirational icon but also as an exampler for ideological concepts and organisational structures. It was always there offering concrete assistance to nascent outfits in training them in guerrilla tactics and providing initial tranche of arms and ammunition!

NSCN(I-M): Strategic and Tactical Thinking

NSCN(I-M), like so many other secessionist entities, has convinced itself that ideological and philosophical base of India can be weakened, and then rent asunder by hammering at its weakest spots. Exploitative policies and domineering ways of its ruling elite will ensure the rise of discontent people and 'nationalities', particularly ethnic and religious minorities, against the Centre which will, by then, be too weak to hold. The fissiparous forces will then just have to pull apart and they all will have their dreamlands for themselves. The neighbours like Pakistan and China too have been working under illusion of bending India through their subversive tactics and use of violent means. India is civilisationally too old and emotionally too cohesive to yield to the designs of such internal and external forces. It is not a surprise that the NSCN(I-M) struck strategic alliance with anti-India forces beyond its borders and tactical understanding with other separatist elements operating within the country. India has the sustaining strength and resilience to face all such challenges to its integrity and emerge victorious in the end. But this has not stopped all the separatist outfits like the NSCN(I-M) from going all out to achieve their aims. Some of the ways and methods employed by the NSCN(I-M) are discussed here.

Combining with and Supporting Like-minded Forces

The existence of certain other ethnic insurgencies and movements in the area gave an opportunity to the NSCN to turn its own war against the Indian State into a war of the nationalities of the Region against a common 'enemy'—

"overbearing, unjust and dominating Indian State". The NSCN(I-M) ideologues perceived that the growing discontent of the different ethnic groups against India would weaken her, which in turn would facilitate its march to its goal of independence. Hence the debate on the desirability of forging a united front with such other outfits. The NSCN(I-M's) logistic support to the insurgent groups like the ULFA, NDFB, NLFT, PLA, etc. within the Region and its moral and ideological support to secessionist terrorism in Punjab (in 1980s) and Jammu and Kashmir far away from its operational area, can be easily understood, aimed as it is at creating a united front against India. The formation of United Liberation Front of the Seven Sisters (ULFSS) in 1993 was the next practical step to concretise this ideology and concept of bonding between the like-minded outfits. As the ULFSS proved a non-starter, the NSCN(I-M) forged another Front on 30 November 1994, consisting of NDFB (Assam), HPC and KYKL (Oken) (both Manipur), HNLA (Meghalaya) United Liberation Volenteers (of Arunachal), ATTF (Tirupura), and some other fringe groups.[22] By bringing all these groups together, Swu and Muivah did pose a security threat to India. The strategic importance of Indo-Burma border area, a topography favourable to the insurgents, presence of ethnic affinities across the border, and long experience of underground movement had enabled NSCN(I-M) to become a magnet and a rallying point for the Region's insurgency outfits. Its understanding with KIA and Intelligence Agencies of Bangladesh (and Pakistan) enabled it to take shelter in these two countries.

Coopting Smaller Outfits

The NSCN(I-M) is not only using smaller outfits for its larger purpose, it even creates some if need be. Following the surrender of A'chik Liberation Matgrik Army (ALMA), a Garo insurgent outfit, on 25 October 1994, it came to be known that the NSCN(I-M) had masterminded the entire outfit.[23] A Garo, while staying at Dimapur, was advised by the NSCN activists to raise an insurgent outfit in Garo Hills. He raised ALMA in 1991, became its General Secretary, and trained his cadres under the NSCN(I-M). During the three years, the two outfits looted banks and committed robberies. 70 per cent of the booty went to the NSCN(I-M) as charges for its services and cost of arms ammunition, and 30 per cent was left with ALMA as reward for its local cover. Unable to cope with the hardships, the ALMA cadres, who had joined for the lure of easy money, surrendered *en masse* in 1994.

When the cadres of the Dimasa National Volunteers of Assam's North Cachar Hills and of the HPC of Mizoram surrendered, ALMA-like arrangements were revealed. The reported NSCN(I-M) links with HNLC and ANVC of Meghalaya, NDFB of Assam,[24] and NLFT of Tripura turned out to be of the same genre. The Mizoram police had established close links between the NSCN(I-M) and HPC (Democratic) insurgents who had abducted

6 NEEPCO employees on 31 March 2000.[25] The two outfits had jointly killed four policemen in an ambush in 1997.

The NSCN(I-M) had similarly coopted PULF, MULTA and ZRA. These three outfits were involved in killings, kidnappings and extortions in the late 1990s, with their bases in Jiribam, in the Central district of Manipur, where they also were being trained by the NSCN(I-M) cadres.[26] Such cooperation served two broad purposes of the NSCN(I-M). First, with threats on multiple fronts the attention of the SF and Intelligence agencies got divided/distracted to the advantage of the major outfit. Second, it enabled the core insurgent outfit to mobilise additional resources from areas beyond its sphere of influence as also to provide the necessary local cover for its operations in those areas, of totally different ethno social milieu.

Naga Issue: International Dimensions

The British officials' exertion to create a "Crown Colony" directly under the White Hall failed essentially because of political exigencies. The aim was to retain a foothold in the area, and use it against the countries of the Region—India, China and Burma—as and if required to serve the political interests of the UK/the West. Even if the Coupland Plan did not materialise, the West still have its interests in the Region. Besides, some neighbouring countries too have been meddling in India's North-East, taking advantage of the unstable situation there.

China's Nefarious Role

The Chinese Communist leaders not only denounced senior Indian leadership at the time of India achieving its Independence, they even continued to muddle her North-East waters. The Chinese took under their wings Indian rebels of all hues, training and equipping them in their camps in China/Burma. The Nagas, Mizos and others made 'pilgrimages' to China to sit at Mao's feet and drink deep the revolutionary philosophy of the Helmsman!

The Chinese intentions of having their foothold in the strategic Himalayan region were obvious when they committed cartographic aggression against India's North-East in the late 1950s. So they focussed their gaze at Nagaland. Kaito Sema, a senior Naga insurgent leader of FGN, flew direct to Beijing from London where he had gone for consultations with Phizo. Even when Kaito had returned from Beijing after finalising the modalities of mutual cooperation between the PRC and FGN, there was always a permanent representative of the FGN in Beijing. The Beijing leadership invited batches of Naga youths to China, and took them to different camps in China to train them in guerrilla warfare. But it was essentially from 1972 that they increased manifold the number of camps for training and equipping the Naga rebels. Batches of Naga, Meitei and Mizo insurgents went to China where they were hailed and hugged as 'brothers', the favourite Communist jargon! They returned with photos in which they posed with the Chinese officials against the Great Wall of China, Tianenman Square, etc. The batch which went to China under Muivah in 1975 was unable to penetrate into Nagaland or Manipur, so they established a Beijing-backed camp in the Sahpa village in North-East Burma, accommodating a large number of Muivah's men. Even since, this area has become a meeting point and training centre for the Indian insurgents. The Naga leadership of this important camp had signed an agreement of "mutual cooperation and assistance" with the Communist Party of China instead of with the Government, allowing the latter to maintain a facade of innocence and correctitude. So the tap was not turned off![27]

Beijing is believed to have organised a meeting of various insurgent groups—Chakmas (of Bangladesh), Nagas, Mizos and Meiteis in 1973 at Bangkok; the venue should indicate collaboration between the Chinese leaders and the CIA, as Bangkok is known to be the South-East Asian Operational Head of the CIA. The aim was to forge organisational set-up consisting of all the insurgent outfits with a common command and common strategy so that the insurgencies in Nagaland, Mizoram, Manipur, and even CHT could be coordinated. When the exercise proved abortive, the Maoists and CIA struck a deal, leaving Beijing to deal separately with each of the insurgent groups.[28]

The Press reported in 1987 that the Chinese had withdrawn support from the Indian insurgents. It proved to be a temporary tactical move. The Chinese were disillusioned when the Mizo and Tripura rebels signed Peace Accords with the Government of India in 1986 and 1988 respectively.

The Chinese support to Indian insurgent outfits from November 1966 onwards was stopped in 1987, but was resumed in 2000.

Pakistan and Bangladesh

On the maxim of enemy's enemy being a friend, Pakistan gave an unabated moral and material support (money, arms and political sinews) to the Naga insurgents from early stages. Besides aiming at weakening India from within, at its strategically sensitive points in the North-East, Pakistan also wanted to compel India to deploy its forces there, thus relieving the pressure in the Kashmir valley which Pakistan had wanted to grab as early as 1947 through armed aggression. Early 1962, Kaito Sema visited Pakistan to arrange for training and arms for Naga cadres in East Pakistan camps and initially, perhaps, in the west. 20 May 1962, Phizo visited Karachi to see for himself the training of his cadres. To express his happiness and gratitude, Phizo announced in London on 7 May 1963 that in case of a plebiscite the Nagas would also have the option of joining Pakistan.

During the 1962-68 period, East Pakistan had trained and armed some 2,500 Naga rebels, and 10 Naga groups visited Pakistan to procure monetary and material help for their war against India.[29] Muivah, after brief visit to Karachi, flew into Bangkok on 19 January 2000, where he was arrested by the Thai police on the charges of travelling on a forged passport and later for jumping bail. Such assistance continued at the behest of the Pak ISI which had built a network of nests in the jungles adjoining Manipur, Bangladesh, Myanmar and Thailand.

[A new Islamic nation will be created on Indian soil in not too distant a future, warns Kissinger and also India's Ex-Director IB. Some analysts feel that Pak ISI and Bangladesh Intelligence are working in cahoots for creation of an eastern flank of fundamentalism, in the bordering districts of Assam, West Bengal and Bihar, dominated by minority communities, mostly migrants ('infiltrators' to some) from East Pakistan/Bangladesh. To wit, this migration started over 150 years ago, in 1840s! But then some Indians dismiss this possibility as a bogey phantasised by the RSS ideologues! But the proponents argue: "Look at the spread of the extremism from Bangladesh to the Rohingya Muslims of Arakan just across its shared border with Burma." Rohingya mujahids have been active in Burma ever since its independence on 4 January 1948.]

Burma

Burma holds a pivotal position in India's CI strategy and in the prevention of flow of drugs through North-East India. It is also the country where India must stem the flood tides of Chinese influence rushing into South Asia and Bay of Bengal. *She* can turn Nelson's eye to the insurgent bases/activities on its soil either as a retaliatory measure (If India can allow Pro-Democracy student camps in Manipur and Mizoram, why cannot she allow I-M camps in its Somra Hills Tract?) or as a tit-for-tat for India's political support for Aung San Suu Kyi. Both the nations have a history of supporting the insurgent outfits of the opposite on selective basis to suit their CI operations against their own groups. Some reports suggested "a deal with NSCN(I-M) wherein the 'M' component and ULFA would be permitted bases in the Kachin State and the Sagaing Division if they supported the Tatmadaw (Burmese Army) against NSCN(K). In its turn, the I component would give up its claim on the Burmese portion of Nagalim" [Defence and Technology, December 2002; Lt Gen SK Pillai (Retd)]. The Tatmadaw sees NSCN(K) as a more serious threat since it is led by a Hemis Naga of Burma and has the larger component of Burmese Nagas in its ranks.

Burma has a history of helping India in its CI operations, barring occasional let ups dictated by its political compulsions. In 1987, the Tatmadaw attacked NSCN(I-M) bases located in KIA-controlled areas. In 1991, when

Tatmadaw signed cease-fire with KIO, I-M had to shift its bases to Bangladesh as the KIA shelter was no more available. Joint India-Burma operations were effective against insurgents of both the countries in post-1993 period, but Tatmadaw was pulled out when India displayed insensitivity towards SLORC by awarding the Nehru Peace Prize to Suu Kyi. Tatmadaw attacked NSCN(K) bases in northern Burma in Oct.-Dec. 1999. Upgraded Indian SF interaction with the Tatmadaw would surely weaken insurgents taking refuge there. [Burma, conscious of need to balance the Chinese influence is stepping up economic cooperation with India eg extension of Indian road network, and signing Indian help for improving Burmese rail lines (July 2004).]

The US Hand

UK reigned supreme till the 1930s in South Asia but world war II and loss of its colonies changed the picture, with the USA supplanting it in this area and even beyond. As early as 1950s, the CIA had extended its activities into Naga Hills, including monetary help to its insurgents. "American spies handed the tribal leaders several million rupees, weapons and secret instructions prepared in Washington."[30] Journalist Dhruva Mazumdar in his *confession of a Journalist,* states that he was paid by the CIA to file reports from the North-East on the movements of Indian Army and "barrack room gossip".[31] Till the early 1971, the US continued to be the chief patron of the insurgent outfits. Bangkok had become the Operational Headquarters of the CIA, from where the arms flowed for mere asking to any adventurist outfit dreaming big against its own nation. "It was the time when Pakistan, particularly its Eastern Wing, provided the insurgents with transit facilities, training centres, and route to Bangkok and Peking. Dacca-Bangkok-London-Pindi-Peking axis was operating, actuated by the common anti-India hatred."[32]

Before the liberation of Bangladesh, the US and some other western nations had conspired to create an Independent (Greater) Bengal, comprising of East Pakistan, West Bengal, Assam, Nagaland, Manipur, Tripura, Sikkim and Bhutan. Lest we forget, the "blue print of this nefarious design had been spelt out long year back in a Dacca datelined dispatch, circulated by Agencies International De Presa (International Press Agency—IPA) on 7 December 1936".[33] The Indian separatist leaders had readily accepted the proposal because it promised the Nagas and Mizos 'Greater Nagaland' and 'Greater Mizoram' respectively as autonomous entities within the framework of 'Greater Bengal'!

International Linkages

The Naga leaders must be given credit that they have not only conducted a violent struggle within India but have also established liaison with some important international organisations like UNHRC (Geneva), the

Unrepresented Nations Peoples' Organisation, UNPO (Hague), and UN Working Group on Indigenous Peoples (UNG-IP) to have its voice heard at the international fora. The NSCN(I-M) became a member of the UNPO which champions the right of self-determination of ethnic minority groups.

Chairman Swu of NSCN(I-M) addressed the UNHRC at Geneva on 24 April 1998, describing the Nagas as distinct people, "a nation of about 3 million people, occupying an area of 100,000 km^2", and allegedly occupied by the Indian and Burmese armed forces.[34] An outlawed Indian outfit succeeded in advocating its secessionist agenda shows UN's intention of creating a platform for the aggrieved communities of the world. India need not worry too much as its negotiations with the Swu-Muivah duo are progressing, even if slowly.

Neutral Thailand is interesting if unique in the sense that all comers, including NSCN(I-M) and ULFA are allowed to dip in the arms stock/market based around the Three Pagodas Pass area. This market services the clandestine international clientele. Purely economics informs Thai policy of permitting these insurgent outfits to function from its soil in an apolitical environment. So, if Thailand provides military hardware and no 'moral back-up', some Western NGOs and Christian Organisations do the exact opposite! Their financial aid has decreased since the 9/11. The UK-based organisations Naga Vigil and Liberation, the Hongkong based Christian Conference of Asia and the Geneva-based World Council of Churches generate awareness of the 'Naga Cause'. Whether they also provide financial aid is uncertain.

In 1987, the NSCN(I-M) shrewdly selected Thailand as its base due to the ease in procurement and dispatch of weapons and all kinds of equipment. It was the first Indian insurgent group to do so. Moreover, NSCN(I-M) has achieved great sophistication in the use of electronic media and projection of its case abroad. For instance, the Nagaland International Support Centre at Amsterdam establishes networks with foreign NGOs like UK-based Naga Vigil, publicises the stand of the NSCN(I-M) and the Human Rights violation of the Indian Security Forces.

Peace Talks

India believes all secessionist movements have to be dealt with politically to find a lasting solution even if use of the state force has to be resorted to thwart the mindless violence unleashed by the separatist outfits. A serious attempt was made by New Delhi at political level when Prime Minister Rao set the ball rolling by meeting Swu and Muivah in Paris on 15 June 1995. Rao laid down the Government's stand: "We must solve the problem through political talks and dialogue." His successor Deve Gowda sent former Union Minister of State Rajesh Pilot in November 1996 for secret meeting with the two leaders in Bangkok, and then met them himself (as Ex-Prime Minister) on 3 February 1997 in Zurich. In May, Prime Minister Gujral sent former Principal Secretary to the Prime Minister, Satish Chandra, and senior IB officials for a meeting with the Duo in Geneva. Prime Minister Vajpayee met them twice: in November 1998 in Paris and on 8 December 2001 in Osaka, Japan.

33 years after the 1964 cease-fire agreements, a fresh bilateral Cease-Fire Agreement was signed between Government of India and NSCN(I-M) on 25 July 1997, effective 1 August 1997. The cease-fire period is extended from time to time, and completed first three years on 31 July 2000. The latest renewal was due on 31 July 2004, for which the rebels were reportedly reluctant for reasons to be discussed a little later here. Since August 1997, Swu and Muivah have been holding talks with New Delhi's emissaries, first Swaraj Kaushal and later former Home Secretary K. Padmanabhaiah.

The peace process entered a new phase when the NSCN(K) also formally announced its unilateral cease-fire on 9 April 2000, and Openly expressed its willingness to hold peace talks with the Centre. But difficulty arises from the fact that the NSCN(I-M) considers itself the sole and only representative of the Nagas and is opposed to the Centre holding talks with any other group. S.C. Jamir, the then Chief Minister, considered close to the NSCN(K) met the Prime Minister in 2000 to plead their case, but without any success.

The public mood was upbeat when the NSCN(I-M) signed cease-fire with the Centre. It got strengthened when the NSCN(K) followed suit. Several social groups expressed themselves for peace, while simultaneously showing disenchantment with the insurgency and violence attached with it.

A piquant situation arose when Muivah was arrested along with lieutenant I. Shimru on 19 January 2000 at Bangkok airport for entering the country on a forged passport, and sentenced to one year's imprisonment. The arrest came exactly on the day when Prime Minister's Special Emissary Padmanabhaiah was all set to leave for third round of talks in Hague on 20 January 2000. NSCN(I-M) refused to hold talks without Muivah's presence, and it rather interestingly held New Delhi responsible for his arrest through pressure on the Thai Government. Even more interestingly, it wanted New Delhi to get Muivah out of jail, given its friendly relations with Bangkok. But New Delhi balked at the prospects of its interfering in the judicial process of another country. The matters got complicated when it was reported that Chief Minister Jamir wanted Muivah to stay where he was because he was convinced that a serious attempt on his life on 29 November 1999 was the handiwork of the NSCN(I-M).[35] NSCN(I-M) on its part considers Jamir the biggest hurdle in the way of settlement of the Naga issue with India.[36]

Around 2000, there were some other complications vitiating the talks. New Delhi found it intriguing that Muivah should be hobnobbing with

Pakistan/ISI during the talks — he had flown in from Pakistan when he was arrested at Bangkok on landing. Was he still in cahoots with the ISI? Was the NSCN(I-M) still collecting arms from Pakistan and getting its cadres trained in Pakistan Camps? Indian Intelligence confirmed two ISI-run camps in Pakistan training 40-50 Nagas during that period. Over 200 cadres were reported to have completed their training in Pakistan during three years (1997-99) since the NSCN(I-M) engaged the Union Government in peace talks. Obviously, the outfit had violated the true conditions.[37] On the top of it, the Army was apprehensive that the outfit was reorganising, stockpiling weapons, and recruiting fresh cadres, making use of the cease-fire period.

The talks had shown little substantive progress in the first 3-4 years. New Delhi felt the Duo had shown no flexibility of approach. The two were allowed to visit Nagaland in March 1998 to assess the situation and consult their cadres. Even after this visit they continued insisting on: (1) Cease-fire must be extended beyond Nagaland. (2) Creation of Greater Nagaland, Nagalim, consisting of Naga inhabited areas of the North-East. (3) The 1951 Phizo conducted plebiscite to be the basis of further negotiations. These incremental conditionalities notwithstanding, New Delhi continued the talks.

The existence of a rival faction, NSCN(K) is another complicating factor. Even a hint of involving it in peace talks by the Government met with a howl of serious protests by the Naga Hoho (it is Kohima based apex tribal Council of Nagas living in different parts of the North-East[38]) and the Nagaland People's Council (NPC). The two organisations are staunchly opposed to involving Jamir's Congress Government in the talks, as it is not a mandated Government of the Nagas since the other parties had boycotted the 1998 elections at the call of these two. The cease-fire between the Army and the NSCN(I-M) had run into rough weather because NSCN(K) lost no chance to snipe at its rivals without a similar truce with them!

There is a third outfit involved in this violent tug-of-the-war, NNC/ FGN. The total number of people who fell to the factional fights during the truce from 1 August 1997 to 22 March 2000, as per the Nagaland Police figures, are 317. Its break down:

NSCN(I-M)	-	61	Government Servants	-	12
NSCN(K)	-	133	Police	-	3
NNC/FGN	-	22	SF/PMF	-	13
Civilians	-	65	Unidentified	-	8

Ultimate Solution?

In June 2001, the Naga Hoho invited B.K. Roy Burman, an eminent anthropologist and an expert on the North-East, to help find a solution to the vexed issue. He strongly feels the solution can be akin to what is being followed in the distant Scandinavian countries for Sami tribes. The Samis are spread over Sweden, Finland, Norway and parts of Russia, but they remain the citizen of the respective countries and their interests are taken care of by the Sami Council, their apex body *(Times of India,* 20-6-01).

Nagalim (=Greater Nagaland)

The Naga insurgents had started their war against India in 1950s to secure an independent Nagaland comprising the present Nagaland, Naga-inhabited areas of Manipur, Assam and Arunachal adjoining the Nagaland borders, and Naga-inhabited areas of Burma. After they signed Truce with New Delhi, it was obvious that they were giving up their dream of a Nagaland outside India. They were always eyeing the Naga areas of Manipur. For a time, they were advocating, with active help from their compatriots of Manipur, creation of Southern Nagaland comprising the districts of Senapati, Ukhrul, Chandel and Tamenglong, within the Indian Union. It was an initial ploy to bifurcate/breakup Manipur, and subsequently integrate Southern Nagaland into Nagaland. They already seem to have gained control over the Tamenglong district dominated by the Zeliangrong Nagas. Finally, it is their demand of Nagalim, to be created by integrating Naga-inhabited areas of Manipur (and to a smaller extent, of Assam and Arunachal) into Nagaland which is proving a stumbling block for the final solution of the Naga imbroglio.

Conceding either of the two alternatives. Southern Nagaland or Nagalim, will certainly bring the Meiteis of Manipur into conflict with the Nagas. The secessionist outfits of Manipur—PLA, PREPAK, RPF and UNLF committed to make Manipur an independent country—would outrightly reject the cession of northern areas of Manipur to Nagaland. These Manipur-based insurgent outfits have formed a new front called the Manipur People's Liberation Front (MPLF) on 1 March 1999 declaring their determination to jointly confront the SF or separatists *(North-East Sun,* 15-31 March 1999). But the Nagas are confident that the 1960 Agreement between them and the Government of India, which had assured them that the contiguous Naga-inhabited area would eventually be integrated into Nagaiand, would give them their desideratum.[39]

The Manipur-Nagaland rift was further widened when the Nagaland Assembly passed a bill demanding the merger of the Naga-inhabited areas of Manipur under the terms of 16-Point Agreement of 1960 the Naga People's Convention signed with the Government of India. Moreover, the hill areas like Ukhrul, Tamenglong, Mao Maram and parts of Churachandpur, and Dimapur-Imphal Road, the life line of Manipur, come under the purview of Nagaland Cease-fire Agreement signed in 1964.[40] Manipur, obviously, will not countenance the presence of NSCN in these areas. How sensitive the Manipuris are about the integrity of their state was obvious when the state went up in flames when Government of India extended the Cease-fire

Agreement beyond the limits of Nagaland in 2001. Manipuris obviously concluded that this was the first step towards the Government conceding Nagalim to the NSCN(I-M)! Hence the apoplexy of violence.

What does the Nagalim demand mean for the neighbouring states in terms of geographical areas claimed from various districts? *See* the table[41] below:

Naga Claims on the Neighbours

Assam		*Manipur*		*Arunachal Pradesh*	
Area: 78,438 km^2		Area: 22,327 km^2		Area: 83,743 km^2	
	km^2		km^2		km^2
Karbi-Anglong	10,434	Ghandel	3,313	Changlang	4,662
N. Cachar Hills	4,888	Ukhrul	4,544	Tirap	2,362
Golaghat	3,502	Senapati	3,271		
Sibsagar	2,668	Tamenglong	4,391		
Jorhat	2,851				
Total area	24,343	Total area	15,519	Total area	7,024

In Assam's case, only parts of the areas of these districts are claimed; say, 50 per cent, i.e., 12,000 km^2. That way the Nagas are claiming over 35,000 km^2 from these three states. The present area of Nagaland is 16,579 km^2. Another estimate puts the claim at 48,500 km^2, an undoubted exaggeration, an opening gambit! Who are the tribes inhabiting these disputed districts? Ukhrul (Tangkhuls), Senapti (Mao, Poumai, Maram), Tamenglong (Zeliangs). Arunachal's Tirap and Changlong districts have a sizeable population of Konyaks.

Peace Talks have Influenced People?

The common people seemed to have had enough of the high-handedness of the NSCN(K) cadres, who shot dead a student on 24 August 2003 "for reportedly questioning the harassment of students in Mokukchung". At his funeral on the 26th, tempers soared high and a crowd of over 10,000 turned violent, killing two of the outfit's cadres (Chairman and Secretary of the Group's Lotha Region). As the mob went on rampage, they set ablaze 8 houses, including that of K's General Secretary Kitovi Zhimoni. The houses belonging to SS Maj Aheto and SS Capt Lanu Ao were also ransacked as the two ran for their lives. This is the first time that the rebels faced the ire of the common man in Nagaland after 3 years. (An incensed crowd had lynched to death 4 I-M cadres in Wokha on 22 January 2000 in eastern Nagaland. In Assam, however, the common people have already lynched about 20 ULFA rebels in the past four years, 1999-2003, apart from handing over at least 50 others to the police.[42])

Close on the heels of the Mokokchung case of 26 August 2003, a furious mob lynched to death in Nagaland's Tuensang town a NSCN(I-M) insurgent on the 28th for assaulting two leaders of the Tuensang and Mon Students Federation (TMSF) while they were returning from a meeting on the 27th. The 28th lynching occurred during a 12-hour *bandh* called by the leaders of the TMSF and the Tuensang Mon Public Organisation to protest against the said assault previous day. On the very date, the 28th, the NSCN(I-M) Kohima issued a press statement asking its cadres to refrain from harassing the members of public and also from collecting 'tax' from any individual or organisation. The statement was seen a clear admission by the outfit that its cadres were indeed harassing the common people and collecting 'tax' despite the cease-fire. The NSCN(I-M) statement comes in the wake of the Ao Senden, the highest body of the AO tribe, making a public appeal (early August) to the people not to pay any taxes to the underground groups, and asking the NSCN cadres to restrict themselves to the designate camps (total 17) created under the ground rules of the cease-fire. Of these 17 camps in Nagaland, ten belong to NSCN(I-M) and the seven to the NSCN(K).[43]

Violence Continues Despite the Cease-fire

On 17 March 2002, 11 ultras of NSCN(I-M) were killed by men of India Reserve Battalion at Pallel in Chandel district of Manipur when they tried to stop an approaching truck and the former opened fire. In the 30-minute encounter, 11 insurgent were killed while one escaped. Four sniper rifles, four AK-47s, three SLRs, two carbines, three 303 rifles, and a hand grenade were recovered from the truck. In a quick reprisal, the rebels abducted the Deputy Commissioner of Chandel, Yambem Thamkishwor from near his office, on the very next day, the 18th. Not only the NSCN(I-M) doubted the genuineness of the encounter, the Manipur Government made the matters worse by announcing rewards for the policemen the next day. During the next few days, the incident developed into a stand-off between the Centre and State. On the 19th, seven Naga tribes in Chandel appealed to the underground United Kuki Liberation Front (UKLF) to release the official on humanitarian grounds. It was a smart move on their part, as it later turned out, the kidnapping was masterminded by the NSCN but jointly executed with the help of its ally UKLF. The NSCN(I-M) not only wanted the culprits to be punished, but also the return of captured weapons. The Centre's Emissary Padmanabhaiah had to be pressed into service to diffuse the crisis "which almost derailed the peace talks". Another version says Manipur's newly elected Congress Chief Minister, Okram Ibobi, determined not to bow down to the NSCN(I-M) demands, asked the Centre to take action against the militants. Padmanabhaiah reportedly told Swu and Muivah that if the DC was not released, the peace process would collapse. Having responded positively to Vajpayee's invitation at Osaka, Japan, on 8 December 2001, to visit India for peace talks, the Duo did not want to test further New Delhi's patience. Hence the unconditional release.

As the present "Truce was in force within the territorial limits of Nagaland', the NSCN(I-M) militants had shifted their activity to the Naga dominated areas in the neighbouring States of Manipur, Assam and Arunachal. The Pallel encounter had been preceded by a 4-hour clash between the I-M and K factions at Sachin village of Changlang district, close to Nagaland. The NSCN(I-M) was at it again on 17 March 2002, making an attempt to blow up a wireless station at Mahadevpur hill in the North Cachar Hills of Assam. The policemen deployed at the centre forced the rebels to retreat after a half-hour long-gun battle. Later 3 militants of this outfit were arrested while trying to cross over to Tripura from the CHT.

In August 2002, the factional clashes claimed four lives i.e., 3 NSCN(K) cadres near Chumukedima in Dimapur district on the 23rd and one NSCN(K) insurgent at Suruhoto in Zunheboto district on the 24th. Lt Gen (Retd) RV Kulkarni, Chairman, Ceasefire Monitoring Group, NSCN(I-M) and the Cease-fire Supervisory Board, NSCN(K) issued a directive to the warring factions to return to their barracks.

In November 2003, 17 members of K faction, including one Deputy Kilonser and a district level Vice-Chairman, defected to their rival I-M side, causing much discomfort to the leaders of the former.

Political Interlocutors

After the December 2001 invitation from Vajpavee for the I-M leaders to visit India, the need for a political 'facilitator' was realised. Mizoram Chief Minister Zoramthanga's name was first proposed by Muivah and later approved by the Centre. His credentials were impeccable. He had assisted Laldenga during the 4-year long Mizo-New Delhi talks. Zoramthanga was present at the Bangkok 6-10 May 2002 Enclave, attended by 41 representatives of Naga social bodies, NGOs, the Church, Student leaders, Naga Hoho, and Nagaland-based NSCN(I-M) *kilonsers* (ministers). It was the second time that I-M leaders held consultations with cross-section of Nagas in Bangkok. (The last one was January 2002 after the Naga Hoho Coordination Committee launched the "Unite and Reconciliation Campaign" in December 2001.) The Bangkok Enclave was preceded by a 2-day (3-4 May 2002) meeting at Kuala Lumpur, Malaysia, between the Naga Duo (then based there) and Indian interlocutors, Padmanabhaiah and K.P. Singh, Director IB *(Hindustan Times,* Chandan Nandy, 4-5-02). In July 2003, Meghalaya Chief Minister D.D. Lapang, openly flayed Zoramthanga for holding parleys with the insurgent outfits, right outside the Advani office in North Block. After meeting Advani on the 11th, he said "no one has been authorised to open second channel of talks with the NSCN(I-M)" *(Times of India,* 12-7-03). Is it a case of sibling rivalry or regional one-up-manship?

For a while during 2002, name of Ex-Speaker P.A. Sangma was in the air as a likely facilitator in the Naga talks. It seems he became a casualty to the intra-regional politics.

With the Manmohan Singh Government having come to power in May 2004, new equations were expected to emerge. After consultations with the Home Ministry, the new Congress Chief Minister Rio of Nagaland said he was awaiting a call from the PMO to leave for Bangkok on 1 July to engage the I-M leaders in peace talk.

Back to the Narrative

Human casualties and arms/ammunition lost during the 1992-2000 period are given in the table below:

Security Force/Police killed/injured and weapons/ ammunitions lost/snatched: 1992-2000

Year	*Security Force/Police*		*Weapons/Ammunition lost*	
	Killed	*Injured*	*Arms*	*Ammunition*
1992	33	52	9	12
1993	85	99	182	9480
1994	92	99	198	12079
1995	57	79	143	8433
1996	62	41	38	1567
1997	112	82	93	2194
1998	63	50	63	2488
1999	58	99	135	7519
2000 (Till 31 July)	23	39	97	1985

Source: Published in open literature.

Swu and Muivah in Delhi: January 2003

The over-4-year-old talks had received a boost with Vajpayee meeting and inviting the two leaders to India for talks. The latter thought the December 2001 meeting was the need of the hour, especially after the 14 June 2001 agreement at Bangkok between the Duo and Padmanabhaiah to extend the Truce beyond Nagaland had faced serious opposition in all the three states. Manipur in particular had plunged into hell fires.

The Government had cleared the decks for the talks when it decided on 15 November 2002 not to re-impose the ban order that expired on the 26th. The Nagaland and Manipur Governments withdrew the arrest warrants, ensuring the Duo safe passage in India. Jamir was against lifting the ban under the Unlawful Activities (Prevention) Act.

The Naga leaders had passed on their 31-point charter to Vajpayee through Padmanabhaiah whom they met in Bangkok in November 2002—two main demands being a separate flag and Greater Nagaland. In a separate letter to the PMO, they made it clear that any settlement would be nullified if the Centre attempts an agreement with the K faction. They alleged that Jamir had been funding and arming the K faction, and sheltering its cadres in his farm houses at Dimapur and Mokokchung as well as in the camps of the Assam Rifles. Jamir is for involving all militant groups in the peace process but the Union Home Ministry has a different view. The I-M faction holds sway in more than 75 per cent of Nagaland while the K faction is active only in 20 per cent. Khaplang, a Hemi Naga from Burma, has been receiving patronage from Burmese Army. The I-M faction's support base consists of the Tangkhuls, Phoms and Angamis while Khaplang draws strength from Hemis, Konyaks and Aos. I-M claims 6,000 cadres against K's 3,500 (1989 figures).

It may be useful to briefly recount the rise of NSCN(I-M) to the top of secessionist pantheon. It is well-known that Khaplang faction had nearly wiped out his rival Muivah and his cadres in a surprise attack in Burmese jungles on 30 April 1988. 230 of his followers, including women and children, escaped into jungle where they were harried by Burmese forces. The survivors scattered in groups and many perished in jungle. Muivah with 33 joined with Swu and started for Nagaland. Further attacks reduced his numbers, and finally Muivah with 7 reached the safety of lower Konyak area. Khaplang and his Deputy, Tali, were accused of spreading the canard about Muivah and Swu's treachery (planning talks and surrender to Indian Government) at the behest of the Indian agents. Rejoinder to the complaint of Rev Y. Chingang Konyak by Tajenyuba Ao in the 1994 issue of the Nagaland Journal is the revealing account of the way the NSCN split. The massacre of the Muivah group was "a terrible set back to the Naga struggle for sovereignty", resulting into a split into Khaplang (Hemi and Konyak) and Muivah-Swu (Tangkhul and Sema) NSCN factions. Feuding since then has been bitter and bloody and has caused inter-tribal tensions and repercussions overground.

Be that as it may, Muivah has staged a strong come-back since 1988. Within a couple of years, NSCN(I-M) had become mainspring of all the North-eastern insurgency movements, taking over its erstwhile benefactor, KIA, which had come to terms with SLORC in Burma. NSCN(I-M) gradually built its base in the Manipur hills among the Tangkhuls and around Kohima, while NSCN(K) coming under pressure from the Burmese Army in Hukawng Valley moved to more familiar and friendly Konyak and Ao areas in Tuensang and Mokokchung regions of Nagaland. Therefore, extortions, threats and elimination of actual and potential "rivals and betrayers" marked the course of both factions. This war of attrition also claimed the life of Lungshim Shaiza, a Tangkhul married to Phizo's niece, Ranno, in the late 1990s. Some years earlier, his brother, Yangmah Shaiza, Ex-Chief Minister, Manipur, had also fallen victim to inter-tribal factional hostility. Signatories to the Shillong Accord had especially been marked by both the factions, and consequently, Kevi Yallay could not attend his brother, Phizo's widely attended and tearful funeral after his body was brought in from England to be interred in Kohima in May 1990.

Localism (love for village) and tribalism (placing one's tribe above the larger collectivity) are among the problems that have dogged "Naga efforts at nation-building, or the concept of *Naganess or Nagahood"*. The 1967 rift between the groups espousing the cause of RGN or FGN was a manifestation of rift between the Semas and Tanghuls. Here is an insightful comment of a sympathetic scholar: "Tribalism was to undo what nationalism had done after years of toil and bloodshed" (Horam, 1988). The same was repeated a decade later in a bitter inter-tribal rivalries between the I-M and K factions. Phizo and his colleagues were severely indicted by the 1988 Manifesto of the NSCN, and the ascendance of the all powerful Angami clan seemed to have received a knocking. The character of the Naga insurgency had changed by the late 1980s. Rural based guerrilla movement had come to town. Though there was large overground, this seemed to have been penetrated at political, administrative and intellectual levels, with sections of community held to ransom by fear of the militant's gun. "Substantial amounts earmarked for development as well as salaries and contract payment are being deviated through taxes, extortions, commissions, and pay-offs. It is generally known that the exchequer is part-financing insurgency, which also draws on the underworld of narcotics and smuggling for funds."

There have been open allegations about both factions enjoying political patronage at the highest level. Nagaland Chief Minister Jamir's name is linked to the Khaplong action. Manipur Chief Minister Rishang Keishing and other ranking Manipuri politicians were accused of helping NSCN(I-M) by no less a person than the then Governor of Manipur, Lt Gen (Retd) VK Nayar, in his official report to the President, recommending President's rule in the State. The report was presented to the Parliament in 1994.

Release on bail on medical grounds of Kheya Hurie, Finance Secretary of the NSCN(I-M) in 1993 caused much resentment within the Security Forces (SF). The leakage of arms from the State Police also dismayed the Army authorities. "Cosy relationship between the underground hankering after easy money and comforts of overground life and politicians glad to have their own hitmen and servitors around are unhealthy symptoms of the same disease." The political debts are/were indeed encashable.

NSCN(I-M) now dominated (early 1990s) insurgency in North-East. Muivah was the man behind the outfit's rise to prominence, though later it came to be known as I-M faction. Its public face certainly was Muivah's. He secured sanctuaries in Bangladesh after the KIA made up with Burmese Army. This change in base and supply area made North Cachar Hills an important transit route, and newer focus of insurgent activities.

NSCN(I-M) succeeded in internationalising its cause by opening offices in a number of countries in South-East Asia, Europe, North America, and by getting admission to the Unrepresented Nations and Peoples Organisation (UNPO), a Hague-based NGO, but nothing to do with UN. Muivah's attending the Conference of the Indigenous People was a step in the same direction. By the mid-1990s, Muivah had a high profile. He had even put in an appearance at a UNHRC session in Geneva in 1993. NSCN(I-M) was in international limelight indeed and Muivah was its familiar face. But by then, there was a flip side to this glow of international arc-lights. There was reports of frustration arising out of sense of futility and fatigue of a never-ending struggle. Whatever the perspective from Bangkok or Amsterdam, the ground realities in India were distorting the idyll! Muivah and Swu were ageing and their younger cadres had lost the elan and fervour of the jungle-hardened guerrillas. "The key figures in NSCN(I-M) have acquired property in Meghalaya, especially in Shillong, where its sympathisers are enrolled as students, which provides a cover for movement into Bangladesh (Darshan Balwally, May 1995). It was not surprising that there were feelers from the outfit for unconditional talks. But the old fears stared them in the face. After all it were the 'rumours' of such talks which had resulted in the K faction vicious attacks on the I-M cadres. Again, they could not forget Muivah rubbishing Phizo and NNC for the Shillong Accord. There was no unity among the Naga insurgent groups.

It is a fact that by mid-1990s, the NSCN was almost functioning as a parallel government on the authority of the gun. The Government servants were paying regular tax to the underground at the rate of 10 per cent of the salary for grade IV, 20 per cent for grades III and II, and 30 per cent for grade I services. An analyst is starkly outspoken: "People in high places do not feel any real sense of accountability for the cheap Delhi money used to finance the 'puppets' and 'subvert' Naga interests."

Besides the ageing leaders and frustration among the cadres, mentioned above, there were other reasons also which disillusioned the insurgent outfits. The Sema and Angamis Hohos were seeking political solution. The Aos criticised the militants for inter-ethnic violence. The Church was anguished over the continuing violence. NSCN(I-M) undoubtedly the leader in the field, was not reaching anywhere. And then the overtures from the Indian Prime Ministers, after long, persistent interaction with the Indian Intelligence, became too alluring. So came the cease-fire in 1997!

NSCN(I-M): Camps in Bangladesh

Mid-2001, a large party of NSCN(I-M) had moved from Nagaland via the Tiddim road, Parva (India-Burma-Bangladesh Trijunction) to Bandarban to collect the arms supplies sent by China from Cox Bazar. 5 of them defected with arms and were arrested by the BSF post at Parva. Their interrogation revealed that the outfit had the following camps:

	Strength
1. Jortan Camp, near Cox's Bazar	250
2. Vaital Camp, near Rangamati	300
3. Galilee Camp, near Alikadam	50
4. Mauni Transit Camp, near Sylhet	
5. Headquarters of NSCN(I-M) at Dhaka. A 4-storey building near New Market.	

For collection of weapons, usually once a year, the route adopted was Cox's Bazar, Alikadam, Kasalang Reserve Forest, Mizoram, Silchar, Jiribam, Tamenglong and Paren. The July 2001 consignment of 35 weapons was brought on foot upto Mizoram near Amchurimukh, whence they were sent by a Gypsy of NSCN(I-M) via Silchar, Jiribam, Tamenglong, Paren and Dimapur. Later it was confirmed that the outfit has a safe house at Aizawl, "obviously given by the State Government. The movement of arms by road too could not take place without that State's patronage [E.N. Rammohan, IPS (Retd), The Naga Insurgency, *USI Journal,* Oct.-Dec. 2003]. He has given some other cases also.

Duo Flies into Delhi and History

On 8 January 2003, Swu (69) and Muivah (66) flew into Delhi and history from Amsterdam. 300 Naga students in their traditional attire braved the chill to receive the Naga leaders, ending their 35-year's exile to talk peace with Prime Minister Vajpayee, his Deputy, Advani, and senior officials. In attendance, unofficially, was a pastor to bless the Naga leaders for their talks. Composition of their delegation: Swu, a devout Christian; Muivah, a Marxist; R.H. Raisingh, the ideologue (some one called him a clone of Govindacharya, once General Secretary of BJP); Azato; Garinder Muivah; and Samson Jojo. Interestingly, Swu and Muivah are perceived as Vajpayee-Advani combination: the one is a moderate, other tough talker.

Both sides expressed satisfaction with the trend of the talks The Naga leaders met the senior leaders of all the parties, and paid homage at Gandhiji's Samadhi. There was one discordant note. Vajpayee's statement to Ibobi Singh that there would be no change in the borders of Manipur was protested by the Naga leaders in their meeting with Padmanabhaiah on 22 January. "They are hurt because the assurance to Manipur came as the Government was holding talks with them." Despite their unhappiness, they did not snap their ongoing dialogue. A silver lining was the declaration by Swu that there "will be no more armed struggle. Nor will we call for the boycott of the elections" due in February 2003 in Nagaland. The Centre was relieved that Muivah had toned down his pro-Chinese rhetoric. From Marxism, the I-M faction's ideology had metamorphosed into Socialism with the power of Christ. The Naga leaders come out as realists and mature thinkers from an answer given by "venerable Scato Swu, a former acting President of the underground and then a nominated MP, to a question from Shekhar Gupta, Editor, *Indian Express,* during the state election of 1982: Why did his people not take over in 1962 and declared independence? Scato's answer in brief was: "Your army had gone away and I had 10,000 men with automatic weapons. If I had blown the whistle.... No, we Nagas are honourable, realistic and fair. We were fighting against you to preserve our tribal culture... Christianity. We had no blood feud with you. It just seemed these might be better preserved in your shadow even without sovereignty than as an independent but Chinese satellite state.... We had been to China and know what they have done to religion. Why, were they going to be more tolerant of our Christianity." Truer words were never spoken![44]

Jamir's Congress lost power in the February 2003 Assembly polls, some thought with not so indirect help from the I-M leaders who sojourned for a fortnight in January for peace talks. Perhaps for this reason, the K faction issued a threat to the newly-elected MLAs of the BJP and National People's Front (NPF), both partners of the ruling Democratic Alliance of Nagaland (DAN), whose Neiphiu Rio replaced Jamir. When the NSCN(K) withdrew the threat, the analysts ascribed it to the outfit's move towards opening of its own formal dialogue with the Centre (like its I-M rival) before the end of 2003.

Besides its K rival, there were other discordant voices against the January 2003 Peace Talks. Adino, President of the fractured, decimated NNC and daughter of Phizo, dubbed the talks as insult to the Nagas, and the I-M "a terrorist outfit from Ukhrul, with no popular support and national mandate". There are 1,35,000 Tangkhaul Nagas in Manipur as against a mere 1,000 in Nagaland. Of the 4,000 Nagas underground, 3,600 are Tangkhuls (2003 figures). Not only Jamir, so many other Naga organisations want the Government to talk to all the Naga outfits. "Look what happened to the 1975 Accord with some elements of the FGN, with Swu, Khaplang and Muivah staying away and raising the NSCN, 5 years later," runs the argument.

Analysts have no doubt that these Delhi Talks were definitely a step forward, "after all, the independence-mouthing Nagas have travelled on the Indians passports".

Some analysts suspect that the NSCN thrives not on the staple of secessionist aspirations, but on the grievances of the Manipur Naga areas. If these areas continue to be in Manipur, it is not only because of the categorical refusal of the State Government to let go of them, but also because of disagreement among the Manipur Nagas themselves, particularly the Tangkhus. A cynical question is: Are they welcome in Nagaland? Another view says the Tangkhuls, scattered across the hills of Manipur but predominantly in the Ukhrul and Tamenglong districts, have always been a nowhere tribe. The dominant Meiteis of Manipur do not consider them Manipuris while the Naga tribes in Nagaland have always regarded them as outsiders.

It is widely accepted that if the Centre were to make peace with Swu and Muivah, it would have dealt a body blow to insurgency in the North-East; for the simple reason that the NSCN(I-M) is today the pivotal force behind insurgent outfits operating in Assam, Manipur, Tripura, and even the nascent ones in Meghalaya.

21st Round. Padmanabhaiah and K.P. Singh had their periodic dialogue—it was 21st round—with the I-M Duo in December 2003 in Bangkok. What added certain significance to this meeting was that it took place in the back drop of Arunachal Chief Minister Gegong Apang's deliberations with Swu and Muivah a fortnight earlier.

On 21 March 2004, Khaplang appealed for an end to the chronic factional fighting among the insurgent groups, and declared that his cadres would not attack rivals for the next 6 months. Analysts view the infighting as a major obstacle to peace in Nagaland as both the factions have cease-fire accords with Government/Indian Army. Khaplang's call came on the 24th anniversary of the NSCN's 1980 declaration of independence for the Naga State.

The peace process received another boost in April 2004 when the State Government released 57 persons belonging to various militant groups [NSCN(I-M) 30, NSCN(K) 26, and NNC 1] and held under the National Security Act (NSA). Even after this release, Nagaland still has 50 NSA detenues.

Congress-UPA Government Takes over

Padmanabhaiah and K.P. Singh had 3-day talks (23-25 June 2004) with the I-M leaders at Amsterdam, the first after the UPA Government took over in May 2004. The UPA Government had announced in its Common Minimum Programme (CMP) that it was committed to maintain territorial sovereignty of the states, especially in the North-East.

After Padmanabhaiah submitted his report on the Amsterdam parleys to the Home Minister Shivraj Patil on the 28th, the Government announced that the peace process with the NSCN(I-M) was on track and the two sides would meet again in a month for the next round of talks at Bangkok. Though they agreed to carry on the dialogue, the Naga leaders refused to come to India, for now. The Duo also did not reportedly agree to extend cease-fire beyond 31 July.

A 4-member delegation of Naga Hoho was in Delhi in (2nd week of) June 2004 to meet the Central leaders and demand unification of all Naga-majority areas in the North-East (read, "Greater Nagaland"). It also wanted reference to maintaining the territorial integrity of North-Eastern states to be removed from the CMP. On the 25th, members of three Naga social organisations (Naga Students Federation, Naga Mothers' Association, and Naga People's Movement for Human Rights) met Prime Minister Manmohan Singh and demanded an expeditious conclusion of peace talks and resolution of the Naga problem. After the meeting, the delegation said that integration of Naga areas would continue to remain a "non-negotiable" issue, irrespective of the outcome of the talks. They also sought the repeal of the Armed Forces (Special) Powers Act and withdrawal of the Disturbed Area Act in Nagaland. These delegations are obviously the mouthpiece of the Naga insurgent groups.

A Wish Fulfilment!

It speaks of resilience of India democratic traditions that a one-time secessionist movement, having fought for independence persistently, doggedly, even virulently for over six decades, is today willing to settle for a Greater Nagaland within the Union! No Indian would be averse to their getting Nagalim if it were not so intermingled with the integrity of three neighbouring States, where passions run high on the issue. Will the rebel leaders display the same mature and realistic stance today as they did in 1962, preferring some connection with India than a 'sovereign' state under godless, ruthless China? They can accept "Scandinavian Solution" for the present, as mentioned above, and try for some adjustments with the neighbouring states subsequently. Nagaland has already some border disputes with Assam and Manipur. They could ask for a commission later.

But there are some minor hurdles here. The iconic personality of the NSCN(I-M) cannot be sure of getting even the Chief Ministership of the present Nagaland, a la Laldenga of MNF, as his tribe has hardly any presence in the state. Then there will be strong opposition from Khaplang and Phizo partisans led by his daughter, Adino, not to speak of the present rulers of Nagaland. Given all this, Swu and Muivah might have to compromise, considering the reality of ageing. A united struggle for Nagalim could still be waged, even after the Agreement. One has nostalgic memories of 1963 when the fighting cadres of militant outfits came overground and were recruited in 111 Bn, BSF, especially raised for the purpose, and whose command was entrusted to a senior rebel commander of his time. He was given the rank of Colonel, later promoted to be a Brigadier, but was universally addressed as

'Commandant Sahab'! The country had never to look over its shoulders about the loyalty of these erstwhile rebels serving as 'soldiers' of the nation they had fought till then. Most of them must have retired by mid-1990s—all by the end of that decade. Is not this the time for one more similar, but unparalleled, bold experiment in India's military annals?

The beautiful memorial at Kohima, raised to commemorate the World War II soldiers who died for a cause, has this unforgettable, poignant inscription facing the visitor at its entrance: "When you go home/Tell them of us and say/For your tomorrow/We gave our today." Since the 1940s, three more generations of the brave Nagas have given their todays! Will the brave, wise men leading the rebels permit their fourth generation to enjoy their tomorrows?

Will it be the Elusive Penultimate Round?

Invited by the new Prime Minister Manmohan Singh, the I-M leaders Swu and Muivah arrived New Delhi and met him on 17 December 2004. They also met the Leader of Opposition L.K. Advani, Home Minister Shivraj Patil, and some other prominent Indians. After these formal calls, the Duo left for Nagaland, reaching Dimapur on the 14th to a rousing reception, having met Jyoti Basu and CM Buddhadeb Bhattacharjee *en route* at Kolkata. It would be after long decades that the Duo would be together in Nagaland during the Christmas.

Thousands of their compatriots converged to Dimapur to greet their leaders. Their plane touched down at 12.40 PM. The 80-year old Aman Muivah was among the welcoming crowd to meet his "little brother" after four decades, as were the other two brothers James and Ashin, and host of cousins. Aman had trudged more than 300 km from his native Somdal village in Ukhrul district to savour the moment.

From Camp Hebron (65 km from Dimapur), where they were staying, they spoke of the need for putting aside past differences with other Naga factions and work with them. The I-M asked the Naga people to be "more realistic and accept that violence would not achieve anything". With unity among the Nagas becoming a kind of pre-condition for a final solution, Muivah and Swu were reported to be all set to prevail upon various Naga organisations like the Naga Hoho, Naga Council and Naga Mothers Association to create a situation, if not exert pressure on the NSCN (Khaplang) to come under one umbrella. In what appeared to be a shot in the arm for political leadership in Delhi, NSCN(K) offered a cease-fire effective 15 December, a day after the arrival of the I-M Duo, "to ensure a peaceful Christmas" in Nagaland, promising to halt all military operations, including rivalry with the I-M, a much desired goal of Naga people after the NSCN had split decades ago. The "K" pointed out that the decision to halt all military operations was taken "despite the fact that the Indian and Myanmari Governments were continuing their operations to destroy NSCN(K) bases on the Indo-Myanmar border" (This indeed was reported and adversely commented upon by certain sections of the Indian Press).

While the I-M leaders were keen to meet Naga NGOs and Naga leaders from all fields, Dr John Murray, Secretary of Naga Hoho, emphasised that unification of the Nagas was necessary as the peace talks with the Prime Minister had reached at a crucial phase. He said all efforts would be made to facilitate one-to-one dialogue between the leaders of two factions of the NSCN. At the public reception organised by the self-styled Government of People's Republic of Nagalim (GPRN), "the parallel government run by the NSCN(I-M) at its Council Headquarters (CHQ) at Hebron", the two leaders called upon every section of the Nagas to come to Camp Hebron and advise on the ongoing peace talks. But when asked by the press at the CHQ if they would hold talks with the K faction before formal negotiations began with the Centre, Muivah was not very welcoming: "We are ready to discuss with anyone who comes forward."

In an ironic situation of optimism about the peace talks with Delhi and calling for cooperation from all sections of Nagas, including 'K', Naga dominated areas in Nagaland and Manipur have been sandwiched in fierce fighting between the I-M and K. A day after the Duo met the Prime Minister and six days before they arrived in Nagaland, their fighters were engaged in a bloody, no-holds-barred battle with the 'K' faction cadres. The vicious attacks continued on the 9th, leaving 10 persons dead. Close to 1,000 persons fled their homes in Tousen, Tamenglong district, seeking shelter with Deputy Commissioner T. Panmei. This has been happening for nearly two decades, and the leaders have been unable to staunch this mutual blood-letting. Unable to curb their egoistic ambitions, can we expect them to unite for a larger Naga cause? These appeals for cooperation to find a solution to the Naga issue seem to be a PR exercise, to impress the gullible!

While in Nagaland till the end of January 2005, the Duo had made public declaration of meeting other separatist outfits, including that of the Kukis (KNA). Nothing of that kind fructified. On the other hand, certain Manipur and Arunachal leaders and organisations met them, advising/requesting the NSCN(I-M) not to press for the Greater Nagaland to avoid any civil strife.

The Naga issue is not a stand-alone case and the Centre cannot discuss it in a vacuum. There is not only serious opposition to the Nagalim demand from the non-Naga groups and the neighbouring three States, there are dissensions within the Naga fold. The criticism of the NNC's Adino has been mentioned earlier. The 'K' is even more harsh in its opposition to the Centre holding talks with I-M only; even the Naga civil society desires all others to join in the talks, including 'K'. When Swu and Muivah arrived in Delhi on 6-12-04, the Kuki students staged vigorous protests against them. Before Swu and Muivah's arrival in Nagaland, powerful bodies of two tribes, viz. Ao Senden and Sumi Hoho, had decided to boycott the reception of the Duo, for a variety of reasons. That all was not well on the home front was evident when the NSCN(K) claimed it had gunned down 10 NSCN(I-M) cadres in Tousen, as mentioned above. In August 2004, CM Tarun Gogoi sought the Centre's intervention to restrain NSCN(I-M) from supporting the cadres of the ULFA, giving them money, shelter and material. He said the growing nexus between the two outfits poses a security threat to India. He said gains from the December 2003 operations to flush out the ULFA cadres from Bhutan had not been proportionate to the resources deployed because of this nexus. He said ULFA "is spreading its camps in Arunachal and Meghalaya, and neighbouring countries such as Bangladesh, Bhutan and Myanmar", and he had informed the Prime Minister and two senior Ministers "of our concern".

After their sojourn in Nagaland, the I-M leaders returned to Delhi on 29-1-05 for detailed, sustained talks with the Centre on the contentious issues. The first session was held on 3-2-05. The I-M delegation led by Muivah called on the Prime Minister on 9-2-05. The second round of talks was held on 10 February 2005 between the 11-member Naga delegation and the Group of Ministers (GOM) led by Oscar Fernandes, MOS (Independent Charge), Statistics and Programme Implementation. The others in the GOM were Prithviraj Chauhan, MOS in the PMO and S. Regupathy, MOS in MHA. With the 6th round of talks due in the first week of April, the Central Team (GOM) of interlocuters was reported to be seeking a meeting with the PM to 'redefine' the; future course of talks as the insurgents had placed all their demands on the table. The GOM wanted a clear direction from the PM on what concessions can be offered to the Nagas. More worrying was the fact that though the GOM was aware of the lethal clashes between the two factions of the NSCN throughout the March in Nagaland, the Centre was unwilling to discuss the clashes with Muivah, even if the MHA was concerned with the muscle-flexing by the NSCN(I-M) cadre.

Fernandes told the *Express* (23-5-05) that to break the deadlock in the Naga talks over the I-M demand of integration of the Naga-inhibited areas of the contiguous states, the Government was considering to have these states (Assam, Manipur and Arunachal) on the high table to know their views on the issue. It was clear that the talks were heading nowhere in the absence of discussions on this vital question. The 9th round of talks was held early June. The MHA decided (end May) to place the (30) demands made by the I-M during the 8 rounds of talks before the Cabinet Committee on Security (CCS).

The two most important issues the MHA wants the CCS to discuss are: (1) Demand for Nagalim, that will require 120,000 Sq km area of the three neighbouring states to be made over to the present State of Nagaland, with an area of 16,579 Sq km. (2) Greater autonomy for Nagaland. The GOM had assured the Naga delegation that it was willing to discuss some other key demands like: (1) Nagas be identified as separate 'Naga Citizens'. (2) An exclusive Planning Commission for Nagaland. (3) Separate flag for the state. (4) State Human Rights Commission. (5) Opening of trade and tourist promotion centres under the new Naga flag. (6) Control over taxation policy. (7) New ethnic names for the ministers and the Assembly. (8) A common defence mechanism. The talks in June 2005 assumed an added importance as the issue of extending the cease-fire, due to expire on 31-7-05, also came up for discussions.

After 12 rounds of talks and 7-month stay in India, the Duo left for Amsterdam, their 'home', on 4 July 2005. Will this series of negotiations prove to be the penultimate round only time will tell, but considering the contentious issues still to be tackled, particularly the Nagalim one, and difficult ('slippery' is a tempting term, but it would be unfair to tag it on to the man who is handling a very difficult assignment on behalf of the brave Nagas) customer that Muivah is, it is unlikely to be so!

Thuingaleng Muivah has a way with the words. He is not only an impressive orator at the public meetings, but also a master of the spoken word. He can blow hot and cold on the alternate days; furious and haughty today, calm, collected, and the reason personified tomorrow. In this department, he is an improvement even on his mentor, the original Great in the insurgency stakes, who was often accused of double-speak in his political pronouncements. Now follow some of the statements made by Muivah during the period under review:

1. "Nagaland was never a part of India, either by conquest or by consent." Refusing to accept Indian sovereignty, he explained he wanted a federal relationship with India. (Hard Talk, BBC, 29-4-05; *Tribune,* 29-4-05)
2. Muivah doubts talks outcome. "Nagas should be ready for any eventuality.... Worse may happen." (*HT,* 12-5-05)
3. "Do not take us and our patience for granted." After the failure of talks, he accused the Centre of dual policy, using force to sabotage peace. He forgets the violence unleashed by his own cadre and blood-letting indulged by his and 'K' cadres. The MHA had reported to the PMO repeated violation of the Truce terms by his NSCN in the period of talks (This was tough talk shortly before the discussions on extension of the Truce beyond 31-7-05)." *(Exp.,* 11-6-05)

4. "India lacks political will, we have the way." Saying the talks were "stuck", he accused New Delhi of being unwilling to address the core issue. "Do not read our patience as a sign of weakness." *(Exp.,* 14-6-05)

5. "In case of external invasion, the disgruntled Nagas can join the other forces against India." (*AA*, 22-6-05)

6. While leaving New Delhi after talks on 4-7-05: "Government has told us about their sincere commitment to resolve the issue. Prime Minister and Madam Sonia Gandhi gave us this serious commitment. We believe their sincerity and thank them" *(AA,* 5-7-05). Addressing over 2000 of his supporters and students at the Palam airport, he said "I'll be back soon" but did not forget to call upon them "to shatter all illusions and carry forward the cause for Nagaland." (*Exp.,* 5-7-05)

7. All the above must be framed in the context of what he said at Dimapur on 14-12-04: "Violence can't be the answer.... We believe in the peaceful ways.... Nagas must be realistic."

Now to some events and non-events pertaining to the issue in hand. H. Khogen Singh, a Manipur analyst says: "The NSCN(I-M) leaders have taken a no-compromise stand on the creation of a Greater Nagaland 'homeland'. This may hinder the success of their meetings with the Centre" *(HT,* 4-2-05). During the period, the NSCN(I-M) suffered a major setback when A.Z. Zami, its senior leader and member of its Steering Committee, defected to its rival 'K' faction, accusing the outfit of "diluting Naga cause" in the name of the ongoing peace talks and also for lack of transparency in the talks between the leadership and the Centre *(Exp.,* 24-5-05). The expected dialogue between the arch rivals, 'K' and I-M, did not take place nor did the three contiguous states come on the High Table.

"Indian currency, joint defence, Indian control of external affairs, Naga control over mineral resources and independence under a Federation of India and Nagaland through a separate agreement are the details of the proposal finetuned over 41 rounds of talks since 1997 by the NSCN leaders Swu and Muivah with New Delhi" (*AA,* 22-6-05). Muivah confirmed that some problems did arise over the issue of joint defence and the Centre's insistence that the NSCN accept a "special status" within the Indian Constitution. Muivah asserted that the "Nagas can defend themselves better than any one else can" and clarified that the NSCN at the best can explore the possibility of a joint defence. The Press confirmed *(Tribune,* 31-7-05 and *Hindu,* 2-8-05) that the NSCN had been offered the "Kashmir type" status.

EXTENDING THE CEASE-FIRE: MAKING AN ISSUE

Even while in India, there were enough indications that Swu and Muivah would act tough on the extension of Truce Agreement due for renewal on 31-7-05. They had obviously rejected to follow the norm of extending it for a year. K. Padmanabhaiah, Centre's interlocutor for the Naga Talks and the IB Chief E.S.L. Narasimhan left 28-7-05 for talks with the I-M Duo in Amsterdam. The 29-30 July talks, the first since they returned from India, was essentially meant for normal annual extension of the Truce for a year. Resorting to pressure tactics after the stalemate in 6-month long Delhi talks, the two leaders offered to extend the cease-fire for 3-month period only while they were in Delhi till 3 July. After the 2-day hard talks, the Indian Duo was able to extract a 6-month extension only, while they wanted a normal 1 year's. This shorter extension is seen by some analysts as an indication of the Naga Talks running into rough weather, and as a "wake-up call", as the Naga leaders warned that in the absence of any headway in the talks during these six months they "Will be forced to go back to the jungle". "This is the last chance that the Centre has to show that it is serious", added the Naga source *(AA,* 1-8-05, *Hindu,* 30-7-05 and *Exp.,* 31-7-05). It may be incidentally added here that at a tripartite Centre-State-NSCN(K) meeting on 28-4-05, the cease-fire with the 'K' was extended by a year.

Sources in the South Block say that Manipur's (2005) decision to declare 18 June as "Manipur Integrity Day" and the Centre's decision of not intervening has added to the disappointment of the Naga leadership. (As a result, the Naga students had imposed a prolonged economic blockade of NH-39 and NH-53, the only life lines of Manipur. Issue discussed earlier.) In the recent round of talks (2004-5) with Padmanabhaiah in Amsterdam, the Naga leaders had expressed concern over the declaration in the Common Minimum Programme (CMP) adopted by the Congress-led UPA (when it assumed power in May 2004) that the "territorial integrity" of the North-East States would be fully protected. The two, 18 June 2005 decision and CMP declaration, come in the way of the Nagas realising their dreamland of Nagalim.

Two points, indicating that the Naga talks are not happily placed after those 12-round, 6-month negotiations (January-June 2005), need to be made. The day (27-7-05) Padmanabhaiah was leaving for Amsterdam for 29-30 July talks with the Naga leaders, the MHA in a report to the PMO said the NSCN(I-M) had violated the cease-fire which was to expire on 31 July. The report says the NSCN(I-M) on the 21st destroyed the bridge over the Irang on NH-53, connecting Silchar and Imphal, the only artery available to the rest of the country to keep Manipur going as the only other life line, NH-39, was under a prolonged economic blockade by the Naga students to protest the 18 June 2005 decision of Manipur. The NSCN(I-M) was actively known to be supporting the student's blockade. Again, Prime Minister will shortly be in Bangkok, the alternate Headquarters of the NSCN(I-M) leadership, for the BIMSTEC meeting, but the official sources ruled out any meeting between him and the Naga leaders *(Hindu,* 30-7-05).

Talks with the NSCN (I-M) are continuing. In fact the latest round was held on 29 March, 2007. The post-mid-2005 narrative on these talks will be discussed in the next chapter, along with some other inter-linked and related issues. During the mid-2007 talks between the Central team led by Oscar Fernandes and the rebels led by the Naga duo and for the first time held at the Naga soil, the two sides decided to extend the ceasefire indefinitely.

NOTES

1. David Galula, *Counter-insurgency Warfare—Theory and Practice,* p. 4.
2. The man behind the Plan was Reginald Coupland, Oxford Professor, who had come to India as Secretary to Sir Stafford Cripps in 1942.
3. Post-1947 Deputy Commissioners were: (1) Imdad Ali, IP, 1947-49, (2) S.J. Duncan, IAS, 1949-52, (3) S.C. Kagti, IAS, 1952-53, (4) S'.N. Barkataki, 1953, (5) S.J.D. Carvalho, IAS, 1953-57.
4. A document published by the Naga Hoho claims that 2000 Nagas were exposed to the outside world for the first time in 1917 during the First World War. These 2000 Nagas served in the European Theatre in the Labour Corps (The break-down: Semas 1000; Lothas, Aos, Rengmas, Chang and Sangtam, 200 each). While sojourning in Paris, the Nagas realised the need to have a common platform. "On return safe at home in 1918, they formed 'Naga Club' with headquarters at Kohima."
5. Anand, 1980, p. 55.
6. *See* Alemchiba (1970), for full text of the Memorandum.
7. n. 6, pp. 162-64.
8. n. 6, pp. 166-69; for full text.
9. DR Mankekar, on the Slippery Slopes of Nagaland, 1967, p. 39.
10. Ghosh, B.B., 1982, p. 163.
11. *Ibid., p.* 166.
12. Y.D. Gundevia, *War and Peace in Nagaland,* 1975, pp. 57-59.
13. Naga Hoho Document, 2001.
14. Kohima, the largest village of Naga Hills, had 948 houses and 4269 people, as per 1971 census.
15. The Head of the NHTA Administration was to be a Commissioner, and the first incumbent was G.S. Puri. U.N. Sarma succeeded him. When the NHTA became *de facto* State of Nagaland on 18 February 1961 with an Interim Council and Executive Council, Sarma took over as its first Chief Secretary.
16. *See* Alemchiba, 1970, pp. 190-95 for full text.
17. Prakash Singh, *Nagaland* (R), 1977, p. 145.
18. Dr M. Aram, *Peace in Nagaland,* 1974, p. 54.
19. M. Horam, *Naga Insurgency,* 1988, p. 243.

20. B. Rahmatullah, *Evolution of National Socialist Council of Nagaland: The Renewal of Insurgency;* Kohima Platform, 25 Feb.-4 Mar., 1982, Vol. V, No. 40, pp. 3-4.
21. n. 18, pp. 306-31.
22. *The North-East Sun,* Valley Insurgents New Front, 15-31 March, 1999, p. 5.
23. *The Shillong Times,* 11-11-93.
24. *North-East Sun,* Ultras give Shillong the Shudders, 15-31 July 1999.
25. *Sentinel,* Guwahati, 22-4-2000.
26. *Ibid.*
27. Sareen, 1980, p. 44.
28. *Ibid.,* p. 52.
29. *Observer of Business and Politics,* Unquiet Hills of the North-East, 17-11-97.
30. Sarin, 1980, p. 15.
31. *Ibid.,* p. 23.
32. n. 27, p. 30.
33. n. 30, p. 24.
34. *North-East Sun,* NSCN Views at Geneva, 1-14 May, 1998, p. 7.
35. *Hindu,* 30-11-99.
36. It seems to be a case of equal and mutual distrust of each other. We have read of a serious attack by NSCN(K) on the cadres of the NSCN (I-M) since it suspected the latter to be involved in serious secret talks with New Delhi. Returning the compliments, NSCN(I-M) did not consider its rival to be genuine freedom fighters, holding them contemptuously to be the creation of Government of India. NSCN(I-M) had stopped treating NNC too as genuine freedom fighter after it sold out the Naga interests through the Shillong Accord.
37. *The Asian Age.* Muivah's Karachi Visit Alarms Centre. 5-2-2000.
38. *The Telegraph,* Nagas in Manipur torn between Hoho and Polls. 28-9-99.
39. n. 16, pp. 211-14.
40. n. 16, pp. 218-22.
41. *Exp.* (1-7-04).
42. *Exp.* (27-8-03).
43. *Exp.* (29-8-03).
44. *Outlook* (20-1-03), *India Today* (20-1-03), *Week* (2-2-03), *Frontline* (26-4-03), and *Exp.* 11 and 23 Jan. 03.

17

Nagaland : Terrorist Outfits and Current Situation Work in Progress

The guns are quiet in the longest-running insurgency in India. The Nagas have been conceded their state in 1963 and they have indeed been governing it themselves ever since. But the NSCN (I-M) want much more than a mere state : Federal status with India. For this purpose, they have observed a cease-fire since Aug 1997 and have been holding talks with New Delhi.

Before going into the situation in Nagaland over the last few years, the following information, consisting of an overview of the situation and some factual data, is deemed useful for its convenient understanding and put it in perspective :

- Nagaland Backgrounder
- National Socialist Council NSCN(I-M)
- National Socialist Council of Nagaland (Khaplang) NSCN(K)
- Nagaland Timeline – 2006
- Nagaland Assessment – 2006

Nagaland Backgrounder

The Nagas comprise some 17 major tribes and over 20 sub-tribes. Some of the major tribes include Ao, Angami, Sema, Lotha, Tangkhul, Konyak, Rengma, and Mao. Each tribe and sub-tribe speaks a different language, though each of these belongs to the Tibeto-Burmese group of languages.

Among all the ethnic groups and tribes living in the Northeast, the Nagas were the first to raise the banner of revolt against the Indian government, on August 14, 1947, under the aegis of the Naga National Council (NNC) led by Angami Zapu Phizo. In July 1948, Phizo was arrested along with some of his associates. They were released in 1949 and Phizo became the President of NNC in 1950. The NNC publicly resolved to establish a sovereign Naga state. In May 1951, the Council held a 'referendum' in which it claimed that 99% of the Naga people supported independence for Nagaland, though this has never been accepted by the government. The NNC boycotted the general elections in 1952 and launched a violent secessionist movement, with Naga insurgents raiding several villages and police outposts. On March 22, 1956, Phizo created an underground government called the Naga Federal Government (NFG) and a Naga Federal Army (NFA). In April that year, the Central Government inducted the army to crush the insurgency in what was, till then, the Naga Hills District of the State of Assam. To deal with the situation, the Armed Forces (Special Powers) Act, 1958, was subsequently enacted. Phizo, however, escaped to the then East Pakistan in December 1956 and, subsequently, to London in June 1960.

After Nagaland attained Statehood on December 1, 1963, a serious attempt was made to bring about a political settlement. In April 1964, a Peace Mission was formed with Jai Prakash Narayan, B.P. Chaliha and Rev. Michael Scott as its members and an Agreement for Suspension of Operation (AGSOP) was signed with the insurgents on September 6. However, the insurgents continued to violate the agreement by indulging in various acts of violence. Six rounds of talks between the insurgents and the Centre resulted in a deadlock and the Peace Mission was dissolved in 1967. In 1972, the Centre banned the NNC, the NFG and the NFA as "unlawful associations" under the Unlawful Activities (Prevention) Act of 1967. The security forces launched a massive counter-insurgency operation and once again brought the situation under control forcing the insurgents to the negotiating table. An agreement known as the Shillong Accord was signed between the Centre and a section of the NNC and the NFG on November 11, 1975. According to the terms of the Accord, the NNC-NFG accepted the Indian Constitution and agreed to come overground and surrender their weapons.

However, a group of about 140 activists of the NNC, who had gone to China for training, repudiated the Shillong Accord and refused to surrender. They formed a new underground organisation called the National Socialist Council of Nagaland (NSCN) under the leadership of Thuengaling Muivah, Isak Chisi Swu and S.S. Khaplang on Myanmarese (Burmese) soil in 1980. With the passage of time, the NSCN emerged as the most radical and powerful insurgent group fighting for the Naga cause, as the NNC-NFG became less active.

The Nagas had always been divided along clan and tribal lines. The majority of the rank and file of the NSCN was from the Konyak tribe, while the command structure was dominated by the Tangkhuls. This created discontent among the Konyaks. There were also apprehensions among the Konyaks and the Myanmerese Nagas that the Tangkhuls were about to strike a deal with the Central Government. These factors resulted in a vertical split in the NSCN in 1988. The Konyaks formed a breakaway faction under the leadership of Khole Konyak and S.S. Khaplang, a Hemie Naga from Myanmar. The Tangkhul faction was led by Isak Swu, a Sema from Nagaland, and Muivah, a Tangkhul from Manipur's Ukhrul district. This was followed by severe inter-factional clashes in which hundreds of activists of the rival groups had been killed.

After the death of Phizo in 1990, there was another split in the NNC. Phizo's daughter Adino, an Angami, and Khudhao Nanthan, a Sema and a close associate of Phizo, constituted separate groups on rival lines. In the winter of 1996-97, Khudhao joined NSCN (IM) and is currently the Vice Chairman of the organization. With this move NSCN (IM) was also able to get the support of the Lothas to which Kudao belongs. All factions of the NSCN and NNC (Adino) have been banned since 1991 under the Unlawful Activities (Prevention) Act, 1967.

The NSCN-IM lays primary emphasis on the point that the Naga region was never a part of India and that Nehru's argument was fallacious when he said that India had "inherited" the Naga area from the British. Both Swu and Muivah argue that "the fate of a people cannot be passed on like an inheritance from one party to another". The NSCN-IM has taken an inflexible stand on this point and insists that their demand is not for 'secession' because they have never been a part of the Indian Union.

Terrorist / Insurgent Groups - Nagaland

Active Terrorist/Insurgent Groups	*Inactive Terrorist/Insurgent Groups*
• National Socialist Council of Nagaland (Isak-Muivah) - NSCN (IM)	• Naga National Council (Adino) – NNC (Adino)
• National Socialist Council of Nagaland (Khaplang) - NSCN (K)	• Revolutionary United Front (RUF)

National Socialist Council of Nagaland - Isak-Muivah

Formation

The National Socialist Council of Nagaland (NSCN) was formed on January 31, 1980 by Isak Chisi Swu, Thuingaleng Muivah and S.S. Khaplang opposing the 'Shillong Accord' signed by the then NNC (Naga National Council) with the Indian Government. Later, differences surfaced within the outfit over the issue of commencing a dialogue process with the Indian Government and on April 30, 1988, the NSCN split into two factions, namely the NSCN-K led by S S Khaplang, and the NSCN-IM, led by Isak Chisi Swu and Thuingaleng Muivah. In the violent clashes between Muivah, Swu and Khaplang on April 30, 1998, about 100 people on both sides were killed.

Objective

The outfit aims to establish a 'Greater Nagaland ('Nagalim' or the People's Republic of Nagaland) based on Mao Tse Tung's ideology. Its manifesto is based on the principle of Socialism for economic development and a spiritual outlook—'Nagaland for Christ'.

Area of Operation

The NSCN-IM primarily consists of Tangkhul Nagas who are in a majority in parts of Nagaland and the hills of Manipur. Its influence inside Manipur is restricted to the four districts of Senapati, Ukhrul, Chandel and Tamenglong. The outfit has also established its presence in Wokha, Phek, Zunebhoto, Kohima, parts of Mokokchung and Tuensang districts of Nagaland. It has also been able to extend its influence to the Naga-inhabited areas of North Cachar Hills and Karbi Anglong districts of Assam and some parts of Arunachal Pradesh.

Leadership and Structure

Thuingaleng Muivah, the General Secretary, and Isak Chisi Swu, Chairman of the NSCN-IM are based in Thailand. I Shimray is another top leader of the outfit. Hungshi is the 'press and publicity secretary' of the group. The outfit also has a military wing — the Naga Army, comprising one brigade and six batallions. There are also several 'town commands' and specialised mobile groups. S Hungshi is the 'Commander-in-Chief' of the Naga Army.

Kraibo Chawang is the 'Deputy Minister (Kilonser), Ministry of Information & Publicity (MIP)' and A K Lungalung is the 'Home Minister', (Kilo-Kilonser) of the outfit. Further, while V. Horam is the 'Deputy Home Minister', V. S. Atem is the 'Convener, Steering Committee'.

On the political front, the NSCN-IM has divided its area of influence into 11 regions, which are organised primarily on tribal considerations. In many areas, it runs a parallel government. There are four major 'Ministries' - defence, home, finance and foreign. Besides, there are five other Ministries including education, information and publicity, forests and minerals, law and justice and religious affairs. The most prominent among the Ministries is the 'Home ministry', which seeks to replace the State government machinery. The heads of 11 administrative regions report to the 'Home Minister' (Kilo Kilonser). The 'administration' deepens down to the town and village levels in the NSCN-IM's areas of influence. R H Raising and Himpa Pochury are 'Home' and 'Defence' 'Ministers', respectively. Angelus Shimrah is the spokesperson of the NSCN-IM.

The outfit has also established a government-in-exile called the Government of the People's Republic of Nagaland (GPRN) which interacts with formal and non-formal world bodies and media. The GPRN sends emissaries abroad to garner support and raise funds for the Naga cause.

It has an estimated 4,500 strong cadre base. It is supported by a section of Aos, Semas, Zeilangs, Anals, Maos and Manipur-based Tangkhul Nagas.

The NSCN (IM) has been passing its annual budget to the tune of Rs 200 million to Rs 250 million each year.

Drug trafficking from Myanmar is reported to be a major source of income for the NSCN-IM, and it also reportedly engages in extortion, bank robberies and other criminal pursuits to obtain finance. In addition, the outfit generates funds through international mobilization. Both the NSCN-IM and the NSCN-K run parallel structures of 'taxation' (extortion) throughout the regions that they dominate.

Linkages

Over the years, the NSCN-IM has developed extensive linkages both within India and outside, and has also been receiving substantial assistance from neighbouring countries. The form of this assistance ranges from supply of arms and ammunition and other logistical support, to provision of safe havens, camping and training facilities. Till 1971, the US was a major provider of arms, finance and intelligence. The erstwhile East Pakistan had also provided assured supplies of money and arms. Till the late 1980s, China also provided support to the organisation. Pakistan's Inter Services Intelligence (ISI) now provides a large component of finance, arms and logistic support to the NSCN-IM.

The NSCN-IM has linkages with the Naga groups operating in Myanmar, and drug trafficking from Myanmar is a major source of income.

NSCN-IM uses money earned through narcotics trade to buy arms and also pay for training of their cadres. The outfit also runs camps for training other militant outfits on a purely mercenary basis. They have established reliable contacts for arms procurement in Thailand and other South East Asian nations, and have very well established links for transportation through Bangladesh and Myanmar. With the funds generated through its various financial operations, as well as from aid provided by the ISI, the NSCN-IM has purchased large stocks of Chinese AK rifles, machine guns, mortars and explosives from black markets in South East Asia and Bangladesh.

Prior to his arrest by Thai authorities in January 2000, Muivah was spotted in Karachi and was believed to have visited some other places as well in Pakistan, besides having met various people there. He was arrested at Bangkok on arrival on a flight from Karachi for travelling on a fake South Korean passport.

A top-NSCN-IM functionary was reportedly dispatched to strike a deal with Chinese officials in the Kunming province to provide them with a 'major arms consignment'; and the NSCN-IM was pleading with the Chinese to use their good offices to secure a passage for the consignment through the territory controlled by the Kachin rebels. Reports of February 2000 indicated that the NSCN-IM have a "full-fledged liaison office" in territories in China across the border with Arunachal Pradesh.

The outfit has also opened up contacts with international organisations like the UN Human Rights Commission in Geneva, Unrepresented Nations People's Organisation (UNPO) at the Hague and the UN Working Group on Indigenous People (UNWGIP)

Insurgents of the National Socialist Council of Nagaland (Isak-Muivah group) are reportedly being trained at two camps in Pakistan.

The NSCN (IM) has a group of its strong supporters in Thailand. Most of them operate front companies—mainly in travel and tourism, real estate and toy manufacture. The NSCN also has a large number of bank accounts in Thailand, Bangladesh and Burma.

NSCN-IM's weapons are smuggled from the Thai-Cambodian border. Reports indicate that Pakistani embassy officials in Thailand provide assistance to the NSCN-IM and other North-Eastern insurgent groups in procuring weapons.

National Socialist Council of Nagaland - Khaplang

Formation

The National Socialist Council of Nagaland - Khaplang (NSCN-K) was formed on April 30, 1988, consequent to an assassination attempt on the General Secretary of what emerged as the rival outfit - NSCN (IM) - Thuingaleng Muivah. Clannish divisions among the Nagas (Konyaks and Tangkhuls) were the primary reason behind the split of the NSCN in 1988. The Konyaks formed the NSCN-K (Khaplang) under the leadership of Khole Konyak and S S Khaplang. The Tangkhul faction, the NSCN-IM (Isak-Muivah), was led by Isak Chisi Swu and T. Muivah.

Leadership

S S Khaplang is the Chairman of the outfit. N Kitovi Zhimomi acts as the General Secretary and Akaho Asumi is the Publicity Secretary.

Objectives

The primary objective of the NSCN-K is the establishment of a 'greater Nagaland' comprising of the Naga dominated areas of the neighbouring States within India, and contiguous areas in Myanmar.

Area of Operation and Structure

The outfit is active in the eastern parts of Nagaland, as well as in the Tirap and Changlang districts of neighbouring Arunachal Pradesh.

It has a cadre strength of approximately 2,000, with a following among the Konyaks of both India and Myanmar, the Pangmeis of Myanmar, the Aos of Mokokchung district, the Phoms and Yimchungers of Tuensang district, the Angamis, the Semas and the Lothas. It commands influence in parts of Nagaland, Tirap and Changlang districts of Arunachal Pradesh, as well as the Hemei and Pangmei settlements in Myanmar.

The NSCN-K runs a government-in-exile called the Government of the People's Republic of Nagaland, NSCN-K. The General Head Quarters (GHQ) of the GPRN/NSCN-K is located in Eastern Nagaland (Myanmar). Kitovi Zhimomi is the self-styled "Prime minister of the Government of the People's Republic of Nagaland".

For generation of finance, the group reportedly indulges in kidnapping, extortion and other terrorist activities. The NSCN-K accounted for 62 civilian and 26 security forces' fatalities during the period 1992 to 2000, and lost 245 of its men over this period.

Linkages

The group is reported to have training camps and its headquarters in Myanmar.

Nagaland Timeline - 2006

January 8	Three militants of the National Socialist Council of Nagaland-lsak-Muivah (NSCN-IM) and the rival Khaplang faction (NSCN-K) are killed in internecine clashes at the Nokyan village in Mon district.
	NSCN-K rules out talks with the Union Government as long as peace talks between the NSCN-IM and the Government continue. Senior leader A. 2. Jami said in Mon: "We had no intention to enter into a cease-fire with the Indian Government. We were pressurized to do so against our will by Naga NGOs."
January 9	Unidentified militants open fire in front of the Nagaland Transport and Communication Minister Imtilemba Sangtam's residence in the ministers' hill area of capital Kohima.
January 11	NSCN-K leader K Mulatonu claims that at least seven Myanmarese Army personnel and three NSCN-K cadres were killed in a gun battle in Myanmar's northern Sagaing division.
January 14	Myanmar Army reportedly begins fresh operations against the NSCN-K in coordination with the Indian Army. Sources in the Ministry of Defence at New Delhi, while confirming reports, say that the operation began about a week ago and the armies of the two countries were working in close co-ordination.
January 18	During a meeting between the officials of the Union Home Ministry and the representatives of the NSCN-K in New Delhi, the outfit asks the Government to strictly enforce the cease-fire ground rules with the NSCN-IM in Nagaland.

	The NSCN-IM and NSCN-K militants clash at Inbung village in the Peren district. Though the NSCN-K claimed that a NSCN-IM militant was killed in the incident, the latter denied it.
January 27	The UNC urges the Union Government and the NSCN-IM to ensure a peaceful and lasting solution to the Naga conflict. It says that Nagas want peace and to that end the Centre must exhibit genuine political will to resolve the issue.
	The NSCN-K warns ULFA not to harbour the NSCN-IM militants in Assam. The outfit's 'chaplee kilonser' (finance minister) Kughalu Mulatonu says that ULFA has been giving shelter to the NSCN-IM militants in areas along Assam's border with Nagaland and Arunachal Pradesh.
January 28	The NSCN-IM decides to defer 'tax collections' for the 'next financial year' in areas it refers to as 'Nagalim' or 'Greater Nagaland'. In a statement it says, "The outfit has deferred its collections of taxes from business establishments and wellwishers throughout 'Nagalim' for the next financial year from April 1, 2006 to March 31, 2007".
January 31	The cease-fire in Nagaland between the Union Government and NSCN-IM is extended by another six months. A joint statement, signed by the Government interlocutor K. Padmanabhaiah and NSCN -IM chief negotiator T. Muivah in Bangkok, said: "In view of the need to maintain the congenial atmosphere for the political negotiations to fructify, it has been mutually decided to extend the ceasefire by six months with effect from February 1."
February 5	The Union Government and NSCN-IM have decided to hold talks on "substantive" issues. Union Minister Oscar Fernandes, who led the Government delegation at the four-day talks with the NSCN-IM in Bangkok, says in New Delhi that the timing of the next round of talks will depend on the outfit. "We have been able to extend the cease-fire by six months. But we were not able to take up issues in a substantive manner. Over the next six months, we will try to hold substantive talks," he says. He further adds, "Whenever they (NSCN-IM) want, we are ready to talk. It will depend on them."
February 8	One NSCN-K cadre, Aman Konyak, is killed in a clash with the rival NSCN-IM near Namsa colony in the Mon district.
February 9	Two NSCN-K cadres, including the outfit's Angami region chairman Neisa Angami alias AKD and his bodyguard, are killed by rival NSCN-IM militants at Rusoma village near Kohima. The NSCN-IM cadres also abduct Neisa Angami's son and daughter-in-law.

February 10	The Ceasefire Monitoring Group chairman, Lt Gen. (retd) R.V. Kulkarni, appeals to both Isak-Muivah and Khaplang factions of the NSCN to exercise restraint.
February 24	An unidentified militant is killed and another sustains injuries during a clash between cadres of the NSCN-IM and the rival NSCN-K at Namsa in the Mon district.
February 28	NSCN-K claims that its cadres have killed 10 Myanmarese soldiers in a gunbatle on at Chumsa village in Myanmar. The outfit's 'chaplee kilonser' (finance minister), Kughalu Mulatonu, says that two cadres are also killed.
	NSCN-K leader K Mulatonu claims that that his group has wrested the Meluri area under Phek district from its rival NSCN-IM.
March 6	NSCN-IM makes it 'mandatory' for non-Nagas living "all over Nagalim (greater Nagaland)" to make identity cards for themselves and their families.
March 7	The Chakhesang Public Organisation, apex body of the Chakhesang tribe, declares prohibiting extortion, movement in combatant uniforms and establishment of camps by any militant outfit of Nagaland within the periphery of their habitation.
March 9	Police recover near the Paramedical Bridge on the outskirts of Kohima city the body of a suspected NSCN-K "tax collector", Vikhoto Zao, who was abducted a day earlier.
March 12	Bodies of two persons, identified as Kobou Kotsu and Atha Puro, who were abducted by the NSCN-IM last week are found near Piphima village on the Dimapur-Kohima national highway.
March 20	Nagaland Chief Minister Neiphiu Rio, while presenting the budget in the Legislative Assembly, said: "It is not possible for any government to prevent this (extortion) completely."
March 29	The NSCN-IM begins a round of consultative meetings with various organisations in the State to frame a strategy for the next round of talks with the Union Government, slated for mid-April in either Bangkok or Amsterdam.
April 6	Two cadres, one each of the NSCN-IM and NNC, are killed in an internecine clash at Porba village in the Phek district.
April 7	An unidentified NSCN -K cadre is killed in an internecine clash with the rival NSCN-IM cadres at Wazeho in the Phek district.
April 15	In a factional clash, two NSCN-IM cadres and one from the NSCN-K are killed at Hongphoi village in the Mon district. Four more militants and a civilian are wounded in the clash.

April 18 Several Phek-based organizations and local leaders urges the Nagaland Government to take up the issue of clashes between the two NSCN factions with the outfits themselves or the Government of India and to ensure that cadres belonging to the two factions moved out of Phek and Chakhesang areas.

April 21 The Union Government extends the cease-fire with the NSCN-K by another year from April 29.

April 27 *Telegraph* reports that NSCN-IM has reportedly affected a major reshuffle in its ranks in the second week of April. Puni Mao is the new 'kilo kilonser' (home minister) taking over from R. Raising, who has been made secretary of the outfit's 'steering committee' and H.U. Huray is the new 'chaplee kilonser' (finance minister), replacing Q. Tuccu.

May 3 SFs arrested the 'joint secretary (home)' of the UPDS, Dhonsing Teron, from an unspecified location in the Dimapur town.

May 6 In a factional clash, two NSCN-K militants, Nukuzo Lohe and Veto, are killed while three others sustained injuries in a pre-dawn attack by the NSCN-IM at Old Phek village in the Phek district.

May 10 A factional clash occurred between cadres of the NSCN-IM and the rival NSCN-K at Kuthur village in the Tuensang district. The clash occurred when about 15 NSCN-K cadres entered Kuthur to rescue two persons reportedly abducted by the NSCN-IM from Yakur village on May 9.

May 12 The NSCN-K has reportedly served an extortion notice amounting to Rupees 30 million to the Oil and Natural Gas Corporation (ONGC) recently. The extortion note was served against the exploration exercise of the ONGC in the Shengtheng area of Nagaland's Mon district.

Nagaland Police arrested four persons, Raju Patel, Chotu Patei, Khuvio Poumai and Phungpha Maipha, and seized two AK rifles from their possession while traveling in a fake army truck loaded with marijuana at Khuzama in the Kohima district.

May 16 Two NSCN-IM cadres are killed while unspecified number of NSCN-Khaplang cadres are wounded in a factional clash between cadres of the rival groups at Athibung in the Perem district.

May 19 Suspected NSCN-IM militants killed a senior functionary of the rival Khaplang faction (NSCN-K) in the Mon district. Nampang Konyak, Education Kilonser (minister) and also convener of the outfit's Council of Kitonsers, is killed at his home. The militants also injured a security guard of the NSCN-K leader and fled with one AK-47 rifle and a US Carbine from the other guards.

The two-day talks between the Union Government and the NSCN-IM begin in Amsterdam. The Indian side is led by Union Minister Oscar Fernandes while a seven-member NSCN-IM team is led by its general secretary Thuingaleng Muivah.

May 20 The two-day peace talks between the Union Government and NSCN-IM concludes in Amsterdam.

May 21 Talking to the media in Amsterdam, the general secretary of the NSCN-IM, Thuingaleng Muivah, threatens to take up arms if the Union Government continues to undermine his outfit. Delhi, he says, should realise that "if its forces go on killing our cadre, betray their commitment to ceasefire and its ground rules, go on supporting the traitors against us, then the Nagas will be compelled to fight back... . Supporting others to undermine us is a treacherous policy. We will not hesitate to take up arms if forced by Government of India's policies." On his outfit's diplomatic forays abroad, Muivah says, "We sent our men to brief others of the progress in the peace talks with India and nothing else. We did not send them to ask for arms. Wherever they go they talk about the need for a solution through peaceful means. This is what our representatives did in London and in China."

May 24 NSCN-K kills two NSCN-IM militants, Shimimi Tangkhul and Leacy Sukhalo, in two attacks at Satakha and Amiphoto Colony respectively in the Zunheboto district.

A factional clash occurs between the rival NSCN factions at Athibung in the Perem district.

May 27 The NSCN-K claims to have killed two rival NSCN-IM cadres and injured two others in an encounter at a place near Longleng in the Tuensang district.

May 30 Two NSCN-IM cadres are wounded in a clash with rival NSCN-K at Lochomi village in the Zunheboto district.

May 31 One NSCN-K cadre, '2nd Lt.' Aloto and a civilian are wounded in a factional clash with rival Isak-Muivah faction at Sheyipu village in the Zunheboto district.

June 1 Unidentified gunmen kill the 'Education Kilonser' (minister) of the Federal Government of Nagaland of the Naga National Council (NNC), Mar Jamir, at a place near BOC area of Kohima town.

June 2	One NSCN-IM cadre, James Tangkhul, is killed in a factional clash with cadres of the rival Khaplang faction at a spot near Zunheboto town.
June 7	Two civilians, Kehubuyi and Sovenulu are wounded when firing broke out between cadres of the NSCN-IM and the NNC at Chosaba village in the Phek district.
June 12	The NSCN-IM asks the Superintendent of Police (SP), Dimapur, Bidhu Shekhar to leave Dimapur district within seven days. The diktat comes in the wake of a notice issued by the SP that appeared in the press, ordering all armed underground cadres to vacate civilian populated areas including towns and villages of Dimapur district within seven days.
June 14	Unidentified gunmen kill an NSCN-IM cadre, Yangthsase Sangtam at Longkhim in the Tuensang district.
	NSCN-IM accuses the Government of India for the factional violence in the State. The outfit's Ceasefire Monitoring Cell Convenor, "Brigadier" Phungthing Shimrang says in Dimapur that the factional violence erupted due to Government of India's failure to restrict the movement of members of other groups.
	Two NSCN faction signs a ceasefire agreement declaring that they will not resort to factional clashes in Sumi dominated areas in Nagaland.
	A factional clash takes place between cadres of rival NSCN factions at Khukiye village and Chisholi village in Nagaland.
June 16	In a notification, the Superintendent of Police of Kiphire district asks all armed cadres of different militant groups in the district to vacate civilian populated areas within ten days.
June 20	One NSCN-IM cadre, Diamond Tangkhul, is killed in a landmine explosion near Athibung in the Peren district.
	Telegraph reports that the Prime Minister Manmohan Singh has told a seven member Congress team from Nagaland that called on him in New Delhi recently that the conflict between the Naga militant factions is a 'law and order problem' which the state home department has to solve on its own instead of blaming Delhi for it.
June 22	Unidentified gunmen kill a civilian, A.S. Mayarping alias Aping, at Phesama Hydrogers in Kohima town.
June 23	NSCN-IM clarifies that the June 14 Zunheboto cease-fire agreement signed between the two NSCN factions is a "farcical imposition" by the NSCN-K.

July 5	NSCN-K kills a rival NSCN-IM cadre, Yongpong Konyak, at Longkhim in the Tuensang district.
July 10	Five NSCN-K cadres are arrested for resorting to indiscriminate firing near the Chief Minister's official residence in Kohima. One AK 47 rifle with 60 live rounds, two .32 pistols with 17 live rounds, one M20 pistol with 18 live rounds, a hand grenade, three mobile sets and cash amounting to INR 18,475 are also recovered from their possession.
July 13	One NSCN-IM cadre, Nzanthungo Lotha, is killed during a shoot out with the rival NSCN-K at Lerie near capital Kohima.
July 19	Nagaland Police arrests 10 People's United Liberation Front (PULF) cadres from Dimapur town.
July 26	NSCN-IM says that it is running out of patience as security forces had killed dozens of its cadres in violation of the 1997 cease-fire agreement. "They have killed around 116 of our boys in cold blood and arrested about 200 of them in the recent past," Phunthing Shimrang, who heads the outfit's cease-fire monitoring cell, tells Reuters at an unspecified place.
July 27	Unidentified gunmen kill a NSCN-IM cadre, Neitho Miachieo, in Kohima.
July 31	The Union Government and NSCN-IM extends the ongoing cease-fire in Nagaland by one more year following a meeting between the representatives of the two sides in Bangkok.
August 6	Nine NSCN-IM cadres defect to the rival NSCN-K faction.
August 9	A NSCN-K cadre, 'corporal' Leshao Khiamniungan, is killed and another seriously wounded in an attack by rival NSCN-IM cadres at Akuluto in the Zunheboto district.
August 13	NSCN-K decides to sever all ties with the Naga Hoho, the Naga Students' Federation and the Naga People's Movement for Human Rights with effect from August 14, whom it accused of deviating from their actual responsibilities and instead acting as political parties "prejudicial to the Naga revolutionary organisations'. It accuses them of acting as auxiliary bodies of the NSCN-IM.
August 16	NSCN-K issues a 'Quit Notice' to the Tangkhuls in Nagaland, accusing them of being "terrorist masterminds". The outfit says that the move would give a fresh fillip to unity efforts and paves the way for permanent peace among the Nagas. It further claimed that Nagas have borne the brunt of the cruelty of the Tangkhuls who are from Manipur.

August 17	Accusing the Naga Hoho, Naga Students' Federation, Naga Mother's Association and Naga People's Movement for Human Rights of directly supporting the rival NSCN-IM, the NSCN-K in a press release states that these organisations do not represent the Nagas. The release states "they should not forget that it was Th. Muivah and Isaac Swu who murdered nearly a thousand of NNC/FGN (read Naga National Council/ Federal Government of Nagaland) workers accusing them to be Shillong Accordists. ...If the IM (read NSCN-IM) signs an agreement for solution within Indian Union, Th. Muivah and Isak will face the same charge sheet they imposed on NNC after Shillong Accord of 1975. Same yardstick will be applied on some NGOs leaders unless they realize their mistakes and keep away from IM sell out plan".
August 18	Nagaland Police arrest two NSCN-IM cadres, Yimlong Chapa Chang and Neilietuo Mepfiio, from the Kohima village gate area of Kohima town. A pistol along with live ammunition is seized from their possession.
August 20	Strongly condemning the NSCN-K diktat to the Tangkhul community to leave Nagaland, the NSCN-IM terms it as an act of "befooling themselves." In a statement made available to the local media, the NSCN-IM says that the NSCN-K is trying to rake up an issue but any issue that aims to fragment the Nagas will never succeed.
August 21	One NSCN-IM cadre, Akam Yimchunger, is killed during a gun battle with NSCN-K at Longkhim in the Tuensang district.
August 22	The Tangkhul Hoho-Nagaland, an apex council of the Tangkhul tribe, urges the NSCN-K to revoke its 'quit notice' served on the Tangkhuls in the interest of peace and unity among the Nagas.
August 25	NSCN-K reiterates its determination to enforce its 'Quit Notice' against the Tangkhuls of Nagaland.
August 26	NSCN-IM cautions NSCN-K for any untoward incident, caused either directly or indirectly, in the aftermath of the 'quit notice' it had served against the Tangkhuls in Nagaland and warnings on several civil society groups like Naga Hoho.
August 28	Cadres of the NSCN-IM and the NSCN-K exchange fire at Angangba village in the Tuensang district.
August 29	Unidentified gunmen assault a NSCN-K cadre, Vikiye Zhimomi, at Aradura locality in capital Kohima.
August 31	One NSCN-IM cadre, Angam Zeliang, is killed in a clash with rival NNC cadres at Phek Basa in the Phek district.

September 1	One unidentified militant is killed and another wounded in a factional clash between rival cadres of the NSCN-IM and the NSCN-K at Asukuto village in the Zunheboto district.
September 5	Three NSCN-IM cadres are killed and several others wounded when a combined force of the NNC and the NSCN-K attack a NSCN-IM camp in the Phek district.
September 5	Unidentified gunmen kill a former NNC cadre, Soloni Poumai, near Ura Academy Hall in the capital Kohima.
September 8	Two NSCN-IM cadres are killed in a fierce gun battle with a combined force of the NSCN-K and the NNC at Phek in the Phek district.
September 11	NSCN-K kills a rival NSCN-IM cadre, Vitoho, at Kholeboto in the Zunheboto district.
September 14	Unidentified gunmen kill a civilian, Akhtar, at Kalibari Road in Dimapur town. Four civilians are wounded when suspected militant exploded a bomb at a shop located at Circular Road in Dimapur town.
	NSCN-K cadre, Aravi, is wounded in a clash with rival NSCN-IM at Yeshulto-Emlo in the Zunheboto district.
September 20	Five NSCN-IM cadres are killed in a factional clash with rival cadres of the NSCN-K at Old Chalkot village in the Peren district.
September 22	Talking to reporters in Kohima, the Inspector General of Assam Rifles (North), Major General S. S. Kumar, discloses that the NSCN-IM is consolidating itself taking advantage of the ongoing cease-fire agreement with the Union Government. "The ceasefire is giving the NSCN an opportunity to consolidate. We have conveyed our concern to the Ministry of Home Affairs... Earlier, there were about 800 cadres of the NSCN-IM. Of late, the figure ranges between 2,000 to 2,500," Kumar disclosed.
September 26	Nagaland Police recovers the bullet ridden bodies of two NSCN-K cadres from a spot near Jotsoma Bye Pass road in the capital Kohima.
September 27	NSCN-IM bans the sale and the bursting of fire crackers in Nagaland.
September 29	A four-year-old boy, Inato Sumi, is killed, while two persons, including a woman, are wounded during a clash between rival cadres of the NSCN-IM and NSCN-K at North Point Colony in the Zunheboto district.

September 30	NSCN-K accuses the Nephiu Rio-led Government of being directly involved with the NSCN-IM in the current factional clash in the Zunheboto district.
October 2	Unidentified militants kill Shimmei Shingnaisui, a 19-year-old student belonging to the Tangkhul tribe of Manipur, in capital Kohima.
	NSCN-K bans the "Tangkhul Naga Long", an apex tribal body of the Tangkhul community, in Nagaland.
October 3	Two militants, one each of the NSCN-IM and the NSCN-K are killed, in a factional clash at a spot between K. Basa and Chisazumi village in the Phek district.
October 5	The NSCN-K claims that five NSCN-IM cadres have defected to its fold.
October 9	At least eight NSCN-K cadres are killed and 10 others sustain injuries when rival NSCN -IM militants attack their mobile camp at Shoixe village in the Zunheboto district.
October 12	The Union Ministry of Home Affairs submits to Myanmar's Government a list of 15 militant camps run by outfits, including NSCN-K.
October 15	One NSCN-IM militant, Lt. Hopson, is shot dead by unidentified gunmen at 5th Mile in the Dimapur district. According to police sources, two unidentified gunmen demanded INR 10,000 from Hopson and later shot him dead on his refusal to pay.
October 19	Peace talks between the Union Government and NSCN-IM in Amsterdam fail following the Government's rejection of the demand for 'self-governance'.
October 21	The dead body of a 'Lance Corporal' of the NSCN-K is recovered from an unspecified place near Jotsoma bye-pass check gate in the Kohima district.
October 27	Three persons are killed following the factional clash between National NSCN-K and IM at Amiphoto in the Zunheboto town.
October 28	A NSCN-IM cadre, identified as Abel Zeliang, is killed by the rival NSCN-K militants during a factional clash at Amiphoto colony in the Zunheboto district.
	A trader, Manoj Chakraborty, was injured when unidentified militants hurled a crude bomb at N. L. Road inside Gurbachans Radios in the Dimapur district. According to police sources, extortion was the reason behind the incident.
November 1	The NSCN-IM accused the former Chief Minister of Nagaland and the present Governor of Goa, S. C. Jamir as the man

behind the 'quit notice' served to the Tangkhul community by the NSCN-K. It also alleged that Jamir once tried to rechristen the Naga Students Federation and the Naga Students Union Delhi to Nagaland Students Union, Delhi.

November 1 1 A NSCN-IM militant was killed and one Khaplang cadre was injured in an internecine clash at Meiuri in the Phek district.

November 1 3 One person belonging to Tangkhul community, identified as Enoch, was killed by the NSCN-K militants at an unspecified place along the National Highway No. 39 near Jotsoma road in the Kohima district. The NSCN-K claimed that the slain person was allegedly an 'informer' of the rival NSCN-IM.

November 14 One NSCN-K militant, identified as '2nd lieutenant' Khetoka Kinimi, was arrested by security force personnel during a search operation at Hong Kong Market in the Dimapur district.

November 17 A senior cadre of the NSCN-IM, 'Major' Lokishe, has defected to the rival Khaplang faction. A statement issued by the NSCN-K military spokesperson Isak Sumi said that Lokishe defected on October 27 after the 'deputy commander-in-chief' of the NSCN-IM, Markson, asked him to assassinate former Sumi Hoho (tribal council of the Sumi tribe) president Huska. Meanwhile, the NSCN-IM, in a circular issued to all its unit battalions informed that Lokishe had defected to the rival faction because of personal reasons.

November 21 A civilian, Raja Diemarey, was killed by unidentified militants at their camp named as Burma in the Dimapur district.

The National Socialist Council of Nagaland-Isak-Muivah (NSCN-IM) has reiterated its demand for 'third party intervention', especially by the Unrepresented Nations and Peoples Organisation, in their peace talks with the Union Government.

November 24 A NSCN-IM militant, 'Sgt.' Limasashi Ao, was shot dead by unidentified militants in an internecine clash at Athibung in the Dimapur district.

November 25 The NSCN-K has asked for a separate board to conduct examinations for the Naga students belonging to the four hill districts of Manipur such as Ukhrul, Tamenglong, Senapati and Chandel. The outfit reportedly opposed the decision of Nagaland Chief Minister Nephiu Rio to allow Naga students to appear for the High School Leaving Certificate examination under the Nagaland Board of School Education.

November 26	One NSCN-IM militant, 'corporal' Yangpak Noke, was killed and another injured by the rival National Socialist Council of Nagaland- Khaplang militants during factional clashes at Zunheboto town and Sukhalu village in the Zunheboto district.
	A clash between the two rival NSCN outfits was reported at New Market Area in the Kohima district. However, no casualty is reported.
November 28	Keviletuo Kiewhuo, the vice president of Naga Hoho (apex tribal council) is assault by unidentified militants at Kohima. Reports added that INR 21,000 and two mobile handsets were snatched from him.
December 1	Four militants are killed during internecine clashes between cadres of the NSCN-IM and the rival Khaplang faction at Inbung and Ahthibung in the Peren district and Zungti village in the Zunheboto district. NSCN-K sources said that its cadres attacked a camp of the IM faction at Inbung killing three of their cadres. One NSCN-K cadre was injured in the incident. An NSCN-IM leader confirmed the attack.
	NSCN-IM militants attack a NSCN-K camp at Athibung. No casualty was reported in the incident.
	A NSCN-K militant is killed at Zungti village during a clash with NSCN-IM cadres. NSCN-IM sources said that an M-21 rifle was recovered by its cadres from the incident site.
December 2	NSCN-K cadres abducted some public leaders and villagers of Kizan village in the Tuensang district.
December 3	A former NSCN-K cadre, Ktyelho Rochill, is shot dead by the rival NSCN-IM militants in the Kohima district.
December 4	A civilian, Tokevi Yeptho, is shot dead by the NSCN-IM militants at an unspecified place between Zunheboto town and Natha Old Village in the Zunheboto district.
December 5	The NSCN-K claimed to have identified two rival NSCN -IM militants, 'lance corp.' Jacob Chakesang and a Zeliang collaborator, who allegedly assaulted the Naga Hoho Vice-President Keviletuo.
	The NSCN-IM reportedly sought a separate 'Naga constitution' under the special federal relationship in the peace talks with the Union Government at Amsterdam, the capital of Netherlands.

The Nagaland Baptist Church Council has reportedly failed to persuade the NSCN-K to revoke the "quit notice" order served on the Tangkhul tribe in Nagaland.

December 10 The NSCN-K reportedly informed all its 'commanders' not to accept any rival NSCN-IM defectors from the Lotha tribe.

December 13 Kiyeshe Aye, a cadre of the NSCN-IM, reportedly defected to the rival NSCN-K faction. The NSCN-K issued a press release welcoming the cadre to their fold.

December 14 A factional clash between NSCN-K militants and the rival Isak-Muivah faction cadres was reported from the New Market area in the Kohima district. Four NSCN-K militants armed with AK-47 assault rifles attacked two NSCN-IM militants who managed to escape and came back subsequently to retaliate. However, there was no casualty reported from the incident site.

An unidentified cadre belonging to the Naga National Council is caught by the public while extorting money from a shop at Dzuvuru in the Kohima district. He was later handed over to the Police.

December 16 Suspected militants of the NSCN-IM killed the 'education kilonser (minister)' of the Naga National Council (NNC)'s Adino faction, Palang Khiamniungan, at Phoolbari in Kohima. This is the second incident in which suspected NSCN-IM militants have killed a senior functionary of the NNC-Adinno. Mar Jamir, also a kilonser, was killed at PR Hill in Kohima on June 1, 2005.

December 19 A NSCN-IM cadre, 'corporal' H. Romeo Poumai, was killed and several others injured after an ambush by the rival Khaplang faction at Bypass Road in Kohima district.

The NSCN-K attacked IM faction militants while the latter were traveling in a vehicle near the dumping slot of Kohima Municipal Council. However, no casualty was reported.

December 20 NSCN-K militants reportedly threatened to eliminate the rival NSCN-IM top leader, Thuingaleng Muivah, if he visits Nagaland. "We have already deployed about 70 fighters around Dimapur town to attack and finish off Muivah if he tries to set foot in Nagaland and if required we shall send more reinforcements to accomplish our mission," said Kughalo Mulatonu, a NSCN-K spokesman.

The Tangkhul Naga Long (the apex body of the Tangkhul tribe) on December 20 requested the NSCN-K to revoke the 'Quit Notice' served to Tangkhuls residing in Nagaland. The President of the Tangkhul Naga Long, Stephen Angkang, and

President of the Tangkhul Naga Villages Headman Association, A.S. Patrick, said that the request was made in the larger interest of the Naga society.

December 26 The NSCN-K reportedly warned Chief Minister Neiphiu Rio, of dire consequences over his alleged nexus with the rival group NSCN-IM. NSCN-K spokesman Kughalu Mulatonu said that his group would not remain a 'lame duck' while Rio patronized the IM faction.

December 29 Two NSCN-K militants, Longtsuo Shitiri and Rabeth Ovung, defected to the rival NSCN-IM group.

Source: http://www.satp.org/satporgtp/countries/india/states/nagaland/timeline/index.html

---

Nagaland Assessment - 2006

In spite of the continuing cease-fire between the Government and the militant outfits, Nagaland continues to witness factional violence, which is an indication of the deepened factional schism between militant outfits and the intransigent nature of the insurgency in the State.

Unabated factional clashes between the two warring factions of the National Socialist Council of Nagaland (NSCN) indicate that the cease-fire agreements signed between the Union Government separately with the Isak-Muivah faction of the NSCN in 1997, and the Khaplang faction of the NSCN-K in 2001 are being violated at will. Worse, efforts to end the abiding and violent confrontation have had no visible impact on the warring factions.

The May 19, 2006-killing of the NSCN-K 'Education Kilonser' (minister), Ngampan Konyak, by the rival NSCN-IM at Mon provoked the NSCN-K to launch a violent campaign codenamed, "Operation Blueland", under which it had stepped up violent attacks against the IM group. On the other side, the IM faction also alerted its armed cadres to reinforce their dominance in different parts of the State. As rebel factions, both claiming to represent the wishes and aspirations of the Nagas, build up their manpower and resources for future mutual carnage, the common people in remote and interior locales, are increasingly worried.

Although the ceasefires with the Union Government still hold formally, escalating factional violence, large-scale extortion and intimidation put a question mark on the very arrangement that supposedly prohibits the movement of armed cadres, armed violence, intimidation and disturbance to peace that are, in fact, endemic. According to the cease-fire agreements, the cadres of each faction are to remain confined to their respective designated camps, but the rule is flouted more often than it is followed. Indeed, the truce has been exploited by militant groups to consolidate and expand. Since the NSCN-IM entered into a formal cease-fire in 1997, it has reportedly raised its cadre strength from 3,000 to 5,000 and nearly doubled its weapon holdings.

The State Government, often described as soft on the militants - especially the NSCN-IM - tends to surrender to their caprice. Nagaland Chief Minister Neiphiu Rio, while presenting the State Budget in the Legislative Assembly in capital Kohima on March 20, 2006, stated: "It is not possible for any Government to prevent this (extortion) completely."

2006 has already seen 36 incident of factional clashes, (till August 21) in which at least 35 militants have been killed (19 of the NSCN-IM, 12 of the NSCN-K and two of the Naga National Council (NNC), and two unidentified). There is no available record of the numbers of injured.

Fatalities in Terrorist Violence - 2006

	Civilians	*Security Force Personnel*	*Terrorist*	*Total*
January	0	0	3	3
February	0	0	4	4
March	2	0	1	3
April	0	0	6	6
May	0	0	7	7
June	2	0	6	8
July	0	0	3	3
August*	0	0	2	2
Total	4	0	32	36

*Data till August 20

Source: Institute for Conflict Management database.

Among the major incidents of violence in 2006 are:

January 8: Three militants of the NSCN-IM and the rival NSCN-K are killed in internecine clashes at the Nokyan village in Mon district.

February 9: Two NSCN-K cadres, including the outfit's Angami region chairman Neisa Angami alias AKD and his bodyguard, are killed by rival NSCN-IM militants at Rusoma village near Kohima.

April 6: Two cadres, one each of the NSCN-IM and NNC, are killed in an internecine clash at Porba village in the Phek district.

April 15: In a factional clash, two NSCN-IM cadres and one from the NSCN-K are killed at Hongphoi village in the Mon district.

May 6: Two NSCN-K militants are killed while three others sustained injuries in a pre-dawn attack by the NSCN-IM at Old Phek village in the Phek district.

May 16: Two NSCN-IM cadres are killed while an unspecified number of NSCN-K cadres are wounded in a factional clash at Athibung in the Peren district.

May 19: NSCN-IM killed the NSCN-K 'Education Kilonser' (minister), Ngampan Konyak, at Mon.

May 27: NSCN-K killed two rival NSCN-IM cadres and injured two others in an encounter at a place near Longleng in the Tuensang district.

The eight year-old cease-fire, beginning August 1997, has led to a significant reduction in insurgency-related fatalities in Nagaland. Between 1992 and 1997, 1,338 persons had been killed in the conflict, averaging 223 per year. Between 1998 and 2004, a further 595 persons have been killed, bringing the average down to 85 per year, still a disturbing number in view of the 'cease fire' that is now in place. During 2005, 40 fatalities were reported from the State. The fatalities in the post-cease fire period have overwhelmingly been the result of turf wars between the NSCN-IM and the NSCN-K. However, the reduced fatalities fail to reflect the ground-level violence which persists across the State, and which affects the widest possible spectrum of the population (Table below).

In 2001, altogether 103 lost their lives, of which 25 (24.27 per cent) were civilians, two (1.94 per cent) were security force (SF) personnel and 76 (73.78 per cent) were militants. It is significant that, between 2002 and 2005 - a period during which both factions of the NSCN were party to a cease-fire -171 persons have been killed in militancy-related violence in the State, of which 113 (66.08 per cent) were militants, 52 (30.40 per cent) were civilians and the rest 6 (3.50 per cent) were SF personnel. With rare exception, most militant deaths have been the result of factional clashes. 2004 saw at least 17 factional clashes, while 2005 witnessed 14.

Comparative Levels of Violence, 2001 -2005

Year	*Civilians*	*Security Force*	*Militants*	*Total*
2001	25	2	76	103
2002	5	2	29	36
2003	3	3	31	37
2004	35	1	22	58
2005	9	0	31	40

Source: Institute for Conflict Management database.

Of the 40 people killed in militancy-related incidents in 2005, there were 31 (77.5 per cent) militants and the rest 9 (22.5 per cent) constituted civilians. In one of the major incidents of the year, at least 10 militants were killed and several others sustained injuries during clashes between the two rival NSCN factions in the Surohuto village of Zunheboto district in March 2005.

The free run of the militants does impact upon the lives of the civilians. On November 8, 2005, Hesso Mao, former Director General of Police of Nagaland, was shot dead by suspected NSCN-K militants at his residence in the capital Kohima. Mao reportedly was served with an extortion demand, which he refused to comply with.

On October 2, SF personnel belonging to the Assam Rifles seized a huge cache of explosives, including 800 detonators, 710 gelatine sticks and six bundles of cordex, each 10 metres long, from Dimapur railway station and arrested one person in this connection. While, on the other hand, on March 19, 2005, the Chief Minister, Neiphiu Rio, told the State Legislative Assembly that three Nagaland Police deserters have joined the NSCN-IM at the outfit's headquarter along with arms and ammunition.

Casualties of Terrorist Violence in Manipur - 2005

	Civilians	*Security Force Personnel*	*Terrorists*	*Total*
January	4	0	0	4
February	0	0	2	2
March	1	0	19	20
April	0	0	1	1
May	0	0	0	0
June	4	0	3	7
July	0	0	0	0
August	0	0	1	1
September	0	0	2	2
October	0	0	2	2
November	1	0	0	1
December	0	0	1	1
Total	10	0	31	41

Source: Institute for Conflict Management database.

Following is a sampling of the major incidents of militant violence in 2005:

- February 25: Two NSCN-IM cadres are killed in an attack by the rival NSCN-K faction at one of the outfit's camps in the Athibung area of Peren district.
- March 24: At least 10 militants are killed and several others sustain injuries during clashes between the two rival NSCN factions in the Surohuto village of Zunheboto district.

- March 27: The NSCN-IM attacks a camp of the rival Khaplang faction in the Zunheboto district. Two militants, one each belonging to both the outfits, are reported to have died in the clash.
- March 29: The NSCN-IM kills four cadres of the NSCN-K during an internecine clash at Yakor village in the Tuensang district.
- September 10: Two NSCN-IM cadres are killed in an internecine clash with the rival NSCN-K at Athibung town in the Peren district.
- October 5: Two NSCN-IM militants are killed in a gun-battle with cadres of the rival NSCN-K at Lapha Lampongbasti in the Mon district.

On September 21, 2001 emerging from negotiations in Amsterdam, the Government of India's chief interlocutor, K. Padmanabhaiah, and NSCN-IM General Secretary, Thuingaleng Muivah, declared a two-year time frame for the 'solution' of the Naga imbroglio. Very few actually believed such an assertion, although it raised some hopes in Nagaland and outside, of an end to the long-standing insurgency. About five years after that declaration, and after numerous rounds of subsequent parleys between both the sides in India and abroad, Nagaland still stands at the crossroads, waiting for peace.

Difficulties became apparent on July 31, 2005, with the NSCN-IM's demand that the cease-fire extension be limited to six months, rather than the usual one-year period. Then, on November 5, IM leader R.H. Raising declared: "There is no point in operating a cease-fire and holding talks without any solution in sight." This statement came less than a month after the October 11, 2005, negotiations in Bangkok, where Muivah had stated, "We are very happy to have the talks with the Indian representatives because both sides are now more serious about all the issues." On November 7, other sympathetic organizations, including the Naga Hoho, the Naga Mothers Association and the Naga Students' Federation put their weight behind the NSCN-IM's position that the talks served no purpose unless they were seen to be leading up to a peaceful solution, creating some consternation in the concerned circles. Finally, on December 19, Muivah issued a veiled threat of the resumption of a bush war in case a tangible solution was not found by January 31, 2006.

The 'threat' to withdraw from the peace process needs to be seen in the context of the failure of the NSCN-IM leadership to make any sort of progress towards its final goal, the integration of the Naga-inhabited areas. On December 15, Muivah, in fact summed up his frustration in the following words. "We Nagas have extended our hand of friendship and India is putting conditions before accepting it. Is this wise? Can we keep coming back again and again, demanding friendship from India? Do Nagas have no honour?" Muivah claimed further that there has been no progress 'from the Indian side' over the last six months of the ceasefire.

There is a pattern to these threats, issued periodically by the NSCN-IM since 1997. These have been used either to keep its arch rival, the Khaplang faction, out of the negotiation process in spite of several demands to broad-base the process; or to wriggle out of difficult positions after the Government has indicated the possibility of a solution short of the IM demand of an integrated Naga territory. Threats have also been used to keep its support base intact, to ensure that the Nagas do not come to view the group as a weak organization, susceptible to the Government's pressure.

The fact remains that, in spite of Muivah's six-month stay in India between January and July 2005 and the three rounds of dialogue [July 29-30, October 10-11 and December 16-17] that followed, very little has been achieved beyond the usual rhetorical assertions. States like Manipur and Assam remain opposed to any dismemberment of their territory to please the NSCN-IM. Union Minister and mediator Oscar Fernandes' October 18 assertion that the NSCN-IM was ready for an interim solution was rebuffed by the outfit.

It would be simplistic to conclude that the Naga peace process, as it stands now, is in the reverse gear. However, the forward movement that was expected is absent. New Delhi has reason to be happy that the NSCN-IM has not really pushed its key demand: that of a sovereign Naga homeland. But, the Government negotiators could not get the NSCN-IM to budge from the next best option that the group thinks is actually feasible - the integration of all Naga-inhabited areas in the Northeast with the existing State of Nagaland to constitute a single politico-administrative unit. It is the logjam over integration demand that stalled the forward movement of the negotiation process.

The Government remains caught in a bind and shied away from telling the NSCN-IM leadership that their demand for integration of the Naga-inhabited areas in the region could not be conceded. New Delhi is aware of the mood of both the State Governments and the people in the States of Assam, Manipur and Arunachal Pradesh - they have made it clear they will not part with any stretch of their territory to appease the Nagas. Obviously, the Government of India cannot attempt to resolve one nagging problem only to open up several new fronts in the already turbulent Northeast.

Terrorist Outfits of Nagaland : Networks

The father of the Naga insurgency, Angami Zapu Phizo, chief of the rebel Naga National Council (NNC), had left the Naga Hills in 1956 to fight for an independent Naga homeland from foreign shores. He travelled through the then East Pakistan and Switzerland to arrive, eventually, in London in 1960, and continued to pursue his dream from the British capital until his death in April 1990. His daughter Adino Phizo, who has succeeded him as the NNC president, is still pushing that demand from her home in , London.[1] A group of around 140 NNC cadres, however, repudiated the Shillong Accord in 1975 and refused to surrender. They formed a new insurgent group called the

National Socialist Council of Nagaland (NSCN) under the leadership of Thuingaleng Muivah, and Isak Chisi Swu in 1980. In 1988, broke the NSCN (Khaplang) faction broke away under away S. S. Khaplang. The significant point to be noted is that the NSCN (IM) formed in 1980 was launched from bases inside Myanmar. With the passage of time, the NSCN (IM) emerged as the most radical and powerful insurgent group fighting for the Naga cause. Clannish divisions among the Nagas (Konyaks and Tangkhuls) resulted in the split of the NSCN in 1988. The Konyaks took the lead in forming the NSCN-K (Khaplang) under the leadership of Khole Konyak and S. S. Khaplang. The faction, led mostly by the Tangkhuls under the leadership of Swu and Muivah, came to be known as the NSCN-IM (Isak-Muivah).

The NSCN, after its formation inside Myanmar and having established itself as a front-ranking insurgent group in India's Northeast, started providing arms training and other logistic support to outfits such as the United Liberation Front of Asom (ULFA), formed in April 1979 to fight for a 'sovereign, Socialist Assam.' The ULFA started sending its cadres for advanced 'military training' at the hands of the Kachin Independence Army (KIA), an anti-Yangon rebel group in Myanmar, from 1988 onwards.

Though NSCN(IM) is in peace talks with the Government of India but it is maintaining its strong linkages with the groups in Thailand, Cambodia and in Bangladesh. It is still busy with its illegal business of drugs and supply of arms to other groups in North East India. The extortion by its cadres still carries on. It always had a soft corner for all the underground organisations, except NSCN(K) in the North East. It wants the situation in this area to remain hot. It would not permit any other group to become stronger than its own group.

While the popular understanding is that Nagaland is now functioning like any other State, in reality, some analysts feel, the NSCN(IM) is ruling Nagaland in totality, having very cleverly marginalised the NSCN(K) and the Hoho group. Their writ runs at all levels (political, administrative, economic and on the society in general), while the common citizens of the state are alienated from them. In addition to their domination within the State, the NSCN (IM) is also nurturing other militant groups in the North East region such as ULFA, KRA, HPC, PLA and so on. It has become something of an umbrella organisation.

A DECADE OF CEASEFIRE IN NAGALAND: WHAT IS THE FUTURE?

This is a brief review of the cease fire from 1997 till the end of the year 2006.

Naga insurgency is one of South Asia's longest running insurgencies that has claimed around 25,000 lives since the country's independence in 1947. Led by Angami Zapu Phizo they were the first to raise the banner of revolt under the aegis of Naga National Council (NNC) when they resolved to establish a Sovereign Naga State. An underground government called Naga Federal Government (NFG) and a Naga Federal Army were raised by Phizo and a full fledged violent movement was launched in 1956. Consequently, Indian army was inducted and 'Armed Forces Special Powers Act, 1958' was enacted to deal with the situation.

Nagaland attained statehood on 01 December 1963. An agreement for suspension of operations was brokered in September 1964 by the Peace Mission comprising of Jai Prakash Narayan, BP Chaliha and Rev. Micheal Scott. However, this did not achieve much and Peace Mission had to be dissolved in 1967 and relentless operations were launched till a major part of the army was deinducted for 1971 war.

After 1971 war, once again relentless operations were launched in 1972 which brought the insurgents to the negotiating table. Consequently, the Shillong Accord was signed between the Government of India and the members of NNC on 11 November 1975. The Shillong Accord was perhaps the most significant achievement towards bringing peace to the insurgency hit state of Nagaland. The representatives of the NNC conveyed their decision of their own volition to accept, without condition, the constitution of India.

However, a group of the NNC, which had gone to China for training, rejected the Shillong Accord and refused to surrender. As a result, National Socialist Council of Nagalim (NSCN) was born on 02 February 1980 with three leaders Isak Chisi Swu, a Sema from Zoneboto, Thuinggaleng Muivah a Tangkhul from Ukhrul in Manipur and SS Khaplang, a Hemi Naga from Myanmar. Geographically, they complemented each other very well. But, there was a vertical split in the NSCN when Khaplang revolted in 1988 as he apprehended that Tangkhul elements led by Muivah were likely to strike a deal with the Government of India compromising the interests of Burmese Nagas. The group led by Khaplang came to be known as NSCN (K), while the one led by Isak Swu and Muivah was called NSCN (IM). Two warring factions were thus formed who were to later carry out insurgent activities not only against the establishment, but also against each other.

Rise in Militancy

The early ninties saw a steady rise in militancy. As security forces stepped up operations against both the factions of NSCN, the casualty figures from 1992 to 1997 started mounting (see table on the next page).

This period also saw bloody clashes between Kukis and Nagas (mainly Tangkhuls) in Ukhrul and Chandel districts of Manipur. Even while Kukis were driven out of North Manipur, they held on to the financial hub of Moreh, a small town at Indo-Myanmar border and smuggling right across it. In order to counter the continuous pressure from Nagas, the Kukis formed Kuki

National Front (KNF), Kuki National Organisation (KNO) and Kuki National Army (KNA)

Insurgency Related Casualties : 1992 - 1997

Year	*Civilians*	*Security Force*	*Terrorist*	*Total*
1992	34	33	29	96
1993	62	43	68	173
1994	110	26	56	192
1995	80	25	108	213
1996	144	48	112	304
1997	104	38	218	360

Source: Institute of Conflict Management database

Faced with depleting strength, NSCN (IM), offered to negotiate for a possible truce with the Government of India. On 31 July 1996, NSCN (IM) set three preconditions for talks with Government of India. These were:

1. Negotiations should focus on sovereignty.
2. Talks should be held in a third country.
3. Third party mediator would be included.

Mr H.D. Devegowda, the then Prime Minister, held initial talks with NSCN (IM) in Geneva on 04 March 1997 and the process of negotiations started which culminated on 24 July 1997, in the signing of a ceasefire agreement between Government of India and NSCN (IM). The agreement finalised a set of 11 ground rules (see Appendix at page 948) to undertake steps for effective implementation of prevailing ceasefire in Nagaland.

As a result of negotiations with the representatives of NSCN (IM), constitution of Cease Fire Monitoring Group (CFMG) was also agreed upon. A CFMG comprising representatives of NSCN (IM), NGOs and persons nominated by the Government of India has been set up at Kohima. Meetings of the CFMG are held at regular intervals. Subsequently, the NSCN (K) also signed the cease fire agreement with Government of India in 2001. This agreement had 15 ground rules (see Appendix at page 949). Significantly, the ceasefire with NSCN(K) is applicable only in the state of Nagaland while the one with NSCN(IM) does not specify the territorial limits. A Cease Fire Supervisory Board (CFSB) was set up for monitoring the ceasefire with NSCN (K).

CFMG as well as CFSB are presently headed by Lt Gen (Retd) RV Kulkarni. Since CFMG and CFSB have not been given any judicial or legal powers, it is unable to check ceasefire violations by both the groups and remains a mute spectator. Many armed cadres of both groups continue to operate outside their designated camps, which is a gross violation of ceasefire ground rules. NSCN (K) has accused Lt Gen (Retd) RV Kulkarni of being partisan towards NSCN (IM) and has refused to attend any meeting of the CFSB since 2001.

Greater Nagaland (Nagalim)

The boundaries of autonomous councils, and separate states have seldom conformed to the distinct ethnic and tribal identities as has been the case with Nagas. As a result, the tribal/ethnic linkages spill over to neighbouring areas of Myanmar, Arunachal, Manipur and Assam.[2] When Nagaland became a full fledged state of Indian Union on 01 December 1963, Naga insurgents (NNC) and some Naga enthusiasts began to claim land beyond the state boundary of Nagaland. This was also reflected in resolutions adopted by Nagaland State Assembly on 12 December 1964, 28 August 1970 and September 1994, urging the Central Government to integrate the contiguous Naga-inhabited areas with Nagaland. While the present state of Nagaland occupies an area of only 16,579 kms, and they would like to add areas from four districts of Ukhrul, Senapati, Tarnenglong and Chandel in the adjacent state of Manipur (22,327sq kms); North Cachar hills areas of Assam (78,438 sq kms) and the districts of Tirap and Changlang of Arunachal Pradesh (83,743 sq kms), making it approximately 120,000 sq kms.[3] A substantial portion of Myanmar has also been included in the proposed Nagalim.

Four years after the cease-fire came into force, Government of India agreed on 14 June 2001 to the long standing demand of NSCN (IM) that the ceasefire in the state of Nagaland since 1997 would also operate 'without territorial limits'. This meant that the ceasefire was to cover not only Nagaland but extend to all Naga-inhabited areas in adjoining states of Manipur, Arunachal Pradesh and Assam. It is also noteworthy that, prior to the signing of this agreement the state governments of Manipur, Arunachal Pradesh, Assam as also the Government of Nagaland were not consulted. This triggered off vehement protests against the extension of ceasefire in other states, especially in Manipur. This was seen as a first step towards acceptance of the demand of Greater Nagaland.[4]

Angry protestors demonstrating against the extension of ceasefire thronged the streets of Imphal and burnt down Manipur Assembly Secretariat building and also the offices of all political parties, Chief Minister's office, Planning Department office, MLA and MP quarters. Demonstrations, *jathas,* sit in *dharnas* and mass depredation continued for six weeks. Not only the Meiteis, but also big sections of Kukis, Kabuis and others joined the agitation. It was remarkable that despite all this tension there were no Naga-Meitei clashes. Ultimately the Government of India conceded the demand of deleting the controversial clause and the ceasefire agreement between the Government of India and NSCN (IM) remained confined to the state of Nagaland.

Consolidation by NSCN

It is a fact that NSCN (IM) has used the period of ceasefire to consolidate and strengthen itself financially and militarily. It has spread its activities on the social, political and economic platforms. In Nagaland, it has gained almost total control on the political system of the state especially after 2003 assembly elections. The state machinery has been completely paralysed and the affairs of the state are being run by the NSCN (IM) by proxy. Government expenditure on the affairs of state is controlled/ monitored by NSCN (IM) functionaries.

Ineffective ceasefire monitoring mechanism has further compounded the problem. NSCN (IM) has also utilised these years of ceasefire by a good measure to extend its influence over the entire Northeast. Today it is the largest and the most influential group in the region and acts like a big brother to a large number of smaller groups. It has reportedly raised its cadre strength from approximately 800 in 1997 to 5000 cadres in 2006 with approximately 3000 weapons (mostly AK).

Extortion remains a fact of life in Nagaland. While the peace talks between the NSCN (IM) and the Government of India, as well as the official ceasefire between the Khaplang faction (NSCN-K) and the Government of India are ongoing, the operations of the Security Forces as also of the insurgents are discontinued. The extortion (tax collection) by all the groups continues vigorously. Both factions of NSCN have been extorting money from government employees as well as the trading community. While the IM faction has fixed 25 per cent of gross salary as the amount to be contributed to the coffers of the outfit annually, the Khaplang group collects 24 per cent from each of the government employees in the state, as well as in all Naga-inhabited areas of neighboring states. Every household in most villages has been paying Rs 120-150. The demands are met mechanically, as any opposition carries an inherent threat of death. Villagers are also obliged to provide the armed cadres food and lodging during their periodic 'area tours'. Such tours by groups of 20-30 armed cadres every couple of months are common.

NSCN (IM) has fully institutionalised the extortion (tax collection) network. Every segment of the society including common man, government officials, businessmen, contractors, transport operators and even rickshaw pullers have to pay the tax to NSCN (IM) regularly and obtain receipt. MLAs and ministers serve at the behest of NSCN (IM) and help by diverting the state funds to the group. Similar activity is done by the Khaplang group in the areas dominated by the group.

Another major source of such revenue consists of collections from the truck drivers passing through Kohima. A sum of Rs 500 is collected from each truck as 'protection money'. The stretch of NH-39, between Kohima and Dimapur provides a perfect setting for this sort of activity. Trucks carrying onions and potatoes from Assam into Nagaland also pay a 'patriotic tax'. At an average, 200 such vehicles ply daily on this route. The NSCN (IM), according to a report of the Union Ministry of Home Affairs (MHA) in 2001, made over Rs. 1,500 million per annum through extortion and other means. In August 2006, within a week of extension of ceasefire, NSCN (IM) served an extortion notice of Rs 50 lakh to Oil India for the supply of petroleum products to Manipur.

The widespread extortion machinery has also given rise to fake cadres who collect money in the name of the established insurgent groups. There are reports suggesting the presence of gangs of unidentified free-lance extortionists who had been extracting money from small traders and businessmen at gunpoint. At least 10 such gangs were caught in October 2006.[5]

Insurgency, over the years, has become a big business in the state. As a matter of fact, rivalry amongst different factions today is primarily over extortion rights over the area rather than on ideological differences[6]. The regular taxation, smuggling and drug money have become a major source of income for the insurgent groups. Funds allocated for developmental and welfare projects are siphoned off by the corrupt politicians to these cadres.

The impact of such 'tax collection' has been significant on the personal lives of civilians, as also on the economy of the state. In every developmental project or any business transaction, after NSCN-IM cut off their lion's share, other groups, NSCN-K and NNC, will also cut their share. When so little amount is left, development is difficult.

Over the years, NSCN(IM) has specialised in the business of creating small ethnic insurgent groups. Not only does it help in spreading its wings in entire Northeast, but it also gives the NSCN rich dividends without having to take part in any action. It sponsored All Tripura Tigers Force in Tripura, National Democratic Front of Bodoland (NDFB) and Dima Halem Daoga (DHD) in Assam. In Meghalaya, a Khasi group called Hynniewtrep National Liberation Council (HNLC) and a Garo group called Achik National Volunteer Council (ANVC). NSCN (IM) has very cleverly networked with their traditional enemies in Manipur, the Kukis, United Kuki Liberation Front (UKLF) and Kuki Revolutionary Army (KRA), and Meitei insurgent group, Kanglei Yawol Kanna Lup (KYKL). However, its animosity with other Nagaland based groups i.e. NSCN (K) and Federal Government of Nagaland (FGN) continues.

The decade long ceasefire provided NSCN (IM) an opportunity to diversify in the illegal trade of arms, ammunition, drugs and timber. The mushrooming of underground outfits in Northeast has resulted in a very high premium on arms and ammunition. NSCN (IM) has the largest network of procuring these from Laos and Cambodia and smuggle these through Bangladesh and Myanmar and then distribute/sell these to different groups. Illegal felling of trees by fictitious contractors in connivance with forest officials goes on with impunity and the proceeds are pocketed by the insurgent groups. Depleting forest cover is the mute testimony of the ecological degradation caused by insurgent outfits.

Ushering of Peace

There has been a significant decrease in the violence in Nagaland ever since the enforcement of ceasefire in August 1997. In the five years preceding the ceasefire (1992 to 1997), 1338 persons were killed in the insurgency related violence in Nagaland, averaging 223 per year. In 1997 alone there were 360 casualties including 218 insurgents and 104 civilians. The number fell drastically in the period following ceasefire (see table below):

Insurgency Related Casualties: 1998 -2001

Year	*Civilians*	*Security Force*	*Insurgents*	*Total*
1998	26	14	72	112
1999	26	4	118	148
2000	13	8	84	105
2001	25	2	76	103

Source: Institute of Conflict Management database

The fatalities in the recent years (2002 to September 2006) have come down to 212, a more than 80% decrease but it is still a disturbing number considering the fact that the ceasefire with both the factions of NSCN is now in place. The casualties during recent years have overwhelmingly been due to the inter-factional clashes between NSCN (IM) and NSCN (K). According to the ceasefire ground rules, the cadres of all factions are to remain confined to their respective designated camps but this rule is usually violated by the insurgents as the ceasefire monitoring mechanism is incapable of enforcing it (see table below):

Insurgency Related Casualties: 2002-2006

Year	*Civilians*	*Security Force*	*Insurgents*	*Total*
2002	5	2	29	36
2003	3	3	31	37
2004	35	1	22	58
2005	9	0	31	40
2006 (upto Sep)	4	0	37	41

Source: Institute of Conflict Management database

Of the 212 fatalities since 2002, 150 (71%) were insurgents belonging to different factions, 56 (27.5%) civilian casualties, again mostly related to inter faction rivalry. It is interesting to note that in the recent past most of the inter- factional clashes have taken place in Phek, Zoneboto and Athibung in Peren usually in the vicinity of NSCN (K)/FGN camps. As such, NSCN (IM) has suffered more fatalities than its rivals.

The casualties to the security forces as also involving action by security forces have almost dried up. The security forces have therefore taken up civic action to provide relief to the deprived society. The public perception of the security forces has undergone a change during the past decade. Strict adherence to ceasefire ground rules and public friendly approach has paid dividends. There has been no allegation of any human rights violation in recent times against the security forces in Nagaland.

Inter-factional Violence

No one would have thought that differences among NSCN (IM), NSCN (K) and FGN would one day become a major hurdle in arriving at a workable solution to the 60 years old Naga conflict. Even while both factions of NSCN are involved in a peace process with Government of India, they have not stopped training their guns on each other and the result has been unending fratricidal violence. The two warring NSCN factions are fighting a bitter turf war for territorial supremacy with an estimated 200 casualties in inter-factional clashes in the past five years. The Naga society today stands divided with tribal alignments with different groups. Some Semas and Tangkhul are aligned to NSCN (IM), Konyaks with Khaplang whereas Angamis and Chakesangs support FGN, thereby deepening the fragmentation of the Naga society.

The church and the Naga Hoho (the apex tribal council of Nagaland) have been attempting to bring all warring underground factions together through a 'reconciliation process', but their efforts have proven futile. The NSCN-K has accused the Naga Hoho, the Naga Students' Federation (NSF), the Nagaland People's Movement for Human Rights (NPMHR), and the Naga Mothers Association (NMA) of a pro-NSCN-IM stance.

To pretend that this divide will not have any impact on the Naga peace process is simply to refuse to call a spade a spade. Unfortunately, differences between the two factions are far too entrenched to yield an easy solution, and it will take more than mere appeals from Naga civil society and the state for them to terminate their internecine war.[6]

Political Level Talks

The political level talks between Government of India and NSCN (IM) are also continuing as part of the peace process. Shri Swaraj Kaushal was initially appointed as the political negotiator on behalf of the Government of

India. However, following his resignation in July 1999, Shri K Padmanabhaiah was appointed as Government of India negotiator. A group of central ministers comprising Mr Oscar Fernandes, Mr Prithviraj Chouhan and Mr S Raghupaty have now been incorporated in the talks by the present Government of India. At least 50 rounds of peace talks in Bangkok, Amsterdam, New Delhi and Nagaland have been held in the past nine years to find solution to one of the longest running insurgencies.

In an interview with BBC in April 2005, Mr Muivah pointed out that, 'While not abandoning its fundamental objective of sovereign Nagalim, NSCN (IM) would for the present focus on the territorial integration of Naga-inhabited areas into political structure[7]. But, integration of these Naga-inhabited areas outside present state of Nagaland is almost impossible as it involves diminution of territories of Assam, Manipur and Arunachal Pradesh.

A significant development during the talks held in July 2006 was the acceptance by both sides that the Constitution would be analysed article-by article to determine which of them would be applicable to Nagaland and which are to be amended. The NSCN (IM) has been demanding a separate constitution like J&K, but the Government is keen to expand existing provisions in Article 371A[8].A major point of negotiations continues to be the form and content of the 'special federal relationship' between India and Nagaland as envisaged by the NSCN (IM). Under the proposed 'special relationship', India and Nagalim would mutually recognise each other's constitution. The Government of India however, has not made any commitment[9].

Since the talks are not transparent and often end with different and diverse statements by both sides, there is very little the people or even the lower-rung rebel leaders know about what was going-on in such negotiations at Bangkok or Amsterdam. There is a very strong reason to broadbase these talks by involving other stake holders i.e. NSCN (K), FGN and the state governments of Nagaland, Manipur, Assam and Arunachal Pradesh. The Central Government should now insist on holding the talks in Nagaland.

There is no gainsaying that so far the peace talks between the Government of India and NSCN (IM) have achieved very little other than periodic extension. Even as NSCN (IM) has been adopting a belligerent posture, but there it does not seem to have a real formula to resolve the issue. Despite the continuous threats by the NSCN (IM) to 'walk away', it appears highly unlikely that it will do so as it has made significant gains because of the ceasefire.

Involvement of International Mediators

Since long NSCN (IM) has been insisting on involving a Dutch non-governmental organization; Kreddha (meaning 'to place trust') in the peace process as a third party facilitator. This organisation is headed by Michael C. Van Walt Praag, former General Secretary of Unrepresented Nations and Peoples Organization (UNPO).

Kreddha's links with the NSCN-IM and its support for the Naga right to 'self-determination' is well-known. Van Praag has been one of the international promoters of the cause of 'Naga independence' and was instrumental in securing some international exposure for the NSCN-IM by its inclusion in the UNPO in 1993. It was during his tenure (1991-98) as the General Secretary, when the UNPO passed a resolution, in January 1995, condemning the Indian and Myanmar Governments for their military action against the group and for what was described as their "forceful invasion and continual occupation of Naga territory and their rampant violations of human rights".

Even as the idea was rejected initially by the Government of India, the recent report published in Nagaland Post of 22 October 2006 confirmed the presence of international experts—Michael van Walt Praag; Anthony Regan, a constitutional adviser in Papua-New Guinea and Yash Ghai, a renowned constitutional lawyer and professor at the University of Hong Kong—at the parleys held during the third week of October 2006. Bhibhu Prasad Routray of Institute of Conflict Management warns that, The involvement of a third party would militate directly against the established Indian policy of rejecting international mediation in internal conflicts, and its impact would reverberate well beyond Nagaland. It is a decision, consequently, that is not likely to be taken lightly.[10]

Naga Society in Transition

The people of Nagaland want peace and prosperity without any fear. They do not approve of mindless killing of innocent civilians and extortion of money. Exposure to outside world through media has changed the perception of an average Naga and a new *Middle Class of Nagas* is emerging. This middle class wants to assure the future of its children, and has become vocal and is beginning to hold the State to account and pushing NSCN (IM) to back foot.

The Chakhesang Public Organisation, an apex body of the Chakhesang tribe, on March 7, 2006, made a declaration prohibiting extortion, movement of cadres in combatant uniform and the establishment of camps within the periphery of the tribe's habitation. Again, on April 17, 2006, several Phek-based organizations under the banner of Phek Area Public Organisation (PAPO) urged the State Government to take up the issue of factional clashes with the rival outfits and the Union Government, and to ensure that cadres belonging to the two rival factions move out of the Phek and the Chakhesang areas. The gathering also condemned the unabated illegal 'tax collection' imposed by the militant groups.

The Chakhesang Baptist Church Council (CBCC) at a meeting held at Pfutsero in the Phek District on May 11 and 12, 2006, said that, in Phek district, innocent citizens had suffered because of threats, intimidation, extortion, and forced taxation imposed by the various militant groups. The church body alleged that the armed factions had forcibly occupied a number of private houses and educational institutions in the District. The meeting described the existing ceasefire with the Union Government as a "public mockery".

In the recent years, media in Nagaland has come of age. Some media organisations have taken a tough stand against mindless killings by insurgent groups and have refused to publish insurgent-sponsored articles. Slowly but surely, the local newspapers have carried articles critical of NSCN. Not only that, the local press today gives much greater coverage to the national, international events, and sports than merely being the mouthpiece of the insurgents. Newspapers today in Nagaland give a far more balanced view than a few years earlier. NSCN (IM) has therefore, been forced to start its own newspaper in July 05. In an opinion poll conducted by Nagaland Post on 21 November 2006 on "who is to be blamed for non adherence of ceasefire?", 78.6% respondents blamed the factions, 7.1% blamed the Centre and 14.3% held the State Government responsible for it. The mood of the society is clearly against the insurgents and in favour of peace.

Nagas of Manipur

The issue of the Nagas of Manipur poses the most formidable obstacle to Naga peace process. The possibility that Manipur may be radically split in negotiations between Government of India and NSCN-IM is a source of enormous anxiety in Manipur. Meiteis today feel embattled and embittered by the identity discourse of the Nagas that threatens a radical diminution of the state's territory. Manipur's anxiety about Naga claims on its territory long precedes the current controversy.

Tangkhuls historically, culturally, linguistically and politically have closer affinity and relationship with Meities of Manipur valley than with the Nagas since pre-colonial ages. Since the foundation of Manipur statehood till date, Tangkhul is the lone tribe that has twice occupied the coveted chief minister's seat of Manipur. In 1994, when Nagaland Assembly called for the unification of all Naga areas. Ironically, it was during the tenure of Reishing Keishing, a Tangkhul, as Chief Minister of Manipur, a declaration in Manipur Assembly was made that, not an inch of Manipur's hill area would be merged with Nagaland. Street protest in Manipur, against the ceasefire began as soon as the present ceasefire came into effect on August 1, 1997. Manipur again erupted into violence after the June 2001 announcement of the ceasefire having 'no territorial limits'.

Tribal Affiliations and Christianity

A tribe essentially refers to .people who live in a specific social formation in their traditional habitat of forests or hills[11]. Nagas claim to have approximately 35 tribes in India.lt may not be out of context to point out that though Naga tribes practiced and observed similar culture and tradition in the past, yet they were not one, nor were they united in the political sense. What created the bond among the disparate Naga tribes to accept each other as part of one family was Christianity.

Despite many good things Christianity brought the Naga people, it was also responsible in large measure for the destruction of the Naga culture and traditions at its very core. The notion of personal salvation encouraged individualism in a society where individualism was indivisible with that of family, clan, *khel*[12] and village. The values by which the Nagas lived were entirely turned upside down. A deep sense of confusion and crisis of identity followed[13].

The age old tribal affiliation is far stronger in the Nagas than religious bonding of Christianity. Carefully crafted *"Nagaland for Christ"* slogan by NSCN (IM) has not helped a great deal. As a matter of fact, the disparate nature of the tribes makes Nagas, vulnerable to division and manipulations. It is a well known fact that there is a growing resentment within NSCN (IM) against the continued domination by Tangkhuls in the hierarchy of the organisation. Quit Tangkhul notice by NSCN (K) in September 2006 was actually aimed at encashing this sentiment and garnering sympathy from the Nagaland based tribes. Five Nagaland based tribes, i.e. Konyaks, Chakesangs, Zealiangrongs, Kheimungan and Yimchangurs have refused to support NSCN (IM).

Should New Delhi take a Tough Stand?

There is a growing sentiment among some sections of Naga society and the security forces that the time is ripe to call the bluff of NSCN (IM). It should not be allowed to carry out its unlawful activities any longer. Even though NSCN (IM) appears to have consolidated in terms of numbers, the training of its cadres certainly is suspect. This is evident from the fact that in the recent inter-factional clashes with NSCN (K) and FGN it has fared poorly. In 2006, NSCN (IM) has lost 32 cadres against 14 of the rival groups[14]. It has failed to make any significant gains in Mon, Tuensang, Phek, Zoneboto and Peren areas. Dissatisfaction amongst the lower rung functionaries is on the rise. Desertion and defection, unheard of in the past, are frequent now.

There appear to be no principled and non-discriminatory efforts to contain the factional violence in Nagaland. Appropriate punitive action as per the law of the land must be taken by the State Government. It is time the Centre reviewed its 'hands off policy and made a proper assessment of the anarchy on the ground. The conditions of the Government's ceasefire with both factions of NSCN have been clearly defined and they cannot be allowed to be habitually violated with impunity. There is also a need to review ceasefire ground rules. The ceasefire monitoring mechanism needs to be strengthened by incorporating the legal and constitutional powers to make it more effective and accountable.

It would be impossible for the government to implement any agreement made with NSCN (IM) alone without involving the other stake holders. Not only NSCN (K) and FGN, but also the state governments of Manipur, Assam, Arunachal Pradesh and above all Nagas must be involved and their sensitivities respected.

Naga peace talks should also focus on disarming of armed cadres on the pattern of 1975 Shillong Accord. Only when the cadres are disarmed, the review of Armed Forces Special Powers Act, 1958 can also be considered. An elaborate plan for the rehabilitation of cadres who give up arms should be worked out keeping in mind their social and economic needs.

Nagaland Government has declared 2006 as the year of agriculture. Ninety per cent of the population of the state depends on agriculture for its survival. The development plan should aim at providing employment in the agro-based projects. There is a vast scope for piggery and poultry farming development in the state. However there is a need for providing support for entrepreneurship at village level. Since Nagaland like other north-eastern states has a high literacy rate, setting up BPOs in Nagaland would not only generate jobs for the Naga youth but shall be highly beneficial to the industry.

The ceasefire ground rules agreed between the Government of India and two factions of NSCN are given in the two appendices below.

Appendix

Ceasefire Ground Rules Between the Union Government and the NSCN-IM, December 1997

1. There would be no offensive operations like ambush, raid and attack leading to death/injury/damage or loss of property against the NSCN by the Indian Army, paramilitary forces and the police;
2. Patrolling by the Indian Army, paramilitary forces and the police would continue to prevent infiltration of militants and arms as earlier;
3. Protection of convoys and patrolling of roads would continue to be undertaken by the Indian Army, paramilitary forces and the police;
4. The Indian Army, paramilitary forces and police would issue instructions to their formations, not to use masks to cover their faces during the period of ceasefire;
5. The NSCN would not undertake offensive operations like ambush raid, sniping, and attack leading to death/injury/damage or loss of property;
6. In the interest of promoting peace process, there would be no parading (either in groups or individually) of NSCN cadres in uniform and/or with arms.
7. There would be no blockade of roads and communications, disruption of economic or developmental activities as well as essential services by the NSCN;

8. It is mutually agreed that no safe haven or sanctuary to any armed group or elements will be maintained by anyone;
9. On the Government of India side, a concern was expressed that forcible collection of money on essential supplies and intimidation of individuals including government officials was taking place in the State. The NSCN representatives stated that their's being a people's organization, they did not resort to such activities;
10. It was further agreed that implementation of these ground rules and modalities will be monitored by a group constituted for this purpose comprising of representatives of NSCN, NGOs and representatives nominated by the Government of India;
11. On the Government of India side a concern was expressed about reports of forced recruitment to armed cadres. The NSCN representatives stated that they have not, and do not resort to forced recruitment

Appendix

Cease-fire Ground Rules Agreed Upon Between the Government of India and the NSCN-K

1. These ground rules will be valid only for the State of Nagaland.
2. Enforcement of ground rules will be the responsibility of the GOI. The GOI and the NSCN will jointly implement the ground rules. Contentious issues relating to the implementation of the ground rules will be resolved by a Cease-Fire Supervisory Board (CFSB) comprising five representatives each of GOI and NSCN and a Chairman to be nominated by the GOI.
3. The NSCN would not undertake offensive operations like ambush, raid, sniping and attack leading to death/injury/damage or loss of property against anybody. The NSCN would also act in a manner as not to cause harassment/damage or loss of property or injury to the civilian population.
4. There would be no offensive operations like ambush, raid and attack leading to death/injury/damage or loss of property against the NSCN by the Indian Army, Paramilitary Forces and the Police. However, the Government of India reserves its right to continue operations against all other militant groups who are not a party to the 'Ceasefire'.
5. NSCN will notify to the CFSB, the list of all their camps. The CFSB would, after due scrutiny, finalise the list of the "designated camps" where all the armed cadres of the NSCN would be located within three months.

6. In the interest of promoting the peace process, there will be no movement in uniform and/or with arms outside "designated camps".
7. Movement of NSCN cadres from one "designated camp" to another will be carried out for mutually agreed purposes and with intimation to the Security Forces and CFSB. The modalities of this would be finalised by the CFSB.
8. The NSCN would refrain from blockade of roads and communications and from any activity which would disturb the functioning of local and, State Governments and of economic or developmental activities as well as essential services.
9. The NSCN will refrain from extending any form of support or assistance to other militant groups.
10. During the course of the cease-fire, the NSCN will refrain from acquiring any additional arms /ammunition military equipment.
11. The NSCN will refrain from extortions, forcible collection of money and supplies and intimidation of individuals including Government officials.
12. The NSCN will refrain from forcible recruitment of armed cadres.
13. Patrolling by the Indian Army, Paramilitary Forces and the Police would continue to prevent infiltration of militants and arms as hithertofore. However, patrolling within one kilometer of the "designated camps" decided after due consultation in the Cease-Fire Supervisory Board (CFSB) will be carried out, with intimation to them. It is noted that no such camps are located/will be located in populated areas, and/or near Highways, Indian Army/Para Military Forces Posts, Police Station/Police Posts etc.
14. Protection of convoys and patrolling of roads would continue to be undertaken by the Indian Army, Para Military Forces and Police.
15. Security Forces will retain the right to enforce measures necessary to uphold the laws of the land and prevent any disturbance to peace.

Source: *Ministry of Home Affairs*

Important Events : Dec. 2006 to Mar. 2007

PM Rules out Integration of Manipur's Naga Areas into Nagaland : 2 Dec 2006

The crucial next round of Indo-Naga talks scheduled to begin on 4 Dec. 2006 in Amsterdam could well mean another impasse following Prime Minister Manmohan Singh's not-too-indirect indication at Imphal on 2 December that effectively rules out the demand for integration of the four Naga-inhabited hill districts of Manipur with Nagaland.

He said at Imphal : "The Government of India is committed to ensuring that nothing is done which will harm the sentiments of the people of State." Minutes before the Prime Minister's assurance, Chief Minister Ibobi Singh had said : "Manipur's integrity cannot be compromised under any circumstances."

FGN Minister Shot Dead : 16 Dec 2006

Unidentified gun men on 16 Dec 2006 shot dead the self-styled Education Kilonser (Minister) of the Federal Government of Nagaland (FGN) L. Palang Khiamniungan near the Nagaland Assembly Secretariat at Kohima.

The gun men involved in the crime are suspected to be from the NSCN(IM). The crime has been committed at a time when the Naga Mothers' Associations and the Nagaland Baptist Church Council are working hard for reconciliation with the slogan : Shed no more blood."

ULFA's No to Demand for Greater Nagaland : 26 Dec 2006

ULFA Chairman Arbinda Rajkhowa in an e-mail statement issued on 26 Dec 2006, said : "The proposed map of the 'Greater Nagalim' includes many parts of Assam, Manipur and Arunachal Pradesh. All these states have registered their protests against the 'Greater Nagalim' design."

He however regretted that protests are more audible in Manipur than in other two states.

It must be noted that Rajkhowa avoided causing any offence to the NSCN(IM). He could not bring himself to outright condemn that outfit whose demand if conceded will result in dismemberment of parts of the three states mentioned above.

Myanmarese offensive against NSCN(K) : 29 Dec 2006

"Myanmar has launched a massive military crackdown against the NSCN(K) separatist group to evict it from its soil. Heavy fighting has been going on between the Junta troops and the NSCN(K) ultras in the district of Hkamti in Myanmar's northern Sagaing Division", said a spokesman of the NSCN(K) on 29 Dec 2006.

NSCN(I-M) Duo in Nagaland : Jan 2007

Chairman of NSCN(Isak-Muivah) Isak Chisi Swu arrived in India (Kolkata) weeks after the arrival of outfit's Gen Sec Thuigaleng Muivah, with a view to carry forward the Naga peace talks. Threatened by the rival NSCN(K) group, Swu arrived in Dimapur amid tight security. He landed unannounced at Kolkata from Bangkok, flew to Guwahati on 3 Jan 2007 and thence travelled by road to Dimapur amid tight security.

Muivah had arrived in New Delhi on 20 Dec 2006.

UN Intervention in Naga Talks Demanded : 5 Jan 2007.

Isak Chisi Swu, Chairman of the NSCN(I-M) on 5 Jan 2007 appealed to the UN Sec Gen Ban Ki-Moon to play the mediator's role in the Naga peace talks with the Indian government.

Swu, who arrived in Nagaland on 3 January after spending two years under a veil of secrecy, wanted the UN to play a proactive role in the 'Indo-Naga' negotiations.

He criticised New Delhi for failing to acknowledge the Naga situation as unique.

NSCN Factions Exchange Fire : 18 Jan 2007

A tribal woman was seriously injured on 18 Jan 2007 in an exchange of fire between the cadres of the two factions—NSCN(IM) and NSCN(K). A jeep load of 'IM' cadres stalked a house in Nagaland where the 'K' men were camping. There was heavy exchange of fire betweem the two groups during which the woman was hit by a stray bullet. Later the 'IM' men fled, and the police arrested six 'K' cadres from the house.

Following the Army crackdown on the hideouts of ULFA militants in Assam, the Assam Rifles guarding the Indo-Myanmar border, has stepped up vigil on it to check fleeing of militants through the market towns of Morch (Manipur) and Namphalong (Myanmar).

Thousands of people are going to Namphalong everyday to purchase foreign goods and visit tourist places. Insurgents in the masquerade of tourists and small traders, have been moving through these two markets and along the border.

The security forces have sealed off the Meghalaya-Bangladesh border also.

Major underground outfits, including ULFA, have announced a boycott of Republic Day celebrations and called a general strike on that day to sabotage official function. This has been the practice during the last so many years.

Truce Monitoring Chief may be Changed : 25 Jan 2007

The tardy peace process with the NSCN(IM) may soon have to face another hurdle if the plan to replace Lt Gen (Retd) RV Kulkarni as the Chairman of the crucial ceasefire monitoring cell in Nagaland becomes a reality, said a source on 25 Jan 2007. The NSCN(IM) has said it would not accept a new incumbent as it would further complicate the ongoing negotiations.

The MHA is in touch with some officials to decide on the replacement. The task of the Chairman is to monitor the implementation of the ceasefire ground rules with both the factions of the NSCN—IM and K—and submit reports to the Centre.

Kulkarni took charge in 2001 after his predecessor PP Srivastava was removed following objections raired by NSCN(IM). A senior functionary of the NSCN(IM) said, "we have also been hearing that efforts are on to replace Kulkarni on health grounds. But it should not be done without our consent."

The chairman's post, which is renewed every year in August, assumes importance in view of the increasing clashes between the two factions. Last year even mortars were used against each other at Zunehboto in the State that resulted in an agitation among the local population.

The NSCN(K) incidentally has begun lobbying hard for Kulkarni's removal and senior cadres have been contacting some Army officers to gauge if they would be interested in the post.

The two leaders—chairman Swu and General Secretary Muivah—who are currently in Nagaland, wished to meet Prime Minister Manmohan Singh soon after their arrival in the capital but could not due to Prime Minister's busy schedule.

No Role for Dutch NGO in Naga talks : MHA : 5 March 2007

The Centre has ruled out any role for the Netherlands-based NGO, Kreddha, in its talks with the NSCN(IM), and insisted that the parleys must be a "bilateral" affair, official sources said at New Delhi on 5 March 2007.

This averment came in the wake of overtures from the NSCN(IM) that Kreddha and its Dutch "Executive President" Michael van Walt van Praag be given a formal role in the talks. Sources in the MHA clarified that rebal group was free to consult the NGO but it cannot have a role in the discussions.

NSCN(IM) Satisfied with the Progress of Talks on 29 Mar 2007

The latest round of talks between the Centre and NSCN(IM) was held at New Delhi on 29 Mar 2007. The latter expressed satisfaction that the Government had discussed several contentious issues it has been raising over the years.

NSCN(IM) also raised some of its key demands that are part of the 30-point charter that it has been pursuing. These includes its concept of Greater Nagalim involving unification of Naga-dominated areas in the region. It also wants its own separate constitution.

The talks scheduled to be spread over three days were wrapped up on 29 March itself, the first day of these talks. The NSCN(IM) said substantial progress has been made. It also expressed hope the next round would be held soon.

Significantly, the talks were held at New Delhi for the first time, a departure from the earlier practice of convening such meetings at a neutral venue like Amsterdam, and, earlier, Bangkok.

The Indian side was represented by Labour Minister Oscar Fernandes, the leader, the official interlocuter, K Padmanabhaiah, Minister of State for

PMO Prithviraj Chavan, Minister of State for Home S. Regupathy, Union Home Secretary VK Duggal and Home Secretary-designate Madhukar Gupta. Top leaders Isaac Chisi Swu and Thiungaleng Muivah were part of the 7-member NSCN(IM) delegation.

NOTES

1. Wasbir Hussain, *Father's Daughter, Sentinel* Guwahati, 31 Aug 2003.
2. Sreeradha Datta, *The North-East Complexities and its Determinants : Ethnic Dimensions of North-East Turmoil*; Shipra Publications, New Delhi, p. 28.
3. Ceasefire Extension in Manipur, Nooral Huda, www.cpim.org, 19 Aug 2001.
4. *Ibid.*
5. *Nagaland Post,* 21 Nov 2006.
6. Vivek Chadha; *Low Intensity Conflicts in India : Nagaland*; Sage Publications, New Delhi, p. 301.
7. MS Prabhakra, "The Long-drawn Naga Dialogue", *The Hindu,* October, 31, 2006.
8. Rajeev Bhattacharya, "Ceasefire agreement with NSCN", *The Indian Express*, Delhi, August 01, 2006.
9. Syed Zarir Hussain, "Needed a roadmap", *The Indian Express,* Delhi, October, 30, 2006.
10. Bhibhu Prasad Routray, "Peace Games", Institute of Conflict Management Website.
11. n. 2
12. A Khel is a group of houses in a Naga village usually belonging to one clan. A village may have three to eight khels.
13. Charles Chasie, "Nagaland in Transition, IIC Quarterly, Monsoon-Winter 2005, p. 255.
14. Source : Institute of Conflict Management, figures from Jan-Sep 2006.
15. *Indian Express,* 6 March 2007.

18

Secessionist Movements of Tripura Playing Politics with Terrorism

It needs notice that Tripura accession to India was not too smooth an affair. It acceded to the Union as late as 15 Oct. 1949, the last to do so in the troubled North-Eastern seven states, and perhaps, the last among the Indian Princely States, with possible exception of an odd one here or there.

Key Statistics : Tripura

Date of formation	21 Jan., 1972
Area	10,491 sq. km.
Population	3,199,203
Capital	Agartala
Major Religions	Hinduism, Christianity, Islam
Main Languages	Bengali, Tripuri, Kokborak, Hindi

The partition cut asunder the State of Tripura from the Mainland, as was the rest of India's North-East. The result was severe market disruption, isolation, and loss of traditional communication infrastructure, pushing the cost of living much above the national norm. Of its total land border of 1001 km, the State shares 839 km (84 per cent) with Bangladesh, leaving a mere 162 km internal border (16 per cent) it shares with Assam and Mizoram. Before the Partition, one had easy land access to Dhaka (150 km away), Chittagong port (75 km), Sylhet (90 km), and Comilla (25 km). Calcutta from Agartala across Bangladesh by rail/road is just 350 km, but travelling through the Siliguri Corridor, as one has to, it is 1645 km away. The Independence fuelled people's aspirations and expectations, as in rest of India, but economic advancement did not meet up with them due to poor communications, scarce local resources and widespread corruption. The situation was even worse in the tribal areas, far-flung and distant. Generous central funds did not produce results to satisfy impatient yearnings for progress and prosperity. The lackluster economy and lackadaisical governance proved fertile ground for extremist elements to spread disaffection. Moreover, initial militancy had roots in the history.

Tripura Insurgency: A Pre-Independence Lineage

The post-1947 influx of refugees/migrants into Tripura has a long history and an honourable ancestry. Tripura, with 10,486 Sq km area and largely hilly, has given shelter to many plainsmen during the long rule of its tribal kings "whose association with the plainsmen was politically motivated". The Tripura kings had not been given a royal status in India till it was bestowed on them by Bengali Brahmins. To begin with, the tribal king of the time brought a good number of the high caste Bengali Brahmins to his kingdom and granted them plains land for settlement. The Brahmins then admitted the king and his close relatives into the higher Hindu castes like the Brahmin and Kshatriyas—the kings mostly to the latter. With this, the Tripura kings stood admitted to the Indian Royalty. As the lands in the hills were not productive enough (with the tribals in the hills subsisting on the jhum cultivation), these migrants to the land were settled in the plains. When the land-hungry plough cultivators flocked to Tripura from the contiguous areas of East Bengal during pre-1947 period, the king allotted the plains lands to them for higher yields. The kings' Bengali association, therefore served two immediate ends : (1) Higher yields through the introduction of plough cultivation. (2) The king's matrimonial relations with other Indian Royal families, courtesy the Brahmins.

The tribals who were a majority in Tripura (including Chakla-Roshanabad in the erstwhile East Pakistan) till 1947, were reduced to a minority due to huge influx of Bengali migrants post-Partition. Wittingly or otherwise, during pre-1947 period, the kings' policies were creating conditions for tribal dissatisfaction, which became acute with the said post-1947 influx. Not only was Tripura's accession to India too smooth an affair (the State acceded as late as 15 October 1949), the king's relations with his tribal subjects too had gone through some turbulent patches. Some fugitives from the 1857 Mutiny had been given sanctuary by certain tribal chief in defiance of the king's wishes as he was under pressure to deliver them to the British to face the law. In 1860, sections of the Jamatia tribes had risen in revolt against the king's officials who were forcibly collecting taxes to be able to pay respectable amount as 'nazarana' to the British Commissioner of Chittagong. The 1939-42 armed revolt of the Reangs was well-known. It was caused by the King Bir Bikram Manikya's decision levying exorbitant rates of house tax to raise funds to enable him to make contributions to the war chest as demanded by the British. These funds were required not only to provide quantities of arms and ammunition to the British Government but also to defray considerable sums of money. The leader of this Reang revolt was their tribal Sardar, Ratan Mani Reang (Kowai). The Reang Revolt can claim certain importance in the history of insurgency in Tripura as "it was the first time the Reangs rose in an organised revolt against the feudal ruler in Tripura".

Post-Independence, in 1948 the peasants at Golaghati near Agartala once stood in an organised manner against a Mahajan (moneylender) that subsequently turned into an armed rebellion against the state power. The historic Golaghati event assumed larger significance due to its politicisation by the CPI. Years before Golaghati, some tribal youth had united and agitated for mass education among the illiterate tribal populace at the remote village of Durga Chaudhury Para on 27 December 1945. In due course, their organisation came to be known to the history as Jansiksha Samiti (JS), dominated by some women Communists. Some analysts aver that it was the JS that sowed the seeds of tribal insurgency against the repression of the tribals by the 'foreigners' in connivance with the state apparatus. Then was born Tripura's Ganamukti Parishad—GMP (People's Liberation Council), espousing political demands like the introduction of democratic "Dewani" Rule.

During the 1940s, the tribal youth led by the CPI took up arms against the feudal rule, avowedly aimed at developing Tripuia's "national identity". With the CPI taking to parliamentary politics, this movement for identity determination suffered a setback and class struggle became dormant. The 1950s and 1960s saw a rash of tribal 'national' movements aimed at preserving their respective ethnic identities and the Centre had to deal firmly with some avowedly secessionist ones. During the last some years came a few adverse situations, mentioned below, which gave fillip to the emergence and spread of insurgent forces:

1. Flood of post-1947 immigration from East Pakistan reduced the tribals to a hapless minority. A concurrent result was that the tribals lost political and economic levers of power to the immigrant plainsmen.
2. When the tribals wanted to give up inefficient jhum cultivation, they found the plains land had become scarce, having been handed/taken over to/by the migrants from East Pakistan.
3. Large scale refugee rehabilitations during the 1950s and early 1960s had disrupted the tribal compactness. The large scale immigration also meant reduced employment avenues for the indigenous tribals and an increasing gap in the living standards of the tribals and non-tribals, which fostered disharmony and conflict.
4. The 'inferior' tribal culture found itself cornered and threatened by the 'superior' culture.

The aforementioned caused widespread discontent among the conscious and politically active tribal youth, who solely blamed the plainsmen and the migrants for their ills. With the CPI taking to parliamentary route, the GMP had lost much of its vigour (as mentioned above), but the crunch came when the Party even denounced the path of armed struggle they had themselves taught to the idealist youth of the GMP. So the tribal youth was completely disillusioned in the 1960s. In 1967, the tribal youth came together to form the TUJS (Tripura Upajati Juva Samiti)—as opposed to the Communist-led mass organisation—as a platform to espouse some regional demands on the ethnic basis. Thereafter, several insurgent outfits of varying sizes, shapes and colours, came the scene, with different longevity.

Land is the Real Cause of the Trouble

To understand the context of this aspect of the problem, a look into Tripura's history is of help. Tripura (earlier Hill Tippera) enjoyed a close nexus with the Bengal plains. Rajmala, the chronicles of Tripura Kings, commencing in the 15th century, were written by the Royal 'Purohits' (Brahmin priests) in Bengali verse *(Imperial Gazetteer,* East Bengal and Assam, 1909). The rulers claimed ancient lineage and engaged in territorial fends. The kingdom pushed as far as Kamarupa, Burma and the Sunderbans at various times. It was overrun by the medieval Muslim rulers in 1633, though Hill Tippera always remained outside the sphere of settled administration. The East India Company took over the plains area (of Tippera) in 1765 along with the 'Dewani' of Bengal and attached them to the Chittagong Division. Hill Tippera however remained a separate State under a Raja whom the British placed on the throne in return for a tribute of elephants and ivory. It was the predominantly tribal Tripura as we know it today, inhabited by a Mongoloid people, speaking Kok-Borok and like the Kacharis, part of the great Bodo race.

The Raja's ownership of extensive estates called Chakla Roshanabad in the districts of Tippera, Noakhali and Sylhet was perhaps one reason for recruitment of Bengali officials, teachers, doctors, and other professionals to administer these estates. The need to augment revenues also led to the Bengali gentry being granted 'talukdari' rights to employ Bengali ryots to cultivate available plains lands. This was the beginning of the Bengali as the language of administration and of the in-migration of Bengalis which was in the subsequent years to become a flood, causing resentment and social dissonance due to the demographic transformation it wrought in (Bhattacharjee, S.R., 1989). Tripura is the only state of the North-East, besides Assam, where tribals are in minority (28.44 per cent in 1981). The state is practically ruled by the Bengali immigrants, the Chief Minister always being a Bengali (Verghese, 1997).

Tripura for long had relations with the adjacent Bengal plains and Hill Tippera was left to the devices of the Raja as long as tribes were quiescent. Even before 1947, the situation had started undergoing a change. In the 18th century, King Ratna Manikya settled 10,000 Bengalis of various professions in Tripura. Practically surrounded by pre-partition Bengal, culture and way of life of the people of the valley have been akin to those of any Bengali village, and most in first place were of Bengali origin. A scholar of the Region thought that "even the tribal people in spite of their own dialects, dances and attire were closer to the people of Bengal". Land for tribal people had never been surplus. But maximum land alienation occurred with the huge population transfer after the partition. Some analyst feel this was one of the reasons behind the birth of tribal violence in the form of Sang-krak in the 1940s, and strident demand to "evict the Bengalis", raised by these tribals. The major task for any Government in Tripura, even before its elevation to statehood in 1972, was to enforce effectively the law to prevent the tribal population, simple and illiterate for the most part, from losing its land to the smarter non-tribal people and to ensure that the lands illegally transferred since 1 January 1969 be returned to their original owners. It was in 1960 that the Tripura Land Revenue and Land Reforms Act was passed with provisions to this effect. Unfortunately, this Act remained unenforced for over a decade, during which "much of the tribal land was alienated". Some amendments to the Act were passed by the Cong (I) Governments in order to strengthen its provisions, one (6th) setting 1969 as the cut-off year. The 6th Amendment was finally passed by the Left Front Government soon after returning to power in April 1993. "Incidentally, the credit for land reforms in Tripura must go to the Left Front which has been in power since 1978, bar a 5-year stint (1988-93). Since October 1993, former tribal owners were asked to approach the Government for restoration of their lost/alienated lands.

Causes of Violence/Insurgency in Tripura

The causes that fostered extremism in Tripura cannot be too different from the ones behind similar extremism in other States of the Region. These were also gone into by the Dinesh Singh Committee set by the Government (MHA) on 8 July 1980 to study the tribal uprising of June 1980 in Tripura, especially the Mandai Massacre.

The Social Science says that the social movements emerge and flourish when groups of people experience relative deprivation, or hold such a perception. It was such a perception perhaps which, to an extent, persuaded sections of the tribal society, both rural and urban, to be vehemently vocal, complaining that the Bengalis had taken away their land, forest, and means of livelihood, and they be expelled. Worse still, the extremist youth seemed to have lost faith in the mainstream political parties and consequently, in the democratic solution to such problems.

The basic cause here seems to be a lack of understanding on the part of the Rulers about the real needs of the tribals and what needs to be done to make them an integral part of the national life, even if some dismiss such postulations as "inane theorisation and banal rhetoric". This school hold that serious efforts made for the economic development have failed to bridge the emotional hiatus as it concentrated on their material and political progress, ignoring the need for psychological and cultural interaction/integration. There is urgent need for greater integration of the tribal societies with the larger entity called India in the psycho-cultural, economic and political fields. They must be the stake-holders in the well-being of the nation at large. First with the British take-over of Assam in the 19th century, and then, the post-1947 improvement of communications, the traders, professionals, (some) politically oriented missionaries, and the land-grabbers penetrated the tribal societies. The problem was compounded by the huge post-1947 influx from East Pakistan, reducing the tribals to a minority in their own home! The deprivation fed the fires of insecurity, and all its attendant ailments. Not only the deprivation must be tackled through necessary political and economic counter measures, but the tribals must be imparted appropriate education and technical training to enable them to face the challenges of the new industrial and technological age. Only then would they be able to manage their own affairs and take a place of pride in the nation's life.

Tripura's economy is basically agrarian and its limited resources are hobbling the rural economic development. Even since 1947, the process of urbanisation has not gone very far due to the fact that no large scale industrialisation has taken place because of lack of the infrastructural facilities. Consequently, there was hardly any transfer of manpower from the agricultural sector to the urban centres. The continuation of that wasteful jhum way in the hills (growing low-yielding variety of crops) is also hobbling the economy. Over 18,000 out of a total of 1,00,000 tribal families are still practicing jhum. Whether through private initiative or official help, the former must quit this ghetto.

Some societal factors also hold back the tribal. Due to tradition, some tribes are unwilling or unable to take to trade or business. Even when the economic plans have expanded job avenues, the tribals at times lose out to the better-equipped migrants, and consequent frustration leads them to the slogan, "Tripura for Tripuris".

The land alienation is admittedly the root cause of the tribal unrest flowing from a sense of deprivation. The settlement of the migrant communities in both the plains and 'tilla' lands in the state created the problem of shortage, even non-availability of land for rehabilitation of 'jhumias' and for distribution among the landless tribals. In a block level survey of indebtedness and land alienation, conducted by the Directorate of Tribal Research, Tripura in 1974, it was found that the indebtedness was directly and positively co-related with the alienation of the tribal land.

The roots of insurgency in this land-locked state lies in the decision of the then Maharaja to abolish the tribal chieftainship and introduce ploughing in farming way back in 1936. Along with it, he also invited tillers from the plains of his state (now forming part of Bangladesh) to the hill tracts and educated Bengalis to this area. There were as many as 19 sects of tribals, 9 of these considered outcastes. The Reangs rose in revolts. But the society, particularly in rural areas, was divided into two hostile camps, following the introduction of ploughing in cultivation. Those who stuck to the traditional jhum were known as "Jamatias" and others who changed over to ploughing were "Navatias". During the World War II, the Maharaja raised the Tripura Rifles (TR) to help the Allied Forces. But the men of the TR deserted and joined the INA of Subhash Bose. Later these men entered into the jungles of Tripura. A section of Communists also infiltrated the state from other parts of Bengal. They were welcomed by the tribal Chieftains. During the 1946 Noakhali (now in Bangladesh) communal riots, the refugees were welcomed into hilly tracts of Tripura. The post-1947 and post-1971 inflow of migrants is too well-known. All this caused a huge resentment and backlash against the migrants.

Militant and Secessionist Outfits

This part deals with the better-known outfits behind the mindless violence in Tripura.

Early Players in the Field

The unchecked influx of immigrants, both outsiders and foreigners, mostly non-tribals, was seen by the tribals as a threat to their ethnic identity, if not their very existence. Therefore, some ethno-centric outfits came into being pledged to the protection of the tribal interest. That is why a group of militant tribals formed Seng-krak in 1947, which was dead set against the influx of refugees into Tripura from across the border. It was outlawed by the Government for its violent activities.

In the successive years were born the Paharia Union, Adivasi Sangh and Tripura Rajya Adivasi Sangh, espousing the tribal causes and aiming to establish the tribal dominance in the State administration. All these organisations merged into a larger entity, creating Adivasi Samsad in 1954. It took up some programmes to enhance the share of tribals in the administration.

Seng-krak

Before changing over to an open phase (armed struggle) in the early 1980s, the tribal movement in Tripura went a long way through an awakening phase. Seng-krak[1], the first militant outfit, was a secret tribal political union formed in 1947. It opposed the influx of refugees and its preaching was anti-Bengalis (Subsequently, the TNV came on the scene to fight for the tribal predominance in the administration). Seng-krak (and TNV) terrorised many refugee colonies to force them out of the state. The first phase of insurgency was supposed to have come to an end with the 1988 Peace Agreement signed by the TNV with the Centre and the state.

Seng-krak (=a clenched first in Kok-Borok, a symbol of protest), having been banned in the late 1940s, first resurfaced in November 1967[2] in Dharmanagar Sub-Division of North Tripur district. Its resurgence was announced by the leaflets, with the red-white-blue flag of the so-called Tripura Tribal Seng-krak Union, pasted along Tripura's northern border with Mizoram and Bangladesh (CHT). The Seng-krak posters had surfaced in the same areas which had earlier been used by the MNF for launching its campaign. The linkage between the two was not known at the time.

By mid-1968, the MNF was training the Seng-krak. The MNF encouraged the Reang guerrilla leaders to attract fresh recruits for more than one reason. First, the MNF was keen to expand its theatre of operations to areas adjoining the Mizo Hills. After the massive military response of the Indian Army took the wind out of the sails of the Mizo insurrection in February 1966, the MNF could envisage the prospect of a protracted struggle. By extending their operations to Manipur and Tripura, the MNF was seeking to stretch the Indian counter-insurgency resources to their limit. Second, the MNF was wedded to the idea of Greater Mizoram by including Mizo inhabited areas of Manipur and Tripura. The Mizos in these areas could be mobilised only if the other local tribals supported them. In return for supporting the Seng-krak, the MNF expected the latter to cede Tripura's Jampui Hills to a Greater Mizoram. Third, the Seng-krak insurgency offered the MNF an opportunity to become the leader of the anti-Indian outfits in the lower stretches of North-Eastern India. The MNF-Senk-krak alliance marked a clear departure from the tradition of guerrilla combat in the violent history of Tripura's insurgency. For the first time, the state witnessed an insurgency with trans-border bases, willing to seek foreign patrons, prepare to kill civilians of a target community, and operate with fraternal insurgent actors and forces on a large scale. Within a couple of years, the Seng-krak died a natural death with the defeat of the Pakistanis and emergence of Bangladesh in 1971.

The group issued some public notices for subscription to certain villages under the jurisdiction of Salema PS in Dhalai district. The Intelligence learnt that it was led by Rajendra Reang/Samprai Deb-Barman and had a 40 to 50 strong cadre. Its aims and operations are similar to those of TTYF.

The ethnic divide was clearly visible by 1997. Every time there is a major strike by the NLFT or ATTF, official Agartala is gripped by fear of retaliatory attacks and reprisals from non-tribals. If the Congress is accused of having used Hrangkhawl's TNV to come to power in 1988, the CPM returned the compliments in 1993, courtesy the ATTF. Chief Minister Dasarath Deb was in fact one of the first to float an organisation—the Tripura Rajya Ganamukti Parishad way back in 1948—to protect tribal interests. The provocation then had been the large scale migration of Bengali Hindus fleeing the newly-created East Pakistan.

Tripura Upajati Juba Samiti (TUJS)

The TUJS was formed in June 1967 by the tribal youth. Its 5 demands were:

1. Restoration of the tribal lands transferred to the non-tribals since 1960.
2. Creation of an Autonomous District Council for the tribals in the state under the 6th Schedule.
3. Reservation of Government jobs for the tribals.
4. Introduction of Roman script for Kok-Borok and its recognition as the state (official) language and as medium of instruction.
5. Reconstitution of the tribal reserves initially created during the Maharaja Regime.

It developed as a political force in its own right and has been launching agitations for the tribal causes. As it grew in size, its younger sections, disenchanted with its peaceful ways, swerved to the militancy to create the secessionist TNV.

As to the environs attending the birth of the TUJS, the defeat of the CPI(M) in both the Parliamentary and Assembly polls in 1967 had created a vacuum in the tribal politics of Tripura. The formation of the youth-based political parties by the Naga, Garo and Khasi tribals had engendered fresh hopes and new aspirations of the younger generation of the Tripura tribals. At a meeting attended by all shades of tribal society, including employees, students, politicians, social workers and youth, tribal problems were discussed and as a result, the TUJS was formed to represent the political face of the more militant among the tribals.[3] Its objectives have been detailed above. The CPI(M) tried to mould the TUJS into its tribal wing, but the latter demurred.

Bijoy Hrangkhawl, who was politically active with the TUJS but was in contact with the more extremist outfits like the Seng-krak and MNF, joined a group of some militants going to the CHT for guerrilla training. Detected and arrested while returning, they were subsequently released for lack of conclusive evidence. Hrangkhawl went on to constitute the Tripura Sena within TUJS which garnered support from the tribal people when some forest areas were dereserved for rehabilitation of the refugees (mostly plainsmen) from Bangladesh.[4] "Throughout its nearly 4 decades of existence, the TUJS has stuck to the twin-track strategy of electoral politics combined with a limited patronage and manipulation of tribal militancy." With the Tripuri tribals' loss of their demographic majority, all-out violent insurgency targeted against the Bengali immigrant majority could boomrang on the tribals with brutal state retaliation as the administration was dominated by the very same majority. Its hobnobbing with the insurgent forces, or more sophistically, limited patronage of militancy, is shrewdly calculated to frighten and pressurise the state and dominant (majority) community to make propitiatory political concessions. In an electoral democracy, where numbers are important, the TUJS leadership must regularly shake its stick at the Government to extract concessions. It has played its hand rather skilfully. To wit, the TUJS in alliance with the Congress wrested power in February 1988 poll from the CPM which had ruled the state for a decade.

Tribal National Volunteers (TNV)

Formed in July 1979 under the leadership of Bijoy Hrangkhawl, it pledged itself to create an Independent tribal state of Tripura through an armed action. With its emergence, Tripura saw the birth of an insurgent movement, publicly avowed to throw out an elected Government.

The TNV cadres trekked to CHT, Bangladesh, to receive guerrilla warfare training. The MNF helped in training and arming the TNV cadres. It put this training to immediate use by raiding police stations and SF outposts, killing policemen and even jawans, looting markets and damaging development projects. At 2.00 AM on 3-8-1979, a gang of miscreants, large number of MNF ultras in uniform included and armed with LMGs, rifles and other small arms, viciously attacked the Birganj PS of South Tripura, killing and injuring some policemen. Anti-immigrants sentiment had been building up in the state during the past few years, especially during 1979, fuelled by the vehement opposition by the Bengali migrants to the tribal demand for creation of an Autonomous District Council. By early 1980, the communal tension was at a high pitch. The vigorous and occasionally violent AASU agitation in Assam, launched in 1979, had inflamed the passions in Tripura also. Something like the great June 1980 tribal uprising was only waiting to happen And it did. There was huge devastation of property and mindless killing of hundreds of men, women and children of mainly migrant communities by the TNV ultras. "Flame of fire spread from village to village, burning thousands of houses and hut, cattle and crops. Numerous villages were laid waste. Lakhs were rendered homeless. Property, moveable and immoveable, was torched, damaged, looted and captured. Women were raped." The Mandai carnage was too horrendous for words.

Further investigations and subsequent revelations persuaded the Intelligence to fix the date of birth of the TNV as 10 November 1978. Two dozen youth from the Jamatia community had assembled that day. Hrangkhawl, who presided over the ceremony, declared himself the President of the new group. The MNF-TNV combine jointly unleashed a series of attacks on the SF along Tripura's northern border with the CHT. But in October 1979, following a joint MNF-TNV attack on Amarpur, Kamalsingh Jamatia, a top TNV leader, was arrested with some documents that gave the State's Left Front Government its first conclusive evidence on Hrangkhawl's involvement with the MNF as also about the formation of a new insurgent movement (designated TNV) in Tripura. With Hrangkhawl fleeing into hiding, the infant outfit slipped into disarray as there was no command structure worth the name. Just when his position seemed shaky, he began to receive feelers from the Chief Minister. He saw it as an opportune happenstance to save his political fortunes. He was prescient enough by then to realise that the independence was a wholly impracticable objective, a mere daydream, and a far better alternative was to rejoin the mainstream and seek redress of the tribal grievances from within the system. Hence his December 1979 letter to the Chief Minister: "There is no conspiracy to secede from India. I fight for total freedom from poverty and expansionist oppression by majority refugees but it does not mean that I declare Tripura independent."[5] He was in touch with the Government/Chief Minister over years before he signed an Agreement on 12 August 1988, in the wake of the Mizo Accord of 1986, which had shown the way.

After prolonged negotiations, a tripartite Agreement was signed on 12 August 1988 by the TNV with the Centre and the State. Its important features were : (1) TNV would give up secessionism and end all violence. (2) Government to enact a constitutional amendment to ensure certain number of seats for the tribals in the State Assembly proportionate to their population. Number of reserved seats were raised from 17 to 20. (3) Government to enact necessary laws to see that the alienated lands are restored to the tribals. (4) Surrendered cadres to be rehabilitated. 8 years of tribal insurgency (its first Phase) was supposed to have come to an end in Tripura with this 1988 Agreement. The Peace Accord was deemed to be a final solvent of all dissonance including insurgent violence in Tripura. But is proved to be a false dawn. The reputation of the TNV and its Supremo, Hrangkhawl seemed to have suffered as a result of this Accord. Other militant outfits surfaced to replace the TNV. The hope of peace engendered by the 1988 Accord was shattered by a violent attack on the Tainani Police Outpost on 11-12-91 by the cadres of the NLFT, the new secessionist outfit pledged to free Tripura "from the Indian Colonial system through guerrilla warfare".

Interestingly, the former TNV rebels organised a peace march programme from 24 March to 20 May 1995 under Hrangkhawl to send an appeal to the tribal extremists to eschew violence and join the democratic mainstream. At the end of it, their delegation called on the Deputy Chief Minister and informed him of the "total disaster in the rural areas". The latter admitted that due to insurgent attacks, the development work in the hills had come to a grinding halt.[6] It was a surreal scene, who was fooling whom?

Not all the TNV cadres were happy with the fact of the TNV laying down its arms. The dissenting hawks and their followers worked overtime to raise two insurgent outfits in the wake of the 1988 Tripartite Agreements: (1) National Liberation Front of Tripura (NLFT) in 1989, and (2) the All-Tripura Tribal Force (ATTF) in 1990.

NLFT and ATTF

Formed in 1989, the NLFT grabbed headlines with its attack on the Tainani Police outpost on 11-12-91, killing one policeman and injuring many more. They made away with 9 rifles and a quantity of ammunition. It was initially led by Dhananjay Reang, and since its split on 10-12-93 by Biswa Mohan Deb-Barman. The outfit, avowedly secessionist, (aiming at liberation of Tripura from India) collects its funds from the public as per the capacity of the person, kidnappings, and the ransoms, dacoities and the looting, and extortions. It obtains its weapons by ambushing SF men and making away with their arms as and when possible, and also through purchases from the arms agents in Bangladesh.

It was known to have training camps in Bangladesh (CHT) where it was trained and armed by that Government. "With its cadre strength placed between 600 and 700, it was reported to have links with certain other extremist outfits of the North-East.

NLFT split in September 2000 mainly due to tribal rivalries accentuated by difference between the Halams (who led a coalition of smaller Tripura tribes in the outfit) and the Deb-barmas (the single largest tribe of Tripura). The schism was the result of the expulsion of Jogendra Deb-barma, Chief of the Political Wing of the NLFT, by the Halam "Prime Minister", Koloi. Jogendra Deb-barma had reportedly formed the Borok National Council of Tripura (BNCT) and had allegedly established contact with certain Meitei insurgent groups in Manipur (www.satp.org/India/Tripura/ Assessment-Tripura.htm). Presently, many of its gun-toting cadres are reported to be involved in snatching small arms and highway robbery. ULFA has supplied them with arms and ammunition[7]. While some NLFT militants have surrendered, those still at large have been busy recruiting the unemployed youth and boasting a cadre strength of over 800, who occasionally resort to ambushes, kidnappings and killings. During a 7-year period (1993-99), the NLFT escalated the blood-soaked horror in the state, including the killing of a large number of civilians, as the table here shows:

Incidents of Violence by NLFT : 1993-99

Year	*No. of incidents*	*Person killed*		
		Civilian	*SF*	*Militant*
1993	31	10	8	3
1994	24	16	6	7
1995	28	34	8	2
1996	26	27	18	4
1997	102	72	44	6
1998	279	130	21	10
1999	313	119	34	12
Total	803	408	139	44

Source: "Tripura Statistics", *North-East Sun,* 1-14 July 2000.

The All Tripura Tribal Force (ATTF) was formed in 1990 by some hawks of the TNV after it laid down arms under the 1988 Accord. It too fought for an Independent Tripura. Through intermediaries, contacts were established between the ATTF and the Tripura Government. After several rounds of talks, a Peace Agreement was signed between the two on 23 August 1993. Under the Agreement, the Government undertook to rehabilitate all the surrendered ATTF rebels, and to provide them jobs and other financial facilities depending upon their qualifications. To start with, all the surrenderees were to be given a monthly incentive of Rs. 500 for a period of not more than 10 months. Most of the ATTF cadres surrendered on 16 September 1993 as required under the Agreement. Till May 1995, as per the official figures, 350 letters of appointment had been issued by the State Government to the outfit's surrendered cadres.

It transpired subsequently that when the ATTF cadres surrendered on 16 September 1993, some under the leadership of Ranjit Deb-Barma defied the orders and subsequently raised another secessionist outfit, All Tripura Tiger Force, and thereby retained the earlier acronym (ATTF) for the new outfit. Later, they consolidated the new outfit and came to occupy an important position in the insurgency stakes in Tripura. It took to violence in September 1993 itself and has continued on the bloody trial ever since.

The ATTF is reportedly the armed wing of the Tripura People's Democratic Front (TPDF), "which is political party of tribals under patronage of the State's Left parties." With an estimated strength of 200 cadres, its activities revolve round its leader, Ranjit Deb-Barma. Aspiring to liberate Tripura from India, it has established close links with militant outfits in Nagaland and Manipur for operational purposes and training of its cadres. Its main sources of finance are extortion, 'tax' collection and kidnapping.

Death and destruction unleashed by it during the 7-year period (1993-2000) are shown in the table below.

Incidents of Violence bv ATTF : 1993-2000

Year	*No. of incidents*	*Person killed*		
		Civilian	*SF*	*Militant*
1993	31	10	8	3
1994	46	10	4	3
1995	90	24	1	5
1996	48	44	10	3
1997	48	95	–	8
1998	68	40	1	4
1999	65	35	7	2
2000 (24 May)	24	11	4	1
Total	389	259	27	26

Source: "Tripura Statistics", *North-East Sun,* 1-14 July 2000.

By 1997, the two groups had a cadre strength of 200 each, but the NLFT was better organised with a nexus with the NSCN(I-M). The ATTF, with its nexus with ULFA and PLA has also set up a few camps in CHT, an area with hardly any Government control—providing a safe haven to all the North-East militants. The NLFT has three base camps in the inaccessible parts of the CHT just opposite Bhandarima area in North District *(Exp.,* 19-5-97).

By early 1999, the battle for supremacy between the NLFT and ATTF had definitely tilted in favour of the former. The ATTF never recovered from a severe setback it suffered in February 1998 when a huge consignment of arms (including 140 AK-series rifles and assorted ammunition) was seized by the Indian Navy in the Andaman Sea in "Operation Leech". The Intelligence found out that ATTF, NSCN(K) and CNA of Burma were set to be the end users of these arms. The NLFT under Vishwamani Deb-barma has 150 cadres against 200 of ATTF under Ranjit Deb-barma. Both had 50 AKs each by early 1999.

On 3 March 2001, the ATTF ambushed a CRPF convoy in South Tripura district, killing 11 CRPF men and two civilians.[8] "It was the last major attack on the SF and a sinister portent". Among the 30 outfits presently operating in Tripura, the NLFT and ATTF have been responsible for most of the terrorist attacks and subversive activities. The MHA banned both, NLFT and ATTF, in April 1997.[9] (Additional information on the organisational and operational aspects of these two terrorist outfits will be found in the next chapter).

Bengali Militant Outfits

Attacks on the Bengali immigrants compelled them to raise rival outfits for their own protection. Amar Bengali (we are Bengalis) or AB, a militant Bengali movement with Anand Margi antecedents had come into being in 1972. It had opposed the idea of an ADC for tribal population and pledged to prevent the 'partition of Tripura' while the TUJS viewed the ADC as a matter of survival (Verghese, 1997, p. 174). Banned during 1972-75, the AB was revived in 1978 to uphold Bengali interests. The United Bengali Liberation Front (UBLF) was formed in October 1999 as a rival terrorist outfit, engaging in a number of reprisal activities. Its actions, no different than those of the tribal outfits, included abduction, extortion, arson, bombing and killing its 'enemies'. In 2000, the UBLF cadres killed 35 tribals.[10] Prior to the birth of these two Bengali outfits, Bengali National Liberation Front was formed to resist the tribals committing atrocities on the Bengalis.[11] Bengalis, earlier reluctant to raise such outfits, now have jumped into the fray; 'having had enough of it', as one told a source. In the near future, the state is likely to see increased dissonance and violent incidents between the tribals and Bengalis.

Bru National Liberation Front (BNLF)

BNLF, based in Mizoram is a nascent outfit dominated by the non-Christian Reangs, a tribal clan living in scattered areas of Tripura, Bangladesh Hill Tract, Mizoram and borders of Hailakandi district of Assam. It was floated in the wake of anti-Reang ethnic violence of October 1997 in Mizoram, in order to protect the interest of the Reangs.[12] Claiming to be emancipator of the entire Reang Community of the Region, its militant activities, including extortion and kidnapping, have mostly been confined to Mizoram and parts of Tripura adjoining the Assam border. In recent times, Mizoram Christians seem to have been its targets of coercion, getting an anti-Christian tag in the process. It is believed the BNLF was raised to counteract the growing supremacy of NLFT, a dominantly Christian-backed insurgency outfit of Tripura—obviously as a strategic management tool to contain extremism in Tripura. The year 2000 saw a series of violent NLFT-BNLF clashes, worst being on 9 July when 70 BNLF cadres were killed by the NLFT ultras at the BNLF Headquarters in Jampui Hills in Bangladesh.[13]

The Bru National Union (BNU) was the precursor of the BNLF. There was widespread tension in western Aizawl after the BNU, a socio-cultural organisations of the Brus (Reangs) in Mizoram, demanded in 1992 the setting up of an ADC in Mizoram, to the west of the Talawng river, along the Bangladesh border. The Mizos of the area in question resented the demand as the Reangs formed less than 30 per cent of this area's population. The Reang youth upped the ante by floating an underground outfit, the BNLF, to press for the same demand of setting up an ADC as also to resist the NLFT excesses against them, as discussed above *(Frontline,* 15-9-2000, *The Dilemma of the Reangs).*

Tripura Resurrection Army (TRA)

After the split of NLFT, its Supremo Dhananjay Reang, formed another extremist outfit, TRA, after camping in Bangladesh, May 1994. No manifesto or declaratory statement on its objectives is known or available. Its area of operations is limited to South Tripura and Dhalai districts. They periodically foment stray incidents like attacks on the SF, kidnappings, etc. After a short camping period in Bangladesh, it engaged itself in consolidating its base in the two years following its formation in 1994. During its stint in Bangladesh camps, it forged links with certain other extremist outfits. It claims a cadre strength of 60-70.

Tripura Tribal Youth Force (TTYF)

Its existence came to light on 3 December 1993 after some of its activists were arrested by the staff of Khowai PS. "With a cadre strength of 30 to 40, it is presently led by Dasratharai Tripura/Uttam Deb-Barman. Its objectives are still unknown." Appearing to be a small time player, it usually engaged in looting, kidnapping and collection of periodic subscriptions only. At times, its cadres are known to have surrendered for pecuniary gains.

Tripura Tribal Volunteer Force (TTVF)

The formation of this extremist group came to light with the arrest of one Subha Mani Deb-Barma of Muraburi (PS Kalyanpur) on 21 October 1993. "With 40-50 cadre, the group is led by Matindra Tripura, Baidya Deb-Barma and Bijoy Deb-Barma.

All Tripura Volunteer Force (ATVF)

Its existence came to notice of the police in September 1994. "With a 50-60 cadre and its objectives still unknown, the group is led by Waishy Lal Halam."

Tripura Liberation Organisation (TLO)

The group caught the attention of the police on 16 January 1994 when it issued some subscription notices to certain villagers under Jirania PS, and also distributed some leaflets. "40-50-cadre group, it is led by Sampak Deb-Barma, Arjun Deb-Barma, and Jumia Deb-Barma." It has issued a 10-point charter of demands to ameliorate the lot of the tribals.

All Tripura Volunteer Association (ATVA) or Ahinksha Tripura Bharat Suraksha Force

The group came to light on 23 June 1994 when it issued subscription notices to some residents of Manu, Chamanu PS. Led by Kalachan Chakma and Biswanath Chakma, it aims to safeguard the Chakma interests in Tripura and to protect them against the depradations of other extremist groups.

Social Democratic Front of Tripura (SDFT)

Its existence came to light on 27 January 1995 when its 3 cadres surrendered at Ram Nagar, PS Bisnalgarh. "It is led by Suren Deb-Barma, Sambhuram Deb-Barma, and some others." It is suspected to be a collaborator of NLFT.

Tripura National Tribal Force (TNTF)

Allegedly patronised by a former TUJS minister who lost April 1993 elections, it was yet to cut its teeth in major attacks.

All Tripura Bengali Force

Like the TNTF, it again was a nascent force in 1993 *(Frontline,* 19-9-93).

Tripura Tribal Democratic Force (TTDF)

The police learnt about the existence of this group on 2 November 1993 when it issued subscription notices to the villages under Killa PS. It was initially led by Jukta Kishore Jamatiya. After the surrender of most of its cadres, a splinter group led by Naik Jamatiya, kept its flag aflutter, and "it is still active in Udaypur and Amarpur Sub-Divisions".

Tripura Security Army (TSA)

Like so many of such smaller entities, it also came to light through the subscription notices issued to certain villages in Longtharai Valley Sub-Division in Dhalai district. "Its activities are not at all prominent."

Religious Groups

During the British days, the Christian missionaries were active in the educational, social, and some were certain, in the political field too. After all they were the only entity allowed entry beyond the Inner Line. Their preachings and education imparted by them had political connotations and some analysts were convinced that the missionaries were engaged in subversive and even "anti-national" activities during the period. Post-1947, the preachers of other faiths too were allowed in the area. In 1990s, the situation became sensitive when certain elements among the Hindus "decided to undo the mischiefs wrought in the area by the missionaries". Portentous aspects of this face-off was the theme of an analysis of the issues:

> "The controversy between the church leaders and Hindu revivalists is more explosive. Nearly a third of the North-Eastern population is Christian. There are 40,000 churches in the Region. The controversy has erupted because of the Hindu activists announcement that they will launch a

campaign to reconvert the people of the North-East to Hinduism. Foreign Christian missionaries are accused of supporting the separatist disturbances.... Leaders of the Nagaland Baptist Convention as well as the Council of Baptist Churches of North-East India had a meeting in Nagaon on 13 July 1998 after which they declared views such as 'There will be battle as we do not have an option', 'There would be a threat to Christianity', etc."[14]

Is a holy war between the two faiths in the offing? The Christians count above 90 per cent in Nagaland, Mizoram and Meghalaya. The Hindu activists fear that the same fate may befall Tripura. So they want to counter the activities of the Church. The target for both the rivals are the tribals constituting 30 per cent of Tripura's populace. Majority of the tribals are Tripuris (Deb-Barma), followed by other tribes like Jamatias, Reangs, Halams, and Mogs.[15] The Reangs displaced from Mizoram and accommodated in the shabby, unhygienic tented colonies have invited the attention of the Hindu activists, who are distributing relief material to the Reang DPs. They see the Reangs as victims of a Christian conspiracy expelled from their homes by a Christian-predominant state just because they happen to be Hindus.

Some recent incidents, unfortunately, have only proved the Hindu fears to be justified. The Tripura Government claims it has irrefutable evidence of some missionaries' complicity with certain separatist terrorist outfits. The state police have uncovered some unsavoury details of direct links between the church and the separatists after an intensive questioning of an important missionary leader, Nagmanlal Halam, Secretary, Noapara Baptist Centre. Halam was arrested when a large quantity of explosive was found in his possession: 60 gelatin sticks, potassium 5 kgs, sulphur 2 kgs and other bomb-making ingredients. Two members of the Centre, arrested earlier, had tipped the police off on the explosives meant for the secessionist outfits like fhe NLFT.'. Some armed NLFT[16] ultras stormed a RSS-run school in Dhalai district on 6 Aug. 1999 and abducted 4 RSS leaders. They demanded Rs. 1 crore as ransom.[17] The NLFT manifesto spells out its objective as "to expand the kingdom of God and Christ in Tripura"[18], which not only fuels the RSS suspicions and confirms its worst fears but also affords grist to the RSS mill. Then the RSS throws a rhetorical question at the Christian friends and foes alike and 'at its own sympathetic constituency: How is it that the Christian missionaries busy doing their work like running schools and churches in the remote interior are never attacked or harmed by the extremists.

Terrorist Incidents and Surrenders : Jan. 1993—Sep. 2005

What follows is a summary of some of the important events and incidents/ cases of violence caused hy the insurgents.

January 93—3 persons killed and many injured in clashes between Amra Bengali and All Tripura Bengali Force (ATBF), two non-tribal groups and Tribal Students Federation and two other tribal groups.

3-4-93—Assembly polls sweep Left Front back to power. Of the 60 seats, CPM alone won 44. Erstwhile rulers, were assigned to scrap heap, winning just 11 seats, Congress (I) 10 and TUJS 1.

1988—3-4-93. During the Cong.-TUJS coalition, some outfits had become powerful: (1) NLFT, led by former Vice-President of the Tl JV, Dhananjay Reang, was openly secessionist. (2) TSV and TRRF, allegedly set up by some leaders of TUJS to "protect themselves against the wrath of their own tribal constituents angry with the coalition Government for its misdeeds." (3) All F was the most talked about, most widespread in geographical terms, and it eschewed secessionism. Congress and TUJS accused CPM of patronising it.

April 1993—The new Chief Minister, Dasarath Deb, declared the problem political rather than administrative, induced large scale surrenders—1500 cadres of ATTF on 16 September; only one-third of these were hard-core militants, the rest, its supporters and collaborators, just stood in the 'surrender' queue to garner the benefits being offered to the 'returnees' by the state [December 1992, one section of militants had changed the name of its group (ATTF was actually the aggregate of some 15 groups operating under that name in a decentralised manner) from the All Tripura Tribal Force to the All Tripura Tiger Force. Ranjit Deb-Barma who had been in the TUJS' Student Wing but had a brief honeymoon with the CPM before going underground, was the President of the new group.] *(Frontline,* 19-11-93). New ATTF was bad news for the Government, as it has secessionist aim and better armed; leader Deb-Barma reportedly directs his group's activities in Tripura from a place 4 km inside Bangladesh across Tripura's Sidai PS. The NLFT enjoyed sanctuary in the Mayani Reserve Forest area of CHT across Tripur's South district.

May 1993—The Left Front restores BJK Tami as DGP, who had been removed by its predecessor.

July 1993—The Government accepted in principle the outstanding tribal demand for a system of Inner-Line Permits to stem further influx of outsiders into the ADC area.

July 1995—Left Front and its ally, Tripura Hill People's Party (THPP) won control of the TTAADC in polls held (on the 26th and 29th) in an atmosphere of violence, with extremist outfits like NLFT, TTVF, Seng-krak and ATTF ambushing police vehicles, attacking distant villages, and kidnapping people. 7 policemen were killed and 5 injured in a 13 July raid.

June 1996—Over 4000 tribal extremists surrendered with pitiable collection of weapons during the 32 months of the present Left Government. At the same time, the insurgency has snow-balled into the ethnic division with the emergence of the Bengali Liberation Front.

Jan.-Dec. 96—Pranab Deb-Barma, a ruling party (CPM) MLA, with his bodyguard, kidnapped in broad day-light from Simma, 30 km from Agartala. He escaped after 11 months, reaching Agartala on 19 December.

4-4-96—6 CSIF men, working with ONGC, killed in an ambush.

12-5-96—7 non-tribals and senior CPM leader, Chandra Mohan Deb-Barma, who tried; to save them, shot dead at Rohitilla market in Khowai Sub-Division, West Tripura district.

28-12-96—The Left Front says the Tripura extremists are getting support from the CIA, ISI and a section of the churches *(Hindu,* 29-12-96).

July 1996—Though tension has been building up in the State for 3 or 4 years with non-tribal people facing abductions and murderous attacks in retaliating against the tribal community in recent times, the present tension is the result of two notices served by the ATTF and Bengal Volunteers (BV), a newly formed organisation of "Bengal Chauvinists". The ATTF notice issued in March said that those who entered Tripura after 1949 and whose names did not appear in the electoral rolls of 1951, would have to leave by 30 June. It called for a 10-day state-wide general strike starting 1st July in support of its demand, naming it "Operation Raukhala (=ouster)".

In its notice, the BV opposed the call and threatened tribal leaders with annihilation. Surprisingly, the NLFT opposed the strike call by the ATTF, and assured that the traffic could move freely along the highway.

Feb. 97—Ultras killed 40 villagers in two attacks in Khowai Sub-Division.

7-5-97—18 CRPF and 1 Home Guard killed in an ambush by NLFT and NSCN(I-M) in Amarpur.

May 97—The official toll alone speaks of some 300 killed by tribal insurgents in the last 15 months *(Exp.,* 18-5-97).

9-6-97—In their second major strike in just over a month, the NLFT ultras opened fire from a hilltop on two trucks carrying personnel of the Territorial Army (TA), General Reserve Engineering Force (GREF), and casual labourers at Chamanu village in Dhalai district, 155 km north of Agartala, killing 1 JCO, 6 TA and 2 GRHF personnel, besides the 9 labourers. They took away their arms, including 11 SLRs.

30-7-97—An ambush laid by the NLFT, 3 Tripura State Rifles men lost their lives at Nuthanbari under Kanchanpur PS.

16 Feb. 98—Left Front retains power in the Assembly poll, though with a reduced majority compared to that of 1993.

Mid-October to Mid-November 1998—With militants on the rampage in the hilly interior areas of Tripura, the situation by now was becoming increasingly tense. The NLFT and ATTF killed 34 persons, including two senior leaders of the CPM (Ananda Mohan Roaja 67, tribal leader and ex-MLA and Shanti Kumar Tripura, 50) and kidnapped 47. Official sources said that in the past 3 years, over 800 people, including Tripura's Health Minister, and Security personnel, have been killed and over 2,000 abducted, many of them have not returned *(Frontline,* 4-12-98).

20-3-98—ATTF gunned down Maj Santosh Pravakar and Naik Khot Shivajee Tukaram in an ambush.

22-3-98—NLFT killed 6 men of Tripura State Rifles at Dhoop Cherra in Khowai Sub-Division.

31-3-98—Tripura's Health and Urban Development Minister and CPM leader Bimal Sinha and his younger brother Bidyut Sinha were gunned down by -20 NLFT ultras near Avanga Ghat, Dhalai River, where he was invited to negotiate the release of his adopted brother Bikram Sinha.

Apr. 98—With 8 more police stations coming under the Disturbed Areas Act, 27 of the state's total 44 police station areas have been brought under the Act since 16 February 1997.

15 August to 20 September 1998—NLFT and ATTF ultras killed 32 persons, including CPM leader Anil Baidya and kidnapped 28. On 24 August, 3 persons, including Kajal Deb-Barma, a 15-year old cricketer, were killed when the NLFT ultras fired indiscriminately on a bus carrying members of the Noabadi Women's Cricket and Football Teams. Ironically, they were returning after playing in tournament organised in memory of CPM leader Khirode Deb-Barma, winner of national award for forging unity between the tribal and, non-tribal people, who was killed by the NLFTX on 9 July 1997. On 16 August, 35 ultras stormed the Narendrapur Tea Estate (TE) in Sadar Sub-Division, killing 5 non-tribals and making away with Rs. 1,18,000. The Tea Association of India threatened to close down 13 of the 23 tea estates, in West Tripura, unless security was ensured. It is noteworthy that for quite sometime the insurgents have been targeting unarmed non-tribal civilians, accentuating the ethnic division.

2 Feb. 1999—6 non-tribal traders were shot dead by the NLFT ultras and they burnt their houses at Kanchanmala and Takarjala areas. In retaliation, 2 tribals were killed by public and 500 huts burnt, 6,000 villagers, both tribal and non-tribal, deserted their houses in and around Kanchanmala. The Congress and TUJS called for a *bandh* on the 3rd. On 12 February, NLFT gunmen set afire several houses of non-tribals in the Garbardi area of West district. These houses were earlier deserted following a week long violence.

March 1999—Large sections of extremists in Tripura, who are not ready to shun the path of violence, continue indiscriminate killing of the non-tribals to realise their declared objective—"Tripura for Tripuris". A recent circular from the NLFT signed by "Major" Thomas Tripura, asked the tribal people of Udaypur Sub-Division "to send at least one member per family for arms training, in order to launch final struggle for a sovereign holy land of tribal Tripura". The tribal youths were asked "not to acquire higher education as it only produces careerists when the motherland needs dedicated soldiers to fight for her freedom". They were warned not to engage Hindu priests for rituals nor 'worship Hindu gods/goddesses.

The NLFT has found out that kidnapping non-tribal students is safer way to raise funds. The four students abducted from Banduar in Udaypur Sub-Division on 19 February, were released 3 days later after their parents paid hefty sum *(Frontline,* 9-4-99).

4-6-99 — Armed rebels intercepted a jeep at Uday Jamadar Para under Takorjala PS, West district and kidnapped 5 passengers.

12-8-99 — NLFT shot dead 5 villagers at Manu in the trouble torn Dhalai district.

26-9-99—20 NLFT ultras killed 8 BSF men in an ambush at Thalcherra in Dhalai district, within four days of killing 5 Assam Rifles men by the same outfit, at Kupilong in South district.

November 1999— On the 14th, 40 ATTF cadres in Army fatigues reached the market of Panchabati village in South Tripura unobtrusively in small groups around 6 PM. 18 people lay dead, when they opened fire with AK-47s after cordoning off the area. Then they staged a mock retreat to the sound of a whistle. As soon the people ventured out of their shelters, they returned to loot and set fire to shops before leaving the ghastly scene. It was all over in 20 minutes.

On the 22nd, the NLFT ambushed a long-range patrol, moving in a jeep and a truck, near Banduar, Udaypur Sub-Division, killing 8 policemen. It was first major attack on SF since the 3 October Lok Sabha polls. Political parties, reacting strongly to these outrages, tried to outdo one another in staging *bandhs*.

In November alone, violence claimed the lives of 30 Bengalis and 8 policemen. With NLFT and ATTF stepping up armed action to drive out non-tribals from the ADC area, "the situation has become explosive" *(Frontline,* 24-12-99).

4 Feb. 2000 — An ailing CPM tribal leader, Dilip Tripura, was shot dead inside the Silacherri Hospital (South district), and his wife injured by some "miscreants". They broke a window and pumped bullets into? Tripura, who with his wife, was under treatment following a 26 January attack on them.

10 Feb. 2000—The Assam Rifles arrested a hardcore NLFT ultra from near Raj Bhavan in Agartala. Believed to have close links with the ISI, trained at a NLFT camp in Khagracheri district of CHT, he was sent here to gather information about vital installations, as a part of the ISI mission to carry out subversive strikes in the state. He had entered Agartala from Akhaura (Bangladesh) on the 10th.

3 April 2000—With unusually high incidents of kidnappings, Tripura accounts for 65 per cent of abductions in the entire North-East. Political parties believe the tribal extremists resort to kidnapping and murder of non-tribals as part of "ethnic cleansing" (Operation Raukhlai) in the tribal dominated areas. With the TTAADC polls exactly a month way, it is feared the run-up might witness a spurt in violence.

Manik Sarkar (Chief Minister) told Home Minister Advani last week that there were 30 militant training camps across the border whence arms, ammunition and funds flowed to the outlawed outfits of Tripura.

The NCP said on an average two persons were kidnapped and one murdered every day. The official data says over the last 7 years, 2,087 persons have been kidnapped and 1,067 murdered. It wanted the entire state declared a "disturbed area". The Left Front cannot accept it since that would result into the President's Rule. The Government's helplessness was shown by a recent incident where the Chairman of the Tripura Horticulture Corporation allegedly sheltered 4 criminals who looted Rs. 10 lakh from a school in Agartala. The four accused and the booty were found in the Chairman's residence. Released on bail on 19-1-2000, he continues in his post, with the Government a mute witness *(Hindu,* 4-4-2000).

12 April 2000—A 24-hour curfew was imposed at 10 PM as ethnic violence continued for the 3rd day in the West district. The shoot-at-sight orders were issued in the Jirania PS area where more than 500 huts belonging to 250 families of both tribals and non-tribals were torched. The violence began on the 10th after a tribal youth sustained a bomb injury at Chakbasta.

15 April 2000—25 NLFT cadres stormed Khas Kalyanpur village, set fire to several houses and shops, and as the villagers were escaping the inferno, shot 12 dead and injured 7. This was the second biggest massacre during the last 4 years, after the 18 people killed at Panchabati year. Kalyanpur (Khowai Sub-Division), 50 km from Agartala, witnessed a series of extremist violence. During December 1996—forcing the Government to promulgate the Disturbed Areas Act in 27 out of the 45 police station areas in the state.

27 April 2000—NLFT cadres shot dead 4 people during the 24 hours: 2 sisters (after being raped) at Garji; Naray Sarkar, brother of a CPM leader at Taidu (both in South Tripura); and a tribal youth, brother of a surrendered extremist, at Ramchandraghat in West Tripura (UNJ, 27-4-2000).

29 April-3 May 2000—The Left Front lost control of the TTAADC in polls held on these days.

May 2000—In a week-long ethnic violence since 18 May, over 50 people, most of them Bengalis, lost their lives—rocking the Khowai and Teliamura areas of West Tripura. Chief Minister Sarkar blamed the vested interests who "have been active for several years to divide the tribals and the Bengalis in the State". He traced the source of this tribal-non-tribal schism to the Partition, "an unscientific division of the country that led to this situation". His rivals in the recently formed Indigenous People's Front of Tripura (IPFT), a party floated with the avowed objective of protecting tribal interest, do not agree. Says IPFT Chief Harinath Deb-Barma: "The Ruling Left Front has been unable to digest its defeat in the recent ADC poll. So, the day we took oath, the violence began. It is the Left Front which is fomenting trouble between the tribals and non-tribals." He further alleges that the ruling Left Front and the new militant group UBLF are working in tandem to create fresh trouble to push the IPFT on the defensive. "The UBLF is a rag-tag outfit comprising fanatical Bengali youth who sees no other way but to take up arms to counter the threat posed by the tribal extremists. The IPFT is certain that it was the UBLF that kickstarted the trouble by killing 6 tribals mid-May. This of course is the politics of this horrendous human tragedy that rendered 2,70,000 people homeless, currently housed in school and office buildings. Most villages have been deserted since most families have fled the area fearing fresh attacks by the NLFT *(Outlook,* 5-6-2000).

May 2000—"Tripura is bleeding again. With tribal militants belonging to the banned NLFT taking a vow to annihilate non-tribal (read, Bengali) people, large-scale violence has broken out in the hilly regions of the State. Attacks on non-tribal people in South and West Tripura have become frequent after the victory of the IPFT, the political wing of the NLFT, in the TTAADC polls held early May."

The above except *(Frontline,* 23-6-2000) sums up the tension-ridden environs in Tripura. Determined to drive out the Bengalis from the area under the TTAADC (Council, for short), the NLFT on 20 May carried out simultaneous attacks at Bagber (housing the refugees who had earlier fled from tribal-dominated villages), Ratiya, and Chakmaghat in Khowai Sub-Division of West Tripura, killing 45 of them. While 60 NLFT ultras killed 25 Bengalis fleeing to Kanchapur (from Bagber), 20 others were killed in ethnic violence across the state between May 20 and 23. "A source at Khowai said that the CRPF personnel deployed near Bagber did not venture out of their camp when the militant struck." With the UBLF, the outlawed militant outfit of Bengali youth preparing itself for a retaliatory forays against the tribal people, "the hilly areas of South and Western Tripura seem dangerously poised for a riot-like situation". These are physical dimensions of the tragedy whose human costs involve painful fallout and more dangerously, the varying political interests and calculations make it explosive!

The latest attacks on them have forced the Bengalis to flee the ADC areas. 30,000 Bengalis have already moved out of the area, say the official sources, and the exodus was continuing. The Government has set up 15 camps to house these refugees. They face an uncertain future of unending travails. Now enters politics. Two parties called a *bandh* on the same day, 23 May; the Left Front to pressure the Centre to send the Army immediately to the state and the Congress (I) to demand' "Central intervention" in view of the intensified insurgency..

Both the Government and Opposition agree that only the joint Centre-State action can stem the blood bath. In three weeks since the Council polls (3 May), 111 people have been killed. The additional 28 CRPF companies and two helicopters deployed during the 1999 Lok Sabha polls have been withdrawn. The Centre has not returned the two Army units withdrawn during the Kargil war. The state asserts the Centre is not allotting additional SF even when it accepts the steady rise in violence compared to declining trend in Assam and Nagaland. Union Home Ministry figures reveal that violent incidents in Tripura grew from 568 in 1998 to 614 in 1999. Till 3 May this year, 286 such incident were reported here. On 22 May, Centre sanctioned some reinforcements for Tripura, the same day the Chief Minister had met Prime Minister Vajpayee and specifically sought the deployment of Army to combat insurgency-related violence. The Centre seemed unwilling to accede, the request as it felt there were already adequate SF (25 battalions in the state—CRPF 15, TSR 6 and AR 4—and 6 of BSF on the border) for the purpose.

In spite of this level of violence, there is no Army deployment in the state, and politics enters the scene here. The Opposition blames the Front that it was reluctant to deploy the Army in the hill areas "for political reasons". Sarkar refutes the suggestion. The sources say the Centre would act after Governor Siddeswar Prasad's tenure ends on 16 June. They suspect the whole state may be brought under the Disturbed Areas Act followed by induction of the Army with independent powers—an arrangement totally unacceptable to the State Government.

8 June 2000—Union Home Secretary (Kamal Pande) said the Centre had sanctioned one additional IRB and two (of the three) BSF battalions for Tripura—all under raising and to be in place before the year-end. He said in the past 7 years, the highest number of 70 ultras were arrested in 1997. Till 31 May this year the SF arrested 41 underground cadre as against 28 last year. The SF killed 23 ultras last year but lost 45 of their own men. 12 SF men lost their lives till 31 May and 6 rebels were killed in encounters during the period.

12 July 2000—The Tripura Assembly today passed unanimously, a private member's resolution moved by the Congress MLA, Prakash Das and amended by Chief Minister Manik Sarkar, condemning forcible conversion from one religion to another in the state (UNI).

14 Sept. 2000—Eight Bengalis killed in a village market in North Tripura. Is it indicative of "Bengali annihilation" campaign? The assailants came from and returned to Sylhet in Bangladesh. It lends credence to Manik Sarkar's remarks that the ISI has taken initiative to unite the ATTF and NLFT. The use of RDX also confirms the suspicions that the ISI is fishing in the troubled waters *(Frontline,* 10-11-2000).

29 September 2000—Satya Narayan Bansal, Delhi RSS Chief, charged the Baptist Church in Tripura with supporting the terrorists in the state and accused its Marxist Government of turning a blind eye to such an act. He said that the NLFT had owned up responsibility for the abduction of four RSS leaders from Ratnamani Ashram, located in the forests of North Tripura, on 6 August, and had demanded Rs. 2 crore for their release (*HT*, 30-9-2000).

Nov.-Dec. 2000—With the NLFT vowing to annihilate the Bengalis and the UBLF bent upon reprisals, large scale violence has broken in the state's hill areas, particularly after the IPFT victory in the May 2000 ADC poll. When the NLFT guerrillas hit Barahaldi, a village of mixed population, on 19 November, 6 people (including 3 women and 2 children) lay dead. In the backlash, Bengalis led by UBLF attacked the neighbouring Falgunjoypara and killed 9 tribals. Several houses were torched on either side. The 3-day curfew was imposed. Both sides called for *bandh* while the left asked for additional forces, the Congress called for dismissal of the State Government for its failure to curb militancy and protect the people. Home Minister Advani said (22 November) that "the Centre has sanctioned the fencing of 839 km Tripura-Bangladesh border.

Manik Sarkar's appeal to people to resist the marauders did receive some response. Hill clans such as Tamatiyas, Reangs, Uchais and Chakmas condemned the NLFT action and asked their members to ignore the ban imposed by the NLFT on their socio-religious practices.

3 March 2001—After a brief lull, NLFT guns boomed again, killing 13 persons including 11 of (4th Battalion) CRPF in an ambush at Bampur under Birganj PS in South Tripura. The ultras decamped with 10 sophisticated weapons (This was the third militant attack on the SF during the past one year. The first one was on 24 March 2000 when 5 BSF men were killed at Siddhicharra in Dhalai district; followed by one on 17 April which killed 3 TSR men at Sonnchnrra in West Tripura). Meanwhile, SF recovered 5 bodies from two separate places in South Tripura, while 3 persons were killed in an encounter between the NLFT and ATTF ultras at Sidhai in West Tripura on 2 March *(Tribune,* 4-3-2001).

17 November 2001—The NLFT abducted 10 labourers in Dhalai district. The SF were combing the area next day to secure their release.

17 Jan. 2002—Two NLFT cadres shot dead in an encounter with SF at Killa in South Tripura.

29 March 2002—SF rescued two civilians from the NLFF hide-out at Nepal tila village in Dhalai district. They had been kidnapped from Manu village on 8 February.

20 August 2002—In bloodiest-ever terrorist attacks in the recent years, 20 Tripura State Rifles (TSR) men were killed and 5 injured in an ambush by the NLFT in Hirapur, West Tripura. They decamped with 17 SLRs and one LMG.

22 August 2002—The police arrested the NLFT leader (Sector Commander) Debashish Reang, in Agartala, believed to be the leader of ambush party which killed 20 TSR men on the 20th.

28 September 2002—Three persons were killed in police firing disperse the workers of the IPFT and Congress who clashed with the police in South Tripura (at Satchand, on the Agartala-Sabroom main road) during their state-wide "rasta roko" agitation.

6 October 2002—Militants, dressed in the Assam Rifles uniform and armed with modern weapons, raided houses in Dharmanagar, the second biggest town of Tripura, killed one resident and abducted 15. The assailants left behind leaflets, announcing a new outfit. Eyewitnesses report that the group comprising tribal, Manipuri and Muslim youths, crossed over to Bangladesh after the outrage *(Hindu,* 7-10-2002).

30 November 2002—Extremist outfits in Tripura have escalated their activities (kidnappings, extortions, etc.) on the eve of the Assembly poll next year, raising the fears that it may not be free and fair. "Revenue collections"—their name for extortions—are in full swing for an independent Tuipura or Twipra (their name, for the state). The ADC has also been using this name for the state. Superibagan, a locality in Tripura, has been renamed as 'Qwaizag'. Such changes in the names are part of a unified programme launched by tribal cultural 'organisations, with support from the AIX: (as also NLFT) to fight the "colonial culture".

The NLFT campaign for a free Tripura is not confined to capturing power at the ADC level (which they did through the IPFT), the next step being "capturing" of the state. That the IPFT is under the direct patronage of the NLFT was crystal clear—when a leading figure of the former, Harinath Deb-Barma, openly admitted recently that the IPFT was being controlled by "unseen threads". The Left Front has alleged that guided by the IPFT, the militants (meaning NLFT) were assaulting, even murdering their workers. The Congress, on the other hand, has charged the ATTF with targeting its workers.

Militants who surrendered recently disclosed that new recruits for the extremist outfits were being trained in the areas adjoining the border with Bangladesh such as Sylhet, Brahmanbaria and CHT. NLFT and ATTF have their headquarters in Dhaka and Chittagong, respectively. Two female surrenderees disclosed that some 50 tribal girls were under training in CHT and they would enter the state before the polls *(Hindu,* 1-12-02).

19 February 2003—Exactly a week before the Assembly Poll, the insurgency has cast its shadow on the process with the NLFT and ATTF calling for its boycott. The Left Front and the Congress-IPPT (Indigenous People's Party .of Tripura) combine are the main contenders for power. Of over 2,300 polling stations to be set up, 124 have been identified as hypersensitive, 353 very sensitive, and 412 sensitive. Three parties—TUJS, TNV and IPFT— merged to form IPPT to fight the poll.

23 February 2003—Sonia Gandhi and Hrangkhawl, IPPT President, share the dais at an Agartala poll meeting. Hrangkhawl, a former militant who made a controversial speech at Geneva in June 2002 demanding right to self-determination for Tripura tribals, will be the unanimous choice for chief ministership if the Left is unseated in the 26th February poll.

15 March 2003—Chief Minister Manik Sarkar, at his first press meet after taking over on the 7th, invited the militants to open talks with the state or the Centre to resolve the 2.5-decade old militancy. He said while the ATTF and NLFT "have set up 51 camps in Bangladesh", the NLFT had also 5 camps in Mizoram. He invited Mizoram Chief Minister Zoramthanga to take initiative and talk to the Tripura militants. He said no dead-line "has been laid down for the ultras to lay down arms nor any decision taken on extending or withdrawing the Disturbed Areas Act, now enforced in 27 of the 51 PS areas" (*TOI*, 16-3-2003).

29 March 2003—NLFT killed 6 Railway Protection Special Force men in an ambush at Sindhu Kumar Para in Dhalai district when they were patrolling the site where the workers were laying railway track to connect Agartala. They made away with 5 rifles.

May 2003—A rou'nd of brutal attacks by NLFT and ATTF in earty May in Tripura left 32 dead, including 7 children and 8 women. First, to start with West Tripura. They stormed 3 predominantly Bengali villages, as part of their campaign to evict all post-1949 migrants from the hills. The attack on 7 May at border village of Jogeswar Nagar (at Samna), where nearly 100 insurgents and foreign criminals killed 20 Bengalis, was worst of its kind in recent years—bordering on the macabre. The ATTF and Muslim fundamentalists from Satchari, where the outfit has it headquarters, "swooped down on the village, set fire to huts, and rained bullets on the residents who rushed out in panic. Those who survived the gunfire were hacked to death. Several children were hurled into the burning houses or shot from close range during the hour-long mayhem" *(Frontline,* 6-6-03). Following night, 9 persons were killed at Mahurchar market. On the 9th, CPM woman leader Rasamala Devbarma was hacked to death at Ashrambari. Jogeswar (45 km from Agartala) is only 500 mtr from the Bangladesh border and the BSF outpost on it!

On the 7th, CPM activist Nilimesh Paul and his wife Alpana Paul were killed at Fatik Ray in Kailashar Sub-Division of North Tripura.

What is particularly disturbing is the fact that the Bangladesh nationals—fundamentalists—are operating jointly with the insurgents. They both came from across the border, committed the carnage, and crossed the border again to reach their base at Satchari where the ATTF insurgents are running a training and operation camp "right under the very nose of the Indian (BSF) SF, as Satchari camp is visible from this side of the border". Across the border is Habibgunj district of Bangladesh.

28 February 2004—3 militants of NLFT (Joshua faction) surrendered to the Assam Rifles with weapons and some IEDs.

8-6-04—NLFT (BM) ultras led by Ranamani Koloy killed one person and kidnapped three others, including a minor girl near Ambassa in Dhalai district.

14-4-04—A 16-strong patrol party of 107 BSF Bn was ambushed by the ATTF cadres at Kalyanpur in the West Tripura, killing 4 men. The patrol was returning from Sonachari.

6-5-04—Montu Koloi (leader of one of the two main NLFT factions) and his 71 cadres surrender before the Governor in Agartala.

13-6-04—NLFT ultras waylaid two trucks carrying traders from Dasda to the weekly market at Kanpui, (North Tripura), abducted 24 of them, and went across the border into the CHT. The incident comes just a day after 5 persons were abducted at Khowai.

21-6-04—Two BSF Assistant Commandants were assaulted and abducted by a mixed group of Bangladeshi and Indian miscreants, at the border village of Mianpara, near Kasba BSF BOP, about 30 km from Agartala. However, the BDR returned the two on the 23rd to the BSF. The incident caused tension in Kamalasagar border area, West Tripura.

21-8-04—The much-awaited peace talk between the Tripura Government and NLFT (Nayanbasi) will be held next month. Nayanbasi Jamatiya had surrendered in April at the instance of the State Government and his 50 cadres are now being looked after by the Government till a rehabilitation plan is chalked out *(Exp.,* 22-8-04).

22 October 2004—Gaganjoy Roaja, son of the late CPM leader Ananda Mohan Roaja, ex-MLA and a policeman were killed while a BSF man and a civilian were wounded by suspected NLFT ultras in Dhalai district *(Hindu,* 24-10-2000).

25-12-04—Bidding farewell to arms, 138 NLFT militants of the Nayanbasi faction, who had recently signed a MOS with the Centre and the state; surrendered before Governor Dinesh Nandan Sahaya at Agartala.

28-12-04—In one of the biggest terrorist strike, the ultras of the illegal NLFT shot dead 17 people including 16 TS jawans in an ambush at Dangabari in South Tripura district. They made away with one LMG, 15 AKs and a huge cache of ammunition from the slain men.

31-3-05—Religious divide claims a life in Mohorbhoge village in West Tripura district. Humayun Kabir fell in love with Kabita Barman and married her. Her parents refused to accept the alliance and beat up Kabir when he came to take Kabita with him on the 30th. Next day, he was found unconscious near her house, and later died.

2-9-05—87 militants of the NLFT and ATTF surrendered before the DGP G.M. Srivastava, with their arms—one LMG, 13 AK and 11 SL rifles, two Chinese rifles, 7 revolvers, 23 Grenades, one 2" mortar, and three radio sets.

EXTREMIST OPERATIONS AND THEIR POLITICS

Presently (2001-2002), 33 extremist groupings are operating in Tripura, most engaged in it for the quick way to make money through terror. It is a well-oiled trade, says the state police. The ATTF and NLFT are notorious for kidnappings and extortion. Lesser-known criminal groups often kidnap a person to 'sell' him to a bigger outfit for a price, who subsequently double/treble the ransom demand. Tripura accounts for 65 per cent of abductions in the North-East.[19] Abduction by terrorists in Tripura has evolved into a well-organised criminal operation. During 2000, a total of 555 incidents of abduction, including 481 by the NLFT[20] and 41 by the ATTF, were reported in the state. There seems to be no ideological underpinnings to the objectives adumbrated by these outfits, as discussed above.

The Intelligence estimated that in the mid-1990s there were 12 extremist groups, besides a number of sub-groups/minor outfits, operating in Tripura, and maintaining their secret camps and bases in jungle in the hill area of Tripura as also in Bangladesh.

Politics of It All

Militancy in Tripura is more closely linked to political parties than ever before. The militant outfits decelerate or accelerate their activities as demanded by the interests of the political parties. It is not that the extremism-politics nexus exists in Nagaland and Manipur only. Replicating the model, the NLFT is allegedly in cahoots with the Congress (I) in the state while the ruling Left Front has similar equation with the ATTF. The terrorism in Tripura, with its disproportionate emphasis on criminal activities like abduction for ransom and extortions, is reported to be substantially nurtured by political patronage.[21] The NLFT had been fighting hard to gain a strategic, political position for itself for quite some time to establish its supremacy over other tribal outfits in Tripura. Initially, it had to perforce depend on the anti-Left political formations mostly controlled by the non-tribals since large sections of Tripura tribals were followers of the Left parties. Naturally, its leaders had to accommodate the wishes of the anti-left political elements. But growing wiser with time, they decided to forge their own overground protege, Indigenous People's Front of Tripura (IPFT)[22], comprising of the Tripura Hill People's Party (THPP), Tripura Tribal National Conference (TTNC), Tripura Tribal Students Federation (TTSF), and Tripura Upajati Karmachari Samiti (TUKS), enabling them to dispense with their dependence on any outside political force. Particularly after the remarkable success of the IPFT in the ADC poll of May 2000[23] when the NLFT played the pivotal if coercive role, its long cherished dream became a reality.

Presently, the anti-Left forces may seem to be gaining ground, something favourable to the NLFT, still any erosion in tribal support to the Left is a far-off dream. As the anti-Left forces depend almost solely on the support of the non-tribals, meaning plainsmen and the Bengali migrants, the NLFT, a tribal outfit, can never hope to gain from this situation as it has been targeting the Bengali-speakers. Persuaded by its success in the first phase of its struggle, the NLFT is concentrating on the unification of the tribals on a single political platform of creating a Borok nation. Such mobilisation may help the NLFT to proceed to its distant goal of capturing political power in the state, but the journey has hardly begun, as there are competing militant outfits in the race.

The hold of the IPFT[24] in the Tripura Tribal Areas Autonomous District Council (TTAADC), the instrument of tribal autonomy first formed in 1982 with limited autonomy under the 5th Schedule, was bound to raise serious questions about the unity/integrity of Tripura. The Left Front Government elevated the TTAADC to full autonomy under the 6th Schedule, effective 1 April 1985. At the given time both moves were seriously opposed by sections of non-tribals, mainly Bengali-speaking, who were not reconciled over the control by the tribals over a large area of the state. Some opposition parties also jumped in the fray for partisan politics, by exploiting the dissatisfaction of the non-tribals/Bengali-speakers, and the-latter remained critical of the Left-Front for their pro-tribal stance. The refrain of their criticism was/is that their "soft policy" was mainly responsible for the tribal Insurgency and its continuance. But there is other side to this "accusation". The Left has the pro-poor image and if they lose support among the tribals following an unduly stringent policy in dealing with the extremists, the terrorist/insurgent outfits enjoying the patronage of the ISI[25] and consequent safe havens in Bangladesh would spread their influence among these tribals. The TTAADC making certain policy decisions disapproved by the

Left-led State Government, would only accentuate the differences between the two, giving a fillip to the extremist tribal opinion which has already apparently taken over the TTAADC "even if through questionable means". Again, as the tribal militancy targets the Bengalis, they too have formed their own extremist outfits to retaliate against the tribals "in their self-defence". The fight on the ethnic lines have cast a shadow on the prospects of early return of peace to the troubled state, besides seriously damaging the social and political harmony between the two sides.

A month long police rebellion in 1992, indicative of poor governance, was a cause of serious concern among the counter insurgency apparatus of the state. Communal riots and arson in North Tripura district on 12 November in the midst of a strike by the State's non-gazetted policemen was a warning of far more serious deterioration in law and order as Chief Minister Samir Ranjan Barman by then had already asked the Army to be put on alert, unable to make the errant policemen, on strike since mid-October, to see reason. The strike had further worsened an already serious situation since not only had the then largest insurgent group, ATTF, been striking with growing frequency but the other rebel group, NLFT, had recently linked up with rebel outfits from Nagaland (NSC-IM) and Manipur (PLA). Root cause of strike was the political interference in its functioning, even if it originated when the police demanded higher wages and right to form a Police Union. The most disturbing fact was that both Congress and CPM leaders had cultivated rival factions in the police force. The political patronage had corrupted the men in uniform and led to a breakdown of discipline *(Exp.*, 4-11-92).

Political realities sometimes come in the way of war against the insurgency, and at times they even smoothen the way for the insurgents. The situation in the State had become so grave by September 2000 that the CPM-led Left-Front Government of Tripura had no option but to invoke the National Security Act to combat the mounting militancy/insurgency in the state's hill areas. "Not a day had passed in the last few months without killings and kidnappings perpetrated by the tribal outfits, essentially the NLFT and ATTF." The Government's writ did not run in many areas where these outfits ruled the roost—literally running a parallel Government. Even more ominous was the fact that these outfits were trying to create a religious and cultural divide between the (Hindu) Bengalis and (Christian) tribals by "banning" the latter from worshipping Hindu deities and participating in Hindu festivals. This situation became all the more explosive when provoked by the tribal violence, there was a Bengali backlash by way of creation of an extremist Bengali outfit, the UBLF. The situation saw a further worsening when the Indigenous People's Front of Tripura (IPFT), NLFT political wing, wrested control of the TTAADC from the Left parties in May 2000, in an election 'rigged' with the help of the NLFT. Bent upon defeating the Left-Front in the elections to the 30-member TTAADC (Council, for short), the NLFT ultras abducted relatives of the candidates of the Left, killed their supporters, burnt the houses of the Bengalis, and threatened voters with dire consequences if they did not vote for IPFT candidates. Even before the poll notification was issued, the NLFT had imposed a "ban" on other parties contesting the polls *(Frontline,* 10-11-2000).

Soon after the IPFT victory in polls, the tug-of-war between the State Government and the Council became intense, with the latter demanding autonomy. The IPFT declared that 20 lakh of the state's 26 lakh Bengalis were "aliens and infiltrators". The war of attrition between the two had begun. In a bid to gain control over the ADC areas, the IPFT-led Council, on coming to power, dissolved all village development committees formed by the Left Government and reconstituted them with people, mostly the NLFT collaborators. To compound matters, the IPFT began to press the State Government to withdraw all Government employees on deputation to the Council and allow the latter to recruit its own staff. Seeking Central intervention for redress of its grievances, an IPFT delegation led by Chief Executive Member Debabrata Koloi met the Prime Minister and Home Minister in Delhi in September 2000 and demanded major amendments to the 6th Schedule to ensure direct flow of funds from the Centre to the Council, by passing the State Government. They also told the Centre the Council did not approve of the 1971 Indira-Mujib Pact, setting 25 March 1971 as the cut-off date for granting citizenship rights to the immigrants; they wanted it to be 15 October 1949, and demanded that all those who entered the state after it be treated as foreigners and deported. The IPFT is already pursuing the "Christian agenda" as openly espoused by the NLFT. Threatened by ultras, thousands of Bengalis have been leaving the hill areas. A circular from the NLFT threatened to close down by force all schools run by Bengalis and Hindu organisations in the hill areas. To show they meant business, the NLFT torched a residential school and a hospital run by the Seva Mission in the remote Ananda Bazar area of North Tripura on 8 September 2000. "Education Minister Anil Sarkar says over 5,00,000 school children in the hill areas face an uncertain situation owing to the militancy." Under rebel pressure about 2,000 schools were closed down in the hills. Sarkar said: "Militants raid schools and kidnap students and teachers. Teachers in most schools are forced to pay 5 per cent of their salary as 'tax' to the insurgents." A senior para military officer told *Frontline:* "The militant outfits have been pursuing the ethnic cleansing in the hills since the IPFT wrested control of the ADC. They cannot take on the SF." So Bengalis are fleeing the hills, being soft targets.

The political scene has changed over the last few years. Earlier the region had only political parties like the CPM and groups like TUJS and TNV. Now it is the militant-backed IPFT holding sway. This points to a possibility that the ISI, helping tribal insurgents from Bangladesh, could operate from within Indian territory, viz from Tripura. The militants want Bengalis out from the ADC area as they are opposed to the demand for a separate Tripura. The size of non-tribal (Bengali) population in the area has gone down from 33 per cent of the total of 1985 to 27 per cent now (2000), due to the militant pressure. They may differ on other issues, all militant outfits are united when it comes to terrorising non-tribals, says Samir Ranjan Barman, ex-Chief Minister. Police records say that in less than 6 months after the ADC polls, 152 people were killed. Extremist-related incidents are on the rise: 342 in 1998, 367 in 1999, and 301 till August 2000. The corresponding figures for the abductions (of mostly non-tribals) are 392, 432 and 367—depicting an upswing. Politics and counter-insurgency cannot go hand-in-hand!

Hitting at the National Sentiment

For the first time, 9 extremist outfits of the North-East, including the ATTF, NLFT (Biswamohan Group), and ULFA gave a joint call for the boycott of Independence Day celebrations across the Region. In run-up to 15 Aug. 2003, the two Tripura extremist outfits staged a series of murderous attacks spread over 4 days on both unarmed civilians and SF, killing 30 Bengalis, including 13 women and 6 children. By repeatedly choosing soft targets for attack (two SC hamlets in the instant case), the ATTF have sent out the message that terror will remain the sole means for achieving their awful objective of ethnic cleansing—expulsion of the overwhelming Bengali majority from Tripura.

These latest attacks squarely raise for political India the issue of the scale and menace of the insurgent camps in Bangladesh. The ATTF, which conducts its training in the CHT, has its Headquarters in Tarabone, Bangladesh, and its Chief, Ranjit Deb-Barman has Dhaka address. Chief Minister Manik Sarkar submitted a detailed report to the Centre in 2000 on the location of extremist base/training camps in Bangladesh and the arms supply arrangements, the latter does not seem to have advised Dhaka strongly enough to evict these Indian insurgent, nor helped Agartala with reinforcements of the SF to adequately meet the threat. As worrying is the linkages two outfits have created in the Region: ATTF with ULFA and Manipur extremists and the NLFT with NSCN(I-M). Yet again, the political considerations seems be messing up an already dangerous conflictual situation. And unfortunately, the country's premier political formation is the guilty party. Not having learnt from its past, an analyst asserts "much worse in relation to the extremist-chauvinist challenge in Tripura has been the role of the Congress. Just as the Party under Rajiv Gandhi joined hands with the extremist TNV in the run-up to February 1988 Poll to wrest power from the Left Front (which it did), it had no compunction in forging ties with the IPFT, the NLFT's overground wing, for the February 2003 contest, though it did not succeed this time. "Such dangerous games where national sovereignty, security and unity are at stake must be stopped immediately", demands the sober *Hindu* editorially (18-8-03).

Use of Religion

The use of religion in the state has further complicated the issue of combating extremism after the conflict has been given ethnic colours. The shrill cry of "Bengali nationalism in danger" has turned the problem into a battle between Hinduism and Christianity. The NLFT has donned the preacher's habit to unify the tribal people under the flag of a single religion, ordaining that all people living in its domain of influence convert to Christianity to ensure protection against any extremist violence. To counter this perceived/genuine threat, the Hindu activists have been spreading their influence among the Bengalis—sharpening the religious hiatus. The common, defenceless people, caught in this cross-fire, feel tempted to offer vocal allegiance to a religious umbrella to protect themselves from the hostile camps. In this backward state, characterised by a least-developed society and underdeveloped economy, Maxism should find it easy to collect faithfuls in droves, but that does not seem to be happening. Amidst the polarisation of the population into rival religious camps, the call for the social and economic reforms seems to have lost its charms. The communal divide is bound to be cynically exploited by the inimical forces, including (and ominously by) the ISI, which will be more dangerous for country's unity than any potential threat posed by the communal forces.

The situation gets further vitiated when inter-tribe differences are added to the religious and ethnic tensions. The Jamatia Hoda, the Supreme Council of the tribe, the third largest in the state, carried on popular opposition to the terrorism. At its 10th conference on 13 December 2000, the Hoda leaders resolved not to pay any kind of "taxes" to any terrorist outfit—not so veiled a reference to the NLFT. The conflict between the two in 2000 had reached a high point when the Jamatia clergy and its community leaders sought Governor's intervention on 16 October to protect their faith amidst the forced conversion drive, constant threats, and intimidation by the NLFT. Besides the Jamatia, the Reang and Uchai were other tribes within the larger anti-terrorism campaign. First week of December 2000 saw the ransacking of at least two Hindu and one Buddhist places of worship by the NLFT ultras, who had earlier issued a directive for cessation of non-Christian ways of worship in the state.[26]

Certain quarters are convinced that the missionaries, have played a role in fanning the ambers of unrest in Tripura. The argument runs that notwithstanding the insurgent violence in these areas the missionaries are able to carry on their normal work of running the schools; hospitals, churches unmolested by those ultras. A Civil Engineer, assigned the duty of constructing a school building for a Mission, expressed his concerns for his personal safety to a journalist, soon after he was told by the Mission to go to his work place on a scooter and no insurgent would touch him. An analyst saw this assurance "as definite proof of indirect relations between the insurgents and Christian Missions". This was dismissed as simplistic conclusion by the other side, with "perhaps it is the good, selfless work by these missionaries which cannot be disregarded even by these desperados".

Costs We Pay

Over the years, insurgency related incidents in Tripura have been growing, from 568 in 1998 to 614 in 1999, and 820 in 2000. Casualties among the civilians mounted to 351 in 2000 from 229 in 1998 and 240 in 1999. The number of terrorists killed in 2000 stood at 37 against 26 in 1998 and 22 in 1999. The SF cut their losses to 17 dead in 2000, compared to 25 in 1998 and 42 in 1999. More militants were arrested (785) in 2000, compared 1998 (399) and 1999 (335).[27] (Figures for the later years will be found in the next chapter).

It is obvious that the worst sufferers of the extremist violence in Tripura, as in all the insurgent situations in other countries, are the poor people, particularly those in the remote interior. Here is a desolate picture of one village as painted by a leading Agartala daily *(Dainik Sambad,* 22-5-95):

> Tetuia is located under Ganganagar Thana of Gandachara Sub-Division. The poverty-stricken area is tribal-dominated and inaccessible. As per official figures, of the 135 families of the village, over 50 have left it as a result of terrorist activities of the tribal insurgents.... Almost all the families are dependent upon the *jhum* along with the practice of animal husbandry. During the last two years, the ultras have been committing repeated atrocities in the area, ruining its economy. The miscreants in the garb of insurgents are looting their corn, domestic fowls and other animals.... Consequently, basic necessities of life—water, health, and education—are not reaching the village.
>
> The agony and travails of people placed in such hopeless situation are not easily comprehensible to people like 'us' living in the comforts of a city life; and both are pithily delineated by Ratanmani Malsoom (a sub-tribe of Tripuri tribe) of Debatamura (Tempai ADC, PO Pitra, South Tripura) in an interview on 9-5-95: "You people living in a town are leading a happy life. We are facing maximum trouble. The insurgents attacks us and collect our food. We are helpless. They threaten to kill us if we inform the police."

During 1995, 366 persons were kidnapped in 365 days. Besides, 31 police and SF men were killed in 68 encounters with the insurgents, compared to 13 death in 40 encounters in 1994. Attacks on NH-44, 198 km Assam-Agartala life line of Tripura, (161 km of which passes through hilly areas) also increased. More importantly, the rebels find the abductions a money-spinning industry, a safer but sure way to make the millions.

Kidnapping Cases: 1993 to 1998

Year	*No. of cases reported*	*Hostages released*	*Hostages killed*	*Hostages missing*
1993	109	85	13	11
1994	216	187	22	7
1995	367	323	21	23
1996	298	248	16	34
1997	126	96	13	17
1998	405	315	18	72

Source: Police Records, Cited *Frontline,* 5-11-99.

To cite just one instance, Yugabrata Chakrabarty, a tea planter, abducted in June 1996, was the first prominent victim of the extremists' "lucrative industry". The ATTF accepted Rs. 30 lakh from his family for his release, but then it said he died of renal failure a few days earlier. The family said they demanded an additional Rs. 10 lakhs to hand over his body *(Frontline,* 5-11-99).

Counter-Insurgency Forces and their Costs

In spite of large number of surrenders, new armed groups have surfaced. Political patronage seems to have encouraged lawlessness and given succour to many outfits. If a Left Party is said to have helped the birth of the ATTF, the rival TUJS allegedly fostered the Tripura Rajya Raksha Bahini (TRRB) and Tripura State Volunteers (TSV) with help from a national political party. The NSCN(I-M) and ULFA have forged links with groups like NLFT, currently the leading insurgent outfit operating in Tripura, and some of its cadres have been trained in Bangladesh and Myanmar. The NSCN(I-M) was reportedly unwilling to offer modern arms to the NLFT since its objectives fell short of an independent Tripura. It was perhaps to counter this averment that the NLFT criticised the July 1995 elections to the TTAADC as unlikely to help the tribals improve their lot, and went on to assert that only independence would meet the aspirations of the Tripuris.

Presently (2001), 6 Tripura State Rifles (TSR), 4 Assam Rifles (AR), and 15 CRPF battalions (Bns) are actively deployed in counter-insurgency role in Tripura. Then, there are 8 battalions of BSF deployed on its international border with Bangladesh and the state also has 8,139 police at its disposal. The state has also raised a Special Task Force (STF) to combat insurgency in the state. The first STF batch completed its training in Nagaland on 8 March 2000.[28] Over 24,000 SF men are deployed in the state to fight the evil. Chief Minister Manik Sarkar told the Assembly in July 2000 that over 1,200 militants were active in state, including 800 with the NLFT, and 400 with the ATTF. Statistically, the ratio of the SF to the militants works out as 20:1. The insurgency is yet not under control, says an analyst. 27 of the 44 police stations have been declared "disturbed" by the Government since February 1997.[29] While demanding more SF in 1999, Chief Minister Manik Sarkar spoke for the entire Region when he told the *Frontline* (27-8-99): "Tripura and other North-Eastern states face serious security risks owing to the operations of the ISI of Pakistan, which has established links with extremist outfits in the Region."

The Centre has plans (October 1998) to raise 12 battalions of India Reserve Police Battalions (IRB) to combat insurgency in the Region—4 for Assam, 2 each for Tripura, Manipur and Arunachal and 1 each for Meghalaya and Mizoram. The Centre also decided to reimburse the entire expenses incurred by North-Eastern states in combating insurgency: Rs. 79 crore to Assam, Rs. 28 crore to Tripura, Rs. 26 crore to Manipur, and Rs. 22 crore to Nagaland.

Hurdles and Road Blocks in the Way

Some events caused concerns among the SF in 1993. Some (September 1993) ATTF returnees who came under attack from active extremists in November vowed to go back underground if. the Government failed to ensure their safety. Moreover some TNV men who had surrendered in the wake of the 1988 Rajiv Gandhi—Bejoy Hrangkhawl Accord "took part in some recent outrages" *(Frontline,* 19-11-93).

Fencing

Chief Minister Manak Sarkar demanded (November 1999) that the Centre start barbed-wire fencing of at least 20-odd vulnerable stretches, totalling 250 km, of its border with Bangladesh. Presently, there is hardly any fencing on this border. Moreover, each BSF battalion mans 100-125 km of the border, against 15 km in J and K.

The Border Road Organisation has (March 2003) completed just 7 km fencing on the state's international border since the work began in 2001. On 3-3-05, the BDR men fired several rounds on the Indian labourers in their first attempt to forcibly prevent the construction of barbed wire along the international border at Subroom in South Tripura district.

Terrorist Outfits and Political Parties: A Sum-up

The faith of the TUJS in democratic ways to redress the tribal grievances was not shared by its extremist fringe which formed the TNV in 1979. The

TNV declared a communal war against the non-tribals, essentially the migrants from East Pakistan. Imbibing deeply the spirit of adventurism, they romanticised about the armed revolution solving all their problems. It was the born-again Maoism in India's North-East. It demanded that all those who entered the state after 1949 when it acceded to India must quit as they were foreigners. To show that they meant business, they staged the horrendous Mandai Carnage in 1980 and subsequently spread the cult of violence, all the while mouthing the slogan 'independence for Tripura'. They spread all over the hill areas and targeted mainly the non-tribal blacksmiths, artisans, carpenters, washermen, barbers, shopkeepers, moneylenders, etc. The TNV ended up with the 1988 Peace Accord. The history has a canny habit of repeating itself, and the extremist fringe of the TNV spawned its twin clones—NLFT and ATTF, as already discussed. In the recent history, in the 1940s, the violent tribal outfit (Sang-krak) had rocked the state. It had collapsed as it lacked ideological moorings. Almost like Sang-krak, the TNV and ATTPLO (All Tripura Tribal People's Liberation Organisation) resorted to violence and armed insurgencies, without firm ideological commitment, barring their, programme of ejecting the foreigners, and expectedly, the latter too dissipated themselves with aimless violence and disappeared like the former. Subsequently, several other militant outfits came into being to fill the space, starting with the ATTF. Others to follow were NLFT, TTVF, TTDF, TTYF, etc. By courtesy, their cadres all can be called 'extremists'. After a while, some of them would stage a surrender drama, getting jobs and some other benefits, including pecuniary gains. Some of these outfits' cadres would indulge in anti-social activities (extortion, looting, abduction for ransom) and disturb the peace in the hills.

At different stages, political parties are reported to have promoted different militant outfits or aligned with them for partisan ends. If the Congress won an election with the help of certain outfit, trouncing the Left Government, the latter equalled the score in the next poll by aligning with some other group. Thus, if the Congress supped with the TUJS, the CPM strengthened its foothold in the tribal areas by mobilising the frustrated tribal youth of the GMP and other outfits against the Congress-TUJS Coalition, particularly the TUJS. It was an open secret that the tribal faction of the CPM built up a strong underground organisation, AATF to weaken and break the TUJS. The frustrated tribal youths were literally let loose to make money by any means. They resorted to populist slogans to widen their support base; viz demanding the introduction of Inner Line Permits and redemarcation of the ADC areas to ensure that the tribal interests and identity are protected. The ATTF launched in different hill areas, sporadic violent activities like looting, arson, burglary, abduction of Government officials and motor vehicles drivers for heavy ransoms—raking in large sums of money. The others followed suit in due course.

Anti non-tribal movement grew as a result of an underground outfit Sang-krak led by Anant Reang. Its one-point demand was: "Deport all non-tribals from Tripura." Some other milestones:

1. *TUJS.* Influenced by the MNF, it continued to gear up the Tripura Sena.
2. *TNV.* It was provided camps in the CHT (Bangladesh) for guerrilla training, courtesy MNF.
3. *1979.* Violence breaks out in Tripura. The situation improved only when the MNF signed the Peace Accord with the Centre. As MNF surrendered, the TNV was crippled. Subsequently, the Tripartite Agreement signed in 1985 was meant to end all the violence in the state, though the gods willed otherwise. The hardliners of the TNV raised ATTF and NLFT and the violence, lethal and mindless, continues till date.

Yearning for Peace and Economic Palliatives

In spite of all the exertions by the Indian polity, the peace presently seems to be a distant goal due to a variety of reasons— social, economic, political and geo-strategic. The economic development will seem to be the only solvent for the ills of not only of Tripura but also of the entire North-East. The ultimate solution lies in SAARC plan for creation of SAFTA by 2010 and integrating economy of India's North-East with ASEAN economy by joining the two by road, rail and air.

Problems of insurgency will have to be resolved politically. But for that, the essential first step is to convince the rebels that they cannot bend India by use of force. It is a fact that the indigenous people have lost out to the immigrants, but the latter indeed have contributed to the economy of the state. Sincere efforts are needed to bring the two closer, reasons for the alienation of the former must be understood sympathetically and remedial measures taken to restore the harmony between the estranged parties, if necessary through all-party endeavour.

The first step to restore the pre-1947 situation in the economic field was taken on 12 July 2001 with the commencement of the long-awaited commercial run of the Dhaka-Agartala direct bus service. Then there is need to increase the trade between Tripura and Bangladesh which presently (2002) stands at Rs. 100 crore.

At the political level, special constitutional rights of the Tripuris' have been ensured and various programmes for the upliftment of the tribal people are under implementation. Efforts are on to isolate the insurgents through counter-insurgency measures. The surrendered terrorists must he rehabilitated purposefully and care must be taken that the process is not misused by the clever to obtain Government largesse.

Bhaumik (whose 1996 book is noted for research it reflects on the North-East) finds it unacceptable that no rebel group raises the issue of land—restoration of tribal lands to the original owners. They raise millions .through empty but alluring rhetoric of independence, which is then blown up in foreign countries by a few 'leaders'! "They behave like mafias—extorting money through abductions—not like guerrillas with a cause." They exploit the poor youth to carry out these abductions. After all, Tripura offers an example of the "sons of the soil becoming outsiders in their own land". The state has hardly any industry despite its being rich in natural gas. It is not surprising that tribal youth strays into crime, with the "kidnap industry" becoming a major money-spinner. Bhaumik suggests (2-8-03) the state go in for a major power project based on its natural gas to meet its electricity needs. Presently, the Dumbur Hydel project[30] in its south produces only 5-7 MW against its peak demand of 110 MW. This Dam, submerging over 40,000 hectares of fertile tribal land, has caused deprivation and consequently the urge to join the rebels among the unemployed youths.

As if to respond to Bhaumik's suggestion, Oil and Natural Gas Corporation (ONGC) Chairman, Subir Raha announced on 6-12-04 that "it will invest Rs. 3,500 crore for a 750 MW gas-fired power plant at Palatana in Tripura, in collaboration with Infrastructure Leasing and Financial Services (ILFS) and Tripura Power Development Corporation. The ONGC will also spend another Rs. 400 crore to drill additional production wells, construct 3 new gas-collection stations, upgrade the 2 existing stations, and lay a pipeline network to transport gas from the wells to the power plant. ONGC has capped production in Tripura at 10 lakh cubic metre (LCM) of gas daily against a capacity of 45 LCM a day in view of poor regional demand and problems of feeding the gas into the national pipeline network. ONGC began operations in Tripura in 1972. Since then, it has developed 8 sub-surface gas reservoirs for commercial production. It is now waiting for New Delhi to take up with Dhaka the issue of a Bangladesh passage for a pipeline to bring gas from the state to the mainland. If Prime Minister Manmohan Singh and Petroleum and Natural Gas Minister Mani Shankar Aiyar, during the 2005 SAARC Summit, can make Dhaka agree to Bangladesh passage for bringing Myanmar gas to India, then the ONGC's Tripura gas can also be hauled across that pipeline simultaneously. [Unfortunately, Bangladesh is not playing along with India. So far (9-9-05), it has been a case of one-sided longing, or is it unrequited love?] The pipeline could be built from Akhaura near Agartala to Bongaon near Kolkata, via Komilla in Bangladesh. Gas from Tripura's fields can be pooled into a pipeline network linking the fields using Konaban, Agartala Dome, Baramura, and Manikyanagar as nodal points (*TOI,* 7-12-04). The two proposed projects (Tripura and Myanmar gas for India passing through Bangladesh) may be seen as distant dreams, but they are certainly worth dreaming about for the sake of Tripura, the North East, and well beyond—South Asia and South-East Asia.

Is the Tide Turning?

The Centre and two factions of the NLFT led by Nayanbasi Jamatiya and Montu Koloi agreed on 15 April 2004 to suspend operations against each other for six months, after the two factions had separate meetings with Home Minister Advani. Efforts are on to bring in the third faction led by Bishwamohan and the ATTF within the gamut of the cease-fire to hammer out an early solution to the 15-year old strife in Tripura. It is only fair to expect that the talks to bring lasting peace to the state would start after the May 2004 General Elections to get a commitment from the new Government at New Delhi. Apart from Jamatiya, other leaders who took part in the meeting are Ananta Deb-Barma, Amulya Deb-Barma and Nilen Jamatiya. The Koloi faction included D. Deb-Barma, Bishnu Prasad Jamatiya and "Capt" Sanjit Deb-Barma (*Exp., TOI, HT,* 16-4-04).

Put together, the two factions have over 300 cadres and over 125 firearms, including AK-47s, LMGs, and SLRs. The meeting was attended by the MHA officials and K.P. Singh, Director IB. The ground rules for suspension of operations and matters concerning the rehabilitation of the cadres post-surrender would be worked out in consultation with the Tripura Government and the NLFT factions, and "the process has started from today".

Murmurs of discontent and disillusionment with the leadership had surfaced long before the 15 April cease-fire. The surrendered ATTF cadres—Sgt Maj Surajit Deb-barma, 33 (April 2003) and Sanjit Deb-barman—said life was monotonous and harsh for them "while their leaders lived in royal style—Ranjit in Dhaka and Chitta Deb-barma, his Deputy, in Chittagong—in palatial comforts, owning luxury cars and visiting five-star hotels.... Some ATTF cadres worked as orderlies for them." How did these leaders live in style? Where does the money come from? For that one has to look at how militancy has become a lucrative trade in the North-East. The Intelligence told the *Week* (25-1-04) that the ATTF and NLFT had wrenched Rs. 6 crore from the people in the last 3 years. "So far as these outfits maintain their reign of terror in the countryside, they will never be short of money." Kidnapping is the biggest money-spinner. Between 1999 and 2003, these outfits kidnapped 1,377 people and several were killed even though the ransom was paid. "In all, 864 were released after hefty ransom was paid", said a police officer. "The militant groups have their zones of influence, from where they collect the levies and also issue receipts. They do not poach on each other's territory."

The intra-NLFT dissensions came into the open with the surrender of Montu Koloi (leader of one of the two main factions), with his 71 cadres on 6

May 2004 before the Governor (Dinesh Nandan Sahai) and the DGP (G.M. Srivastava) in Agartala. It followed the 15 April meeting with the Home Minister, when the rebel leaders said the Constitution has enough provisions to redress the tribals' grievances. But there has to be a more mundane face to this sudden realisation. "The tribals were fed up of paying a monthly 'tax' of Rs. 20, besides rice/edibles to the rebels" *(Week,* 30-5-04), and frustrated with the insecurity of their existence. Early January, Nayanbasi sent a letter from his Bangladesh perch to the Government, expressing his desire to surrender. His demands included a political post for himself, and amnesty for all NLFT cadres as well as for the Tripura State Rifles renegade Rashid Mian. The state will find it difficult to accede the last request as Rashid had connived with the ultras and killed 3 colleagues in North Tripura last year. If the leaders are looking for jobs in PSUs, there are precedents. Earlier, TNV's Hrangkhawl and AATFS's Lalit Deb-barma were given such jobs when they laid down arms.

Certain leaders of NLFT are not too keen on the peace with India, e.g., NLFT-N's senior commander Joshua Deb-barma and leader of third faction, Biswamohan Deb-barma. The tide does not seem to be turning—at least not as yet.

In fact, the peace is proving too elusive in Triputa. It is a complex situation there : tribal versus non-tribal, intra-tribal, indegenous verus immigrant majority, and worst of all, terrorist outfits mixed up with the politicians. The next chapter looks at the secessionist/terrorist outfits and post-2005 situation in Tripura.

NOTES

1. Verghese (1997), p. 171.
2. Bhaumik (1996), p. 126.
3. Sarin (1980), p. 133.
4. n. 1, pp. 172-73.
5. *The Tripura Star,* Agartala, 13-12-79, reproduced Hrangkhawl's letter to Chief Minister Nripen Chakrabarty.
6. The *Tripura Observer,* Agartala, 21-5-95.
7. Panna Lal Dhar, *Ethnic Unrest in India and Her Neighbours,* 1998, p. 123.
8. *Hindu,* 4-3-2001.
9. "Reign of Terror", *The North-East Sun,* 1-14 Oct. 1999.
10. www.satp.org\India\Tripura\Assessmnent-Tripura.htm.
11. n. 7, p. 125.
12. *Sentinel,* Guwahati 18-7-2000, "NLFT Massacres 70 BNLF Cadres in Bangladesh".

13. *Ibid.*
14. J.N. Dixit, ex-Foreign Secretary, *Indian Express,* 15-10-98.
15. For more details, *see North-East Sun,* 1-14 April 2001.
16. www.swordoftruth.com/swordoftruth/archives/cstit.htr
17. n. 9.
18. n. 16.
19. *The Hindu,* 4-4-2000.
20. NLFT abducted 24 Jamatias in February 2001 but when the community leaders issued a threat, the kidnapped were released. As the Jamatias, second largest community in Tripura after Deb-barmas, protested against the excesses of the NLFT, the latter has declared a war against the former *(North-East Sun,* 1-14 March 2001).
21. n. 10.
22. The IPFT won 18 of the 28 seats in the May 2000 poll of the TTAADC, gaining an absolute majority: The Governor can nominate 2 members to the ADC. Bar a 5-year tenure (1988-93) of the Congress (I)-TUJS alliance, ADC has been ruled by the CPM-led Left Front since 1982. The performance of the IPFT in the 1995 Elections to the ADC, was by far the most emphatic, when it won all but one of the 24 seats in contention. The lone seat went to the TUJS *(Frontline,* 9-6-2000).
23. To enable the backward tribals in the state to manage their own affairs, the Tribal Autonomous District Council was set up in 1979, under the 5th Schedule, It was disbanded on 19 March 1985 and replaced on 1 April IVXI by the TTAADC set up under the 6th Schedule (*Frontline,* 24-12-99).
24. Gaining control of the TTAADC, the IPFT has started working to develop its distinct identity. The Council decided to form its own police stations and police force without the consent of the State Government. This and some other issue brought the two on collision course, that naturally hampered the achievement of the main objective behind the setting up of the TTAADC *(North-East Sun,* 1-14 March 2001).
25. The DGP Tripura claims that the Government has definite information about the presence of the ISI agents in the state. The police caught an ISI agent in Khowai area of the West district (n. 9).
26. n. 10, cited Dinesh Kotwal, IDSA, *Challenges in Tripura,* 21-7-01.
27. n. 10 and "Tripura Statistics", *North-East Sun,* 1-14 July 2000, p. 11.
28. *The Statesman,* 9-3-2000 and *Hindu,* 9-6-2000.
29. n. 9.
30. Bhaumik suggests that since the Dumbur yields only 5 MW and has submerged over 40,000 hectares of fertile tribal land, it should be closed and that land be reclaimed and handed back to the 25,000 or so landless tribal families, whose jhum harvest yield lasts them for barely 4 months a year. These are the families from which the insurgents have emerged.

19

Tripura : Terrorist Outfits and Current Situation

Situation in Tripura continues to be murky as ever with the terrorist outfits splitting due to personality clashes. NLFT continues to be a major force, establishing trans-border linkages in Myanmar and Bhutan, and the ATTF continues to be ambivalent on the question of entering into negotiations with the Government.

The following information on Tripura situation and some terrorist organisations is considered helpful to understand some of the events and incidents unfolding lately in the State :

- Tripura Backgrounder.
- A table of terrorist groups in the state.
- All Tripura Tiger Force (ATTF).
- National Liberation Front of Tripura (NLFT).
- Tripura Liberation Organisation Front (TLOF).
- United Bengali Liberation Front (UBLF).

Tripura Backgrounder

The indigenous people of Tripura comprise of 19 tribes, including the Tripra, Reang, Jamatia, Kaipeng, Naotia, Koloi, Halam, Hrangkhal, Mog and Bangcher. Kok Borok is the lingua franca of the tribal people and other dialects spoken in Tripura are of Tibeto-Burmese group.

Tripura was a princely state that acceded to the Indian Union on October 15, 1949. It became a Union Territory on November 1, 1956 and a full-fledged State on January 21, 1972.

The genesis of insurgency in Tripura can be traced to the massive influx of Bengali refugees from East Pakistan following partition. The indigenous people, who accounted for 95 per cent of the population of Tripura in the

1931 census, had been reduced to just 31 per cent at the time of the 1991 census. This has led to serious discontent among the tribals, who have become a minority in their own land.

In addition to land, control of trade and business, government jobs are now in the hands of the immigrants. In order to protect their rights, some tribes formed a political front called *Tripura Upajati Juba Samiti* (TUJS) in June 1967. They demanded an autonomous district council under the Sixth Schedule of the Constitution, adoption of Kok Borok as official language and the restoration of tribal lands allotted to non-tribals.

By 1970, some elements had come to believe that only armed action could secure their demands, and the *Tripura Sena* (Tripura Army) was created. Subsequently, in December 1978, the Tripura National Volunteers (TNV) was formed under the leadership of Bijoy Hrangkhal to fight for an independent tribal Tripura state. To assuage tribal feelings, the State Government passed the Tripura Tribal Areas Autonomous District Council Act in 1979. However, it was strongly opposed by a section of the Bengali population. To counter the pressures from the tribal extremists, they also launched a militant organisation called *Amra Bangali* (We Are Bengalis). Consequently, violent communal clashes broke out in several parts of the State in which about 1,800 people lost their lives and over 3,600 dwellings were burnt. In June 1980, the Army was inducted in the State, and the situation was brought under control.

The TNV, with its stronghold in the Jampui area bordering Mizoram, had close links with the Mizo National Front (MNF). But with the signing of the Mizo Accord in 1986 and the subsequent surrender of the MNF to the authorities, the TNV's ability to continue the armed struggle was severely curbed. On August 12, 1988, the TNV signed a Memorandum of Settlement with the State Government and its members laid down arms and came overground. The main point of the agreement was the restoration of alienated lands to the tribal people. However, there were persistent complaints that the agreement had not been implemented. New militant outfits had since come into being and there has been a resurgence of militancy in the State.

Tripura Terrorism Statistics : 1993-98

	1993	*1994*	*1995*	*1996*	*1997*	*1998*	*Remarks*
No. of Cases Reported	115	232	395	313	103	433	
Reported Missing	93	197	388	257	98	349	
Hostages Released	13	15	14	12	6	13	
Hostages Killed	14	8	15	29	27	98	
Total 1993-98	235	452	812	611	234	893	

Terrorist / Insurgent Groups - Tripura, India

Proscribed Terrorist/ Insurgent Groups	*Active Terrorist/Insurgent Groups*	*Inactive Terrorist/ Insurgent Groups*
1. All Tripura Tiger Force (ATTF)	1. Borok National Council of Tripura (BNCT)	1. All Tripura Bengali Regiment (ATBR)
2. National Liberation Front of Tripura (NLFT)		2. All Tripura Bharat Suraksha Force (ATBSF)
		3. All Tripura Liberation Organisation (ATLO)
		4. All Tripura National Force (ATNF)
		5. All Tripura Volunteer Force (ATVF)
		6. Bangla Mukti Sena (BMS) National Militia of Tripura (NMT)
		7. Socialist Democratic Front of Tripura (SDFT)
		8. Tripura Armed Tribal Commando Force (TATCF)
		9. Tiger Commando Force (TCF) Tripura Defence Force (TDF)
		10. Tripura Liberation Force (TLF)
		11. **Tripura Liberation Organisation Front (TLOF)**
		12. Tripura Mukti Police (TMP)
		13. Tripura National Army (TNA)
		14. Tripura National Democratic Tribal Force (TNDTF)
		15. Tripura Rajya Raksha Bahini (TRRB)
		16. Tripura State Volunteers (TSV)
		17. Tripura Tribal Action Committee Force (TTACF)
		18. Tripura Tribal Democratic Force (TTDF)
		19. United Bengali Liberation Front (UBLF)

All Tripura Tiger Force (ATTF)

Formation

The All Tripura Tiger Force (ATTF) was originally founded as All Tripura Tribal Force on July 11, 1990, by a group of former Tripura National Volunteers (TNV) terrorists, who under the leadership of Ranjit Debbarma dissociated themselves from a faction of the TNV led by Lalit Debbarma which surrendered arms in accordance with the August 1988 Accord concluded between the TNV and the Union Government.

According to the ATTF, the outfit rechristened itself as All Tripura Tiger Force by substituting the word 'Tribal' with 'Tiger' sometime in 1992.

It was initially a small group of tribal extremists who operated in pockets of North and South Tripura districts. Gradually, it began mobilising manpower by recruiting tribal youth and enhancing the firepower of its cadres. And by year 1991, it emerged as a formidable terrorist group in Tripura.

However, more than 1,600 cadres surrendered by March 1994, under an amnesty scheme offered by the State Government. A group of ATTF cadres which did not surrender revived the ATTF. It was subsequently banned in April 1997 under the Unlawful Activities (Prevention) Act, 1967.

Over the years, the ATTF either formed or was associated with fringe terrorist/criminal groupings such as the Tripura Tribal Youth Force (TTYF), the Tripura Liberation Organization (TLO), the Tripura Young Rifle (TYR), the Tripura Lion Force (TLF) and the Tripura National Army (TNA). Most of these groups, however, have ceased to exist.

Objective

According to the available literature, the outfit's objectives are:

1. Expulsion of all Bengali-speaking immigrant settlers who entered Tripura after 1956.
2. Restoration of land to tribals under Tripura Land Revenue and Land Reforms Act, 1960.
3. Removal of names of migrants who entered Tripura after 1956 from the electoral roll.

Leadership and Structure

The outfit is headed by its President, Ranjit Debbarma. Chitta Debbarma alias Bikash Koloi is the Vice-President and Upendra Debbarma is its Organisation Secretary. Malinjoy Reang functions as the outfit's Publicity Secretary, while Subodh Debbarma is its Communication Secretary. Asit Debbarma is the outfit's Finance Secretary.

According to State police sources, the community-wise break-up in the ATTF is as follows. Debbarma - 70 per cent, Jamatia - 10 percent, Reang - 10 per cent, Tripuri - 5 per cent and others - 5 per cent. About 90 per cent of the top ranking ATTF cadres are Hindus and the rest are Christians.

The political wing of the ATTF - Tripura Peoples' Democratic Front (TPDF) - has reportedly set up a parallel government in the remote areas of the State.

The outfit's cadre strength is reported to be about 600.

The ATTF headquarters is located at Tarabon in Bangladesh. It also serves as the makeshift headquarters of Arabinda Rajkhowa, chairman of the United Liberation Front of Asom (ULFA).

Linkages

ATTF cadres are reported to have received training in the Chittagong Hill Tracts (CHT) of Bangladesh and the outfit has a number of bases there. More than 70 per cent of ATTF cadres are reportedly located in Bangladesh.

Ranjit Debbarma, the ATTF President, has taken refuge in Bangladesh. According to official sources, he is known to have bought a four-storied building in Dhaka in the second half of year 2003. He also owns a motor garage and also runs a travel network in Dhaka.

On September 22, 2003, Chief Minister Manik Sarkar disclosed the location of 16 ATTF camps/ safe houses operational in Bangladesh. They are:

1. Satcherri (Headquarters of the ATTF)
2. Parakutal (TPDF camp)
3. Kelenga (Agriculture farm of ATTF)
4. Barchu Halai
5. Silai Halai
6. Thaipong Halai (Communication Centre)
7. Biswamanipara
8. Dalucherra
9. Khasiapunji
10. Takhirai
11. Taraban
12. Matiranga
13. Khagrachhari
14. Laugang
15. Dhaka (Safe houses)
16. Chittagong (Safe houses)

Over the years, the ATTF has established linkages with other terrorist groups operating in India's northeast, such as:

- National Socialist Council of Nagaland-Khaplang (NSCN -K)
- United Liberation Front of Asom (ULFA)
- People's Liberation Army (PLA)
- United National Liberation Front (UNLF)
- People's Revolutionary Party of Kangleipak (PREPAK)
- Revolutionary Peoples Front (RPF)
- National Liberation Front of Arunachal Pradesh (NLFA)

Dialogue for Peace

The ATTF has resisted official attempts for a negotiated settlement of the insurgency. On April 22, 2004, however, the outfit's 'President', Ranjit Debbarma, laid down three conditions for the peace process to commence:

- Those who entered Tripura after 1949 and whose names did not figure in the Voters List of 1952 should be declared as foreigners;
- The issue of sovereignty should be point of discussion in the peace talks; and
- A representative of the Unrepresented Nations and Peoples Organization (UNPO) should be present during the peace talks.

The move was welcomed by Chief Minister Manik Sarkar. However, no progress in this front has taken place thus far.

National Liberation Front of Tripura (NLFT)

Formation

The National Liberation Front of Tripura (NLFT) was formed on March 12, 1989, with Dhananjoy Reang (former Vice-President of the Tripura National Volunteers) as its 'chairman'. Reang after being 'expelled' from the NLFT in 1993 formed a separate outfit, the Tripura Resurrection Army (TRA), but surrendered in the year 1997. After Reang's removal, Nayanbasi Jamatiya became leader of the outfit and later Biswamohan Debbarma took over. However, another split occurred in September 2000 following differences between the Halam and Debbarma tribal members of the NLFT. Thus, the Borok National Council of Tripura (BNCT) was formed by Jogendra alias Joshua Debbarma. Personal ambitions of the leaders and parochial religious considerations are believed to have caused yet another split in 2001 when Nayanbasi Jamatiya and Biswamohan Debbarma parted ways from the parent outfit to have factions of the NLFT under their respective leaderships. Further, the fourth split is said to have occurred in June 2003 when Biswamohan Debbarma was deposed allegedly at the behest of NLFT's patrons inside Bangladesh and Mantu Koloi was placed as the leader of that faction. Debbarma is reported to have subsequently set up separate camps on the Tripura-Bangladesh border with his followers.

The NLFT was outlawed in April 1997 under the Unlawful Activities (Prevention) Act, 1967, following its involvement in terrorist and subversive activities. It is also proscribed under the Prevention of Terrorism Act (POTA), 2002.

Split

The NLFT split into two groups, one headed by Biswamohan Debbarma and the other by Nayanbasi Jamatiya, in February 2001. Following the expulsion of Nayanbasi Jamatiya and Joshua Debbarma from the NLFT, nearly 125 cadres of the group formed a parallel outfit under the leadership of Nayanbasi Jamatiya. Police records based on interrogation reports of surrendered/arrested cadres reveal that the split occurred as a result of:

(*a*) Reluctance of the Central Executive Committee of NLFT led by Biswamohan Debbarma to nominate Joshua Debbarma as the King of Tripura Kingdom;

(*b*) Misappropriation of funds by senior leaders;

(*c*) Lavish lifestyles led by the senior leadership; and

(*d*) Forcible conversion of tribal cadres/civilians to Christianity.

Leadership

Nayanbasi Jamatiya and Biswamohan Debbarma have been heading two factions since year 2001. In June 2003, 'General Secretary' Mantu Koloi was reportedly made leader of the faction Biswamohan had been heading. Earlier, internal bickering within the NLFT had led to a spate of violent internecine clashes in Tripura and at the outfit's camps in Bangladesh. Senior leaders such as Utpanna Tripura and Mukul Debbarma are believed to have been killed in such violence. However, other leaders of the undivided NLFT included 'Vice President' Kamini Debbarma, 'Publicity Secretary' Binoy Debbarma, 'Chief of Army' Dhanu Koloi, and 'Finance Secretary' Bishnu Prasad Jamatiya. While the Debbarma faction reportedly has an estimated strength of 550 cadres, the Nayanbasi faction comprises approximately 250 cadres.

According to the State police sources, community-wise break-up in the NLFT is as follows. Debbarma - 40 per cent, Jamatiya - 30 percent, Reang - 10 per cent, and others - 20 per cent. About 90 per cent of the top ranking NLFT cadres are Christians.

Objectives

The purported objective of the NLFT is to establish an 'independent' Tripura through an armed struggle following the liberation from 'Indian neo-colonialism and imperialism' and furtherance of a 'distinct and independent identity'.

Headquarters and Linkages

The headquarters of NLFT is located at Sajak, a camp in the Khagrachari district of Bangladesh. Approximately 65-armed NLFT cadres are permanently stationed in seven huts at the headquarters. Another NLFT camp is in the Mayani Reserve area, also in the Khagrachari district. There are three huts here where 10-12 NLFT terrorists are present. Boalchari, the 'general family headquarters camp' of the NLFT is located in Khagrachari near the Sajak camp. Family members of top NLFT leaders reportedly stay at this camp.

Besides the camps mentioned above, the NLFT also has camps in the Chittagong Hill Tracts (CHT), Sylhet, Maulavi Bazar, Habibganj and Comilla areas of Bangladesh. According to official sources, the outfit has approximately 21 camps in these areas. Alikadam, a 'major' training camp for the NLFT, is located in the Bandarban district. This camp is also used to procure and store arms from the Cox's *Bazaar* port in southeastern Bangladesh.

Usmanpur is yet another camp used for transit. This camp is located in the Habibganj district under Chunarughat police station limits. The outfit reportedly carries out strikes from this camp in the Khowai East and Khowai West regions of West Tripura district.

Details of other camps used by NLFT for subversive activity against India are as following:

1. Tailongbasti Transit Camp: Located in the Moulabibazar district, this camp is two km northwest of the Indo-Bangladesh border in Kamalpur, in an area dominated by the Debbarma clan. The camp is allegedly used for strikes in the Kamalpur and Kailasaher sub-divisions on Tripura.
2. Niralapunji: Located two kilometers southeast of the Indo-Bangladesh border at Kamalpur in the Moulabibazar district, the outfit uses this camp for attacks in the Srimangal town.
3. Kurma / Khasiapunji: The Nayanbanshi Jamatia faction of NLFT uses this camp that is located four-km north of the Indo-Bangladesh border in Kamalpur.
4. Cox's *Bazaar*: A rented transit house has been set up by NLFT in the Sripur area for procurement of arms from this port town.
5. 'Safe House' in Chittagong: Earlier there was a NLFT 'safe house' in Chittagong Road No. 8, in a three-storied building bearing a signboard of the Bangladesh Urban Development Centre. The safe house then shifted to Chittagong Road No. 1 in a Government housing centre in Halisahar. The Biswamohan Debbarma faction was using this safe house that has modern communication systems including mobile telephones, computers and satellite televisions. Latest status of the 'house' following the reported removal of Biswamohan Debbarma is not yet known.
6. Mog Bazar, Dhaka: This 'safe house' in a three-storied building was rented after the NLFT vacated their New Eskaton Road house in

Dhaka. This is another major communication centre of the NLFT. According to the Bangladesh Rural Phone Authority, they had recently sanctioned a mobile phone with ISD (international phone call) facility at this address.

NLFT has further links with the Inter Services Intelligence Agency (ISI), Pakistan's external intelligence agency and its counterpart in Bangladesh, the Directorate General of Field Intelligence (DGFI). During 1997-98, NLFT leaders are reported to have visited Pakistan to receive training and arms from the ISI. The ISI had allegedly arranged the passport and visas for the NLFT leaders.

NLFT has also developed trans-border linkages in Myanmar and Bhutan. Besides these, according to Tripura police, the NLFT has also linkages with the Nagaland-based National Socialist Council of Nagaland- Isak-Muivah (NSCN-IM), the Manipur-based Kanglei Yawol Kanna Lup (KYKL) and the National Democratic Front of Bodoland (NDFB), which is active in Assam.

Tripura Liberation Organisation Front (TLOF)

The Tripura Liberation Organisation Front (TLOF) was formed in early 1992 by a break away faction of Tripura National Volunteers (TNV). It seeks to liberate' Tripura from 'Indian colonial exploitation' through armed struggle. The outfit suffered a major setback in June 1992 when 218 of its activists surrendered to the authorities.

United Bengali Liberation Front (UBLF)

The United Bengali Liberation Front (UBLF) came into existence in October 1999. The proclaimed objective of the outfit is protection of the Bengali population in the State from attacks by other terrorist outfits such as the National Liberation Front of Tripura (NLFT). Thus, its formation, in a way, demonstrated the clash of interests between the dominant Tribal population and the non-Tribes. The NLFT has, reportedly, carried out targeted attacks against the latter. One such instance cited is the May 20, 2000-massacre in which 15 non-Tribals were killed and approximately 13 injured in the West Tripura district.

At present important leaders of the group include Biplab Das and Bijon Basu among others. The UBLF militants have a *modus operandi* under which, an attack is always carried out against the Tribes in the State generally, by throwing bombs from a distance. This operation strategy is different from that of the NLFT or the All Tripura Tiger Force (ATTF) in the sense that UBLF terrorists move about in small groups and single out their victims at isolated spots. Their target could be a moving vehicle or a small conglomeration of tribes away from the settlement.

The group reportedly has been making efforts to establish linkages with the United Liberation Front of Asom (ULFA) and National Democratic Front of Bodoland (NDFB). It is through such organisations that it allegedly tries to reach out sympathisers in the neighbouring countries like Bangladesh. However, official sources have not indicated any clear evidences as regards the same, thus far.

The UBLF is not a proscribed outfit under the Prevention of Terrorism Act, 2002, but has been banned by the State Government for its involvement in the activities of selective killings. The UBLF terrorists are also alleged to be involved in activities such as kidnappings, extortion, arson besides the killing of Tribes. Media reports quoting intelligence sources also suggest that the group raises funds from the Kolkata-based business groups, sympathetic to it, who deal in tea, rubber, timber and construction work in Tripura. Moreover, UBLF militants are also reported to be extorting money from State Government employees. UBLF has also reportedly secured a large amount of arms and ammunition, which include AK-47 and AK-56 assault rifles from other terrorist groups operating in the Northeast and tried to procure more weapons and high power explosives from Bangladesh in the past. Media reports have also indicated UBLF has been trying to follow the example of terrorist outfits like ULFA in imparting training to its cadres in camps on the international border along with Bangladesh. In this regard it has also been reported to have urged even the Bangladeshi government for help, primarily appealing to the common ethnic link.

Major Incidents

2001

- A representative of the Unrepresented Nations and Peoples Organization (UNPO) should be present during the peace talks.
- September 28: Suspected UBLF terrorists kill two and injure two others at Maharanipur in West Tripura. April 26:8 UBLF terrorists arrested in Tripura.
- October 18: UBLF terrorists kill three, including a woman in South Tripura.

2000

- September 29: UBLF terrorists kill two tribals in a bomb attack at Teliamura in West Tripura.
- June 18: UBLF terrorists kill 3 and injure three others in a bomb attack in North Tripura district.
- May 19: UBLF terrorists kill 8 tribals including two women and a child and injure 11 others in West Tripura district.
- April 19: UBLF local action group commander, Biplab Das arrested by the Security Forces (SFs) in Hawaibari West Tripura.

A tribal youth killed in North Tripura district by the suspected UBLF terrorists. SFs arrest 19 UBLF supporters in this connection.

- March 1: Two tribals killed at Kathalcherra, North Tripura by suspected UBLF terrorists. Four others injured in a separate attack.
- February 6: Suspected UBLF kill Sub-Divisional Officer's (SDO) personal bodyguard and injure the driver.

Tripura Terrorist Outfits and Their Network

Tripura is a state which is distinctly different, from other states of northeast India in respect of their culture, traditions and political setup. The main problem that has been plaguing the state is the communal violence, which originated due to demographic inversion wherein the local tribals who were in majority (70%) in the state in 1931 were reduced to a minority (30%) by 1991. This situation arose because of heavy influx of expatriates from Bangladesh both Bengalese and Muslims.

All Tripura Tiger Force whose leadership functions from Dhaka, has nexus with ULFA, PLA and National Liberation Front of Tripura (Nayanbshi) [NLFT(N)] and NSCN(K). The NLFT(N) has established linkages with ATTF, UNLF, NSCN(K), ULFA and PLA. NLFT(Biswa Mohan) have linkages with ATTF, UNLF, NSCN(K), ULFA and PLA.

Within the changing global context of counter-terrorism and perspectives on South Asia, Bangladesh is certainly and increasingly on the back-foot, with its official position *vis-a-vis* Indian insurgent groups increasingly losing the cover of credible deniability. In addition to the volumes of evidence accumulated by Indian authorities, the case against Bangladesh is also gradually being independently validated. For instance, the location of the NLFT hideout that was reported in Bangladesh media as having been raided by the BDR on January 2, 2004 tallies with a location mentioned in the list of 194 Indian insurgent camps inside Bangladesh submitted by the BSF to its Bangladesh counterpart, the BDR, in January 2004. The Indian list stated that the NLFT had a transit camp at Thakurgaon under Chunarughat Police Station in the Habiganj District of Bangladesh. Again, the very fact that Dhaka did not deny the raid and subsequent capture of six NLFT cadres goes against its official position that there are neither camps nor any Indian insurgent cadres operating from Bangladeshi territory.

Current Scenario : Mid-2006 to Early 2007

Tripura Frequented as a Corridor : 22 Jun 2006

That Tripura is increasingly becoming popular among the North-East insurgents as a corridor for east-west traffic was proved once again when the police on 22 Jun 2006 arrested 10 Meghalaya insurgents at the Hirachera Tea Garden in Kailashahar, after they had sneaked in from Bangladesh on their way to Shillong.

They were arrested when the police raided the garden area. The arrested insurgents included a senior leader of the Hynnientrep National Liberation Council, West Syngkli. No arms and ammunition was recovered from them.

"Eleven Tripura ultras hold key to Malegaon" Police : 16 Jul 2006

The Tripura police believe that the alleged mastermind of the 11 Jul 2006 copycat strikes, Zahibuddin Ansari alias Zabi, the prime accused in the Malegaon arms haul case, could have been hiding in the State. He probably fled Mumbai the day after the blasts.

A BSF Inspector, posted at Kamalpur close to the Bangladesh border, told Mumbai's Dalai district police that he had seen/recognised Ansari from the photographs on television after the blasts.

Superintendent Dalai Police Arindam Nath told the press on 16 July that 11 member of a "hardline" Islamic sect had been rounded up on 13 June from near the Bangladesh border. All of them were from Mumbra in Thane district of Maharashtra. A special team of Maharashtra police left for Tripura to interrogate them. This group told the Tripura interrogators that one of their associates, Faizal Ansari, admitted to a private clinic, had left for Mumbai on 12 July, the day after the blasts Ansari, an autorikshaw driver from Thane, police was told, had fractured his hand in a road accident on 16 June. He came to Agartala on the 26th after the pain intensified. The BSF Inspector's description of Ansari matched that of Ansari's photograph.

The police came across a series of calls made from a local booth to the UK, Bangkok, UAE, and Germany. They are being questioned about these ISD calls. Port Blair police arrested six Bangladeshi nationals from Portmouth village in South Andamans on 15 July during combing operations in the wake of the blasts.

The Bangladeshis were found working "illegally" for a building contractor. It turned out that a tout had brought them from Kolkata and they did not report at the immigration counter.

Incidentally, the Mumbai police had raided 250 establishments on 16 Jul 2006.

Two CRPF Men Killed in NLFT Ambush : 24 Oct 2006

Two CRPF men were killed in an ambush sprung by the terrorists belonging to the outlawed NLFT on 24 Oct 2006.

The CRPF squad was patrolling the insurgency-affected Ganganagar area of Dhalai district, 95 km north of Agartala. The heavily-armed militants, perched on a road-side hill tops, sprayed bullets from their automatic weapons, killing the two (Shyamdev Das, 38 and Shravan Kumar, 40) on the spot.

The insurgents took away one AK-47, one SL rifle and "huge cache of communication".

The NLFT and ATTF, another banned militant outfit, are rebel groups fighting for an independent tribal homeland in Tripura. They are operating from their bases in the neighbouring Bangladesh and carry out 'hit and run' guerrilla strikes on both security forces and civilians.

This attack on the CRPF men was the second on the paramilitary forces in 5 days. The NLFT ultras mowed down two Tripura State Rifles (TSR) men on 20 Oct in West Tripura and escaped with two AK-47s of their victims.

Some analysts aver the militant activities seem to be indicative of the declining graph in Tripura as during 2006 (till 24 October) 21 civilians have been killed and 20 kidnapped in contrast to the respective figures of 228 and 174 for 2005, 2004, and 2003 collectively.

"Tripura Ultras face Cash Crunch" : State Police : Dec 2006

DGP, Tripura, GM Shrivastava, addressing the press on the occasion of the Police Week on 1 Dec 2006 said that lack of funds has pushed Tripura insurgents on the backfoot. He ascribed it to the resistance from the public and an increased pressure from the police. So the insurgents are finding it difficult to garner subscriptions, as also collecting funds through ransom for the kidnapped persons.

The make his claim pleansible, he gave the figures for the 2006 and 2005

	2006 (Till 30 November)	*2005*
Killed	13	30
Kidnapped	25	62
Total	38	92

Such averments, rather assertions by the police chiefs should not be taken at their face value. As a rule, such self-congratulatory claims, particularly on some celebratory occasions, as this one indeed was, should be analysed more carefully.

INPT on Verge of Split Again : 9 Dec 2006

The regional political party, the Indigenous Nationalist Party of Tripura (INPT) is facing another split. One of its dissident MLAs is all set to float a new outfit with the support of some disgruntled leaders from his party and reportedly backed by a section of the ruling CPI(M).

The erstwhile Tripura Upajati Juba Samity (TUJS) transformed into INPT after amalgamation with the Tripura National Volunteers (TNV), a militant outfit, in 2001and emerged as the strongest regional party in the State when they won six seats in the State Assembly elections in 2003 in alliance with the Congress.

The alliance broke when the INPT decided to go along with the BJP-led NDA in 2004 parliamentary elections.

Glossary

Aung	An autocratic chief among the Konyaks, as also in the hierarchy of the Naga Federal Government.
Bakerwals	Cowherds owning and tending grazing cattle—more commonly the goats.
Chapori	Sand bank; small island in the rivers.
Char	River island; a highland formed in the river by deposits of silt.
Damdami Taksal	The Sikh seminary once headed by Jarnail Singh Bhindranwale.
Dhok	Summer huts built by cowherds on the hill tops.
Fatwa	A religious decree by Muslim clerics.
Hadith	A nine-volume compilation of the words and deeds of Prophet Mohammad, authored by Imam Mohd al-Bukhari.
Hafiz	Individual who knows the Quran by memory.
Hat/Haat	A market, where shops are usually in sheds or temporary shelters. In the North-East the haats spring along the roads/main approach of the villages and towns on a fixed day on weekly basis where the villagers from the neighbourhood flock with their wares and do frisk business either on the barter basis or in cash.
Jhum	Land cultivated by 'Jhumming', in which a given area is cleared of jungle, which is then burnt and the resultant ashes are then dug into the soil. The land is then sown for a cycle of 3 to 4 years, depending upon the fertility of the soil, after which the land is allowed to remain fallow for 4 to 7 years. Thus each area comes under the cultivation in a cyclic rotation. Popularly known as slash-and-burn type of cultivation and being wasteful, it has been discouraged as a policy by the concerned state governments and replaced by permanent or wet rice-terrace-cultivation where ever feasible. Considerable areas still remain under jhum.
Jihad	Holy war.

Lingdow or Lyngdoh	A Garo priest: head of an administrative unit. In the later period, Lyngdohs came to be identified with the ruling classes.
Madaris	Plural term for Madrassa.
Madrassa	Islamic seminary.
Mujahid	Holy warrior.
Mujahideen	Plural term for Mujahid.
Nazrana	A tribute, an offering, or gifts paid by the native rulers to the visiting British dignitaries like the viceroys, governors etc. It could be in cash or kind. The term comes from the Mughal period when the local chieftains paid *nazrana* to the king or the subedar of the province.
Paiks	Foot soldiers armed with swords and shields who were provided with land in return for military service in the Ahom rule in Assam. During the peace time, they were mandated to render service to the state for a given period (3 months initially, 4 in the later days) in a year for construction of the roads, tanks, other public works etc. Each member of the roalty and rich classes like the land lords was allotted a given number of paiks to cultivate their lands and render other services. When the British after taking over Assam in 1826, abolished the paik system, the roalty and the landed gentry were set on the road to ruin.
Qari	Individual skilled in the rules that govern the recitation of Quran.
Siropa	Robe of honour presented to prominent personalities at a Sikh temple (Gurudwara).
Syiem or Siem	Syiem is the vernacular for chief (king) of a Khasi state in Khasi Hills, presently in Meghalaya.

Bibliography

Alexander, Yanah and Robert G picord	1991	In the Camera's. Eye : News coverage of Terrorist Events.
Anand, VK	1980	Conflict in Nagaland.
Begin, M	1948	The Rivolt.
Bell, J Bower	1971	The Myth of Guerrilla (New York, Alfred A Knopf).
Bhattacharjee, SR	1989	Tribal insurgency in Tripura.
Bhattacharya, Sanjukta and Das, Rochana	1998	Perspectives on India's North-East.
Blum, Yehuda Z	1974	"The Beirut Raid (late 1960s) and the International Double Standards : A Reply to Prof Richard A Falk." The Arab-Irrael Conflict, Vol. II (ed John Norton Moore, Princeton, New Jersey).
Chatterjee, Suniti, K.	1974	Kirata Jinakriti.
CIA	1976	International and Transnational Terrorism : Diagnosis and Prognosis (Washington DC).
Copelond, Miles	1975	Beyond Cloak and Dagger : Inside the CIA (New York, Pinnacle Pooks).
Das, A	1991	Middle class in Assam.
Das, PS	1993	Assamese and Outsiders.
Datta-Ray, B	1989	Tribal identity and tensions in North-East India.
Encyclopaedia, Britannica	1984	15th Edition (London).
Falk, Richards A	1970	"The Beirut Raid (late, 1960s) and the International Law of Retaliation" in Great issues of International Politics (ed Morton A Kaplan, Checago).
Fanon, Frantz	1966	The Wretched of the Earth.
Fay, Sidney B	1966	The Origins of the World War (New York).

Freedman, Roger	1976	"Soviet Policy towards Inter-national Terrorism" in International Terrorism ed. Yonah, Alexander.
Gozier, Brian, ed.	1972-73	"Annual of Power and conflict, a Survery of political violence and International Influence" (London, Institute for Study of Conflict).
Guevara, Ernesto (Che)	1968	The Diary of Che Guevara, New York, Bantam Book. (His full name : Ernesto Guevara De La Serna, June 1928-Oct. 1967).
Guevara, Che	1968	Guerrilla Warfare (New York).
Guha, RC	1999	Savaging the Civilised : Verrier Elwin-His tribals and India.
Gurr, Robert Ted	1971	Why Men Rebel (Princeton, New Jersey).
Huntington, Samuel	1971	"Civil Violence and the Process of Development", in Civil Violence and the International System (London, IISS).
Hutchinson Marth Genshaw	1972	The Concept of Revolutionary Terrorism (Journal of Conflict Resolution, Vol. 16, No 3).
Jenkins, Brian	1975	International Terrorism : A New Code of Conduct (Los Angeles, Crescent Publications).
Jenkins, Brian	1975	High Technology Terrorism and Surrogate Warfare : The Impact of New Technology on Low Level Violence`(Rand Corporation).
Jenkins, Brian and Johnson, Jenera	1975	International Terrorism : A Chronology, 1968-74 (Rand Corporation).
Karim, Maj Gen., Afsar	1991	Counter-Terrorism: The Pakistan Factor (New Delhi, Lancer International)
Lok Sabha Debate	25 Mar. 1966	Vol. I, 11, Column 7893-94.
Laquena, Walter, Z	1985	"Diversties of violence and the Current World System" in Civil Violence and International Politics (IISS, London).

Lenin, VI	1902	Why Social Democrats must declare a determined and relentless war on the Social Revo-lutionaries (in Lenin Reader, ed Stefan Possony, Chicago, 1966).
Man in India	125(4)	Dec 1945.
Misra, Udayan	1988	North-East India : Quest for identity.
Nag, AK	1984	Mizo dilemma.
Naunihal Singh	1989	The World of Terrorism.
Netanyahu, Benjamin (ed)	1986	Terrorism : How the West can win?
Nibedan, Nirmal	1981	North-East India : The ethnic explosion.
Pakam B (ed)	1997	Insurgency in North-East India.
Phadnis, Urmila	1989	Ethnicity and Nation Building in South Asia.
Raghavaiah V	1971	Tribal Revolts.
Segre, DV and Alder, JR	July-Aug 1973	"The Ecology of Terrorism", in Survivor, Vol. XV, No 4.
Santhanam, K, and others (Sreedhar, Sudhir Saxena and Manish)	2002	Jihadis in Jammu and Kashmir: A Portrait.
Sarin, HK	1980	Insurgency in North-East : A study of Sino-American Role.
Sarin, VIK	1980	India's North-East in flames.
Singh, KS (ed.)	1983	Tribal movements in India.
Tarapot, Phanjoubam	1993	Insurgency move-ments in North-East India.
Taylor, AJP	1950	The Struggle for Mastery in Europe, 1948-68.
Templer, Gen, Gerald	1952	Malayan Separatist Cam-paign.
William, A and Hannay, DJ	Apr., 1974	International Terrorism : The Need for a Fresh Perspective (International Lawyer, Vol. 8, No. 2.

Index

F

G

H

N

W

Y

Z